EURAIL® GUIDE

How To Travel Europe And All The World By Train

TWENTY-SECOND (1992) Edition

By Kathryn M. Turpin and Marvin L. Saltzman

Editor - Roger J. B. Turpin

385.22
E

Publishing History

First Edition	1971	96 pages	Twelfth Edition	1982	816 pages
Second Edition	1972	168 pages	Thirteenth Edition	1983	816 pages
Third Edition	1973	288 pages	Fourteenth Edition	1984	816 pages
Fourth Edition	1974	384 pages	Fifteenth Edition	1985	816 pages
Fifth Edition	1975	384 pages	Sixteenth Edition	1986	816 pages
Sixth Edition	1976	432 pages	Seventeenth Edition	1987	816 pages
Seventh Edition	1977	432 pages	Eighteenth Edition	1988	816 pages
Eighth Edition	1978	768 pages	Nineteenth Edition	1989	816 pages
Ninth Edition	1979	768 pages	Twentieth Edition	1990	816 pages
Tenth Edition	1980	816 pages	Twenty-First Edition	1991	816 pages
Eleventh Edition	1981	816 pages	Twenty-Second edition	1992	816 pages

Copyright History

Library of Congress Catalog Number: 72-83072
ISBN: 0-912442-22-0
US ISSN: 0085-0330

Published by
Eurail® Guide Annual
27540 Pacific Coast Highway
Malibu, California 90265, U.S.A.

IMPORTANT NOTES

Always without exception before commencing each journey doublecheck the departure and arrival times given in our book or in any timetable, as they are subject to change without prior notice. Changes will usually be minor and have no effect on the trips described in this book. We do not want you to miss a train or to be stranded.

Departure and arrival times in this book are given in 24-hour time. A departure at 01:10 PM is shown as 13:10. Midnight is 24:00. Time between Midnight and 01:00 AM is shown as 00:01 to 00:59.

All schedules shown are daily, unless designated otherwise.

Unless indicated otherwise, the departure and arrival times in our book are for the period of late May to late September. In most cases, these schedules change slightly during September-May.

Where we state that departures from a city are "at frequent times", this means at least once each hour between the 2 time periods indicated.

Trips in all of the European (and many other) countries appear in this sequence: (1) one-day excursion roundtrips or circle trips from a base city to interesting destinations and information on what to see and do there, (2) scenic train rides, many of which can be made as a one-day roundtrip or circle trip, and (3) international rail service (trips to adjoining countries).

The schedules for one-day roundtrip excursions do not always reflect all the departure times from either the base-city or the destination-city. Only those departure times involved in making a one-day roundtrip are shown. On a particular route, there frequently are later departure times from the base-city and earlier departure times from the destination-city than are shown, none of which would be applicable to a one-day roundtrip.

Many cities have 2 or more railstations. Wherever this is so, we note the name of the applicable railstation (in parenthesis) after the name of the city. For Austria, Germany and Switzerland, where no name is shown after the name of the city, the station is always "Hauptbahnhof".

The number appearing at the start of a schedule is the Thomas Cook Timetable number, such as 481 in the example below:

Bergen - Oslo 481

| Dep. Bergen | 07:30 |
| Arr. Oslo | 14:05 |

Every year hundreds of readers send us suggestions, each of which is checked and answered. Many are added to the next annually-revised edition. If you have discovered rail travel facts helpful to others, please send them to us.

INDEX

An index of 2,102 cities, resorts and places of interest to tourists appears on pages 808-815.

PRICES

Unless designated otherwise, all prices appearing in Eurail Guide are in US dollars.

RAIL TRIP CATEGORIES

Trips in all of the European (and many other) countries appear in this sequence: (1) one-day excursion roundtrips or circle trips from a base city to interesting destinations and information on what to see and do there, (2) scenic train rides, many of which can be made as a one-day roundtrip or circle trip, and (3) international rail service (trips to adjoining countries).

COUNTRIES WITHOUT PASSENGER TRAIN SERVICE

AFGHANISTAN
BAHRAIN
BHUTAN
BRUNEI
BURKINA FASO (UPPER VOLTA)
BURUNDI
CENTRAL AFRICAN REPUBLIC
CHAD
EL SALVADOR
GAMBIA
GUYANA
GUYANE
JORDAN
KUWAIT
LAO PEOPLE"S DEMOCRATIC REP.
LEBANON
LESOTHO

LIBERIA
LIBYA
MAURITIUS
NIGER
OMAN
QATAR
REUNION
RWANDA
SIERRA LEONE
SOMALI REPUBLIC
SURINAM
SWAZILAND
UNITED ARAB EMIRATES
URUGUAY
YEMEN, ARAB REPUBLIC
YEMEN, PEOPLE'S DEMOCRATIC REP.

ALPHABETICAL LIST OF COUNTRIES

TABLE OF CONTENTS

TRAVELING SWITZERLAND'S RHONE VALLEY BETWEEN BERNE AND ISELLE

Chapter 1

THE JOY OF TRAIN TRAVEL

In the 22 years since Eurail® Guide's first (96-page) edition, the many advantages that European train travel offered back in 1971 have continually increased and improved.

The 36 Trans Europ Express trains that were in service in 1980 have been replaced since then by a fleet of 92 much faster and more frequent EuroCity trains plus dozens of ultra-speed TGV trains (up to 238 miles per hour).

All EuroCity trains comply with strict standards of speed, puntuality, comfort, air-conditioning and food. TGV trains are described on page 121 (see "World's Fastest Trains").

We have claimed for 22 years that the least expensive, safest, most convenient, interesting and pleasant way to travel and really see the world is by train.

Eurail® Guide accents "pleasant", because our book is about joyous adventure. Our goal since 1971 has been to make worldwide train travel easy and pleasurable for our readers.

It will always be true that when traveling by train, your departure is not delayed by weather, as it can be when traveling by airplane or automobile.

You still leave and arrive in the center of a city, saving the time, effort and expense involved with going back and forth to distant airports. In fact, in Europe and Japan, many high-speed trains actually get you from a hotel in one city to a hotel in another city faster than by airplane when the distance is 250-350 miles.

The cost of an uncomfortable and non-airconditioned mini car for 350 miles per day travel in Europe can come to more than $80 (U.S.) per day — rental, very high taxes on the rental charge (in 1991 as much as 25% in Sweden, 22% in France, 22% in Denmark, 21% in Austria, 20% in Norway, 19% in Italy, 17.5% in Britain) . . . plus insurance, servicing, overnight parking fees ($10–$20 per night), substantial drop-off charge, and astronomic gasoline prices.

Sample price-per-gallon in 1991: $4.86 (U.S.) in Italy, $4.45 in Sweden, $4.02 in France, $3.98 in Portugal, $3.72 in Belgium, $3.11 in England !

Kemwell's rental cost alone (*before* sales tax) in 1991 for its smallest car (a manual-shift Fiat Panda, or similar) per week when drop-off was in the same country as start of rental (Unlimited milage and including sales tax and collision waiver) were: $409 (U.S.) in Norway, $359 Sweden, $319 Ireland, $309 Denmark, $299 France, $289 Italy, and $279 in Austria, Britain, Greece and Spain. For an automatic transmission Mercedes-Benz (or similar), the 1991 one-week rental prices were: $1,319 (U.S.) in Italy, $1,149 Denmark, $1,039 Norway, $1,009 Sweden, and $949 Austria.

Highway tolls are another cost of auto touring. In Italy, during recent years, motorists had to pay $33(U.S.) in road tolls for the 350-mile drive from Menton (at the French-Italian border) to Florence. *Consumer Reports Travel Letter* said in 1991 that extensive driving in France or Italy "will add $5–$15 to your daily cost".

By contrast, one can travel on high-speed, air-conditioned trains with any of more than 80 bargain European train passes for $12–$40 per day. (See detailed list on our Inside Back Cover.) The first-class 15-day Eurailpass at $430 in 1992 or the first-class Eurail Saverpass or the first-class Eurail Flexipass (see page 18) represent a fantastic bargain by comparison, as do also the many European national and regional train passes listed throughout Chapters 6 and 7.

In train travel, you reach thousands of interesting destinations not accessible by airplane. You eliminate the worries, frustrations and delays of socked- in airports, flat tires, the requirement to check-in early at airports, the interminable waiting for baggage to be unloaded, driving into the crowded streets of an unfamiliar city, coping with strange traffic laws and the many other problems, expenses and inconveniences connected with airplane and auto travel.

From London to Tokyo, you find at principal railstations a wide variety of services and goods: food, information on local tours, assistance in obtaining lodging, money exchange, waiting rooms where you can relax, shoe repair, etc.

If you plan your routes well, you will see an array of visual delights that airplane passengers never see: indescribable seashores, vineyards tinted by afternoon sunlight, castles that have been straddling their hilltops for centuries, raging rivers, breathtaking waterfalls, Alpine summits, remote villages founded before Christ, fjords, forests, lovely orchards and pastures — a feast of colorful pictures to enjoy long after the trip ends.

At the end of a train trip, you arrive at your destination relaxed and rested.

There is no waiting for the next city to have the use of lavatory facilities. Usually, a cup of coffee or bottle of beer is only a 2-minute walk away. During the trip you can get up from your seat, stretch, take a stroll through the train.

Only train travel affords the opportunity of meeting and conversing with the people in the area you are visiting and also with tourists from other parts of the world. Since 1959, among the fellow passengers with whom we have shared train rides have been Amsterdam businessmen, students from California, Italian army officers, gregarious Yugoslav geologists, an Uruguayan cardiologist, North Dakota farmers, a Chinese woman doctor from Canada, a family from Brazil, a young Russian woman returning home from a trade fair in Germany, and a professor of language from Boston.

Every year since the first Eurail® Guide in 1971, each annually-revised and expanded edition of our book has been the product of a large "family".

Our daughter Kathryn proposed the idea for Eurail® Guide when she was traveling Europe on a 3-month Eurailpass in 1970. We published our first annual edition in early 1971 as 96 pages, and the book has been growing ever since then.

Kathryn and I, in writing each new edition, are aided and abetted by Barbara, who uncovers errors, suggests improvements and causes endless revisions the classic dissatisfied editor to whom authors become permanently indebted once the travail is over.

Kathryn has traveled at different seasons and has taken different routes than those Barbara and I have traveled, giving each edition a variety of experiences and strikingly different viewpoints. For one thing, no stranger has offered to carry my suitcases or take me to dinner.

Many others have provided information and extraordinary assistance, for which we express our gratitude: Andy Lazarus, A.J. Lazarus Associates . . . Dagobert M. Scher, the North American Assistant General Manager of Rail Europe, and his aides, Susan Alcorn and Michelle Topper . . . Michael Fox, BritRail Travel International . . . and Donna Bouchard, CIT/Italian Rail .

Other important members of the Eurail® Guide family are the scores of readers who each Fall write us as we are preparing the next edition to tell us where they have traveled and describe their experiences.

Comments about your train journeys will be greatly appreciated. Write us what you liked and disliked . . . out-of-the-way places you visited and recommend . . . and anything else you believe would help other travelers plan future trips.

Send your notes to: Eurail Guide Annual, 27540 Pacific Coast Highway, Malibu, California 90265, U.S.A.

In the following pages, we identify basic problems in train travel worldwide, show how these can be overcome, and tell you all you need to know in order to travel the world by train safely, economically and pleasantly.

(M.L.S.)

Postscript: Never plan to travel without finding out if the countries you are going to tour have low-price train passes.

And when those countries have train passes, make sure to know before you leave home if any pass you want to buy has to be purchased before you leave home or can be bought only after you arrive in the country you will be touring.

All of the train passes offered throughout the world when this edition of Eurail® Guide went to press are described in our book.

Chapter 2

WHETHER TO EURAILPASS

Since 1959 Western European railroads have offered the travel bargain called Eurailpass, sold throughout the world except in Europe and North Africa.

All of the 6 different Eurailpasses entitle one to unlimited first or second- class train travel plus free or reduced fare on many buses and boats in these 17 countries: Austria, Belgium, Denmark, Finland, France, Germany, Greece, Holland, Hungary, Irish Republic, Italy, Luxembourg, Norway, Portugal, Spain, Sweden, and Switzerland.

In Europe, first-class cars (and the first-class portion of mixed-class cars) are marked outside by a yellow line running above the windows.

All Eurailpasses are non-refundable if lost or stolen. If you present an un-used Eurailpass to a Eurailpass office before it becomes valid, 85% of the purchase price will be refunded.

There are Eurail Aid Offices in several European cities (listed on the map that is given with each Eurailpass), where a lost validated Eurailpass can be replaced if the buyer presents the validation slip and a police report of loss or theft. If reported within one year after issue date, a lost or stolen pass will be re-issued at a charge of $25 (U.S.).

You must start to use any Eurailpass within 6 months after buying it. For example, if purchased on February 1, first use must be prior to August 1.

All Eurailpasses become valid on the first day they are used, after first having been recorded at the ticket office of the station from where the first journey begins.

Prices in this chapter are U.S. dollars.

The phrase "unlimited travel" means exactly that. You can literally travel 24 hours a day for the entire period a pass is valid. Countless travelers have used 3 and 4 times the price of their pass, saving hundreds of dollars their itinerary would have cost if they had used ordinary tickets.

The bargain does not end there. Tickets for the high-speed EuroCity, Inter- City and super-speed TGV trains cost more than space on an ordinary, slower train on the same route, charging a supplement ranging from $3.00(U.S.) to $18.00. Eurailpasses include unlimited use of EC, IC and TGV trains without having to pay any supplement.

Many of the EC, IC and TGV trains require reservations, the price of which is normally included in the supplement. However, Eurailpass travelers must still pay the $3(U.S.) fee for each seat reservation, although the cost of the supplement is covered by the pass.

In addition to the money-saving feature, Eurailpass adds precious time to a travel schedule. Many travelers feel that never having to stand in a ticket-selling line when you have a Eurailpass or Eurail Youthpass is enough reason to have the pass. It can take up to 30 minutes for purchasing each ticket along the way.

(With or without a pass, if reserved seats are required or desired it is necessary to allocate time for the separate Seat Reservation Line when you have not made reservations before starting your trip. More information about reservations appears on pages 30-35.)

On the other hand, Eurailpass is not always an economy. Some European itineraries are less expensive using regular train tickets or using one or a combination of the many national and regional rail passes described in this book (France Railpass, German Flexipass, Benelux Tourrail, etc.).

The only way to find out if a Eurailpass or the numerous other passes will save you money on your trip is to compare their price with the total prices of tickets for your particular itinerary.

There are over 100,000 miles of European train travel you can make with a pass. It is impossible for us to give you the fare and travel time for every possible trip in Europe.

However, we provide you in our Chapter 17 "Route Chart" (pages 784-807) a list of more than 700 train trips that most people touring the 17 Eurailpass countries might take, with the first-class fare and travel time for each of them.

If you are considering traveling the heavily-crowded second-class, compute second-class fares at two-thirds of the first-class fares shown. That will come close to actual second-class ticket prices. While second-class usually is more crowded than first-class, often the disadvantage of having to stand because all the seats are occupied can be overcome by arriving early at the railstation.

The first step in using the Chapter 17 Route Chart is to make a list of your itinerary. It is advisable to schedule any part of your trip that is not in the 17 Eurailpass countries (such as England, Yugoslavia, etc.) either before or after the days you are touring the countries in which Eurailpass is valid so as to avoid consuming Eurailpass days and in order to buy the least expensive Eurailpass for your trip. Next, consult the Route Chart and note the first-class fare for each leg of your trip that can be covered by Eurailpass.

Keep in mind that even though you purchase your Eurailpass weeks or months in advance of starting your trip, the Eurailpass validity period does not begin until the first day you actually use the pass, which must be within 6 month after the date it was issued.

It's a good idea to protect yourself from having your pass rendered partly or wholly invalid because the validity dates were entered incorrectly. The Eurailpass must be validated at the ticket office of the station at your first departure. At that time, the clerk writes on the pass both the first and last day it can be used. Before he does this, write a note with what you believe are the validity dates, show it to him, and ask him if he agrees with those dates. Only when he says your dates are correct, or explains why they are not, should you hand your pass to him for the dates to be entered on it.

Once the clerk has written validity dates on the face of your Eurailpass, those dates cannot be changed because any alteration of the dates invalidates the pass. That is why it is wise to have him agree on the correct dates *before* he writes anything.

If one fails to have the Eurailpass validated before boarding the first train ride, the train conductor can do no harm. There is a $15 fee, plus departure, validation.

After your Eurailpass has been validated, remove the "proof of purchase" stub from the 2-part pass. From then on, as you would do with a line of traveler's checks after purchasing them, keep that stub separate from the pass. It is this stub that is required for a replacement in case the pass itself is lost or stolen.

Eurailpasses are accepted by those trains running between airports and cities: Amsterdam, Barcelona, Bilbao, Brussels, Dusseldorf, Geneva, Frankfurt, Malaga, Paris, Pisa, Vienna and Zurich.

EURAILPASS PRICES

All prices shown in this chapter are U.S. dollars.

The 1992 prices for the consecutive-days Eurailpass are: $430 for 15 days, $550 for 21 days, $680 for one month, $920 for 2 months and $1,150 for 3 months. Children 4 to under 12 pay half-fare. Children under 4 travel free.

An average 21-day itinerary is $200-$300 more expensive with first-class tickets than with a Eurailpass. (A *frantic* itinerary can be $500-$700 more expensive.) And, a Eurailpass gives you the convenience of not having to stand in time-consuming lines to purchase tickets.

Depending on the itinerary, it can be the least expensive formula to buy a combination of Eurailpass and train tickets. For example, when traveling by train over a 21-day period with the $76 Geneva-Zurich ride on the last day, it saves $54 to buy a 21-day Eurailpass and a ticket for the 22nd day ($550+$76=$626) instead of buying a $680 one-month Eurailpass.

On the other hand, if the trip on the 22nd day is $130 or more (Vienna-Paris is $226 in 1992), it will save money to buy a one-month Eurailpass *even though it is being used only 22 days.*

Eurail Flexipass Same privileges as the Eurailpass, but travel days need not be consecutive. The 1992 prices are: $280 for any 5 days within a 15-day period, $450 for 9 days within 21 days, and $610 for 14 days within a month. (Example: June 12 through July 11.) Children 4 to under 12 pay half-price.

Eurail Saverpass. This 15-day pass for unlimited first-class travel allows three or more people to travel together April 1, 1992 to September 30, 1992 for $340 per person, with the same privileges as the standard Eurailpass. Only 2 persons need travel together October 1 to March 31. There is a 50% discount for children age 4 to under 12, who also count toward the minimum group number.

Euraildrive Pass Same privileges as the Eurailpass. Features 4 days of unlimited first-class train travel plus 3 days of a Hertz rental car with unlimited mileage, tax, basic liability insurance and drop-off (providing that drop-off is within the same country as that in which the car is rented). There is also an option to buy up to 5 additional days of either train travel and/or car rental. This pass (up to 17 days of travel) must be used within 21 days.

The 1992 per-person price for 2 or more persons when using the category of smallest car is $269.

An option for single travelers is available at $439.

The Chapter 17 Route Chart (pages 784-807) makes it easy for you to compute the ticket price for your trip and then determine *whether* to buy a Eurailpass, which Eurailpass will save you the most money, and how to schedule your train trips so as to fit them into the validity period of your Eurailpass.

Figures in the Route Chart for travel time between 2 cities represent the longest time for each trip. The time stated for many routes is for a night train, and there is a shorter-time day train on which you could make the same journey. Or there may be 2 or more trains running during the day, one of which is a fast express that makes the trip in less time than what is indicated in the Chapter 17 Route Chart.

Despite such differences, the time shown in the Eurail® Guide Route Chart, as a rule, will be no more than 10% greater than the fastest time between 2 cities.

The Eurail® Guide Route Chart is accurate enough to help you decide whether you want to make a particular trip in one day or break it up into 2 or more shorter trips.

THE 5 MOST SCENIC RAIL TRIPS IN EUROPE

In Chapter 6 (16 of the 17 Eurailpass countries) plus Hungary in Chapter 8 (the 17th) and in Chapter 7 (the 4 BritRailpass areas: England, Wales, Scotland, Northern Ireland) we show 3 types of rail trips for each country:

One-day excursion roundtrips or circle trips from a base city to interesting destinations plus information on what to see and do there . . . scenic train rides, many of which can be made as a one-day roundtrip or circle trip . . . and international rail service (trips to adjoining countries).

Below are what we consider are the 5 most scenic train rides in Europe.

The pages on which they appear are shown in parentheses.

Milan-Zurich (257). Zurich-Milan (365).

Locarno-Camedo (349), a part of these 3 rides:

> Bern-Locarno (335)
> Brig-Locarno (339)
> Milan-Locarno (235)

Geneva-Lausanne-Brig-Spiez-Bern-Geneva (342)

Bergen-Oslo (289)

Oslo-Dombas-Andalsnes (293)

EURAIL YOUTHPASS

This pass is for unlimited *second*-class train travel in the same 17 countries (see page 16) which honor the first-class Eurailpass. In 1992, the $470 (U.S.) price for a one-month Eurail Youthpass is a $210 savings compared to the $680 one-month first-class Eurailpass. The $640 two-month Eurail Youthpass is a $280 savings compared to the $920 two-month first-class Eurailpass.

Second-class space is very acceptable on trains in Austria, Belgium, Denmark, Finland, France, Germany, Holland, Irish Republic, Luxembourg, Norway, Sweden and Switzerland.

The buyer of a Eurail Youthpass must prove he or she is under 26 years of age on the first day of using the pass.

EURAIL YOUTH FLEXIPASS

The 1992 price for unlimited *second*-class train travel any 15 days in a 2-month period (example: June 16 to August 15) is $420 (U.S.).

All Eurailpasses can be purchased from a travel agent or directly from the following places:

U.S.A. and CANADA

ATLANTA, GA.
German Rail Inc.
3400 Peachtree Rd., NE (30326)

BOSTON, MA.
German Rail Inc.
625 Statler Office Bldg. (02116)

CHICAGO, IL.
Rail Europe
11 E. Adams St. (60603)

German Rail Inc.
9575 W. Higgins Road
Rosemont, IL (60018)

FORT LAUDERDALE, FL.
Rail Europe
800 Corporate Dr. (33334)

IRVING, TX
German Rail Inc.
222 W. Las Colinas (75039)

LOS ANGELES, CA.
CIT (Italian State Railways)
6033 W. Century Blvd., (90045)

German Rail Inc.
11933 Wilshire Blvd. (90025)

MONTREAL, P.Q., CANADA
CIT (Italian State Railways)
1450 City Councillors St. (H3A 2E6)

Rail Europe
643 Notre Dame Ouest (H3C 1H8)

NEW YORK, N.Y.
CIT (Italian State Railways)
594 Broadway (10012)

Rail Europe
610 Fifth Ave. (10020)

German Rail Inc.
747 Third Ave. (10017)

SAN FRANCISCO, CA.
Rail Europe
360 Post St. (94108)

German Rail Inc.
240 Stockton St. (94108)

SANTA MONICA, CA.
Rail Europe
100 Wilshire Blvd. (90401)

TORONTO, ONT., CANADA
C.I.T. Tours, Inc.
111 Avenue Road (M5R 3J8)

Rail Europe
2087 Dundas East
Mississauga, Ont. (L4X 1M2)

German Rail Inc.
1290 Bay St. (M5R 2C3)

VANCOUVER, B.C., CANADA
Rail Europe
409 Granville St. (V6C 1T2)

WHITE PLAINS, N.Y.
Rail Europe
226-230 Westchester Ave. (10604)

ELSEWHERE

AUSTRALIA: CIT Australia Pty. Ltd., Ltd., Concorde International Travel, National Australia Bank Travel Service, Thomas Cook Pty. Ltd.; **BAHREIN:** Thomas Cook Overseas Ltd.; **EGYPT:** Thomas Cook Overseas Ltd.; **HONG KONG:** Hong Kong Student Travel Bureau, Lufthansa German Airlines, Thomas Cook Hong Kong Ltd.; **INDIA:** Travel Corporation India Pvt. Ltd.; **INDONESIA:** Pantravel Travel & Tourism Service; **ISRAEL:** European World Representatives; **JAPAN:** Japan Travel Bureau, Travel Plaza International; **KOREA:** Seoul Travel Service, Ltd.; **MALAYSIA:** Boustead Thomas Cook Sdn. Bhd.; **NEW ZEALAND:** Atlantic & Pacific Travel International, Ltd., Thomas Cook Pty. Ltd.; **PAKISTAN:** American Express International, Inc., **PHILIPPINES:** PCI Travel Corporation, Thomas Cook Inc.; **SAUDI ARABIA:** Tarfa Tours & Travel, Alrajhi Wings for Travel and Tourism; **SINGAPORE:** American Express International Inc., Thomas Cook Boustead Pte., Ltd.; **SOUTH AFRICA:** Global Tours S. Africa (Pty) Ltd., World Travel Agency (Pty) Ltd.; **SRI LANKA:** Aitken Spence Travels Ltd.; **TAIWAN:** American Express International Inc., Federal Transportation Ltd.; **THAILAND:** DITS Travel (Diethelm International Transport Services, Ltd.); **U.A.E.:** Thomas Cook A.L. Rostamini (Pvt) Ltd.

SECOND-CLASS SPACE

The 3 price alternatives that passengers 26 or older have when traveling the 17 Eurailpass countries by train are: first-class tickets, Eurailpass, or second-class tickets. (Passengers *under* 26 have the fourth option of Eurail Youthpass.)

Even though second-class tickets are very close to only 66% of the first- class price, the cost of a typical itinerary using second-class tickets *is more expensive than traveling first-class on trains with a Eurailpass !*

OTHER PASSES AND DISCOUNTS

There are alternative economies to use besides Eurailpass and Eurail Youthpass when traveling Europe by train. These are the special discount tickets, coupons, passes, etc. which various countries issue individually. Details on all of them appear in this book under the listing of each country.

Some of these discount tickets can be purchased outside Europe. Others may be purchased *only* in the issuing country itself. **Since these regulations change frequently, it is suggested that you first contact the office nearest your residence.**

The U.S. and Canadian offices are listed here.

AUSTRIA
Austrian National Tourist Office

500 No. Michigan Ave., Suite #1950, Chicago, IL. 60611
11601 Wilshire Blvd., Suite #2480, Los Angeles, CA. 90025
1010 Ouest Rue Sherbrooke, Suite #1410, Montreal, Que. H3A 2R7
500 Fifth Ave., Suite #2009-2022, New York, N.Y. 10110
2 Bloor Street East, Suite #3330, Toronto, Ont. M4W 1A8
200 Granville St., Suite #1380, Vancouver, B.C. V6C 1S4

BELGIUM
Reservations and tickets for Belgian trains are provided by the offices of Rail Europe, addresses for which appear under "France" on page 23.

DENMARK
Scandinavian Tourist Boards

8929 Wilshire Blvd., Suite #300, Beverly Hills, CA. 90211
150 No. Michigan Ave., Suite #2110, Chicago IL. 60601
655 Third Ave., New York, N.Y. 10017

FINLAND
Finnish Tourist Board

1900 Avenue of the Stars, Suite #1070, Los Angeles, CA. 90067
655 Third Ave., New York, N.Y. 10017

FRANCE
Rail Europe

11 East Adams St., Chicago, IL. 60603
800 Corporate Dr., Fort Lauderdale, FL. 33334
2087 Dundas East, Mississauga, Ont. L4X 1M2, Canada
643 Notre Dame Ouest, Montreal H3C 1H8
360 Post St., San Francisco, CA. 94108
100 Wilshire Blvd., Santa Monica, CA. 90401
409 Granville St., Vancouver, B.C., V6C 1T2, Canada
226-230 Westchester Ave., White Plains, N.Y. 10604

GERMANY
German Rail Inc.

3400 Peachtree Road N.E., Suite #1229, Atlanta GA. 30326
625 Statler Office Bldg., Boston, MA. 02116
222 W. Las Colinas, Suite #1050, Irving, TX. 75039
11933 Wilshire Blvd., Los Angeles, CA. 90025
747 Third Ave., New York, NY. 10017
9575 W. Higgins Road, Suite #505, Rosemont, IL. 60018
240 Stockton St., 6th Floor, San Francisco, CA. 94108
1290 Bay St., Toronto, Ont. M5R 2C3, Canada

GREAT BRITAIN
BritRail Travel International

1500 Broadway, New York, N.Y. 10036-4015
250 Eglinton Avenue East, Toronto, Ont. M4P 3E1

GREECE
Greek National Tourist Organization

168 No. Michigan Ave., Chicago, IL. 60601
611 W. 6th St., Los Angeles, CA. 90017
1233 De la Montagne, Montreal, P.Q. H3G 1Z2, Canada
645 Fifth Ave., New York, N.Y. 10022
Upper Level, 1300 Bay St., Toronto, Ont. M5R 3K8, Canada

HOLLAND
Netherlands Board of Tourism

225 No. Michigan Ave., Suite #326, Chicago, IL. 60601
355 Lexington Ave., New York, N.Y. 10017
90 New Montgomery St., Suite #305, San Francisco, CA. 94105
25 Adelaide St. East, Suite #710, Toronto, Ont. M5C 1Y2, Canada

24

IRELAND
Irish Tourist Board

757 Third Ave., New York, N.Y. 10017
160 East Bloor St., Suite #934, Toronto, Ont. M4W 1B9, Canada

ITALY
Italian State Railways

6033 W. Century Blvd., Suite #980, Los Angeles, CA 90045
1450 City Councillors St., Suite #750, Montreal, P.Q. H3A 2E6, Canada
594 Broadway, Suite #307, New York, N.Y. 10012
111 Avenue Road, Concourse Level, Toronto, Ont. M5R 3J8, Canada

LUXEMBOURG
Luxembourg National Tourist Office

801 Second Ave., New York, N.Y. 10017

NORWAY
Scandinavian Tourist Boards

8929 Wilshire Blvd., Suite #300, Beverly Hills, CA. 90211
150 No. Michigan Ave., Suite #2110, Chicago, IL. 60601
655 Third Ave., New York, N.Y. 10017

POLAND
Polish National Tourist Office

333No. Michigan Ave., Chicago, IL. 60601
Orbis Polish Travel Bureau, Inc. 342 Madison Ave., New York, N.Y. 10173

PORTUGAL
Portuguese National Tourist Office

590 Fifth Ave., New York, N.Y. 10036
60 Bloor St. West, Suite #1005, Toronto, Ont. M4W 3B8, Canada

SPAIN
National Tourist Office of Spain

8383 Wilshire Blvd., Suite #960, Beverly Hills, CA. 90211
845 N. Michigan Ave., Suite #915E, Chicago, IL. 60611
1221 Brickell Ave. , Suite #1850, Miami, FL. 33131
665 Fifth Ave., New York, N.Y. 10022
102 Bloor St. West, Suite 1400, Toronto, Ont. M5S 1M8, Canada

SWEDEN
Scandinavian Tourist Boards

8929 Wilshire Blvd., Suite #300, Beverly Hills, CA 90211
150 No. Michigan Ave., Suite #2110, Chicago, IL 60601
655 Third Ave., New York, N.Y. 10017

SWITZERLAND
Swiss National Tourist Office

150 No. Michigan Ave., Suite 2930, Chicago, IL. 60601
222 No. Sepulveda Blvd., Suite #1570, El Segundo, CA. 90245
608 Fifth Ave., New York, N.Y. 10020
260 Stockton St., San Francisco, CA. 94108
154 University Ave., Toronto, Ont. M5H 3Y9, Canada

EURAILPASS BONUSES
In addition to unlimited train travel, the Eurailpasses provide the following free bonuses or reduced prices for boat trips, buses and private railways.

Many bonuses are not listed in the Eurailpass brochure, such as discounts on some of Norway's fjord boats and some of Switzerland's cable cars. Always show your Eurailpass before purchasing any bus, boat, cable car or train ticket. Many rides that are not covered completely will allow a discount when you have a Eurailpass.

AUSTRIA Two rack railways: (1) Puchberg am Schneeberg-Hochschneeberg and (2) St. Wolfgang-Schafbergspitze. The Danube cruise between Passau and Vienna. Reduction of 50% on Lake Constance, Linz-Passau (and v.v.), and Vienna-Budapest ships.

DENMARK These ferry crossings: Aarhus-Kalundborg, Knudshoved-Halskov, Nyborg-Korsor, Fynshav-Bojden, Rodby Faerge-Puttgarden (Germany), Helsingor- Helsingborg (Sweden) and Frederikshavn-Goteborg (Sweden).

A 50% reduction on the Flyvebadene Company hydrofoil between Copenhagen and Malmo (25% for Eurail Youthpass), and a 30% reduction on the Color Line for the ship between Hirtshals and Kristiansand (Norway).

FINLAND Two cruises: (1) Helsinki-Stockholm and (2) Turku-Aland Islands- Stockholm. Also buses which operate as train substitutes.

FRANCE Irish Ferries ships LeHavre-Rosslare, Cherbourg- Rosslare, and (late June to late August) LeHavre-Cork. (Port taxes are extra, payable in French francs.)

Also, the Digne-Nice (and v.v.) rail trip.

GERMANY Free sightseeing cruises on: (1) Rhine (between Cologne and Mainz), and (2) Mosel (between Koblenz and Cochem). Eurail Youthpass holders must pay an extra charge on Express-steamers. Everyone must pay an extra charge on hydrofoils.

Three ferry crossings: Puttgarden to Rodby Faerge (Denmark), Warnemunde-Gedser (Denmark), and Sassnitz-Trelleborg (Sweden).

Two free bus rides: "Romantic Road" (Frankfurt-Munich and vice versa) and "Castle Road" (Mannheim-Nuremberg and vice versa). Also other bus lines of Regionale Omnibus Verkehrsgesellschaften der Deutschen Bundesbahn.

Reduction of 50% on (1) Ferries from Lubeck-Travemunde to Trelleborg (Sweden), (2) Cruises on Lake Constance, and (3) Steamer day trips Passau-Linz (and v.v.). Reduction of 25% on the Garnish-Zugspitze (Schneefernerhaus) mountain railroad and on some cable cars in the summit area.

Reduced fares on the Freiburg (Breisgau)-Schauinsland mountain railroad.

26

GREECE The ferry crossing from Patras to Brindisi (see note under "Italy" on page 217.)
     A 30% reduction is allowed on Adriatica di Navagazione Line for ships Piraeus-Venice (and v.v.) and Piraeus-Alexandria (and v.v.).

ITALY The ferry crossing from Brindisi to Patras (see notes under "Italy" on page 217).
     A 30% reduction on Adriatica di Navagazione's cruises Venice-Piraeus (and v.v.) and Venice-Alexandria (and v.v).

WARNING ! SEE PAGE 217

Don't be diverted at the Patras or Brindisi railstations from Hellenic Mediterranean Line or Adriatica di Navagazione Line (the only ferries that honor Eurailpass) to other ships that charge large fees after deceiving passengers into believing their ships accept Eurailpass, extorting the charges when it is too late for passengers to leave their ferry and go to the other docks. The proper lines charge pass holders $11 (U.S.) between June 10 and September 30. Reservations ($3 each) are advisable when using Eurailpass.

*   *   *

IRELAND Irish Ferries ships Rosslare-LeHavre, Rosslare-Cherbourg and (late June to late August) Cork-Le Havre. Port taxes are extra, payable in Irish pounds. Another bonus is travel on all (except to and from Northern Ireland) Expressway buses operated by Irish Railroads, a system that connects major Irish cities.

NORWAY A 30% reduction on the boat trip between Kristiansand and Hirtshals (Denmark) on Color Line steamships.

SWEDEN These 5 boat trips: (1) Stockholm-Helsinki, (2) Stockholm- Aland Islands-Turku, (3) Helsingborg-Helsingor (Denmark), (4) Goteborg-Frederikshavn (Denmark), and (5)Trelleborg-Sassnitz (Germany).
     A 50% reduction (25% for Eurail Youthpass) on the Flyvebadene Company hydrofoil Malmo-Copenhagen, and 50% reduction on the Trelleborg ferry to Lubeck-Travemunde (Germany).

SWITZERLAND Boats on the lakes of Biel, Brienz, Geneva, Luzern, Murten, Neuchatel, Thun and Zurich. Boats on the Rhine (Schaffhausen- Kreuzlingen) and on the Aare (Biel/Bienne-Solothurn). A 50% reduction on Lake Constance boats Romanshorn-Friedrichshafen and Rorschach-Lindau.

YOUTH INTERNATIONAL EDUCATIONAL EXCHANGE CARD

Persons under 26 years old, whether students or not, can obtain substantial discounts worldwide for hotels, transportation, museums and restaurants (as well as transatlantic airfares) with a YIEE Card.

Send U.S.-$7 (which includes postage and handling), date of birth, a passport-size photo, the country of your citizenship, and an envelope with your address to: Campus Holidays, Dept. E-92, 242 Bellevue Ave., Upper Montclair, NJ 07043. Be sure to request a copy of the free brochure "Discounts for Youth Travel".

Housing including full English breakfast at approximately $35 (U.S.) per night in resident halls at British universities (all convenient to railstations) and at $18 per night in youth hostels throughout Britain and Ireland is available from Campus Holidays, address above. Telephone: (201) 744-8724 or toll-free (800) 526-2915. Lodging is generally available July through September. Some universities provide lodging also during Christmas-New Year's Day and the Easter/Spring break (year-round in London).

A directory listing all cooperating campuses along with directions for reaching each campus from the respective railstation is included with the vouchers.

RAIL EUROP SENIOR

Sold to persons 60 and over who prove they are *permanent residents of one of the participating countries*. Valid for one year.

Offers discount of 50% for first or second-class tickets on the railways of Belgium, France, Germany, Great Britain, Greece, Holland, Irish Republic, Luxembourg, Portugal, Spain and Switzerland. Discount of 30% on the railways of Austria, Denmark, Finland, Hungary, Italy, Norway, Sweden and Yugoslavia.

Sold at main railstations of the 20 issuing countries. The 1992 price in France is 55 francs.

Purchasers must first buy from one of the participating countries its national senior citizen discount card. In France, for example, the Carte Vermeil which costs 165 francs in 1992.

Use of Rail Europ Senior is limited by each of the participating countries. For example, in France a traveler using Rail Europ Senior cannot start a train ride between Noon Friday and noon Saturday, or between noon Sunday and noon Monday, or on certain holidays, or during various periods of heavy traffic.

The limitations are different in each of the participating countries.

INTER-RAIL CARD

Unlimited second-class train travel for one month. (Example: January 14 to February 13.) Can be purchased only in Europe and Morocco. Sold only to persons under 26 years old who prove they have resided at least 6 months in the issuing country. The bearer can travel half-fare in the issuing country and free on the railways of the other 20 countries.

The validity period begins on the first day the card is used, and that day must be within 2 months after the card is purchased. The card also allows discounts on several ship services (North Sea, Irish Sea, English Channel, Spain-Morocco, France-Corsica, Italy-Sardinia), and also on some Swiss private railways.

Must be paid for in the currency of the country that issues it. The 1992 price in France is 1,793 francs. Can be purchased for any number of consecutive months.

Sold at most railstations in Austria, Belgium, Bulgaria, Denmark, Finland, France, Germany, Great Britain, Greece, Holland, Hungary, Ireland, Italy, Luxembourg, Morocco, Norway, Poland, Portugal, Romania, Spain, Sweden, Switzerland, Yugoslavia and the European area of Turkey.

EUROTRAIN

Discounts up to 40 % on train and ship tickets to over 2,000 destinations in all of eastern and western Europe (22 countries), Turkey and Morocco for anyone under 26 years old on the first day of travel, regardless of residence. A ticket is valid for 2 months and allows as many stopovers as desired.

Available from Eurotrain, Dept. E-92, 52 Grosvenor Gardens, London SW1W 0AG.

STUDENT TRAVEL DISCOUNTS WITH
INTERNATIONAL STUDENT IDENTITY CARD

This Card is a passport to low-cost travel for students over the age of 12. Bearers of the Card are entitled to discounts on rail, air, bus and ferry travel, museums, theaters, cinemas and other places of interest in approximately 60 countries. More than a million are issued every year. Those issued in the U.S.A. carry basic accident/sickness insurance which includes emergency evacuation insurance coverage up to $10,000 (U.S.) and features a 24-hour toll-free Traveler's Assistance hotline. The toll-free number helps students replace lost traveler's checks or passports, or locate an English-speaking doctor or lawyer.

There is no maximum age limit for the Card itself. However, some transportation companies (airlines, steamships, etc.) and other vendors have their own age restriction.

Upon buying the Card, students receive with it a brochure listing worldwide discounts and benefits. Even if a student discount is not posted, holders of the Card should always ask about a discount before paying the full price.

Developed and regulated by the International Student Travel Confederation, the Card carries the owner's full name, birthdate, citizenship, school name and photo. In the U.S.A., it is available through Council Travel and hundreds of college/university campuses authorized by the Council on International Educational Exchange: CIEE,Dept. E-92, 205 E. 42nd St., New York, NY 10017. For an application and the location of an issuing office near you, call (800) 438-2643 from 09:00 to 20:00 EST.

The 1992 Card is valid from September 1, 1991 through December 31, 1992 and is available for $14(U.S.) Applications must also include a passport-size photo (with name printed on back), proof of current student status (copy of transcript, letter from registrar, or copy of bill showing payment of enrollment fees), and a note indicating birthdate, citizenship and the U.S. address to which the card should be mailed. For insurance purposes, applicants must provide the name, address and phone number of a beneficiary.

A free catalog describing other products and services of CIEE is available on request by phoning (212) 661-1414, extension 1109.

Chapter 3

HOW TO PLAN A RAIL INTINERARY

There are 3 dimensions to every train tour: the number of days one can allot, interesting destinations and scenic routes.

Whenever time and budget permit, the minimum trip to Europe should be 23 days. That includes the day you fly away and the day you fly back. Out of the 21 remaining days, you can figure that what is left of your first day in Europe (after going from the airport to your hotel) is good for little more than recovering from the combination whammy of travel fatigue and time change. Very few people are immune to the temporary disablement of jet lag, and most travelers are well advised to go to bed and postpone any appreciable activity until the second day in Europe. That leaves only 20 active days for sightseeing, and it's difficult to really see even a fraction of Europe in that time.

We recommend staying a minimum of 2 or 3 nights in most cities you visit, with only occasional one-nighters mixed in the itinerary. Even the sturdiest develop a psychosis when they spend too many consecutive nights each in a different hotel room. Besides, if you travel mostly by day as we suggest in order to see the countryside and have some opportunity to visit with fellow passengers, you will arrive in a city late in the day. If you leave there the next morning, you certainly are not going to see much in that city.

On a 2-night basis, you can cover 10-11 different cities during your 21 full days in Europe. Reducing a trip to 14 days means reducing the number of cities where you stop to 5 or 6. If 14 days is your limit, the 15-day Eurailpass and some fast footwork will still let you have a happy tour and cover a great deal of Europe.

After deciding on the length of time one has to tour, the next step in itinerary planning is to pick the places to be visited, and most people have several cities in mind, usually more than time, energy and distance will allow.

The common-sense approach is to consult a map and visualize from it what is practical and what is impractical in putting together a list of places to see. Part of this narrowing-down process depends of course on what interests you the most.

Every hamlet in Europe has some art, but if it's the greatest masterpieces you want to see, you go to cities such as Paris and Florence, not to Avignon or Oslo. If your interest is Alpine scenery, you are going to concentrate on Bern and Salzburg, not on Barcelona or Copenhagen.

Knowing the travel time between each point on your itinerary is essential unless you are indifferent to 15-hour journeys that bring you into a destination after Midnight. The timetables in this book give you that information on more than 9,000 different rail trips.

At this point, you have determined how many days you will be in Europe, where you want to go, and where you can go in that time. You should now consider the combination of using special trains along with the most rewarding routes.

For example, the journey from Paris to Marseille can be made on any one of a dozen ordinary trains instead of riding on a high-speed TGV. A traveler has the same choice on many railway routes all over the world, between riding a commonplace, slow train or having an encounter with extraordinary rail travel.

RESERVATIONS — HOTEL AND TRAIN

Once you have composed the elements of days, cities, trains and routes, you are ready to consider whether you want to reserve hotels in advance.

When traveling to places we haven't been either before or recently, we rely on recommendations by friends who enjoyed particular hotels recently and whose tastes are similar to ours. The "recently" qualification is important, because a hotel's quality changes from time to time. We do not recommend hotels or restaurants. Management of both change (and quality along with it) between our annually-revised editions. It is always best to consult a competent travel agent who has current input from clients recently returning.

As in most other things, there is a great deal of luck connected with traveling. We prefer to maximize the odds in favor of our comfort and security when we travel and, as most travel writers urge readers to do, we reserve hotel space well in advance. We also reserve train seats whenever we want to be on a particular train on a certain date.

The objection to such reservations has a great deal of merit. It is that you cannot be a footloose, carefree vagabond, lingering where unexpected attractions are discovered and making impetuous detours as the spirit moves one or abruptly departing sooner than you had planned to do when someplace fails to come up to expectations.

The sturdier one is, physically and psychologically, the stronger that argument is. There is no question that for those of us forced by the circumstances of daily life to lead ordered routines, there are few lawful activities that offer as great an opportunity to achieve freedom from a structured existence as does traveling by train.

While not quite infinite, the random choices one can make spontaneously are considerable. The feature that many people find irresistible about European trains is how easily one can decide an hour after starting a ride to one destination to leave that train and head elsewhere. Depending on how strongly this motive moves you, how fundamentally lucky you are in most matters and what you are willing and able to endure, advance hotel reservations may not be important for you.

On the other hand, if you ever have played an entire night of poker without holding one winning hand, or if you arrive in Copenhagen on the opening day of a World Bank Conference (no room within 20 miles) and your next stop was Paris where the International Motor Salon opened on the day of your arrival and the most popular horse race on the Continent was being run the next day (no room within 30 miles), and your next stop was Dijon where the first 2 hotels you phoned ahead to were sold-out even though nothing special was happening that October week in Dijon, you might want to weigh the whole proposition.

From May through early October, European and non-European tourists pack all classes of hotels in leading European cities. Trade shows and business conventions pick up the slack instantly in September, October, March and April. A hotel in Bordeaux (not Paris or Rome, mind you) wrote us on July 13 that it was booked for the 2 nights we had requested: October 2 and 3 !

If you travel Europe without advance room reservations from March through October, it is wise to arrive in your destination city early in the day. Rooms available because of no-shows or last-minute cancellations frequently are taken before mid-afternoon.

Upon arriving without a hotel reservation, go at once to the tourist accommodations desk in the train station. For a fee of $1 to $2.00, one of its employees will phone hotels and do his or her best to find you a room that comes close to your specifications. In certain cities (Amsterdam, Bergen, Brussels, etc.), this convenient service is not offered at the station but can be found at the city tourist office, sometimes only across from the railstation, sometimes quite a distance from it.

In the peak Summer touring months you will find long lines and if, as is usually the case, your stay is brief, you will have to devote previous sightseeing time to obtaining a room.

When traveling in groups of 2 or more, this ploy is effective: one person remains at the station guarding the luggage while the other canvasses the area near the station to find a room. Many non-Europeans are unaware that stations even in the smallest cities have waiting rooms with comfortable, upholstered chairs. If you follow this system, be sure to use the shelter of these waiting rooms. All over Europe, you will find many hotels within a radius of 2 or 3 blocks from the railstation.

A third system has been used successfully by many — to stay in the suburbs and not even attempt to find a hotel room in major cities, provided the suburb is linked by train with the city you want to tour.

Pick a town of moderate size about 30-45 minutes train travel time away from a major metropolis.

TRAIN RESERVATIONS

Your second consideration is whether to reserve train seats, for which the charge ranges from $2 (U.S.) to $8 per ride — when reservation is made in Europe.

Reservations for seats on Europe's greatest trains can be made as much as 2 months in advance, and many Europeans grab spaces on them soon after they become reservable. Casual tourists discover a few days before they want to travel on a special train that it is completely sold-out.

Reservations are mandatory on many of the best and fastest European trains. That is why we have been recommending since 1971 reserving seats even before you arrive in the countries you plan to travel.

Most European trains do not require reservation of seats — with the exception of the French TGVs, some of the EuroCity trains that go from one country to another, and overnight trains. Such trains accept reservations 2 months in advance of travel date.

If your Eurailpass, one of the French national passes or tickets for French trains are purchased from one of the North American offices of Rail Europe (addresses listed on page 23 under "France"), those offices will make reservations for train trips in France and in most (but *not* all) other European countries — both on trains which *require* reservation and also on those trains that merely *offer* reserved seats.

Rail Europe charges $8 (U.S.) per person, per train (including cable fee). They send their reservations to customers by Express Mail, for which there is a handling charge.

The North American offices of Italian State Railways (page 24) make reservations for train trips in Italy and in most (but *not* all) other European countries when only your Eurailpass is purchased from them — both on trains which *require* reservation and also on those trains that merely *offer* reserved seats. They do **not** make reservations in connection with Italian passes or ordinary train tickets.

Their fee is $3 (U.S.) per person, per train, plus a cable fee — $10 (U.S.) for the first train requested, and $5 (U.S.) for each additional train. The maximum number of reservations they will make is 3 trains per pass. However, 2 people traveling together can*not* reserve 6 trains.

Even though the holder of a Eurailpass who makes a seat reservation after arriving in Europe is exempt from the reservation fee, this does not apply to Italy's special "Pendolino" trains for which a large supplement ($6 to $28) is charged. Those supplements, however, include both a reservation fee and a meal.

If your Eurailpass, one of the German national passes or tickets for German trains are purchased from one of the North American offices of GermanRail (U.S.A. and Canadian offices listed on page 23), their offices will reserve up to 3 trains that *require* reservation — at a charge of $10 (U.S.) per person, per train ($5 plus $5 cable fee). Exceptions to this limit are possible "according to the size of the party and time of travel."

The North American offices of all European railways are listed on pages 22–25.

It is always advisable to have the office that issues you the Eurailpass cable your reservation requests to Europe. This can result in your obtaining seats which otherwise might have been sold to others if your request had been sent by mail.

If, on the other hand, you wait to reserve train space at each departure station, keep in mind that at most European stations you must get in one line for a ticket and in a different line for a seat reservation. If you have a Eurailpass (described in Chapter 2), you eliminate having to wait in the ticket line, often a long wait.

As a matter of fact, you face long waits in 5 different lines — and part of the trick of making the most of your limited time is to avoid standing in any, and hopefully all, of these lines: information, ticket purchase, seat reservation, hotel accommodation and baggage checkroom.

We will cover how you can avoid needing information in the "Timetables" section of Chapter 4. If you use Eurailpass (Chapter 2), you never need to buy a ticket and therefore completely omit the time wasted standing in the ticket purchase line. The solution to the hotel accommodation line, of course, is to make those reservations before you leave home. The baggage check-room problem is discussed in Chapter 5.

There is a way to reduce the amount of time spent in either the ticket or seat reservation lines. These lines are far shorter Monday-Thursday than they are on the weekend (when the natives are traditionally restless), and in mid-morning, rather than during the lunch hours or at early evening in the height of the commuter rush hours. During the mid-June to mid-September tourist season, it is often advantageous to have the hotel concierge or the one who runs your pensione get your reservation for you from someone they know at the station.

If you don't make reservations before leaving home and wait to do so until you arrive in the country you are going to tour, be sure to do it as much in advance as possible, preferably upon your arrival in the departure city. Requirements for reservations vary from country to country and, within a country, from city to city. In Italy, for example, reservations cannot be made less than 2 hours before a departure in some cities. Milan requires 3 hours notice. Rome requires 5 hours notice.

Say your trip is New York to Paris, then train to Geneva and train from Geneva to Rome. Make the Paris-Geneva reservation your first day in Paris, and make the Geneva-Rome reservation a few minutes after you arrive at the Geneva depot.

It has become increasingly difficult since 1989 to make train reservations before arriving in Europe. We concluded in 1991 that obtaining reservations after arriving in Europe is usually preferable — and that obtaining at one time all the reservations for your complete itinerary at a travel agency in the first European city you visit is far easier than making reservations one-by-one as you journey.

The travel agency can sell you all of your tickets and/or make all of both your seat and sleeper reservations.

This advice does not mean you must have seat reservations. They are required only on a few trains. However, anyone traveling on main routes in peak tourist months without reserved space will probably make the trip standing in the aisle and being brushed-up against approximately every 30 seconds by passengers ambling up and down the corridor. Keep in mind that Europeans can, and do, reserve train seats 2 months in advance.

We rode a very ordinary train from Bordeaux to Tours on an October Monday morning. It was completely sold-out.

If, as we urge you to do in Chapter 5, you eat your train meals in your compartment rather than in the restaurant-car, there is something else you can and should do when you make your seat reservation: *specify the window seat.*

On most European trains these are the only seats that have a fold-out table. Moreover, you see the sights better from a window seat. In some compartments, the seats next to the sliding door also have a fold-out table.

Another variation in seat reservations is that on nearly all European trains you can reserve seats in a compartment in which smoking is either prohibited or permitted. Depending on what your preference is, this can make a great deal of difference in enjoying your trip.

And still another reservation to keep in mind is specifying on which side of the train you want to be seated. Often there is a decided sightseeing advantage on one side and a corresponding disadvantage on the alternate side.

Obviously, if you are traveling along the Riviera, the view of the Mediterranean is possible only on the left side if you are traveling West, and on the right side if your route is going East.

After logic tells you which side of the train offers the best view, the first step is to inquire while making your seat reservation if there is seating on that side. If so, ask for seats accordingly.

Reservation clerks in many European cities speak little or no English. It will save you much time and insure against getting an incorrect reservation if you hand the clerk a note indicating your destination, departure time and day of departure. But be sure to follow the European custom of showing the day of the month first, followed by the number of the month. In Europe, July 8 is 8/7.

If you wanted to take a train to Milan, leaving at 1:50 PM on July 8, your note would read "Milan — 13:50 — 8/7".

Finally, here are 7 great tips to keep in mind. Having made a seat reservation, when you leave your compartment to go to the W.C., dining car or merely to stretch, leave some object on your seat — newspaper, hat, something to inhibit seat-grabbers from settling down in your space during your absence. While it is true that the conductor will aid you in removing an interloper, finding the conductor, explaining the problem and using his intervention is somewhat more bothersome than simply preventing the event.

Do not waste time trying to make a seat reservation for a train trip within Belgium, Holland, Luxembourg or Switzerland. Those countries sell seat reservations only for rides going from them into another country. However, finding a seat on trains of those countries is not a problem except on peak travel days.

Next, on a business day even though the reservation clerk claims all seats on a certain train are taken, you can nevertheless occasionally hop aboard and find an empty seat. This is due to the custom of many European business men, when undecided as to which train they are taking or on which day they are making a trip, to make several advance reservations so as to cover all bases — and then forfeit their reservation fee on all trains other than the one they finally do take. This practice accounts for some seats being marked "reserved" which are not used.

If traveling without seat reservations, be careful you do not take a reserved seat while all the unreserved ones are being occupied.

Check the seat chart outside each compartment before you sit down. If the rightful owners claim your seat later, you may have to stand during the entire ride.

If the required advance time for making a seat reservation has run out, seek the conductor and, in your most charming manner, tell him what your destination is and ask him to help you find a seat. As a class, conductors are remarkably courteous and cooperative and many we have observed welcome the opportunity to use their authority constructively.

Never, never discard a train ticket until after your trip has been completed and you have left the arrival station. You will frequently ride a train for hours without being asked to show a ticket or pass. Then, after you get off the train you discover you are required to show your ticket or pass at the exit of the arrival station. If you have thrown yours away, you will end up having to buy a second one. Best bet is to always hold onto your ticket, whether or not a conductor checks it.

PREPARATION FOR AUTUMN TOURING

One thing that is nearly always overlooked in itinerary planning is to prepare in advance for one very important contingency connected with traveling off- season. If you travel Europe anytime after early September — and Fall is outstanding for touring Europe — you'll find that English-language city sightseeing tours are discontinued as the volume of American tourists decline, particularly in places such as Avignon, Verona, Rouen, Tours, etc.

Autumn travelers can solve that problem by taking advantage of the fact that nearly every city in Europe, even a hamlet such as Honfleur, has a tourist office which will give you a comprehensive folder that includes a fine city map, an interesting description of principal things to see and often a suggested 2 or 3-hour walking tour that allows a visitor to find on his own the worthwhile historic sites, museums, churches, palaces and all the other local highspots he would have been shown on the discontinued motorcoach sightseeing tour.

The only hitch is that by early September many city tourist offices run out of the current year's supply of these useful folders. To insure against the disappointment of arriving somewhere and finding that neither a city tour nor printed material to use in lieu of a tour is available, there is a precaution you can take.

In the early part of the year, write to the cities you plan to visit and ask them while their supply is still good to mail you a copy of all literature and tourist maps they have, and specify you want the English-language (or whatever your preference) version, since this material is usually printed in several languages.

Then, if you arrive in a town that Fall after the last bus tour of the season, you're all set to see the sights without a guide, and at your own leisurely pace.

Simply address your request to "Tourist Office". You'll be surprised how much this easy preparation will add to your travel enjoyment.

Birnbaum Travel Guides

Any one of the 36 titles in this outstanding series of skillfully edited travel books makes a perfect combination with Eurail® Guide, providing tons of crisply written, current information about hotels, restaurants, shopping and a myriad of vacation activities — physical and cerebral — such as golf, tennis, skiing, snorkeling, the most memorable museums and monuments to visit, as well as detailed driving routes to exiting sites and sights.

Each of these guides is completely revised and updated annually, and they offer more sources for airline and accommodations discounts than any other travel guides.

Travel Europe

This monthly newsletter (published since 1983) is a boon to anyone needing information about getting to Europe (special fares) and what to see and do there: special events, new tour packages, tips on river cruising, shopping, restaurants, money exchange and hotels.

The 1992 subscription price is $20 for one year, $35 for 2 years. The publisher has promised us subscribers will get a complete refund if not satisfied with the first issue received. Write to: Travel Europe, P.O. Box 9918-E, Virginia Beach, VA. 23450, USA.

Chapter 4

DON'T MISS THE TRAIN !

MULTI-STATION CITIES

Determine beforehand whether your departure or transfer city has more than one railstation. If so, next make sure that the train on which you are going to continue your trip will depart from the same station at which you are arriving. The easiest way to do that is to consult Thomas Cook European Timetable. If you are making a transfer, then be certain that there is adequate time to get from one station to the other in the following European cities with more than one railstation:

Antwerp	Dublin	Lodz	Prague
Athens	Dunkerque	London	Ramsgate
Barcelona	Essen	Lyon	Rome
Basel	Exeter	Madrid	Rotterdam
Belfast	Folkestone	Malmo	San Sebastian
Belgrade	Geneva	Manchester	Seville
Berlin	Genoa	Marseille	Southampton
Bilbao	Glasgow	Milan	Stockholm
Boulogne	Halsingborg	Moscow	Tilbury
Brussels	Hamburg	Munich	Tours
Bucharest	Harwich	Naples	Turin
Budapest	Hendaye	Newhaven	Venice
Calais	Irun	Oporto	Vienna
Casablanca	Le Havre	Orleans	Warsaw
Cologne	Leningrad	Oslo	Weymouth
Como	Liege	Paris	Wiesbaden
Copenhagen	Lisbon	Portsmouth	Zurich
Dover	Liverpool		

As can be seen from the preceding list, there are 70 European cities which have 2 or more railroad stations. Immediately upon arriving in any of these multi-station cities, find out from which station your train departs for your next destination. Do not rely on getting that information an hour or so before your departure from someone such as your hotel clerk or taxi or bus driver.

TIMETABLES

The venerable Thomas Cook European Timetable has been published (under 7 other titles) since 1873 (except from 1939 to 1945). Its younger sibling, the Overseas Timetable, was started in 1981, prompted by the interest in train travel outside Europe that had been generated 7 years earlier by Eurail® Guide. Both timetables are published in England.

The European Timetable (covering Britain and the Continent) is supposed to be published the first day of each month but sometimes misses the mark. The Overseas Timetable, covering the rest of the world, is issued every other month, starting with January.

In addition to train, boat and bus schedules, these publications also provide information on types of food service and sleeping accommodations offered. Their extensive array of symbols for such services and other information are translated into ordinary language at the start of each edition, under "Explanation of Signs".

Summer European train schedules appear in the June, July, August and September "European Timetable" issues. The latter contains an advance Winter supplement. Similarly, the February through May issues contain an advance Summer service supplement.

Both publications can be obtained in North America from Dept. "E", Forsyth Travel Library, P.O. Box 2975, Shawnee Mission, KS. 66201, or by telephoning Dept. "E" at 800-FORSYTH, Monday-Saturday, 09:00-16:30 Central Time, and charging the purchase against a Visa or Master Charge credit card.

Both the "European Timetable" and "Overseas Timetable" each costs $23.95 (U.S.), plus $4 for shipping. Cook's "Rail Map of Europe" costs $9.95 (U.S.) plus $2 for shipping.

A combined purchase of the "European Timetable" and the "Rail Map of Europe" costs $31.95 plus $4.50 for priority shipping.

A "World Rail Map" costs $9.95, plus $2 for shipping.

FTL has an extensive list of travel publications, maps of all countries and hundreds of cities, atlases, etc.

Because many countries do *not* offer their own timetables, or run short of them, Cooks is valuable for carrying along on a trip as well as for studying at home while planning an itinerary. Numerous readers tell us that having a copy while touring allows them to make impromptu changes in travel plans on the spur of the moment.

As Cooks says in each edition, the services shown are subject to alteration, and **travelers should re-check departure times upon arriving in each station**. Our standard train travel procedure upon arriving anywhere is to first provide for shelter, when we have not made advance reservations. The second item we dispose of is deciding what train we are taking to the next city on our itinerary. Third, we make our seat reservation then and there for that departure. Having done this, we are now carefree for the balance of our time in that city.

Cook publications are incomplete condensations of much more extensive national timetables that all major countries publish. Inexpensive and complete national timetables can be purchased at railstations in many countries.

Cooks depends on sometimes unreliable individuals for timetable changes in underdeveloped countries whose governments are unmoved by Cook's pleas for official information.

The "Eurail Timetable-Horaire Eurail-Eurail Fahrplan" contains most connections betwen important cities in Western Europe. It is sold at major European railstations.

There are 3 other timetables, specialized and far more condensed than Cooks, that you may find useful. All are distributed free. One, offered by French National Railroads (see North American addresses on page 22), is the very useful 24-page mini-folder called "Les Trains d'Affaires" ("businessman's trains", not as romantic as it sounds!). Containing May-September schedules, it has timetables for many trains that connect French cities both with each other and with cities in other countries.

The second is a 672-page Intercity timetable that is issued by Germany's Deutsche Bundesbahn / Reichsbahn.

The third publication is the 156-page "Through Europe By Train", valid for 12 months from the end of every May. It has timetables for rail trips originating from 108 major cities to various destinations. It is available in the United States from: Eurailpass, P.O. Box 10383, Stamford, CT. 06904-2383.

In Canada, from: Eurailpass Distribution Centre, C.P. 300, Succursale R., Montreal H2S 3K9.

SUMMER AND WINTER SCHEDULES

In most European countries, a Summer timetable goes into effect on the last Sunday of May or the first Sunday of June, remaining in effect until and including the last Saturday in September.

Winter schedules usually start on the Sunday following the last Saturday of September and run until and including the Saturday preceding the last Sunday of May of the following year.

British timetables differ from the Continental pattern. Summer timetables for British rail service begin on the first Monday of May. Changes occur on various dates, first in October and then again in January.

Unless designated otherwise, the departure and arrival times given in this book are for the Summer tourist season and apply to trips that will be made from late May to late September. In most cases, these schedules change only slightly during September-May.

CAR-SLEEPER EXPRESS SERVICE

Europe's "Car-Sleeper Express Service" becomes more popular every year. You can sleep in a couchette or sleeping compartment on the same train that carries your auto...or you can ship your car ahead on an "Auto Express" while you ride on another train, and find your car waiting for you at your destination.

Started by FrenchRail in 1957, this service is now offered as well by Austria, Belgium, Britain, Holland, Italy, Spain and West Germany.

It links cities in those countries and also in Portugal, Switzerland and Yugoslavia. In recent years, it annually has moved 500,000 people and more than 160,000 cars.

TRAIN-SPLITTING

How can one fail to admire the superhuman efficiency of Europe's vast international rail systems? Thousands of trains daily transport millions upon millions of people and yet achieve a dependability factor that is nearly perfect. An important part of this remarkable capacity is the technique of avoiding unnecessary duplication of personnel and equipment by the methods of switching cars and timing transfers so that when one must take 2 or more trains to get from one place to another the time between each segment of a trip is very brief.

The foreign tourist is inclined to wrongly regard these positive factors as an undue bother when, actually, only a minimum effort and preparation is required in order to have the advantage of travel speed and flexibiity along with reasonable ticket prices.

This is how simple it is to prevent a mix-up. Before you leave the station to go to the track, find out if the car in which you will be starting your journey is going all the way to your destination without being switched to some other train or if you must transfer from this train to another train en route to your destination.

If your car is to be switched to another train, find out the name of the city where the switching will occur, the time it will take place, and the name of the stop just prior to the switching point.

Next, you're at the correct track, your train is ready to board, and your last step is to get onto the correct car. Where a train originally consists of cars that are eventually going to different destinations, each car is clearly marked with the name of the city where it originated and the name of the city where it will terminate. Frequently, the sign will also designate, as the example below does, some of the cities en route where stops will be made.

VENEZIA

Bologna — Firenze

ROMA

This sign shows that the car began in Venice, stops at Bologna and Florence, and terminates in Rome. Next to the steps leading up into a car, either the numeral "1" or "2" appears, designating first-class or second-class seats. You may find an entirely first-class car coupled to an entirely second-class car, both cars marked with the same origin-destination sign. Or, a single car may be marked "1" at one end and "2" at the other end, indicating that part of this car is first-class and part is second-class.

A car change can occur while you are several cars away from your seat (and from your baggage, since it usually stays either in your compartment or at the end of your car). You may have so little time to get back to your car that you end up going one direction while your suitcases are heading, without you, for the place you had intended to go.

If you have determined in advance when and where your car is being switched and have also boarded the correct car, you are prepared for the change by being in your car when the change occurs. The following story illustrates the hazard we want you to avoid and may induce you to follow some practical recommendations we offer at the end of the vignette.

An officer in the U.S. Army Transportation Corps, who is an expert on both military and personal travel, Lt. Col. Will B. Allanson, wrote us about an experience he suffered when he was a novice: "I and my family had just arrived in France, for our first time in Europe, in the Summer of 1964. Within 5 days of our arrival, my boss asked me to make a busines trip to an army installation in Germany. Thinking it would be nice to let the family catch an initial glimpse of Europe too, I bought tickets for them and off we went from Paris on a rapide headed for Frankfurt.

"At about 11:30, the train stopped at the little town of Bar-le-Duc. My children were beginning to get hungry, and there was no dining-car. Leaning out of the window of our car, the last car on the train, I spied a sandwich hawker up near the locomotive. I jogged up the track to him, bought some sandwiches and, not being certain how long the train would remain stopped, I boarded it near the locomotive. As I started walking through the train, heading back toward my car, the train started up.

"I got about as far as what had been the middle of the train . . . and there was no more train ! It had been split.

"All I knew was that I was heading off towards an unknown direction, without my family, at approximately 80 mph.

"I had done just about everything wrong there was to do. First, of course, was leaving my car. Next, I had most of the travel money on me, leaving my wife practically penniless. But she had the trump she had my ticket and my passport.

"Well, my wife was on her way to Frankfurt, heading Northeast, while I was heading due East to Nancy. I borrowed a timetable from the conductor and figured out that I could get off in Nancy and from there take another train to Metz. In Metz, I could then catch a train that would be following my wife's train by 2 hours.

"I did this and, in Metz, found my wife and kiddies (who had gotten off their train to wait for me) practically in a pool of tears. Other passengers in my wife's compartment were Frenchmen who, alarmed at my not returning, had guessed what had happened and urged my wife to get off in Metz and wait for me there."

This experience taught Col. Allanson these rules: Don't stray from your car while stopped in a station. When 2 or more people are traveling together, each should carry his own money, his own passport and his own ticket or train pass. On our travels, we divvy-up not only U.S. one-dollar bills and the currency of the country we're in, but we also carry separate traveler's checks in each name.

TRAIN-CHANGING

Frequently you will find that while you cannot take a train directly to some point, it is quite easy to get there by using a series of 2 or more trains. And in many cases the connections are very convenient, so that you change from one train to another with only a short waiting period at the transfer station. For example, there is no direct train from Zurich to popular Locarno, but the Zurich-Milan train arrives in Bellinzona at 12:33, and a train for Locarno departs Bellinzona 3 minutes later, at 12:36.

The track for the Bellinzona-Locarno train is next to the track on which you arrive from Zurich, making this change effortless. Even if the Zurich- Milan train is running a few minutes late — and you will be amazed how rarely trains in Western Europe are even slightly off schedule — your walk from one train to another on this connection is about 10 feet, and they will hold a local train such as the Bellinzona-Locarno one for you to make a train change when the principal train is running late.

On the other hand, international trains from eastern countries (Turkey, Greece, Yugoslavia, etc.) usually arrive late due to delays at border-crossings.

The problem in train-chainging for which you should prepare, by being ready to step off the first train as soon as it pulls into the transfer station, is that if the transfer station is a large one you may find you are arriving on Track #2 and departing from Track #21, a considerable distance and invariably involving first descending into the underground walkway that connects all tracks, passing through it, and then climbing up the steps leading to your departure track. This transfer problem is compounded if your first train arrives late and the second train is an express train which cannot detain its scheduled departure time.

Normally, your first train will arrive on schedule, and you have more than enough time to make the change. However, it is best to inquire on board the first train from its conductor the number of the track on which you are arriving and the number of the track from which your departing train leaves and also to be ready at the exit door of your arriving train some minutes before it pulls into the transfer point.

The word for "track" in Europe is: Gleis (Austria, Germany and Switzerland), Spor (Holland and Belgium, which also uses Voie), Spor (Norway), Spart (Sweden), Quai (France), Binario (Italy), Anden (Spain), Voie (Luxembourg), and Perron (Denmark).

Most train stops in Europe are efficiently very brief, 2 or 3 minutes. This is one of the reasons you can go from place to place so rapidly on European trains. Where a stop is fairly generous, say 20 minutes or more, it is often because some car on your train is being swtiched to another train and possibly also to another track in that station.

Unwary passengers are apt to get out of the train at a stop and wander away, discovering too late that their train has left without them ! When we have the urge to stretch our legs, get some fresh air and look at the trackside activity, we never go more than a few feet away from the door of the train car. That way, if our car is being switched or the stop is merely a momentary one, we can jump back aboard.

Chapter 5

VALUABLE TRAIN TRAVEL TIPS

We have included in this chapter the many facts we wish we had known when we first traveled by train many years ago. They will make your journeys easier and happier.

PRECAUTIONS BEFORE LEAVING HOME

Make photocopies of your airline ticket, passport identification page, driver's license, and the credit cards you take with you. Leave one set of photocopies at home and take another set with you, in a separate place from the original documents.

Leave a list of the serial numbers of your traveler's checks at home. Take a copy of that list on your trip, but separate from the checks. As you cash each check, tally the ones that remain unredeemed.

Learn about the local laws and customs in the areas you plan to visit by consulting your library, a travel agent, airline or the tourist bureau of those countries.

Pack an extra set of eyeglasses. Keep it and any medicines you need (as well as a copy of prescriptions and generic names of those drugs) in your carry-on luggage. Leave medicines in their original labeled containers so as to make customs processing easier. If any medications contain narcotics, carry a letter from your physician attesting to your need to take them. Leave a copy of your medical and dental records with a relative or friend.

Put your name and address *inside* each piece of your luggage, and then lock them.

Leave a copy of your itinerary with a relative or friend should they need to contact you in case of an emergency.

Find out if your insurance policies cover you for theft, loss, accident and illness while you are in another country.

PREVENTING YOUR HOME FROM BEING BURGLARIZED

Don't have the post office hold your mail while you are away. *Don't* stop delivery of your newspaper. Both acts advertise your absence and invite burglary of your home. Instead, arrange for someone to collect your mail and newspaper once a day.

Leave the key to your home with someone who can inspect the interior daily to check on water leaks, escaping gas, and signs that someone has made an unauthorized entry. If you will be away one week, have your lawn cut the day before you leave. If your absence will be more than 7 days, arrange for the lawn to be cut at least every 14 days. An overgrown lawn signals burglars that the home is unoccupied.

Ask a neighbor to place one of his or her filled trash cans in front of your house on the day trash is picked-up and to have one car in your driveway or in front of your home.

Use 3 or more electrical timers to turn on lights in your home at various times from dusk to dawn.

Move valuables to a bank deposit box or to a friend's home: unnecessary credit cards, expensive jewelry, irreplaceable family objects.

DAY OR NIGHT

There are some advantages to traveling by night train. You can hop from one place to another without sacrificing daytime activities in either the departure city or the arrival city. Also, the holder of a Eurailpass (by going at night in a regular sitting compartment, not in an extra-fare couchette or sleeping compartment) can make a substantial contribution to a budget trip by dispensing with room rent.

On some trains the seats in the regular sitting compartments can be adjusted so that you can get your seat and the one facing you to either come together or nearly meet, and many who are fortunate enough to be in a compartment that is not full are able to stretch out, using the facing seat. This is the crafty technique for eliminating room rental at night that many students and other economy prone tourists have used successfully. However, if the seat opposite you has another passenger, both of you are going to spend the night sitting up.

The offsetting drawbacks to taking a night train, however, are considerable. The best way of meeting and conversing with Europeans and tourists from other parts of the world is to be on a train, but that opportunity is slim when you travel at night. And equally important, you miss the scenery en route.

Then, too, if you are in a generally excited state when you travel and don't sleep well on trains, that's another negative to weigh.

Train sleeping accommodations vary from one European country to another, but generally they consist of Couchette Compartments (berths) or Sleeping Car Compartments (beds).

A blanket and a pillow are provided for each berth in a couchette compartment. There is no way to tuck the blanket in. It just slides around during the night. You can stretch out, but you may not undress.

First-Class couchette is a berth in a compartment with 4 berths (2 rows of 2 berths each). The 1992 price for each berth is $14 (U.S.), plus a first-class ticket or train pass.

Most second-class couchettes are in a compartment with 6 berths (4 berths on a few trains). With either a first or second-class ticket or train pass, the 1992 price per berth is: $20 in a 4-berth compartment, $14 in a 6-berth compartment.

Sleeping car compartments are available in either a "small" or a "big" size. All have a power plug and a wash basin. The *small* compartments convert to one, 2 or 3 beds. The 1992 price Paris-Zurich for one-bed (small compartment) is a *first*-class ticket plus $100 (U.S.). For a big compartment: $140. Compartments with 2 and 3 beds require a *second*-class ticket plus $60 and $40 per person.

Sleeping compartment cars have a toilet at both ends of the car.

Neither Couchettes nor Compartments are included in the Eurailpass or any national train passes.

If you survive the vibrations, and you don't mind missing the scenery and camaraderie that goes with daytime travel, you can absolutely count on being awakened sometime between 2:00 AM and 5:00 AM by the voice of a stationmaster bellowing over the public address system at some stations where your train stops along the way.

EATING ON TRAINS

Food in train dining cars is expensive, and the choice is limited. In restaurant cars of de luxe trains, the lunch is a fixed menu, very good and very caloric. On ordinary trains, the restaurant car food is adequate quality . . . and also high-priced.

Here is a sampling of recent prices in U.S. dollars — for food only, *before tip or tax.* Lunch on the Amsterdam-Paris "Etoile du Nord" was $45 (crayfish, duck or lamb chop, potatoes Lyonnaise, vegetables, cheeses and rolls, pastry). Dinner Oslo-Bergen on "Bergen Express" was $35 (salad, salmon with boiled potatoes, beer). Dinner Paris- Lisbon on "Sud Express" was $30 (vegetable soup, wild turkey with rice, fava beans, flan and fruit, coffee).

Both budget travelers and many of those who can afford the meals served on trains buy their food at a market or delicatessen (ah, those great French charcuteries !) before they get on the train — ranging from a hunk of cheese and some bread to a really sensational assortment of salads, meats, pates, fruits and wine.

Before we made the 12-hour ride from Copenhagen to Amsterdam, we bought a dozen, delicious smorre-brod sandwiches a block from the Copenhagen station. The variety included shrimp, salmon, ham, chicken and beef, all garnished with tasty cucumbers, asparagus, tomatoes, etc. We ate some of them for lunch and the others for dinner that day. Total cost, 4 meals, 2 persons: $30(U.S.).

And we had the convenience of eating when we felt hungry rather than when we could get a table in the restaurant-car, where lunch and dinner for the 2 of us would have cost over $90.

On the trip from Dijon to Geneva, we feasted on 5 different salads and pates we bought for $14.00 in the supermarket at the big department store in Dijon where we shopped an hour before train time. On another trip, a charcuterie across from the station in Tours was the source for a delightful $13.00 assortment of meat, olives, salads, cheese, bread and custard that 2 of us had for lunch on the way to Rouen.

On many trains, you must reserve a seat in the restaurant car for the entire trip if you want lunch or dinner.

The meals are larger and heavier than we want, particularly at Noon, and the odor of cooked food for a whole trip is unpleasant to us. We much prefer on such 3-4 hour runs either to wait until we reach our destination and eat a late lunch (or dinner) after arriving there, or to bring our own food onto the train and eat when we are hungry and in our compartment.

If you find the features of "picnicking" attractive, you can ask your hotel or pensione to pack a lunch for you, or you can purchase food either at a store near the station, in a restaurant at the station, from a food market inside the station or, along the way, from vendors that push carts up and down the platforms at many station stops.

Not only is the latter the most inferior food, but our experience is that the train always moves out just as the vendor rolls his cart toward our window.

You will find restaurants and food stores located in many principal railstations. Food stores in the Copenhagen, Stuttgart, Vienna. Zurich and many other railstations offer meat, cheeses, salads, breads, pastries, etc. that are excellent.

Whatever your source of bring-along food, don't forget the note under "Reservations" (pages 30-35) to reserve the window-seat, with its fold-out table, that is convenient and comfortable for dining.

If you want train food, make sure before you start the trip that the train you are taking has light refreshments, buffet or a restaurant car. You can check this in the Eurail® Guide trip timetable footnotes and confirm it at the railstation.

BAGGAGE

Karl Baedeker wrote in 1891, in the 14th edition of his *Switzerland — Handbook For Travelers*: "The traveler will save both time and money by planning his tour carefully before leaving home. A superabundance of luggage infallibly increases the delays, annoyances and expenses of travel. To be provided with enough luggage, and no more, may be considered the second golden rule for the traveler."

The criticism we hear most often about rail travel in Europe concerns the problems of storing and handling suitcases. Don't count on being able to get a porter. Many small cities don't have them. Nearly all the large cities with porters have too few.

Some stations provide self-service carts, but the stations which do so don't have enough of them at peak times.

An effective procedure if you travel in pairs is for one of you to guard your luggage while the other hurries toward the station to find a cart and returns to the track with it.

When boarding a train, you want to avoid the difficulty of hauling your luggage down the narrow corridors of several cars. Before your train arrives, examine the train diagram on the platform.

The sequence of cars and the platform location for each car are shown for all long- distance trains. Then place yourself and your luggage at the correct site for boarding your car.

On some trains, there is a storage area for luggage at one or at both ends of the car. On most trains, you have to store your baggage on a rack above your seat.

The racks are very high. Lifting a 30-pound (or heavier) weight above one's head can be a physical strain for the elderly, those who have a physical disability or even for an average healthy person who weighs less than 140 pounds — which covers most women.

In some compartments the seat construction is such that a small suitcase can be stored under the seats.

For these reasons, it is much better to travel with 2 small, relatively light-weight suitcases per person than with one monstrous case. The small ones are easier to lift, and there's a better chance of being able to store them on the floor under the seat.

Some trains have a baggage car. Using it is always inconvenient, and although the charge is fairly small — about $6 (U.S.) per piece, with a limit of 66 pounds each — it is more expensive than having your cases with you in your own car or in your compartment. Also, unless you verify that your luggage is going on the same train you are riding, it may go on another train — possibly arriving a day or 2 days after you arrive.

If you want luggage to arrive at the destination prior to your arrival, you can arrange to send it in advance and it will be held in the "checked luggage" room at your destination. Usually, no charge is made for the first 2 or 3 days of storage there, after which a small daily fee must be paid.

When your bag is in the baggage car, you don't have access to its contents. Also, you may have to wait up to 30 minutes for your cases to be unloaded if they happen to be in the rear of the baggage car.

Waiting for cases to be unloaded, in turn, delays you in getting to the room reservation desk at the tourist accommodation office inside the depot — a delay that can cost you getting a decent room that night, since every minute counts in obtaining an available room during peak travel days. Waiting at the baggage car also delays you in getting into what is often a very long line for taxis.

We were riding on the elegant, crack "Settebello" (before it was removed from service). It was mandatory to have your luggage in its baggage car. Shortly before arriving at the Milan destination, we strolled down the length of the train, passing through the baggage car as we did so. In the baggage car, a passenger was paying the porter several dollars.

When the train finally reached Milan, and we were outside the baggage car with 60 other people, trying to get our luggage, we then understood the transaction we had observed earlier.

The suitcases of the tipping passenger had been placed in advance at the door of the baggage car so that his cases were the first to be unloaded. He had his suitcases a moment after the train stopped. It was 25 minutes later when the last suitcase had been unloaded.

In the interim, some other passengers who were trying to make an imminent flight at the Milan airport became so frantic to get their luggage that they had climbed onto the baggage car and began fighting with the baggage clerk.

While some trains equipped with baggage cars require you to store your luggage in them, on other trains it is optional. When that is the case, always keep your luggage with you and avoid using the baggage car.

Another luggage problem is storing suitcases at a railroad station, both necessary and convenient when you want to avoid being burdened either upon arriving, while you search for lodging, or when departing if, as often happens, you must give up your room several hours before your train leaves and you want to sightsee in that interval.

Very savvy travelers obtain a locker in the station the night before their departure so as to be sure of having the use of one the following morning.

Although there are baggage check-rooms at nearly all major railstations, using a check-room instead of a rental locker eats up precious time you could have used more pleasantly and productively because there frequently are long lines both when you leave your luggage and again when you are claiming it.

If you use check-rooms instead of rental lockers, be sure to leave yourself adequate time prior to your train's departure to retrieve your suitcases.

The most convenient and safest method of storing luggage is to place it in a 24-hour rental locker. Unfortunately, the lockers present their own set of problems. Several European stations we have checked-out have too few lockers.

Furthermore, rental lockers in European stations are usually in 2 sizes. If you are carrying both a small and large case, you may find several small lockers available but not be able to locate one large locker. Again, we urge you to carry small suitcases.

Another wise maneuver is to have small change on hand for each destination. Remember, the lockers in each country are geared to the local coins. You cannot use a kroner for a locker in France, or a franc for one in Denmark !

CUSTOMS PROCEDURES AND DUTY-FREE PURCHASES

Items at "duty-free" shops in major airports are not always a bargain. Often, the merchandise in a duty-free shop is priced higher than in an ordinary store in the same city.

Only by comparison shopping can you be sure whether it is worthwhile buying at the duty-free shops.

Furthermore, upon returning to your home country you will often find that you must pay a duty on your "duty-free" purchases. "Duty-free" means only that the airport store from which you made a purchase did not have to pay a duty when it bought the article.

To know what can and cannot be brought back to the country of your residence and what the duty tax (if any) you will have to pay when returning home with articles purchased abroad, learn about your country's import regulations before you start your trip to another country.

Residents of the U.S.A. can obtain a copy of "Know Before You Go", a helpful booklet, by writing to: U.S. Customs Service, Custom Information Section, 6 World Trade Center, New York, N.Y. 10048.

Only a fool tries to smuggle through customs an article on which there is an embargo or to avoid paying duty for one which is subject to import tax. If caught, the penalty when entering the United States can be a combination of having the article seized, paying a penalty in the amount of the U.S. value, and criminal prosecution.

For example, you buy a $1,000 piece of jade in Hong Kong. In 1991, there was an exemption of $400(U.S.) on goods entering the U.S. that were purchased anywhere outside the U.S. other than the U.S. Virgin Islands, American Samoa and Guam. After that first $400, the flat duty for the next $1,000 was 10% (or $100 for the first $1,400). You owe a duty of $60: ($1,000 less $400 = $600 at 10%).

In trying to avoid this $60 tax, you could lose the jade, be forced to pay a fine of $1,000 and go to jail.

The duty on purchases in excess of $1,400 was at variable rates, ranging from 2.5% for passenger autos and up to 25.5% for wool sweaters.

The exemption for purchases made in U.S. Virgin Islands, American Samoa and Guam was $1,200. There was a 5% duty on the next $1,000 — and then variable rates for everything over $2,200.

It is almost a certainty that the salesperson who sells you any item of value or one which cannot legally be brought into your country will report your name and your purchase to your country's authorities in that country a few minutes after concluding the transaction.

The informer receives a good reward for enabling the customs people at your home port to be expecting you.

To avoid delays and difficulty when you return to your home country, it is advisable before leaving home to register with your Customs Service any major foreign-made items (cameras, watches, etc.) you take on your trip.

Always keep your sales slips, invoices or other evidence of purchase. These are essential when presenting a declaration upon re-entering your home country.

If you carry narcotic medicines or injection needles, have a statement from your physician about them.

Do not try to bring home fruits, vegetables or plants that cannot be cleared by your country's Agriculture Department. Without such clearance, it is a certainty such items will be confiscated.

AIRPORT-CITY RAIL CONNECTIONS

An increasing number of cities in Europe have fast rail service to and from their outlying airports: Amsterdam (18 minutes), Barcelona (18), Brussels (20), Frankfurt (14), London (50 minutes from Heathrow, 30 minutes from Gatwick), Malaga (12), Paris (37 minutes from De Gaulle, 35 minutes from Orly), Rome (24), Vienna (25) and Zurich (11). See Table #5 in Cook's "European Timetable".

LOST MONEY AND PASSPORTS

Having your money or passport stolen or losing them is certain to spoil your trip.

The best precaution is to carry little cash, have traveler's checks instead, and to keep the record of both your traveler's checks and passport number in a different location than you carry the checks and passport. Also guard your return airport ticket as closely as you guard cash, traveler's checks and passport.

Each year, approximately 3,000 U.S. passports are stolen and another 11,000 are lost. There is a big market for American and European passports in Latin America and Asia.

Here are the steps to take when your passport is taken or missing:

First, notify the police of the country in which you are traveling. At the moment you are without your passport, you are in that country illegally. Next, get a copy of the police report and take it to the local office of your country's *consulate*. Do not waste time going to your country's embassy. It is your consulate, not your embassy, that will assist you by issuing you a replacement passport.

Obtaining a replacement is expedited if you can provide the passport number. It frequently takes 3-4 business days (up to 6 or 7 days if weekends or holidays intervene) before the consulate receives a reply from a telegram sent to your country's capital, the procedure when you do not know your passport number.

If, in addition to the passport number, you also have a certified copy of your birth certificate or certificate of citizenship, the consulate usually can issue a new passport the same day without cabling your capital.

When your new passport is prepared, you must again provide 2 photos of yourself.

The trip delay, missed connections, taxis (to police, consulate, photographer, return trip to the consulate, going to the airline to change your ticket), additional hotel days and various fees to your consulate can amount to a great expense.

OVERCOMING JET LAG

When your trip involves a 5-9 hour time change, many of the early days of your trip to another country can be drastically impaired.

There are ways you can greatly reduce the effects of "jet lag" and have more fun on your trip.

On the flight, drink a great deal of water to overcome dehydration resulting from cabin air conditioning. Do not drink alcoholic beverages. Eat very lightly. Dress comfortably by wearing loose clothing. Exercise as much as possible in flight.

Both SAS and Lufthansa once had concise booklets which described exercises that can be performed on a crowded airplane, while you are sitting. Do the motions involved in rowing a boat and picking apples from an overhead branch. Rise up and sit down repeatedly. Raise your knees to your elbows, alternately. Nod your head and turn it vigorously from side to side. Turn your hands at the wrist while spreading and closing your fingers. Lift your heels up and then place them down vigorously while placing pressure on your toes. With toes up, rotate your feet in large circles.

DAY ROOMS

Many non-Europeans are unfamiliar with an extremely convenient service available at some railstations called "Day Rooms". With this accommodation, the tenant has privacy, a place to change clothes and, sometimes, bath facilities. Some day rooms have a bed.

The advantages of a railstation day room over a conventional hotel room are that it is usually cheaper and it is located at the station.

WHAT WEATHER TO EXPECT

These descriptions of weather patterns are helpful in planning what season is most comfortable for visiting the areas listed.

NORTH AMERICA AND EUROPE   Spring is April-June, Summer July-September, Fall October-December. Winter January-March.

MEXICO AND CENTRAL AMERICA   Very rainy May-October.

SOUTH AMERICA, AUSTRALIA AND NEW ZEALAND   Spring is October-December, Summer January-March, Fall April-June, Winter July- September.

ASIA   Year-round tropical heat in Hong Kong, India, Indonesia, Malaysia, Philippines, Singapore, Thailand, South Pacific islands, anywhere that is near the Equator. Typhoon season is June-September in Japan, August to mid-October in Taiwan. The monsoon months in India are June-August. The rainy season in most of Asia is May-September (June-November in the Philippines).

NORTH AFRICA   Extremely hot, except December-February in Egypt.

MIDDLE EAST   Israel has mild Mediterranean temperature year round. Iran, Iraq, Jordan, Lebanon and Syria have the same 4 seasons as North America and Europe.

LAST MINUTE CHECKLIST

Here are several important tips that can greatly increase the pleasure of your travel.

Carry as little luggage as possible. You will arrive at many railstations where it is a long walk from the train to the taxis (often requiring walking up and down stairs) and find there are neither porters nor carts.

If the luggage you take is a burden, bring along a folding cart of your own.

Take a container of drinking-water on any long trip. Most trains do not provide drinking-water.

Pack soft-ply toilet paper, wash-and-dry packets, and plastic bags. The bags are useful for storing left-over food items, wet soap and laundry that was not completely dry at the start of that day's journey.

When traveling in pairs, it is easier to pass a suitcase through the train window, into or from your compartment, than it is to carry luggage through the length of a crowded, narrow corridor. Unfortunately, the windows of many new air-conditioned train cars cannot be opened.

SIGNS — THE INTERNATIONAL LANGUAGE

The signs shown on next 3 pages appear in railstations and elsewhere all over the world. They help overcome language problems.

53

At the Train Station. It won't surprise you to learn that most every station is located in the center of town and is the focal point for all public transportation. A number of hotels are also in the immediate vicinity. What might surprise you is the number and variety of services available on the inside. You can find practically everything—from post office and telegraph bureau to barber and beauty shop, from bookstore and newsstand to gift shop, money exchange, and restaurants. But what will impress the foreign traveler most is the highly efficient information system with which almost every station overcomes the language barrier. Here's the most multi-lingual of visual aids you should look for . . .

Ladies' Rest Room	Men's Rest Room	Waiting Room	Telegram
Barber - Beauty Parlor	Bath	Drinking Water	Restaurant
		Post office	Telephone
		Smoking permitted	No smoking

Language. Don't worry. Europeans like to practice their conversational English, especially on trains. For detailed information, consult the English-speaking staff at tourist offices, information bureaus, and hotels. At the railroad stations, pictograms lead you not only to the information desk but to any other facility you may be looking for. There are also the highly visible and efficient timetables posted inside the railroad station for get-it-yourself train information. Once you acquire the knack of reading them (and we shall tell you how, later on), they will get you on the right train at the right time on the right track.

Information

Temporary Luggage Storage. At almost every large station you'll find coin-operated lockers. Else, use the special baggage storage indicated by a pictogram and/or the legend: CONSIGNE DES BAGAGES... GEPAECKAUFBEWAHRUNG... CONSIGNA DE EQUIPAJES... DEPOSITO BAGAGLIO. You'll get a claim check which you have to present when you pick your luggage up again.

Baggage check room

Locker

Checking Your Luggage Through. Time and circumstances permitting, take your bulky luggage or bicycle along on your train, but not with you. Wherever international border crossings and train regulations don't stand in your way, avoid the hassle by checking your extra pieces through to your destination, to ride in the luggage-car. The right counter for this service is indicated by a pictogram.

Luggage registration office

Door-to-Door Luggage Service. If you really want to travel light in France or Germany—with a claim check instead of luggage—find out whether your train station in the city you're in is one of those which pick up your luggage where you're staying and deliver it at your next stay. If that's the case, the small service fee is worth every penny of it.

Baggage Claim

Border and Customs Control. Be in your seat. Immigration officials will inspect your passport and whatever visa or other required documents right in your compartment, while the train moves across border points. You will be asked whether you have anything to declare, but as a foreign tourist in transit, especially with a EURAILPASS or STUDENT-RAILPASS, you will be given the appropriate considerations.

Customs

Changing Money. A railroad station is a good place to exchange the bills and coins of one currency for another. Look for the sign where the action is: BUREAU DE CHANGE...GELDWECHSEL...WECHSELSTUBE...OFICINA DE CAMBIO...OFFICIO CAMBEIO...UFFICIO CAMBIO ...or just follow the pertinent pictogram.

Currency exchange

Which Ticket Window for What. At larger stations tickets for domestic and international travel are purchased at different windows. But as a EURAILPASS or STUDENT-RAILPASS holder, you have your ticket already. So all you'll really want is either the information or reservation window or desk—except in Spain, where you must get a boarding pass at the station before you can board a train.

Tickets

Services for Businessmen. If you are combining pleasure with business, there are a number of TEE and Intercity trains on which you can hire a secretary, send telegrams or make telephone calls, make car-rental reservations ahead of arrival, or reserve a taxi to pick you up at your destination.

Rent-a-car

Taxi stand

Your Helpful Porter. You'll recognize him by his uniform or official badge. You can usually find one as your cab pulls up to the station. If not, look for him inside. Consult the proper pictogram to find the porters' room. You can rely on your porter to get you to the right track, train, and car. He will put you in a smoker or non-smoker, as you wish, will try his best to find a vacant window-seat, and will place your luggage into the overhead rack.

Call for porter

Washroom Facilities. You can freshen up in a "W.C." (Water Closet) at either end of your car. In most long distance trains next to the "WC" are separate Washrooms. And remember not to drink the tap water; it is not potable.

Rest rooms

A Seat Reservation. Even though you can travel on a European train in most cases without a seat reservation, it's always nice to have a reserved seat—at a window, if possible, or where you want your lunch or dinner served (yes, advance reservations can be made on some TEE trains for meals to be served in your seat). EURAILPASS and STUDENT-RAILPASS holders must pay for seat reservations, but it's very little for a lot of convenience.

Reservation

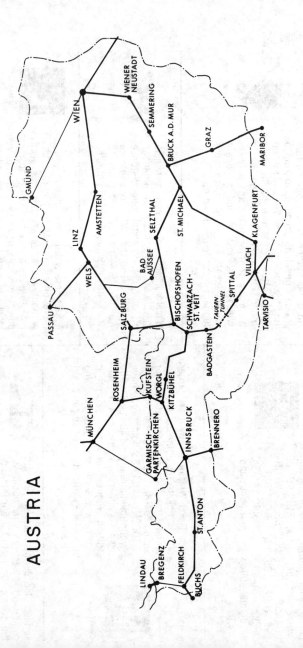

AUSTRIA

Chapter 6   EURAILPASS EUROPE

AUSTRIA

Children under 6 travel free. Half-fare for children 6-14. Children 15 and over must pay full fare.

Special through tickets are required for "privilege trains", trains which cross German or Italian borders without border formalities (customs, passport and currency control) when traveling from one part of Austria to another part of Austria. These trains do not allow passengers to board or leave the train in Germany or Italy.

The second-class couchette cars on most Austrian internal routes and on some international services have 4 berths per compartment instead of 6. A supplement of 33% over the price of a couchette in a 6-berth compartment is charged for them. Inquire about this when reserving a couchette.

The signs you will see at railstations in Austria are:

ABFAHRT	DEPARTURE
ANKUNFT	ARRIVAL
AUSGANG	EXIT
AUSKUNFT	INFORMATION
BAHNHOF	STATION
BAHNSTEIG	PLATFORM
DAMEN	WOMEN
EINGANG	ENTRANCE
FAHRKARTEN-SCHALTER	TICKET OFFICE
FAHRPLAN	TIMETABLE
GEPACKAUFBEWAHRUNG	BAGGAGE CHECKROOM
GLEIS	TRACK
HERREN	MEN
PLATZ RESERVIERUNG	SEAT RESERVATION
RAUCHER	SMOKING COMPARTMENT
SCHLAFWAGEN	SLEEPING CAR
SPEISEWAGEN	RESTAURANT CAR

AUSTRIAN HOLIDAYS

A list of holidays is helpful because some trains will be noted later in this section as not running on holidays. Also, those trains which operate on holidays are filled, and it is necessary to make reservations for them long in advance.

January 1	New Year's Day		Corpus Christi Day
January 6	Epiphany	August 15	Assumption Day
	Easter	October 26	National Holiday
	Easter Monday	November 1	All Saints Day
May 1	Labor Day	December 8	Immaculate Conception
	Ascension Day	December 25	Christmas Day
	Whit Monday	December 26	St. Stephen's Day

58

SUMMER TIME

Austria changes to Summer Time on the last Sunday of March and converts back to Standard Time on the last Sunday of September.

AUSTRIA's TRAIN PASSES

European East Pass   See page 456.

Senior Citizen Half-Fare   In 1992, women 60 and over and men who are 65 and older can buy train and bus tickets at half-price after purchasing a Senior Citizen's Identification for 220 Austrian schillings, available at all railstations and major post offices in Austria, and also at the Hauptbahnhof stations in Frankfurt, Munich and Zurich.

The ID (valid for one calendar year) can also be obtained by mail by sending a travelers check in the amount of $25 (U.S.) or equivalent, a photostat of the passport page which has a picture and states the holder's age, plus one passport-size photo to: OeBBVerkehrseinnahmen- und Reklamationsstelle, Mariannengasse 20, A-1090 Wien, Austria.

This discount is *not* valid on municipal transit lines (subway, trolley, bus).

Bundesnetzkarte (Network Pass)   Sold only in Austria. Unlimited train travel in all of Austria. The 1992 *first-class* prices are: 5,100 Austrian schillings for one month, AS-40,800 for one year. *Second-class*: AS-3,400 and AS-27,200.

Regional-Netzkarten   Sold only in Austria. Unlimited train travel in any one of the country's 18 provinces for any 4 days within a 10-day period. The 1992 prices are: 600 Austrian schillings for *first-class*, AS-450 for *second-class*.

Kilometer Bank   Sold only in Austria. Valid for *both* first and second-class seats. May be used by 1-6 persons traveling together on trips of over 70 km one way. Can be used in first or second-class. The conductor deducts trip distance for each passenger age 16 or older. Only half the distance is charged for each child age 6–15. No charge for children under age 6.

The 1992 prices are: 1,800 Austrian schillings for 2,000 km, AS-2,750 for 3,000 km, AS-3,600 for 4,000 km, and AS-4,550 for 5,000 km.

The maximum kilometers charged against this pass for any one trip are 600. Any number of kilometers above that are free.

For *first-class* use, one kilometer is counted as 1.5 kilometers.

Rabbit Card   Vouchers that are exchangeable at your first stop in Austria can be purchased from travel agencies, Rail Europe and German Rail in the U.S.A. (see "France" and "Germany" on page 23), and at all major railstations in Germany, Holland, Italy and Switzerland. Unlimited travel on all Austrian Federal Railway, state and private rail lines throughout Austria. Valid any 4 days out of a 10-day period that starts with date of purchase.

The 1992 prices for passengers age 26 and older are: $136 (U.S.) for *first-class*, $91 for *second-class*. For passengers who are under 26 on first day of travel: $84 and $56.

EURAILPASS BONUSES IN AUSTRIA

Two rack railways: (1) Puchberg am Schneeberg-Hochschneeberg (see page 72) and (2) St. Wolfgang-Schafbergspitze (see page 64). The Danube cruise between Passau and Vienna. Reduction of 50% on Lake Constance, Linz-Passau (andv.v.v), and Vienna-Budapest ships.

ONE-DAY EXCURSIONS AND CITY-SIGHTSEEING

Here are 31 one-day rail trips that can be made comfortably from Innsbruck, Linz, Salzburg and Vienna, returning to them in most cases before dinnertime. Notes are provided on what to see and do at each destination. The number after the name of each route is the Cook's timetable.

Innsbruck

Marvelous Winter resort. Gateway to many cable railway trips (Hungerburg, Hafelekar, Igls, Patscherkofel). See the 28 bronze statues around the enormous and magnificent tomb of Maximilian I in the 16th century Court Church and the effigy of King Arthur there. The silver altar at the Silver Chapel.

The roof (2,657 gold plated tiles) on Goldenes Dachl, built in 1500. The Museum of Tyrolean Folk Art, considered the most important collection of costumes and rustic furniture in Austria. The 18th century Roman-style Triumphal Arch. Reisenrundgemalde, a huge circular fresco depicting the Battle of Bergisel. The splendid views of the city and surrounding mountains from Bergisel Kaiserjager, containing the museum of the Tyrolean Imperial Light Infantry.

The excellent art collection of Archduke Ferdinand II at Schloss Ambras, open daily except Tuesday in Summer. The Alpen Zoo. The 18th century Imperial Palace. The paintings and furniture at the Tyrolean Regional Museum in the Arsenal of Emperor Maxmillian I.

Linz

Visit the schloss (castle) where Emperor Fredrich III lived, with its Upper Austrian Regional Museum collections of prehistoric and Roman antiquities, medieval armor and weapons, musical instruments and regional arts and crafts, open Tuesday-Saturday 10:00-18:00, Sunday 10:00-16:00.

Martinskirche, one of Austria's oldest churches. The medieval, Renaissance and Baroque exhibits in the City Museum at 7 Bethlehemstrasse, open Monday-Friday 09:00-18:00, Saturday and Sunday 15:00-17:00.

Take the 20-minute tram ride from the Urfahr section to Postlingberg, a hill on the south side of the Danube, to visit the Town Hall and see the view from there.

Kremsmunster, an enchanting small town established in 777, is a 30-minute drive south of Linz. Visit it in order to see the treasures in the monastery. It houses a fabulous library as well as an exceptional museum of natural history and early scientific instruments, a picture gallery, an art gallery, a fine collection of stained glass, and an armory.

Among its more than 100,000 rare books, 886 incunabula (books produced before movable type was invented in the 16th century), and 910 old manuscripts are the 2 famous "jewels" of the 230-foot-long library: the 8th and 9th century splendidly illuminated parchments called Codex Millenarius Major and Codex Minor. All 4 large rooms of the library are furnished with beautiful baroque bookcases.

Salzburg

Do not miss seeing the most amusing place in Europe, the 17th century Hellbrunn Palace. The 16th century 200-pipe barrel organ (played 3 times every day) in the 12th century fortress, 500 feet above the town (Festung Hohensalzburg) where 40-minute guided tours start every 15 minutes 09:00-17:30 daily in July and August. The traditional Music Festival (last week of July until the end of August).

Guided tours of the incredibly opulent rooms in The Residenz, the 17th century city palace of Salzburg's archbishops, start at 10:00, 10:30, 11:00, 11:30, 13:00, 13:30, 14:00, 14:30 and 15:00, Monday-Friday. The gallery of paintings in The Residenz (including Titian and Rembrandt) is open daily 10:00-17:00.

The painted ceilings in the 17th century Festspeilhaus. The collection of Mozart musical instruments and family memorabilia in the Mozart Museum, his birthplace (9 Getreidegasse), open daily 09:00-19:00. The vast musical library at Bibliotheca Mozartiana. St. Sebastian's Cemetery (Linzergasse 41). The 17th century Cathedral. The Universitatskirche. The Gothic cloister in the 9th century Benedictine Abbey of St. Peter.

The Glockenspiel Tower particularly at 07:00, 11:00 and 18:00 for the carillon concerts. The ancient marketplace, Alter Markt. The marble Angel Staircase and the Salzburger Barock-Museum in the 17th century Schloss Mirabell, and the marvelous gardens there. The superb collection of prehistoric objects, fossils and meteorites at the Natural History Museum.

Take the cable car to the top (5,800 feet) of Untersberg for a breathtaking view of Salzburg and the Alps. There are other good views of the city and river from Hettwer Bastion and also from the top of Monchsberg, Kapuzinerberg and Gaisberg.

Vienna (Wien)

The main tourist office (38 Kartnerstrasse) is open daily 09:00-19:00.

There is 30-minute train service [Table 738] from *Vienna (Nord) to the city's Schwechat Airport (Flughafen)* daily at 05:51, 06:15 and hourly from 07:28 to 21:28. Monday-Friday except holidays: at 05:13, 16:00 and 16:59.

Rail service *from the Airport to Vienna (Nord)* departs the Airport daily at 06:38, 07:24 and hourly from 08:03 to 22:03. Monday-Friday except holidays: at 05:08. Daily except Sundays and holidays: at 05:31, 06:15, 07:03 and 07:12.

There is 35-minute train service [Table 738] *from Vienna (Westbahnhof) to the Airport* daily at 06:00, 06:45 and hourly from 07:15 to 19:15, plus 21:15. Rail service *from the Airport to Vienna (Westbahnhof)* is hourly from 07:00 to 18:00, plus 19:15, 20:00 and 23:00.

For a glimpse at the world's most beautiful horses and extraordinary riding skill, see the Spanish Riding School. The view from the top of the south steeple of the 13th century Saint Stephen's Cathedral, reached by climbing 365 steps. That steeple is open daily 09:00-16:30.

Another great view is from the top of the Donauturm (Danube Tower). or from the hills in the Vienna Woods. Vienna's most elegant shopping streets are 2 pedestrian malls that run south and east from St. Stephen's: Karntnerstrasse and Graben. Three-hour boat trips on the Danube Canal operate daily except Monday at 10:00, 13:00 and 16:30 from Schwedenbrucke, a bridge that is a 15-minute walk from St. Stephen's.

See the Opera House. The Art Gallery. The Burgtheater. The Rathaus (City Hall). The gigantic Ferris Wheel and the miniature railway in the Prater amusement park.

Guided tours of some of the 1,400 rooms in Schonbrunn Castle, Vienna's Versailles, are offered daily 09:00-12:00 and 13:00-16:00. It is a 20-minute ride from Burgring on streetcar # 58.

Visit Tierpark, the zoo, in the Schonbrunner Schlosspark. The 2 museums of modern art, one in Palais Liechtensten, the other in Schweizer Garten. See the crown jewels of the Holy Roman Empire and the Austrian Empire, in the Imperial Apartments at the Hofburg (Imperial Palace), open Monday-Saturday 08:30-16:00 and Sunday 08:30-12:30.

The collection of great paintings (Titian, Rubens, Rembrandt) and Egyptian, Greek, Etruscan and Roman antiquities at the Museum of Art History on Ringstrasse , open Tuesday and Friday 10:00-21:00, Wednesday and Thursday 09:00-18:00, Saturday and Sunday 09:00-18:00.

The many art museums in Belvedere Palace (medieval, baroque and modern art), open Tuesday-Saturday from 10:00 to varying afternoon hours, Sunday 09:00-12:00. The 20 centuries of memorabilia in the Historical Museum in the Karlsplatz, open Tuesday- Friday 10:00-16:00, Saturday 14:00-18:00, Sunday 09:00-17:00.

The Sigmund Freud Museum at 19 Berggasse, where the founder of psychoanalysis lived and practiced for many years, open Monday-Friday 09:00-13:00, Saturday and Sunday 09:00-15:00.

The many art museums in Belvedere Palace, open Tuesday-Sunday 10:00-16:00. The beautiful Austrian National Library at 1 Josefplatz. The great churches: Peterskirche and Karlskirche.

The finest collection of Durer paintings in the world and one of the world's largest graphics collections (1,000,000 prints from 5 centuries and 45,000 drawings) at the Albertina, 1 Augustinerstrasse, open Monday, Tuesday and Thursday 10:00-16:00, Wednesday 10:00-18:00, Friday 10:00-14:00, Saturday and Sunday 10:00-13:00.

The paintings of Kandinsky and other moderns at the Museum of the 20th Century in Schweizer Garten (near the Southeast Railroad Terminal), open daily except Wednesday 10:00-18:00. Works by Austrian painters and sculptors since World War II at the Museum of Modern Art in the Liechtenstein Palace, 1 Furstengasse, open daily except Tuesday 10:00-18:00.

The great paintings (Hieronymus, Bosch, Rubens, Titian, Van Dyck) at the Academy of Fine Arts, 3 Schillerplatz, open Tuesday, Thursday and Friday 10:00-14:00, Wednesday 10:00-13:00, Saturday and Sunday 09:00-13:00.

The treasures of the Holy Roman Empire, including the 10th century crown, at the Imperial Treasury, open Monday, Wednesday, Thursday and Friday 10:00-16:00, Saturday and Sunday 09:00-16:00 (November-March) or 09:00-18:00 (April-October).

Treasures collected by the Hapsburgs (including paintings by Pieter Bruegel the Elder and Rubens) at the Museum of Fine Arts on Maria-Theresien-Platz, open Tuesday-Friday 10:00-18:00, Saturday and Sunday 09:00-16:00 (November-March) or 09:00-18:00 (April- October).

The Austrian Baroque Museum and the Museum of Austrian Medieval art are located in the Lower Belvedere.

Vienna's largest outdoor food market (Naschmarkt) runs between Rechte Wienzeile and Linke Wienzeile.

Sightseeing flights over Vienna operate from the Schwechat Airport.

Take trolley car # 38 from Schottentor (in central Vienna) to **Grinzing**, the wine-tasting village. Continue from there on bus # 38A to the small Church of St. Joseph on the top of the 1,585-feet high **Kahlenberg**, from where Hungary and Czechoslovakia can be seen on clear days.

In the following timetables, where a city has more than one railstation we have designated the particular station after the name of the city (in parentheses). **Where no station is designated for cities in Austria, Switzerland and West Germany, the station is "Hauptbahnhof".**

Innsbruck - Bregenz - Innsbruck 800

Dep. Innsbruck	07:02 (1)	09:02 (1)	Dep. Bregenz	12:17 (1)	14:17 (1+2)
Arr. Bregenz	09:44	11:44	Arr. Innsbruck	14:58	16:58

(1) Restaurant car. (2) Plus other departures from Bregenz at 16:17 (1), 17:18 (1), 18:17 (1), 20:17 (1) and 21:38, arriving Innsbruck 18:58, 19:51, 20:58, 22:58 and 00:34.

Sights in **Bregenz**: Divided into 2 sections, features of the lower town include the lakeshore, the shopping district and the Voralberg Museum. The upper town has churches. Situated on the shore of the Bodensee (Lake Constance), easy day trips can be made from here to Innsbruck, Munich, Salzburg and Zurich.

The annual Music Festival (light opera and ballet on an unusual water stage in the lake) runs mid-July to mid-August. Take the funicular to the top (3,200 feet) of Pfander Mountain for a spectacular view of Bodensee, the Rhine River and the town of Lindau (see notes about Lindau under "Munich-Lindau", page 371). The funicular runs 08:30-20:00 (until 22:00 in mid-Summer). Steamboats are operated on the lake from early April to early October.

Innsbruck - Igls - Innsbruck

Four miles from Innsbruck by suburban railway. A great ski resort.

Innsbruck - Kitzbuhel - Innsbruck 800

Dep. Innsbruck	08:25 (1)	09:20 (2)	10:25 (1)	11:20 (2)	12:25 (1)	13:20 (2)
Arr. Kitzbuhel	09:30	10:25	11:30	12:25	13:21	14:25

Sights in **Kitzbuhel**: This is one of the major winter resorts in the Alps. Cable cars take you from Kitzbuhel to many mountaintops. The city has one museum, some old churches.

Dep. Kitzbuhel	12:29 (1)	13:34 (2)	14:29 (1)	15:48 (2)	16:29 (2)	17:34 (1+3)
Arr. Innsbruck	13:35	14:40	15:35	16:51	17:35	18:40

(1) Restaurant car. (2) Light refreshments. (3) Plus other departures from Kitzbuhel at 18:29 (1), 19:34 (2), 20:29 (1), 21:34 (2) and 22:29 (1).

Innsbruck - Mayrhofen - Innsbruck 800

Dep. Innsbruck	09:20	-0-	10:25	11:20	12:25	13:20 (2)
Arr. Jenbach	09:38	-0-	10:43	11:38	12:43	13:38

Change from a standard-gauge train to a narrow-gauge train. Table 805

Dep. Jenbach	09:50	10:30 (1)	10:50	11:50	12:50	13:50
Arr. Mayrhofen	10:47	12:10	11:47	12:47	13:47	14:47

Sights in **Mayrhofen**: This is a popular Winter resort, with horse sleighs.

Dep. Mayrhofen	12:20	12:47 (1)	13:20	14:20	15:20	16:20 (3)
Arr. Jenbach	13:11	14:06	14:13	15:11	16:13	17:11

Change from a narrow-gauge train to a standard-gauge train. Table 800

Dep. Jenbach	13:14	-0-	14:20	15:15	16:20	17:15
Arr. Innsbruck	20 minutes later					

(1) Steam train. (2) Plus another departure from Innsbruck at 14:25, arriving Mayrhofen 15:47 by ordinary narrow-gauge....16:20 by steam train. (3) Plus other departures from Mayrhofen at 17:00 (1), 17:20, 18:20 and 19:20.

Innsbruck - Munich - Innsbruck 782

Dep. Innsbruck	06:34 (1)	08:43 (1)	09:41 (2)
Arr. Munich	09:51	11:51	12:38

Sights in **Munich:** See notes about sightseeing in Munich on pages 375-376.

Dep. Munich	14:00	15:00 (1)	18:00 (3)
Arr. Innsbruck	16:39	18:40	20:53

(1) Change trains in Mittenwald. (2) Restaurant car. (3) Change trains in Garmish.

Innsbruck - St. Anton - Innsbruck 800

Dep. Innsbruck	07:02 (1)	08:02	09:02 (1)	11:02 (1)	11:55	12:44 (1)
Arr. St. Anton	08:20	09:25	10:20	12:20	13:33	13:53

Sights in **St. Anton:** A popular ski center since 1907, located at the eastern end of the 6-mile-long Arlberg Tunnel. The enormous number of ski lifts here offer a great variety of slopes.

Dep. St. Anton	11:35 (1)	12:03 (1)	13:35 (1)	15:35 (1)	17:35 (1)	18:39 (1+2)
Arr. Innsbruck	12:58	13:16	14:58	16:58	18:58	19:51

(1) Restaurant car. (2) Plus other departures from St. Anton at 19:35 (1), 21:35 (1), 22:03 (1) and 23:13.

Innsbruck - Salzburg - Innsbruck (via Zell am See) 800

The route via Zell-am-See is one of the most scenic rides in Austria, as well as a trip to an interesting destination. Exceptionally beautiful views of gorges, lakes, mountains and rivers.

All of these trains have a restaurant car.

Dep. Innsbruck	06:25 (1+2)	07:02 (2)	08:25 (1)	09:02 (2)	10:25 (1+3)
Dep. Zell-am-See	08:20	-0-	10:20	-0-	12:20
Arr. Salzburg	09:51	09:00	11:51	11:00	13:51

Sights in **Zell-am-See:** Minutes by bus from year-around glacier skiing.

Sights in **Salzburg:** See notes about sightseeing in Salzburg on page 60.

Dep. Salzburg	13:00	14:08 (1)	15:00 (2)	16:08 (1)	17:00 (2+4)
Dep. Zell-am-See	-0-	15:41	-0-	17:41	-0-
Arr. Innsbruck	14:58	17:35	16:58	19:35	18:58

(1) Of the 2 routes between Innsbruck and Salzburg, this train takes the more interesting one (via Zell-am-See), one of the most scenic rail trips in Austria. (2) Via Kufstein. (3) Plus other departures from Innsbruck at 11:02 (2) and 11:24 (2), arriving Salzburg 13:00 and 13:22. (4) Plus other Salzburg departures at 18:14 (1), 19:00 (2), 20:02, 20:08 (1) and 21:20 (2), arriving Innsbruck 21:35, 20:58, 21:49 and 23:12.

Linz - Munich - Linz 61

All of these trains charge a supplement and have a restaurant car.

Dep. Linz	07:48	10:46	Dep. Munich	16:25	19:25
Arr. Munich	10:35	13:36	Arr. Linz	19:19	22:14

Sights in **Munich**: See notes about Munich on pages 375-376.

Linz - Salzburg - Linz 800

Most of these trains have a restaurant car.

Dep. Linz	Frequent times from 05:34 to 23:15
Arr. Salzburg	1 to 2 hours later

Sights in **Salzburg**: See notes about sightseeing in Salzburg on page 60.

Dep. Salzburg	Frequent times from 04:53 to 21:51
Arr. Linz	1 to 2 hours later

Linz - Vienna - Linz 800

Most of these trains have a restaurant car.

Dep. Linz	Frequent times from 04:30 to 23:15
Arr. Vienna (Westbf.)	1½ to 2 hours later

Sights in **Vienna**: See notes about sightseeing in Vienna on page 60.

Dep. Vienna (Westbf.)	Frequent times from 04:40 to 23:30
Arr. Linz	1½ to 2 hours later

Salzburg - Zell am See - Innsbruck - Salzburg 800

The route via Zell-am-See is one of the most scenic rides in Austria, as well as a trip to an interesting destination. Exceptionally beautiful views of gorges, lakes, mountains and rivers.

All of these trains have a restaurant car.

Dep. Salzburg	07:00 (1)	08:08 (2)	09:00 (1)	10:08 (2)	11:00 (1)
Dep. Zell-am-See	-0-	09:41	-0-	11:41	-0-
Arr. Innsbruck	09:02	11:35	10:58	13:35	12:58

Sights in **Zell-am-See**: Minutes by bus from year-around glacier skiing.
Sights in **Innsbruck**: See notes about sightseeing in Innsbruck on page 59.

Dep. Innsbruck	12:25 (2)	14:25 (2)	15:02 (1)	16:25 (2)	17:02 (1+3)
Dep. Zell-am-See	14:20	16:20	-0-	18:20	-0-
Arr. Salzburg	15:51	17:51	17:00	19:51	19:00

(1) Via Kufstein. (2) Of the 2 routes between Salzburg and Innsbruck, this train takes the most interesting one (via Zell-am-See), one of the most scenic rail trips in Austria. (3) Plus other departures from Innsbruck at 18:25 (2), 19:02 (1), 20:25 (2) and 21:14 (1), arriving Salzburg 21:51, 21:00, 23:51 and 23:12.

Salzburg - Kitzbuhel - Salzburg 800

All of these trains have a restaurant car.

Dep. Salzburg	08:08	10:08	12:08	14:08
Arr. Kitzbuhel	10:29	12:29	14:29	16:29

Sights in **Kitzbuhel**: See notes about Kitzbuhel under "Innsbruck-Kitzbuhel" on page 62.

Dep. Kitzbuhel	13:32	15:32	17:32	19:32
Arr. Salzburg	15:51	17:51	19:51	21:51

Salzburg - Linz - Salzburg 800

Most of these trains have a restaurant car.

Dep. Salzburg	Frequent times from 05:05 to 21:51
Arr. Linz	80 minutes later

Sights in **Linz**: See notes about sightseeing in Linz on page 59.

Dep. Linz	Frequent times from 05:34 to 23:15
Arr. Salzburg	80 minutes later

Salzburg - Munich - Salzburg 780

All of these trains charge a supplement and have a restaurant car, unless designated otherwise.

Dep. Salzburg	07:15 (1)	08:02 (1)	09:05	10:05	12:09
Arr. Munich	09:10	09:48	10:35	11:35	13:36

Sights in **Munich**: See notes about sightseeing in Munich on pages 375-376.

Dep. Munich	12:25	13:25	15:25	16:25	17:52 (2)
Arr. Salzburg	13:55	14:55	16:55	17:53	19:40

(1) No supplement charged. No restaurant car. (2) Plus other Salzburg departures at 13:05 and 15:07, arriving Munich 14:35 and 16:36. (3) Plus other Munich departures at 19:25, 20:50 (1), 21:52 and 23:10, arriving Salzburg 20:55, 22:45, 23:40 and 01:01.

Salzburg - Schafbergspitze - Salzburg

A very scenic one-day trip that includes views of the 8-mile-long **Wolfgangsee (Lake Wolfgang)**, the warmest lake in Austria (79 degrees in Summer). The cogwheel train climbs 5,682 feet to the top of the **Schafberg**, from where there are glorious views of 13 lakes and many mountains.

Bus. Austrian timetable 3000

Dep. Salzburg	06:45 (1)	08:15	09:15 (1)	11:25	13:15
Arr. Strobl	07:59	09:19	10:29	12:39	14:29
Change buses					
Dep. Strobl	08:15	09:40	10:40	12:45	14:40
Arr. St. Wolfgang	08:30	09:55	10:55	13:00	14:55

Change to steam rack railway 813

Dep. St. Wolfgang	08:35	10:00	11:45	13:25	15:05
Arr. Schafbergspitze	09:14	10:39	12:24	14:04	15:44

* * *

Dep. Schafbergspitze	09:16	10:50	14:19	17:36
Arr. St. Wolfgang	09:56	11:37	14:59	18:18

Change to bus. Austrian timetable 3000

Dep. St. Wolfgang	10:05 (2)	12:10	15:05	20:00
Arr. Strobl	10:20	12:25	15:20	20:15
Change buses				
Dep. Strobl	10:41	12:41	15:41	20:33
Arr. Salzburg	11:55	13:55	16:55	21:40

(1) Daily, except Sundays and holidays. (2) Daily, except Saturday and Sunday.

Salzburg - Vienna - Salzburg 800

Marvelous views of the Alps and pretty farmland on this ride.

All of these trains have a restaurant car.

Dep. Salzburg	06:05	07:00	08:05	09:00	10:05	11:00
Arr. Vienna (Westbf.)	09:25	09:45	11:25	12:05	13:25	14:05

Sights in **Vienna**: See notes about sightseeing in Vienna on page 60.

Dep. Vienna (Westbf.)	13:35	14:40	15:40	16:00	17:00	18:00(1)
Arr. Salzburg	16:35	17:55	18:55	19:00	20:00	21:00

(1) Plus other Vienna departures at 18:40, 19:40, 20:40 and 21:25, arriving Salzburg 21:55, 22:55, 00:12 and 00:33.

Vienna - Baden - Vienna

A local tram runs at frequent time from the center of Vienna to Baden and v.v.

Sights in **Baden**: Only 16 miles from Vienna, Baden is an alternative to staying in Vienna.

Famous since the 1st century for the curative powers of its hot sulphur springs. Many of the rooms in hotels here have a faucet in the bathroom that carries mineral water. See the Baroque Trinity Column. Try your luck in the Casino in Kurpark.

Visit the house where Beethoven lived, at 10 Rathausgasse, open daily except Thursdays, May-September, 09:00-11:00 and 15:00-17:00.

Vienna - Graz - Vienna 820

All of these trains have light refreshments.

Dep. Vienna (Sudbf.)	06:30	08:30	09:06	10:30	12:30
Dep. Bruck a.d. Mur	08:20	10:20	10:55	12:20	14:20
Arr. Graz	08:55	10:55	11:28	12:55	14:55

* * *

Dep. Graz	13:05	15:05	16:55	17:05	19:05 (1)
Dep. Bruck a.d. Mur	13:43	15:43	17:30	17:43	19:43
Arr. Vienna (Sudbf.)	15:33	17:33	19:20	19:33	21:33

(1) Plus another departure from Graz at 21:05, arriving Vienna 23:33.

Sights in **Graz**: A 2 ½-hour motorcoach sightseeing tour of Graz starts from in front of the Opera House weekdays at 10:00, June through September

From the main square (Hauptplatz) with its many markets of vegetables, fruits and flowers, go to the arcades with shops in the 17th century Luegghaus. Then to the City Hall (Rathaus) to see the city's symbol, a carved white panther.

Follow Neutorgasse to the Joanneum (state Museum of Styria), one of the world's oldest museums, to see its archaeological collection, library, paintings and exhibits of Styrian crafts (09:00-12:00 daily, 14:30-17:00 Monday, Wednesday and Friday).

Continue on Landhausgasse and Herrengasse to the splendid Renaissance Landhaus. Next door, in the 4-story, 17th century Styrian Armory (Zeughaus) is an exhibit of 17th century armor (for both men and horses) said to be the best and largest collection in Europe (same hours as the Joanneum). Its 32,000 weapons include complete suits of armor, guns, helmets, swords, lances, shields and breastplates.

Walk on Opernring to the outstanding Opera House and then through marvelous Stadtpark with its fantastic double-spiral Gothic staircase and cross the Glacis to visit the city's oldest church, 13th century Leekirche, the Church of the Teutonic Order.

Pass the castle and see the Diocesan Museum and Treasury in the 15th century Cathedral. Across a narrow street is the 17th century Mausoleum of Emperor Ferdinand II and his mother (Maria of Bavaria), open 11:00-12:00 and 14:00-15:00 from May to September, only 11:00-12:00 the rest of the year.

Don't miss the folk dance by carved wood figures performing at 11:00 and 18:00 on the 400-year-old clock in Glockenspielplatz. Nearby is the 116-foot-high belfry which has a 4-ton bell that the people here call "Liesl". See the exhibits of regional costumes, tools, folk art, etc. in the Volkskundemuseum (Folk Art Museum of Styria) open Monday, Wednesday and Friday 14:30-17:00.

Cable cars leave every 15 minutes from 38 Kaiser Franz Josef Kai for the 350 foot ascent to the top of Schlossberg (Castle Hill), from where there is a great view of Graz, its suburbs, the Mur Valley and the Alps.

Drink Schilcher (the local rose wine) and Steiermark beer. Local food specialties to sample are: Steierische Wurzelfleisch (pork shoulder), Sulmtaler Krainer (smoked pork sausage) and Steierische Brettljause (a dish of bacon, sausage, cheese, peppers and tomatoes served on a wooden platter).

Take the tram to **Eggenberg** to see the hunting museum in the 17th century castle there. Go to the top of Castle Hill (Schlossberg) by foot or funicular for a great view of Graz and tour the Bell Tower and Clock Tower, where the big hands show the hour and the small hands the minutes.

Take a local bus to nearby **Stubing**, which has the largest open-air museum in Austria (ancient wood churches, peasants' homes). Another tour goes to **Koflach**, where a stud farm that is an auxiliary of Vienna's Spanish Riding School has been breeding thorough-bred horses since 1798.

Vienna - Linz - Vienna 800

Most of these trains have a restaurant car.

Dep. Vienna (Westbf.)	Frequent times from 04:40 to 23:30.
Arr. Linz	2 hours later.

Sights in **Linz**: See notes about sightseeing in Linz on page 59.

Dep.Linz	Frequent times from 04:30 to 23:15.
Arr. Vienna (Westbf.)	2 hours later.

Vienna - Melk - Vienna   Train Ride + Danube Boat Trip

The Melk-Vienna boat is covered by Eurailpass.

Train 800			Danube Steamship 756	
Dep. Vienna (Westbf.)	07:35	12:26	Dep. Melk	14:30 (1)
Arr. Melk	08:14	13:38	Arr. Vienna	20:00 (2)

(1) Operates from mid-May to mid-September. (2) Arrives at Vienna's Schiffahrtzentrum (the main landing next to the U-Bahn station Vorgartenstrasse, Line U1).

Sights in **Melk**: Walk from the railstation up the hill to the Abbey, built in 1133 but completely reconstructed 1702 to 1736. English-language guided tours are offered sometimes. There is a splendid view of the Danube from the terrace.

At the top of the stone Emperor's Stairway is the 644-foot-long Emperor's Corridor, off which are several rooms whose doors are made of highly decorated rare wood and in which many treasures are displayed. Also on this floor are the magnificently decorated Marble Hall (actually faux marble stucco), the gilded bookcases of inlaid wood in the Library (over 85,000 books and 1,200 manuscripts from the 9th to the 15th centuries), and the Abbey church with a pulpit made entirely of gold.

A restaurant at the Abbey serves a hearty lunch. For the return trip to Vienna by boat, go to the main river dock, not to the dock below the abbey.

Vienna - Salzburg - Vienna 800

All of these trains have a restaurant car, unless designated otherwise. Most of these trains charge a supplement which includes a reserved seat.

Dep. Vienna (Westbf.)	06:00	07:35	09:00	09:35	10:40	11:40
Arr. Salzburg	09:00	10:35	11:58	12:35	13:55	14:55

Sights in **Salzburg**: See notes about sightseeing in Salzburg on page 60.

Dep. Salzburg	13:51	15:00	15:51	17:00	17:51	19:05 (1)
Arr. Vienna (Westbf.)	17:25	18:25	19:25	20:25	21:25	22:25

(1) Plus other Salzburg departures at 21:00 and 21:57, arriving Vienna 00:05 and 00:58.

Vienna - Sopron - Vienna 847

A day-trip into Hungary.

Dep. Vienna (Sud)	07:40 (1)	Dep. Sopron	19:33 (1)	21:15
Arr. Sopron	08:51	Arr. Vienna (Sud)	20:43	22:33

(1) Second-class only.

Sights in **Sopron**: A 900-year-old architectural treasure, with 240 perfectly preserved historic buildings. The Castle has a Roman foundation and a Norman basement. Visit the 13th century Goat Church and Church of St. Michael. The 15th century synagogue. St. George Church. Holy Ghost Church. The 16th century Lyceum. The 18th century Trinity Statue. The rococo Erdody Palace. Many museums: Liszt, Stonework, Pharmacy, Guild History, and Fabricius House.

SCENIC RAIL TRIPS

Innsbruck - Brennero 74 + 381

The beautiful mountain scenery here can be seen either on an easy one-day roundtrip from Innsbruck or as a portion of the Innsbruck-Verona-Milan route.

For the first way:

Dep. Innsbruck	06:37	08:39 (1)	09:40	12:43	15:22 (1)
Arr. Brennero	35–50 minutes later				

* * *

Dep. Brennero	07:56 (2)	09:56 (3)	12:04 (2)	14:04 (2)	16:32
Arr. Innsbruck	35–50 minutes later				

Here is the schedule for going from Innsbruck to Italy:

381

Dep. Innsbruck	06:37 (4)	08:39 (2)	09:40	11:22 (2)	15:22 (2)	17:22 (2+6)
Dep. Brennero	07:40	09:22	10:42	12:14	16:14	18:14
Arr. Bolzano	09:24	10:54	12:30	13:31	17:33	19:39
Arr. Verona	11:08	12:26	14:21	15:14	19:14	21:18

(1) Supplement charged for first-class. Restaurant car. (2) Runs daily, except Saturday and Sunday. (3) Runs Saturday and Sunday. (4) Change trains in Bolzano. (5) Carries a sleeping car. Also has couchettes. (6) Plus other departures from Innsbruck at 19:24 (4), 22:22 (5) and 23:40 (5), arriving Verona 00:40, 02:34 and 03:47.

Innsbruck - Buchs 800

The excellent mountain scenery here can be seen either on an easy one-day roundtrip from Innsbruck or as a portion of the Innsbruck-Zurich route.

These trains charge a supplement and have a restaurant car, unless designated otherwise

For the first way:

Dep. Innsbruck	06:44	08:02 (1)	14:44
Arr. Buchs	09:08	10:52	17:08

* * *

Dep. Buchs	10:53	12:44	20:52
Arr. Innsbruck	13:16	15:13	23:20

(1) No supplement or restaurant car.

Here is the schedule for going from Innsbruck to Switzerland.

310

Dep. Innsbruck	06:44	08:02 (1)	12:44	14:44	16:53	18:44
Arr. Buchs	09:13	11:13	15:13	17:13	19:22	21:13
Arr. Zurich	10:26	12:26	16:26	18:26	20:41	22:26

(1) No supplement or restaurant car.

Innsbruck - Bruck an der Mur - Vienna

This indirect route from Innsbruck to Vienna, traveling south of the main line (via Linz), offers excellent mountain scenery. As the schedules below indicate, a stopover of up to 10 hours in Bruck an der Mur is possible.

All of the trains Innsbruck-Bruck an der Mur have light refreshments. The trains Bruck an der Mur-Vienna have a restaurant car or light refreshments.

830

Dep. Innsbruck	07:20	09:20	11:20	13:20	15:20	17:20
Arr. Bruck an der Mur	12:40	14:40	16:40	18:40	20:40	22:40

Sights in **Bruck an der Mur**: Located in the Styrian Alps, at the meeting of the Mur and Murz rivers, on the main route between Vienna and Graz. See the 17th century Wrought Iron Well, the outstanding example of Styrian ironwork. The 15th and 16th century houses. The Parish Church.

820

Dep. Bruck an der Mur	Frequent times from 06:43 to 22:43
Arr. Vienna (Sudbf.)	50 minutes later

Innsbruck - Feldkirch - Innsbruck 800

Very good mountain scenery. As the schedules shown below indicate, a stopover of 2-8 hours in Feldkirch is possible.

All of these trains have a restaurant car, unless designated otherwise.

Dep. Innsbruck	07:02	08:02 (1)	09:02	11:02	13:02	15:02
Arr. Feldkirch	09:14	10:32	11:15	13:14	15:14	17:14

Sights in **Feldkirch**: A medieval town, next to the Swiss border. See the Old Town and Marketplace. The 12-foot-thich walls at the 16th century Schattenburg Castle. The local museum, open daily except Wednesday afternoon.

Dep. Feldkirch	10:43	11:11	12:43	14:43	16:43	18:43
Arr. Innsbruck	12:58	13:16	14:58	16:58	18:58	20:58

(1) No restaurant car.

Innsbruck - Garmisch - Zugspitze 782

The outstanding mountain scenery here can be seen either on an easy one-day roundtrip from Innsbruck or as a portion of the Innsbruck-Munich route (page 63).

For the first way:

Dep. Innsbruck	06:34 (1)	07:40	08:43 (1)	09:41	11:04	13:45 (1)
Arr. Garmisch	08:24	09:09	10:22	11:09 (2)	12:24 (2)	15:17

Change trains.

The following schedule allows one to ride one cable route to the summit of Zugspitze and ride a different cable route back to Garmisch.

787

Dep. Garmisch	08:35	09:35	10:35	11:35	12:35	15:35
Arr. Eibsee	09:13	10:13	11:13	12:13	13:13	16:13

Change to cable railway.

Dep. Eibsee	Every 30 minutes from 08:00 to 17:30
	(until 18:00 during July and August)
Arr. Zugspitze	10 minutes later

(1) Change trains in Mittenwald. (2) As the Garmisch departures show, there is time to lunch in Garmisch and take a later train to Eibsee and Zugspitze. See departures above.

Use a different cable railway in returning to Garmisch.

Dep. Zugspitze	Every 30 minutes from 08:30 to 17:00
	(until 18:00 during July and August)
Arr. Schneefernerhaus	4 minutes later

* * *

787 Train

Dep. Schneefernerhaus	10:00	11:00	13:00	14:00	15:00	17:00
Arr. Garmisch	11:20 (1)	12:20 (1)	14:20	15:20	16:20	18:20

Change trains. 782

Dep. Garmisch	11:26 (2)	12:27 (2)	14:26	16:05 (3)	16:35 (2)	18:26 (2+4)
Arr. Innsbruck	12:55	14:02	15:58	17:40	18:40	20:01

(1) As the Garmisch departures show, there is time to lunch in Garmisch and take a later train to Innsbruck or Munich. (2) Change trains in Mittenwald. (3) Restaurant car. (4) Runs Monday-Friday, except holidays. Plus another departure from Garmisch at 19:29, arriving Innsbruck 20:53.

Here is the schedule for continuing on from Garmisch to Munich.

782

Dep. Garmisch	11:34	12:27	13:34	14:27	15:34	16:27 (1)
Arr. Munich	12:51	13:51	14:51	15:51	16:51	17:53

(1) Plus other departures from Garmisch at 17:34, 18:31, 19:34 and 20:27.

Innsbruck - Salzburg - Innsbruck

The good canyon, lake, river and mountain scenery on this route can be seen either on an easy one-day roundtrip from Innsbruck (see details under "Innsbruck - Zell am See - Salzburg - Innsbruck" on page 63), or as a portion of the Innsbruck-Vienna route (see below).

Innsbruck - Vienna 800

Here are the schedules for going across Austria.

All of these trains have a restaurant car unless designated otherwise.

Dep. Innsbruck	07:02	09:02	11:02	13:02	15:02	17:02 (1)
Arr. Vienna (Westbf.)	12:25	14:25	16:25	18:25	20:25	22:25

(1) Plus another departure from Innsbruck at 19:55, arriving Vienna 00:58.

Linz - Selzthal - Amstetten - Linz

The Selzthal-Amstetten portion of this easy one-day circle trip affords fine river, canyon and mountain scenery. There are good views of the colorful **Enns Valley**.

All of the Linz-Selzthal and v.v. trains have light refreshments. All of the Selzthal-Amstetten and v.v. trains are second-class only. All of the Amstetten-Linz and v.v. trains have a restaurant car.

830

Dep. Linz	08:40	10:40	12:40	14:40
Arr. Selzthal	10:16	12:16	14:16	16:16

Change trains.
825

Dep. Selzthal	10:19	12:19	14:19	16:19
Arr. Amstetten	12:48	14:48	16:48	18:48

Change trains.
800

Dep. Amstetten	12:55	14:55	16:55	18:55
Arr. Linz	13:32	15:32	17:32	19:32

The same trip can be made in reverse, using this schedule:

800

Dep. Linz	08:27	10:27	12:27	14:27
Arr. Amstetten	09:02	11:02	13:02	15:04

Change trains.
825

Dep. Amstetten	09:10	11:10	13:10	15:10
Arr. Selzthal	11:41	13:41	15:41	17:41

Change trains.
830

Dep. Selzthal	11:44	13:44	15:44	17:44
Arr. Linz	13:20	14:20	17:20	19:20

Salzburg - Zell am See - Innsbruck

There are exceptionally beautiful views of canyon, lakes, mountains and rivers on one of the most scenic rides in Austria. Schedules for this trip appear earlier in this section under both "Innsbruck-Salzburg" on page 63 and "Salzburg- Innsbruck" on page 64.

Salzburg - Gmunden - Stainach - Salzburg

There is fine mountain and lake scenery on the Gmunden-Stainach portion of this circle trip.

800			830		
Dep. Salzburg	06:05 (1)	12:05 (1)	Dep. Stainach	09:55 (3)	15:52 (3)
Arr. Attnang	06:50	12:50	Arr. Salzburg	11:55	18:00
Change trains.					
815					
Dep. Attnang	07:13	13:14 (2)			
Dep. Gmunden	07:29	13:31			
Dep. Bad Ischl	08:14	14:12			
Dep. Hallstatt	08:39	14:38			
Dep. Bad Aussee	09:07	15:07			
Arr. Stainach	09:43	15:45			
Change trains.					

(1) Restaurant car. (2) Second-class only. (3) Light refreshments

Sights in **Gmunden**: A colorful little town. Artistic pottery has been made here since the 15th century. See the porcelain-tiled clocktower of the Renaissance Town Hall in the main square (Rathausplatz). Stroll from there along the beautiful flowerbeds and chestnut trees of the Esplanade to the yacht harbor and lakeshore beach. Walk on the breakwater to the Ort Chateau, built on a small island.

Sights in **Bad Ischl**: A popular mineral water spa since 1822. This is the center of the Salzkammergut resort region. Visit the home of composer Franz Lehar, now a museum. The Imperial Villa.

Sights in **Hallstaat**: The colorful houses (blue, red, yellow or beige), every balcony and window festooned with flowers. It is a short walk to several waterfalls. See the collection of neatly piled , gaily decorated skulls of generations of villagers in the charnel house. There is not enough land here for a cemetery.

Sights in **Bad Aussee**: This was the center of the salt region in the 15th century. Still popular for health-inducing brine baths. Both a Summer resort and Winter sports area. There are many picturesque lakes here.

Salzburg - Vienna

Marvelous views of the Alps and pretty farmland. See schedules on page 66 (and Vienna-Salzburg on page 68).

Salzburg - Villach - Salzburg 820

The excellent canyon and mountain scenery on this ride can be seen either on an easy one-day roundtrip from Salzburg or as a portion of the Salzburg-Venice route.

For the first way:

Dep. Salzburg	07:08 (1)	09:08 (2)	11:08 (2)	13:08 (2)	15:08 (3)
Arr. Villach	09:43	11:43	13:43	15:43	17:44

* * *

Dep. Villach	10:19 (3)	12:19 (3)	14:19 (2)	16:19 (2)	18:19 (2)
Arr. Salzburg	12:53	14:53	16:53	18:53	20:53

(1) Light refreshments. (2) Restaurant car. (3) Supplement charged for first-class. Restaurant car

Here is the schedule for going from Salzburg to Italy:

75		75	
Dep. Salzburg	09:08	Dep. Villach	12:00 (1)
Arr. Villach	11:43	Arr. Venice (Mestre)	15:18
Change trains.		Change trains.	
		Dep. Venice (Mestre)	16:01
(1) Restaurant car.		Arr. Venice (S.L.)	16:10

The very scenic Klagenfurt-Udine-Trieste portion of the Vienna-Trieste route is described under "Vienna-Trieste" with complete schedules on page 75. A departure from Salzburg can connect with that trip at Villach.

Vienna - Puchberg am Schneeberg - Hochschneeberg - Vienna

52d (Unsere Bahn)

Dep. Vienna (Sud)	06:55	07:55	09:55	10:55 (1)	11:55 (1)	13:55
Arr. Wiener Neustadt	07:30	08:30	10:30	11:30	12:30	14:30
Change trains.						
Dep. Wiener Neustadt	07:36	08:36	10:36	11:36	12:36	14:36
Arr. Puchberg	08:26	09:26	11:26	12:26	13:26	15:26
Change trains. 52e (Unsere Bahn)						
Dep. Puchberg	08:50	-0-	11:40	-0-	-0-	15:45 (3)
Arr. Hochschneeberg	10:19 (2)	-0-	13:03 (2)	-0-	-0-	17:13 (2)

Sights in **Puchberg**: Located at the foot of the mountain called Schneeberg, the eastern edge of the Alps. A Summer and Winter resort. Popular for water cures and weight-loss treatment.

Sights in **Hochschneeberg**: At 5,900 feet, there are good views and a restaurant at the peak.

Dep. Hochschneeberg	13:44	-0-	15:46	-0-	-0-	17:50 (3)
Arr. Puchberg	15:11	-0-	17:21	-0-	-0-	19:17
Change trains. 52d (Unsere Bahn)						
Dep. Puchberg	15:37	16:37	17:37	18:37	-0-	19:37
Arr. Wiener Neustadt	16:23	17:23	18:23	19:23	-0-	20:23
Change trains.						
Dep. Wiener Neustadt	16:30	17:30	18:30	19:30	-0-	20:30
Arr. Vienna (Sud)	17:00	18:05	19:05	20:05	-0-	21:05

(1) Deparures after 09:55 can return to Vienna from Hochschneeberg (at 17:50) only on Friday and Saturday. (2) Return journey to Puchberg must be booked *on arrival*. (3) Runs Friday and Saturday.

Vienna - Bruck an der Mur - Innsbruck

This indirect route from Vienna to Innsbruck, traveling south of the main line (via Linz), offers excellent mountain scenery. The schedules allow a stopover in Bruck an der Mur.

All of these trains have a restaurant car.

820

Dep. Vienna (Sudbf.)	09:30	11:30
Dep. Bruck an der Mur	11:24	13:24
Arr. Bischofshofen	16:09	18:09
Change trains. 800		
Dep. Bischofshofen	16:53	18:58
Arr. Innsbruck	19:35	21:35

Sight in **Bruck an der Mur**: See "Innsbruck-Bruck an der Mur" on page 70.

Vienna - Klagenfurt - Udine - Trieste

The marvelous farm and lake scenery on this route includes seeing **Worthersee**, a lake fed by warm springs that is very popular for swimming and boating, and the beautiful coastline from Udine to Trieste.

The great Worthersee resort area is open June through mid-September. The region around Klagenfurt has attractive lakes, rolling hills and wildlife parks.

Even if you don't stay there, at least watch for that area a few minutes before the stop at Klagenfurt. An early departure from Vienna is recommended in order to be able to see the Adriatic shore approach-ing Trieste in the afternoon sunlight, as we have done.

The comfortable local train from Udine hurtles downhill too fast to permit picture-taking, but you will have a memory of that truly beautiful scene forever. Have a seat on the right-hand side of the train for the best possible view.

Not only is Trieste a worthwhile one-day stopover, it is also ideal as a base for several short rail trips into Yugoslavia such as Villa Opicina, Sezana, Pivka, Postojna and Ljubljana. While staying in Trieste, it is also easy to make a one-day rail excursion to see the sights in Udine (page 76).

75		75	
Dep. Vienna (Sudbf.)	07:24 (1)	Dep. Udine	14:35
Arr. Klagenfurt	11:16	Arr. Trieste	15:43
Dep. Villach	11:45		
Arr. Udine	14:02		
Change trains.			

(1) Supplement charged. Restaurant car. (2) Runs daily except Sundays and holidays. Second-class only.

Sights in Trieste: City buses go to Miramare Castle, Maximilian and Charlotte's lovely seaside palace. Charlotte returned here after their tragic brief time as rulers of Mexico, made insane by Maximillan's death. The Piazza deli'Unita is reminiscent of Piazza San Marco in Venice. The 15th century Castello di San Giusto. The 14th century Cathedral of San Giusto. The ruins of a Roman amphitheater. The Civic Museum of History and Art. It is a scenic 30-minute bus trip (#45, from Piazza G. Oberdan) to visit **Grotta Gigante**, a cave large enough to contain St. Peter's Cathedral.

If you are starting from Salzburg rather than Vienna, the Udine-Trieste route can be seen by making a connection in Villach, shown here:

820		75	
Dep. Salzburg	09:08 (1)	Dep. Udine	14:35 (2)
Arr. Villach	11:43	Arr. Trieste	15:43
Change trains.			
75		(1) Restaurant car.	
Dep. Villach	11:45	(2) Runs daily except Sundays and	
Arr. Udine	14:02	holidays. Second-class only.	
Change trains.			

Now for the one-day excursion to Udine:

Trieste - Udine - Trieste 388

Dep. Trieste	06:55	08:08	10:15 (1)	12:20	13:15 (1)	14:10 (2)
Arr. Udine	08:12	09:15	11:50	13:25	14:46	15:15

Sights in **Udine**: The collection of paintings in the Civic Museum and Gallery, a 20-minute walk from the railstation. Do they still have in Room 32 Vollett's "Crepuscolo" and Cormaldi's "La Donna e lo Specchio" ?

Tiepolo's paintings are featured in both the Bishop's Palace and the Cathedral. Visit Piazza della Liberta.

Dep. Udine	13:15 (2)	14:35 (2)	15:35	17:20 (1)	19:04	19:35 (1+3)
Arr. Trieste	14:22	15:43	16:40	18:52	20:13	21:08

(1) Second-class only. (2) Runs daily, except Sundays and holidays. (3) Plus another departure from Udine at 20:45, arriving Trieste 22:00.

DANUBE CRUISE

This service operates daily from mid-May to mid-September..

843			
Dep. Vienna (Schif.)	08:00	Dep. Linz	08:45
Arr. Durnstein	13:35	Arr. Durnstein	15:45
Arr. Linz	22:55	Arr. Vienna (Schif.)	20:00

Sights in **Durnstein**: This small, fortified town is at the foot of a ridge surrounded by vineyards. Richard the Lion Hearted was held for for an enormous ransom in the Castle, from which there is a wonderful view of Durnstein and the valley below it.

The town's Parish Church and its main street are interesting.

INTERNATIONAL ROUTES FROM AUSTRIA

The Austrian gateways for travel to Germany (and on to Copenhagen) are Innsbruck, Salzburg and Vienna. Vienna is also the access point for travel to Poland and Czechoslovakia (and on to Russia), Hungary, Romania and Yugoslavia (and on to Bulgaria, Greece and Turkey). Innsbruck, Salzburg and Vienna are also starting points for trips to Italy. Innsbruck is also the gateway to Switzerland (and on to Belgium, France, Holland and Luxembourg).

Innsbruck - Munich 782

Dep. Innsbruck	07:40 (1)	08:43 (1)	09:41 (2)	11:04	13:45	15:55 (4)
Arr. Munich	11:14	11:51	12:38	13:31	16:51	18:53

(1) Change trains in Mittenwald. (2) Supplement charged. Restaurant car. (3) Change trains in Garmish. (4) Plus other departures from Innsbruck at 17:04 and 18:27 (3), arriving Munich 19:54 and 21:51.

Vienna - Salzburg - Munich 61

If you are starting this trip in Salzburg, arrive at the Salzburg railstation sufficiently in advance of departure time to complete the German Customs clearance that takes place before boarding the train. There are departures fom Salzburg in addition to those shown here, at frequent times from 07:46 to 01:42 (Table 780).

Dep. Vienna (West)	06:00 (1)	09:00 (1)	16:00 (1)	18:00 (1)	19:40 (2+5)
Dep. Salzburg	09:05	12:09	19:05	21:05	23:07
Arr. Munich (Hbf.)	10:35	13:36	20:36	22:35	00:28 (3)

(1) Supplement charged for first-class. Restaurant car. (2) Carries a sleeping car. Also has second-class couchettes. Coaches are second-class only. Restaurant car Vienna-Salzburg. (3) Arrives at Munich's Ost railstation. (4) Has first-class coach and second-class couchettes. (5) Plus another departure from Vienna at 22:30 (4) and from Salzburg at 03:45 (4), arriving Munich 05:50.

Vienna - Prague - Berlin 87

Dep. Vienna (F.J. Bf.)	07:17 (1)	10:24 (3)	14:07 (3)	17:12	20:00 (4+6)
Arr. Prague (Hlavni)	12:15 (2)	15:44	19:34	23:08	-0-
Arr. Berlin (Licht.)	-0-	21:44	-0-	-0-	08:44

(1) Departs from Vienna's Sudbahnhof railstation. Restaurant car. (2) Arrives at Prague's Holesovice railstation. (3) Restaurant car. (4) Departs from Vienna's Westbahnhof railstation. Carries a sleeping car. Also has couchettes. Coach is second-class only. (5) Carries a sleeping car. Also has couchettes and a first-class coach. (6) Plus another departure from Vienna at 20:40 (5), arriving Prague 02:14, Berlin 08:08.

Vienna - Warsaw (or Kiev) - Moscow

	88	88	48
Dep. Vienna (Sudbf.)	16:00 (1)	21:00 (1)	21:25 (4)
Dep. Zebrzydowice	-0-	-0-	04:00 (2)
Arr. Warsaw (Wschodnia)	-0-	-0-	08:29
Dep. Warsaw (Wschodnia)	-0-	-0-	12:18 (4)
Dep. Brest	-0-	-0-	19:48 (4)
Arr. Kiev	20:33 (2)	06:18 (2)	-0-
Arr. Minsk	-0-	-0-	23:35
Arr. Moscow (Byel.)	-0-	-0-	10:08 (3)
Arr. Moscow (Kievski)	10:00 (3)	19:41	-0-

(1) Carries only sleeping cars. (2) Day 2. (3) Day 3. (4) Vienna-Warsaw: Carries a sleeping car. Also has couchettes and a coach. Warsaw-Moscow: Carries *only* sleeping cars. Light refreshments from Zebrzydowice to Warsaw. Restaurant car from Brest to Moscow.

Vienna - Budapest - Bucharest 32 + 82

Dep. Vienna (Westbf.)	-0-	-0-	08:30 (4)	19:05 (3)
Dep. Vienna (Sudbf.)	07:15 (1)	08:03 (2)	-0-	-0-
Arr. Budapest (Deli)	10:03	-0-	-0-	-0-
Arr. Budapest (Keleti)	-0-	11:08	11:48	21:28
Arr. Bucharest (Nord)	-0-	-0-	-0-	15:00

(1) Restaurant car. (2) Reservation required. Restaurant car. (3) Carries a sleeping car. Also has couchettes. Restaurant car Vienna-Budapest. (4) Plus other departures *for Budapest* from Vienna (Westbf.) at 10:05 (1), 12:30 (1), 14:20 (1) and 15:20 (1)....and another from Vienna (Sudbf.) at 16:00.

Vienna - Belgrade and Athens

Many of these trains do not have either food or beverage service.

	82	88	933
Dep. Vienna (Sudbf.)	08:03 (1)	19:05 (3)	20:10 (5)
Arr. Belgrade	16:40	06:57 (3)	08:32

Change trains.

	970	88 + 970
Dep. Belgrade	21:45	07:35
Dep. Thessaloniki	11:30 (2)	21:50
Arr. Athens	18:45	05:45 (4)

(1) Reservation required. Restaurant car. (2) Day 2 from Vienna. (3) Direct train. No train change in Belgrade. Carries a sleeping car. Also has couchettes. (4) Day 3 from Vienna. (5) Carries a sleeping car. Also has couchettes.

Vienna - Belgrade and Istanbul 65

This train has a second-class coach car that runs direct to Istanbul, with no train change in Belgrade.

Dep. Vienna (Sudbf.)   20:10 (1)

During Summer Time, set your watch back one hour.

Arr. Belgrade   08:32   Day 2

Change trains and railstations (about 1-mile distance).

Dep. Belgrade (Centar)   09:00 (2)   Day 2

All year, set your watch forward 2 hours.

Arr. Istanbul   07:00   Day 3

(1) Carries a sleeping car. Also has couchettes. (2) Reservation required. Has couchettes daily. Caries a sleeping car Wednesday, Saturday and Sunday. Restaurant car 18:40 – 23:00.

Innsbruck - Verona and Milan 74 + 381

Dep. Innsbruck	08:39 (1)	17:22 (1)	23:40 (2)
Arr. Verona (P.N.)	12:26	21:18	03:47
Dep. Verona (P.N.)	12:39	21:31	04:15
Arr. Milan (Cen.)	14:13	23:00	05:50

(1) Supplement charged. Restaurant car. (2) Carries a sleeping car. Also has couchettes. Train splits in Verona. Be sure to board Innsbruck-Milan car.

Innsbruck - Verona - Bologna - Florence - Rome 74 + 381

Dep. Innsbruck	01:38 (1)	06:37	09:40 (2)	11:22 (3)
Arr. Verona (P.N.)	05:52	11:25	14:21	15:14
Arr. Bologna	07:55	13:25	16:14	17:27
Arr. Florence (S.M.N.)	09:10	-0-	-0-	18:35
Arr. Rome (Ter.)	-0-	-0-	-0-	20:45

Dep. Innsbruck	15:22 (4)	22:22 (1)	23:40 (6)
Arr. Verona	19:14	02:34	03:47
Arr. Bologna	21:30	04:21	05:30
Arr. Florence (S.M.N.)	-0-	05:46 (5)	-0-
Arr. Rome (Ter.)	-0-	08:33	-0-

(1) Reservation required. Carries a sleeping car. Also has couchettes. (2) Reservation required. Light refreshments. (3) Reservation required. Supplement charged. Restaurant car. (4) Supplement charged. Restaurant car. (5) Arrives at Florence's Campo di Marte railstation. (6) Carries a sleeping car . Also has couchettes.

Vienna - Nurnberg - Frankfurt - Cologne 64

All of these trains charge a supplement and have a restaurant car, unless designated otherwise.

Dep. Vienna (Westbf.)	08:00	10:00	12:00	14:00 (1)
Arr. Nurnberg	13:06	15:06	17:06	19:06
Arr. Frankfurt	15:38	17:38	19:38	21:38
Arr. Cologne	18:05	20:05	22:05	00:09

(1) Plus other departures from Vienna at 19:00 and 22:30 (both trains carrying a sleeping car and also having couchettes), arriving Cologne 04:50 and 09:21.

Vienna - Salzburg - Munich - Stuttgart - Strasbourg - Paris 61

This train carries a sleeping car and also has couchettes. Coaches are second-class only. Restaurant car Vienna-Salzburg.

Dep. Vienna (Westbf.)	19:40	Arr. Stuttgart	02:55
Dep. Linz	21:34	Arr. Strasbourg	05:00
Arr. Salzburg	22:55	Arr. Nancy	06:41
Arr. Munich (Ost)	00:28	Arr. Paris (Est)	09:29

Vienna - Venice 75 + 45

Dep. Vienna (Sudbf.)	07:24 (1)	13:11 (2)	19:45 (3)	22:30 (4)
Arr. Venice (Mestre)	15:18	-0-	03:50	-0-
Change trains.				
Dep Venice (Mestre)	16:01	-0-	04:29	-0-
Arr. Venice (S.L.)	16:10	21:57	04:38	08:32

(1) Supplement charged. Restaurant car. (2) Direct train to Venice's Santa Lucia railstation. No train change in Mestre railstation. Restaurant car. (3) Carries a sleeping car. Also has couchettes. (4) Direct train to Venice's Santa Lucia railstation. No train change in Venice's Mestre railstation. Carries a sleeping car. Also has couchettes.

Innsbruck - Zurich 57+ 310

There is marvelous Alpine scenery on this route. About 2½ hours before reaching Zurich, the train passes through one of Europe's longest rail tunnels, the 6.3-mile long Arlberg.

Dep. Innsbruck	02:44 (1)	06:44 (2)	08:02	12:44 (2)	14:44 (2+3)
Arr. Zurich	06:26	10:26	12:26	16:26	18:26

(1) Carries a sleeping car. Also has couchettes. (2) Supplement charged. Restaurant car. (3) Plus other departures from Innsbruck at 16:53 (2) and 18:44 (2), arriving Zurich 20:41 and 22:26.

BENELUX

BELGIUM, NETHERLANDS and LUXEMBOURG

Children under 6 travel free on Belgium's trains, children 6-11 pay half-fare, children 12 and over must pay full fare.

Children under 4 travel free on Holland's trains, children 4-9 pay half-fare, children 10 and over must pay full fare.

Children under 4 travel free on Luxembourg's trains, children 4-11 pay half-fare, children 12 and over must pay full fare.

An 18-minute train ride between Amsterdam's Central railstation and Schipol Airport runs frequent times 00:15 to 23:38. Airport to Amsterdam: 00:09 to 23:52 [table 222]

There is 19-minute train service from Brussels (Central) and 16-minute train service from Brussels (Nord) to that city's National Airport every 30 minutes from 05:39 to 23:14. Same frequency (06:09-23:46) for the trip from the Airport to Brussels [table 201].

There is frequent bus service between Luxembourg's Gare Centrale and the city's Findel Airport [table 5].

The signs you will see at railstations in Belgium, Holland and Luxembourg are:

	BELGIUM and LUXEMBOURG	HOLLAND
Arrival	Arrivee	Aankomst
Departure	Depart	Vertrek
Exit	Sortie	Uitgang
Information	Renseignements	Inlichtingen
Luggage Check-Room	Consigne	Hetbagagedepot
Men	Messieurs	Heren
Restaurant Car	Wagon-Restaurant	Restauratie-Wagen
Sleeping Car	Wagon-Lit	Slaapcoupe
Smoking Compartment	Fumeurs	Rokers
Station	Gare	Station
Timetable	Horaire	Spoorboekje
Track	Quai	Spoor
Women	Dames	Dames

SUMMER TIME

Belgium, Holland and Luxembourg change to Summer Time on the last Sunday of March and convert back to Standard Time on the last Sunday of September.

82

BENELUX

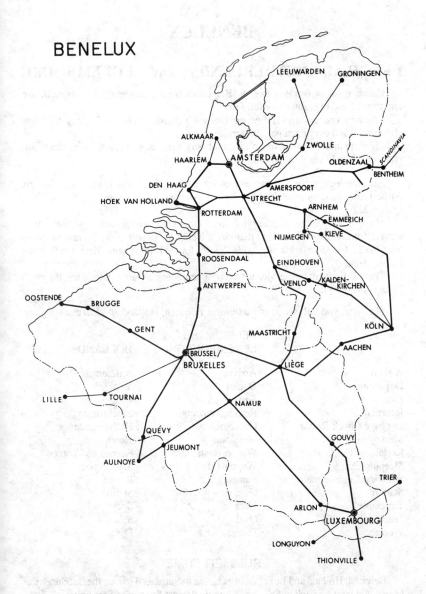

A list of holidays is helpful because some trains will be noted later in this section as not running on holidays. Also, those trains which operate on holidays are filled, and it is necessary to make reservations for them long in advance.

BELGIUM'S HOLIDAYS

NOTE: When any holiday falls on Sunday, the following day is also a holiday.

January 1	New Year's Day	July 21	Independence Day
	Easter	August 15	Assumption Day
	Easter Monday	November 1	All Saints Day
May 1	Labor Day	November 11	Armistice Day
	Ascension Day		(World War I)
	Whit Sunday	December 25	Christmas Day
	Whit Monday		

HOLLAND'S HOLIDAYS

January 1	New Year's Day	May 1	Labor Day
	Good Friday		Ascension Day
	Easter		Whit Monday
	Easter Monday	December 25	Christmas Day
April 30	Queen's Birthday	December 26	Boxing Day

LUXEMBOURG'S HOLIDAYS

January 1	New Year's Day		Whit Monday
	Shrove Monday	June 23	National Holiday
	Easter	August 15	Assumption Day
	Easter Monday	December 25	Christmas Day
May 1	Labor Day	December 26	Boxing Day
	Ascension Day		

EURAILPASS BONUSES

A 35% reduction on the normal fare for the Ostend-Dover ferry operated by Regie belge des Transports Maritimes. Reduced fare tickets are available only in Ostend and Dover. There are no Eurailpass bonuses in Holland or Luxembourg.

BENELUX TOURRAIL PASS

This pass is for any 5 days of unlimited travel out of a 17-day period on all the rail lines of Belgium, Holland and Luxembourg, plus railway buses in Luxembourg. Sold at the railstations of all 3 countries and also by the U.S. and Canadian offices of the Netherlands Board of Tourism and Rail Europe (see "Holland" and "France" on page 23). The 1992 *First-class* prices are: $154 (U.S.) for passengers age 26 and older, $109 for those 12–25 years old, $54 for children 4–11. *Second-class*: $103, $74 and $36. Children under 4 travel free when not occupying a separate seat.

BELGIUM'S TOURRAIL

Sold at Belgian railstations. Unlimited train travel in Belgium for any 5 days out of a 17-day period.

For adults 26 years of age and older. (For younger persons, see "Junior" card, below.)

The 1991 *first*-class prices were: 3,740 Belgian francs. *Second*-class: Bf-2,490. Children under 6 travel free.

BELGIUM'S JUNIOR TOURRAIL CARD

Sold at Belgian railstations. Unlimited train travel in Belgium for any 5 days out of a 17-day period for persons 6 to under 26 years old.

The 1991 *first*-class price was: 2,690 Belgian francs. *Second*-class: Bf-1,790.

BELGIUM'S HALF-FARE CARD

Sold at Belgian railstations. Entitles the traveler to unlimited first-class and second-class train travel at half-fare for one month. The 1991 price was 550 Belgian francs. Validity period starts on the day chosen by the holder of the card.

ONE-DAY HOLLAND TOURS

Netherlands Railways offers during the Spring and Summer months nearly 100 one-day excursions from Amsterdam to interesting destinations. Eurailpass holders pay only for the non-rail portions of these trips and for admission fees.

An example is the day-trip that starts with a train ride from Amsterdam to Utrecht, coffee and cake, bus to **Maliebaan,** admission there to both the Railway Museum and to the Van Speelklok Museum of automatic musical in- struments (music boxes, street organs, etc.), and the train ride back to Amsterdam.

HOLLAND'S LEISURE CARD

Valid for one year. Provides 40% discount on a one-way train ticket and the "One-Day Rover" train pass (see page 85) and discounts of 25% to 30% on sightseeing excursions, car rentals and domestic flights. The 1992 price is $15(U.S.) plus $2.50 for postage and handling.

Can be purchased at VVV Tourist offices in Amsterdam, Apeldoorn, Arnhem, Breda, Maastricht, Middelburg, Rotterdam and The Hague. Also at the travel agencies in the railway stations of Amsterdam (Cen.), Arnhem, Eindhoven, Groningen, Haarlem, Leiden, Maastricht, Nijmegen, Rotterdam (Cen.), Schipol Airport, The Hague (Cen.) and Utrecht (Cen.) . . . as well as at offices of Netherlands Board of Tourism in Chicago, London, New York, San Francisco and Toronto. Through travel agencies in Japan.

U.S.A. and Canadian offices are listed under "Holland" on page 23.

HOLLAND'S ROVER TICKETS

These rail passes are sold in 4 versions. All are available in Holland at railstations and accredited travel agencies. *The 7-Day Rover pass is also sold in the U.S.A. at: Netherlands Board of Tourism, 225 No. Michigan Avenue, Suite 326, Chicago, IL 60601.* The buyer must provide a passport number and the date of the first day the ticket will be used. Children 4 to under 12 travel at 40% discount. Children under 4 travel free.

One-Day Rail Rover   One day of unlimited train travel for distances of over 210 kilometers (130 miles), valid until 4:00 the next morning. Through March of 1992, the prices for both adults and children are: first-class 81 Dutch florins, second-class Dfl-54 less 40% discount on either first-class or second-class to holders of Holland's Leisure Card (see page 84). And less 40% discount for *un*accompanied children 4 to under 12. (The "Children's Railrunner"at Dfl-1.00 is more economical for accompanied children age 4–11.)

7-Day Rail Rover   Seven consecutive days of unlimited train travel. Through March of 1992, the prices for both adults and children are: first-class Dfl-194, second-class Dfl-129.

A pass for unlimited use of all city transit services (buses and streetcars), available *only in combination with the 7-Day Rover,* is valid for the same 7 days at an additional $13 (U.S.).

Multirover   One day of unlimited first-class or second-class train travel. During June, July and August, it is valid all day, any day. From September through May: valid after 09:00 Monday-Friday, all day on Saturdays, Sundays and holidays. Priced for 2–6 people. For children age 4 –11, the "Children's Railrunner" at Dfl-1.00 is more economical.

The first-class prices through March of 1992 are: Dfl-124 for 2 passengers, Dfl-150 for 3, Dfl-160 for 4, Dfl-190 for 5, and DFL-210 for 6. Second- class: Dfl-82, Dfl-99, Dfl-112, Dfl-125 and Dfl-138.

Zomertour Plus   Unlimited train travel for any 3 days out of a 10-day period during July and August. The 1992 prices are: Dfl-79 for one person, Dfl-99 for 2 persons. An additional pass covering municipal transportation costs Dfl-14 for one person, Dfl-20 for 2 persons.

HOLLAND RAIL PASS

Unlimited train travel for 3 days out of a 10-day period. Must be purchased before arriving in Holland. Sold in the U.S.A. at: Netherlands Board of Tourism, 225 No. Michigan Avenue, Suite 326, Chicago IL 60601.

The prices through March, 1992 are: $66.50 (U.S.) for first-class, $53 for second-class. Children up to 11 years of age pay $2.00 for either class.

LUXEMBOURG'S SPECIAL TICKETS

Valid on both trains and all public buses, including Luxembourg-City buses. *Not* valid for journeys departing from or arriving at border stations. Children under age 6 travel free.

Prices shown are *second-class*. A supplement of 60 Luxembourg francs is charged for first-class.

Short-Distance Ticket   Valid for one-hour trips. The 1992 price is Lf-30. A book of 10 tickets cost Lf-240.

One-Day Network Ticket   Valid from time first used on one day until 08:00 the next morning. The 1992 price is Lf-120. A book of 5 tickets cost Lf-480.

One-Month Ticket   The 1992 price is Lf-1,200.

LUXEMBOURG'S SENIOR CITIZEN HALF-FARE

A 50% reduction on both first and second-class *train* tickets for people over age 65. Presentation of identity card or passport required as proof of age. Not valid for journeys departing from or arriving at border stations.

ONE-DAY EXCURSIONS AND CITY-SIGHTSEEING

Here are 59 one-day rail trips that can be made comfortably from 3 major Benelux cities (Amsterdam, Brussels and Luxembourg City), returning to them in most cases before dinner time. (Five of these trips offer, in addition to interesting destinations, scenic fields of flowers in bloom mid-March through May.) Notes are provided on what to see and do at each destination. The number after the name of each route is the Cook's timetable. Three other one-day trips are recommended for exceptional scenery.

Schedules for international connections conclude this section.

Amsterdam

Trains depart Amsterdam's Central, RAI and Zuid railstations for Schipol (the airport) and from Schipol to Amsterdam at frequent times during all 24 hours. The journey takes 18 minutes.

The Tourist Office in the Central railstation is open daily 08:45-23:00 from Easter to September 30.

Your city sightseeing in Amsterdam should include the Rijkmuseum (State Museum) collection of Rembrandt, Rubens, Goya and El Greco paintings (42 Stadhouderskade). Also exhibited there are Dresden china, delftware, tapestries, prints, furniture, dollhouses and sculpture.

See the works of Chagall, Cezanne, Picasso, Calder, Pollack, Rodin, Braque and Warhol at the Stedelijkmuseum (Municipal Museum), 13 Paulus Potterstraat. A complete spectrum of Van Gogh paintings plus several by Gauguin and Toulouse-Lautrec at the Museum Vincent van Gogh (7-11 Paulus Potterstraat). The display of Indonesian and Far Eastern art and anthropology at the Tropical Museum.

The exhibit of 300 ship models, many atlases and charts, and 5,000 books in the National Shipping Museum (1-7 Kattenburgplein). Rembrandt's house (4-6 Jodenbreestraat). The Flea Market, near Rembrandt's house. Exhibits depicting the city's history since its founding in 1270, at the Amsterdam Historical Museum (92 Kalversraat).

The history of Jews in Holland since 1590, at the Jewish Historical Museum (4 Nieumarkt). The altar and organ at the attic church of the 17th century Amstelkring Museum (40 Oudezijds Voorburgwal), the last of the "hidden" Catholic churches in Holland, with interesting 17th and 18th century furniture.

All 9 museums are open Tuesday-Saturday 10:00-17:00 and on Sundays and holidays 13:00-17:00.

Visit the Anne Frank House (263 Prinsengracht), open Monday-Saturday 9:00-17:00 and on Sundays and holidays 10:00-17:00. Take a 75-minute ride in a glass-roofed canal boat, starting at the piers in front of Central railstation or at Stadhouderskade, near the Rijksmuseum.

Royal Palace. The Tower of Tears. Nieuwe Kerk on the Dam, open Monday-Saturday 10:00-17:00, Sunday 12:00-15:00. Mint Tower. Free samples when ending the tour of Heineken Brewery, Monday-Friday starting at 10:00. The Flower Market (Bloemenmarkt), open Monday-Friday. Several diamond-cutting factories.

The Theater Museum (168 Herengracht), open Tuesday-Friday 10:00-17:00, Sundays and holidays 11:00-17:00. See Willet Holthuyen Museum (5 Herengracht), a classical 17th century canal house, elegantly furnished in the style of Holland's Golden Age. Open Monday-Saturday 09:30-17:00, Sundays and holidays 13:00-17:00.

Take an inexpensive half-day bus tour to the heart of the tulip district. It is near Aalsmeer, less than 45 minutes from Amsterdam. Visit the daily Aalsmeer Flower Auction, close to Amsterdam's Schipol Airport. The peak time at the auction is 08:00-10:00.

Brussels

Sightseeing starts in Grand Place, the ornate town square with many gilded buildings. Inside Hotel de Ville (Town Hall), there is a tapestry museum open daily in Summer, Monday-Friday in Winter. Next to it is a reproduction of a 17th century brewery. See the 15th century Notre Dame des Victoires church and the 17th century Flemish houses in nearby Place du Grand Sablon.

The marvelous Place Parc de Bruxeles gardens and lakes. The Royal Palace, at one end of this park, is open daily except Monday 09:30-16:00 for about 6 weeks during Summer. The Belgian Parliament is located at the other end of the park.

One of the world's best collections of 15th and 16th century Flemish and Dutch paintings (Rubens, Brueghel, Bosch) is exhibited at the Museum of Ancient Art & Modern Art on Rue de la Regence, open daily except Monday 10:00-17:00.

Nearby, the collection of rare musical instruments in the Royal Conservatory of Music at the Petit Sablon (also on Rue de la Regence), open Tuesday, Thursday and Saturday 14:30-16:30, Sunday 10:30-22:00, Wednesday 20:00-22:00.

The collection of paintings by both medieval masters (one section devoted entirely to Bruegel) and also those of later centuries through the 19th, in the Beaux Arts Museum at 3 Rue de la Regence. Then go through a short passageway to the new (1984) Modern Art Museum (Henry Moore, Dali, Magritte, Delvaux). Both museums are open daily except Monday 10:00-17:00.

See the impressive array of African art in The Royal Museum of Central Africa, 12km east, in Tervuren Park & Arboretum. The view from the Palais de Justice. The Law Courts. The tapestries in the 13th century Cathedral of St. Michael.

The Brussels City Museum. The Museum of Arms and Armor. The museum of sculptures by Constantin Meunier, whose work depicts the dignity of laborers. The Postal Museum. The Royal Greenhouses. The Brueghel Museum, in the house where the painter lived his last 6 years.

The Railway Museum, on the mezzanine of Brussels' Nord railstation. The Art Nouveau pieces in the Horta Museum at 25 Rue Americaine, open daily except Mondays and holidays 14:00-17:30.

The most famous gourmet food emporium here is the Rob store at Boulevard de la Woluwe 28. (Take the subway from the center of town to the Tomberg stop and then bus #42, which stops in front of Rob.) Fruits from all over the world, an assortment of 25 ordinary and exotic pates (baby boar !), eel cooked in green sauce, snails marinated in wine sauce, numerous fish (live trout, Scotch salmon, Norwegian lobsters), 600 different wines, 35 types of mustard, chocolates galore.

A bus can be taken 10 miles to **Waterloo.**

Luxembourg City

The Citadel, with its 53 forts connected by 16 miles of tunnels. Fish Market, site of the city's oldest buildings. The State Museum, open daily except Monday 10:00-12:00 and 14:00-18:00. The Palais Grand-Ducal. The splendid view from the bridge that crosses the River Alzette. The Palais Municipal, on the Place d'Armes. The Municipal Art Gallery, open daily except Monday during Summer, only on Saturday and Sunday the rest of the year. City Hall. The old quarter, Pfaffenthal, with its medieval buildings. The Fort of Three Acorns. Malakoff Tower. The Church of St. Michael.

The Three Towers, marking the outer limits of the town in 1050. Notre Dame Cathedral. The 4th century Chapel of St. Quirinus, one of the oldest shrines in Christendom. The Museum of History and Art. General Patton's grave in the U.S. Military Cemetery, 3 miles away, at **Hamm.**

In the following timetables, where a city has more than one railstation we have designated the particular station after the name of the city (in parentheses).

ONE-DAY EXCURSIONS AND CITY-SIGHTSEEING

On day trips from Amsterdam that we have designated "H-L", you will see in the area between Haarlem and Leiden, from mid-March through May, fields of tulips, narcissus, crocus and other bulb flowers in bloom. The region is known as the "Champs de Fleurs" (Fields of Flowers).

Amsterdam - Alkmaar - Amsterdam 223

Dep. Amsterdam   every 30 minutes from 07:22 to 23:22
Arr. Alkmaar   30 minutes later

Sights in **Alkmaar**: The Friday Cheese Market, from the end of April until the end of September, 10:00-12:00. The organ at St. Lawrence Church.

Dep. Alkmaar   every 30 minutes from 08:08 to 23:38
Arr. Amsterdam   30 minutes later

Amsterdam - Alkmaar - Haarlem - Amsterdam 223

It is easy to visit both Alkmaar and Haarlem in a single day-trip.

Dep Amsterdam   twice each hour   Dep. Haarlem   twice each hour.
Arr. Alkmaar   30 minutes later.   Arrive Amsterdam 19 minutes later.
   Change trains.
Dep. Alkmaar   twice each hour.
Arr. Haarlem   28 minutes later.

Sights in **Haarlem**: See notes on page 95.

Amsterdam - Amersfoort - Amsterdam   225

Dep. Amsterdam   Frequent times from 06:32 to 23:32
Arr. Amersfoort   34 minutes later

Sights in **Amersfoort**: A beautiful citadel town with many canals and ancient streets. Popular among antique collectors and for taking side trips to **Spakenburg** (a quaint fishing village on the old Zuider Zee), **Laren** (to visit the Singer Museum), **Zeist** (to see the beautifully-furnished castle there), **Baarn** (to visit Palace Soestdijk, the residence of the former Queen Juliana, **Muiden** (to see the 15th century moated castle, Muiderslot).

Dep. Amersfoort   Frequent times from 06:22 to 23:26
Arr. Amsterdam   34 minutes later

Amsterdam - Antwerp - Amsterdam   76

Dep. Amsterdam   Frequent times from 06:22 to 20:26
Arr. Antwerp (Cen.)   2 hours and 20 minutes later

Sights in **Antwerp**: To the right of the railstation is one of the best zoos in the world, set in a beautiful garden. It is open daily 08:30-17:00. Walk through the maze of streets called Grote Markt (art galleries, bakeries, fruit stalls, antique shops).

You can watch diamonds being cut and polished at Diamond Land, 33 Appelmanstraat, open daily except Sunday 09:00-18:00. There is a good exhibit of the history of diamonds at the Provincial Museum of Safety, 28-30 Jezusstraat, open Wednesday-Saturday 10:00-17:00, with demonstrations on Saturday 14:00-17:00.

Visit the Cathedral, open April through mid-October: Monday-Friday 12:00-17:00, Saturday 12:00-15:00, Sunday 13:00-17:00. The rest of the year: Monday 14:00-17:00, Saturday 12:00-15:00, Sunday 13:00-17:00.

Flemish, Italian, French, Dutch and German masterpieces in the Gallery of Fine Arts, open daily except Monday 10:00-17:00. Rubens House, with many of his paintings, at 9-11 Wapper, open daily 10:00-17:00. The 16th century printing shop in the Plantin-Moretus Museum. The Marine Museum.

The Mayer van den Bergh Museum. The Folklore Museum. Town Hall. Guild Houses. Vieille Bourse (the Old Stock Exchange). The Rockox Mansion. The view of Antwerp from the 24th floor of Torengebouw.

Now a classy suburb of Antwerp, **Middelheim** was first settled in the 14th century. See there the more than 300 statues (by Henry Moore, Vic Gentil, Charles Leplae and many other great sculptors) in the 30-acre Middelheim Open-Air Museum of Sculpture, founded in 1950. It is 30 minutes by bus #17, #27 or #32, from Antwerp's Central railstation. The bus driver will tell you where to get off, and the walk to the sculpture park is 15 minutes from there, passing many splendid mansions.

One can begin circling the park-museum by starting either toward the left of the entrance (in the direction of the statue of Balzac) or to the right, along a tree-shaded stream and through a lawn that has many statues.

The park (admission free) is open daily 10:00 to sunset about 17:00 in Winter, 21:00 in Summer.

Dep. Antwerp (Cen.)   Frequent times from 06:54 to 23:54
Arr. Amsterdam   2 hours and 20 minutes later

Amsterdam - Apeldoorn   225

| Dep. Amsterdam (Cen.) | 2 minutes after every hour from 07:02 to 20:02 |
| Arr. Apeldoorn | 1 hour and 4 minutes later |

Sights in **Apeldoorn:** From the railstation, take buses #102, #104 and #106 to the Het Loo Palace. Set in a 27,000-acre Royal Forest, the palace was a private residence for the Dutch royal family until it became a state museum in 1971.

Both the lavish, enormous palace and the geometric patterns of its extraordinary gardens are well worth visiting. Seventeenth century tapestries, magnificent furniture, exceptional Delft pottery and fine paintings (Rembrandt, Vermeer, van Ruisdael) are exhibited in the palace.

| Dep. Apeldoorn | 26 minutes after everry hour from 06:26 to 22:26 |
| Arr. Amsterdam (Cen.) | 1 hour and 6 minutes later |

Amsterdam - Arnhem - Amsterdam   230

| Dep. Amsterdam (Cent.) | Frequent times from 06:02 to 23:49 |
| Arr. Arnhem | 60-70 minutes later |

Sights in **Arnhem:** The nearly 3-square-mile Netherlands Open-Air Museum, a collection of several farm villages, depicting rural lifestyles from the 18th to early 20th centuries. Colored arrows direct visitors to one, 2 and 4-hour tours. Open April-October, Monday-Friday 09:00 - 17:00, Sunday 10:00 - 17:00. At the craft exhibits, wood shoes are chiseled, bread is baked, baskets and paper are made. See a blacksmith at his forge. Don't fail to try the little pancake balls called "poffertjes", and then eat some pannekoeken (traditional Dutch pancakes) and wafelen (waffles).

Also visit the 16th century Grootekerk (Ptotestant Church) and the extensively-restored Eusebiuskerk, a Gothic church. See the Duivelshuis (devil's house). The best collection of Van Gogh is at the Kroller-Muller Museum in the nearby National Park. Special buses go the several miles from the railstation to the museum and surrounding 13,300-acre national park during June, July and August. The museum is open Tuesday-Saturday 10:00–17:00, Sunday 11:00–17:00.

| Dep. Arnhem | Frequent times from 05:30 to 23:37 |
| Arr. Amsterdam | 60-70 minutes later |

Amsterdam - Bonn   64 + 700

All of these trains are EuroCity or InterCity, which require reservation and have a restaurant car or light refreshments. EC trains charge a supplement.

Change trains at Cologne in both directions.

| Dep. Amsterdam (Cen.) | 06:02 | 07:08 | 08:00 | | |
| Arr. Bonn | 09:17 | 10:47 | 11:47 | | |

Sights in **Bonn**: See notes about Bonn under "Cologne-Bonn" on page 381

| Dep. Bonn | 12:39 | 14:39 | 16:39 | 17:39 | 18:39 |
| Arr. Amsterdam (Cen.) | 15:51 | 17:51 | 19:51 | 21:51 | 23:57 |

Amsterdam - Brussels - Amsterdam 205

Dep. Amsterdam	06:22	07:00	07:24	08:26 (4)
Arr. Brussels (Nord)	09:21	09:49	10:21	11:21
Arr. Brussels (Cen.)	09:28	-0-	10:26	11:26
Arr. Brussels (Midi)	09:30	09:56	10:30	11:30

Sights in **Brussels**: See notes about sightseeing in Brussels on page 88.

Dep. Brussels (Midi)	13:29 (1)	14:10	15:10	16:10 (5)
Dep. Brussels (Cen.)	-0-	14:14	15:14	16:14
Dep. Brussels (Nord)	13:36	14:19	15:19	16:19
Arr. Amsterdam	16:34	17:08	18:08	19:08

(1) Restaurant car. (2) Runs daily, except Sundays and holidays. Restaurant car. (3) Light refreshments. (4) Plus other departures from Amsterdam at 08:53(2), 09:26, 10:26 and 10:49, arriving Brussels (Nord) 11:30, 12:21, 13:21 and 13:46. (5) Plus other departures from Brussels (Midi) at 17:10, 17:54 (3), 18:10, 19:10, 19:51, 20:13, 21:10 and 21:20 (1), arriving Amsterdam 20:08, 21:01, 21:08, 22:08, 22:35, 23:08, 00:10 and 23:59.

Amsterdam - Cologne 230

All of these trains charge a supplement and have a restaurant car, unless designated otherwise

Amsterdam	06:02	07:08	08:00	09:08	11:08
Arr. Cologne	08:42	09:42	10:57	11:57	13:42

Sights in **Cologne**: See notes about Cologne on page 372.

Dep. Cologne	13:17 (1)	15:17	17:17	18:02	19:02(2)
Arr. Amsterdam	15:51	17:51	19:51	20:51	21:51

(1) No restaurant car. (2) Plus another departures from Cologne at 21:17, arriving Amsterdam 23:57.

Amsterdam - Delft - Amsterdam (H-L) 220

Dep. Amsterdam (Cen.)	Frequent times from 00:43 to 23:26
Arr. Delft	60 minutes later

Sights in **Delft**: The tourist information office (on the main square) pro- vides a brochure that describes a walking tour which includes all of the city's principal sights.

See the 14th century New Church, where members of the Dutch royal family are buried. The Mausoleum of William the Silent at the 15th century New Church. The 17th century Prinsenhof (Princes Court), housing the Municipal Museum. Tetar van Elven Museum, containing the works of Vermeer and Pieter de Hoogh. Old Church. The Grain Market. Town Hall. The Old Delft Canal.

The Delft Pottery Factory ("De Porceleyne Fles") at 196 Rotterdamsweg is open May-September 09:00-17:00 Monday-Saturday and 13:00-18:00 on Sun- day. It is open 09:00-17:00 Monday-Saturday from October through April. Its tour includes visiting a showroom, a shop and exhibits of antique tiles and mural ceramics.

Dep. Delft	Frequent times from 00:26 to 23:58
Arr. Amsterdam (Cen.)	60 minutes later

Amsterdam - Den Haag - Amsterdam (H-L) 220

Dep. Amsterdam   2-3 times each hour from 05:31 to 23:26
Arr. Den Haag (H.S.)   45-50 minutes later

Sights in **Den Haag**: Binnenhof, a complex of palaces and courtyards, including the 13th century Hall of Knights (an 118-by-56-foot banquet hall where Holland's Parliament meets every September), and Gevangenpoort, Holland's 14th century prison.

Mauritshuis, a great art gallery (Rembrandt, Vermeers, Rubens) The finest collection in the world of 19th century Dutch art, at the Gemeente Museum. The collection of Rembrandts at the Bredius Museum. The Peace Palace. The Hidden Church, at 38 Molenstraat. The Mesdag Museum. The Costume Museum. Municipal Museum. The miniature city of Madurodam, with everything on a scale of 1/25th life size.

The marvelous paintings in the Johan de Witt Huis at Kneuterdijk 6, open Monday-Saturday 10:00-17:00, and on Sundays and holidays 11:00-17:00. The more than 1,000 puppets and marionettes at the Puppet Museum. The 5 miles of wide, beautiful beach.

Dep. Den Haag (H.S.) 2-3 times each hour from 05:39 to 00:38
Arr. Amsterdam   45-50 minutes later

Amsterdam - Den Haag + Utrecht - Amsterdam (H-L)

It is possible to visit both Den Haag (see sightseeing notes above) and Utrecht in one day.

220

Dep. Amsterdam   Frequent departures from 05:31 to 23:26
Arr. Den Haag (**H.S.**) 45-50 minutes later
   Change trains *and* railstations.
   225
Dep. Den Haag (**Cen.**) Frequent times from 07:35 to 22:03
Arr. Utrecht   40 minutes later

Sights in **Utrecht**: The 13th century Dom Cathedral, and the view from the top of its 465 steps (300 feet high). In fall, winter and spring the tower is open only on weekends. Nearby is the Music Box and Street Organ Museum on Achter de Dom, open Tuesday-Saturday 11:00-16:00. Next door is the Museum of Contemporary Art at 14 Achter de Dom.

The museum of mechanical instruments, at 38 Lange Nieuwstraat. The Netherlands Railway Museum, at 6 Van Oldenberneveltlaan, open Tuesday- Saturday 10:00-17:00, Sundays 13:00-17:00. The 11th century St. Peter's Church. The paintings and Viking ship in the Centraal Museum at 1 Agnietenstraat, open Tuesday-Saturday 10:00-17:00, Sundays and holidays 14:00-17:00.

The ancient fish market, Vis Markt, an institution at the same location since the 12th century. The largest medieval art collection in Holland, at the Museum of Religious Art in Het Catherijneconvent (St. Catherine's Church and Convent).

The collection of 180 musical instruments ("from music box to barrel organ") displayed at the van Speeldos tot Pierement Museum. The Gold, Silver and Clock Museum. The Museum of Contemporary Art. The Museum of the Insurance Business.

Nearby interesting villages: **Breukelen**, for which New York's Brooklyn was named (castles, 17th century mansions), **Oudewater** (famous for its stork colony and 3-aisle church), and **Loenen** (known for its 18th century houses and their lovely gardens).

230

Dep. Utrecht   Frequent times from 06:17 to 00:20
Arr. Amsterdam   30 minutes later

For those who prefer the direct trip to Utrecht and to have more time there, refer to notes under "Amsterdam-Utrecht" on page 98.

Amsterdam - Dusseldorf - Amsterdam 230

All of these trains charge a supplement and have a restaurant car, unless designated otherwise.

Dep. Amsterdam (Cen.)	06:02	07:08	08:00	09:08
Arr. Dusseldorf	08:19	09:19	10:31	11:31

Sights in **Dusseldorf**: See notes about Dusseldorf under "Cologne-Dusseldorf" on page 382

Dep. Dusseldorf	13:39 (1)	15:39	17:39	18:26 (2)
Arr. Amsterdam (Cen.)	15:51	17:51	19:51	20:51

1) No restaurant car. (2) Plus other departures from Dusseldorf at 19:26 and 21:39, arriving Amsterdam 21:51 and 23:57.

Amsterdam - Enkhuizen - Amsterdam 223

Local trains run every 30 minutes 07:19–23:19 for the 66-minute trip north from Amsterdam's Central railstation. Trains depart Enkhuizen every 30 minutes 08:38–23:08 for the 66-minute trip back to Amsterdam.

It is a 4-minute walk from the Enkhuizen railstation to its ferry dock. Boats depart every 15 minutes to the 700-acre Zuider Zee Open Air Museum, open summer months 10:00–17:00.

This museum consists of 130 houses, portraying life and work from 1880 to 1932. Allow at least 2 hours to tour it. Then take a 10-minute walk to the Binnenmuseum, an indoor complex of 15 exhibition halls displaying fine examples of furniture, fishing boats, toys and other items. It is open mid-February to December 31: Monday-Saturday 10:00–17:00, Sunday 12:00–17:00.

Amsterdam - Gouda - Amsterdam 227

Dep. Amsterdam   24 minutes after each hour, from 07:24 to 22:24
Arr. Gouda   50 minutes later

Sights in **Gouda**: Stained-glass in Sint Janskerk. The 15th century Town Hall. The famous Thursday cheese market.

Dep. Gouda   18 minutes after each hour, from 06:18 to 23:18
Arr. Amsterdam   50 minutes later

Amsterdam - Haarlem - Amsterdam 235

Dep. Amsterdam (Cen.)	Twice each hour, from 08:34 to 22:04
Arr. Haarlem	14 minutes later

Sights in **Haarlem**: It is only a few minutes' walk from the railstation to town center, Grote Markt, where jousting tournaments took place in the Middle Ages. Nearby is the 14th century Town Hall and many cafes.

Works by Franz Hals and many other great painters plus Delft tiles, Flemish wallpaper made of gilded and painted panels of leather, silver tankards and candlestands, pikes and swords, and stained and painted glass windows at the Frans Hals Museum at 62 Groot Heiligland (Note the address. That is the only mark outside the building !). This museum is only a 20-minute walk from the railstation, or take buses 1, 2, 3, 5, 6, 70 or 71.

In St. Bavo's, Holland's most beautiful church, hear the massive 5,000-pipe Baroque organ (ivory and tortoise shell keyboard) built in 1738 by Christiaan Muller. Mozart played it when he was 10 years old. It can be heard Sundays at 10:00 and 19:00, also at free concerts Tuesday at 20:15.

The World Clock at 88 Wagenweg. Teyler's Museum at 16 Spaarme (open Tuesday-Saturday 10:00-17:00), to see 16th to 20th century Dutch, Italian and French paintings as well as antique musical instruments, telescopes and globes.

Dep. Haarlem	Twice each hour, from 07:12 to 21:12
Arr. Amsterdam (Cen.)	14 minutes later

Amsterdam - Hoorn 223

Dep. Amsterdam	Frequent times	Dep. Hoorn	Frequent times
Arr. Hoorn	40 minutes later	Arr. Amsterdam	40 minutes later

Sights in **Hoorn**: The full-scale enactment of 17th century trades and crafts in Hoorn's "Old Dutch Market" takes place in the Rodesteen Square on Wednesdays mid-June to mid-August: folk dances and stalls with basket weaving, net mending and the making of wood shoes. Daily from mid-June to mid-August (plus Saturdays and Sundays from mid-August through mid-September), a steam train with antique coaches operates between Hoorn and **Medemblik**.

See Hoorn's 17th century mansions and warehouses. The collection of paintings and antiques in the West Friesian Museum. The 17th century Weighhouse. The 16th century Hospital of St. John. The 2 medieval churches: Noorderkerk and Oosterkerk. The 16th century St. Mary Tower and East Gate, remains of the original fortification. The 17th century almshouse, St. Pietershof.

Amsterdam - Leiden - Amsterdam (H-L) 220

Dep. Amsterdam	Frequent times during all 24 hours
Arr. Leiden	33 minutes later

Sights in **Leiden**: Pieterskerk, the church where the Pilgrim fathers worshipped for 10 years before setting sail for America in 1620. The University. The Royal Arms Museum. The National Museum of Antiquities. The Municipal Museum. The National Ethnological Museum.

Dep. Leiden	Frequent times during all 24 hours
Arr. Amsterdam	33 minutes later

Amsterdam - Maastricht - Amsterdam 235

Most of these trains have light refreshments.

Dep. Amsterdam   06:32 (1)   Plus frequent times daily until 21:32
                                       and daily except holidays at 22:02

Arr. Maastricht   2 ½ hours after departing Amsterdam

Sights in **Maastricht**: The 6th century St. Servatius Church, oldest church in Holland, where Charlemagne occasionally attended mass. There is a large statue of him in the rear of the church. Shoppers from not only nearby Dutch cities but even from Belgium, France and Germany come to the Market Day (produce and pastries) at Town Hall Square, Fridays   08:00-13:00.

See the carved wood columns of the choir in the 10th century Basilica of Our Gracious Lady. The many 17th and 18th century houses on the Stokstraat Quarter, each having a plaque that shows the construction date, the owner's name and his trade. Some of the old houses are now antique shops, art galleries and boutiques. Try the local Limburger cheese and gingerbread in one of the sidewalk cafes on famous Vrijthof Square.

A bus departs from the railstation for the short trip to the Mount St. Peter caves, consisting of 200 miles of labyrinths where people hid during a Spanish invasion in 1570. It was originally a sandstone quarry, worked from Roman times until the end of the 19th century. Since 1584, famous visitors (Napoleon, Archduke Ferdinand of Spain, Voltaire, Sir Walter Scott) have scratched their signatures on the walls of the very cold and very damp caves.

Dep. Maastricht   Frequent times from 07:30 to 21:31
Arr. Amsterdam   2 ½ hours later

(1) Runs Monday-Friday, except holidays.

Amsterdam - Paris - Amsterdam   76

Dep. Amsterdam (Cen.)	07:00 (1)	Dep. Paris (Nord)	18:36 (2)
Arr. Paris (Nord)	12:56	Arr. Amsterdam (Cen.)	23:59

(1) Light refreshments. (2) Supplement charged. Runs daily, except Saturday. Light refreshments entire trip. Restaurant car 18:36-21:08.

Sights in **Paris**: See notes about Paris on pages 125-128.

Amsterdam - Rotterdam - Amsterdam (H-L) 220 + 227

Dep. Amsterdam   Frequent times during all 24 hours
Arr. Rotterdam (Cent.)   60-70 minutes later

Sights in **Rotterdam**: The Netherlands Tourist Information Bureau has offices all over Holland. Look for its "VVV" sign.

Don't miss the view of the city and port from the top of the 340-foot high Euromast, open daily 09:00-22:00 March 15 - October 14, and 09:00-18:00 October 15 - March 14. Nearby, Heineken's Brewery (Crookswigksingle 50).

The fantastic collection of 15th to 19th century Flemish and Dutch pain- tings and a wing of modern sculpture and art (Van Gogh and Kandinsky to the present day) as well as objects of glass, pewter, silver, lace, furniture and tiles in the Boymans-van Beuningen Museum (Mathenesserlaan 18-20).

Devices used by smugglers to defraud customs, at the Profesor van der Poel Tax Museum (Parklaan 14). The collection of globes, ships and atlases in the Maritime Museum (Leuvhaven 1). Many old vessels there can be visited.

The 75-minute boat trip in the harbor, one of the world's largest ports, departing every 45 minutes from Willemsplein Landing.

Stroll through the noteworthy Lijnbaan shopping center. Hear a free lunchtime concert every day at De Doelen, an enormous complex of music and congress halls, just across from Central railstation.

Unwind in the 10,000-acre Zuiderpark, Plaswijck Park, Zuiderparkgordel, Het Park, and the Kralingse Bos (woods). See the wide variety of trees in Arboretum Trompenburg.

Visit the collection of elephants, orangutans, tigers (Sumatran, Siberian and Bengal), great apes, reptiles and seals in the Blijdorp Zoo (open 09:00-17:00).

Enjoy many statues located throughout the city, particularly Mastroianni's "Kiss", at the Central Railroad Station. Visit "De Ster", a working windmill (spice and snuff grinding) near Kralingse Lake.

The collection of folk art of primitive cultures from the non-Western world at the Museum of Ethnology (Willemskade 25). Complete 17th, 18th and 19th-century interiors at the Rotterdam Historical Museum in the Schielads Huis (Korte Hoogstraat 31). Many art galleries, including Lijnbaan Centrum (Linjbaan 165) and Kunstzaal (Zuidplein 120). The Henrik Chabot Museum. The 14th century church, St. Laurenskerk.

Nearby **Delfshaven** is the port from which the Puritans started their voyage to the New World, sailing from there on July 22, 1620, before boarding the Mayflower off the English coast. That group spent its last night praying in Delfshaven's Reformed Church, now called Pelgrimvaderskerk (Pilgrim Fathers' Church). A stained-glass window and a plaque there commemorate the Pilgrims' sailing. Visit the "De Dubbelde Palmboom" Museum (with everyday objects used centuries ago in Rotterdam) and a pewter workshop in the Sack Carriers guildhouse.

The enormous hydraulic project of the Haringvliet sluices can be seen in nearby **Stellendam**.

Dep. Rotterdam (Cent.)   Frequent times during all 24 hours
Arr. Amsterdam   60-70 minutes later

Amsterdam - Rotterdam + Den Haag - Amsterdam (H-L) 220

This circle trip allows seeing only a few of the sights in Rotterdam (see notes in preceding listing) and in Den Haag (see notes earlier in this section), but one can see something of both Rotterdam and Den Haag in this one-day trip.

Dep. Amsterdam (Cen.)	Frequent times during all 24 hours
Arr. Rotterdam (Cen.)	65 minutes later
Dep. Rotterdam (Cen.)	Frequent times from 05:14 to 00:12
Arr. Den Haag (Hbf.)	16-24 minutes later
Dep. Den Haag	Frequent times from 05:39 to 00:38
Arr. Amsterdam (Cen.)	35-55 minutes later

Amsterdam - Utrecht - Amsterdam (H-L) 230 + 235

Dep. Amsterdam	Frequent times from 06:02 to 23:49
Arr. Utrecht	36-44 minutes later

Sights in **Utrecht**: see notes about sightseeing in Utrecht under "Amsterdam - Den Haag + Utrecht - Amsterdam" on page 93.

Dep. Utrecht	3-4 times each hour from 06:17 until 00:03
Arr. Amsterdam	36-44 minutes later

Amsterdam - Zwolle - Amsterdam 225

All of these trains have light refreshments.

Dep. Amsterdam	Hourly, from 07:32 to 23:32
Arr. Zwolle	80 minutes later

Sights in **Zwolle**: Hear the famous Schnitger Organ in the magnificent St. Michael's Church. There are many beautiful buildings in this more than 700-year old town on the Ijssel River. This is a popular base for taking side trips to **Hattem** (great for local arts and crafts) and **Giethoorn** (the Venice of Holland, where everything moves on water).

Dep. Zwolle	Hourly, from 08:49 to 22:48
Arr. Amsterdam	80 minutes later

Brussels - Aachen - Brussels 200

All of these trains have light refreshments, unless designated otherwise.

Dep. Brussels (Midi)	06:48	07:48	09:48	11:48
Dep. Brussels (Cen.)	06:52	07:52	09:52	11:52
Dep. Brussels (Nord)	06:57	07:57	09:57	11:57
Arr. Aachen	08:43	09:43	11:43	13:43

Sights in **Aachen**: Charlemagne's 8th century treasury at the Cathedral contains an extraordinary collection of German medieval ecclesiastical gold and silver, including the Shrine of the Virgin Mary, completed in 1236. The Grand Coronation Chamber in Town Hall.

Dep. Aachen	13:03	14:09 (1)	16:03	17:03	19:03	21:03
Arr. Brussels (Nord)	14:48	15:50	17:48	18:48	20:48	22:48
Arr. Brussels (Cen.)	14:52	-0-	17:52	18:52	20:52	22:52
Arr. Brussels (Midi)	14:55	15:56	17:55	18:55	20:55	22:55

(1) Does not have light refreshments.

Brussels - Amsterdam - Brussels 205

Dep. Brussels (Midi)	Frequent times from 07:10 to 21:20
Dep. Brussels (Cen.)	4 minutes after departing Midi station
Dep. Brussels (Nord)	4 minutes after departing Central station
Arr. Amsterdam	3 hours after departing Brussels (Midi)

Sights in **Amsterdam**: See notes about sightseeing in Amsterdam on page 87.

Dep. Amsterdam	Frequent times from 06:22 to 20:26 plus 22:15
Arr. Brussels (Nord)	3 hours later
Arr. Brussels (Cen.)	4 minutes after arriving Nord station
Arr. Brussels (Midi)	4 minutes after arriving Central station

Brussels - Antwerp - Brussels 205

Dep. Brussels (Midi)	Frequent times from 06:42 to 23:30
Dep. Brussels (Cen.)	4 minutes later
Dep. Brussels (Nord)	4 minutes after departing Central station
Arr. Antwerp (Cen.)	45 minutes after departing Brussels (Midi)

Sights in **Antwerp**: See notes about sightseeing in Antwerp under "Amsterdam-Antwerp-Amsterdam" on page 90.

Dep. Antwerp (Cen.)	Frequent times from 06:19 to 23:19
Arr. Brussels (Nord)	40 minutes later
Arr. Brussels (Cen.)	4 minutes after arriving Nord station
Arr. Brussels (Midi)	4 minutes after departing Central station

Brussels - Bruges - Brussels 200

Dep. Brussels (Nord)	Dep. Brussels (Nord) Frequent times from 05:48 to 22:48
Dep. Brussels (Cen.)	4 minutes after departing Nord station
Dep. Brussels (Midi)	7 minutes after departing Central station
Arr. Bruges	60 minutes after departing Brussels (Midi)

Sights in **Bruges**: The splendid view from the top of the 255-foot-high 13th century Belfry (365 steps), with its famous 47-bell carillon, in the city's main square, Markt. The Belfry's tower is closed 12:00-14:00. The Tourist office is in the nearby Government Palace. (Many cafes are located in this area.)

At the 12th century Basilica of the Holy Blood, a phial said to contain a few drops of Christ's blood is displayed on Fridays. It was brought to Bruges in 1150 from the Second Crusade. Also there: a fine display of gold, silver and copper artwork. Open daily, except 12:00-14:30.

See the lace, pottery, gold pieces, musical instruments and weapons in the 15th century mansion that houses the Gruuthuse Museum. The small museum in the 13th century Saint Saviour's Cathedral. The black slate and gilded brass 16th century effigies and Michelangelo's white carrara marble Madonna with Child statue in the Church of Our Lady. Behind the Church, the Dutch masterpieces at the Groeninge Museum (open daily 09:30-12:00 and 14:00-17:00).

The collection of Old Flemish School paintings at the Hans Memling Museum, in a section of the 13th century Hospital of St. John (open 09:00-12:30 and 14:00-18:00 in Summer, 09:00-12:00 and 14:00-16:00 the rest of the year). Paintings and silverwork at the Archer's Guild of St. Sebastian. Ter Buerze, the world's first stock exchange, now a bank, on the corner of Acadamiesstraat and Vlamingstraat.

St. John's, the most beautiful of Belgium's 140 functioning windmills, built in 1770. Nearby is the beach resort **Knokke-Heist** (many hotels, shops and nightclubs).

Canal boats leave from several docks for half-hour cruises with English-language guides.

Dep. Bruges	Frequent times from 05:46 to 22:50
Arr. Brussles (Midi)	One hour later
Arr. Brussels (Cen.)	10 minutes after arriving Midi station
Arr. Brussels (Nord)	3 minutes after arriving Central station

Brussels - Cologne (Koln) - Brussels 200

Dep. Brussels (Midi)	06:48	07:48	09:48	11:48
Dep. Brussels (Cen.)	4 minutes after departing Midi station			
Dep. Brussels (Nord)	5 minutes after departing Central station			
Arr. Cologne	09:37	10:36	12:35	14:37

Sights in **Cologne**: See notes about sightseeing in Cologne on page 372.

Dep. Cologne	13:17	15:17	16:17	18:17	20:17
Arr. Brussels (Nord)	15:50	17:48	18:48	20:48	22:48
Arr. Brussels (Cen.)	-0-	17:52	18:52	20:52	22:52
Arr. Brussels (Midi)	15:56	17:55	18:55	20:55	22:55

Brussels - Gent - Brussels 200

Dep. Brussels (Nord)	Frequent times from 05:48 to 22:48
Dep. Brussels (Cen.)	4 minutes after departing Nord station
Dep. Brussels (Midi)	5 minutes after departing Central station
Arr. Gent (St. Pieters)	40-50 minutes after departing Nord station

Sights in **Gent**: Located at the confluence of the Lys and Scheldt rivers. Flanked by many canals lined with 15th century gabled buildings.

The Tourist Office, located in the 14th century Town Hall, is near the 14th century Belfry and the 15th century Cloth Hall, where a 20-minute sound and light program commemorates ancient Gent. Two-hour walking tours start at the Tourist Office. A 30-minute boat tour on the canals gives a fine perspective of Gent's past.

See the superior collection of paintings at the Fine Arts Museum. The collection of furniture at the Museum of Decorative Arts. The reproductions of medieval Gent homes, ironwork, costumes and weapons at the Byloke Museum.

The fantastic altarpiece in St. Bavo's Cathedral. West from it is Graseli, the city's oldest port, lined by famous guild houses. Gent's other medieval harbor, Koornlei, is on the opposite bank from Graseli. Many of the old houses there were restored and reconstructed at the beginning of the 20th century.

See the foreboding dungeons and torture chambers in the 12th century Gravensteen (Castle of the Counts), modeled 8 centuries ago on forts visited by Philip of Alsace when he led Crusaders in Syria. Sint Jorishof, built in 1228 and operated as a hotel since the 15th century. It is believed to be the oldest hotel in Europe, with 70 rooms in the original building.

The largest indoor plant and flower show (nearly 7 acres) is held in Gent in April, every 5 years. The 31st show takes place in 1995.

Dep. Gent (St. Pieters)	Frequent times from 05:46 to 23:15
Arr. Brussels (Midi)	30-35 minutes later
Arr. Brussels (Cen.)	6 minutes after arriving Midi station
Arr. Brussels (Nord)	3 minutes after arriving Central station

Brussels - Liege - Brussels 200

Dep. Brussels (Midi)	Frequent times from 05:48 to 22:18
Dep. Brussels (Central)	4 minutes later
Dep. Brussels (Nord)	6 minutes after departing Brussels (Central)
Arr. Liege (Guillemins)	72 minutes after departing Brussels (Midi)

Sights in **Liege**: There are many museums on and near Rue Feronstree. The wonder- ful collection of illuminated manuscripts, ancient Roman pottery, tapestries, medieval sculpture and ancient coins in the Musee Curtius (do not miss seeing the enormous twin fireplaces in the large hall on the second floor). In a building at the rear of the Curtius is the Musee du Verre, which has an incredible collection of ancient Egyptian and Roman glassware.

See the exhibit of very beautiful guns in the Musee d'Armes, on nearby Quai de Maestricht. The clocks, tapestries, wood paneling, chandeliers, leather covered walls, porcelain, kitchen utensils and furniture in the Musee d'Ansembourg. The collection of impressionist and expressionist paintings (Courbet, Corot, Chagall, Gauguin and Picasso) at the Musee des Beaux-Arts. The Aquarium.

The columned courtyard at the Palais des Princes-Eveques. Stroll La Roture, the city's old quarter. Visit the colorful Sunday market at La Batte. Shop the boutiques on Rue Pont de I'lle and Rue Vinave de I'lle.

Dep. Liege (Guillemins)	Frequent times from 05:46 to 22:02
Arr. Brussels (Nord)	60-70 minutes later
Arr. Brussels (Central)	6 minutes after arriving Nord station
Arr. Brussels (Midi)	3 minutes after arriving Central station

Brussels - Luxembourg - Brussels 210

Dep. Brussels (Midi/Zuid)	22 minutes after each hour, from 05:22 (1) to 20:22
Dep. Brussels (Cen.)	6 minutes after departing Brussels Midi-Zuid
Dep. Brussels (Nord)	3 minutes after departing Brussels Central
Arr. Luxembourg	2 ½ hours after departing Brussels Midi/Zuid

Sights in **Luxembourg**: See notes on page 89.

Dep. Luxembourg	31 minutes after each hour, from 06:31 (2) to 20:31
Arr. Brussels (Nord)	2 ¼ hours later
Arr. Brussels (Cen.)	5 minutes after arriving Brussels Nord
Arr. Brussels (Midi/Zuid)	4 minutes after arriving Brussels Central

(1) The 05:22 departure runs Monday-Friday, except holidays. Additional departures from Midi/Zuid station at 07:15 and 12:20 (both require reservation and have a restaurant car) do not stop at Central station. (2) There are additional departures from Luxembourg at 08:14, 12:06, 16:59 and 20:06 which require reservation and (except for the 20:06) do not stop at Brussels Central. Both the 12:06 and the 20:06 have a restaurant car.

Brussels - Namur - Brussels 210

Dep. Brussels (Midi)	Frequent times from 06:22 to 22:36
Dep. Brussels (Central)	4 minutes later (1)
Dep. Brussels (Nord)	6 minutes after departing Brussels Central
Arr. Namur	One hour after departing Brussels Midi

Sights in **Namur**: The silver art in Sisters of Our Lady Convent. The fortress. The baroque 18th century Cathedral. The Diocesan Museum. The extremely elegant Casino, featuring gastronomic feasts.

Dep. Namur	Frequent times from 06:20 to 22:24
Arr. Brussels (Nord)	47 minutes later
Arr. Brussels (Central)	6 minutes after arriving Nord station (1)
Arr. BRussels (Midi)	4 minutes after arriving Central station

(1) A few trains do not stop at Brussels' Central railstation.

Brussels - Paris - Brussels 76

Dep. Brussels (Midi)	07:10 (1)	08:10	10:10 (2)	11:51 (3)
Arr. Paris (Nord)	09:36	11:13	12:56	14:19

Sights in **Paris**: See notes about sightseeing in Paris on pages 125-128.

Dep. Paris (Nord)	14:46 (2)	16:47	17:36 (4)	18:36 (5+7)
Arr. Brussels (Midi)	17:40	19:38	20:08	21:08

(1) Supplement charged. Restaurant car. September - June: runs daily, except Sunday. July and August: runs Monday-Friday. (2) Light refreshments. (3) Supplement charged. Runs daily, except Sundays and holidays. Restaurant car. (4) Reservation required. Sup. charged. First-class only. Restaurant car. Early July to early September: runs Mon.-Fri. Early September to early July: runs daily. (5) Supplement charged. Runs daily, except Sat. Restaurant car. (6) Operates early September to late June. Runs daily except Friday and Sunday. (7) Plus another Paris departure at 19:28 (6), arriving Brussels 22:33.

Brussels - Tournai - Brussels 214

Dep. Brussels (Nord)	57 minutes after each hour, from 05:57 to 22:57
Dep. Brussels (Midi)	10 minutes later
Arr. Tournai	53 minutes after departing Midi station

Sights in **Tournai**: One of Belgium's leading art towns. Pick up a free map and brochure at the city tourism center, at Vieux-Marche-aux-Poteries 14, open Monday-Friday 09:00-19:00, Saturday and Sunday 10:00-13:00 and 15:00-18:00. English-speaking guides are available ($21-U.S. for a 2-hour tour in 1988).

Tournai is best seen on foot, and the place to start is at the Grand Place, a square that is lined with reconstructed medieval guild houses, of which the Cloth Hall is dominant. Nearby is the 236-foot-high 12th century Belfry. Its 16th century 43-bell carillon is played daily at 11:30.

Visit the 12th century 435-foot-long Romanesque Cathedral, particularly to see its 13th centuryIle-de-France Gothic choir and many fine paintings in several of its chapels. The remains of two 12th century murals there are extraordinary.

Also see the 13th century gilded copper Shrine of Our Lady, decorated with silver figures that depict scenes from the life of the Virgin . . . and a 7th century Byzantine cross studded with rubies, emeralds and pearls with what is said to be a fragment of the cross on which Jesus died imbedded in its back.

From Easter until the end of September, the Cathedral is open 08:30-18:00. The rest of the year: 08:30-16:30. Its Treasury is open from Easter until the end of September 10:00-12:00. Rest of the year: 10:00-12:00 and 14:30-16:30. Walk across the Scheldt River and see the earliest examples in Western Europe of bourgeouis houses of the Romanesque period as well as 14th and 15th century Gothic houses. From the Pont des Trous (one of the oldest bridges in Europe), view the 5 mammoth Cathedral towers at dusk, silhouetted against the sky.

Dep. Tournai	43 minutes after each hour, from 05:43 to 22:43
Arr. Brussels (Midi)	53 minutes later
Arr. Brussels (Nord)	10 minutes after arriving at Midi station

Luxembourg - Basel - Luxembourg 63

A departure at 05:28 from Luxembourg in 1990 made this excursion more practical than it was in 1991.

Both of these trains.

Dep. Luxembourg	10:00	Dep. Basel (SNCF)	16:25
Arr. Basel (SNCF)	13:39	Arr. Luxembourg	19:56

Sights in **Basel**: Superb Holbein, Delacroix, Gaugin, Matisse, Ingres, Courbet and Van Gogh paintings in the Kunstmuseum on St. Alban Graben. The collection of 18th century clothing, ceramics and watches in the Kirschgarten. The Historical Museum in the Franciscan church in Barfusserplatz. Shop on Freiestrasse.

See the 16th century Town Hall. The fishmarket. The 15th century New University. Take a boat excursion from the pier in the back of Hotel Three Kings. See the view of the city from the Wettstein Bridge. Visit Munsterplatz.

Luxembourg - Bonn - Luxembourg   707

Dep. Luxembourg	08:26	09:40 (1)	Dep. Bonn (Hbf.)	14:31	16:31 (3+4)
Arr. Trier	09:10	-0-	Arr. Trier	16:37	-0-
Change trains.			Change trains.		
Dep. Trier	09:16	-0-	Dep. Trier	16:43	-0-
Arr. Bonn (Hbf.)	11:23	12:51 (2)	Arr. Luxembourg	17:27	19:22

(1) Operates late June to early September. Direct train. No train change in Trier. (2) Arrives at Bonn's Beuel railstation. (3) Operates all year. Direct train. No train change in Trier. (4) Plus other departures from Bonn at 18:31 and 20:31, arriving Luxembourg 22:29 and 00:24.

Sights in **Bonn**: See notes under "Cologne-Bonn" on page 381.

Luxembourg - Brussels - Luxembourg   210

Dep. Luxembourg	31 minutes after each hour, from 06:31 to 20:31 plus 08:14 (1) and 12:06 (1+2)
Arr. Brussels (Nord)	2 hours and 10 minutes later
Arr. Brussels (Cen.)	5 minutes after arriving Brussels Nord
Arr. Brussels (Midi)	4 minutes after arriving Brussels Central

Sights in **Brussels**: See notes about sightseeing in Brussels on page 88.

Dep. Brussels (Midi)	22 minutes after each hour, from 06:22 to 20:22 plus 07:15 (1+2), 12:20 (1+2), 16:09 (1+2), 19:00 (1) and 22:18 (1)
Dep. Brussels (Cen.)	4 minutes after departing Brussels Midi
Dep. Brussels (Nord)	5 minutes after departing Brussels Central
Arr. Luxembourg	2 hours, 20 minutes after departing Brussels Midi

(1) Reservation required. Does not stop at Brussels Central. (2) Restaurant car .

Luxembourg - Clervaux - Luxembourg   217

The best view (from the viaduct) as you depart Luxembourg City is from the left-hand side of the train.

Dep. Luxembourg	08:08	10:08	12:08 (1)
Arr. Clervaux	08:55	10:55	12:55

Sights in **Clervaux**: This is the Ardennes area, where the Battle of the Bulge was fought in December, 1944. It is a 15-minute walk from the railstation, along the river, to the center of town. You cross a bridge over the river in order to get to the office of the miniature golf course. This is also the tourist information office, open from late March to late September 10:00-12:00 and 14:00-18:00.

You can obtain a copy of the description they provide about the "Family of Man" exhibition of Edward Steichen photos. This world-famous American photographer was born in Luxembourg. Then, go to see that collection at DeLannoi Castle, which also has the Battle of the Bulge Museum and its monument—one of General Patton's U.S. army tanks. It also has an exhibit of castle models.

The Castle is open 10:00-17:00 June through September (13:00-17:00 on Sundays and bank holidays the rest of the year). It is pleasant to lunch at the Castle's restaurant.

See the view from the Benedictine Abbey of St. Maurice.

Dep Clervaux	10:44	12:44	14:44	17:42 (1)	19:31	20:44
Arr.. Luxembourg	11:38	13:38	15:38	18:34	20:25	21:36

(1) Reservation required.

Luxembourg - Cologne (Koln) - Luxembourg 707

Dep. Luxembourg	08:26	09:40 (1)	Dep. Cologne	15:51 (1)	18:23 (2)
Arr. Trier	09:10	-0-	Arr. Trier	-0-	21:14
Change trains.			Change trains.		
Dep. Trier	09:16	-0-	Dep Trier	-0-	21:43
Arr. Cologne	11:45	13:14	Arr. Luxembourg	19:10	22:29

(1) Operates late June to early September. Direct train. No train change in Trier. (2) Runs Monday-Friday, except holidays.

Sights in **Cologne:** See notes about sightseeing in Cologne on page 372.

Luxembourg - Dusseldorf - Luxembourg

707			700		
Dep. Luxemb'g	05:36 (1)	08:26 (3)	Dep. Dusseldorf	15:44 (2)	18:27 (4)
Arr. Koblenz	07:40	10:38	Arr. Koblenz	-0- (2)	19:42
Change trains.			Change trains.		
700			707		
Dep. Koblenz	08:13 (2)	10:46	Dep. Koblenz	-0- (2)	20:19 (3)
Arr. Dusseldorf	09:31	12:12	Arr. Luxemb'g	19:22	22:29

(1) Runs daily, except Sundays and holidays. (2) Direct train via Cologne. Restaurant car. (Source: Lux.) (3) Change trains in Trier. (4) Runs daily, except Saturday.

Sights in **Dusseldorf:** See notes under "Cologne-Dusseldorf" on page 382.

Luxembourg - Frankfurt - Luxembourg

707			700		
Dep. Luxemb'g	05:36 (1)	06:37 (3+4)	Dep. Frankfurt	13:50 (2)	14:50 (2+5)
Arr. Koblenz	07:40	09:40	Arr. Koblenz	15:11	16:11
Change trains.			Change trains.		
700			707		
Dep. Koblenz	07:47 (2)	09:47 (2)	Dep. Koblenz	15:19 (3)	17:19
Arr. Frankfurt	09:09	11:09	Arr. Luxemb'g	17:27	19:22

(1) Runs daily, except Sundays and holidays. (2) Supplement charged. Restaurant car. (3) Change trains in Trier. (4) Plus another departure from Luxembourg at 08:26 (3), arriving Frankfurt 12:09. (5) Plus another departure from Frankfurt at 18:38 (2), arriving Luxembourg 22:29.

Sights in **Frankfurt:** See notes about sightseeing in Frankfurt on page 373.

Luxembourg - Koblenz - Luxembourg   707

These schedules show that a stopover in Trier is possible in both directions.

Dep. Luxembourg	05:36 (1)	06:37(1)	08:26 (2)	09:40 (3)	10:34	12:26(2)
Arr. Trier	06:18	07:25	09:10	10:26	11:16	13:10
Arr Koblenz	07:40	09:40	10:38	11:55	12:38	14:38

Sights in **Trier**: See "Luxembourg-Trier" on page 109.

Sights in **Koblenz**: A pedestrian tunnel goes from the ront of the railstation to the city tourist information office, open mid-June to mid-October Monday-Saturday 08:30-20:00, Sunday 13:30-19:00. For a small fee you can obtain; hotel reservations, a city map and a "Tour of the City" brochure. See where the Moselle and Rhine rivers meet. Visit the Old Town, St. Castor's Church and the Middle Rhine Museum.

Dep. Koblenz	11:19	15:19 (2)	16:56 (3)	17:19	20:19 (2)	22:19(4)
Dep. Trier	12:42	16:43	18:20	18:39	21:43	23:39
Arr. Luxembourg	13:22	17:27	19:10	19:22	22:29	00:24

(1)Runs daily, except Sundays and holidays. (2) Runs daily, except Sundays and holidays. Change trains in Trier. (3) Operates late June to early September. (4) Runs daily, except Saturday.

Luxembourg - Liege - Luxembourg   217

Dep. Luxembourg	08:08	10:08	12:08 (1)
Arr. Liege (Guillemins)	10:34	12:34	14:34

Sights in **Liege**: See notes under "Brussels-Liege" on page 101

Dep Liege (Guillemins)	13:08	16:08 (1)	17:47	19:08
Arr. Luxembourg	15:38	18:34	20:25	21:36

(1) Reservation required.

Luxembourg - Mainz - Luxembourg
707

Dep. Luxembourg	05:36 (1)	06:37 (2)	08:26 (2)	10:34
Arr. Koblenz	07:40	09:40	10:38	12:38

Change trains.
700

Dep. Koblenz	07:53 (2)	09:53 (3)	10:53 (3	12:53 (3)
Arr. Mainz	08:42	10:42	11:42	13:42

Sights in **Mainz**: The art collection in the Cathedral. The Museum of the Central Rhineland. The rare books in the World Museum of Printing in the Romischer Kaiser. The restored Baroque mansionns on the Schillerplatz and Schillerstrasse, in the Kirschgarten. Old Town. The sculptures in the Diocesan Museum.

Dep. Mainz	14:18 (3)	16:18 (3)	19:18 (3)	21:18 (3)
Arr. Koblenz	15:05	17:05	20:05	22:05

Change trains
707

Dep. Koblenz	15:19 (2)	17:19	20:19 (2)	22:19 (4)
Arr. Luxembourg	17:27	19:22	22:29	00:24

(1) Runs daily, except Sundays and holidays. (2) Change trains in Trier. (3) Supplement charged. Restaurant car. (4) Runs daily, except Saturday.

Luxembourg - Metz - Luxembourg 173 + 176
Dep. Luxembourg   05:28 (1)   07:08   08:52 (2) 10:00 (2) 13:07
Arr. Metz   45 minutes later

Sights in **Metz**: The fantastic railstation here looks like a castle because it was built for Kaiser Wilhelm II when he was Germanifying this region. The imperial apartments in the station were arranged for the Kaiser to enjoy his obsession with train-spotting.

See the oldest church in France, the 4th century Pierre-aux-Nonains.

The largest stained-glass windows in the world, in the 16th century Cathedral of Saint Etienne. The Cathedral was formed by the joining of two 12th century churches into a single building. Its contemporary Marc Chagall and Jacques Villon stained-glass are exceptional.

See the Gallo-Roman antiquities in the city's Museum. Walk across the 13th century Porte des Allemands (Gate of the Germans).

Dep. Metz   11:14 (2) 13:53 (3) 16:04 (2) 19:12 (2) 20:01 (2+4)
Arr. Luxembourg 45 minutes later

(1) Runs daily, except Sundays and holidays. Restaurant car. (2) Restaurant car. (3) Runs daily, except Sundays and holidays. Light refreshments. (4) Plus other departures from Metz at 21:42 (2) and 23:02.

Luxembourg - Mulhouse - Luxembourg 176
Both of these trains have a restaurant car.

Dep. Luxembourg   10:00 | Dep. Mulhouse   16:48
Arr. Mulhouse   13:13 | Arr. Luxembourg 19:56

Sights in **Mulhouse**: France's largest collection of antique cars, and one of the best collections in the world of old autos. The Musee Nationale de l'Automobile exhibits about 500 cars ranging from an 1878 steam-powered Jacquot to a magnificent 12-liter Bugati Royale. It is open daily except Tuesday 10:00-18:00.

The Museum of Fabric Printing (Musee de l'Impression sur Etoffes) has displays of textile arts (at 3 Rue des Bonnes-Gens). There are 8,000,000 fabric samples as well as drawings of printed and woven fabrics in its 1,700-volume library. April-December the museum is open daily 10:00-12:00 and 14:00-18:00. January-March: same hours, but closed on Tuesday.

Luxembourg - Paris - Luxembourg 173
Dep. Luxembourg   05:28 (1)   07:08   08:52 (2)
Arr. Paris (Est)   09:08   10:52   12:35

Sights in **Paris**: See notes about Paris on pages 125-128.

Dep. Paris (Est)   17:17 (2)   18:49 (3)   19:47
Arr. Luxembourg   20:45   22:30   23:48

(1) Runs daily, except Sundays and holidays. Restaurant car. (2) Restaurant car. (3) Runs daily, except Saturday.

Luxembourg - Saarbrucken - Luxembourg — *via Trier*   707

These schedules allow stopping-over in Trier for sightseeing on the ride to Saarbrucken. (For sights in Trier, see "Luxembourg-Trier" on page 109.)

Dep. Luxembourg	06:37 (1)	08:26	09:40 (2)	10:34	12:26
Arr. Trier	07:25	09:10	10:26	11:16	13:10
Change trains.					
Dep. Trier	07:40	09:39 (1)	10:39	11:39	13:39
Arr. Saarbrucken	08:50	10:45	11:40	12:46	14:46

Sights in **Saarbrucken**: The Electors' Palace. Ludwigskirche. The Saarland Museum. The City Hall.

These schedules allow stopping-over in Trier for dinner en route back to Luxembourg:

Dep. Saarbrucken	11:12	15:12	17:12	20:09	22:09
Arr. Trier	12:18	16:18	18:18	21:08	23:10
Change trains.					
Dep. Trier	12:39	16:43	18:39	21:43	23:39 (3)
Arr. Luxembourg	13:22	17:27	19:22	22:29	00:24

(1) Runs daily, except Sundays and holidays. (2) Operates late June to early September. (3) Runs daily, except Saturday.

Luxembourg - Saarbrucken — *via Metz*

These schedules allow stopping-over for sightseeing in Metz en route to Saarbrucken. (See notes about Metz under "Luxembourg-Metz" on page 107.

	173	173	173	176
Dep. Luxembourg	05:28 (1)	07:08 (2)	08:52 (1)	10:00
Arr. Metz	06:13	07:53	09:34	10:43
Change trains.				
	170	170	173	173
Dep. Metz	07:25 (3)	08:26 (3)	09:52 (1)	11:55
Arr. Saarbrucken	09:03	09:53	10:49	12:49

These schedules allow stopping-over in Metz for lunch or dinner en route back to Luxembourg:

	173	173	173	173
Dep. Saarbrucken	12:24 (2)	13:10	17:10	19:10
Arr. Metz	13:31	14:03	18:09	20:03
Change trains.				
	173	173	176	173
Dep. Metz	13:53 (4)	16:04 (1)	19:12	21:42
Arr. Luxembourg	14:36	16:49	19:56	22:30

(1) Restaurant car. (2) Runs daily, except Sundays and holidays. (3) Operates late June to early September. (4) Runs daily, except Sundays and holidays. Light refreshments.

Luxembourg - Strasbourg 176 + Government timetable

Both of these trains have a restaurant car.

| Dep. Luxembourg | 10:00 | Dep. Strasbourg | 17:47 | 19:52 (1) |
| Arr. Strasbourg | 12:08 | Arr. Luxembourg | 19:56 | 22:30 |

(1) Runs daily, except Saturday. Change trains in Metz at 21:18 (table 173).

Sights in **Strasbourg**: See notes about sightseeing in Strasbourg on page 128.

Luxembourg - Trier 707 + Government timetable

| Dep. Luxembourg | 08:26 | 10:34 | 12:26 | 14:34 |
| Arr. Trier | 09:10 | 11:16 | 13:10 | 15:16 |

Sights in **Trier**: There are more Roman monuments here than in any other German city: the 4th century Porta Nigra (Black Gate), 2nd and 4th century baths, a 1st century amphitheater, and the 4th century Roman palace, Palastula (with its throne room of Roman emperors), now a Lutheran church. See the "Holy Coat of Trier", said to be Christ's robe, in the Romanesque Cathedral, started in the 6th century.

Roman and medieval relics in the Municipal Museum. Peter's Fountain in the market square and, nearby, the 17th century Electoral Palace and 18th century Kasselstatt Palace.

| Dep. Trier | 13:43 | 16:43 | 18:39 | 21:43 |
| Arr. Luxembourg | 14:47 | 17:27 | 19:22 | 22:29 |

Luxembourg - Vianden 217 + Government timetable

The Ettelbruck-Viandin bus leaves from the front of the Ettelbruck railstation. Re-check the bus schedules ! !

Dep. Luxembourg	08:08	09:37	12:08	14:08
Arr. Ettelbruck	08:29	10:11	12:34	14:29
Change to bus.				
Dep. Ettelbruck	08:53	10:18	13:14	14:51
Arr. Vianden	09:15	10:43	13:42	15:14

Sights in **Vianden**: Leave the bus at the first stop, the Hotel Oranienburg. At the end of the day, don't fail to board the bus at Gare Routiere (the bus station) for the ride back to Ettelbruck. Most of the attractions in Vianden are closed 12:00-14:00.

Walk uphill from the Hotel Oranienburg to the large and very interesting castle, open daily March-December, only weekends in January and February.

Leave the castle at 12:00 and have lunch before visiting the home of Victor Hugo. Take the chairlift across the river to the top of a hill from which there are good views of the castle, dam and valley. After descending, walk across the top of the dam.

See the rococo altar in the 13th century Church of the Trinitarians. Visit the exhibits of folklore and ancient household items in the Museum of Rustic Arts.

Bus

Dep. Vianden	14:50	16:23	18:00	20:12
Arr. Ettelbruck	15:22	16:55	18:40	20:55
Change to train.				
Dep. Ettelbruck	15:27	17:01	19:57	21:10
Arr. Luxembourg	16:03	17:39	20:25	21:38

SCENIC RAIL TRIPS

Most of the scenic rail trips of the Benelux countries are in Holland, and all of those are included in the list of one-day roundtrips from Amsterdam preceding this section. They are the train rides between Amsterdam and Delft (page 92), Den Haag (page 93), Leiden (page 95), Rotterdam (page 96) and Utrecht (pages 93 and 98).

The scenery on these trips is best from mid-March through May: fields of tulips, narcissus, crocus and other bulb flowers in bloom. The region is known as "Champs de Fleurs" (Fields of Flowers).

Three other scenic trips in the Benelux countries are listed in this section. All are noteworthy for beautiful river scenery.

Liege - Jemelle

This fine farm and river scenery can be seen by taking an indirect route from Brussels to Luxembourg.

200

Dep. Brussels (Midi)	10:18	11:18	12:18	13:18
Dep. Brussels (Cen.)	4 minutes after departing Midi station			
Dep. Brussels (Nord)	6 minutes after departing Central station			
Arr. Liege (Guill.)	11:40	12:40	13:40	14:40
Change trains.				

215

Dep. Liege (Guill.)	11:49	13:05	13:49	14:49 (1)
Arr. Namur	12:27	13:52	14:27	15:27
Change trains.				

210

Dep. Namur	13:12 (2)	14:22	15:22	16:22
Dep. Jemelle	-0-	15:00	16:00	17:00
Arr. Luxembourg	14:49	16:11	17:11	18:11

215

Dep. Liege	15:49	16:49 (1)	17:49	18:39 (2)
Arr. Namur	16:27	17:27	18:27	19:18
Change trains.				

210

Dep. Namur	17:09 (2)	18:22	19:22	20:22
Arr. Jemelle	-0-	18:58	19:58	20:58
Arr. Luxembourg	18:50	20:11	21:11	22:11

(1) Runs Monday-Friday, except holidays. (2) Reservation required. Restaurant car.

Luxembourg - Liege 217

Excellent farm and river scenery on this easy one-day roundtrip. See page 106 for timetables.

Namur - Dinant 210

This is a spur off the Brussels-Luxembourg route. The great farm and river scenery here can be seen either by breaking-up the ride from Brussels to Luxembourg (or vice versa) . . . .or as an easy one-day roundtrip from Brussels.

For the first way:

Dep. Brussels (Midi)	08:42 (1)	09:42 (1)	Dep. Luxembourg		08:31
Dep. Brussels (Cen.)	08:46	09:46	Arr. Namur		00:19
Dep. Brussels (Nord)	08:53	09:53	Change trains.		
Arr. Namur	09:42	10:42	Dep. Namur		10:47 (1)
Arr. Dinant	10:13	11:13	Arr. Dinant		11:13
Change trains.			Change trains.		
Dep. Dinant	11:27 (1)	14:27 (1)	Dep. Dinant		14:27 (1)
Arr. Namur	11:55	14:55	Dep. Namur		15:00
Change trains.			Arr. Brussels (Nord)		15:49
Dep. Namur	12:22	15:22	Arr. Brussels (Cen.)		15:56
Arr. Luxembrg	14:11	17:11	Arr. Brussels (Midi)		16:00

(1) Mid-June to early September: runs daily. Early September to mid-June: runs Monday-Friday, except holidays.

Here is the Brussels one-day roundtrip 210

All of these trains run daily mid-June to early September. All of them run Monday-Friday except holidays early September to mid-June.

Dep. Brussels (Midi)	08:42	09:42	Dep. Dinant	14:27	16:27
Dep. Brussels (Cen.)	08:46	09:46	Arr. Namur	15:00	17:00
Dep. Brussels (Nord)	08:53	09:53	Arr. Brussels (Nord)	15:49	17:49
Arr. Namur	09:42	10:42	Arr. Brussels (Cen.)	15:56	17:56
Arr. Dinant	10:13	11:13	Arr. Brussels (Midi)	16:00	18:00

INTERNATIONAL ROUTES FROM BELGIUM

The Belgian gateway for rail travel to London, Amsterdam, Basel (and on to Zurich and Milan), Cologne (and on to Hamburg and Copenhagen) and Paris (and on to Madrid) is Brussels.

Brussels - Amsterdam 205

Many of these trains have light refreshments.

Dep. Brussels (Midi)	10 minutes after each hour, from 06:10 to 21:10 (1)
Dep. Brussels (Cen.	4 minutes after departing Midi station
Dep. Brussels (Nord)	4 minutes after departing Central station
Arr. Amsterdam	3 hours later

(1) Plus additional additional departures from Midi station (that do not stop at Brussels' Central station) at 13:29, 17:54 and 21:20, arriving Amsterdam 3 hours later.

Brussels - Basel - Milan 63

Dep. Brussels (Midi)	07:15 (1)	12:20 (2)	16:09 (3)	19:00 (5)	22:19 (6)
Dep. Brussels (Nord)	8 minutes after departing Midi station				
Dep. Brussels (Q.L.)	10 minutes after departing Nord station				
Arr. Basel (S.N.C.F.)	13:39	18:25	22:39	01:40	05:25
Arr. Milan (Cen.)	19:35	-0-	04:00 (4)	07:40	-0-

(1) Restaurant car Brussels-Basel. Light refreshments Basel-Milan. (2) Reservation required. Restaurant car Brussels-Basel. (3) Reservation required. Carries a sleeping car. Also has couchettes. Restaurant car Brussels-Basel. (4) Arrives at Milan's Lambrate railstation. (5) Carries a sleeping car. Also has couchettes. (6) Reservation required. Carries a sleeping car. Also has couchettes.

Brussels - Cologne (Koln) 200

Dep. Brussels (Midi)	06:48	07:48	09:48	11:48	13:48
Dep. Brussels (Cen.)	06:52	07:52	09:52	11:52	13:52
Dep. Brussels (Nord)	06:57	07:57	09:57	11:57	13:57
Arr. Cologne	09:37	10:36	12:35	14:37	16:35

Dep. Brussels (Midi)	15:48	16:55 (1)	18:09 (2)	18:48 (1)	19:48 (1+3)
Dep. Brussels (Cen.)	15:52	-0-	18:13 (2)	18:52 (1)	19:52
Dep. Brussels (Nord)	15:57	17:03 (1)	18:18 (2)	18:57 (1)	19:57
Arr. Cologne	18:37	19:45	20:42	21:40	22:40

(1) Reservation required. Light refreshments. (2) Supplement charged. Restaurant car. (3) Plus another departure from Brussels Midi at 21:40, arriving Cologne 00:28.

Brussels - London   via Oostende   (Jetfoil) 52

The schedules shown below are for late May to late September, unless designated otherwise.

Dep. Brussels (Nord)	06:48	09:46 (1)	11:35 (2)	14:46 (1)	17:46 (3)
Dep. Brussels (Midi)	06:59	09:59	11:45	14:59	17:59
Arr. Oostende	08:09	11:09	12:48	16:09	19:09

Change to boat.

Dep. Oostende	08:25	11:30	13:15	16:45	19:30 (3)

Set your watch back one hour, except from late September to late October.

Arr. Western Docks	09:05	12:10	13:55	17:25	20:10
Arr. London (Vict.)	11:06	14:06	15:54	19:23	22:04

(1) Light refreshments   (2) Supplement charged. Restaurant car.   (3) Operates early July to late September. Light refreshments.

Brussels - London   via Oostende   (Regular Ferry) 52

The schedules shown below are for late May to late September.

Dep. Brussels (Nord)	07:48	11:48	22:46
Dep. Brussels (Midi)	07:59	11:59	22:59
Arr. Oostende	09:09	13:09	00:09

Change to a boat.

Dep. Oostende	10:00	13:45	02 :00

Set your watch back one hour, except from late September to late October.

Arr. Western Docks	13:00	16:45	05:00
Arr. London (Vict.)	15:06	19:00	07:37

Brussels - Luxembourg 218

See "Brussels-Luxembourg" on page 102.

Brussels - Paris   76

All of these trains charge a supplement and have a restaurant car, unless designated otherwise.

Dep. Brussels (Nord)	01:25 (1)	-0-	-0-	09:49 (3)
Dep. Brussels (Midi)	01:53	07:10 (2)	08:10	10:10
Arr. Paris (Nord)	06:25	09:36	11:13	12:56

Dep Brussels (Nord)	11:30 (4)	13:46 (3)	-0-	-0-
Dep. Brussels (Midi)	11:51	14:02	16:10	17:10 (5)
Arr. Paris (Nord)	14:19	17:09	18:59	19:44

Dep. Brussels (Nord)	-0-	18:43 (3)	-0-	-0-
Dep. Brussels (Midi)	18:10 (6)	19:10	20:22 (7)	-0-
Arr. Paris (Nord)	20:44	22:06	23:05	-0-

(1) Has couchettes. No supplement. No restaurant car. (2) Early July to early September: runs Monday-Friday. Early September to early July: Runs daily, except Sunday. (3) Light refreshments. No supplement. (4) Runs daily, except Sunday. (5) Early July to early September: runs Monday-Friday. Early September to early July: Runs daily, except Saturday. (6) Runs daily, except Saturday. (7) No supplement charged. No restaurant car.

INTERNATIONAL ROUTES FROM HOLLAND

Amsterdam is the Dutch gateway for rail travel to London, Basel (and on to Zurich and Milan), Cologne, Hamburg (and on to Copenhagen) and Paris (and on to Madrid). Notes on the route to London appear under "London-Amsterdam" on page 428.

Amsterdam - Brussels 205

Dep. Amsterdam	Frequent times from 06:22 to 22:15
Arr. Brussels (Nord)	3 hours later
Arr. Brussels (Cent.)	4 minutes after departing Nord station
Arr. Brussels (Midi)	4 minutes after departing Central station

Amsterdam - Cologne (Koln) - Mainz - Basel 68

Many castles are seen in the Koblenz-Mainz area as the train travels alongside the Rhine River. En route to Basel, sit on the left-hand side for the best views of marvelous Rhine River scenery.

All of these trains charge a supplement and have a restaurant car, except the night train.

Dep. Amsterdam	06:02	07:08	08:00	09:08	11:08 (1)
Dep. Duisburg	08:08	09:08	10:19	11:19	13:08
Arr.. Cologne	08:42	09:42	10:57	11:57	13:42
Dep. Koblenz	09:50	10:50	11:50	12:50	15:50
Arr. Mainz	10:41	13:41	12:41	13:41	16:41
Arr. Basel (Bad.)	13:37	14:37	15:37	16:37	19:37
Arr. Basel (S.B.B.)	13:45	14:45	15:45	16:45	19:45

(1) Plus another departure from Amsterdam at 20:05. It carries a sleeping car and also has couchettes.....arriving Duisburg 23:04, Cologne 23:47, Koblenz 00:54, Mainz 01:48, Basel (Bad.) 06:17, and Basel (S.B.B.) 06:26.

Amsterdam - Bremen - Hamburg - Copenhagen 67

Dep. Amsterdam	07:02 (1)	20:10 (2)
Arr. Bremen	-0-	00:49 (3)
Arr. Hamburg	12:06 (1)	01:53 (3)
Arr. Copenhagen	17:20	07:25 (3)

(1) Change trains in Osnabruck at 10:04 and in Hamburg at 12:06. (2) Has couchettes. (3) One hour later from early September to mid-june.

Amsterdam - Luxembourg 63

Change trains in Maastricht.

Dep. Amsterdam	12:32
Dep. Maastricht	15:18
Arr. Luxembourg	18:34

Amsterdam - London via Hoek van Holland (regular ferry) 66

Dep. Amsterdam	09:32 (1)	19:49 (1)
Arr. Hoek van Holland	10:57	21:13
Change to ferry.		
Dep. Hoek van Holland	12:00	22:30 (2)
Set your watch back one hour.		
Arr. Harwich	17:45	06:45
Change to train		
Dep. Harwich	18:45 (1)	07:45 (1+3)
Arr. London (Liverpool)	20:00	09:00

(1) Light refreshments. (2) Reservation required. (3) On Sunday, depart Harwich at 07:25.

Amsterdam - Brussels - Paris 76

Dep. Amsterdam	07:00 (1)	08:53 (2)	10:49 (1)	12:26 (3)
Dep. Antwerp (Berch.)	09:15	10:58	13:13	14:52
Dep. Brussels (Nord)	09:49	11:30	13:46	15:21
Dep. Brussels (Cen.)	-0-	-0-	-0-	15:26
Arr. Brussels (Midi)	09:56	11:37	13:54	15:30 (3)
Dep, Brussels (Midi)	10:00	11:51 (2)	14:02	16:10
Arr. Paris (Nord)	12:56	14:19	17:04	18:59
Dep. Amsterdam	13:26 (3)	14:26 (3)	15:53 (1)	16:48(7)
Dep. Antwerp (Berch.)	15:52	16:52	18:10	19:15
Dep. Brussels (Nord)	16:21	17:21	18:43	-0-
Dep. Brussels (Cen.)	16:26	17:26	-0-	-0-
Arr. Brussels (Midi)	16:30 (3)	17:30 (3)	18:50	19:54
Dep. Brussels (Midi)	17:10 (4)	18:10 (5)	19:10	20:22 (7)
Arr. Paris (Nord)	19:40	20:44	22:06	23:05

(1) Light refreshments. (2) Supplement charged. Runs daily, except Sunday. Light refreshments to Brussels. Restaurant car Brussels-Paris. (3) Change trains in Brussels at Midi station. Light refreshments. (4) First-class only. Supplement charged. Restaurant car. Early July to early September: runs Monday-Friday. Early September to early July: runs daily, except Saturday. (5) Supplement charged. Runs daily, except Saturday. Restaurant car. (6) Has couchettes. (7) Plus another departure from Amsterdam at 22:15 (6), arriving Brussels (Nord) 01:20, Paris 06:25.

INTERNATIONAL ROUTES FROM LUXEMBOURG

Luxembourg City is a gateway for rail travel to London, Amsterdam, Basel (and on to Zurich and Milan), Brussels, Cologne, Koblenz (and on to Frankfurt), and Paris. (Notes on the routes from Amsterdam, Brussels and Paris to London appear in Chapter 7, on page 428.)

Luxembourg - Amsterdam 63

This train operates all year. From late September to late May, change trains in Maastricht

Dep. Luxembourg	12:08
Arr. Maastricht	15:22
Arr. Amsterdam	18:01

Luxembourg - Basel

	16	63	63	63	63
Dep. Luxembourg	01:18 (1)	10:00 (2)	14:59 (2)	19:00 (2)	21:45 (1)
Arr. Basel (SNCF)	05:25	13:39	18:25	22:39	01:30

(1) Carries a sleeping car. Also has couchettes. (2) Restaurant car.

Luxembourg - Brussels 210

Dep. Luxembourg	04:15	05:31 (1)	06:31	07:07 (1)	08:14 (2+4)
Arr. Brussels (Nord)	07:06	08:11	09:11	09:33	10:40
Arr. Brussels (Cen.)	-0-	08:16	09:16	09:37	-0-
Arr. Brussels (Midi)	07:17	08:20	09:20	09:41	10:48

(1) Runs Monday-Friday, except holidays. (2) Reservation required. (3) Reservation required. Restaurant car. (4) Plus other departures from Luxembourg at 31 minutes after each hour from 08:31 to 20:31 . . . also at 12:06 (3), 16:59 (3) and 20:06 (3).

Luxembourg - Cologne 707

Dep. Luxembourg	06:37 (1)	08:26	09:40 (2)	10:34 (3)	12:26 (4)
Arr. Trier	07:25	09:10	-0- (2)	-0- (3)	13:10
Change trains.					
Dep. Trier	07:47 (1)	09:16 (3)	-0-	-0-	13:16
Arr. Cologne	10:34	11:45	13:14	13:45	15:45

(1) Runs daily, except Sundays and holidays. (2) Direct train. No train change in Trier. Operates late June to early September. (3) Direct train. No train change in Trier. (4) Plus other departures from Luxembourg at 14:34 (3), 15:24 and 18:28 (1), arriving Cologne 17:45, 19:45 and 21:45.

Luxembourg - Paris 173 *via Metz*   177 *via Rheims*

	173	177	173	173	173
Dep. Luxembourg	05:28 (1)	06:00 (2)	07:08	08:52 (3)	13:07 (5)
Dep. Rheims	-0-	10:03	-0-	-0-	-0-
Dep. Metz	06:17	-0-	08:02	09:49	14:16
Arr. Paris (Est)	09:08	11:27	10:52	12:36	17:09

(1) Runs daily, except Sundays and holidays. Restaurant car. (2) Runs daily, except Sundays and holidays. Change trains in Longwy. (3) Restaurant car. (4) Change trains in Longwy. (5) Plus other departures from Luxembourg at [177] 17:18 (4) and [173] 17:29, arriving Paris 21:55 (via Rheims) and 21:02 (via Metz).

FRANCE

Children under 4 travel free. Half-fare for children 4–11. Children 12 and over must pay full fare.

French rail tickets purchased *in* France are valid for travel any day within 2 months from the date of purchase. Train tickets obtained *before arrival* in France are valid for 6 months, and it is *no*t required that a ticket purchased outside France be validated.

Before boarding a train, passengers are required to *validate tickets purchased in France* in one of the many orange-colored machines located at the entrance to the platforms. Tickets are spot-checked on the trains. A person holding a non-validated ticket is subject to a fine.

Semi-Couchettes

Some compartments on French trains have 8 semi-inclined bunks (instead of seats) on these routes: Paris–Brest, Paris–Bordeaux, Paris–Hamburg, Paris–Quimper, Paris–Strasbourg, Paris–Ventimiglia, and Rheim–Nice. For reservation purposes, these "Cabine 8" bunks are treated as seats and no supplement is charged.

The signs you will see at railstaions in France are:

ARRIVEE	ARRIVAL
CONSIGNE	BAGGAGE CHECKROOM
DAMES	WOMEN
DEPART	DEPARTURE
ENTREE	ENTRANCE
FUMEURS	SMOKING COMPARTMENT
GARE	STATION
HORAIRE	TIMETABLE
LOCATION DE PLACE ASSISE	SEAT RESERVATION OFFICE
MESSIEURS	MEN
QUAI	PLATFORM
RENSEIGNEMENTS	INFORMATION
SORTIE	EXIT
VOIE	TRACK
VOITURE-LIT	SLEEPER CAR
VOITURE-RESTAURANT	RESTAURANT CAR

CONNECTIONS WITH BRITAIN
See pages 426–427.

SUMMER TIME

France changes to Summer Time on the last Sunday of March and converts back to Standard Time on the last Sunday of September.

EURAILPASS BONUSES

Irish Ferries ships Le Havre-Rosslare, Cherbourg-Rosslare, and (late June to late August) Le Havre-Cork. Port taxes and cabin accommodations are *not* covered.

The bus (7-franc charge) that transports passengers from le Havre railstation to the boat pier takes people on a first-come-first-served basis. When the bus is filled, people left at the railstation must take a taxi to the pier.

On arrival in Ireland, the bus service there (taking passengers from Rosslare pier to the Rosslare railstation) accommodates *all* passengers, and at no charge.

Another bonus is the Digne–Nice and v.v. rail line (see page 159 for trip details).

FRENCH HOLIDAYS

A list of holidays is helpful because some trains will be noted later in this section as *not* running on holidays. Also, those trains which operate on holidays are filled, and it is necessary to make reservations for them long in advance. *When at all possible, avoid train travel in France on holidays !*

January 1	New Year's Day		Pentecost
	Easter		Pentecost Monday
	Easter Monday	July 14	National Day
May 1	Labor Day		(Bastille Day)
May 8	Victory Day (WW II)	August 15	Assumption Day
	Ascension Day	November 1	All Saints' Day
	Joan of Arc Day	November 11	Armistice Day (WW I)
		December 25	Christmas Day

FRANCE'S TRAIN PASSES

Sold everywhere in the world, *except* in France — at travel agencies and offices of Rail Europe (U.S.A. and Canadian addresses shown under "France" on page 23).

France Railpass   Unlimited train travel for any 4 days within a month. The 1992 prices are: $175 (U.S.) for *first*-class, $125 for *second*-class. Up to 5 more days can be added at $38 per day for *first*-class, $27 per day for *second*-class. Half-fare for children age 4–11.

Both passes include these bonuses: Free roundtrip train service between Orly or Charles de Gaulle Roissy airports and downtown Paris, a one-day Metropass valid in second-class within the city limits on the Paris subway and bus systems, 50% discount on the Nice-Digne scenic private rail line, 15% discount on the "Train + Auto" car rental system available at more than 20 railstations and airports, 15–20% discount on the entrance fee to several museums, and a gift from the Printemps Department Store.

France Rail'N Drive   Unlimited 4 days of train travel plus 3 days of car rental (any 7 days) within one month. Prices vary (a) whether for one person or for 2 or more persons, and (b) the category of car. A third passenger needs to pay only for a 4-day France Railpass.

The 1992 prices per person for 2 persons (using the smallest size car) are: $199 (U.S.) for *first*-class train, $159 for *second*-class. Up to 5 more days of train travel can be added at $38 per day for *first*-class, $27 per day for *second*-class. Up to 5 more days of car rental can be added at $35 per day.

(Description of passes continues on page 121.)

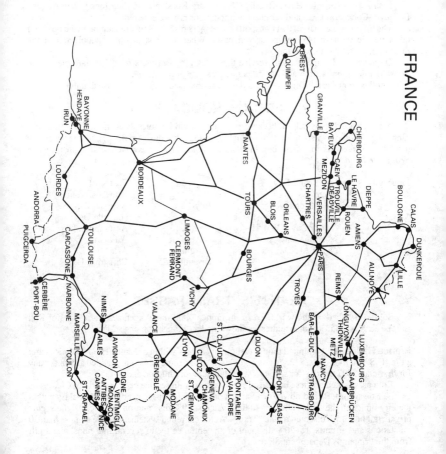

FRANCE

All prices include Value Added Tax, unlimited mileage, basic liability insurance, and free drop-off within continental France. (The car can be driven in other countries but must be dropped-off in France.) Avis has more than 500 rental locations in France.

Reservations for cars should be made from the country where you reside at least 7 days in advance. (In the U.S.A., phone 1-800-331-1084.) For making reservation after arriving in France, phone 05-05-22-11 at least 24 hours in advance.

France Rail'N Fly   Unlimited 4 days of train travel plus one day of air travel anywhere in France (any 5 days) within one month. The 1992 prices are: $249 (U.S.) for *first*-class, $199 for *second*-class. for children age 2–11: $160 or $135.

Up to 5 more days of train travel can be added at $38 per day for *first*-class, $27 per day for *second*-class. For children 2–11: $19 or $13.50. One additional day of air travel can be added at $75 for *either* first or second-class, for either adult or child.

Carte Vermeil   Can be purchased *only* in France, at major railstations. Available to persons 60 and over. Allows purchase of both first and second-class train tickets at 50% discount for travel from Monday 12:00 to Friday 15:00 and from Saturday 12:00 to Sunday 15:00. The discount is *not* given on certain holidays.

Valid for one year. The 1991 price was 165 francs.

BritFrance Pass   Unlimited train travel in both Britain and France, plus one Hovercraft roundtrip Dover–Boulogne or Dover–Calais and v.v. (or on regular cross-channel ferries when Hovercraft cannot operate because of bad weather).

Sold at travel agencies and also offices of BritRail Travel International and Rail Europe (U.S.A. and Canadian offices shown under "Great Britain" and "France" on page 23) — everywhere in the world, *except* in Britain and France.

The 1992 prices for any 5 days within 15 days are: $335 (U.S) for *first*-class, $249 for *second*-class, and $199 for youths age 12–25. For any 10 days in one month: $505, $385 and $299. Half-fare for children age 4–11.

BritFrance Rail'N Drive   Unlimited 5 days of train travel plus 3 days of car rental (any 8 days) within one month. Prices vary (a) whether for one person or for 2 or more persons, and (b) the category of car. A third passenger needs only to pay for a 5-day BritFrance Pass (above). The 1992 prices per person for 2 persons (using the smallest size car) are: $399 (U.S.) for *first*-class, $315 for *second*-class.

WORLD'S FASTEST TRAINS

Since 1981, France has operated the world's fastest trains, the "Trains a Grande Vitesse", which have run at 320 miles per hour and are operated at the top speed of 186mph on the 126-mile Paris–LeMans line, making that trip in 55 minutes versus 100 minutes for other trains. The Paris–Lyon TGV has a maximum speed of 238mph. *Seat reservation is required for most TGV trains —particularly on peak days and at peak hours. Standing is not allowed on them.*

Although normal fares are charged at off-peak times, a supplement is charged for those TGV that run at the busiest times. The supplement for passholders is only the small $3 reservation fee.

The usual composition for a TGV is 386 seats: 111 in first-class, 275 in second-class. Each TGV has a bar. Meals are brought to seats in some of the first-class cars.

The 1982 service (Paris–Lyon, Paris–Dijon and Paris–Geneva) was expanded in 1983 to include Paris–Marseilles, Paris–Montpelier and Paris–Annecy–Grenoble. A TGV service Paris–Lausanne (with cross-platform transfer in Lausanne for trains to Milan) began in 1984. Service Paris–Grenoble started in 1985, Paris-LeMans and Paris–Tours in 1989.

ONE-DAY EXCURSIONS AND CITY-SIGHTSEEING

Here are 68 one-day rail trips that can be made comfortably from French cities, returning to them in most cases before dinnertime. Notes are provided on what to see and do at each destination. The number after the name of each route is the Cook's timetable.

Avignon

This walled city, the tourist capital of Provence, can be entered through 14 different gates. You can obtain a city map or a personal guide at the Syndicat d'Initiative (41 Cours Jean-Jaures). During the 14th century, Avignon was briefly the world headquarters of the Catholic Church when it was unsafe for a series of French popes to be in Rome. Take the one-hour tour of the Palace of the Popes, open daily 09:00–11:15 and 14:00–16:30. Next to it is the 12th century Cathedral of Notre-Dame-de-Doms.

Outside the Palace you can board a trackless 2-car train pulled by a gasoline- powered locomotive and climb to the top of the hill overlooking the Palace for a view of the city and the Rhone Valley.

See the art in the museum in the 13th to 16th century Italian-school religious paintings in the museum in the 14th century Petit Palais, open daily except Tuesday 9:30–11:30 and 14:00–18:00. Other medieval buildings worth seeing are the 12th century St. Ruf Church and the 14th century gothic St. Didier Church. See the Roman sculptures and mosaics (some dating back 3,000 years) in the Lapidary Museum (housed in the 17th century Jesuit Church), open daily except Tuesday 10:00–11:55 and 14:00–18:00.

The collection of ironwork in the Calvet Museum on Rue Joseph Vernet. The ancient Roman Triumphal Arch and the Amphitheater that was built during the reign of Augustus Caesar. Cross the Rhone River by walking or driving over the bridge to Villeneuve-les-Avignon and see the view of Avignon from the other side of the river.

All-day bus tours from Avignon to many interesting places in this area can be taken from in front of the railstation. One tour includes Roman ruins at **St. Remy**, the village of **Les Baux** (sculptured during the Middle Ages from the top of a stone hill), and the Roman theatre in **Arles**.

Bordeaux

Information about tours of the port and an excellent city map for making a walking tour of Bordeaux are available at the Tourist Office, 12 Cours du 30 Juillet. The opera, parks, hotels, Roman ruins and 18th century mansions are in the northern sector of the city. Museums, churches and fine shops are in the southern part of Bordeaux.

See the Maritime Museum, on the Quai de la Douane. Wonderful Louis XV houses on Rue Fernand Philippart. The modern stained-glass in the 14th century St. Michel Church on Place Dubourg. The view of Bordeaux from the top of that church's tower. The large 15th century belltower, Grosse Cloche. The 13th century Gothic St. Andre's Cathedral. The art in the Musee des Beaux Arts, open daily except Tuesday 10:00–12:00 and 14:00–18:00.

The fans with mother of pearl, ivory and silver handles (plus Medieval furniture, costumes and ceramics) in the Musee des Arts Decoratifs (39 Rue Bouffard), open daily except Tuesday 14:00–18:00.

Do not miss seeing the array of fruits, cheeses, wild game and many exotic foods at the market on Place des Grands Hommes. The fantastic carved plants and the swan boat in the Jardin Public. The Maison des Vins at 1 Cours du 30 Juillet, where you can obtain information on visiting nearby famous wineries.

See the lovely 18th century Opera House. The Grand Theatre. The Museum of Painting and Sculpture. The Numismatic Museum. The Museum of Old Bordeaux. The Bonie Museum of Far Eastern Art.

Lyon

Occasionally, 2 trains depart from the same track at Lyon's Perrache railstation, heading in opposite directions. Be sure to stand at the correct end (North or South) of the track in order to board the train you want to ride. Check the departure signs at the underground passageway. Do not rely merely on a track number when departing from Perrache railstation !

Next to the North passageway of Track "A" is a take-out restaurant, handy for provisioning your trip.

A metropolitan train connects Lyon's Brotteaux and Perrache railstations. The ride is 15 minutes.

Try to keep from eating at the spectacular Nouvelle Les Halles food market: 65 tantalizing stalls of meat, poultry, fish, produce, cheese, bread, pastry, coffee, tea, spices, wine and candy, plus small restaurants and a florist. Open 07:00–19:00 Monday–Saturday and 07:00–12:00 on Sunday.

Here, you can buy pheasants in plumage, partridges, wild ducks, quail, snipe, frog legs, 4 varieties of oysters, shrimp, eel, cod and sole. There are goose, duck and game pates. Do not fail to sample the 3 Lyon specialties: Morteau de Jesu (pork meat in a pig's foot casing), the peppery pink and white salami, and the garlicky Lyon sausage.

The wine here is magnificent. It has been said that Lyon has 3 rivers: the Rhone, the Saone, and the Beaujolais.

Stroll for a few hours through the winding streets of the 3-block wide half-mile long ancient section (Vieux Lyon) and see the magnificent 15th century Renaissance mansions. Much information is available in the booklet "Guide du Vieux Lyon" sold everywhere in the city.

Take the funicular to the 19th century Basilica of Notre Dame de la Fourviere to see the extraordinary mosaics on its floors, walls and nave. The view from either the terrace behind it or from the observatory above it is marvelous.

Then walk downhill to the Gallo Roman Museum (open daily except Monday and Tuesday 09:30–12:00 and 14:00–18:00), built into the side of a hill next to several Roman ruins. Its exhibits include objects from prehistory to the end of the Roman Empire, as well as elaborate floor mosaics and scale models of ancient Lyons.

Walking further downhill brings you to the Cathedral of St. Jean, which has 13th century stained glass and a 500-year-old astrological clock that performs a tableau at 12:00, 13:00, 14:00 and 15:00. In the nearby Palais Gadagne are the History Museum and the Puppet Museum, both open daily except Tuesday 10:45–18:00.

The historical exhibits cover the period from where the Gallo Roman Museum leaves off, including carved Renaissance furniture, prints, Nevers glazed pottery, and documents from the French Revolution. The adjoining Puppet Museum at 10–14 Rue de Gadagne, honors Laurent Mourguet, a destitute weaver who took up extracting teeth and, in seeking to attract customers with a puppet show, invented the character Guignol. It is open daily except Tuesday 10:45–18:00.

In the modern area, take Bus #13 from the railstation, through the main shopping streets, to the Place de la Croix Rousse and then walk to Place des Terreaux to see the 17th century City Hall, the 19th century Opera House and The Fine Arts Museum. This museum, featuring works of Rodin, Renoir, Gauguin, Monet, Delacroix, Courbet and Corot, is open daily except Monday and Tuesday 10:30–18:00. Do not miss seeing the Italian fountain with its 4 bronze horses, sculptured by the same Bartholdi who created the Statue of Liberty.

The Musee des Tissus (34 Rue de la Charite), open daily except Monday 10:00–17:30, houses a nearly 2,000-year-old collection of Oriental and European silks and velvets. It displays Persian carpets hung in a room that is 28-feet high. Next door, there is a good collection of silver objects, kitchen utensils, Louis XIV furniture, tapestries and enamels in The Museum of Decorative Arts, open daily except Monday 10:00–12:00 and 14:00–17:30.

Visit The Museum of Printing and Banking (13 Rue de la Poullaillerie), open daily except Monday and Tuesday 09:30–12:00 and 14:00–18:00. The Museum of Medicine in Hotel-Dieu on Rue de l'Hopital, closed Monday.

Marseille

Most of the museums in Marseille are closed Tuesday.

There are fancy shops on Canebiere, the main street. Visit the dungeon from which the Count of Monte Cristo escaped, at Chateau d'If, reached by launch from the Quai des Belges. The Maritime Museum, on the ground floor of the Palais de la Bourse (Stock Exchange). The Fine Arts Museum and Natural History Museum, in the Palais de Longchamps. The Roman Docks Museum.

The Museum of Old Marseille. The Museum of Mediterranean Archaeology and the Lapidary Museum, both in the Park of Borely. There are fine views of the harbor from Fort St. Jean and Fort St. Nicolas.

Nice

Most of the museums in Nice are closed Monday or Tuesday.

See the priceless antiques, lavish carpets and exceptional paintings and sculptures in the Hotel Negresco at 37 Promenade des Anglais. The Jules Cheret Museum of Fine Arts, 33 Avenue des Baumettes (behind the Promenade des Anglais), has many of Cheret's paintings as well as those of Dufy, Picasso and several other artists.

The Matisse Museum, 164 Avenue des Arenes, has guided tours in English. See the War Memorial. The view of the Bay of Angels from the Naval Museum, in the Bellanda Tower. The Marc Chagall National Museum, a short walk down the hill from the Arenes station. The Roman Baths. The Terra Amata Prehistory Museum. The exhibit of 15,000 species of seashells at the Musee Internationale de Malacologie. Take the lift to the Colline du Chateau fortress ruins.

Try the Nicoise cuisine: *pissaladiere* (the local pizza), *socca* (a pancake), *ratatouile* (sauteed eggplant, onions, tomatoes and squash), *le poulrt farci aux figues* (roast chicken stuffed with fresh figs), and of course *salade nicoise*.

Paris

There is rail service [Table 100] between Nord station (and 4 other Paris stations) and Charles-de-Gaulle Airport every 15 minutes from 05:00 to 24:00 for this 37-minute trip.

Rail service is also available [Table 100] between 5 Paris subway stations and Orly Airport every 15 minutes from 05:00 to 21:30 and every 30 minutes from 21:30 to 24:00 for this 35-minute trip.

Bus service connects these Paris railstations:
(1) From Austerlitz to Est, Nord and St. Lazare. (2) From Lyon to Est, Nord and St. Lazare. (3) From Nord to Lyon and Austerlitz. (4) From Est to Austerlitz, Nord and St. Lazare.

See the Montmartre area and Sacre Coeur. Eiffel Tower. The equestrian statues and Obelisk, at Place de la Concorde. The good views from the platform at the Arch of Triumph. The stained-glass at St. Chapelle. The Treasure Museum inside Notre Dame Cathedral, open daily except Sundays and holidays 10:00–17:00. The Louvre (open Monday and Wednesday 09:00–21:45, Thursday–Sunday 09:00–18:00). Luxembourg Palace and Gardens. Stroll the Champs Elysee. Visit Galleries Lafayette, the most beautiful department store building in the world.

The collection of modern art at Pompidou Center (closed Tuesday), near Galleries Lafayette. The Musee of the Renaissance, in the 16th century Chateau d'Ecouen Castle, with its antique tapestries, ceramics, arms, furniture, outstanding carved white fireplace and painted ceilings, open daily except Tuesdays 09:45–12:30 and 14:00–17:15.

The 150 works of such impressionist painters as Renoir, Matisse, Cezanne, Picasso and Utrillo at the Orangerie Museum. The Army Museum, at Hotel des Invalides. The Rodin Museum, at Hotel Biron, closed Tuesday.

The excellent views of Paris from the top of the 650-foot high Tour Mont- parnasse. The Postal Museum, closed Thursday. Beautiful tapestries in the museum at Hotel de Cluny, closed Tuesday. The Museum of African and Oceanic Art. The Botanical Garden.

Marvelous costumes in the Musee de la Mode et du Costume, 10 Ave. Pierre Premier de Serbie. Open daily except Monday 10:00–17:40. Remnants from Paris' 3rd century Roman through 18th century periods (all of them discovered when an underground parking lot was built in the 1970's in front of Notre Dame Cathedral) are exhibited at the Archaeological Museum.

See the electronic exhibits at Musee Branly. Chinese and Japanese artifacts at Musee D'Ennery. The Museum of French Bread. The Museum of Police History. The Musical Instruments Museum. The Mint Museum. The medical display at Musee de Val-de-Grace.

The large poster collection in the Musee de l'Affiche, 18 Rue de Paradis, open daily except Tuesdays 12:00–18:00. The Tiepolo ceilings, fantastic staircase, excellent paintings (Rembrandt, Reynolds, Manet, Monet and many other Impressionists) in the Musee Jacquemart-Andre, 12 Rue Louis-Boilly. Open daily except Monday 13:30–17:30.

Paintings and engravings illustrating the history of Paris, along with 17th and 18th century furniture in the Musee Carnavalet, 23 Rue de Sevigne, open daily except Monday 10:00-17:40. The flower markets on the Ile de la Cite, the rue de Buci, and rue Mouffetard in the Latin Quarter. The Flea Market, near the Place de la Republique, and the Sunday Flea Market at Porte Clignacourt.

The collection of sculptures of composers, the ballet slippers of Nijinski and Pavlova, and opera costumes, scores and photos in the Museum at the Opera, Place de l'Opera, open daily except Sunday 10:00-16:30 and during intermissions of performances.

Near the Opera, at 25 Boulevard des Capucines, is the Musee Cognac-Jay, which has an exhibit of lorgnettes, snuff boxes, letter openers and sewing kits, all of them in porcelain, precious metals and jewels, and the furniture and art that were the property of a man who owned department stores in the 19th century. Open daily except Mondays and holidays 10:00-17:00.

The Wine Museum, 3 Rue des Eaux, is open daily except Monday 14:00-18:00. The Eugene Delacroix Museum, 6 Place Furstenberg, is open daily except Tuesday 09:45-17:15. The Rodin Museum, 77 Rue de Varenne, is open daily except Tuesday 10:00-17:00. (Visitors are not admitted after 16:30.) In addition to the sculptor's famous bronze and marble works, some of his favorite paintings are also displayed. Strolling in the garden there is allowed.

The Jewish Art Museum, 42 Rue des Saules, is open Monday–Thursday 15:00-18:00. The collection of naive art in the Le Halle St. Pierre Musem, 1 Rue Ronsard, can be viewed daily 10:00-18:00.

See the exhibit of 19th century player pianos, violins and banjos in the Museum of Mechanical Musical Instruments at Impasse Berthaud, open Saturdays, Sundays and holidays 14:00-19:00.

The display of more than 8,000 instruments and machines (16th to 20th centuries) in the National Technical Museum at 270 Rue St. Martin, open Tuesday–Saturday 13:00-17:30, Sunday 10:00-17:15. The Tobacco Museum, 12 Rue Surcouf, is open daily except Sunday 11:00-18:00.

The Pasteur Museum, 25 Rue du Docteur-Roux, is open daily except Saturdays, Sundays and holidays 14:00-17:30. The Honore de Balzac Museum, 47 Rue Raynouard, is open daily except Mondays and holidays 10:00-17:40.

See the enormous collection of uniforms, weapons, war trophies, flags, books, manuscripts and paintings in the Army Museum at Les Invalides. The museum and the Eglise du Dome (containing Napoleon's Tomb) are open daily 10:00-18:00 April–September and 10:00-17:00 October-March. A fine sound-and-light show is presented there every night April–September.

At the Galerie des Monnaies, Medailles et Antiques (in the National Library at 58 Rue de Richelieu) there are exhibits from its collection of 400,000 historic coins, 15th–17th century sculptures, magnificent ancient cameos, 1800-year-old Roman silver goblets and plates, historic globes and maps, and oriental arts. Open daily 13:00-17:00 (18:00 on Sunday).

The Sevres Museum's collection of 18th century porcelain, the most beautiful porcelain ever produced. Open daily, except Tuesdays and holidays, 10:00-12:30 and 13:30-17:00. Take the metro to the Pont de Sevres station and walk across the bridge. The museum is the large gray building on the other side of the Seine.

Information about tours sponsored by the Department of Historical Monuments (botanical gardens, the Latin Quarter, churches that are architecturally interesting, private homes) can be obtained at the Caisse Nationale des Monuments Historiques, at 62 Rue Saint-Antoine.

Completed in 1987, the restored classic d'Orsay railstation has been a museum (Musee d'Orsay) of 19th century art since then. Its outstanding collection of Impressionists is its main attraction: Monet, Van Gogh, Renoir, Pissarro.

*　　*　　*

A great food store that welcomes tourists is Hediard, across Rue Tronchet, at 21 Place de la Madeleine. It has a world-wide reputation for quality. Next to it is La Maison de Truffe (19 Place de la Madeleine), where truffles, foie gras and caviar are the specialties. On the other side of it (17 bis Place de la Madeleine), the Creplet-Brussol dairy store features 250 varieties of cheese.

Caviar Kaspia (17 Place de la Madeleine) sells fine caviar from Iran and the Soviet Union. Marquise de Sevigne (32 Place de la Madeleine) has been making fine chocolate for nearly 100 years.

*　　*　　*

The Marais district, the ancient section of Paris, a maze of narrow 16th century streets, is overlooked by many tourists.

It can be examined by starting at the Pompidou Center and walking along Rue Rambuteau to Rue des Francs-Bourgeois a street named in the 15th century, describing its poor residents who were exempt from paying taxes.

Interesting documents (the order sending Marie Antoinette to the guillotine, the 1944 law giving French women the right to vote, etc.) can be seen in the History of France Museum at 60 Rue des Francs-Bourgeois, open daily except Tuesdays and holidays 14:00-17:00.

Among the many elegant town mansions (called "hotels" in the 15th century) worth seeing in the Marais are Hotel d'Albret, Hotel de Fourcy, and Hotel de Lamignon (all on Rue des Francs-Bourgeois). Then see Hotel Merle and Hotel de Chatillon (along Rue Payenne), and follow the signs leading to Hotel Sale on Rue de Thorigny, housing the Picasso Museum, open Wednesday 10:00–22:00, Thursday–Monday 10:00–17:15.

There is an extraordinary collection of stuffed animals, furniture carved with animal figures, and silver encrusted riflea at the Hunting and Nature Museum, in the Hotel Gueneguad at 60 Rue des Archives, open daily except Mondays and holidays 10:00–17:30.

By walking down Rue du Parc Royal, you pass the pink and white Hotel Duret de Chevry. Turn right to go down Rue de Sevigne so as to pass by Hotel Le Peletier St. Fargeau and Hotel Carnavalet, now a museum of French interior design, open daily except Monday 10:00–17:40.

Then visit the Victor Hugo House (6 Place des Vosges), open daily except Mondays and holidays 10:00–17:40. Next, walk down Rue de Birague and onto Rue St. Antoine in order to see Hotel Sully (at Number 62).

By walking Rue Mahler until it reaches Rue des Rosiers, you arrive at the center of the Jewish district and the most famous delicatessen in Paris, Jo Goldberg's, at Number 7. Nearby is the Art Deco synagogue on Rue Pavee. Rue Simon-le-ranc will lead you back to the Pompidou Center.

*   *   *

At the 14-acre Pere Lachaise Cemetery are the graves of Edith Piaf, Gertrude Stein, Alce B. Toklas, Colette, Sarah Bernhardt, Isadora Duncan, Simone Signoret, Frederick Chopin, Oscar Wilde, Honore de Balzac, Ferdinand de Lesseps (promoter of the Suez Canal), and Jean Francois Champollion (interpreter of the Rosetta stone).

Opened in 1804, it is the oldest of the 4 cemeteries in Paris. It is open mid-March to mid-November Monday–Saturday 07:30–18:00, the rest of the year 08:30–17:30. On Sundays and holidays: mid-November to mid-January 09:00–18:00, the rest of the year 08:30–17:30.

*   *   *

Swimmers can chose from a wide variety of pools in this city. The 50-meter Piscine Georges-Vallerey, built for the 1924 Olympic Games, has a transparent roof that is opened in good weather. It is located next to the Porte des Lilas metro station.

The underground Piscine Suzanne Berlioux at Les Halles, near the Pompidou Center, is another modern 50-meter facility.

Aquaboulevard de Paris is an indoor-outdoor amusement park (sand beaches, wave machines, slides. toboggans, mock tropical islands and lagoons) is near the Balard metro station. The former Piscine Pontoise re-opened after renovations in 1990 with the new name Piscine du Quartier Latin.

Strasbourg

An historical pawn, Strasbourg was French until 1872. German 1871–1918, French 1918–1940, German 1940-1944, and has been French since 1944.

On Rue de la Rape, see the city's majestic 13th century Cathedral of Notre- Dame. All of its windows are 12th, 13th and 14th century stained-glass.

Its famous 60-foot high astronomical clock, which calculates eclipses, sunrises and sunsets into eternity, comes alive on the hour and quarter-hour, when figures appear from and return into its interior.

The clock's major performance is at 12:30. It is then that the "Four Ages of Man" pass before "Death", and the 12 Apostles move past the figure of Jesus. As he blesses them, a mechanical rooster flaps its wings and crows 3 times.

There is an extraordinary view of the city from a platform 217 feet above the street, at the top of the Cathedral's 328-step spiral staircase. April-September, a fabulous sound-and-light show is presented inside the Cathedral: illuminated stained-glass windows, bells tolling, organ music.

There are 3 good museums in the 18th century Chateau des Rohans (next to the Cathedral): a collection of Monet, Renoir, El Greco, Goya and Tintoretto in its Art Gallery; the relics in the Archaeological Museum; and a display of clocks, ironwork, earthenware and porcelain in its Museum of Decorative Arts.

Next to the Rohans is a 14th century building that houses wonderful 11th to 17th century Alsatian art in the Musee de l'Oeuvre Notre-Dame. Next to it is the Modern Art Museum.

All of these museums are open daily except Tuesday 10:00–12:00 and 14:00–18:00.

Take a one-hour sightseeing minitrain ride that starts at the south side of the Cathedral. Runs every half-hour, late March to the end of October. There are also cruises on the Rhine (90 minutes, 3 hours, and 11 hours) starting in front of the Palais des Rohans, 2 blocks from the Cathedral.

Walk around Place Kleber. Sample the world's best pate de fois gras. Stroll down Rue du Bain-aux-Plantes, an alley where herbs once were sold.

See the rooms dating from the early 17th century (furnished with marvelous utensils, stoves, wooden molds and pottery from the same era) at the Musee Alsacien, 23 Quai St. Nicholas.

Tours

Much of the old city was destroyed in the 1944 bombings. The German occupiers were forced to retreat, resulting in liberation of Tours. Take a 90-minute walk by departing the Tours railstation along Boulevard Heurteloup to Rue Nationale, then turn right and go up one side of Rue Nationale to the bridge, returning along the opposite side of Rue Nationale, cross Boulevard Heurteloup, go one block further, turn left onto Rue de Bordeaux, taking it directly back to the railstation.

See the fine collection of paintings in the Musee des Beaux-Arts.

A pamphlet called "The Loire Valley by Train" may be obtained from the information desk at many French railstations. It shows schedules of trains from Tours (*not provided in Cook*) that stop at stations near 12 different castles.

The train to **Azay-le-Rideau** continues to **Chinon**. Another train goes to **Amboise**, **Chaumont** (Onzain), **Blois** and **Beaugency**. A third goes to **Villandry** (Savonnieres), **Langeais**, **Samur** and **Angers**. A fourth train goes to **Loches** and a fifth goes to **Chenonceaux**.

These train rides range from 10 to 70 minutes in each direction. Most are less than 30 minutes. There are also bus tours from Tours to the castles.

In the following timetables, where a city has more than one railstation we have designated the particular station after the name of the city (in parentheses).

Note that **Paris has 9 railstations**: Austerlitz, Bercy, Charolais, Est, Lyon, Montparnasse, Nord, Tolbiac and Vaugirard. Don't assume that the station for your departure from Paris is the same as the station where you arrived. Doing so may cause you to miss your train.

Always double-check the station for any departure from Paris !

Avignon - Antibes - Avignon 54

| Dep. Avignon | 06:04 (1) | 06:30 (2) |
| Arr. Antibes | 10:05 | 10:39 |

Sights in **Antibes**: The exhibit of 231 Picasso paintings at the special Picasso Museum in Grimaldi Castle, on Place Mariejol. Open daily except Tuesday 10:00–12:00 and 15:00–18:00.

| Dep. Antibes | 18:15 (3) | 18:40 (4) | 18:57 (5) |
| Arr. Avignon | 22:38 | 22:56 | 22:35 |

(1) Late June to late August, runs daily. Late August to late June, runs Friday and Saturday. (2) Operates early September to late June. Runs daily except Friday and Saturday. (3) Late June to late Augus, runs daily. Late August to late June, runs Friday and Sunday. (4) Light refreshments. (5) Operates early September to late June. Runs Monday–Friday

Avignon - Arles - Avignon 151

| Dep. Avignon | 07:56 (1) | 09:45 | 12:03 (2) | 15:03 |
| Arr. Arles | 20 minutes later |

Sights in **Arles**: The ancient Roman cemetery, Alyscamps, that contains 400,000 sarcophagi, hand-carved granite caskets. The 21,000-seat Roman arena. The Forum, built during Augustus' rule. The Thermae, from Constantine's era.

The 12th century Cloister in the marvelous Romanesque Church of Saint-Trophime.

| Dep. Arles | 12:30 (3) | 14:52 | 17:53 | 20:13 (4) | 21:58 (5) | 22:35 (4) |
| Arr. Avignon | 20 minutes later |

(1) Runs daily except Sunday and holidays. (2) Mid-August to mid-July, runs daily. Mid-July to mid-August, runs Monday, Saturday and Sunday. (3) Runs daily *except* during September. September: runs Saturday and Sunday only. Light refreshments. (4) Runs daily. Light refreshments. (5) Late June to early September, runs daily. Early September to late June, runs Friday and Sunday.

Avignon - Lyon - Avignon 151

| Dep. Avignon | 06:56 | 07:38 (1) | 08:00 (2) | 10:35 |
| Arr. Lyon (Part Dieu) | 09:04 | 09:26 | 10:18 | 12:37 |

Sights in **Lyon**: See notes about sightseeing in Lyon on page 123.

| Dep. Lyon (Part Dieu) | 12:02 (3) | 13:50 | 14:06 (3) | 17:17 (3) | 18:44 (6) |
| Arr. Avignon | 13:58 | 15:54 | 16:02 | 19:16 | 20:40 |

(1) TGV. Reservation required. Supplement charged. Early September to early July: runs Monday–Friday. Early July to early September: runs Monday only. Light refreshments. (2) Daily except Sunday and holidays. (3) Light refreshments. (4) TGV. Reservation required. Supplement charged. Light refreshments. (5) TGV. Reservation required. Supplement charged. Restaurant car. (6) Plus other departures from Lyon at 19:00 (4), 21:01, 22:03 (5), 23:10 and 23:43 (3), arriving Avignon 20:49, 23:09, 23:56, 01:09 and 01:41.

Avignon - Marseille - Avignon 151

| Dep. Avignon | 07:56 (1) | 08:05 (2) | 09:45 | 10:52 (3) | 11:41 (4) | 12:03 (5) |
| Arr. Marseille (St. Ch.) | 50–60 minutes later |

Sights in **Marseille**: See notes about Marseille on page 124.

Dep. Marseille (St. Ch.)	13:58 (6)	14:39 (7)	16:46 (6)	17:10	17:31 (8)	18:20 (9)
Arr. Avignon	50–60 minutes later					

Dep. Marseille (St. Ch.)	19:25 (7)	21:14 (10)	21:48 (7)	22:55 (11)	22:59	23:21 (12)
Arr. Avignon	50–60 minutes later					

(1) Daily except Sunday and holidays. (2) Operates early September to late June. Runs Monday–Friday. (3) TGV. Reservation required. Supplement charged. Runs Monday–Friday. (4) TGV. Reservation required. Supplement charged. Operates mid-August to mid-July. (5) Mid-August to mid-July: runs daily. Mid-July to to mid-August: runs Monday, Saturday and Sunday. (6) TGV. Reservation required. Supplement charged. Light refreshments. (7) Light refreshments. (8) TGV. Reservation required. Supplement charged. Restaurant car. (9) TGV. Reservation required. Supplement charged. Runs daily except Saturday. Restaurant car. (10) Late June to early September: runs daily. Early September to late June: runs Friday and Sunday. (11) Operates late June to late August. Runs Saturday and Sunday. (12) Operates late June to late August. Runs daily.

Avignon - Monaco (Monte Carlo) - Avignon

151		164	
Dep. Avignon	07:56	Dep. Monaco	19:28
Arr. Marseille	09:10	Arr. Nice	20:00
Change trains. 164		No train change.	
Dep. Marseille	09:14	Dep Nice	20:17
Arr. Nice	11:41	Arr. Marseille	22:41
Change trains.		Change trains. 151	
Dep. Nice	11:50	Dep. Marseille	22:59
Arr. Monaco	12:10	Arr. Avignon	00:05

Avignon - Nimes - Avignon 162

Dep. Avignon	07:35 (1)	09:40	11:00 (1)	11:48 (2)	12:14	14:06 (3)
Arr. Nimes	25 minutes later					

Sights in **Nimes:** Many Roman ruins in excellent condition, such as the 1st century amphitheater (seating 24,000 people) in the center of the city, used in recent years for bullfights to entertain Spanish migrant workers. The construction of the arena was done by fitting large stones together without the use of mortar.

Also see the beautiful 1st century rectangular temple, Maison Carree, and its collection of Roman sculptures. The view of Nimes from the oldest Roman building, Tour Magne, on a hill outside the city. A few miles away is the enormous Pont du Gard Roman aqueduct.

Visit the collection of Iron Age and Roman objects in the Archaeological Museum. Stroll through the 18th century Garden of the Fountain.

Dep. Nimes	11:56	12:47 (2)	13:29 (4)	14:29 (2)	15:05 (5)	16:30 (6)
Arr. Avignon	25 minutes later					

Dep. Nimes	17:17 (7)	17:44	18:29	18:50 (8)	18:58 (6)	20:09 (10)
Arr. Avignon	25 minutes later					

(1) Runs daily except holidays. (2) TGV. Reservation required. Supplement charged. Light refreshments. (3) TGV. Reservation required. Supplement charged. Restaurant car. (4) Daily except Sunday and holidays. (5) Light refreshments. (6) Runs Monday–Friday except holidays. (7) TGV. Reservation required. Supplement charged. Early July to early September: runs Tuesday–Friday. Early September to Early July: runs daily exzcept Sunday. Restaurant car. (8) TGV. Reservation required. Supplement charged. Runs daily except Saturday. Light refreshments. (9) Runs daily except Saturday. (10) Plus other Nimes departures at 20:09, 20:29 (9), 22:17 and 22:37.

Avignon - Orange - Avignon 151

Dep. Avignon	08:00 (1)	10:23	12:32	15:13
Arr. Orange	15 minutes later			

Sights in **Orange**: See the 10,000-seat Roman Theater and the ancient walls of the old city. The Roman Triumphal Arch.

Dep. Orange	11:46 (2)	14:46	15:38	21:03 (3)
Arr. Avignon	15 minutes later			

(1) Runs daily except Sunday and holidays. (2) Mid-August to mid-July: runs daily. Mid-July to mid-August: runs Monday, Saturday and Sunday. (3) Daily except Saturday.

Bordeaux - Bayonne and Biarritz - Bordeaux 137

Dep. Bordeaux (St. Jean)	07:24	11:10 (1)	11:54 (2)
Arr. Bayonne	09:23	12:47	13:44
Arr. Biarritz	09:34	12:57	13:55

Sights in **Bayonne**: This is the Cote Basque's leading port and private yacht harbor. See the cathedral. The Basque Museum. Chateau-Viex. The Museum Bonnat. Exhibits tracing Basque history and customs (farm tools, household objects, costumes) in the Musee Basque, at 1 Rue Marengo.

Sights in **Biarritz:** France's snootiest beach resort since 1854. Golf, tennis and every type of water sport are popular here. There are many spas offering thalassotherapy. See the food market.

A small grocery store called Maison Arosteguy stocks 120 types of Scotch whiskey and what has been described as "a dizzying array" of Armagnacs.

Dep. Biarritz	14:46 (3)	16:38 (4)	17:05 (5)	18:03 (2)	18:40 (6+8)
Dep. Bayonne	14:56	16:48	17:17	18:14	18:57
Arr. Bordeaux (St. Jean)	16:30	18:23	19:16	20:33	21:25

(1) TGV. Reservation required. Supplement charged. Daily except Sunday and holidays. Restaurant car. (2) Sunday only. (3) TGV. Reservation required. Supplement charged. Light refreshments. (4) TGV. Reservation required. Supplement charged. Runs Sunday only. (5) Daily, except holidays. (6) Daily except Sunday and holidays. (7) Operates early July to early September. (8) Plus other departured from Biarritz at 18:59 (20, 19:43 (7), 20:24 (2) and 22:51 (7), arriving Bordeaux 20:39, 22:02, 22:46 and 00:16.

Bordeaux - Carcassone - Bordeaux 139

Bordeaux (St. Jean)	06:37 (1)	08:23 (2)	11:54 (1)
Arr. Carcassone	09:50	12:47	15:06

Sights in **Carcassone:** The most interesting walled city in France and Europe's best preserved relic of the Middle Ages. It is actually double-walled. The inner wall, built by the Romans in the 2nd century, bears 29 towers. The 13th century French outer wall has 17 towers and barbicans (fortified castles).

Nearby are the ruins of 5 other walls, to the South, erected by France in medieval days as additional protection from attack by the Spaniards. As you stand on the walkways at the top of the French wall, it is easy to imagine yourself shooting arrows through the narrow slits or dropping hot oil on the marauders below.

See the Narbonnaise Gate and drawbridge. Nearby is a bust of Dame Carcas, for whom the city is named. Carcassone had been under siege by Charlemagne. She gathered the little grain the starving people had and scattered it to livestock in view of the soldiers who were by then weary of the months they had been waiting for the people inside the impregnbable walls to capitulate.

Her bold act convinced the soldiers that the people could last much longer, and Charlemagne abandoned his attempt to starve-out the town.

Inside the Basilica of St. Nazare are many stone carvings depicting scenes from the fort's history, magnificent stained-glass windows regarded by many as the finest in southern France, and the rectangular tombstone of Bishop Radulph. Also see the 12th century Countal Castle.

| Dep. Carcassone | 12:32 | 16:59 (3) | 20:17 (3) |
| Arr. Bordeaux (St. Jean) | 15:52 | 21:53 | 23:35 |

(1) Light Refreshments. (2) Light refreshments. Change trains in Toulouse (arr. 11:03–dep. 11:29). (3) Light refreshments. Change trains in Toulouse (arr. 17:52–dep. 19:16).

Bordeaux - Limoges - Bordeaux 140

| Dep. Bordeaux (St. Jean) | 06:20 (1) | 07:47 (2) | 12:00 |
| Arr. Limoges | 08:32 | 10:45 | 14:35 |

Sights in **Limoges**: Tours of the famous porcelain and enamel factories are free, by applying to the Syndicat de la Porcelain, 7 Rue du General Cerez. Visit the Adrien Dubouche Museum, with its great collection of ceramics. The Municipal Museum, to see its display of china made in Limoges from the 12th century to the present. The Cathedral of Saint Etienne.

| Dep. Limoges | 11:44 (1) | 16:52 | 21:04 (1) |
| Arr. Bordeaux (St. Jean) | 13:56 | 20:19 | 23:22 |

(1) Light refreshments. (2) Runs daily, except Sundays and holidays. Change trains in Perigueux at 09:06.

Bordeaux - Lourdes - Bordeaux 137

| Dep. Bordeaux | 07:24 (1) | 11:10 (2) | 11:54 (3) | 13:12 (4) | 15:03 (9+13) |
| Arr. Lourdes | 10:11 | 13:37 | 14:48 | 15:54 | 17:31 |

Sights in **Lourdes**: A 14-year-old girl, Bernadette Soubirous, had numerous visions here in 1858, in the Massabielle grotto. The underground spring in the grotto is believed by many to have miraculous qualities. About 3,000,000 people come here every year, many of them disabled or diseased and hoping to be cured.

The immense underground church seating 20,000 was innaugurated in 1958.

On the other side of the torrent called Gave de Pau there is an interesting 14th century castle which was used as a prison from 1643 until the early 19th century.

| Dep. Lourdes | 14:59 (5) | 16:21 (6) | 17:39 (7) | 19:38 (8) | 22:51 (9+14) |
| Arr. Bordeaux | 17:23 | 19:16 | 20:05 | 22:46 | 01:06 |

(1) Operates late June to early September. (2) TGV. Reservation required. Supplement charged. Daily except Sunday and holidays. Restaurant car. (3) Sunday only. Change trains in Dax at 13:13. (4) Light refreshments. (5) TGV. Reservation required. Supplement charged. Light refreshments or restaurant car. (6) Daily except Sunday and holidays. (7) TGV. Reservation required. Supplement charged. Sunday only. Restaurant car. (8) Sunday only. (9) Operates late June to early September. (10) Daily except Friday. (11) Friday only. Light refreshments. (12) Early July to early September: runs daily. Early September to early July: daily except Sunday and holidays. (13) Plus other departures from Bordeaux at 17:01 (5), 18:29 (10), 19:15 (11) and 20:51 (5), arriving Lourdes 19:24, 21:50, 22:07 and 23:13. (14) Plus other departures from Lourdes (for those wishing to spend the night here) at 07:51 (12), 08:58 (4) and 11:29, arriving Bordeaux 10:15, 11:43 and 13:53.

134

Bordeaux - Nantes - Bordeaux   134

Dep.Bordeaux (St. J.)	06:46 (1)	10:26 (1)	
Arr. Nantes	11:06	14:24	
	*	*	*
Dep. Nantes	13:45 (1)	18:14 (1)	19:35 (2)
Arr. Bordeaux (St. J.)	18:02	22:12	23:25

(1) Light refreshments. (2) Late June to early September: runs daily, except Friday. Early September to late June: runs Friday and Sunday.

Sights in **Nantes**: This was a commercial center under the Romans. The Normans pillaged the town in 834. After having been partly destroyed in World War II, its railway was placed underground.

This is an important seaport and shipbuilding center. See the extraordinary white marble Renaissance tomb of Francois II, duke of Brittany, in the Cathedral that was bombed during World War II. The church was restored, only to have its roof almost entirely destroyed by fire in 1972. The tomb was not harmed.

Tour the medieval castle that was rebuilt in 1466, Chateau des Ducs de Bretagne and its museums (entrance on the Rue des Etats). Guided tours are offered every half-hour, daily during July and August from 10:00–12:00 and 14:00–18:00. The rest of the year there are only 3 tours a day, and the castle is closed on Tuesday. The castle is surrounded by a moat and has a drawbridge at its entrance.

Visit the Jules Verne Museum (the author was born in Nantes in 1828), open daily except Tuesday 10:00–12:00 and 14:00–17:00. See the exceptional paintings in the Fine Arts Museum (10 Rue Georges Clemenceau), open daily except Tuesday and national holidays 10:00–12:00 and 13:00–17:45.

Stroll through the Passage Pommeraye, a decorative 3 level shopping arcade. Visit the Jardin des Plantes, a botanical garden and formal French park, with grottos, waterfalls, statues, ponds, 400 varieties of camelias, and 19th century greenhouses, containing many orchids.

There are 3-hour boat cruises on the **Erbe River**, leaving from 24 Quai de Versailles at 12:30 (Lunch), 14:30 and 20:00 (dinner).

Bordeaux - Narbonne - Bordeaux   139

All of these trains have light refreshments.

Dep. Bordeaux (St. Jean)	06:37	08:23 (1)	Dep. Narbonne	19:48
Arr. Narbonne	10:20	12:47	Arr. Bordeaux (St. Jean)	23:35

Sights in **Narbonne**: The Cloister adjacent to the Palace of the Archbishops. The choir of the incomplete Cathedral of Saint-Just.

(1) Change trains in Toulouse at 11:03.

Bordeaux - Toulouse - Bordeaux   139

Dep. Bordeaux (St. Jean)	05:47 (1)	06:37	08:23 (2)	11:00	11:46
Arr. Toulouse (Matabiau)	08:50	08:57	11:03	13:01	14:12

Sights in **Toulouse**:The Basilica of Saint Sernin, displaying the remains of 128 saints, including 6 of the apostles and a thorn from the Crown of Thorns. It also has 7 extraor- dinary 11th century marble bas reliefs and the Meigeville Door, a 12th century sculpture of apostles watching Christ ascend to heaven surrounded by angels.

The museum on the history of art and an exceptional collection of busts of Roman emperors at Musee Saint Raymond on Place St. Sernin. The Roman and medieval sculptures in the Musee des Augustins, 21 Rue de Metz. The beautiful 14th century Church of the Jacobins.

Popular art of the region and the history of Toulouse, at the Musee du Vieux-Toulouse, 7 Rue du May.

Chinese, Japanese and Indian art at the Musee Georges Labit, 43 Rue des Martyrs de la Liberation. St. Etienne Cathedral. Two 16th century homes: Hotel de Bernuy and Hotel d'Assezat, and the view of the city from the tower of the latter.

The Office de Tourisme (Donjon du Capitole, Square Charles de Gaule, 31000 Toulouse) offered in 1991 a 2–hour walking tour at 09:30 and 15:00 for $6 (U.S.), as well as an $8 city bus tour at 15:00.

Obtain the tourist office's brochure describing 16 different one-day bus sightseeing excursions to nearby interesting places ($21 each in 1991). All of these trips start at 08:00 and arrive back in Toulouse between 19:00–20:30.

One of these tours goes to the 16th century Chateau de Saint-Genies-Bellevue; to Cordes, a 13th century walled town, to see marvelous Gothic houses and the quality arts and crafts sold at 14th Marketplace; to see more than 600 works of Toulouse-Lautrec in Albi, where he was born in 1864; then to Chateau Latours for tasting Gaillac wine.

Every year, from the end of June to late September, both an international Piano Festival featuring noted soloists and a series of orchestral concerts (jazz to Beethoven) are presented in Toulouse.

Barges can be rented to tour the 17th century Canal du Midi all the way to the Mediterranean. Visitors can also rent motorboats and rowboats.

Dep. Toulouse (Matabiau)	13:27 (2)	16:35	16:57 (2)	19:12	21:14 (1)
Arr. Bordeaux (St. Jean)	15:52	18:33	19:07	21:53	23:35

(1) Runs daily, except Sunday and holidays. (2) Light refreshments.

136

Bordeaux - Tours - Bordeaux   136

Dep. Bordeaux (St. Jean)	07:11 (1)	10:19 (1+2)
Arr. St. Pierre-des-Corps	09:40	12:55
Change trains.		
Dep. St. Pierre-des-Corps	09:43	12:58
Arr. Tours	09:50	13:05

Sights in **Tours**: See page 129.

Dep. Tours	14:43	16:14	19:39
Arr. St. Pierre-des-Corps	14:50	16:20	19:45
Change trains.			
Dep. St. Pierre-des-Corps	14:53 (3)	16:23 (4)	19:48 (1+5)
Arr. Bordeaux (St. Jean)	17:22	18:48	22:22

(1) TGV. Reservation required. Supplement charged. Restaurant car. (2) Change trains in Poitiers at 12:04. (3) Runs daily except Friday. TGV. Reservation required. Supplement charged Light refreshments. (4) TGV. Reservation required. Supplement charged. Light refreshments. (5) Early July to early September: daily except Friday. Early September to early July: daily except Friday and Sunday.

Dijon - Beaune - Dijon   149

Dep. Dijon	07:40 (1)	09:07	11:27	12:01 (2)	14:40 (2)
Arr. Beaune	20 minutes later				

Sights in **Beaune**: The wine capital of Burgundy. Popular for its old houses along narrow, cobbled streets. Famous for Burgundian food: coq au vin, game birds, terines of veal and pork, snails, salamis, sausages, terines of salmon and sole. Hotels and restaurants here are booked months in advance.

Visit the many great wineries in this locale, such as Chateau de Meursault, Marche aux Vins and Maison Patriarche. Persuade your hotel to sell you $100 tickets to one of the 17 "grand dinners" at the Clos de Vougeot, sponsored by the Confrerie des Chevaliers de Tastevin. See the priceless art collection in the 15th century Hotel-Dieu. The other attractions there are the 28 red-canopied and red-curtained beds that were used 5 centuries ago, the original 15th century furnishings in the 160-foot-long Paupers' Room, the ancient pharmacy and kitchen, fantastic tapestries and rare pewter.

See the 15th century tapestries in the Notre Dame Church.

Many hot-air balloon trips are available in this area.

Dep. Beaune	13:26 (3)	14:22 (3)	15:23 (1)	17:16	17:56	20:05	21:44
Arr. Dijon	20 minutes later						

(1) Light refreshments. (2) Runs daily, except Sun. and holidays. (3) Runs Mon.–Fri., except holidays.

Dijon - St. Claude - Dijon   157

Dep. Dijon	06:35 (1)	08:52 (2)	Dep. St. Claude	15:37 (3)	16:52
Arr. St. Claude	09:30	11:42	Arr. Dijon	18:30	19:14

(1) Runs daily, except Sundays and holidays. (2) TGV. Reservation required. Supplement charged. Restaurant car. Change trains in Mouchard at 09:39. (3) Daily except Sundays and holidays. Change trains in Dole at 18:06. (TGV. Reservation required. Light refreshments).

Sights in **St. Claude**: The 15 manufacturers of smoking pipes who are located here have made this "the pipe capital of France". They produce 1,600,000 briar pipes annually. A walk down Rue du Pre and its extension, Rue du Marche, takes you past many pipe shops to the Pipe Museum, at 1 Rue Gambetta, visited by 35,000 people June–September (the only months the museum is open), 09:30–11:30 and 14:00–19:00.

Across from the Pipe Museum is St. Claude's Cathedral.

The Genod factory, at 13 Fauborg Marcel, allows visitors daily except Saturdays, Sundays and holidays 09:30–11:30 and 14:00–18:00. One of the pipe shops, La Tabatiere at 8 Rue du Pre, has pipes ranging in price from $5 (U.S.) to $1,400.

Limoges - Les Eyzies de Tayac 138

Dep. Limoges	05:40(1)		Dep. Les Eyzies	12:00
Arr. Les Eyzies	07:49		Arr. Limoges	14:22

(1) Runs daily, except Sundays and holidays.

Sights in **Les Eyzies de Tayac:** This is the prehistoric capital of Europe. The tourist information office and the famous cave paintings are a short walk from the railstation.

Lyon - Annecy - Lyon 167

En route, the train splits. Some cars go to Annecy, others to Grenoble. Be sure to sit in a car marked "Annecy" (pronounced Ahn-see).

Dep. Lyon (Part-Dieu)	06:59	09:12 (1)
Arr. Annecy	08:51	11:15

Sights in **Annecy**: This is a beautiful lake resort. See the 12th century Island Palace. The shops in the old quarter.

Dep. Annecy	11:43	16:00	17:17	19:04 (2)
Arr. Lyon (Part-Dieu)	13:48	18:07	19:32	21:07

(1) Light refreshments. (2) Supplement charged.

Lyon - Dijon - Lyon 149

Dep. Lyon (Perrache)	05:35 (1)	06:43 (2)	08:16	-0-	-0-
Dep. Lyon (Part-Dieu)	05:44	06:52	-0-	09:34	12:41 (3)
Arr. Dijon	07:29	08:35	10:30	11:13	14:32

Sights in **Dijon**: Town Hall, formerly the palace of those swashbuckling dukes of Burgundy and now one of the richest museums in France. The Church of Notre Dame. The 13th century Cathedral of St. Benigne archaeological museum. The Palace of Justice. The Magnin Museum. The 14th century Chartreuse de Champmol, with its famous chapel portrait and Moses Fountain. Rude Museum.

Don't fail to have lunch in Dijon, France's food and wine capital.

Dep. Dijon	12:17	15:45	16:57	19:18	20:43 (4)
Arr. Lyon (Part-Dieu)	14:01	17:44	18:39	-0-	22:25
Arr. Lyon (Perrache)	-0-	17:56	-0-	21:37	22:36

(1)Runs Monday–Friday, except holidays. (2) Runs daily except Sunday and holidays. (3) Light refreshments. (4) Daily except Saturday. Light refreshments

Lyon - Geneva 159

There are many scenic gorges on this ride.

Dep. Lyon (Perrache)	07:30	09:24	12:13
Dep. Lyon (Part-Dieu)	07:39	09:33	12:23
Arr. Geneva (Cornavin)	09:38	11:26	14:16

Sights in **Geneva:** See notes about sightseeing in Geneva on page 311.

Dep. Geneva (Cornavin)	16:30	19:45	21:54
Arr. Lyon (Part-Dieu)	18:18	21:42	23:39
Arr. Lyon (Perrache)	18:27	21:51	-0-

Lyon - Grenoble - Lyon 154

Dep. Lyon (Part-Dieu)	07:06 (1)	07:46 (2)	08:48 (3)	10:12	12:06 (4+10)
Arr. Grenoble	08:24	09:16	09:58	11:47	13:20

Sights in **Grenoble**: The information office outside the railstation offers maps, guides and city bus tickets. See the monumental Calder sculpture at the railstation. The very rich (Utrillo, Picasso, Ruben) art museum in the 16th century Palace of Justice. The contemporary art museum's collection of Delaunay, Picasso, Matisse and many surrealists.

Fine paintings in the Musee des Beaux Arts at Place de Verdun (Corot, Renoir, Monet, Roualt, Picasso, Utrillo). The Stendahl Museum, devoted to Grenoble's native son and greatest writer, whose real name was Henri Beyle. The Museum of the Resistance, in the house where Stendahl was born on Rue Jean-Jacques Rousseau. At the Municipal Library, the "Catholicon" (printed by Gutenburg in 1460), Stendahl's manuscripts, and more historic papers.

The geometrical gardens and 3 fountains in Place Victor Hugo, Grenoble's prettiest square, locale of expensive shops and sidewalk cafes. The Natural History Museum, in the Jardine des Plantes. The 17th century Church of St. Laurent. The City Gardens.

Take the cable car ride up to Guy Pape Park for a marvelous view of the city below and the fields surrounding Grenoble. While at the top, visit the military museum in the 19th century fort, the Bastille, and the Auto Museum.

Walk back to Grenoble, downhill, through the Jardine des Dauphines.

Another walk on the way down leads to a collection of Alpine artifacts from the past (antique cradles, beds, chests, backpacks, school rooms) at the Musee Dauphinois, in a 17th century cloister.

Dep. Grenoble	12:09 (5)	13:04	14:43 (4)	16:04	17:45 (4)
Arr. Lyon (Part-Dieu)	13:33	14:29	15:56	17:29	18:56

* * *

Dep. Grenoble	18:01	19:16 (7)	20:33 (8)	20:53	21:55
Arr. Lyon (Part-Dieu)	19:20 (6)	20:44	21:45	22:42 (9)	23:24

(1) Runs Monday-Friday, except holidays. (2) Departs from Lyon's Perrache railstation. Runs daily except Sunday and holidays. (3) TGV. Reservation required. Supplement charged. Runs Monday-Friday, except holidays. Restaurant car. (4) TGV. Reservation required. Supplement charged. Runs daily. Light refreshments. (5) Runs daily, except Sunday and holidays. (6) Arrive 19:50 on Friday and Sunday. (7) Runs daily, except Saturday. (8) TGV. Reservation required. Supplement charged. Runs Sunday only. Light refreshments. (9) Arrives at Lyon's Perrache railstation. (10) Plus other departures from Lyon at 12:56 (5) and 14:14, arriving Grenoble 14:19 and 15:30.

Lyon - Marseille - Lyon 151

Dep. Lyon (Part-Dieu)	-0-	09:03 (1)	-0-	12:02 (3)
Dep. Lyon (Perrache)	07:26	-0-	09:59 (2)	-0-
Arr. Marseille (St. Ch.)	10:51	11:46	13:03	15:00

Sights in **Marseille**: See "Avignon-Marseille" on page 131.

Dep. Marseille (St. Ch.)	14:39 (3)	16:18 (4)	17:10	18:20 (5+10)
Arr. Lyon (Per.)	-0-	-0-	-0-	-0-
Arr. Lyon (Part-Dieu))	17:38	19:35	20:35	21:07

(1) TGV. Reservation required. Supplement charged. Runs Monday-Friday. Restaurant car.
(2) Mid-July to mid-August: runs Monday, Saturday and Sunday. Mid-August to mid-July: runs daily. (3) Light refreshments. (4) Early July to early September: runs Friday, Saturday and Sunday. Early September to early July: runs Friday and Sunday. (5) TGV. Reservation required. Supplement charged. Runs daily, except Saturday. Restaurant car. (6) Runs Sunday only. Light refreshments. (7) Late June to early September: runs daily. Early September to late June: runs Friday and Sunday. (8) Arrives at Lyon's Perrache railstation. (9) Arrives at Lyon's Part-Dieu railstation. (10) Plus other departures from Marseille at 19:25 (3), 20:21 (6), 21:14 (7) and 21:48 (3), arriving Lyon 23:02 (8), 23:14 (9), 00:55 (8) and 01:08 (8).

Lyon - Paris - Lyon 150

All of these trains are TGV, require reservation, charge a supplement and have a restaurant car or light refreshments.

Dep. Lyon (Per.)	05:40 (1)	06:20 (2)	07:49	08:49 (3)	09:50 (4)
Dep. Lyon (P-D)	05:50	06:30	08:00	09:00	10:00
Arr. Paris (Lyon)	08:06	08:34	10:10	11:02	12:00

Sights in **Paris**: See page 125.

Dep. Paris (Lyon)	14:00 (5)	15:00 (5)	16:00 (1)	17:00 (5)	17:27 (6+11)
Arr. Lyon (P-D)	16:07	17:00	18:08	19:04	19:31
Arr. Lyon (Per.)	16:17	17:10	18:18	19:14	19:44

(1) Runs Mon.-Fri., except holidays. (2) Operates early September to early July. Runs Mon.-Fri. First-class only on Friday. (3) Runs daily, except Sun. and holidays. (4) Operates early September to early July. Runs daily. (5) Runs daily. (6) Operates early September to late July. Runs Mon.-Fri. (7) Operates early September to early July. Runs daily. (8) Operates early September to early July. Runs Mon.-Thurs. (9) Runs daily, except some days in July and August. (10) Early July to early September: runs Mon.- Fri. Early September to early July: runs daily, except Sat. (11) Plus other departures from Paris at 18:00 (7), 19:00 (8), 20:00 (9) and 21:00 (10), arriving Lyon (P-D) 20:04, 21:04, 22:00 and 23:04.

Lyon - Tours - Lyon 128

All of these trains have light refreshments.

Dep. Lyon (Perrache)	06:36	-0-
Dep. Lyon (Part-Dieu)	06:46	09:14
Arr. Tours	11:40	14:10

Sights in **Tours**: See "Paris-Blois-Tours- Paris" on page 145.

Dep. Tours	15:52	18:21
Arr. Lyon (Part-Dieu)	20:48	23:16
Arr. Lyon (Perrache)	20:58	23:27

Lyon - Vienne - Lyon 151

Dep Lyon (Perrache)	07:26	12:31
Arr. Vienne	18 minutes later	

Sights in **Vienne**: Many good Roman ruins. The Temple of Augustus and Livia, a large amphitheater, and the pyramid which once marked the center of a Roman coliseum. Ancient jewels and bronze and ceramic relics on exhibit at the Museum of Fine Arts. Try to dine at one of the world's most famous restaurants, Pyramide, open daily except Tuesday and closed November through mid-December.

Dep. Vienne	14:17 (1)	17:53	21:30 (2)	22:30	22:43
Arr. Lyon (Perrache)	18 minutes later				

(1)Arrives at Lyon's Part-Dieu station. (2)Runs daily, except Saturday.

Marseille to Aix-en-Provence 166

Dep. Marseille (St. Ch.)	08:15	09:30	11:28 (1)	12:08	14:05
Arr. Aix-en-Provence	35-40 minutes later				

Sights in **Aix-en-Provence**: See the remarkable Vasarely Museum and the 18th century quarter of the city.

Dep. Aix-en-Provence	11:29	13:07	15:05	15:56	16:20 (2)
Arr. Marseille (St. Ch.)	35-40 minutes later				

(1) Runs daily, except Sundays and holidays. (2) Plus other departures from Aix-en-Provence at 17:20, 18:12, 19:20, 19:53, 20:32 and 21:40.

Marseille - Antibes - Marseille 164

Dep. Marseille	09:14	10:57	13:13
Arr. Antibes	11:20	13:17	15:22

Sights in **Antibes**: See notes under "Avignon-Antibes" on page 130.

Dep. Antibes	13:59	14:53 (1)	16:54	18:01 (2)	18:40 (1)	20:17 (3)
Arr. Marseille	16:09	17:00	19:09	20:12	21:37	22:41

(1) Light refreshments. (2) Daily, except holidays. Light refreshments, except Sunday. (3) Plus other Antibes departures at 20:42 and 22:48, arriving Marseille 23:11 and 01:05.

Marseille - Cassis - Marseille SNCF timetable 508

Dep. Marseille (St. Ch.)	11:15	12:09	14:42
Arr. Cassis	30 minutes later		

Sights in **Cassis:** A fishing village and beach resort. There are many small restaurants here offering "the catch of the day" prepared so as to please any gourmand. The activities in Cassis are topless sunbathing, sailing, swimming, snorkeling, diving and fishing.

Dep. Cassis	12:29	13:09	13:42	14:26	16:35 (1)
Arr. Marseille (St. Ch.)	30 minutes later				

(1) Plus other departures from Cassis at 18:06, 19:07, 20:45 and 21:54.

Nice - Antibes - Nice 164

| Dep. Nice | Frequent times from 05:44 to 00:15 |
| Arr. Antibes | 16-30 minutes later |

Sights in **Antibes**: See notes under "Avignon-Antibes" on page 130.

| Dep. Antibes | Frequent times from 05:35 to 23:44 |
| Arr. Nice | 16-30 minutes later |

Nice - Cannes (and Grasse) - Nice 164

| Dep. Nice | Frequent times from 05:44 to 00:15 |
| Arr. Cannes | 40 minutes later |

Sights in **Cannes:** Stroll along Promenade de la Croisette to see the beautiful beach and splendid yachts, all the way to the Palm Beach Casino. Take boat rides on the Bay of Cannes or to the **St. Honorat** and **St. Marguerite** islands. On the latter, you can visit the prison that held the Man in the Iron Mask.

There is also a short boat trip to **Lerins**, where the 5th century Monastery of the Cistercians is located. It is said that St. Patrick began his evangelical tour of Europe from there. Visit the 10th century castle, Castrum Canois, on a mountain that overlooks Cannes. It houses the Museum of Mediterranean Civilization.

La Napoule is a few miles west of Cannes. The attraction there is theChateau de la Napoule Art Foundation, one of the finest art galleries on the Riviera, open daily except Tuesday, with guided tours in the afternoon.

Sights in **Grasse:** Take the 50-minute bus ride from Cannes' railstation to nearby Grasse, the perfume capital of France. Many of the 35 perfume factories there are open to visitors. One of them, Parfumerie Fragonard, is only a 5-minute walk from the Grasse bus terminal. Near it is a Perfume Museum. The nearby hillsides are covered with wildflowers and jasmine every Spring.

| Dep. Cannes | Frequent times from 05:20 to 23:30 |
| Arr. Nice | 40 minutes later |

Nice - Marseille - Nice 164

Dep. Nice	06:00	06:38 (1)	08:14 (1)	08:55 (1+3)
Arr. Marseille (St. Ch.)	08:31	09:08	11:13	11:36

Sights in **Marseille**: See notes about Marseille on page 124.

Dep. Marseille (St. Ch.)	13:13	15:07	15:52 (1)	16:39 (1+4)
Arr. Nice	15:48	17:34	18:30	19:05

(1) Light refreshments. (2) Supplement charged. Reservation advisable. Light refreshments. (3) Plus other Nice departures at 10:55 (1) 11:24 (2) and 11:59, arriving Marseille 13:07, 13:43 and 14:29. (4) Plus other Marseille departures at 17:04 (1), 17:25 (1), 18:45 (1), 20:35 (1) and 22:03, arriving Nice 19:53, 20:16, 21:28, 23:02 and 00:25.

Nice - Monaco (Monte Carlo) - Nice 164

| Dep. Nice | Frequent times from 06:05 to 00:35 |
| Arr. Monaco | 20-25 minutes later |

* * *

| Dep. Monaco | Frequent times from 05:23 to 23:51 |
| Arr. Nice | 20-25 minutes later |

Nice - Saint Raphael - Nice 164

Dep. Nice	Frequent times from 06:00 to 22:07
Arr. St. Raphael	60 minutes later

Sights in **Saint Raphael**: An excellent Riviera beach resort. Good golfing, hiking and sailing here. There is a gambling casino.

Dep. St. Raphael	Frequent times from 06:46 to 23:34
Arr. Nice	60 minutes later

Paris - Angers - Paris 123

All of these trains are TGV, require reservation, charge a supplement and have light refreshments, unless designated otherwise.

Dep. Paris (Mont.)	07:50 (1)	08:50	09:50	11:25	
Arr. Angers (St. L.)	09:19	10:19	11:22	12:58	

Sights in **Angers**: Located on Promenade du Bout du Monde (Walkway of the World's End), is the massive 13th century castle (Chateau d'Angers), with its 17 towers. It houses the world's finest collection of medieval and Renaissance tapestries. Don't fail to see the supreme tapestry, "The Apocalypse".

It was 430 feet long and about 20 feet high when it was woven in the 14th century, unbelievably produced in less than 7 years. What we can view today is 350 feet long and 15 feet high 8,600 square feet. What remains are 67 of the original 84 panels and 4 of the original 6 scenes showing a bearded figure sitting on a stone dais.

The Angers tapestry illustrates the text of the Book of Revelation, complete with the 4 horsemen (the last of which is death), followed by hell.

It is in the second half of the tapestry that we are shown the ultimate destruction (Judgment Day): shipwrecks, rains of fire, many-headed beasts (including a dragon that has 7 heads and 10 horns), the fall of Babylon, the extinction of both the sun and the moon, and the descent of Jerusalem from heaven to earth, where it becomes the eternal dwelling of those who are blessed. The miracle of the tapestry is its survival.

Dep. Angers (St. L.)	12:08	14:14	15:18	18:09	19:30 (2)
Arr. Paris (Mont.)	13:40	15:50	16:50	19:45	21:10

Dep. Angers (St. L.)	20:14 (3)	21:01 (3)	21:04 (4)	21:14 (5)
Arr. Paris (Mont.)	21:50	23:36	22:35	22:50

(1) Operates late August to mid-July. Runs daily, except Sundays and holidays. (2) Runs Sunday only. (3) Runs daily, except Sundays and holidays. *No* light refreshments. (4) Runs Monday-Friday, except holidays. *No* light refreshments. (5) Runs Sunday only. *No* light refreshments.

Paris - Basel - Paris 57

Dep. Paris (Est)	07:30 (1)	08:39	17:04 (2)	22:40 (3)	
Arr. Basel (SNCF)	12:13	14:04	21:35	05:35	

Sights in **Basel**: See notes about Basel on page 310.

Dep. Basel (SNCF)	00:25 (3)	08:16 (2)	12:48	16:48 (4)	18:30
Arr. Paris (Est)	06:47	12:59	18:05	21:29	23:39

(1) Supplement charged. Runs daily, except Sunday. Light refreshments. (2) Supplement charged. Restaurant car. (3) Has first and second-class couchettes. Coach is second-class only. (4) Supplement charged. Runs daily, except Saturday. Light refreshments.

Paris - Bayeux - Paris 120

All of these trains have light refreshments, unless designated otherwise.

Dep. Paris (St. Laz.)	06:55 (1)	09:02	11:29 (2)	12:40 (3)
Arr. Bayeux	09:28	11:25	13:55	15:32

Sights in **Bayeux**: The world-famous 230-foot long, 20-inch wide embroidered tapestry, sewn by Queen Mathilda (wife of William the Conqueror) and her friends for 10 years after the 1066 Battle of Hastings, both to commemorate the Norman conquest of England and her husband becoming king of England.

On public view in Bayeux since 1077, it consists of 58 scenes that include 626 people, 37 ships, 33 buildings and 730 animals while also depicting 11th century life.

The battle waged by Duke William of Normandy involved transporting 10,000 Normans across the English Channel in 400 ships.

One of the world's greatest works of art, "Queen Mathilda's Tapestry" has been exhibited daily 09:00-19:00 (except Christmas and New Year's Day) in a museum which opened in 1983 after 2 years of construction. As many as 2,300 people enter the museum on some days, including hordes of schoolchildren that begin arriving at 10:00.

The tapestry is mounted on a horseshoe-shaped frame, sealed inside unbreakable glass. Its humidity and temperature are regulated. Except for the light directed at the tapestry, the rest of the hall is entirely dark. A 15-minute description can be heard over earphones in many languages.

Other local attractions are the World War II Battle of Normandy Museum (next to the British Military Cemetery) and the 3-spired Notre Dame Cathedral. There are views of a magnificent seascape from its high center tower.

Dep. Bayeux	15:06 (4)	15:13 (5)	16:14 (6)	16:56 (7)	18:06 (8+11)
Arr. Paris (St. Laz.)	17:41	18:13	19:07	19:54	20:42

(1) Early July to early September: runs daily except Saturday. Early September to early July: runs daily, except Sunday. (2) Runs Saturday only. (3) Runs Saturday only. No light refreshments. (4) Operates early September to late June. (5) Operates late June to early September. Runs daily. (6) Operates early September to late June. Runs Sunday only. (7) Operates early July to early September. Runs Sunday only. (8) Supplement charged. Runs daily except Sundays and holidays. (9) Runs Sunday only. No light refreshments. (10) Supplement charged. . Runs daily except Friday and Sunday. No light refreshments. (11) Plus other Bayeux departures at 19:11 (9) 19:51 (9) and 20:15 (10), arriving Paris 22:10, 22:44 and 23:08.

Paris - Bayeux - Caen - Paris 120

All of these trains have light refreshments, unless designated otherwise.

As shown below, it is possible to combine a visit from Paris to both Bayeux and Caen in one day.

Dep. Paris (St. Lazare)	06:55 (1)	Dep. Bayeux	15:06 (2)
Arr. Bayeux	09:28	Arr. Caen	15:31

(Footnotes and return trip appear on page 144.)

Sights in **Bayeux**: See notes above.

Sights in **Caen**: Although much was destroyed here during the 1944 Nor- mandy invasion battle, numerous historical buildings have been preserved. Hotel d'Escoville, he "Chateau". The 11th century Abbaye aux Hommes and Abbaye aux Dames. The Museum. The church of Saint Sauveur. The Palace of Justice. For lunch, try these regional specialties: *tripes, berlingots, cider, Calvados.*

Dep. Caen	20:21 (3)	20:41 (4)	20:45 (5)	21:49 (6)
Arr. Paris (St. Laz.)	22:47	22:50	23:08	00:18

Here are schedules for having more time in Caen.

All of these trains have light refreshments , unless designated otherwise.

Dep. Paris (St. Laz.)	06:55 (1)	08:06 (2)	09:02	
Arr. Caen	09:13	10:43	11:25	

* * *

Dep. Caen	14:16 (7)	15:33 (2)	16:06 (7)	17:22 (6+11)
Arr. Paris (St. Laz.)	16:37	17:41 (8)	18:37	19:54

(1) Early July to early September: runs daily, except Saturday. Early September to early July: runs daily, except Sunday. (2) Runs daily. (3) Runs Friday only. (4) Runs Monday only. (5) Runs Tuesday, Wednesday, Thursday and Saturday. (6) Runs Sunday only. No light refreshments. (7) Runs daily, except Sundays and holidays. (8) Arrive 18:13 late June to early September. (9) Supplement charged. Runs daily, except holidays. (10) Runs daily, except Friday and Sunday. (11) Plus other Caen departures at 18:32 (9), 19:17 (6), 19:37 (6), 20:21 (3), 20:41 (10) and 21:49 (6), arriving Paris (St. Laz.) 20:42, 22:01, 22:10, 22:47, 23:06 and 00:18.

Paris - Blois - Paris 135

Dep. Paris (Aust.)	07:33 (1)	09:20 (1)
Arr. Blois	09:08	10:59

Sights in **Blois**: St. Louis Cathedral. Church of Saint Nicolas. Church of Saint Vincent. Church of Saint Saturin, and its curious cemetery. The Alluye Manor.

Visit the Castle of Blois, the palace of Catherine de Medici during the 16th century. From late March to late September, a sound-and-light show is presented there every evening. The other 2 fine Chateaux here are Chambord and Bracieux (Herbault-en-Sologne). For lunch in Blois, try the regional specialties: Rillettes, Loire fish, great local wines and cheeses.

Dep. Blois	13:39 (2)	15:42	16:40	17:28	19:42 (3+5)
Arr. Paris (Aust.)	15:14	17:16	18:31	19:03	21:43

(1) Light refreshments. (2) Runs daily, except Sundays and holidays. (3) Runs Sunday only. (4) Runs Friday only. (5) Plus other departures from Blois at 20:20 (4) and 21:09 (3), arriving Paris 21:56 and 22:47.

Paris - Blois - Tours - Paris 135

As shown below, it is possible to combine a visit from Paris to both Blois and Tours in one day.

Dep. Paris (Aust.)	07:33 (1)	Dep. Blois	12:56
Arr. Blois	09:08	Arr. Tours	13:36

(1) Light refreshments.

Sights in **Blois**: See "Paris-Blois" on page 144.

Sights in **Tours**: See "Bordeaux-Tours" on page 136.

Dep. Tours	17:29	Dep. Orleans	19:39
Arr. Orleans	19:10	Arr. Paris (Aust.)	20:51
Change trains.			

Paris - Tours - Paris 133

Here are schedules for having more time in Tours than when combining a trip from Paris to both Blois and Tours.

All of these trains are TGV, require reservation, charge a supplement and have light refreshments. They travel at 186 miles per hour on some portions of this route.

Dep. Paris (Mont.)	06:55 (1)	07:25 (2)	07:55 (2)	09:00 (3)	10:45 (3+7)
Arr. Tours	08:01	08:35	09:01	10:07	11:50
		*	*	*	

Dep. Tours	12:48 (3)	15:38 (3)	17:47 (3)	19:08 (4)	20:04 (5)
Arr. Paris (Mont.)	13:55	16:45	18:55	20:15	21:15

Dep. Tours	20:27 (3)	21:48 (5)	22:22 (6)
Arr. Paris (Mont.)	21:35	22:55	23:30

(1) Operates early September to late June. Runs daily except Sundays and holidays. (2) Runs daily, except Sundays and holidays. (3) Runs daily. (4) Runs daily, except holidays. (5) Runs Sunday only. (6) Runs Monday–Friday except holidays. (7) Plus another departure from Paris at 12:15 (3), arriving Tours 13:25.

Paris - Bordeaux - Paris 136

All of these trains are TGV, require reservation and charge a supplement.

Dep. Paris (Mont.)	06:50 (1)	07:10 (2)	07:55 (2)	08:15 (3+10)
Arr. Bordeaux (St. Jean)	09:48	10:24	11:08	11:46

Sights in **Bordeaux**: See notes about Bordeaux on page 122.

Dep. Bordeaux (St. Jean)	16:34 (4)	17:27 (4)	18:03 (5)	19:27 (6+11)
Arr. Paris (Mont.)	19:50	20:30	21:35	22:30

(1) Operates from early September to early July. Runs Monday–Friday. Restaurant car. (2) Runs daily, except Sundays and holidays. Restaurant car. (3) Runs daily, except holidays. Light refreshments. (4) Runs daily. Light refreshments. (5) Late June to early September: runs daily. Early September to late June: runs daily except Sundays and holidays. Restaurant car. (6) Early July to early September: runs daily except Sundays and holidays. Early September to early July: runs daily except Saturday. Restaurant car. (7) Runs daily. Restaurant car. (8) Early September to early July: runs daily except holidays. Early July to early September: runs Monday–Friday, except holidays. Restaurant car. (9) Runs Sunday only. Light refreshments. (10) Plus another Paris departure at 10:00 (7), arriving Bordeaux 12:58. (11) Plus other Bordeaux departures at 20:07 (8) and 20:43 (9), arriving Paris 23:00 and 23:45.

Paris - Bourges - Paris 141

Dep. Paris (Austerlitz)	06:15	08:52 (1)	09:07 (2)
Arr. Vierzon	08:17	-0- (1)	10:58
Change trains.			
Dep. Vierzon	08:21	-0-	12:10
Arr. Bourges	08:50	11:27	12:40

Sights in **Bourges**: A key gateway to the chateau area of the Loire Valley. Bourges is a living history museum.

The beautifully preserved stained glass windows in the Cathedral of St.-Etienne are a dazzling play of red against magenta and deep blue, located in a narrow halll that is 387 feet long, 136 feet wide, and an amazing 130 feet high. "Spellbinding" is the only way to describe these windows that depict the Bible's great morality stories. The Cathedral's restored 17th century organ is the best one of France.

The l'Archeveche Garden is near the Cathedral. See the medieval houses below the Cathedral on a stroll along the town's winding, cobbled streets.

Visit the 15th century Palace of Jacques Couer, open daily 9:00-12:00 and 14:00-18:00 (closes at 17:00 November–March). See the collection of Roman artifacts and antique ceramics at the Musee de Berry in the 15th century Hotel Cujas (4 Rue des Arenes), open daily except Tuesday 10:00-12:00 and 14:00-18:00 (Sunday: only 14:00-18:00).

The Museum of Decorative Arts in the 16th century Hotel Lallemant (6 Rue Bourbonnoux), open daily except Tuesday 10:00-11:30 and 14:00-16:30.

The Municipal Garden and the garden at the City Hall, formerly the residence of a 17th century archbishop.

Dep. Bourges	16:02 (3)	17:55 (1)	18:34 (1)	19:53 (4)
Arr. Vierzon	-0-	-0- (1)	-0- (1)	20:24
Change trains.				
Dep. Vierzon	-0-	-0-	-0-	20:46
Arr. Paris (Austerlitz)	18:25	20:20	20:51	22:40

(1) Direct train. No train change in Vierzon. (2) Runs daily, except Sundays and holidays. (3) Runs daily, except Saturday. Direct train. No train change in Vierzon. (4) Runs daily, except Saturday.

Paris - Brussels - Paris 76

Dep. Paris (Nord)	07:07 (1)	07:47 (2)	10:20 (2)	
Arr. Brussels (Midi)	09:38	10:48	13:18	

Sights in **Brussels**: See notes about Brussels on page 88.

Dep. Brussels (Midi)	14:02 (3)	16:10	17:10 (4)	18:10 (1+5)
Arr. Paris (Nord)	17:04	18:59	19:40	20:44

(1) Supplement charged. First-class only. Runs Monday-Friday. Restaurant car. (2) Light refreshments. (3) Operate late June to late July. Runs Monday, Friday, Saturday and Sunday. (4) First-class only. Early July to early September: runs Monday–Friday. Early September to early July: runs daily, except Saturday. (5) Plus other departures from Brussels (Midi) at 19:10 (2) and 20:22, arriving Paris 22:06 and 23:05.

Paris - Chantilly - Paris SNCF Timetable 220

Dep. Paris (Nord)	Frequent times from 06:30 to 21:41
Arr. Chantilly	30-40 minutes later

Sights in **Chantilly:** (Pronounced "Shawnteeyee") The 16th century castle, actually 2 chateaux, has been called "the most beautiful house in France". It stands in a lake and is surrounded by magnificent gardens and a large forest.

Of the 2 routes from the railstation to the castle, the shortest distance (and most pleasant stroll) is to walk 30 minutes via a trail through tall trees and then across the large lawn infield of the racecourse, locale during the first 2 weeks of June every year for a very elegant horse-racing meet.

The 2 attractions are the chateau's Conde Museum and its Living Museum of the Horse. Among the fine objects exhibited in the Conde are priceless collections of art spanning 1,000 years; 13,000 books beginning with 10th century manuscripts, paintings (Delacroix, Fouquet, Ingres, Rembrandt, Clouet, Raphael, Rosselli, Greuze) and furniture; all on an estate of 17,000 acres that contain forests, farms, a racetrack with stadium, and a golf course.

Between April and September 30, the chateau is open daily except Tuesday 10:30-18:00 (until 17:00 the rest of the year).

Between April 1 and October 31, the Grand Stables are open daily except Tuesday 10:30-17:00 (13:00-17:00 the rest of the year). Riders wearing 18th century costumes perform at 12:00, 15:00 and 17:00 April 1 to October 31 (at 14:30 and 16:00 the rest of the year).

See the spectacle of the Tuesday and Saturday fox hunts.

Dep. Chantilly	Frequent times from 06:10 to 22:46
Arr. Paris (Nord)	30-40 minutes later

Paris - Chartres - Paris 125

Dep. Paris (Montpar.)	09:00 (1)	10:00 (1)	10:05 (2)	11:14	12:59 (3)
Arr. Chartres	50–60 minutes later				

Sights in **Chartres:** The main attraction is the magnificent 13th century Cathedral, third largest in the world, exceeded in size only by St. Peter's and Canterbury. Its stained-glass is unrivalled. Other sights: The Former Collegiate Church. The Church of Saint Aignan. The Church of Saint Martin-au-Val. The Church of Saint Foy.

Dep. Chartres	11:25	14:03	15:10 (1)	16:55 (1)	18:31 (5)
Arr. Paris (Montpar.)	50–60 minutes later				

(1) Operates late June to late August. Light refreshments. (2) Runs daily, except Saturday. (3) Runs daily, except Sundays and holidays. (4) Runs Sunday only. (5) Plus other departures from Chartres at 19:34 (3), 20:22 (4), 21:48 (4), 22:27 (4), 22:47 (3) and 23:05 (4)

Paris - Cologne (Koln) - Paris 62

Both of these trains charge a supplement and have a restaurant car.

Dep. Paris (Nord)	07:27		Dep. Cologne	17:07
Arr. Cologne	12:38		Arr. Paris (Nord)	22:10

Sights in **Cologne**: See notes about sightseeing in Cologne on page 372.

148

Paris - Compiegne - Paris 106

| Dep. Paris (Nord) | 07:00 (1) | 12:14 | 13:46 (2) | | |
| Arr. Compiegne | 50-60 minutes later | | | | |

Sights in **Compiegne**: Town Hall. Vivenel Museum. Hotel Dieu. The 7th century Beauregard Tower. The "Clairere de l'Armistice" in Compeigne Forest, where Marshal Foch signed the 1918 armistice for France...and Adolph Hitler received the June 21, 1940 surrender of France.

| Dep. Compeigne | 10:28 | 13:10 | 19:08 | 20:09 (3) | 21:56 (4) |
| Arr. Paris (Nord) | 50-60 minutes later | | | | |

(1) Runs daily, except Sundays and holidays. (2) Runs Saturday only. (3) Runs Sunday only. (4) Runs daily, except Saturday.

Paris - Dijon - Paris 157

All of these trains are TGV, require reservation, charge a supplement and have a restaurant car or light refreshments.

| Dep. Paris (Lyon) | 07:14 | 10:28 (1) | 12:25 | 14:20 | |
| Arr. Dijon | 08:50 | 12:06 | 14:01 | 15:56 | |

Sights in **Dijon**: See notes under "Lyon-Dijon" on page 137.

| Dep. Dijon | 14:48 | 16:55 | 18:34 | 19:37 | 21:09 (3) |
| Arr. Paris (Lyon) | 16:28 | 18:35 | 20:19 | 21:17 | 22:49 |

(1) Runs Monday-Friday, except holidays. (2) Runs Sunday only. (3) Plus another departure from Dijon at 21:53 (2), arriving Paris 23:33.

Paris - Evreux - Paris 120

| Dep. Paris (St. Laz.) | 08:06 (1) | 09:21 (2) | 10:30 | 11:58 (3) | 12:47 (4) |
| Arr. Evreux | 09:10 | 10:31 | 11:29 | 12:55 | 13:43 |

Sights in **Evreux**: The Cathedral of Notre Dame, a jumble of architectural styles due to having been built over a period of 6 centuries: from the 11th to the 17th. Goldsmith work in the Church of Stain Taurin. The ancient Eveche. The tower of The Clock. For lunch, try the Norman cuisine.

| Dep. Evreux | 13:36 (1) | 15:34 (5) | 17:03 (6) | 18:31 (7) | 18:45 (8+10) |
| Arr. Paris (St. Laz.) | 14:45 | 16:37 | 18:13 | 19:40 | 19:54 |

(1) Light refreshments. (2) Operates early July to early September. Runs Monday–Friday except holidays. (3) Runs daily, except Sundays and holidays. (4) Runs daily, except Saturday. (5) Runs daily, except Sundays and holidays. Light refreshments. (6) Operates early July to early September. Runs daily. (7) Operates all year. Runs Sunday only. (8) Early July to early September: runs Monday–Friday. Early September to early July: runs daily. Light grefreshments. (9) Operates all year. Runs Tuesday, Wednesday, Thursday and Saturday. (10) Plus other departures from Evreux at 19:11 (7), 20:35 (7), 21:26 (7), 22:06 (9) and 23:10 (7), arriving Paris 20:27, 21:47, 22:44, 23:08 and 00:18.

Paris - Fontainebleau - Paris 151a

| Dep. Paris (Lyon) | Frequent times from 06:00 to 22:33 |
| Arr. Fontainebleau-Avon | 42 minutes later |

Take the 10-minute bus ride from the railstation to the palace, open 08:00 to sunset, daily except Tuesdays.

Sights in **Fontainebleau:** It is advisable to plan on an entire day here for seeing the magnificent 16th century palace that many kings of France occupied, and the parks and gardens surrounding it. There are guided tours of the palace 10:00-12:30 and 14:00-18:00. Many visitors bring a picnic lunch.

| Dep. Fontainebleau-Avon | Frequent times from 05:17 to 21:50 (1) |
| Arr. Paris (Lyon) | 30-40 minutes later |

(1) Plus other departures from Fontainebleau on Sundays at 21:59 and 22:35.

Paris - Granville - Paris 119

| Dep. Paris (Montpar.) | 07:14 (1) | 08:16 (2) |
| Arr. Granville | 10:42 | 12:09 |

Sights in **Granville:** This is a lively seaside town near Mont.-st.-Michel (see "Paris to Mont.-st.-Michel" on page 150) with remarkably high tides and sandy beaches. The marina here can accommodate 1,000 yachts. The Regional Nautical Center offers instructions in sailing and wind surfing.

The Aquarium (with exhibits of sea life, shells and mineral stones) is along the walk to the lighthouse. The **Chausey Islands** can be seen from the shore, and there is daily boat service to them.

Visit the Church of Notre Dame. Try your luck in the Casino.

| Dep. Granville | 14:19 (1) | 14:29 (2) | 18:10 (3) | 19:18 (4) |
| Arr. Paris (Montpar.) | 17:43 | 18:27 | 21:53 | 22:16 |

(1) Runs Monday-Friday, except holidays. (2) Runs Saturday and Sunday. (3) Runs daily, except holidays. (4) Runs Sunday only. Light refreshments.

Paris - Limoges - Paris 138

Dep. Paris (Aust.)	06:15	07:30 (1)	09:07 (2)	10:03 (3)	10:10 (4)
Arr. Limoges	10:12	10:31	12:43	13:06	13:35

Sights in **Limoges**: See notes under "Bordeaux-Limoges" on page 134.

Dep. Limoges	14:45 (5)	16:42 (5)	18:03 (6)	18:34 (7)	19:43 (7+9)
Arr. Paris (Aust.)	18:09	20:51	21:42	22:31	23:12

(1) Supplement charged. Runs daily, except Sundays and holidays. Restaurant car. (2) Light refreshments. (3) Operates early September to late June. Light refreshments. (4) Operates late June to early September. Light refreshments. (5) Light refreshments. (6) Mid-July to early September: runs daily. Early September to mid-July: runs daily except Saturday. (7) Runs Sunday only. (8) Supplement charged. Runs daily. Restaurant car. (9) Plus another Limoges departure at 20:55 (8), arriving Paris 00:01.

Paris - Lyon - Paris 150

All of these trains are TGV, require reservation, charge a supplement and have a restaurant car or light refreshments.

Dep. Paris (Lyon)	06:45 (1)	07:00	07:30	08:00	08:20 (2+10)
Arr. Lyon (P.D.)	08:45	09:00	09:30	10:08	10:20

Sights in **Lyon**: See notes on page 123.

Dep. Lyon (P.D.)	13:48 (3)	14:49	15:46 (4)	16:50	17:49
Arr. Paris (Lyon)	16:04	17:04	18:00	19:10	20:04

Dep. Lyon (P.D.)	18:30 (5)	19:50	20:13 (6)	21:35 (7)	
Arr. Paris (Lyon)	20:50	22:04	22:27	23:59	

(1) Runs Mon.-Fri.,except holidays. (2) Operates early September to early July. Runs daily, except Sunday. (3) Operates early September to early July. Runs daily. (4) Early July to early September: runs daily. Early September to early July: runs daily, except Fri. and Sat.. (5) Operates early September to early July. Runs daily, except Sat. (6) Operates early September to early July. Runs Sunday only. (7) Operates all year. Runs Sunday only. (8) Operates early September to early July. Runs Mon.-Fri.. (9) Operates early July to early September. Runs daily. (10) Plus other departures from Paris at 10:00, 11:00 (8) and 11:55 (9), arriving Lyon (P.D.) 12:07, 13:00 and 14:03.

Paris - Nancy - Paris 173

Dep. Paris (Est)	06:54 (1)	07:52 (2)	08:01 (3)	08:49 (4)	10:52 (5)
Arr. Nancy	09:36	10:26	11:22	11:29	13:29

Sights in **Nancy:** The Ducal Palace, with its museum of this city's 2,000-year history at 64 Grande Rue, open daily except Tuesdays and holidays 10:00-12:00 and 14:00-18:00.

Its exhibits include a room on the history of Jews in this region. The Church of the Cordeliers. The 14th century Porte de la Craffe, oldest monument in Nancy. The wrought-iron grillwork and fountains in Place Stanislas. Lovely 18th century houses on Place de la Carriere.

Visit the model rooms of early 20th century interior decor at the Musee de l'Ecole, 36-38 Rue Sergent Blandan, open daily except Tuesdays and holidays. April-September: 10:00-12:00 and 14:00-18:00. October-March: 10:00-12:00 and 14:00-17:00.

Much work by Emile Galle, Jacques Gruber, Eugene Vallin and other Art Nouveau artisans is exhibited there: glass bowls, tables, fireplaces, tooled leather wall coverings, inlaid bed headboards and footboards, inlaid chests, Galle's fantastic glass mushroom lamp, and the extraordinary Louis Majorelle grand piano, inlaid with irises and waterlillies.

Majorelle's house, a few blocks away at 1 Rue Majorelle (open Monday-Friday except holidays 8:30-12:00 and 13:00-18:00), is well worth visiting to see the exterior and interior ceramic work and the Gruber stained glass windows there.

Visitors can also see examples of Galle and Daum vases, lamps and other glass objects at the Musee Beaux-Arts, Place Stanislas, open daily except Tuesdays and holidays 10:00-12:00 and 14:00-18:00.

Pepiniere is a 57-acre park with gardens, a small zoo, and a restaurant.

Dep. Nancy	13:37 (2)	14:36 (6)	17:22 (7)	18:35 (8)	18:57 (9+11)
Arr. Paris (Est)	16:10	18:00	20:10	21:11	22:07

(1) Reservation required, and substantial supplement charged for first-class. Operates early September to early July. Runs daily, except Sundays and holidays. Light refreshments. (2) Runs daily. Restaurant car. (3) Runs daily, except holidays. Light refreshments. (4) Runs daily, except Sundays and holidays. Light refreshments. (5) Operates early September to early July. Runs daily, except Sundays and holidays. Light refreshments. (6) Runs daily. Light refreshments. (7) Runs daily, except Saturday. Supplement charged. (8) Reservation required, and substantial supplement charged for first-class. Operates early September to early July. Runs daily, except Saturday. (9) Mid-July to early September: runs Monday-Friday, except holidays. Early September to mid-July: runs daily, except Saturday. (10) Mid-July to early September: runs Friday and Sunday. Early September to mid-July: runs daily, except Saturday (11) Plus other Nancy departures at 19:35 (2) and 20:30 (10), arriving Paris 22:10 and 23:20.

Paris - Neuilly - Paris

Take the Metro from Paris' Champs-Elysees station. **Neuilly** is the fourth stop.

The attraction here is The Museum of Women at 12 Rue de Centre, open daily except Sunday 14:30-18:00. The one guided tour starts at 15:00. Among the exhibits is the lavishly decorated bed used by France's most famous prostitute during the reign of Napoleon III, the Marchioness de La Paiva. While the bed cost her 10,000 gold francs, she recovered this expense quickly. She charged her clients 10,000 gold francs a night.

There is also the corset that Marie Antoinette wore in prison while waiting to be guillotined, a bronze cast of ballet dancer-choreographer Katherine Dunham's feet, a silk jacket that belonged to the last empress of China, a letter written by Nobel prize-winner Marie Curie, and many other curiosities.

Paris - Rheims - Paris 115

| Dep. Paris (Est) | 07:16 (1) | 08:01 (2) | 11:03 | 12:52 (2) |
| Arr. Rheims | 08:47 | 08:48 | 12:36 | 14:28 |

Sights in **Rheims**: See the 13th century Cathedral of Notre Dame (open daily 7:30-19:30), longer and higher than Notre Dame in Paris. Most of this city was destroyed in World War I, and restoration of the Cathedral was not completed until 1938.

See church treasures in the Palais du Tau (2 Place du Cardinal-Lucon), open 10:00-12:00 and 14:00-18:00. The Porte Mars 13th century Arch. Saint Remi Basilica (open daily 8:00-18:30). Nearby, the great collection of 16th-19th century weapons in the St. Remi Museum (53 Rue Simon), open daily 14:00-18:30.

The Church of St. Jacquet. The museum at the Church of St. Denis.

See champagne processed. The public is invited to visit the Taitinger and Pommery caves.

| Dep. Rheims | 12:25(1) | 16:09 (3) | 17:12 (3) | 17:55 (4+7) |
| Arr. Paris (Est) | 14:02 | 17:38 | 18:50 | 19:33 |

(1) Runs daily. Light refreshments. (2) Runs daily, except Sundays and holidays. (3) Runs Monday-Friday, except holidays. (4) Runs Saturday and Sunday. (5) Runs daily. (6) Runs Sunday only. (7) Plus other departures from Rheims at 18:09 (3), 20:27 (5) and 20:55 (6), arriving Paris 19:38, 21:55 and 22:21.

Paris - Rouen - Paris 115

| Dep. Paris (St. Laz.) | 07:39 (1) | 07:55 (2) | 08:15 (3) | 09:15 (4+12) |
| Arr. Rouen (Rive Dr.) | 08:50 | 09:02 | 09:47 | 10:26 |

Sights in **Rouen**: Walk out of the railstation and then down Rue de Jeanne D'Arc about 1½ miles. Turn right onto Rue de la Grosse Horloge and continue a short distance to the remodeled ancient, large central market, Vieux Marche, the place where Joan of Arc was tied to a stake and burned. This is now the Church of St. Joan, built in 1977. It is in the shape of an upside-down boat and has magnificent stained-glass windows that were saved from the Church of Saint-Vincent, bombed during World War II. Try the regional specialty (terrine of duck) in one of the nearby restaurants.

Then, go back along Rue de la Gross Horloge (crossing Rue de Jeanne D'Arc). Straight ahead is the gigantic, ornate clock for which the street was named. The clock presents a spectacle of moving figures when each hour strikes.

Past the famous clock is the Cathedral, with its renowned Carillon of 56 bells. Nearby, see the sculptures on the doors of the Church of Saint-Maclou.

See the stained-glass windows in the Church of St Godard and the Church of St. Patrice.

Visit the remains of a building located below the Palace of Justice. It was either an 11th century Jewish school or a synagogue. See the Hebrew graffiti written on the walls there more than 900 years ago, the elaborate carved columns and the 2 inverted Lions of Judah. It is open only on Saturdays.

The rose window of the Gothic Church of St. Ouen. The collection of fine faience ware for which Rouen was once famous, in the Museum of Fine Arts. The Gallo-Roman artifacts in the Museum of Antiquities. The late Gothic and Renaissance Bourgtheroulde mansion. The collection of old street signs and other ironwork pieces in the Musee Le Secq.

From Rouen, it is an easy bus trip to the colorful harbor at **Honfleur**. Take a taxi to **Giverny**, to visit the home and spectacular garden of painter Claude Monet.

Dep. Rouen (Rive Dr.)	12:48 (5)	14:12 (3)	14:26 (1)	15:00 (5)
Arr. Paris (St. Laz.)	14:01	15:44	15:37	16:12

Dep. Rouen (Rive Dr.)	16:57 (4)	17:30 (6)	17:57 (7)	18:26 (8+13)
Arr. Paris (St. Laz.)	18:15	18:57	19:09	19:59

(1) Runs Sunday only. (2) Supplement charged. Late August to early July: runs daily, except Sundays and holidays. Early July to late August: runs Monday and Saturday. (3) Runs daily, except Sundays and holidays. (4) Runs daily. Light refreshments. (5) Runs daily, except Sundays and holidays. Light refreshments. (6) Runs Monday–Friday, except holidays. (7) Late August to early July: runs Monday–Friday. Early July to late August: runs Friday only. (8) Runs Sunday only. (9) Reservation required. Runs Sunday only. (10) Reservation required. Runs daily, except Sundays and holidays. (11) Runs Friday, Saturday and Sunday. (12) Plus other departures from Paris at 10:43 (9), 10:52 (10) and 12:00 (3), arriving Rouen 12:02, 12:02 and 13:35. (13) Plus other departures from Rouen at 18:49 (11), 19:46 (8), 20:10 (1), 21:07 (1), 21:18 (3) and 21:59 (1), arriving Paris 20:01, 21:20, 21:26, 22:38, 22:37 and 23:11.

Paris - Strasbourg - Paris 173

This ride is along the Marne, with clear views of the area near famous World War I battlefields.

Dep. Paris (Est)	06:54 (1)	07:52 (2)	08:01 (3)		
Arr. Strasbourg	10:57	11:41	12:50		

Sights in **Strassbourg**: See notes about Strasbourg on page 128.

Dep. Strasbourg	16:03 (4)	17:05 (5)	17:27 (6)	18:20 (2)	19:07 (7)
Arr. Paris (Est)	20:10	21:11	22:07	22:10	23:20

(1) Reservation required and substantial supplement charged for first-class. Operates early September to early July. Runs daily, except Sundays and holidays. (2) Runs daily. Restaurant car. (3) Runs Sunday only. Light refreshments. (4) Supplement charged. Runs daily, except Saturday. (5) Reservation required and Substantial supplement charged for first-class. Operates early September to early July. Runs daily, except Saturday. (6) Operates early July to early September. Runs daily. (7) Early September to early July: runs daily, except Saturday. Early July to early September: runs Friday and Sunday.

Paris - Tours - Paris

This one-day excursion appears immediately following "Paris-Blois-Tours-Paris" on page 145.

Paris - Trouville and Deauville - Paris 120

Dep. Paris (St. Laz.)	07:44 (1)	08:29 (2)	10:30 (3)	12:17 (4)
Arr. Trou Deau	09:49	10:52	12:50	14:14

Sights in **Trouville**: There is no chance of obtaining hotel rooms here in Summer without advance reservation. One of France's most beautiful swimming beaches. A gambling casino. Marvelous seafood.

(Sightseeing notes, return trip and footnotes appear on page 154)

Sights in **Deauville**: One of France's most beautiful swimming beaches. Two race-tracks. Lovely gardens. To explore the Norman countryside, you can rent a car at the Deauville railstation.

Take a bus 6 miles to **Honfleur**, the beautiful fishing village that inspired many Impressionist pantings. Very crowded in July and August. Stroll along the bank of its old harbor on the English Channel. Visit the Eugene Bodin Museum (paintings of the Saint Simeon school) and the Marine Museum in the 14th century Church of St. Etiene.

Dep. Trou Deau	13:25 (5)	15:39 (6)	17:27 (7)	18:25 (8+12)
Arr. Paris (St. Laz.)	15:34	17:41	19:40	20:35

(1) Operates early July to early September. Runs daily, except holidays. (2) Runs Saturday and Sunday. (3) Runs Saturday only. Light refreshments. (4) Operates late June to early September. Runs daily, except Sundays and holidays. (5) Operates early July to early September. Runs daily. Light refreshments. (6) Operates early July to early September. Runs daily. (7) Runs Sunday only. Light refreshments. (8) Supplement charged. Runs Sunday only. (9) Runs Sunday only. (10) Operates July and August. Runs Saturday only. (11) Operates July and August. Runs Monday-Friday, except holidays. (12) Plus other departures from Trou Deau at 19:01 (9), 19:08 (10), 19:22 (11) and 19:51 (9), arriving Paris 21:36, 21:27, 21:25 and 22:44.

Paris - Troyes - Paris 171

Dep. Paris (Est)	07:08 (1)	08:39 (2)	12:40 (2)	13:30 (3)
Arr. Troyes	08:38	10:12	14:11	14:54

Sights in **Troyes**: This is the Champagne area. The most interesting places here are located along the 30-minute walk from the railstation to St. Pierre Cathedral, which has marvelous 13th, 14th and 16th century stained glass.

See the museum of tools used in French crafts at the 16th century Hotel de Mauroy, on Rue de la Trinite. The 16th century religious art and the hosiery museum, both at the Musee de l'Hotel de Vauluisant. The mansions of Autry, des Ursins and Marisy. The Museum of Fine Arts, with its solid collection of 17th-18th century paintings and 13th-14th century sculptures.

The 12th century manuscripts in the Library. The Pharmacy Museum. The Archaeology Museum. The Natural History Museum

Dep. Troyes	12:11 (4)	16:37 (2)	17:53 (5)	19:14 (6)	19:23 (1+8)
Arr. Paris (Est)	13:40	18:05	19:36	21:06	21:06

(1) Runs daily, except Sundays and holidays. (2) Runs daily. Light refreshments. (3) Supplement charged. Runs Saturday and Sunday. Light refreshments. (4) Runs daily, except Sundays and holidays. (5) Runs daily, except Saturdays and holidays. (6) Runs Sunday only. (7) Runs Sunday only. Light refreshments. (8) Plus other departures from Troyes at 20:33 (6), 20:57 (7) and 22:14 (2), arriving Paris 22:17, 22:20 and 23:39.

Paris - Versailles - Paris SCNF Timetable 350

Dep. Paris (Mont.)	Frequent times from 06:29 to 23:40
Arr. Versailles	30 minutes later

Versailles is also reached by suburban trains that stop in Paris at the Pont St. Michel, Invalides and Pont d'Alma stations.

Sights in **Versailles**: The fabulous palace where Louis XV lived like a king, and the elegant 250 acres of gardens here. Open daily except Mondays and public holidays. Bring a picnic lunch and eat in the gardens, by the mile-long Grand Canal.

During the time of Louis XV, about 5,000 members of the nobility lived in the palace's private apartments. Versailles became a museum in 1837.

Among its highlights are: the 237-foot-long by 33-foot-wide Hall of Mirrors (in which 17 mirror-lined arcades reflect 17 corresponding arched windows), throne room, queen's chambers, chapel, theater, the apartments of Madame de Pompadour and Madame du Barry, and the rooms named for Venus, Mercury, Diana and Mars.

The private apartment of the king can be seen only as a part of the guided tours of the palace, which start at various times from 9:45 to 15:30. However, most of the great rooms, such as the Hall of Mirrors and the king's bedroom, can be visited without a guide from 9:45 until the palace closes at 17:00. Visitors can purchase a book here which makes it possible to see and appreciate the palace without a guide.

Dep. Versaille	Frequent times from 05:37 to 23:44
Arr. Paris (Mont.)	30 minutes later

If you visit Versaille in the morning, it is possible to also see Chartres (page 147) in early afternoon. Ther are frequent trains for the 30-minute ride from Versaille to Chartres. See page 147 for schedules Chartres-Paris.

TRIPS TO THE RIVIERA

Unless designated otherwise, all of these trains are TGV, require reservation, charge a supplement and have light refreshments.

Paris - Marseile - Paris 151

Dep. Paris (Lyon)	07:00 (1)	07:40	10:23	11:42	12:55	13:29 (7)
Arr. Marseille (St. Ch.)	11:46	12:37	15:03	16:22	17:39	18:10

* * *

Dep. Marseille (St. Ch.)	06:42 (2)	08:06	08:44	12:13	13:58	14:58 (3+8)
Arr. Paris (Lyon)	11:33	12:49	13:39	16:59	18:40	19:46

(1) Runs Monday-Friday, except holidays. (2) Operates early September to early July. Runs Monday-Friday. (3) Operates early July to early September. Runs daily, except Saturday. (4) Operates early September to early July. Runs daily, except Saturday. (5) A non-TGV train that carries a sleeping car and has couchettes. Light refreshments. (6) Runs daily, except Saturday. (7) Plus other departures from Paris at 15:40, 16:49, 17:47, 18:35 (4) and 20:30 (5), arriving Marseille 20:25, 21:44, 22:35, 23:24 and 04:47. (8) Plus other departures from Marseille at 16:46, 17:31, 18:20 (6) and 21:48 (5), arriving Paris 21:43, 22:22, 23:20 and 06:24.

Paris - Nice - Paris 151

Dep. Paris (Lyon)	07:30	10:41 (1)	15:05 (2)	20:30 (3)
Arr. Nice	14:26	17:38	22:02	04:47

* * *

Dep. Nice	10:08	15:18 (1)	18:18 (3)
Arr. Paris (Lyon)	17:09	22:16	06:24

(1) Restaurant car. (2) Operates late June to early September. (3) A non-TGV train that carries a sleeping car and has couchettes. Light refreshments.

SCENIC RAIL TRIPS

Chamonix - Vallorcine - Chamonix 268

Good mountain scenery on this short ride. It is easy to combine this with the one-day roundtrip from Geneva to Chamonix, described on page 344.

Dep. Chamonix	07:54	09:11	10:10 (1)	11:34	13:44 (2)	15:18 (4)	-0-
Arr. Vallorcine	30 minutes later						

* * *

Dep. Vallorcine	08:35	09:50 (1)	11:09	13:08	14:58 (3)	15:58	17:13 (5)
Arr. Chamonix	30 minutes later						

(1) Operates late June to early September. (2) Operates most of June and most of September. (3) Operates early June to late September. (4) Plus other departures from Chamonix at 16:34, 17:31, 18:09 and 19:18. (5) Plus other departures from Vallorcine at 18:23, 19:16 and 19:56 (1).

Limoges - Toulouse - Limoges 138

Recommended for mountain scenery. This can be seen either as an easy one-day roundtrip between Limoges and Toulouse or as a portion of the route from Paris to Toulouse via Limoges.

Dep. Limoges	06:23 (1)	10:33 (2)	12:48 (3)	13:12 (4)	13:38 (3)
Arr. Toulouse (Mat.)	09:57	13:45	16:31	16:50	16:55

Sights in **Toulouse**: See notes about Toulouse under "Bordeaux-Toulouse" on page 135.

Dep. Toulouse (Mat.)	11:05 (5)	14:39 (6)	-0-	17:45 (7)	18:02 (8)
Arr. Limoges	14:41	18:01	-0-	20:53	22:15

(1) Early July to early September: runs daily. Early September to early July: runs Sunday only. (2) Supplement charged. Runs daily, except Sundays and holidays. Restaurant car. (3) Operates late June to early September. Light refreshments. (4) Operates early September to late June. Light refreshments. (5) Light refreshments. (6) Mid-July to early September: runs daily. Early September to late June: runs daily, except Saturday. (7) Supplement charged. Runs daily. Restaurant car. (8) Runs Monday-Friday, except holidays.

Here is the schedule for the Paris-Toulouse route:

138

Dep. Paris (Aust.)	07:30 (1)	09:07 (2)	10:03 (3)	10:10 (4)	13:24 (5)
Dep. Limoges	10:33	12:48	13:12	13:38	16:56
Arr. Toulouse (Mat.)	13:45	16:31	16:50	16:55	20:30

* * *

Dep. Toulouse (Mat.)	06:17 (6)	07:37 (7)	09:09 (6)	10:23 (9)	11:05 (5+11)
Dep. Limoges	-0-	10:56	12:35	13:56	14:45
Arr. Paris (Aust.)	11:30	14:02	16:15	17:27	18:09

(1) Supplement charged. Runs daily, except Sundays and holidays. Restaurant car. (2) Operates late June to early September. Light refreshments. (3) Operates early September to late June. Light refreshments. (4) Operates late June to early September. Light refreshments. (5) Light refreshments. (6) TGV. Reservation required. Supplement charged. Runs daily, except Sundays and holidays. (7) Suplement charged. Runs daily, except Sundays and holidays. (8) Operates early July to late August. Runs daily, except Sunday and Monday. (9) Runs Sunday only. (10) Supplement charged. Runs daily. Restaurant car. (11) Plus other departures from Toulouse at 14:39 (5) and 17:45 (10), arriving Paris 21:42 and 00:01.

Lyon - Geneva 159

This trip is noted for scenic canyons. See details on page 138.

Marseille - Grenoble - Marseille 165

Excellent mountain scenery.

This roundtrip can be made only on a Friday.

Dep. Marseille (St. Ch.)	06:38	08:41	Dep. Grenoble	18:15 (1)
Arr. Grenoble	13:05	15:10	Arr. Marseille (S. C.)	21:25

(1) Runs Friday only.

Marseille - Nimes - La Bastide - Clermont Ferrand

The train follows a beautiful river valley between La Bastide and Clermont Ferrand.

163		145	
Dep. Marseille (St. Ch.)	06:05 (1)	Dep. Clermont Ferrand	12:55 (2)
Arr. Nimes	07:11	Dep. La Bastide	15:51
Change trains. 145		Arr. Nimes	17:37
Dep. Nimes	07:35	Change trains. 163	
Dep. La Bastide	09:41	Dep. Nimes	17:55 (3)
Arr. Clermont Ferrand	12:38	Arr. Marseille (St. Ch.)	19:10

(1) Runs Monday only. (2) Restaurant car. (3) Light refreshments.

Narbonne - Carcassone 139

Outstanding farm and vineyard scenery. Easy to make as a one-day roundtrip or can be covered in the short route from Narbonne to Toulouse and Bordeaux.

Dep. Narbonne	06:51	08:41	09:50	12:01	12:50 (1)
Arr. Carcassone	40-45 minutes later				

Sights in **Narbonne**: The Cloister adjacent to the Palace of the Archbishops. The choir of the incomplete Cathedral of Saint-Just.

Sights in **Carcassone**: See notes under "Bordeaux-Carcassone" on page 133.

Dep. Carcassone	09:52 (1)	12:19 (1)	12:49 (1)	15:08 (1)	18:03 (2)
Arr. Narbonne	40-45 minutes later				

(1) Light refresments. (2) Plus other departures from Carcassone at 19:47 (1) and 21:54 (1).

Here is the daytime viewing schedule for the Narbonne-Bordeaux route:

All of these trains have light refreshments.

Dep. Narbonne	07:03	09:20	15:14 (1)
Dep. Carcassone	10:20	12:32	15:45
Dep. Toulouse (Matabiau)	11:12	13:27	16:35 (1)
Arr. Bordeaux (St. Jean)	13:28	15:52	18:33

* * *

Dep. Bordeaux (St. Jean)	06:37	08:23 (2)	12:35	14:45
Dep. Toulouse (Matabiau)	09:04	11:29 (2)	14:19	17:12
Dep. Carcassone	09:52	12:19	15:08	18:03
Arr. Narbonne	10:20	12:47	15:36	18:31

(1) Change trains in Toulouse at 16:28. (2) Change trains in Toulouse at 11:03.

Nice - Cuneo 353

There is spectacular scenery on the 74-mile long Nice-Cuneo rail route through the Alps and the **Roya Valley**, a service that first became operational in 1928. Severe damage during World War II caused it to be closed in 1940, and it was not re-opened until the Winter of 1979. An outstanding feat of engineering, this line is a succession of very high viaducts, bridges and 60 tunnels that span 27 miles of this route, interspersed with sections that look down into deep valleys. This route has attracted many tourists.

Dep. Nice	07:52 (1)	12:15	Dep. Cuneo	16:16
Arr. Cuneo	10:45	15:30	Arr. Nice	19:11

(1) change trains in Breil-sur-Roya at 09:00. Depart Breil-sur-Roya 09:06.

Nice - Digne - Nice 193

This is a very scenic ride up the beautiful **Var Valley** on a self-propelled single car narrow-gauge train. One-way cost $17.50 (U.S.) in 1990, roundtrip $35. Half-fare for holders of Eurailpass or any French pass. There is a great drop in temperature between sea-level Nice and 1,955-foot-high Digne.

Dep. Nice (Sud)	06:15 (1)	08:35	09:35	12:30	17:00
Arr. Digne	09:30	11:59	12:54	15:41	20:15

Sights in **Digne**: A popular mineral bath resort. See the 15th century Cathedral of Saint Jerome. Many fruit orchards. Digne is famed for the lavender cultivated here.

Dep. Digne	06:40	10:55	13:45	16:10	17:30
Arr. Nice (Sud)	10:04	14:05	16:57	19:27	20:43

(1) Runs daily, except Saturday and Sunday.

Lyon - Torino (and Rome) 152

The Culoz-Modane portion of this trip offers outstanding lake and mountain scenery. The train goes through the 8.5-mile long Mont Cenis Tunnel, constructed in 1871.

Dep. Lyon (Per.)	06:49	12:34	Dep. Torino (P.N.)		16:48
Dep. Lyon (P-D)	06:59	12:44	Dep. Modane		18:19
Dep. Culoz	-0-	13:44	Arr. Culoz		20:11
Arr. Modane	09:38	15:37	Arr. Lyon (P-D)		21:07
Arr. Torino (P.N.T)	11:13	17:20	Arr. Lyon (Per.)		21:17

Toulouse - Limoges - Toulouse 138

Recommended for mountain scenery. This route can be seen either as an easy one- day roundtrip between Toulouse and Limoges or as a portion of the ride from Toulouse to Paris.

Dep. Toulouse (Mat.)	07:37 (1)	09:09 (2)	10:23 (3)	11:05 (4)	13:00 (5)	14:33 (4)
Arr. Limoges	10:54	12:32	13:52	14:41	16:28	18:01
		*	*	*		
Dep. Limoges	12:48 (6)	13:12 (7)	13:38 (6)	16:56 (4)	20:53 (8)	
Arr. Toulouse (Mat.)	16:31	16:50	16:55	20:30	00:02	

Here is the schedule for the Toulouse-Paris ride:

Dep. Toulouse (Mat.)	07:37 (1)	09:09 (2)	10:23 (3)	11:05 (4)	13:00 (5)	14:39 (4)
Dep. Limoges	10:54	12:32	13:52	14:41	16:28	18:01
Arr. Paris (Aust.)	14:02	16:15	17:27	18:09	20:51	21:35

(1) Supplement charged. Runs daily, except Sundays and holidays. (2) Operates early July to late August. Runs daily, except Monday and Sunday. Light refreshments. (3) Runs Sunday only. (4) Light refreshments. (5) Runs Friday and Sunday. Light refreshments. (6) Operates late June to early September. Runs daily. Light refreshments. (7) Operates early September to late June. Runs daily. Light refreshments. (8) Runs daily, except Sunday. Supplement charged. Restaurant car Monday–Thursday.

INTERNATIONAL ROUTES FROM FRANCE

The French gateway for rail travel to Amsterdam, Bern (and on to Zurich and Vienna), Brussels, Cologne, Geneva, London and Madrid is Paris. **Notes on the routes to London appear in Chapter 7, pages 426-427.**

From Marseille, there is rail service to Barcelona and Genoa (and on to Milan and Rome). From Paris, there are trains to Amsterdam, Barcelona, Bern, Brussels, Cologne, Geneva, Genoa, Lisbon, Madrid, Milan and Rome.

Nice - Marseille - Narbonne - Barcelona

163

Dep. Nice	-0-	-0-	11:56 (2)
Dep. Marseille	09:20 (1)	12:45 (2)	14:42
Arr. Narbonne	-0- (1)	15:12	17:35
Change trains.			

162

Dep. Narbonne	-0-	16:24	19:04 (2)
Arr. Port Bou	13:18	17:58	20:45
Change trains.			

416

Dep. Port Bou	13:22 (3)	18:08 (3)	21:05 (3)
Arr. Barcelona (P. de G.)	15:53	21:27	23:32

(1) Direct train to Port Bou. No train change in Narbonne. Light refreshments. (2) Light refreshments. (3) Second-class only.

Marseille - Nice - Genoa - Milan - Rome 78

There is marvelous Mediterranean coastal scenery on this route.

Dep. Marseille (St. Ch.)	-0-	05:00 (1)	05:13	06:15
Dep. Nice	07:15	08:08	08:32	09:10
Dep. Ventimiglia	08:50	09:50 (1)	10:10	10:55
Arr. Genoa (P.P.)	11:33	12:16	12:48	13:30
Arr. Milan (Cen.)	13:40	-0-	-0-	15:40
Arr. Rome	-0-	18:15	19:20	-0-

Dep. Marseille (St. Ch.)	16:39 (1)	-0-	-0-
Dep. Nice	19:10	20:10 (2)	23:12 (3)
Dep. Ventimiglia	20:10	21:40	01:00
Arr. Genoa (P.P.)	22:10	00:17	03:30
Arr. Milan (Cen.)	23:59	-0-	05:40
Arr. Rome	-0-	07:10	-0-

(1) Light refreshments Marseille-Milan. Supplement charged Ventimiglia-Milan. (2) Carries a sleeping car. Also has couchettes. (3) Has couchettes.

Paris - Amsterdam 76

See "Amsterdam-Paris" on page 96.

Paris - Basel 57

See "Basel-Paris" on page 142.

Paris - Bern 55

Both of these trains are TGV, require reservation, charge a supplement and have a restaurant car.

Dep. Paris (Lyon)	07:14 (1)	18:06
Arr. Bern	12:02	22:37

(1) Change trains in Frasne at 10:13.

Paris - Bordeaux - Lisbon 28

Reservation required. Supplement charged. Restaurant car Irun-Lisbon. Has couchettes Paris-Lisbon and Paris-Porto.

Dep. Paris (Austerlitz)	09:30	Dep. San Sebastian		19:01
Dep. Bordeaux (St. J.)	14:16	Set watch back one hour.		
Dep. Bayonne	15:56	Arr. Pampilhosa		07:48 (1)
Dep. Irun	18:40	Arr. Lisbon (S. Apol.)		10:49

(1) The cars for Porto depart Pampilhosa at 08:25, arriving Porto 09:51.

Paris - Bordeaux - Madrid 58

Dep. Paris (Aust.)	10:00 (1)	15:55 (1)	18:05 (4)	20:00 (5)
Dep. Bordeaux (St. J.)	13:01	18:56	22:36	00:24
Arr. St. Jean de Luz	-0-	20:59	-0-	-0-
Arr. Irun	15:12	21:16	-0- (4)	-0- (5)
Change trains.				
Dep. Irun	15:50 (2)	23:00 (3)	-0- (4)	-0- (5)
Arr. Madrid (Cham.)	23:05	08:30	09:50	08:32

(1) Departs from Paris' Montparnasse railstation. TGV. Resservation required. Supplement charged.
(2) Supplement charged. Light refreshments. (3) Carries sleeping car. Also has couchettes. (4) Direct train. No train change in Irun. Supplement charged. Has second-class couchettes. Light refreshments. (5) 'Paris-Madrid Talgo" [Table 25]. This train began in 1990 carrying one "Gran Clase" sleeping car, the most luxurious sleeping car in Europe. Each of its large single and double compartments has a shower and a toilet. Direct train to Madrid. No train change in Irun. Supplement charged. Restaurant car and buffet car. Also has ordinary sleeping compartments and 4-berth tourist compartments. No coach seats.

Sights in **St. Jean de Luz**: A harbor, facing the Bay of Biscay.

Paris - Brussels - Amsterdam 76

Dep. Paris (Nord)	07:07 (1)	07:47 (2)	10:07 (3)	10:20 (2)	11:29 (4+11)
Arr. Brussels (Midi)	09:38	10:48	13:11	13:18	13:58 (5)
Arr. Amsterdam	-0-	14 :02	-0-	16:34	17:08

(1) First-class only. Sup. charged. Runs Mon.-Fri. Restaurant car. (2) Light refreshments. (3) Operates late June to early September. (4) Sup. charged. Runs daily, except Sun.. Restaurant car Paris-Brussels. (5) Change trains in Brussels. Depart Brussels 14:10 (light refreshments). (6) Sup. charged.Early July to early September: runs Mon.-Fri. Early September to early July: runs daily. (7) Sup. charged. Runs daily, except Sat. Restaurant car. (8) Operates early September to late June. Runs daily, except Friday and Sunday. (9) Late June to early September: runs daily . Early September to late June: runs Friday and Saturday only. (10) Has couchettes. (11) Plus another departure from Paris at 13:43, arriving Brussels 16:40, change trains, depart Brussels 17:10 (2), arriving Amsterdam 20:08. . . 14:46 (2), arriving Brussels 17:40, Amsterdam 21:01. . . 16:47 (2), arriving Brussels 19:38, Amsterdam 22:35 . . . 17:36 (6), arriving Brussels 20:08, change trains, depart Brussels 20:13, arriving Amsterdam 23:08. . . 18:36 (7), arriving Brussels 21:08, Amsterdam 23:59. . . 19:28 (8), terminating in Brussels 22:33. . . 19:40 (9), terminating in Brussels at 22:33. . . and 23:19 (10), arriving Brussels 04:30, Amsterdam 08:05.

Paris - Cologne (Koln) 62

Dep. Paris (Nord)	07:27 (1)	13:43 (2)	16:39 (1)	18 :40 (1)	23:12 (3)
Arr. Cologne	12:38	19:45	21:57	00:24	05:52

(1) Supplement charged. Restaurant car. (2) Light refreshments. (3) Carries a sleeping car. Also has couchettes.

Paris - Geneva 159

All of these trains are TGV, require reservation and charge a supplement.

Dep. Paris (Lyon)	07:35 (1)	10:36 (1)	14:32 (2)	17:40 (1)	19:13 (1)
Arr. Geneva (Corn.)	11:08	14:05	18:15	21:11	22:45

(1) Restaurant car. (2) Light refreshments.

Paris - Dijon - Lyon - Torino - Milan - Genoa - Rome - Naples

	60	60	60	34	60
Dep. Paris (Lyon)	10:47 (1)	-0-	15:00 (1)	18:47 (6)	20:56 (7+9)
Dep. Dijon	-0-	-0-	-0-	21:17	23:48
Arr. Lyon (P-D)	-0-	-0-	17:00 (4)	-0-	-0-
Dep. Lyon (P-D)	-0-	-0-	17:14 (5)	-0-	-0-
Arr. Chambery	14:04 (2)	-0-	18:36	23:49	02:28
Dep. Chambery	14:15	-0-	18:39 (5)	23:52	02:48
Arr. Torino (P.N.)	17:20	-0-	21:20 (5)	02:51 (6)	06:10 (7)
Change trains.					
Dep. Torino (P.N.)	17:53	17:35 (3)	21:30 (5)	03:05 (6)	06:35 (7)
Arr. Milan (Cen.)	19:40	-0-	23:00	-0-	-0-
Arr. Genoa (P.P.)	-0-	19:19	-0-	04:37	08:29
Arr. Pisa	-0-	21:22	-0-	06:30 (6)	10:48 (7)
Arr. Rome (Ter.)	-0-	-0-	-0-	09:35	14:27
Arr. Naples (Cen.)	-0-	02:33	-0-	-0-	16:55

(1) TGV. Reservation required. Supplement charged. (2) Change trains in Chambery. (3) This train has only sleeping cars and couchettes. (4) Change trains in Lyon. (5) Direct train to Milan. No train change in Torino. Supplement charged. Light refreshments. (6) Direct train to Rome. No train change in Torino. Train has only sleeping cars and couchettes. Light refreshments Paris-Chambery. and Pisa-Rome. (7) Direct train to Naples. No train change en route. Carries a sleeping car. Also has couchettes. Light refreshments Paris-Dijon and Torino-Naples. (8) Direct train to Milan. No train change in Torino. Coaches are second-class only. Carries a sleeping car. Also has couchettes. (10) Plus another departure from Paris at 22:22 (8), departing Dijon 01:17, arriving Torino (Porto Susa) 07:13, Milan 08:45.

THE FERRY-CROSSING TO IRELAND

Paris - Le Havre - Rosslare and Paris - Cherbourg - Rosslare

Covered by Eurailpass. Operated by Irish Ferries Companiy.

Reserving and paying extra for a cabin with private toilet ($71 (U.S.) in 1991) is essential in Summer, when many passengers outnumber the seats on the vessel and must sit on the deck for this 21-hour trip.

Days of operation and departures times vary during 6 different periods of the year. For 1992 schedules and reservations, contact the North American agent: Lynott Tours Inc., 350 Fifth Avenue, New York, NY 10118. Telephone: (800) 221-2474.

GREECE

Children under 3 travel free if they do not occupy a separate seat.

The signs you will see at railstations in Greece are:

ANDRON	MEN
GRAMMH	TRACK
EISODHOS	ENTRANCE
EXODHOS	EXIT
GRAPHEION TON EISITIRION	TICKET OFFICE
GYNAIKON	WOMEN
IMATOPHYLAKION	CHECKROOM
PLIROPHORIA	INFORMATION
STATHMO	STATION

GREEK HOLIDAYS

January 1	New Year's Day	May 1	Labor Day
January 6	Epiphany	August 15	Virgin Mary's Day
	Ash Monday	October 28	National Day
March 25	Independence Day	December 25	Christmas
	Greek Good Friday	December 26	Boxing Day
	Greek Good Saturday		
	Greek Easter		
	Greek Easter Monday		

SUMMER TIME

Greece changes to Summer Time on the last Sunday of March and converts back to Standard Time on the last Sunday of September.

GREECE'S TRAIN PASSES

Sold worldwide outside Greece by travel agencies and Rail Europe (U.S.A. and Canadian offices listed under "France" on page 23).

Greek Rail Pass   Unlimited *first-class* train travel. The 1992 prices for one person are: $66 (U.S.) for any 5 days within 15 days, $119 for any 10 days within one month. The price per person for 2 or more persons: $56 and $99. Half-fare for children 4 –11.

Greek Rail'N Drive   Unlimited *first-class* train travel plus car rental. Prices vary (a) whether for one person or for 2 or more persons, and (b) the category of car. A third passenger needs to only pay for the Greek Rail Pass.

The 1992 prices per person for 2 or more persons (using the smallest size car) are: $129 (U.S.) for any 5 days of rail plus any 3 days of car rental within 15 days....or $175 for any 10 days of rail plus any 3 days of car rental within one month.

EURAILPASS BONUSES IN GREECE

The ferry crossing from Patras to Brindisi (see note under "Italy" on page 217).

There is also a 30% reduction on Adriatica di Navagazione Line for ships between Piraeus-Venice (and v.v.) and Piraeus-Alexandria (and v.v.).

GREECE

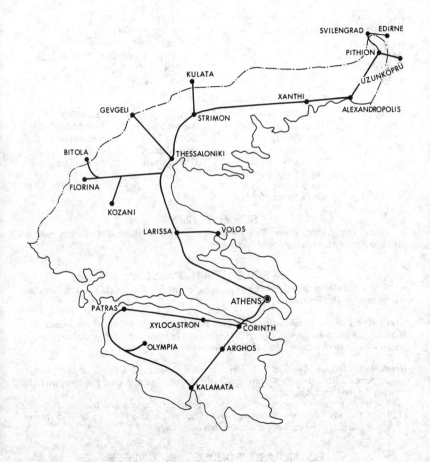

ONE-DAY EXCURSIONS AND CITY-SIGHTSEEING

Here are 8 one-day rail trips that can be made comfortably from Athens and Thessaloniki, returning to them in most cases before dinnertime. Notes are provided on what to see and do at each destination. The number after the name of each route is the Cook's timetable.

Details on 2 longer rail trips in Greece follow the one-day excursions. Schedules for international connections conclude this section.

Athens (Athinai)

From 07:30 to sunset, and from 21:00 to 24:00 on nights of a full moon, visit the Parthenon, the elegant temple of the Wingless Victory and the Erechtheion at the ancient Acropolis. The monuments there can be seen 07:30–16:45 daily. The adjacent museum is closed Tuesday. Then walk northwest to the partly restored ancient Agora to see the best preserved Doric temple in Athens, the Hephaistos, also known as the Thesseion.

Also near the Acropolis are: The old theater of Dionyssos. The gravestones and sculptures in Kerameikos, the city's ancient cemetery. The Corinthia-style columns of the Temple of Olympian Zeus. Hadrian's Arch. The all-marble Athenian Stadium, where the Olympic Games were revived in 1896. The Clock of Kyrrestos, showing the prevailing wind on each of its 8 sides, standing in Aerides Square, named for the function of the clock. The Roman Forum.

Walk downhill to the Monastiraki area, where the daily "Flea Market" is held. See the view of Athens from the white chapel of Agios Georgios on the Hill of Lycabettus, climbed either by foot or by cable car.

Athens' best-known museums are the National Archaeological Museum at 1 Tositza Street; the collection of ancient coins at the Numismatic Museum, next to the Archaeological Museum; the Acropolis Museum (noted above), the Byzantine Museum at 22 Vassilis Sophias Avenue (closed Monday), for its collection of icons; the Museum of Greek Popular Art (closed Monday); the Museum of the Ancient Agora excavations in the Stoa, an ancient commercial community at Attalus (closed Tuesday).

The work of contemporary Greek painters and sculptors in the National Gallery at 60 Vas Constantinou (closed Monday). The more than 2,000 items relating to the social and religious customs of Romanlot and Sephardic Jews in the Jewish Museum (third floor at 36 Amalias Avenue, open daily except Saturday 09:00–13:00. Displays include the reconstructed interior of a provincial synagogue, religious articles, costumes and objects of everyday life.

The 28 exhibit rooms at the fantastic Benaki Museum in central Athens (Vasilisis Sophias Avenue at Koumbari Street), arranged chronologically, cover the entire spectrum of Greek culture from the early Bronze Age to the start of the 20th century: gold, ornaments, jewelry, portraits, statues, embroidery, icons, rare 17th and 18th century bibles, and 8 centuries (10th to 18th) of Islamic art that includes ceramics, textiles and wood carvings. The Benaki is open daily except Tuesday 08:00 to 14:00.

Figurines of white marble from the Cycladic islands (in the Aegean Sea), created 5,000 years ago, in the Goulandris Museum of Cycladic Art (4 Neophytou Douka Street), open Monday-Friday 10:00-16:00, Saturday 10:00–15:00.

A collection of weapons since the Neolithic Age in the War Museum (Vasilisis Sophia Avenue at Rizari Street), open Tuesday-Saturday 09:00–14:00, Sunday 9:30–14:00. Nineteenth century arts and crafts (woodcarving, needlework, naive painting) at the Museum of Greek Folk Art (17 Kydathineon Street), open daily except Monday 10:00–14:00.

The collection (from the Archaic period through the Middle Ages) of stone sculptures, ceramics, bronzes and exceptionally beautiful icons in the Canellopoulos Museum (below the Acropolis, at Theorias and Panos streets), closed Tuesday, open other weekdays 08:45–15:00, Sundays 09:30–14:30.

There are sound-and-light performances in English at Pnyx Hill every night at 21:00. When it ends, cross the road and see native dances of Greece, performed nightly at 22:15 on the Hill of Philopappus.

For Greek arts and handicrafts (ceramics, hand-woven fabrics, alabaster articles, embroideries, hand-carved wood furniture), shop on the streets around Syntagma Square, the center of the city.

Athens - Arghos - Athens 980

Sit on the right-hand side of the train en route to Arghos in order to see best the view of the canal that connects the Aegean and Ionian Seas, about 80 minutes after leaving Athens. The train crosses a 108-foot long bridge, 200 feet above the water. It is a short walk or inexpensive taxi ride from the Arghos railstation to the town center.

Dep. Athens	07:25	09:05	11:30	13:07	22:10
Arr. Arghos	10:13	12:04	15:06	16:49	01:23

Sights in **Arghos:** The Museum, with its archaeological exhibits. From there, it is a 15-minute walk to the ancient theater, carved into the hillside, and to some Roman ruins. A 5-mile taxi ride to the 800 B.C. ruins of Tiryns is well worth the small fare. At the birthplace of Hercules you will see the ruins of Greece's oldest recognizable temple: underground galleries polished for many centuries by the woolly backs of innumerable sheep who sought shelter there during storms. Massive Cyclopean walls.

Dep. Arghos	14:49	19:02	02:39
Arr. Athens	17:49	21:37	05:30

Athens - Corinth (Korinthos) - Athens 980

Watch 80 minutes after departing Athens for the same view described above, under "Athens-Arghos". The arrival in Corinth is in the "modern" Corinth, built after the 1858 earthquake.

Dep. Athens	07:25	08:26	09:31	10:00	12:01	13:00 (2)
Arr. Corinth	09:11	10:10	11:08	11:55	14:02	14:49

Sights in **Corinth**: The 2500-year old Temple of Apollo. The Kato Pirini Fountain. The rostrum from which St. Paul preached Christianity to the Corinthians.

Dep. Corinth	10:44	11:58	13:16	13:47	15:53	16:39 (2)
Arr. Athens	12:54	13:50	15:02	15:45	17:49	18:47

(1) Operates late June to late September. (2) Plus other departures from Corinth at 19:11, 19:59, 21:00 and 22:54 (1).

Athens - Kalamata - Athens 980

Dep. Athens	07:25	09:31	12:01	13:51	22:38
Arr. Kalamata	14:38	15:48	19:34	21:15	05:37

Sights in **Kalamata**: The exhibits at the Museum in the Kyriakos mansion, ranging from Stone Age weapons to Venetian mirrors and coins as well as relics from the 1821 War of Independence. The Byzantine-style Church of Aghii Apostoli. The splendid view from the Frankish castle and, descending from there, see the handmade silk articles at the Convent. Aghios Haralambos, one of the finest Byzantine churches in the area, is a short distance east of the Convent. Stroll along the seafront.

Dep. Kalamata	06:30	08:25	10:35	15:20	20:40
Arr. Athens	13:50	15:45	17:49	21:37	06:51

Athens - Pirghos - Olympia - Athens

Most of this trip is alongside the sea, through green fields of citrus and olive trees. Between Athens and Corinth, the train goes across a bridge that spans the Korinthos Canal, which separates northern Greece from Peloponesia.

All of the trains Pirghos–Olympia and v.v. are second-class only.
980

Dep. Athens	08:26	13:00	21:38
Arr. Pirghos	14:10	19:00	04:15
Change trains. 977			
Dep. Pirghos	14:14	19:10	06:30
Arr. Olympia	14:59	19:46	07:06

Sights in **Olympia**: The first Olympic Games (776 B.C.) were held here and continued here every 4 years for the next 12 centuries. See the Stadium. The fine Olympic Museum, with its marvelous Hermes of Praxiteles sculpture. The temples of Hera and Zeus.

Dep. Olympia	07:30	10:38	13:16	16:04	19:55
Arr. Pirghos	08:08	11:15	13:52	16:45	20:31
Change trains. 980					
Dep. Pirghos	09:17	11:40	14:15	16:59	23:59
Arr. Athens	15:02	18:47	21:14	22:56	06:51

Athens - Patras - Athens 980

Dep. Athens	07:00	08:26	10:00	13:00	15:03	18:28 (2)
Arr. Patras	11:31	12:21	14:43	17:09	20:00	22:20

Sights in **Patras**: Cross the street in front of the railstation to the park. Then walk from the Trion Fountain along Ayiou Nijulauo to the steps that ascend to the Patras Acropolis for a fine view of Patras, the surrounding mountains and the port, third largest of Greece.

(Timetable continues on page 168.)

After descending the steps, go to the left along Georgiou Street to the old Roman Theater, the Odeon.

Another walk from the Trion Fountain is to the Archaeological Museum to see its collection of exhibits from the Mycenean, Geometric, Archaic and Roman periods. Also worth seeing are the Venetian castle and Greece's largest church, St. Andrews's.

See the Clock of Patras, made entirely of flowers. Visit the century-old Achaia Clauss Winery, the leading producer of Greek wines.

| Dep. Patras | 02:15 | 06:30 | 08:10 | 11:10 | 14:00 | 16:32 (3) |
| Arr. Athens | 06:51 | 10:41 | 12:54 | 15:02 | 18:47 | 21:14 |

(1) Operates late June to late September. (2) Plus another departure from Athens at 21:38, arriving Patras 02:09. (3) Plus other departures from Patras at 18:45 and 20:35 (1), arriving Athens 22:56 and 00:40.

Athens - Piraeus - Athens   892a

Subway trains depart every few minutes from the southbound section of a combined north-and-south platform at Athens' Omonia Square railstation for the 20-minute ride to Piraeus. Be certain, at the same platform, you are not boarding the northbound train for Kifissia. There is also ordinary train service from Athens to Piraeus.

Sights in **Piraeus**: One of the largest ports on the Mediterranean. Ships sail daily from here to almost all the Aegean islands and to many other Greek ports. The 2 small adjoining ports of Zea and Mikrolimano are for pleasure craft. Bus #20 goes to those ports. The bus terminal is to the left of the railstation.

See the neo-classical style Municipal Theater and the exhibits in the Archaeological Museum. The Maritime Museum, closed Monday, exhibits 13,000 items reflecting 5,000 years of Greek seafaring. Plays are performed at the open-air Theater of Kastella in the Summer.

Athens - Thessaloniki   970

| Dep. Athens (Larissa) | 00:30 (1) | 07:20 (2) | 10:00 | 13:00 (3+8) |
| Arr. Thessaloniki | 08:25 | 13:38 | 17:37 | 19:11 |

Sights in **Thessaloniki**: Second largest city in Greece. See the ruins of the Roman Baths, north of the Church of Agios Demetrios. The Roman Market and Theater. Nymphaion, the ancient circular building. The Arch of Galerius. The unique mosaics in the 4th century Rotunda, at the intersection of Agiou Georgiou and Filippou streets.

The 2 surviving early Christian churches: the 4th century Ahiropiitos and the 5th century Osios David. The 15th century White Tower. The collection of pre-historic to Byzantine items in the Archaeological Museum on YMCA Square. Articles from the past 3 centuries at the Folklore and Ethnological Museum, 68 Vasilisais Olgas.

| Dep. Thessaloniki | 07:00 (4) | 08:20 (2) | 11:30 | 13:00 (4+9) |
| Arr. Athens (Larrissa) | 13:10 | 16:20 | 18:45 | 19:14 |

(1) Carries a sleeping car. Also has couchettes. (2) Supplement charged. Light refreshments. (3) Reservation required. Light refreshments. (4) Reservation required. Supplement charged. Light refreshments. (5) Carries a sleeping car. Also has couchettes. Light refreshments. (6) Reservation required. (7) Light refreshments. (8) Plus other departures from Athens at 14:40 (2), 17:00 (4), 22:00 (5), 23:00 (1) and 23:55 (6), arriving Thessaloniki 22:25, 23:15, 05:38, 06:30 and 07:50. (9) Plus other departures from Thessaloniki at 17:00 (4), 21:00 (7), 21:50 (1) and 23:00 (5), arriving Athens 23:16, 05:10, 05:45 and 06:50.

Thessaloniki - Kavala - Thessaloniki

974

Dep. Thessaloniki	07:30	09:05 (1)	12:08 (1)	14:45 (2)
Arr. Drama	10:12	12:54	15:46	18:06
Change (G.T.O. advice)				
Dep. Drama	10:30	13:00	16:00	18:30
Arr. Kavala	11:00	13:30	16:30	19:00

Sights in **Kavala**: The view from the Byzantine Fort. The colossal 16th century aqueduct, Kamares. Imaret, the group of Moslem buildings constructed a short time prior to the 1821 War of Independence. The ancient relics in the Archaeological Museum. Beautiful beaches.

Dep. Kavala	08:30	12:00	15:00	19:00
Arr. Drama	09:00	12:30	15:30	19:30
Change to train. 974				
Dep. Drama	09:29	12:50 (2)	16:01	19:36
Arr. Thessaloniki	13:08	16:04	20:11	22:19

(1) Light refreshments. (2) Supplement charged. Light refreshments.

SCENIC RAIL TRIPS

Thessaloniki - Katerini - Athens   970 + Greek Timetable

About one hour after departing Katerini (Thessaloniki-Athens), you can see on the right side of the train 9000-foot high **Mt. Olympus**, home of the ancient Greek gods. Thirty minutes later, the train passes through **Tembi Valley** and goes along **Pinios River**. From **Domokos** to **Tithorea**, the train winds along **Mt. Orthrys** and **Mt. Iti**, providing a panoramic view of many valleys and high mountains and, at one point, of the sea in the distance.

Dep. Thessaloniki	07:00 (1)	08:20 (2)	13:00 (1)	17:00 (3)	21:00 (4+7)
Arr. Katerini	08:08	09:34	14:10	18:12	22:21
Arr. Athens (Larissa)	13:10	16:20	19:14	23:16	05:07
Dep. Athens (Larissa)	06:30 (1)	13:00 (5)	14:40 (2)	17:00 (1)	22:00 (6+8)
Arr. Katerini	12:51	18:01	21:13	22:07	04:09
Arr. Thessaloniki	14:00	19:10	22:25	23:19	05:16

(1) Reservation required. Supplement charged. Light refreshments. (2) Supplement charged. Light refreshments. (3) Reservation required. Supplement charged. (4) Light refreshments. (5) Reservation required. Light refreshments. (6) Carries first and second-class sleeping cars. Also has second-class couchettes. Light refreshments. (7) Plus other departures from Thessaloniki at 21:55 (6) and 23:00 (6), arriving Athens 06:03 and 06:45. (8) Plus other departures from Athens at 22:30 (6) and 00:01 (6), arrving Thessaloniki 05:56 and 08:00.

Athens - Pirghos - Athens

See notes and timetables on page 167.

INTERNATIONAL ROUTES FROM GREECE

Athens is Greece's gateway to Italy and Yugoslavia (and on to Western Europe) as well as to Turkey (and on to the Middle East).

Athens - Belgrade + Munich or Venice

	945	945	65	
Dep. Athens	00:30 (1)	10:00 (1)	23:00 (4)	-0-
Dep. Thessaloniki	09:10	18:30	07:20	-0-

Set your watch back one hour from late September to early April, 2 hours from early April to late September.

Arr. Belgrade	21:22	06:08	-0-	
Change trains.				
		930		930
Dep. Belgrade	-0-	07:50 (2)	-0-	20:00 (1)
Arr. Munich	-0-	-0-	08:46	-0-
Arr. Venice (S.L.)	-0-	22:19 (3)	-0-	11:39

(1) Carries a sleeping car. Also has couchettes. (2) Light refreshments until 18:05. (3) Arrives at Venice Mestre railstation. (4) Direct train to Munich. Does not call on Belgrade. Reservation required. Carries a sleeping car. Also has couchettes.

Athens - Patras - Brindisi 980

The Patras-Brindisi boat trip is covered by Eurailpass and Eurail Youthpass but only if you go on Adriatica di Navagazione.

WARNING: The employees of other lines intimate that their ships honor the 2 passes and then charge fees after the boat leaves the pier.

With or without a Eurailpass or Eurail Youthpass, a reservation theoretically can be made on day of departure or day before departure but it is very unlikely that space will be available (particularly during July and August) unless a reservation is made many weeks in advance of departure date.

Those gambling on making a reservation after arriving in Patras can make application January 1 to June 9 and October 1 to December 31 only at the Adriatica di Navagazione embarkation office, located at Othonos Amalias Street 8.

From June 10 to September 30, those without advance reservations can apply also to any Patras travel agency that displays in its window the green badge "Eurail Information - Eurailpass".

Holders of advance reservations must go at all times directly to the Adriatica di Navagazione embarkation office to have their tickets checked, settle port taxes due and obtain the required Embarkation Ticket. That office is open 09:00–13:30 and 16:00–22:00.

Advance reservations before you start your trip can be made by contacting Extra Value Travel, 683 So. Collier Blvd., Marco Island, Florida 33937, U.S.A. Telephone: (813) 394-3384.

Another fee is charged for such special accommodations as aircraft type seats, pullman berths and cabins. There is also a port tax of 180 Drachmas that is not covered by Eurailpass and must be paid in Drachmas.

Passengers without advance reservations must obtain the Embarkation Ticket at least 2 hours prior to the ship's departure time. The ships reserve the right to cancel a reservation when that is not done and to give the space to a standby passenger.

Readers reported to us in 1990 that conditions on the boat were unsatisfactory.

For a view first of the Corinthian Canal and then the Corinthian Gulf, sit on the right side of the train Athens-Patras.

Notes about sightseeing in **Patras** appear on page 168.

Dep. Athens	07:00	08:26	10:00	13:00	15:03 (2)
Arr. Patras	11:31	12:21	14:43	17:09	20:00

It is a 20-minute walk from the railstation to the harbor. a taxi costs about $4.00 .

For sailing dates, check Cook's Table 1490.

Dep. Patras Harbor	18:00	22:00	
Arr. Brindisi	10:30	17:00	Both arrivals are on day 2

(1) Operates late June to late September. (2) Plus other departures from Athens at 15:58 (1), 18:28 and 21:38, arriving Patras 20:20, 22:20 and 02:09.

Athens - Istanbul   974

The train that ran at 06:30 every day in 1990 (arriving Istanbul 08:40 on day 2) did not run in 1991.

Dep. Athens
Arr. Istanbul

172

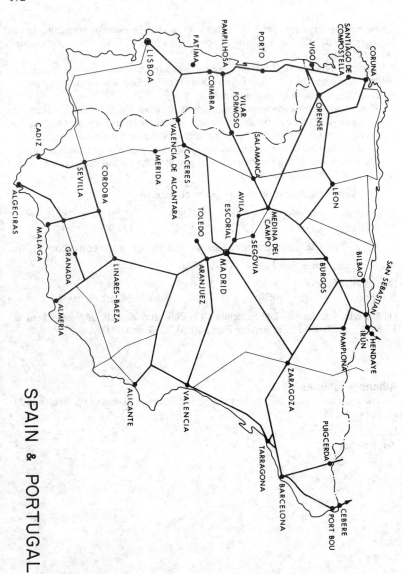

SPAIN & PORTUGAL

IBERIAN PENINSULA (SPAIN AND PORTUGAL)

Children under 4 travel free in Portugal and Spain if they do not occupy a separate seat. Half-fare for children 4-11 includes use of a separate seat. Children 12 and over must pay full fare.

Spain and Portugal have the broadest gauge railroad tracks in Western Europe (5' 6" versus 4' 8½″ in France and the other Western European countries). It is therefore necessary in most crossings from Spain into France (at Irun/Hendaye, Port Bou/Cerbere, or La Tour-de-Carol) to change trains. A few trains running between Spain and France are adaptable to either gauge.

First-class sleeping cars in Spain have single-berth and 2-berth compartments. Second- class sleeping cars have 3-berth tourist compartments, except the Paris-Madrid and Barcelona Talgos, which have tourist compartments with 4 berths. There is a supplemental charge for air-conditioned sleeping cars. Neither berths nor this supplement are covered by Eurailpass. Some Spanish trains have second-class couchette cars, with 6-berth compartments, as are also available in other Western European countries.

First-class sleeping cars in Portugal have single and double-berth compartments. Second- class Portuguese sleeping cars have 3-berth compartments.

Many Spanish train tickets include the price of a lunch or dinner. It is wise to determine this in advance of a trip.

For most Spanish trains, **it is necessary to reserve a seat and have one's ticket stamped with the train number and departure date**. Even when traveling with a Eurailpass or a Spanish pass, an endorsed ticket should be obtained for trains requiring them.

Do *not* discard a ticket during the journey. Frequently, the ticket is collected at the termination of a ride. If it is not presented at the destination railstation, the passenger must purchase a second ticket.

It is wise to retain rail tickets all over the world until after exiting the destination railstation so as to avoid having to pay twice for one journey.

Every year, some tourists using Eurailpass or a Spanish pass report being ejected from a Spanish train either just before its departure or at a station en route to their destination for failing to obtain the required endorsed tickets.

A person using a Eurailpass has been indoctrinated with the idea that he or she need not have either a ticket or (when riding an ordinary train) a seat reservation. This is confirmed on all of one's travels in Europe *outside* Spain.

Unaware of the Spanish Railway regulation, the passenger blithely steps aboard a train in Spain without having the ticket and seat reservation required there and a ticket can be obtained without charge upon presenting a Eurailpass or a Spanish pass.

If the train is not exceptionally crowded that day and the conductor appears before the train departs, the passenger is told to get off the train, go back into the railstation, and obtain the required endorsed ticket. Frequently, the notice to do this is given so close to the departure time that the train leaves before the passenger is able to return to it.

If the train departs before the conductor has discovered the omission of an endorsed ticket, often the passenger is forced to leave the train at the next stop to obtain a ticket. If that stop is typically brief, the train leaves that station before the passenger is able to return to the train.

The justification for the Spanish ticket-and-reservation requirement is that Spain's first-class fares are substantially lower than those of other countries. For example, the charge for the 8-hour Madrid-Barcelona run is about 60% of what French National Railroads charges for the 7-hour trip from Paris to Avignon or what Norwegian State Railways charges for the 8 ½ -hour Bergen-Oslo trip. The demand for Spain's limited number of express train seats far exceeds the supply. Only by issuing endorsed tickets can they control the situation.

The Spanish name for Spanish National Railways is "Red Nacional de los Ferrocarriles Espanoles". Abbreviation: RENFE. Reservations can be made at RENFE offices both in the major railstations and at numerous locations outside the station, as well as at various travel agencies in Spanish cities.

Making train reservations in Spain is very easy. More than 90% of the stations in Spain are hooked-up with a computer in Madrid, making it usually possible to arrange at one time all of your reservations for train trips in Spain. Reservations can be made as much as 2 months in advance. Timetable information can be obtained at offices of RENFE and at Spanish travel agencies.

Tell the clerk at the train information window your departure date, train number (which you can find in the railstation on the list of departures) and/or departure time, destination and number of seats required.

You will be handed a form which you then take to a ticket window, where you will be handed a seat reservation computer card. It will show either an exact seat number or the symbol "SR" ("Seat Reserved") under the column "Asiento".

If it is marked "SR", the conductor will tell you which seat to occupy after you board the car designated on the reservation computer card.

Do *not* board a Spanish non-local train without a seat reservation !

To ride without a Eurailpass or a Spanish pass on Spanish trains classified "Rap", one must pay a supplement. An even higher supplement must be paid when riding a train classified "Talgo", "E.L.T." or "T.E.R.", all of which are air-conditioned. A Eurailpass or a Spanish pass entitles the bearer to ride these special trains without having to pay their supplemental charges, the same as when riding EuroCity or InterCity trains.

In Spain, Rail Club Lounges are special railstation waiting rooms that have television, a bar, telephones, magazines and daily newspapers. These lounges are located at Madrid's Chamartin and Atocha, Barcelona's Sants, Valencia's Termino and in Bilbao, and at the railstation in Cordova, Malaga, Vigo and Zaragoza.

These lounges are available to passengers who are ticketed for international trains: Madrid-Paris, Barcelona-Geneva, Barcelona-Paris, Barcelona-Bern . . . and also for domestic travelers holding first-class tickets for sleeping compartments, for coach seats on any Talgo or InterCity train

In order to avoid waiting in the wrong line for Spanish tickets and seat reservations, take note of these signs you will find in large Spanish railstations:

TRENES DE SALIDA INMEDIATE	trains ready to depart
VENTA PARA HOY	trains leaving later in the day
VENTA ANTICIPADA	for trains leaving on a future day

Other **Spanish** railstation signs:

ANDEN	PLATFORM
ASIENTO	SEAT
BILLETTE	TICKET
CABALLEROS	MEN
COCHE-CAMA	SLEEPING CAR
COCHE-LITERA	COUCHETTES
COCHE-COMEDOR	RESTAURANT CAR
ENTRADA	ENTRANCE
ESTACION	STATION
HOMBRES	MEN
HORARIOS DE TRENES	TIMETABLES
LARGO RECORRIDO	LONG DISTANCE
LLEGADA	ARRIVAL
OFICINA DE INFORMACION	INFORMATION OFFICE
RESERVA	SEAT RESERVATION
SALA DE CONSIGNA	BAGGAGE CHECKROOM
SALIDA	DEPARTURE (EXIT)
SENORAS	WOMEN
TREN CON SUPLEMENTO	TRAIN WITH SURCHARGE
VIA	TRACK

Signs you will find in **Portuguese** railstations:

CARRUAGEM-CAMA	SLEEPING CAR
CARRUAGEM-RESTAURANTE	RESTAURANT CAR
CHEGADA	ARRIVAL
ESTACAO	STATION
HOMENS	MEN
HORARIO DOS CAMINHOS	TIMETABLES
PARTIDA	DEPARTURE
PLATAFORMA	PLATFORM (TRACK)
SAIDA	EXIT
SENHORAS	WOMEN

SPANISH HOLIDAYS

A list of holidays is helpful because some trains will be noted later in this section as *not* running on holidays. Also, these trains which operate on holidays are filled, and it is necessary to make reservations for them long in advance.

January 1	New Year's Day		Ascension Day
January 6	Epiphany		Corpus Christi Day
March 19	Saint Joseph's Day	June 29	St. Peter and St. Paul
	Maundy Thursday	July 18	National Holiday
	Good Friday	July 25	Saint James' Day
	Easter	August 15	Assumption Day
	Easter Monday (Barcelona)	October 12	Columbus Day
April 1	Victory Day	November 1	All Saints Day
May 1	St. Joseph Artisan Day	December 8	Immaculate Conception
		December 25	Christmas Day

PORTUGUESE HOLIDAYS

January 1	New Year's Day	August 15	Assumption of Our Lady
	Shrove Tuesday	October 5	Anniversary of the
	Good Friday		Proclamation of the
	Easter		Portuguese Republic
May 1	Labor Day	November 1	All Saints Day
	Corpus Christi Day	December 1	Restoration of Independence
June 10	Day of The Race	December 8	Immaculate Conception
	(Portuguese National Day)	December 25	Christmas
	Saint Anthony's Day (Lisbon)		

SUMMER TIME

Portugal is one hour earlier than Spain all year. Portugal is on the same time as England nearly all year, except for a few weeks in the Spring and Fall. Both Portugal and Spain change to Summer Time on the last Sunday of March and convert back to Standard Time on the last Sunday of September. During Summer Time, when it is 12:00 in England, it is 12:00 in Portugal and 13:00 in Spain.

SPAIN'S TRAIN PASSES

Spain Railpass and Spain Flexipass are sold both in Spain (at travel agencies and the offices of RENFE — the Spanish Railway) and also outside Spain worldwide by travel agencies and Rail Europe (U.S. and Canadian offices listed under "France" on page 23). Purchasers must prove by passport that they are *not* residents of Spain.

High season is May 16 to September 14. Low season is the rest of the year. Half-fare for children 4–11.

Spain Railpass   Unlimited train travel (*not* including supplements charged for some trains). The 1992 High Season *first*-class prices are: $320 (U.S.) for 8 days, $520 for 15 days and $620 for 21 days. *Second*-class: $230, $370 and $480. Low Season *first*-class prices are: $256, $416 and $496. *Second*-class: $184, $296 and $384.

Spain Flexipass   Unlimited train travel . The 1992 High Season *first*-class price are: $240 (U.S.) for any 4 days within 15 days, and $500 for any 9 days within 21 days. *Second*-class: $180 and $380. Low Season *first*-class: $192 and $400. *Second*-class: $144 and $304.

Spain Rail'N Drive   Four days of unlimited train travel plus 3 days of car rental (any 7 days) within 15 days. Prices vary (a) as to season, (b) whether for one person or for 2 or more persons, and (c) the category of car. A third passenger needs to pay only for a 4-day flexi train pass.

The 1992 prices per person for 2 persons (using the smallest size car and travelling in the Low Season) are: $259 (U.S.) for *first*-class, $209 for *second*-class. Up to 5 more days of car rental can be added at $40 per day.

All of the following are sold only in Spain, at main railstations and travel agencies.

Family Pass   For families of at least 3 persons, a discount is given on train tickets for "Blue Days" (approximately 300 days a year — a calendar is provided at railstation information offices). The passholder pays full fare. All adults except the passholder receive 50% discount on tickets. For children 12 to under 25, the discount is 50%. Children 4-11: 75%. Valid for one year from date of purchase. Proof by marriage certificate or any other certifying documents is required. The 1992 price is 300 pesetas.

Gold Pass   (Senior Citizen and Disabled Person Discount) For persons 60 and older and disabled persons of any age —*and who are residents of Spain*. Seniors must first purchase a "Tarjeta Dorada" (Gold Card) for 300 pesetas at any railstation or Renfe ticket office. Proof of age (passport, etc.) required. With the Gold Card, there is a 50% discount *only* on "Blue Days" (see "Family Pass" above) for single trips of 100 kilometers (63 miles) or more, or roundtrips of at least 200 km., but does *not* cover supplements charged for some trains.

Youth Pass   The "Tarifa Joven" is for travelers 12 to under 26 years old. Valid May 1 to December 31 for any train, for both first-class and second-class coach space, and *also* for sleeping accommodations. Can be used *only* on "Blue Days" (see "Family Pass", page 177). This 50% discount applies only to single trips of 100 kilometers (63 miles) or more, or roundtrips of at least 200 km, *and also covers any supplements charged for some trains*. Must be used within 2 months after beginning use. The 1992 price is 3,000 pesetas.

Roundtrip Discount   A 20% discount on both first-class and second-class roundtrips of 20 kilometers (12.6 miles) or more. Discount is available only on "Blue Days" (see "Family Pass", page 177). The return ride can be made up to 2 months after the initial departure. No discount is given on the supplement charged for special fast trains.

PORTUGAL'S TRAIN PASSES

Portuguese Flexipass   Unlimited *first*-class train travel. The 1992 prices are: $89 (U.S.) for any 4 days whithin 15 days, $139 for any 7 days whithin 21 days.

Portuguese Rail'N Drive   Unlimited 3 days of *first*-class train travel plus 3 days of car rental (any 6 days) within one month. Prices vary (a) whether for one person or for 2 or more persons, and (b) the category of car. The 1992 prices per person for 2 persons (using the smallest size car) is: $129 (U.S.). Up to 5 more days of car rental can be added at $40 per day.

All of the following are sold only in Portugal, at main railstations and travel agencies:

Tourist Ticket   Unlimited train travel for any class. The 1991 price was: 15,200 escudos for 7 days, Esc-24,200 for 14 days, and Esc-34,600 for 21 days.

Senior Citizen Discount   Persons 60 or older pay half-fare.

Family Ticket   For 3 or more persons. Valid only for trips of more than 149 km. (92 miles). Passports and documents proving family relationship must be presented. One person must pay full fare. Half-fare for others who are age 13 or older. One-quarter fare for children 4-12. Children under 4 travel free.

EURAILPASS BONUSES

There are no Eurailpass bonuses in Portugal or Spain.

ONE-DAY EXCURSIONS AND CITY SIGHTSEEING

Here are 67 one-day rail trips that can be made comfortably from 13 major Spanish and Portuguese cities, returning to them in most cases before dinner-time. Notes are provided on what to see and do at each destination. The number after the name of each route is the Cook's timetable.

The 13 base cities are: Barcelona, Cordoba, Granada, Leon, Lisbon, Madrid, Porto, Regua, San Sebastian, Seville, Tarragona, Valencia and Vigo.

This section concludes with details on 12 rail trips recommended for exceptional scenery plus 6 trips to/from Madrid, the schedules for 2 other major routes (Barcelona-Valencia and Lisbon-Seville), and the international rail connections from Portugal and Spain.

Barcelona

There is rail service (Table 413) between the center of Barcelona (Sants railstation) and the city's airport every 30 minutes from 06:12 to 22:42. The rail service from the airport to the city is every 30 minutes from 06:00 to 22:30.

Local trains, not requiring seat reservations, depart from Barcelona's underground Paseo de Garcia and Sants railstations. Faster express trains, requiring seat reservations, also depart from Paseo de Garcia and from Sants, as well as from Barcelona's Termino station.

Your sightseeing here can be divided into covering 4 separate areas of Barcelona. In the Gothic Quarter: The cloisters in the 14th century Cathedral (La Seu), the Episcopal Palace, Palacio de la Generalidad, many elegant 14th and 15th century palaces, the Federico Mares Museum. The Picasso Museum.

In the Montjuich area: the Museum of Catalan Art in the National Palace, the collection of El Greco, Velasquez and Rembrandt paintings at the Archaeological Museum in Palacio Real, handicrafts and architecture representing every region of Spain in the Spanish Village.

In the Tibidado area: Pedralbes Palace, Pedralbes Monastery, and the view all the way to Montserrat and the Pyrenees.

In the modern city center: Stroll the mile-long Ramblas, from Plaza de Cataluna to Plaza Puerta de la Paz at the waterfront, with its Columbus monument. You will enjoy seeing the numerous stalls selling hundreds of varieties of birds, the many stands with flowers and plants, the very large central food market, cafes offering tapas (the local and varied between-meal snacks), and at least half the population of Barcelona. Visit the Picasso Museum, for exhibits of his early Impressionist works. Another rewarding walk, in the opposite direction, is along beautiful Paseo de Gracia, from Plaza de Cataluna to Avenida del Generalismo Franco (also called "Diagonal", its original name), to see luxury shops, decorative sidewalks designed by Dali, and several buildings created by Barcelona's most radical and inventive architect, Antonio Gaudi.

In Plaza Gaudi, you must see the uncompleted and absolutely unique church, La Sagrada Familia, the architect's most important work. It was started in 1884. Because of lack of funds, Barcelonians believe construction will not be finished until 100 years from now.

What has been constructed in the last 100 years is well worth seeing: the 4 lofty towers (nearly 300 feet tall), the Nativity and Passion facades with the Tree of Life supported by the central arch, and the wrought-iron plants in the side chapels of the completed crypt.

Although public transportation is not available to the Gaudi-designed park, Parque Guell, we suggest you take a taxi there to see it and to see the view of Barcelona from its elevated plaza. The paths in this park are decorated with concrete pillars that imitate trees and vines. Also see the colorful undulating bench surfaced with broken ceramic pieces, on the plaza. And the gigantic tiled frog fountain on the steps leading down from the park's plaza.

Regular city tours include only the church and one apartment building designed by Gaudi. A guided tour of most of his projects is offered by the Municipal Tourist Office (Avenida Paralelo 202) for both individuals and groups.

Lisbon

Santa Apolonia is Lisbon's railstation for departure to Madrid and beyond (to France and the rest of Europe). It has currency exchange and hotel reservation services.

See the beautiful Avenida de Liberdade. The Tower of Belem (monument to Portugal's sailors). The view from the bi-cultural St. George's Castle, built by the Visigoths in the 5th century and by the Moors in the 9th century. Largo das Portas do Sol (Sun Gateway), one of the 7 gates into the ancient Arab City. Santa Cruz quarter. Alfama Quarter. Salazar Bridge.

The lovely Praco de Rossio. The marvelous collection of tapestries, jewelry, ceramics, and Dutch, Spanish and Italian paintings in the Ancient Art Museum. The more than 3,000 art treasures (Rembrandt, Fragonard, Corot, many Impressionists, Egyptian sculpture, Persian art) in the Gulbenkian Museum.

Edward VII Park. The Zoological Garden. The Botanical Garden. The Museum of Modern Art. The Municipal Museum. The greatest collection in the world of royal coaches in the Belem Palace at Praca Afonso de Albuquerque. The Flea Market. The Military Museum. The collection of 17th and 18th century Portuguese and Indo-Portuguese furnishings in the Museum of Decorative Arts.

The Maritime Museum, in the West wing of Jeronimos Monastery. Jeronimo's Church. The Cathedral. House of Facets, its front entirely faced with dark stones that have been cut into diamond-like facets.

Madrid

There is train service connecting Madrid's Chamartin and Atocha stations. A Eurailpass *can* be used on it. At Chamartin station, look for the track marked "Linea de Atocha y Guadalajara". At Atocha, go to the separate small station, a short walk from the main station. "Atocha- Apeadero" is a lower level at Atocha railstation.

See the Prado Museum, with its breathtaking collection of great paintings (open Tuesday- Saturday 09:00-19:00, Sunday 09:00-14:00). Puerta del Sol. The Goya Pantheon. Plaza Mayor. San Miguel Basilica. San Isidor Cathedral.

Two-hour, guided tours of the Royal Palace take you nearly a mile through 52 sumptuously furnished rooms on the main floor. Open Monday-Saturday 09:30-12:45 and 18:00-17:45, Sundays and holidays only 09:30-12:45.

CAUTION: the Palace is closed to the public about 60 days a year for official functions. Check in advance about the day you plan to tour it.

At the Palace, you will see more than 400 antique clocks (keeping perfect time), paintings (Velasquez and Goya), and 15th and 18th century Flemish tapestries. Then, spend more hours seeing the magnificent Armory. Also, visit the Carriage Museum, near the west gate.

The Music Museum has 5 instruments made by Stradivari. Other fascinating rooms in the Palace are the State Apartments and Chapel, Apartments of Queen Maria Cristina of Hapsburg, the Private Apartments, Royal Pharmacy, Library, Numismatic Museum and Music Museum.

Additional interesting sights in Madrid are the Botanical Garden. The Bullfighting Museum. Descalzas Reales Convent. The Archaeological Museum. The Folk Museum. The Americas Museum. Retiro Park. University City. Plaza de Espana, with its stone monument to Cervantes. The Royal Tapestry Factory, closed Sunday during August.

For the best food in Spain, and it is moderately priced, dine at Restaurante Botin, at Calle de Cuchilleros 17. Every dish is marvelous. Their specialties are roast suckling pig and roast baby goat. These and many other foods are cooked there with oak wood in the original 16th century tiled oven. Botin is run by a very handsome gentleman, Antonio Gonzalez Jr. His family has operated Botin for more than 90 years.

San Sebastian

Excellent beaches. The Goya and El Greco collection at San Sebastian Picture Gallery. Santa Maria Church. San Telmo Museum. The Aquarium and Oceanographic Museum in Sea Palace, open daily 10:00 – 13:30 and 15:00 – 20:00. The picturesque fishing village nearby. Mount Urgull.

Seville

The city of Don Juan and Carmen. You must not miss seeing Corpus Christi Cathedral, largest Gothic cathedral in the world and the site of Columbus' tomb.

The 14th century Alcazar Palace with its magnificent chambers, particularly the room where foreign ambassadors were received. Its colorful mosaics and tiles, delicate wrought-iron and carved wood ceilings are spellbinding. You can see nearby Segovia from the tower of Isabella's castle. Allow time to stroll through the elaborate gardens there: bronze and marble statues, lovely fountains and the extraordinary Pavillion of Carlos V.

On one side of the Alcazar is a university, formerly Antigua Fabrica de Tobacos, the tobacco factory Bizet immortalized in his opera, Carmen. On the other side of the Alcazar is Barrio de Santa Cruz, with its ancient buildings and narrow streets. Once a refuge for Jews fleeing the Inquisition, now it is a fashionable residential section of Seville.

You can enjoy spending many hours in Maria Luisa Park, seeing the beautiful buildings, gardens, pools and fountains there. Particularly noteworthy is the magnificent Plaza de Espana.

Other notable sights in Seville: The 12th century La Giralda Tower, a minaret when the Moors ruled here (open only on Sundays and holidays 11:00 – 14:00). The 12-sided Tower of Gold. Meander along the city's cobbled streets to see many picturesque homes.

RESERVATIONS ARE STRONGLY ADVISED
ON ALL SPANISH TRAINS !!

In the following timetables, where a city has more than one railstation we have designated the particular station (in parentheses).

Barcelona - Blanes - Barcelona 416

Go to the "Estacion de Cercanias" (suburban section of Barcelona's Termino railstation) to board the train for Blanes. Seat reservations are not required for this ride. Board well before departure time to avoid standing for 70 minutes.

All of these trains are second- class only.

Take a bus or taxi from Blanes' railstation to the center of the village. It is a half- mile walk there from the station.

Dep. Barcelona (Sants)	Frequent times from 05:47 to 21:58
Arr. Blanes	90 minutes later

Sights in **Blanes**: Stroll the waterfront. See the Aquarium and Botanical Garden, near the location of the daily fish auction, at 17:00. The Gothic fountain. The Church of Santa Maria. The view of the Bay of Blanes from the ruins of the castle on San Juan Mountain. it is a short drive to many popular beaches: Santa Catalina, Fanals, Lloret and Tossa.

Sights in **Lloret de Mar**: See the remains of the Tower of the Moors. The colored tiles that decorate the Church of San Roman. The 11th century castle at the beach. There is an active nightlife here (discotheques, nightclubs and casinos).

Sights in **Tossa de Mar**: Exhibits of Roman archaeology, modern paintings and sculptures (Catalan and foreign), and a 1933 painting of the town by Marc Chagall in the Town Museum, open 10:00 – 13:00 and 17:00 – 20:00. See the view from the lighthouse.

Dep. Blanes	Frequent times from 06:30 to 21:11
Arr. Barcelona (Sants)	90 minutes later

Barcelona - Girona - Barcelona 416

All of these trains are second-class only, unless designated otherwise.

Dep. Barcelona (Sants)	07:23 (1)	08:10	09:55 (2)	10:10	10:58 (3)
Dep. Barcelona (P. de G.)	-0-	08:16	10:01	10:16	-0-
Arr. Girona	08:56	09:59	11:03	11:50	13:12

Sights in **Girona**: The collection of paintings, sculptures, ceramics, glass objects, coins and silverware at the Art Museum in the former Episcopal Palace, open 10:00 – 13:00 and 16:30 – 19:00. Exhibits of local history and art in the Museum of the History of the city, open Monday – Saturday 10:00 – 14:00 and 17:00 – 19:00, Sundays and holidays 9:30 – 14:30.

The Museum in the magnificent 14th century Cathedral has such outstanding exhibits as the 11th century Tapestry of Creation. the 10th century Book of the Apocalypse, and the 10th century Arab chest of Hisham II, the oldest Hispanic-Arab work of silver. It is open daily 10:00 – 13:00 and 15:30 – 18:00.

The Provincial Archaeological Museum is open daily 10:30– 13:00 and 16:30 – 19:00.

Visit the 12th century Arab Baths. See Sobreportes, the ancient gate. Stroll on the narrow 17th century streets.

(Timetable continues on page 182.)

182

Dep. Girona	11:41	13:29	14:19	15:19	15:46 (4)
Arr. Barcelona (P. de G.)	13:13	15:11	15:53	17:04	-0-
Arr. Barcelona (Sants)	13:17	15:16	15:58	17:09	17:57

(1) Supplement charged. Has a first-class coach. Light refreshments. (2) Reservation required. Supplement charged. Restaurant car. (3) Plus another departure from Barcelona (Sants) at 12:15, arriving Girona 14:01. (4) Plus other departures from Girona at 17:09, 18:26, 19:42 (1), 20:04 (2), 20:40 and 21:59, arriving Barcelona (Sants) 18:51, 20:22, 21:15, 21:18, 22:27 and 23:37.

Barcelona - Lerida - Barcelona   410

It is advisable to make a reservation for this ride well in advance of departure date. Although departures are from other stations, go to Triunfo station to make this reservation. On boarding, find a seat on the left-hand side so as to have a good view of the restored 13th century hilltop Seo Antigua Cathedral before the arrival in Lerida.

All of these trains charge a supplement and are air- conditioned. Reservation advisable.

Dep. Barcelona (Paseo de Gracia)	07:17 (1)	10:51 (2)	11:17 (1)
Dep. Barcelona (Sants)	07:30	11:00	11:25
Arr. Lerida	09:20	13:03	13:46

Sights in **Lerida**: The Archaeological Museum, in the Antiguo Hospital de Santa Maria, where the tourist office is located. A walking tour is easy with the city map available there. See the old Byzantine-Gothic-Moorish 13th century Cathedral. The Palacio de la Paheria. Stroll the maze of narrow streets in the interesting old section on the right bank of the Segre River, and visit the 12th century Alcazaba (castle).

Dep. Lerida	15:37 (1)	16:15 (2)	20:06 (2)	20:53
Arr. Barcelona (Sants)	18:00	18:30	22:00	22:50
Arr. Barcelona (Paseo de Gracia)	18:08	18:44	-0-	22:54

(1) Light refreshment. (2) Restaurant car.

Barcelona - Montserrat - Barcelona   Spanish timetable

This trip is not covered by Eurailpass.

| Dep. Barcelona (P. Espanya) | Frequent times from 05:20 to 20:10 |
| Arr. Martorell-Enllac | 50-60 minutes later |

Change to cable car.

| Dep. Martorell-Enllac | Frequent times |
| Arr. Monistrol (Monastery) | 5 minutes after departing Martorell-Enllac |

Sights in **Montserrat**: The 9th century Monastery, still occupied by hundreds of Benedictine monks, is 3700 feet above a valley. It ranks with Zaragoza and Santiago de Compostela as one of the most important pilgrimage sites in Spain. See the Grotto of the Virgin, the Mirador, the Chapel of San Miguel and the Chapel of Santa Cecilia. Then take a funicular to the Grotto of San Juan Garin and an aerial tram to the 4,000-foot-high Hermitage of San Jeronimo, from where you will have a view of the Eastern Pyrenees.

| Dep. Monistrol (Monastery) | Frequent times |
| Arr. Martorell-Enllac | 5 minutes later |

Change to train.

| Dep. Martorell-Enllac | Frequent times from 06:35 to 21:39 |
| Arr. Barcelona (P. Espanya) | 50-60 minutes later |

Barcelona - Sitges - Barcelona

Frequent local trains run from Barcelona's Paseo de Gracia and Sants stations to Sitges, a 30-minute trip.

Sights in **Sitges:** The 18th century furnishings at Casa Llopis. Antique dolls collected from every part of Europe, in the Lola Anglada Museum. El Greco paintings at the Cap Ferrat Museum.

Barcelona - Tarragona - Barcelona

Frequent local trains run from Barcelona's Paseo de Gracia and Sants stations to Tarragona, a 90-minute trip.

Sights in **Tarragona:** Relics of pre-Roman, Roman, Visigothic and Moorish cultures.

It is a short, but severely uphill, walk from the railstation to the long promenade, Balcon del Mediterraneo, from which there is a marvelous view of the sea. Two strolling streets start at each end of the "balcony". The first is Rambla del Generalismo. The other is Rambla de San Carlos.

We suggest you rest a while at one of the many sidewalk cafes on either Rambla. Then, start your walking tour of Tarragona by going 2 blocks from the "balcony", down Rambla de San Carlos to where it intersects with San Augustin. Turn right (the street name changes to "Mayor") and walk one- quarter mile to the 12th century Cathedral, worth seeing for its large and architecturally unique Cloisters, influenced by Roman, Gothic and Moorish styles.

Next, return to Rambla de San Carlos and turn right. Walk down it 2 blocks until it intersects with Abalto. Turn right and walk uphill, alongside the Roman wall.

You will then be on the semi-circular Paseo Arqueologico walk, from which there are excellent views of the countryside surrounding Tarragona.

At the end of this walk, bear to the right and come downhill on Avenida de la Victoria for 5 minutes until you reach Plaza del Rey. There, you can visit both the museum in the 1st century B.C. Pretoria and also the marvelous mosaics and ancient coins in the Archaeological Museum.

Across from Plaza del Rey is the Roman Amphitheater. Having completed a circle, you will again be at Balcon del Mediterraneo, and it is all downhill to return to the railstation.

Granada - Malaga - Granada   439

Between Bobadilla and Malaga, the train travels through the spectacular **El Chorro Gorge**.

All of these trains are second-class only.

Dep. Granada	08:15	Dep. Malaga	13:45	18:35
Arr. Bobadilla	10:11	Arr. Bobadilla	15:01	19:37
Change trains.		Change trains.		
Dep. Bobadilla	10:15	Dep. Bobadilla	15:15	19:40
Arr. Malaga	11:14	Arr. Granada	17:28	21:39

Sights in **Malaga**: Winter sun. The 9th century Alcazaba Moslem palace and the ruins of Gibralfaro Castle, 2 fortresses which made Malaga a major stronghold in the Middle Ages. The Fine Arts Museum. Sagrario, an unusual rectangular church that was originally a mosque. The Cathedral

Lisbon - Algarve Resorts

The 100-mile Algarve (Lisbon-Vila Real de Santo Antonio) coastline, famous for its many popular resorts, consists of several centuries-old fishing villages and offers championship golf courses, tennis, horseback riding and all the watersports (windsurfing, fishing, water skiing, yachting).

Lisbon - Vila Real   449

All of these trains have light refreshments. There is 15-minute ferry service **Vila Real** to **Ayamonte** (Spain) every 30 minutes. Summer: 08:00 – 23:30. Winter: 09:00 – 18:00

Boat			Train		
Dep. Lisbon			Dep. Vila Real	-0-	06:33 (6)
(Ferry Ter.)	07:40	07:40 (2)	Dep. Faro	-0-	07:50
Arr. Barreiro	08:10	08:10	Dep. Albufeira	-0-	08:23
Change to train.			Dep. Lagos	07:15 (5)	-0-
Dep. Barreiro	08:25	08:25	Arr. Tunes	08:20 (3)	08:29
Arr. Tunes	12:12	12:12 (3)	Dep. Tunes	08:42	08:42
Dep. Tunes	12:17	12:25	Arr. Barriero	12:25	12:25
Arr. Lagos	-0-	13:32	Change to boat.		
Arr. Albufeira	12:24	-0-	Dep. Barriero	12:35	12:35
Dep. Faro	12:58	-0-	Arr. Lisbon		
Arr. Vila Real	14:03	-0-	(Ferry Ter.)	13:05	13:05

(1) Plus another Lisbon departure for Vila Real at 00:10. Plus other Lisbon departures for Tunes, Albufeira and Faro at 14:10, 18:00 and 00:10. (2) Plus other departures for Tunes and Lagos at 14:10 (3), 18:30 (3) and 00:10 (4). (3) Change trains in Tunes. (4) Direct train. No train change in Tunes. (5) Plus other departures from Lagos at 13:45, 17:00 and 00:15. (6) Plus other departures from Via Real at 16:15 and 23:48.

Sights in **Lagos**: This historic town was the center for the Portugal-Africa trade. See the marvelous tiles in the Baroque Chapel of San Antonio.

Sights in **Albufeira**: The Moorish ambiance here is striking. This is a very "arty" place. Has a colorful market.

Sights in **Faro**: The ancient church. The old quarter.

Lisbon - Setubal and Lisbon - Evora   448

All of these trains are second-class only.

Boat					
Dep. Lisbon (Ferry Ter.)	06:45	07:55	08:25	09:35	11:05
Arr. Barreiro	07:15	08:25	08:55	10:05	11:35
Change to train.					
Dep. Barriero	07:25	08:37	09:35	10:45	12:05
Arr. Setubal	08:18	-0-	10:27	11:28	12:51
Arr. Casa Branca	-0-	10:01 (1)	-0-	-0-	-0-
Arr. Evora	-0-	10:43	-0-	-0-	-0-

Sights in **Setubal**: The paintings in the Town Museum. Next to it, the lovely Church of Jesus. The view from the 16th century Saint Philip's Castle, while having lunch there. Many sardine canneries, some of them open to the public. The Maritime Museum. Take an inexpensive taxi ride to the nearby (5½ miles) Palmela Castle.

Sights in **Evora**: Portugal's "Museum City". The Tourist Information Office faces the main square, Praca Do Giraldo. See the beautiful Temple of Diana, oldest Roman remains on the Iberian Peninsula. Visit the excellent regional museum in what was once the Bishop's Palace. The 17th century monastery, now an inn called Pousada dos Loios. The Church of St. Francis, where the walls are decorated with the skulls and bones of nearly 5,000 monks.

Dep. Evora	-0-	-0-	14:10 (1)	-0-	19:25 (1+4)
Dep. Casa Branca	-0-	-0-	15:05	-0-	20:18
Dep. Setubal	12:39	13:17	-0-	16:52 (3)	-0-
Arr. Barriero	13:28	14:10	15:45	17:37	21:40
Change to boat.					
Dep. Barreiro	13:40	14:15	15:55	17:45	21:50
Arr. Lisbon (Ferry Ter.)	30 minutes later				

(1) Change trains in Casa Branca. (2) Runs Monday–Friday, except holydays. (3) Plus other Setubal departures at 18:50 (2), 19:35, 21:10 and 22:00. (4) Plus other Evora departures at 19:25 (1) and 22:08 (1).

Lisbon - Coimbra - Lisbon 445

All of these trains have light refreshments.

Dep. Lisbon (S. Apol.)	07:20 (1)	08:40 (1)	11:10 (2)	11:35 (3)
Arr. Coimbra	09:27	10:39	13:09	14:07

Sights in **Coimbra:** Walk uphill to the 13th century Old Cathedral, one of the finest Romanesque buildings in Portugal. Continue to the treasures at the Machado do Castro Museum. At the top of the hill is the 13th century University, where you must see the gilded carved stone and wood and the Baroque library. Also see the silver shrine in the magnificent interior of the New Convent of St. Clara. The Almedina Gate. Nearby, the Roman ruins at **Conimbriga.** Try the local food specialty, roasted suckling pig (leitao).

Dep. Coimbra	13:50 (3)	15:49 (1)	17:19 (3)	18:19 (1)	20:14 (4)	20:45 (3)
Arr. Lisbon (S. Apol.)	16:20	17:50	19:50	20:20	22:23	23:15

(1) Reservation required. Supplement charged. (2) Runs daily, except Sundays and holidays. Reservation required. Supplement charged. (3) Reservation advisable. (4) Reservation required.

Lisbon - Estoril and Cascais - Lisbon

Dep. Lisbon (Cais do Sodre)	Every 20-30 minutes
Arr. Estoril	29 minutes later
Arr. Cascais	4 minutes after departing Estoril

Sights in **Estoril:** Portugal's major beach resort. Try your luck in the gambling Casino.

Sights in **Cascais:** Bloodless bullfights on Summer Sundays. Surf fishing. Wednesday is market day, on the street that veers right from the railstation. There are taxis that will take you to Sintra (see "Lisbon-Sintra" on page 186.)

Dep. Cascais	Every 20-30 minutes
Dep. Estoril	4 minutes later
Arr. Lisbon (Cais do Sodre)	29 minutes after departing Estoril

Lisbon - Fatima - Lisbon

Cook did not carry this route in 1991. Journey time was 1 ½ – 2 hours in prior years.

Dep. Lisbon (S. Apol.)
Arr. Fatima

Sights in **Fatima:** Millions of pilgrims have come here from all over the world to worship at one of the world's most famous Marian Shrines. Pope Paul VI was here on May 13, 1967.

Dep. Fatima
Arr. Lisbon (S. Apol.)

Lisbon - Figueira da Foz - Lisbon   444

| Dep. Lisbon (Rossio) | 07:40 | 13:00 (1) | 17:48 (1) | 19:25 (2) |
| Arr. Figueira da Foz | 11:19 | 16:30 | 21:27 | 22:42 |

Sights in **Figueira da Foz:** The Casa do Paco Museum, with what is said to be the world's greatest collection of Delft tiles. Try your luck in the Casino Oceano.

| Dep. Figueira da Foz | 07:10 (2) | 13:30 (1) | 18:12 | -0- |
| Arr. Lisbon (Rossio) | 10:11 | 16:52 | 21:40 | -0- |

(1) Reservation advisable. (2) Reservation required.

Lisbon - Porto (Oporto) - Lisbon   445

All of these trains have buffet or light refreshments.

| Dep. Lisbon (S. Apol.) | 07:00 (1) | 07:20 (2) | 08:40 (3) | 08:50 (4) |
| Arr. Porto (Campanha) | 10:00 | 10:54 | 12:00 | 13:10 |

Sights in **Porto**: The more than 80 wine stores occupying all of the Vila Nova de Gaia quarter. The 12th century Cathedral. The 3 great bridges: Dom Louis, Dona Maria and Ponte da Arrabida. Portugal's oldest chapel, Sao Martinho de Cedofeita. The gilded woodcarvings in the Church of San Francisco.

The Church of the Clerigos, with its 10-story tower. The city's many beautiful gardens. The 15th century Church of Santa Clara. The Moorish Hall of the Stock Exchange. The 14th century convent-fortress, Leca do Bailio Abbey. The fine paintings, sculpture, porcelain and jewelry at the Soares dos Reis Museum. The folklore objects of this region in the Ethnological Museum.

| Dep. Porto (Campanha) | 14:30 (3) | 15:30 (4) | 17:00 (3) | 18:45 (2) | 18:55 (4) | 20:20 (1) |
| Arr. Lisbon (S. Apol.) | 17:50 | 19:50 | 20:20 | 22:23 | 23:15 | 23:20 |

(1) Runs daily, except Sundays and holidays. Reservation required. Supplement charged. (2) Reservation required. (3) Reservation required. Supplement charged. (4) Reservation advisable.

Porto - Braga - Porto   446

Change trains in Nines, unless designated otherwise.

| Dep. Porto (Cam.) | 06:27 (1) | 07:32 (2) | 08:24 | 09:42 | 10:32 (3) | 12:07 (1) | 13:15 |
| Arr. Braga | 08:16 | 09:01 | 10:15 | 11:18 | 11:51 | 13:18 | 14:52 |

Sights in **Braga**: The most interesting buildings are on the narrow street that runs from Arco da Porta Nova to the Praca da Republica. (It changes its name along the way.)

See the beautiful Santa Barbara Gardens. The treasury at the Cathedral (gold and ivory crosiers, also damask and velvet vestments embroidered with heavy gold thread). The museum in the Casa dos Biscainhos. The terraced gardens that ascend uphill to the church of Bom Jesus.

| Dep. Braga | 12:45 | 13:28 | 15:36 | 16:40 | 17:25 (4) | 17:33 (1) | 18:18 (5+6) |
| Arr. Porto (Cam.) | 14:12 | 15:07 | 16:48 | 18:13 | 18:30 | 19:16 | 20:09 |

(1) Direct train. No train change in Nines. (2) Reservation advisable. Light refreshments. (3) Reservation advisable. (4) Direct train. Reservation required. Light refreshments. (5) Runs daily, except Saturday. (6) Plus other departures from Braga at 19:27, 21:02 (1+5), 21:27 (5) and 22:11 (2), arriving Porto 21:00, 22:40, 23:14 and 23:36.

Lisbon - Sintra - Queluz - Lisbon

| Dep. Lisbon (Rossio) | Frequent times |
| Arr. Sintra | 45 minutes later |

Sights in **Sintra**: An old town, nestled on a mountaintop. There are many antique and craft shops on this village's winding, narrow streets. Take the "Sintra-Vila" bus from the railstation to the city's tourist office, where guide books and maps are available.

Use inexpensive taxis to see the view from the 19th century Palacio de Pena, the Moorish Castle, the Palacio Real and the marvelous gardens at the Palacio de Monserrate. The palaces are closed on Tuesday.

Dep. Sintra   Frequent times
Arr. Queluz   20 minutes later

Sights in **Queluz**: The beautiful gardens, the monument to Maria I and the exquisite restaurant at the 18th century Palacio de Queluz, a miniature Versailles.

Dep. Queluz   Frequent times
Arr. Lisbon (Rossio)   21 minutes later

Madrid - Aranjuez - Madrid

	420	420	420	425	425	420
Dep. Madrid (Ch.)	08:00 (1)	-0-	09:00 (1)	09:31 (2)	10:30 (3)	-0-
Dep. Madrid (Atocha)	-0-	09:00	09:12	09:45	10:42	11:00 (2)
Arr. Aranjuez	08:41	09:39	09:41	10:25	11:14	11:41

Sights in **Aranjuez**: The Museum of Royal Robes, the luxurious interiors of the Porcelain Room (walls and cielings covered with red and green figures depicting Chinese and Japanese themes), the intricately chiseled Moorish interior of the Arab Chamber, the more than 200 drawings from the Ching Dynasty in the Chinese Print Room, and the Throne Room all in the Royal Palace, which has guided tours that are usually in Spanish. See the bed of Queen Isabella II, inlaid with carvings, floral decorations and bronze ornaments.

There are guided tours of the magnificent furnishings in the 18 rooms at the 18th century Casa del Labrador, where a 19th century clock in the form of Hadrian's Column is exhibited in the sculpture gallery. (A ruby and pearl-studded star strikes the hour by spiraling up and down the column.) Platinum, gold and bronze decorations are displayed in the Platinum Chamber. There are many silk wall tapestries in this palace.

The Pastere and Island gardens. The collection of royal ships in the Casa de Marinos.

	420	425	420	420	425	425
Dep. Aranjuez	13:24 (3)	13:41 (1)	15:45 (4)	17:41 (2)	18:35 (3)	19:50 (2+5)
Arr. Madrid (Atocha)	14:10	14:13	16:25	18:20	-0-	20:32
Arr. Madrid (Ch.)	-0-	14:28	-0-	-0-	19:33	20:47

(1) Suppplement charged. Light refreshments. (2) Second-class only. (3) Buffet or light refreshments. (4) Runs daily, except Saturday. (5) Plus other Aranjuez departures [table 420] at 20:17 and 22:14, arriving Madrid (Atocha) 21:00 and 22:51.

Madrid - Avila - Madrid   435

Dep. Madrid (Atocha)	06:30 (1)	-0-	08:04 (3)	09:15 (4)
Dep. Madrid (Cham.)	06:44	08:00 (2)	08:18	09:30
Arr. Avila	08:30	09:24	10:04	11:11

Sights in **Avila**: There are bus and inexpensive taxi services from Avila's railstation to the city center, about one mile from the station. Take a stroll on the 1 1/2-mile long 11th century walls that circle Avila to see best the 88 semi-circular towers and more than 2,300 battlements (11:00-13:00 and 16:15-18:00, closed weekday afternoons from October through April).

Also see the El Greco painting and the enormous (nearly 200 pounds) silver monstrance in the fortress Cathedral. The baroque 17th century Convent of St. Teresa. The Basilica of St. Vincent.

Dep. Avila	13:43 (2)	15:36	18:36 (4)	19:17 (5)	20:04 (2+6)
Arr. Madrid (Cham.)	15:10	17:13	20:10	20:50	21:30
Arr. Madrid (Atocha)	15:41	17:29	20:25	-0-	-0-

(1) Runs Monday–Friday, except holidays. (2) Supplement charged. Light refreshments. (3) Runs Saturdays, Sundays and holidays. (4) Second-class only. (5) Supplement charged. Restaurant car. (6) Plus another departure from Avila at 21:43 (4), arriving Madrid (Cham.) 23:10.

Madrid - Burgos - Madrid   435

Both of these trains require reservation, charge a supplement, are air-conditioned and have light refreshments.

Dep. Madrid (Ch.)	08:00	Dep. Burgos	18:42
Arr. Burgos	11:40	Arr. Madrid (Ch.)	21:55

Sights in **Burgos**: The many interesting chapels in the magnificent 13th century Cathedral of Santa Maria, where the remains are of Spain's greatest hero, El Cid, and those of his wife. The Archaeological Museum. Stroll 15 minutes on Paseo del Espolon, from the 14th century Arch of Santa Maria to the statue of El Cid.

To see the Royal Monastery of Las Huelgas, only a few minutes outside Burgos, take a bus from Plaza de Jose Antonio.

Madrid - Cuenca - Madrid   420

Dep. Madrid (Ato.)	09:00	10:00 (1)	Dep. Cuenca	15:30 (1)	18:31
Arr. Cuenca	11:36	14:14	Arr. Madrid (Ato.)	18:20	21:00

(1) Second-class only.

Sights in **Cuenca**: The Tourist Information Office (Calderon de la Barca 28) is only a 5-minute walk from the railstation.

Strolling down the winding lanes and narrow footpaths is marvelous. See the old houses hanging from sheer cliffs in this 15th century setting. The best modern art museum in Spain, Museo de Arte Abstrato. Wonderful El Greco paintings and 15th and 16th century altarpieces in the cathedral. A few steps away from the Cathedral, the collection of coins, statues and Roman mosaics at the Archaeological Museum in a restored 14th century granary.

Paleolithic red paintings of bison, wild boars, horses and archers at La Pena del Escrito National Monument.

Madrid - Escorial - Madrid   435

Dep. Madrid (Ato.)	09:15 (1)	12:05 (1)	Dep. Escorial	16:30	19:30 (1)
Dep. Madrid (Ch.)	09:30	12:20	Arr. Madrid (Ch.)	17:13	20:10
Arr. Escorial	10:14	13:07	Arr. Madrid (Ato.)	17:29	20:25

(1) Second-class only.

Sights in **Escorial**: Burial place of Spanish kings and queens. The Royal Monastery of San Lorenzo del Escorial, an enormous granite fortress (300 rooms), has more than 1,600 paintings (many of the finest Velasquez and El Greco) and murals, and it houses the Charter Hall Royal Library, containing 60,000 volumes.

See the Phillip II Apartments, the Throne Room, Apartments of the Bourbon kings, Whispering Hall, Casita del Principe, and the Basilica.

The Basilica was intended to copy St. Peter's in Rome, filled with gilt and marble carvings. Its 4 enormous pillars are 100 feet in circumference and support a cupola more than 300 feet high. Life-size bronze figures (royal families) surround the 100-foot-high altar.

The 18th century Prince's Cottage has 9 elaborately furnished rooms. Don't miss seeing the famous cross by Benvenuto Cellini and paintings by El Greco, Ribera and Velasquez in the church.

The circular, domed Royal Pantheon, crypt for most of the Spanish kings since the 17th century. Thirty feet underground, it contains 26 charcoal-gray marble coffins, in 5 tiers, and is illuminated by Italian baroque candelabra. Lesser royalty rest in white marble coffins in other rooms.

In planning a visit here, keep in mind that this enormous 16th century building covers 8 acres. It is open 10:00–13:00 and 15:30–18:30 (18:00 in Winter).

Also visit the nearby monumental Valley of the Fallen, memorializing those who died in Spain's civil war. A 492-foot-high cross of concrete faced with stone marks this crypt containing more than 100,000 bodies. Its 900-foot-long Basilica is a tunnel into the mountain. You can ride to the top of the cross in an elevator.

Madrid - Salamanca - Madrid 435

All of these trains are second-class only.

Dep. Madrid (Principe Pio)	09:30	Dep. Salamanca	17:00	19:35 (1)
Arr. Salamanca	13:12	Arr. Madrid (Principe Pio)	20:30	23:11

(1) Runs Sunday only.

Sights in **Salamanca:** The Convent of San Sebastian. The House of Shells. The 15th and 16th century houses around the beautiful Plaza Mayor. The oldest university in Spain. The church and cloister at St. Stephens Monastery.

Madrid - Segovia - Madrid

Train service was discontinued in 1991.

Madrid - Toledo - Madrid 433

Seat reservations are not required or obtainable for this ride. Board well before departure time to avoid standing for entire ride. The walk from Toledo's railstation to the center of that city is long. It is best to take a bus or taxi.

Dep. Madrid (Cham.)	-0-	09:05	10:35 (1)	12:06	-0-
Dep. Madrid (Atocha)	08:05 (1)	09:20	10:50	12:20	13:50
Arr. Toledo	09:25	10:27	12:07	13:19	15:06

Sights in **Toledo**: The most spectacular Cathedral in Spain (750 stained-glass windows, priceless church clothing, jeweled ornaments, hundreds of tapestries, and paintings by Goya, El Greco, Velasquez, Tintoretto, Murillo and Titian). The house of El Greco, with a superb collection of his paintings. The 15th century Palace of the Duchess of Lerma. The Church of Santo Tome, containing El Greco's "Burial of the Count of Orgaz".

The Sefardi Museum in the 14th century El Transito Synagogue. The Provincial Museum of Archaeology and Fine Arts in the 16th century Hospital de Santa Cruz. The Army Museum in the Alcazar (fortress).

(Timetable continues on page 190.)

The Museum of Santa Cruz. Cristo de la Luz, the church first built in the 11th century as a Mosque (on the site of the ruins of a Visigothic church). It was then converted into a Catholic church in the 12th century. The works of Spain's leading modern sculptor, in the Vitorio Macho Museum.

Dep. Toledo	12:40	13:45 (1)	15:45 (1)	17:00	18:05	19:15 (2)
Arr. Madrid (Atocha)	13:41	15:02	17:03	18:10	19:13	20:16
Arr. Madrid (Cham.)	14:02	15:21	-0-	18:27	19:32	20:33

(1) Second-class only. (2) Plus other departures from Toledo at 20:50 (1) and 22:05 (1), arriving Madrid (Atocha) 22:02 and 23:36.

Madrid - Valladolid - Madrid   435

Dep. Madrid (Atocha)	06:30 (1)	-0-	08:04 (3)	09:15 (4)	10:35 (2+5)
Dep. Madrid (Cham.)	06:44	08:00 (2)	08:18	09:30	-0-
Arr. Valladolid	09:47	10:30	11:21	12:30	13:03

Sights in **Valladolid**: The National Museum of (Wood) Sculpture in San Gregorio College, founded in the 15th century by the confessor to Isabella, one of the finest museums in Spain, open Tuesday–Saturday 10:00–14:00 and 16:00–19:00. Its life-size 15-16th century carvings are famous for their emotive and natural expressions, swirling draperies, and their realistic, vivid colors.

These sculptures were carved for religious processions and also to fill many of the magnificent and very complex altars that still remain in churches and museums throughout Spain. Visit the adjacent Church of San Pablo.

Sculptures, carvings and massive gold and silver objects are exhibited at the Cathedral in a museum that is open Tuesday–Friday 10:00–13:30 and 16:30–19:00; on Saturdays, Sundays and holidays 10:00–14:00.

See Vivero Palace, where Ferdinand and Isabella were married in 1474. The magnificent ceilings and wood sculptures at the National Museum of Sculpture, in the 15th century Colegio de San Gregorio. The wood sculptures in the 15th century Convent of Santa Clara. The 15th century Palace of Santa Cruz.

Cervantes' House, where he spent the last years of his life. Simancas Castle, 7 miles from Valladolid. Charles V converted the castle into a storehouse for state records. It holds 8,000,000 documents that provide a history of Spanish administration from the 16th through the 20th century.

Dep. Valladolid	14:25	17:15 (4)	18:04 (2)	18:57 (2)	20:35 (4)
Arr. Madrid (Cham.)	17:13	20:10	20:50	21:30	23:10
Arr. Madrid (Atocha)	17:29	20:25	-0-	-0-	23:25

(1) Runs Monday–Friday, except holidays. (2) Reservation required. Supplement charged. Light refreshments or restaurant car. (3) Runs Saturdays, Sundays and holidays. (4) Second-class only. (5) Departs from Madrid's Principe Pio railstation.

Madrid - Zaragoza - Madrid   410

All of these trains require reservation and charge a supplement.

Dep. Madrid (Chamartin)	07:00 (1)	09:50 (1)	11:00 (2)
Arr. Zaragoza (Portillo)	10:01	13:20	14:19

Sights in **Zaragoza**: The Tapestry Museum in the Cathedral. The Exchange. Aljaferia, an 11th century Moorish palace. The Basilica de Pilar. The Goya and El Greco paintings at the Museo de Pintura.

Dep. Zaragoza (Portillo)	14:50 (2)	15:35 (1)	17:20 (3)	18:30 (2)	20:00 (1)
Arr. Madrid (Chamartin)	18:15	19:00	20:58	21:45	23:08

(1) Reservation required. Supplement charged. Light refreshments. (2) Reservation advisable. Supplement charged. Air-conditioned. Restaurant car. (3) Light refreshments.

San Sebastian - Bayonne - San Sebastian

	435	28
Dep. San Sebastian (Amara)	07:31 (1)	09:12 (3)
Arr. Hendaye	08:15	-0- (3)
Change trains.		
	137	
Dep. Hendaye	09:38 (2)	-0- (3)
Arr. Bayonne	10:10	12:07

Sights in **Bayonne**: The Cote Basque's leading port and private yacht harbor. The Cathedral. The Basque Museum. The Museum Bonnat. Chateau-Vieux.

	137	28	137	137
Dep. Bayonne	14:38 (2)	15:56 (3)	16:29 (4)	20:36 (2)
Arr. Irun	15:12	-0- (3)	17:09	21:16
Change trains.				
	435		435	435
Dep. Irun	15:55 (1)	-0- (3)	18:35 (5)	23:00
Arr. San Sebastian (Amara)	16:06	18:59	19:04	23:30

(1) Second-class only. (2) TGV. Reservation required. Supplement charged. (3) Direct train San Sebastian-Bayonne and v.v. No train change in Hendaye. Reservation required. Supplement charged. (4) Operates late June to late August. (5) Operates mid-July to early September. (6) Runs Monday–Friday.

San Sebastian - Bilbao - San Sebastian 429

*This second-class narrow-gauge rail trip is **not** covered by Eurailpass.*
Other (slower) trains run on this route at frequent times not listed in Cook.

| Dep. San Sebastian (Amara) | 07:21 | Dep. Bilbao (Concordia) | 13:40 | 20:35 |
| Arr. Bilbao (Concordia) | 09:41 | Arr. San Sebastian (Amara) | 15:55 | 22:42 |

Sights in **Bilbao**: The Fine Arts Museum. The Biscay Historical Museum. The Begona Sanctuary.

San Sebastian - Burgos - San Sebastian 435

| Dep. San Sebastian (Amara) | 08:28 (1) | 08:48 (2) | 09:04 | |
| Arr. Burgos | 11:21 | 12:05 | 12:29 | |

Sights in **Burgo**s: See notes under "Madrid-Burgos" on page 188.

| Dep. Burgos | 16:07 | 17:21 (2) | 18:35 (1) | 21:48 (3) |
| Arr. San Sebastian (Amara) | 19:28 | 20:27 | 21:27 | 01:33 |

(1) Reservation advisable. Supplement charged. Light refreshments. (2) Light refreshments.
(3) Reservation advisable. Supplement charged. Restaurant car. Second-class only.

San Sebastian - Pamplona - San Sebastian 412

All of these trains have light refreshments.

| Dep. San Sebastian (Nor.) | 09:45 (1) | Dep. Pamplona | 16:17 | 17:59 (1) |
| Arr. Pamplona | 11:22 | Arr. San Sebastian (Nor.) | 18:29 | 19:47 |

(1) Supplement charged.

Sights in **Pamplona**: The 14th century Gothic Cathedral, with its cloisters and Diocesan Museum. The Navarre Museum. The running of the bulls through the city's streets, every year between July 6 and July 15.

Seville - Cadiz - Seville 426

| Dep. Seville (S.Justa) | 06:35 (1) | 08:17 (1) | 11:30 | | |
| Arr. Cadiz | 09:00 | 10:35 | 13:18 | | |

Sights in **Cadiz**: The African environment. The Fine Arts Museum. The Museum of Archaeology and Art. The Cathedral, with its monumental Silver Tabernacle, decorated with almost 1,000,000 jewels. The Historical Museum.

| Dep. Cadiz | 13:30 (2) | 15:10 | 17:45 (1) | 20:00 | 22:10 |
| Arr. Seville (S.Justa) | 15:05 | 16:59 | 19:54 | 20:23 | 00:07 |

(1) Light refreshments. (2) Supplement charged. Restaurant car.

Seville - Cordoba - Seville   426

Dep. Seville (S. Justa)	07:40 (1)	08:53 (2)	11:57 (3)	14:00 (4)
Arr. Cordoba	09:34	10:10	13:34	16:00

Sights in **Cordoba**: One thousand years ago, this was the most important city west of Constantinople (today's Istanbul). Its 200,000 houses *then* were double those of today. See the array of marble, jasper, onyx and granite on the 80 marble columns in the 8th century Mosque, built on top of what was first a Roman temple and later a Catholic church, before the Moors seized Cordoba.

Following the recapture of the city by the Spaniards and in the conversion of the building to a church again, most of the original 1,000 marble columns were removed to provide space for a nave and a high altar. Called "Mezquita", its interior is illuminated by 4,000 bronze and copper lamps. Its ceiling is carved cedar. Its mosaics are made from 35 tons of glass bits. The Mosque is closed from 12:00 to 16:00, and the Alcazar palace fortress is closed from 12:00 to 17:00.

Also see the 14th century Synagogue. The Fine Arts Museum. The Museum of Julio Romero de Torres. The Museum of Cordoban art, with its Bullfight Museum. The Provincial Archaeological Museum, one of the most important archaeological collections in Spain. The Roman Bridge, built in the time of Emperor Augustus. The home of the Marques de Viana, with its 14 flower-filled patios.

Dep. Cordoba	13:30 (1)	16:04 (3)	18:05 (2)	18:25 (1)	19:38 (2+6)
Arr. Seville (S. Justa)	15:42	17:46	19:34	20:28	20:58

(1) Second-class only. (2) Supplement charged. Restaurant car. (3) Light refreshments. (4) Runs daily, except Sundays and holidays. Second-class only. (5) Runs daily except Saturday. Supplement charged. Light refreshments. (6) Plus other departures from Cordoba at 20:35 (1) and 21:35 (5), arriving Seville 22:49 and 22:56.

Seville - Granada - Seville   427

Both of these trains are second-class only.

Dep. Seville (S.Bernardo)	07:45	Dep. Granada	17:40
Arr. Granada	12:12	Arr. Seville (S. Bernardo)	21:53

Sights in **Granada**: The indescribable Alhambra complex, consisting of the Royal Palace, adjacent Partal Gardens, the 9th century Alcazaba watchtower fortress and, a quarter of a mile away, the Generalife (summer palace of Moorish caliphs), one of Europe's greatest gardens.

At the Royal Palace, be sure to see the Court of the Mexuar, the Hall of the Ambassadors, the Court of the Myrtle Trees, the Hall of the Two Sisters, the Court of the Lions, the Royal Baths and the Daraxa courtyard. The Mocarabes Gallery and Abencerrrajes Gallery are near the Court of the Lions.

The Partal Gardens are a series of terraces featuring roses, poinsettias, orange and lime trees, lilies, bouganvillea and carnations.

Also in Granada, see the crypts of Ferdinand and Isabella in the Cathedral's Royal Chapel. The Fine Arts Museum and Hispano-Moorish Museum in Charles V's Palace. The Royal Hospital. Casa Castril.

Seville - Jerez - Seville 426

Dep. Seville (S. Justa)	06:35 (1)	08:17 (1)	11:30
Arr. Jerez	07:48	09:41	12:35

Sights in **Jerez**: A 3,000-year old city, famous for its horses, beautiful women and sherry wine. Its renowned Andalusian horses, bred from Spanish mares and stallions which the Moorish invaders brought here more than 1,500 year ago, do not date as far back as the wine does.

Phoenicians started the vineyards here in 1100 B.C. Later Romans began the vinting of sherry. Many of the best wineries offer tours that conclude with tasting.

See the annual September Wine Festival. Its opening ceremony takes place on the steps that lead into the 17th century Collegiate Church of Santa Maria. Next to it is the 11th century Moorish fort, the Alcazar.

Also visit the 15th century San Dionisio Church. See the exhibit of Punic, Roman and Arabic pottery, tombstones, household implements and statues in the Archaeological Museum that occupies 2 small rooms inside Chapter House on tiny Plaza de la Asuncion, across from San Dionisio Church.

Look for the 7th century BC Corinthian helmet, believed to be the oldest Greek artifact ever found in Spain.

Dep. Jerez	14:07 (2)	18:28 (1)	20:41	23:01
Arr. Seville (S. Justa)	15:05	19:54	22:08	00:07

(1) Light refreshments. (2) Supplement charged. Restaurant car.

Seville - Merida - Seville 430

Schedules have not permitted a one-day excursion Seville-Merida since 1983.

Both of these trains are second-class only.

Dep. Seville (P.A.)	16:30	Dep. Merida	10:00
Arr. Merida	20:25	Arr. Sevile (P.A.)	14:10

Sights in **Merida**: During the 400 years this city was ruled by Romans, the population was 100,000 — nearly 3 times today's population. Come here to see the 2,000-year old antiquities. Puente Romano, the longest bridge ever built by Romans (82 arches, more than half a mile long).

The mosaic floors in the restored, large 9th century fort, covering 2 city blocks. The 6,000-seat Roman theater (where plays are still performed) and 14,000-seat Roman amphitheater. Trojan's Arch. The Temple of Diana.

The collection of statues (including Augustus, his adopted son Tiberius, and his grandson Claudius), coins, tombstones, pottery and tools at the Archaeological Museum in the 17th century Santa Clara Church. The ancient Arab "Alcazaba", now a monastic church.

The church of Santa Eulalia. The bullfights, mid-March to mid-October.

Sevile - Malaga (via Bobadilla) - Seville   427

All of these trains are second-class only.

Dep. Seville (S.B.)	07:45	12:05	Dep. Malaga	13:45	18:35
Arr. Bobadilla	10:07	14:42	Arr. Bodilla	15:01	19:37
Change trains.			Change trains		
Dep. Bobadilla	10:15	15:10	Dep. Bobadilla	15:25	19:42
Arr. Malaga	11:14	16:32	Arr. Seville (S.B.)	17:58	21:53

HERE IS A SECOND ROUTE FROM SEVILLE TO MALAGA
Seville - Malaga (via Cordoba) - Seville

These schedules do not permit a practical one-day roundtrip excursion. Staying overnight one or more nights in Cordoba is recommended.

See page 193 for other Seville-Cordoba schedules.

Dep. Seville (S. Justa)	08:53 (1)	11:57 (2)	15:20 (3)	-0-
Arr. Cordoba	10:10	13:34	16:45	-0-
Change trains. 427				
Dep. Cordoba	13:20 (4)	16:14 (2)	18:36 (5)	19:07 (1)
Arr. Malaga	16:32	19:00	21:30	21:20

Sights in **Malaga**: See notes under "Granada-Malaga" on page 183.

Dep. Malaga	08:25 (5)	11:00 (2)	15:00 (3)	18:15 (7)
Arr. Cordoba	10:38	13:24	17:03	21:04
Change trains. 426				
Dep. Cordoba	-0-	13:30 (4)	18:05 (1)	21:34 (7)
Arr. Seville (S. Justa)	-0-	15:42	19:34	22:56

(1) Supplement charged. Restaurant car. (2) Light refreshments. (3) Supplement charged. Restaurant car. (4) Second-class only. (5) Supplement charged. Light refreshments. (6) Runs daily, except Friday and Saturday. Light refreshments. (7) Runs daily, except Saturday. Supplement charged. Light refreshments.

Seville - Torremolinos - Seville
427

| Dep. Seville (S.B.) | 07:45 (1) |
| Arr. Malaga | 11:14 |

(1) Second-class only. Change trains in Bobadilla at 10:13.

Change to electric train.   431

| Dep. Malaga | Every 30 minutes from 06:03 to 22:33 |
| Arr. Torremolinos | 24 minutes later |

Sights in **Torremolinos**: Characters from all over the world, on and around this resort's 5-mile beach.

Dep. Torremolinos	Every 30 minutes from 06:59 to 23:59
Arr. Malaga	24 minutes later
Change trains. 427	
Dep. Malaga	See "Malaga-Seville" schedules above
Arr. Seville	See "Malaga-Seville" schedules above

Tarragona - Tortosa - Tarragona 415

Dep. Tarragona	07:30 (1)	08:23 (2)	09:57 (2)	11:49 (3)	12:37 (4)
Arr. Tortosa	08:43	09:09	10:49	12:45	13:26

Sights in **Tortosa**: St. Louis College, founded in 1554 by Charles V for Moors converting to Christianity. The Cathedral. The Bishop's Palace.

Dep. Tortosa	14:32 (4)	15:55 (1)	17:16 (1)	18:12 (3)	18:34 (1+6)
Arr. Tarragona	15:23	17:32	18:19	18:58	20:24

(1) Second-class only. (2) Supplement charged. Light refreshments. (3) Operates late June to early September. Light refreshments. (4) Supplement charged. Restaurant car. (5) Operates late June to early September. (6) Plus other Tortosa departures at 20:04 (1) and 20:35 (2), arriving Tarragona 20:58 and 21:28.

Valencia - Alicante - Valencia 421

Dep. Valencia (Ter.)	08:00 (1)	Dep. Alicante (Ter.)	17:07	19:25 (2)	20:15 (1)
Arr. Alicante (Ter.)	10:17	Arr. Valencia (Ter.)	20:13	22:00	22:40

(1) Light refreshments. (2) Second-class only. Light refreshments.

Sights in **Alicante**: The avenue lined with date palms, part of the complete African atmosphere. The huge Moorish castle. Take the 26-mile bus trip to Elche to see the only palm forest in Europe.

Alicante - Benidorm - Denia - Alicante 418

There is marvelous scenery on a one-class narrow-gauge train that runs from Alicante, via **Benidorm**, to **Denia** and time to take it (13:15–18:05) before returning to Valencia. *Not covered by Eurailpass.* A special tourist train called "Limon Express" (for which Cook does not carry a timetable) operates between Benidorm and **Gata de Gorgos**. *Not covered by Eurailpass.*

Valencia - Cuenca - Valencia 420

Dep. Valencia (Ter.)	08:39 (1)	11:10 (2)	Dep. Cuenca	14:16 (2)	18:30 (1)
Arr. Cuenca	11:42	15:28	Arr. Valencia (Ter.)	18:12	21:15

(1) Light refreshments. (2) Second-class only.

Sights in **Cuenca**: See notes under "Madrid-Cuenca" on page 188.

Valencia - Murcia - Valencia 421

All of these trains require a train change in Alicante, unless designated otherwise.

Dep. Valencia (Ter.)	08:00 (1)	Dep. Murcia	15:58 (2)	16:45 (3)	18:10 (1)
Arr. Murcia	12:40	Arr. Valencia (Ter.)	20:13	22:00	22:40

(1) Valencia-Alicante and v.v.: Supplement charged. Light refreshments.Alicante-Murcia and v.v.: Second-class only. (2) Direct train. No train change in Alicante. (3) Murcia-Alicante: Supplement charged. Light refreshments. Alicante-Valencia: Second-class only and light refreshments.

Sights in **Murcia**: The Moorish granary. The 14th century Gothic-Romanesque Cathedral. Glass, pottery and leather factories.

SCENIC RAIL TRIPS

Here are 16 exceptionally scenic rail trips in Spain and Portugal.

Barcelona - La Tour-de-Carol - Villefranche - Perpignan - Barcelona

Passengers on the famous La Tour-de-Carol to Villefranche narrow-gauge service (called "The Yellow Train") may ride either in modern cars, an antique car or a completely open car, which John Zucker of New York City recommends for best glimpses of beautiful Pyrenees mountain scenery.

This very scenic route can be traveled either as a one-day circle trip from Barcelona (see schedules below) or when going from Spain to France. (A direct train Perpignan-Marseille [Table 162] departs Perpignan 19:26.)

You pass the popular **Mont-Louis** and **Font-Romeu** ski resorts and then ride alternately along very narrow ledges and also on very high bridges as the line criss-crosses gorges before arriving in the ancient walled-city of **Villefranche-de-Conflans**, a few miles from the **Vernet les Bains** sulfur-bath spa. The train-change in Villefranche is an easy cross-platform transfer.

THE ONE-DAY CIRCLE TRIP

414			161		
Dep. Barcelona (Sants)	06:05 (1)	09:19 (1)	Dep. Villefranche	17:16	-0-
Arr. La Tour	10:12	13:00	Arr. Perpignan	18:04	-0-
Change to narrow-gauge			Change trains.		
"Yellow Train"			162		
143			Dep. Perpignan	18:09 (3)	18:56
Dep. La Tour	10:42 (1)	13:31 (1)	Arr. Port Bou	-0- (3)	19:38
Dep. Font-Romeu	11:43	14:31 (2)	Change trains.		
Arr. Villefranche	12:57	16:28	416		
Change trains.			Dep. Port Bou	-0-	21:05
			Arr. Barcelona (P. de G.)	-0-	23:32
			Arr. Barcelona (Sants)	21:18	23:37

(1) Second-class only. (2) Change trains in Font-Romeu. (3) Table 78. Direct train to Barcelona. No train change in Port Bou. Reservation required. Supplement charged. Restaurant car.

Barcelona - Massanet - Blanes - Barcelona   416

Fine coastline and mountain scenery on this easy one-day circle excursion. As this schedule shows, it is possible to layover in Massanet or Blanes for dining before returning to Barcelona.

(Via Granollers)   Second-class only.

Dep. Barcelona (Sants)	06:50	08:10	12:15	13:10	14:45	15:40	17:20
Arr. Massanet	08:08	09:29	13:33	14:28	16:01	16:52	18:44

*   *   *

(Via Blanes)   Second-class only.

Dep. Massanet	08:13	09:13	10:43	12:13	12:42	14:13 (1)
Dep. Blanes	08:30	09:30	11:00	12:30	12:28	14:30
Arr. Barcelona (Sants)	09:57	10:57	12:27	13:57	14:27	15:57

(1) Plus other departures from Massanet at 16:13, 17:42, 18:43, 19:13 and 19:43.

Barcelona - Zaragoza - Madrid 410

There are many ancient towns, castles, mountains and gorges to see on this route.

All of these trains require reservation and charge a supplement.

Dep. Barcelona (Sants)	08:30 (1)	11:00 (2)	15:00 (2)	21:30 (3)	21:50 (3)	23:00 (4)
Arr. Zaragoza	12:38	14:45	18:25	02:32	03:56	03:38
Arr. Madrid (Cham.)	16:35	18:15	21:45	07:40	08:30	08:00

(1) Light refreshments. (2) Supplement charged. Restaurant car. (3) Carries a sleeping car. Also has second-class couchettes. Light refreshments. (4) Carries only sleeping cars and a restaurant car. No couchettes or coaches.

Barcelona - Puigcerda

There is beautiful Pyrenees mountain scenery on this portion of the Barcelona-Toulouse route. As shown below, this trip also can be made as a one-day excursion from Barcelona.

All of these trains are second-class only, unless designated otherwise.

414

Dep. Barcelona (Sants)	06:05	09:19	15:22
Arr. Puigcerda	10:06	12:54	18:52
Arr. La Tour-de-Carol	10:12	13:00	18:59
Change trains. 144			
Dep. La Tour-de-Carol	10:40	13:27	19:19
Arr. Toulouse (Mat.)	13:13	16:31	22:17

HERE IS THE EASY ONE-DAY EXCURSION 414

All of these trains are second-class only.

The schedule above for Puigcerda plus a departure from Barcelona (Sants) 12:19— Barcelona (P. Cat.) at 12:24 ...arriving in Puigcerda at 15:30.

* * *

Dep. Barcelona (Sants)	06:05	09:19	12:19	14:19
Arr. Puigcerda	10:06	12:54	15:35	17:24
Arr. La Tour-de-Carol	10:12	13:00	-0-	17:30

* * *

Dep. La Tour-de-Carol	10:50	13:33	-0-	18:25
Dep. Puigcerda	10:57	13:40	16:35	18:35
Arr. Barcelona (Sants)	14:43	17:22	20:52	22:13

Barcelona - Tarragona

This trip is noted for excellent scenery along the Mediterranean coastline. Complete schedules can be found on page 183.

Barcelona - Valencia 425

There are good views of the Mediterranean shoreline on this ride.

Schedules appears on page 206.

Cordoba - Malaga - Cordoba   427

Scenic canyons can be seen on this trip, an easy one-day excursion from Cordoba.

Dep. Cordoba	06:18 (1)	07:36 (2)
Arr. Malaga	09:24	10:30

Sights in **Malaga**: See notes under "Granada–Malaga" on page 183.

Dep. Malaga	13:45 (3)	15:00 (4)	18:15 (5)	19:05 (1)	19:35 (3)	21:45 (1)
Arr. Cordoba	16:52	17:03	21:04	21:45	22:54	00:26

(1) Light refreshments. (2) Runs Monday-Friday. Restaurant car Monday, Wednesday and Friday. Second-class only and light refreshments on Tuesday and Thursday. (3) Second-class only. (4) Supplement charged. Air-conditioned. Restaurant car. (5) Runs daily, except Friday and Saturday. Restaurant car Tuesday, Thursday and Sunday. Second-class only and light refreshments on Monday and Wednesday.

Granada - Almeria   425

Excellent mountain scenery on this one-day roundtrip.

All of these trains are second-class only.

Dep. Granada	08:10	13:20	Dep. Almeria	13:15	16:45
Arr. Almeria	11:26	16:18	Arr. Granada	16:57	19:57

Leon - Oviedo - Leon   440

Very good mountain scenery on this one-day roundtrip.

Sights in **Leon**: The stained-glass windows in the Cathedral and the 11th century Church of San Isidoro.

Dep. Leon	06:35 (1)	07:20 (2)	13:30 (3)	14:47 (4)	17:32 (5)	19:19 (4)
Arr. Oviedo	08:53	10:08	16:13	16:55	19:44	21:30

* * *

Dep. Oviedo	08:55 (6)	13:35 (3)	14:20 (7)	18:55 (3)	20:58 (1)	23:35
Arr. Leon	10:55	16:05	16:24	21:40	23:06	02:00

(1) Second-class only. Light refreshments. (2) Runs Monday–Friday, except holidays. Second-class only. (3) Second-class only. (4) Supplement charged. Runs Monday–Friday, except holidays. Restaurant car. (5) Supplement charged. (6) Supplement charged. Light refreshments. (7) Supplement charged. Restaurant car.

Leon - Monforte   440

The Leon-Monforte portion of the Leon-Vigo route is recommended for mountain scenery.

All of these trains have light refreshments.

Dep. Leon	07:40	14:05	Dep. Monforte	11:58	20:25
Arr. Monforte	11:05	17:25	Arr. Leon	15:21	23:57

Lisbon - Porto - Vigo - Santiago de Compostela . . . Lisbon

This table shows both extending the Leon-Vigo trip (above) from Vigo to Santiago de Compostela and also the route from Lisbon to Santiago. Notes on this marvelous attraction appear under "Madrid-Santiago" on page 204. Notes about Porto and complete Lisbon-Porto schedules appear on page 186.

445		439	
Dep. Lisbon (S. Apol.)	08:50 (1)	Dep. Santiago	08:49
Arr. Porto (Campanha)	13:10	Arr. Vigo	10:25
Change trains. 446		Change trains. 446	
Dep. Porto (Campanha)	14:00 (1)	Dep. Vigo	13:40 (1)
Set watch forward one hour		Set watch back one hour	
Arr. Vigo	19:10	Arr. Porto (Campanha)	16:48
Change trains. 439		Change trains. 445	
Dep. Vigo	20:35	Dep. Porto (Campanha)	17:00 (1)
Arr. Santiago	22:40	Arr. Lisbon (S. Apol.)	20:20

(1) Reservation advisable. Light refreshments.

Porto - Viana do Castelo - Vigo 446

Schedules allow stopping over in Viana on the Porto-Vigo route.

Reservation is advisable for all of these trains. All of these trains have light refreshments.

Dep. Porto (Camphanha)	07:32	14:00	18:07
Arr. Viana do Castelo	09:17	15:48	19:48
Arr. Vigo	12:40	19:10	23:15

Sights in **Viana do Castelo**: A pretty, little fishing resort. Walk along the twisting road lined with pine and eucalyptus trees, up to the Basilica of Santa Luzia for marvelous views (or take the funicular).

See a collection of ceramics for which Portugal is famous, at the Municipal Museum. The renaissance buildings in the Praca da Republica. The church of Sao Domingos.

Dep. Vigo	07:25	13:40	20:35
Arr. Viana do Castelo	08:35	15:10	21:56
Arr. Porto (Camphanha)	10:19	16:48	23:40

Porto - Regua - Porto 447

There is good river scenery on this easy one-day roundtrip.

Dep. Porto (S. Bento)	08:45	10:40 (1)	12:15 (2)	14:25 (1)	16:15
Dep. Porto (Campanha)	08:52	10:49	12:23	14:36	16:23
Arr. Regua	11:15	12:59	14:48	16:44	18:37
		* * *			
Dep. Regua	11:20 (1)	13:16	14:50 (1)	17:54	19:07
Arr. Porto (Campanha)	13:27	15:18	16:37	19:55	21:32
Arr. Porto (S. Bento)	13:35	15:25	-0-	20:02	21:41

(1) Reservation advisable. Light refreshments. (2) Runs daily, except Sundays and holidays.

Madrid - Barcelona 410

Many ancient towns, castles, mountains and gorges to see on this route.

Dep. Madrid (Cham.)	11:00 (1)	11:45 (2)	15:20 (1)	21:45 (3+5)
Arr. Barcelona (Sants)	18:30	20:05	22:00	07:10

(1) Supplement charged. Restaurant car. (2) Light refreshments. (3) Carries a sleeping car. Also has couchettes. Light refreshments. (4) Reservation advisable. Supplement charged. Carries only sleeping cars and a restaurant car. No coach seats. (5) Plus other departures from Madrid at 22:30 (3) and 23:10 (4), arriving Barcelona (Sants) 08:45 and 08:00.

THE MAJORCA ONE-DAY RAIL TRIP

If you are planning on visiting the island of Majorca, you will enjoy this trip.

This narrow-gauge, easy one-day trip goes through olive groves before tunneling through a mountain and emerging high above **Soller**. At the tunnel exit, the train stops for 10 minutes to allow passengers to enjoy the view before the train spirals downhill to Soller. A quaint tram makes the short ride from Soller to the seaside **Puerto de Soller**.

Palma - Soller   424

*This ride is **not** covered by Eurailpass or Eurail Youthpass.*

Dep. Palma	08:00	10:40	13:00	15:15	19:45
Arr. Soller	55 minutes later				

* * *

Dep. Soller	06:45	09:15	11:50	14:10	18:30
Arr. Palma	55 minutes later				

THE TRIP TO ANDORRA

Barcelona   to   La Tour-de-Carol   to   Andorra la Vella

All of these trains are second-class only.

414 Train

Dep. Barcelona (Sants)	06:12	-0-	14:19
Arr. La Tour-de-Carol	10:12	-0-	17:30

Change to a bus (weather permitting).   192

Dep. La Tour-de-Carol	10:45 (1)	11:35 (2)	18:10 (3)
Arr. Andorra la Vella	13:00	13:40	20:10

Sight in **Andorra la Vella**: Capital of the quaint, tiny (50,000 population) co-principality, governed jointly by the French government and the Spanish Bishop of Urgel. Both the Spanish peseta and the French franc are legal currency here.

The country's main export is postage stamps, created for philatelists. Small ski resorts and duty-free shops are the main attraction for the 6,000,000 tourists who come here every year. Located in the eastern Pyrenees, the country's mountain peaks reach heights of 9,800 feet.

Lying in one of Andorra's 6 valleys, this is the market town for the entire country (179 square miles). Catalan (the language of the Barcelona area), Spanish and French are spoken here.

Dep. Andorra la Vella	07:30 (1)	08:10 (2)	14:30 (3)
Arr. La Tour-de-Carol	10:00	10:30	17:00

Change to train.   414

Dep. La Tour-de-Carol	-0-	10:50	18:25
Arr. Barcelona (Sants)	-0-	14:43	22:13

(1) Operates May 1 to October 31. (2) Operates November 1 to April 30. (3) Operates July 1 to September 30.

THE MADRID ROUTES

Madrid is the hub of the Iberian Peninsula, with spokes going from it to the major cities of Spain and Portugal: Barcelona, Bilbao, Cordoba, Lisbon, San Sebastian, Santiago de Compostela, Seville and Valencia.

Where city sightseeing notes are not indicated in the following schedules, they can be found on pages 178–180 (Valencia, page 206).

Here are the schedules for reaching those cities from Madrid:

Madrid - Barcelona

Covered under the description of scenic trips, on page 201.

Madrid - Bilbao   412

Dep. Madrid (Chamartin)	09:24 (1+2)	22:30 (3)
Arr. Castejon de Ebro	14:45	04:38
Change trains.		
Dep. Castejon de Ebro	16:58 (2)	05:50 (4)
Arr. Bilbao (Abando)	20:40	09:50

Sights in **Bilbao**: This is the largest Basque city. A major port and industrial city.

Dep. Bilbao (Abando)	08:45 (2)	19:00 (4)
Arr. Castejon de Ebro	12:35	22:50
Change trains.		
Dep. Castejon de Ebro	13:37 (4)	01:20 (3)
Arr. Madrid (Chamartin)	18:43 (1)	08:30

(1) Depart / Arrive Madrid Vallecas railstation. (2) Supplement charged. Light refreshments. (3) Carries a sleeping car. Coaches are second-class only. (4) Light refreshments.

Madrid - Lisbon   44

Both of these trains charge a supplement and have light refreshments.

Dep. Madrid (Chamartin)	13:50 (1)	23:00 (2)
Dep. Madrid (Atocha)	14:13	-0-
Set your watch back one hour.		
Arr. Lisbon (S. Apolonia)	21:10	08:45

*   *   *

Dep. Lisbon (S. Apolonia)	12:15 (1)	21:25 (2)
Set your watch forward one hour.		
Arr. Madrid (Atocha)	21:15	-0-
Arr. Madrid (Chamartin)	21:32	08:50

(1) Reservation advisable. (2) Reservation required. Carries a sleeping car. Also has couchettes.

Madrid - San Sebastian 435

All of these trains charge a supplement, unless designated otherwise.

Dep. Madrid (Cham.)	07:00 (1)	08:00 (1)	15:30 (1)	18:15 (2)	22:35 (3)
Arr. San Sebastian	13:30	14:28	21:24	01:29	07:26

Sights in **San Sebastian**: See notes on page 180.

Dep. San Sebastian	02:24 (4)	08:28 (1)	15:28 (1)	16:08 (1)	23:32 (4)
Arr. Madrid (Cham.)	09:50	15:00	21:55	23:08	08:30

(1) Light refreshments. (2) Has couchettes. Coaches are second-class only. Restaurant car 18:15 – 22:51. (3) No supplement. Carries a sleeping car. Also has couchettes. Coaches are second-class only. (4) Has couchettes. Coaches are second-class only. Restaurant car 05:01–09:50

Madrid - Santiago de Compostela 441

In addition to this route, there is a good circle trip: Lisbon–Santiago–Vigo–Porto–Lisbon (see page 200).

All of these trains have a restaurant car.

Dep. Madrid (P. Pio)	-0-	22:00 (2)	Dep. Santiago	09:15 (3)	12:15 (4+5)
Dep. Madrid (Ch.)	13:30 (1)	-0-	Arr. Madrid (Ch.)	22:00	21:15
Arr. Santiago	20:48	07:33	Arr. Madrid (P. Pio)	18:15	-0-

(1) Reservation advisable. Supplement charged. (2) Carries a sleeping car. Also has couchettes. Coach seats are second-class only. (3) Supplement charged. Runs Saturday only. Change trains in Orense. (4) Supplement charged. Runs daily, except Saturday. Change trains in Orense. (5) Plus another Santiago departure at 22:36 (2), arriving Madrid (Principe Pio) 08:45.

Sights in **Santiago de Compostela**: One of the 3 most sacred places in Christendom, ranking equally with Jerusalem and Rome since 812. It is believed that this is the repository of St. James (Santiago), a cousin of Jesus, son of Mary's sister, and the first follower of Jesus to attain martyrdom.

After witnessing the crucifixion, James came to Spain in A.D. 44, converted 9 Iberians to Christianity, was visited at Zaragoza by the Virgin Mary, returned to the Holy Land, and was beheaded there by King Herod Agrippa.

The legend which has generated the pilgrimage to Santiago de Compostela for the past 1,100 years is that, after the decapitation in Jerusalem, his body was disinterred and found to have the head intact. The body was brought to Spain's West Coast in A.D. 44.

Eight centuries later, a hermit saw a bright star (stela) over a vacant field (compo). Excavations were conducted, and the remains of James were found. Since that event, pilgrims have come to this shrine by horse and in vehicles, as well as on foot (from as far as Scandinavia) to pray and meditate here.

You would stop here to see the majestic Cathedral built in the 12th century.

See its beautiful Baroque sculptured Obradoire facade. The carved Romanesque 12th century Door of Glory. Touch the grooves left in the central pillar by the fingers of millions of pilgrims over the centuries.

Visit the Archaeological Museum in its basement, the art pieces in its Treasury, the collection of tapestries with designs by Goya and Rubens in the many halls of the Cathedral's Tapestry Museum.

Also see the gigantic 6-foot tall, 118-pound brass censer in the Library of the Cathedral.

In the early pilgrimage years, it was difficult for priests to tolerate the odor of worshippers from afar who had gone unbathed for weeks and months. The censer here, called Botafumeiro (smoke-thrower), masked the noxious odors.

A custom that originated in the early days of pilgrimages here is perpetuated today. On feast days, this censer is brought into the Cathedral, filled with incense, hung by ropes from the dome 104 feet above the floor, and swung in an arc, barely passing over the heads of people standing in the Cathedral.

It is easy to explore Santiago de Compostela on foot. See the marvelous view of the town from Alameda Park. Santa Maria del Sar, one of the more than 40 churches here, is a splendid example of 12th century Romanesque architecture.

Madrid - Seville 426

See 1992 "Thomas Cook European Timetable".

The introduction of high-speed trains on this route in 1992 was too late for the timetable to appear in this year's edition of Eurail® Guide. This trip has been reduced from 6 hours to 3 hours. When planning it, be sure to obtain the new schedules.

Known as AVE (Tren de Alta Velocidad Española), these trains travel some stretches at 186 miles per hour. They go between Madrid's Atocha railstation and Seville's Santa Justa station (on the ground of *World Expo '92*, taking place April-October this year).

AVE's are air-conditioned and their restaurant cars have telephones and a boutique. When this edition of Eurail® Guide was being printed at the end of 1991, Spain planned 10 to 14 departures in each direction.

Madrid - Valencia - Madrid 420

All of these trains charge a supplement, unless designated otherwise.

Dep. Madrid (Cham.)	07:05 (1)	-0-	09:30 (3)	12:00 (4)	14:00 (5)	-0- (8)
Dep. Madrid (Atocha)	N/A	09:00 (2)	09:41	12:11	N/A	15:45 (6)
Arr. Valencia (Ter.)	11:25	14:35	14:00	16:20	18:30	21:15

(Sightseeing, return trip and footnotes appear page 206.)

Sights in **Valencia**: See the Holy Grail, the chalice used at the Last Supper, exhibited in the 13th century Cathedral. The great art collection in the Convent of Pio V. The Orange Court at the 15th century Lonja del Mercado. The popular beaches: Arenas, Nazaret and Pinedo y Saler. The scent of the vast surrounding orange groves, perfuming the night.

Dep. Valencia (Ter.)	07:00 (1)	08:39 (6)	09:00 (3)	12:00 (4)	13:30 (3)	15:25 (2+9)
Arr. Madrid (Atocha)	11:08	14:10	13:08	16:08	N/A	21:00
Arr. Madrid (Cham.)	11:20	-0-	13:20	16:20	17:20	-0-

(1) Runs daily, except Sundays and holidays. Light refreshments (2) *No* supplement charged. (3) Light refreshments. (4) Restaurant car. (5) Runs daily, except Saturday. Light refreshments. (6) *No* supplement charged. Light refreshments. (7) *No* supplement charged. Carries a sleeping car. Also has couchettes. Coach is first-class only. (8) Plus other departures from Madrid (Chamartin) at 16:30 (3), 18:00 (3), 19:30 (3) and 23:40 (7), arriving Valencia 20:55, 22:20, 23:40 and 07:50. (9) Plus other departures from Valencia at 15:25 (2), 16:30 (3), 18:00 (3), 19:30 (3) and 23:10 (7), arriving Madrid 21:00 (Atocha), 20:38 (Atocha), 22:20 (Cham.), 23:40 (Cham.) and 07:50 (Cham.).

Barcelona - Valencia - Barcelona   415

Dep. Barcelona (P. de G.)	-0-	-0-	-0-	-0-
Dep. Barcelona (Sants)	07:00 (1)	07:25 (2)	09:00 (2)	10:48 (3)
Arr. Valencia (Termino)	10:48	11:18	12:55	15:15

Dep. Barcelona (P. de G.)	-0-	-0-	16:22 (1)	-0-
Dep. Barcelona (Sants)	11:41 (4)	15:30 (2)	16:30	17:30 (5)
Arr. Valencia (Termino)	15:38	19:25	20:50	21:59

Dep. Barcelona (P. de G.)	18:52 (2)	-0-	-0-
Dep. Barcelona (Sants)	19:00	19:45 (6)	22:00 (8)
Arr. Valencia (Termino)	23:00	00:45 (7)	02:38 (7)

Sights in **Valencia**: See "Madrid-Valencia" above.

Dep. Valencia (Termino)	03:09 (7+8)	06:05 (5)	06:25 (6+7)	07:00 (2)
Arr. Barcelona (Sants)	07:35	11:10	11:35	11:00
Arr. Barcelona (P. de G.)	-0-	-0-	-0-	11:10

Dep. Valencia (Termino)	09:16 (2)	11:30 (2)	12:16 (4)	15:00 (9)
Arr. Barcelona (Sants)	13:30	15:42	16:30	19:30
Arr. Barcelona (P. de G.)	-0-	-0-	-0-	-0-

Dep. Valencia (Termino)	16:00 (2)	17:10 (1)	17:30 (10)	18:10 (2)
Arr. Barcelona (Sants)	19:55	21:30	22:08	22:30
Arr. Barcelona (P. de G.)	20:05	-0-	22:16	-0-

(1) Supplement charged. Restaurant car. (2) Supplement charged. Light refreshments. (3) Operates late June to early September. Light refreshments. (4) Reservation advisable. Supplement charged. Restaurant car. (5) Light refreshments. (6) Operates early July to early September. Coaches are second-class only. Light refreshments. (7) Depart / Arrive Valencia's Cabanyal railstation. (8) Carries a sleeping car. Also has couchettes. Light refreshments. (9) Operates late June to early September. (10) Second-class only.

INTERNATIONAL ROUTES FROM PORTUGAL

The route to southern Spain is Lisbon-Seville.

The 2 routes to France and beyond are Lisbon-Madrid (page 203) and Lisbon-Hendaye on the "Sud Express" which goes north of Madrid, via Pampilhosa and Medina del Campo.

Lisbon - Seville

The only practical way to make this trip in 1991 was very indirect: Lisbon-Madrid-Seville.

Lisbon - Madrid

Schedules for this trip appears under "The Madrid Routes" on page 203.

Lisbon - Biarritz - Bayonne - Bordeaux - Paris 28

The 60-minute stop in Hendaye is for changing the train's wheels to conform with the narrower track in France.

Reservation required. Supplement charged. Has couchettes Lisbon-Paris. Restaurant car Lisbon-Hendaye. Light refreshments Hendaye-Paris.

Dep. Lisbon (S. Apol.)	14:45
Dep. Vilar Formoso	22:10

Set your watch forward one hour.

Arr. Salamanca	01:19
Arr. San Sebastian	09:07
Arr. Hendaye	10:30
Dep. Hendaye	11:30
Arr. Biarritz	11:55
Arr. Bayonne	12:07
Arr. Bordeaux	14:02
Arr. Paris (Austerlitz)	19:03

INTERNATIONAL ROUTES FROM SPAIN

Reservations for travel from Spain to other countries on night trains are complex, taking often as long as one month to obtain. Normally, day trains are *not* such a problem.

When traveling by train from another country to Spain, if you want to travel later from Spain back into France and/or beyond France, it is advisable to book the trip out of Spain *before you enter Spain.*

If this is not possible, then we suggest that immediately after you clear Spanish customs (leaving France) that you go as soon as possible to the reservation booth in the Spanish arrival city to reserve space for your train trip back into France.

The Spanish gateway for rail travel to London, Paris, Brussels and Amsterdam is Madrid. (Notes on the route to London, via Paris, appear on pages 426 and 427).

From Barcelona, there is rail service to southwestern France (via Toulouse) and to southeastern France (Avignon, Marseille and Nice), from where there are connections to Italy, Austria and Switzerland (and on to Germany and Denmark)....plus Barcelona-Zurich and Barcelona-Milan on the fabulous "Pablo Casals" (see page 209).

Seville - Lisbon

The only practical way to make this trip in 1991 was very indirect: Seville-Madrid-Lisbon.

Madrid - Lisbon

Schedules for this trip appear under "The Madrid Routes" on page 203.

Madrid - Paris

The "Madrid-Paris Talgo" (the 19:35 departure below) began in 1990 to carry one "Gran Clase" sleeping car, the most luxurious sleeping car in Europe. Each of its large single and double compartments has a shower and toilet. The train also has ordinary sleeping compartments and 4-berth tourist compartments. There are *no coach seats.* The train has light refreshments. It is a direct train to Paris: *no train change* in Hendaye.

	58	58	25+58
Dep. Madrid (Cham.)	08:00 (1)	18:15 (2)	19:35 (3)
Arr. Hendaye	15:00	-0- (2)	-0- (3)
Dep. Hendaye	16:15 (1)	-0- (2)	-0- (3)
Arr. Paris (Mont.)	21:30	-0-	-0-
Arr. Paris (Aust.)	-0-	10:30	08:30

(1) The connection in Hendaye with a TGV running Hendaye-Paris occurs only on Sunday. Madrid-Paris: a supplement is charged and light refreshments are available. (2) Direct train. *No train change in Hendaye.* Reservation required. Supplement charged. Has couchettes. Restaurant car 18:15 – 21:46. Light refreshments Day 2 from 05:59 to 10:30. (3) See note about "Madrid-Paris Talgo" at the beginning of this trip description.

Barcelona - Avignon - Geneva   178

Dep. Barcelona (Ter.)	09:55 (1)	19:40 (2)	Dep. Avignon	15:23 (1)	02:50 (2)
Arr. Avignon	15:21	02:48	Arr. Geneva (Corn.)	19:42	07:25

(1) Reservation advisable. Restaurant car. (2) Has couchettes.

Barcelona - Toulouse - Paris

414

Dep. Barcelona (Sants)	06:05 (1)	09:19 (1)	15:22 (1)
Arr. La Tour-de-Carol	10:12	13:00	18:59
Change trains. 144			
Dep. La Tour-de-Carol	10:40	13:27	19:19 (2)
Arr. Toulouse (Mat.)	13:13	16:14	22:17 (2)
Change trains. 138			
Dep. Toulouse (Mat.)	14:39 (3)	17:45 (4)	22:38 (2)
Arr. Paris (Aust.)	21:42	00:01	06:48

(1) Second-class only. (2) Direct train to Paris. No train change in Toulouse. Has couchettes. (3) Light refreshments. (4) Supplement charged. Restaurant car.

Barcelona - Torino - Milan 178

The "Pablo Casals" began in 1990 to carry one "Gran Clase" sleeping car, the most luxurious sleeping car in Europe. Each of its large single and double compartments has a shower and toilet. The train also has ordinary sleeping compartments and 4-berth tourist compartments. There are *no coach seats*. The train has a restaurant car.

Dep. Barcelona (Sants)	20:15	Dep. Torino	07:36
Arr. Torino	07:33	Arr. Milan (Cen.)	09:00

Barcelona - Geneva - Lausanne - Bern - Zurich 178

Another route of the fabulous "Pablo Casals" (see description in preceding trip, above).

Dep. Barcelona (Sants)	20:15	Dep. Lausanne	06:43
Arr. Geneva (Cor.)	05:52	Arr. Bern	07:51
Dep. Geneva (Cor.)	06:07	Dep. Bern	07:55
Arr. Lausanne	06:40	Arr. Zurich	09:15

REPUBLIC OF IRELAND

Children under 5 travel free. Half-fare for children 5–15. Children 16 and over must pay full fare.

SUMMER TIME

Ireland changes to Summer Time on the last Sunday of March and converts back to Standard Time on the last Sunday of October.

EURAILPASS BONUSES IN IRELAND

See page 26.

IRISH TRAIN PASSES

Rambler Pass Unlimited travel in the Irish Republic. Sold at rail and bus stations throughout Ireland and also at CIE Tours, 108 Ridgedale Ave., Morristown, N.J. 07960.

The 1992 adult prices for only rail *or* bus are: $96 (U.S.) for any 8 days within 15 days, $144 for any 15 days within 30 days. Children age 5–15: $48 and $72. For *both* rail *and* bus, the 1992 adult prices are: $125 for any 8 days within 15 days, $184 for any 15 days within 30 days. Children age 5–15: $63 and $93.

Student and Youth Rambler Pass Available to persons 14 to 26 years old. Must be purchased from CIE Tours before arriving in Ireland (see address under "Rambler Pass" above). Covers *both* rail *and* bus travel. The 1992 prices are: $116 (U.S.) for any 8 days within 15 days, $160 for any 15 days within 30 days, and $ 240 for 30 *consecutive* days.

Emerald Isle Card Covers all scheduled rail services of Irish Rail and Northern Ireland Railways....all scheduled long-distance services of Bus Eireann and Ulster Bus....plus city buses in Belfast, Cork, Dublin, Galway, Limerick and Waterford. Sold both in Ireland (at the CIE offices in Dublin and Limerick City, and by Ulsterbus) and also outside Ireland at CIE Tours and at travel agencies.

The 1992 adult prices are: $168 (U.S.) for any 8 days within 15 days and $288 for any 15 days within 30 days. Children age 5–15: $85 and $144.

4-Day Rail Pass Unlimited train travel any 4 days within 8 days. The 1992 prices are: $72 (U.S.) for adults, $40 for children age 5–15.

ONE-DAY EXCURSIONS AND CITY SIGHTSEEING

Here are 8 one-day rail trips that can be made comfortably from Belfast, Cork, Dublin, Galway and Limerick, returning to them in most cases before dinnertime. Notes are provided on what to see and do at each destination. The number after the name of each route is the Cook's timetable.

Dublin - Belfast - Dublin 615

Dep. Dublin (Con.)	08:00(1)	10:30 (2)	11:00 (1)	13:00 (3)	15:00 (4+6)
Arr. Belfast (Cen.)	10:15	13:05	13:15	15:20	17:15
		* *	*		
Dep. Belfast (Cen.)	08:00 (1)	09:00 (3)	10:15 (2)	11:00 (1)	15:00 (4+7)
Arr. Dublin Con.)	09:55	11:20	12:40	13:15	17:15

(1) Runs daily, except Sun. and holidays. Restaurant car. (2) Runs Sun. only. Light refreshments. (3) Runs daily, except Sun. and holidays. Light refreshments. (4) Runs daily, except holidays. Restaurant car Mon.-Sat., except holidays. (5) Runs daily, except Sun. and holidays. Change trains in Dundalk. (6) Plus other Dublin departures at 18:20 (4), 18:33 (5), 19:50 (2) and 20:15 (3). (7) Plus other Belfast departures at 17:00 (3) and 18:00 (4), arriving Dublin 19:20 and 19:55 (20:25 on Sunday).

Dublin   Capital of the Irish Republic. See the outstanding Bronze Age gold ornaments, the 9th century Derrynaflan Chalice and the 12th century Cross of Cong, in the National Museum, open Tuesday-Saturday 10:00-17:00 and Sunday 14:00-17:00. The collection of paintings (Rubens, Rembrandt, Goya. Reynolds, Gainsborough) at the National Gallery of Art, open Monday-Saturday 10:00-18:00 and Sunday 14:00-17:00.

The 8th century Book of Kells, a richly illuminated bible regarded as one of the most beautiful books ever made, on view in the Old Library of Trinity College. The Hugh Lane Municipal Gallery of Modern Art.

The pulpit from which Jonathan Swift preached, at the 12th century St. Patrick's Cathedral, and a performance of the young boys' choir there. The collection of oriental manuscripts at Chester Beatty Library. The Zoo, in the 1,760-acre Phoenix Park. The 13th century Dublin Castle. Leinster House. The restored 12th century Christ Church Cathedral.

The 18th century mansions on St. Stephen's Green. Window-shop on Grafton Street. Stroll on O'Connell Street. See the historic General Post Office, site of the 1916 uprising. The Georgian houses on Parnell Square. The house where George Bernard Shaw was born. Take a tour of the facilities of the Irish Sweepstakes. A tour of Guinness's Brewery.

Belfast   This is the capital of Northern Ireland. A major port. See the elegant Queen's University. The collection of antique locomotives and train cars in the Transport Museum. The richly marbled interior of the 19th century City Hall. The beautiful Grand Opera House. Across the street, the decorative interior of the Crown Bar.

Palm House and the collection of modern Irish paintings, silver and glass and exhibits of the history, geology and botany in Ulster Museum, both at the Botanic Gardens. Tour the Harland and Wolff Shipyard, location of the world's largest drydock and where many of the world's great ocean liners were built.

See the display of everything produced in Ulster factories (old farm implements, stage-coaches, a schooner, antique locomotives and train cars, modern aircraft) at the 180-acre open-air Ulster Folk and Transport Museum, a complex of 18 exhibit buildings. It also has cottages in styles spanning several centuries (some with original furniture), water-powered mills, and demonstrations of such traditional crafts as spinning and thatching.

Genealogical research can be done at the Public Record Office, 66 Balmoral Avenue as well as by mail with the Irish Genealogical Association, 164 Kingsway, Dunmurry, Belfast BT17 9AD.

Birth and death records since 1864 and copies of marriage registrations since 1922 can be obtained at General Register Office, Oxford House, 49-55 Chichester Street, Belfast BT1 4HL.

Dublin - Cork - Dublin   617

This is a train ride through Ireland's lush southern area.

There is bus service from Cork railstation to Cork airport 07:20 daily except Sundays and holidays....and daily every hour 08:20-22:20. From Cork airport to the railstation: 07:00 and 24:00 daily except Sundays and holidays....and daily every hour 08:00-23:00.

All of these trains have light refreshments, unless designated otherwise.

Dep. Dublin (Heu.)	07:30 (1)	08:20 (2)	09:00 (3)	10:40 (4)	13:25 (5+11)
Arr. Cork (Kent)	10:05	10:55	12:15	13:45	16:25 (5)

(Timetable continues on page 213)

IRELAND

Dep. Cork (Kent)	05:20 (6)	07:30 (7)	08:22 (8)	09:00 (5)	11:15 (7+12)
Arr. Dublin (Heu.)	08:40	10:00	11:10	12:10 (5)	14:20

(1) Runs Mon.-Fri., except holidays. (2) Runs Sat. only. (3) Runs daily, except holidays. Departs 08:50 on Sun. Change trains in Mallow. (4) Runs daily, except holidays. Departs 10:25 on Sun. (5) Runs daily, except holidays. Departs and arrives 15 minutes later on Sun.. (6)Runs daily, except Sun. and holidays No light refreshments. Second-class only. (7) Runs daily, except Sun. and holidays. (8) Runs daily, except Fri. and Sun. Change trains in Mallow. (9) Runs Sun. only. Change trains in Mallow. (10) Runs Sun. only. (11) Plus other departures from Dublin at 13:25 (5), 14:40 (7), 17:30 (7), 18:25 (8), 19:00 (7), 19:15 (9), 20:50 (7) and 21:25(10). (12) Plus other departures from Cork at 14:30 (10), 14:45 (7), 17:30 (7), 18:20 (10), 18:50 (10) and 18:55 (7).

Cork - Killarney - Tralee - Cork 617

There is much beautiful scenery throughout this fertile area.

Dep. Cork	11:15 (1)	15:00 (1)	18:55 (3)	20:00 (2)
Arr. Mallow	11:42	15:30	19:20	20:30
Change trains.				
Dep. Mallow	11:45 (1)	16:00 (2)	20:23 (2)	20:37 (3)
Dep. Killarney	12:39	16:54	21:17	21:31
Arr. Tralee	13:15	17:30	21:55	22:15

* * *

Dep. Tralee	07:30 (4)	09:55 (2)	14:25 (3)	17:35 (2)
Dep. Killarney	08:03	10:31	14:59	18:08
Arr. Mallow	08:59	11:35	15:56	19:01
Change trains.				
Dep. Mallow	09:39 (4)	11:45 (3)	15:59 (3)	19:35 (3)
Arr. Cork	10:05	12:15	16:25	20:00

(1) Runs daily, except Sundays and holidays. Second-class only. Light refreshments. (2) Runs daily, except Sundays and holidays. Second-class only. (3) Runs daily, except Sundays and holidays. Light refreshments. (4) The Mallow-Cork trains runs Monday-Friday, except holidays.

Sights in **Killarney**: It is 85 miles from Shannon Airport. See the sculpture by Seamus Murphy, called The Shy Woman of Kerry. The marvelous garden and the exhibit of early crafts and housing at Muckross House, a 19th century mansion on the outskirts of Killarney. Shop here for linens, glassware and crocheted women's clothing.

Take the 112-mile, all-day "Ring of Kerry" bus sightseeing trip, a popular excursion. You will see many lakes and mountains.

Dublin - Galway - Dublin 616

The are many beautiful lakes in this area.

All of these trains run daily except Sundays and holidays and have light refreshments, unless designated otherwise.

Dep. Dublin (Heu.)	07:55 (1)	09:30 (2)	11:00	14:05	18:35 (4)
Arr. Galway	11:05	12:30	13:45	17:00	21:05

Sights in **Galway:** The 14th century St. Nicholas' Church. The ruins of a 13th century Franciscan friary. The 13th century town walls.

Dep. Galway	08:00	09:05 (2)	11:35	15:10 (1)	18:10 (2+5)
Arr. Dublin (Heu.)	10:25	11:45	14:15	18:15	21:10

(1) Second-class only. (2) Runs Sundays only. Second-class only. (3) Runs Sundays only. No light refreshments. (4) Plus other Dublin departures at 18:50 (2) and 20:05 (3), arriving Galway 21:35 and 23:30. (5) Plus another Galway departure at 18:25 (1), arriving Dublin 21:25.

Dublin - Kilkenny - Dublin 614

Dep. Dublin (Heuston)	07:40 (1)	09:55 (2)	11:35 (3)	15:00 (1)	18:10 (1)	18:15 (2)
Arr. Kilkenny	09:31	11:41	13:11	16:48	19:50	20:01

*   *   *

Dep. Kilkenny	08:25 (1)	10:35 (2)	11:38 (1)	16:05 (3)	18:55 (2)	19:09 (1)
Arr. Dublin (Heuston)	09:55	12:10	13:25	17:50	20:35	21:00

(1) Runs daily, except Sun. and holidays. Light refreshments. (2) Runs Sun. only. (3) Runs daily, except Sun. and holidays.

Sights in **Kilkenny**: The formal gardens and the 150-foot-long hall at Kilkenny Castle. The 13th century Saint Canice Cathedral, one of the loveliest in Ireland from that era. The 13th century Kytler's Inn, now a restaurant. The 19th century Saint Mary's Cathedral.

Dublin - Limerick - Dublin 618
There is bus service between Limerick and Shannon Airport.

Dep. Dublin (Heuston)	07:30 (1)	09:00 (2)	10:25 (3)	10:40 (2+6)
Arr. Limerick	09:30	11:45	13:20	13:09

*   *   *

Dep. Limerick	07:00 (2)	08:00 (2)	08:30 (4)	09:40 (3+7)
Arr. Dublin (Heuston)	09:25	10:00	10:35	12:30

(1) Runs Mon.-Fri., except holidays. (2) Runs daily, except Sun. and holidays. (3) Runs Sun. only. (4) Runs daily, except Sun. and holidays. Light refreshments. (5) Runs daily. Departs 15:00 on Sun. and holidays. (6) Plus other departures from Dublin at 14:40 (2), 17:40 (4), 17:45 (2), 18:40 (3) and 20:50 (2). (7) Plus other departures from Limerick at 11:50 (2), 15:10 (5), 15:30 (2) and 17:50 (3).

THE FERRY-CROSSINGS TO FRANCE

Rosslare - LeHavre - Paris and Rosslare - Cherbourg - Paris
Covered by Eurailpass. Operated by Irish Ferries Company.

Reserving and paying extra for a cabin with private toilet ($71–U.S. in 1991) is essential in Summer, when many passengers outnumber the seats on the vessel and must sit on the deck for this 21-hour trip.

Days of operation and departure times vary during 6 different periods of the year. For 1992 schedules and reservations, contact the North American agent: Lynott Tours Inc., 350 Fifth Avenue, New York, NY 10118. Telephone: (800) 221-2474.

RAIL CONNECTIONS WITH ENGLAND
See pages 426 and 427.

ITALY

Except for EuroCity trains: Children under 4 travel free. Half-fare for children 4—11. Children 12 and over must pay full fare.

Italy has 4 types of fast trains: Pendolino (first-class only), EuroCity, Intercity and Rapido. Passengers using individual tickets (not traveling with first-class Italian passes or one of the first-class Eurailpasses) must pay a supplemental charge when riding on all Pendolinos and most of the other 3.

Pendolinos have been the poshest trains in Europe since 1990. In order to accommodate curves at very high speeds, Pendolinos tilt — using the motion of a pendulum. The supplement for them includes the seat reservation fee and a meal.

Reservation is required for all EuroCity and most Intercity trains.

Sleeping-car service is offered by Wagon-Lits Company in first-class compartments, second-class compartments, first-class couchette and second-class couchette. All of these should be reserved in advance.

Few Italian trains offer full meal service.

The signs you will see at railstations in Italy are:

ARRIVI	ARRIVAL
BINARIO	TRACK
CARROZZA LETTI	SLEEPING CAR
CARROZZA RISTORANTE	RESTAURANT CAR
DONNE	WOMEN
ENTRATA	ENTRANCE
ORARIO FERROVIARIO	TIMETABLE
PARTENZE	DEPARTURE
PIATTAFORMA	PLATFORM
PRENOTAZIONE POSTI	SEAT RESERVATION
SCOMPARTIMENTO PER FUMATORI	SMOKING COMPARTMENT
STAZIONE FERROVIARIO	RAILSTATION
UFFICIO BAGAGLI	BAGGAGE CHECKROOM
UFFICIO BIGLIETTO	TICKET OFFICE
UOMINI	MEN
USCITA	EXIT

ITALIAN HOLIDAYS

A list of holidays is helpful because some trains will be noted later in this section as *not* running on holidays. Also, those trains which operate on holidays are filled, and it is necessary to make reservations for them long in advance.

January 1	New Year's Day		Proclamation of the Republic
January 6	Epiphany		(First Monday in June)
	Easter	August 15	Assumption Day
	Easter Monday		Victory Day (World War I)
April 25	Liberation Day		(First Monday in November)
May 1	Labor Day	December 8	Immaculate Conception
		December 25	Christmas Day
		December 26	St. Stephen's Day

ITALY

SUMMER TIME

Italy changes to Summer Time on the last Sunday of March and converts back to Standard Time on the last Sunday of September. Many Italian trains and international trains originating or terminating in Italy have different schedules during Summer Time than they do the balance of the year.

EURAILPASS BONUSES IN ITALY

A 30% reduction from the fare for the Venice-Piraeus (and v.v.) and Venice–Alexandria (and v.v.) boat trips.

The Brindisi-Patras boat trip (see schedules on page 218) is covered by the Eurailpasses — but only if you go on Adriatica di Navagazione Line or Hellenic Mediterranean Line.

WARNING: The employees of other lines intimate that their ships honor the 2 passes and then charge fees after the boat leaves the pier.

With or without a Eurailpass, a reservation theoretically can be made on day of departure or day before departure — but it is very unlikely that space will be available (particularly during July and August) unless a reservation is made many weeks in advance of departure dates.

Those gambling on making a reservation after arriving in Brindisi can make application January 1–June 9 and October 1–December 31 only at the Adriatica di Navagazione embarkation office, located at Maritime Station, a 15-minute walk from Brindisi's Central railstation, along Corso Umberto and Corso Garibaldi. Taxis are available at the railstation.

From June 10 to September 30, those without advance reservations can apply also to any Brindisi travel agency that displays in its window the green badge "Eurail Information — Eurailpass".

Holders of advance reservations must go at all times directly to the Adriatica di Navagazione embarkation office to have their tickets checked, settle port taxes due and obtain the required Embarkation Ticket. That office is open 08:30–13:00 and 15:30–22:30.

Advance reservations before you start your trip can be made by contacting Extra Value Travel, 683 South Collier Boulevard, Marco Island, Florida 33937, U.S.A. Telephone: (813) 394-3384.

Another fee is charged for such special accommodations as aircraft type seats, pullman berths and cabins. There is also a port tax of 7,000 Lira that is *not* covered by Eurailpass and must be paid in Lira.

Passengers with advance reservation must obtain the Embarkation Ticket at least 2 hours prior to the ship's departure time. The ships reserve the right to cancel a reservation when that is not done and to give the space to a standby passenger.

The trains from northern Italy to Brindisi, timed to connect with the ferry departures, are frequently late. For that reason, it is *advisable* to arrive Brindisi the day before a ferry departure to Patras.

Readers reported to us in 1990 that conditions on the boat were unsatisfactory.

Brindisi - Patras - Athens   For sailing dates, see Cook's Table 1490.

Dep. Brindisi Harbor	20:00	22:30
Arr. Patras	13:00	18:00

It is a 20-minute walk from Patras' dock to its railstation. A taxi costs about $7 (U.S.)

Change to train.   980

For a view of the Corinthian Gulf and then the Corinthian Canal, sit on the left side of the train.

Dep. Patras	14:00	18:45
Arr. Athens	19:21	23:21

ITALIAN TRAIN PASSES

When ordering any number of train tickets or any train pass *except Eurailpass* from the Italian State Railways (U.S.A. and Canadian offices listed on page 24), there is a $20 processing fee per order for ordinary tickets and a $10 fee per pass on all Italian train passes.

Anyone who purchases an Italian train pass may obtain a 10% discount on city sightseing and excursion tours by presenting the pass at any Compagnia Italiana Turismo (CIT) office in Florence, Milan, Naples, Rome and Venice.

Both the Italian Train Pass and Italy Flexi Railcard offer unlimited travel on all Italian trains (including InterCity and EuroCity trains), including free seat reservations — *which can be made only in Italy*. Sleeper and couchette services are *not* included. Both passes are available at travel agencies worldwide *outside* Italy and at all offices worldwide of CIT. Validity dates must be marked on these passes at the station where the holder is boarding the train for the first use of the pass.

Italian Tourist Ticket   The 1992 *first*-class prices are: $226 (U.S.) for 8 days, $284 for 15 days, $330 for 21 days, and $396 for 30 days. For *second*-class: $152, $190, $220, and $264. The 15, 21 and 30-day tickets can be extended to double their initial period. Half-fare for children 4-12 years old. Children under 4 travel free.

Italy Flexi Railcard   The 1992 *first*-class prices are: $170 (U.S.) for any 4 days within 9 days, $250 for any 8 days within 21 days, and $314 for any 12 days within 30 days. For *second*-class: $116, $164 and $210.

Kilometric Ticket   Permits travel up to a maximum of 20 single trips totaling 3,000kms (1,875 miles) within a 2-month period. When used on a train that charges a supplement, the passengers using the Ticket must pay the supplement. Can be used by more than one person at a time, to a maximum of 5 persons. When a child 4–12 years old travels on this ticket, only half the mileage used is counted. Children under 4 travel free. Available before you leave home at both Italian State Railways (U.S.A. and Canadian offices listed on page 24) and from travel agents worldwide. Also available in Italy at all railstations and from Italian travel agencies.

The 1992 prices are: $264 (U.S.) for *first*-class, $156 for *second*-class.

ONE-DAY EXCURSIONS AND CITY SIGHTSEEING

Comprehensive maps which make it easy to find the worthwhile sights there can be obtained in most Italian cities in offices marked "Azienda Autonoma di Turismo" or "Ente Provinciale di Turismo", located on a principal street.

Here are 70 one-day rail trips that can be made comfortably from Agrigento, Bologna, Catania, Florence (Firenze), Genoa, Messina, Milan, Naples (Napoli), Palermo, Rome and Torino (Turin), returning to those cities in most cases before dinnertime. Notes are provided on what to see and do at each destination. The number after the name of each route is the Cook's timetable.

Bologna

See the dissection theater in the ancient medical school. The fantastic inlaid wood panels in the Chorus at San Domenico Church. (Be sure to turn on the electric lights there in order to get a good look at the marvelous woodwork.) The Church of San Petronio. The Art Gallery. Neptune's Fountain, where Piazza Maggiore and Piazza Nettuno connect.

The 2 leaning towers in Piazza di Port Ravegnana: 165-foot tall Garisenda and the 330-foot high Asinelli. Climb the 486 steps of the Asinelli for the splendid view from the top of the tower. Visit the churches on Santo Stefano. The Municipal Archeological Museum. The Communale, Podesta, Mercanzia, Re Anzio and Bevilacqua palaces. Try the marvelous Bolognese food.

Florence (Firenze)

The 14th century Cathedral of Santa Maria del Fiore (open daily 07:00–12:00 and 14:30–18:00) is where most visitors begin sightseeing in Florence. Ascend its 292-foot high belltower for a great view of the city. Across from the Cathedral, see the magnificent sculptured bronze Ghiberti doors ("Gates of Paradise" was Michelangelo's description) on the octagonal Baptistry of San Giovanni (open 09:30–12:30 and 14:30–17:30).

See the 14th-19th century furniture and utensils representing domestic life in those eras, in the Davanzati Palace.

There is much more to see, in 2 different directions from the Cathedral-Baptistry complex. Facing the Baptistry, you proceed North on Via Ricasoli to visit Area #1. You go South, toward the Arno River, for the sightseeing in Area #2.

Area #1: See the Michelangelo sculptures and breathtaking marble floors, walls and crypts at the Medici Chapel. The street behind the Chapel is lined with vendors. On the other side of the street is an enormous food market where game with colorful furs and feathers make an unusual display.

An easy walk from the Chapel is the Academia (closed Monday), housing the stupen- dous statue of David. Nearby is the Fra Angelico Museum in the Church of San Marco, with its interesting frescoes and monk's cells.

Across the street from the Academia, you can board a city bus for the 20-minute ride uphill to the village of Fiesole, where there are Etruscan ruins, a Roman amphitheater, a 13th century Cathedral, the Convent of St. Francis, and a splendid view of Florence.

Area #2: The Piazza della Signoria and, next to it, the thousands of great art treasures in the 29 exhibit rooms of the Palazzo degli Uffizi (open Tuesday-Saturday 09:00-19:00, Sunday 09:00-13:00). Nearby is the Franciscan Church of Santa Croce, where Michelangelo, Machiavelli, Rossini and Galileo are buried. Also see the sculptures (Donatello's bronze David and the della Robbia glazed terra cottas) at the Bargello Palace and Museum, in a 13th century palace. Next, cross to the other side of the Arno River, over the Ponte Vecchio (lined with tiny jewelry shops) to visit the outstanding paintings, statues, tapestries and furniture in the 28 exhibit rooms and galleries of the Palazzo Pitti (closed Monday).

The Pitti is a complex of 5 different museums. The Palace itself contains the Palatine Gallery (noted for its Raphaels), the Modern Art Gallery, and the Silver Museum. Two other museums are located in the Boboli Gardens behind the Palace: the Costume Museum and the Porcelain Museum, both of which are open only on Tuesday, Thursday and Saturday (hours during May and June are 09:00–19:00).

The Medici Chapel, Academia, Bargello, Uffizi and Pitti are open Tuesdays–Saturdays 09:00–14:00 and Sundays and feast days from 09:00–13:00.

Genoa

Italy's largest port. See the house where Columbus was born. St. Lawrence Cathedral. *Do not fail* to walk down the 15th century streets near the waterfront, too narrow for a tour bus and unfortunately not seen by many visitors to Genoa. The incredible Monumental Cemetery, with its vast number of dramatic statues of many of the people buried there. The landscaped hillside with colorful plants painting a flowering tapestry of Columbus' fleet: the Nina, the Pinta and the Santa Maria.

The 16th century palaces on Via Garibaldi. The 17th century palaces on Via Balbi. The Cathedral of San Lorenzo, constructed from 1099 to 1250.

Milan

The Duomo Cathedral, holding more than 20,000 people, begun in 1386 and taking 5 centuries to complete. There are more than 3,000 statues on its exterior. Then go through the incredibly beautiful shopping arcade, the Galleria Vittorio Emanuele, to La Scala Opera House—one of the world's greatest theaters, accommodating 3,600 people, it was first constructed in 1776. Its opera museum is open Tuesdays–Saturdays 09:00–12:00 and 14:00–18:00.

Exhibited in the museum are old paintings and engravings of the opera house before its destruction by bombs in 1943 and its reconstruction in 1946, portraits of many famous singers, several of Verdi's pianos and such other Verdi memorabilia as his manuscripts and death mask.

Opposite La Scala, behind a statue of da Vinci, is the 16th century Palazzo Marino, now the City Hall. Just past the gate (Porta Nuova) at the end of Via Manzoni are the Museum of Natural History, the Zoo and the Planetarium.

See da Vinci's "Last Supper" at Santa Maria delle Grazie. It can be viewed Tuesday-Saturday 09:00–13:30 and 14:00–18:30, and on Sunday 09:00—15:00. *Do not fail to see* the enormous and elaborate crypts at the Monumental Cemetery. Visit the Palazzo Dugnani, on Via Manin, to see the Tiepolo ceiling fresco there.

It is a short taxi ride from the Dugnani to the enormous Castello Sforzesco, which has a vast collection of paintings (including Michelangelo's last work, the Rondanini Pieta) and exhibits of harpsichords, wrought iron, tapestries and ceramics. The Castle is open daily except Monday 09:30–12:00 and 14:30–17:00.

See the collection of sculpture, Flemish and Persian tapestries, paintings, scientific instruments, glass and armor at Museo Poldi-Pezzoli, at 12 Via Manzoni, open Tuesday-Sunday 09:30–12:30 and 14:30–17:30. Many great paintings (Raphael, Tiepolo, Canaletto) are exhibited in the Accademia di Brera on Via Brera, open Tuesday- Saturday 09:00–14:00, and on Sunday 09:00–13:00.

Both the Modern Art Gallery (16 Via Palestra) and the Archaeological Museum (15 Corso Magenta) are open Wednesday–Saturday 09:30–12:30 and 14:30—17:30; on Sunday 09:30–13:00. There are marvelous paintings by Raphael, Caravaggi and Botticelli in the Ambrosian Library, open Mondays–Fridays except holidays 10:00–12:00 and 15:00–17:00 and Saturdays, Sundays and holidays 15:00–17:00.

Gourmets will want to visit the fantastic food store called Peck's, at No. 9 Via Spadari, opened in 1892 by a Czechoslovak named Frank Peck. It is the Italian equivalent of Hediard, described under "Paris" in the section of this chapter on France. What you will see at Peck's are: large wedges of parmigiano and reggiano cheese, Italian wines, roasts, loins, saddles and breasts of white veal, caviar, numerous cold seafood salads, mussels, langouste, squid, lobster, celery remoulade, pates, head cheese, scampi, sturgeon, hot vegetable dishes (baked fennel, baby zucchini, asparagus milanese), roasted quail skewered with sausages and wrapped in bacon, tripe in tomato sauce, a wide range of pasta (green ravioli al forno, tortellini, ravioli alla contadina), paella with saffron rice, white mushrooms in oil, many sausages and many fish (herring, smoked salmon, smoked eels, smoked trout).

If that is not enough, across the street from Peck's is a famous pork store, La Bottega del Maiale, with an enormous display of whole baby pigs, pork parts (loins, ears, fillets, tongue, liver) and such sausages as sopresa Calabra, salame Toscana, coppa, cacciatorini, stagionata, capocolla and finocchiona.

Next door to the pork store is Peschere Spadari, a great fish store, selling nearly everything that swims: scampi, Channel sole, mackerel, scampi, squid, mussels. A short distance down the street, at No. 1 Via Speroni, is a large cheese store.

Naples

Most museums in Naples are closed on Monday. See the view from Certosa de San Martino monastery and, inside, its National Museum. The 13th century Castel Nuovo. The National Library. The Archaeological Museum, with its great Grecian and Roman sculptures. The Capodimonte Park, Palace and Art Gallery. The Teatro San Carlo, home of Neapolitan opera. The Royal Palace and scores of other palaces. The Botanical Garden. There are good views of Naples Bay from the gardens of the Duca di Martina Museum of Ceramics at the Villa Floridiana. Splendid views of Mount Vesuvius from the quay at Santa Lucia. Nearby **Herculaneum** (now called (**Ercolano**) is as interesting as Pompeii.

Rome

Visit St. Peter's, the most wonderful work by man in all the world. Take an elevator to the dome for views of Vatican City and Rome. Tour the Vatican to see the Sistine Chapel, Raphael Rooms, Pio-Clementino Museum, Picture Gallery, Tapestry Gallery, Map Gallery and Candelabra Gallery (all of them closed on Sunday, except the last Sunday of each month).

See Capitoline Hill. The Roman Forum. Palatine Hill. The Imperial Fora.

Marcellus Theatre. The Jewish Synagogue. The Temple of Avesta. Aventine Hill. St. Paul's Gate. The view of Rome from the Villa Borghese Park. The Protestant cemetery, with the graves of Keats and Shelley. The Colosseum. The Arch of Constantine. The Basilica of St. Paul Outside the Walls. Michelangelo's statue of Moses in the Church of St. Peter in Chains. The Pantheon. The mosaics at the Baths of Caracalla.

Castel Sant'Angelo (closed Monday). Trevi Fountain. The Zoo. The Etruscan Museum (closed Monday). The Napoleon Museum (closed Monday). The Spanish Square, Steps and Fountain. The National Modern Art Gallery (closed Monday). Diocletian's Baths.

The House of the Vestal Virgins. Marvelous views of Rome from Janiculum Hill. The Monument to Vittorio Emanuele. The Bernini sculptures in the Borghese Gallery (Villa Borghese), open daily 09:00–13:30. The magnificent Velazquez portrait of Pope Innocent X in the Doria Gallery (Piazza del Collegio Romano), open Tuesday, Friday, Saturday and Sunday 10:00–13:00.

Works of Raphael, Caravaggi and other Renaissance artists in the Palazzo Barberini Gallery (Via Quattro Fontane), open Tuesday-Saturday 09:00–14:00, Sunday 09:00–13:00. Displays of Etruscan art at the National Museum of Villa Giulia (Piazza di Villa Giulia), open daily except Monday 09:00–19:00, holidays 09:00–13:00. Exhibits of ancient Rome at the National Museum of Rome (in the Baths of Diocletian), open Tuesday–Saturday 09:00–14:00, Sunday 09:00–13:00. The Museum of Folklore (Piazza Sant' Egidio, in Trastevere), open Tuesday–Sunday 09:00–13:00, also Thursday evenings 17:00–19:30.

In the following timetables, where a city has more than one railstation we have designated the particular station after the name of the city (in parentheses).

Bologna - Florence - Bologna 374

Exceptional mountain scenery on this easy one-day roundtrip.

The train goes through the 11.5-mile long Apennine Tunnel, Italy's longest tunnel. Some trains stop almost midpoint in the tunnel at an underground station called **Precedenze**. Residents of a small village at the crest of the mountain, in order to return home, must climb 1,863 steps inside a diagonal shaft that was used for constructing the tunnel.

Dep. Bologna	Frequent times from 03:37 to 22:42
Arr. Florence (S.M.N.)	70 minutes later

Sights in **Florence**: See notes about sightseeing in Florence on page 219.

Dep. Florence (S.M.N.)	Frequent times from 03:30 to 23:54
Arr. Bologna	70 minutes later

Bologna - Milan - Bologna 374

Dep. Bologna	07:42	08:07 (1)	08:37	09:14 (2)	09:19 (3)	09:38
Arr. Milan (Cen.)	09:50	09:55	10:25	10:45	11:00	11:57

Sights in **Milan**: See notes about sightseeing in Milan on page 220.

Dep. Milan (Cen.)	15:00 (3)	15:55 (4)	16:05	17:00	17:55 (5)	18:00 (7)
Arr. Bologna	16:49	17:38	18:16	18:47	19:38	20:14

(1) Reservation *advisable*. Supplement charged. Light refreshments. (2) "Pendolino" (see page 215). Reservation *required*. Supplement includes reservation and meal. First-class only. Runs daily, except Sundays and holidays. (3) Reservation *advisable*. Supplement charged. (4) Reservation *required*. Supplement charged. Restaurant car. (5) Reservation *required*. Supplement charged. Light refreshments. (6) "Pendolino" (see footnote 2). Runs daily, except Saturday. (7) Plus other departures from Milan at 19:30 (6), 19:55, 20:35, 21:05, 22:10 and 22:55, arriving Bologna 20:57, 21:53, 22:35, 22:54, 00:47 and 01:33.

Bologna - Parma - Bologna 374

Dep. Bologna	Frequent times from 06:06 to 20:38
Arr. Parma	50-65 minutes later

* * *

Dep. Parma	Frequent times from 06:48 to 23:49
Arr. Bologna	50-65 minutes later

Sights in **Parma:** The 19th century Teatro Reggio opera house. Nearby, the Lombardi Museum in the Palazzo di Riserva. The restored Palazzo della Pilotta, which houses the Farnese Theater, National Gallery, Palatina Library and the National Museum of Antiquities.

The latter, Italy's most modern museum, has an outstanding collection of Etruscan, Roman, medieval and Renaissance works of art, including larger-than-life-size statues of members of the Julian-Claudian family (Britannicus, the 2 Drussii, Livia and Claudius) that are familiar to viewers of the "I Claudius" television program.

More than 40,000 rare books are displayed in the Library (Biblioteca). Particularly interesting are the De Rossi collection of Oriental manuscripts and the Bodoni Museum, a complete collection of all the volumes of the great 19th century typographer for whom it is named.

Visit the Cathedral to view the marvelous Assumption of the Virgin fresco by Corregio in the dome. Also the Camera di Corregio, a room near the Cathedral he frescoed in 1518. The 12th century sculptures by Benedetto Antelami, in the 5-story red marble Baptistry, one of Italy's finest buildings. See the early 19th century sculpture by Lorenzo Bartolini in the Madonna della Steccata church. Toscani's room at the Conservatory.

Bologna - Pisa - Bologna

374

Dep. Bologna	07:46 (1)	08:00	09:42 (2)	10:30	11:42 (3)	12:42 (1)
Arr. Florence (S.M.N.)	08:51	09:10	10:46	11:40	12:46	13:46

Change trains. 370

Dep. Florence (S.M.N.)	09:00	10:00	11:00	12:00	13:00	14:00
Arr. Pisa	09:51	10:53	11:53	12:53	13:53	14:53

The #1 Bus takes you from the Pisa railstation to the Piazza del Duomo in 10 minutes.

* * *

Dep. Pisa	13:46	14:46	15:46	16:46	17:46	18:46 (5)
Arr. Florence (S.M.N.)	14:38	15:38	16:38	17:38	18:38	19:38

Change trains. 374

Dep. Florence (S.M.N.)	15:19 (4)	16:19 (1)	17:19 (4)	18:19 (2)	19:17 (2)	20:18 (5)
Arr. Bologna	16:22	17:22	18:22	19:22	20:22	21:22

(1) Reservation *required*. Supplement charged. Light refreshments. (2) Reservation *required*. Supplement charged. Restaurant car. (3) Runs daily, except Sundays and holidays. Reservation *required*. Supplement charged. Light refreshments. (4) Reservation *required*. Supplement charged. (5) Plus other Pisa departures at 19:10 and 22:02....arriving Florence 20:08 and 23:35....departing Florence 20:25 and 23:54....arriving Bologna 21:28 and 01:23.

Sights in **Pisa**: The Piazza del Duomo, with 4 major attractions. Walk up the spiral stairs of the Leaning Tower to its roof and see the view from there. A few feet from the base of the Tower is the majestic 11th century striped marble Cathedral. Key features of it are the magnificent bronze entrance doors and, inside, paintings, statues, mosaics, a fantastic pulpit, and Galileo's lamp. While watching the lamp swing, Galileo timed each arc by his pulse and observed that every swing, long or short, took the same time span. By that, he postulated "the isochronism of the pendular movement".

Next, walk the short distance from the Cathedral to the beautiful, enormous 11th century circular marble Baptistry to see its font and its 6 columns of porphyry, marble and oriental granite. Three of the columns rest on carved lions. Biblical scenes are carved on each panel.

A very short walk from the Baptistry is a large building with a cemetery in its central court. Each section of the building exhibits many frescoes. See the 50-foot by 19-foot "Triumph of Death" in the North Gallery.

Before the train from Florence reaches Pisa, it stops 2 minutes in **Campiglia Marittima**, which has a large statue of a mongrel dog at its railstation. The dog (named Lampo) appears to watch the procession of arriving and departing trains.

Lampo ("flash of lightning") liked train travel as much as we do. He learned the train schedules and took a trip every day more than 3,000 train trips in his lifetime.

Owned by the assistant stationmaster, Lampo escorted his master's daughter to school every morning. For that reason, he made short rail trips on schooldays, longer journeys on weekends. Always, he would go only such distances and make the necessary connections so as to return home every day before dawn.

Prior to Lampo's death in 1961 (under a freight train), he had become known not only by every trainman in Italy but by the Italian public as well, through reports of his love of train travel that appeared on Italian television and in Italy's newspapers.

Local railway workers say only a person with a printed timetable could have equaled the dog's feat, when he once went past his stop on a certain trip and then managed to return home by taking a complex series of connecting trains to get back to Campiglia Marittima.

Bologna - Ravenna - Bologna   376

| Dep. Bologna | 06:13 | 08:21 | 10:25 (1) |
| Arr. Ravenna | 07:33 | 09:33 | 11:22 |

Sights in **Ravenna**: The marvelous 5th century monuments, the Mausoleum of Galla Placidia and the Orthodox Baptistry. Just behind the Mausoleum, see the mosaics at the Church of San Vitale. Great mosaics also in Sant'Appollinare Nuovo Church, where it is helpful to use binoculars or even an opera glass in order to see those mosaics that are at the top of the walls. There are more dazzling mosaics in the Archiepiscopal Chapel.

See the ivory pulpit in the Archbishop's Palace. Dante's Tomb. The Museum of Antiquities. The exhibits at the Academy of Fine Arts.

| Dep. Ravenna | 13:00 | 14:31 | 17:30 | 20:10 |
| Arr. Bologna | 14:43 | 15:44 | 18:52 | 21:21 |

(1) Operates early June to late September.

Bologna - Rome   374

| Dep. Bologna | 06:00 (1) | 07:40 (2) | 07:46 (3) | 08:24 (2) | 09:12 (2+8) |
| Arr. Rome (Ter.) | 09:50 | 10:15 | 11:20 | 11:00 | 11:46 |

Sights in **Rome**: See notes about Rome on page 221.

| Dep. Rome (Ter.) | 15:15 (4) | 16:10 (5) | 17:00 (5) | 18:00 (3) | 19:00 (6+9) |
| Arr. Bologna | 18:30 | 19:22 | 20:22 | 21:22 | 21:34 |

(1) Reservation *required*. Supplement charged. Second-class only. (2) "Pendolino" (see page 215). Reservation *required*. Supplement includes reservation and meal. First-class only. (3) Reservation *required*. Supplement charged. Light refreshments. (4) Reservation *required*. Supplement charged. (5) Reservation *required*. Supplement charged. Restaurant car. (6) "Pendolino" (see footnote 2). Runs daily, except Saturday. (7) Second-class only. (8) Plus another departure from Bologna at 09:22 (3), arriving Rome 12:45. (9) Plus other departures from Rome at 19:15, 19:45 (2), 20:00 (2) and 20:25 (7), arriving Bologna 22:47, 22:17, 22:32 and 00:35.

Bologna - Siena - Bologna

374			355 c		
Dep. Bologna	06:30 (1)	09:42 (2)	Dep. Siena	15:40 (1)	18:40 (1+4)
Arr. Florence (S.M.N.)	07:42	10:46	Arr. Florence (S.M.N.)	17:13	20:00
Change trains. 355 c			Change trains. 374		
Dep. Florence (S.M.N.) 08:10 (1)	11:42 (1)		Dep. Florence (S.M.N.) 17:27 (3)	20:25 (1)	
Arr. Siena	09:50	13:25	Arr. Bologna	18:30	21:28

(1) Second-class only. (2) Reservation *required*. Supplement charged. Restaurant car. (3) Reservation *required*. Supplement charged. (4) Plus another departure from Siena at 19:38 (1), departing Florence 21:42, arriving Bologna 22:47.

Sights in **Siena:** The pervasive color, named for Siena, that dominates this hill town. The view of Italy's most unique square, Piazza del Campo, from the top of the Mangia Tower of the Palazzo Publico (with its marvelous 14th century murals) or from a window of the Palazzo Publico (open daily except Sunday 9:00-13:00), where records in unbelievably beautiful calligraphy going back to the 12th century are exhibited with 15th century costumes and fine frescoes. The Pisano sculpture and mosaic floors at the Cathedral, on Piazza del Duomo. The paneled Duccio Crucifixion in the Museum of the Cathedral. Climb from there to the top of Facciatone, the skeleton for a new cathedral whose construction ceased when the Black Death of 1348 ravished Siena.

Pinacoteca, the art museum, on a street that is down from the Cathedral. Fontebranda, the old fountain with 3 arches. The ancient houses along Via degli Archi, Vicolo della Fortuna, and Vicolo delle Scotto, all of these streets radiating out from the Piazza del Campo.

Bologna - Venice - Bologna 390

Dep. Bologna	06:03	07:40	08:40	11:32 (1)	11:40	12:40
Arr. Venice (S.L.)	08:10	09:46	10:42	13:15	13:42	14:42
			* * *			
Dep. Venice (S.L.)	13:20	14:20	14:45 (1)	16:20	17:20	18:10 (2+3)
Arr. Bologna	15:23	16:30	16:23	18:23	19:23	20:03

(1) "Pendolino" (see page 215). Reservation *required*. Supplement includes reservation and meal. First-class only. (2) reservation *required*. Supplement charged. Restaurant car. (3) Plus other departures from Venice at 18:26, 19:20. 20:20 and 20:55, arriving Bologna 20:30, 21:23, 22:23 and 23:08.

Sights in **Venice**: After the obligatory gondola ride, stand at either end of Piazza San Marco and try to cope with the enormity and beauty of the most impressive square in the world. Next visit St. Mark's Cathedral, the most wonderful Byzantine structure in Europe. Next door, see the Doge's Palace. Then relax at one of the outdoor cafes on St. Mark's Square and take in the wonder of it all while waiting for the figures on the enormous 15th century clock to emerge and strike the bell.

For another view of St. Mark's Square and the entire Lagoon, go to the top of the Bell Tower. Walk through the colorful, narrow streets of shops to the 16th century Rialto Bridge and, standing there, watch the canal traffic. The Rialto is lined with stores selling jewelry, linens, hand-blown glass, clothing, gloves and fabrics. After crossing over the Bridge, walk a short distance to the extraordinary fish market, which is the most lively 07:00—11:00 and particularly on Friday.

Among the score of churches to see in Venice are: San Giuliano, Santa Maria Formosa, Santa Maria dei Miracoli, San Giovanni e Paolo, San Francesco della Vigna, San Zaccaria, Santo Stefano, Santa Maria Gloriosa dei Frari, Santa Maria del Carmine, San Sebastiano, Madonna dell'Orto and Santi Apostoli. There are also 5 synagogues here: the German (oldest), Spanish (most beautiful), Levantine, Italian and Canton.

See the Archaeological Museum (closed Monday) in the Old Library. The many beautiful palaces on the Grand Canal. The exquisite 18th century decor of the most beautiful small opera house in the world, the Gran Teatro La Fenice.

A 15-minute boat ride takes you to the Lido, Venice's beach resort and site of its largest gambling casino. It is only a 3-minute boat ride to the beautiful, white Church of Santa Maria della Salute, built on more than one million wood pilings.

It is a 15-minute boat ride to the island of **Murano** to watch glass-blowing and visit the Glassworks Museum (closed Tuesday) in Palazzo Giustiniani. Boats for Murano leave from the Fondamenta Nuove vaporetto dock. We recommend you get off the boat at the second stop, tour the Glassworks Museum, and then walk past many interesting shops to the first landing for the return ride to Venice. The Glassworks Museum displays ancient Roman work and many excellent glass pieces from the Middle Ages

To see lacemaking (tablecloths, handkerchiefs, bedspreads, dresses) and buy fine lace, take a 30-minute boat ride to **Burano**. It is only a few minutes by boat from Burano to **Torcelo**, a small island of orchards, vineyards and artichoke farms. The 11th century basilica there has splendid mosaics. Another sight on Torcello that interests some tourists is the display of the small skeleton of the martyr Santa Fosca in a glass coffin at the church there that is named for her.

Bologna - Verona - Bologna   381

Dep. Bologna	06:44	08:00 (1)	08:44	10:30 (1)	11:45	12:44
Arr. Verona	08:16	10:05	10:38	12:26	13:30	14:35

Sights in **Verona:** The large and excellently preserved first century Arena. Then take Via Mazzini (Verona's main shopping street) to Piazza della Herbe (Herb Square), where you will find a marvelous display of fruits, vegetables, live pet birds, and dead game birds. Only a few minutes walk from there, the Veronese marble lobby of the Hotel Due Torri is worth seeing.

At Piazza dei Signori are the tombs of the Della Scala Family, once rulers of Verona. La Scala Opera House in Milan is named after them. See the paintings in the Church of Sant'Anastasia. Visit the Cathedral and the Museum of Art in Castelvecchio, on Corso Cavour.

The main attraction in Verona, since Shakespeare, has always been Juliet's balcony, at Via Cappelo 17-25 (Shakespeare's "Capulet".)

Dep. Verona	12:40 (2)	13:29	14:36	15:43	17:29	19:29	21:33
Arr. Bologna	14:00	15:20	16:14	17:26	19:20	21:20	23:35

(1) Reservation *required*. Supplement charged. Restaurant car. (2) Reservation *required*. Supplement charged. First-class only.

Florence - Arezzo - Florence   374

Dep. Florence (S.M.N.)	06:55 (1)	08:50	09:00 (1)	10:00	10:33 (1)	11:05 (3)
Arr. Arezzo	07:38	10:02	09:44	11:02	11:16	12:02

Sights in **Arezzo:** The 15th century Piero frescoes of the Legend of the True Cross that can be seen 12:00–14:30 and 19:00–21:30 in the Church of San Francesco. The carvings on the facade of the 11th century Church of Santa Maria della Pieve. Behind Pieve, the marvelous Piazza Grande, with its palaces. There are many other fine palaces on Corso Italia.

The musical scale and staff of 4 lines was invented in the 10th century by Guido Monaco of Arezzo. The Piazza Guido Monaco is named for him.

See the 16th century stained glass and the great Renaissance organ in the Cathedral. The collection of Etruscan and Roman artwork in the Archaeological Museum at the Convent. The enormous fortress, Medicea, built in the 16th century by the Medicis. A library and museum is maintained in the home where Petrarch was born.

| Dep. Arezzo | 13:46 | 15:46 | 17:46 |
| Arr. Florence (S.M.N.) | 14:40 | 16:45 | 18:40 |

(1) Reservation *required*. Supplement charged. Light refreshments. (2) Runs daily, except Sundays and holidays. (3) Plus another departure from Florence at 13:05 (2).

Florence - Assisi - Florence
374

Dep. Florence (S.M.N.)	08:50		11:05		12:15 (1)
Arr. Terontola	10:30		12:30		-0- (1)
Change trains. 368					
Dep. Terontola	10:45 (2)		12:50 (2)		-0- (1)
Arr. Assisi	11:51		13:51		14:50

Sights in **Assisi**: St. Francis' tomb in the 13th century Basilica on the Hill of Paradise, and the many outstanding paintings there, considered to be the greatest museum of Italian Renaissance mural painting. St. Claire's Church. The medieval Castle. Piazza del Commune. The upper and lower churches at the Convent of St. Francis, with their many frescos. Prison Hermitage. The 16th century Church of Santa Maria degli Angeli. The 12th century Cathedral of St. Ruffino. The 14th century La Rocca Maggiore fortress. The Temple of Minerva.

Dep. Assisi	14:12 (3)	16:12 (3)	16:53 (2)	18:53
Arr. Terontola	-0- (3)	-0- (3)	18:06	20:08
Change trains. 374				
Dep. Terontola	-0- (3)	-0- (3)	18:30	20:26
Arr. Florence (S.M.N.)	16:45	18:40	19:50	21:50

(1) Runs daily, except Sundays and holidays. Direct train. No train change in Terontola. (2) Second-class only. (3) Runs daily. Direct train. No train change in Terontola.

Florence - Bologna - Florence   374
Exceptional mountain scenery on this easy one-day roundtrip. The train goes through the 11.5-mile long Apennine Tunnel, Italy's longest tunnel.

| Dep. Florence (S.M.N.) | 07:23 (1) | 08:22 (2) | 09:19 | 10:19 (3) | 11:24 (4) |
| Arr. Bologna | 08:30 | 09:11 | 10:43 | 11:22 | 12:26 |

Sights in **Bologna**: See notes about Bologna on page 219.

| Dep. Bologna | 12:42 (4) | 14:12 | 14:42 (3) | 15:30 | 16:26 (5+9) |
| Arr. Florence (S.M.N.) | 13:46 | 15:16 | 15:46 | 16:40 | 17:20 (6) |

(1) Reservation *advisable*. (2) "Pendolino" (see page 215). Reservation *required*. Runs daily, except Sundays and holidays. Supplement includes reservation and meal First-class only. Departs and arrives Florence's Rifredi railstation. (3) Reservation *required*. Supplement charged. Restaurant car. (4) Reservation *required*. Supplement charged. Light refreshments. (5) "Pendolino" (see footnote 2). (6) Arrives at Florence's Rifredi railstation. (7) "Pendolino" (see footnote 2). Runs daily, except Saturday. (8) Arives at Florence's Campo di Marti railstation. (9) Plus other Bologna departures at 16:42 (4), 17:42 (3), 18:42 (3), 19:42 (4), 20:07 (3), 21:00 (7), 21:36 (8), 22:30 and 23:02 (8).

Florence - Livorno - Florence

On the 14:41 and 15:55 departures from Livorno, there is time to taxi 10 minutes from Pisa's station to the Leaning Tower and return to the station for a later departure to Florence.

370			355		
Dep. Florence (S.M.N.)	07:55 (1)		Dep. Livorno	14:41	15:55 (2)
Arr. Pisa	08:58		Arr. Pisa	14:53	16:04
Change trains. 355			Change trains. 370		
Dep. Pisa	09:36		Dep. Pisa	15:46 (1)	16:46 (1)
Arr. Livorno	09:48		Arr. Florence (S.M.N.)	16:38	17:38

(1) Second-class only. (2) Plus other Livorno departures at 16:47 and 17:55, departing Pisa 17:46 (1) and 18:46 (1), arriving Florence 18:38 and 19:38.

Sights in **Livorno**: The old and new forts, both from the 16th century. The marble statue of Ferdinand. Tacca's 17th century bronze statues of "The Four Moors". Villas once occupied by Shelley and Byron. Italy's Naval Academy. The paintings and the Communal Library, both in the Civic Museum.

Florence - Milan - Florence   374

Dep. Florence (S.M.N.)	06:58 (1)	07:23	08:22 (2)	09:19	10:19 (3)
Arr. Milan (Centrale)	09:55	10:25	10:45	12:55	13:10

Sights in **Milan**: See notes about sightseeing in Milan on page 220.

Dep. Milan (Centrale)	14:55 (1)	15:55 (3)	16:55 (3)	17:55 (1)	19:30 (4+6)
Arr. Florence (S.M.N.)	17:46	18:48	19:46	20:50	21:54 (5)

(1) Reservation *required*. Supplement charged. Light refreshments. (2) "Pendolino" (see page 215). Reservation *required*. Supplement includes reservation and meal. First-class only. Departs and arrives Florence's Rifredi railstation. Runs daily, except Sundays and holidays. (3) Reservation *required*. Supplement charged. Restaurant car. (4) "Pendolino" (see footnote 2). Runs daily, except Saturday. (5) Arrives at Florence's Rifredi station. (6) Plus another departure from Milan at 20:35, arriving Florence 23:52.

Florence - Padua - Florence   390

Dep. Florence			Dep. Padua	15:59 (1)	18:47 (1+3)
(S.M.N.)	09:33 (1)	10:37 (2)	Arr. Florence		
Arr. Padua	11:46	12:40	(S.M.N.)	18:16	21:11

(1) Reservation *required*. Supplement charged. Restaurant car. (2) "Pendolino" (see page 215). Reservation *required*. Supplement includes reservation and meal. First-class only. Departs from Florence's Rifredi railstation. (3) Plus another departure from Padua at 20:57, arriving Florence 23:40.

Sights in **Padua**: The 13th century university on the Via 8 Febraio. Scrovegni Chapel. The Church of Eremitani. The Basilica of Sant'Antonio, with several statues by Donatello.

Florence - Parma - Florence   374

Dep. Florence (S.M.N.)	06:58 (1)	07:23 (2)	10:19 (3)	11:24 (4)
Arr. Bologna	08:03	08:30	11:22	-0- (4)
Change trains.				
Dep. Bologna	08:20	09:38	11:38	-0- (4)
Arr. Parma	09:13	10:29	12:30	13:17

Sights in **Parma**: See notes about Parma under "Bologna-Parma" on page 223.

Dep. Parma	14:21	15:21	16:30	17:22	18:24	19:21 (5)
Arr. Bologna	15:14	16:14	17:25	18:16	19:20	20:14
Change trains.						
Dep. Bologna	15:30	16:42 (1)	17:42 (3)	18:42 (3)	19:42 (1)	20:25
Arr. FLorence (S.M.N.)	16:40	17:46	18:48	19:46	20:50	22:02

(1) Reservation *required*. Supplement charged.Light refreshments. (2) Reservation *advisable*. (3) Reservation *required*. Supplement charged. Restaurant car. (4) Direct train. No train change in Bologna. Reservation *required*. Supplement charged. Light refreshments. (5) Plus another departure from Parma at 21:21, arriving Bologna 22:15, arriving Florence 23:52.

Florence - Perugia - Florence
374

Dep. Florence (S.M.N.)	08:50	11:05	12:15 (1+2)
Arr. Terontola	10:30	12:32	-0- (1)
Change trains. 368			
Dep. Terontola	10:45	12:50	-0- (1)
Arr. Perugia	11:28	13:27	14:29

Sights in **Perugia:** The Municipal Palace, to see the magnificent carved and inlaid wood panels in the Library, the chapel of the Stock Exchange, and the great paintings in the National Gallery (Pinacoteca). On display to the left of the main door of the Stock Exchange chapel is the white onyx ring with which the Virgin Mary was married.

Also visit the 13th century Church of San Ercolano. Galleng Palace, with its Foreign University. The Pisano sculptures at the Fontana Maggiore in beautiful Piazza 4 Novembre. The fine collection of Tuscan paintings in the museum of the 13th century Palazzo dei Priori. Stroll along Maesta della Volte, Via dei Priori (to the Oratory of San Bernardino), Via Bagliona and Corso Vannucci, the main street.

Dep. Perugia	14:34 (1+3)	16:34 (1+3)	17:21	19:18
Arr. Terontola	-0- (1)	-0- (1)	18:06	20:08
Change trains. 374				
Dep. Terontola	-0- (1)	-0- (1)	18:30	20:26
Arr. Florence (S.M.N.)	16:45	18:40	19:50	21:50

(1) Direct train. No train change in Terontola. (2) Runs daily, except Sundays and holidays. (3) Runs daily.

Florence - Pisa - Florence 370

Dep Florence (S.M.N.)	Frequent times from 05:55 to 22:30
Arr. Pisa	50-60 minutes later

Sights in **Pisa**: See notes about Pisa under "Bologna-Pisa" on page 223.

Dep. Pisa	Frequent times from 04:15 to 23:46
Arr. Florence (S.M.N.)	50-60 minutes later

Florence - Ravenna - Florence

374			376		
Dep. Flor. (S.M.N.)	06:58 (1)	08:22 (2)	Dep.Ravenna	13:00	14:31 (6)
Arr. Bologna	08:03	09:11	Arr. Bologna	14:43	15:44
Change trains. 376			Change trains. 374		
Dep. Bologna	08:21 (3)	10:25 (4)	Dep. Bologna	15:30	16:42 (5)
Arr. Ravenna	09:33	11:22	Arr. Flor. (S.M.N.)	16:40	17:46

(Footnotes appear on page 230)

(1) Res. *required*. Sup. charged. (2) "Pendolino" (see page 215). Res. *required*. Sup. includes reservation and meal. First-class only. Runs daily, except Sundays and holidays. (3) Second-class only. (4) Operates early June to late September. (5) Res. *advisable*. Sup. charged. Light refreshments. (6) Plus other Ravenna departures at 17:30 and 20:10....departing Bologna 19:42 (5) and 22:30....arriving Florence 20:50 and 23:40.

Sights in **Ravenna**: See notes under "Bologna-Ravenna" on page 224.

Florence - Rome - Florence   374

Dep. Florence (S.M.N.)	06:55 (1)	07:15	08:50	09:00 (1)		
Arr. Rome (Ter.)	09:05	09:40	12:35	11:20		

Sights in **Rome**: See notes about Rome on page 221.

Dep. Rome (Ter.)	16:10 (1)	16:30	17:00 (2)	18:00 (1)	18:25	19:10 (3)
Arr. Florence (S.M.N.)	18:10	19:50	19:08	20:09	21:50	20:49 (4)

Dep. Rome (Ter.)	19:15	20:55	21:30 (5)	21:55	22:15
Arr. Florence (S.M.N.)	21:33	23:45	00:50	01:05	01:40 (6)

(1) Res. *advisable*. Sup. charged. Light refreshments. (2) Res. *advisable*. Restaurant car. (3) "Pendolino" (see page 215). Res. *required*. Sup. includes reservation and meal. First-class only. (4) Arrives at Florence's Rifredi railstation. (5) Departs at Rome's Tiburtina railstation. (6) Arrives at Florence's Campo di Marte railstation.

Florence - Siena - Florence   355 c

All of these trains are second-class only.

Dep. Florence (S.M.N.)	06:40	08:10	11:42	13:30		
Arr. Siena	08:04	09:50	13:25	15:10		

Sights in **Siena**: See notes about Siena under "Bologna-Siena" on page 225.

Dep. Siena	13:35	15:40	18:40	19:38	21:15	22:40
Arr. Florence (S.M.N.)	15:05	17:13	20:00	21:17	22:33	00:18

Florence - Verona - Florence
374

Dep. Florence (S.M.N.)	07:23	09:24 (1)	11:24 (2)	
Arr. Bologna	08:30	-0- (1)	12:26	
Change trains. 381				
Dep. Bologna	08:44	-0- (1)	12:44	
Arr. Verona (P.N.)	10:50	12:36	14:43	

Sights in **Verona**: See notes under "Bologna-Verona" on page 226.

Dep. Verona (P.N.)	15:26 (1)	15:43	17:29	19:29
Arr. Bologna	-0- (1)	17:26	19:20	21:20
Change trains. 374				
Dep. Bologna	-0- (1)	17:42 (3)	19:42 (4)	22:30
Arr. Florence (S.M.N.)	18:35	18:48	20:50	23:40

(1) Reservation *required*. Supplement charged. Direct train. No train change in Bologna. Restaurant car. (2) Reservation *advisable*. Supplement charged. Light refreshments. (3) Reservation *required*. Supplement charged. Restaurant car. (4) Reservation *advisable*. Supplement charged. Light refreshments.

Genoa - Bologna - Genoa 354

| Dep. Genoa (Piazza Principe) | 06:56 | 16:18 | 18:18 |
| Arr. Bologna | 10:05 | 19:20 | 21:27 |

Sights in **Bologna**: See notes about sightseeing in Bologna on page 219.

| Dep Bologna | 06:22 | 13:38 | 17:38 |
| Arr. Genoa (Piazza Principe) | 09:27 | 16:48 | 20:48 |

Genoa - Cremona - Genoa
356

Dep. Genoa (P.P.)	05:48	09:23 (1)	12:05
Arr. Milan (Centrale)	07:40	10:52	13:45
Change trains. 362			
Dep. Milan (Centrale)	08:20	12:05	14:10
Arr. Cremona	09:31	13:04	15:11

Sights in **Cremona**: One of Italy's most impressive squares, the Piazza del Commune, with its octagonal Baptistry, 12th century Duomo Cathedral, Loggia de Militi, and the Gothic Torrazzo (tallest bell tower in Italy).

Cremona is where the art of violin-making reached its apex, with the works of Amati, Stradivari and Guarneri. It is possible to watch young violin makers following that great tradition by visiting La Scuola Internazionale de Liuteria, in a renovated 16th century palace.

At the City Museum every day at 11:00, an outstanding violin made by Stradivari is played by the museum curator. Located near the Liuteria are many shops which will make a special violin to order. On view at the City Hall are 2 original Stradivari, 2 Amatis and a Sacconi.

Dep. Cremona	12:42	16:04	19:58	-0-
Arr. Milan (Centrale)	13:50	17:08	21:00	-0-
Change trains. 356				
Dep. Milan (Centrale)	14:05	18:05	21:15	22:05
Arr. Genoa (P.P.)	15:53	19:53	23:10	23:53

(1) Reservation *required*. Supplement charged. Restaurant car.

Genoa - Milan - Genoa 356

| Genoa (P.P.) | 07:05 (1) | 07:48 | 09:05 (1) | 09:23 (2) | 10:55 |
| Arr. Milan (Centrale) | 08:45 | 09:40 | 10:45 | 10:52 | 12:45 |

Sights in **Milan**: See notes about sightseeing in Milan on page 220.

| Dep. Milan (Centrale.) | 14:15 | 15:05 (1) | 16:05 | 17:05 (1) | 18:05 (3) |
| Arr. Genoa (P.P.) | 16:09 | 16:42 | 17:53 | 18:42 | 19:53 |

(1) Reservation *advisable*. Supplement charged. Light refreshments. (2) Reservation *required*. Supplement charged. Restaurant car. (3) Plus other departures from Milan at 18:15 (2), 19:05 (1), 19:55 (1), 20:05, 21:15 and 22:05, arriving Genoa 19:50, 20:42, 21:27, 21:53, 23:10and 23:53.

Genoa - Nice 164 + 356

| Dep. Genoa (P.P.) | 05:55 | 08:23 (1) | Dep. Nice (Ville) | 19:10 (1) | 23:12 (2) |
| Arr. Nice (Ville) | 10:10 | 11:20 | Arr. Genoa (P.P.) | 22:10 | 03:30 |

(1) Reservation *advisable*. Supplement charged. Light refreshments. (2) Has couchettes.

Sights in **Nice**: See notes about Nice on page 124.

Genoa - Parma - Genoa 354

Dep. Genoa (P.P.)	06:56	Dep. Parma	14:32	18:32
Arr. Parma	09:06	Arr. Genoa (P.P.)	16:48	20:48

Sights in **Parma:** See notes under "Bologna-Parma" on page 223.

Genoa - Pisa - Genoa 355

There is exceptional mountain and Mediterranean coastline scenerey on this ride. Many marble mountain quarries can be seen between **La Spezia** and **Viareggio**.

Dep. Genoa (P.P.)	07:05	07:53	08:32 (1)	09:57 (2)	12:20 (1)
Dep. La Spezia	08:28	09:22	09:53	11:13	13:34
Dep. Viareggio	09:16	10:10	10:30	11:47	14:14
Arr. Pisa (Cen.)	09:33	10:27	10:48	12:03	14:30

Sights in **Pisa:** See notes about Pisa under "Bologna-Pisa" on page 223.

Dep. Pisa (Cen.)	14:56(1)	15:43 (1)	17:03	17:56 (2)	19:03	19:24 (5)
Dep. Viareggio	15:12	16:00	17:19	-0-	19:20	19:42
Dep. La Spezia	15:58	16:40	18:09	18:43	20:12	20:19
Arr. Genoa (P.P.)	17:29	17:53	19:37	20:00	21:37	21:45

(1) Light refreshments. (2) Reservation *advisable*. Supplement charged. Light refreshments. (3) "Pendolino" (see page 215). Reservation *required*. Supplement includes reservation and meal. First-class only. (4) Arrives at Genoa's Brignole station. (5) Plus other departures from Pisa at 19:44 (2), 20:57 and 21:40 (3), arriving Genoa at 21:51, 23:27 and 23:30 (4).

Genoa - Rome 355

Dep. Genoa (P.Prin.)	01:03 (1)	-0-	07:05	09:57 (3)	12:20 (4)
Dep. Genoa (Brig.)	01:11	06:15 (2)	07:12	10:05	12:28
Arr. Rome (Ter.)	07:10	10:25	13:35	15:10	18:15

Dep. Genoa (P.Prin.)	12:56 (4)	14:57 (5)	15:15	16:57 (3)	18:00 (6+11)
Dep. Genoa (Brig.)	13:05	15:08	15:21	17:05	18:08
Arr. Rome (Ter.)	19:20	20:10	21:40	22:10	23:15

(1) Carries a sleeping car. Also has couchettes. (2) "Pendolino" (see page 215). Reservation *required*. Supplement includes reservation and meal. First-class only. (3) Reservation *advisable*. Supplement charged. Light refreshments. (4) Light refreshments. (5) Reservation *advisable*. Supplement charged. (6) Reservation *advisable*. Supplement charged. Restaurant car. (7) Has only sleeping cars and couchettes. No coach cars. (8) Operates late June to mid-September. Has couchettes. (9) Arrives at Rome's Ostiense railstation. (10) Has couchettes. (11) Plus other departures from Genoa (P. Prin.) at 20:58 (8), 22:46 (10) and 23:04, arriving Rome 02:25 (9), 04:07 (9) and 04:15 (9).

Genoa - Torino - Genoa 355

Dep. Genoa (P.P.)	06:51	08:19	09:10	09:58 (1)	12:07 (2+5)
Arr. Torino (P.N.)	08:53	10:25	11:10	11:50	13:52

Sights in **Torino**: The marvelous facade of the Porta Nuova railstation, built in the 1860's. The beautiful Piazza Carlo Felice park, near the railstation.

Piazza San Carlo (considered second only to St. Mark's in Venice), dominated by a large statue (called "the bronze horse") of Emanuele Filiberto, hero king of the mid-16th century. In Piazza dello Statuto, the large monument dedicated to the completion of the Frejus rail tunnel between Italy and France in the late 19th century.

The imposing Palazzo Madama, with its enormous marble staircase and Royal Armory, in Piazza Castello, which is the heart of the city. (It is a museum.) The Museo Egizio in Palazzo Carignano, the third most important (after London and Cairo) Egyptian collection in the world.

The university in Piazzo Carlo, where Erasmus of Rotterdam earned his doctorate in 1506. The view from the top of Mole Antonelliani, on Via Montebello. Parco del Valentino, with its splendid gardens and buildings.

The frescos in the Castello del Valentino. It is an easy walk from the Castle to Borgo Medievale, a village built in 1884 to depict the lifestyle of this area in the year 1400. The Church of the Great Mother of God, patterned after Rome's Pantheon.

The 17th century Royal Palace. Near it, the black and white marble Chapel of the Holy Shroud in the Church of San Lorenzo. An urn holding what is believed to be the shroud placed on Jesus when he was taken from the cross is the major attraction there. The Auto Museum on Corso Unita d'Italia, with models going back to 1893.

| Dep. Torino (P.N.) | 13:20 (3) | 15:20 (1) | 16:20 (2) | 17:05 | 18:30 (1+6) |
| Arr. Genoa (P.P.) | 14:54 | 16:54 | 17:57 | 19:10 | 20:05 |

(1) Reservation *advisable*. Supplement charged. Light refreshments. (2) Reservation *advisable*. Supplement charged. Restaurant car. (3) Reservation *advisable*. Supplement charged. (4) Operates late June to mid-September. (5) Plus another departure from Genoa at 12:24, arriving Torino 14:47. (6) Plus other departures from Torino at 19:05 (4), 20:35, 21:10, 22:10 and 23:05, arriving Genoa 20:53, 22:26, 22:57, 23:59 and 00:57.

Milan - Bologna - Milan 374

Most of these trains charge a supplement and have either a restaurant car or buffet.

| Dep. Milan (Cen.) | 06:55 (1) | 07:00 (2) | 07:55 (3) | 08:00 | 09:05 (3) | 09:55 (2+6) |
| Arr. Bologna | 08:21 | 08:49 | 09:38 | 10:14 | 10:48 | 11:38 |

Sights in **Bologna**: See notes about Bologna on page 219.

| Dep. Bologna | 13:26 (4) | 14:07 (3) | 14:38 | 15:16 (4) | 16:10 (2) | 17:26 (2+7) |
| Arr. Milan (Cen.) | 15:10 | 15:55 | 16:53 | 17:00 | 18:00 | 19:10 |

(1) "Pendolino" (see page 215). reservation *required*. Supplement includes reservation and meal. First-class only. (2) Reservation *advisable*. Supplement charged. Light refreshments. (3) reservation *advisable*. Supplement charged. Restaurant car. (4) Reservation *required*. Supplement charged. Restaurant car. (5) "Pendolino" (see footnote 1). Runs daily, except Saturday. (6) Plus other departures from Milan at 10:32 (2), 11:00 (3) and 11:55 (2), arriving Bologna 12:38, 12:49 and 13:49. (7) Plus other departures from Bologna at 18:26 (3), 19:26 (3), 20:26 (3), 20:38, 21:54 (2) and 22:35 (5), arriving Milan 20:10, 21:10, 22:30, 23:00, 23:40 and 00:05.

Milan - Como - Milan 290

Reservation is required or advisable on most of these trains. All of them charge a supplement.

| Milan (Cen.) | Frequent times from 07:05 to 21:25 |
| Arr. Como (S.G.) | 35-45 minutes later |

Sights in **Como**: Take Bus #4, marked "Piazza Cavour", from the railstation to reach both the lakeshore and the cable car which ascends the 2300-foot high **Mount Brunate** in 7 minutes. At the peak, there is a wonderful view of **Lake Como** and the Alps.

| Dep. Como (S.G.) | Frequent times from 06:50 to 22:53 |
| Arr. Milan (Cen.) | 35-45 minutes later |

Milan - Cremona - Milan 362

Dep. Milan (Cen.)	08:20	12:05	Dep. Cremona	12:42	16:04 (1)
Arr. Cremona	09:29	13:02	Arr. Milan (Cen.)	13:50	17:08

(1) Plus another departure from Cremona at 19:58, arriving Milan 21:00.

Sights in **Cremona**: See "Genoa- Cremona" on page 231.

Milan - Florence - Milan 374

Dep. Milan (Cen.)	06:55 (1)	07:55 (3)	09:05 (3)	09:55 (3)	10:32 (4)
Arr. Florence (S.M.N.)	09:20 (2)	10:46	11:56	12:46	13:46

Sights in **Florence:** See notes about sightseeing in Florence on page 219.

Dep. Florence (S.M.N.)	14:09 (5)	15:19 (6)	16:19 (4)	17:19 (4)	18:19 (3+9)
Arr. Milan (Cen.)	17:00	18:10	19:10	20:10	21:10

(1) "Pendolino" (see page 215). Reservation *required*. Supplement includes reservation and meal. First-class only. (2) Arrives at Florence's Rifredi railstation. (3) Reservation *advisable*. Supplement charged. Restaurant car. (4) Reservation *advisable*. Supplement charged. Light refreshments. (5) Reservation *required*. Supplement charged. Restaurant car. (6) Reservation *advisable*. Supplement charged. (7) Reservation *required*. Second-class only. (8) Arrives at Milan's Lambrate railstation. (9) Plus other departures from Florence at 19:17 (3) and 20:44 (7), arriving Milan 22:30 and 23:50 (8).

Milan - Genoa - Milan 356

Dep. Milan (Cen.)	06:40 (1)	07:05	08:05	09:30	12:05
Arr. Genoa (P.P.)	08:10	08:53	10:00	11:25	13:53

Sights in **Genoa**: See notes about sightseeing in Genoa on page 220.

Dep. Genoa (P.P.)	13:48 (2)	14:50	15:48	17:05 (1)	17:50	18:41 (3)
Arr. Milan (Cen.)	15:40	16:40	17:45	18:45	19:45	20:40

(1) Reservation *advisable*. Supplement charged. Light refreshments. (2) Light refreshments. (3) Plus other departures from Genoa at 19:48, 21:05 (1), 21:59 and 22:25 (1), arriving Milan 21:40, 22:45, 23:45 and 23:59.

Milan - Locarno - Milan

The Camedo-Locarno portion of this trip is one of the 5 most scenic rail trips in Europe, with outstanding mountain, gorge and river scenery.

270

Dep. Milan (Cen.)	07:23 (1)	09:20 (2)	11:07 (2)	13:25 (3)
Arr. Domodossola	09:00	10:42	12:33	14:55

Change trains. Walk outside the Domodossola railstation and go to the underground track in order to board the Centovalli narrow-gauge local railway.

272

Dep. Domodossola	09:05 (1)	11:12 (1)	13:15 (1)	15:18 (1)
Dep. Camedo	10:06	12:14	14:18	16:22
Arr. Locarno	10:38	12:45	14:50	16:55

Sights in **Locarno**: Stroll the gardens along the shore of **Lake Maggiore** and take the funicular ride to **Orselin** to see the art treasures in the Madonna del Sasso (Madonna of the Rock) church high above the village and, from there, the fine view of Locarno and Lake Maggiore. From Orselin, ride the cable-car to 4,400-foot-high **Cardada**. Then take the chair lift from **Cardada** to **Cimetta**, more than a mile high.

In nearby **Ascona**, see the frescoes depicting scenes of the Old and New Testament in the 14th century church of Santa Maria Misericordia and the adjoining cloisters of Collegio Papio.

Dep. Locarno	11:01 (1)	13:13 (1)	15:10 (1)	16:04	17:20	19:04
Dep. Camedo	11:34	13:48	15:43	16:39	17:55	19:40
Arr. Domodossola	12:34	14:52	16:44	17:44	18:58	20:48

Change trains. Walk from the underground Centovailli track, up to the main Domodossola railstation.

270

Dep. Domodossola	13:20 (2)	15:22 (1)	17:45 (3)	18:13	20:13 (2)	21:04 (1)
Arr. Milan (Cen.)	14:40	16:55	18:15	19:35	21:35	22:40

(1) Light refreshments. (2) Reservation *required*. Supplement charged. Light refreshments. (3) Reservation *advisable*.

CRUISING THE BORROMEAN ISLANDS ON LAKE MAGGIORE

An overnight stay in Locarno is worthwhile, in order to have a complete day for touring the **Borromean Islands** on Lake Maggiore.

Isola Madre is a fantastic garden island. See the 18th century palace and stroll through the lush gardens there (palm trees, orange and grapefruit trees, magnolias, roses, camelias, azaleas, and many gold and silver Chinese pheasants).

On **Isola Bella**, the fascinating and very unique 17th century palace where European leaders met in 1925 to sign the Locarno Pact is the attraction. You will be enchanted by the palace's 6-room Neptune Grotto, decorated with enormous plaster seashells, walls that simulate white coral, and floors that are mosaics of small pebbles. Stroll through the lavish 10-terrace garden.

From 1974 through 1990, we carried timetables for visiting the islands, and we regret that a timetable has not been available from Italian tourist authorities since 1990. For all of those 17 years, we recommended a route which made it possible to visit in one day (from 08:00 to 17:00) Isola Madre and Isola Bella, with a lunch stop on Isola dei Pescatori. We hope any readers who tour Lake Maggiore will advise us about current boat schedules.

Milan - Lugano - Milan 290

Dep. Milan (Cen.)	07:20 (1)	08:25 (2)	09:25 (3)	10:25 (2)	11:25 (3)	12:35 (1)
Arr. Lugano	08:54	09:54	10:54	11:54	12:54	13:54

Sights in **Lugano:** Take the cable car from the railstation to Piazza Cioccaro. Walk downhill from there to the city center, Piazza Riforma. See the view of the city from the Cathedral of San Lorenzo. The collection of over 400 masterpieces (Rubens, Goya, Durer, Raphael, Tiepolo, Tintoretto, and some Americans) in the Thyssen Art Gallery of La Villa Favorita, open only from Easter to October.

Stroll the shore of lovely **Lake Lugano.**

Take one of the many boat trips on the lake (visit the casino at **Campione**; the ceramic, clothing and craft shops at Gandria). Also take the cogwheel train to the 5300-foot top of **Mt. Generoso** and the chair-lift to the slightly higher top of **Mt. Lema.**

Dep. Lugano	14:06 (3)	15:32 (3)	16:06 (3)	17:06 (1)	18:06 (3+4)
Arr. Milan (Cen.)	15:39	16:35	17:35	18:35	19:35

(1) Reservation *advisable*. Supplement charged. Light refreshments. (2) Reservation *advisable*. Supplement charged. Restaurant car. (3) Reservation *required*. Supplement charged. Restaurant car. (4) Plus other departures from Lugano at 19:06 (2), 20:06 (2), 21:17 (2) and 22:06 (2), arriving Milan 20:35, 21:30, 22:40 and 23:35.

Milan - Rome and Rome - Milan 374

Dep. Milan (Cen.)	06:55 (1)	07:55 (2)	09:05 (2)	09:55 (4+5)	10:32 (4)
Arr. Rome (Ter.)	11:00	12:49 (3)	14:05	14:55	16:15
Dep. Milan (Cen.)	12:55 (6)	14:55 (4)	15:55 (6)	16:55 (2)	19:30 (7+14)
Arr. Rome (Ter.)	17:55	19:55 (3)	21:00	21:55	23:55
		*	*	*	
Dep. Rome (Ter.)	06:40 (8)	08:10 (6)	09:00 (4)	10:13 (3+6)	11:10 (9)
Arr. Milan (Cen.)	10:45	13:10	14:35	15:10	16:10
Dep. Rome (Ter.)	12:00 (6)	13:10 (10)	14:10 (4)	15:15 (10)	16:10 (2+15)
Arr Milan (Cen.)	17:00	18:10	19:10	20:13 (11)	21:10

(1) "Pendolino" (see page 215). Res. *required*. Sup. includes reservation and meal. First-class only. (2) Res. *advisable*. Sup.. Restaurant car. (3) Depart/Arrive Rome's Tiburtina railstation. (4) Res. *advisable*. Sup.. Light refreshments. (5) Runs daily except Sun. and holidays. (6) Res. *required*. Sup.. Restaurant car. (7) "Pendolino" (see footnote 1). Runs daily except Sat.. (8) "Pendolino" (see footnote 1). Runs daily except Sun. and holidays. (9) Res. *advisable*. Sup.. Light refreshments. (10) Res. *advisable*. Sup.. (11) Arrives at Milan's Lambrate station. (12) Carries a sleeping car. Also has couchettes. (13) Operates early September to early August. (14) Plus other Milan departures at 20:35 (12), 21:05, 22:55 (12), and 23:30 (12+13). (15) Plus other Rome departures at 17:00 (2), 20:00 (7), 20:55 (11+12), 21:55 (11+12), 22:35 (12) and 23:30 (12).

Milan - Torino - Milan 352

| Dep. Milan (Cen.) | 07:10 (1) | 08:10 | 09:30 (2) | 11:30 (1+3) | 12:10 |
| Arr. Torino (P.N.) | 08:47 | 09:57 | 11:04 | 13:03 | 13:57 |

Sights in **Torino**: See notes under "Genoa-Torino" on page 233.

| Dep. Torino (P.N.) | 13:10 (1) | 13:53 | 15:10 (1) | 15:53 | 16:53 (4) |
| Arr. Milan (Cen.) | 14:45 | 15:40 | 16:45 | 17:40 | 18:40 |

(1) Res. *advisable*. Sup. charged. Light refreshments. (2) Res. *advisable*. Sup. charged. (3) Depart/ Arrive Milan's Porta Garibaldi railstation. (4) Plus other Torino departures at 17:53 , 19:10 (1), 19:53, 21:30 (1), 21:45 and 23:00, arriving Milan 19:40, 20:45, 21:40, 23:00, 23:45 and 00:45.

Milan - Venice - Milan 352

| Dep. Milan (Cen.) | 06:00 | 06:50 (1) | 08:00 | 08:57 (2) | 09:10 | 11:50 |
| Arr. Venice (S.L.) | 09:12 | 09:40 | 11:12 | 11:48 | 12:18 | 15:03 |

Sights in **Venice**: See notes under "Bologna-Venice" on page 225.

Dep. Venice (S.L.)   Frequent times from 05:15 to 00:05
Arr. Milan (Cen.)   3 hours later

(1) Reservation *advisable*. Supplement charged. Light refreshments. (2) Departs from Milan's Porta Garibaldi station.

Milan - Verona - Milan 352

| Dep. Milan (Cen.) | 07:00 (1) | 08:00 | 09:10 | 11:50 | 12:00 (2) |
| Arr. Verona (P.N.) | 08:27 | 09:39 | 10:44 | 13:32 | 13:41 |

Sights in **Verona**: See notes about Verona under "Bologna-Verona" on page 226.

Dep. Verona (P.M.)   1Frequent times from 05:40 to 22:10
Arr. Milan (Cen.)   1½ hours later

(1) Reservation *required*. Supplement charged. Restaurant car. (2) Restaurant car.

Naples - Bari - Naples 400

| Dep. Naples (P. Garibaldi) | 06:46 | Dep. Bari | 17:00 |
| Arr. Bari | 10:42 | Arr. Naples (P. Garibaldi) | 21:15 |

Sights in **Bari**: See notes about Bari on page 242.

Naples - Pompeii - Naples 392

The standard-gauge trains that depart from Naples' Centrale railstation, (shown below) are covered by Eurailpass.

The narrow-gauge trains that leave from Naples' F.S. railstation are operated by Circumvesuviana Railway (Table 401) and are not covered by Eurailpass.

Salerno is as convenient a base for visiting Pompeii as Naples is.

| Dep. Naples (Cen.) | 07:10 | 10:33 | 13:10 | 14:10 | 15:10 |
| Arr. Pompeii | 25 minutes later |

Sights in **Pompeii:** See where 20,000 people were living and how they lived 1900 years ago when this city was buried within a few minutes under a volcanic rain of ashes from nearby (still active) Vesuvius, when it was young and strong.

| Dep. Pompeii | 11:36 | 14:39 | 15:42 | 17:20 | 19:32 | 20:35 |
| Arr. Naples (Cen.) | 25 minutes later |

238

Naples - Rome - Naples 394

Dep. Naples (Cen.)	06:46	07:05	07:15	-0-	08:15
Dep. Naples (P.G.)	-0-	-0-	-0-	-0-	-0-
Dep. Naples (Mer.)	-0-	-0-	-0-	07:50 (1)	-0-
Dep. Naples (C. Fl.)	-0-	-0-	-0-	07:54	-0-
Arr. Rome (Ter.)	09:00	09:20	09:55	09:32	11:00

Sights in **Rome**: See notes about Rome on page 221.

Dep. Rome (Ter.)	13:40 (1)	13:45 (2)	14:20	15:55 (3)	16:20 (4)
Arr. Naples (C. Fl.)	15:14	-0-	-0-	-0-	-0-
Arr. Naples (Mer.)	15:20	-0-	-0-	17:45	-0-
Arr. Naples (P.G.)	-0-	-0-	-0-	17:56	-0-
Arr. Naples (Cen.)	-0-	16:05	17:05	-0-	19:00

(1) "Pendolino" (see page 215). Reservation *required*. Supplement includes reservation and meal. First-class only. (2) Light refreshments. (3) Reservation *advisable*. Supplement charged. Light refreshments. (4) Plus other departures from Rome Termini at frequent times from 17:20 to 23:30, including a "Pendolino" at 19:25.

Rome - Anzio - Rome 393a

All of these trains are second-class only.

Dep. Rome (Ter.)	08:05	09:43 (1)	11:55	13:05	14:05	14:45
Arr. Anzio	50-60 minutes later					

Sights in **Anzio**: Has been a beach resort since ancient times. Many Americans visit the nearby military cemeteries, holding those killed in the January 22, 1944 Allied invasion.

Dep. Anzio	12:59	14:14 (2)	15:11	16:08	18:18	19:16 (3)
Arr. Rome (Ter.)	50-60 minutes later					

(1) Departs from Rome's Tiburtina railstation. (2) Runs daily, except Sundays and holidays. (3) Plus other departures from Anzio at 20:21, 21:46 and 23:03.

Rome - Assisi - Rome 368

Dep. Rome (Ter.)	06:57 (1)	07:25	10:00 (1)			
Arr. Foligno	08:27	09:17	11:37			
Change trains						
Dep. Foligno	08:35 (2)	09:35	12:00			
Arr. Assisi	08:49	09:49	12:10			

Sights in **Assisi**: See notes under "Florence-Assisi" on page 227.

Dep. Assisi	13:01 (2)	14:52	15:41 (2)	16:52	18:52	20:51
Arr. Foligno	13:19	15:06	15:58	17:06	19:05	21:02
Change trains						
Dep. Foligno	13:41	15:41	16:29 (1)	17:29 (1)	19:41	21:32 (1)
Arr. Rome (Ter.)	15:35	17:35	18:07	19:20	21:35	23:05

(1) Reservation *required*. Supplement charged. (2) Second-class only.

Rome - Florence - Rome   374

Dep. Rome (Termini)	06:40 (1+2)	07:20 (4)	08:10 (4)	08:55 (1+8)
Arr. Florence (S.M.N.)	08:20 (3)	09:24	10:10	10:35 (3)

Sights in **Florence**: See notes about sightseeing in Florence on page 219.

Dep. Florence (S.M.N.)	12:55 (5)	13:55 (6)	15:55 (4)	16:55 (6+9)
Arr. Rome (Termini)	14:55	16:15	17:55	18:55

(1) "Pendolino" (see page 215). Reservation *required*. Supplement includes reservation and meal. First-class only. (2) Runs daily, except Sundays and holidays. (3) Arrives/Departs Florence's Rifredi railstation. (4) Reservation *advisable*. Supplement charged. Restaurant car. (5) Runs daily, except Sundays and holidays. Reservation *advisable*. Supplement charged. Light refreshments. (6) Reservation *advisable*. Supplement charged. Light refreshments. (7) Runs daily, except Saturday. (8) Plus other Rome (Ter.) departures at frequent times from 09:00 to 23:30, including a "Pendolino" at 19:10 (1+3) and 20:00 (1+3). (9) Plus other Florence departures at frequent times from 17:55 to 21:20, including a "Pendolino" at 21:54 (1+3+7).

Rome - Genoa   355

Dep. Rome (Ter.)	-0-	-0-	-0-	-0-	06:55 (4)
Dep. Rome (Ost.)	00:20 (1)	01:19	03:30 (2)	05:27 (3)	-0-
Arr. Genoa (Brig.)	05:46	06:15	08:46	10:32	12:06
Arr. Genoa (P.Prin.)	05:54	06:25	08:56	10:42	12:14

Dep. Rome (Ter.)	08:55 (5)	09:10	12:20 (6)	14:50 (5)	16:15 (7)
Dep. Rome (Ost.)	-0-	09:18	-0-	-0-	-0-
Arr. Genoa (Brig.)	14:08	15:33	17:45	19:52	21:35
Arr. Genoa (P.Prin.)	14:16	15:40	17:53	20:00	21:45

(1) Carries a sleeping car. Also has couchettes. (2) Has couchettes. (3) Operates late June to mid-September. Has couchettes. (4) Reservation *advisable*. Supplement charged. Restaurant car. (5) Reservation *advisable*. Supplement charged. Light refreshments. (6) Light refreshments. (7) Plus other departures from Rome (Termini) at 16:35 (5), 17:10, 23:15 (1) and 23:30 (1), arriving Genoa (P. Principe) 21:51, 23:27, 05:13 and 05:26.

Rome - Naples - Rome   392 + 394

Dep. Rome (Ter.)	07:00 (1)	07:20	08:50	09:05	12:20
Arr. Naples (Mer.)	08:49	-0-	-0-	-0-	-0-
Arr. Naples (P.G.)	09:01	-0-	-0-	-0-	-0-
Arr. Naples (Cen.)	-0-	10:00	10:57	11:45	14:58

Sights in **Naples**: See notes about sightseeing in Naples on page 221.

Dep. Naples (Cen.)	13:00 (1)	13:52 (3)	14:15	15:15 (4)	16:00(5+7)
Arr. Rome (Ter.)	15:05 (2)	16:07 (2)	16:55	17:55	17:40

(1) Reservation *advisable*. Supplement charged. Light refreshments. (2) Arrives at Rome's Tiburtina railstation. (3) Light refreshments. (4) Departs from Naples'Piazza Garibaldi railstation. (5) Departs from Naples'Mergalina railstation. "Pendolino" (see page 215). Reservation *required*. Supplement includes reservation and meal. First-class only. (6) Arrives at Rome's Ostiense railstation. (7) Plus other departures from Naples' Centrale at 17:15, 17:58, 18:15, 18:48, 19:54 (1+4), 20:15 and 21:28, arriving Rome's Termini 19:55, 20:15, 20:50, 20:05, 21:55, 22:55 and 00:15 (6).

Rome - Perugia - Rome   368

Dep. Rome (Ter.)	06:57 (1)	07:25	10:00 (1)		
Arr. Foligno	08:31	09:22	11:39		
Change trains.					
Dep. Foligno	08:35 (2)	09:35	12:00		
Arr. Perugia	09:23	10:15	12:32		

Sights in **Perugia**: See notes under "Florence-Perugia" on page 229.

Dep. Perugia	12:33 (2)	14:31	15:15 (2)	17:00 (3)	18:31	20:31
Arr. Foligno	13:19	15:06	15:58	-0- (3)	19:05	21:04
Change trains.						
Dep. Foligno	13:41	15:41	16:29 (1)	-0- (3)	19:41	21:32 (1)
Arr. Rome (Ter.)	15:35	17:35	18:07	19:20	21:35	23:05

(1) Reservation *required*. Supplement charged. (2) Second-class only. (3) Direct train. No train change in Foligno. Reservation *required*. Supplement charged.

Rome - Pisa - Rome   355

Dep. Rome (Ter.)	06:55 (1)	07:10	08:55 (2)	09:10	11:10 (3)
Arr. Pisa	10:01	11:02	12:06	13:05	14:53 (4)

Sights in **Pisa**: See notes about Pisa under "Bologna-Pisa" on page 223.

Dep. Pisa	12:40	14:40 (3)	15:31 (3)	17:06 (1)	19:02 (5+6)
Arr. Rome (Ter.)	16:40	18:15	19:20	20:10	22:10

(1) Reservation *advisable*. Supplement charged. Restaurant car. (2) Reservation *advisable*. Supplement charged. (3) Light refreshments. (4) The Leaning Tower is only 10 minutes by bus or taxi from the railstation. (5) Reservation *advisable*. Supplement charged. Light refreshments. (6) Plus another departure from Pisa at 20:09 (1), arriving Rome 23:15.

Rome - Pompeii - Rome

Trains departing Rome's Termini railstation at 07:00, 08:00, 08:30, 08:50 and 09:00 arrive 2 hours later at Naples' Centrale or Piazza Garibaldi stations. Garibaldi is next to Centrale. A travelator provides transportation from Centrale to the F.S. station, from which it is a short walk to the Circumvesuviana station.

The ride from Circumvesuviana station to Pompeii is only 30 minutes, arriving there about 4 hours after having departed Rome.

Departures from Pompeii at 14:31, 15:31, 16:31, 17:21 and 18:31 bring one back to Rome at 18:55, 19:55, 20:50, 21:35 and 22:55.

Sights in **Pompeii**: See notes under "Naples-Pompeii" on page 237.

Rome - Rimini - Rome

368			393		
Dep. Rome (Ter.)	07:25	10:00 (1)	Dep. Rimini	16:01	18:11
Arr. Falconara	11:06	13:11	Arr. Falconara	17:10	19:15
Change trains. 393			Change trains. 368		
Dep. Falconara	11:38	13:38	Dep. Falconara	17:45	19:49 (1)
Arr. Rimini	13:00	15:00	Arr. Rome (Ter.)	21:35	23:05

(1) Reservation *required*. Suppplement charged.

Sights in **Rimini**: Malatesta Temple. Sigismondo's Castle. The Bridge of Tiberius over the Marecchia River. The Arch of Augustus. Frescoes in St. Augustin's Church. Remains of a Roman amphitheater.

Rome - Spoleto - Rome 368

Dep. Rome (Ter.)	06:57 (1)	07:25	10:00 (1)
Arr. Spoleto	08:13	08:59	11:20

Sights in **Spoleto:** Roman ruins. The enormous 14th century Rocca (fortress). The central mosaic, magnificent 15th century Lippi fresco, and 8 rose windows in the Cathedral. The 14th century arched bridge, Ponte delle Torri, that holds the aqueduct which still supplies Spoleto its water.

The tourist office in Piazza della Liberta has many brochures, including a town map and 3 half-day walking itineraries.

Dep. Spoleto	13:59	15:59	16:47 (1)	17:47 (1)	19:57	21:49 (1)
Arr. Rome (Ter.)	15:35	17:35	18:07	19:29	21:35	23:05

(1) Reservation *required*. Supplement charged.

Rome - Florence - Venice and Venice - Florence - Rome 390

Dep. Rome (Ter.)	-0-	07:20 (1)	08:55 (2)	-0-	
Dep. Florence (S.M.N.)	07:15	09:33	10:37 (3)	11:29	
Arr. Venice (S. Lucia)	10:42	12:18	13:15	14:42	
Dep. Rome (Ter.)	11:50 (4)	13:50 (5)	-0-	18:00 (6+10)	
Dep. Florence (S.M.N.)	13:59	15:59	18:25	20:18	
Arr. Venice (S. Lucia)	16:58	19:08	21:42	23:18	

(1) Reservation *required*. Supplement charged. Restaurant car. Change trains in Venice's Mestre railstation. (2) "Pendolino" (see page 215). Reservation *required*. Supplement includes reservation and meal. First-class only. (3) Depart from Florence's Rifredi railstation. (4) Reservation *advisable*. Supplement charged. Restaurant car. (5) Reservation *required*. Supplement charged. First-class only. Change trains in Venice's Mestre railstation. (6) Reservation *advisable*. Supplement charged. Light refreshments. (7) Does not operate in August. Runs daily, except Saturday. (8) Carries a sleeping car (9) Carries a sleeping car. Also has couchettes. Change trains in Venice's Mestre railstation. (10) Plus other Rome departures at 19:45 (2+7), 19:15 (8), 22:15 (9) and 23:10 (9)....and another Florence departure at 21:27 (2+3+7).

ROUTES TO THE TOE OF ITALY

Here (pages 242 and 243) is the rail route to southern Italy: along the Adriatic and Ionian seacoasts, from Pescara to Brindisi and on to Reggio di Calabria...and north from Reggio to Pescara.

See pages 244-245 for the route to southern Italy along the Tyrrhenian seacoast from Rome to Naples and on to Reggio di Calabria...and north from Reggio to Rome.

Pescara - Foggia - Barletta - Bari - Brindisi -Taranto - Catanzaro - Reggio di Calabria

This trip offers beautiful coastal scenery along both the Adriatic (Pescara-Bari) and the Mediterranean (Taranto-Reggio di Calabria).

393

Dep. Pescara	02:12	03:09 (1)	-0-	05:00	05:43	12:22 (2+9)
Dep. Foggia	04:30	05:31	-0-	07:23	08:04	14:28
Dep. Barletta	05:08	06:09	-0-	08:02	08:42	15:04
Arr. Bari	06:03	06:47	-0-	08:39	09:21	15:39
Dep. Bari	06:29	07:10	08:33 (3)	09:00	09:42	15:59
Arr. Brindisi	08:03	08:55	-0-	10:36	11:11	17:10
Change trains. 403						
Dep. Brindisi	08:24 (4)	10:11	-0-	14:66	12:30 (5)	17:23
Arr. Taranto	09:35	11:19	09:48	12:54	14:04	18:39
Change trains. 397						
Dep. Taranto	10:00 (6)	-0-	10:00 (6)	-0-	15:38 (6)	23:24 (1)
Arr. Catanzaro	13:36	-0-	13:36	-0-	19:10	03:25
Arr. Reggio	15:50	-0-	15:50	-0-	21:23	06:10

(1) Has couchettes. (2) Reservation *required*. Supplement charged. Light refreshments. (3) Direct train Bari-Reggio [table 397]. Reservation *advisable*. Supplement charged. Plus other direct trains at 14:00 (reservation *advisable*, supplement charged) and 21:21 (has couchettes), arriving Taranto 15:26 and 23:12, arriving Catanzaro 19:10 and 03:25, arriving Reggio 21:23 and 06:10. (4) Second-class only. (5) Plus another Brindisi departure at 19:18, departing Taranto 23:24 (1), arriving Reggio 06:10. (6) Reservation *advisable*. Supplement charged. (7) Has only sleeping cars and couchettes. No coach cars. (8) Reservation *advisable*. Supplement charged. Light refreshments. (9) Plus other Pescara departures at 03:57 (7), 04:21 and 16:22 (8), arriving Brindisi 09:43, 10:02 and 21:09.

Sights in **Bari**: Much wine, olive oil and almonds in this area. Bari is actually a complex of 3 different cities. The "old town" is a peninsula which was the ancient port, rivaling Venice 900 years ago. Both the 11th century St. Nicola Basilica and the 12th century Romanesque Cathedral are located there.

"New Bari", built in the 19th century, is where the Archaeological Museum, the Picture Gallery, concert halls and fine restaurants are located. Industrial Bari encircles the other 2 areas (factories, oil refineries, low-income apartments).

Don't fail to visit the rebuilt Norman Castle.

Sights in **Barletta**: The 13th century S. Sepolcro Church. The Norman castle. The 12th century Gothic Cathedral.

Sights in **Brindisi:** Many Crusaders set out from here for Jerusalem. See the Roman column that marks the end of the Appian Way. The Civic Museum in the 11th century circular S. Giovanni al Sepolcro Church. Frederick II's 13th century castle. The rebuilt 11th century Cathedral.

Sights in **Catanzaro**: The Baroque S. Domenico Church. The paintings in the Museum.

Sights in **Foggia**: Much wool has been marketed here for centuries. See the ancient records of sheep tax at the Library. The city has an Art Gallery, a Museum and a Cathedral.

Sights in **Pescara**: A nice beach resort on the Adriatic coast.

Sights in **Reggio di Calabria**: A very popular tourist resort. Founded by the Greeks in 720 B.C. See the fine archaeological collection in the Museo Nazionale della Magna Grecia. The 15th century Aragonese Castle. The reconstructed Romanesque-Byzantine Cathedral. There are many Greek and Roman ruins in this area.

Sights in **Taranto**: A swing bridge connects the "old" city (on an island) with the new Taranto on the mainland. See the 15th century Aragonese castle. The 14th century S. Domenico Maggiore Church. The exhibit of Greek vases and statues in the Museo Nazionale. The early 19th century Arsenal. The 11th century Cathedral.

THE NORTHBOUND TRIP

397

Dep. Reggio	07:00 (1)	-0-	-0-	-0-	-0-	15:02 (1+7)
Dep. Catanzaro	09:20	-0-	-0-	-0-	-0-	17:21
Arr. Taranto	12:51	-0-	-0-	-0-	-0-	21:04
Change trains. 403						
Dep. Taranto	13:00	06:16 (2)	06:53	10:02	12:43	21:20
Arr. Brindisi	-0-	07:26	08:06	11:04	14:02	-0-
Change trains. 393						
Dep. Brindisi	-0-	07:41 (3)	09:07	13:34 (3)	15:57 (5+8)	-0-
Arr. Bari	14:36	08:58	11:31 (4)	14:58	17:35	22:41 (4)
Dep. Bari	-0-	09:18	11:50 (3)	15:10	18:00	23:42 (5)
Dep. Barletta	-0-	-0-	12:29	15:40	18:34	00:14
Arr. Foggia	-0-	10:30	13:23	16:22	19:32	01:01
Arr. Pescara	-0-	12:26	15:37	17:32	21:45	03:21

(1) Reservation *advisable*. Supplement charged. (2) Second-class only. (3) Reservation *advisable*. Supplement charged. Light refreshments. (4) Change trains in Bari. (5) Has couchettes. (6) Carries a sleeping car. Also has couchettes. (7) Plus another Reggio departure at 23:18 (5), departing Taranto 06:30, arriving Brindisi 08:22. (8) Plus other Brindisi departures at 18:19, 18:36, 20:10 (6) and 21:45 (5), arriving Pescara 23:45, 00:35, 01:56 and 03:21.

Rome - Naples - Villa San Giovanni - Reggio di Calabria and v.v. 392

There is great coastal scenery between Salerno and Reggio.

Dep. Rome (Ter.)	-0-	-0-	-0-	-0-
Dep. Rome (Tib.)	02:36 (1)	03:10	04:19 (3+4)	04:28 (4)
Dep. Naples (Cen.)	04:55	05:20 (2)	07:00	06:38 (2)
Dep. Salerno	05:39	06:16	07:41	07:32
Arr. V.S. Giovanni	10:25	10:40	12:23	12:00
Arr. Reggio di Cal.	10:43	11:10	12:37	12:21

Dep. Rome (Ter.)	07:00 (5)	08:55	13:00 (5)	13:45 (8)
Dep. Rome (Tib.)	-0-	-0-	-0-	-0-
Dep. Naples (Cen.)	09:05 (6)	11:04 (2)	15:05 (6)	16:17
Dep. Salerno	09:45	12:01	15:49	17:01
Arr. V.S. Giovanni	13:35 (7)	16:00	19:48	21:43
Arr. Reggio di Cal.	14:58	16:21	20:05	22:00

Dep. Rome (Ter.)	15:55 (5)	17:15 (9)	19:35 (10)	20:45 (11)
Dep. Rome (Tib.)	-0-	-0-	-0-	-0-
Dep. Naples (Cen.)	18:00 (6)	19:12	21:57	23:05
Dep. Salerno	18:40	19:52	22:36	23:47
Arr. V.S. Giovanni	23:35	23:11	02:35	03:35
Arr. Reggio di Cal.	23:52	23:25	-0-	-0-

Dep. Rome (Ter.)	22:00 (1)	22:35 (12)	23:30 (1)	-0-
Dep. Rome (Tib.)	-0-	-0-	-0-	-0-
Dep. Naples (Cen.)	00:17	00:50	01:52	-0-
Dep. Salerno	-0-	01:30	02:32	-0-
Arr. V.S. Giovanni	05:51	05:20	08:39	-0-
Arr. Reggio de Cal.	06:09	05:41	09:06	-0-

(Footnotes appear on page 245.)

THE NORTHBOUND RETURN TRIP

Dep. Reggio di Cal.	01:30 (12)	05:20 (4)	07:20 (5)	08:30 (8)
Dep. V.S. Giovanni	02:10	05:33	07:36	08:48
Dep. Salerno	06:53	09:00	11:16	13:35
Arr. Naples (Cen.)	07:36	09:41 (6)	11:56 (6)	14:13
Arr. Rome (Tib.)	-0-	-0-	-0-	-0-
Arr. Rome (Ter.)	09:20	11:50	14:00	16:54 (3)

Dep. Reggio di Cal.	11:37 (7)	13:05 (8)	15:00 (5)	17:00
Dep. V.S. Giovanni	12:12 (5)	13:40	15:17	17:40
Dep. Salerno	16:04	17:54	19:10	21:52
Arr. Naples (Cen.)	16:42 (6)	18:45 (2)	19:50 (6)	22:44
Arr. Rome (Tib.)	-0-	-0-	-0-	-0-
Arr. Rome (Ter.)	18:45	20:55	21:55	01:07 (3)

Dep. Reggio di Cal.	18:32 (4)	19:42 (1)	20:25 (1)	-0-
Dep. V.S. Giovanni	18:50	20:00	21:03	00:40 (10)
Dep. Salerno	00:17	01:14	03:28	-0-
Arr. Naples (Cen.)	00:56	01:52	04:16	06:00
Arr. Rome (Tib.)	-0-	04:13	-0-	-0-
Arr. Rome (Ter.)	03:18 (3)	-0-	06:50	08:50

(1) Carries first and second-class sleeping cars. Also has first and second-class couchettes and coaches. (2) Departs/Arrives Naples' Campi Flegrei railstation. (3) Departs/Arrives Rome's Ostiense railstation. (4) Has couchettes. (5) Reservation advisable. Supplement charged. Light refreshments. (6) Departs/Arrives Naples' Piazza Garibaldi railstation. (7) Change trains in V.S. Giovanni. (8) Light refreshments. (9) "Pendolino" (see page 215). Reservation *required*. Supplement includes reservation and meal. First-class only. (10) Reservation *required*. Carries first and second-class sleeping cars. Also has first and second-class couchettes. Coaches are first-class only. (11) Train has only sleeping cars and couchettes. No coaches. (12) Carries first and second-class sleeping cars. Also has second-class couchettes and coaches.

THE RAIL TRIP TO SICILY

Rome - Naples - Messina - Palermo
and
Rome - Naples - Messina - Taormina - Catania - Siracusa   392+406

This trip includes a 35-minute ride on the ferry boat that runs between Villa S. Giovanni and Messina (Maritima).

There is beautiful seacoast scenery Messina-Siracusa portion of this journey.

Dep. Rome (Ter.)	-0-	-0-	-0-	-0-
Dep. Rome (Tibur.)	-0-	-0-	-0-	-0-
Dep. Naples (Cen.)	01:06 (1)	02:45 (2)	03:52	-0-
Dep. Naples (C. Fleg.)	-0-	-0-	-0-	04:30
Dep. Naples (P. Gari.)	-0-	-0-	-0-	-0-
Arr. Messina (Mari.)	0735	08:50 (3)	10:15 (3)	10:50
Arr. Palermo	-0-	12:55	14:15	-0-
Arr. Taormina	08:51	10:17	11:37	12:01
Arr. Catania	09:45	11:10	12:26	12:58
Arr. Siracusa	11:15	12:48	14:00	14:50

Dep. Rome (Ter.)	-0-	04:28 (4)	07:00 (5)	08:55
Dep. Rome (Tibur.)	03:10	-0-	-0-	-0-
Dep. Naples (Cen.)	-0-	-0-	-0-	-0-
Dep. Naples (C. Fleg.)	15:20	06:38	-0-	11:04
Dep. Naples (P. Gari.)	-0-	-0-	09:05	-0-
Arr. Messina (Mari.)	12:00 (3)	13:25 (3)	14:45 (3)	17:20 (3)
Arr. Palermo	16:25	18:05	18:30	21:30
Arr. Taormina	12:55	14:55	15:53	18:35
Arr. Catania	13:58	15:45	16:36	19:26
Arr. Siracusa	15:38	17:18	17:55	20:50

Dep. Rome (Ter.)	19:35 (6)	20:45 (2)	-0-	22:35 (7)
Dep. Rome (Tibur.)	-0-	-0-	-0-	-0-
Dep. Naples (Cen.)	21:57	23:05	00:31 (5)	00:50
Dep. Naples (C. Fleg.)	-0-	-0-	-0-	-0-
Dep. Naples (P. Gari.)	-0-	-0-	-0-	-0-
Arr. Messina (Mari.)	03:55	04:55	06:15	06:40
Arr. Palermo	08:00	-0-	-0-	11:00
Arr. Taormina	-0-	06:14	07:26	08:03
Arr. Catania	-0-	07:06	08:15	09:00
Arr. Siracusa	-0-	08:45	10:00	10:30

THE NORTHBOUND TRIP

Dep. Siracusa	07:52 (5)	08:48 (9)	12:27	15:15 (2)
Dep. Catania	09:03	10:16	14:03	16:50
Dep. Taormina	09:40	11:00	14:48	17:34
Dep. Palermo	07:30 (8)	08:30 (8)	12:06 (8)	-0-
Dep. Messina (Mari.)	11:00 (8)	12:20 (8)	16:20	18:55
Arr Naples (P. Gari.)	16:42	-0-	-0-	-0-
Arr. Naples (C. Fleg.)	-0-	18:45	-0-	-0-
Arr. Naples (Cen.)	-0-	-0-	22:44	00:45
Arr. Rome (Tibur.)	-0-	-0-	01:07 (4)	03:00
Arr. Rome (Ter.)	18:45	20:55	-0-	-0-

Dep. Siracusa	18:04 (10)	-0-	-0-	-0-
Dep. Catania	19:50	-0-	-0-	-0-
Dep. Taormina	20:40	-0-	-0-	-0-
Dep. Palermo	14:03 (8)	15:45 (2)	15:55	19:05 (12)
Dep. Messina (Mari.)	22:10 (8)	19:30	20:10	23:29
Arr Naples (P. Gari.)	-0-	-0-	-0-	-0-
Arr. Naples (C. Fleg.)	-0-	-0-	-0-	-0-
Arr. Naples (Cen.)	04:02 (11)	00:18	02:26	06:00
Arr. Rome (Tibur.)	-0-	03:36	04:41	-0-
Arr. Rome (Ter.)	-0-	-0-	-0-	08:50

Dep. Siracusa	20:20 (2)	20:55 (7)
Dep. Catania	22:00	22:30
Dep. Taormina	22:50	23:16
Dep. Palermo	-0-	20:40 (8)
Dep. Messina (Mari.)	00:20	00:45
Arr Naples (P. Gari.)	-0-	-0-
Arr. Naples (C. Fleg.)	-0-	-0-
Arr. Naples (Cen.)	06:34	06:53
Arr. Rome (Tibur.)	-0-	-0-
Arr. Rome (Ter.)	09:00	09:20

(1) Has couchettes. (2) Train has only sleeping cars and couchettes. *No* coach cars. (3) Train splits in Messina: one section goes to Palermo, the other section to Taormina, Catania and Siracusa. (4) Departs/Arrives Rome's Ostiense railstation. (5) Reservation *advisable*. Supplement charged. Light refreshments Rome-Palermo and Palermo-Rome. (6) Reservation *required*. Supplement charged. Carries first and second-class sleeping cars. Also has first and second-class couchettes. Coach cars are first-class only. (7) Carries a sleeping car. Also has couchettes. (8) Train from Siracusa, Catania and Taormina combines in Messina with train from Palermo. (9) Light refreshments. (10) Has couchettes. (11) Terminates in Naples. (12) Reservation *required*. Train has only sleeping cars and couchettes. *No* coach cars.

Sights in **Messina**: The Cathedral and the Annunciata dei Catalani Church, both rebuilt in the 12th century by Norman occupiers. The beautiful astronomical clock in the modern Bell Tower, next to the Cathedral. The art in the Museo Nazionale. The Botanical Gardens.

Sights in **Catania**: Founded 729 B.C. by Greek settlers. Now a very busy seaport and a popular Winter beach resort. Whatever could happen to a city happened here in the 16th and 17th centuries: famines, civil wars, epidemics, pirate raids, earthquakes, and the eruption of Mt. Etna in 1693, after which Catania was almost completely rebuilt. The dark gray color of the city results from the use of volcanic matter in constructing buildings.

See the Greek and Roman theaters, aqueducts and baths. The excellent collection of art and archaeological relics in the Civic Museum of the 13th century Castello Ursino. The tomb of the composer Vincenzo Bellini in the rebuilt 11th century Cathedral, also containing relics of St. Agatha. Sicily's largest church, San Nicolo. Next to it, the Benedictine San Nicolo Monastery, started in the 14th century.

The medieval manuscripts in the library of the University. The royal chapel, Collegiata. The 18th century palaces circling the Piazza del Duomo, with its Elephan Fountain. The museum at the birthplace of Bellini. The Astronomical Observatory.

Sights in **Siracusa**: Settled by Greeks in 734 B.C., 5 years after the founding of nearby Catania. An earthquake that destroyed much of Catania leveled Siracusa in 1693, after which Siracusa was rebuilt.

A comprehensive tour of Siracusa starts by visiting on the hill of Neapolis the Roman Amphitheater (which held 15,000 people attending gladiator fights), constructed during the reign of Augustus, before the birth of Christ. This structure was severely stripped in 1526 for the building of the city's defensive walls.

Above the Amphitheater is the 600-foot-long altar of Hieron II, where 450 oxen were simultaneously sacrificed on pagan religious days. Nearby is the ancient Paradise Quarry in which the cave called "the ear of Dionysius" is located. Next to it is the 5th century B.C. Greek Theater, where Plato and Aeschylus performed.

Behind the Theater is the "Grotto of the Nymphs". The views are wonderful from the walkway to the Paradise Grotto and from the Viale Rizzo, looking down into the Greek Theater and out toward the harbor. The archaeological area is open daily except Monday 09:00-17:00 (later in Summer).

Five miles further, on the hill of Epipoli overlooking Siracusa, is the Castle of Euryalus, the mightiest and most complete fortress of Greek times.

Returning downhill, along Corso Gelone, you come to the ruins of the Roman Forum, at Piazzale Marconi. Go along Corso Umberto I and cross the Ponte Nuovo to reach the island of **Ortygia**. There, in Piazza Pancali, are the remains of the Temple of Apollo, which the conquering Arabs turned into a mosque.

Other sights in Ortygia are the 16th century Santa Maria dei Miracoli church, the 15th century arch (Porta Marina), the Maniace Castle, and the 13th century Bellomo Palace, which houses a museum of medieval and modern art. The 17th century Palazzo del Municipo (Town Hall), the 18th century Palazzo di Benevantano del Bosco.

The National Archaelogical Museum, which has one of the most important collections (Greek, Roman and Byzantine) of sarcophagi, pottery, coins and bronzes in Italy. Its most famous treasure is the 2nd century B.C. Venus Landolina sculpture.

The ancient Cathedral is dominated by the Doric columns of the original Temple of Minerva, where many works of art are exhibited.

Sights in **Palermo**: This city was entirely Arabic in ancient times. It is the modern capital of Sicily. Severely damaged by bombs in July of 1943. Most museums and galleries here are closed on Monday. Their hours are 09:00 to 12:30 or 13:30. Most of them re-open from 15:00 to 18:00 on certain days. All are open Sunday 09:00 to 12:00 or 13:00.

See the exhibits of carretti (Sicilian horsecarts) and many other phases of traditional Sicilian life (bridal dresses, fishing boats, whips used for self-flagellation during Holy Week processions) at the Pitre Ethnological Museum. The fine archaeological collection in the Museo Nazionale on Via Roma. The Risorgimento Museum at Piazza San Domenico. The International Museum of Marionettes (located at Via Butera 1), open daily 10:00-13:00 and 17:00-19:00.

Watch tin, copper and iron being shaped into utensils in the stalls along Via dei Calderai, near Piazza Bellini. See tombs of important Sicilians, in the San Domenico Church.

The 800-year old Cathedral and, next to it, The Archepiscopal Palace, both on Vit- torio Emanuele. Nearby, the marvelous Oriental garden at the Church of San Giovanni degli Eremiti, a converted mosque.

See statues of former Spanish rulers in the Quattro Canti (Four Corners), a small octagonal piazza. Near it are 2 very interesting street markets, Vucciria and Il Capo. Located on a small, twisting street, Vucciria offers Sicilian pastries, cheeses and many foods that are exotic to non-Mediterranean tastebuds: fried lungs and spleen, sea urchins, pork sausage encased in the skin of a pig's foot.

The great array of food at Il Capo (which starts at the intersection of Via Volturno and Via Carini) includes squash, cheese, mounds of tomato paste, grapes, melons, sword- fish, eggplant as well as shirts, blouses, sweaters, leather handbags, etc.

See the antiques sold at Il Papireto, the flea market. Decorative tiles, Italian Victorian furniture, filigree jewelry, coins, religious art.

One of the most splendid opera houses in Europe, the Teatro Massimo, built in 1897. The 12th century Royal Palace. The Cuba and Zisa palaces. The catacombs under the Convent of the Capuchin Friars.

There are dazzling mosaics at the 12th century Sala di re Roggero, open to the public on Monday, Friday and Saturday mornings if no official meetings of the Regional Assembly are taking place. This is only one of the many local churches and palaces built when Norman knights returned to Europe from the Crusades, ending Saracen rule of Sicily. Additional ancient mosaics can be seen in the Martorana Church in Piazza Bellini.

Don't fail to see other Norman mosaics in the Palace of the Norman Kings and at the 12th century Arabic-Norman Palatine Chapel in nearby **Monreale**, a 5-mile bus ride (#9) from Palermo. It is one of the most outstanding architectural achievements in Italy, open in the morning on Wednesday and Sunday, all other days 09:00-13:00 and 15:00-17:30 (hours vary in Winter). Also the excellent mosaics in the 12th century Cathedral there.

Take the #14 or #77 bus to the bathing beach, Mondello. There are half-day bus excursions and local train service to **Segesta** and **Selinunte**, sites of substantial Greek ruins.

A local train leaves almost hourly for the 15-minute ride to **Bagheria**, where the eccentric 18th century Villa Palagonia and the beautiful Villa Valguarnera are located.

There is hydrofoil service in the Spring and Summer to 2 interesting islands. The Blue Grotto on **Ustica** attracts many visitors. The Archaeological Museum on **Lipari** is worthwhile. From Lipari, there is boat service to other nearby islands: **Alicudi, Filicudi, Salina, Stromboli** (immortalized by Ingrid and Roberto with more passion off the silver screen than they invested in the motion picture) and **Vulcano**.

Passenger ships run from Palermo to Tunisia.

TRAIN ROUTES IN SICILY
(including One-Day Excursions)

Messina - Milazzo - Palermo 405

Dep. Messina	04:33 (1)	05:30	06:18 (2)	07:27	09:35	12:40
Dep. Milazzo	05:05	06:00	06:50	08:04	10:12	13:12
Arr. Palermo	08:00	09:00	09:40	11:00	12:55	16:25

Dep. Messina	14:07 (3)	14:15	15:20 (4)	16:37	18:10	20:45
Dep. Milazzo	14:39	14:59	15:50	17:08	18:47	21:20
Arr. Palermo	17:35	18:05	18:30	20:00	21:30	23:55

Sights in **Milazzo**: Founded 7 centuries before Christ. An important naval victory over the Carthaginians was won by the Romans in Milazzo's bay more than 2,200 years ago. See the 13th century Norman castle and the 16th century Spanish walls at the old town, on a hill above the modern city.

Sights in **Palermo**: See notes about Palermo on page 249.

Dep. Palermo	03:48 (3)	06:15	07:30 (4)	08:30	11:30 (3)	12:06
Dep. Milazzo	07:10	09:01	09:51	11:03	14:40	15:00
Arr. Messina	08:05	09:35	10:25	11:40	15:20	15:40

Dep. Palermo	13:30	14:00	15:45 (2)	15:55	18:10	19:05 (5+6)
Dep. Milazzo	16:09	17:28	18:18	18:48	20:59	21:57
Arr. Messina	16:42	18:15	18:50	19:30	21:35	22:40

(1) Reservation *required*. Supplement charged. First-class only. (2) Second-class only. (3) Runs daily, except Sundays and holidays. (4) Reservation *advisable*. Supplement charged. Light refreshments. (5) First-class only. (6) Plus another departure from Palermo at 20:40, departing Milazzo 23:22, arriving Messina 23:59.

Messina - Taormina - Catania - Siracusa 406

There is beautiful seacoast scenery on this route.

Dep. Messina (Cen.)	05:45	07:30	08:15	12:00	14:15	15:25 (1)	18:05 (2)	20:50
Arr. Taormina	06:14	08:03	08:51	12:55	14:55	15:53	18:35	21:22
Arr. Catania	07:18	09:13	09:58	14:20	15:52	16:40	19:34	22:13
Arr. Siracusa	08:45	10:30	11:15	15:38	17:18	17:55	20:50	23:20

Sights in **Taormina**: A year-around resort, with very mild Winter weather, consisting mainly of 3 streets, each on a different level, connected to each other by many stairways, all on one side of Mont Venere. One funicular provides access to the beaches below the little town (4,000 population).

Stroll and shop for pottery, embroidery and carved wood figures along Corso Umberto, the main street. See the 3rd century Roman theater, facing Mt. Etna. The medieval great halls in the 15th century Palazzo Corvaja. The 14th century Palace of the Duke of St. Stephen. The 13th century Cathedral.

Sights in **Catania:** See notes about sightseeing in Catania on page 248.

Sights in **Siracusa**: See notes about sightseeing in Siracusa on page 248.

Dep. Siracusa	06:40 (3)	07:52 (1)	08:48 (2)	10:43 (3)	12:27	16:54 (4)
Arr. Catania	08:06	09:03	10:16	13:00	14:03	18:38
Arr. Taormina	08:43	09:40	11:00	13:42	14:48	19:24
Arr. Messina (Cen.)	09:28	10:23	11:38	14:30	15:38	20:05

(1) Reservation *advisable*. Supplement charged. (2) Light refreshments. (3) Change trains in Catania. (4) Plus other Siracusa departures at 18:04 and 20:55, arriving Messina 21:25 and 23:58.

Palermo - Agrigento - Palermo   407

Dep. Palermo	06:05	07:35	09:15	10:58	13:00	14:20	16:05 (1)
Arr. Agrigento	08:00	09:55	11:25	13:10	15:10	16:44	18:25

Sights in **Agrigento**: Founded by Greeks in 581 B.C. See the extremely fine Greek ruins: 7 Doric temples in the Valley of the Temples, many ancient aqueducts and cemeteries. The 14th century Cathedral. The 13th century churches: S. Nicola, Santa Maria dei Greci and S. Spirito. Baroque palaces. There is an especially good Archaeological Museum here.

Dep. Agrigento	06:42	08:10	10:00	11:30	13:25	14:20	16:55 (2)
Arr. Palermo	08:48	10:20	12:10	13:35	15:30	16:50	19:00

(1) Plus other departures from Palermo at 17:15 and 21:00, arriving Agrigento 19:40 and 23:25.
(2) Plus other Agrigento departures at 17:55 and 20:10, arriving Palermo 19:55 and 22:18.

Palermo - Caltanissetta - Palermo   407

Dep. Palermo	06:00 (1)	08:15	12:00	13:45	15:15 (1)	19:12
Arr. Caltan. (Xirbi)	07:31	09:54	14:03	15:30	17:03	21:03

Sights in **Caltanissetta**: The Greek, Arabic and Norman ruins at the Pietrarossa Castle. The excellent archaeological collection in the Civic Museum. The Baroque Cathedral and Palazzo Moncada.

Dep. Caltan. (Xirbi)	07:37 (1)	10:00	15:50 (1)	18:35	21:07
Arr. Palermo	09:10	11:30	17:25	20:20	22:52

(1) Runs daily, except Sundays and holidays.

Palermo - Catania - Palermo   407

Dep. Palermo	06:00 (1)	08:15	12:00	13:45	15:15 (1)	19:12
Arr. Catania	09:15	11:45	16:04	17:18	19:12	22:54

Sights in **Catania**: See notes about sightseeing in Catania under "Naples—Messina– Catania" on page 248.

Dep. Catania	05:50 (1)	08:05	14:10 (1)	16:46	19:12
Arr. Palermo	09:10	11:30	17:25	20:20	22:52

(1) Runs daily, except Sundays and holidays.

252

Palermo - Siracusa   392

Dep. Palermo	07:30 (1)	08:30	12:06	20:40
Arr. Siracusa	15 minutes later			

Sights in **Siracusa**: See notes about Siracusa on page 248.

Dep. Siracusa	10:30	17:18	20:50
Arr. Palermo	15 minutes later		

(1) Reservation *advisable*. Supplement charged.

Palermo - Trapani - Palermo   405

Dep. Palermo	06:52 (1)	09:00	10:15	13:00	13:50	14:45	17:15 (2)
Arr. Trapani	09:20	11:15	12:20	14:50	15:54	17:12	19:25

Sights in **Trapani**: A major Carthaginian and Roman naval base in the 3rd century B.C. See the outstanding 14th century Santuario dell'Annunziata, rebuilt in the 18th century. The 14th century Santa Agostino Church. The excellent sculpture and paintings in the Museo Nazionale Pepoli. The 17th century Cathedral. The Baroque Palazzo della Giudecca. The 15th century Santa Maria di Gesu Church.

Dep. Trapani	04:50 (1)	08:00	09:25	11:00	12:50	16:10	17:15 (3)
Arr. Palermo	07:38	10:10	11:35	13:32	15:10	18:22	19:10

(1) Second-class only. (2) Plus other departures from Palermo at 18:48 and 20:10, arriving Trapani 21:15 and 22:20. (3) Plus another departure from Trapani at 20:25, arriving Palermo 22:36.

Agrigento - Caltanissetta - Agrigento   407

Dep. Agrigento	06:25 (1)	10:15	14:03	16:32
Arr. Caltanissetta (Cen.)	07:56	11:40	16:08	18:30
Arr. Caltanissetta (Xirbi)	10 minutes after arriving Centrale station			

Sights in **Caltanissetta**: See "Palermo–Caltanissetta" on page 251.

Dep. Caltanissetta (Xirbi)	-0-	12:10	13:07	19:57 (2)
Dep. Caltanissetta (Cen.)	00:15	12:28	13:47	20:20
Arr. Agrigento	01:30	14:18	15:35	21:50

(1) Runs daily, except Sundays and holidays. (2) Second-class only.

Catania - Caltanissetta - Catania   407

Dep. Catania	05:50 (1)	08:05	09:40	10:15	13:30 (3)
Arr. Caltanissetta (Xirbi)	07:32	09:55	12:05	13:02	15:24

Sights in **Caltanissetta**: See "Palermo–Caltanissetta" on page 251.

Dep. Caltanissetta (Xirbi)	07:36 (1)	08:09 (1)	09:59	11:51	14:08 (4)
Arr. Catania	09:15	10:00	11:45	13:50	16:04

(1) Runs daily, except Sundays and holidays. (2) Second-class only. (3) Plus other departures from Catania at 14:10 (1), 16:46, 17:48 (2), 19:12 and 22:18, arriving Caltanissetta 15:45, 18:30, 19:52, 21:02 and 00:15 (Centrale station). (4) Plus other departures from Caltanissetta at 15:35, 16:22, 17:08 (1), 18:44 and 21:08, arriving Catania 17:18, 19:05, 19:12, 21:20 and 22:54.

THE MALTA CRUISE

Reggio di Calabria, Catania and Siracusa are gateways for the boat trip to Malta.

1465

Dep. Reggio	08:30 (1)	Dep. Malta	08:45 (2)
Dep. Catania	13:00	Arr. Siracusa	14:00
Dep. Siracusa	16:30	Dep. Catania	17:45
Arr. Malta	21:30	Arr. Reggio	22:00

(1) Runs Tuesday, Friday and Sunday. (2) Runs Monday, Wednesday and Saturday.

SCENIC RAIL TRIPS

Arona - Brig 270

There is beautiful lake and mountain scenery on this portion of the Milan–Lausanne route.

Dep. Milan (Cen.)	07:23 (1)	09:20 (2)	10:05 (1)	14:00 (2)	15:25 (4)	16:10 (5)
Dep. Arona	08:16	10:02	11:03	-0- (3)	16:06	17:00
Dep. Brig	09:51	11:14	12:29	15:52	17:30	18:31
Arr. Lausanne	11:28	12:38	14:09	17:15	18:52	19:52

(1) Light refreshments. (2) Reservation *required*. Supplement charged. Restaurant car. (3) Does *not* stop in Arona. (4) Reservation *advisable*. Supplement charged. Restaurant car. (5) Reservation *advisable*. Supplement charged. Light refreshments.

Bologna - Florence 374

Excellent mountain scenery on this ride.

The train goes through the 11.5-mile long Apennine Tunnel, Italy's longest tunnel.

Complete schedules appear under the "Bologna–Florence" (page 222) and "Florence–Bologna" (page 227) one-day excursions.

Bolzano - Brennero

Beautiful views of medieval castles and wild alpine mountain scenery on this portion of the route from Verona to Innsbruck, and on to Munich (see "Verona-Munich" on page 254).

Sights in **Bolzano**: Has been Italian since only 1919. The language spoken here (called "Bozen" during the nearly 6 centuries it was ruled by the Hapsburgs, from 1363 until World War I) is German.

Take at least one of the 3 funiculars that climb up the Alps. See the 16th to 18th century house on both Bindnergasse and Silbergasse. The vegetable and fruit market on Piazza delle Erbe. The 18th century Neptune fountain.

The exceptional carved altar depicting the Nativity, in the Holy Virgin Chapel of the Franciscan church. The frescoes at both the Cathedral and the Dominican church.

Stroll along the Talvera River first to the 13th century Maretsch Castle and then to Runkelstein Castle, whose lovely frescoes can be seen on guided tours Tuesday–Saturday, 10:00–12:00 and 15:00—18:00.

Buses are available to make short trips of less than an hour to many vineyard villages. Traminer and Gewurztraminer are produced in this area.

Verona - Innsbruck - Munich 74 + 381

Dep. Verona (P.N.)	08:40 (1)	10:35 (1)	12:38 (2)	13:50 (3)
Dep. Bolzano	10:22	12:18	14:20	15:47
Arr. Fortezza	11:08	-0- (4)	15:05	16:41
Dep. Brennero	12:04	14:04	16:04	17:50
Arr. Innsbruck	12:37	14:37	16:37	18:28
Arr. Munich	14:30	16:30	18:30	20:30

(1) Reservation *advisable*. Supplement charged. Restaurant car. (2) Reservation *required*. Supplement charged. Restaurant car. (3) Light refreshments. (4) Does not stop in Fortezza.

Fortezza - Dobbiaco

Very good mountain scenery on this spur off the Bolzano–Brennero route, appearing above. The following schedule shows how the Verona–Innsbruck–Munich trip can accommodate this en route detour.

381			383		
Dep. Verona (P.N.)	08:40 (1)	10:35 (1+4)	Dep. Dobbiaco	12:43 (2)	14:33 (3)
Arr. Fortezza	10:20	12:16	Arr. Fortezza	13:47	-0-
Change trains. 383			Change trains. 381 + 74		
Dep. Fortezza	11:18 (2)	12:40 (2)	Dep. Fortezza	15:05 (1)	-0-
Arr. Dobbiaco	12:17	13:42	Dep. Fortezza	15:05 (1)	-0-
			Arr. Innsbruck	16:37	17:08
			Arr. Munich	18:30	-0-

(1) Reservation *advisable*. Supplement charged. Restaurant car. (2) Second-class only. (3) Direct train to Innsbruck. No train change in Fortezza. (4) Plus another departure from Verona at 12:38, arriving Dobbiaco 13:42, departing Dobbiaco 14:33, arriving Innsbruck 17:08, Munich 20:30.

Torino - Cuneo - Breil - Nice 353

There is spectacular scenery on the 74-mile-long Cuneo–Nice rail route through the Roya Valley and the Alps, a service that first became operational in 1928. Severe damage during World War II caused it to be closed in 1940, and it was not re-opened until the Winter of 1979.

An outstanding feat of engineering, this line is a succession of very high viaducts, bridges and 60 tunnels that span 27 miles of this route, interspersed with sections that look down into deep valleys. This route has attracted many tourists.

Dep. Torino (P.N.)	08:43 (1)	09:03 (2)	14:27 (3)
Arr. Cuneo	-0-	10:21	15:55
Change trains.			
Dep. Cuneo	-0-	10:29	16:16 (4)
Arr. Breil	11:00	12:05	-0-
Change trains.			
Dep. Breil	11:07	12:45	-0-
Arr. Nice	12:02	13:37	19:11

(1) Direct train to Breil. *No* train change at Cuneo. (2) Second-class only. (3) Departs from Torino's Porta Susa railstation. Runs daily, except Sundays and holidays. (4) Direct train to Nice. *No* train change in Breil.

Sights in **Cuneo:** The 10th century Cathedral. The 13th century Church of San Francesco. The marvelous viaduct over the Stura di Demonte. The Civic Museum in the 18th century Palazzo Audiffredi. The 18th century Town Hall.

The magnificent Cuneo-Breil scenery can also be seen on the following easy one-day roundtrip from Torino.

Torino - Cuneo - Torino 353

Dep. Torino(P.N.)	09:03 (1)	12:30	Dep. Breil	12:12 (2)	16:52 (2)
Arr. Cuneo	10:21	13:34	Arr. Cuneo	13:38	18:18
Dep. Cuneo	10:29	14:03	Dep. Cuneo	13:50	18:30 (3)
Arr. Breil	12:05	15:30	Arr. Torino (P.N.)	14:57	19:44

(1) Second-class only. Change trains in Cuneo. (2) Change trains in Cuneo. (3) Second-class only.

Another route for viewing the breathtaking Cuneo-Breil scenery is the next one- day circle-trip from Genoa, in 2 directions.

Genoa - Torino - Cuneo - Ventimiglia - Genoa and v.v.

355		356	
Dep. Genoa (P.P.)	09:58 (1)	Dep. Genoa (P.P.)	08:23 (1)
Arr. Torino (P.N.)	11:50	Arr. Ventimiglia	10:25
Change trains. 353		Change trains. 353	
Dep. Torino (P.N.)	12:30	Dep. Ventimiglia	11:35
Arr. Cuneo	13:34 (2)	Arr. Breil	12:12
Dep. Breil	15:35	Arr. Cuneo	13:38 (2)
Arr. Ventimiglia	15:57	Arr. Torino (P.N.)	14:57
Change trains. 356		Change trains. 355	
Dep. Ventimiglia	16:55	Dep. Torino (P.N.)	15:20 (1+4)
Arr. Genoa (P.P.)	19:30	Arr. Genoa (P.P.)	16:54

(1) Reservation *advisable*. Supplement charged. Light refreshments. (2) Change trains in Cuneo. (3) Reservation *advisable*. Supplement charged. Restaurant car. (4) Plus other departures from Torino at 16:20 (3), 17:05, 18:10, 18:30 (1), 20:35, 21:10 and 22:10, arriving Geneva 17:57, 19:10, 20:18, 20:05, 22:26, 22:57 and 23:59.

Brindisi - Taranto - Reggio

There is splendid coastline scenery on this trip.

403		397	
Dep. Brindisi	08:24 (1)	Dep. Taranto	10:00 (2)
Arr. Taranto	09:35	Arr. Reggio (Cent.)	15:50
Change trains.			

(1) Second-class only. (2) Reservation *advisable*. Supplement charged.

Genoa - Pisa

There is exceptional mountain and Mediterranean coastline scenery on this ride. Complete schedules appear under the "Genoa–Pisa" one-day excursion on page 232.

Genoa - Nice - Cannes - Marseille 164 + 255

A close look at more than 100 miles of outstanding seashore resorts along the Mediterranean's Ligure coastline: the Savona and San Remo beaches (on the Italian Riviera) and the Monaco, Nice, Antibes, Cannes and St. Raphael beaches (on the French Riviera).

Dep. Genoa (P.P.)	05:55	08:23 (3)	16:13	18:05
Arr. Nice	10:10 (1)	11:20	19:45	22:00
Dep. Nice	10:55 (2)	11:24	20:00	22:20
Dep. Cannes	11:19	11:48	20:34	22:47
Arr. Marseille (St. Ch.)	13:07	13:43	22:41	01:00

(1) Change trains in Nice. (2) Light refreshments. (3) Supplement charged. Light refreshments.

Milan - Barcelona 78

The "Pablo Casals" began in 1990 to carry one "Gran Clase" sleeping car, the most luxurious sleeping car in Europe. Each of its large single and double compartments has a shower and toilet. The train also has ordinary sleeping compartments and 4-berth tourist compartments. There are *no* coach seats. The train has a restaurant car. This is a direct train to Barcelona. No train changes in Marseille, Narbonne or Port Bou.

Dep. Milan (Cen.)	06:40 (1)	18:05 (4)	20:00 (5)
Arr. Marseille	13:43	-0-	-0-
Change trains.			
Dep. Marseille	14:42 (2)	-0-	-0-
Arr. Narbonne	17:35	-0-	-0-
Change trains.			
Dep. Narbonne	17:37 (3)	-0-	-0-
Arr. Barcelona (Sants)	21:18	09:46	09:10

(1) Suplement charged. Light refreshments. (2) Light refreshments. (3) Supplement charged. Restaurant car (4) Does not call on Marseille or Narbonne. Direct train to Port Bou. Change trains in Port Bou at 06:31. Has couchettes. (5) "Pablo Casals" (see description above the timetable).

Milan - Bern 280

The Brig-Bern portion of this ride is one of the 5 most outstanding scenic rail trips in Europe, with a fabulous array of lakes, mountains and rivers.

All of these trains require reservation and charge a supplement.

Dep. Milan (Cen.)	07:23 (1)	11:07 (1)	13:25	17:25 (2)	19:05
Dep. Brig	10:01	13:15	15:38	19:55	21:33
Arr. Bern	11:38	14:43	17:08	21:26	23:10

(1) Restaurant car. (2) Light refreshments.

Milan - Locarno

Great gorge, mountain and river scenery is seen from a narrow-gauge local train over the Domodossola-Locarno portion of this route. This Centovalli (one hundred valley) ride is one of the 5 most outstanding scenic rail trips in Europe. Complete schedules appear under the "Milan–Locarno" one-day excursion on page 235.

Milan - Genoa

Great views of marble quarries, mountains, farms and the Mediterranean coast, all in 1½ hours. An easy one-day roundtrip. See schedules under one-day excursions on page 234.

Milan - Zurich   69

This is one of the 5 most outstanding scenic rail trips in Europe.

A feast of beautiful farms, lakes, mountains, rivers and vineyards. You go through the 9.3-mile long Gotthard Tunnel. Before it was opened to traffic in 1882, there was no direct rail route from Italy to eastern Switzerland through the Alps.

Prior to entering the Gotthard, the train goes through the beautiful Ticino Valley.

Immediately upon exiting the first of a series of 9 tunnels, you first see the small, white Wassen Church on your right, 170 feet below the track. The next time the church comes into view, after exiting tunnel #4, the church is to your left and nearly level with the track.

Later, after exiting tunnel #6, you have a third view of the church, again to your left, this time nearly 230 feet above the track, but you will see it there only if you look far ahead and before being alongside the church. (The train is in the Kirchberg Tunnel when it is directly alongside the church.)

The turns inside 3 semi-circular tunnels in this area (Leggistein, Wattinger and Pfaffensprung) are engineered so well that there is no sensation of the curves that the train is making inside those tunnels.

Try this interesting experiment: make a pendulum of any object, holding the top of a weighted string, chain or handkerchief against the inner face of a train window (a left-hand window when inside Leggistein, and a right-hand window when inside Wattinger and Pfaffensprung). As the train goes around a curve, the weighted bottom will move away from the window.

The Mediterranean climate on the Italian end of the tunnel is usually much warmer than the Alpine temperature on the Swiss end. The train makes 3 gradients at 45–50 miles per hour.

Dep. Milan (Cen.)	07:05 (1)	08:25 (2)	09:25 (2)	10:25 (3)	
Dep. Chiasso	-0-	09:30	10:30	11:30	
Arr. Zurich	10:57	12:57	14:53	14:57	
Dep. Milan(Cen.)	12:25	14:25	16:25	17:20 (1)	19:25 (1)
Dep. Chiasso	13:30	15:12	17:30	18:17	-0-
Arr. Zurich	16:57	18:57	20:57	21:50	23:36

(1) Reservation *required*. Restaurant car Milan-Zurich. (2) Reservation *required*. Restaurant car Chiasso-Zurich. (3) Restaurant car Chiasso-Zurich.

Milan - Tirano - St. Moritz - Chur - Zurich

This is an alternate route from Milan to Zurich. Many rivers and lakes are seen between Milan and Tirano. The descent from St. Moritz to Chur is spectacular.

357

Dep. Milan (Cen.)	05:10 (1)	08:00	09:00	12:05
Arr. Tirano	08:23	10:20	11:44	14:42
Change trains. 333				
Dep. Tirano	08:40	10:30 (2)	12:24	15:30
Arr. St. Moritz	10:58	12:56 (2)	14:56	17:56
Change trains. 330				
Dep. St. Moritz	11:00 (3)	13:00 (2)	15:00	18:00 (4)
Arr. Chur	13:06	15:06	17:06	20:06
Change trains. 310				
Dep. Chur	13:15 (5)	15:15 (5)	17:15 (5)	20:13 (4)
Arr. Zurich	14:50	16:50	18:50	21:50

(1) Runs daily, except holidays. Departs 06:00 on Sunday. (2) Direct train to Chur. *No* train change in St. Moritz. (3) Runs daily. Light refreshments on Saturdays, Sundays and holidays. (4) Restaurant car. (5) Light refreshments.

Naples - Brindisi 403

Very good mountain scenery on this route, the gateway for the cruise to Greece..

Since 1986, some of these trains have required changing to a bus for the Battipaglia–Grassano and v.v. portion of the Naples–Taranto, Taranto–Naples route and other trains for the Battipaglia–Taranto and v.v. portion while the rail line is being electrified.

Dep. Naples (Cen.)	14:30 (1)	18:00 (2)	Dep. Brindisi	04:18	06:16
Arr. Taranto	19:34	22:29	Arr. Taranto	05:20	07:32
Change trains.			Change trains.		
Dep. Taranto	19:41	22:49	Dep. Taranto	06:00 (1)	07:50 (1)
Arr. Brindisi	20:43	23:55	Arr. Naples (Cen.)	10:00	12:25 (2)

(1) Bus Naples-Taranto and vice versa. (2) Depart/Arrives at Naples' Piazza Garibaldi railstation.

Naples - Siracusa

There is wonderful Mediterranean coastline scenery on this trip. See details earlier in this section, under "Connections To Sicily" on page 246.

Naples - Sorrento 401

There is excellent Mediterranean coastline scenery on this ride.

Dep. Naples (Circumvesuviana) and Naples (F.S.) at one or 2 times per hour from 04:51 until 22:48 for the 55–65 minute ride to Sorrento.

* * *

Dep. Sorrento at one or 2 times every hour from 04:13 to 22:41 for the ride back to Naples. (There are stops in both directions at Pompeii.) A travolator provides transportation between Naples' F.S. station and Naples' Centrale station.

Naples - Taranto

There is very good mountain scenery on this route.

400		397	
Dep. Naples (P. Gari.)	06:46	Dep. Taranto	14:38
Arr. Bari	10:42	Arr. Bari	16:52
Change trains. 397		Change trains. 400	
Dep. Bari	12:27 (1)	Dep. Bari	17:00
Arr. Taranto	13:42	Arr. Naples (P. Gari.)	21:15

(1) Reservation *advisable*. Supplement charged. Light refreshments

Reggio Calabria - Taranto - Brindisi

There is excellent coastline scenery on this ride, which allows a sightseeing stopover in Taranto. See notes about what to see and do in Taranto on page 243.

Brindisi is the gateway for the cruise to Greece.

397					
Dep. Reggio Calabria (Cen.)	07:00 (1)	15:02 (1)			
Arr. Taranto	12:51	21:04			
Change trains. 403					
Dep. Taranto	13:28	14:38	16:29	17:31	19:41	21:32
Arr. Brindisi	14:59	15:52	17:47	18:40	20:43	22:44

(1) Reservation *advisable*. Supplement charged.

Rimini - Pescara - Brindisi 393

The excellent scenery on this route includes olive groves, vineyards and superb beaches on the Adriatic coastline. This can be broken into a 2-day trip by *stopping in Pescara one night and then continuing on to Brindisi the next day.*

Also, this trip can be extended by continuing on from Brindisi to Reggio di Calabria, a ride that offers fine coastline scenery (see page 242).

Dep. Rimini	09:00 (1)	10:01 (2)	14:01 (3)	15:01 (4)
Arr. Pescara (Cen.)	12:05	12:19	16:19	17:32
Dep. Pescara (Cen.)	12:10 (1)	12:22 (2)	16:22 (3)	17:35 (4)
Arr. Brindisi	17:31	17:15	21:14	23:54

(1) Operates late June to early September. (2) Reservation *required*. Supplement charged. Light refreshments. (3) Reservation *advisable*. Supplement charged. Light refreshments. (4) Reservation *advisable*. Supplement charged. Light refreshments. Change trains in Bari at 20:54, departing Bari at 22:26.

Rome - Foligno - Terontola - Foligno - Rome   368

Between Foligno and Terontola, there are magnificent views of vineyards, olive groves, the hillside towns of **Spello** and **Assisi, Lake Trasimente**, and the city of **Perugia**.

These Schedules allow a sightseeing stopover in Foligno or Perugia.

Dep. Rome (Ter.)	06:57 (1)	07:25	10:00 (1)	13:25
Arr. Foligno	08:29	09:20	11:37	15:16
Change trains				
Dep. Foligno	08:35 (2)	10:46 (2)	12:00	16:00
Dep. Perugia	09:25	11:30	12:34	16:34
Arr. Terontola	10:08	12:09	13:17	17:17

Sights in **Foligno**: An ancient Roman city that was badly damaged by earthquake in 1832 and then by heavy bombing during World War II. See the restored 12th century Cathedral. The archaeological museum and picture gallery, in the 14th century Palazzo Trinci.

Sights in **Perugia**: see notes under "Florence-Perugia" on page 229.

Dep. Terontola	10:45 (2)	13:45	15:45	17:45	19:45
Dep. Perugia	11:30	14:31	16:31	18:31	20:31
Arr. Foligno	12:10	15:06	17:06	19:05	21:04
Change trains.					
Dep. Foligno	13:41	15:41	17:29 (1)	19:41	21:32 (1)
Arr. Rome (Ter.)	15:35	17:35	19:20	21:35	23:05

(1) Reservation *required*. Supplement charged. (2) Second-class only.

Rome - Pescara

There is excellent mountain scenery on this trip. See "Rome–Pescara" on page 240 for timetable.

Udine - Trieste

This portion of the Venice-Trieste ride has excellent scenery of the Adriatic coastline. Sit on the right side for best viewing. The schedules allow a sightseeing stopover in Udine.

390

Dep. Venice (S. L.)	07:00	08:55	11:00	12:20 (1)	14:00 (3)
Arr. Udine	08:55	10:36	12:55	14:30	15:50
Change trains. 388					
Dep. Udine	09:35	12:25 (1)	13:15 (2)	14:35 (2)	16:45 (1+4)
Arr. Trieste (Cen.)	10:50	13:31	14:22	15:43	18:18

(1) Second-class only. (2) Runs daily, except Sundays and holidays. (3) Plus another departure from Venice at 15:00, arriving Trieste 18:52. (4) Plus other departures from Udine at 17:20 (2), 19:04, 19:35 (2), 20:45 and 23:00, arriving Trieste 18:52, 20:13, 21:08, 22:00 and 00:28.

Sights in **Udine**: see notes under "Trieste-Udine" on page 76.

INTERNATIONAL ROUTES FROM ITALY

The primary Italian gateway for rail travel to Switzerland, western Germany, Luxembourg, Belgium, Holland and northeastern France (Paris) is Milan. A secondary gateway for rail travel from Italy to Switzerland is from Torino, via Aosta, to either Brig or Geneva.

There is rail service to southern France (Nice, Marseille and Avignon), Paris, and to Spain from Milan and Genoa.

The gateways for travel to Austria, Germany and Denmark are Verona and Venice.

Venice is also the starting point for trips to Yugoslavia, Czechoslovakia, eastern Germany and the rest of Eastern Europe (Bulgaria, Greece, Romania, Hungary, Poland and Russia).

Milan - Genoa - Nice - Marseille - Barcelona   78

"Pablo Casals" (departing Milan 20:00) began in 1990 carrying one "Gran Clase" sleeping car, called by Cook "probably the most luxurious sleeping car in Europe". Each of its large single and double compartments has both a shower and a toilet. Travel on this train is *not* covered by Eurailpass or Spanish passes.

Dep. Milan (Cen.)	06:40 (1)	14:05	-0-	20:00 (7)
Dep. Genoa (P. Principe)	08:23	16:13	18:05 (6)	-0-
Arr. Nice	11:20 (2)	19:45	22:00	-0-
Dep. Nice	11:56 (3)	20:00	22:20	-0-
Arr. Marseille	14:25	22:41	01:00	-0-
Arr. Montpellier	16:18 (2)	00:38 (2)	03:11	-0-
Dep. Montpellier	16:37 (4)	02:42 (5)	03:16	-0-
Arr. Port Bou	19:01	05:25 (2)	05:45 (2)	-0-
Arr. Barcelona	21:18	09:46	09:46	09:10

(1) Supplement charged. Light refreshments Milan-Marseille. (2) Change trains. (3) Light refreshments. (4) Supplement charged. Restaurant car Montpellier-Barcelona. (5) Has couchettes Montpellier-Port Bou. (6) Has couchettes Genoa-Port Bou. (7) "Pablo Casals" (see note above the timetable.). Supplement charged. Train has only sleeping cars. (No coaches.) Offers 4 different classes of accommodation: Gran Clase, single, double and 4-berth tourist compartments. Restaurant car.

Milan - Zurich   277

See page 257.

Milan - Luzern - Basel   290

Dep. Milan (Cen.)	07:20 (1)	09:25 (2)	11:25 (2)	13:30 (2)	15:25 (2)
Arr. Luzern	11:39	13:39	15:39	17:39	19:39
Arr. Basel (S.B.B)	12:53	14:53	16:53	18:53	20:53

Dep. Milan (Cen.)	17:25 (1)	18:25	19:25 (3)	22:40 (4)	22:45 (5)
Arr. Luzern	21:39	22:39	-0-	-0-	-0-
Arr. Basel (S.B.B.)	22:52	23:59	00:50	03:34	03:56

(1) Reservation *required*. Supplement charged. Light refreshments. (2) Reservation *required*. Supplement charged. Restaurant car. (3) Runs Saturdays, Sundays and holidays. Reservation *required*. Supplement charged. Restaurant car. Change trains in Zurich at 23:24, departing Zurich 23:37. (4) Departs from Milan's Lambrate railstation. Operates late June to mid-September. Carries first and second-class sleeping cars. Also has second-class couchettes. Coach cars are second-class only. (5) Carries first and second-class sleeping cars. Also has second-class couchettes. Coach cars are second-class only.

Torino - Aosta Gateways to Switzerland

(1) Via Le Grand St. Bernard

Torino - Aosta - Martigny - Brig or Lausanne

All of the Torino-Aosta trains are second-class only.

355 e

Dep. Torino (Place Narbonne)	06:30 (1)	10:05	13:00
Arr. Aosta	08:51	12:43	15:04

Change to a bus.
273

Dep. Aosta (Place Narbonne)	10:00 (2)	14:15 (2)	16:30 (3)
Arr. Le Grand St. Bernard	11:15	15:30	-0-

Change buses.

Dep. Le Grand St. Bernard	12:36	16:36	-0-
Arr. Orsieres	13:25	17:25	18:08

Change to a train.

Dep. Orsieres	13:34	17:34	18:34
Arr. Martigny	14:03	18:03	19:03

Change trains.
270

Dep. Martigny	14:25 (4)	18:25	19:21 (4)
Arr. Brig	15:29	19:23	20:12

OR

Dep. Martigny	14:09	18:07	19:34
Arr. Lausanne	15:05	19:05	20:28

(1) Runs daily, except Sundays and holidays. (2) Operates mid-June to mid-September.
(3) Via the St. Bernard Tunnel. Direct bus. No bus change in Le Grand St. Bernard.
(4) Light refreshments.

(2) Via Mt. Blanc Tunnel

Torino - Aosta - Chamonix - Geneva

A layover in Chamonix (11:30-17:50) allows for sightseeing there. See page 344 for what to see and do in Chamonix.

355 e

Dep. Torino (Place Nar.)	06:30 (1)	09:01	10:05	-0-
Arr. Aosta	08:51	10:59	12:43	-0-

Change to bus.
191

Dep. Aosta	09:40 (2)	11:30 (2)	13:05 (3)	14:25 (2)
Arr. Chamonix	11:30	13:10	14:40	17:25

Change to train.

All of the Chamonix-Geneva train changes are "cross-platform", each taking less than one minute.

167

Dep. Chamonix	12:01	13:46	-0-	17:50 (2)
Arr. St. Gervais	12:41	14:26	-0-	18:29
Change trains				
Dep. St. Gervais	12:54	14:40	-0-	18:37 (4)
Arr. La-Roche-sur-Foron	13:47	15:24	-0-	-0-
Change trains.				
Dep. La-Roche-sur-Foron	13:49	15:32	-0-	-0-
Arr. Geneva (Eaux-Vives)	14:20	16:03	-0-	19:50

(1) Runs daily, except Sundays and holidays. (2) Operates early July to early September. (3) Operates early February to mid-April. (4) Direct train to Geneva. *No train change* in La-Roche-sur-Foron.

ROUTES TO OTHER COUNTRIES

Milan - Genoa - Nice - Cannes - Marseille - Avignon - Lyon - Paris

356 + 151 + 164

Dep. Milan (Cen.)	00:05 (1)	-0-	06:40 (5)	-0-	14:05
Dep. Genoa (P.P.)	02:37	05:55	08:23	13:00 (7)	16:13
Arr. Nice	08:25	10:10 (3)	11:20	18:13	19:45
Dep. Nice	08:55 (2)	12:52 (4)	11:24	18:18	20:00
Dep. Cannes	09:30	-0-	11:48	18:58	20:34
Arr. Marseille (St. Ch.)	11:36 (1)	-0-	13:43 (3)	21:37	22:41 (3)
Change trains.					
Dep. Marseille (St. Ch.)	11:46 (1)	-0-	14:58 (6)	21:48	22:59 (8)
Arr. Avignon	12:48	-0-	15:50	-0-	00:05
Arr. Lyon (Part Dieu)	14:50	-0-	-0-	01:08	02:29 (9)
Arr. Dijon	16:39	-0-	-0-	03:13	04:21
Arr. Paris (Lyon)	19:16	19:51	19:46	06:24	-0-

(1) Direct train to Paris. No train change. Has couchettes. (2) Light refreshments Nice-Paris. (3) Change trains. (4) TGV. Reservation *required.* Supplement charged. First-class only. Light refreshments. (5) Reservation *required.* Supplement charged. Light refreshments. (6) TGV. Reservation *required.* Supplement charged. Early July to early September: runs daily. Early September to early July: runs daily, except Saturday. (7) Change trains in Ventimiglia at 16:00, departing Vintimiglia 17:28 on "Cote D'Azur", which carries a sleeping car and also has couchettes. No train change in Marseille. (8) Carries a sleeping car. Also has couchettes. (9) Arrives at Lyon's Perrache railstation.

Rome - Genoa - Torino - Paris and Milan - Torino - Paris

	24	34	60	60	29
Dep. Rome (Ter.)	16:15 (1)	19:10 (2)	23:15 (3)	-0-	-0-
Dep. Genoa (P.P.)	22:04	00:13	05:17	-0-	-0-
Dep. Milan (Cen.)	-0-	-0-	07:10 (4)	09:30	21:10
Arr. Torino (P.N.)	23:58	01:53	07:25 (5)	11:04 (9)	22:41 (11)
Dep. Torino (P.N.)	00:15	02:08	08:57 (6)	12:25 (10)	22:44 (3+11)
Arr. Lyon (P.D.)	-0-	-0-	13:03 (7)	-0-	-0-
Dep. Lyon (P.D.)	-0-	-0-	13:30 (8)	-0-	-0-
Dep. Dijon	06:03	07:40	-0-	-0-	04:34
Arr. Paris (Lyon)	08:52	10:07	15:34	18:59	07:22

(1) Departs from Rome's Ostiense railstation. Carries a sleeping car. Also has couchettes. Light refreshments Rome-Torino. (2) Carries a sleeping car . Also has couchettes. Light refreshments 05:02–10:07 on day 2. (3) Carries a sleeping car. Also has couchettes. (4) Light refreshments Milan-Lyon. Arrives Torino 08:47. (5) Passengers from Rome and Genoa change to the Milan-Paris train. (6) Light refreshments Torino-Lyon. (7) Change to a TGV for the Lyon-Paris ride. (8) TGV. Reservation *advisable.* (9) Change trains in Torino. (10) Change trains in Chambery at 15:11. (11) Arrive/Depart Torino's Porta Susa railstation.

Rome - Venice - Budapest - Kiev - Moscow

75			88		
Dep. Rome (Ter.)	22:15 (1)	Day 1	Dep. Budapest (Keleti)	20:15 (2)	Day 2
Dep. Venice (S.I.)	06:10	Day 2	Arr. Kiev	20:33	Day 3
Arr. Budapest (Keleti)	19:08	Day 2	Arr. Moscow (Kiev)	10:00	Day 4
Change trains.					

(1) Carries a sleeping car. Also has couchettes. Restaurant car. (2) Train has only sleeping cars. No coach cars.

Verona - Innsbruck - Munich 74

Dep. Verona (P.N.)	00:18 (1)	02:27 (2)	08:40 (3)	10:35 (3)
Arr. Innsbruck	04:24	06:37	12:37	14:37
Arr. Munich (Hbf.)	06:35	08:31	14:30	16:30

Dep. Verona (P.N.)	12:38 (3)	13:50 (4)	17:10 (3)
Arr. Innsbruck	16:37	18:28	20:58
Arr. Munich (Hbf.)	18:30	20:30	22:40

(1) Reservation *required*. Carries a sleeping car. Also has couchettes. (2) Carries a sleeping car. Also has couchettes. Coach is second-class only. (3) Reservation *required*. Supplement charged. Restaurant car. (4) light refreshments.

Venice - Belgrade (Beograd) 35 + 46 + 930

Dep. Venice (Santa Lucia)	-0-	16:55 (2)
Dep. Venice (Mestre)	07:07 (1)	-0-
Arr. Zagreb	15:34	01:31
Arr. Belgrade	20:59	06:45

(1) Reservation *required*. Light refreshments Zagreb-Belgrade. (2) Carries a sleeping car. Also has couchettes.

Venice - Salzburg 75 + 390 + 820

Dep. Venice (S. Lucia)	07:00 (1)	11:30 (3)	20:50 (4)	23:52 (5)
Arr. Villach (Hbf.)	11:16	16:00	-0-	03:52 (6)
Change trains.				
Dep. Villach (Hbf.)	12:19 (2)	16:19	-0-	05:00 (7)
Arr. Salzburg	14:53	18:53	04:15	08:47

(1) Restaurant car. (2) Reservation *advisable*. Supplement charged. Restaurant car. (3) Change trains in Venice's Mestre railstation at 11:39. Depart Mestre 12:27 (2). (4) Direct train to Salzburg. No train change in Villach. (5) Change trains in Venice's Mestre railstation at 23:58. Carries a sleeping car. Also has couchettes. (6) Arrives 04:20 on Monday, Tuesday, Wednesday and Thursday. (7) Second-class only.

Venice -Vienna (Wien) 390

Dep. Venice (S. Lucia)	07:00 (1)	11:00	20:50 (1+3)	23:52
Arr. Venice (Mestre)	-0-	11:09	-0-	23:58
Change trains.				
Dep. Venice (Mestre)	-0-	12:27 (2)	-0-	00:50 (3)
Arr. Vienna (Sudbf.)	15:47	20:40	06:51	08:57

(1) Direct train to Vienna. *No* train change in Venice's Mestre railstation. (2) Reservation *required*. Supplement charged. Restaurant car. (3) Carries a sleeping car. Also has couchettes.

266

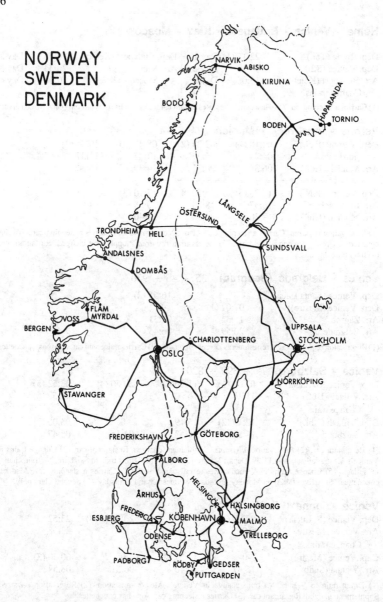

NORWAY
SWEDEN
DENMARK

NARVIK
ABISKO
KIRUNA
HAPARANDA
BODÖ
BODEN
TORNIO
LÅNGSELE
ÖSTERSUND
TRONDHEIM
HELL
SUNDSVALL
ANDALSNES
DOMBÅS
FLÅM
MYRDAL
VOSS
BERGEN
UPPSALA
CHARLOTTENBERG
STOCKHOLM
OSLO
STAVANGER
NORRKÖPING
FREDERIKSHAVN
GÖTEBORG
ÅLBORG
HELSINGÖR
ÅRHUS
HÄLSINGBORG
FREDERICIA
KÖBENHAVN
ESBJERG
MALMÖ
ODENSE
TRELLEBORG
PADBORG
RÖDBY
GEDSER
PUTTGARDEN

SCANDINAVIA (Denmark, Finland, Norway, Sweden)

Children under 4 travel free on trains in Denmark and Norway, under 6 in Finland, and under 12 in Sweden.

SCANRAILPASS

Unlimited travel on all trains and several ferries throughout Denmark, Finland, Norway and Sweden — such as Stockholm-Turku, Rodby-Puttgarden and Trelleborg-Sassnitz. Also allows 50% discount on such ferries as Copenhagen-Malmo, Stockholm–Helsinki and Bergen-Flam.

Sold worldwide by travel agencies, tour operators, and Rail Europe (U.S.A. and Canadian offices listed under "France" on page 23).

The 1992 *first*-class prices are: any 4 out of 15 days $179 (U.S.), any 9 out of 21 days $299, and any 14 days within a month $459. For *second*-class: $145, $239 and $349. Half-fare for children age 4–11. Children under 4 travel free.

SCANRAIL'N DRIVE

Unlimited 4 days of train travel plus 3 days of car rental (any 7 days) within 15 days.... or 9 days of train travel plus 3 days of car rental (any 12 days) within 21 days. Prices vary (a) whether for one person or for 2 or more persons, and (b) the category of car. A third passenger needs to pay only for a Scanrailpass.

The 1992 prices per person for 2 persons (using the smallest size car) with the 7-day pass are: $259 (U.S.) for *first*-class train, $225 for *second*-class. With the 12-day pass: $385 and $319. Up to 5 more days of car rental can be added to either pass at $50 per day.

NORDTOURIST RAIL TICKET

Sold only in Denmark, Finland, Norway and Sweden. Unlimited travel for 21 days on all government railways and most ferries, plus 50% discount on other ferries (such as Helsinki-Stockholm and Copenhagen-Oslo).

The 1992 *adult* prices are: $323 (U.S.) for *first*-class, $241 for *second*-class. Youths age 12–25: $241 and $180. Children age 4–11: $161 and $121. Children under 4 travel free.

MIDNIGHT SUN CALENDAR

An average June day has over 17 hours of daylight in Copenhagen and almost 19 in Helsinki, Oslo and Stockholm. Above the Arctic Circle, the whole disc of the sun remains visible throughout the night for periods of 30 to 120 days, depending how far north a city is. Some of the best vantage points are:

NORWAY					SWEDEN				
Green Harbor	April	21	– Aug	23	Bjorkliden	May	26	– July	19
North Cape	May	14	– July	30	Abisko	May	31	– July	14
Hammerfest	May	17	– July	28	Kiruna	May	31	– July	14
Tromso	May	21	– July	23	Gallivare	June	2	– July	12
Harstad	May	26	– July	19	Boden	June	4	– July	10
Narvik	May	26	– July	19					
Svolvaer	May	26	– July	19	FINLAND				
Bodo	June	5	– July	9	Utsjoki	May	22	– July	24
Trondheim	June	8	– July	6	Kilpisjarvi	May	27	– July	18
Andalsnes	June	5	– July	3	Pallastunturi	May	30	– July	15

Gallivare, Kiruna and Abisko are on the rail route from Boden to Narvik. Andalsnes, Trondheim and Bodo can be reached by train service from Oslo. Trondheim also can be reached by rail from Stockholm.

268

DENMARK

Children under 4 travel free. Half-fare for children 4–11. Children 12 and over must pay full fare. Denmark's 2 categories of fast trains are "IC" (Intercity Trains) and "EC" (EuroCity Trains). Seats are reservable on "IC" and "EC" trains, and reservation is *required* Copenhagen-Frediricia-Aalburg, Copenhagen-Fredericia-Herning and Copenhagen-Fredericia-Esbjerg. Ferry service to England operates from Esbjerg.

The signs you will see at railstations in Denmark are:

AFGANG	DEPARTURE
ANKOMST	ARRIVAL
BANEGARDEN	RAILSTATION
BILLETKONTORET	TICKET OFFICE
DAMER	WOMEN
GARDEROBEN	CHECKROOM
HERRER	MEN
INDGANG	ENTRANCE
KOREPLAN	TIMETABLE
LYNTOG	FAST INTERCITY TRAIN
OPLYSNING	INFORMATION
PLADSBESTILLINGEN	RESERVATIONS
PERRON	TRACK
RYGEKUPE	SMOKING COMPARTMENT
SOVEVOGN	SLEEPING CAR
SPISEVOGN	RESTAURANT CAR
TIL PERRONERNE TO	THE PLATFORMS
TOG AFGAR	DEPARTURE TIMETABLE
TOG ANKOMMER	ARRIVAL TIMETABLE
UDGANG	EXIT

DANISH HOLIDAYS

A list of holidays is helpful because some trains will be noted later in this section as *not* running on holidays. Also, those trains which operate on holidays are filled, and it is necessary to make reservations for them long in advance.

January 1	New Year's Day	June 5	Constitution Day
	Maundy Thursday		(from Noon)
	Good Friday		Whit Sunday
	Easter		Whit Monday
	Easter Monday	December 24	(From Noon)
	Prayer Day	December 25	Christmas Day
	(4th Fri. after Easter)	December 26	Boxing Day
	Ascension Day		

SUMMER TIME

Denmark, Finland, Norway and Sweden change to Summer Time on the last Sunday of March and convert back to Standard Time on the last Sunday of September. Finland is one hour ahead of Denmark, Norway and Sweden all year.

EURAILPASS BONUSES IN DENMARK

See page 25.

DENMARK'S TRAIN PASSES

All of Denmark's passes must be purchased in Denmark.

Landsrabatkort (Rebate Card) Allows a 50% discount on train and ferry tickets. The 1991 prices were: Dk-336 for 3 months, Dk-504 for 6 months, and Dk-672 for 12 months. Half-fare for children under 12.

10-Ride Pass Allows discount of about 20% on either first or second-class tickets. Can be used by several persons.

Cheap Days Discount Allows discount of about 20% on *first-class* tickets only, on distances of over 100kms (62 miles). Valid all year on Tuesday, Wednesday, Thursday and Saturday.

Child's Discount One child plus one adult traveling a minimum of 100kms in *second-class* only pay the price of 2 children's tickets. On a "cheap day" (see above), the price is even lower. Children under 4 travel free. Half-fare for children 4-11.

65-Ticket Persons 65 and older receive discounts of 25-40% on both first and second-class tickets, depending on the day of the week. Valid most days except Fridays, Sundays, the Wednesday before Easter, Maundy Thursday, Easter Monday, Common Prayer Eve, Ascension Eve, and Dec. 22 to Jan. 2.

Group Ticket Discounts of 20% and more on tickets. The group must be a minimum of 3 adults.

ONE-DAY EXCURSIONS AND CITY-SIGHTSEEING

Here are 12 one-day rail trips that can be made comfortably from Copenhagen and Odense, returning to them in most cases before dinnertime. Notes are provided on what to see and do at each destination.

Copenhagen

City tours start from Town Hall Square, in front of the Palace Hotel. To get to the Mermaid or Amalienborg Castle (changing of the guard daily at 12:00) on your own, take bus #1 or #6. For brewery visits, take bus #6 to Carlsberg, or take bus #1 to Tuborg.

Also see Thorvaldsen Museum, with his sculptures and tomb. Tivoli Gardens. Christiansborg Palace, where the Danish Parliament meets. The Danish Resistance Museum. The Zoo. Windowshop in the walking area, Stroget.

The vast collection in the National Museum (12 Frederiksholms Kanal) reflecting Danish life from the Ice Age to today, open daily except Monday. From mid-June to mid-September: 10:00–16:00. From mid-September to mid-June: 11:00–15:00 Tuesday-Friday and 12:00–16:00 on Saturday and Sunday.

Danish and European paintings (an excellent Matisse collection) at the Royal Museum of Fine Arts, on Solvgade, open daily 10:00–17:00. An exhibit of superb French Impressionists and also Egyptian, Greek, Roman and French sculptures at Glyptotek (behind Tivoli Gardens), open daily except Monday. From May through September: 10:00–16:00. From October through April: 12:00–15:00 (10:00–16:00 on Sunday).

The Toy Museum is open all year Wednesday-Sunday 10:00-16:00. There is a good collection of weapons and uniforms in the Royal Arsenal. From May through September: 13:00–16:00 on weekdays, 10:00–16:00 on Sunday. From October through April: 13:00–15:00 on weekdays, 11:00–16:00 on Sunday.

The City Museum, at 59 Vesterbrogade. The view from the top of Town Hall's 350-foot-high tower. Borsen, the oldest stock exchange in the world, still functioning.

The gilded spiral staircase of the Old Saviour's Church (Vor Frelsers Kirke), and the view at the top, from its tower. Regensen, a residential university since 1623. Thorvaldsen's marble statues of Christ and the Apostles in Our Lady's Church (Vor Frue Kirke).

The picturesque buildings along Nyhavn Canal. The line of foreign naval ships along Langelinie Promenade.

The crown jewels and other possessions of Danish monarchs in the museum at Rosen- borg Palace (open daily in Summer, only on Tuesday, Friday and Sunday the rest of the year), particularly the pearl-encrusted saddle of Christian IV. Nearby, the 25-acre Botanical Garden and the National Art Gallery.

The Frilandsmuseet open-air museum of Danish houses and farms in suburban **Sorgenfri**, open daily except Monday 10:00–17:00. The collection of modern art (Giacometti sculptures, painters of the Cobra group and post-1950 art) at the Louisiana Museum, 20 minutes away, in nearby Humlebaek (see page 274).

In the following timetables, where a city has more than one railstation we have designated the particular station after the name of the city (in parentheses).

Copenhagen - Alborg - Copenhagen 450

All of these trains require reservation.

Dep. Copenhagen	07:00	08:00	09:00	
Arr. Alborg	12:45	13:45	14:45	

Sights in **Alborg**: This thousand-year old town is the most important in the north Jutland area. You will find many medieval houses, down the lanes that wind off the modern boulevards. The early 15th century Monastery of the Holy Ghost. The early 16th century Aalborghus Castle. The outstanding Jens Bang House. The 12th century St. Botolph Cathedral.

Dep. Alborg	15:54	16:54	17:54	18:54 (1)
Arr. Copenhagen	21:48	22:48	23:48	00:48

(1) Runs daily, except Saturday.

Copenhagen - Aarhus - Copenhagen

There are 2 ways to make this trip. The first is by train between Copenhagen and Kalundborg, then by boat between Kalundborg and Aarhus. The boat has a smorgasbord cafeteria, and the scenery on the cruise is good.

The second way to Aarhus, entirely by train, is via Fredericia.

It makes an interesting day to go to Aarhus by the combination of train and boat via Kalundborg and return to Copenhagen by train via Fredericia.

Boat - via Kalundborg 451

The tickets for the ferry must be purchased before boarding the train.

Train			Boat		
Dep. Copenhagen (H.)	07:25 (1)	10:25	Dep. Aarhus (Pier)	13:00 (2)	16:00 (3)
Arr. Kalundborg	08:54	11:54	Arr. Kalundborg	16:10	19:10
Change to boat.			Change to train.		
Dep. Kalundborg	09:00 (1)	12:00	Dep. Kalundborg	16:25 (2)	19:25
Arr. Aarhus (Pier)	12:05	15:05	Arr. Copenhagen (H.)	17:45	20:45

(1) Runs daily, except Sundays and holidays. (2) Late June to early August: runs daily, except Sundays and holidays. Early August to late June: runs Monday-Friday, except holidays. (3) Plus another Aarhus departure at 20:00 on Sunday only, arriving Copenhagen 00:45.

Sights in **Aarhus**: Board the train at the Aarhus pier and take it to Aarhus' railstation. Don't fail to visit the 17th century Clausholm Castle and its Italian garden. The owners have been restoring their home since 1965 in order to make its extraordinary interior accessible to the public.

The magnificent decor, paintings, tapestries and furnishings of the Castle are worth going to Aarhus.

It is a one-hour drive from the city to the Castle, which is open only Easter to October 15. In Spring and Autumn, it is open only on Saturday and Sunday. From June 1 to August 15, Clausholm is open daily 11:00–17:00.

See the 60 completely furnished medieval houses and the 400-year-old mayor's residence at the Old Town open-air museum (Den Gamle By) in the Botanical Gardens. The 15th century Cathedral, noted for the magnificent tones of its twin organs and for the altar's woodcarvings. The ancient University. The Tivoli Friheden amusement park in Marselisborg Woods.

Take bus #6 from the railstation to see the great collection of primitive relics (Stone Age to Viking Era) in the Prehistoric Museum at **Moesgaard**, open daily in Summer 10:00–17:00. It is closed Mondays the rest of the year.

Train - via Fredericia 450

All of these trains require reservation.

Dep. Copenhagen (H.)	06:00 (1)	07:00	08:00	09:00	10:00
Arr. Aarhus	10:14	11:14	12:14	13:14	14:14
		*	*	*	
Dep. Aarhus	13:27	14:27	15:27	16:27	17:27 (3)
Arr. Copenhagen (H.)	17:48	18:48	19:48	20:48	21:48

(1) Runs daily, except Sundays and holidays. (2) Runs daily, except Saturday. (3) Plus other departures from Aarhus at 18:27, 19:27 and 20:27 (2), arriving Copenhagen 22:48, 23:48 and 00:48.

272

Copenhagen - Alborg - Aarhus - Copenhagen 450

It is possible to visit both Alborg and Aarhus in one day by using the following schedule.

All of these trains require reservation.

Dep. Copenhagen (H.)	06:00 (1)	07:00	
Arr. Aarhus	10:14	11:14	

Sightsee in **Aarhus** (see page 271).

Dep. Aarhus	13:18	14:18	
Arr. Alborg	14:45	15:45	

Sightsee in **Alborg** (see page 270).

Dep. Alborg	16:54	17:54	18:54 (2)
Arr. Copenhagen (H.)	22:48	23:48	00:48

(1) Runs daily, except Sundays and holidays. (2) Runs daily, except Saturday.

Copenhagen - Frederickshavn and Frederickshavn - Copenhagen 450

All of these trains require reservation.

Dep. Copenhagen (H.)	06:00 (1)	07:00	08:00	09:00 (5)
Dep. Odense	08:35	09:35	10:35	11:35
Dep. Fredericia	09:13	10:13	11:13	12:13
Dep. Arhus	10:18	11:18	12:18	13:18
Arr. Alborg	11:45 (2)	12:45	13:45 (2)	14:45
Arr. Frederickshavn	13:02	13:55	15:02	15:55

Signts in **Frederickshavn**: The military museum at the 17th century fort. The museum in the 18th century manor house called Bangsbo.

Dep. Frederickshavn	04:40 (1)	05:39 (1)	06:40	07:16 (1+6)
Arr. Alborg	05:50 (2)	06:45 (2)	07:50	08:30 (2)
Dep. Arhus	07:27	08:27	09:27	10:27
Dep. Fredericia	08:33	09:33	10:33	11:33
Arr. Odense	09:08	10:08	11:08	12:08
Arr. Copenhagen (H.)	11:48	12:48	13:48	14:48

(1) Runs daily, except Sundays and holidays. (2) Change trains. (3) Runs daily, except Saturday. (4) Train has only sleeping cars and couchettes. (5) Plus other departures from Copenhagen every hour from 10:00 to 16:00, Plus 17:00 (2) and 23:30 (4). (6) Plus other Frederickshavn departures at 08:49, 09:38, 10:49, 11:38, 12:49, 13:38, 14:49, 15:38 (3), 16:49, 17:38 (3) and 22:10 (4).

Copenhagen - Helsingborg - Copenhagen   463

Train

Dep. Copenhagen (H.)	07:25	07:55	08:25	08:55	09:25	09:55 (1)
Arr. Helsingor	08:20	08:50	09:20	09:50	10:20	10:50
Change to ferry						
Dep. Helsingor	08:30	09:10	09:30	10:10	10:30	11:10
Arr. Helsingborg	25 minutes later					

Sights in **Helsingborg:** Stained-glass windows, depicting the city's 900 years of history, in the Radhuset (Town Hall). Karnan, the 14th century fort with walls up to 15 feet thick, one of the best preserved Medieval buildings in Scandinavia. To reach it, take the elevator at the left of The Terrace, from the Main Square.

See the view of the Sound from Rosengarden, and the beautiful roses there. The Municipal Museum. The magnificent pulpit in the 15th century Mariakyrkan (Church of St. Mary). The handsome Concert Hall in Stadsbiblioteket (Town Library). The bronze statue in Hamntoget (Harbor Square).

Ferry

Dep. Helsingborg	13:10	13:30	14:10	14:30	15:10	15:30 (2)
Arr. Helsingor	13:35	13:55	14:35	14:55	15:35	15:55
Change to train						
Dep. Helsingor	13:44	14:14	14:44	15:14	15:44	16:14
Arr. Copenhagen (H.)	14:39	15:09	15:39	16:09	16:39	17:09

(1) Plus other departures from Copenhagen at 10:25, 10:55 and 11:25, arriving Helsingborg 1½ hours later. (2) Plus other departures from Helsingborg at 10 and 30 minutes after each hour until 21:30 (less frequent after 21:30), arriving Copenhagen 1½ hours later.

Copenhagen - Helsingor - Copenhagen   463

Dep. Copenhagen (H.)	07:09 (1)	07:25	07:55	08:09 (1)	08:25	08:55 (2)
Arr. Helsingor	55 minutes later					

Sights in **Helsingor:** Kronborg Castle (of Shakespeare's Hamlet). The stained-glass, depicting the town's history, in the Council Chamber of the Radhus (Town Hall). If time allows you to visit only Helsingor or Hillerod (described in the next listing), do *not* choose Helsingor. Fredericksborg Castle at Hillerod is by far the more interesting of the two.

Dep. Helsingor	12:01 (1)	12:14	12:44	13:01 (1)	13:14	13:44 (3)
Arr. Copenhagen (H.)	55 minutes later					

(1) Runs Monday to Friday, except holidays. (2) Plus other departures from Copenhagen at the same frequencies until 12:55. (3) Plus other departures from Helsingborg at the same frequencies until 18:44, plus every 30 minutes from 19:14 to 23:44.

Copenhagen - Hillerod - Copenhagen   STB (1991)

This is an excellent one-day trip by local commuter train on which Eurailpass is valid. We recommend leaving Copenhagen (Central) at 08:54 or 09:54 for the 50-minute ride. It is a 25-minute walk from the **Hillerod** railstaion, through the village, past the lake and market square, to Fredericksborg Castle and its National Historic Museum of both worldwide art and Danish history. You could spend many days enjoying its contents. A full morning will fly by.

The Castle is open 10:00–17:00 May through September, 10:00–16:00 in October, and 10:00–15:00 November through March.

Market days in Hillerod are Monday, Thursday and Saturday (09:00–13:00).

You can eat lunch at the Castle's restaurant or in the village on your walk back to the railstation, for departures to Copenhagen every hour at 8 minutes past the hour (05:08–00:08.

Copenhagen - Humlebaek - Copenhagen STB (1991)

Dep. Copenhagen	Frequent times from 05:25 to 00:55
Arr. Humlebaek	30 minutes later

Sights in **Humlebaek**: Exhibits of Giacometti sculptures, painters of the "Cobra" group, and post-1950 art (Warhol, Picasso, Lichtenstein, Calder) in the Louisiana Museum of Modern Art, open daily except Wednesday 10:00–17:00, on Wednesday 10:00–22:00. It is a 15-minute walk from the railstation to the Museum.

Dep. Humlebaek	Frequent times from 05:05 to 00:05
Arr. Copenhagen	30 minutes later

Copenhagen - Malmo - Copenhagen 1215

This popular roundtrip ferry-boat ride to Sweden's West Coast is inexpensive (1992: $38 (U.S.) for first-class, $26 for second-class), and a 50% discount from first-class is given to holders of a Eurailpass, 25% discount from second-class for Eurail Youthpass.

There are 16-22 sailings daily from Copenhagen (Havnegade) and Malmo for this 45-minute cruise.

Sights in **Malmo**: The Art, Archaeology, Military, Technical and Carriage Museums, all in the Castle. Town Hall. St. Peter's Church. The Sailor's House (3 Fiskehamnsgatan). The 17th and 18th century houses on Lilla Torg (Small Square).

Copenhagen - Odense - Copenhagen 450

En route, the train drives onto a ferry for the 65-minute boat ride between Korsor and Nyborg. Passengers can leave the train and stroll on the boat for fine views of the shoreline.

All of these trains require reservation.

Dep. Copenhagen (H.)	Every hour from 07:00 to 20:00
Arr. Odense	2½ hours later

Sights in **Odense**: The home of Hans Christian Andersen, now a museum, on Hans Jensenstraede. You can visit another Andersen Museum at Munkemollestraede 3. Also see the National Railway Museum in the Dannebrogsgade. The 13th century Cathedral of St. Knud.

Dep. Odense	Every hour from 06:08 to 22:08
Arr. Copenhagen (H.)	2½ hours later

Copenhagen - Roskilde - Copenhagen   450

Dep. Copenhagen (H.)   Frequent times from 07:00 to 20:00
Arr. Roskilde   18 minutes later

Sights in **Roskilde:** The 40 tombs of Denmark's kings and queens, a 500-year old clock, and the post on which such royalty as Peter the Great and the 20th century Duke of Windsor marked their heights (some of them with humorous exaggeration), all in the red brick Cathedral. Open for tours weekdays April-September 09:00–17:45 and October-March 10:00–15:45. Also on Sundays and holidays 12:30–17:45 June-August and 12:30–15:45 September-May.

Also see the exhibits of 5 ancient boats (39 to 59-feet long) in the Viking Ship Museum. Open daily 09:00—17:00 April-October, 10:00–16:00 November-March. It is a 20-minute walk from the town center.

The town center and the Cathedral are a short walk from the railstation. The tourist office (near the Cathedral) supplies an excellent English-language brochure, a city map, and a printed description of a walking tour that includes the town's most important sights.

Dep. Roskilde   Frequent times from 08:26 to 23:26
Arr. Copenhagen (H)   18 minutes later

SCENIC RAIL TRIPS

Odense - Fredericia - Odense   450

There is fine coastline scenery on this easy one-day roundtrip. This can also be seen as a portion of the Copenhagen-Frederickshavn route (page 272).

All of these trains require reservation.

Dep. Odense   35 minutes after each hour, from 07:35 to 22:35
Arr. Fredericia   35 minutes later

* * *

Dep. Fredericia   33 minutes after each hour, from 06:33 to 22:33 (1)
Arr. Odense   39 minutes later

(1) Plus another departure from Fredericia at 23:33 daily except Saturday.

INTERNATIONAL ROUTES FROM DENMARK

Copenhagen is the gateway for travel from Denmark, Norway and Sweden to Western Europe, starting with its connections to Berlin and Hamburg, and then on from those cities to the rest of Western Europe.

Copenhagen - Berlin 80

The trains are carried by Gedser-Warnemunde, (a 2-hour trip) by ferries that have a restaurant.

Dep. Copenhagen (H.)	06:41 (1)	12:41 (2)	22:30 (3)
Dep. Gedser	09:15	15:20	01:00
Arr. Berlin (Licht.)	15:03	21:13	07:10

(1) Restaurant car on train 12:05–15:03. (2) Light refreshment on train Copenhagen-Berlin. (2) Carries a sleeping car. Also has couchettes.

Copenhagen - Hamburg 460

The trains are carried Rodby-Puttgarden (a 65-minute trip) by ferries that have a restaurant.

Dep. Copenhagen (H.)	07:20 (1)	09:20 (1)	11:20	12:20 (2)	13:20
Dep. Rodby Ferry	09:30	11:30	14:30	14:30	15:30
Arr. Hamburg (Hbf.)	12:31	14:31	17:34	17:34	18:31

Dep. Copenhagen	15:20	16:20 (1)	17:20 (3)	19:05 (4)	20:05(4+7)
Dep. Rodby Ferry	17:30	18:30	19:30	21:30	22:30
Arr. Hamburg (Hbf.)	20:31	21:31	22:31	00:41	01:36

(1) Reservation advisable. Supplement charged. (2) Operates early June to late September. (3) Light refreshments. (4) Carries a sleeping car. Also has couchettes. (5) Operates mid-June to late August. Has couchettes. (6) Has couchettes. (7) Plus other Copenhagen departures at 21:05 (4), 22:05 (5) and 23:45 (2+6), arriving Hamburg 02:41, 04:10 and 06:25.

Copenhagen - Oslo 466 + 487

All of these trains require reservation.

Dep. Copenhagen (H.)	07:15 (1)	09:45 (1)	12:35 (2)	21:15 (3)
Arr. Oslo (Sen.)	17:10	20:10	22:10	07:10

(1) Light refreshments. (2) Light refreshments 14:35–22:10. (3) Carries a sleeping car. Also has couchettes. Coach car is second-class only.

Copenhagen - Stockholm 465

Dep. Copenhagen (H.)	10:35 (1)	14:35 (1)	22:35 (2)	23:15 (4)
Arr. Stockholm (Cen.)	18:59	22:47	07:17 (3)	08:17

(1) Reservation required. Restaurant car. (2) Carries a sleeping car. Also has couchettes. Mid-June to mid-August: carrries first and second-class coach cars. Mid-August to mid-June: carries only second-class coach cars. (3) Arrives one hour later mid-August to mid-June. (4) Operates mid-June to mid-August. Train has only coach cars.

FINLAND

Travel on Finnish trains titled "Rap" or "IC" requires payment of a supplement. The tracks in Finland are constructed with the wide Russian gauge of 5'0". This makes for spacious cars. The rail service extends as far north as Lapland. Service is maintained during severe Winter weather.

All major Finnish name express trains are equipped with radiotelephones for passengers to use. Finland's national timetable is called Suomen Kulkuneuvot.

The signs you will see at railstations in Finland are:

AIKATAULUT	TIMETABLE
LAHTO	DEPARTURE
LAITURILTA	TRACK
LIPPULUUKKU	TICKET OFFICE
MAKUUVAUNU	SLEEPING CAR
MATKALIPPUJEN MYYNTI	RESERVATIONS
MIEHILLE	MEN
NAISILLE	WOMEN
NEUVONTA (TOIMISTO)	INFORMATION
ODOTUSSALI	CHECKROOM
RAUTATIEASEMALLE	RAILSTATION
RAVINTOLAVAUNU	RESTAURANT CAR
SAAPUMINEN	ARRIVAL
SISAAN	ENTRANCE
TUPAKOITSEVILLE	SMOKING COMPARTMENT
ULOS	EXIT

FINLAND'S TRAIN PASSES

Finnrailpass Unlimited rail travel. Can be purchased worldwide and at railstations and ports of arrival in Finland. Sales agents in North American are Holiday Tours of America (40 E. 49th St., New York, N.Y. 10017) and Scantours Inc. (1535 Sixth St., Suite #205, Santa Monica, CA 90401). The 1992 *first*-class prices are: $176 (U.S.) for 8 days, $274 for 15 days, and $345 for 22 days. For *second*-class: $118, $183 and $230. Half-fare for children age 6–17. Twenty percent reduction for groups.

Senior Citizens Rail Card Available at railstations. Buyer must pay 50 Finnish marks and provide photo. Allows persons over 65 a 50% discount on each trip that is at least 48 miles. *Not* valid on certain holidays or from 12:00 Friday to 12:00 Saturday, and from 12:00 Sunday to 06:00 Monday.

Group Reduction Groups of 3 or more persons traveling together on a trip of at least 48 miles are allowed discounts of 20% on ticket prices, 25–50% discount for groups of 10 or more.

Child Reduction Tickets are half-price for children 6–17.

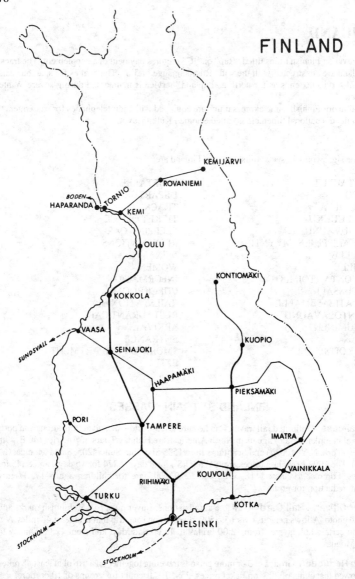

FINLAND

FINNISH HOLIDAYS

A list of holidays is helpful because some trains will be noted later in this section as *not* running on holidays. Also, those trains which operate on holidays are filled, and it is necessary to make reservations for them long in advance.

January 1	New Year's Day		Whit Saturday
	Epiphany		Whit Sunday
	Good Friday	June	Midsummer Eve
	Easter		Midsummer's Day
	Easter Monday		All Saint's Day
May 1	May Day	December 6	Independence Day
	Ascension Day	December 25	Christmas Day
		December 26	Boxing Day

EURAILPASS BONUSES IN FINLAND

These cruises on the Silja Line: Helsinki-Stockholm and Turku-Aland Islands-Stockholm.

Buses which are used as a substitute for a train.

ONE-DAY EXCURSIONS AND CITY-SIGHTSEEING

Here are 7 one-day rail trips that can be made comfortably from Helsinki, returning there in most cases before dinnertime. Notes are provided on what to see and do at each destination. The number after the name of each route is the Cook's timetable.

Helsinki

Helsinki's single most inspiring sight is Temppeliaukio Church, known since its 1969 dedication as the "Rock Church". This fantastic structure was quarried on its site, out of the bedrock in the middle of one of the oldest residential districts of Helsinki. Because the area occupied by worshipers is below the street level, all that can be seen as you walk toward the church is a low rock wall and the massive (70-foot diameter) copper dome.

Also see the large tubular steel sculpture, symbolizing music, in Sibelius Park. Tapiola, the model "new town". Finlandia Hall. The National Museum (closed Mondays September through May). The floral cemetery. The onion towers on the Greek Orthodox Uspenski Cathedral.

It is best to visit Market Square before Noon, to see the flowers, fish and mountains of berries. Also see the Town Hall. The Empress Stone obelisk. (Ferries from a pier near the obelisk go every hour to the island Suomenlinna Fortress.) See the impressive columns of Parliament House. The University Library and the Cathedral, in Senate Square.

The paintings and sculptures in the National Art Gallery. The National Theater. The Elaintarhantie shopping complex, opposite the railstation. The Botanical Gardens, in Elaintarha Park. The Linnanmaki amusement center, closed Mondays. The collection of Finnish wood houses at the open-air Museum of Seurasaari.

The Ateneum Art Gallery. The Gallen-Kallela Museum. The art and furniture at the Helsinki Municipal Museum. Old-fashioned and modern farm tools and implements in the Agricultural Museum. The Military Museum (Maurinkatu 1.) There are good views of the South Harbor and the waterfront from Observatory Hill (Tahtitornin Vuori).

Take the #6 tram to Arabia and see the original site of Helsinki, Old Town. Take the ferry from North Harbor to the Korkeasaari Island Zoo. See the displays in the Architectural Museum of Finland (Puistokatu 4).

Helsinki - Hameenlinna - Helsinki

All of these trains have light refreshments, unless designated otherwise.

	497	497	497	497	497	497
Dep. Helsinki	07:00	08:00	09:00 (1)	10:00	11:00	12:00 (2+4)
Arr. Hameenlinna	65 minutes later

Sights in **Hameenlinna**: The medieval castle. Ahvenisto Tower. The Art Museum. The City Museum.

	497	497	497	497	492	497
Dep. Hameenlinna	11:44	12:44 (3)	13:44	14:44	15:44	17:14 (5)
Arr. Helsinki	74 minutes later

(1) Runs daily, except Sundays and holidays. (2) Runs daily, except Saturday. (3) Reservation required. Restaurant car. (4) Plus another Helsinki departure at 13:00. (5) Plus other Hameenlinna departures at 18:48, 19:44 (1) and 22:44 (2).

Helsinki - Hanko - Helsinki   493 + Finnish timetable

A beautiful ride through woods and along lakes,

All of the trains Helsinki-Karjaa and v.v. have light refresments.

Dep. Helsinki	07:02	09:02	12:02
Arr. Karjaa	07:59	10:01	13:01

Change to local train.

Dep. Karjaa	08:10	10:10	13:10
Arr. Hanko	08:52	10:52	13:52

Sights in **Hanko**: The southernmost town in Finland. The tourist office is open all year Monday-Friday, 09:00–16:00 and in Summer also on Saturday 09:00–16:00, Sunday 11:00–15:00. Take a 2-hour cruise, leaving from the eastern harbor, operating June through mid-August. There is good fishing here. See the statue dedicated to the many Finns who disembarked from here to migrate to the United States between 1880 and 1930. Dance or try your luck at the Casino.

Dep. Hanko	16:10	18:45	21:10
Arr. Karjaa	16:52	19:27	21:52

Change to a standard train.

Dep. Karjaa	17:02	19:42	22:02
Arr. Helsinki	18:02	21:02	23:02

Helsinki - Lahti - Helsinki   498

All of these trains have light refreshments.

Dep. Helsinki	07:04	08:04	10:26	11:26	13:26	
Arr. Lahti	08:23	09:23	11:46	12:46	14:46	

* * *

Dep. Lahti	12:07	15:10	17:30	18:30	20:32	21:30
Arr. Helsinki	13:30	16:34	18:54	19:54	21:56	22:44

Sights in **Lahti**: A Winter sports center. The tourist office (closed Sunday) is in the rear of the Town Hall (intersection of Vesijarvenkatu and Aleksanterinkatu). See the view from the top of the 90-meter high ski jump, its elevators operating June through September, 10:00–19:30. It is only a 10-minute walk from the Town Hall.

Visit the Art Gallery. The Ethnographic Museum. The Radio Museum, open Sundays 13:00–15:00. In Summer, there are open-air concerts at the Mukkula Tourist Center. Shop here for marvelous Finnish glassware.

Helsinki - Riihimaki - Helsinki   492 + 497 + 498

Dep. Helsinki   Frequent times from 07:00 to 23:30
Arr. Riihimaki   50 minutes later

Sights in **Riihimaki**: The wood-working mills of H. G. Paloheimo. The glass factories of Riihimaen Lasi Oy. The Museum Peltosaari. The Municipal Museum.

Dep. Riihimaki   Frequent times from 06:00 to 23:05
Arr. Helsinki   50 minutes later

Helsinki - Rovaniemi   492

A trip to Lapland.

Dep. Helsinki	07:00 (1)	10:00 (1)	19:22 (2)	20:22 (3)	21:22 (2)
Arr. Rovaniemi	16:40	20:05	07:42	08:28	09:04

* * *

Dep. Rovaniemi	07:00 (1)	13:00 (1)	19:20 (2)	20:10 (3)	21:05 (2)
Arr. Helsinki	16:58	22:58	07:30	08:10	08:27

(1) Light refreshments. (2) Carries a sleeping car. Coach seats are second-class only. Light refreshments. (3) Runs Friday and Sunday. Carries a sleeping car. Coach seats are second-class only. Light refreshments.

Helsinki - Savonlinna   498

Dep. Helsinki	07:04 (1+2)	13:26 (3)	17:04 (2+4)	19:04 (5)
Arr. Savonlinna	11:44	18:45	21:42	00:11

Sights in **Savonlinna**: A charming town in the Lake Region, near the Russian border. The Tourist Office (Olavinkatu 35) is open in Summer daily 07:15–22:00. There is an English-language guided tour at Olavinlinna, a medieval castle. Shop for food at the open-air market.

Dep. Savonlinna	06:07 (5)	07:47 (2+4)	10:30 (6)	16:52 (2+7)
Arr. Helsinki	11:30	12:30	16:34	21:56

(1) Light refreshments. (2) Change trains in Parikkala about one hour before arriving (or departing) Savonlinna. (3) Runs daily, except Saturday. Light refreshments. Change to a bus in Parikkala about one hour before arriving Savonlinna. (4) Supplement charged. Restaurant car. (5) Direct train to Savonlinna. No train change in Parikkala. Runs daily, except Sunday. Light refreshments. (6) Bus service Savonlinna-Parikkala. Light refreshments Parikkala-Helsinki. (7) Runs daily, except Sunday. Light refreshments.

Helsinki - Tampere - Helsinki   492 + 497

All of these trains have light refreshments, unless designated otherwise.

Dep. Helsinki	07:00	08:00	09:00 (1)	10:00	11:00 (2)
Arr. Tampere	2 hours later				

Sights in **Tampere**: The aquarium, planetarium, children's zoo, amusement park, observation tower and planetarium at the Sarkanniemi Recreation Center. The more than 30,000 objects exhibited in the Hame Museum, particularly the handwoven rugs and tapestries. Many excellent artworks, frescoes and the altarpiece in the Cathedral, completed in 1907. The fine modern architecture of Kaleva Church. The National history Museum. The Haihara Doll Museum. The largest church bells in Finland, at the Orthodox Church.

See a performance at Tampere's Summer Theater in Pyynikki Park, from a seat in the unique bowl-shaped auditorium that rotates 360 degrees. Everyone sitting in the last row at the beginning of a performance also has a front-row seat during the show.

| Dep. Tampere | 12:00 (3) | 12:56 | 13:56 | 15:00 | 16:26 (4) |
| Arr. Helsinki | 2 hours later | | | | |

(1) Runs daily, except Sundays and holidays. (2) Runs daily, except Saturday. (3) Reservation required. Supplement charged. Restaurant car. (4) Plus other departures from Tampere at 18:04, 18:56 (1), 20:56 and 21:56 (2).

Helsinki - Turku - Helsinki   493
All of these trains have light refreshments.

| Dep. Helsinki | 07:02 | 09:02 | 12:02 |
| Arr. Turku (Stn.) | 09:12 | 11:27 | 14:27 |

Sights in **Turku:** A "Turku Card", good for city buses, museum admissions and discounts in restaurants and shops is sold at the City Tourist Office, near Market Square, at Kasityolaiskatu 4.

See the Provincial Museum and the marvelous Banquet Hall in the 13th century Castle, a short walk from the Silja Lane railstation, only a few minutes ride past the Main railstation. The Castle is open 10:00–18:00 May–September, 11:00–15:00 the rest of the year. The great organ (6,057 pipes) in the 13th century Cathedral.

The composer's instruments and personal possessions in the Sibelius Museum. The cobbled marketplace (fruits, flowers, fish and produce), Monday Saturday 08:00-14:00

| Dep. Turku (Stn.) | 13:47 | 15:47 | 17:00 | 19:35 | 20:50 |
| Helsinki | 16:02 | 18:02 | 19:18 | 22:02 | 23:02 |

INTERNATIONAL ROUTES FROM FINLAND

Helsinki is the gateway both to Russia (Leningrad, and on to Moscow) and Western Scandinavia (Stockholm, and on to Oslo and Copenhagen). Oulu is the starting point for trips to northern Sweden (Boden) and northern Norway (Narvik).

Helsinki - Leningrad   495
This train requires reservation and has a restaurant car.

| Dep. Helsinki | 13:12 | Arr. Leningrad | 19:40 |

Helsinki - Moscow   495 + 902
This train carries a sleeping car and a restaurant car.

| Dep. Helsinki | 18:10 | Arr. Moscow | 08:50 |

Helsinki - Stockholm

The price for the cruise across the Gulf of Bothnia (Turku-Stockholm) on the comfortable and pleasant Silja Line ships was $50 (U.S.) in 1991. This passage *is* covered by Eurailpass. The fare for a sleeping cabin is *not* covered by Eurailpass. Food on the ship is varied and delicious.

We recommend the daytime sailing in order to see the thousands of tiny islands on the ride through this extremely interesting archipelago. During the daytime cruise, there is a good smorgasbord for both lunch and dinner. On the night cruise, a live band plays music in the ship's nightclub. On both day and night cruises, the major activity is duty-free shopping.

493 Train			1250 Ship		
Dep. Helsinki	07:02 (1)	18:38 (1)	Dep. Turku (Abo)	10:00 (2)	21:30 (4)
Arr. Turku (Harbor)	09:27	20:57	Arr. Stockholm (Var.)	19:00 (3)	07:00
Walk to Abo Pier.					

(1) Light refreshments. (2) Does not operate January to mid-February. Mid-February to mid-May: runs daily except Monday. Mid-May to mid-August: runs daily. Mid-August to late December: runs daily, except Monday. (3) Arrives 20:15 on Saturday and Sunday mid-February to mid-May, daily mid-May to mid-August, Saturday and Sunday mid-August to late December. (4) Does not operate January to mid-February. Mid February to mid-May: runs Saturday and Sunday. Mid-May to mid-August: runs daily. Mid-August to late September: runs Saturday and Sunday.

Helsinki - Oulu - Haparanda - Boden - Narvik

All of the Helsinki-Kemi trains have light refreshments.

492					
Dep. Helsinki	07:00 (1)	10:00	16:00 (4)	19:22 (5)	21:22 (5)
Arr. Oulu	13:52	17:07	22:35	04:20	05:31

Sights in **Oulu:** The Art Museum. The Zoological Museum. The Cathedral. The Water Tower, on top of Puolivalinkangas, open May-October. Picturesque, ancient waterfront warehouses. The Church and Open Air Museum. Kastelli Church.

Dep. Oulu	14:04	-0-	-0-	-0-	05:45
Arr. Kemi	15:09	-0-	-0-	-0-	07:00
Change to bus. 496					
Dep. Kemi	15:32 (2)	-0-	-0-	-0-	11:32 (6)
Arr. Haparanda	17:17	-0-	-0-	-0-	13:37
Set your watch back one hour.					
Dep. Haparanda	18:30 (3)	-0-	-0-	-0-	13:30
Arr. Boden	20:35	-0-	-0-	-0-	15:35
Change to train. 476					

We recommend stopping-over in Boden for the night so as to travel Boden-Narvik during the daylight hours in order to be able to see the fine mountain scenery on that route. You cross the Arctic Circle going from Boden to Narvik.

Dep. Boden	08:40 (7)	13:15 (8)	-0-	-0-	-0-
Arr. Narvik	15:05	20:12	-0-	-0-	-0-

(1) Runs daily Helsinki-Oulu, but Haparanda-Boden runs only Saturdays, Sundays and holidays. (2) Bus service Kemi-Tornio. Change to train in Tornio at 16:25. (3) Runs Saturdays, Sundays and holidays. (4) *This schedule is for those who want to layover in Oulu.* Reservation required. Supplement charged. Restaurant car. (5) Carries a sleeping car. Coach is second-class only. Light refreshments. (6) Bus service Kemi-Tornio. Change to train in Tornio at 12:14. (7) Reservation required. Restaurant car until 11:55. (8) Reservation required. Second-class only. Restaurant car.

NORWAY

Children under 4 travel free. Half-fare for children 4–15. Children 16 and over must pay full fare.

Norway has the most number of scenic rail trips of any Scandinavian country and the most glorious places in which to experience the wonder of the Midnight Sun.

Norwegian State Railways has one coach on the Oslo-Bergen and Bergen-Oslo runs (and similar service on other long-distance routes) designed for conveying handicapped persons and other passengers requiring special care, such as mothers traveling with young children.

These special cars have a compartment accommodating 2 wheel chairs that are lifted aboard. An 8-seat compartment in these cars, equipped for mothers and their infants, is provided with a baby-chair, bottle heater, and other equip-ment helpful when caring for small children. This compartment is adjacent to a space with fitted toilets and a diaper-changing table. The car also has oxygen tanks, a stretcher and a small wheel chair for handicapped persons to use in moving about inside the train.

From Dombas and on north, you are in the land of the Midnight Sun. (See "Midnight Sun Calendar" on page 266.)

The signs you will see at railstations in Norway are:

ANKOMIST	ARRIVAL
AVGANG	DEPARTURE
BANESTASJONEN	RAILSTATION
BILLETLUKEN	TICKET OFFICE
DAMER	WOMEN
GARDEROBEN	CHECKROOM
HERRER	MEN
INFORMASJON	INFORMATION
INGANG	ENTRANCE
RESERVASJONSLUKEN	RESERVATIONS
ROKERE	SMOKING COMPARTMENT
SOVEVOGN	SLEEPING CAR
SPISEVOGN	RESTAURANT CAR
SPOR	TRACK
TIL PLATTFORMENTE	TO THE PLATFORMS
TOGTABELL	TIMETABLE
UTGANG	EXIT
VEKSLIGSKONTOR	CURRENCY EXCHANGE
VINDUSPLASS	WINDOW SEAT

NORWEGIAN HOLIDAYS

A list of holidays is helpful because some trains will be noted later in this section as *not* running on holidays. Also, those trains which operate on holidays are filled, and it is necessary to make reservations for them long in advance.

January 1	New Year's Day		Ascension Day
	Maundy Thursday	May 17	Constitution Day
	Good Friday		Whit Monday
	Easter	December 25	Christmas Day
	Easter Monday	December 26	Boxing Day
May 1	Labor Day		

EURAILPASS BONUSES

A 30% reduction on the fares of the Color Line Steamship Company for the cruise between Kristiansand and Hirtshals (Denmark).

NORWAY'S TRAIN PASSES

All of Norway's passes must be purchased at railstations in Norway.

Mini-Price Tickets A one-way, *second*-class train ticket of unlimited distance in Norway for approximately $66 (U.S.) in 1992. No stopovers are allowed except to change trains. Valid only on Monday–Thursday. An ordinary second-class ticket for the Oslo-Trondheim-Bodo 1,282 km trip (797 miles) costs $115 (U.S.) in 1992. This $230 roundtrip can be covered with 2 Mini-Price Tickets for only $132.

Senior Citizen Discount Persons over 67 years old are allowed a 50% discount on both first-class and second-class tickets. Must obtain an ID card, available at railstations.

ONE-DAY EXCURSIONS AND CITY-SIGHTSEEING

Here are 11 one-day rail trips that can be made comfortably from Bergen, Oslo and Stavanger, returning to them at or shortly after dinnertime. Notes are provided on what to see and do at each destination. The number after the name of each route is the Cook's timetable.

In the following timetables, where a city has more than one railstation, we have designated the particular station after the name of the city (in parentheses).

Oslo

Free admission to many Oslo museums, 50% discount on sightseeing tours, free travel on city buses, discounts on car rentals, and special prices at many restaurants are provided in 1991 with "Oslo Card". Sold at the Tourist Infomation office in Oslo's City Hall, its 1991 price is 90 Norwegian Kroner for one day, NK-130 for 2 days, NK-150 for 3 days. Half-fare for children 4–15.

Walk from the railstation, up Karl Johansgate, to the Royal Palace. En route, you will pass the National Theater. Behind it is the underground suburban train station. See the massive mural, in the post World War II City Hall, commemorating the Nazi occupation of Norway.

From the pier behind City Hall, take a 4-minute boat ride to Bygdoy to see the 4 interesting museums there: Viking ships (daily 10:00-18:00), the balsa Kon Tiki and reed Ra II rafts used by Thor Heyerdahl to recreate ancient voyages (daily 10:00-18:00); Roald Amunden's polar exploration ship Fram in the National Maritime Museum (daily 10:00-20:00); and the outdoor collection of 170 historical buildings brought to Oslo from all over Norway along with more than 80,000 items exhibited in the Norwegian Folk Museum.

The walk from the Maritime Museum to the Viking ships and the Folk Museum takes only 20 minutes.

The best way to reach Bygdoy is by public ferry from Pier 3, opposite the City Hall, or by Bus #30 from the center of town.

Later, see the bronze and granite sculptures of Gustav Vigeland in Frogner Park. Its highlight is a 55-foot-high monolith that has 121 intertwined figures. The Vigeland Museum at Nobelsgate 32. The Edvard Munch Museum (Tuesday–Saturday 09:00–22:00, Sunday 11:00–22:00). The Historical Museum. Norway's largest art collection, at the National Gallery. Oslo Cathedral.

Visit Aker Brygge (pier), a huge entertainment, shopping and residential project. The Museum of Applied Art. The 12th century, stone Gamle Aker Church (open Tuesday and Thursday in Summer).

The Resistance Museum and Defense Museum (commemorating the German occupation of Norway during World War II) in the Hjemmefront, at the 14th century Akershus Castle and Fortress, only a 5-minute walk from City Hall.

The Sonja Henie-Nils Onstad collection of modern paintings at Henie-Onstad Art Center   (Monday-Saturday 09:00–22:00, Sunday 11:00–22:00). Marvelous views from the Ski Jump and Ski Museum at Holmenkollen. Take the trolley to the Merchant Marine Academy at Sjomannsskolen.

Take Bus #36 from Town Hall Square for a one-hour ride to **Sundvollen**. Beautiful Tyri Fjord scenery.

Oslo - Goteborg - Oslo   487

All of these trains have light refreshments.

Dep. Oslo (Sen.)	07:30 (1)	Dep. Goteborg	15:10 (1)	17:33
Arr. Goteborg	11:59	Arr. Oslo (Sen.)	20:10	22:10

(1) Reservation required.

Sights in **Goteborg**: See notes about Goteborg on page 301.

Oslo - Hamar - Oslo 483

Be sure to sit on the right-hand side for the best view of the fantastic scenery along the western shore of **Lake Mjosa**. Norway's largest lake (75 miles long).

All of these trains have light refreshments. Most are second-class only.

Dep. Oslo (Sen.)	08:00 (1)	09:00	11:00
Arr. Hamar	09:26	10:44	12:42

Sights in **Hamar**: The enormous outdoor Hedmark Museum complex of more than 40 buildings, most of them from the 18th and 19th century, brought here from other places. One of the buildings is a house built in 1871 in North Dakota, U.S.A., by a Norwegian emigrant.

Also visit the 7 ½-acre Railway Museum, open May-September, to see many early coaches and locomotives as well as Norway's first railstation.

Dep. Hamar	13:16 (1)	14:54	16:53	18:54	20:49 (1)
Arr. Oslo (Sen.)	14:46	16:46	18:46	20:46	22:16

(1) Reservation required. Has first-class coach seats.

Oslo - Lillehammer - Oslo 483

All of these trains have light refreshments. Most are second-class only.

Dep. Oslo (Sen.)	08:00 (1)	09:00	11:00
Arr. Lillehammer	10:09	11:37	13:40

Sights in **Lillehammer**: The Sandvig collection of more than 100 old buildings and craftwork demonstration at the 100-acre open-air Maihaugen Museum, open daily 11:00–19:00 from late June to early August and 11:00–14:00 the rest of the year. See the "White Swan" paddle-wheel steamboat, Skibladner, at the city's dock.

Dep. Lillehammer	12:32 (1)	14:02	16:00	17:55	20:04 (1)
Arr. Oslo (Sen.)	14:46	16:46	18:46	20:46	22:16

(1) Reservation required. Has first-class coach seats.

Oslo - Vinstra - Oslo 483

All of these trains have light refreshments. Most are second-class only.

Dep. Oslo (Sen.)	08:00 (1)	09:00	11:00
Arr. Vinstra	11:05	12:47	14:50

Sights in **Vinstra:** A mountain resort. Home of the legendary Peer Gynt. See the memorial over his grave in the village church. Cross-country skiing is popular here.

Dep. Vinstra	11:30 (1)	12:52	16:40	18:08 (2)	18:59 (1)
Arr. Oslo (Sen.)	14:46	16:46	20:46	22:07	22:16

(1) Reservation required. Has first-class coach seats. (2) Runs Sunday only.

THE FJORD TRAIN ROUTE

Oslo - Drammen - Tonsberg - Sandefjord - Larvik - Skien - Nordagutu - Oslo   488

This one-day excursion offers great views of several fjords (starting with the Oslofjord), wooded countryside, and lovely lakes. As the schedules indicate, stops can be made for sightseeing in several of the towns on this route.

All of these trains have light refreshments.

Oslo (Sen.)	06:24	09:00	11:00	13:00	14:00
Arr. Drammen	07:04	09:37	11:37	13:37	14:37
Arr. Tonsberg	07:59	10:30	12:30	14:30	15:31
Arr. Sandefjord	08:19	10:54	12:54	14:54	15:54
Arr. Larvik	08:38	11:12	13:12	15:12	16:19
Arr. Skien	09:21	11:56	13:56	15:56 (2)	17:00
Dep. Skien	09:25	12:20 (1)	-0-	16:12	-0-
Arr. Nordagutu	09:58	12:52	-0-	16:44	-0-
		*	*	*	
Dep. Nordagutu	-0-	10:20	13:05	-0-	16:45 (3+5)
Arr. Skien	-0-	10:52 (2)	13:35 (2)	-0-	17:17
Dep. Skien	09:40	11:40	13:40	15:40	17:40 (4)
Dep. Larvik	10:23	12:23	14:23	16:23	18:23
Dep. Sandefjord	10:39	12:39	14:39	16:39	18:39
Dep. Tonsberg	11:02	13:02	15:02	17:02	19:02
Dep. Drammen	12:03	14:03	16:03	18:03	20:03
Arr. Oslo (Sen.)	12:43	14:43	16:43	18:43	20:43

(1) From Skien: runs daily, except Saturday. (2) Change trains in Skien. (3) From Nordagutu: runs daily, except Saturday. (4) From Skien: runs daily. Plus another departure from Skien at 19:40, arriving Oslo 22:43. (5) Plus another departure from Nordagutu at 20:05 (2), arriving Oslo 23:43.

Sights in **Drammen**: The activity along the busy docks. Many attractive old buildings. Watching the Drommensfjorden meet the Drammen River.

Sights in **Tonsberg**: Norway's oldest town. See today's whaling ships and the ruins of an ancient Viking castle, Tonsberghus. Also, the Vestfold Museum, the 12th century St. Michael's Church, the 12th century Sem Church, and the 13th century Royal Castle.

Sights in **Sandefjord**: The main port for Norway's whaling ships. See the whaling monument in the square. The Whaling Museum. Nearby are the mouth of the Oslofjorden and the head of the Sandefjorden.

Sights in **Larvik**: The Museum. The fjord.

Sights in **Skien**: The large sawmill operations. The meeting of Skien River and Lake Hjelle.

SCENIC RAIL TRIPS

Bergen to Oslo . . . and The Stalheim-Flam Detour   481

Indisputably, the most scenic rail route in Europe. There are several ways to make the detour, either in a single day or by adding one or 2 days to the Bergen-Oslo trip (see page 290).

The most carefree way to make the detour in a single day is to check baggage direct from Bergen to Oslo, rather than be bothered with it all day.

"Norway In A Nutshell"

The easiest way to take the Myrdal-Flam scenic train ride is to buy the one-day "Norway In A Nutshell" package, which costs 295 Norwegian Kroner in 1992 (NOK-155 for children under 16). Sold in the U.S.A. by Passage Tours of Scandinavia. Telephone: (800) 548-5960 or (305) 776-7070.

The tour price includes the train ride Bergen–Myrdal, the "Flam Line" cogwheel train Myrdal-Flam, the fjord boat trip Flam–Gudvangen, the bus Gudvangen–Voss, and the train from Voss back to Bergen. When this package is purchased in Norway, a Eurailpass can be used for the 3 train rides. This reduces the price by about 50%.

Sights in **Bergen**: Visit Torget, a fish market that has been operating for 9 centuries (weekdays: 08:30–15:00). See Bergenhus Fortress, with its 13th century Hakon Hall. The 12th century Mariakirken (St. Mary's Church). Europe's most modern aquarium and the collection of 19th century houses in Gamle Bergen (Old Bergen). Edvard Grieg's home in **Troldhaugen**.

Take the 5-minute funicular ride to the top of 2,000-foot-high **Mt. Floien**. See the Hanseatic Museum. The Maritime Museum. The Arts and Crafts Museum. The Bryggen Museum. The Leprosy Museum. Take the cable car to the top of **Mt. Ulriken**.

It is only 22 minutes for the bus ride and short walk to see the 13th century Fana Church and Fantoft, the 12th century Stave Church.

THE DIRECT ROUTE

All of these trains require reservation.

481

Dep. Bergen	07:30 (1)	10:30 (1)	14:30 (2)	15:30 (3)	22:45 (4+5)
Arr. Oslo (Sen.)	14:10	17:55	20:48	22:12	07:00
		* * *			
Dep. Oslo (Sen.)	07:30 (1)	10:30 (1)	14:30 (2)	15:42 (1)	23:00 (4+6)
Arr. Bergen	14:07	18:10	20:45	22:36	07:20

(1) Light refreshments. (2) Runs daily, except Saturday. Light refreshments. (3) Restaurant car. (4) Carries a sleeping car. Coach seats are second-class only. (5) Plus a second train on Sunday at 22:36 that carries a sleeping car and has a second-class coach, arriving Oslo 06:25. (6) Plus a second train on Sunday at 23:36 that carries a sleeping car and has a second-class coach, arriving Bergen 07:52.

The complete Bergen-Oslo line was opened in 1909 as the only year-round land transportation between Norway's 2 larges cities. It was electrified in 1964. Terrain and climate both caused construction problems which prior to then had never been encountered in building a railway line. The 300-mile length of track must pass through 200 tunnels and 18 miles of snow sheds in addition to crossing more than 300 bridges.

The first 40 minutes after leaving Bergen is along the lovely Sorfjorden. Travelers are frustrated by the interruptions of viewing the scenery caused by the many snow sheds.

However, it would be impossible for the trains to operate daily year round on this route and stick to a strict timetable if it were not for these structures.

When taking the Voss-Stalheim–Flam–Myrdal detour we have been recommending since 1971, you omit the 63-minute Voss–Myrdal portion of the main Bergen–Oslo line.

Voss - Stalheim - Flam - Myrdal Detour

The Gudvangen-Flam cruise on the Sognefjord (called "King of the Fjords") is the most scenic fjord trip in Norway.

481		481	
Dep. Bergen	07:30 (1)	Dep. Oslo (Sen.)	07:30 (1)
Arr. Voss	08:34	Arr. Myrdal	12:21
Change to bus. (Nor.)		Change to narrow-gauge train (481a)	
Dep. Voss	09:45	Dep. Myrdal	12:33
Arr. Stalheim	10:25	Arr. Flam	13:25
Dep. Stalheim	10:35	Change to fjord boat.	
Arr. Gudvangen	11:20	Dep. Flam	14:30 (2)
Change to fjord boat.		Arr. Gudvangen	16:35
Dep. Gudvangen	11:31 (2)	Change to bus. (Nor.)	
Arr. Flam	13:30	Dep. Gudvangen	16:50
Change to narrow-gauge train (481a)		Arr. Voss	18:10
Dep. Flam	15:00	Change to train. 481	
Arr. Myrdal	15:41	Dep. Voss	18:15 (4)
Change trains. 481		Arr. Bergen	19:25
Dep. Myrdal	17:16 (3)		
Arr. Oslo (Sen.)	22:12		

(1) Reservation required. Light refreshments. (2) Operates June, July and August. (3) Reservation required. Restaurant car. (4) Second-class only.

Sights in **Voss**: The 13th century church. The restored farmhouses and other buildings in the outdoor folk museum.

NOTE: On the Oslo-Bergen route (right-hand column above), there are only 6 minutes to change trains in Myrdal. *In mid-Summer, hundreds of people compete for the few seats on the Flam Line train.* Bus tour groups which board the Flam Line in Vatnahalsen (3 minutes after Myrdal) have to stand, which is very difficult on this route.

En route Bergen-Oslo, the one-hour bus ride from Voss to **Stalheim** passes (on your left) the spectacular Tvinde waterfall. At Stalheim there is only a Norwegian village museum and a hotel. But what an elegant place Stalheim Hotel is, managed superbly by handsome Reidar Chris Thomassen and his charming wife, Ingrid.

There is a view here of such magnificence that Kaiser Wilhelm II came to Stalheim annually for 25 years to look at it. Then there is a smorgasbord lunch that alone makes taking a trip from anywhere in the world to this Scandinavian oasis worthwhile. We always allow 2½ hours for this outstanding meal and stay overnight in Stalheim.

The land here has been farmed since 400 A.D. Some facility for food and lodging has existed here since 1647 when mail was carried by Norway's "pony express" from Bergen to Oslo, and Stalheim was one of the stations for changing horses and riders, right up until 1900.

An inn was operated at Stalheim before 1700. The first hotel here, constructed in 1885, burned in 1900. A second hotel, built in 1901, met the same fate in 1902. Another hotel, constructed and used first in Voss, was moved to Stalheim in 1906, enlarged in 1912, and burned down in 1959.

The present Stalheim Hotel was built in the Winter of 1959–60 and enlarged in 1967 to its present capacity of 130 units, ranging from single rooms to doubles and then suites consisting of a double room plus sitting-room with fireplace. Stalheim can accommodate 219 guests, and it is filled nearly every day in its April-September operation.

The terrace of the hotel provides a view over the Naro, Brekke and Jordal valleys, the Sivle and Stalheim waterfalls, and the conical peak of Mt. Jordal.

Two mounds on the right-hand side of the hotel's terrace date from 800 A.D. These were opened in 1890, revealing the remains of a woman who had been buried with her frying-pan, loom, bronze brooches and bracelets and the remains of a man, with his sword, axes and other utensils.

These relics were given to the museum in Bergen. The mounds have been reconstructed, and photos of the relics are displayed in the hotel's entrance hall.

Of those who start lunch at Stalheim at 12:00, few finish before 14:30. The remainder of the afternoon can be used enjoying the after-lunch euphoria in the spacious main lobby or on the large terrace. A leisurely stroll through the Open Air Museum on the hill behind the hotel is an enjoyable way to fill part of the afternoon and prepare oneself for dinner.

A walk down the narrow country road in September when delicious and accessible wild raspberries are in profusion is another pleasant diversion.

The hotel will arrange a tour of the ancient village museum. The owner of Stalheim, Kaare Tonneberg, gives an excellent commentary on the old log buildings, the lives that were led in them, the white mansion of the landowner who built it in 1726, and the contents of all the structures. These objects dramatize the contrasting life-style between the rich and the poor of that era. Among the contents are antique Norwegian furniture, arms, glass, silver, pewter and brass, some of which are also displayed in the hotel lobby.

If your schedule does not allow staying overnight at Stalheim, from mid-June to mid-August a boat leaves Gudvangen (only a 30-minute bus ride from Stalheim) at 16:50 and 19:50 for a cruise along the Sognefjord, all in Midnight Sun daylight, arriving Aurland at 18:15 and 21:20.

To get the most out of the Stalheim-Flam detour, remain at Stalheim for an excellent dinner that night and have the enormous "cold table" breakfast the next morning. The traditional Norse breakfast (cereals, fruits, fish, cold and hot meats, salads, cheeses, breads and beverages) originated in the days when a farmer doing heavy physical work in sub- freezing temperatures had to be sustained by one meal from dawn until sunset.

We tourists are fortunate that most Norwegian hotels have perpetuated this eating tradition long after most of the people in Norway have come to work in heated factories or offices 7 hours a day !

You can leave Stalheim by bus on Day 2 at 10:35 to connect with the Gudvangen–Flam boat ride on the **Sognefjord**, starting at 11:20 for arrival in Flam at 13:25. Snacks and beverages are available on the boat, or you can have lunch after you reach **Flam** at the excellent Hotel Fretheim, which is usually very crowded.

Short strolls from either of these bring you to the foot of several interesting waterfalls, or you can swim in Fretheim's heated pool.

On the morning of the following day, start the 12½-mile "Flam Line" railway ride to Myrdal (Table 481a) at 11:00, arrive Myrdal 11:41, change to the 12:28 departure for Oslo, and arrive Oslo 17:55.

The 41-minute Flam-Myrdal trip is one of the 5 most beautiful train rides in Europe.

"Flam Line" goes along the **Aurlandsfjord**, a branch of the Sognefjord. Watch for sturdy, wild mountain goats that often cluster on huge granite boulders only a few feet from the track. There is an ascent of 2,845 feet from sea level in the first 12 miles. This railway has the greatest incline of any Norwegian track, 5.5 percent at one stretch.

The descent is so steep that the train takes a longer time to go downhill than it does to go up. It has 5 different braking systems, any one of which is sufficient to stop the train.

The mountainside is so steep along one stretch that the train has to go through reverse tunnels. In one particular short distance, the track must go on 3 different levels on one side of Kjosfossen Gorge and on 2 levels on the other side of the Gorge. There are 20 tunnels with a combined length of 3.7 miles in the 12 ½ -mile route.

The train proceeds slowly or stops completely at the finest scenic sections in order for passengers to have the best possible views of magnificent scenery and of a road that was built in 1895 to supply materials for building the railway. This road has 21 hairpin bends. Along another stretch, the train crosses a 110-yard-long embankment and stops there for several minutes so that passengers can get off and walk closer to the enormous raging Kjos waterfall that cascades close to the train. Its force is marvellous to see and hear.

The first stop en route from Myrdal to Oslo is at **Finse**, highest elevation (4,267 feet) of the entire Bergen–Oslo line. Workers are stationed permanently at Finse to fight snow on the tracks 9 months out of the year and repair the snow sheds during the 3-month Spring-Summer-Autumn there.

Between Finse and Oslo, the scenery changes from glacier to ski resorts, waterfalls, and then beautiful valley farms and fast-moving rivers.

If time does not permit going to Stalheim, you can leave Bergen (late May to mid-September) at 08:10. Arrive Flam at 13:30. Depart on the "Flam Line" train at 15:00 or (early June to early September) at 15:30. Arrive Myrdal at 15:41 or 16:16. Connect in Myrdal with the train that departed Bergen at 15:30. Depart Myrdal on that train at 17:16 (reservation required). Arrive Oslo at 22:12. Despite the late arrival, you will see all of the interesting scenery between Myrdal and Oslo in daylight if you are taking this trip in Summer.

Oslo to Bergen   with Myrdal-Flam Detour   481

Depart Oslo (Sentral) 07:30, 10:30, 14:30 or 15:42. If you eliminate the Myrdal-Flam-Stalheim-Voss detour, you arrive Bergen 14:07, 18:10, 20:45 or 22:36. All of these 4 Oslo departures require reservation and have light refreshments.

If you want to take the Myrdal-Flam-Myrdal detour, depart Oslo 07:30, change to the "Flam Line" in Myrdal at 12:21, arrive Flam 13:25, depart Flam 15:00, arrive back in Myrdal at 15:41, change to the train departing Myrdal 16:13, arrive Bergen at 18:10.

For taking the 2 or 3-day Myrdal-Flam-Stalheim-Voss detour, depart Oslo at either 07:30, 10:30 or 14:30. The 15:42 Oslo departure does *not* stop at Myrdal.

The 07:30, 10:30 and 14:30 Oslo departures arrive Myrdal 12:21, 16:05 and 19:06. (The 14:30 runs daily except Saturday.) Change trains. "Flam Line" departs Myrdal at 12:33 and also 16:20 and 19:15 (running daily except Saturday) for the splendid 50-minute ride to Flam. Spend the night in Flam.

On the morning of Day 2, leave Flam Pier 08:45 for the boat trip on Sognefjord. Arrive Gudvangen 10:45. Take a bus to Stalheim for the great Smorgasbord lunch there. Either the same day or (if you stay overnight in Stalheim) the next day, go by bus from Stalheim to Voss, and then by train from Voss to Bergen.

Dep. Voss	06:00 (1)	08:45 (2)	12:15 (3)	13:04 (4)	14:45 (5)	17:04 (4+7)
Arr. Bergen	07:20	09:55	13:25	14:07	16:01	18:10

(1) Reservation required. Second-class only. (2) Runs daily, except Sundays and holidays. (3) Runs Monday–Friday, except holidays. (4) Reservation required. Light refreshments. (5) Second-class only. (6) Reservation required. Runs daily, except Saturday. Light refreshments. (7) Plus other departures from Voss at 18:15 (5), 19:45 (6) and 21:31 (4), arriving Bergen 19:25, 20:45 and 22:36.

Hotel Grand Terminus is a 2-minute walk from the Bergen railstation.

If time does not permit going to Stalheim on Day 2, you can depart Flam by fjord boat [table 481a] at 15:25 (mid-May to mid-September), arriving Bergen at 20:30 the same day.

Oslo - Dombas - Andalsnes   483

This 71-mile "Rauma Line" detour off the "Dovre Line" (Oslo to Trondheim) is, mile for mile, one of the 5 greatest scenic rides in Europe.

Even for one who is not going further north than Dombas, the 2-day roundtrip is well worth the time involved. There is no question that the route is worth seeing twice, and from 2 perspectives.

Be sure to obtain a free brochure at Oslo's Central railstation before beginning the trip. We would enjoy riding "Rauma Line" every day of our lives. Depart Oslo (Sentral) at 09:00 or 14:27. Arrive Andalsnes 15:35 or 21:00. In the Summer, you can read a newspaper there by sunlight at Midnight.

Soon after the train leaves Dombas it crosses the granite Jora Bridge, which spans a 120-foot deep gorge. At **Bjorli,** the Romsdal Valley comes into view, and you will see (at least in late Spring and early Summer) unmatched foaming torrents of thawed- glacier water, rushing at 80 miles an hour down vertical mountain slopes and through the boulder-strewn Rauma River bed.

The descent from Bjorli involves a double spiral through 2 circular mountain tunnels, first the 1,550-yard-long Stavem Tunnel, then through the 500-yard-long Kylling Tunnel.

Between these 2 tunnels, at **Verma** railstation, there is a monument that commemorates the opening of the Rauma Line by King Haakon in 1924. Along the opposite side of the Rauma River are small, well-kept farms, lush from the benefit of the warmth of the Gulf Stream, which keeps temperatures moderate along most of the coast of Norway.

The train next crosses Kylling Bridge, 200 feet above a thundering run of the Rauma River through a steep, narrow gorge. You are now approaching the valley floor.

Near **Flatmark,** you cross Foss Bridge and see Bridal Veil, best known of the numerous waterfalls on this route. At **Marstein** railstation, the sun is visible only 7 months of the year due to the combination of the tall surrounding mountains and the arc of the sun at this latitude.

After passing along the glaciated foot of the majestic Romsdalshorn Montain, whose peak rivals the Matterhorn as a climber's challenge, one can see on the left the highest vertical rock face in northern Europe, the "Troll's Wall" (Trollveggen), which is 3,000 feet high.

The "Rauma Line" reaches sea level in the Romsdall Valley before ending at **Andalsnes** (population 2,500) on the shore of Isfjord, at the head of the Romsdallfjord.

There is a bus connection between Andalsnes and **Alesund.** At Alesund, one can make flights to Oslo, Bergen or Trondheim, or make coastal express boat trips to Bergen or Trondheim.

The Rauma River is fished by sportsmen for salmon and trout.

To return to Oslo, depart Andalsnes 10:10. Change trains in Dombas at 11:43. Depart Dombas 11:53. Arrive Oslo 16:46. . . or, depart Andalsnes 16:20, change trains in Dombas at 17:57, depart Dombas 18:07, arrive Oslo 22:16. Both trains require reservation and have light refreshments.

The Oslo-Andalsnes-Oslo roundtrip can be made without stopping overnight in Andalsnes. There is a night departure from Andalsnes at 23:15 [483], arriving Oslo the next morning at 07:16. What a shame, to take this ride at night !

The only overnight lodging we know of in **Andalsnes** is at the 65-room Grand Hotel Bellevue. Advance room reservations are recommended.

There is a 2-hour bus/ferry connection [483] from Andalsnes to **Molde**, Norway's "town of roses" located on a fjord and surrounded by 87 beautiful snowcapped peaks. In Molde, see the many ancient wood buildings from the 11th century. The Romsdal Museum, largest Norwegian provincial museum. The floral decorations in the modern concrete and glass Town Hall. The view of the Norwegian Sea and the countryside from the Varden Restaurant, 1300 feet above the town. An International Jazz Festival (music, art, poetry and theatrical events) has been held in Molde the first week of August every year since 1960.

Take the Eide bus 18 miles to visit the grottos and caves at the Troll's Church and the waterfall that tumbles against a marble mountain.

Oslo - Andalsnes - Trondheim - Bodo - Narvik

This is a marvelous 5-day rail trip up Norway's Gulfstream-warmed coastline. There is very good mountain and lake scenery Oslo–Trondheim, and excellent mountain, lake and seacoast scenery Trondheim-Bodo.

Keep in mind when reading the timetables that there is constant daylight on this route during June and July.

A transplanted herd of gigantic musk oxen live along the Dombas–Trondheim route, Day 2 of this journey. On one of our trips, we saw a mother and baby grazing late at night on a grassy slope near the train track.

The scenery of forests, rich valleys, waterfalls, rivers and farms is lovely almost all the way to the crossing of the Arctic Circle, on the ride from Trondheim to **Bodo**.

Passengers are given a brochure with details about the Arctic Circle trip. Announcements during the ride over a public address system alert passengers to approaching points of interest. A steward or hostess is on board to provide information.

Upon reaching the stone monument that marks the Arctic Circle, the train stops there for 5 minutes, allowing passengers adequate time to take photographs.

We were fortunate that it was snowing on our first crossing of the Arctic Circle one June, giving the trip the feeling of a polar environment. A few hours later, as the train's route came close to the coastline, and when we were considerably north of the Arctic Circle, the weather was sunny and warm.

Because of the sunny, balmy weather that day, there was no sensation of being so far north, nor was there in Narvik the next day, by which time we were 700 miles above the Arctic Circle.

The northernmost rail service from Oslo is to Bodo. Passage from Bodo to Narvik is via an all-day bus trip through beautiful countryside interspersed by 3 ferry-boat crossings.

There are schedules on this page for a recommended rail trip from Oslo to Narvik, and then (page 296) from Narvik across northern Norway to northern Sweden and then south to Stockholm. On the trip from Narvik to Sweden (Boden), you cross the Arctic Circle north-to-south, although without the interesting ceremony that is presented on the south-to-north Trondheim-Bodo ride.

Day 1 table 483			Day 3 in Trondheim	
Dep. Oslo (Sen.)	09:00 (1)			
Arr. Dombas	13:51		Day 4 table 489	
Change trains.			Dep. Trondheim	08:30 (3)
Dep. Dombas	13:58		Cross the Arctic Circle.	16:10
Arr. Andalsnes	15:35		Arr. Bodo	19:20
Day 2 table 483			Day 5 Bus.	
Dep. Andalsnes	16:20		Dep. Bodo	07:45 (4)
Arr. Dombas	17:57		Arr. Narvik	14:35
Change trains.				
Dep. Dombas	19:11 (2)			
Arr. Trondheim	21:50			

(1) Second-class only. Light refreshments. (2) Reservation *required*. Light refreshments. (3) Reservation *advisable*. Restaurant car. (4) Food is available at occasional stops.

Keep in mind that during late June, all of July and most of August, the Midnight Sun allows you to see the scenery all the way to Trondheim, despite the 22:20 arrival time there. The light is not blinding, but you can read a newspaper by it straight through the night.

Deleting Overnight in Andalsnes and Trondheim

Here are schedules for those wishing to continue on from Andalsnes to Narvik without spending 21 hours in Andalsnes or a night in either Trondheim or Bodo and who don't mind missing a daytime view of the Andalsnes-Dombas "Rauma Line". The bus Fauske-Narvik is *not* covered by Eurailpass. Its cost in 1991 was 200 Norwegian kroner.

483			483		
Dep. Oslo (Sen.)	09:00 (1)	14:27 (1)	Dep. Dombas	19:11 (1)	04:12 (2)
Arr. Dombas	13:51	19:07	Arr. Trondheim	21:50	07:20
Change trains.			Change trains. 489		
Dep. Dombas	13:58	19:17	Dep. Trondheim	23:00 (2)	08:30 (3)
Arr. Andalsnes	15:35	21:00	Cross the Arctic Circle.		
Return to Dombas.			Arr. Fauske	09:05	18:30
Dep. Andalsnes	16:20	23:15	Change to a bus		
Arr. Dombas	17:57	01:05	Dep. Fauske	09:30	19:00
Change trains.			Arr. Narvik	14:35	00:10

(1) Light refreshments. (2) Reservation required. Carries sleeping car. Coach is second-class only. (3) Reservation advisable. Restaurant car.

Sights in **Trondheim**: This is the gateway for northern cruises. See the old Nidaros Cathedral, the largest medieval structure in Scandinavia. The 18th century rococo Striftsgarden royal residence. The Bishop's Palace. The open-air Folk Museum, open daily 10:00–18:00. The dazzling array of unusual musical instruments in the Ringve Museum of Musical History (including an Eskimo drum made from a walrus stomach, a Tibetan trumpet, a violin made of matches).

Sights in **Narvik:** The second (after Murmansk) most northern rail passenger terminus in the world.

Founded in 1901 at the western tip of **Ofot Fjord** to provide an ice-free port for the mid-Winter export of iron ore from Swedish mines which cannot ship via the frozen Bay of Bothnia during Winter.

For the most breathtaking view of Midnight Sun sky, fjords, mountains and the town of Narvik, take the 10-minute walk from Grand Hotel Royal to the base of the cable that lifts you 2,000 feet in 13 minutes to the top of **Mt. Fagernesfjell**.

Food and beverages are sold in the Fjellsheimen restaurant on the peak, an ideal site for taking spectacular photos and watching the sun revolve clockwise around the horizon.

A crucial British-German naval battle (commemorated at a small museum in the center of town) was fought in Narvik's fjords during World War II. Destroyed in 1940, Narvik was completely rebuilt after the war.

The Direct Trip

Oslo - Trondheim and Trondheim - Oslo 483

Dep. Oslo (Sen.)	08:00 (1)	14:27 (2)	16:00 (1)	23:00 (3)
Arr. Trondheim	14:45	21:50	22:35	07:20
		* * *		
Dep. Trondheim	08:10 (1)	09:05 (2)	15:35 (1)	22:35 (3)
Arr. Oslo (Sen.)	14:46	16:46	22:16	07:16

(1) Reservation required. Light refreshments. (2) Light refreshments. (3) Reservation required. Carries a sleeping car. Coach seats are second-class only.

Narvik - Boden - Stockholm 476

There is fine mountain scenery Narvik-Kiruna.

Day 6 (see 5-day Oslo-Narvik trip on page 295)

This train requires reservation, carries a sleeping car and also has couchettes.

Dep. Narvik	13:40	
Arr. Kiruna	16:45	
Arr. Boden	20:45	
Arr. Stockholm (Cen.)	10:56	Day 7 of the Oslo-Narvik-Stockholm trip.

Oslo - Kritiansand - Stavanger   482

There is excellent mountain scenery between Kristiansand and Stavanger.

Dep. Oslo (Sen.)	08:12 (1)	15:12 (2)	22:30 (3)
Arr. Kristiansand	13:20	19:40	04:00
Arr. Stavanger	16:45	22:45	07:37

Sights in **Stavanger**: Many old streets and houses in this 1100-year old town. See the market of fruits, vegetables, flowers and fish. The 11th century Cathedral. Outside the city, see the prehistoric Viste Cave. Try a deep-sea fishing trip.

Dep. Stavanger	07:25 (2)	13:40 (1)	22:00 (3)
Arr. Kristiansand	10:10	16:42	01:25
Arr. Oslo (Sen.)	14:49	21:52	07:18

(1) Second-class only. Reservation required. Light refreshments. (2) Reservation required. Light refreshments. (3) Reservation required. Runs daily, except Saturday. Carries a sleeping car. Coach is second-class.

Stavanger - Kristiansand - Stavanger   482

From Stavanger, it is an easy one-day roundtrip to see the fine mountain scenery en route to Kristiansand.

All of these trains require reservation and have light refreshments.

Dep. Stavanger	07:25	13:40		Dep. Kristiansand	13:35	19:50
Arr. Kristiansand	10:10	16:42		Arr. Stavanger	16:45	22:45

Voss - Granvin

This spur off the Bergen-Oslo route affords great farm, mountain and river scenery. It is an easy one-day roundtrip.

481 Train

Dep. Bergen	04:00 (1)	-0-	10:30 (2)	13:30 (1)	15:30 (3)
Arr. Voss	10:10	-0-	11:40	14:40	16:33
Change to bus.	490				
Dep. Voss	10:20 (4)	-0-	13:40	-0-	17:25 (5)
Arr. Granvin	10:40	-0-	14:20	-0-	17:45
		*	*	*	
Dep. Granvin	10:45 (4)	-0-	17:20	-0-	20:25 (5)
Ar. Voss	11:20	-0-	18:00	-0-	21:00
Change to train.	481				
Dep. Voss	12:15 (6)	13:04 (2)	18:15 (1)	19:45(2+5)	21:31 (2)
Arr. Bergen	13:25	14:07	19:25	20:45	22:36

(1) Second-class only. (2) Reservation required. Light refreshments. (3) Reservation required. Restaurant car. (4) Runs daily, except Sundays and holidays (5) Runs daily, except Saturday. (6) Second-class only. Runs Monday–Friday, except holidays.

INTERNATIONAL ROUTES FROM NORWAY

Bergen is Norway's starting point for *cruises* to England. Oslo is the gateway for *rail* trips to Sweden (Stockholm, and on to Finland) and Denmark (Copenhagen, and on to Germany and the rest of Western Europe).

Bergen - Newcastle 1050

The arrivals in Newcastle are on Day 2 after departing Bergen.

Dep. Bergen	11:00 (1)	11:00 (2)	13 :00 (3)	17:00 (4)
Dep. Stavanger	17:15	18:00	19:15	23:59
Arr. Newcastle (Tyne)	10:00	12:00	12:00	19:00

(1) Operates early June to late September. Runs Wednesday only. (2) Operates late February to early June and late September to late December. Runs Monday only. (3) Operates early June to late September. Runs Friday only. (4) Operates late February to early June and late September to late December. Runs Thursday only.

Narvik - Boden - Haparanda - Kemi - Oulu - Helsinki

This is the way to see all of the Narvik-Helsinki route during what are the average person's waking hours: take the 08:30 departure from Narvik, spend that night in Boden, take the 09:00 departure from Boden, spend that night in Oulu (refer to page 283 for what to see and do in Oulu), and on Day 3 or later depart Oulu at either 07:20, 09:55 or 12:52, arriving Helsinki 13:54 or 19:58 the same day.

All of these trains are second-class only, unless designated otherwise

476

Dep. Narvik	08:30 (1)	13:40 (1)			
Arr. Boden	16:05	20:45			

Change trains.   496

Dep. Boden	09:00 (2)	13:40 (3)			
Arr. Haparanda	11:15	15:56			
Dep. Haparanda	11:20	16:00			

Set your watch forward one hour.

Arr. Tornio	12:27	17:07			

Change to a bus. (Train ticket is valid.)

Dep. Tornio	13:17 (2)	17:12 (2)			
Arr. Kemi	13:52	17:52			

Change to a train.   492

Dep. Kemi	14:22 (4)	21:23 (5)	22:43 (5)	-0-	-0-
Arr. Oulu	15:39	22:33	23:57	-0-	-0-
Dep. Oulu	16:03	22:50	00:12	07:20 (6)	09:55 (4+7)
Arr. Helsinki	22:58	07:30	08:27	13:54	16:58

(1) Reservation required. (2) The Tornio-Kemi bus service does not run on Sundays or holidays. (3) Runs Monday–Friday, except holidays. (4) Has both first and second-class coaches. Light refreshments. (5) Carries a sleeping car. Coach seats are second-class only. Light refreshments. (6) Reservation required. Supplement charged. Restaurant car. (7) Plus another Oulu departure at 12:52 (4), arriving Helsinki 19:58.

Narvik - Boden - Stockholm

Schedules for this trip appear under "Scenic Rail Trips" on page 296.

Oslo - Stockholm   470

Dep. Oslo (Sen.)	06:50 (1)	10:55 (2)	15:47 (3+4)	22:50 (4+5)
Arr. Stockholm	13:23	17:23	22:23	06:47

(1) Reservation required. Runs Monday-Friday, except holidays. Restaurant car.
(2) Reservation required. Restaurant car. (3) Reservation required. Light refreshments. (4) Mid-June to mid-August: runs daily. Mid-August to mid-June: runs daily, except Saturday. (5) Carries a sleeping car all year. Mid-June to mid-August also has couchettes.

Oslo - Copenhagen   466

All of these trains require reservation.

Dep. Oslo (Sen.)	07:30 (1)	10:00 (1)	14:00 (1)	22:40 (2)
Arr. Helsingborg	14:58	18:16	21:45	05:55
Arr. Copenhagen (H.)	16:50	20:15	23:24	08:50

(1) Light refreshments. (2) Carries a sleeping car. Also has couchettes. Coach is second-class only.

SWEDEN

Children under 12 travel free in coach cars. Half-fare for children 12–15. Children 16 and over must pay full fare.

The signs you will see at railstations in Sweden are:

ANKOMST	ARRIVAL
AVGANG	DEPARTURE
BILJETTLUCKAN	TICKET OFFICE
DAMER	WOMEN
GARDEROBEN	CHECKROOM
HERRAR	MEN
JARNVAGSSTATIONEN	RAILWAY STATION
INGANG	ENTRANCE
INFORMATIONSDISKEN	INFORMATION
LIGGPLATSVAGN	COUCHETTE CAR
PLATSBILJETTER	RESERVATIONS
RESTAURANGVAGN	RESTAURANT CAR
SOVVAGN	SLEEPING CAR
SPAR	TRACK
TILL SPAREN	TO THE PLATFORMS
UTGANG	EXIT
VAXELKONTORET	CURRENCY EXCHANGE

SWEDISH HOLIDAYS

A list of holidays is helpful because some trains will be noted later in this section as *not* running on holidays. Also, those trains which operate on holidays are filled, and it is necessary to make reservations for them long in advance.

January 1	New Year's Day		Ascension Day
	Epiphany		Whit Monday
	Good Friday		Midsummer Day
	Easter		All Saint's Day
	Easter Monday	December 25	Christmas Day
May 1	Labor Day	December 26	Boxing Day

EURAILPASS BONUSES IN SWEDEN

These boat trips: Goteborg–Fredrickshavn, Helsingborg–Helsingor, Stockholm—Helsinki, Stockholm–Turku and Stockholm–Aland Islands–Turku. There is also a 50% reduction of the fares of the ferries between Malmo and Lubeck- Travemunde (Germany) and between Trelleborg and Sassnitz (Germany). From Stockholm or Oslo, Sassnitz is the most direct gateway to Berlin, with both day and night trains operating Sassnitz-Berlin.

SWEDEN'S TRAIN PASSES

All of Sweden's passes are sold *only* in Sweden, at main railstations and travel agencies.

Monday-Thursday and Saturday Discount   Sweden's "normal prices" for train tickets apply only to travel on Friday and Sunday. Passengers traveling on all other days receive a discount. While ticket prices are based on the length of the ride, the maximum charge in recent years was for 900 kilometers (560 miles). The *maximum* charge for a one-way first-class ticket on Friday or Sunday in 1992 is 688 Swedish Kroner. For second-class: SEK-430.

Inlandsbanan Pass   Unlimited travel on the very scenic Inland Railway covering the Ostersund-Gallivare midnight sun area. Allows unlimited stopovers en route close to fishing, hiking and sightseeing areas. Members of the train crew and the staff at railstations offer guidance and advice. Sold at Swedish railstations and travel agencies.

The trains do not have sleeping compartments, couchettes or a restaurant car. At several stops local residents come on board to sell what Swedish Tourism claims are "excellent meals at a range of budget".

The price is 50% of the one-way or roundtrip regular fare. Example: The Ostersund-Gallivare-Ostersund roundtrip fare is reduced from 298 Swedish Kroner to SEK-149. Half- fare for children age 12–15 years. Children under 12 travel free.

Senior Citizen Discount   Persons 65 and older can buy first or second-class tickets at 30% discount. Valid every day. Age must be verified (passport, etc).

ONE-DAY EXCURSIONS AND CITY SIGHTSEEING

Here are 9 one-day rail trips that can be made comfortably from Stockholm and Goteborg, returning to them in most cases before dinnertime. Notes are provided on what to see and do at each destination. The number after the name of each route is the Cook's timetable.

Goteborg

A great seaport. The one-hour sightseeing bus tour leaves from Stora Teatern. There are one-hour boat trips covering the 7-mile harbor and its canals, leaving from Kungsportsbron. See the view of the harbor and city from the Sailor's Tower near the Maritime Museum at Gamla Varvsparken. The Liseberg amusement park. The magnificent City Theater, Concert House and Art Museum, all in the large square, Gotaplatsen. Antikhallarna, Scandinavia's largest permanent antiques and collectors market.

The view from Ramberget, highest point on the Hisingen side of Goteborg. The Botanical Garden. The 07:00 fish auction, weekdays, at Scandinavia's largest fish market. The 17th century Elfsborg Fortress. The historical and archaeological collections at the Goteborg Museum, located in the city's oldest (1643) building. Art from all over the world, at the Rohss Museum. Slottsskogen Zoo. The view of the harbor and city from the top of Sjomanjtornet, a 193-foot high tower.

Stockholm

Maps, literature and advice can be obtained at the Stockholm Tourist Association in Sweden House (Hamngatan 27), in the central business-shopping district (open Monday–Friday 08:30–18:00, Saturday and Sunday 08:00–17:00).

Bus connections to the city's airport are available at a terminal across the street from the Central railstation. Stockholm's subways depart from the same level as the Tourist Information

302

Office in Central railstation. A Tourist Ticket, good for rides on both buses and subways, is sold for 2 periods: one day and 3 days. These can be purchased at the Tourist Information Office in Central railstation.

Bus #47 can be taken from across the street from Central railstation to the 75-acre Skansen amusement park, open 08:00–23:30 June through August. Its prime attraction is the Wasa Museum (open daily 09:30–19:00 June through mid-August), where a 17th century battleship is on exhibit. This ancient ship sank in Stockholm harbor at the moment she set forth on her first voyage as flagship of the Swedish Navy and rested in 100 feet of water from 1628 until it was raised in 1956, restored and turned into a museum.

Also popular are Skansen's Zoo and its outdoor museum of life in early Stockholm (more than 150 buildings from the 18th and 19th centuries).

At the Royal Palace, the treasury and Armory are open in Summer 10:00–16:00. The king's silver throne in the Hall of State can be seen 12:00–15:00. Also see the Bernadotte and Festival suites. The historic and art treasures in the Royal Chapel. The Changing of the Guard in the courtyard takes place daily at 12:10.

Other sights: the 15th century Storkyrkan Cathedral, with its sculpture of St. George and the Dragon, is a short walk from the Palace. The tall old houses and Stock Exchange on Stortorget, the city's oldest square. The modern architecture in Skarholmen, a suburb

The collection of Carl Milles statues at Millesgarden sculpture park. The Nordic Museum. Fine views of the city and the archipelago from the 504-foot-high Kaknas television tower, open May through August 09:00–24:00. The National Museum of Fine Arts, open daily 10:00–16:00 (see the 9 Rembrandts on the second floor). Rosendal Palace, closed Monday. The Chinese Pavilion, Court Theater and Museum, all at Drottingholm Palace, open April through October.

Do not miss seeing the Golden Hall, Blue Hall, Prince's Gallery, Terrace and the view from the Tower, all at Town Hall (1 Hantverkgatan), one of Europe's most famous buildings, where guided tours are offered daily at 10:00 (plus 12:00 on Sundays and holidays). The Nobel festivities take place there.

Goteborg - Kalmar - Goteborg   467

This roundtrip cannot be made on Saturdays.

| Dep. Goteborg | 08:04 | Dep. Kalmar | 17:20 (1) |
| Arr. Kalmar | 12:44 | Arr. Goteborg | 21:52 |

(1) Runs daily, except Saturday.

Sights in **Kalmar**: The moat, courts and towers of the Castle. A bus trip to the nearby glassworks.

Stockholm - Eskilstuna - Stockholm   466 a

| Dep. Stockholm | 07:12 (1) | 09:36 (2) | 10:36 (1) | 13:36 (3) |
| Arr. Eskilstuna | 09:00 | 11:13 | 12:13 | 15:13 |

Sights in **Eskilstuna:** The 6 Rademacher Forges that are more than 300 years old, on display in the center of town. Eskilstuna is the capital of Sweden's steel industry. Also see the wooden Fors Church and the statue of the 10th century English missionary, Saint Eskil, for whom the town was named in 1659, one year after Reinhold Rademacher built the forges which launched the local industry.

The Zoo and Amusement Park. The 12th century church. The wonderful collection of Scandinavian art in the Art Museum. Take a local bus 8 miles to Sundbyholm Castle. Shop for gold, iron and copper souvenirs.

Dep. Eskilstuna	12:35 (3)	15:35 (1)	16:35 (2)	20:35 (4)
Arr. Stockholm	14 :17	17:17	18:17	22:17

(1) Runs Monday-Friday, except holidays. (2) Runs Saturdays, Sundays, and holidays. (3) Runs daily. (4) Runs Sunday only.

Stockholm - Gavle - Stockholm   476

All of these trains require reservation and have a restaurant car.

Dep. Stockholm (Cen.)	05:43 (1)	07:13	08:13	10:43	12:13
Arr. Gavle	07:41	09:04	10:04	12:39	14:05

Sights in **Gavle:** The Swedish Railway Museum.

Dep. Gavle	11:22	12:39	15:55	16:36	17:54 (2+3)
Arr. Stockholm (Cen.)	13:17	14:47	17:53	18:44	19:56

(1) Runs daily, except Sundays and holidays. (2) Runs daily, except Saturday. (3) Plus another departure from Gavle at 20:32, arriving Stockholm 22:26.

Stockholm - Goteborg - Stockholm   469

All of these trains require reservation and have a restaurant car.

Dep. Stockholm (Cen.)	06:30 (1)	07:06 (2)	08:00 (3)	08:12	09:00 (4)
Arr. Goteborg (Cen.)	09:55	11:45	11:23	12:45	12:59

Sights in **Goteborg:** See notes about sightseeing in Goteborg on page 301.

Dep. Goteborg (Cen.)	15:10	17:05	19:10 (5)
Arr. Stockholm (Cen.)	19:47	21:47	23:47

(1) Supplement charged. Mid-June to mid-August: runs daily. Mid-August to mid-June: runs Monday–Friday, except holidays. (2) Runs daily, except Sundays and holidays. (3) Supplement charged. Mid-June to mid-August: runs daily. Mid-August to mid-June: runs Saturday only. (4) Operates mid-June to mid-August. Runs daily, except Sunday. (5) Runs daily, except Saturday.

Stockholm - Malmo - Stockholm   465

This trip is impratical as a one-day Stockholm excursion.

All of these trains require reservation and have a restaurant car.

Dep. Stockholm (Cen.)	06:42 (1)	08:06	10:06	12:30	14:06	15:35 (2+6)
Arr. Malmo (Cen.)	13:03	14:53	16:45	18:55	20:53	21:23

Sights in **Malmo:** See notes under "Copenhagen-Malmo" on page 274.

Dep. Malmo (Cen.)	06:20 (3)	07:05	09:05	11:00	13:17	15:03 (7)
Arr. Stockholm (Cen.)	12:35	13:53	15:53	17:53	19:35	21:53

(1) Runs daily, except Sundays and holidays. (2) Runs daily, except Saturday. (3) Operates mid-August to mid-June. Runs daily, except Sundays and holidays. (4) Early August to early July: runs daily, except Saturday. Early July to early August: runs Friday and Sunday only. (5) Runs daily, except Saturday. Carries a sleeping car. Also has couchettes. Coach is second-class only. (6) Plus other Stockholm departures at 16:47 (4) and 21:07 (5), arriving Malmo 22:50 and 07:05. (7) Plus other Malmo departures at 16:35 (2) and 22:05 (5), arriving Stockholm 22:47 and 08:26.

Stockholm - Borlange - Mora - Stockholm 478

There is excellent lake and mountain scenery Borlange-Mora.

For a one-day roundtrip, the 09:13 Stockholm departure should be taken only Monday–Thursday.

Dep. Stockholm (Cen.)	06:03 (1)	09:13 (2)	Dep. Mora	13:50 (3)	18:02 (4)
Dep. Borlange	08:56	11:50	Dep. Borlange	15:29	19:41 (5)
Arr. Mora	10:37	13:30	Arr. Stockholm (Cen.)	18:14	22:14

(1) Reservation required. Restaurant car. Runs daily, except Sundays and holidays. (2) Reservation required. Restaurant car. Mid-June to mid-August: runs daily. Mid-August to mid-June: runs Friday, Saturday and Sunday. (3) Reservation required. Restaurant car. Mid-June to mid-August: runs daily, except Saturday. Mid-August to mid-June: runs Friday and Sunday. (4) Runs Monday–Thursday. Second-class only. Change trains in Borlange at 19:38. (5) Reservation required. Restaurant car. Runs Monday–Thursday.

Sights in **Mora**: The outdoor museum of 40 timber buildings, some 600 years old. The collection of Anders Zorn, Swden's most famous painter.

Stockholm - Norrkoping - Stockholm 465

All of these trains require reservation and have a restaurant car, unless designated otherwise.

Dep. Stockholm (Cen.)	06:05 (1)	06:42 (2)	08:06	09:06 (3)	10:06	10:30 (7)
Arr. Norrkoping	07:59	08:25	10:05	11:05	12:05	12:22

Sights in **Norrkoping**: The amazing collection of more than 25,000 cactus plants in beautiful Karl Johans Park. Take the short sightseeing trip by boat, from the pier at the end of this park.

See the 3,000-year old Bronze Age carvings and also the display of roses in Himmelstalund Park, to the right of the railstation. On the other (east) side of the railstation, visit the ruins of the star-shaped Johannisborg Fort. See the Lindo Canal.

Hear the bell-chiming at 13:00 in front of the Radhuset (Council House). See Hedvigs Kyrka, the German Church.

See the demonstration of antique textiles (from rugs to doilies) and textile machinery in the museum of old factory buildings and tour the restored residence of the factory owner, the Stadsmuseet, a short walk from the railstation. Also exhibited there are interesting scale models of the city as it was in various past centuries.

Dep. Norrkoping	11:54	13:54	14:54	15:54	16:56	17:00 (4+8)
Arr. Stockholm (Cen.)	13:53	15:53	16:53	17:53	18:59	19:17

(1) Runs Monday-Friday, except holidays. (2) No restaurant car on Sundays and holidays. (3) Runs daily, except Sundays and holidays. (4) Runs Monday-Friday, except holidays. Reservation not required. No restaurant car. (5) Runs daily, except Saturday. (6) Runs Sunday only. (7) Plus other departures from Stockholm at 11:06 (4), 12:30 and 13:06, arriving Norrkoping 13:05, 14:20 and 15:01. (8) Plus other departures from Norrkoping at 17:44, 18:54 (5), 19:54, 20:54 (2) and 21:54 (6), arriving Stockholm 19:35, 20:53, 21:53, 22:47 and 23:53.

Stockholm - Rattvik - Stockholm 478

All of these trains require reservation and have a restaurant car.

Dep. Stockholm (C.)	06:03 (1)	09:13 (2)	Dep. Ratvik	14:23 (3)	16:12 (4+6)
Arr. Rattvik	10:03	12:56	Arr. Stockholm (C.)	18:14	20:14

Sights in **Rattvik**: The rustic arts museum.

(1) Runs daily, except Sundays and holidays. (2) Mid-June to mid-August: runs daily. Mid-August to mid-June: runs Friday, Saturday and Sunday. (3) Mid-June to mid-August: runs daily, except Saturday. Mid-August to mid-June: runs Friday and Sunday. (4) Runs Saturday only. (5) Runs daily, except Saturday. Monday–Thursday: change trains in Borlange at 19:38. (6) Plus another Ratvik departure at 18:35 (5), arriving Stockholm 22:14.

Stockholm - Uppsala - Stockholm 476 + 478

Many of these trains require reservation. Most run daily and have a restaurant car or light refreshments. A few of these trains run daily, except Sundays and holidays.

Dep. Stockholm (Cen.)	Frequent times from 05:43 to 23:33
Arr. Uppsala	40-50 minutes later

Sights in **Uppsala:** The largest church in Scandinavia, Uppsala Cathedral, a short walk from the railstation. Sweden's largest library, Carolina Rediviva, with more than 20,000 hand-illuminated medieval manuscripts, including the only book in existence that is written in pure Gothic, the famous Codex Argentus, the 5th century Silver Bible. The Great Hall of State in the old red Castle, open 11:00–18:00 from mid-May to mid-September. The 18th century Linnaeus Garden at 27 Svartsbacksgatan (open May–December 09:00–21:00) was created for the study of plant species by Karl von Linne, Sweden's "Prince of Botanists". The present collection numbers 1,300 plants. It was Linne who originated the system of sexual plant classification and the dual nomenclature for natural science.

Take a bus marked "Gamla Uppsala" for a 2-mile ride to see relics of heathen worship going back to the 5th century.

Dep. Uppsala	Frequent times from 05:56 to 22:03
Arr. Stockholm (Cen.)	40-50 minutes later

INTERNATIONAL ROUTES FROM SWEDEN

Stockholm is the gateway for rail trips to northern Norway (Trondheim and Narvik) and to northern Finland (Oulu), as well as by boat to Helsinki, and on to Leningrad. It is also the gateway for travel to southern Norway (Oslo, and on to Bergen or Stavanger). Malmo is the starting point for rail travel to Denmark, (Copenhagen, and on to Germany and the rest of Western Europe).

There is fine lake scenery on the Ostersund-Storlien portion of this route.

Stockholm - Trondheim

476

Dep. Stockholm (Cen.)	07:13 (1)	-0-	12:13 (4)	22:13 (6)
Arr. Ostersund	13:23	-0-	18:37	-0-
Arr. Storlien	15:58	-0-	21:25	09:30

Change trains or change to a bus.   485

Dep. Storlien	16:30 (2)	16:50 (3)	21:35 (5)	09:45 (5)
Arr. Trondheim	18:50	19:20	23:25	11:45

(1) Reservation required. Restaurant car until Ostersund. (2) Bus. Runs Sunday only. (3) Bus. Runs daily, except Sundays and holidays. (4) Reservation required. Restaurant car until Storlien. (5) Train. Second-class only. (6) Carries a sleeping car. Also has couchettes. Coach is second-class only.

Stockholm - Copenhagen   465

All of these trains require reservation and have a restaurant car, unless designated otherwise.

Dep. Stockholm (C.)	06:42 (1)	10:30	14:06 (2)	22:00 (3)
Arr. Copenhagen (H.)	14:50	18:50	23:24	06:58

(1) No restaurant car. (2) Change trains in Hassleholm and Helsingor. (3) Carries a sleeping car. Also has couchettes. Coach is second-class only.

Stockholm - Helsinki   Boat and Train

This is the short route to Helsinki, *across* the Gulf of Bothnia. (See page 307 for the long route, *around* the Gulf "Stockholm-Oulu-Helsinki".

The price for the cruise across the Gulf of Bothnia on the comfortable and pleasant Silja Line ships was $50 (U.S.) in 1991. This passage *is* covered by Eurailpass. The fare for a sleeping cabin is *not* covered by Eurailpass. Food on the ship is varied and delicious.

We recommended the 08:15 sailing in order to see the thousands of tiny islands on the ride through this extremely interesting archipelago. During the daytime cruise, there is a good smorgasbord for both lunch and dinner.

A small band plays music in a delightful bar area. Movies are shown in a small theater.

There is a duty-free shop on board. The ships ferry autos.

The ferries departing Stockholm at 20:00 and 21:15 have a limited number of *free* bunk beds in an area like a dormitory. Because there are less bunks than passengers, those knowing of the bunks arrive at the dock many hours before departure, position themselves toward the front of the line, and race directly to the bunk area when boarding starts.

All of the Turku-Helsinki trains have light refreshments.

1238 Boat

Dep. Stockholm (Var.)	08:15 (1)	08:15 (2)	20:00 (3)	21:15 (2)
Arr. Turku (Harbor)	19:00	20:15	08:00	08:00

Walk to either railstation.
493

Dep. Turku (Harbor)	19:17	20:40	-0-	08:40
Dep. Turku (Stn.)	19:35	20:50	-0-	09:23
Arr. Helsinki	22:02	23:02	-0-	11:02

(1) Runs Tuesday–Friday mid-February to mid-May and mid-August to late December. (2) Runs Saturday and Sunday mid-February to mid-May, daily mid-May to mid-August, Saturday and Sunday mid-August to late December. (3) Operates mid-February to mid-May and mid-August to late December. Runs Monday–Friday.

Stockholm - Narvik   475 + 476

There is good mountain scenery on the Kiruna-Narvik portion of this trip.

Both of these trains require reservation, carry a sleeping car and have couchettes.

Dep. Stockholm (Cen.)	17:43 (1)	20:13 (2)
Arr. Lulea	-0-	11:08
Arr. Boden	07:57	12:38
Arr. Kiruna	11:55	16:50
Arr. Narvik	15:06	20:12

(1) Restaurant car Stockholm-Kiruna. (2) Restaurant car Stockholm-Lulea. Change trains in Lulea. Depart Lulea 12:15.

Stockholm - Oslo   470

Dep. Stockholm (Cen.)	08:42 (1)	15:30 (2)	23:07 (3)
Arr. Oslo (Sen.)	15:00	21:50	07:35

(1) Reservation required. Light refreshments. (2) Reservation required. Restaurant car. Mid-June to mid-August: runs daily. Mid-August to mid-June: runs daily, except Saturday. (3) Mid-June to mid-August: runs daily, carries a sleeping car and also has couchettes. Mid-August to mid-June: runs daily except Saturday and carries a sleeping car.

Stockholm - Oulu - Helsinki

By stopping-over one night in Oulu, the Oulu-Helsinki trip can be made the next day in daylight by departing Oulu 07:20, 09:55 or 12:52.

476

Dep. Stockholm (Cen.)	17:43 (1)	20:13 (5)
Arr. Boden	07:57	10:28

Change trains.   496

Dep. Boden	09:00 (2)	13:40 (6)
Arr. Haparanda	11:15	15:56

Change trains.

Dep. Haparanda	11:20 (2)	16:00 (6)

Set your watch forward one hour.

Arr. Tornio	12:27	17:07

Change to a bus. (Train ticket is valid.)

Dep. Tornio	13:17 (3)	17:12 (3)
Arr. Kemi	13:52	17:52

Change to a train.   492

Dep. Kemi	14:22 (4)	21:23 (7)	-0-	-0-	-0-
Arr. Oulu	15:39	22:33	-0-	-0-	-0-
Dep. Oulu	16:03	22:50	07:20 (8)	09:55 (4)	12:52 (4)
Arr. Helsinki	22:58	07:30	13:54	16:58	19:58

(1) Reservation required. Carries a sleeping car. Also has couchettes. Coach seats are second-class only. (2) Second-class only. (3) Runs daily, except Sundays and holidays. (4) Light refreshments. (5) Reservation required. Carries a sleeping car. Also has couchettes. Restaurant car. (6) Runs Monday–Friday, except holidays. Second-class only. (7) Carries a sleeping car. Coach seats are second-class only. Light refreshments. Plus another Keni departure at 22:43 (same services), arriving Helsinki 08:27. (8) Reservation required. Restaurant car.

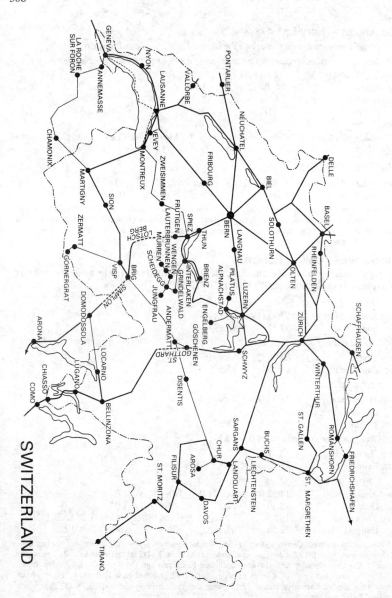

SWITZERLAND

SWITZERLAND

See "Swiss Family Card" below for children's free fare.

The signs you will see at railstations in Switzerland are those you would see in France, Germany or Italy, depending on the section. French is the language south and southwest of Bern. Italian is dominant in the southeast corner of the country. Elsewhere, the prevailing language is German. There are free timetables at the railstations.

Ride on one of the luxurious air-conditioned Intercity trains. They have both first-class and second-class space, give a smoother ride and are more comfortable than ordinary Swiss trains, while the ticket price for them is the same.

A traveler with a confirmed flight reservation for a departure from Zurich's or Geneva's aiport can check bags at a special counter in the railstation at nearly 100 Swiss cities.

Unencumbered with luggage, the passenger using "Fly Luggage Service" rides a train from places such as Bern, Locarno and Luzern directly to the airport, checks-in at the airport's "Express" counter, boards the airplane, and claims the luggage at the end of the flight. The time required for baggage deposit in advance of train departure varies from one Swiss railstation to another. Be sure to obtain that information before departure day. Because of U.S.A. security procedures, "Fly Luggage Service" is not available to passengers who are departing on a U.S. airline.

SWITZERLAND'S TRAIN PASSES

These passes are good for unlimited travel on all trains covered by Eurailpass, *plus* many expensive trains that do *not* honor Eurailpass, and on lake steamers and postal buses *not* covered by Eurailpass . . . plus local subways, buses and trams in 25 major Swiss cities.

Rail Europe is the sales agent of all Swiss train passes (see "France" on page 23 for list of U.S. and Canadian offices).

Swiss Family Card   Any number of children under 16 years old, while traveling with one adult (not necessarily a parent). who has either an ordinary ticket or any Swiss train pass, travel free.

Swiss Pass   Sold worldwide, including in Switzerland. In addition to the services described above, also provides either free travel or discounts up to 50% on many extremely scenic and very expensive privately-owned mountain railroad and aerial cable car routes that are *not* covered by a Eurailpass. Valid for consecutive days.

The 1992 *first*-class prices are: $239 (U.S.) for 8 days, $289 for 15 days, and $389 for one month. *Second*-class: $159, $189 and $269.

Swiss Flexipass   Allows unlimited travel any 3 days within a 15-day period. Includes everything covered by Swiss Pass. The 1992 *first*-class price is: $199 (U.S.). For *second*-class: $129.

Swiss Card   A free one-day trip from any entry point (airport or border station) to any single destination in Switzerland and a free one-day trip from any place in Switzerland to any departure point. In addition, the holder can purchase an unlimited number of both roundtrip and one-way tickets for Swiss trains postal buses and lake steamers at 50% discount (25% discount on some mountain railroads). Valid for one month, the 1992 prices are: *first*-class $109 (U.S.), *second*-class $79.

Swiss Rail'N Drive   Three days of unlimited train travel plus 3 days of car rental (any 6 days) within 15 days. Prices vary (a) whether for one person or for 2 or more persons, and (b) the category of car. A third passenger needs to pay only for a 3-day Swiss Flexipass.

The 1992 prices per person for 2 persons (using the smallest size car) are: $265 (U.S.) for *first*-class, $195 for *second*-class. Up to 5 more days of car rental can be added at $45 per day.

All prices include for rail travel: all of the Swiss government railways, most of the private mountain railroads and aerial cable cars (except some short routes), lake steamers and distance buses, plus local railways, buses and trams in 25 major Swiss cities. All prices for Hertz auto rental include Value Added Tax, unlimited mileage, basic liability insurance, and free drop-off in Switzerland. The car can be driven into other countries but must be dropped-off in Switzerland.

SUMMER TIME
Switzerland changes to Summer Time on the last Sunday of March and converts back to Standard Time on the last Sunday of September.

EURAILPASS BONUSES IN SWITZERLAND
Boat trips on the Rhine from Schaffhausen to Kreuzlingen and also on the Aare from Biel/Bienne to Solothurn and on the lakes of Biel, Brienz, Geneva, Luzern, Murten, Neuchatel, Thun and Zurich.

SWISS HOLIDAYS
A list of holidays is helpful because some trains will be noted later in this section as not running on holidays. Also, those trains which operate on holidays are filled, and it is necessary to make reservations for some Inter-City, Euro City and TGV trains.

January 1	New Year's Day		Ascension Day
January 2			Whit Monday
	Good Friday	December 25	Christmas Day
	Easter Monday	December 26	

ONE-DAY EXCURSIONS AND CITY-SIGHTSEEING
Here are 129 one-day rail trips that can be made comfortably from cities in Switzerland, returning to them in most cases before dinnertime. Notes are provided on what to see at each destination. The number after the name of each route is the Cook's timetable. The 13 base cities are: Basel, Bern, Brig, Chur, Geneva, Interlaken, Lausanne, Locarno, Luzern, St. Moritz, Spiez, Zermatt and Zurich. When no station is designated for cities in Austria, Switzerland and West Germany, the station is "Hauptbahnhof".

Basel (Appears as *Bale* in French timetables)
The superb Picasso, Holbein, Delacroix, Gauguin, Matisse, Ingres, Courbet and Van Gogh paintings in the Kunstmuseum. The Historical Museum in the Franciscan Church in Barfusserplatz. The Municipal Casino. The collection of 18th century clothing, ceramics and watches in the Kirschgarten mansion. Shop on Freiestrasse. See the 16th century Town Hall. The fishmarket. The 15th century New University.

The beautiful Munsterplatz. Fifteenth century tapestries in the 14th century Barfuserkirche. The tombs of Queen Anne and Erasmus of Rotterdam at Munster, the 13th century Cathedral. Nearby, the Folk Art Museum.

The more than 100,000 rarities from every continent (particularly those from New Guinea and the South Seas) in the Ethnological Museum at Augustinerstrasse 2. In the same complex, the extraordinary geological section at the Museum of Natural History.

The Jewish Museum of Switzerland, at Kornhausgasse 18, where Theodore Herzl presided over the first Zionist Congress, in 1897. One of the world's greatest collection of animals, at the Zoo (Binningerstrasse 40), open 08:00–18:30 in Summer, 08:00–17:30 in Winter. Switzerland's largest, it is a short stroll from the SNCF and SBB railstations. Or, take Trolleys #4 and #7 from the stations.

Take a boat excursion from the pier in the back of the Hotel Three Kings. See the view of the city from the Wettstein Bridge.

Bern

The capital of Switzerland. See the comic antics of the denizens of the Bear Pit. How they love figs ! The Rose Gardens, north of the Bear Pit. The performance every hour of the 16th century clock tower, the Zytglockenturm. The nearby old arcaded streets. Lunch on the terrace of the Casino restaurant and enjoy the view from there of the River Aare. The Art Museum, with the largest Klee collection in the world.

Climb the 254 steps to the top of one of the towers of the Cathedral for a marvelous view. Play chess with people-size chessmen on the huge slate chessboard near the Cathedral. The elaborate statue honoring the world postal system, without which it would be impossible to have one country handle and deliver to an addressee a mailing for which another country had been paid the postage by the addressor.

One of the world's largest stamp collections, at the Swiss PTT Museum. The view of the Alps from the terrace of the Federal Palace, and the nearby open-air flower and produce market (Tuesday and Saturday mornings). The Swiss Alpine Museum. The Natural History Museum. Prison Tower. Holy Ghost Church. The Botanical Gardens. The many window-boxes with flowering geraniums throughout the streets in the city center.

Geneva

The 6-minute train ride [table 250] *from* the airport to the center of Geneva runs 05:39 to 23:46. From the center of Geneva *to* the airport, it runs 06:14 to 23:12.

Walk from the railstation, down Rue du Mont Blanc, to the shore of Lake Leman. See the enormous Jet d'Eau (water fountain). Walk on the bridge across the lake to the Jardin Anglais. It has a fabulous clock of living flowers and plants and a monument to international Protestantism. It is on that side of the lake you will find the city's old narrow streets and, in St. Peter's Cathedral, the pulpit from which Calvin preached. See the view of Geneva and Lake Leman from the top of the Cathedral's North Tower, a climb of 153 steps.

In modern Geneva: Palais des Nations, today the European headquarters of the United Nations Organization. The chinaware collection in the Ariana Museum, open daily except Monday during Summer. The Far East art (Japanese jade, Chinese porcelain, many pieces from Sri Lanka) at the Baur Collection. The Botanical Garden. The Museum of Historic Musical Instruments, open Tuesday, Thursday and Friday. The Ethnographic Museum, closed Monday.

The Art and History Museum, 2 rue Charles-Galland (Bus #1 from the railstation) has an archaeological collection, paintings, decorative art and sculptures, open daily except Monday 10:00-17:00. The National History Museum, 11 route de Malagnou (Bus #5 from the railstation), one of the most modern museums in Europe, open Tuesday- Sunday 10:00–12:00 and 14:00–18:00, on Monday 14:00–18:00. Nearby, at 15 route de Malagnou, is the Watch and Clock Museum, open daily except Monday 10:00–12:00, also every day 14:00–16:00.

The Voltaire Museum, 25 rue des Delices (Bus #6 from the railstation), open Monday-Friday 14:00–17:00. The world-famous Davidoff's Cigar Store on rue de Rive, open Monday-Friday 08:00–18:00 and Saturday 08:00-18:30, where the No. 2 coronas sold for $6.60 (U.S.) each in 1982. Also in stock there: enormous ebony and mahogany humidors.

Luzern

Walk across the 14th and 15th century bridges spanning the Reuss River and see the 120 paintings on the ceiling of Kappelbrucke depicting Luzern's history and the 45 "Dance of Death" paintings inside the Spreuerbrucke.

See the immense 30-foot high, 42-foot long Lion of Luzern, carved in 1821 into a sandstone cliff which became in 1872 the entrance to the Glacier Gardens outdoor museum. The lion commemorates the bravery of those Swiss soldiers who defended Marie Antoinette during the French Revolution.

You will see at the Glacier Museum the absolute proof that palm trees grew here 20,000,000 years ago when this area was tropical. A bank manager, planning to augment his income by turning a meadow into a vineyard, blasted this area so as to make a wine cellar in the rock. A geologist friend spotted a bowl-like recess in the sandstone and convinced the banker to cease the blasting. The 11 round holes found there were made by the erosion from ice-age waterfalls.

The old railway cars, locomotives, trolley cars, buses, autos, many scale models, and the simulated ride in an engine cab at the Swiss National Transport Museum at Lidostrasse 5, largest museum of its kind in Europe. There is also a very interesting model of the Gotthard Tunnel (see "Zurich-Logano" on page 359). The museum is open 09:00–18:00 March-October, 10:00–16:00 November–February. Next door is a Planetarium. See the exhibit of model railways nearby. The Art Museum, near the railstation. The August Music Festival.

The giant (12,000 square foot) canvas Grand Panorama, depicting the Winter campaign of the 1870-71 Franco-Prussian War.

Zurich

There is 12-minute rail service [Table 310] *from* the airport to Zurich's Hauptbahnhof (Main Railstation) from 06:05 to 23:21. From Zurich's Hauptbahnhof *to* the airport, it runs 06:26 to 23:22. A cruise on Lake Zurich is covered by Eurailpass. Board the boat at the lake end of Bahnhofstrasse.

Here is a great 2-hour walk: Upon arriving at the main Zurich railstation, take the escalator down one level and enjoy a snack or meal in Shopville, the enormous underground shopping center beneath Bahnhof Platz, the square in front of the station. Come up from Shopville on the other side of Bahnhof Platz. Walk one mile down one side of Bahnhofstrasse, lined with smart stores. When this city's Fifth Avenue ends at the shore of Lake Zurich, take in the lakeside promenade before returning to the railstation by walking along the opposite side of Bahnhofstrasse that you walked earlier.

Upon returning to the station, go all the way through it, cross Museumstrasse, and visit the National Museum to see its collection of medieval and Renaissance art, prehistoric artifacts, elaborately carved ancient peasant furniture and much more. Open Tuesday-Friday and Sunday 10:00–12:00 and 14:00–17:00, on Saturday 14:00–16:00.

Other sights: The Bellevue Platz amusement center. The paintings and sculptures at the Kunsthaus. African and Asian art at the Rietberg Museum. Kunstgewerbemuseum (The Museum of Applied Arts): handicrafts, architecture and industrial design. The Zoo. The Botanical Garden. The 5 Chagall stained-glass windows (red, blue and green) in the 13th century Fraumunsterkirche.

Basel - Baden Baden - Basel 755

All of these trains have a restaurant car.

Dep. Basel (S.B.B.)	09:15	11:15	13:15
Dep. Basel (Bad. Bf.)	7 minutes after departing Badischer railstation		
Arr. Baden-Baden	10:40	12:40	14:40

Sights in **Baden-Baden:** Praised for its hot salt springs since the Romans discovered the curative water in this area nearly 2,000 years ago. The illnesses treated here include rheumatism, abnormal blood pressure, metabolic disturbances, respiratory ailments, and problems caused by lack of physical exercise.

Nearly 300 prominent European families once had their permanent homes here. Fantastic landscape. The Oos Valley has been called the most beautiful valley in the world. Exotic trees include the Japanese maple, American tulip, East Asian ginkgo, Chinese trumpet, magnolia and fig. The colors of many deciduous trees make Autumn glorious here.

See the Louis XIII and Louis XIV decor of the halls in the casino. The fancy boutique shops. Exhibitions of international art in the Staatliche Kunsthalle (City Art Gallery).

Motorized vehicles are not permitted in the central area of Baden-Baden. There is a constant schedule of balls, fashion shows and concerts. Food specialties here are Grunkernsuppe (a vegetable soup), game pate, pike dumplings, Blaufelchen (a kind of whitefish, from Lake Constance), raspberry schnapps and kirsch with smoked bacon, bread baked by charcoal, and pate of truffled goose-liver from nearby Strasbourg.

Dep. Baden-Baden	15:15	16:46	19:15	22:20 (1)
Arr. Basel (Bad Bf.)	16:37	18:37	20:38	23:45
Arr. Basel (S.B.B.)	7 minutes later			

(1) Runs daily, except Saturday.

Basel - Bern - Basel 250

Dep. Basel (S.B.B.)	07:01 (1)	07:23 (1)	08:01 (2)	08:11	09:01 (1+4)
Arr. Bern	08:15	08:45	09:12	09:36	10:12

Sights in **Bern**: See notes about sightseeing in Bern on pages 310–311.

Dep. Bern	11:48 (2)	12:48 (2)	13:48 (1)	14:48 (2)	15:48 (1+5)
Arr. Basel (S.B.B.)	12:59	13:59	14:59	15:59	16:59

(1) Light refreshments. (2) Restaurant car. (3) Change trains in Olten. (4) Plus other departures from Basel at 10:01 (1), 11:01 (2) and 12:01 (2), arriving Bern 11:12, 12:12 and 13:12. (5) Plus other departures from Bern at 16:48 (2), 17:48 (1), 18:48 (1), 19:48 (1), 20:48 (2), 21:34 (1), 22:51 (3), and 23:45 (3), arriving Basel at 17:59, 18:59, 19:59, 20:59, 21:59, 22:45, 00:31 and 01:11.

Basel - Interlaken - Basel 280

All of these trains have light refreshments, unless designated otherwise.

Dep. Basel (S.B.B.)	07:01 (1)	08:01 (2)	09 :01 (1)	10:01 (3)	11:01 (4+9)
Arr. Interlaken (West)	09:16	10:16	11:16	12:16	13:16
Arr. Inerlaken (Ost)	5 minutes later				

Sights in **Interlaken**: A fine Summer resort and health spa. Take the funicular to **Heimwehfluh** for a marvelous view of the mountains.

Dep. Interlaken (Ost)	12:39	13:39 (1)	14:39 (5)	15:39 (6)	16:39 (3+10)
Dep. Interlaken (West)	5 minutes later				
Arr. Basel (S.B.B.)	14:59	15:59	16:59	17:59	18:59

(1) Light refreshments to Bern. Change trains in Bern. (2) Restaurant car. (3) Light refreshments. (4) Restaurant car to Bern. Change trains in Bern. (5) Change trains in Bern. Light refreshments Bern–Basel. (6) Change trains in Bern. Restaurant car Interlaken–Bern. Light refreshments Bern–Basel. (7) Change trains in Bern. Light refreshments Interlaken–Bern. Restaurant car Bern–Basel. (8) Change trains in Bern. (9) Plus another departure from Basel at 12:01 (4), arriving Interlaken (West) 14:16. (10) Plus another departure from Interlaken (Ost) at 17:39 (7), 18:39 (5), 19:39 (2) and 20:37 (8), arriving Basel 19:59, 20:59, 21:59 and 23:10.

Basel - Luxembourg - Basel 63 + 176

Dep. Basel (SNCF)	08:23 (1)
Arr. Luxembourg	11:57

Sights in **Luxembourg**: See notes about Luxembourg on page 88.

Dep. Luxembourg	14:59 (1)	19:00	21:45
Arr. Basel (SNCF)	18:25	22:39	01:40

(1) Restaurant car.

Basel - Luzern - Basel 290

Dep. Basel (S.B.B.)	06:00	07:07 (1)	08:07 (1)	08:51 (1)	09:51 (3)
Arr. Luzern	70 minutes later				

Sights in **Luzern**: See notes about sightseeing in Luzern on page 311.

Dep. Luzern	09:56	10:56 (1)	11:46 (1)	12:56 (2)	13:46 (2+4)
Arr. Basel (S.B.B.)	70 minutes later				

(1) Light refreshments. (2) Restaurant car. (3) Plus other departures from Basel at 10:07 (2), 10:51 (2), 11:51, 12:07 (2), and 12:51 (1) (4) Plus other departures from Luzern at 14:56 (2), 15:46 (2), 15:56, 16:56 (1), 17:46 (2), 17:56, 18:56 (1), 19:46 (2), 19:56, 20:56 (1), 21:46 (1) and 22:46.

Basel - Rheinfelden - Basel 268

Dep. Basel (S.B.B.)	Every hour from 07:41 to 23:32.
Arr. Rheinfelden	15 minutes later

Sights in **Rheinfelden**: This has been a world-famed health spa since 1844. There are tours of the Cardinal and Feldschlosschen breweries. Visit the island park on the Rhine River.

Dep. Rheinfelden	Every hour from 07:39 to 22:55.
Arr. Basel (S.B.B.)	15 minutes later

Basel - Strasbourg - Basel 63 + 176

Dep. Basel (SNCF)	08:23 (1)	09:22 (2)	11:14	13:22 (1)
Arr. Strasbourg	09:43	10:41	12:38	14:36

Sights in **Strasbourg**: See notes under "Paris-Strasbourg" on page 128.

Dep. Strasbourg	17:08 (1)	17:14	17:41	21:01 (3)
Arr. Basel (SNCF)	18:25	18:44	19:16	22:30

(1) Restaurant car. (2) Runs Monday-Friday, except holidays. (3) Plus other departures from Strasbourg at 21:01 and 00:17, arriving Basel 22:30 and 01:40.

Basel - Zurich - Basel 310

Dep. Basel (S.B.B.)	Frequent times from 05:52 to 00:02
Arr. Zurich	60 minutes later

Sights in **Zurich**: See notes about sightseeing in Zurich on page 312.

Dep. Zurich	Frequent times from 06:37 to 00:03
Arr. Basel (S.B.B.)	60 minutes later

Bern - Basel - Bern 250

Dep. Bern	Frequent times from 06:48 to 23:45
Arr. Basel (S.B.B.)	70–80 minutes later

Sights in **Basel:** See notes about Basel on page 310.

Dep. Basel (S.B.B.)	Frequent times from 05:50 to 00:02
Arr. Bern	70 –80 minutes later

Bern - Geneva - Bern 250

Dep. Bern	06:15 (1)	07:18 (2)	07:38 (1)	08:18 (2)	08:38 (1+3)
Arr. Geneva (Corn.)	08:02	09:02	09:25	10:02	10:34

Sights in **Geneva:** See notes about sightseeing in Geneva on page 311.

Dep. Geneva (Corn.)	11:48 (2)	12:15 (1)	12:48 (2)	13:48 (2)	14:15 (1+4)
Arr. Bern	13:42	14:22	14:42	15:42	16:22

(1) Light refreshments. (2) Restaurant car. (3) Plus other Bern departures at frequent times from 09:18 to 23:26. (4) Plus other Geneva departures at frequent times from 14:58 to 22:58.

Bern - Interlaken - Bern 280

Dep. Bern	06:56	07:28	08:28	09:28 (1)	10:28 (2)
Arr. Interlaken (West)	07:44	08:16	09:16	10:16	11:16
Arr. Interlaken (Ost)	5 minutes later				

Sights in **Interlaken:** See notes under "Basel-Interlaken" on page 313.

Dep. Interlaken (Ost)	Frequent times from 05:31 to 22:37
Dep. Interlaken (West)	5 minutes after departing Ost railstation
Arr. Bern	55 minutes after departing Interlaken (Ost)

(1) Restaurant car. (2) Plus other departures from Bern at frequent times from 11:28 to 23:28.

Bern - Lausanne - Bern 250

Dep. Bern	Frequent departures from 06:15 to 23:26
Arr. Lausanne	70 minutes later

Sights in **Lausanne:** The Cathedral. The Castle of St. Maire. City Hall. The Federal Palace of Justice. There are 13 museums here, including the collection of photographs at Musee Cantonal de l'Elysee (18 Avenue de l'Elysee), and the Pipe Museum (7 Rue de l'Academie).

Dep. Lausanne	Frequent departures from 05:31 to 23:45
Arr. Bern	70 minutes later

Bern - Fribourg - Lausanne - Bern 250

It is possible to stop and sightsee in both Fribourg and Lausanne on the same one-day excursion.

| Dep. Bern | 08:18 | 08:38 | 09:18 | 10:18 | 10:38 | 11:18 | 12:18 |
| Arr. Fribourg | 23 minutes later | | | | | | |

Sights in **Fribourg**: The 17th century altar in the Church of the Augustines. Farmers and their wives in traditional local dress, at the Wednesday and Saturday markets. The many stone fountains in the winding streets that lead to the 16th century Town Hall.

| Dep. Fribourg | 10:41 | 11:01 | 11:41 | 12:41 | 13:01 | 13:41 | 14:41 |
| Arr. Lausanne | 45 minutes later | | | | | | |

Sights in **Lausanne**: See notes under "Bern-Lausanne" on page 315.

| Dep. Lausanne | Frequent times from 05:31 to 23:45 |
| Arr. Bern | 70 minutes later |

Bern - Fribourg - Bern 250

Here are the schedules for a one-day excursion involving only Fribourg.

| Dep. Bern | Frequent times from 06:18 to 23:26 |
| Arr. Fribourg | 20 minutes later |

Sights in **Fribourg**: See notes in preceding listing.

| Dep. Fribourg | Frequent times from 06:18 to 00:33 |
| Arr. Bern | 20 minutes later |

Bern - Luzern - Bern 265

Outstanding farm and forest scenery as you travel through Switzerland's beautiful Emmental (valley of the Emme River).

| Dep. Bern | 06:48 | 07:31(1) | 07:48 | 08:31(1) | 09:48 | 10:31 | 11:48 (2) |
| Arr. Luzern | 08:12 | 08:46 | 09:12 | 09:46 | 11:12 | 11:46 | 13:12 |

Sights in **Luzern**: See notes about sightseeing in Luzern on page 311.

| Dep. Luzern | 11:13(1) | 11:46 | 13:13(1) | 13:46 | 15:13 | 15:46 | 17:13 (3) |
| Arr. Bern | 12:29 | 13:12 | 14:29 | 15:12 | 16:29 | 17:12 | 18:29 |

(1) Light refreshments. (2) Plus other departures from Bern at 12:31, 13:48, 14:31 (1), 15:48, 16:31 (1), 17:31, 18:31 (1), 19:25, 20:31 (1) and 22:45. (3) Plus other departures from Luzern at 18:13 (1), 19:13, 20:13, 21:01, 22:01 and 22:45.

Bern - Langnau - Luzern - Bern 265

It is possible to stop and sightsee in both Langnau and Luzern on the same one-day excursion.

| Dep. Bern | 07:31(1) | 08:31(1) | 10:31 | 12:31 | 14:31(1) |
| Arr. Langnau | 25 minutes later | | | | |

Sights in **Langnau**: The antique household utensils and local industry products (linen-weaving, tanning, embroidery) in the museum housed in a 16th century wood building.

| Dep. Langnau | 09:00 (1) | 11:00 | 13:00 | 15:00 (1) | 17:00 (1) |
| Arr. Luzern | 09:46 | 11:46 | 13:46 | 15:46 | 17:46 |

Sights in Luzern: See notes about sightseeing in Luzern on page 311.

| Dep. Luzern | 13:13 (1) | 15:13 | 17:13 | 18:13 (1) | 19:13 | 20:13 | 21:01 (2) |
| Arr. Bern | 14:29 | 16:29 | 18:29 | 19:29 | 20:29 | 21:29 | 22:15 |

(1) Light refreshments. (2) Plus other Luzern departures at 22:01 and 22:46, arriving Bern 23:20 and 00:25.

Bern - Langnau - Bern 265

Here are the schedules for a one-day excursion involving only Langnau.

| Dep. Bern | 07:31 (1) | 08:31 (1) | 10:31 | 12:31 | 14:31 (1) |
| Arr. Langnau | 30 minutes later |

Sights in Langnau: See notes under "Bern-Langnau" on page 316.

| Dep. Langnau | 10:01 (1) | 12:01 (1) | 14:01 (1) | 16:01 | 18:01 | 19:01 (1+2) |
| Arr. Bern | 30 minutes later |

(1) Light refreshments. (2) Plus other Langnau departures at 20:01, 21:48 and 22:53.

Bern - Neuchatel - Bern 255

| Dep. Bern | Frequent time from 06:05 to 23:46 |
| Arr. Neuchatel | 40–60 minutes later |

Sights in **Neuchatel:** The 16th and 17th century houses, fountains and towers. Painted, carved 16th century statues. The exhibit of androids, a seated draftsman, scribe and musician, that have been performing since 1774 and attracting tourists from all over the world since then.

After many years of recommending a visit to the Suchard chocolate factory, we received a letter from the Suchard people telling us it *does not offer tours during July and August* when its employees take vacations and it slows down production during those months. At any time of year, Suchard requires advance notice "of at least a couple of days" before it can provide a factory tour. For chocolate maniacs such as we are, if a tour of Suchard is imperative try phoning them at (038) 21-11-55.

Failing the Suchard tour, see the city's museum of mechanical dolls and music boxes. Take a stroll up winding streets, past elegant Renaissance and 17th century houses, to the hilltop Castle. Visit the Fine Art Museum. Take the funicular to the top (3,839 feet) of Chaumont for a view of the Alps.

Boat rides on the 3 lakes (Neuchatel, Biel and Morat) *are* covered by Eurailpass.

Try the great Fondue Neuchatelois, made from white wine and kirsch schnapps. On the first Sunday of October, the local grape harvest is celebrated with a colorful Parade and Battle of Flowers. On this day, wine flows from the city's outdoor fountains instead of water.

| Dep. Neuchatel | Frequent times from 07:02 to 23:10 |
| Arr. Bern | 40–60 minutes later |

Bern - Zurich - Bern 250

Most of these trains have a restaurant car or light refreshments.

| Dep. Bern | Frequent times from 04:51 to 23:45 |
| Arr. Zurich | 60–90 minutes later |

Sights in **Zurich:** See notes about sightseeing in Zurich on page 312.

| Dep. Zurich | Frequent times from 04:45 to 0:03 |
| Arr. Bern | 60–90 minutes later |

Chur - Andermatt - Chur 320

Not covered by Eurailpass. The 1991 prices for a roundtrip ticket *without* a Swiss Pass: 94 Swiss francs for first-class, Sfr-58.40 for second-class. *With* a Swiss Pass: Free.

Dep. Chur	05:45	06:50	08:11	09:45	12:55	14:55 (3)
Arr. Disentis	07:17	08:15	09:32	11:08	14:17	16:17

Change trains.

Dep. Disentis	07:23	08:25	10:23	11:34	14:24	16:30
Arr. Andermatt	08:28	09:39	11:23	12:45	15:31	17:45

Sights in **Andermatt**: A great ski resort. See the rock crystal altar crucifix and other treasures in the baroque St. Peter and St. Paul Church.

Dep. Andermatt	08:28	10:30 (2)	12:18	14:18	16:18	18:18
Arr. Disentis	09:32	11:36	13:37	15:26	17:26	19:25

Change trains.

Dep. Disentis	09:40	11:40	13:40	15:40	17:40	19:40
Arr. Chur	11:03	13:03	15:03	17:03	19:03	21:03

(1) Daily except Sundays and holidays (2) Light refreshments. (3) Plus another departure from Chur at 16:55, arriving Andermatt 19:45.

Chur - Arosa - Chur 324

These are cogwheel trains that leave from the front of the Chur railstation. A very scenic ride.

Not covered by Eurailpass. The 1991 prices for a roundtrip ticket: 30.80 Swiss francs for first-class, Sfr-19.20 for second-class. *With* a Swiss Pass: Free.

Dep. Chur	06:31	08:13	09:00	09:55	10:55	11:55	12:55 (1)
Arr. Arosa	61 minutes later						

Sights in Arosa: Great Summer and Winter sports. Fantastic mountain scenery.

Dep. Arosa	07:45	09:05	10:05	11:05	12:05	13:05	14:05 (2)
Arr. Chur	61 minutes later						

(1) Plus other departures from Chur every hour 13:55–22:55. (2) Plus other departures from Arosa every hour 15:05–21:05.

Chur - Filisur - St. Moritz - Chur 330

Most of these trains have light refreshments.

Dep. Chur	06:45	08:08	09:00	09:52	10:52 (1+3)
Arr. Filisur	08:00	09:15	10:14	11:00	12:00
Arr. St. Moritz	09:07	10:18	11:18	11:58	12:58

Dep. St. Moritz	11:00 (1)	12:00	13:00	14:00 (1+4)
Arr. Filisur	12:02	13:02	14:02	15:02
Arr. Chur	13:06	14:06	15:06	16:06

(1) Runs daily. Light refreshments only on Saturdays, Sundays and holidays. (2) Restaurant car. (3) Plus other Chur departures at 11:52(2), 12:52, 13:52(1), 16:52(1), 17:52(2), 18:52, 19:52 and 20:52. (4) Plus other St Moritz departures at 05:50, 07:10, 08:05, 09:00, 14:00(1), 15:00, 16:00, 17:00, 18:00(2) and 20:00(1).

Sights in **Filisur:** Near a very high railway bridge, Filisur is located in a narrow valley. The Hotel Grischuna, close to the railstation, has some rooms with a view of the village and the valley. Train fans might prefer other rooms that face the rail line.

It is only a 30-minute walk to the edge of the roaring **Landwasser River**, where you can look up at the trains going over the bridge.

Sights in **St. Moritz:** See notes about St. Moritz on page 330.

Chur - Zurich - Chur 310
All these trains have meal service or light refreshments.

Dep. Chur	06:13(1)	07:15(1)	08:15(2)	09:15(1)	10:23 (2)	11:15(1)
Arr. Zurich	07:51	08:50	09:50	10:50	11:50	12:38

Sights in **Zurich:** See notes about Zurich on page 312.

Dep. Zurich	11:10 (1)	12:10 (1)	13:10 (1)	14:10 (1)	15:10 (2)	16:10 (2+3)
Arr. Chur	12:45	13:37	14:45	15:37	16:45	17:37

(1) Light refreshments. (2) Restaurant car. (3) Plus other departures from Zurich at 17:10 (1), 18:10 (2), 19:10 (1), 20:10 (1), 21:10 (1) and 22:10.

Geneva - Annecy - Geneva 167
The train changes in La Roche-sur-Foron are easy cross-platform transfers.

Dep. Geneva (Eaux-Vives)	08:26	12:50		
Arr. La Roche-sur-Foron	08:53	13:42		
Change trains.				
Dep. La Roche-sur-Foron	09:01	13:50		
Arr. Annecy	09:47	14:25		

Sights in **Annecy**: Pronounced "Ahn–see". This is a beautiful lake resort. See the 12th century Island Palace. The shops in the old quarter.

Dep. Annecy	11:20	14:53	18:31	
Arr. La Roche-sur-Foron	11:55	15:30	19:17	
Change trains.				
Dep. La Roche-sur-Foron	11:58	15:32	19:20 (1)	
Arr. Geneva (Eaux-Vives)	12:36	16:03	19:50	

(1) Operates early July to early September.

Geneva - Basel - Geneva 260

Dep. Geneva (Corn.)	07:54 (1)	09:07 (2)	09:25	10:54 (1)	11:25 (1)
Arr Basel (S.B.B.)	10:36	12:01	12:35	13:36	14:36

Sights in **Basel**: See notes about Basel on page 310.

Dep. Basel	13:23 (1)	15:23 (1)	16:23 (3)	17:23 (1)	17:59 (4+6)
Arr. Geneva (Corn.)	16:06	18:06	19:06	20:06	21:16

(1) Light refreshments. (2) Restaurant car. (3) Change trains in Biel at 17:30. Depart Biel 17:35(1). (4) Restaurant car 17:59–19:04. Change trains in Biel at 19:09. Depart Biel 19:33 (2). (5) Change trains in Biel at 22:30. Depart Biel 22:33 (2). (6) Plus other departures from Basel at 18:23, 19:23, 20:23 and 21:23 (5), arriving Geneva 21:34, 22:37, 23:34 and 00:34.

Geneva - Bern - Geneva 250

All of these trains have a restaurant car, unless designated otherwise.

Dep. Geneva (Corn.)	06:25	06:58	07:58	08:58	09:58
Arr. Bern	08:22	08:42	09:42	10:42	11:42

Sights in **Bern**: See notes about sightseeing in Bern on pages 310–311.

Dep. Bern	12:18	12:38 (1)	13:18	14:18	14:38 (1+4)
Arr. Geneva (Corn.)	14:02	14:34	15:02	16:02	16:44

(1) Light refreshments. (2) No restaurant car or light refreshments. (3) Plus other departures from Geneva at 10:25(1), 10:58, 11:58, 12:25(1) and 12:58. (4) Plus other departures from Bern (all with restaurant car) every hour 15:18–21:18, plus 22:21 and 23:26(2).

Geneva - Dijon - Geneva 250

Dep. Geneva (Corn.)	06:25	11:48 (1)	
Arr. Lausanne	07:05	12:32	
Change trains. 157			
Dep. Lausanne	07:32 (2)	12:46 (2)	
Arr. Dijon	09:42	14:44	

Sights in **Dijon**: See notes about Dijon on page 137.

Dep. Dijon	14:03 (3)	15:58 (3)	19:46 (2)
Arr. Lausanne	16:06	18:06	21:57
Change trains. 250			
Dep. Lausanne	16:28 (1)	18:28 (1)	22:28 (1)
Arr. Geneva	35 minutes later		

(1) Restaurant car. (2) TGV. Reservation required. Supplement charged. Restaurant car. (3) TGV. Reservation required. Supplement charged. Light refreshments.

Geneva - Grenoble - Geneva 165

Dep. Geneva (Corn.)	09:44	10:34	11:27 (1)
Arr. Grenoble	11:39	12:47	13:29

Sights in **Grenoble**: See notes under "Lyon–Grenoble" on page 138.

Dep. Grenoble	15:12	17:35 (1)	18:31 (2)
Arr. Geneva (Corn.)	17:18	19:42	20:44

(1) Supplement charged. Restaurant car. All cars are air-conditioned. (2) Operates late June to early September.

Geneva - Lausanne - Montreux - Geneva 251

As these schedules indicate, a stopover in Lausanne en route to Montreux is possible.

Dep. Geneva (Corn.)	07:48	08:48 (1)	09:48 (1)	10:48	11:48 (2)
Arr. Lausanne	08:30	09:30	10:30	11:30	12:30
Arr. Montreux	23 minutes later				

Sights in **Lausanne:** See "Bern-Lausanne" on page 315,

Sights in **Montreux**: The casino offers gambling, a cabaret and a disco. The 13th century Chillon Castle, about 1½ miles from Montreux, was immortalized by Byron. Its dungeon, used as a model for many movies, is the attraction. Board the bus to Chillon across from the Montreux railstation.

Dep. Montreux	11:08 (1)	12:08 (1)	13:08 (1)	14:08 (1)	15:08 (3)
Dep. Lausanne	11:30	12:30	13:30	14:26	15:26
Arr. Geneva (Corn.)	50 minutes later				

(1) Light refreshments. (2) Plus other departures from Geneva at 12:48 (1), 13:48 (1)and 14:48 (1). (3) Plus other departures from Montreux at frequent times from 16:08 to 22:08.

Montreux - Gstaad - Zweisimmen - Montreux 275

This is the scenic route of both the "Panoramic Express" and "Superpanoramic Express". See details about these special Observation Trains as well as the scenery and interesting places on this line under "Geneva - Montreux - Zweisimmen - Geneva" (pages 345–346)

Reservations for "Superpanoramic Express" are accepted only for groups, but individuals may ride if there are any vacant seats.

Dep. Montreux	08:56 (1)	09:00	10:00 (2)	11:00	12:20 (3)
Dep. Gstaad	10:11	10:30	11:18	12:30	13:42
Arr. Zweisimmen	10:36	11:00	11:45	13:00	14:10

Sight in **Gstaad**: A *very* expensive ski village.

Dep. Zweisimmen	10:43 (1)	12:00	14:00	15:15 (2)	16:00 (4)
Dep. Gstaad	11:16	12:32	14:32	15:44	16:32
Arr. Montreux	12:30	14:00	16:00	17:02	18:00

(1) Reservation required. Supplement charged. "Superpanoramic Express". Runs Saturdays, Sundays and holidays. (2) Reservation required. Supplement charged. "Panoramic Express". Runs daily. (3) Plus other Montreux departures at 14:20 (2) and 15:00, arriving back in Montreux at 18:38 and 20:00. (4) Plus other Zweisimmen departures at 16:50, 17:15(1), 18:00 and 20:00, arriving Montreux at 18:38, 19:00, 20:00 and 22:00.

Geneva - Lyon - Geneva 159

Occasionally, 2 trains depart from the same track at Lyon's Perrache railstation, heading in opposite directions. Be sure to stand at the correct end (North or South) of the track in order to board the train you want to ride. Check the departure signs at the underground passageway. Do not rely merely on a track number when departing from Perrache railstation !

Next to the North passageway of Track "A" is a take-out restaurant, handy for provisioning your trip.

Dep. Geneva (Corn.)	06:37	10:22	12:44	
Arr. Lyon (Part-Dieu)	08:30	12:12	14:35	
Arr. Lyon (Per.)	9 minutes later			

Sights in Lyon: See notes about sightseeing in Lyon on pages 122–123.

Dep. Lyon (Per.)	12:13	17:10	19:21	21:32 (1)
Dep. Lyon (Part-Dieu)	9 minutes later			
Arr. Geneva (Corn.)	14:16	19:12	21:29	23:30

(1) Runs Friday and Sunday only.

322

Geneva - Neuchatel - Geneva 260

Dep. Geneva (Corn.)	07:54 (1)	08:54 (1)	09:07 (2)	09:54 (1)	10:54 (1+3)
Arr. Neuchatel	09:04	10:04	10:34	11:04	12:04

Sights in **Neuchatel:** See notes under "Bern-Neuchatel" on page 317.

Dep. Neuchatel	12:55 (1)	13:55 (2)	14:55 (1)	15:55 (2)	16:55 (1+4)
Arr. Geneva (Corn.)	14:06	15:06	16:06	17:06	18:06

(1) Light refreshments. (2) Restaurant car. (3) Plus other departures from Geneva at 11:54(2) and 12:54(1).
(4) Plus other departures from Neuchatel at 17:55(1), 18:55(1), 19:26(2), 19:55(2), 21:01, 22:01 and
23:01(2).

Geneva - Zurich - Geneva 250

All of these trains have a restaurant car, unless designated otherwise.

Dep. Geneva (Cor.)	05:58	06:58	07:58	08:58	09:58	10:58
Arr. Zurich	08:57	09:57	10:57	11:57	12:57	13:57

Sights in **Zurich:** See notes about sightseeing in Zurich on page 312.

Dep. Zurich (Hbf.)	Every hour from 06:00 to 21:03
Arr. Geneva (Cor.)	3 hours later

Interlaken - Bern - Interlaken 280

Dep. Interlaken (Ost)	Every hour from 05:31 to 22:37
Dep. Interlaken (West)	5 minutes after departing Ost railstation
Arr. Bern	53 minutes after departing Interlaken (Ost)

Sights in **Bern:** See notes about sightseeing in Bern on pages 310–311.

Dep. Bern	Every hour from 06:56 to 23:28
Arr. Interlaken (West)	48 minutes after departing Bern
Arr. Interlaken (Ost)	5 minutes later

Interlaken - Lausanne - Interlaken 250

Dep. Interlaken (Ost)	06:39 (1)	07:39	08:11 (2)	08:39 (2)	09:39 (3)
Dep. Interlaken (West)	5 minutes later				
Arr. Bern	07:38	08:32	09:05	09:32	10:32

Change trains.

Dep. Bern	08:18 (1)	08:38 (2)	09:18 (1)	10:18 (1)	10:38 (2)
Arr. Lausanne	09:26	09:50	10:26	11:28	11:50

Sights in **Lausanne:** See "Bern - Lausanne" on page 335.

Dep. Lausanne	12:34 (1)	13:10 (2)	13:34 (1)	15:10 (2)	15:34 (1+4)
Arr. Bern	13:32	14:22	14:42	16:22	16:42

Change trains.

Dep. Bern	13:56	14:28 (2)	15:28 (2)	16:28 (2)	17:28 (1)
Arr. Interlaken (West)	14:44	15:16	16:16	17:16	18:16
Arr. Interlaken (Ost)	5 minutes later				

(1) Restaurant car. (2) Light refreshments. (3) Plus other Interlaken (Ost) departures at 10:39 (2) and
11:39 (1), arriving Bern 13:26 and 13:50. (4) Plus other Lausanne departures at 17:10 (2), 17:34 (1),
19:10 (2), 19:34 (1), 20:34 (1) and 21:34 (1), arriving Interlaken (West) 19:16, 20:19, 21:19, 22:19, 23:19
and 00:22.

Interlaken - Murren - Jungfraujoch - Interlaken 288

This one-day trip covers the heart of the Bernese Oberland area. *It is not covered by Eurailpass.* The 1991 total price of tickets *without* a Swiss Pass: 164 Swiss francs for first-class, and Sfr-156.20 for second-class. *With* a Swiss Pass: Sfr-86.40.

All of the train changes shown here take less than one minute.

Hiking and trout fishing are Summer activities in **Murren**. Both it and **Wengen** are postcard Alpine villages. There have been top ski resorts in this area since 1906. **Jungfraujoch** is the highest (11,333 feet) railstation in Europe. From there, you can see the Jungfrau, Eiger and Monch peaks. The highest waterfall in Europe (2,000-foot drop) is spectacular there in late Spring and early Summer.

Dep. Interlaken (Ost)	08:55 (1)	Dep. Scheidegg	12:02
Arr. Lauterbrunnen	09:20	Arr. Jungfraujoch	12:53
Change to funicular.		Change trains	
Dep. Lauterbrunnen	09:30	Dep. Jungfraujoch	13:00 (2)
Arr. Murren	09:58	Arr. Scheidegg	13:47
Return to Lauterbrunnen.		Change trains.	
Dep. Murren	10:00	Dep. Scheidegg	14:02
Arr. Lauterbrunnen	10:28	Arr. Grindelwald	14:55
Change to a train.		Arr. Interlaken	16:00
Dep. Lauterbrunnen	10:35		
Dep. Wengen	11:20		
Arr. Scheidegg	11:45		
Change trains.			

(1) Plus other circle trips departing Interlaken at 09:31, 09:55, 10:31, 11:31 and 12:31, arriving back in Interlaken at 16:00, 16:26, 17:00, 18:00 and 19:00. (2) Plus other departures from Jungfraujoch (via Grindelwald) at 13:30, 14:00, 14:30, 15:00, 15:30, 16:00, 17:00 and 18:00 (1), arriving Interlaken (Ost) at 16:26, 17:00, 17:26, 18:00, 18:26, 19:00, 19:26 and 20:12.

Interlaken - Luzern - Interlaken 285

Dep. Interlaken (Ost)	06:32	07:35	08:44	09:35	10:44 (1)
Arr. Luzern	08:36	09:36	10:36	11:36	12:36

Sights in **Luzern**: See notes about sightseeing in Luzern on page 311.

Dep. Luzern	11:24	12:24	13:24 (1)	14:24	15:24 (2+3)
Arr. Interlaken (Ost)	13:16	14:25	15:16	16:25	17:16

(1) Restaurant car. (2) Light refreshments. (3) Plus other departures from Luzern at 16:24, 17:24 (2), 18:24, 19:09 and 20:09, arriving Interlaken 18:25, 19:20, 20:25, 21:25 and 22:25.

Lausanne - Sion - Lausanne 251

Dep. Lausanne	08:09	08:58 (1)	09:32 (2)	09:55 (2)	10:32 (3)
Arr. Sion	09:02	09:51	10:41	11:03	11:41

Sights in **Sion**: Ruins of the 13th century Valere Castle and the 4th–11th century religious art in the museum there. The world's oldest operable pipe organ, carved and painted wood chests and 15th century frescoes in the Church of Our Lady of Valere, open daily except Monday, 9:00–12:00 and 14:00–18:00.

The collection of Roman antiquities in the Cantonal Archaeological Museum on rue des Chateaux. Paintings by artists of this area in the Majorie Fine Arts Museum. Both museums are open daily except Monday 9:00–12:00 and 14:00–18:00.

The astronomical clock and carved doors of the 17th century City Hall. The ancient Tour de Sorciers (Tower of the Wizards). The 9th century Romanesque bell-tower of the Cathedral. Supersaxo, the 16th century mansion of a Renaissance nobleman.

Dep. Sion	13:17 (2)	13:54 (2)	14:17	14:54 (2)	15:17 (2+4)
Arr. Lausanne	14:28	15:05	15:28	16:05	16:28

(1) Supplement charged. Restaurant car. (2) Light refreshments. (3) Plus other departures from Lausanne at 11:13 (1), 11:32, 11:55 (2) and 12:32. (4) Plus other departures from Sion at frequent times from 15:44 to 22:31.

Luzern - Andermatt - Luzern

The Goschenen-Andermatt-Goschenen portion of this one-day excursion (a thrilling ride in the Schollenen Gorge) is by rack railway and is *not* covered by Eurailpass. The 1991 price of a roundtrip ticket *without* a Swiss Pass is 18 Swiss francs for first-class, Sfr-11.20 for second-class. *With* a Swiss Pass: free.

290

Dep. Luzern	08:14	10:14 (1)	12:14 (2)	14:14 (1)	
Arr. Goschenen	09:45	11:45	13:45	15:45	

Change trains. 286

Dep. Goschenen	09:55	11:55	13:55	15:55	
Arr. Andermatt	10:06	12:06	14:06	16:06	

Sights in **Andermatt**: A great ski resort.

Dep. Andermatt	10:50	12:50	14:50	16:50	18:50 (3)
Arr. Goschenen	11:05	13:05	15:05	17:05	19:05

Change trains. 290

Dep. Goschenen	11:14 (2)	13:14 (2)	15:14 (1)	17:14 (1)	19:14 (1)
Arr. Luzern	12:46	14:46	16:46	18:46	20:46

(1) Light refreshments. (2) Restaurant car. (3) Plus another departure from Andermatt at 19:14, departing Goschenen 22:00 and arriving Luzern 23:43.

Luzern - Basel - Luzern 277

Dep. Luzern	06:46 (1)	07:56	08:56	09:56	10:56 (2)
Arr. Basel (S.B.B.)	07:52	09:09	10:09	11:09	12:09

Sights in **Basel**: See notes about sightseeing in Basel on page 310.

Dep. Basel (S.B.B.)	10:51 (3)	11:51	12:07 (4)	12:51 (2)	13:51 (5)
Arr. Luzern	12:04	13:04	13:12	14:04	15:04

(1) Runs daily, except Sundays and holidays. Light refreshments. (2) Light refreshments. (3) Restaurant car. (4) Supplement charged. Restaurant car. (5) Plus other departures from Basel at frequent times from 14:07 to 23:02.

Luzern - Bern - Luzern 265

Most of these trains have light refreshments.

Dep. Luzern	07:13	08:13 (1)	09:13	11:13	11:46	13:13
Arr. Bern	08:29	09:29	10:29	12:29	13:12	14:29

Sights in **Bern**: See notes about sightseeing in Bern on pages 310-311.

Dep. Bern	12:31	14:31	15:48	16:31	17:31	18:31	20:31 (2)
Arr. Luzern	13:46	15:46	17:12	17:46	18:49	19:46	21:52

(1) Runs Saturdays, Sundays and holidays. (2) Plus another departure from Bern at 22:45, arriving Luzern at 00:16.

Luzern - Interlaken - Luzern 285

Dep. Luzern	06:03	07:24 (1)	08:24	09:24 (2)	10:24 (3)
Arr. Interlaken (Ost)	08:25	09:16	10:25	11:16	12:25

Sights in **Interlaken**: See notes under "Basel-Interlaken" on pages 313-314.

Dep. Interlaken (Ost)	10:44 (1)	11:35	12:44 (2)	13:35	14:44 (4)
Arr. Luzern	12:36	13:36	14:36	15:36	16:36

(1) Restaurant car. (2) Light refreshments. (3) Plus other departures from Luzern at frequent times from 11:24 to 20:09. (4) Plus other departures from Interlaken at frequent times from 15:35 to 20:35.

Luzern - Neuchatel - Luzern

265

Dep. Luzern	06:09 (1)	07:13 (2)	08:13 (3)	09:13 (2)	09:56 (4)
Arr. Bern	07:29	08:29	09:29	10:29	11:36

Change trains.

255

Dep. Bern	08:21	09:21	10:21	11:21	12:21
Arr. Neuchatel	08:57	09:57	10:57	11:57	12:57

Sights in **Neuchatel:** See notes under "Bern-Neuchatel" on page 317.

Dep. Neuchatel	13:02	14:02	15:02	16:02	17:02	18:02 (5)
Arr. Bern	13:38	14:38	15:38	16:38	17:38	18:38

Change trains.

265

Dep. Bern	14:31 (2)	15:48	16:31 (2)	17:31	18:31 (2)	19:25
Arr. Luzern	15:46	17:12	17:46	18:49	19:46	21:04

(1) Runs Monday–Friday, except holidays. (2) Light refreshments. (3) Runs Sat., Sun. and holidays. (4) Plus other departures from Luzern at 11:46 and 13:13 (2), arriving Neuchatel at 13:57 and 14:57. (5) plus other departures from Neuchatel at 19:02, 20:02 and 21:05, arriving Luzern at 21:50, 22:59 and 00:16.

Luzern - Schwyz - Luzern 290

Dep. Luzern	08:14	10:14 (1)	12:14 (2)	14:14 (1)
Arr. Schwyz	50 minutes later			

Sights in **Schwyz:** Visit the Staatsarcivmuseum (National Archive Museum), to see the 13th century Oath of Eternal Alliance, the document which marks the founding of Switzerland. This village's name became the name of the country (Schweiz). The Museum is one mile (uphill) from the railstation. A bus meets every train. There are also nicely restored 17th and 18th century patrician homes here.

Dep. Schwyz	12:01 (2)	14:01 (2)	16:01 (1)	18:01 (1)	20:01 (1)	22:54
Arr. Luzern	50 minutes later					

(1) Light refreshments. (2) Restaurant car.

Luzern - Zurich - Luzern 315

Most of these trains have light refreshments.

Dep. Luzern	Frequent times from 05:30 to 22:04
Arr. Zurich	50 minutes later

Sights in **Zurich**: See notes about sightseeing in Zurich on page 312.

Dep. Zurich	Frequent times from 07:07 to 00:09
Arr. Luzern	50 minutes later

Zurich - Andermatt - Zurich

The Goschenen-Andermatt-Goschenen portion of this one-day excursion (a thrilling ride down the **Schollenen Gorge**) is by rack railway and is *not* covered by Eurailpass. The 1991 prices of a roundtrip ticket *without* a Swiss Pass were: 18 Swiss francs for first-class, Sfr-11.20 for second-class. *With* a Swiss Pass: free.

All of the trains **Zurich** - *Gochenen* *and vice-versa, have light refreshments, unless designated otherwise.*

290

Dep. Zurich	06:33 (1)	07:30	09:03	11:03	
Arr. Goschenen	08:10	09:08	10:45	12:45	
Change trains. 286					
Dep. Goschenen	08:14	09:16	10:55	12:55	
Arrr. Andermatt	10 minutes later				

Sights in **Andermatt**: A great ski resort.

Dep. Andermatt	11:50	13:50	15:50	16:27	17:50
Arr. Goschenen	12:05	14:05	16:05	16:42	15:05
Change trains. 290					
Dep. Goschenen	12:14	14:14	16:14	16:47	18:10
Arr. Zurich	13:57	15:57	17:57	18:31	19:45

(1) No light refreshment.

Zurich - Arosa - Zurich

310

Dep. Zurich	06:30	07:33 (1)	08:10	09:10 (2)	10:10 (2)	11:10 (2)
Arr. Chur	08:02	08:51	09:37	10:45	11:37	12:45
Change trains. 324						

The Chur–Arosa cogwheel train leaves from the front of the Chur railstation. This is a very scenic ride *not* covered by Eurailpass. The 1991 prices for this roundtrip *without* a Swiss Pass were: 30.80 Swiss francs for first-class, Sfr-19.20 for second-class. *With* a Swiss Pass: Free.

| Dep. Chur | 08:13 | 09:00 | 09:55 | 10:55 | 11:55 | 12:55 |
| Arr. Arosa | one hour later | | | | | |

Sights in **Arosa**: Great Summer and Winter sports. Fantastic mountain scenery.

| Dep. Arosa | 10:05 | 11:05 | 12:05 | 13:05 | 14:05 | 15:05 (3) |
| Arr. Chur | 11:07 | 12:07 | 13:07 | 14:07 | 15:07 | 16:07 |

Change trains. 310

| Dep. Chur | 11:15 (2) | 12:23 (2) | 13:15 (2) | 14:23 (2) | 15:15 (2) | 16:23 (2) |
| Arr. Zurich | 12:50 | 13:50 | 14:50 | 15:50 | 16:50 | 17:50 |

(1) Restaurant car. (2) Light refreshments. (3) Plus other departures from Arosa (parenthesis designate Chur-Arosa service) at 16:05 (2), 17:05 (2), 18:05 (2), 19:05 (1), 20:05 and 21:05, arriving Zurich 18:50, 19:50, 20:50, 21:50, 22:50 and 23:50.

Zurich - Baden - Zurich 250 + 310

| Dep. Zurich | Frequent times from 06:25 to 23:37 |
| Arr. Baden | 15 minutes later |

Sights in **Baden**: See page 313 for sightseeing information at Baden.

| Dep. Baden | Frequent times from 06:15 to 00:28 |
| Arr. Zurich | 15 minutes later |

Zurich - Basel - Zurich 310

Many of these trains have a restaurant car or light refreshments.

| Dep. Zurich | Frequent times from 05:55 to 23:37 |
| Arr. Basel (S.B.B.) | 60–70 minutes later |

Sights in **Basel**: See notes about Basel on page 310.

| Dep. Basel (S.B.B.) | Frequent times from 05:12 to 23:32 |
| Arr. Zurich | 60–70 minutes later |

Zurich - Bern - Zurich 250

Many of these trains have a restaurant car or light refreshments.

| Dep. Zurich | Frequent times from 06:00 to 00:03 |
| Arr. Bern | 90 minutes later |

Sights in **Bern**: See notes about Bern on pages 310-311.

| Dep. Bern | Frequent times from 04:51 to 23:45 |
| Arr. Zurich | 90 minutes later |

Zurich - Chur - Zurich 310

Many of these trains have a restaurant car or light refreshments.

| Dep. Zurich | Frequent times from 06:30 to 22:10 |
| Arr. Chur | 90 minutes later |

Sights in **Chur**: This 2100-year old village is located at what has been a strategic pass in the Alps since Roman times. Walk from the station up through the small business area to a hilltop church and see the unusual cemetery there. The modern portion of it has rows of graves that are solidly decorated with living, blossoming plants.

Also see the fine stained-glass and the 12th century carved altar in the 15th century Cathedral. The Bishop's Palace. A one-hour walking tour of Chur is made easy by following red and green footprints painted on the sidewalks. The footprints are matched to a map available at the city's tourist office.

Dep. Chur	Frequent times from 06:13 to 22:13
Arr. Zurich	90 minutes later

Zurich - Landquart - Davos - Zurich
310

Dep. Zurich	07:23 (1)	08:00	09:00 (2)	10:00 (2)	11:00 (2)
Arr. Landquart	08:39	09:25	10:33	11:25	12:33
Change trains. 327					
Dep. Landquart	08:56	09:40	10:40	11:40	12:40
Arr. Klosters	09:34	10:18	11:18	12:18	13:40
Arr. Davos (Platz)	10:02	10:46	11:46	12:46	13:46

A **scenic circle-trip** *that avoids repeating the above route by returning to Zurich via Filisur and Thusis is shown on page 359.*

Sights in **Davos**: One of the world's most popular ski resorts. Also popular for its skating rinks, hiking trails, a sled run, horse-drawn sleigh rides, indoor swimming, hang-gliding, horseback riding and ice hockey.

Take the 22-minute ride on the Parsenn cable railway, once described by Vogue Magazine as "the Rolls Royce of mountain railways", to the ridge of **Weissfluh**. A cable car ascends from there to the summit, the start of the different ski runs to **Serneus**, **Sass** and **Klosters**.

A general-fare ticket (Sfr-223 for adults, Sfr-134 for children in 1991) allows unlimited use of the entire network of funicular railways, ski lifts and cable cars for 6 days. It also covers the buses that run every 15 minutes from one end of Davos to the other.

Dep. Davos (Platz)	12:05	13:05	14:05	15:05	16:05 (5)
Dep. Klosters	29 minutes after departing Davos				
Arr. Landquart	13:17	14:17	15:17	16:17	17:17
Change trains. 310					
Dep. Landquart	13:26 (2)	14:34 (2)	15:26 (2)	16:34 (2)	17:26 (2)
Arr. Zurich	14:50	15:50	16:50	17:50	18:50

(1) Restaurant car. (2) Light refreshments. (3) Light refreshments Landquart-Zurich. (4) Restaurant car Landquart-Zurich. (5) Plus other departures from Davos at 17:05 (3), 18:05 (3), 19:05 (4), 19:55 and 20:55, arriving Zurich 19:50, 20:50, 21:50, 22:50 and 23:50.

Zurich - Frankfurt - Zurich 73
Both of these trains have a restaurant car.

Dep. Zurich	07:37	Dep. Frankfurt		18:10
Arr. Frankfurt	11:49	Arr. Zurich		22:23

Sights in **Frankfurt**: See notes about Frankfurt on page 374.

Zurich - Geneva - Zurich 250
Most of these trains have a restaurant car or light refreshments.

Dep. Zurich	Frequent times from 06:06 to 21:06
Arr. Geneva (Corn.)	3 hours later

Sights in **Geneva:** See notes about sightseeing in Geneva on page 311.

Dep. Geneva (Corn.)	Frequent times from 06:07 to 20:58
Arr Zurich	3 hours later

Zurich - Interlaken - Zurich 250

All of these trains have light refreshments, unless designated otherwise.

Dep. Zurich	06:25	08:29	10:29	11:29	
Arr. Interlaken (Ost)	09:21	11:21	13:21	14:21	

Sights in **Interlaken**: See notes about sightseeing in Interlaken under "Basel–Interlaken" on page 313.

Dep. Interlaken (Ost)	13:39	14:39	15:39 (1)	17:39	18:39 (1+2)
Arr. Zurich	16:31	17:31	18:31	20:31	21:31

(1) No light refreshment. (2) Plus another departure from Interlaken at 19:39. Restaurant car to Bern. Change trains in Bern at 20:32. Depart Bern at 21:42. Restaurant car to Zurich. Arrive Zurich 22:57.

Zurich - Lugano - Zurich 290

Dep. Zurich	06:24 (1)	06:33	07:03 (2)	08:03 (2)	09:03 (4+5)
Arr. Lugano	09:15	09:45	10:03	11:03	12:21

Sights in **Lugano**: See notes under "Milan-Lugano" on page 236.

Dep. Lugano	12:41 (4)	13:57 (4)	14:41 (4)	15:57 (2)	16:41 (3+6)
Arr. Zurich	15:57	16:57	17:57	18:57	19:57

(1) Reservation required. Supplement charged. Restaurant car. (2) Restaurant car. (3) Light refreshments. (4) Reservation required. Restaurant car. (5) Plus other departures from Zurich at 10:03 (2) and 11:03 (3), arriving Lugano 13:03 and 14:21. (6) Plus other Lugano departures at 17:57 (5), 18:42 (2), 19:41 and 20:31 (4), arriving Zurich 20:57, 21:50, 23:03 and 23:36.

Zurich - Luzern - Zurich 315

Most of these trains have light refreshments.

Dep. Zurich	Frequent times from 06:42 to 23:40
Arr. Luzern	50 minutes later

Sights in **Luzern**: See notes about sightseeing in Luzern on page 311.

Dep. Luzern	Frequent times from 05:30 to 23:08
Arr. Zurich	50 minutes later

Zurich - Milan - Zurich 69

Dep. Zurich	06:24 (1)	07:03 (1)	08:03 (1)	10:03 (2)
Arr. Milan (Cen.)	10:30	11:35	12:35	14:35

Sights in **Milan**: See notes about Milan on pages 220–221.

Dep. Milan (Cen.)	14:25	16:25	17:20 (1)	19:25 (1)
Arr. Zurich	18:57	20:57	21:50	23:36

(1) Restaurant car. (2) Light refreshments.

Zurich - Munich - Zurich 84

All of these trains have a restaurant car.

| Dep. Zurich | 07:07 | Dep. Munich | 15:00 | 17:58 |
| Arr. Munich | 11:25 | Arr. Zurich | 19:21 | 22:21 |

Sights in **Munich**: See notes about Munich on pages 375–376.

Zurich - Neuchatel - Zurich 260

| Dep. Zurich | 07:06 (1) | 08:06 (2) | 09:06 (1) | 10:06 (2) | 11:06 (3) |
| Arr. Neuchatel | 08:59 | 09:53 | 10:59 | 11:53 | 12:59 |

Sights in **Neuchatel**: See notes under "Bern-Neuchatel" on page 317.

| Dep. Neuchatel | 12:01 (1) | 13:06 (2) | 14:01 (1) | 15:06 (2) | 16:01 (1+4) |
| Arr. Zurich | 13:53 | 14:53 | 15:53 | 16:53 | 17:53 |

(1) Light refreshments. (2) Restaurant car. (3) Plus another Zurich departure at 12:06 (2), arriving Neuchatel 13:55. (4) Plus other Neuchatel departures at 17:06 (2), 18:01 (1), 19:06 (2), 20:01 and 21:06 (1), arriving Zurich 18:53, 19:53, 20:53, 21:53 and 22:53

Zurich - Rheinfelden - Zurich 310

Change trains in Brugg, unless designated otherwise.

Dep. Zurich	06:40 (1)	07:12 (1+2)	08:00	09:00	10:00 (4)
Dep. Brugg	-0-	-0-	08:30	09:30	10:30
Arr. Rheinfelden	07:37	08:11	09:01	10:01	11:01

Sights in **Rheinfelden**: A world-famed health spa since 1844. There are tours of the Cardinal and Feldschlosschen breweries. Visit the island park on the Rhine River.

| Dep. Rheinfelden | 12:46 (1+3) | 13:56 | 14:56 | 15:56 (1+2+5) |
| Arr. Zurich | 65 minutes later | | | |

(1) Direct train. *No* train change in Brugg. (2) Runs Monday–Friday, except holidays. (3) Runs daily, except Sundays and holidays. (4) Plus other departures from Zurich at 11:00, 12:00, 13:00 and 14:00. (5) Plus other departures from Rheinfelden at 17:56, 18:56, 19:56, 21:05 (1) and 23:45 (1).

Zurich - St. Moritz - Zurich

310			330		
Dep. Zurich	07:33 (1)	08:10	Dep. St. Moritz	13:00 (1)	14:00 (3+4)
Arr. Chur	08:51	09:37	Arr. Chur	15:06	16:06
Change trains.			Change trains.		
330			310		
Dep. Chur	09:00 (2)	09:52 (2)	Dep. Chur	15:15 (2)	16:23 (2)
Arr. St. Moritz	11:18	11:58	Arr. Zurich	16:50	17:50

(1) Restaurant car. (2) Light refreshments. (3) Runs daily. Light refreshments only on Saturdays, Sundays and holidays. (4) Plus other departures from St. Moritz at 15:00, 16:00 (2), 17:00 (2), 18:00 (1) and 20:00 (3).....departing Chur 17:15 (2), 18:23 (2), 19:15 (2), 20:13 (1) and 22:13.....arriving Zurich 18:50, 19:50, 20:50, 21:50 and 23:50.

Sights in **St. Moritz:** The lovely scenery of the Alps, reflected on the Lake of St. Moritz. The curative waters. Great Summer sports (swimming, sailing, fishing, golf, mountain climbing) as well as Winter sports. The creme de la creme of the international jet set is here December to April.

See the collection of porcelain stoves, furniture and carved woodwork in the Engadine Museum, open Monday-Saturday 09:30-12:00 and 14:00-17:00, also on Sunday 10:00-12:00. Many paintings of this beautiful area by Giovanni Segantini in the Segantini Museum, open Monday-Saturday 09:30–12:00 and 14:00–16:00, on Sunday 14:30–16:00.

Zurich - Schwyz - Zurich 290

| Dep. Zurich | 07:30(1) | 08:03(2) | 09:03(1) | 10:03(2) | 11:03(1) | 13:03(2) | |
| Arr. Schwyz | one hour later | | | | | | |

Sights in **Schwyz:** See notes under "Luzern–Schwyz" on page 326.

| Dep. Schwyz | 11:01 | 12:01(2) | 13:01(1) | 14:01(2) | 15:01(1) | 16:01(2) | 17:01(1+3) |
| Arr. Zurich | one hour later | | | | | | |

(1) Light refreshments. (2) Change trains in Arth Goldau. (3) Plus other departures from Schwyz at 17:36 (1), 19:01 (1), 20:01 (2) and 22:01.

Zurich - Solothurn - Zurich 260

All of these trains have light refreshments.

| Dep. Zurich | Frequent times from 06:06 to 23:03 |
| Arr. Solothurn | 60 minutes later |

Sights in **Solothurn:** Switzerland's oldest town. (It and Trier, in Germany, are the 2 oldest towns north of the Alps.) This is the best preserved Baroque town in Switzerland, located in the **Aare Valley**, at the foot of the **Jura Mountains**. Everything worth seeing here can be reached by walking the town's narrow streets: the town's many fine statues, 11 churches and chapels, 11 ornamental fountains . . . and the 11 steps leading to the entrance of the Cathedral of St. Ours which has 11 bells, 11 towers and 11 altars.

Solothurn became in 1481 the *eleventh* canton to join the Swiss Federation !

See the outstanding ancient art here. Holbein's Madonna in the Museum. Traces of the 4th century Roman wall. Farmers selling flowers, fruits and vegetables in the town center every Wednesday and Saturday. The marvelous Assumption over the high altar in the Jesuit church.

The bulb domes on the twin towers of the Town Hall. The comprehensive collection of arms and armor in the Old Arsenal Museum, said to be the second largest collection of weapons in Europe. It has 400 suits of armor among its exhibits. The Italian belltower of the Cathedral.

| Dep. Solothurn | Frequent times from 05:41 to 22:56 |
| Arr. Zurich | 60 minutes later |

Zurich - Stuttgart - Zurich 69

| Dep. Zurich | 07:13 | 09:13 | | |
| Arr. Stuttgart | 10:20 | 12:20 | | |

Sights in **Stuttgart:** See notes under "Frankfurt–Stuttgart" on page 388.

| Dep. Stuttgart | 12:43 (1) | 14:43 (1) | 16:42 (2) | 18:43 |
| Arr. Zurich | 15:47 | 17:47 | 19:47 | 21:47 |

(1) Restaurant car. (2) Light refreshments.

Zurich - Winterthur - Zurich 300

Dep. Zurich   Frequent times from 06:18 to 23:15
Arr. Winterthur   22 minutes later

Sights in **Winterthur**: More art treasures than any other place in Switzerland, at the country's National Gallery in the Am Roemerholz mansion. Great Austrian, German and Swiss paintings.

Dep. Winterthur   Frequent times from 06:27 to 23:36
Arr. Zurich   22 minutes later

Zurich - Zug - Zurich 315

Dep. Zurich   Frequent times from 07:07 to 00:09
Arr. Zug   26 minutes later

Sights in **Zug**: This village is located on the northeast shore of the 14-mile long Lake Zug. See the spires and massive towers of the 15th century Church of St. Oswald. The stained-glass for which this area is noted and also gold and silver work, embroidery and wood carvings in the Museum at the 16th century Town Hall.

The view from the peak of the **Zugerberg**, 4000 feet above the town. From there, one can see the peaks of Rigi and Pilatus.

Try the local specialties: *rotel* (a tasty salmon-like fish from the lake), the local cherries that are used for producing the liqueur kirsch, and the local cake, kirsch-torte, laced with the cherry liqueur.

Dep. Zug   Frequent times from 06:28 to 23:32
Arr. Zurich   26 minutes later

SCENIC RAIL TRIPS IN SWITZERLAND

Basel - Schaffhausen - Basel 762

An easy one-day roundtrip, to see the marvelous Rhine Falls.

Dep. Basel (Bad Bf.)	08:16	10:16	12:16	14:16	16:16
Arr. Schaffhausen	09:28	11:28	13:28	15:28	17:28

Sights in **Schaffhausen**: See notes under "Zurich–Schaffhausen" on page 362

Dep. Schaffhausen	11:37	13:37	15:37	17:37	19:37
Arr. Basel (Bad Bf.)	12:48	14:48	16:48	18:48	20:48

Bern - Brig - Bern 280

An easy one-day roundtrip that affords a view of **Rhone Valley** and **Lonza Valley** canyons, lakes and mountains plus the Lake Thun scenery at Spiez about which we enthuse in the "Geneva–Spiez" trip described on page 342 . . .and going through the 9-mile Lotschberg Tunnel and over the Bietschtal Bridge. This structure takes the train 255 feet above the ravine it crosses.

We recommend a stop in Spiez and a stroll there on either the outbound or home- bound leg of the trip.

Dep. Bern	06:22 (1)	07:22 (1)	08:22 (1)	08:51 (1)	09:22 (1)	10:22 (1+3)
Arr. Spiez	06:52	07:52	08:52	09:21	09:52	10:52
Dep. Spiez	06:54	07:54	08:54	09:23	09:54	10:54 (4)
Arr. Brig	07:59	08:59	09:59	10:21	10:59	11:59

Sights in **Brig**: Switzerland's largest private residence, the 17th century Stockalper Castle, built by a very successful businessman.

Dep. Brig	08:01 (1)	09:01 (1)	10:01 (2)	11:01 (1)	12:01 (1)	13:01 (1+5)
Arr. Spiez	09:05	10:05	11:05	12:05	13:05	14:05
Dep. Spiez	09:07	10:07	11:07	12:07	13:07	14:07 (6)
Arr. Bern	31 minutes after departing Spiez.					

(1) Light refreshments. (2) Restaurant car. (3) Plus other departures from Bern at frequent times from 11:22 to 20:22. (4) Plus other departures from Spiez at frequent times from 11:54 to 20:54. (5) Plus other departures from Brig at frequent times from 13:15 to 21:33. (6) Plus other departures from Spiez at frequent times from 14:14 to 22:39.

Bern - Brig - Domodossola - Bern

To see all of the scenery and Lotschberg Tunnel noted above under "Bern–Brig" plus having the experience of going through the 11.9-mile Simplon (Europe's longest rail tunnel), make the Bern–Domodossola portion of the Bern–Milan trip.

The Simplon is actually 2 tunnels, one southbound and a 65-foot longer bore for the separate northbound tunnel.

280

Dep. Bern	06:50 (1)	08:51 (1)	10:22 (2)	11:22 (2)	12:22 (3+4)
Arr. Brig	- 0 -	- 0 -	11:59	12:59	13:59
Change trains.					

270

Dep. Brig	- 0 -	- 0 -	12:38	13:41	14:38
Arr. Domodossola	08:50	11:00	13:07	14:18	15:07

* * *

Dep. Domodossola	09:15 (1)	12:45 (1)	13:41	15:08 (1)	15:22
Arr. Brig	- 0 -	- 0 -	14:18	- 0 -	15:50
Change trains.					

280

Dep. Brig	- 0 -	- 0 -	15:01 (3)	- 0 -	16:01 (2)
Arr. Bern	11:38	14:43	16:38	17:08	17:38

(1) Direct train. No train change in Brig. Restaurant car or light refreshments. (2) Light refreshments. (3) Restaurant car. (4) Plus another departure from Bern at 14:17 (1), arriving Domodossola 16:18. For the return to Bern, depart Domodossola at 18:00, change trains in Brig at 18:28, depart Brig at 19:01 (3), arriving Bern 20:38.

Bern - Interlaken - Brienz - Interlaken - Bern

There is fine canyon, lake and mountain scenery on this easy one-day roundtrip.

Most of the trains Bern–Interlaken and v.v. have light refreshments.

280					
Dep. Bern	07:28	08:28	09:28 (1)	10:28	11:28 (2+3)
Arr. Interlaken (Ost)	08:21	09:21	10:21	11:21	12:21
Change trains. 285					
Dep. Interlaken (Ost)	08:44	09:35	10:44	11:35	12:44
Arr. Brienz	09:00	09:58	11:00	11:58	13:00
		*	*	*	
Dep. Brienz	09:01	10:02	11:01	12:02	13:01
Arr. Interlaken (Ost)	09:16	10:25	11:16	12:25	13:16
Change trains. 280					
Dep. Interlaken (Ost)	09:39	10:39	11:39 (1)	12:39	13:39 (2)
Arr. Bern	10:32	11:32	12:32	13:32	14:32

(1) Restaurant car. (2) Light refreshments. (3) Plus other departures from Bern (that allow the same roundtrip) at 12:28 (2), 13:28, 14:28 (2), 15:28, 16:28 (2) and 17:28 (1), arriving back in Bern 15:32, 16:32, 17:32, 18:32, 19:32 and 20:32.

Bern - Interlaken - Wengen - Jungfrau - Grindelwald - Interlaken - Bern

This easy one-day trip covers the heart of the Bernese Oberland area and offers very good gorge, lake and mountain scenery. There have been popular ski resorts in this area since 1906.

The Interlaken-Jungfraujoch-Interlaken portion of this excursion is *not* covered by Eurailpass. The 1991 prices *without* a Swiss Pass were: 140.40 Swiss francs for first-class, Sfr-132.60 for second-class. *With* a Swiss Pass: Sfr-86.40.

At **Jungfraujoch**, passengers alight to look down on the great Jungfrau glacier and stroll in the "Ice Palace" carved inside the glacier. Jungfraujoch is the highest (11,333 feet) railstation in Europe. Fabulous views of the Jungfrau, Eiger and Monch peaks can be seen from the revolving restaurant, which rotates completely every 50 minutes. The highest waterfall in Europe (2,000-foot drop) is spectacular in late Spring and early Summer.

We suggest, for variety, you go from Interlaken to Jungfraujoch *via Wengen* and then return to Interlaken *via Grindelwald*.

280		
Dep. Bern	07:28	08:28
Arr. Interlaken (Ost)	08:21	09:21
Change trains.		
288		
Dep. Interlaken (Ost)	08:31	09:31
Arr. Wengen	09:14	10:24
Arr. Scheidegg	09:45	10:55
Change trains.		
Dep. Scheidegg	10:02	11:02
Arr. Jungfraujoch	10:53	11:58
Sight see in Jungfraujoch		

288		
Dep. Jungfraujoch	12:00	13:00
Arr. Scheidegg	12:47	13:47
Change trains.		
Dep. Scheidegg	13:02	14:02
Arr. Grindelwald	13:55	14:55
Change trains.		
Dep. Grindelwald	14:48	15:18
Arr. Interlaken (Ost)	15:26	16:00
Change trains.		
280		
Dep. Interlaken (Ost)	15:39	16:39
Arr. Bern	16:32	17:32

Bern - Lausanne - Brig - Spiez - Bern

Excellent canyon, lake and mountain scenery on this easy one-day circle trip. This is a portion of the "Geneva–Spiez–Geneva" trip shown on page 342. There is time for a stopover in Lausanne and/or Spiez. You go through the 9-mile Lotschberg Tunnel after leaving Brig.

250

Dep. Bern	06:38 (1)	07:18 (2)	09:18 (2)	10:18 (2)	11:18 (2+4)
Arr. Lausanne	07:50	08:26	10:26	11:26	12:26

Change trains. 270

Dep. Lausanne	07:55	08:32	10:32	11:32	12:55 (3)
Arr. Brig	09:53	10:19	12:23	13:23	14:35

Change trains. 280

Dep. Brig	10:01 (2)	11:01 (3)	13:01 (3)	14:01 (3)	15:01 (2)
Arr. Spiez	11:05	12:05	14:05	15:05	16:05
Dep. Spiez	11:07	12:07	14:07	15:07	16:07
Arr. Bern	11:38	12:38	14:38	15:38	16:38

(1) Daily except Sundays and holidays. (2) Restaurant car. (3) Light refreshments. (4) The same circle trip can be made in daylight by leaving Bern at 12:18 (2) 12:38 (3), 13:18 (2) and 14:18 (2)....depart Lausanne 13:55, 14:32 (3), 15:32 (3) and 15:55....depart Spiez 17:07, 18:07, 18:33 and 19:07....arriving back in Bern 17:38, 18:38, 19:04 and 19:38.

Bern - Locarno - Bern

Complete notes on the Domodossola–Locarno portion of this easy one-day roundtrip, one of the 5 most scenic rail journeys in Europe, appear under "Brig–Domodossola—Locarno" on page 339.

280

Dep. Bern	06:50 (1)	07:22 (2)	08:22 (2)	10:22 (2)	12:22 (2)
Arr. Brig	08:20	08:59	09:59 (2)	11:59 (2)	13:59 (2)
Arr. Domodossola	08:50	09:42	10:42	13:07	15:07

Change trains. Walk from the Domodossola station and go to the underground Centovalli track. *Hurry!*

272

Dep. Domodossola	09:05 (3)	10:16 (3)	11:12 (3)	13:15 (3)	15:18 (3)
Arr. Locarno	10:38	11:50	12:45	14:50	16:55

Sights in **Locarno**: See notes under "Milan–Locarno" on page 235.

Dep. Locarno	11:01 (4)	13:13 (4)	15:10 (4)	16:04	17:20	19:04
Arr. Domodossola	12:34	14:52	16:44	17:44	18:58	20:48

Change trains. Walk from the underground Centovalli track, up to the main Domodossola station. *Hurry!*

280

Dep. Domodossola	12:45 (1)	15:08	17:18 (5)	18:00 (6)	19:15 (7)	21:00
Dep. Brig	13:15	15:38	18:01 (5)	19:01 (6)	19:55	21:33
Arr. Bern	14:43	17:08	19:38	20:38	21:26	23:10

(1) Restaurant car Bern-Domodossola and v.v. (2) Change trains in Brig. Light refreshments Bern-Brig. (3) Light refreshments first hour of trip. (4) Light refreshments last hour of trip. (5) Change trains in Brig. Light refreshments Brig-Bern. (6) Change trains in Brig. Restaurant car Brig-Bern. (7) Light refreshments Domodossola-Bern.

Bern - Luzern - Alpnachstad - Pilatus

Very nice canyon, lake and mountain scenery on this easy one-day roundtrip that can include a stopover in Luzern. There are good views and several restaurants at the peak of **Pilatus.**

Note in the footnotes that the Pilatus Rack Railway trip (Alpnachstad–Pilatus–Alpnachstad) operates *only* May through November . . . and it is *not* covered by Eurailpass. The 1991 price *without* a Swiss Pass for the one-class roundtrip was: 49 Swiss francs. *With* a Swiss Pass: Sfr-36.75.

269				292		
Dep. Bern	07:31 (1)	08:31 (1+3)		Dep. Pilatus Kulm	11:30	13:04 (4)
Arr. Luzern	08:49	09:46		Arr. Alpachstad	12:10	13:44
Change trains. 264				Change to ordinary train. 264		
Dep. Luzern	09:09	10:09		Dep. Alpachstad	12:25	14:25
Arr. Alpnachstad	09:31	10:50		Arr. Luzern	12:50	14:50
Change to rack railway. 292				Change trains. 269		
Dep. Alpnachstad	09:32	10:55		Dep. Luzern	13:13 (1)	15:13
Arr. Pilatus Kulm	10:12	11:25		Arr. Bern	14:29	16:29

(1) Light refreshments. (2) Operates July 1 to August 31. (3) Plus other departures from Bern at 10:31 and 12:31, arriving Pilatus Kulm 12:34 and 14:34. (4) Plus other departures from Pilatus Kulm at 15:07 and 17:52 (2), arriving Bern 18:29 and 21:12.

Bern - Spiez - Bern 280

Great canyon, lake and mountain scenery on this easy one-day roundtrip. This is a portion of the "Geneva–Spiez–Geneva" trip listed on pages 342-343. Plenty of time to stroll in Spiez and enjoy the beauty of Lake Thun and the mountains above it.

Dep. Bern	Frequent times from 06:22 to 23:28
Arr. Spiez	30 minutes later

* * *

Dep. Spiez	Frequent times from 05:58 to 23:01
Arr. Bern	30 minutes later

Bern - Spiez - Brig - Lausanne - Bern

Marvelous canyon, lake, mountain and river scenery on this easy one-day circle trip. This is the reverse of the "Bern–Lausann–Spiez–Bern" ride listed earlier in this section. A stroll in Spiez is a nice way to break the journey. You go through the 10-mile Lotschberg Tunnel after leaving Spiez.

All of these trains have light refreshments, unless designated otherwise.

280					
Dep. Bern	07:22	08:22	09:22	10:22	11:22 (2)
Arr. Spiez	07:52	08:52	09:52	10:52	11:52
Dep. Spiez	07:54	08:54	09:54	10:54	11:54
Arr. Brig	08:59	09:59	10:59	11:59	12:59
Change trains. 270					
Dep. Brig	09:07	10:36	11:15	12:29	13:07
Arr. Lausanne	11:05	12:28	13:05	14:06	15:05

(Timetable continues on the next page)

Change trains.   250

Dep. Lausanne	11:34 (1)	12:34 (1)	13:10	14:34 (1)	15:10 (3)
Arr. Bern	12:42	13:42	14:22	15:42	16:22

(1) Restaurant car. (2) Plus another Bern departure at 12:22 (1), arriving Bern 17:42. (3) Plus other departures from Lausanne at frequent times from 16:34 to 23:45.

Brienz - Rothorn - Brienz   283

This is a cogwheel line. It goes through forests, mountains and meadows to the magnificent view from the 7,714-foot-high peak of **Rothorn**, from which there is an excellent 4-hour walk on a good mountain path to **Brunig**. There ia a superb network of well-maintained hiking trails in this area.

Not covered by Eurailpass. The 1991 price for a one-class roundtrip ticket *without* a Swiss Pass was 51 Swiss francs. *With* a SwissPass: Sfr-38.25.

Dep. Brienz	08:05	09:05	09:35 (1)	10:15	11:15	13:05	14:15 (3)
Arr. Rothorn	50-60 minutes later						

                              *   *   *

Dep. Rothorn	09:05	10:10	11:20	13:00	13:40	14:45	15:45 (4)
Arr. Brienz	60-70 minutes later						

(1) Operates July 1 to August 31. (2) Operates early June to late September. (3) Plus other departures from Brienz at 15:15 and 16:15 (2). (4) Plus other departures from Rothorn at 16:45 and 17:20 (2).

Brig - Andermatt - Disentis - Brig   320

Fine canyon and mountain scenery on this easy one-day roundtrip. A stopover can be made (8:25-19:07) in Andermatt, a great ski resort.

This trip is a portion of the "Glacier Express" route. See details about reservations and prices under "St. Moritz–Zermatt and Zermatt–St. Moritz" on page 355.

Sit on the right side for best views from Brig, on the left side from Disentis.

This trip is *not* covered by Eurailpass. The 1991 roundtrip ticket price for an ordinary train (not "Glacier Express", which charges a supplement) *without* a Swiss Pass was 98 Swiss francs for first-class, Sfr-61 for second-class. *With* a Swiss Pass: Free.

Dep. Brig	06:27	08:50 (1)	10:18 (2)	10:30 (3)	12:18 (2)
Arr. Andermatt	08:25	10:22	12:13	11:58	14:13
Arr. Disentis	09:32	11:36	13:37	12:58	15:28

Sights in **Disentis**: The stained glass in the Cathedral

Dep. Disentis	10:23 (3)	12:12 (3)	13:41 (3)	14:24	16:30
Dep. Andermatt	11:30	13:25	14:45	15:32	17:48
Arr. Brig	13:15	15:01	16:13	17:40	19:33

(1) Light refreshments. (2) Change trains in Andermatt. (3) "Glacier Express". See details about reservations and prices under "St. Moritz–Zermatt" on page 355. Plus another "Glacier Express" at 11:45, arriving Disentis at 14:45.

Brig - Arona - Brig 270

Beautiful lake and mountain scenery on this easy one-day roundtrip, which can also be seen as a portion of the Lausanne–Milan route. This ride takes you through Europe's longest (19.8km or 11.9 miles) tunnel, the Simplon.

It is the third longest tunnel in the world, after Japan's Seikan Tunnel (33.4 miles, between Tappi and Yoshioka) and Japan's Daishimizu Tunnel (13.4 miles, btween Tokyo and Niigata).

Dep. Brig	08:22	09:34	09:45	10:31 (1)	14:38 (2)	15:49 (1)
Arr. Arona	09:46	10:55	11:24	11:52	16:01	17:12

* * *

Dep. Arona	10:02 (3)	11:03 (2)	11:49 (1)	14:10	16:06 (1)	17:00 (2+4)
Arr. Brig	11:12	12:27	13:13	15:36	17:28	18:28

(1) Supplement charged. Restaurant car. (2) Light refreshments. (3) Reservation required. Supplement charged. Restaurant car. (4) Plus other departures from Arona at 17:41, 18:15 (1) and 19:57, arriving Brig 19:20, 19:45 and 21:30.

Here is the schedule for the Lausanne-Milan route.

55

Dep. Lausanne	08:09	08:58 (1)	11:13 (1)	12:55 (3)	16:13 (1)
Dep. Brig	09:34	10:31	12:38	14:36	17:41
Arr. Arona	10:56	11:54	-0- (2)	16:02	18:48
Arr. Milan (Cen.)	11:45	12:40	14:40	16:55	19:35

(1) Supplement charged. Restaurant car. (2) Train does not stop in Arona. (3) Light refreshments.

Brig - Bern - Brig 280

An easy one-day roundtrip that affords a view of Rhone Valley and Lonza Valley farms, canyons, lakes and mountains plus the Lake Thun scenery at Spiez about which we enthuse in the "Geneva–Spiez" trip described on page 342 . . . and going through the 10-mile-long Lotschberg Tunnel and over the Bietschtal Bridge. This structure takes the train 255 feet above the ravine it crosses.

We recommend a stop in Spiez and a stroll there on either the outbound or homebound leg of this trip.

For best views, sit on the right side Brig to Spiez, on the left side Spiez to Brig.

Dep. Brig	07:01 (1)	08:01 (2)	09:01 (1)	10:01 (2)	11:01 (2+3)
Arr. Spiez	08:05	09:05	10:05	11:05	12:05
Dep. Spiez	08:07	09:07	10:07	11:07	12:07
Arr. Bern	30 minutes after departing Spiez.				

* * *

Dep. Bern	09:22 (2)	10:22 (2)	11:22 (2)	12:22 (1)	13:22 (1+4)
Arr. Spiez	09:52	10:52	11:52	12:52	13:52
Dep. Spiez	09:54	10:54	11:54	12:54	13:54
Arr. Brig	66 minutes after departing Spiez.				

(1) Restaurant car. (2) Light refreshments. (3) Plus other departures from Brig that allow daylight viewing in Summer months at frequent times from 12:01 to 19:01. (2) Plus other departures from Bern at frequent times from 14:17 to 20:22.

Brig - Domodossola - Locarno - Domodossola - Brig

We call the Domodossola–Locarno portion of this one-day roundtrip one of the 5 most scenic rail trips in Europe. It is a spectacular narrow-gauge local train ride offering great gorge, mountain and river scenery on the Centovalli (one hundred valleys) route.

Be sure to have your passport with you. On this trip, you go from Switzerland to Italy, then Switzerland, back to Italy, and then again to Switzerland.

This ride takes you through Europe's longest (19.8km or 11.9 miles) tunnel, the Simplon (between Brig and Domodossola). It is the third longest tunnel in the world, after Japan's Seikan (33.4 miles, between Tappi and Yoshioka) and Japan's Daishimizu Tunnel (13.4 miles, between Tokyo and Niigata).

The 90-minute, 35-mile Locarno–Domodossola trip does not start from the Locarno railstation. You catch what looks like a trolley car at the central Locarno bus stop, across from the train station. Stops en route include **Intragna**, with its many churches; **Verdasio**, which has a train connection to the mountain town of **Rasa; Palagnedra,** which has a lake; **Camedo** (see notes on page 349); and **Druogno**, the highest point on this scenic route.

See detailed notes about Locarno on page 235, under "Milan–Locarno–Milan".

All of the trains Domodossola-Locarno and v.v. shown below have light refreshments, unless designated otherwise.

When changing trains in Domodossola, keep in mind that trains to and from Brig are located at street level. Trains to and from Locarno are on an underground track, connected by a walkway to the street level.

270

Dep. Brig	08:22	09:08	09:45	12:38	14:38
Arr. Domodossola	08:50	09:42	10:17	13:07	15:07

Change trains. 272

Dep. Domodossola	09:05	10:16	11:12	13:15	15:18
Arr. Locarno	10:38	11:50	12:45	14:50	16:55

* * *

Dep. Locarno	13:13	15:10	16:04 (1)	17:20 (1)
Arr. Domodossola	14:52	16:44	17:44	18:58

Change trains. 55

Dep. Domodossola	15:22 (2)	16:58 (2)	18:00	19:15
Arr. Brig	30 minutes later			

(1) No light refreshments. (2) Supplement charged.

Brig - Spiez - Interlaken - Brienz - Interlaken - Brig

Very good canyon, lake and mountain scenery on this easy one-day roundtrip.

For best views, sit on the right side Brig to Spiez, on the left side Spiez to Brig. Between Brig and Spiez, the train goes through the 10-mile-long Lotschberg Tunnel and over the Bietschtal Bridge. This structure takes the train 255 feet above the ravine it crosses.

(The timetable for this trip appears on page 340)

Most of the trains Brig-Spiez and v.v. below have light refreshments or a restaurant car.

280		
Dep. Brig	09:01	10:01
Arr. Spiez	10:05	11:05
Change trains. 280		
Dep. Spiez	11:01	12:01
Arr. Interlaken (Ost)	11:21	12:21
Change trains. 285		
Dep. Interlaken (Ost)	11:35	12:44
Arr. Brienz	11:58	13:00

285		
Dep. Brienz	12:02	13:00
Arr. Interlaken (Ost)	12:25	13:16
Change trains. 280		
Dep. Interlaken (Ost)	12:39	13:39
Arr. Spiez	12:59	13:59
Change trains. 280		
Dep. Spiez	13:54	14:54
Arr. Brig	14:59	15:59

Brig - Interlaken - Wengen - Jungfrau - Grindelwald - Brig

There is excellent canyon, lake and mountain scenery on this easy one-day roundtrip. See "Bern-Jungfraujoch" on page 334.

The Interlaken-Jungfraujoch-Interlaken portion of this trip is *not* covered by Eurailpass. The 1991 prices of tickets *without* a Swiss Pass were 140.40 Swiss francs for first-class, Sfr-132.60 for second-class. *With* a Swiss Pass, both the Interlaken-Wengen and Grindelwald–Interlaken portions were free, and the one-class Wengen–Scheidegg, Scheidegg–Jungfraujoch–Scheidegg and Scheidegg–Grindelwald portions were at 25% discount, making the entire trip cost Sfr-86.40.

It is for variety that we suggest you go from Interlaken to Jungfraujoch *via Wengen* and then return to Interlaken *via Grindelwald*.

Most of the trains Brig-Spiez and v.v. below have light refreshments or a restaurant car.

280		
Dep. Brig	08:01	09:01
Arr. Spiez	09:05	10:05
Change trains. 260		
Dep. Spiez	10:01	11:01
Arr. Interlaken (Ost)	10:21	11:21
Change trains. 288		
Dep. Interlaken (Ost)	10:31	11:31
Arr. Wengen	11:14	12:24
Arr. Scheidegg	11:45	12:55
Change trains.		
Dep. Scheidegg	12:02	13:02
Arr. Jungfraujoch	12:53	13:53
Sightsee in Jungfraujoch.		

288		
Dep. Jungfraujoch	14:00	15:00
Arr. Scheidegg	14:47	15:47
Change trains.		
Dep. Scheidegg	15:02	16:02
Arr. Grindelwald	15:55	16:55
Change trains.		
Dep. Grindelwald	16:18	17:18
Arr. Interlaken(Ost)	17:00	18:00
Change trains. 280		
Dep. Interlaken (Ost)	17:39	18:39
Arr. Spiez	17:59	18:59
Change trains. 280		
Dep. Spiez	18:54	19:54
Arr. Brig	19:59	20:59

Brig - Zermatt - Gornergrat - Zermatt - Brig

Great canyon and mountain scenery on this easy one-day roundtrip that includes an outstanding 5½–mile narrow-gauge cogwheel train ride to Gornergrat (10,200 feet) for a close view of the **Gorner Glacier**, the **Matterhorn** (14,692 feet) and more than 50 other peaks.

This trip is *not* covered by Eurailpass. The 1991 prices of rountrip tickets *without* a Swiss Pass were 130 Swiss francs for first-class, Sfr-100 for second-class. *With* a Swiss Pass, the Brig–Zermatt–Brig trip is free and the Zermatt–Gornergrat–Zermatt trip is at 25% discount, making the entire trip Sfr-37.50.

300

Dep. Brig	Frequent times from 06:10 to 20:23
Arr. Zermatt	90 minutes later

Change trains. Swiss timetable.

Dep. Zermatt	Frequent times from 07:05 to 18:00
Arr. Gornergrat	45 minutes later

                        *   *   *

Dep. Gornergrat	Frequent times from 07:55 to 19:07
Arr. Zermatt	45 minutes later

Change trains. Swiss timetable.

Dep. Zermatt	Frequent times from 06:00 to 21:10
Arr. Brig	90 minutes later

Lausanne - Zermatt - Gornergrat - Lausanne

Nice canyon, lake, mountain and river scenery on this easy one-day roundtrip. The Visp–Zermatt–Gornergrat roundtrip is *not* covered by Eurailpass.

The 1991 prices of roundtrip tickets for an *ordinary* train (not "Glacier Express", which charge a supplement) *without* a Swiss Pass were 126 Swiss francs for first-class, Sfr-97 second-class. *With* a Swiss Pass, the Visp–Zermatt–Visp trip is free and the Zermatt–Gornergrat–Zermatt trip is at 25% discount, making the entire trip cost Sfr-37.50.

270

Dep. Lausanne	06:55	07:32	08:32	09:32 (1)	10:32	12:32
Arr. Visp	08:33	09:14	10:17	11:14	12:14	14:14

Change trains. **320**

Dep. Visp	08:36	09:36	10:36	11:36	12:36	14:36
Arr. Zermatt	09:45	10:47	11:45	12:47	13:47	15:47

Change trains. Swiss timetable.

Dep. Zermatt	10:00	11:12	12:00	13:12	14:00	16:00
Arr. Gornergrat	10:43	11:55	12:43	13:55	14:43	16:43

                        *   *   *

Dep. Gornergrat	11:55	13:07	14:19	15:55	17:07	17:55
Arr. Zermatt	12:39	13:51	15:03	16:39	17:51	18:37

Change trains. **320**

Dep. Zermatt	13:10	14:10	15:10	17:10	18:10	19:10
Arr. Visp	14:21	15:21	16:21	18:21	19:21	20:21

Change trains. **270**

Dep. Visp	14:43 (1)	15:42 (1)	16:36 (1)	18:43	19:43	20:43
Arr. Lausanne	16:28	17:27	18:28	20:28	21:28	22:28

(1) Light refreshments.

Chur - Brig - Zermatt - Gornergrat - Zermatt

There is fabulous Rhone Valley scenery on this ride plus crossing Oberalp Pass (6,700 feet) and going through the 8-mile long Furka Tunnel on the Chur-Brig portion. This trip crosses the highest bridges in Europe and includes the outstanding cogwheel train ride to Gornergrat (10,200 feet) for a close view of the Matterhorn (14,692 feet) and more than 50 other Alpine peaks.

This trip is *not* covered by Eurailpass. The 1991 prices for this trip on an ordinary train (not "Glacier Express", which charges a supplement) *without* a Swiss Pass were: 197 Swiss francs for first- class, Sfr-141 for second-class. *With* a Swiss Pass, the Chur-Zermatt portion was free, and the Zermatt–Gornergrat–Zermatt roundtrip was at 25% discount, making the entire trip Sfr-37.50.

See details about "Glacier Express" reservations and prices under "St. Moritz-Zermatt" on page 355.

320

Dep. Chur	09:03 (1)	-0-	-0-	-0-	10:55 (1)	12:16 (1)
Arr. Zermatt	14:45	-0-	-0-	-0-	16:45	17:45

Change to a narrow-gauge train.   Swiss timetable.

Dep. Zermatt	15:12	15:36	16:00	16:24	-0-	18:00
Arr. Gornergrat	15:55	16:19	16:43	17:07	-0-	18:43

* * *

Dep. Gornergrat	16:19	16:43	17:07	17:55	-0-	19:07
Arr. Zermatt	45 minutes later					

(1) "Glacier Express". See details about reservations and prices under "St. Moritz–Zermatt" on page 355.

Chur - St. Moritz - Chur 330

Marvelous canyon, lake and mountain scenery on this easy one-day roundtrip. It is a very scenic ride involving going through double spiral tunnels and across the amazing Landwasser Viaduct.

All of these trains have light refreshments every day, unless designated otherwise.

Dep. Chur	06:45	08:08	09:00	09:52	10:52 (1)	11:52 (4)
Arr. St. Moritz	09:07	10:18	11:18	11:58	12:58	13:58

* * *

Dep. St. Moritz	10:00 (2)	11:00	12:00	13:00	14:00 (1)	15:00 (5)
Arr. Chur	12:06	13:06	14:06	15:06	16:06	17:06

(1). Light refreshments only on Saturdays, Sundays and holidays. (2) "Glacier Express". See details about reservations and prices under "St. Moritz–Zermatt" on page 355. (3) Restaurant car. (4) Plus frequent other departures from Chur 12:52-20:52. (5) Plus other departures from St. Moritz 16:00, 17:00, 18:00 (3) and 20:00 (1).

Geneva - Lausanne - Brig - Spiez - Bern - Lausanne - Geneva

One of the 5 most scenic rail trips in Europe.

The succession of beautiful scenes defy verbal description: 15 miles of terraced vineyards and Lake Geneva shoreline between Geneva and Lausanne. Great river scenery en route from Martigny to Brig.

Upon leaving Brig, take a seat on the side of the train that faces the Brig railstation. In the 52 miles between Brig and Thun, the train goes through 37 tunnels (including the 10-mile Lotschberg) and crosses the top of 25 bridges and viaducts. The 866-foot-long **Kander Viaduct** is 92-feet high.

Upon emerging from the Lotschberg Tunnel, there is such beautiful farm and mountain scenery around tiny **Kandersteg** and **Fruitigen** that you want to get off the train and spend the rest of your life there.

It is only a 15-minute downhill walk from the Spiez railstation to the castle overlooking Lake Thun, the most beautiful lake scene on this planet. If the view of Lake Thun and the mountains reflected on its surface does not thrill you, pack up and go home because you will not find any landscape more beautiful in this world. From here, you can see the peaks of Jungfrau, Eiger, Monch and Finsteraarhorn.

You can return to Geneva (via Bern) either by boarding a train in Spiez or by first taking the 45-minute boat ride (covered by Eurailpass) from Spiez to **Thun** village and then boarding the train in Thun. It is a 10-minute downhill walk from the Spiez railstation to the Spiez pier. The lake steamer ties up 100 feet from Thun's railstation.

On the way back to Geneva from Bern, you pass through the same lake and vineyard scenery you saw between Lausanne and Geneva that morning, at the start of this fabulous one-day trip.

The schedules shown below allow a brief stopover in Bern.

270

Dep. Geneva (Corn.)	07:48	08:20 (1)	08:48 (2)	10:34 (1)	10:48
Dep. Lausanne	08:32	08:58	09:32	11:13	11:32
Arr. Brig	10:19	10:22	11:23	12:36	13:23

Change trains. 280

Dep. Brig	– 0 –	11:01 (2)	12:01 (2)	13:15 (3)	14:01 (2)
Arr. Spiez	– 0 –	12:05	13:05	14:13	15:05
Dep. Spiez	– 0 –	12:07	13:07	14:14	15:07
Dep. Thun	– 0 –	12:18	13:18	14:24	15:18
Arr. Bern	– 0 –	12:38	13:38	14:43	15:38

Change trains. 250 *All of these trains have a restaurant car.*

Dep. Bern	– 0 –	13:18	14:18	15:18	16:18 (4)
Arr. Lausanne	– 0 –	14:26	15:26	16:26	17:26
Arr. Geneva (Corn.)	– 0 –	15:02	16:02	17:02	18:02

(1) Supplement charged. Restaurant car. (2) Light refreshments. (3) Restaurant car. (4) Plus other Geneva departures at 12:18 (2), 12:48 (2) and 13:48 (2)....Departing Brigg at 15:01(3), 15:38 and 17:01 (3).... Departing Bern at 17:18 (3), 18:18 (3) and 19:18 (3)....Arriving back in Geneva at 19:02, 20:02 and 21:02. Plus other Bern depatures at 17:18 (3), 18:18 (3), 19:18 (3), 20:18 (3), 20:38, 21:18 and 23:26

Here are the Lake Thun (Spiez-Thun) boat schedules (covered by Eurailpass) to combine with departures from Thun village for Bern.

281 Boat

Dep. Spiez	13:17 (1)	13:49	15:17 (1)	16:03 (1)	16:43 (3)
Arr. Thun (Pier)	14:02	14:53	16:04	16:48	17:38

It is a 2-minute walk from the boat pier to the train.

280 Train

Dep. Thun (Stn.)	14:12	15:12	16:12	17:12	17:44
Arr. Bern	20 minutes later				

(1) Has restaurant. (2) Light refreshments. (3) Plus other boat departures from Spiez at 17:04 (2), 18:03 (1), 19:17 (1) and 20:11, connecting in Thun with trains that arrive Bern 18:32, 19:32, 20:32 and 21:26.

Geneva - Chamonix (Mt. Blanc) - Geneva 167

Be sure to have your passport with you on this trip filled with fantastic mountain scenery, as you will be going from Switzerland to France. From Chamonix, take the 2-mile-high cable-car ride that goes nearly to the top of the tallest mountain in Europe, the 15,771-foot **Mt. Blanc**, towering almost 10,000 feet above Chamonix, for a view of Alpine peaks extending 80 miles.

After descending, there is just time to also take the narrow-gauge train to see the "Sea of Ice" glacier bed (which does not operate in Winter). The tombstones in the small cemetery, a 5-minute walk from the railstation, are fascinating. Nearly one-fourth of the headstones read "died on the mountain" climbers and their rescuers.

Dep. Geneva			Dep. Chamonix	13:46	17:50
(Eaux Vives)	08:00	08:26 (1)	Arr. St. Gervais	14:30	18:27
Arr. St. Gervais	09:16	09:58	Change trains.		
Change trains.			Dep. St. Gervais	14:40 (1)	18:37
Dep. St. Gervais	09:26	10:45	Arr. Geneva		
Arr. Chamonix	10:06	11:24	(Eaux Vives)	16:03	19:50

(1) Change trains in La Roche-sur-Foron.

Geneva - Martigny - Chamonix - Geneva 167

This one-day circle trip avoids the repetition involved in the Geneva-Annemasse- Chamonix-Geneva roundtrip described in the previous listing and also allows time for the activities in Chamonix described above. The scenery Martigny-Vallorcine-Chamonix is fantastic !

270			268		
Dep. Geneva			Dep. Vallorcine	09:50 (2)	11:09
(Corn.)	06:48	07:48	Arr. Chamonix	10:27	11:51
Arr. Martigny	08:20	09:20	Change trains.		
Change trains.			167		
268			Dep. Chamonix	13:46 (3)	17:50 (4)
Dep. Martigny	08:38	09:58 (1)	Arr. Geneva		
Arr. Vallorcine	09:39	11:06	(Eaux-Vives)	16:03	19:50
Change trains.					

(1) Change trains in Le Chatelard. (2) Operates late June to early September. (3) Change trains in St. Gervais and La Roche-sur-Foron. (4) Change trains in only St. Gervais.

Geneva - Lausanne - Geneva

Here is a short trip packed with fine scenery of 15 miles of terraced vineyards, nearly the entire route following the lovely shoreline of Lake Geneva. Complete schedules are listed under the "Geneva–Lausanne" one-day excursion on page 320.

Geneva - Lyon - Geneva 159

The first 1½ hour from Geneva is noted for scenic canyons.

Occasionally, 2 trains depart from the same track at Lyon's Perrache railstation, heading in opposite directions. Be sure to stand at the correct end (North or South) of the track in order to board the train you want to ride. Check the departure signs at the underground passageway. Do not rely merely on a track number when departing from Perrache railstation !

Next to the North passageway of Track "A" is a take-out restaurant, handy for provisioning your trip.

Dep. Geneva (Corn.)	06:37	10:22	12:44	16:30
Arr. Lyon (Part-Dieu)	08:30	12:12	14:37	18:18
Arr. Lyon (Perrache)	9 minutes after departing Part-Dieu railstation			

*   *   *

Dep. Lyon (Perrache)	09:24	12:13	17:10	19:21
Dep. Lyon (Part-Dieu)	9 minutes after departing Perrache railstation			
Arr. Geneva (Corn.)	11:26	14:16	19:12	21:29

Geneva - Martigny - Geneva 251

This is a scenic trip of intermediate length, longer than the Geneva–Lausanne ride and shorter than the Geneva–Brig–Bern–Geneva circle trip. Very good canyon, lake, mountain and vineyard scenery.

Dep. Geneva (Corn.)	06:48	07:48	08:48 (1)	09:48	10:48 (2)
Arr. Martigny	08:20	09:20	10:20	11:20	12:20

*   *   *

Dep. Martigny	09:34 (1)	10:41 (1)	11:34 (1)	12:34 (1)	13:16 (1+3)
Arr. Geneva (Corn.)	11:12	12:12	13:12	14:12	14:43

(1) Light refreshments. (2) Plus other departures from Geneva at frequent times from 11:48 to 22:58.
(3) Plus other departures from Martigny at frequent times from 13:34 to 21:34.

Geneva - Montreux - Zweisimmen - Spiez - Bern - Geneva

This narrow-gauge variation on the scenic trip described earlier (Geneva–Brig–Bern—Geneva) runs parallel and north of the Martigny–Brig route. You miss going through the Lotschberg Tunnel, but you are able to see all of the Geneva–Lausanne vineyard and Lake Geneva scenery plus Lake Thun (Spiez) and a possible stopover in Bern, en route back to Geneva.

There is time to leave the train in Spiez, take the lake boat from Spiez to Thun, and then take the train from Thun to Bern. See notes under the "Geneva–Brig–Bern–Geneva" scenic trip on pages 342-343.

The ascent from Montreux to Zweisimmen is very scenic as the train climbs from the shore of Lac Leman to Les Avants in a series of hairpin bends. The funicular ride from **Les Avants** to **Sonloup** is worth stopping over in Les Avants and rejoining the Montreux-Zweisimmen route later in the day. **Gstaad** is a very expensive ski resort.

We recommend departing Montreux on "Panoramic Express" or "Superpanoramic Express". The comfortable coaches of these special narrow-gauge Observation Trains have glass domes and large side windows for viewing the marvelous scenery. Refreshments are available from vending machines in their bar car.

For "Superpanoramic", reservations are accepted only for groups. Individuals may ride it if there are any vacant seats.

There are seats in the front car, which has an elevated cab for the engineer. The next car is a bar car which seats 45 passengers. The third and last car is the locomotive.

Regardless which train you ride, sit on the right side Montreux-Zweisimmen for best views.

270

Dep. Geneva (Corn.)	08:48 (1)	09:48	10:48	11:48	12:48 (1)
Arr. Montreux	09:51	10:51	11:51	12:51	13:51

Change trains.   275

Dep. Montreux	10:00 (2)	11:00	12:20	13:00	14:00 (3+4)
Arr. Les Avants	10:22	11:22	12:42	13:22	– 0 –
Dep. Gstaad	11:18	12:30	13:42	14:30	15:18
Arr. Zweisimmen	11:45	13:00	14:10	15:00	15:45

Change trains.

Dep. Zweisimmen	12:21	13:05	14:21	15:05	16:05
Arr. Spiez	12:57	13:51	14:57	15:51	16:51

Change trains.   280

Dep. Spiez	13:07 (1)	14:01 (1)	15:07 (1)	16:01	17:01 (1)
Dep. Thun	13:18	14:12	15:18	16:12	17:12
Arr. Bern	13:38	14:32	15:38	16:32	17:32

Change trains.   250

Dep. Bern	14:18 (3)	15:18 (3)	16:18 (3)	17:18 (3)	18:18 (3+5)
Arr. Geneva (Corn.)	16:02	17:02	18:02	19:02	20:02

(1) Light refreshments. (2) "Panoramic Express". See details in text before this timetable on page 345. (3) "Superpanoramic". See details in text before this timetable on page 345. (4) Plus another departure from Montreux at 14:20 (2), arriving Spiez 16:57. (Easy connection with 17:01 departure from Spiez.) (5) Plus other departures from Bern at 18:38, 19:18 (3), 20:38, 21:18 (3) and 22:21 (3), arriving Geneva 20:35, 21:02, 22:02, 22:37, 23:02 and 00:09.

Geneva - Nyon - Geneva 250

See the magnificent views of **Lac Leman** (the Lake of Geneva) and the Alps, particularly of Mont Blanc, from **Nyon**, a medieval hilltop village on the shore of Lac Leman.

Dep. Geneva (Corn.)	Frequent times from 04:49 to 23:40
Arr. Nyon	14 minutes later

Sights in **Nyon**: Sailboating is popular here.

Dep. Nyon	Frequent times from 06:00 to 01:06
Arr. Geneva (Corn.)	14 minutes later

Interlaken - Mt. Pilatus - Interlaken

Great canyon and mountain scenery on this easy one-day narrow-gauge roundtrip. There are good views and several restaurants at the peak of Pilatus.

The Alpnachstad–Pilatus–Alpnachstad rack railway portion operates only May through November and is *not* covered by Eurailpass. The 1991 price of a one-class roundtrip ticket *without* a Swiss Pass was 49 Swiss francs. *With* a Swiss Pass: Sfr-36.75.

285 + Swiss 470

Dep. Interlaken (Ost)	08:44	09:35	10:44(1)	11:35	12:44(1)	13:35	14:44
Arr. Giswil	09:54	10:54	11:54	12:54	13:54	14:54	15:54

Change trains.

Dep. Giswil	10:06	11:06	12:06	13:06	14:06	15:06	16:06
Arr. Alpnachstad	10:30	11:30	12:30	13:30	14:30	15:30	16:30

Change to rack railway for the ride to the top of Mt. Pilatus. table 294

Dep. Alpnachstad	10:55	11:35	13:09	13:49	14:32	16:00	17:18(2)
Arr. Pilatus Kulm	11:25	12:05	13:39	14:19	15:02	16:30	17:48

               *   *   *

Dep. Pilatus Kulm	12:10	13:04	14:27	15:07	17:52 (2)
Arr. Alpnachstad	12:50	13:44	15:07	15:47	18:25

Change to a standard train.   285 + Swiss 470

Dep. Alpnachstad	13:29	14:29	15:29	16:29	18:29
Arr. Giswil	13:51	14:51	15:51	16:51	18:51

Change trains

Dep. Giswil	14:00(1)	15:00	16:00(3)	17:00	19:00
Arr. Interlaken (Ost)	15:16	16:25	17:16	18:25	20:25

(1) Restaurant car. (2) Operates July 1 to August 31. (3) Light refreshments.

Interlaken - Luzern - Interlaken

A very scenic 48-mile panorama of the Alps on this easy one-day excursion.
Schedules appear under "Interlaken-Luzern" on page 323.

Interlaken - Spiez - Bern - Spiez - Interlaken 280

Excellent canyon, lake and mountain scenery on this easy one-day roundtrip that includes visiting Lake Thun and a possible stopover in Bern. See earlier notes about Spiez and taking a boat on Lake Thun from Spiez to Thun village, under "Geneva–Brig–Bern–Geneva" on page 342.

Dep. Interlaken (Ost)	07:39	08:11	08:39	09:39	10:39	11:39 (1)
Dep. Interlaken (West)	5 minutes later					
Dep. Spiez	08:01	08:33	09:01	10:01	11:01	12:01
Dep. Thun	08:12	08:44	09:12	10:12	11:12	12:12
Arr. Bern	20 minutes later					

See notes about **Bern** on page 310

Dep. Bern	Frequent times from 06:56 to 22:28
Arr. Interlaken (West)	45–60 minutes later
Arr. Interlaken (Ost)	5 minutes after arriving West station

(1) Restaurant car.

Interlaken - Spiez - Brig - Spiez - Interlaken 280

Nice canyon, lake and mountain scenery on this easy one-day roundtrip which includes visiting Lake Thun and going through the 10-mile Lotschberg Tunnel.
The schedules below allow time to stopover in Spiez.

Most of the trains Spiez-Brig and v.v. have light refreshments.

Dep. Interlaken (Ost)	06:39	08:11	08:39	09:39	10:39	11:39
Dep. Interlaken (West)	5 minutes later					
Arr. Spiez	07:04	08:31	08:59	09:59	10:59	11:59
Change trains.						
Dep. Spiez	07:22	08:54	09:23	10:54	11:54	12:54 (1)
Arr. Brig	08:20	09:59	10:21	11:59	12:59	13:59

Sights in **Spiez**: See notes under "Geneva–Brig–Bern–Geneva" on page 342.

Sights in **Brig**: See notes under "Bern-Brig" on page 333.

Dep. Brig	Frequent times from 05:39 to 21:33
Arr. Spiez	minutes later
Change trains.	
Dep. Spiez	Frequent times from 07:29 to 23:01
Arr. Interlaken (West)	15 minutes later
Arr. Interlaken (Ost)	5 minutes after arriving West station

(1) Restaurant car.

Interlaken - Jungfraujoch - Interlaken 288

Great canyon and mountain scenery on this easy one-day roundtrip. This spectacular route ends at Europe's highest (11,333 feet) railstation. It includes 2 stops in the tunnel through Mount Eiger, for viewing through "windows" which the railroad's builders cut in the face of the cliff.

At **Jungfraujoch**, passengers alight to look down on the great Jungfrau glacier and stroll in the "Ice Palace" carved inside the glacier. Fabulous views can be seen from the revolving restaurant, which rotates completely every 50 minutes. For variety, we show how to go from Interlaken to Jungfraujoch *via Wengen*, and then return to Interlaken *via Grindelwald*.

Grindelwald sits at 3400-feet altitude. The majestic peaks that rise around this village are: **Jungfrau** (13,642 feet), **Eiger** (13,026), **Wetterhorn** (12,142), **Breithorn** (12,409), **Monch** (13,449), **Schreckhorn** (13,380), **Gspaltenhorn** (11,277) and **Tschingelhorn** (11,736).

This trip is *not* covered by Eurailpass. The 1991 price of a tickets *without* a Swiss Pass were: 140.40 Swiss francs for first-class, Sfr-132.60 for second-class.

With a Swiss Pass, both the Interlaken–Wengen and Grindelwald–Interlaken portions were free, and the one-class Wengen–Scheidegg,–Scheidegg-Jungfraujoch–Scheidegg and Scheidegg–Grindelwald portions were at 25% discount making the entire trip cost Sfr-86.40.

(Via Wengen)

Dep. Interlaken (Ost)	07:37	08:31	08:55	09:31	09:55	10:31	11:31 (1)
Arr. Scheidegg	08:55	09:45	10:10	10:55	11:20	11:45	12:55
Change trains.							
Dep. Scheidegg	09:02	10:02	10:28	11:02	11:28	12:02	13:02

Arr. Jungfraujoch	09:55	10:53	11:27	11:58	12:24	12:53	13:53
		*	*	*			
Dep. Jungfraujoch	10:30	11:00	12:30	13:00	14:00	14:30 (2)	
Arr. Scheidegg	11:22	11:47	13:21	13:47	14:47	15:22	
Change trains. **(via Grindelwald)**							
Dep. Scheidegg	11:32	12:32	13:32	14:02	15:02	15:32	
Arr. Interlaken (Ost)	13:26	14:26	15:26	16:00	17:00	17:26	

(1) Plus other departures from Interlaken at 12:31, 13:31 and 14:31, arriving back in Interlaken 18:00, 19:00 and 19:26. (3) Plus other departures from Jungfraujoch at 15:00, 15:30, 16:00, 17:00 and 18:00, arriving Interlaken 18:00, 18:26, 19:00, 19:26 and 20:21.

Lausanne - Brig - Lausanne 270

Enjoy the fine canyon, lake, mountain and river scenery on this easy one-day roundtrip.

Dep. Lausanne	Frequent times from 06:55 to 22:32
Arr. Brig	1½ –2 hours later

* * *

Dep. Brig	Frequent times from 05:28 to 21:42
Arr. Lausanne	1½ –2 hours later

Lausanne - Brig - Spiez - Bern - Lausanne

Marvelous canyon, lake, mountain and river scenery on this easy one-day roundtrip, a portion of the "Geneva–Lausanne–Spiez–Bern–Geneva" scenic trip listed on page 342 and to which you can refer for complete schedules and sightseeing details.

Locarno - Camedo - Locarno 272

One of the 5 most scenic rail trips in Europe. Fantastic canyon, river and mountain scenery. Hillside farms that are nearly vertical. The ride is called "Centovalli", and you *will* see a hundred valleys. This trip can be made either as an easy one-day roundtrip or as a portion of these routes: Milan–Locarno (page 234), Bern–Locarno (page 335), Brig–Locarno (page 339), Luzern–Locarno (page 351), and Locarno–Brig (page 350).

Please note that this trip does *not* start from the Locarno *railstation*. You catch what looks like a trolley car at the *central bus stop, across from the train station.*

At **Camedo,** a small hotel (Osteria Grutly) is only a 5-minute walk from the railstation. Walter Stern had lunch there in 1991 before taking a train back to Locarno. The granite slab roofs on the houses in this area are unique.

Dep. Locarno	07:30	08:53	10:05	11:01	13:13	15:10 (1)
Arr. Camedo	08:01	09:26	10:38	11:32	13:46	15:41
			*	*	*	
Dep. Camedo	10:06	11:18	12:14	14:18	16:22	17:38
Arr. Locarno	45 minutes later					

(1) Plus other departures from Locarno at 16:04 and 17:20 that allow a roundtrip, arriving back in Locarno 18:10 and 19:55.

Locarno - Domodossola - Brig - Domodossola - Locarno

Very good canyon, mountain and river scenery on this one-day roundtrip that includes the wonderful **Centovalli** ride described in the previous trip plus going through the 12-mile Simplon, longest main line rail tunnel in the world. Be sure to take your passport on this trip from Switzerland to Italy, Switzerland, back to Italy and then again to Switzerland.

The Domodossola–Brig (and v.v.) portion of this route takes you through Europe's longest (19.8km - 11.9 miles) tunnel, the Simplon. It is the world's second-longest tunnel, after Japan's Daishimizu Tunnel between Tokyo and Niigata (22.3km - 13.4 miles).

The 90-minute, 35-mile Locarno-Domodossola trip does *not* start from the Locarno *railstation*. You catch what looks like a trolley car at the central Locarno bus stop, *across from the train station*. Stops en route include **Intragna**, with its many churches; **Verdasio**, which has a train connection to the mountain town of **Rasa**; **Palagnedra**, which has a lake; **Camedo** (see notes on page 349); and **Druogno**, highest point on this scenic route.

272			270		
Dep. Locarno	08:53	10:05 (1)	Dep. Brig	12:38 (2)	14:38 (3)
Arr. Domo.	10:28	11:42	Arr. Domo.	13:07	15:07

Change trains. Walk from the underground Centovalli track, up to the main Domodossola station. *Hurry!*

Change trains. Walk outside the Domodossola station and go to the underground Centovalli track. *Hurry!*

270			272		
Dep. Domo.	10:44	11:58 (2)	Dep. Domo.	13:15 (4)	15:18 (4)
Arr. Brig	11:12	12:27	Arr. Locarno	14:50	16:55

(1) Light refreshments from 10:40 to 11:42. (2) Reservation required. Supplement charged. (3) Light Refreshments. (4) Light refreshments first hour of trip.

Luzern - Brunnen - Luzern 292

Here is an excellent one-day roundtrip boat ride on Lake Luzern, that is covered by Eurailpass.

All of these boats have a restaurant, unless designated otherwise.

Dep. Luzern (Stn. Quay)	09:05 (1)	09:30	10:20	11:15 (1+5)
Arr. Brunnen	10:54	11:45	12:30	12:50

* * *

Dep. Brunnen	12:46 (1)	13:42	14:45 (2)	15:56 (1+6)
Arr. Luzern (Stn. Quay)	14:54	16:20	16:50	18:35

(1) Paddle steamer. Runs daily. (2) Runs daily. Paddle steamer on Sunday. (3) Runs daily all year. July and August: paddle steamer daily. September to June: paddle steamer only on Sunday. (4) Light refreshments. (5) Plus other departures from Luzern at 11:25 (1), 13:15 (3), 14:15 (4) and 15:20 (4).   (6) Plus other departures from Brunnen at 17:26 (3) and 18:50 (4).

Luzern - Interlaken - Luzern

Great canyon and mountain scenery on this easy one-day roundtrip. Complete schedules are listed under "Luzern-Interlaken-Luzern" on page 325.

Luzern - Interlaken - Brig - Domodossola - Locarno - Luzern

This circle route includes going through the 9-mile Lotschberg Tunnel, the 12-mile Simplon and the 9-mile St. Gotthard, as well as seeing the beautiful Centovalli scenery between Domodossola and Locarno.

285			272		
Dep. Luzern	07:24 (1)		Dep. Domodossola	13:15	
Arr. Interlaken (Ost)	09:16		Arr. Locarno	14:50	
Change trains. 280			Change trains		
Dep. Interlaken (Ost)	09:39		290		
Arr. Spiez	09:59		Dep. Locarno	15:03 (3)	
Change trains.			Arr. Bellinzona	15:20	
Dep. Spiez	10:54 (2)		Change trains.		
Arr. Brig	11:59		Dep. Bellinzona	15:22 (4)	
Change trains. 270			Arr. Luzern	17:39	
Dep. Brig	12:38 (1)				
Arr. Domodossola	13:07				

(1) Restaurant car. (2) Light refreshments. (3) Plus other departures from Locarno at 15:34 (2), 17:03 (1) and 17:34 (2), arriving Luzern 18:46, 19:39 and 20:46. (4) Supplement charged. Restaurant car.

Luzern - Interlaken - Jungfraujoch - Interlaken - Luzern

There is marvelous canyon, lake and mountain scenery on this easy one-day roundtrip. See details about Jungfraujoch under "Interlaken-Jungfraujoch" on page 348.

For variety, we suggest you go from Interlaken to Jungfraujoch via Wengen, and then return to Interlaken via Grindelwald. The Interlaken–Jungfraujoch portion is not covered by Eurailpass. The 1991 prices of tickets *without* a Swiss Pass were 140.40 Swiss francs for first-class, Sfr-132.60 for second-class. *With* a Swiss Pass, both the Interlaken–Wengen and Grindelwald–Interlaken portions were free, and the one-class Wengen–Scheidegg, Scheidegg–Jungfraujoch–Scheidegg and Scheidegg–Grindelwald portions were at 25% discount making the entire trip cost Sfr-86.40.

For the best views, sit on the right-hand side Luzern–Meiringen, on the left side Meringen–Interlaken. For the return ride, sit on the right Interlaken–Meiringen and on the left Meiringen–Luzern.

285		288		
Dep. Luzern	08:24	Dep. Jungfraujoch	13:00	14:00
Arr. Meiringen	09:41	Arr. Scheidegg	13:47	14:47
Arr. Interlaken (Ost)	10:25	Change trains 288		
Change trains. 288		Dep. Scheidegg		
Dep. Interlaken (Ost)		(via Grindelwald)	14:02	15:02
(via Wengen)	10:31	Arr. Interlaken (Ost)	16:00	17:00
Arr. Scheidegg	11:45	Change trains. 285		
Change trains. 288		Dep. Interlake (Ost)	16:44 (1)	17:35
Dep. Scheidegg	12:02	Arr. Meiringen	17:12	18:13
Arr. Jungfraujoch	12:53	Arr. Luzern	18:36	19:36

(1) Restaurant car.

352

Luzern - Interlaken - Spiez - Brig - Andermatt - Goschenen - Luzern

Here is a marvelous one-day circle trip, crammed with outstanding scenery. Although this schedule allows only 50 minutes in Spiez, if you take a packed lunch from Luzern there are benches outside the Spiez railstation where you can sit while eating and have a fabulous view of the village, Lake Thun and the mountains reflected on its surface.

From Spiez to Brig, there is a good view of the Matterhorn from the right side of the train. Walk to the front of the Brig railstation to board the train to Andermatt.

En route from Brig to Andermatt, you see the beautiful Rhone Valley and go through the 8-mile long Furka Tunnel. The Brig–Andermatt–Goschenen portion of this trip is *not* covered by Eurailpass. The 1991 ticket prices for an ordinary train (not for "Glacier Express", which charges a supplement) *without* a Swiss Pass were 147 Swiss francs for first-class, Sfr-91 for second-class. *With* a Swiss Pass: Free.

285		
Dep. Luzern	08:24	09:24 (1)
Arr. Interlaken (Ost)	10:25	11:16
Change trains. 280		
Dep. Interlaken (Ost)	10:39	11:39
Arr. Spiez	10:59	11:59
Change trains. 280		
Dep. Spiez	11:54 (1)	12:54 (2)
Arr. Brig	12:59	13:59
Change trains.		

320		
Dep. Brig	13:45 (3)	14:18 (5)
Arr. Andermatt	15:24	– 0 –
Change trains. 286		
Dep. Andermatt	15:50	– 0 –
Arr. Goschenen	16:05	16:42
Change trains. 290		
Dep. Goschenen	16:14 (4)	17:14 (1)
Arr. Luzern	17:39	18:46

(1) Light refreshments. (2) Restaurant car. (3) "Glacier Express". See details about reservations and prices under "St. Moritz - Zermatt" on page 355. (4) Change trains in Arth Goldau at 17:08. Depart Arth Goldau 17:14. (5) Direct train to Goschenen. No train change in Andermatt...plus other Brig departures at 15:18 (5) and 16:18 (5), arriving Luzern 19:39 and 20:46.

Luzern - Mt. Pilatus - Luzern 292 + 294

See the fine canyon and mountain scenery on this easy one-day roundtrip. The Alpnachstad–Pilatus–Alpnachstad rack railway portion operates only from May to the end of November and is *not* covered by Eurailpass. The 1991 price for a one-class roundtrip ticket *without* a Swiss Pass was 49 Swiss francs. *With* a Swiss Pass: Sfr-36.75. There are good views and several restaurants at the peak of Pilatus.

Dep. Luzern	08:09	09:09	10:09	11:09	12:09	13:09	14:09 (1)
Arr. Alpnachstad	08:27	09:27	10:27	11:27	12:27	13:27	14:27

Change to rack railway for the ride to the top of Mt. Pilatus.

Dep. Alpnachstad	08:50	09:32	10:55	11:35	13:09	13:49	14:32
Arr. Pilatus Kulm	09:20	10:02	11:25	12:05	13:39	14:19	15:02

* * *

Dep. Pilatus Kulm	09:27	10:05	11:30	12:10	13:04	14:27	15:07 (2)
Arr. Alpnachstad	10:07	10:45	12:10	12:50	13:44	15:07	15:45

Change to standard trains.

Dep. Alpnachstad	10:32	11:32	12:32	13:32	14:32	15:32	16:32
Arr. Luzern	18 minutes later						

(1) Plus another departure from Luzern at 15:10, arriving Pilatus Kulm 16:30. (2) Plus another departure from Pilatus Kulm at 16:35, arriving Luzern 17:32.

This is the way to travel *both* sides of Pilatus: take the electric bus that goes from the Luzern railstation to **Kriens**, get off at the stop *before* Kriens (marked by a sign that has a drawing of a cable car), go up that side of Pilatus by gondola and tramway. Return to Luzern by the cogwheel from Pilatus to Alpnachstad. This 2-way route can also be done in reverse.

Luzern - Engelberg - Mt. Titlis - Luzern 293

There is very good canyon and mountain scenery on this easy one-day roundtrip. The Engelberg–Titlis–Engelberg rack railway is *not* covered by Eurailpass and does not operate late October to early December. The 1991 price of a one-class roundtrip ticket *without* a Swiss Pass was 56 Swiss francs. *With* a Swiss Pass: Sfr-42.

Engelberg is a popular ski resort. It also has more than 20 miles of level walking and hiking paths, toboggan runs, a gambling casino and indoor swimming pools.

There are great views from the restaurant on the top of **Mt. Titlis**. See the 11th century illuminated manuscripts in the Benedictine monastery.

Dep. Luzern	07:24	08:14	09:14	10:14	11:14	12:14 (1)
Arr. Engelberg	08:23	09:13	10:13	11:13	12:13	13:13

Change to the funicular.

Dep. Engelberg	Frequent times
Arr. Mt. Titlis	60 minutes later

* * *

Dep. Mt. Titlis	Frequent times
Arr. Engelberg	60 minutes later

Change to the train.

Dep. Engelberg	10:44	11:44	12:44	13:44	14:44	15:44	16:44 (2)
Arr. Luzern	60-65 minutes later

(1) Plus other departures from Luzern at frequent times from 13:14 to 19:23 for return to Luzern *from Engelberg.* (2) Plus other departures from Engelberg at 17:44, 18:44, 19:48 and 20:48.

Luzern - Engelberg - Mt. Titlis - Luzern - Mt. Pilatus - Luzern

From May through October, *all 3* mountains can be ascended in one day by following this schedule.

293		294	
Dep. Luzern	07:24	Dep. Luzern	13:09 (3)
Arr. Engelberg	08:23	Arr. Alpnachstad	13:29
Change to the funicular.		Change to the rack railway. 294	
Dep. Engelberg	08:30 (1)	Dep. Alpnachstad	13:49
Arr. Mt. Titlis	09:30 (1)	Arr. Pilatus Kulm	14:19
* * *		* * *	
Dep. Mt. Titlis	10:00 (1)	Dep. Pilatus Kulm	14:27 (5)
Arr. Engelberg	11:00 (1)	Arr. Alpnachstad	15:07
Change to the train. 293		Change to the train. 294	
Dep. Engelberg	11:44 (2)	Dep. Alpnachstad	15:20
Arr. Luzern	12:45	Arr. Luzern	15:40

(Footnotes appear on page 354.)

Neither the Engelberg-Titlis nor Alpnachstad-Pilatus one-class roundtrips are covered by Eurailpass. The 1991 ticket prices for them without a Swiss Pass totaled 105 Swiss francs. With a Swiss Pass: Sfr-78.75.

(1) Estimated. Cook Timetables does not publish Engelberg-Titlis schedules. (2) Plus other Engelberg departures at frequent times (see "Luzern–Engelberg" timetable on page 353.). (3) Plus another Luzern departure at 14:09, arriving Pilatus 15:02. (4) Operates July and August. (5) Plus other Pilatus departures at 15:07, 17:52 (4), and 21:45 (4), arriving Luzern 16:50, 17:50 and 22:50.

Luzern - Mt. Rigi (via Arth Goldau) - Luzern

The excellent canyon and mountain scenery on this route (unlike the route via Vitznau that follows) is entirely by train. This is an easy one-day roundtrip. The rides between Arth Goldau and Rigi are *not* covered by Eurailpass. The 1991 price for a one-class roundtrip ticket *without* a Swiss Pass was 44 Swiss francs. *With* a Swiss Pass: Sfr-33.

290

Dep. Luzern	10:14	11:19	12:14	13:19	14:14	15:19 (1)
Arr. Arth Goldau	10:40	11:44	12:40	13:44	14:40	15:44

Change to rack railway. 296

Dep. Arth Goldau	11:03	12:03	13:03	14:03	15:03	16:03
Arr. Rigi Kulm	11:38	12:38	13:38	14:38	15:38	16:38

* * *

Dep Rigi Kulm	12:10	13:10	14:10	15:10	16:10	17:10 (2)
Arr Arth Goldau	12:54	13:54	14:54	15:54	16:54	17:54

Change to standard train. 290

Dep. Arth Goldau	13:14	14:20	15:14	16:20	17:14	18:20
Arr. Luzern	30 minutes later				

(1) Plus another Luzern departure at 16:14, arriving Rigi Kulm 17:38. (4) Plus other Rigi Kulm departures at 18:10 and 19:10, arriving Luzern 19:39and 20:46.

Luzern - Mt. Rigi (via Vitznau) - Luzern

There is very nice canyon, lake and mountain scenery on this easy one-day roundtrip that includes a boat ride (*covered by Eurailpass*) on Lake Luzern. From Vitznau to Mt. Rigi, the train climbs 4,000 feet in 4¼ miles. Over 450,000 passengers take this ride every year. There is good skiing at **Rigi** in the Winter. This line was constructed in 1871.

The Vitznau–Rigi ride is *not* covered by Eurailpass. The 1991 price of the (one-class) roundtrip ticket for the Vitznau–Rigi portion *without* a Swiss Pass was 44 Swiss francs. *With* a Swiss Pass: Sfr-33. *All of the boats have a restaurant or light refreshments.*

292 Boat

Dep. Luzern (Stn. Qy.)	09:05 (1)	09:30	10:20	11:25 (1)	12:00	13:15 (2+4)
Arr. Vitznau (Pier)	10:00	10:27	11:36	12:30	12:51	14:15

Change to rack railway adjacent to the quay. 296

Dep. Vitznau	10:10	10:45	11:45	12:40	13:30	14:20
Arr. Rigi Kulm	10:40	11:15	12:15	13:10	14:00	14:50

* * *

Dep. Rigi Kulm	10:45	11:40	12:40	14:15	15:00	16:05 (5)
Arr. Vitznau	11:25	12:20	13:10	14:55	15:40	16:45

Change to boat adjacent to the railstation. 292

Dep. Vitznau (Pier)	11:33	12:52	13:47(1)	15:10	15:48 (2)	17:01
Arr. Luzern (Stn. Qy.)	55–70 minutes later					

(1) Runs daily. Paddle steamer. (2) Runs daily. Paddle steamer only on Sundays. (3) July and August: Runs daily. September to June : Runs Sundays only. (4) Plus other departures from Luzern at 14:15 and 16:15 (3), arriving Rigi Kulm 15:45 and 17:30. (5) Plus another departure from Rigi Kulm at 17:45, arriving Luzern 20:46.

St. Moritz - Tirano - St. Moritz 333

Great mountain scenery on this easy one-day narrow-gauge roundtrip into Italy. (Take your passport !) It is absolutely breathtaking. The track goes through the Bernina Pass, making this Europe's highest main rail line, reaching 7,400 feet at **Bernina Hospiz**. Buy a lunch in St. Moritz to eat on the train.

Dep. St. Moritz	07:45	09:05	10:00	11:05	12:00 (1)	15:00 (1)
Arr. Tirano	10:22	11:28	12:24	13:30	14:28	17:28
			* * *			
Dep. Tirano	10:30	11:30	13:05	14:05	15:30	17:30
Arr. St. Moritz	12:56	13:56	15:56	16:27	17:56	19:56

(1) In good weather, carries an open sightseeing car in July and August.

St. Moritz - Zermatt and Zermat - St. Moritz STO timetable

Many ordinary trains which do not require reservation, are *not* packed, and have seats that are as comfortable as those of "Glacier Express" run every day. Their only disadvantage is that they require changing trains 4 times: in Chur, Disentis, Andermatt and Brig.

All of the schedules below are for the direct-ride, luxury, "Glacier Express", *for which a reservation is required.* During the summer, seats in its elegant 34-seat restaurant car are usually reserved several months in advance. Reservations both for assigned seats and also for lunch in the elegant 34-seat paneled restaurant car can be made as much as 2 months in advance of travel date through a travel agency or the Swiss Tourist offices (addresses on page 25). Passengers may also have food served at their seats from a mini-bar that is rolled down the aisle.

Sit on the left side for the best views. There is marvelous gorge, mountain and Rhone Valley scenery on this ride, which crosses 291 bridges (including Europe's highest ones) and goes through 91 tunnels, including the 9-mile-long Furka, as the train traverses the 6,700-foot Oberalp Pass.

This "Albula Line" is one of the world's greatest feats of railroad engineering. Its **Landwasser Viaduct** towers over a rampaging Alpine stream. Some of its tunnels are spirals inside the mountains, tunnels that you exit traveling in the same direction as you entered them, but at either a higher or lower level.

Whithout either a Eurailpass or a Swiss pass, in 1991 first-class cost $127 (U.S.) for one-way, $206 roundtrip. Second-class was $81 and $132.

With a Eurailpass, one-way was $44 or $29, roundtrip was $53 or $33. With a Swiss pass, the trip was *free*.

Dep. St. Moritz	– 0 –		08:30 (1)	09:05 (3)	10:00 (4)
Dep. Chur	09:02 (1+2)		10:55 (2)	10:53 (2)	12:16
Dep. Disentis	10:21		12:12	12:15	13:41
Dep. Andermatt	11:30		13:25	13:30	14:45
Dep. Brig	13:23		15:23	15:23	16:23
Arr. Zermatt	14:45		16:45	16:45	17:45

(Timetable continues on page 356.)

*   *   *

Dep. Zermatt	08:54 (1)	10:10 (1)	10:10 (3)	12:10 (1)
Dep. Brig	10:30	11:45	11:48	13:45
Dep. Andermatt	12:00	13:30 (2)	13:40 (2)	15:32 (6)
Dep. Disentis	13:10 (5)	15:05	14:55	16:45
Arr. Chur	14:18	16:13	16:02	17:55
Arr. St. Moritz	16:58	17:58	17:48	19:46 (7)

(1) Operates early June to late October. (2) Restaurant car Chur-Andermatt and v.v.. (3) Operates late October to early June. (4) Operates early June to late October. Restaurant car St. Moritz-Disentis. (5) Restaurant car Disentis-Chur. (6) Restaurant car Andermatt-Davos Platz. (7) Arrival in Davos Platz.

Sights in **Zermatt**: Access to the Matterhorn. Great skiing in woods, pastures and hills. Displays of the challenges that mountaineers face are exhibited at the Alpine Museum. There are many hiking trails here, so easy that neither special shoes nor gear is necessary. Although each trail climbs about 2,000 feet, they are effortless because the incline is spread over many miles. Because autos have to park several miles away, the air here is pristine.

Sights in **Disentis**: The stained glass in the Cathedral.

Zermatt - Gornergrat - Zermatt 281

This is a great cogwheel train ride to the 10,200-foot high Gornergrat for a close view of the Matterhorn (14,692 feet) and more than 50 other Alpine peaks.

This ride is *not* covered by Eurailpass. The 1991 price of a one-class rountrip ticket *without* a Swiss Pass was 50 Swiss francs. *With* a Swiss Pass: Sfr-37.50.

| Dep. Zermatt | Frequent times from 07:05 to 18:00 |
| Arr. Gornergrat | 45 minutes later |

*   *   *

| Dep. Gornergrat | Frequent times from 07:55 to 19:07 |
| Arr. Zermatt | 45 minutes later |

Zurich - Sargans - Vaduz - Zurich The Trip To Liechtenstein

There is fine scenery along the shores of **Lake Zurich** and **Lake Walen** on this easy one-day roundtrip.

It is only a 30-minute *bus ride* from Sargans to **Vaduz**, in the tiny country of Liechtenstein. Buses leave Sargans' railstation every 20 minutes for the 27-minute ride to Vaduz.

All of the trains Zurch–Sargans and v.v. have light refreshments.

310

Dep. Zurich	07:10	08:10	09:10	10:10	11:10	12:10
Arr. Sargans	08:21	09:13	10:19	11:13	12:19	13:13
Change to bus. 323						
Dep. Sargans	08:33	09:33	10:33	11:28	12:33	13:53
Arr. Vaduz	09:00	10:00	11:00	12:00	13:00	14:20

357

			*	*	*		
Dep. Vaduz	13:05	14:05	15:05	16:05	17:05	18:05 (1)
Arr. Sargans	13:34	14:34	15:34	16:34	17:34	18:34

Change to train. 268

Dep. Sargans	13:39	14:45	15:39	16:45	17:39	18:45
Arr. Zurich	14:50	15:50	16:50	17:50	18:50	19:50

(1) Plus other departures from Vaduz at 19:00, 20:00, 21:00 and 22:00, arriving Sargans 20:41, 21:50, 22:50 and 23:50.

Sights in **Vaduz**: Capital of the principality of Liechtenstein, a country that is 16 miles long by 4 miles wide, nestled between Switzerland and Austria. The extensive network of walking paths is very popular. Many excellent restaurants here.

See the collection of paintings by Rubens and other old masters at the National Art Gallery, open daily (April–October: 10:00–12:00 and 13:30–17:30. November–March: 10:00–12:00 and 14:00–17:30.) The exhibits of prehistoric and Roman articles: ancient weapons, coins, wood carvings, folk art and handicrafts, items from the area's medieval castles and other historical artifacts in the National Museum, open May-September daily 10:00–12:00 and 13:30–17:30. October-April: daily except Monday, 14:00–17:30.

The Postage Stamp Museum is open daily all year 10:00–12:00 and 14:00–18:00.

Zurich - Chur - Arosa - Chur - Zurich

See the good canyon, lake and mountain scenery on this easy one-day roundtrip. There is time for a stopover in Chur, as shown by the schedules below.

The Chur–Arosa–Chur roundtrip is *not* covered by Eurailpass. The 1991 prices for tickets *without* a Swiss Pass were: 30.80 Swiss francs for first-class, Sfr-19.20 for second-class. *With* a Swiss Pass: Free.

Most of the Zurich-Chur and Chur-Zurich trains have a restaurant car or light refreshments.

310

Dep. Zurich	07:33	08:10	09:10	10:10	11:10	12:10	13:10
Arr. Chur	08:51	09:37	10:45	11:37	12:45	13:37	14:45

Change trains. 324

Dep. Chur	09:00	09:55	10:55	11:55	12:55	13:55	14:55
Arr. Arosa	60 minutes later						

			*	*	*		
Dep. Arosa	10:05	11:05	12:05	13:05	14:05	15:05	16:05
Arr. Chur	11:07	12:07	13:07	14:07	15:07	16:07	17:07

Change trains. 310

Dep. Chur	11:15	12:23	13:15	14:23	15:15	16:23	17:15 (1)
Arr. Zurich	12:50	13:50	14:50	15:50	16:50	17:50	18:50

(1) Plus other departures from Chur at 18:23, 19:15, 20:13 and 21:13, arriving Zurich 19:50, 20:50, 21:50 and 23:50.

Zurich - Chur - Zermatt - Gornergrat - Zermatt

There is fabulous Rhone Valley scenery on this ride plus crossing Oberalp Pass (6,700 feet) and going through the 8-mile long Furka Tunnel on the Chur–Brig portion.

This trip includes going over the highest bridges in Europe and, by departing Zurich at 07:10 or 09:10, you can include the outstanding cogwheel train ride to Gornergrat (10,200 feet) for a close view of the Matterhorn (14,692 feet) and more than 50 other Alpine peaks.

The Chur–Zermatt, Zermatt–Gornergrat and Gornergrat–Zermatt portions of this trip are *not* covered by Eurailpass.

The 1991 prices of tickets for those rides *without* a Swiss Pass were: 197 Swiss francs for first-class, Sfr-141 for second-class. *With* a Swiss Pass, the Chur–Zermatt portion was free, and the Zermatt–Gornergrat–Zermatt roundtrip was at 25% discount, making the entire trip Sfr-37.50.

All of the Chur–Zermatt trains in this timetable are "Glacier Express", for which reservation is required. *For services, prices and reservations, see "St. Moritz–Zermatt" on page 355.*

Do not let this timetable discourage you. This trip is easier to make than it was for us to prepare the table !

310			Swiss timetable		
Dep. Zurich	07:10 (1)	09:10 (1)	Dep. Zermatt	14:48	17:12
Arr. Chur	08:47	10:45	Arr. Gornergrat	15:31	17:55
Change trains.	320			* * *	
Dep. Chur	09:03 (2)	10:55 (2)	Dep. Gornergrat	15:55	16:19 (3)
Arr. Zermatt	14:45	16:45	Arr. Zermatt	16:40	16:59
Change trains.					

(1) Light refreshments. (2) "Glacier Express". See details about reservations and prices under "St. Moritz – Zermatt" on page 355. (3) Plus other departures from Gornergrat at 16:43, 17:07, 17:55 and 19:07.

Sights in **Chur**: See notes about Chur on page 328.
Sights in **Disentis**: See notes about Disentis on page 356.
Sights in **Brig**: See notes about Brig on page 333.
Sights in **Zermatt**: See notes about Zermatt on page 356.

Zurich - Davos - Filisur - Thusis - Zurich

In order to make a scenic *circle-trip* that avoids repeating the Landquart-Filisur route in the Zurich-Davos roundtrip shown on page 328, return to Zurich from Filisur via Thusis.

The Davos-Filisur portion of this trip is *not* covered by Eurailpass. The 1991 prices *without* a Swiss pass were: 12.20 Swiss francs for first-class, Sfr-7.60 for second-class. *With* a Swiss Pass: Free.

310					
Dep. Zurich	07:23 (1)	08:10	09:10 (2)	10:10 (2)	11:10 (2+5)
Arr. Landquart	08:39	09:25	10:33	11:25	12:33
Change trains.	327				
Dep. Landquart	08:56	09:40	10:47	11:40	12:47
Dep. Klosters	09:52	10:20	11:43	12:20	13:43
Arr. Davos	10:24	10:46 (3)	12:13 (3)	12:46 (3)	14:13 (3)
Arr. Filisur	10:51	11:51	12:51	13:51	14:51

Change trains. 330

Dep. Filisur	– 0 –	12:02 (1)	13:02 (2)	14:02 (2)	15:02 (4)
Dep Thusis	– 0 –	12:37	13:37	14:37	15:37
Arr. Chur	– 0 –	13:06	14:06	15:06	16:06

Change trains. 310

| Dep. Chur | – 0 – | 13:15 (2) | 14:23 (2) | 15:15 (2) | 16:23 (2) |
| Arr. Zurich | – 0 – | 14:50 | 15:50 | 16:50 | 17:50 |

(1) Restaurant car. (2) Light refreshments daily. (3) Change trains. (4) Runs daily. Light refreshments only on Saturdays, Sundays and holidays. (5) Plus other departures from Zurich at 12:10 (2) and 13:10 (4), arriving back in Zurich 18:50 and 19:50 .

Sights in **Davos**: See notes under " Zurich-Landquart-Davos" on page 328.

Sights in **Filisur**: See notes under "Chur-Filisur" on page 318.

Zurich - Landquart - Davos - Landquart - Zurich

Excellent canyon, lake and mountain scenery may be viewed on this easy one-day roundtrip. See page 328 for timetable.

Zurich - Bellinzona - Lugano 290

The Zurich – Lugano portion of the Zurich-Milan route (one of the 5 most scenic rail trips in Europe) can be seen on a one-day roundtrip from Zurich. (The "Zurich–Milan" timetable appears on page 365.) A feast of beautiful farms, lakes, mountains, rivers and vineyards. You go through the 9.3-mile long Gotthard Tunnel.

Before the Gotthard was opened to traffic in 1882, there was no direct rail route from eastern Switzerland through the Alps to Italy. For 7 years and 5 months, 2500 men worked in 3% shifts day and night to build this engineering marvel. Immediately after exiting the third of a series of 9 tunnels, the train passes the small, white **Wassen** Church to your right, and about 230 feet above the track. The next time the church comes into view, after leaving Wassen Station, it is also to your right, and nearly level with the track. Later, after exiting tunnel #7, you have a third view of the church, this time to your left and 170 feet above the track.

The turns inside 3 semi-circular tunnels in this area (Pfaffensprung, Wattinger and Leggistein) are engineered so well that there is no sensation of the curves that the train is making inside those tunnels.

Try this interesting experiment: make a pendulum of any object, holding the top of a weighted string, chain or handkerchief against the inner face of a train window (a left-hand window when inside Pfaffensprung and Wattinger, a right-hand window when inside Leggistein). As the train goes around a curve, the weighted bottom will move away from the window.

Climate on the Swiss side of the tunnel is usually much cooler than the Mediterranean temperature on the Italian end. There is a beautiful descent from the Italian end of the tunnel down the Ticino Valley. The train makes 3% gradients at 45–50 miles per hour.

At Bellinzona, the line forks. One branch goes to Locarno, the other to Lugano and Milan.

Dep. Zurich	07:03 (1)	08:03 (1)	09:03 (2)	10:03 (1)	11:03 (2)
Arr. Bellinzona	09:33	10:33	11:52	12:33	13:51
Arr. Lugano	10:03	11:03	12:21	13:03	14:21

Sights in **Bellinzona**: The view of the Ticino Valley from Montebello Castle. The museum in the Sasso Castle. The church of St. Peter and Stephen. Castello Grande. The Saturday morning market.

(Timetable continues on page 360.)

Sights in **Lugano**: See notes under "Milan–Lugano" on page 236.

Dep. Lugano	10:41 (2)	11:57 (2)	12:41 (2)	13:57 (2)	14:41 (2+4)
Dep. Bellinzona	11:08	12:27	13:08	14:27	15:08
Arr. Zurich	13:57	14:57	15:57	16:57	17:57

(1) Restaurant car. (2) Light refreshments. (3) Reservation required. Restaurant car. (4) Plus other departures from Lugano at 16:41 (2), 17:57 (1), 18:42 (1), 19:41 and 20:31 (3), arriving Zurich 19:57, 20:57, 21:50, 23:03 and 23:36.

Zurich - Mt. Rigi - Zurich

The Arth Goldau-Mt. Rigi-Arth Goldau roundtrip portion of this trip is *not* covered by Eurailpass. The 1991 price of a one-class roundtrip ticket *without* a Swiss Pass was 44 Swiss francs. *With* a Swiss Pass: Sfr-33.

290

Dep. Zurich	08:03 (1)	09:03 (2)	10:03 (1)	11:03 (2)	12:03 (2+3)
Arr. Arth Goldau	08:45	09:45	10:45	11:45	12:45

Change to rack railway.

296

Dep. Arth Goldau	09:03	10:03	11:03	12:03	13:03
Arr. Rigi Kulm	09:38	10:38	11:38	12:38	13:38

                           *   *   *

296

Dep. Rigi Kulm	10:10	11:10	12:10	14:10	15:10 (4)
Arr. Arth Goldau	10:54	11:54	12:54	14:54	15:54

Change from rack railway to a standard train

290

Dep. Arth Goldau	11:15	12:15 (1)	13:15 (2)	15:15 (2)	16:15 (2)
Arr. Zurich	11:57	12:57	13:57	15:57	16:57

(1) Restaurant car. (2) Light refreshments. (3) Plus other departures from Zurich at 13:03 (2), 14:03 (2) and 15:03 (2) that arrive back in Zurich at 17:57, 18:31 and 18:57. (4) Plus other Rigi Kulm departures at 15:40, 16:40, 17:10, 18:10 and 19:10, arriving Zurich 17:57, 18:31, 18:57, 19:57 and 20:57. All of these journeys have restaurant car or light refreshments on Arth Godau-Zurich.

Zurich - Luzern - Mt. Pilatus - Luzern - Zurich

There is fine canyon and mountain scenery on this easy one-day roundtrip.

The Alpnachstad–Pilatus–Alpnachstad rack railway portion operates *only from May to the end of November* and is *not* covered by Eurailpass. The 1991 price of a one-class roundtrip ticket *without* a Swiss Pass was: 49 Swiss francs. *With* a Swiss Pass: Sfr-36.75.

There are good views and several restaurants at the top of Pilatus.

315

Dep. Zurich	07:07	08:07	09:07	10:07	11:07	12:07 (3)
Arr. Luzern	07:56	08:56	09:56	10:56	11:56	12:56

Change trains. Table 292

Dep. Luzern	08:09	09:09	10:09	11:09	12:09	13:09
Arr. Alpnachstad	08:29	09:29	10:29	11:29	12:29	13:29

Change to rack railway. Table 294

Dep. Alpnachstad	08:50	09:32	10:55	11:35	13:09	13:49
Arr. Pilatus Kulm	09:20	10:02	11:25	12:05	13:39	14:19

* * *

Dep. Pilatus Kulm	09:27	10:05	11:30	12:10	14:27	15:07 (4)
Arr. Alpnachstad	10:07	10:45	12:10	12:50	15:07	15:47

Change to standard train. Table 292

Dep. Alpnachstad	10:30	11:30	12:30	13:30	15:30	16:30
Arr. Luzern	10:50	11:50	12:50	13:50	15:50	15:50

Change trains. Table 315

Dep. Luzern	Frequent times from 05:30 to 23:08
Arr. Zurich	50 minutes later

(1) Operates late May to late September. (2) Operates July and August. (3) Plus other departures from Zurich (footnotes pertain to Alpnachstad-Pilatus portion) at 13:07, 14:07, 15:07 (1) and 17:05 (2), arriving Pilatus Kulm 15:02, 16:30, 17:10 and 19:35. (4) Plus other Alpnachstad departures at 16:35, 17:52 (2) and 21:45 (2), arriving Zurich 18:53,19:53 and 23:57.

Zurich - Romanshorn - St. Gallen (St. Gall) - Zurich

There is excellent lake and mountain scenery on this easy one-day circle roundtrip that visits **Lake Konstanz**.

Sights in **St. Gallen:** The history of lacemaking and embroidery from the 16th century to the present, and lacework worn by European nobility, at the Gewerbemuseum (Embroidery Museum). The paintings in the Historisches Museum. The 100,000 volumes (including illuminated manuscripts), more than 1,000 years old, in the rebuilt rococo library of the ancient abbey. The twin-towered baroque 18th century Cathedral. Near it, many old houses decorated with frescoes and oriel windows, in the city's old quarter.

300

Dep. Zurich	08:10	09:10 (1)	10:10 (1)	11:10 (2)	12:10 (1+3)
Arr. Romanshorn	09:21	10:21	11:21	12:21	13:21

Take time for a boat ride on Lake Konstanz. Table 311

Dep. Romanshorn	10:08	– 0 –	12:08 (2)	– 0 –	13:32 (2)
Arr. St. Gallen	10:35	– 0 –	12:35	– 0 –	13:57

Change trains. Table 300

Dep. St. Gallen	10:41 (1)	– 0 –	12:41 (1)	– 0 –	14:41 (1)
Arr. Zurich	11:53	– 0 –	13:53	– 0 –	15:53

(1) Restaurant car. (2) Light refreshments. (3) Plus other departures from Zurich at 13:10 (1), 14:10 and 15:10 (1)....with only 2 departures from Romanshorn, at 16:08 (2) and 18:08 (2), arriving back in Zurich 17:53 and 19:53.

Romanshorn - Friedrichshafen 313

This is the ferry service between Romanshorn and Friedrichshafen (50% discount with Eurailpass). *All of these boats have a restaurant.*

| Dep. Romanshorn | 09:36 | 10:36 | 11:36 | 12:36 | 13:36 | 14:36 (1) |
| Arr. Friedrichshafen | 40-45 minutes later | | | | | |

*   *   *

| Dep. Friedrichshafen | 10:43 | 11:43 | 12:43 | 13:43 | 14:43 | 15:43 (2) |
| Arr. Romanshorn | 40-45 minutes later | | | | | |

(1) Plus other departures from Romanshorn at 15:36, 16:36, 17:36, 18:36 and 19:36. (2) Plus other departures from Friedrichshafen at 16:43, 17:43, 18:43 and 19:43.

Zurich - Schaffhausen - Zurich 302

A trip to see the marvelous **Rhine Falls**.

| Dep. Zurich | Frequent times from 06:32 to 23:36 |
| Arr. Schaffhausen | 38 minutes later |

Sights in **Schaffhausen**: Tumultuous waterfalls. The gold and silver room in the Allerheiligen Museum. The Thursday market. Many restored medieval buildings.

Take the uphill path, through vineyards, a 15-minute walk to the hilltop castle, for the view from there. Ride the cable car to the summit of 8,215-foot-high **Mt. Santis** for a spectacular view of many Alpine peaks, including Germany's Zugspitze.

Take the 90 minute river boat to **Stein am Rhein** to see the 11th century Hohenklingen Castle, the museum at the 11th century St. George Monastery, the ruins of Tasgetium (a Roman fort), and the stained glass, wood walls and medieval firearms on the top floor of the 16th century Town Hall.

| Dep. Schaffhausen | Frequent times from 06:06 to 23:23 |
| Arr. Zurich | 38 minutes later |

A GLORIOUS WEEK IN SWITZERLAND

Here is a great 7-day circle itinerary of Switzerland that gives you, in the span of one week, a visit to most of the country's major cities plus a view of much of Switzerland's great scenery. (The rides to Jungfraujoch and Mt. Rigi are *not* covered by Eurailpass.)

Day 1 Geneva, Montreux, Zweisimmen, Spiez (Lunch). Lake Thun boat to Interlaken.
Day 2 Interlaken, Jungfraujoch, Grindelwald (lunch), Interlaken.
Day 3 Interlaken, Luzern.
Day 4 Luzern, Vitznau, Mt. Rigi (lunch), Arth-Goldau, Lugano.
Day 5 Lugano, Bellinzona, Locarno.
Day 6 Locarno, Domodossola, Bern.
Day 7 Bern to Geneva or Zurich.

A MAGNIFICENT ONE-DAY TRIP

Here are several of the most scenic rail trips in Europe, combined in a single day.

All of these rides are covered by Eurailpass.

Table				
280	Dep. Spiez	07:54 (1)	Arr. Brig	08:59
270	Dep. Brig	09:08	Arr. Domodossola	09:42
272	Dep. Domodossola	10:16 (1)	Arr. Locarno	11:50
290	Dep. Locarno	12:03	Arr. Bellinzona	12:22
290	Dep. Bellinzona	13:28 (2)	Arr. Luzern	15:39
285	Dep. Luzern	16:24	Arr. Interlaken (Ost)	18:25
280	Dep. Interlaken (Ost)	18:39	Arr. Spiez	18:59

(1) Light refreshments. (2) Restaurant car.

THE "GOLDEN PASS" ROUTE
Luzern - Interlaken - Spiez - Zweisimmen - Montreux - Lausanne

There are snowcapped Alpine peaks, flowering meadows, and sparkling mountain streams on this marvelous one-day trip. As the timetables show, a layover in Spiez is possible.

285		275		
Dep. Luzern	08:24	Dep. Spiez	11:08	12:03 (1)
Arr. Interlaken (Ost)	10:25	Arr. Zweisimmen	11:55	12:39
Change trains.		Change trains.		
280		Dep. Zweisimmen	12:00	12:50
Dep. Interlaken (Ost)	10:39	Arr. Montreux	14:00	14:38
Arr. Spiez	10:59	Change trains. 270		
Change trains.		Dep. Montreux	14:08	14:44
		Arr. Lausanne	14:28	15:05

(1) Plus other departures from Spiez at 13:08, 14:03 (includes "Panoramic Express" Zweisimmen-Montreux — Reservation required...see page 345) and 15:08...changing trains in Zweisimmen 14:00, 15:15 and 16:00...changing trains in Montreux 16:08, 17:07 and 18:08...arriving Lausanne 16:28, 17:25 and 18:28.

INTERNATIONAL ROUTES FROM SWITZERLAND

The Swiss gateways for travel to West Germany are Basel (to Cologne), Geneva (to Frankfurt), and Zurich (to Munich). Zurich is also the starting point for the train trip to Austria (Innsbruck, and on to Vienna and East Europe) and for train travel to Italy (Milan and beyond).

Basel is also a starting point for trips to Belgium, Holland and France (Paris, and on to London or Madrid).

Geneva (via Aosta, and on to Torino) as well as Bern and Brig (via Domodossola) are also departure cities for rail rides to Italy (Milan, and beyond).

There is also rail service from Geneva to Paris, and from Geneva to southern France (Avignon) and on to Spain (Barcelona).

Basel - Cologne - Amsterdam

Sit on the right side of the train for best views of the marvelous Rhine River scenery.
Most of these trains have a restaurant car

	36	63	68	68	68
Dep. Basel (SBB)	– 0 –	08:23 (1)	09:15	12:15	13:15 (2+4)
Dep. Basel (Bad.)	05:08	– 0 –	09:22	12:22	13:22
Arr. Cologne	10:21	– 0 –	13:59	16:59	17:59 (2)
Change trains. 68					
Dep. Cologne	– 0 –	– 0 –	15:17	17:17	18:02
Arr. Amsterdam (Cen.)	– 0 –	18:01	17:51	19:51	20:51

(1) Depart from Basel's SNCF railstation. (2) Direct train. No train change in Cologne. (3) Carries a sleeping car. Also has couchettes. (4) Plus other Basel (S.B.B.) departures at 14:15 (2), 16:59 and 23:25 (2+3)....arriving Cologne 18:59, 20:59 and 05:45....arriving Amsterdam 21:51, 23:57 and 09:40. Also [Table 700] other Basel departures (Terminating in Cologne) every hour from 14:15 to 18:15.

Basel - Copenhagen 68

Dep. Basel (SBB)	09:15 (1)	17:33 (4)	23:17 (5)
Dep. Basel (Bad.)	09:22 (2)	17:53	23:40
Arr. Hamburg (Hbf.)	15:51	03:53 (4)	08:01
Change trains.			
Dep. Hamburg (Hbf.)	17:11 (3)	04:04 (4)	08:11 (3)
Dep. Puttgarden	09:05	06:05	10:05
Arr. Copenhagen	22:20	09:25	13:20

(1) Restaurant car Basel-Copenhagen. (2) Change trains in Mannheim at 11:26. (3) Light refreshments until Puttgarden. (4) Direct train. No train change in Hamburg. Carries a sleeping car. Also has couchettes. (5) To Hamburg: Carries a sleeping car. Also has couchettes.

Zurich - Munich 84

Dep. Zurich	07:07 (1)	09:39 (1)	12:39 (1)	15:39 (2)	18:39 (1)
Arr. Munich	11:25	13:59	17:00	20:09	23:02

(1) Restaurant car. (2) Light refreshments.

Zurich - Innsbruck - Salzburg - Vienna 57

About 2½ hours out of Zurich, the train passes through one of Europe's largest tunnels, the 6.3-mile long Arlberg. There is a very beautiful view of Alpine scenery as the train comes out of the tunnel.

Dep. Zurich	07:20 (1)	09:33 (1)	13:33 (1)	23:11 (2)
Arr. Innsbruck	11:16	13:16	17:16	02:47
Arr. Salzburg	13:22	15:22	19:22	04:45
Arr. Vienna (West.)	16:30	18:30	22:30	08:05

(1) Supplement charged. Restaurant car. (2) Carries a sleeping car. Also has couchettes. Has a Hungarian restaurant car.

Bern - Brig - Milan 280

This trip takes you on the marvelous scenic route via Spiez (see "Geneva–Spiez" on page 342) and through both the 10-mile long Lotschberg Tunnel Bern–Brig) and the 11.9-mile long Simplon (Brig–Milan), longest tunnel in Europe and world's third longest, after Japan's Seikan Tunnel (33.4 miles, between Tappi and Yoshioka) and Japan's Daishimizu Tunnel (13.4 miles, between Tokyo and Niigata).

Dep. Bern	06:50 (1)	08:51 (2)	14:17 (1)	15:22 (2)	18:43 (2)
Arr. Brig	08:20	10:21	15:47	16:59	20:49
Arr. Milan (Cen.)	10:45	12:35	17:55	19:15	22:40

(1) Restaurant car. (2) Light refreshments.

Zurich - Milan 69

See detailed notes about the wonderful scenery on this route (one of the 5 most scenic rail trips in Europe) under "Zurich–Lugano" on page 359.

Dep. Zurich	06:24 (1)	07:03 (1)	08:03 (1)	10:03 (2)	12:33 (1+3)
Arr. Milan (Cen.)	10:30	11:35	12:35	14:35	16:35

(1) Restaurant car. (2) Light refreshments. (3) Plus other departures from Zurich at 14:03 (2), 16:03 (1) and 18:10 (1), arriving Milan 18:35, 20:35 and 22:40.

Basel - Luxembourg - Brussels

	63	63	63	63	16
Dep. Basel (S.N.C.F.)	04:20 (1)	08:23 (2)	13:22 (2)	16:25 (2)	23:59 (3)
Arr. Luxembourg	08:04	11:57	16:49	19:56	04:05
Arr. Brussels (Q.L.)	10:29	14:17	19:10	22:22	-0-
Arr. Brussels (Nord)	10:40	14:27	19:20	22:34	07:06
Arr. Brussels (Midi)	8 minutes after arriving Nord railstation.				

(1) Carries a sleeping car. Also has couchettes. (2) Restaurant car. (3) Departs from Basel's S.B.B. railstation. Carries a sleeping car. Also has couchettes.

Geneva - Milan - Venice 55

Dep. Geneva (Corn.)	08:20 (1)	10:34 (2)	12:18 (3)	15:34 (2)	17:48 (3)
Arr. Milan (Cen.)	12:40 (1)	14:40	16:55	19:55	22:40
Change trains.					
Dep. Milan (Cen.)	13:00 (1)	15:05	18:00	20:00	00:20
Arr. Venice (S.L.)	15:48	17:56	21:00	23:12	04:22

(1) Direct train. No train change in Milan. Supplement charged. Restaurant car. (2) Supplement charged. Restaurant car. (3) Light refreshments.

Geneva - Paris 159

All of these trains are TGV and have a restaurant car. (See page 121).

Dep. Geneva (Corn.)	07:09	10:02	13:01	16:50	19:29
Arr. Paris (Lyon)	10:39	13:34	16:38	20:31	23:09

Zurich - Bern (or Basel) - Geneva - Avignon - Barcelona 78

The "Pablo Casals" (19:33 departure from Zurich) began in 1990 to carry one "Gran Clase" sleeping car, the most luxurious sleeping car in Europe. Each of its large single and double compartments has a shower and toilet. The train also has ordinary sleeping compartments and 4-berth tourist compartments. There are *no* coach seats. The train has a restaurant car. Travel is not covered by either Eurailpass or Spain's rail passes. A supplement is charged. This is a direct train. No train change in Port Bou.

Dep. Zurich	-0-	-0-	19:33 (4)
Dep. Bern	-0-	-0-	20:48
Dep. Basel	-0-	18:23 (2)	-0-
Dep. Geneva (Cor.)	11:27 (1)	21:54	22:46
Dep. Avignon	15:44	01:45	-0-
Arr. Narbonne	17:32	03:39	-0-
Arr. Port Bou	-0-	05:25	-0-
Change trains.			
Dep. Port Bou	-0-	05:55 (3)	-0-
Arr. Barcelona (Sants)	21:18	09:46	09:10

(1) Supplement charged. Restaurant car. Direct train. No train change in Port Bou. (2) Has couchettes. (3) Second-class only. (4) "Pablo Casals". See description above.

Aosta - Torino Gateways to Italy

(1) Via San Bernardo Tunnel
Lausanne or Brig to Martigny and Martigny - Aosta - Torino

270 (Train)			270 (Train)		
Dep. Lausanne	06:55	15:32 (1)	Dep. Brig	06:48 (1)	15:35 (1)
Arr. Martigny	07:45	16:23	Arr. Martigny	07:36	16:26

* * *

273 (Bus)			
Dep. Martigny (Stn.)	08:00	16:30	-0-
Arr. Aosta (P. Narbonne)	10:05	18:35	-0-
Change to a train. 355e			
Dep. Aosta	13:05 (2)	18:52 (3)	20:52
Arr. Torino (Piazza Narbonne)	16:34	20:51	22:47

(1) Light refreshments. (2) Second-class only. (3) Runs daily, except Sundays and hollidays.

(2) Via Mt. Blanc Tunnel
Geneva - Chamonix -Aosta - Torino

All of the train changes Geneva–Chamonix are cross-platform, taking less than one minute.

167						
Dep. Geneva (Eaux-Vives)	06:40	08:00 (2)	08:26	11:10 (3)	14:43	
Arr. La Roche-sur-Foron	07:20	-0- (2)	08:55	11:48	15:17	
Change trains.						
Dep. La Roche-sur-Foron	07:31 (1)	-0- (2)	09:10	11:57 (4)	15:37	
Arr. St. Gervais	08:19	09:16	09:58	12:40	16:26	
Change trains.						
Dep. St. Gervais	08:29	09:26	10:45	13:00	16:47	
Arr. Chamonix	09:08	10:06	11:24	13:39	17:28	
Change to a bus. 191						
Dep. Chamonix	09:15 (5)	10:05 (6)	15:00 (7)	16:15 (6)	17:30	19:30 (6)
Arr. Aosta	11:40	11:40	17:00	18:00	19:30	21:35

(1) Late June to early September: runs daily. Early September to late June: runs daily, except Saturday.
(2) Operates late June to late August. Direct train to St. Gervais. No train change in La Roche-sur-Foron.
(3) Runs Saturday and Sunday. (4) Light refreshments. (5) Mid-December to mid-April and early July to mid-September: runs daily. Rest of year: runs daily, except Sunday. (6) Operates early July to mid-September. (7) Operates early February to mid-April and early July to mid-September.

Change to a train. 355e

Dep. Aosta (P. Narbonne)	13:05	14:12		18:52 (1)	20:52
Arr. Torino (P. Narbonne)	16:34	16:02		20:51	22:47

(1) Runs daily, except Sundays and holidays.

A good break in this journey is to spend the night in Aosta and continue on to Torino the next day. Here are the schedules for the other departures from Aosta:

Dep. Aosta (P. Narbonne)	05:14	06:04	07:57	09:08	16:29
Arr. Torino (P. Narbonne)	07:23	08:30	09:45	10:59	19:50

GERMANY

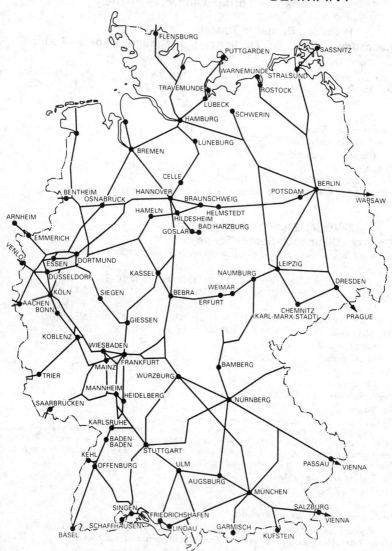

GERMANY

Children under 4 travel free. Half-fare for children 4–11. Children 12 and over pay full fare.

Where no station is designated for cities in Germany, the station is "Hauptbahnhoff".

Fast InterCity and EuroCity trains, connecting 50 important cities along 5 major rail routes, have easy cross-platform connections in such cities as Cologne, Wurzburg, Mannheim and Dortmund. The DM-6 supplement charged for IC and EC trains includes the cost of a seat reservation.

Where a timetable footnote indicates that a supplement is charged by a particular train, a passenger using a Eurailpass or German Flexipass does not have to pay the extra charge. (All of those passes are also valid on all commuter rail services in major German cities.) The IC supplement must be paid when using the Inter-Rail Card, available only to residents of Europe.

Some of the InterCity trains have top speeds of 125 mph. A "conference compartment" in them can be rented for the cost of 4 first-class tickets. Worldwide telephone calls can be made from all IC trains.

When entering or leaving Germany on an international train, the customs, passport and currency control are usually performed in the train. Because of this, passengers traveling across Germany (such as from Amsterdam to Copenhagen) are required to travel in a special car or compartment.

Porter service may be reserved in advance at many railstations, including those at the Dusseldorf and Frankfurt airports. A program began in 1987 to install conveyor belts at stairways in 130 railstations as well as escalators which can accommodate baggage carts in all major stations..

The signs you will see at railstations in Germany are the same as those listed earlier in this chapter, under "Austria" on page 57.

SUMMER TIME

Germany changes to Summer Time on the last Sunday of March and converts back to Standard Time on the last Sunday of September.

GERMAN HOLIDAYS

A list of holidays is helpful because some trains will be noted later in this section as not running on holidays. Also, those trains which operate on holidays are filled, and it is necessary to make reservations for them long in advance.

January 1	New Year's Day	June 17	Commemorating the
	Good Friday		East Berlin Uprisings
	Easter	August 15	Assumption Day
	Easter Monday	November 1	All Saints Day
May 1	Labor Day	December 25	Christmas
	Ascension Day	December 26	Holiday
	Whit Monday		

EURAILPASS BONUSES IN GERMANY

See page 25.

GERMANY'S TRAIN PASSES

EuroCity and InterCity supplements are included in the prices listed below for German Flexipass, German Junior Flexipass and German Rail & Drive. All of these are sold at travel agencies worldwide and at many German railstations and airports.

Travelers arriving in Germany by airplane can validate all of these passes (and also Eurailpasses) at the airport rail ticket office after exiting the customs area, and can use these passes for the rail trip from the airport to the city.

German Flexipass   Unlimited train travel in Germany during one month from the first day the pass is used. The 1992 *first*-class prices are: 5 days $240 (U.S), 10 days $360, 15 days $450. For *second*-class: $160, $240 and $300. A "twin fare" applies to the second person when 2 people travel toguether: $184, $192, and $240

German Junior Flexipass   Unlimited *second*-class train travel in Germany during one month from the first day the pass is used — *for passengers under 26 years old on the first day of travel*. The 1992 prices are: 5 days $110 (U.S), 10 days $145, and 15 days $180.

Rail & Drive Pass   Combines *any* 3 days of car rental with *any* 5-day, 10-day or 15-day German Flexipass. Prices vary according to whether car rental is for a single traveler or for 2 people, which class of Flexipass, and which of 4 categories of car is rented. The 1991 price for 2 people with a *second*-class Flexipass renting the *smallest-car* category was $185 (U.S).

National Netzkarte   *Sold only in Germany*. Unlimited train travel through all of Germany for one month. The 1991 prices were: *first*-class DM-1,860 and *second*-class DM-1,240.

Area Netzkarte   *Sold only in Germany*. Unlimited train travel in *one specified area* of Germany for one month. In 1991: *first*-class DM-813, *second*-class DM-542.

Tourenkarte   *Sold only in Germany*, after presentation of a roundtrip ticket that covers a distance of at least 250 km (155 miles). Allows *second*-class train travel for any 10-day period within 21 consecutive days over a network of approximately 1,000 km (621 miles) of rail lines. The 1991 prices were: 1 person DM-50, 2 persons DM-70, one family DM-85.

Family Railpass   *Sold only in Germany*. Valid one year. Members of the same family receive 50% discount on tickets when at least 2 of the persons listed in the pass travel together. The 1991 price was DM-130.

Senior Citizen Railpass   *Sold only in Germany*. Valid one year. Persons 60 years old or more receive 50% discount on tickets. In 1991, Pass "A" (Monday-Thursday and Saturday) was DM-75. Pass "B" (every day) was DM-110.

Junior Railpass   *Sold only in Germany.* Valid one year. Non-students 18–22 years old and students under 27 receive 50% discount on tickets. The 1991 price: DM-110.

Pocket-Money Rail Pass   *Sold only in Germany.* Valid one year. Persons 12–17 years old receive 50% discount on tickets. The 1991 price: DM-40.

Tramper Ticket   *Sold only in Germany.* Non-students under 23 years old and students under 27 have *one month* of unlimited rail travel. The 1991 price: DM-246.

ONE-DAY EXCURSIONS AND CITY-SIGHTSEEING

Here are 94 one-day rail trips that can be made comfortably from cities in Germany, returning to them in most case before dinnertime. Notes are provided on what to see and do at each destination. The number after the name of each route is the Cook's timetable. Details on 11 other rail trips recommended for exceptional scenery and schedules for international connections conclude this section.

Sightseeing tours to Chemnitz (formerly Karl Marx Stadt), Dresden and Potsdam start in Berlin at Parkplatz Rankestrasse, near the Kurfurstendamm. For reservations, contact Deutsches Reiseburo, Kurfurstendamm 17, Berlin W.30, Germany.

The 8 base cities for one-day excursions are Berlin, Cologne (Koln), Dresden, Frankfurt/Main, Hamburg, Hannover, Leipzig and Munich (Munchen).

Berlin

Two-hour and 4-hour tours of West Berlin begin at 10:00 and occur at frequent intervals during the day, from 220 Kurfurstendamm, 216 Kurfurstendamm, and opposite from the bombed-out Gedachtniskirche (Memorial Church).

The stroll down tree-lined Kurfurstendamm is almost mandatory, to observe the city's fine stores, theaters, cafes, movie houses and bars. See the Zoo (started in 1843) and Aquarium, one of Europe's oldest and best animal exhibits, open daily until dusk. The New National Gallery, at Potsdamerstrasse 50, open daily except Monday 09:00–17:00.

The bust of Nefertiti and other important items in the Egyptian Museum at 70 Schloss Strasse, closed Friday. The rooms and gardens of Charlottenburg Castle, closed Monday, opposite the Egyptian Museum. The 1936 Olympic Stadium. The German History Museum, in the reconstructed Reichstag Building, on Paul-Lobe Strasse, open daily except Monday 10:00-17:00. The tent-shaped Philharmonic Hall. Take a boat ride on the Havel River.

See modern paintings at Brucke Museum, Bussardsteig 9, open Monday-Friday 11:00–17:00. Masterpieces by Durer, Cranach the Elder and Holbein the Younger, at the Dahlem Museum, Arnimallee 23-27, open Tuesday-Sunday 09:00–17:00. Models of everything that floats, flies or rolls, at the Transport Museum, Trebbinerstrasse 9, open Tuesday-Friday 09:00–18:00 and on Saturday and Sunday 10:00–18:00.

Exhibits about many modern architects in the Bauhaus Museum, Klingelhoferstrasse 13, open daily except Tuesday 11:00-17:00. The best collection of Durer drawings in Germany is at the Kupferstichkabinett.

Visit the sixth floor (called Feinschmecker Etage — "the gourmet's floor") of Kaufhaus des Westens (called KaDeWe "Kah-day-vay" by local people), a large department store on Tauentzienstrasse. It is the largest food store in Europe: 500 sales clerks dispensing 30,000 different products. Fruits and vegetables sold there include limes from Brazil, rare wild mushrooms from France and Poland, avocados from Israel, tiny beans from Kenya, tomatoes from Spain, apples from Hungary.

They sell 1,500 kinds of meats (250 varieties of salami). Then there are also eels, crawfish, catfish and carp. Live lobsters are delivered to the store in tank trucks. You will also find 400 types of bread. Three separate counters for 1,800 varieties of cheese from France, Italy and other countries. Eighteen kinds of herring salad. It also has 28 restaurants, counter services and stand-up bars.

Store hours are: 9:00–18:30 on Monday, Tuesday, Wednesday and Friday; 9:00–20:30 on Thursday; 9:00–14:00 on most Saturdays.

The Weissbierstube Restaurant in the Berlin Museum is acclaimed for its bounteous buffet tables. Both the Restaurant and the Museum are open daily except Mondays 11:00-18:00.

To see East Berlin, take the elevated railway from West Berlin's Zoo railstation to its Friedrichstrasse station. On leaving Friedrichstrasse station, turn right and walk 3 blocks to reach Berlin's famous boulevard, Unter den Linden, and the enormous Soviet embassy. A few blocks further, at the end of the boulevard, is the classical Brandenburg Gate and the ruins of the Berlin Wall.

Also see the reconstructed St. Hedwig's Cathedral. The National Gallery. The 18th century State Opera. The tremendous collection of Oriental, Greek and Roman antiquities, the Market Gate of Milet and the impressive Pergamon Altar, all at the Pergamon Museum on Bodestrasse, open Wednesday and Thursday 09:00-18:00 and Friday 10:00-18:00.

The Palace of the Republic. Bode Museum. The Altes Museum. The tiny 14th century church, Marienkirche. The Museum of German History.

Cologne (Koln)

All museums are closed on Monday.

It is a 10-minute bus ride from the Cologne/Bonn Airport to the center of Cologne.

Your city-sightseeing in Cologne should include, above all, the Cathedral, very near the railstation. Started in 1248 and not completed until 1880, it houses the world's largest reliquary, containing relics of the 3 kings, the Magi, as well as a splendid collection of illuminated books, vestments, ivories and liturgical articles. These can be seen Monday-Saturday 09:00–17:00, Sundays and holidays 12:30–17:00.

The best time to be inside the Cathedral is at the Sunday 10:00 mass, when the ceremony starts with a procession of church elders dressed in robes of burgundy, crimson and rose, and wearing white, embroidered, starched linen. If you climb the 502 steps to the top of the spire, past the 9 giant bells, you will see a magnificent view of Cologne, The Rhine River and the Rhine Valley.

Near the Cathedral, explore ancient Cologne. The Praetorium, a palace for Roman governors several centuries before Christ, located in the basement of the Town Hall, open daily 10:00–17:00. Its entrance, difficult to find, is across from the Restaurant-Bar-Cafe Oldtimer at 110 Kleine Budengasse. See the 3rd century Dionysus mosaic (once the dining hall floor of a Roman house) in the Roman Museum, open Tuesday–Sunday 10:00–20:00.

Also on view there is an outstanding collection of Roman glass, cooking utensils and 4th century jewelry. Visit the 3rd century Roman tower.

See the collection of paintings by Cologne masters of the 13th–17th and 19th centuries in the Wallraf Richartz Museum (1 Bischofsgartenstrasse, between the Cathedral and the Hauptbahnhoff), open Tuesday, Wednesday and Thursday 10:00–20:00. On Friday, Saturday and Sunday 10:00–18:00. Modern art is exhibited in the Ludwig Museum (same address and hours).

The Zoo. The 15th century Gurzenich. The Metropolitan Historical Museum. The Town Hall. St. Pantaleon Church. St. Andreas Church. Relics and treasures in the Golden Room at the Church of St. Ursula. The luxury shops on Hohestrasse and Schildergasse.

Dresden

Major works of Raphael, Rembrandt, Rubens, Tintoretto, Van Eyck, Vermeer and other great 16th and 17th century painters at the Picture Gallery in the Semper Building of Zwinger Palace. Another excellent collection of paintings in the National Gallery.

Hear the Silberman organ (235 years old in 1990) at the cathedral, Hofkirche. Visit the baroque Opera House. The Zoo in Stadtpark (also called Volkspark). The Block House. Dresden Palace. The Japanese Castle. The treasures at the Albertinium Museum. The Palace of Culture. Take the cable car to Weisser Hirsch for the view of Dresden from the top of that hill.

It is a 17-mile ride by suburban railway from Dresdent to **Meissen**. See the 15th century castle (Albrechtsburg) and the Cathedral there. Shop in Meissen for Dresdent china and Albrecht porcelain.

Frankfurt

There is frequent rail service from Frankfurt's Hauptbahnhof railstation to the city's airport and vice versa (11-minute travel time) every 20 minutes from 05:14 to 23:33. Frequent trains per hour continue beyond the airport station to Mainz and Wiesbaden. Trains also depart the airport at frequent times for Bonn, Cologne, Dortmund, Dusseldorf, Koblenz, Ludwigshafen, Luxembourg, Mannheim, Nurnberg, Trier and Wurzburg.

Bus tours that cover in 2 ½ hours the city's most interesting places depart daily from the south side of the main railstation at 10:00 and 14:00. Most museums in Frankfurt are closed on Monday.

See Goethe's house. Next to it, the Goethe Museum (books, pictures, furniture and manuscripts associated with the writer) in the Grosser Hirschgraben, open Monday-Saturday 09:00-18:00, Sunday 10:00-3:00.

The Zoo, one of the world's greatest, at Am Tiergarten, open 08:00-19:00 in Summer, 08:00-18:00 in October, 08:00-17:00 in Winter. Its Exoticarium (aquarium and reptile house) is open until 22:00. Buses #10, #13 and #15 go to the Zoo.

The emperor's coronation hall in the Romer complex at medieval Romerberg Square. The wonderful doors in the 13th century Leonhardskirche. The 13th century chapel of Saalhof in the remains of the palace of Frederick Barbarossa. Cloth Hall. The Botanical Garden. The pews and murals in the Cathedral of St. Bartholomew. The Church of St. Nicholas. The Church of St. Paul. Senckenberg Museum, the largest natural history museum in West Germany, open 09:00–16:00. The collection of Dutch primitives and 16th century German masters at the Stadel Art Institute and Municipal Gallery, open daily except Monday 10:00–17:00. The Liebighaus Exhibition of Sculpture.

The Museum of Plastic Art. The changing exhibits of European silver, porcelain, furniture and glass from the Middle Ages to the present time and also an Asian collection (3rd to 19th century) at the Museum of Arts and Crafts. The Henninger Tower in Sachsenhausen, the old quarter of the city (across the Main River, near the commercial district). The Postal Museum. The major shopping streets: Zeil and Kaiserstrasse.

The palm trees, other tropical plants, and Alpine gardens in the city's central park, Palmengarten. Nine miles away in **Offenbach**, center of West Germany's leather industry, is the German Leather Museum, open daily 10:00–17:00.

Hamburg

Most museums in Hamburg are closed Monday. See the port, one of the busiest in the world. There are splendid views of the enormous port from Stintfang Hill. Visit Hagenbeck Zoo, the first cageless zoo in the world, at Stellingen Gardens. St. James Church, with its famous organ, built in 1693. Rathausmarkt Square. The models of Old Hamburg, the port and the city's railway system, in the Museum of the History of Hamburg.

The Counting Houses in the business quarter, around Burchardplatz. The notorious Reperbahn. The view of the city from the Michel Tower of St, Michaelis Church. The Museum of Decorative Arts. The Art Gallery. The Botanical Garden. The "Sight and Sound" performances during Summer in the Planten un Blomen park. Take a flight over the city from Fuhlsbuttel Airport.

Hannover

The bus ride between Langenhagen Airport and Hannover's railstation takes 30 minutes. The bus terminal is located next to Track #14.

See the collection of art (from the Middle Ages to the beginning of the 20th century) in the Niedersachsische Landesgalerie. Modern painting and sculpture in the Sprengel Museum (Max Beckmann, Paul Klee, Pablo Picasso).

For an interesting 2-hour walking tour of Hannover, obtain the detailed brochure available at both of the railstation's 2 tourist information offices. Walk out of the station to the statue in front of it and start to follow the painted red line which leads to Passerelle (a pedestrian mall), the 19th century Opera House, the old city wall, Town Hall, and Hannover's oldest (16th century) half-timbered structure.

See the bronze doors by Marcks at Market Church. The outstanding collection of Egyptian antiquities in the Kestner Museum. The prehistoric objects in the Museum of Lower Saxony.

Take a short walk from the Central railstation to the station under Kropke Cafe and, from there, Tram #1 or #2 to the absolutely fantastic baroque Royal Gardens of Herrenhausen. Its ornamental fountains perform in Summer Monday-Friday 11:00–12:00 and 15:30–16:30. On Saturdays and Sundays, they can be seen 10:00–12:00 and 15:30–17:30.

Next to Herrenhausen is the natural park, Georgengarten. Nearby, see the exotic plants in the greenhouses at Berggarten.

Take streetcar #6 from the Central railstation to Hannover's outstanding Zoo.

Leipzig

Concentrate on the area around Market Place. Visit the Museum of the History of Leipzig in the Renaissance Old Town Hall. The 17th century stock exchange (Alte Bourse), rebuilt in 1963. The weighinghouse (Alte Waage), where taxes were levied on imported goods. Auerbachs Keller, the old tavern on which Goethe based the locale of his Faust drama. Bach's tomb, at St. Thomas Church. The Museum of Fine Arts.

West of Market Place is the church where Johann Sebastian Bach is buried. Bach composed in that church the last 27 years of his life. Also see Gohliser Schlosschen, a rococo palace. Gohlis, the home of the poet Schiller. The Opera House in Karl Marx Platz. It is impossible to find a room in Leipzig during the semi-annual (March and September) trade fairs that attract visitors from all over the world.

Munich (Munchen)

A metropolitan train connects Munich's Hauptbahnhof and Ostbanhof railstations. It is a 10-minute bus ride between Munich's Riem Airport and the Hauptbahnhof railstation, where the city's monthly program of events (theaters, museums, exhibits, concerts, plays, etc.) can be obtained. The program is also sold at newsstands.

Most museums in Munich are closed on Monday. There are more than 50 — on coins, ethnology, theater, applied arts, hunting and fishing, folk music, graphic arts, mineralogy, Egyptian art, toys, fire fighting, beer making, prehistory, porcelains, paleontology, puppets, photography, even chamber pots.

See the works of Durer, El Greco, Raphael, Holbein, Rembrandt and many other great 14th to 18th century painters at Alte (Old) Pinakothek, at 27 Barer Strasse, open Tuesday-Sunday 09:00–16:30, and on Tuesday and Thursday 07:00–21:00. The Neue (New) Pinakothek at 29 Barer Strasse (same days and hours as the "Old" museum) has a collection of 19th and 20th century artists. The paintings of Kandinsky, Marcs and Klees in the Lenbachhaus, at 33 Luisen Strasse, open daily except Monday 10:00-18:00.

The 15th century Frauenkirche Cathedral, and the view of Munich from its north tower . . . and then later the view of Frauenkirche from the top of Neue Rathaus (New City Hall), where at 11:00 every day the mechanical figures in its bell tower perform a tournament of knights, a medieval royal wedding, and a dance. There are other fine views of Munich from Olympia Tower.

The paintings of Cezanne, Gauguin, Renoir and other impressionists at the Haus der Kunst at 1 Princregenten Strasse, open daily except Monday 09:00-16:30. On Thursday, it is also open 19:00-21:00. See Wittelsbach Fountain.

The fine exhibits and planetarium at Deutsches Museum, considered the best scientific museum in the world, open daily 09:00–17:00. It is across the Ludwigsbrucke, on an island in the **Isar River**. Displays of 16,000 items.

The view of the Alps from the top of Peterskirche. The best collection of tapestries and wood carvings in Germany, at the Bavarian National Museum. Munich's most famous beer palace, Hofbrauhaus.

The Schatzkammer in the Residenz palace (which houses the enormous Festaal and many museums that are open Tuesday-Saturday 10:00–16:30, Sunday 10:00–13:00), and the flower gardens in the park north of it. Words cannot describe the fabulous beauty of the Festaal.

The decorations in and rococo architecture of the 18th century Asamkirche on Sendlinger Strasse. Schack Gallery. Theatinerkirche (in 17th century Italian baroque style) on Odeonsplatz.

At Schloss (Castle) Nymphenburg: the porcelain in the showrooms of Nymphenburger Porzellan Manufaktur, open daily except Monday 10:00–12:00 and 13:30–16:00. Also visit the park outside the castle. Located on the outskirts of Munich, Nymphenburg can be reached by taking the U-1 subway to the end of that line (Rotkreutzplatz) and transfering to the #12 streetcar. Alternate lines from the center of Munich are streetcars #17 or #21, or buses #41 or #42.

See the history of Munich in the Isartorplatz Museum. The impressive Renaissance Michalskirche on the Neuhauserstrasse pedestrian mall. Ancient Greek and Roman sculpture in the Glyptothek (Konigsplatz 3), open Tuesday, Wednesday, Friday and Sunday 10:00-16:30, on Thursday 12:00–20:30. Nearby, the Staatliche Antikensammlungen (State Collection of Antiquities) at Konigsplatz 1, open Tuesday and Thursday–Sunday 10:00–16:30, on Wednesday 12:00–20:30.

The collection of Medieval art and sculpture, arts and crafts, applied arts, folk art and folklore at the Bayerisches Nationalmuseum (Bavarian National Museum), at Prinzregenstrasse 3, open daily except Monday 09:30–17:00. Nearby, an exhibit of late 19th century Herman painters in Schackgalerie at Prinzregenstrasse 9, open daily except Tuesday 09:00–16:30.

Visit Schwabing, the Latin quarter. The palaces on Ludwigstrasse. The history of Bavarian Motor Works (aircraft, motorcycles, automobiles) in the BMW Museum, open daily 09:00–16:00.

Infamous Dachau is a 40-minute ride by commuter train #S-2 or bus #11. Although there are no guides at Dachau, an exhibit there details the operation of the concentration camp, and an English-language film is shown at 11:30 and 15:30.

Since 1870, an Alois Dallmayr food store has offered gourmet delicacies in Munich. It added a restaurant in 1978. As Fauchon's in Paris does, Dallmayr (15 Dienerstrasse) has a vast section of imported foods. Its most notable feature, however, is the enormous array it offers of West Germany's finest lunch meats, 22 varieties of smoked fish, and 27 types of bread.

Nearly everything edible can be found at Dallmayr's: local and imported fruits, cooked meats and poultry, live fish swimming in marble tanks, wines, more than 50 different salads, 200 different chocolates, 120 different sausages, 18 types of ham, and they also sell special cigars.

If you eat none of the splendid food there, at least see the statues, marble pillars and mounted deer heads that decorate the interior of the store. Another famous food emporium is Kafer's, at 73 Prinzregenten, Germany's largest delicatessen and caterer. Both stores have an excellent restaurant.

The Viktualienmarkt, behind St. Peter's Church, is one of Europe's largest outdoor food markets. Two blocks long, it has operated since 18:07: fruits, vegetables, poultry, cheeses, herbs, breads, pastries, wines, plants and flowers. It is open Monday-Friday 07:00–18:30, Saturday 07:00–17:00. Friday and Saturday are its busiest days. It is closed on Sundays.

An excursion bus departs at 08:30 from Neptunbrunnen Eisenstrasse 1 for **Neuschwanstein** and **Hohenschwangau Castles**, returning to Munich at 18:30. Fantastic Alpine and lake scenery.

In the following timetables, where a city has more than one railstation we have designated the particular station after the name of the city (in parentheses).

Where no station is designated for cities in Austria, Switzerland and Germany, the station is "Hauptbahnhoff".

Berlin - Chemnitz (formerly Karl Marx Stadt) - Berlin   731

Reservation is advisable for all of these trains.

Dep. Berlin (Schoneweide)	06:32	10:20
Dep. Berlin (Schonefeld)	06:49	10:37
Arr. Chemnitz	09:59	13:59

Sights in **Chemnitz**: This was an East German post-World War II showplace new city before the 1990 unification of West and East Germany.

Dep. Chemnitz	15:15	18:15
Arr. Berlin (Schonefeld)	18:30	21:30
Arr. Berlin (Schoneweide)	18:48	21:48

Berlin - Dresden - Berlin   730

All of these trains have a restaurant car, unless designated otherwise.

Dep. Berlin (Licht)	06:02 (1)	07:53 (2)	08:41 (2)	09:53 (3)	12:00 (2)
Arr. Dresden (Hbf.)	08:36	10:24	11:10	12:39	14:33

Sights in **Dresden**: See notes about sightseeing in Dresden on page 373.

Dep. Dresden (Hbf.)	12:48 (3)	13:41 (4)	14:48	15:48 (4)	16:48 (5)
Arr. Berlin (Licht.)	15:26	16:14	17:14	18:14	19:18 (1)

(1) Depart/Arrive Berlin's Schonewiede railstation. Reservation *advisable*. (2) Reservation *advisable*. Restaurant car. (3) Reservation *advisable*. Light refreshments. (4) Reservation *required*. Restaurant car. (5) Plus other Dresden departures at 19:18 (4) and 20:18 (4), arriving Berlin 21:44 and 22:44.

Berlin - Erfurt - Berlin   720

Reservation is advisable for all of these trains.

Dep. Berlin (Lichtenberg)	05:30 (1)	06:47 (2)	10:17 (1)
Dep. Berlin (Schonefeld)	05:55	07:13	10:43
Arr. Erfurt	09:32	10:36	14:11

Sights in **Erfurt**: The exquisite Gothic and German Renaissance houses. The Cathedral, where Martin Luther was ordained in 1507. The bridge, on which 33 houses stand. St. Severin Church.

(The return trip and footnotes appear on page 378)

Dep. Erfurt	13:24 (2)	16:23 (1)	18:11 (1)	19:42 (4)
Arr. Berlin (Schonefeld)	17:00	19:42	21:24	23:00
Arr. Berlin (Lichtenberg)	17:18 (3)	20:08	21:50	23:26

(1) Light refreshments. (2) Restaurant car. (3) Arrives at Berlin's Schoneweide railstation.
(4) Runs Sundays and holidays only. Restaurant car.

Berlin - Frankfurt 710

Reservation is advisable for all of these trains. All of them charge a supplement and have a restaurant car.

Dep. Berlin (Hbf.)	05:26	07:18	09:18	11:18	15:18 (3)
Arr. Frankfurt (Hbf.)	11:58	13:58	15:58	17:58	21:59

See notes about **Frankfurt** on page 373.

Dep. Frankfurt (Hbf.)	06:00 (1)	08:02	12:02	14:02	16:02 (4)
Arr. Berlin (Hbf.)	12:27	14:27	18:27	20:27	22:27

(1) Runs daily, except Sunday. (2) Carries a sleeping car. Also has couchettes. Light refreshments. (3) Plus other Berlin departures at 17:18 and 22:20 (2), arriving Frankfurt 23:59 and 07:11. (4) Plus other Frankfurt departures at 18:02 and 22:16 (2), arriving Berlin 00:27 and 07:03.

Berlin - Hamburg 655

Reservation is advisable for all of these trains, and all of them have a restaurant car.

Dep. Berlin (Hbf.)	05:46 (1)	08:08 (1)	08:53	12:31 (1)	14:55	18:21 (1)
Dep. Berlin (Fried.)	06:00	08:22	09:06	12:44	15:10	18:34
Dep. Berlin (Zoo)	16:13	08:34	10:00	12:57	15:35	18:45
Arr. Hamburg (Hbf.)	09:43	12:00	13:53	16:20	19:33	22:01

See notes about **Hamburg** on page 374.

Dep. Hamburg (Hbf.)	06:23 (1)	08:13	10:33 (1)	14:03 (1)	16:24 (2)
Arr. Berlin (Zoo)	09:44	12:06	14:07	17:37	21:10
Arr. Berlin (Fried.)	09:55	12:23	14:23	17:49	21:24
Dep. Berlin (Hbf.)	10:07	12:27	14:37	18:02	21:38

(1) Supplement charged. (2) Plus other Hamburg departures at 17:43 and 18:58 (1), arriving Berlin (Hbf.) 22:17 and 22:52.

Berlin - Hannover 670

Reservation is advisable for all of these trains. All of the day trains charge a supplement and have a restaurant car, unless designated otherwise.

Dep. Berlin (Hbf.)	00:22 (1)	05:36	-0-	06:41	07:18 (2)
Dep. Berlin (Fried.)	00:36	05:50	-0-	06:55	07:32
Dep. Berlin (Zoo)	00:56	06:02	06:30	07:07	07:44
Arr. Hannover	04:42	09:58	10:21	10:58	11:58

See notes about **Hannover** on page 374.

Dep. Berlin (Hbf.)	08:41	10:41	12:41	14:41	15:18 (2+4)
Dep. Berlin (Fried.)	08:55	10:55	12:55	14:55	15:32
Arr. Berlin (Zoo)	09:07	11:07	13:07	15:07	15:44
Arr. Hannover	12:58	14:58	16:58	18:58	19:58

(1) Carries a sleeping car. Also has couchettes. (2) Change trains in Braunschweig. (3) *No* supplement. (4) Plus other Berlin (Hbf.) departures at 16:41, 17:18 (2), 18:54 (3) and 23:18 (1), arriving Hannover 20:58, 23:30, 20:58 and 03:49.

Berlin - Leipzig - Berlin 739

Reservation is advisable on all of these trains.

Dep. Berlin (Licht.)	06:30 (1)	08:00 (2)	09:00 (1)	-0-	11:47 (1)
Dep. Berlin (Sch'feld)	06:55	08:25	09:25	10:38 (3)	12:13
Arr. Leipzig	09:09	10:19	11:40	12:57	14:25

Sights in **Leipzig:** See notes about sightseeing in Leipzig on page 375.

Dep. Leipzig	13:40 (2)	15:36 (1)	17:00 (1)	18:20 (1)	19:50 (1+4)
Arr. Berlin (Sch'feld)	15:36	17:24	19:00	20:12	21:36
Arr. Berlin (Licht.)	16:02	17:50	19:38	20:38	22:01

(1) Light refreshments. (2) Restaurant car. (3) Departs from Berlin's Schoneweide railstation. (5) Plus another departure from Leipzig at 21:12, arriving Berlin (Lichtenberg) 23:45.

Berlin - Munich and Munich - Berlin

Reservation is advisable on all of these trains.

	741	740	740	740	741
Dep. Berlin (Hbf.)	05:12 (1)	-0-	09:03 (2)	-0-	13:48 (1+5)
Dep. Berlin (Licht.)	-0-	06:00 (2)	-0-	11:47 (2+4)	-0-
Dep. Berlin (Sch'feld)	-0-	06:25	-0-	12:13	-0-
Arr. Munich	15:07	15:22	18:52	21:22	00:04

See notes about **Munich** on page 375

	741	741	740	741	741
Dep. Munich	06:29 (1)	09:49 (1)	12:37 (1)	14:49 (2)	22:12 (3+6)
Arr. Berlin (Sch'feld)	-0-	-0-	21:36	-0-	-0-
Arr. Berlin (Licht.)	-0-	-0-	22:01	-0-	-0-
Arr. Berlin (Hbf.)	16:46	19:47	-0-	00:57	08:14

(1) Restaurant car. (2) Light refreshments. (3) Carries a sleeping car. Also has couchettes. (4) Plus another Berlin (Lichtenberg) departure at [740] 19:17 (2), arriving Munich 06:00. (5) Plus another Berlin (Hbf.) departure at [741] 20:50 (3), arriving Munich 07:07. (6) Plus another Munich departure at [740] 23:08 (3), arriving Berlin (Schonefeld) 08:18, Berlin (Lichtenberg) 08:44.

Berlin - Potsdam - Berlin 670

There are frequent trains from Berlin's Friedrichstrasse and Zoo stations 05:26 to 00:22 for this 50-minute ride. From Potsdam:04:55 to 00:40.

Sights in **Potsdam:** The Concert Room and the great paintings in the Picture Gallery at the 18th century Sans Souci Palace. The 17th century Palace, Cecillienhof, where Truman, Attlee and Stalin signed the Potsdam Agreement in 1945.

Berlin - Rostock - Berlin 736

Reservation is advisable on all of these trains.

Dep. Berlin (Lichtenberg)	06:25 (1)	08:51	10:36 (2)
Arr. Rostock	09:10	11:23	13:36

Sights in **Rostock**: East Germany's largest seaport. See St. Mary's Church. The ancient Town Hall.

Dep. Rostock	12:05 (1)	15:54	18:18 (1)	20:40
Arr. Berlin (Lichtenberg)	15:03	18:51	21:15	23:38

(1) Restaurant car. (2) Light refreshments.

Berlin - Stralsund - Berlin 735

Reservation is advisable on all of these trains.

Dep. Berlin (Licht.)	06:57 (1)	07:04 (1)	08:40 (2)	10:31 (2)
Arr. Stralsund (Hbf.)	10:00	10:22	11:28 (3)	13:31

Sights in **Stralsund**: Many old red-brick buildings and churches along the city's quaint Hanseatic streets.

Dep. Stralsund (Hbf.)	13:58 (1+3)	14:53 (2)	15:46 (2+3)	18:00 (2)	18:44 (1+3+4)
Arr. Berlin (Licht.)	16:45	18:10	18:40	21:05	22:00

(1) Restaurant car. (2) Light refreshments. (3) Departs/Arrives Stralsund's Rugendamm railstation.
(3) Plus another Stralsund departure at 20:49, arriving Berlin 23:43.

Berlin - Warnemunde - Berlin 736

Reservation is advisable on all of these trains.

Dep. Berlin (Licht.)	00:13 (1)	06:25 (2)	14:11 (2)
Arr. Warnemunde	03:25	09:40	17:35

Sights in **Warnemunde**: A famous beach resort. A ferry connection to Denmark.

Dep. Warnemunde	03:44 (1)	11:39 (2)	17:45 (2)
Arr. Berlin (Licht.)	07:10	15:03	21:16

(1) Carries a sleeping car. Also has couchettes. Coach is second-class only. (2) Restaurant car.

Berlin - Weimar - Berlin 720

Reservation is advisable on all of these trains.

Dep. Berlin (Lichtenberg)	05:30 (1)	06:47 (2)	10:17 (1)
Dep. Berlin (Schonefeld)	05:55	07:13	10:43
Arr. Weimar	09:11	10:14	13:50

Sights in **Weimar**: The marvelous atmosphere of the era when German princes lived here.

Dep. Weimar	13:40 (2)	16:40 (1)	18:27 (1)	21:42 (1)
Arr. Berlin (Schonefeld)	17:00	19:42	21:24	00:54
Arr. Berlin (Lichtenberg)	17:18 (3)	20:08	21:50	01:20

(1) Light refreshments. (2) Restaurant car. (3) Arrives at Berlin's Schoneweide railstation.

Cologne - Amsterdam - Cologne 230

Reservation is advisable for all of these trains. All of them charge a supplement and have a restaurant car, unless designated otherwise.

Dep. Cologne	07:17	09:17	11:17	
Arr. Amsterdam	09:54	11:51	13:51	

Sights in **Amsterdam:** See notes about Amsterdam on page 87.

Dep. Amsterdam	15:08	17:00	19:08	20:56 (1)
Arr. Cologne	17:42	19:42	21:42	00:28

(1) *No* supplement charged. (2) *No* restaurant car.

Cologne - Bonn - Cologne 700 + 706

Dep. Cologne	Frequent times from 06:11 to 00:49
Arr. Bonn	22 minutes later

Sights in **Bonn**: The government buildings in the capital of West Germany, including Bundeshaus where its legislature meets. Beethoven-Halle and the museum at Bonngasse 20, where Beethoven was born in 1770. Drachenfels Mountain and the castle ruins that Byron immortalized. The 13th century Remigius Church. Jesu Church. The view of the Rhine and Siebengebirge from Alte Zoll. The university in the Electors' Castle. Poppelsdorf Castle. The Rhineland Museum. The Collegiate Church and Cloister.

Dep. Bonn	Frequent times from 04:25 to 01:50
Arr. Cologne	22 minutes later

Cologne - Brussels - Cologne 200

Reservation is advisable for these trains, unless designated otherwise.

Dep. Cologne	05:08 (1)	06:45 (2)	07:08	08:10	09:14 (3)
Arr. Brussels (Nord)	07:55	09:23	09:43	10:43	11:27
Arr. Brussels (Cen.)	-0-	-0-	09:47	10:47	11:34
Arr. Brussels (Midi)	08:07	09:36	09:55	10:52	11:42

Sights in **Brussels**: See notes about Brussels on page 88.

Dep. Brussels (Midi)	11:48 (4)	13:48 (4)	15:48 (4)	16:55 (5)	18:09 (3+6)
Dep. Brussels (Cen.)	11:52	13:52	15:52	-0-	18:13
Dep. Brussels (Nord)	11:57	13:57	15:57	17:03	18:18
Arr. Cologne	14:37	16:35	18:37	19:45	20:42

(1) Reservation not available. (2) Reservation not available. Second-class only. (3) Supplement charged. Restaurant car. (4) Supplement charged. (5) Reservation required. Light refreshments. (6)Plus other departures from Brussels Midi/Zuid at 18:48 (4), 19:48 (4) and 21:40 (1), arriving Cologne 21:40, 22:40 and 00:28.

382

Cologne - Dortmund - Cologne 660 + 670

Dep. Cologne   Frequent times from 05:03 to 23:35
Arr. Dortmund   70 minutes later

Sights in **Dortmund**: The view of the city from the top of the Television Tower. Westphalia Park. The Ostwall Museum.

Dep. Dortmund   Frequent times from 06:16 to 22:23
Arr. Cologne   70 minutes later

Cologne - Dusseldorf - Cologne 700

There is frequent rail service between Dusseldorf's railstation and its airport. Travel time is 12 minutes (Table 683).

Dep. Cologne   Frequent times from 05:03 to 00:35
Arr. Dusseldorf 24–28 minutes later

Sights in **Dusseldorf:** Many sensational modern buildings, replacing the 85 of the city that was destroyed in World War II. See the Paul Klee collection at Kunsttammlung Nordhein-Westfallen. The Aquarium at the Museum- bunker am Zoo.

The collection of 18th century Meissenware and 20th century art (Kadinsky, Chagall, Braque, etc., with 90 works by Paul Klee) at the 18th century Jagerhof Castle in the 30-acre Hofgarten (park), open daily except Monday 10:00–17:00 (until 20:00 on Wednesday).

The large collection of Goethe memorabilia (30,000 items: first editions, paintings, manuscripts) at the Goethe Museum, also in Hofgarten, open daily except Monday 10:00–17:00. An enormous collection of paintings in the Kunstmuseum.

The more than 4,000 manuscripts in the Heinrich Heine Institute, Bilkerstrasse 14, open daily except Monday 10:00–17:00. Near Altstadt ("Old Town"), stroll the half-mile long shopping street, Konigsallee (called "the Ko").

Take the 75-minute boat trip on the Rhine to **Zons**. Boats leave every 60 minutes from 13:3 –17:30 from the Rathausufer, at the edge of Old Town.

Take the 30-minute tram ride (#1 and #18, from Jan-Welem-Platz) to the 18th century Benrath Castle, surrounded by spectacular English-style and French- style gardens.

Sample the 8 local beers in Old Town and try the local food specialties: *reibekuchen*, a potato pancake; *halve hahn*, a caraway cheese eaten with mustard on *roggelchen*, small loaves of rye bread; *spanferkel brotchen*, slices of roast suckling pig served on a roll; *bratwurst* with hot mustard; and *blutwurst*, a black pudding served with raw onions.

Dep. Dusseldorf Frequent times from 05:36 to 23:27
Arr. Cologne   24–28 minutes later

Cologne - Frankfurt - Cologne 700

All of these trains have a restaurant car or light refreshments.

Dep. Cologne   Frequent times from 06:54 to 21:25
Arr. Frankfurt   2–2½ hours later

Sights in **Frankfurt**: See notes about sightseeing in Frankfurt on page 373.

Dep. Frankfurt   Frequent times from 06:10 to 21:50
Arr. Cologne   2–2½ hours later

Cologne - Hamburg - Cologne 660

Reservation is advisable for all of these trains. All of them charge a supplement and have a restaurant car.

Dep. Cologne	06:10	07:09 (1)	08:09	09:09
Arr. Hamburg (Hbf.)	10:06	11:06	12:06	13:06

Sights in **Hamburg**: See notes on page 374.

Dep. Hamburg (Hbf.)	13:52	14:52	15:52	16:52 (4)	17:52	18:52(2+3)
Arr. Cologne	17:50	18:50	19:50	20:50	21:50	22:50

(1) Runs daily, except Sunday. (2) Runs daily, except Saturday. (3) Plus another departure from Hamburg at 19:52, arriving Cologne 23:50.

Cologne - Heidelberg - Cologne 700

Reservation is advisable for all of these trains. All of them charge a supplement and have a restaurant car.

Dep. Cologne	06:30	07:30	08:30	09:30	10:30
Arr. Heidelberg	09:04	10:04	11:04	12:04	13:04

Sights in **Heidelberg**: Take a short cable-car ride from the town center to see the gardens, Library, Great Terrace, Fat Tower, Elizabeth Gate, Freidrich's Wing, the Otto-Heinrich Wing, the Mirror Room Wing, the 10-room German Pharmaceutical Museum and the Great Vat (said to be the world's largest wine barrel, holding 55,000 gallons), all at Heidelberg Castle.

Visit Germany's oldest (13th century) university, immortalized in "The Student Prince" opera. The astounding 16th century carved wood Altar of the Twelve Apostles in the Kurpfalzisches Museum. The Jesuit Church. The Church of the Holy Ghost, where visitors often hear impromptu organ concerts.The 16th century wood-carved Windsheim Altar (Christ and the Twelve Apostles) plus many rooms furnished with period pieces and paintings in the Palatine Museum at the Palais Morass. Knight's Mansion. Student's Jail.

From Easter into October, there are boat trips on the **Neckar River** that begin each morning and afternoon, with views of many medieval villages and fortresses.

It is only a 20-minute bus ride to **Neckargemund**, where you can wander ancient cobbled streets and see the view of the river and the countryside from Zum Ritter, a restaurant operating since 1579.

Dep. Heidelberg	13:54	14:54	15:54	16:54	17:54	18:54 (1)	19:54
Arr. Cologne	16:29	17:29	18:29	19:29	20:29	21:29	22:29

(1) Runs daily, except Saturday.

Cologne - Koblenz - Cologne   700

(There is a description on page 408 of a marvelous scenic trip from Cologne to Koblenz and Bullay and back to Cologne which does not permit much time for sightseeing in Koblenz.)

Reservation is advisable for all of these trains. Most of them charge a supplement and have a restaurant car.

Dep. Cologne	Frequent times from 06:30 to 00:49
Arr. Koblenz	60 minutes later

Sights in **Koblenz**: Where the Rhine and Moselle rivers meet. See Old Town. St. Castor's Church. The Middle Rhine Museum. Stolzenfels Castle. The 18th century Prince Electors' Palace. The regional and Rhenish museums in the 19th century Ehrenbreitstein Fortress. The wine village.

The 13th century Old Castle. The 18th century Mint Master's House. The 18th century Baroque Franconian Royal Palace. The 13th century Romanesque Church of Our Lady. The 15th century Altes Kaufhaus. The 16th century Schoffenhaus.

Dep. Koblenz	Frequent times from 03:43 to 23:16
Arr. Cologne	60 minutes later

Cologne - Luxembourg - Cologne   707

Reservation is advisable for all of these trains.

Dep. Cologne	06:11	08:11 (1)	10:11
Arr. Luxembourg	09:22	11:27	13:22

Sights in **Luxembourg**: See notes about Luxembourg on page 88.

Dep.Luxembourg	12:26 (1)	14:34	15:24 (1)	17:35 (1)
Arr. Cologne	15:45	17:45	19:45	21:45

(1) Change trains in Trier.

Cologne - Mainz - Cologne   Boat   705

Here is a way to combine a cruise on the Rhine with a scenic rail trip.

Have lunch and Rhine wine on board just before arriving Mainz. Early in the trip, you can see Drachenfels Castle, near Bonn. During the Koblenz-Bingen portion of this cruise, you will see the best scenery on the Rhine, many hilltop castles, and the Lorelei.

Dep. Cologne (Rheingarten)	09:00 (1)	-0-	-0-
Dep. Bonn	09:40	-0-	-0-
Dep. Koblenz	11:05	11:00 (2)	12:30 (2)
Dep. Bingen	12:28	16:20	17:50
Arr. Mainz	13:10	18:45	20:15

(1) Hydrofoil boat express service. *Not* covered by Eurailpass. Operates mid-April to late October. Runs daily, except Monday. (2) Operates late June to early September. Runs daily.

Sights in **Mainz:** The art collection in the 1,000-year-old Cathedral. Adjacent to it is the Gutenberg Museum, with the first printed bible and where a movie on the inventor's life can be viewed. Also visit the Museum of the Central Rhineland. Rare books in the World Museum of Printing in the Romischer Kaiser. Restored Baroque mansions on the Schillerplatz and Schillerstrasse, in the Kirschgarten. Old Town. Sculptures in the Diocesan Museum.

Then for the train ride back to Cologne:

Reservation is advisable for all of these trains. All of them charge a supplement and have a restaurant car.

700

Dep. Mainz	14:18	19:24	21:18	22:24
Arr. Koblenz	15:05	20:11	22:05	23:12
Arr. Bonn	15:34	20:40	22:34	23:43
Arr. Cologne	15:59	21:05	22:59	00:09

Here is the schedule for visiting Mainz by taking the train both ways:

700

Dep. Cologne	Frequent times from 06:30 to 21:25
Arr. Mainz	2 hours later

* * *

Dep, Mainz	Frequent times from 07:16 to 22:21
Arr. Cologne	2 hours later

Cologne - Mannheim - Cologne   700

Reservation is advisable for all of these trains. All of them charge a supplement and have a restaurant car, unless designated otherwise.

Dep. Cologne	06:30	07:00	07:30	08:00	08:30 (1)
Arr. Mannheim	08:52	09:23	09:52	10:23	10:52

Sights in **Mannheim:** The Squared Town. The first thing that strikes you about Mannheim is its "Squareness". Built to be a fortified town, it was designed as a chessboard of 144 residential blocks, each known by a letter and number that identifies its position on the grid.

See the Fine Arts Museum. The Reiss Municipal Museum. The Cathedral, Europe's largest Romanesque Church. The Water Tower. The old Town Hall and parish church in the Marketplatz. The Castle.

Dep. Mannheim	Frequent departures from 05:50 to 20:36
Arr. Cologne	2½ hours later

(1) Plus other frequent departures from Cologne at 09:00 to 20:00.

Cologne - Siegen - Cologne 685

Dep. Cologne	07:19	08:19	09:19	10:19	11:19	12:19	13:19
Arr. Siegen	08:48	09:48	10:48	11:48	12:48	13:48	14:48

Sights in **Siegen:** The Upper Castle, with its Reubens paintings (he was born here) in the Siegerland Museum, which also offers the history of this region and a tour of the old iron mine under the Castle's cellar. See the crypts of the Princes of Nassau-Orange in the Castle.

Dep. Siegen	11:10	12:10	13:10	14:10	15:10	16:10	17:10 (1)
Arr. Cologne	12:39	13:39	14:39	15:39	16:39	17:39	18:39

(1) Plus other departures from Siegen at 18:10, 19:10, 20:08, 21:10 and 22:10.

Cologne - Trier - Cologne 707

Dep. Cologne	07:23	08:11	09:23	Dep. Trier	15:18	15:44	16:46 (1)
Arr. Trier	10:06	10:37	12:06	Arr. Cologne	17:45	18:34	19:45

(1) Plus other departures from Trier at 17:44 and 19:18, arriving Cologne 20:34 and 21:45.

Sights in **Trier**: See notes under "Luxembourg–Trier" on page 108.

Dresden - Berlin - Dresden 730

Reservation is advisable for all of these trains.

Dep. Dresden (Hbf.)	05:48 (1)	06:48 (2)	07:48 (1)	08:48	11:18 (3)
Arr. Berlin (Licht.)	08:25	09:14	10:26	11:14	13:51

Sights in **Berlin:** See notes on page 371.

Dep. Berlin (Licht.)	12:46 (1)	14:11 (4)	15:17 (4)	15:53	17:41 (4)	19:00 (4+5)
Arr. Dresden (Hbf.)	15:44	16:42	17:47	18:39	20:10	21:43

(1) Light refreshments. (2) Runs daily, except Sundays and holidays. (3) Reservation required. Restaurant car. (4) Restaurant car. (5) Plus other departures from Berlin at 20:47, 21:53 and 23:00, arriving Dresden 23:21, 00:38 and 01:28.

Dresden - Chemnitz (formerly Karl Marx Stadt) - Dresden 740

Reservation is advisable for all of these trains.

Dep. Dresden (Hbf.)	06:51	07:30 (1)	09:23 (2)	11:30	12:52 (3)
Arr. Chemnitz	08:17	09:00	10:52	12:57	14:19

Sights in **Chemnitz:** An East German post-World War II showplace *new* city.

Dep. Chemnitz	12:21	13:23 (3)	14:21 (1)	16:21	17:20	19:25 (1+4)
Arr. Dresden (Hbf.)	13:46	14:48	15:43	17:48	18:49 (2)	20:49

(1) Light refreshments. (2) Departs/Arrives Dresden's Neustadt railstation.light refreshments. (3) Restaurant car. (4) Plus other Chemnitz departures at 21:06 (3), 21:38 (1) and 23:07 (1), arriving Dresden 22:32, 23:03 and 00:37 (2).

Dresden - Leipzig - Dresden 725

Reservation is advisable for all of these trains.

Dep. Dresden (Hbf.)	06:33 (1)	07:33 (2)	08:33	09:33 (1)	11:11 (1)
Dep. Dresden (Neu.)	06:41	07:41	08:41	09:41	11:19
Arr. Leipzig	08:26	09:12	10:13	11:26	12:57

Sights in **Leipzig**: See notes about sightseeing in Leipzig on page 375.

Dep. Leipzig	12:55	14:42	15:37	17:09 (1)	18:43 (1)
Arr. Dresden (Neu.)	14:36	16:24	17:24	18:44	20:26
Arr. Dresden (Hbf.)	10 minutes later				

Dep. Leipzig	19:29 (3)	20:18 (4)	20:40 (2)	21:09 (1)	22:26 (1)
Arr. Dresden (Neu.)	21:07	21:54	22:10	22:54	00:08
Arr. Dresden (Hbf.)	10 minutes later				

(1) Light refreshments. (2) Supplement charged. Restaurant car. (3) Operate mid-June to early September. (4) Operates late June to early September.

Frankfurt - Basel - Frankfurt 700

Reservation is advisable for all of these trains. These trains have a restaurant car, unless designated otherwise.

Dep. Frankfurt (Hbf.)	06:39 (1)	07:19 (3)	09:46 (1)	10:46 (4)
Arr. Mannheim	-0- (2)	-0- (2)	10:25	11:25

Change trains.

Dep. Manheim	-0- (2)	-0- (2)	10:32 (1)	11:32 (1)
Arr. Basel (Badisch.)	09:38	11:09	12:37	13:38
Arr. Basel (S.B.B.)	7 minutes later			

Sights in **Basel**: See notes about Basel on page 310.

Dep. Basel (S.B.B.)	14:15 (1)	15:15 (1)	16:15 (1)	17:15 (1)	17:33 (3+6)
Dep. Basel (Badisch.)	7 minutes later				
Arr. Mannheim	16:26	17:26	18:26	19:26	-0- (2)

Change trains.

Dep. Mannheim	16:34 (1)	17:34 (1)	18:34 (5)	19:34 (1)	-0- (2)
Arr. Frankfurt	17:13	18:13	19:13	20:13	21:47

(1) Supplement charged. (2) Direct train. No train change in Mannheim. (3) Light refreshments. (4) Runs daily, except Sunday. Supplement charged. (5) Runs daily, except Saturday. Supplement charged. (6) Plus other departures from Basel at 18:15 (1) and 19:15 (1+2), arriving Frankfurt 21:13 and 22:19.

Frankfurt - Bremen - Frankfurt

Reservation is advisable and a supplement is charged for all of these trains. Unless designated otherwise, the Frankfurt-Hannover (and v.v.) trains have a restaurant car — and the Hannover-Bremen and (v.v.) trains have light refreshments.

710

Dep. Frankfurt	06:17 (1)	07:17	08:17	09:17	10:17	
Arr. Hannover	08:38	09:38	10:38	11:38	12:38	
Change trains.	655					
Dep. Hannover	08:43 (2)	09:43	10:43	11:43 (3)	12:43	
Arr. Bremen	09:39	10:39	11:39	12:40	13:39	

Sights in **Bremen**: It is an easy walk, down Bahnhofstrasse, from the railstation to the fine buildings in Market Square and to the 17th century Rathaus (Town Hall), Liebfrauenkirche, and the 11th century Cathedral, with its ancient crypt. From Market Square, walk down Bottcherstrasse to see the Porcelain Carillon and the Atlantis House, decorated with Zodiac signs. The collection of Durer paintings in the Kunsthalle.

Visit the Overseas Museum. Rampart Walk. The Focke Museum of Folklore. The Municipal Weights and Measures Office. Martini Church, from which 75-minute harbor cruises depart frequently every day in Summer. See the old workshops, inns and houses in the Schnoor residential area.

Dep. Bremen	13:20 (3)	14:20 (4)	15:20	16:20	17:20 (4)	18:20 (5)
Arr. Hannover	14:15	15:15	16:15	17:15	18:15	19:15
Change trains.	710					
Dep. Hannover	14:20	15:20 (4)	16:20	17:20	18:20 (4)	19:20
Arr. Frankfurt	16:42	17:42	18:42	19:42	20:42	21:42

(1) Runs daily, except Sunday. (2) Runs daily, except Sundays and holidays. (3) No supplement. (4) Runs daily Bremmen–Hannover, but the Hannover–Frankfurt train does *not* run Saturday. (5) Plus another Bremen departure at 19:20, arriving Frankfurt 22:42.

Frankfurt - Brussels - Frankfurt 64

Dep. Frankfurt	06:50 (1)	08:50(1+2)	Dep. Brussels (Midi)	15:48 (4)	16:55 (4+6)
Arr. Cologne	09:05	11:05	Arr. Cologne	18:38	19:45
Change trains.			Change trains.		
Dep. Cologne	09:14 (1)	11:17 (3)	Dep. Cologne	18:54 (5)	19:54 (1)
Arr. Brussels (Midi)	11:42	13:55	Arr. Frankfurt	21:09	22:09

(1) Reservation advisable. Supplement charged. Restaurant car. (2) Runs daily, except Sundays and holidays. (3) Reservation advisable. Light refreshments. (4) Light refreshments. (5) Runs daily, except Saturday. Reservation advisable. Another train departs daily at 19:54 (1), arriving Frankfurt 22:09. (6) Plus another Brussels departure at 18:09 (1), arriving Frankfurt 23:09.

Sights in **Brussels**: See notes about Brussels on page 88.

Frankfurt - Cologne - Frankfurt 700

From Mainz to Bonn, the cliffs on both sides of the Rhine are topped by ruins of ancient castles. This portion of the river is crowded with barges, sailboats, recreational motorboats, ferries and cruise ships.

Reservation is advisable for all of these trains. All of them charge a supplement and have a restaurant car, unless designated otherwise.

Dep. Frankfurt	06:50	07:50	08:50 (1)	09:50	10:50	
Arr. Cologne	09:05	10:05	11:05	12:05	13:05	

Sights in **Cologne**: See notes about sightseeing in Cologne on page 372.

Dep. Cologne	12:54	13:54	14:54	15:54	16:54	17:54 (5)
Arr. Frankfurt	15:09	16:09	17:09	18:09	19:09	20:09

(1) Runs daily, except Sunday. (2) Runs daily, except Saturday. (3) No supplement. Light refreshments. (4) No supplement. Neither restaurant car nor light refreshments. (5) Plus other departures from Cologne at 18:54 (2), 19:54, 20:38 (3), 20:54 and 21:25 (4), arriving Frankfurt 21:09, 22:09, 22:55, 23:09 and 23:26.

Frankfurt - Dusseldorf - Frankfurt 700

Reservation is advisable and supplement is charged for all of these trains. All of them have a restaurant car, unless designated otherwise.

Dep. Frankfurt	06:50	09:50	10:50		
Arr. Dusseldorf	09:31	12:31	13:31		

Sights in **Dusseldorf**: See "Cologne-Dusseldorf" on page 382.

Dep. Dusseldorf	13:27	15:27	16:27	18:27 (1)	20:06 (2)
Arr. Frankfurt	16:09	18:09	19:09	21:09	22:55

(1) Runs daily, except Saturday. (2) Light refreshments.

Frankfurt - Essen - Frankfurt 700

Reservation is advisable and supplement is charged for all of these trains. All of them have a restaurant car, unless designated otherwise.

Dep. Frankfurt	06:50	07:50 (2)	09:50		
Arr. Essen	09:57	11:37	12:57		

Sights in **Essen**: One of the leading German collections of 18th, 19th and 20th century art (Menzel, Delacroix, Renoir, Gaugin, Vlaminck, Kandinsky, Klee, Rothko, Rodin) at the Folkwang Museum. The 10th century Cathedral and its collection of priceless 10th and 11th century processional crosses, the 9th century Golden Madonna (oldest Western statue of the Virgin Mary), and the sword of Cosmas and Damian, the martyr saints.

The chronicle of the Krupp family and business in the Annex at Villa Hugel, former residence of the Krupp family. The 12th century castle, Burg Altendorf. The Four Horsemen bronze door on the 11th century Marktkirche, Protestant since 1563.

Dep. Essen	15:01	16:01	18:01 (3)	19:31 (4)	20:01 (5)
Arr. Frankfurt	18:09	19:09	21:09	22:55	23:05

(1) No supplement. No restaurant car. (2) Change trains in Cologne at 10:05. Depart Cologne 10:35 (1). (3) Runs daily, except Saturday. (4) No supplement. Light refreshments. (5) Plus another departure from Essen at 20:21 (1), arriving Frankfurt 23:51.

Frankfurt - Hamburg - Frankfurt 710

Reservation is advisable and supplement is charged for all of these trains. All of them have a restaurant car.

Dep. Frankfurt (Hbf.)	06:17 (1)	07:17	08:17	09:17	10:17
Arr. Hamburg (Hbf.)	09:51	10:51	11:51	12:51	13:51

Sights in **Hamburg**: See notes on page 374.

Dep. Hamburg (Hbf.)	14:07 (2)	15:07	16:07	17:07 (2)	18:07
Arr. Frankfurt (Hbf.)	17:42	18:42	19:42	20:42	21:42

(1) Runs daily, except Sunday. (2) Runs daily, except Saturday.

Frankfurt - Hannover - Frankfurt 710

Reservation is advisable and supplement is charged for all of these trains. All of them have a restaurant car.

Dep. Frankfurt	06:17 (1)	07:17	08:17	09:17	10:17	
Dep. Hannover	08:38	09:38	10:38	11:38	12:38	

Sights in **Hannover**: See notes about sightseeing in Hannover on page 374.

Dep. Hannover	14:20	15:20 (2)	16:20	17:20	18:20 (2)	19:20 (3)
Arr. Frankfurt	16:42	17:42	18:42	19:42	20:42	21:42

(1) Runs daily, except Sunday. (2) Runs daily, except Saturday. (3) Plus another Hannover departure at 20:20, arriving Frankfurt 22:42.

Frankfurt - Heidelberg - Frankfurt 700

Reservation is advisable for all of these trains.

Dep. Frankfurt	Frequent times from 05:16 to 21:50
Arr. Heidelberg	one hour later

Sights in **Heidelberg**: See notes under "Cologne-Heidelberg" on page 383.

Dep. Heidelberg	Frequent times from 05:50 to 23:05
Arr. Frankfurt	one hour later

Frankfurt - Kassel - Frankfurt 710

Reservation is advisable for all of these trains. All of them charge a supplement and have a restaurant car.

Dep. Frankfurt (Hbf.)	07:17	08:17	09:17	10:17	11:17 (1)	12:02
Arr. Kassel (Wil.)	08:42	09:42	10:42	11:42	12:42	13:30

Sights in **Kassel:** Take the bus #13 to see the enormous 233-foot high copper statue of Hercules, the 19th century Wilhelmshohe Castle, and the art museums (Rembrandt, Durer, Rubens) inside the Castle. Open daily except Monday, March–October, 10:00–17:00. Also see the collection of Brothers Grimm memorabilia in the City Museum. They wrote their fairy tales here. Other interesting sights are the 18th century Orangery Palace in Karlsaue Park. The paintings in the Landesmuseum. The Tapestry Museum. The Fredericianum Museum. The world's only Wallpaper Museum.

Dep. Kassel (Wil.)	13:16	14:29	15:16	16:29	17:16	18:16 (3)
Arr. Frankfurt (Hbf.)	14:42	15:58	16:42	17:58	18:42	19:42

(1) Runs daily, except Sunday. (2) Runs daily, except Saturday. (3) Plus other departures from Kassel at 19:16 (2), 20:29, 21:16 and 22:29, arriving Frankfurt 20:42, 21:59, 22:42 and 23:59.

Frankfurt - Luxembourg - Frankfurt

Reservation is advisable and a supplement is charged for all of the Frankfurt-Koblenz (and v.v.) trains — and all have a restaurant car. Reservation is advisable for all of the Koblenz-Luxembourg and (v.v.) trains.

700			707		
Dep. Frankfurt	07:50	09:50	Dep. Luxembourg	14:34	17:35 (2)
Arr. Koblenz	09:11	11:11	Arr. Koblenz	16:38	20:38
Change trains. 707			Change trains. 700		
Dep. Koblenz	09:19 (1)	11:19	Dep. Koblenz	16:47	20:47
Arr. Luxembourg	11:27	13:22	Arr. Frankfurt	18:09	22:09

(1) Change trains in Trier at 10:37. Depart Trier 10:43. (2) Or depart Luxembourg 18:28 (daily, except Sundays and holidays). Both the 17:35 and 18:28 departures require changing trains in Trier (at 18:32 or 19:10). depart Trier at 19:18.

Sights in **Luxembourg**: See notes about Luxembourg on page 88.

Frankfurt - Mainz - Frankfurt 700

Reservation is advisable for all of these trains. All of them charge a supplement.

Dep. Frankfurt	07:50	08:50 (1)	09:50	10:50	12:50	13:50
Arr. Mainz	30 minutes later					

Sights in **Mainz**: See notes under "Cologne-Mainz" on page 384.

Dep. Mainz	Frequent times from 05:40 to 23:26
Arr. Frankfurt	30 minutes later

(1) Runs daily, except Sunday.

Frankfurt - Mannheim - Frankfurt 700

Reservation is advisable for all of these trains. All of them charge a supplement and have a restaurant car.

Dep. Frankfurt	07:46 (1)	08:46	09:46	10:46 (1)	11:46	12:46
Arr. Mannheim	40 minutes later					

Sights in **Mannheim**: See notes under "Cologne-Mannheim" on page 385.

Dep. Mannheim	12:34	13:34	14:34	15:34	16:34	17:34 (2)
Arr. Frankfurt	40 minutes later					

(1) Runs daily, except Sunday. (2) Plus other Mannheim departures at 18:16, 19:34, 20:34, 21:36 and 22:20.

Frankfurt - Munich - Frankfurt 700

Reservation is advisable for all of these trains. All of them charge a supplement and have a restaurant car.

Dep. Frankfurt	06:14 (1)	07:46 (2)	08:46	09:46		
Arr. Munich	09:45	11:20	12:20	13:20		

Sights in **Munich**: See notes about Munich on page 375.

Dep. Munich	12:41	14:41	15:41 (3)	16:41	17:41	18:19 (3)
Arr. Frankfurt	16:13	18:13	19:13	20:13	21:13	22:38

(1) Runs Monday–Friday, except holidays. (2) Runs daily, except Sunday. (3) Runs daily, except Saturday.

Frankfurt - Nurnberg (and Bayreuth) - Frankfurt 770

Reservation is advisable for all of these trains. All of them charge a supplement and have a restaurant car, unless designated otherwise.

Dep. Frankfurt	07:21 (1)	08:21	09:21	10:21	11:21
Arr. Nurnberg	09:47	10:40	11:47	12:40	13:47

Sights in **Nurnberg**: The bronze and silver Sebaldusgrab, excellent stained glass and the carved tomb of the Saint for whom it is named in the 13th century St. Sebaldus Church. Take a guided tour of the Kaiserburg (Imperial Castle), Burggrafenburg and Imperial Stables in the fort. See the Albrecht Durer Haus, with copies of his paintings. The kitchen is as it was, when the artist lived there from 1509 to 1528. It is open daily except Monday 10:00–13:00 and 14:00–17:00. The Rosette window, wood carving and statues in St. Lorenz Kirche.

Visit the 14th century Frauenkirche in the marketplace, where the moving figures in the clock perform every day at 12:00. Then lunch at a bratwurst restaurant. One is located next to St. Sebaldus Church; another is behind the rebuilt 17th century Rathaus (City Hall). There are guided tours of 14th century catacombs (torture chamber and dungeons) in the Rathaus.

The Alstadt Museum. The collection of toys, doll houses and other works in the German National Museum. The 40 gold figures of artists, emperors, philosophers, prophets and popes around the 14th century Schoner Brunnen (Beautiful Fountain) at Hauptmarkt, where farmers sell their produce from stalls.

On the little island in the Pegnitz River is the Holy Ghost Hospital, locale of the legendary Till Eulenspiegel. Disguised as a doctor, this is where the 14th century peasant clown told the man in charge of the hospital that he could cure all the patients in one day. The hospital authorities believed Till was a miracle worker when the patients rose from their beds and left the hospital after he whispered in each one's ear. He told the patients: "Those of you who are the most sick are going to be burned into a powder the hospital will use to heal the others."

Visit the collection of porcelains and the model of Old Nurnberg at Fembo House (The City Historical Museum), 15 Burgstrasse, open daily except Monday 10:00–17:00. The best collection of old trains in West Germany (including Germany's first locomotive) is in Nurnberg's Transport Museum, open Monday-Saturday 10:00–17:00 (closes at 16:00 in Winter) and Sunday 10:00–13:00. Toys from all over the world are exhibited at Spielzeug Museum, open daily except Monday 10:00–17:00.

From Nurnberg, it's a short trip (see timetable on page 388) to Bayreuth, site of a 5-week annual (over 100 years) Wagner opera festival at Festspielhaus, every year from late July to late August at 16:00.

Marvelous sights in **Bayreuth**: Haus Wahnfried, Wagner's home. The breathtaking opera house. The Orangerie castle, open daily 10:00–11:30 and 13:30–15:00. Eremitage Park.

Dep. Nurnberg	12:20 (2)	13:19	14:11	15:19	16:11	17:19	18:11 (4)
Arr. Frankfurt	15:20	15:38	16:38	17:38	18:38	19:38	20:38

(1) Runs daily, except Sunday. (2) No supplement. (3) Runs daily, except Saturday. (4) Plus other Nurnberg departures at 19:19, 20:11 (3) and 21:17.

Here are the connections between Nurnberg and Bayreuth:

740

Dep. Nurnberg	09:57 (1)	12:52 (2)	Dep. Bayreuth	13:52	15:25 (2)	16:13 (3)
Arr. Bayreuth	11:12	14:15	Arr. Nurnberg	15:03	16:39	17:23

(1) Runs daily, except Sundays and holidays. (2) Runs Monday-Friday, except holidays. (3) Plus other Bayreuth departures at 17:45, 20:39 and 21:45 (2).

Frankfurt - Siegen - Frankfurt 685

Dep. Frankfurt	07:58	09:58 (1+2)	Dep. Siegen	13:54	15:54(3)
Arr. Giessen	08:38	10:38	Arr. Giessen	14:51	16:51
Change trains.			Change trains.		
Dep. Giessen	09:08	11:08	Dep. Giessen	15:14	17:14
Arr. Siegen	10:05	12:05	Arr. Frankfurt	16:02	18:02

(1) Light refreshments. (2) Plus another Frankfurt departure at 11:58, arriving Siegen 14:05. (3) Plus other Siegen departures at 17:54 and 19:54, arriving Frankfurt 20:02 and 22:02.

Sights in **Siegen**: See notes under "Cologne-Siegen" on page 386.

Frankfurt - Strasbourg - Frankfurt

700			755 a		
Dep. Frankfurt	07:50	09:50	Dep. Strasbourg	15:18	17:18(1)
Arr. Offenburg	09:53	11:53	Arr. Offenburg	15:47	17:45
Change trains. 755 a			Change trains. 700		
Dep. Offenburg	10:10	12:10	Dep. Offenburg	16:06	18:06
Arr. Strasbourg	10:40	12:40	Arr. Frankfurt	18:09	20:09

(1) Plus other Strasbourg departures at 19:18 and 20:45, arriving Frankfurt 21:47 and 00:09.

Frankfurt - Stuttgart - Frankfurt 700

Reservation is advisable for all of these trains. All of them charge a supplement and have a restaurant car.

Dep. Frankfurt	07:46 (1)	08:46	09:46	10:46	11:46
Arr. Stuttgart	09:08	10:08	11:08	12:08	13:08

Sights in **Stuttgart**: Outstanding contemporary architecture, built since World War II. The Schillerplatz flower and vegetable market (Tuesday, Thursday and Saturday). Also on Schillerplatz, Swabian art and culture from the Middle Ages to Art Nouveau, at the Wuerttemberg Provincial Museum in the Altes Schloss. Europe's most modern planetarium, opened in 1977.

The largest Picasso collection in Germany, at the State Gallery. The Daimler-Benz Automobile Museum, admission only by advance appointment. The Museum of Natural History, in Rosenstein Palace. The Wilhelms Palace, residence of the last king of Wuerttemberg, Wilhelm II. The Wilhelma Zoo (over 1,000 kind of animals) and Botanical Garden at the Summer residence of Wilhelm I, built in Moorish style in 1853.

Liederhalle, with its 3 concert halls. The birthplace of the philosopher Hegel at Eberhardstrasse 53. The 4,000 paintings (14th–20th century) in the State Gallery, at Konrad Adenaur Strasse 32.

Dep. Stuttgart	12:53	13:53	14:53	15:53	16:53	17:53 (2)
Arr. Frankfurt	14:13	15:13	16:13	17:13	18:13	19:13

(1) Runs daily, except Sunday. (4) Plus other departures from Stuttgart at 18:53 and 19:53.

Frankfurt - Wiesbaden 708

Reservation is advisable and a supplement is charged for all of these trains.

Dep. Frankfurt	06:53	08:53	10:53	12:53	14:53	16:53	18:53
Arr. Wiesbaden	28 minutes later						

Sights in **Wiesbaden:** One of Europe's top mineral bath resorts. See Brunnenkolonnade, the longest colonnade in Europe.

Dep. Wiesbaden	07:39	08:39	11:39	13:39	15:39	17:39	19:39
Arr. Frankfurt	28 minutes later						

Hamburg - Berlin - Hamburg   665

All of these trains have a restaurant car.

Dep. Hamburg (Alt.)	06:08 (1)	07:58 (2)	Dep. Berlin (Hbf.)	18:21
Dep. Hamburg (Hbf.)	06:23	08:13	Arr. Hamburg (Hbf.)	22:01
Arr. Berlin (Hbf.)	10:07	12:27	Arr. Hamburg (Alt.)	22:14

(1) Reservation advisable. Supplement charged. (2) Reservation advisable.

Sights in **Berlin**: See notes about Berlin on page 371.

Hamburg - Bremen - Hamburg   660

Reservation is advisable for all of these trains. All of them charge a supplement and have a restaurant car.

Dep. Hamburg (Alt.)	07:38	08:38	09:38	10:38	11:38	
Dep. Hamburg (Hbf.)	14 minutes later					
Arr. Bremen	08:46	09:46	10:46	11:46	12:46	

Sights in **Bremen**: See notes under "Frankfurt–Bremen" on page 388.

Dep. Bremen	12:12	13:12	14:12	15:12	16:12	17:12 (2)
Arr. Hamburg (Hbf.)	13:06	14:06	15:06	16:06	17:06	18:06
Arr. Hamburg (Alt.)	13 minutes later					

(1) Runs daily, except Saturday.   (2) Plus other departures from Bremen at 18:12, 19:12, 20:12 (1), 21:12, 22:12 and 23:12.

Hamburg - Hannover - Hamburg   710

Reservation is advisable for all of these trains. Most of them charge a supplement. All have a restaurant car or light refreshments.

Dep. Hamburg (Alt.)	Frequent times from 05:33 to 22:38
Dep. Hamburg (Hbf.)	14 minutes later
Arr. Hannover	85 minutes after departing Hamburg (Hbf.)

Sights in **Hannover**: See notes about Hannover on page 374.

Dep. Hannover	Frequent times from 04:40 to 22:49
Arr. Hamburg (Hbf.)	85 Minutes later
Arr. Hamburg (Alt.)	14 minutes after departing Hbf.

Hamburg - Lubeck - Hamburg   661

| Dep. Hamburg (Hbf.) | Frequent times from 07:15 to 23:16 |
| Arr. Lubeck | 40 minutes later |

Sights in **Lubeck**: All museums here are closed Monday. April-September, they are open other days 10:00–17:00, October-March 10:00–16:00. It is an easy walk from the railstation down Konrad Adenauer Strasse, over the Puppenbrucke bridge, and straight ahead to the museum of the city's history in Holstentor, the immense 15th century fort. Particularly interesting there is the model of the town as it was in 1650.

Nearby, just off Holstenstrasse, is the 15th century St. Peter's Church. There is a marvelous view of the city and its harbors from the top of the church's 165-foot-high tower. Also see the elegant chapel in the 14th century St. Mary's Church. Across the square from it is Buddenbrookshaus, at 4 Mengstrasse, where Thomas Mann was born. Although it is now a bank, some of the upstairs rooms can be visited during the hours the bank is open.

There are dozens of interesting alleys and little passageways here with lovely cottages, shops and restaurants. See the mansions on Grosse Petersgrube, Engelsgrube, Fischergrube and Mengstrasse. See the 19th and 20th century paintings, handicrafts and sculptures in the Bennhaus, a magnificent 18th century merchant's house. The city's main museum is in St. Anne's Convent.

Cruise boats that go around the city and harbor leave from the front of Hotel Jensen (Trave Landing) daily in Spring, Summer and Fall every half hour from 10:00 to 18:00.

| Dep. Lubeck | Frequent times from 05:35 to 24:00 |
| Arr. Hamburg (Hbf.) | 40 minutes later |

Hannover - Berlin - Hannover 670

Reservation is advisable for all of these trains. All of them charge a supplement and have a restaurant car, unless designated otherwise.

| Dep. Hannover | 05:49 | 07:28 (1) | 09:02 | | |
| Arr. Berlin (Hbf.) | 10:27 | 12:27 | 13:17 | | |

Sights in **Berlin**: See notes about Berlin on page 371.

| Dep. Berlin (Hbf.) | 14:41 | 15:18 (1) | 16:41 | 17:18 (1) | 18:54 (2) |
| Arr. Hannover | 18:58 | 19:58 | 20:58 | 21:58 | 23:30 |

(1) Change trains in Braunscheig. (2) No supplement. No restaurant car.

Hannover - Bremen - Hannover 655

| Dep. Hannover | 07:47 | 08:43 (1) | 08:47 | 09:43 (2) | 09:47 | 10:43 (2+4) |
| Arr. Bremen | 09:04 | 09:39 | 10:04 | 10:39 | 11:04 | 11:39 |

Sights in **Bremen**: See notes about Bremen under "Frankfurt–Bremen" on page 388.

| Dep. Bremen | 13:54 | 14:20 (2) | 14:54 | 15:20 (2) | 15:54 | 16:54 (5) |
| Arr. Hannover | 15:10 | 15:15 | 16:10 | 16:15 | 17:10 | 18:10 |

(1) Runs daily, except Sundays and holidays. Light refreshments. (2) Reservation advisable. Supplement charged. Light refreshments. (3) Reservation advisable. (4) Plus other Hannover departures at 10:47, 11:43 (2), 11:47 and 12:43 (2). (5) Plus other departures from Bremen at 17:20 (2), 17:54, 18:20 (2), 18:52, 19:20 (2), 19:54, 20:19 (2), 20:54, 21:18 (3), 22:07 (3), 22:35 and 23:44.

Hannover - Celle - Hannover 710

Reservation is advisable for all of these trains.

| Dep. Hannover | Frequent times from 04:56 to 23:46 |
| Arr. Celle | 25 minutes later |

Sights in **Celle**: The beautifully decorated chapel and wonderful French Garden at the 13th century Duke's Palace. The 14th century Marienkirche. The exhibit of the local life and farm culture in the Bomann Museum. The heavy wood-beamed ceilings and quality wood panelling in the 14th century Rathaus (Town Hall), oldest tavern in Northern Germany. The Lower Saxony stud farm, home of the famous Hannoverian horses.

The 480 half-timbered houses, some dating back to the 15th century, many with carved beams. The Apiary Museum at the Institute for Bee Research. The nearby Wienhausen Monastery. Regional food specialties are *heidschnuckenbraten* (roasted lamb), *meissendorfer spiegelkarpfen* (carp) and *burgdorfer spargel* (asparagus). There are steamer cruises on the **Aller River.**

| Dep. Celle | Frequent times from 06:49 to 21:35 |
| Arr. Hannover | 25 minutes later |

396

Hannover - Dortmund - Hannover 670

Reservation is advisable for all of these trains. All of them charge a supplement and have a restaurant car.

Dep. Hannover	07:01	08:01	09:01 (1)	10:01	11:01	12:01
Arr. Dortmund	08:33	09:33	10:33	11:33	12:33	13:33

Sights in **Dortmund**: See notes about Dortmund on page 382.

Dep. Dortmund	13:27	14:27	15:27	16:27	17:27	18:27 (4)
Arr. Hannover	14:59	15:59	16:59	17:59	18:59	19:59

(1) Runs daily, except Sunday. (2) Runs daily, except Saturday. (3) No supplement charged. No restaurant car. (4) Plus other departures from Dortmund at 19:27 (2), 20:27, 21:10 (3) and 22:27.

Hannover - Dusseldorf - Hannover 670

Reservation is advisable for all of these trains. All of them charge a supplement and have a restaurant car.

Dep. Hannover	08:01	10:01
Arr. Dusseldorf	10:25	12:25

Sights in **Dusseldorf**: See notes about Dusseldorf on page 382.

Dep. Dusseldorf	14:33	15:40 (1)	16:33	17:33	19:40	20:09 (2+3)
Arr. Hannover	16:59	18:22	18:59	19:59	22:22	23:09

(1) Light refreshments. (2) No supplement. No restaurant car. Coach is second-class only. (3) Plus another Dusseldorf departure at 21:33, arriving Hannover 23:59.

Hannover - Frankfurt - Hannover 710

Reservation is advisable for all of these trains. All of them charge a supplement and have a restaurant car.

Dep. Hannover	06:20 (1)	07:20	08:20 (1)	09:20	10:20
Arr. Frankfurt	08:42	09:42	10:42	11:42	12:42

Sights in **Frankfurt**: See notes about Frankfurt on page 373.

Dep. Frankfurt	13:17	14:17	15:17	16:17	17:17	18:17 (3)
Arr. Hannover	15:38	16:38	17:38	18:38	19:38	20:38

(1) Runs daily, except Sunday. (2) Runs daily, except Saturday. (3) Plus other Frankfurt departures at 19:17 (2) and 20:17, arriving Hannover 21:38 and 22:38.

Hannover - Goslar - Hannover 677

Dep. Hannover	06:42 and every hour until 19:42 + 21:42
Arr. Goslar	77 minutes later

Sights in **Goslar**: The many 13th–16th century half-timbered buildings and 19th century houses. The Eagle Fountain. The five 13th century churches. The chandeliers of reindeer horns in the 15th century Town Hall. The 16th century towers and old city walls. The 11th century Imperial Palace. The museums of natural science and antiquities.

Goslar is a popular base for touring the Harz Mountains.

Dep. Goslar	07:01 and every hour until 19:01 + 21:01
Arr. Hannover	73 minutes later

Hannover - Hamburg - Hannover 710

Reservation is advisable for all of these trains. All of them charge a supplement and have a restaurant car, unless designated otherwise.

Dep. Hannover	07:40	08:06 (1)	08:40 (2)	09:40	10:30	11:40
Arr. Hamburg (Hbf.)	08:51	09:51	09:51	10:51	11:46	12:51

Sights in **Hamburg:** See notes on page 374.

Dep. Hamburg (Hbf.)	14:12	15:07	16:07	17:12 (2)	18:07	19:07 (3)
Arr. Hannover	70 minutes later					

(1) No supplement. Light refreshments. (2) Runs daily, except Saturday. (3) Plus another departure from Hamburg at 20:07, arriving Hannover 21:19.

Hannover - Hameln - Hannover   674

Dep. Hannover	06:46 and every hour until 22:46
Arr. Hameln	47 minutes later

Sights in **Hameln:** Every Sunday at Noon (mid-May through mid-September), see the reenactment of the Pied Piper leading children through the Town Square. Approximately 80 actors in historical costumes participate in the 30-minute performance.

Take the 90–minute guided walking tour (10:00–11:30) from the tourist information office. A stroll through the surrounding woods is pleasant. Or, try a steamboat trip on the **Weser River**.

Dep. Hameln	08:25 and every hour until 22:25
Arr. Hannover	47 minutes later

Hannover - Hildesheim - Hannover   677

Dep. Hannover	06:42 and every hour until 21:42
Arr. Hildesheim	30 minutes later

Sights in **Hildesheim**: The supposedly 1,100-year old rose tree (probably 300--500 years old) which survived World War II bombings that literally destroyed the city, on the grounds of the 11th century Cathedral.

The Cathedral houses marvelous 11th century art, particularly the 2 wings of the bronze door cast in 1015, showing 8 scenes from the Old and New Testaments.

Also see the Egyptian and Greco-Roman objects, as well as the collection of episcopal silverware and Chinese porcelain, in the Roemer und Pelizaeus Museum. The 12th century painted ceiling in the 11th century St. Michael's Church. The 15th century Tempelhaus.

The Gothic Town Hall. The collection of 15th century books and official records dating back to the 12th century at the Stadtarchiv.

Take a local train for the short ride to **Nordstemmen** and then it is a 20-minute walk from that railstation to see the medieval castle, Schloss Marianburg.

Dep. Hildesheim	06:44 and every hour until 21:44
Arr. Hannover	30 minutes later

Hannover - Kassel - Hannover   710

There is beautiful **Fulda River Valley** scenery 20 minutes before arriving in Kassel.

Reservation is advisable for all of these trains. All of them charge a supplement and have a restaurant car.

Dep. Hannover	07:31	08:31	09:31	10:31	11:31
Arr. Kassel (Wil.)	63 minutes later				

Sights in **Kassel**: See notes under "Frankfurt-Kassel" on page 390.

Dep. Kassel (Wil.)	13:24 and every hour until 21:24
Arr. Hannover	60 minutes later

Hannover - Luneburg - Hannover 710

Reservation is advisable for all of these trains. Most of them charge a supplement and have a restaurant car or light refreshments.

Dep. Hannover   Frequent times from 04:56 to 22:49
Arr. Luneburg   55–70 minutes later

Sights in **Luneburg**: The 18th century crane at the waterfront. Guided tours of Town Hall, constructed over 5 centuries (1300-1800). The 17th century Ducal Palace. The view of the town from Kalkberg (Chalk Mountain).

The 15th–16th century wood carvings and paintings and the 16th–18th century organs in the 3 churches that have survived out of the city's 14 original churches: St. Johannis, St. Michaelis and St. Nicolai. There are magnificent tombs of the town's most important citizens inside St. Johannia, the oldest church here. The sound of its organ is unique.

Don't miss seeing the 12th century Monastery, slightly more than one mile northeast of the town.

Dep. Luneburg   Frequent times from 06:14 to 23:20
Arr. Hannover   55–70 minutes later

Leipzig - Berlin - Leipzig 739
Reservation is advisable for all of these trains.

Dep. Leipzig	06:19	07:20 (1)	08:17 (3)	10:21 (4)	11:30 (5)
Arr. Berlin (Schonef.)	08:18	09:12	10:12	12:12	13:22
Arr. Berlin (Licht.)	08:44	09:30 (2)	-0-	12:38	13:49

Sights in **Berlin**: See notes on page 371.

Dep. Berlin (Licht.)	14:02 (2)	15:29	16:00	17:08(2+3)	19:17 (6)
Dep. Berlin (Schonef.)	14:19	15:54	16:25	17:25	19:43
Arr. Leipzig	16:33	17:47	18:37	19:27	22:02

(1) Light refreshments. (2) Depart/Arrive at Berlin's Schoneweide railstation. (3) Restaurant car. (4) Runs daily, except Monday. (5) Runs Monday only. (6) Plus another departure from from Berlin's Lichtenberg railstation at 21:11 (1) and Berlin's Schonefeld at 21:37 (1), arriving Liepzig 23:49.

Leipzig - Chemnitz (formerly Karl Marx Stadt) - Leipzig 724

Dep. Leipzig	07:53	09:56	11:45	Dep. Chemnitz	13:17	15:17	17:17(1)
Arr. Chemnitz	09:28	11:30	13:15	Arr. Leipzig	14:41	16:39	18:41

(1) Plus other departures from Chemnitz at 19:17 and 22:03, arriving Leipzig 20:41 and 23:31.

Sights in **Chemnitz**: An East German post-World War II showplace new city.

Leipzig - Dresden - Leipzig 725
Reservation is advisable for all of these trains.

Dep. Leipzig	06:30	07:05	08:15	09:48	10:48
Arr. Dresden (Neu.)	08:09	08:37	09:58	11:29	12:24
Arr. Dresden (Hbf.)	11 minutes later				

Sights in **Dresden**: See notes about Dresden on page 373.

Dep. Dresden (Hbf.)	13:03	14:03	15:03	16:03 (1)	17:03 (2)
Dep. Dresden (Neu.)	8 minutes later				
Arr. Lzeipzig	14:49	15:47	16:50	17:46	18:52

(1) Restaurant car. (2) Plus other departures from Dresden Neustadt at 18:03, 19:33, 21:30 and 21:48, arriving Leipzig 19:48, 21:28 and 23:26.

Leipzig - Erfurt - Leipzig 720
Reservation is advisable for all of these trains.

Dep. Leipzig	07:10	08:36 (1)	09:30 (2)	10:48 (1)	11:50 (1)
Arr. Erfurt	08:44	10:10	10:52	12:19	13:24

Sights in **Erfurt**: See "Berlin–Erfurt" on page 377.

Dep. Erfurt	14:30 (1)	15:30 (1)	16:39 (1)	19:03 (2)	20:20 (1)	22:00(3)
Arr. Leipzig	16:10	17:11	18:28	20:30	22:12	23:47

(1) Light refreshments. (2) Supplement charged. Restaurant car. (3) Plus another Erfurt departure at 23:03 (2), arriving Leipzig 00:32.

Leipzig - Naumburg - Leipzig 720
Reservation is advisable for all of these trains. All of them have light refreshments, unless designated otherwise.

Dep. Leipzig	07:10 (1)	08:36	10:48	11:50	13:07
Arr. Naumburg	53 minutes later				

Sights in **Naumburg**: A gem of a Medieval village.

Dep. Naumburg	11:58	15:19	16:20	17:28	21:08	22:50(1)
Arr. Leipzig	53 minutes later					

(1) No light refreshments.

Leipzig - Rostock - Leipzig 665
Reservation is advisable for all of these trains.

Dep. Leipzig	06:30	Dep. Rostock	15:46	18:00
Arr. Rostock	12:29	Arr. Leipzig	22:08	00:09

Sights in **Rostock**: Eastern Germany's largest seaport. St. Mary's Church. The ancient Town Hall.

Leipzig - Schwerin - Leipzig 665
Reservation is advisable for all of these trains.

Dep. Leipzig	06:30	10:40 (1)	Dep. Schwerin	17:05	19:13
Arr. Schwerin	11:16	15:36	Arr. Leipzig	22:08	00:09

(1) Light refreshments.

Sights in **Schwerin**: The Opera House. The fine castle.

Munich - Augsburg - Munich   760

Reservation is advisable and a supplement is charged for most of these trains. Most of them have a restaurant car or light refreshments.

Dep. Munich (Hbf.)   Frequent times from 06:15 to 22:07
Arr. Augsburg   30–40 minutes later

Sights in **Augsburg**: An ancient castled city, complete with splendid Gothic gate, moat, tower and ramparts. The Tourist Information Office, 7 Bahnhofstrasse, is open Monday-Friday 09:00–18:00, Saturday 09:00–13:00.

See the palatial, 8-story, 17th century City Hall. Next to it is the 11th century Perlachturm, a belltower. The oldest (12th century) Romanesque stained-glass in the world, great 11th century bronze doors, 4 altarpieces by Holbein and a huge 11th century bronze portal with scenes from the Old Testament in the 10th century Cathedral.

Just north of the Cathedral, on Frauentorstrasse, is the Mozart Museum (closed on Tuesday) in the house where the composer's father lived.

Schaezlerpalais, at 46 Maximilianstrasse, is an 18th century 60-room mansion that houses the Municipal Art Collections (Rubens, Rembrandt, Veronese, Tiepolo) and has a richly ornamented rococo ballroom on the second floor. The ballroom leads to an adjacent building that has a dazzling collection: Lucas Cranach, Holbein the Elder, Albrecht Durer. Both museums are open daily except Monday 10:00–16:00.

Also see the 15th century Basilica of St. Ulrich and St. Afra, the largest and most impressive church in Augsburg. The collection of manuscripts and drawings in the Municipal Library. The city's three 16th century fountains. Maximilianstrasse is considered by many to be the best Renaissance street in Germany.

Dep. Augsburg   Frequent times from 06:51 to 23:08
Arr. Munich (Hbf.)   30–40 minutes later

Munich - Bamberg - Munich   741

Reservation is advisable for all of these trains.

Dep. Munich (H.)	06:29(1)	07:49(2)	09:49(3)	Dep. Bamberg	16:11(1)	19:09(4)	21:14(2)
Arr. Bamberg	09:23	10:22	12:25	Arr. Munich (H.)	18:52	21:50	00:04

(1) Light refreshments. (2) Supplement charged. Restaurant car. (3) Restaurant car. (4) Supplement charged. Light refreshments.

Sights in **Bamberg**: A major port on the Rhine-Main-Danube Canal that connects the North Sea with the Black Sea. One of the few towns not damaged in World War II.

Visit the Town Hall, located in the center of the bridge that crosses the Regnitz River. The 16th century Geyerworth Castle.

Walk 10 minutes up the hill to Domplatz (Cathedral Square), location of the 13th century Imperial Cathedral, to see many masterpieces of German medieval and early Renaissance sculpture (especially the 13th century life-size Knight of Bamberg astride his horse)....the 16th century tomb of Henry II with sculpted bas-relief panels showing scenes from his and his wife's life....the dazzling carved wood Marienaltar....the tile floors, frescoes and 18th century French tapestries in the Neue Residenz, the 15th and 16th century German paintings in the Museum there, and its 18th century rose garden.

The Cathedral is open dawn to sunset, daily except holidays. The Neue Residenz is open 09:00–12:00 and 13:30–17:00 (16:00 October through March). See the paintings of more than 600 different medicinal herbs in the ceiling of St. Michael, an 11th century church.

Munich - Bayreuth - Munich

Reservation is advisable for all of the Munich-Nurnberg (and v.v.) trains.

770			740		
Dep. Munich (Hbf.)	07:49 (1)	08:18 (2)	Dep. Bayreuth	15:25 (5)	16:13 (6)
Arr. Nurnberg	09:37	10:03	Arr. Nurnberg	16:39	17:23
Change trains. 740			Change trains. 770		
Dep. Nurnberg	09:57 (3)	10:55 (4)	Dep. Nurnberg	16:53 (2)	17:53 (2)
Arr. Bayreuth	11:12	12:18	Arr. Munich (Hbf.)	18:34	19:36

(1) Supplement charged. Light refreshments. (2) Supplement charged. Restaurant car. (3) Runs daily, except Sundays and holidays. Restaurant car. (4) Restaurant car. (5) Runs Monday–Friday, except holidays. (6) Plus other Bayreuth departures at 17:45 (4), departing Nurnberg 19:58 (1), arriving Munich 21:50....and 20:39, departing Nurnberg 22:03 (4), arriving Munich 00:04.

Sights in **Bayreuth**: Sight of a 5-week annual (over 100 years) Wagner opera festival at Festpielhaus, every year from late July to late August, at 16:00. See Haus Wahnfried, Wagner's home. The breathtaking opera house. Eremitage Park. The Orangerie castle, open daily 10:00–11:30 and 13:30–15:00.

Munich - Frankfurt - Munich 700 + 770

Reservation is advisable for all of these trains. All of them charge a supplement and have a restaurant car.

Dep. Munich (Hbf.)	06:19	07:41 (1)	08:41	09:41		
Arr. Frankfurt	10:38	11:13	12:13	13:13		

Sights in **Frankfurt**: See notes about sightseeing in Frankfurt on page 373.

Dep. Frankfurt	15:46	16:46	17:46	18:46	19:46 (2)	20:10 (3)
Arr. Munich (Hbf.)	19:20	20:20	21:20	22:20	23:20	00:12

(1) Runs daily, except Sunday. (2) Runs Sunday only. (3) Runs daily, except Saturday.

Munich - Heidelberg - Munich 760

Reservation is advisable for all of these trains. All of them charge a supplement and have a restaurant car.

Dep. Munich (Hbf.)	06:49	08:49	09:49			
Arr. Heidelberg	09:54	11:52	12:52			

Sights in **Heidelberg**: See notes under "Cologne-Heidelberg" on page 383.

Dep. Heidelberg	14:06 (1)	15:06	16:06	17:06	18:06	20:06
Arr. Munich (Hbf.)	17:12	18:12	19:12	20:12	21:12	23:12

(1) Runs daily, except Sunday. (2) Runs daily, except Saturday.

Munich - Innsbruck - Munich   782

Dep. Munich (Hbf.)	08:00	09:00	10:00	11:00
Arr. Mittenwald	09:39	10:46	11:49 (1)	12:47 (1)
Dep. Mittenwald	09:46	11:01	11:58	13:06
Arr. Innsbruck	10:38	11:55	12:55	14:02

Sights in **Innsbruck**: See notes about Innsbruck on page 59.

Dep. Innsbruck	13:45	15:04	15:55	17:04	17:50	18:27
Arr. Mittenwald	14:44	15:59	16:55 (1)	17:56	18:52	19:30
Dep. Mittenwald	14:56	16:02 (2)	17:03	18:03	19:06	19:56 (3)
Arr. Munich (Hbf.)	16:51	17:53	18:53	19:54	20:51	21:51

(1) Change trains in Mittenwald. (2) Change trains in Garmish at 16:23. Departs Garmish 16:27. (3) Change trains in Garmish at 20:01. Depart Garmish 20:27.

Munich - Lindau - Munich   775

There are good views of the Allgau region and fine mountain scenery on this easy one-day roundtrip.

Dep. Munich (H.)	06:58 (1)	09:00 (2)	Dep. Lindau	14:38 (1)	15:16	16:28 (4)
Arr. Lindau	09:22	11:18	Arr. Munich (H.) 17:06		18:10 (3)	19:10 (3)

(1) Reservation advisable. Supplement charged. Restaurant car. (2) Reservation advisable. Light refreshments. (3) Arrives at Munich's Starnberger railstation. (4) Plus other departures from Lindau at 17:43 (2), 18:18 and 20:39 (1), arriving Munich 20:09, 21:10 (3) and 23:02.

Sights in **Lindau**: An island resort town in the Bodensee (Lake Constance), third largest lake in central Europe and actually a part of the Rhine River. Departure times for the sightseeing boat can be obtained at the tourist information office across from the railstation.

See the 13th century lighthouse, Mangturm. The beautiful 15th century Old Town Hall on the Reichplatz. The Fountain of Linavia. The casino. The collection of furniture, arms, paintings and folk art in the 18th century mansion that now houses an art museum called Stadtische Kunstsammlungen, open Tuesday-Saturday 09:00–12:00 and 14:00–17:00, also Sunday 10:00–12:00.

The 15th century homes on Hauptstrasse, a pedestrian-only road. Enjoy a mid-day repast at one of the many sidewalk cafes along that street. The only existing wall mural by Hans Holbein The Elder can be seen in the 11th century St. Peter's Church. Visit the wine tavern in the 16th century Pulverturm (Gun Powder Tower). Walk on the breakwater to the New Lighthouse and climb its 108-foot-high tower for a breathtaking view of the Alps.

Munich - Mainz - Munich   700

Reservation is advisable for all of these trains. All of them charge a supplement and have a restaurant car.

Dep. Munich (Hbf.)	06:49	08:49	09:49
Arr. Mainz	10:46	12:46	13:46

Sights in **Mainz:** See notes under "Cologne-Mainz" on page 384.

Dep. Mainz	14:14	15:14	16:14	17:14	18:44 (1)
Arr. Munich (Hbf.)	18:12	19:12	20:12	21:12	22:20

(1) Change trains in Mannheim at 19:23. Depart Mannheim 19:28.

Munich - Mannheim - Munich   760

Reservation is advisable for all of these trains. All of them charge a supplement and have a restaurant car.

Dep. Munich (Hbf.)	Frequent times from 06:41 to 18:41
Arr. Mannheim	3 hours later

Sights in **Mannheim**: See notes under "Cologne–Mannheim" on page 385.

Dep. Mannheim	Frequent times from 06:57 to 19:28
Arr. Munich (Hbf.)	3 hours later

Munich - Nurnberg - Munich   770

Reservation is advisable for all of these trains. All of them charge a supplement and have a restaurant car.

Dep. Munich (Hbf.)	07:21	08:18	09:21	10:18	11:21		
Arr. Nurnberg	09:03	10:03	11:03	12:03	13:03		

Sights in **Nurnberg**: See notes under "Frankfurt–Nurnberg" on page 392.

Dep. Nurnberg	13:53	14:53	15:53	16:53	17:53	18:53	19:58 (1+2)
Arr. Munich (Hbf.)	15:36	16:34	17:36	18:34	19:36	20:34	21:50

(1) Light refreshments. (2) Plus other departures from Nurnberg at 20:53 and 22:03, arriving Munich 22:34 and 00:04.

Munich - Oberammergau - Munich

There is very good mountain and lake scenery on the Murnau-Oberammergau portion of this trip.

All of the Murnau-Oberammergau (and v.v.) trains are second-class only.

782

Dep. Munich (Hbf.)	08:00	09:00	10:00	11:00	12:00	
Arr. Murnau	08:52	09:56	10:52	11:56	12:52	

Change trains.   768

Dep. Murnau	09:06	10:06	11:00	12:14	13:06
Arr. Oberammergau	40 minutes later				

Sights in **Oberammergau**: Every year ending in zero (1990, 2000, etc.), the famous Passion Play. Three hundred years ago the villagers here promised to produce this play every 10 years if the Black Plague ended. In the interval between decades, you can still see the unique theater and enjoy this interesting woodcarving capital of Bavaria. There is time to take a bus trip and see the lapis lazuli, gilt and crystal in King Ludwig II's glorious palace, Schloss Linderhof.

768

Dep. Oberammergau	10:57	12:11	13:07	15:07	16:07	17:07	18:10 (1+2)
Arr. Murnau	11:36	12:50	13:37	15:47	16:45	17:47	18:50

Change trains.   782

Dep. Murnau	11:58	12:54	13:58	15:58	16:54	18:01	18:58
Arr. Munich (Hbf.)	12:51	13:51	14:51	16:51	17:53	18:53	19:54

(1) Bus that connects with train in Murnau. (2) Plus another Oberammergau departure at 19:56 (1), arriving Munich 21:51.

Munich - Regensburg - Munich 740

Dep. Munich (Hbf.)	06:37 (1)	07:06		08:37 (2)	09:08	10:37 (2)	11:08
Arr. Regensburg	07:57	08:46		09:57	10:46	11:57	12:46
			*	*	*		
Dep. Regensburg	13:20 (1)	14:00 (1)	15:06		16:00 (2)	17:06	18:00 (3)
Arr. Munich (Hbf.)	14:42	15:22	16:40		17:22	18:40	19:22

(1) Reservation advisable. Restaurant car. (2) Reservation advisable. Light refreshments.
(3) Plus other Regensburg departures at 19:06, 20:00 (2), 21:06 and 22:00.

Sights in **Regensburg:** Founded by the Celts in about 500 B.C. It was made into an impregnable fort by the Romans in 179 A.D. How amazing that it still exists, intact ! Its location on the Danube River made this city Germany's gateway to the Balkans and the Orient for several centuries.

Undamaged during World War II, this is the largest (130,000 population) and most perfectly preserved medieval city in Germany.

Because most of the streets here are too narrow for modern vehicles and also because its size is only one mile by a half-mile, Regensburg is ideal for strolling. A half-day guided walking tour is offered by the municipal tourist office, located in the 14th century Rathaus (City Hall). Many guided tours of the City Hall's ornate rooms are offered daily.

The ancient Roman 23-foot-high wall surrounding the city is built of enormous limestone blocks without mortar, and it runs more than a mile long. Christian tombstones here date back to the 4th century. The city's forum, temples, mint, and pottery and tile factories served a population of 12,000 in Roman times. This was also one of the most important cities in the German Holy Roman Empire from the 10th through the 18th centuries.

You will not even scratch the surface in a one-day visit. In order to see all of the 26 Romanesque and Gothic churches and the wonderful artwork displayed in them would require several weeks . . . and there is much more than those churches to see here.

Walk over the 12th century Steiner Brucke (Stone Bridge), one of the greatest engineering marvels of the Middle Ages. Riverboat rides on the Danube start near the Stone Bridge.

Visit St. Peter's Cathedral to see its lacework spires and its collection of sacral art dating back to the Middle Ages and the Renaissance, especially the 13th century gem-and-pearl-encrusted crucifix.

Hear the boys' choir (called "cathedral sparrows", they sing both secular and liturgical songs) in the adjacent Niedermunster. Famous since the year 975, the choir can be heard Sundays and holidays at the 9:00 a.m. mass.

See the 20 medieval tower houses (some are 12 stories high), especially the 13th century Goldener Turm on Wahlenstrasse and the Bamberger Turm on Watmarkt, near the City Hall. The Golden Cross, a magnificent hotel since the 16th century.

The Municipal Museum at Dachauplatz has several paintings by Albrecht Altdorfer, considered to be the world's first landscape painter and founder of the Danubian School in the 16th century. The collection there also includes Celtic, Roman, early German and medieval artifacts.

The 9th and 10th century sculptures and tombs in the 5th century St. Emmeramskirche are notable. There are many illuminated manuscripts and more than 200,000 ancient books in the adjacent abbey.

The enormous monastery at St. Emmerams's (named for a martyred 7th century missionary monk) is presently the palace of the princes of Thurn-und-Taxis. After Napoleon secularized the abbey in 1808, that family bought it and converted it into their palace. It is worth visiting to see the priceless art in its many lavishly decorated rooms.

The Thurn-und-Taxis family invented postal service in the 15th century and used a network of stage coaches. There is a very interesting stable museum across from St. Emmeram's, with exhibits of silver and gold harnesses, equestrian paintings and 19th century coaches.

Also near this church is the Diozesan Museum, which houses 1,000 years of ecclesiastical art.

The Shipping Museum is located on the other side of the Danube River. Weinstube zur Stritzelback at No. 6 Watmarkt has been an inn since the 13th century. (Stritzel is a salty roll.)

There is an exhibit of 17th century mathematical instruments, astronomical tools and manuscripts that were used by the mathematician and astronomer Johann Kepler at No. 5 Keplerstrasse, the house in which he died in 1630.

Sample the chocolate pralines called "Barbara's kisses" at Cafe Prinzess (No. 2 Rathausplatz), Germany's oldest pastry shop and coffeehouse. It opened in 1686.

Try the fist-sized, white radishes that the locals eat as beer snacks.

Munich - Salzburg - Munich   780

Reservation is advisable for most of these trains. Most of them charge a supplement and have a restaurant car.

Dep. Munich (Hbf.)	07:25	08:25	09:25	09:52	10:50 (1)	
Arr. Salzburg	08:55	09:55	10:55	11:40	12:45	

Sights in **Salzburg**: See notes about Salzburg on page 60.

Dep. Salzburg	13:05	14:18	15:18 (1)	16:18	18:05	19:05 (2)
Arr. Munich (Hbf.)	14:35	16:06	17:10	18:06	19:35	20:36

(1) Reservation not available. No supplement. No restaurant car. (2) Plus other Salzburg departures at 20:18, 21:05 and 22:18, arriving Munich 22:00, 22:35 and 24:00.

Munich - Stuttgart - Munich   760

Reservation is advisable for all of these trains. All of them charge a supplement and have a restaurant car.

Dep. Munich (Hbf.)	Frequent times from 06:45 to 22:07
Arr. Stuttgart	2–3 hours later

Sights in **Stuttgart:** See notes under "Frankfurt-Stuttgart" on page 393.

Dep. Stuttgart	Frequent times from 05:02 to 21:59
Arr. Munich	2–3 hours later

Munich - Tegernsee and Schliersee - Munich 1000

Take a local train from Starnberger Bahnhof (the northern annex of Munich's Central station) for this 36-mile ride.

At the northern end of Tegernsee (an exceptionally beautiful lake) is **Gmund**, not to be confused with the 2 Austrian villages also named Gmund. A mile away from this Gmund is a smaller lake, **Schliersee**. It is only a 4-mile walk around Schliersee.

There is a lovely view of the lake from the ruins of Hohenwaldeck Castle and also from one of the many benches along the lake's shore. Sports (tennis, sailing, swimming)are very popular in this area.

The Taubenstein mountain railway goes to an area that provides extensive mountain hiking. Wandering through the Weissachau wildlife preserve, with its rare flowers, is worthwhile. Local food specialties in this region are white sausage, liver loaf, big white radishes and spicy Miesbacher cheese.

Sights in **Tegernsee**: The concerts (May–September) in the enormous Baroque dining hall of the Castle. The large collection of rustic furniture, weapons, craft utensils, traditional costumes and ancient books in the Tegernsee Museum. Try the beer in the Hofbrauhaus, located in the Museum building. Ludwig Schieffer of Cologne tells us the beer there is better than which is sold at Munich's famous Hofbrauhaus.

See the drawings, illustrations, sketches and caricatures by Olaf Gulbransson at the Kurpark Museum. Visit the lakeside gambling casino at Wiessee, across the lake.

Take the 10-minute boat trip (every half hour) across the lake to Wiessee. Both Tegernsee and Wiessee have been popular for centuries for their curative mineral waters, laden with iodine and sulphur. Swimming in the pristine lake is marvelous.

Take the cable car from nearby **Rottach-Egern** to the top of **Wallberg** for a view of the Tegernsee Valley and Austria's highest peak, the **Grossglockner**.

Munich - Ulm - Munich 760

Reservation is advisable for all of these trains. All of them charge a supplement and have a restaurant car or light refreshments.

Dep. Munich   Frequent times from 06:15 to 22:07
Arr. Ulm   70–80 minutes later

Sights in **Ulm**: The Bakery Museum (tools, library, artwork pertaining to bread) on Fuersteneckerstrasse. The display there includes breads made in ancient Egypt and in the Middle Ages. Open Monday-Friday 10:00–12:00 and 15:00–17:30.

The 14th century Gothic Cathedral has one of the highest towers in the world (528 feet) and a ceiling that is 100 feet above the central nave. When you hear an organ recital here (8,000 pipes !), you will experience an incredible affect from the exceptional acoustics. Don't miss seeing the magnificent 15th century carving on the choir stalls.

The views of the Alps while climbing the 528-feet-high tower are breathtaking. (You don't have to make the entire ascent.)

The 17th century Schworhaus, where Town Council members once took their oaths to perform their duties (where they were "sworn in").

Arts and crafts from this region are displayed in the Ulmer Museum, open Tuesday–

Saturday 10:00–12:00 and 14:00–17:00, Sunday 10:00–13:00 and 14:00–17:00. See the 15th century fountain, Fischkasten, at the Marktplatz. Also on that square is the 14th century Town Hall with an exceptional astronomical clock on its east wall.

Visit Metzgerturm, Ulm's 14th century leaning tower. Cross the bridge to New Ulm and walk along the Jahnufer promenade to see good views of the old city.

Dep. Ulm	Frequent times from 06:05 to 22:56
Arr. Munich	70–80 minutes later

Munich - Wurzburg - Munich 770

Reservation is advisable for all of these trains. All of them charge a supplement and have a restaurant car.

Dep. Munich (Hbf.)	06:19	07:21	08:18	09:21	10:18
Arr. Wurzburg	09:06	10:06	11:06	12:06	13:06

Sights in **Wurzburg**: Vineyards and wineries galore. The tourist information center is located in Falcon House, on the square where bratwurst, vegetables, fruits and flowers are sold. See the Main-Franconia Museum (sculptures, wine presses, etc.) in the 13th century Miarienberg Fortress.

The view of the city from the restaurant at the Fortress. The rococo garden in the nearby Schloss Veitshochheim. The 12 statues of saints on the Old Main Bridge. Pilgrimage Church. The Tiepolo ceiling and the Emperor's Hall, in the Residenz. Neumunster Church. The Cathedral. The fine sculptures in the Mainfrankisches Museum at the Festung. Take a boat trip on the River Main to see **Randersacker** and **Sommerhausen**, both of them located in one of Germany's most important wine regions. Pfuelben, Sonnenstuhl and Tuefelskeller are among the leading wineries here.

Sights in **Randersacker**: There are many scenic walking tours near the **Main River** and through vineyards. Stroll the narrow Medieval streets lined with baroque houses. Many sculptures here (madonnas and pietas). See the Balthasar garden-pavilion. Try the delicious franconian meat and sausages. Fishing and many other watersports here.

Sights in **Sommerhausen:** Famous since the Middle Ages for winemaking. Its coat-of-arms features a radiant sun above a cluster of grapes. Its old town walls, gates and towers make it one of the most beautiful towns in the region. Sailing and motorboating are popular here. Visit the Rechteren-Limpurgsche Castle. The ancient City Hall.

Dep. Wurzburg	12:52	13:52	14:52	15:52	16:52	17:52	18:52 (1)
Arr. Munich (Hbf.)	15:36	16:34	17:36	18:34	19:36	20:34	21:36

(1) Plus other Wurzburg departures at 19:52 and 22:34, arriving Munich 22:34 and 00:17.

Munich - Zurich - Munich 84

Reservation is advisable for all of these trains.

Dep. Munich (H.)	06:58 (1)	09:00 (2)	Dep. Zurich	15:39 (2)	18:39 (1)
Arr. Zurich	11:21	13:21	Arr. Munich (H.)	20:09	23:02

(1) Supplement charged. Restaurant car. (2) Light refreshments.

Sights in **Zurich:** See notes about Zurich on page 312.

SCENIC RAIL TRIPS

Cologne - Koblenz - Bullay - Cologne   707

There is beautiful farm, mountain and vineyard scenery on this easy one-day trip through the Moselle Valley. Very good river scenery on the Koblenz-Bullay portion.

Reservation is advisable for all of these trains.

Dep. Cologne	08:11	10:11	12:11	14:11
Dep. Koblenz	09:19	11:19	13:19	15:19
Arr. Bullay	50 minutes later			

		*	*	*	
Dep. Bullay	09:55	11:55	13:55	15:55
Arr. Koblenz	10:38	12:38	14:38	16:38
Arr. Cologne	57 minutes later			

Cologne - Mainz

See the fine mountain, vineyard and Rhine river scenery. Complete schedules appear under the "Cologne–Mainz-Cologne" one-day excursion on page 384.

Cologne - Giessen - Frankfurt - Koblenz - Cologne

View excellent mountain scenery on this ride, which can be made as a circle trip from either Cologne or Frankfurt (see page 409).

685

Dep. Cologne	08:19	10:19	12:19
Arr. Giessen	10:51	12:51	14:51
Change trains.			
Dep. Giessen	11:14	13:14	15:14
Arr. Frankfurt	12:02	14:02	16:02

Change trains.   700

Dep. Frankfurt	12:38 (1)	14:50 (1)	16:50 (1)	17:50 (1)	18:50 (1)	19:05 (1+2)
Dep. Koblenz	14:13	16:13	18:13	19:13	20:13	21:13
Arr. Cologne	15:05	17:05	19:05	20:05	21:05	22:05

(1) Reservation advisable. Supplement charged. Restaurant car. (2) Plus another Frankfurt departure at 20:50 (1), arriving Cologne 23:05.

Frankfurt - Koblenz - Cologne - Giessen - Frankfurt

Here is the Frankfurt version of the circle trip shown on the previous trip:

700

Dep. Frankfurt	07:50 (1)	09:50 (1)	11:50 (1)	13:50 (1)
Dep. Koblenz	09:13	11:13	13:13	15:13
Arr. Cologne	10:05	12:05	14:05	16:05

Change trains. 685

Dep. Cologne	10:19	12:19	14:19	16:19
Arr. Giessen	12:51	14:51	16:51	18:51

Change trains.

Dep. Giessen	13:14	15:14	17:14	19:14
Arr. Frankfurt	14:02	16:02	18:02	20:02

(1) Reservation advisable. Supplement charged. Restaurant car.

Freiburg - Donaueschingen

The train runs through the heart of the Black Forest. Very good mountain scenery on this spur of the Frankfurt–Basel route.

68			757 + 758		
Dep. Frankfurt	10:46 (1)	11:46 (3)	Dep. Donau.	15:47 (2)	17:47 (2)
Arr. Freiburg	13:01	14:01	Arr. Freiburg	17:17	19:17
Change trains. 757 + 758			Change trains. 68		
Dep. Freiburg	13:12 (2)	14:42 (2)	Dep. Freiburg	19:03 (3)	20:29 (3)
Arr. Donau.	15:11	16:17	Arr. Basel (Bad.)	19:40	21:08
			Arr. Basel (S.B.B.)	19:45	21:13

(1) Change trains in Mannheim. Reservation is advisable and supplement is charged for all of these Frankfurt-Mannheim and Mannheim-Freiburg trains. (2) Change trains in Neustadt. (3) Reservation advisable. Supplement charged. Restaurant car.

Koblenz - Giessen 688

There is fine river scenery on this easy one-day roundtrip. This area can also be seen by taking an *indirect route* from Koblenz to Frankfurt. For the first way:

Dep. Koblenz	08:42 (1)	10:42 (1)	12:42	14:42 (2)
Arr. Giessen	10:38	12:38	14:38	16:38
		*	* *	
Dep. Giessen	11:15 (1)	13:15	15:15 (2)	17:15
Arr. Koblenz	13:11	15:13	17:17	19:11

Here is the long route to Frankfurt which offers the same scenery:

688

Dep. Koblenz	08:42 (1)	10:42 (1)	12:42	14:42 (2)	16:42 (2)
Arr. Giessen	10:38	12:38	14:38	16:38	18:38
Change trains. 710					
Dep. Giessen	10:58 (3)	12:58 (3)	14:58 (3)	16:58 (3)	18:58 (3)
Arr. Frankfurt	11:38	13:38	15:38	17:38	19:38

(1) Runs daily, except Sundays and holidays. (2) Runs daily, except Saturday. (3) Reservation advisable. Light refreshments.

Here is the schedule for the reverse of the Koblenz-Frankfurt trip on page 409:

710

| Dep. Frankfurt | 08:21 (1) | 10:21 (1) | 12:21 (1) | 14:21 (1) | 16:21 (1) |
| Arr. Giessen | 09:00 | 11:00 | 13:00 | 15:00 | 17:00 |

Change trains. 688

| Dep. Giessen | 09:15 (2) | 11:15 (2) | 13:15 | 15:15 (3) | 17:15 |
| Arr. Koblenz | 11:11 | 13:11 | 15:13 | 17:17 | 19:11 |

(1) Reservation advisable. Light refreshments. (2) Runs daily, except Sundays and holidays. (3) Runs daily, except Saturday.

Munich - Garmisch - Innsbruck - Munich

There is fine mountain scenery on this easy one-day circle trip.

782

Dep. Munich (Hbf.)	08:00	09:00	10:00	11:00	13:00	14:21 (2)
Arr. Garmish	09:16	10:23	11:16	12:23	14:23	15:51
Arr. Mittenwald	09:39	10:46	11:49 (1)	12:47 (1)	14:46 (1)	16:31
Arr. Innsbruck	10:38	11:55	12:55	14:02	15:58	17:40

Change trains. 74

| Dep. Innsbruck (via Kufstein) | 10:39 (3) | 12:41 (4) | -0- | 14:41 (4) | 16:41 (5) | 18:37 (6+7) |
| Arr. Munich (Hbf.) | 12:30 | 14:30 | -0- | 16:30 | 20:30 | 20:30 |

(1) Change trains in Mittenwald. Depart Mittenwald 15 minutes later. (2) Restaurant car. (3) Reservation advisable. (4) Reservation advisable. Supplement charged. Restaurant car. (5) Reservation *required*. Supplement charged. Restaurant car. (6) Reservation advisable. Light refreshments. (7) Plus another Innsbruck departure at 21:03 (4), arriving Munich 22:40.

Garmisch - Zugpitze - Garmisch 787

The following schedule allows one to take one route to the summit of Zugspitze and a different route back to Garmisch.

Cog train.

| Dep. Garmisch | 07:35 | 08:35 | 09:35 | 10:35 | 11:35 | 12:35 | 13:35 | 14:35 | 15:35 |
| Arr. Eibsee | 08:13 | 09:13 | 10:13 | 11:13 | 12:13 | 13:13 | 14:13 | 15:13 | 16:13 |

Change to cable car.

| Dep. Eibsee | 08:30 | 09:30 | 10:30 | 11:30 | 12:30 | 13:30 | 14:30 | 15:30 | 16:30 |
| Arr. Zugspitze | 08:40 | 09:40 | 10:40 | 11:40 | 12:40 | 13:40 | 14:40 | 15:40 | 16:40 |

Change to cable cars.

| Dep. Zugspitze | 08:45 | 09:45 | 10:45 | 11:45 | 12:45 | 13:45 | 14:45 | 15:45 | 16:45 |
| Arr. Schneefernerhaus | 08:49 | 09:49 | 10:49 | 11:49 | 12:49 | 13:49 | 14:49 | 15:49 | 16:49 |

Change to cog train.

| Dep. Schneefernerhaus | 09:00 | 10:00 | 11:00 | 12:00 | 13:00 | 14:00 | 15:00 | 16:00 | 17:00 |
| Arr. Garmisch | 10:20 | 11:20 | 12:20 | 13:20 | 14:20 | 15:20 | 16:20 | 17:20 | 18:20 |

Munich - Nurnberg - Heilbronn - Heidelberg

This schedule follows the route of the "Castle Road" and "Romantic Road" bus trips. (See pages 414 and 415.)

770

Dep. Munich	07:49 (1)	09:49 (2)	11:21 (3)
Arr. Nurnberg	09:37	11:42	13:03

Change trains.
745

Dep. Nurnberg	09:45 (1+4)	11:55 (5)	13:45 (1+6)
Arr. Heilbronn	11:56	14:24	15:45

Sights in **Heilbronn**: More than 80% of the pre-World War II buildings in this city of 110,000 in the heart of Germany's wine country was obliterated by Allied bombing planes in 1944. The Wine Festival (one week in September) attracts 300,000 people every year.

Change trains.
744

Dep. Heilbronn	13:19	15:19	17:19
Arr. Heidelberg	14:34	16:34	18:34

(1) Reservation advisable. Light refreshments. (2) Reservation advisable. Restaurant car. (3) Reservation advisable. Supplement charged. Restaurant car. (4) Change trains in Crailsheim. (5) Runs Monday–Friday, except holidays. Change trains in Schwabisch. (6) Runs Monday–Friday, except holidays. Change trains in Crailsheim.

Munich - Salzburg

This route offers good mountain scenery and is an easy one-day roundtrip. See schedules earlier in this section, under "One-Day Excursions" on page 405.

Offenburg - Konstanz - Offenburg   755 + 762

This trip is recommended for exceptional mountain scenery.

Dep. Offenburg	07:00 (1)	07:55 (1)	08:37	09:55 (1)	10:37	11:55 (1)
Arr. Konstanz	09:17	10:11	11:18	12:11	13:18	14:11

Dep. Offenburg	12:37	13:55 (1)	14:37	15:55 (1)
Arr. Konstanz	15:18	16:11	17:18	18:11

* * *

Dep. Konstanz	09:51 (1)	10:45	11:51 (1)	12:45	13:51 (1)	14:45
Arr. Offenburg	12:04	13:18	14:04	15:18	16:04	17:18

Dep. Konstanz	15:51 (1)	16:42	17:51 (1)	18:45	19:51 (1)	20:57 (1)
Arr. Offenburg	18:04	19:18	20:04	21:15	22:04	23:09

(1) Reservation advisable. Light refreshments.

Offenburg - Singen - Schaffhausen - Offenburg

Excellent Black Forest scenery on this route. This trip can also be made as a detour en route from Frankfurt to Basel.

755

Dep. Offenburg	07:00 (1)	08:37	10:37	12:37	14:37
Arr. Singen	08:54	10:52	12:52	14:52	16:52

Change trains. 762

Dep. Singen	09:19	11:19	13:19	15:19	17:19
Arr. Schaffhausen	09:35	11:35	13:35	15:35	17:35
		*	*	*	
Dep. Schaffhausen	11:30	13:30	15:30	17:30	19:30
Arr. Singen	11:45	13:45	15:45	17:45	19:45

Change trains. 755

Dep. Singen	12:14 (1)	14:14 (1)	16:14 (1)	18:14 (1)	20:14 (1)
Arr. Offenburg	14:04	16:04	18:04	20:04	22:04

(1) Reservation advisable. Light refreshments.

Here is the detour from the Frankfurt-Basel ride:

700			762		
Dep. Frankfurt	07:50	09:50 (1)	Dep. Singen	13:19	15:19
Arr. Offenburg	09:53	11:53	Dep. Schaffhausen	13:37	15:37
No train change. 755			Arr. Basel (Bad.)	14:48	16:48
Dep. Offenburg	09:55 (1)	11:55 (1)			
Arr. Singen	11:48	13:48			
Change trains.					

(1) Reservation advisable. Light refreshments.

Wurzburg - Zurich

There is exceptional Black Forest scenery on this ride.

744

Dep. Wurzburg	10:11	12:11	14:11
Arr. Stuttgart	12:34	14:34	16:33

Change trains. 69

Dep. Stuttgart	12:43 (1)	14:43 (2)	16:42 (3)
Arr. Zurich	15:47	17:47	19:47

(1) Reservation advisable. Restaurant car. (2) Reservation advisable. (3) Reservation advisable. Light refreshments.

RHINE RIVER CRUISES

A variety of cruising on the Rhine is offered. The complete 5-day *down*stream route (from Basel to Amsterdam or Rotterdam) and the complete 6-day *up*stream route (Amsterdam or Rotterdam to Basel) are offered April to October.

A shorter portion (Rotterdam-Strasbourg and vice versa) is also available April to October. It is 4 days downstream and 5 upstream.

Still another service (3 days downstream and 4 upstream), between Amsterdam or Rotterdam and Mainz, is offered April to September.

On any of these, passengers may stop-over at points en route and resume the journey later (Cologne, Koblenz, etc.).

The most popular stretch of the Rhine (Koblenz to Mainz and Frankfurt) is covered by the Eurailpass. This is the portion famed for scenic vineyards and hilltop castles. The *entire* Rhine trip is *not* covered by Eurailpass. However, with a Eurailpass there is *no* charge for either the boat trip or train ride Mainz–Cologne or Cologne–Mainz.

The scenery between Mainz and Koblenz can be seen as well from a train as from a boat because the track on this run goes along the river bank.

Here are the schedules for taking the boat *Mainz-Cologne* and returning to Mainz by train the same day:

705 (Boat)		700 (Train)	
Dep. Mainz	08:45 (1)	Dep. Cologne (Hbf.)	20:00 (2)
Arr. Koblenz	13:50	Dep. Koblenz	20:53
Arr. Cologne (Rheing'n)	18:50	Arr. Mainz	21:42

(1) Operates late June to early September. (2) Reservation advisable. Supplement charged. Restaurant car.

Here are the schedules for taking the boat *Cologne-Mainz* and returning to Cologne by train the same day:

705 (Boat)		700 (Train)	
Dep. Cologne (Rheing'n)	09:00 (1)	Dep. Mainz	14:18 (2)
Arr. Koblenz	11:00	Dep. Koblenz	15:07
Arr. Mainz	13:10	Arr. Cologne (Hbf.)	15:59

(1) Operates mid-April to late October. Runs daily, except Monday. Supplement charged. (2) Reservation advisable. Supplement charged. Restaurant car. Plus other departures from Mainz at frequent times from 14:24 to 22:24.

THE ONE-DAY RHINE HYDROFOIL CRUISE

Cologne - Mainz - Cologne   705

Operates mid-April to late October. Runs daily, except Mondays.

Dep. Cologne	09:00	Dep. Mainz	14:25
Dep. Koblenz	11:05	Dep. Koblenz	16:20
Arr. Mainz	13:10	Arr. Cologne	18:05

SCENIC BUS TRIPS COVERED BY EURAILPASS

Both of these extremely popular bus trips are covered by Eurailpass: "Romantische Strasse" (**Romantic Road**) and "Burgenstrasse" (**Castle Road**). Advance seat reservations should be made at least 3 days before travel date. They can be obtained at no cost by writing to: Deutsche Touring GmbH, Am Roemerhof 17, D-6000 Frankfurt/M. 90, Germany, or by phoning: (069) 790-32-48. Be sure to indicate the dates you want to journey, which of the 2 different lines you want to travel, where you will start and end your trip, and the number of seats you want.

Passengers are allowed to break the journey at as many stops as they desire on both bus lines, and we recommend some specific places to do so in the text that follows. If that is your plan, be sure to provide all the specific dates this will involve when requesting a reservation.

The 2 lines connect in **Rothenburg**, making it easy to ride on all or part of both trips. Lodging in Rothenburg is good quality, but the supply is small and the demand very great. The Encyclopedia Britannica calls Rothenburg "probably the finest surviving example of a medieval town". It has been there for 1,000 years. Its 30 watchtowers and many dungeons, churches, patrician homes, ornamental fountains and market squares are perfectly preserved.

The town's most important buildings are on the old Market Square: Town Hall, Virgin's Pharmacy (Marienapotheque), the lovely stone fountain (Herterichbrunnen), the ancient city council drinking hall, and the mechanical clock that performs at 11:00, 13:00 and 14:00.

The Meistertrunk Legend When the town was under siege in the 17th century, the commander of the victorious Imperial Army was given his first taste of wine by the inhabitants. He offered to spare the lives of the city officials if any of them could empty in one drink the content of a tankard holding almost one gallon. One burgermeister rose to the challenge, accomplished the feat, and even quaffed more. The 3.24 liter Meistertrunk tankard is on display in the town's Reichstadt Museum. The legend is recreated every year in a pageant held on Whitsunday, 7 weeks after Easter.

Statues of the 7 deadly sins and 7 virtues adorn the Baumeisterhaus, on Schmiedgasse, near Market Square. This chiseled house is well worth seeing. The torture museum at the Dominican Nunnery is another attraction in the town.

Rothenburg has 15 hotels with 11 to 145 rooms each. It is an ideal stopover either for breaking the Romantische Strasse ride into 2 days or for transferring from or to the Burgenstrasse ride.

Also a recommended stopover on the Romantische Strasse ride is **Dinkelsbuhl**, another finely preserved medieval town with a surfeit of gates, bastions, towers, a moat equipped with floating swans and a sharp sense of ancient history. Its major pageant is every July, complete with sword dances and historic tableaux.

Augsburg is an ancient castled city. See notes under "Munich–Augsburg" on page 400.

CASTLE ROAD 771

This bus trip operates from mid-May to late September.

Dep. Mannheim	07:30		Dep. Rothenburg	16:30
Dep. Heidelberg	08:00		Arr. Heidelberg	20:15
Arr. Rothenburg	12:27		Arr. Mannheim	20:40

ROMANTIC ROAD 771

The portion of this bus trip which has the principal sights is Wurzburg–Augsburg (and v.v.). A stewardess-guide is provided for that part of the 2 schedules shown below.

Dep. Frankfurt	08:15 (1)	-0-		Dep. Munich	09:00 (1)	-0-
Dep. Wurzburg	10:15	09:00 (3)		Dep. Fussen	-0-	08:15 (3)
Arr. Rothenburg	11:35 (2)	12:00 (2)		Dep. Augsburg	10:20	11:10
Dep. Rothenburg	13:45	13:30		Arr. Dinkelsbuhl	12:35 (2)	13:10 (2)
Arr. Dinkelsbuhl	14:45 (2)	14:30 (2)		Dep. Dinkelsbuhl	14:15	14:40
Dep. Dinkelsbuhl	15:30	15:00		Arr. Rothenburg	15:15 (2)	15:35 (2)
Arr. Augsburg	17:35	16:55		Dep. Rothenburg	17:00	17:00
Arr. Fussen	-0-	19:35		Arr. Wurzburg	18:09	19:20
Arr. Munich	18:55	-0-		Arr. Frankfurt	19:55	-0-

(1) Operates mid-March to late October. (2) Meal stop. Time to stroll. (3) Operates mid-May to early October.

SPECIAL RAIL TRIP FROM FUSSEN

For a marvelous extension from Fussen, here is a train trip that offers superb scenery: alpine meadows, deep river gorges, mountains. One of the most spectacular one-day rail routes in Europe.

Bus. German table.						
				782		
Dep. Fussen	09:30	13:20		Dep. Garmisch	13:11	15:16
Arr. Reutte	10:05	13:48		Arr. Innsbruck	14:49	16:39
Change to train.				Change trains.		
782				**800**		
Dep. Reutte	12:00 (1)	14:08		Dep. Innsbruck	15:02 (2)	17:02 (2)
Arr. Garmisch	12:57 (1)	15:06		Arr. Salzburg	17:00	19:00
Change trains						

(1) Direct train Reutte-Innsbruck. No train change in Garmish. (2) Reservation advisable. Supplement charged. Restaurant car.

INTERNATIONAL ROUTES FROM GERMANY

The German gateway for travel to Amsterdam and Brussels (and on to London) is Cologne. Notes on the route to London appear on page 428. Frankfurt and Cologne are the access points to Paris (and on to Barcelona and Madrid). Frankfurt is also the starting point for travel to Basel and Zurich (and on to Milan and Genoa) . . . as well as to Warsaw.

Munich and Nurnberg are gateways for trips to Vienna (and on to Belgrade and Budapest), and Bologna (and on to Rome or Venice). Nurnberg and Berlin are departure points for getting to Prague. Berlin and Hamburg are the gateways to Copenhagen (and on to Oslo and Stockholm).

Berlin - Copenhagen 80

Dep. Berlin (Lichtenberg)	00:13 (1)	06:25 (2)	14:11 (3)
Arr. Copenhagen	08:28	15:00	23:00

(1) Carries first and second-class sleeping car. Also has second-class couchettes. Coach is second-class only. Restaurant on ferry 04:00–06:05. (2) Light refreshments on train. Restaurant on ferry 10:20–12:15. (3) Restaurant car on train 14:11–17:35. Restaurant on ferry 18:20–20:15.

Berlin - Prague 87 + 730

Reservation is advisable for all of these trains

Dep. Berlin (Licht.)	00:41 (1)	02:47 (1+2)	07:53 (2)	08:41 (2)	12:00 (2)
Dep. Berlin (Sch'fld)	01:07	03:13	08:19	09:07	12:25
Arr. Prague (Hole.)	07:01	08:50	13:28	14:27	17:57
Arr. Prague (Hlavni)	-0-	-0-	-0-	14:41	-0-

Dep. Berlin (Licht.)	14:11 (2)	15:17 (2)	17:41 (2)	20:47 (1)	23:00 (1)
Dep. Berlin (Sch'fld)	14:37	15:43	18:07	21:13	23:25
Arr. Prague (Hole.)	20:38	21:09	23:30	-0-	05:10
Arr. Prague (Hlavni)	-0-	21:29	-0-	02:48	-0-

(1) Carries a sleeping car. Also has couchettes. (2) Restaurant car.

Berlin - Warsaw 850

	850	23	17	850
Dep. Berlin (Zoo)	-0-	06:10 (2)	07:01 (3)	-0-
Dep. Berlin (Hbf.)	00:16 (1)	06:58	08:03	10:48
Arr. Warsaw (Centralna)	09:15	16:10	16:50	20:50
Arr. Warsaw (Wschodnia)	09:29	16:24	17:04	21:04

	850	850	850
Dep. Berlin (Zoo)	-0-	-0-	-0-
Dep. Berlin (Hbf.)	15:33 (4)	21:16 (5)	22:36 (1)
Arr. Warsaw (Centralna)	22:50	07:00	07:40
Arr. Warsaw (Wschodnia)	23:04	07:14	07:54

(1) Operates early June to late September. Train has only first and second-class sleeping cars. *No* coaches (2) Reservation required. Time shown is for period late June to late September. Second-class only. Light refreshments. (3) Second-class only. Light refreshments. (4) Light refreshments. (5) Departs from Berlin's Lichtenberg railstation. Reservation required. Carries a sleeping car. Also has couchettes.

Cologne - Amsterdam   64

Sit on the right-hand side for best views of the marvelous Rhine River scenery.

Reservation is advisable for all of these trains. All of them charge a supplement and have light refreshments, unless designated otherwise.

Dep. Cologne	07:17 (1)	09:17	11:17	13:17	15:17	17:17	18:02 (1)	19:02 (1+2)
Arr. Amsterdam	09:54	11:51	13:51	15:51	17:51	19:51	20:51	21:51

(1) Restaurant car. (2) Plus another departure from Cologne at 21:17, arriving Amsterdam 23:57.

Cologne - Basel - Zurich   68

Dep. Cologne	10:00 (1)	12:00 (1)	15:00 (1)	23:59 (3)
Arr. Basel (S.B.B.)	14:45	16:45	19:45 (2)	06:26
Arr. Zurich	16:00	18:00	22:23	08:15

(1) Reservation advisable. Supplement charged. Restaurant car. (2) Change trains in Basel. Depart Basel 21:27 (1). (3) Carries a sleeping car. Also has couchettes.

Cologne - Brussels   62 + 200

Reservation is advisable and a supplement is charged for most of these trains.

Dep. Cologne	05:08 (1)	07:08	08:10	09:14 (2)	11:17 (4)
Arr. Brussels (Nord)	07:58	09:46	10:46	11:30	13:46
Arr. Brussels (Cen.)	-0-	09:50	10:50	11:37	13:50
Arr. Brussels (Midi)	08:07	09:55	10:55	11:42	13:55

(1) Reservation not available. No supplement. (2) Restaurant car. (3) No supplement. (4) Plus other departures from Cologne at 12:17, 13:17 (3), 15:17, 16:17, 18:17 and 20:17, arriving Brussels Nord 14:46, 15:46, 17:46, 18:46, 20:46 and 22:46.

Cologne - Paris   62

Dep. Cologne	00:07 (1)	05:46 (2)	08:05 (3)	13:17 (4)	17:07 (3)
Arr. Paris (Nord)	06:55	11:21	13:18	18:59	22:10

(1) Carries a sleeping car. Also has couchettes. Light refreshments. (2) Coach is second-class only. (3) Reservation advisable. Supplement charged. Restaurant car. (4) Reservation advisable. Light refreshments.

Munich - Bologna - Florence - Rome   74

Dep. Munich (Hbf.)	07:40 (1)	09:30 (2)	13:30 (3)	20:30 (4)	23:30 (4)
Arr. Bologna	16:14	17:27	21:30	04:21	07:55
Arr. Florence (S.M.N.)	-0-	18:35	-0-	05:46 (5)	09:10
Arr. Rome (Ter.)	-0-	20:45	-0-	08:33	-0-

(1) Reservation *required*. Light refreshments. (2) Reservation *required*. Supplement charged. Restaurant car. (3) Reservation advisable. Supplement charged. Restaurant car. (4) Reservation *required*. Carries a sleeping car. Also has couchettes. (5) Arrives at Florence's Campo di Marte railstation.

Munich - Salzburg - Vienna   61

Dep. Munich (Hbf.)	04:28 (1)	07:25 (2)	09:25 (2)	16:25 (2)	19:25 (2+4)
Arr. Salzburg	05:53	08:55	10:55	17:53	20:55
Arr. Vienna (Westbf.)	09:25	12:05	14:05	21:05	00:05

(1) Departs from Munich's Ost railstation. Restaurant car. (2) Reservation advisable. Supplement charged. Restaurant car. (3) Has couchettes. (4) Plus another Munich departure at 23:10 (3), arriving Salzburg 01:01, Vienna 06:32.

BRITAIN

Chapter 7

ENGLAND, WALES and SCOTLAND

Children under 5 travel free. Half-fare for children 5–15. Children 16 and over must pay full fare.

On British trains, first-class sleeping cars have single compartments; second-class sleeping cars have 2-berth compartments. Sleeping-car passengers are served morning tea and biscuits free of charge. Generally, overnight passengers may remain in sleeping cars at destinations the next morning until 07:30.

Britain's 1,800 "Inter-City" trains, linking more than 200 towns each weekday, average 98 to 100 miles per hour on some routes.

Reservations are required on the fast day trains. If there are vacant spaces, the conductor at the departure platform can allocate available places.

British Rail usually makes repairs to train lines on Sundays, as late as 16:00. If you plan to travel by train here on a Sunday, it is advisable to telephone the railstation and confirm the time for routes you intend to use.

BRITAIN'S TRAIN PASSES

BritRail Pass   The BritRail Pass, similar to Eurailpass (which does *not* cover Britain), provides unlimited rail travel in England, Scotland and Wales. Youth-Pass (limited to ages 16 to under 26) is for standard-class space. The 1992 prices (in U.S. dollars) are:

	8 Days	15 Days	22 Days	One Month
First-class	$ 319.00	$ 479.00	$ 599.00	$ 689.00
Standard-class	209.00	319.00	399.00	465.00
Child 5-15				
First-class	159.50	239.50	299.50	344.50
Standard-class	104.50	159.50	199.50	232.50
Youth 16-25				
Standard-class	169.00	255.00	319.00	375.00
Senior Citizen 60 +				
First-class	289.00	429.00	539.00	619.00
Standard-class	189.00	289.00	359.00	419.00

These passes do not cover travel in the Irish Republic or in Northern Ireland. They *cannot* be purchased in Britain. They can be purchased worldwide through the offices of British Rail Travel International, its representatives, and travel agencies outside Britain. Validate these passes at the railstation's "Travel Centre" before starting your first trip with them. The rail official will mark your pass with that day's date and also the appropriate expiration date.

It is a good idea to protect yourself from having your pass rendered partly or wholly invalid because the validity dates were entered incorrectly.

Before the rail official writes on the pass the first and last day it can be used, you should write a note with what you believe are the correct validity dates, show it to the seller, and ask if he or she agrees with those dates.

(Be sure to follow the European custom of showing the day of the month first, followed by the number of the month. In Europe, July 8 is 8/7. If you wanted to take a train to Edinburgh, leaving London at 2:00 PM on July 8, your note for a reservation would read: "Edinburgh 14:00 8/7".) Only when the official says your dates are correct, or explains why they are not, should you have the dates entered on your pass.

Flexipass   Valid any 4 of 8 consecutive days, any 8 of 15 consecutive days, or any 15 days in one month. (For "Youth", the 15-day pass can be used within two months.) Same conditions and purchase locations as BritRail Pass (page 419). The 1992 prices (in U.S. dollars) are:

	4 Days	8 Days	15 Days
First-class	$ 269.00	$ 379.00	$ 549.00
Standard-class	179.00	255.00	369.00
Child 5-15			
First-class	134.50	189.50	274.50
Standard-class	89.50	127.50	184.50
Youth 16-25			
Standard-class	145.00	199.00	295.00
Senior Citizen 60 +			
First-class	239.00	339.00	495.00
Standard-class	159.00	229.00	329.00

BritFrance Pass   Unlimited train travel in both Britain and France, plus one Hovercraft roundtrip Dover-Boulogne or Dover-Calais and v.v. (or on regular cross-channel ferries when Hovercraft cannot operate because of bad weather).

Sold at travel agencies and also offices of BritRail Travel International and Rail Europe (U.S.A. and Canadian offices shown under "Great Britain" and "France" on page 23) — everywhere in the world, *except* in Britain and France.

The 1992 prices for any 5 days within 15 days are: $335 (U.S.) for *first*-class, $249 for *standard*-class, and $199 for youths age 12–25. For any 10 days in one month: $505, $385 and $299. Half-fare for children age 4–11.

BritFrance Rail'N Drive   Unlimited 5 days of train travel plus 3 days of car rental (any 8 days) within one month. Prices vary (a) whether for one person or for 2 or more persons, and (b) the category of car. A third passenger needs to pay only for a 5-day rail pass (above).

The 1992 prices per person for 2 persons (using the smallest size car) are: $399 (U.S.) for *first*-class, $315 for *standard*-class.

All-Line Rover   Sold only in Britain, at BritRail Travel Centres. Unlimited train travel plus the ferries to the Isle of Wight (see page 436). The *first*-class prices until May 9, 1992 are: £ 320 for 7 days, £ 500 for 14 days. For *standard*-class: £ 200 and £ 320. Children age 5–15 receive a discount of 34%.

Area Rovers   Sold at main railstations and at British Rail Travel Centres in the area of the ticket. *Not* valid in some cases before 09:00 Monday-Friday. A map of the region is provided with each pass.

7-Day Regional Rovers

Unlimited first and standard-class train travel. These passes allow persons age 60 and older, disabled passengers and an adult accompanying a disabled person to travel at discount first-class, when first-class seats are available. All of them and children age 5–15 are allowed a 34% discount. (Children using the 34% discount are limited to standard-class seats.)

The regions and adult prices until May, 1992 are: Freedom of Wales £ 45, North and Mid Wales £ 30, North East £ 52, North West £ 39.50, Coast and Peaks £ 39.50, Heart of England £ 39.50, East Midlands £ 39.50, East Anglia £ 29.50, South West £ 45, Cornish £ 30, Devon £ 30, and Severn-Avon-Wessex £ 30.

For Scotland, the prices after May 10, 1992 are: North Highland £ 39 (not valid on train arriving Aberdeen or Inverness before 09:00 Monday – Friday), Heart of Scotland £ 40 (not valid on trains arriving Aberdeen, Edinburgh, Glasgow, Haymarket or Inverness before 09:15 Monday – Friday), and West Highland £ 39.

Freedom of Scotland is £ 69 for 7 days, £ 105 for 15 days (not valid on trains arriving Aberdeen, Edinburgh, Glasgow, Haymarket or Inverness before 09:15 Monday – Friday).

Flexi Regional Rovers

Same discounts as for 7-day Rovers, The regions and adult prices until May, 1992 are: North East £ 38 for any 4 in 8 days, North West £ 29.50 for any 3 in 7 days, North Country £ 38 for any 4 in 8 days, Coast and Peaks £ 29.50 for any 3 in 7 days, Heart of England £ 29.50 for any 3 in 7 days, East Midlands £ 29.50 for any 3 in 7 days, East Anglia £ 19.50 for any 3 in 7 days, Cornish £ 19 for any 3 in 7 days, Devon £ 22 for any 3 in 7 days, and Severn-Avon-Wessex £ 22 for any 3 in 7 days.

For Scotland, the prices after May 10, 1992 are: Freedom of Scotland £ 55 for any 4 in 8 days, £ 95 for any 10 in 15 days. Festival Cities £ 18.50 for any 3 in 7 days (not valid before 09:15 Monday – Friday or on trains departing Edinburgh, Glasgow or Haymarket 16:25 – 17:40.

Young Persons Railcard   Allows 33% discount on rail tickets and Rover passes (see above), subject to several conditions as to hours, days and minimum fares. Available to everybody age 16 – 23 and students over 23 who are studying over 15 hours a week for at least 20 weeks a year at a school in the United Kingdom.

Sold at British railstations and travel agencies upon proof of age (birth certificate or passport) or an application form that has been signed and stamped by the student's teacher. tutor or department head. The 1991 price was £ 16. Valid for one year.

London Extra   *Cannot be purchased in England.* Unlimited travel on trains in Southeast England plus a London Visitor Card (see below) for same duration. Does *not* include airport transfers. The 1992 adult *first*-class prices are $105 (U.S.) for 3 days, $125 for 4 days, $185 for 7 days. For children age 5–15 : $53, $63 and $93. The 1992 adult *standard*-class prices are: $79 (U.S.), $99 and $149. For children age 5–15 : $40, $50 and $75.

London Visitor Travelcard   Can be purchased worldwide. Valid for unlimited travel on London's buses and subways, plus discounts on the admission prices at such attractions as London Transport Museum, London Zoo, Madame Tussaud's, Kensington Palace, Tower Bridge and the Cabinet War Rooms. (A version sold in Britain does not include discounts at historical sites.)

The 1992 adult prices prices are: $20 (U.S.) for 3 days, $26 for 4 days, $45 for 7 days. Children age 5–15 : $10, $12 and $20.

SCOTLAND'S RAIL PASS

All of the Scottish Rover passes (see "Flexi Regional Rovers" on page 421) are sold at main railstations and Travel Centres in the area of the "ticket". All of these allow 33% discount for children 5–15. Children under 5 travel free.

Scottish Travelpass   Unlimited train travel plus many ferries and discounts on many buses. The 1992 prices are: £ 80 for 8 days, £ 120 for 15 days. Sold at main British railstations and in North America by: Scots-American Travel Advisors, 26 Rugen Drive, Harrington Park, N.J. 07640, U.S.A. Telephone: (201) 768-5505.

COMBINING BRITAIN AND THE CONTINENT

When planning to travel both in Britain and on the European Continent, keep in mind that the maximum value of combining a British train pass with a Eurailpass is achieved by scheduling Britain for either the start or end of a tour. For example, to start a tour in Amsterdam and have one's itinerary then go to Paris, London, and then return to the continent for additional Eurailpass traveling would require a longer (and more expensive) Eurailpass because of consuming Eurailpass days while in Britain.

Conversely, to start a tour in London, followed by travel on the Continent, and then concluding with more travel in Britain will require a longer and more expensive British pass since the days spent on the Continent will consume British pass days.

We present in this chapter descriptions of 4 categories of rail service. First, the train connection services between London and the Continent (Paris, Brussels and Amsterdam). Next, 41 one-day rail trips that can be made comfortably out of London, with departure and arrival times, on-board-services, and what to see and do at each destination before returning to London, in most cases at dinnertime.

Third, readers will find itineraries for 4 long trips from and to London: Cork, Shannon Airport, Dublin and Edinburgh. This chapter concludes with details on 12 rail trips in Scotland from Aberdeen, Edinburgh, Glasgow and Inverness. Several of those routes are very scenic.

Before commencing any journey, always — without exception — doublecheck the times in this book or in any published timetable, as they are subject to change without prior notice. Eurail® Guide has made every effort possible to publish correct departure and arrival times, but schedules are subject to constant change.

Changes will usually be minor and have no effect on the trips recommended in this book. However, "a miss is as good as a mile" applies to being one-minute late for a departure. WE DO NOT WANT YOU TO BE STRANDED !

The extensive notes in this book about train times are intended to both help you *plan* your itinerary and are also useful after your trip begins (if you bring Eurail® Guide along !) for making impromptu last-minute travel plans.

WARNING: Many cities have 2 or more railstations. London has 8 railstations. We take pains to tell you for every trip in this book the name of the railstation from which your train departs, by noting the station in parenthesis immediately after the name of the city, such as: London (King's Cross). *PAY HEED !*

All of London's railstations are interconnected by subway service, providing far easier and quicker transfers than by surface streets. For example, when entering England by rail from France, at Dover, you will come into Victoria station. To continue on to Edinburgh, it is necessary to first transfer by subway (Circle line) from Victoria (along to Thames River) to King's Cross station , on the opposite side of London from Victoria station.

A brief description of the areas served by London's 8 major railstations:

CHARING CROSS STATION   This station services suburban commuters between London and Folkestone, and between London and Hastings. It connects at Dover (Priory station) with Hovercraft service to and from France.

EUSTON STATION   A part of Central England and the northwestern area of Britain are reached from Euston station, starting with Coventry and Birmingham, and then running through Stafford, Chester, Liverpool, Manchester and Blackpool, on into Glasgow. Also, Holyhead, gateway to Dublin.

KING'S CROSS STATION   Northeastern England (Leeds, York, Hull, Newcastle) and Edinburgh are reached by trains from King's Cross station. Newcastle is the gateway to Norway. Hull is a gateway to Denmark, Germany and Holland.

LIVERPOOL STREET STATION   This station services the area immediately northeast of London: Colchester, Cambridge, Ipswich, Harwich (gateway to Holland, Germany, Austria, Yugoslavia and Norway), Norwich and King's Lynn.

PADDINGTON STATION   The area in southern England, west from Weymouth (Exeter, Plymouth and Penzance), is reached out of Paddington station as is also that portion of southwestern England running north to Bristol, Swansea, Fishguard (gateway to Rosslare, at the southeastern tip of the Republic of Ireland), Gloucester, Worcester, Hereford and Oxford.

ST. PANCRAS STATION   Trains going due north from London to Leicester, Derby, Nottingham and Sheffield leave from St. Pancras station.

VICTORIA STATION   The London airport for charter flights is Gatwick, which is serviced from 05:30 to 23:00 by a train every 15 minutes (and hourly from 01:00 to 05:00) for the 40-minute ride to and from London's Victoria station. The transfer from airplane to train, or vice versa, is entirely indoor as the railstation at Gatwick is a part of the airport.

Victoria station services the small area of Southern England just East of but not including Portsmouth: Worthing, Brighton, Newhaven, Eastbourne, Hastings and Dover (gateway to France, Spain, Belgium, Switzerland, Italy, Austria and Yugoslavia).

WATERLOO STATION   Services South Central England: Southampton, Bournemouth and Weymouth.

424

HEATHROW – LONDON UNDERGROUND CONNECTION

Opened in mid-1977, the subway service between Heathrow (London's airport for scheduled airlines) and central London allows one to take a direct train beteen Heathrow and any station on Piccadilly Line (starting at Kings Cross railstation) every 4–10 minutes 05:30–23:30 Monday–Saturday except holidays, and 07:30–23:30 on Sundays. Journey time is 50–58 minutes.

GATWICK – LONDON TRAIN CONNECTION

Trains make this 30-minute trip from both Gatwick Airport (both commercial and charter flights) and Victoria railstation every 15 minutes 05:30–22:00 daily. The London airport for charter flights is Gatwick, which is serviced from 06:00 to 24:00 by a train every 15 minutes (and hourly from 01:00 to 05:00) for the 40-minute ride to London's Victoria station.

The transfer from airplane to train, or vice versa, is entirely indoor as the railstation at Gatwick is a part of the airport.

SUMMER TIME

Britain changes to Summer Time on the last Sunday of March and converts back to Standard Time on the last Sunday of October.

DAYS OF THE WEEK VARIANCES

For the time schedules given in this book, "daily" means Monday through Sunday. Where Sunday departure and arrival times are specified in conjunction with a list of daily schedules, this refers to *additional* service on Sunday, not to substitute service.

In other words, if a daily schedule lists departures at 10:00 and 11:12, and the Sunday schedule indicates a departure at 13:05, there are 3 departures on Sunday: at 10:00, 11:12 and 13:05.

Conversely, if Monday-Friday or Monday-Saturday schedules show departures at 10:00 and 11:12, and there is a listing of a Sunday departure at 13:05, then the only departure on Sunday for that trip is 13:05.

The same treatment applies to "Saturday only" schedules in connection with times given as "Monday–Friday" or as "daily".

SUMMER AND WINTER SCHEDULES

In most European countries, Winter schedules usually start on the Sunday following the last Saturday of September and runs through the Saturday preceding the last Sunday in May of the following year.

British timetables differ from the Continental pattern. Summer timetables for British rail service begin on the second Monday in May. There are two changes in Winter schedules, occuring on the first Monday in October and on the first Monday in January.

Unless designated otherwise, the departure and arrival times given in this chapter are for the Summer season and apply to trips that are made from early May to early October.

HOLIDAY TRAVEL

Nearly all train, bus and subway services cease on holidays. The main holidays on which to avoid travel are all "Bank" holidays (whose dates vary) and the period from December 25 through January 1. If you cannot avoid intra-city travel on a holiday, it is advisable to reserve a taxi by telephone the day prior.

LONDON

The capital of England. See the changing of the guard at Buckingham Palace. Downing Street, official residence of the Prime Minister. The Tower of London. London Bridge. The Houses of Parliament. The Wellington Museum (Aiseley House) and Wellington Arch. Hyde Park. Tate Gallery. The London Transport Museum at 39 Wellington Street, Covent Garden, is open daily 10:00–18:00.

The Kensington Gardens complex of Royal Albert Hall, the Science Museum, Geological Museum, Natural History Museum, and the Victoria and Albert Museum (closed on Fridays). Piccadilly Circus. The National Gallery and National Portrait Gallery.

The British Museum. Dickens' House (closed Sunday). St. Paul's Cathedral. Gray's Inn. The Imperial War Museum. The Royal Botanic Gardens (Kew). Regent's Park. Westminster Abbey. Nelson's Monument in Trafalgar Square. St. James's Palace. St. James's Park. The 53-acre Green Park.

Admiralty Arch.The Museum of London. The Royal Academy. The Museum of Mankind. The Sunday orators at Speaker's Corner. Marble Arch. Lambeth Palace, the residence of the Archbishop of Canterbury.

The dragon at Temple Bar Memorial. Mansion House, the residence of the Lord Mayor of London. Tower Bridge. The South Bank Arts Centre complex of National Theatre, Queen Elizabeth Hall, Royal Festival Hall, and Hayward Gallery.

The Victoria Tower. Whitehall, the compound of government offices. The beautifully uniformed sentries outside The Horse Guards.

One of the world's greatest food stores, in Harrods Department Store, presents a spectacle of more than 500 cheeses, 120 different breads, 21 kinds of butter, produce from California, and a meat hall 90 feet long by 60 feet wide containing hams, pork, sausages, beef and lamb. There is also venison, shellfish, poultry, salmon (smoked and fresh), tinned foods from all over the world, eggs, teas from everywhere, caviars, wine, and the list goes on forever.

Don't miss London's other great food store, in Fortnum and Mason (also a complete department store), operating since 1707 on Picadilly Circus. Open 09:30–18:00, daily except Sunday. The food and wine salesmen there wear morning coats.

'Fortnums', as Londoners call it, has 3 restaurants. "The Fountain", in the basement, has an American-style soda fountain. It is open 09:30–24:00, very popular for after-theater snacks. "The Patio", on a mezzanine, offers the same light menu as "The Fountain" but also has grilled meats. It is open 09:30–16:30. The elegant fourth-floor "St. James" offers more extensive and more expensive food, open 11:30–18:00.

For a different view of food, visit Smithfield Meat Market, England's largest meat and poultry market, covering over 10 acres and employing almost 3,000 people. On a busy day, it sells in 19 hours more than 4,000 tons of meat, poultry and game: grouse, ducks, partridges, rabbits, pheasant, hams, green bacon, Danish bacon, smoked bacon, Irish bacon, lamb, beef and many exotic imported meats. Open Monday-Friday 05:00–12:00.

Near Smithfield is the very interesting 12th century St. Bartholomew the Great Church. Stroll the entire area: St. John's Lane, Charterhouse Street and many narrow alleys for a look at the London of 300 years ago.

For a different view of London, explore the city on a Sunday, by foot. Walk along Whitechapel Road to see the (still working) foundry where the Liberty Bell was cast. From Whitechapel, it's an easy walk to the Tower of London and the St. Katherine marina.

426

CONNECTIONS WITH THE CONTINENT

The shortest route from England to the Continent is Dover to Calais or Boulogne.

The validity of one's BritRail Pass stops or starts, as the case may be, at the British shore. Similarly, the validity of one's Eurailpass stops or starts at the Continental port where your boat ride begins or ends.

In all cases, the channel boat fare is *not covered* by either pass. However, the Brit France Pass (page 420) *does* include a Hovercraft roundtrip Dover–Boulogne-Dover and Dover–Calais–Dover, as well as Boulogne–Dover–Boulogne and Calais–Dover–Calais.

Regular ferries run the following routes: Dover–Calais, Dover–Oostende, Folkestone–Boulogne, Harwich–Hoek van Holland and Newhaven–Dieppe.

Hovercraft service, faster and more expensive, is provided Dover–Boulogne, Dover–Calais, Dover–Oostende, Newhaven–Dieppe, Portsmouth–Cherbourg, and Ramsgate–Dunkerque.

Both regular ferries and hovercraft carry autos. *All of the regular ferries have a restaurant.*

London - Paris via Newhaven and Dieppe and v.v. 50

Dep. London (Vic.)	08:25	20:40	Dep. Paris (St. Laz.)	10:43	22:13
Arr. Newhaven Harbour	09:45	21:55	Dep. Rouen (Rive Dr.)	12:12	23:46
Change to a ferry.			Arr. Dieppe	13:05	00:38
Dep. Newhaven Harbour	10:15	22:30	Change to a ferry.		
Set your watch forward			Dep. Dieppe	13:45	01:45
one hour, except			Set your watch back		
late Sept. to late Oct.			one hour, except		
Arr. Dieppe	15:15	03:30	late Sept. to late Oct.		
Change to a train.			Arr. Newhaven Harbour	16:45	04:45
Dep. Dieppe	15:53	04:47	Change to a train.		
Arr. Rouen (Rive Dr.)	16:45	05:35	Dep. Newhaven Harbour	17:20	05:25
Arr. Paris (St. Laz.)	18:15	07:01	Arr. London (Vic.)	18:33	06:40

London - Paris via Portsmouth and Le Havre (regular ferry) and v.v.

Frequent trains make the 83-108 minute ride London(Waterloo) to Porthmouth and v.v..
1030 Ferry

Dep. Portsmouth	08:30 (1)	14:45 (2)	23:00

Set your watch forward one hour, except late September to late October.

Arr. Le Havre	15:15	21:30	07:00
Change to train. 115			
Dep. Le Havre	17:02	-0-	07:57
Arr. Paris (St. Laz.)	19:09	-0-	10:00

* * *

Dep. Paris (St. Laz.)	-0-	12:34 (3)	17:48
Arr. Le Havre	-0-	14:45	20:03
Change to a ferry. 1030			
Dep. Le Havre	08:30 (1)	16:45 (2)	23:00

Set your watch back one hour, except late September to late October.

Arr. Portsmouth	13:15	21:30	06:15

(1) Runs daily, except Monday. (2) Departs one hour later from late September to lat October. (3) Runs daily, except Sundays and holidays. Light refreshments.

OTHER CHANNEL-CROSSING SCHEDULES

London - Paris via Calais or Boulogne and v.v. 50

Schedules shown here are for early June to late September.

All of the trains from French ports to Paris and v.v. have light refreshments, unless designated otherwise.

Train

Dep. London (Vic.)	09:10	10:00	11:30	13:30	14:30
Arr. Folkestone			13:00		
Arr. Dover (West.)	10:45	11:28		15:00	16:00
Change to ferry.					
Dep. Folkestone			13:30		
Dep. Dover (West.)	11:15	12:30 (1)		16:15 (1)	16:30
Set your watch forward one hour.					
Arr. Boulogne		14:30	16:20	18:15 (1)	
Arr. Calais	13:45				19:00
Change to train.					
Dep. Boulogne		15:07	16:54	19:02 (2)	
Dep. Calais	14:20				19:40
Arr. Paris (Nord)	17:21	17:35	19:33	21:27	22:48

Train

Dep. Paris (Nord)	08:02	10:43	12:20 (2)	14:17	16:22 (2)
Arr. Calais		13:55			
Arr. Boulogne	10:26		14:45	16:55	18:55
Change to ferry.					
Dep. Calais		14:45			
Dep. Boulogne	11:30		15:30 (1)	17:30	19:30 (1)
Set your watch back one hour.					
Arr. Dover (West.)		15:15	15:30 (1)		19:30 (1)
Arr. Folkestone	12:20			18:20	
Change to train.					
Dep. Dover (West.)		15:55	16:40		20:40
Dep. Folkestone	12:55			18:55	
Arr. London (Vic.)	14:24	17:30	18:07	20:24	22:04

(1) Hoverspeed catamaran. Reservation required. Supplement charged. Depart/Arrive Dover's Eastern Docks. A free bus transfers passengers railstation-docks and v.v.. (2) No light refreshments.

London - Brussels via Oostende (Jetfoil) 52

Reservations are advisable on all of these trains. A light refreshment trolley goes through the ferry.

Passengers from London *must* check-in at the Jetfoil Lounge in Victoria railstation and obtain the Jetfoil boarding card at least 20 minutes before train departs.

Change to jetfoil in Dover.

Dep. London (Vict.)	07:45	11:10	13:30	16:10
Dep. Dover Docks	09:35	13:25	15:30	18:25
Set your watch forward one hour.				
Arr. Oostende	12:15	16:05	18:10	21:05
Change to train.				
Dep. Oostende	12:34 (1)	16:34	18:34 (1)	21:34
Arr. Brussels (Midi)	13:43	17:43	19:43	22:43
Arr. Brussels (Nord)	12 minutes later			

(1) Light refreshments.

London - Brussels via Oostende (regular ferry) 52

Times shown below are for Summer service (early June to late September). Change to a ferry in Dover. All of the ferries have a restaurant.

Dep. London (Vict.)	09:00	13:00	20:35
Arr. Dover Docks	10:27	14:28	22:14
Set your watch forward one hour.			
Arr. Oostende	15:45	19:45	03:45
Change to train.			
Dep. Oostende	16:34	20:30 (1)	05:32 (1)
Arr. Brussels (Midi)	17:43	21:37	06:45
Arr. Brussels (Nord)	12 minutes later		

(1) Light refreshments.

London - Amsterdam via Hoek van Holland (regular ferry) and v.v. 66

Change to ferry in Harwich Parkeston Quay (en route to Amsterdam) and in Hoek van Holland (en route to London).

All of the trains have light refreshments.

Dep. London (Liverpool Street)	09:25	19:25
Dep. Harwich	11:30	21:30 (1)
Set your watch forward one hour, except from late Sept. to late Oct.		
Arr. Hoek van Holland	19:00	07:00
Arr. Amsterdam (Cen.)	21:32	09:37
	* * *	
Dep. Amsterdam (Cen.)	09:32	19:49
Arr. Hoek van Holland	10:57	21:13
Dep. Hoek van Holland	12:00	22:30 (1)
Set your watch back one hour, except from late Sept. to late Oct.		
Arr. Harwich	17:45	06:45
Arr. London (Liverpool Street)	20:00	09:00

(1) Ferry reservation required.

ONE-DAY EXCURSIONS FROM LONDON

Here are 39 one-day rail trips that can be made comfortably, returning to London in most cases at dinnertime. Notes are provided on what to see and do at each destination.

The notation "frequent times" in these schedules means at least one departure (and usual- ly more) every hour.

London - Bath - London 530

Dep. London (Pad.)	07:15 (1)	08:15 (2)	08:30 (3)	09:15 (2)	10:15 (1+6)
Arr. Bath	08:37	09:32	10:06	10:32	11:32

Sights in **Bath**: For interesting walking tours here, go to the Tourist Information Centre and purchase "Official Guidebook" and "Walks Around Bath". During Summer, guide 1½-hour tours on foot (at no charge) start at the churchyard of the abbey.

Visit the Roman baths. Antique shops arround Abbey Green. The Costume Museum in the Assembly Rooms. The Pump Room. The Royal Crescent Row of town houses. Queen Square. The shops on Pulteney Bridge. The Circus.

The American Museum at Claverton Manor, open daily except Monday 14:00–17:00. The collection of Eltonware and Nailsea glass in the 14th century Clevedon Court manor house, open Wednesday, Thursday and Sunday 14:30–17:30. There is much elegant 18th century architecture here.

Bath is a great base for seeing many of the best sights in England. Several good, inexpensive motorcoach tours go to Gloucester, Salisbury, Stonehenge and Cheddar Gorge. These buses stop for photo-taking along the way.

Dep. Bath	12:12 (4)	12:27 (2)	13:12 (4)	13:27 (5)	14:12 (4+7)
Arr. London (Pad.)	14:09	14:01	15:08	14:50	15:55

(1) Runs Monday–Friday, except holidays. (2) Runs daily, except Sundays and holidays. (3) Runs daily, except Saturdays and holidays. (4) Runs Sunday only. (5) Runs Saturday only. (6) Plus other departures from London at frequent times from 11:15 to 23:15. (7) Plus other departures from Bath at frequent times from 14:27 to 22:27.

London - Birmingham -London 540

Dep. London (Eus.)	07:10 (1)	07:30 (2)	08:00 (3)	08:30 (2)	09:10 (1+6)
Arr. Bir. (New St.)	08:56	09:18	09:48 (4)	10:17	10:49

Sights in **Birmingham**: The Tourist Information Centre has brochures on walking tours. The Cadbury Company's "World Chocolate Experience" museum at its factory here features an exhibit on the history of chocolate. Visitors can sample a chocolate drink made from an ancient Aztec recipe, see chocolate being made, and sample chocolate at the factory's restaurant, ice cream parlor and souvenir shop.

See the restored 18th century water mill, Sarehole Mill. The 17th century house furnished as it was in its era, Blakesley Hall. The first (1734) English locomotive can be seen at the Science Museum.

Dep. Bir. (New St.)	12:18 (5)	12:48 (5)	13:18 (5)	13:48 (2)	14:18 (2+7)
Arr. London (Eus.)	14:04 (4)	14:38	15:08 (4)	15:43	16:07 (4)

(1) Runs Monday-Friday, except holidays. (2) Runs daily, except Sundays and holidays. (3) Runs daily, except holidays. (4) Arrives 40 minutes later on Sunday. (5) Runs daily, except Sundays and holidays. Restaurant car. (6) Plus other departures from London at frequent times from 09:30 to 20:40. (7) Plus other Birmingham departures at frequent times from 14:48 to 22:18.

London - Bournemouth - London   ABC page 58

Most of these trains have light refreshments.

Dep. London (Wat.)	Frequent times from 07:45 to 22:45
Arr. Bournemouth	Monday–Saturday: 2 hours later
	Sunday: 2 ½ hours later

Sights in **Bournemouth**: A large seaside resort. Stroll through Pavillion Rock Garden. There are 3 gambling casinos. Many lovely parks and gardens.

Dep. Bournemouth	Frequent times from 06:35 to 21:45
Arr. London (Wat.)	Monday–Saturday: 2 hours later
	Sunday: 2 ½ hours later

London - Brighton - London   ABC page 61

Dep. London (Victoria)	Frequent times from 05:47 to 23:59
Arr. Brighton	55–70 minutes later

Sights in **Brighton**: Walk from the railstation down Queen Street to the seashore and the Aquarium at Palace Pier. See the antique shops in the many alleys, called "The Lanes". The Regency architecture prevalent here. The Royal Pavillion. The ornate chandelier in Banquet Hall.

Dep. Brighton	Frequent times from 05:50 to 23:35
Arr. London (Victoria)	55–70 minutes later

London - Bristol - London   530

Dep. London (Paddington)	Frequent times 06:45 to 23:59 (from 08:00 on Sunday)
Arr. Bristol (Temple Meads)	90 minutes later

*   *   *

Dep. Bristol (Temple Meads)	Frequent times 05:45 to 22:15 (from 08:00 on Sunday)
Arr. London (Paddington)	90 minutes later

Sights in **Bristol**: A famous seaport. Everything here is either a short walk or can be reached by bus. The city operates 1½-hour guided walking tours June, July and August from the Exchange on Corn Street at 11:00 on Monday and Tuesday, at 14:30 on other days. Some of Bristol can be seen from a tour boat at the harbor. That tour operates daily at 12:00, 14:00, 15:00 and 16:00.

See the many excellent Georgian buildings on Royal York Crescent, Cornwallis Crescent, Windsor Terrace, West Mall, Caledonia Place, Queen Square and Berkeley Square. The Christmas Steps, built in 1669. The 12th century St. James' Church.

The John Wesley Chapel, world's first Methodist preaching house, with a bronze statue of Wesley in the courtyard. The 11th century St. Mary-le-Port Church. St. John's Church. The 13th century St. Mary Redcliffe, one of England's largest churches. The 12th century Cathedral.

The exhibit of period furniture in the 18th century Georgian House. The view from the top of Cabot Tower, on Brandon Hill. The collection of porcelain, models of early sailing ships and paintings of the waterfront in the Bristol Museum and Art Gallery, open every day 10:00–17:00. See the beautiful gardens and the rare animals (including the Okapi and the white tigers) at the Zoo. Brunel's Clifton Suspension Bridge, built in 1864, straddling Avon Gorge, 245 feet above the water. Tour Brunel's iron steamship, The Great Britain (the first ocean screw steamship, launched in 1843), returned to Bristol in 1970 from the Falkland Islands. It is open 10:00–18:00.

London - Cardiff - London   530

Dep. London (Paddington)	Frequent times from 07:00 to 23:59
Arr. Cardiff (Central)	2 hours later

Sights in **Cardiff**: Llandaff Cathedral. Cardiff Castle. The National Museum of Wales, featuring Welsh handicraft and art. It is a short train ride from Cardiff's Queen Street railstation to **Caerphilly**, whose castle is nearly as large as Windsor Castle and has many interesting exhibits.

Dep. Cardiff (Central)	Frequent times from 05:55 to 21:39
Arr. London (Paddington)	2 hours later

London - Bristol - Cardiff - London

As these schedules indicate, it is easy to visit both Cardiff and Bristol in one day.

These schedules are for travel daily, except Sundays and holidays.

530		530	
Dep. London (Pad.)	08:15	Dep. Cardiff (Cen.)	16:25 (1)
Arr. Bristol (T.M.)	09:46	Arr. London (Pad.)	18:32
Sightsee in Bristol			
532		(1) Plus other departures from	
Dep. Bristol (T.M.)	12:38	Cardiff at 17:25, 18:25, 19:25	
Arr. Cardiff (Cen.)	13:22	and 21:25.	

London - Cambridge - London   585

Dep. London (King's X)	07:15 (1)	08:48 (1)	09:48 (1)	10:48 (1)	11:20 (2+3)
Arr. Cambridge	70–80 minutes later				

* * *

Dep. Cambridge	Frequent times from 06:58 to 22:22
Arr. London (King's X)	70–80 minutes later

(1) Runs daily, except Sundays and holidays. (2) Runs Sunday only. (3) Plus other departures from London at frequent times from 11:48 to 18:10, plus 20:15 (1).

Sights in **Cambridge**: To see buildings that have housed great colleges for more than 700 years, take bus #101 to Market Street. See King's College Chapel and Queen's College. Visit the Wren Library at Trinity College. The medieval and renaissance armor, weapons, tapestries and manuscripts in the Fitzwilliam Museum on Trumpington Street.

The Botanical Gardens. On Castle Street, see the Folk Museum and the modern paintings and sculpture at Kettles Yard Art Gallery. Hire a boat at Mill Bridge or Anchor Inn, and paddle along the idyllic Cam River. Four miles away is the American Cemetery.

London - Canterbury - London

For this 2-hour ride, there are frequent departures both from London's Waterloo and Charing Cross railstations to Canterbury's West railstation. There are also frequent departures from London's Victoria station to Canterbury's East station. The walk from Canterbury's *West* station to the famous Cathedral allows you to view interesting buildings.

Canterbury's *East* railstation is nearer the Cathedral and therefore more convenient to use for returning to London after visiting the Cathedral than the West station. A departure from Canterbury's East station will take you to London's Victoria station. Or, you can depart from Canterbury's West station, arriving London's Waterloo or Charing Cross stations.

Sights in **Canterbury**: Guided tours (Monday–Friday) start at 14:15 at a kiosk in Longmarket, a pedestrian area next to Christ Church Gate.

See the great Cathedral, housing the tomb of Thomas a Becket. Medieval inns (Falstaff, Beverlie, Olive Branch). The cemetery, where Christopher Marlowe and Joseph Conrad are buried. The Old Weaver's House, built in 1500. Excavated Roman ruins. Plays, ballet, cricket.

London - Sevenoaks - Chartwell - London   500

There are many departures daily from London's Charing Cross railstation for the 45-minute ride to Sevenoaks. Take a taxi for the 7-mile trip from Sevenoaks to Chartwell.

Sights in **Chartwell:** The country house that Winston Churchill bought in 1922, where he painted and wrote his books during the years he was out of power. You will see here the best collection of Churchilliana in the world: his collection of eccentric hats, his World War II "jump suit", Knight of the Garter uniform, many of his paintings, and a model of the Invasion Day harbor at Arromanches. Also the brick wall and cottage he built with his own hands on a small part of the 79 acres there. The main house is open Wednesday, Thursday, Saturday and Sunday from April to mid-October.

London - Chester - London   555

Dep. London (Euston)	06:30 (1)	08:50 (2)	09:45 (1)	11:35 (1)	
Arr. Chester	09:53	11:52	12:18	14:07	
		*	*	*	
Dep. Chester	14:53 (3)	15:20 (2)	16:39 (2)	17:56 (3)	18:26 (4)
Arr. London (Euston)	17:45	18:12	19:30	20:43	22:07 (5)

(1) Runs daily, except Sundays and holidays. Departs 10 minutes earlier on Saturday. (2) Runs Sunday only. (3) Runs daily, except Sundays and holidays. (4) Runs daily, except holidays. (5) Arrives 21:18 on Sunday.

Sights in **Chester**: The 2-mile-long Roman Wall. The excellent collection of Roman artifacts (glass, tools, coins, weapons, tombstones) at Grosvenor Museum. The "Rows", long covered balconies (to protect shoppers from rain) that are full-length streets above the streets of Chester. These are lined with shops. Also see St. Werburgh's Cathedral. The castle overlooking the **River Dee**. The marvelous carving of animals and historic scenes on the front of the 17th century Bishop Lloyd's House on Watergate Street. The antique shops on Lower Bridge Street and Watergate Street. The 16th century mansion, Stanley Palace. The 30-minute slide show of Chester's history, in the British Heritage Centre.

Sightseeing bus tours start in Market Square, opposite the Tourist Office at the Victorian Gothic Town Hall. Guided *walking* tours of 1 to 3 hours cost £1.80 for adults in 1990 (95 pence for children). Leave from the Tourist Information Office at the Town Hall at 10:45 (May-October: daily. November–April: daily, except Sunday)....and at 14:30 (April–October: daily. November–March: daily, except Sunday).

The 130-acre open-space Zoo, just north of the city, attracts nearly 1,000,000 people a year.

London - Chichester - London ABC page 72

This service is daily. Most of the trains Monday–Saturday have light refreshments.

Dep. London (Vic.)	Frequent times 08:17 – 21:17 (until 23:21 Monday–Saturday)
Arr. Chichester	About 100 minutes later

Sights in **Chichester**: The Marc Chagall stained glass window and the John Piper Holy Trinity tapestry in the 12th century Norman Cathedral. The 2nd century Roman wall. The 16th century arcaded Market Cross. Two miles west, the museum and mosaic floors in the 3rd century Palace at Fishbourne, the largest Roman residence in Britain.

The Palace is open daily, March through October. The attractive mosaic floors in the 1st century Roman villa at **Bignor**, 2 miles east, open daily except Monday, March through October.

Dep. Chichester	Frequent times 09:15 – 20:15 (until 21:15Monday–Saturday)
Arr. London (Vic.)	About 100 minutes later

London - Coventry - London 540

Dep. London (Eus.)	07:10 (1)	07:30 (2)	08:00 (2)	08:30 (2)	09:10 (1)	09:30 (3+7)
Arr. Coventry	08:22	08:47	09:18	09:47	10:16	10:47

Sights in **Coventry**: Completely rebuilt since the Nazi air attacks, Coventry was the site of Lady Godiva's notorious horseback ride. See the Graham Sutherland tapestry, the abstract stained-glass windows and the enormous engraved glass wall at the new (1962) Cathedral.

Dep. Coventry	12:10 (3)	12:40 (3)	13:10 (3)	13:40 (3)	14:10 (2)	14:40 (2+8)
Arr. London (Eus.)	13:34	14:04	14:38	15:08	15:43	16:07

(1) Runs Monday-Friday, except holidays. (2) Runs daily, except Sundays and holidays. (3) Runs daily, except Sundays and holidays. Restaurant car. (4) Runs daily, except holidays. (5) Runs Sunday only. (6) Runs Friday, Saturday and Sunday. (7) Plus other departures from London at 10:00 (3), 10:30 (3), 11:00 (3), 11:30 (3), 12:00 (2), 12:30 (1), 13:00 (3) and 13:30 (3). (8)Plus other departures from Coventry at 15:10 (3), 15:40 (2), 16:10 (3), 16:40 (4), 17:10 (4), 17:40 (4), 18:10 (4), 18:40 (4), 19:11 (5), 19:40 (4), 20:10 (4), 20:40 (2), 21:10 (6), 21:41 (2), 22:01 (5), 22:41 (4) and 22:55 (2).

London - Dover - London ABC page 10

Dep. London (Vic.)	08:23 (1)	09:23 (1)	10:20 (1)	11:20 (1)
Arr. Dover (Priory)	10:43	11:41	12:00	13:00

Sights in **Dover**: It is a short walk downhill from the Priory railstation to the village. Or, you can ride a bus. See the legendary white cliffs. The mighty castle. The busy harbor. The museum in the 4th century Roman painted house.

Dep. Dover (Priory)	14:52 (2)	15:39 (3)	15:52 (4)	16:09 (5)	16:39 (5+6)
Arr. London (Vic)	16:34	17:33	17:33	18:02	18:35

(1) Runs daily. (2) Runs daily, except Sundays and holidays (3) Runs Sunday only. (4) Runs Mondy–Friday, except holidays. (5) Runs Saturday only. (6) Plus other Dover departures at 17:09 (2), 17:24 (3), 17:39 (2), 17:52 (5), 18:24 (3), 18:39 (2), 19:39 (1), 20:39 (1), 21:21 (3), 21:39 (2), 22:09 (2) and 22:21 (3).

London - Exeter - London   (main line via Reading)

(Paddington station) 510

Dep. London (Pad.)	07:35 (1)	08:02 (3)	09:05 (3)	09:20 (4)	09:35 (1)
Arr. Exeter (St. David's)	10:16 (2)	10:51	11:13	12:01	11:53

Dep. London (Pad.)	10:35 (5)	10:50 (4)	11:05 (3)	11:35 (6)	12:05 (3+12)
Arr. Exeter (St. David's)	12:33	13:32	13:12	13:47	14:09

Sights in **Exeter**: The 11th century Cathedral, with its 300-foot nave and row of statutes. Rougemont Castle. The Mint. The underground water channel at Princesshay. The paintings and oak paneling in Exeter Guildhall.

The exhibit of boats from all parts of the world at the very interesting Maritime Museum.

Dep. Exeter (St. David's)	14:00 (5)	14:35 (7)	15:00 (1)	15:36 (9)
Arr. London (Pad.)	16:15	17:01 (8)	17:11	18:17 (10)

Dep. Exeter (St. David's)	16:35 (5)	17:17 (4)	17:28 (1)	17:56 (4)	18:29 (11+13)
Arr. London (Pad.)	18:58	19:50	19:43	20:40	20:59

(1) Runs daily, except Sundays and holidays. (2) Arrives 09:39 on Saturday. (3) Runs Saturday only. (4) Runs Sunday only. (5) Runs daily, except Sundays and holidays. Restaurant car. (6) Runs Monday–Friday, except holidays. Restaurant car. (7) Runs daily, except Saturdays and holidays. (8) Arrives 17:28 on Sunday. (9) Runs daily, except holidays. (10) Arrives 18:58 on Sunday. (11) Runs Saturday and Sunday only. (12) Plus other departures from London at 12:20 (3) and 12:35 (1), arriving Exeter 14:58 and 14:51. (13) Plus other departures from Exeter at 18:56 (4), 19:35 (5) and 20:06 (4), arriving London 21:43, 22:02 and 22:58.

OR

London - Exeter - London   (via Salisbury)

(Waterloo Station)   511

Most of these trains have light refreshments.

Dep. London (Waterloo)	07:52 (1)	08:40 (2)	09:15 (1)	10:40 (4+7)
Arr. Exeter (Central)	11:11	12:13 (3)	12:36	14:39
Arr. Exeter (St. David's)	5 minutes later			

* * *

Dep. Exeter (St. David's)	15:48 (4)	16:22 (2)	17:22 (4)	17:38 (5+8)
Dep. Exeter (Central)	5 minutes later			
Arr. London (Waterloo)	19:16	19:50 (3)	21:16	21:25

(1) Runs Saturday only. (2) Runs daily, except Saturday. (3) Arrives 20 minutes later on Sunday. (4) Runs Sunday only. (5) Runs daily, except Sundays and holidays. (6) Runs Monday-Friday, except holidays. (7) Plus other London departures at 11:00 (6) and 11:15 (2). (8) Plus another Exeter (St. David's) departure at 18:35 (4).

London - Greenwich - London suburban train

Sights in **Greenwich**: Take the Docklands Light Railway, opposite the Tower of London, for the 20-minute ride to the "Island Gardens" terminus. Walk from it through the pedestrian tunnel that goes under the Thames River, ending next to the famous 1870 clipper ship Cutty Sark. Near the Cutty Sark, see the 53-foot Gypsy Moth sailboat which Chichester sailed solo around the world in 1966–67. Both Cutty Sark and Gypsy Moth are open May-September 14:30–18:00 daily.... October–April 11:00–17:00 Monday–Saturday and 14:30–17:00 Sunday.

Visit the Royal Observatory's museum of navigation, astronomy and chronometry (astrolabes, hourglasses, clockwork planetariums, quadrants, chronometers). See the Meridian Building's brass strip which marks the division of the eastern and western hemispheres. All distances and time worldwide are measured from this, the prime meridian.

See the marvelous exhibits (ship models, scientific instruments, marine paintings, chronometers, naval uniforms) in the National Maritime Museum.

Both the Royal Observatory and the Maritime Museum are open Monday–Friday 10:00–17:00 (October–April) and 10:00–18:00 (May–September), Saturday 10:00–18:00 all year, and Sunday 14:30–18:00 all year.

See the enormous Painted Hall in the Royal Naval College, open daily except Thursday 14:30–17:00. Lunch in one of the good "pubs" at the riverside.

For the return to London, a boat ride on the Thames is an enjoyable alternative to the train.

London - Hampton Court - London ABC table 50

| Dep. London (Waterloo) | Frequent times from 06:20 to 23:25 |
| Arr. Hampton Court | 35 minutes later |

Sights in **Hampton Court**: This is the riverside Palace built by Cardinal Wolsey and then given to Henry VIII, after he expressed his desire to have it. Walk through the ancient maze.

| Dep. Hampton Court | Frequent times from 06:08 to 23:42 |
| Arr. London (Waterloo) | 35 minutes later |

London - Hastings - London ABC table 16

Dep. London (Char. X)	08:00 (1)	08:15 (1)	09:15 (1)	09:45 (2)	10:45 (2)	11:20 (3)	11:50 (2)
Arr. Hastings	09:40	09:42	10:42	11:26	12:26	12:44	13:26

Sights in **Hastings**: This is where William became the Conqueror, of the Saxons. Take buses #5, #252, #485 or #486 to see the ancient battlefield. Visit the old fishing harbor and stroll the 3-mile promenade along the beach. Obtain a printed description of the Castle at the Tourist Information Center, 4 Robertson Terrace.

See the 243-foot-long tapestry in Town Hall, illustrating the 81 greatest events of British history since 1066: the battle of Hastings, the Boston Tea Party, the first television broadcast, etc.

Dep. Hastings	13:55 (2)	14:39 (3)	14:55 (2)	15:39 (3)	15:55 (2)	16:39 (2+4)
Arr. London (Char. X)	15:33	16:03	16:42	17:10	17:50	18:18

(1) Runs daily. Departs 15 minutes earlier on Sunday. (2) Runs daily. (3) Runs daily, except Sunday. (4) Plus other departures from Hastings at frequent times from 17:36 to 22:05 (to 21:39 on Sunday).

London - Isle of Wight (Yarmouth) - London   (via Lymington)

There are 148 miles of well-posted footpaths on Wight, including a 60-mile path along the entire coastline of this island that measures 13 miles at its widest by 23 miles at its longest. Also several bus lines. Many quiet beaches. Good fishing.

Twenty-two orchid species grow here. See the dinosaur bones in the Museum of Wight Geology over the Public Library. Carisbrooke Castle. Quarr Abbey, near Ryde. Take the boat trip that starts at Alum Bar.

ABC table 60 (Train)			ABC table 61 (Ferry)		
Dep. London (Wat.)	07:45 (1)	07:45 (2)	Dep. Yarmouth	13:30 (1)	14:00 (2+3)
Arr. Brockenhurst	09:20	09:52	Arr. Lym. Pier	14:00	14:30
Change trains. ABC 61			Change to train		
Dep. Brockenhurst	09:25	09:57	Dep. Lym. Pier	14:10	14:38
Arr. Lym. Pier	09:36	10:08	Arr. Brockenhurst	14:18	14:47
Change to ferry.			Change trains. ABC 60		
Dep. Lym. Pier	09:45	10:15	Dep. Brockenhurst	14:23	14:58
Arr. Yarmouth	10:15	10:45	Arr. London (Wat.)	16:05	16:48

(1) Runs daily, except Sundays and holidays. (2) Runs Sunday only. (3) Plus other Yarmouth departures every day hourly until 18:30.

London - Kings Lynn - London   585

Some trains Cambridge-King's Lynn were temporarily replaced by bus in 1990 while the rail line was being electrified.

Dep. London (Kings X)	08:48 (1)	09:48 (3)	10:48 (4)	11:48 (1)
Arr. Cambridge	09:46	10:46	11:46	12:46
Change trains.				
Dep. Cambridge	10:07 (2)	11:07	11:52	13:07 (2)
Arr. Kings Lynn	11:06 (2)	12:06	12:51	14:06 (2)

Sights in **Kings Lynn**: The "Town Trail" brochure, available at the City Information Center, is very helpful for touring the winding, twisting streets here in one of England's most historic towns.

See the attractive merchants' houses on Queen Street. The King John Cup and one of the oldest paper books in the world (the Red Register), at the Treasury in the 15th century Town Hall. The country market, every Tuesday near Duke's Head Hotel and every Saturday opposite Town Hall.

Dep. Kings Lynn	14:32 (3)	14:45 (5)	15:32 (3)	15:45 (5)	16:27 (4+7)
Arr. Cambridge	15:33	15:45	16:36	16:43	17:28
Change trains.					
Dep. Cambridge	15:42	16:30	16:39	17:30	17:44
Arr. London (Kings X)	16:41	17:37	17:41	18:38	18:43

(1) Runs daily, except Sundays and holidays. (2) Fifteen minutes earlier on Saturday. (3) Trip to/from Kings Lynn runs Monday–Friday, except holidays. (4) Trip to/from Kings Lynn runs Saturday only. (5) Runs sunday only. (6) Runs Saturday only. (7) Plus other Kings Lynn departures at 16:30 (3), 16:45 (5), 17:27 (4), 17:30 (3), 17:45 (5), 19:18 (1), 19:45 (5) and 21:07 (4)....arriving London 18:36, 19:37, 20:19, 20:38, 22:22 (2), 22:58 and 23:47.

London - Leicester - London 560

Most of these trains have light refreshments or a restaurant car.

Dep. London (St. Pan.)	07:00 (1)	07:30 (1)	08:00 (2)	08:30 (3)	09:00 (2+7)
Arr. Leicester	08:19	08:44	09:10	09:45 (4)	10:11

Sights in **Leicester**: The Jewry Wall, to see outstanding Roman ruins. The Church of St. Mary de Castro.

Dep. Leicester	12:30 (1)	13:00 (3)	13:30 (1)	14:00 (3)	14:30 (5+8)
Arr. London (St. Pan.)	13:46	14:12 (4)	14:53	15:16 (4)	15:42 (4)

(1) Runs daily, except Sundays and holidays. (2) Runs Monday–Friday, except holidays. (3) Runs daily, except holidays. (4) Arrives 40 minutes later on Sunday. (5) Runs daily, except Saturdays and holidays. (6) Runs Sunday only. (7) Plus other London departures at 09:30 (1), 10:00 (1), 10:30 (3), 11:00 (1), 11:30 (3), 12:00 (1) and 12:30 (5). (8) Plus other Leicester departures at 15:00 (3), 15:30 (1), 16:00 (5), 16:30 (3), 17:00 (3), 17:30 (5), 18:00 (3), 18:30 (3), 19:00 (6), 19:30 (1), 20:00 (3), 21:00 (3) and 22:00 (3).

London - Lincoln - London 570 + 574

All of these schedules require changing trains in Newark.

Dep. London (Kings X)	07:05 (1)	08:10 (1)	09:25 (1)	10:10 (1)	11:10 (1)
Arr. Lincoln (Cen.)	09:21	10:25	11:22	12:06	13:08

Sights in **Lincoln**: The wonderful Cathedral. Newport Arch. Roman relics in the City and County Museums. The houses on High Bridge.

Dep. Lincoln (Cen.)	12:03 (1)	12:55 (3)	13:30 (1)	14:22 (3)	14:55 (3+5)
Arr. London (Kings X)	14:30	15:25	15:26	16:35	17:21

(1) Runs daily, except Sundays and holidays. (2) Runs Monday-Friday, except holidays. (3) Runs Sunday only. (4) Runs Saturday only. (5) Plus other departures from Lincoln at 15:11 (1), 16:08 (2), 17:09 (3), 18:19 (3), 18:51 (2), 19:06 (4) and 19:30 (3), arriving London 17:27, 17:59, 19:30, 20:31, 20:57, 21:32 and 22:00.

London - Norwich - London 580

Most of these trains have light refreshments.

Dep. London (L'pool)	07:30 (1)	08:00 (2)	08:30 (3)	09:30 (4)	10:30 (3+8)
Arr. Norwich	09:20	09:35	10:17	11:17	12:15

Sights in **Norwich**: Norwich Grammar School. (Its alumni include Lord Nelson.) The Cathedral. The collection of lace, pottery, teapots, paintings and coins at the Museum in the Castle, built in 1068 by William the Conqueror.

Walk down the Elm Hill alley. See the view of Norwich from the Castle. Assembly House. The Strangers Hall. The 16th century house on the 12th century High Bridge.

Dep. Norwich	12:55 (3)	13:55 (3)	14:55 (3)	15:55 (3)	16:20 (5+9)
Arr. London (L'pool)	14:50	15:50	16:50	17:50	18:05

(1)Runs Saturday only. (2) Runs Monday–Friday, except holidays. (3) Runs daily, except holidays. (4) Runs daily. (5) Runs Sunday only. (6) Runs daily, except Sundays and holidays. (7) Runs daily, except Sundays and holidays. Restaurant car. (8) Plus another London departure at 11:30 (6), arriving Norwich 13:15. (9) Plus other Norwich departures at 17:05 (7), 17:55 (3), 18:55 (3), 20:20 (5) and 20:40 (2), arriving London 18:50, 19:50, 20:50, 22:15 and 22:31.

London - Nottingham - London 560

Dep. London (St. Pan.)	07:30 (1)	08:30 (2)	09:30 (3)	10:30 (4)	11:30 (2+13)
Arr. Nottingham	09:09	10:10	11:13	12:08 (5)	13:04

Sights in **Nottingham**: The Duke of Newcastle's castle. which was a new Newcastle castle in 1679 . . . with its art collection. The great council house. The Natural History Museum in Wollaton Hall.

Dep. Nottingham	12:23 (6)	13:07 (7)	13:37 (2)	14:05 (8)	14:37 (9+14)
Arr. London (St. Pan.)	14:12 (5)	14:46	15:16	16:28	16:23

(1) Runs daily, except Sundays and holidays. (2) Runs Monday-Friday, except holidays. Restaurant car or light refreshments. (3) Runs daily, except Sundays and holidays. Restaurant car Monday–Friday. Light refreshments Saturday. (4) Runs daily, except holidays. Restaurant car Monday–Friday. Light refreshments on Saturday and Sunday. (5) Arrives 50 minutes later on Sunday. (6) Runs daily, except Saturdays and holidays. Light refreshments. (7) Runs Saturday only. Light refreshments. (8) Runs Sunday only. Light refreshments. (9) Runs daily, except Sundays and holidays. Light refreshments. (10) Runs daily, except Saturdays and holidays. Restaurant car Monday–Friday. Light refreshments Sunday. (11) Runs daily. Light refreshments. (12) Runs daily, except holidays. (13) Plus other departures from London at 12:00 (7), 12:30 (6) and 13:30 (9), arriving Nottingham 13:42, 14:13 and 15:08. (14) Plus other departures from Nottingham at 15:37 (10), 16:07 (7), 16:37 (6), 17:37 (11), 18:38 (8), 19:07 (9) and 20:37 (12), arriving London 17:12, 17:51, 18:19, 19:23, 20:24, 20:57 and 22:29.

London - Oxford - London 525

All of these trains have light refreshments.

Dep. London (Pad.)	08:20 (1)	09:20 (2)	09:50 (3)	10:20 (2)	11:15 (1+5)
Arr. Oxford	60-70 minutes later				

Sights in **Oxford**: Daily guided tours by open-top, double-decker bus depart the railstation every 15 minutes until approximately 17:30. The 1991 price was £ 5.

This is the home of one of the greatest universities in the world, comprising 23 different colleges. Start your stroll at the center of Oxford (Carfax Tower), where the Information Center is located. There is bus service from the railstation to Carfax Tower.

Begin by walking south from Carfax Tower, down St. Aldates Street to Folly Bridge, the Cathedral and the numerous portraits (John Wesley, William Penn, Lewis Carroll, William Gladstone) at Christ Church College. Founded by Cardinal Wolsey and Henry VIII, it is the largest and most splendid of all the colleges here.

Later, see Merton College and Corpus Christi before continuing on to Oriel and then into High Street. See Bodleian Library, which has a copy of every book published in England. See the decorative bookcases in the library of Queen's College. Most popular among visitors is Magdalen College, with its beautiful main quadrangle.

At 20:55, hear "Great Tom's" 101 strokes every night as the heavy bell calls the original number of Osney Abbey's students to return to their rooms before the nightly closing of its gates.

Dep. Oxford	Frequent times from 06:00 to 22:25
Arr. London (Pad.)	60-70 minutes later

(1) Runs daily, except holidays. (2) Runs daily, except Sundays and holidays. (3) Runs Monday-Friday, except holidays. (4) Runs Sunday only. (5)Plus other departures from London at 12:03 (4), 12:20 (2), 12:45 (4), 13:20 (2) and 13:40 (4).

NEARBY BLENHEIM PALACE   Churchill's Birthplace

To see lovely Blenheim Palace, take a bus in Oxford from Gloucester Green bus station for the 8-mile trip to **Woodstock**. This magnificent 18th century structure was the birthplace of Winston Churchill in 1874.

A gift from Britain to the Duke of Marlborough after this ancestor of Churchill defeated the French in 1704 at Blenheim in Bavaria, the beautiful 300-room mansion is open daily March–October, with guided tours 11:30–17:00.

Letters, documents, photos, even a lock of Churchill's hair (at the age of 5) are exhibited in the tiny room where he was born prematurely and unexpectedly on November 30, 1874, in his mother's seventh month of pregnancy.

Other rooms throughout the palace have more memorabilia: some of Churchill's paintings (see "London-Chartwell" on page 432), recordings of his speeches, his letters, etc. A visit here is worthwhile if only to see the 180-foot-long library, with its marvelous Willis pipe organ.

There is time in the same day to visit nearby Bladon Churchyard. A simple tombstone there that reads merely "Winston Leonard Spencer Churchill 1874/1965" marks the burial place (alongside his American mother Jenny Spencer) of the greatest Englishman of the last 1,000 years.

London - Penzance - London   515

Reservation is advisable for all of these trains.

Dep. Lon. (Pad.)	07:35 (1)	07:45 (2)	08:20 (3)	09:05 (1)	10:20 (3)	10:35 (4)
Arr. Penzance	12:40	13:19	14:06	14:08	16:00	15:30 (5)

Dep. Lon. (Pad.)	11:35 (1)	12:20 (3)	12:35 (6)	13:35 (7)	14:20 (3)	14:35 (6+18)
Arr. Penzance	16:39	18:04	17:57	19:30 (8)	20:00	19:42

* * *

Dep. Penzance	04:57 (1)	05:21 (11)	06:46 (4)	08:00 (1)	08:40 (9)	09:40 (9)
Arr. Lon. (Pad.)	09:54	10:00	11:45	13:15	13:35 (10)	14:57 (10)

Dep. Penzance	10:45 (3)	12:36 (11)	13:39 (1)	14:45 (11)	15:45 (12)	16:30 (4+19)
Arr. Lon. (Pad.)	16:08	18:17 (10)	18:48	19:43	20:59	22:02

(1) Runs Sat. only. (2) Runs Mon.–Fri., except holidays. Restaurant car. (3) Runs Sun. only. (4) Runs daily, except Sun. and holidays. (5) Arrives 15:00 on Saturday. (6) Runs daily, except Sun. and holidays. (7) Runs Fri. and Sat. (8) Arrives 18:45 on Sat.. (9) Runs daily, except holidays. Restaurant car Mon.–Fri. (10) Arrives 40–50 minutes later on Sun. (11) Runs daily, except holidays. (12) Runs Sat. and Sun. (13) Runs daily, except Sat. and holidays. (14) Runs Fri. only. (15) Runs daily, except Sat. Restaurant car. (16) Runs daily, except holidays. Carries a sleeping car. (17) Runs Sat. only. Carries a sleeping car. (18) Plus other London departures at 15:35 (6), 17:35 (13), 18:05 (1), 18:35 (14), 19:35 (15) and 23:35 (16), arriving Penzance 20:53, 22:29 (10), 23:11, 23:34, 01:03 and 08:24. (19) Plus other Penzance departures at 17:15 (3), 21:15 (17) and 22:15 (6), arriving London 22:58, 05:00 and 05:31.

Penzance and the rest of Cornwall deserve a stay of several days, although Penzance can be visited on a one-day train excursion from London. Sights in **Penzance**: Take the walk described in the free brochure called "A day in Chapel Street, Abbey Street and Quay Street" and visit Egyptian Shop, the Admiral Benbow Inn, the Nautical Museum and Morrab Gardens. See the view of Mount's Bay from Bolitho Gardens.

It is only a 10-mile bus trip to **Land's End**, the westernmost edge of England and a beautiful seascape of waves crashing against the granite cliffs. In another direction, it is also only a 10-mile bus ride to **St. Ives**, a quaint fishing village and the location of The Hepworth Gallery, containing the work of Britain's best-known sculptress. (Both buses leave from the terminal next to the railstation.)

Go a mere 3 miles by city bus to **Marazion** and then by small motorboat to visit **St. Michael's Mount**, a tiny island only a half-mile offshore. There has been a church at the summit since 1135. The castle has been occupied by the St. Aubyn family from 1659 to the present day. Visitors are allowed to enter most of the rooms of the castle and are provided a brochure describing its history and the many interesting contents: furniture, costumes, guns, maps, portraits, banners.

Penzance is also the gateway to the more than 100 **Isles of Scilly**. The largest island is the 3-miles-by-2-miles St. Mary's. For information, about the 2½-hour ferry-boat ride to it (600 passengers), contact Isles of Scilly Steamship Company, Quay St., Penzance, Cornwall TR18 4BD, United Kingdom.

A 20-minute helicopter flight operated by British International Helicopters departs Monday–Saturday hourly from 07:50 to 17:50 Penzance-St. Mary's Island and Penzance–Tresco Island.

The northern half of **Tresco**, dominated by the ruins of the 16th century King Charles Castle and the 17th century Cromwell's Castle, is windswept and treeless. Its southern half, lush and semitropical, has wide beaches, a roofless 16th century stone fort from which there are beautiful views, and the marvelous Abbey Gardens with its collection of restored figureheads salvaged from ships that were wrecked in this area.

There is boat service from Tresco to **St. Mary's**, the commercial center of the archipelago, where the main attractions are a 16th century Star Castle and a museum open every day except rainless Sundays 09:30–12:30, 13:30–16:30 and 19:30–21:00 (old rowboats, Roman pottery, stone tools).

St. Mary's also offers sandy beaches (washed by frigid water). many beautiful gardens of sub-tropical plants, coastal walks, nature trails, and a 9-hole golf course along the seacoast. Small launches can be taken to the other inhabited islands: **Bryher**, **St. Agnes** and **St. Martin's**.

London - Portsmouth - London ABC 56

These departures are daily except holidays.

Dep. London (Waterloo)	08:20	09:20	10:20	11:20	12:20
Arr. Portsmouth (Hbr.)	10:06	11:05	12:05	13:05	14:05

Sights in **Portsmouth**: England's great naval base. See Lord Nelson's flagship H.M.S. Victory, which won the battle of Trafalgar over the combined Spanish and French fleets. The nearby Victory Museum (Nelson relics, good marine paintings, ship models) at the Naval Yard. Nearby is Henry VIII's man-of-war, "Mary Rose", raised in 1982 from the seabed where it had lain since it sank in 1545.

The Dickens Museum at the house where the author was born, 393 Commercial Road. Many fine 17th and 18th century houses on Lombard Street and High Street.

Dep. Portsmouth (Hbr.)	14:20	15:13	16:06	17:06	18:06	19:06 (1)
Arr. London (Waterloo)	16:01	17:01	17:30	18:29	19:30	20:31

(1) Plus other departures from Portsmouth at 19:57, 20:57, 21:32 (Sunday only) and 22:18.

London - Isle of Wight (Shanklin) - London (via Portsmouth)

As these schedules indicate, it is easy to visit both Portsmouth and the Isle of Wight in one day by stopping-over in Portsmouth at 08:24, 09:38 or 09:59....until 11:20, 11:50 or 12:20.

ABC 56

Dep. London (Wat.)	06:50 (1)	08:10 (1)	08:50 (2)	09:50 (3)	10:50 (3)
Arr. Portsmoth (Hbr.)	08:24	09:38	10:13	11:13	12:13
Change to ferry. ABC 57					
Dep. Portsmouth (Hbr.)	08:45	09:50	10:20	11:20	12:20
Arr. Ryde Pier Head	09:00	10:15	10:35	11:35	12:35
Change to train.					
Dp. Ryde Pier Head	09:02	10:22	10:42	11:42	12:42
Arr. Shanklin	09:27	10:46	11:06	12:06 (4)	13:06 (4)

There are full-day and half-day bus tours of the island, starting from Ryde Esplanade.

Sights in **Ryde**: Six miles of pretty beaches. many nice gardens. Take the 9-mile island train from Ryde Pier to Shanklin . En route is Ryde Esplanade, a working-class resort. A 3-mile steam railway roundtrip from there offers pretty views.

Sights in **Shanklin**: One of Britain's loveliest towns. Ten minutes' walk from the railstation there are views of the sea and farms from East Cliff Promenade. On the way back to Shanklin, walk through the Chine (deep ravine) to the mile-long beach and see lovely Old Village. Buses (on Carter Avenue, 2 blocks from the railstation) go to Cowes on the north coast. Near Cowes is Osborne House, queen Victoria's summer mansion, which can be toured from the day after Easter through early October.

Dep. Shanklin	13:51 (5)	14:11 (3)	15:11 (3)	15:51 (1)	16:11 (3+5)
Arr. Ryde Pier Head	14:16	14:36	15:36	16:16	16:39
Change to ferry.					
Dep. Ryde Pier Head	14:20	14:45	15:45	16:20	16:55
Arr. Portsmouth (Hbr.)	14:45	15:10	16:00	16:45	17:10
Change to train. ABC 56					
Dep. Portsmouth (Hbr.)	15:06	15:13	16:06	17:06	17:13
Arr. London (Wat.)	16:29	17:03 (6)	17:30	18:29	19:03

(1) Runs daily, except Sundays and holidays. (2) Runs daily, except holidays. Departs 08:25 on Sunday. (3) Runs daily, except holidays. (4) Arrives 40 minutes later on Sunday. (5) Runs Monday–Friday. (6) Arrives 17:29 on Sunday. (7) Runs Saturday and Sunday. (8) Runs Saturday only. (8) Plus other departures from Shanklin at 17:14 (3), 18:14 (3), 18:54 (5), 19:14 (7), 19:34 (8), 20:19 (1) and 21:24 (7), arriving London 19:30, 20:31, 21:33, 21:45, 22:31, 00:12 and 00:12.

London - Rochester - London ABC 9

| Dep. London (Victoria) | Frequent times from 07:23 to 23:53 (23:05 on Sunday) |
| Arr. Rochester | 60 minutes later |

Sights in **Rochester**: The 17th century Bull Hotel, where Charles Dickens' characters, Pickwick and his friends, spent the first night of their long and memorable trip.

See the little house at 11 Ordinance Terrace, where Dickens lived from the time he was 4 until he was 9 years old, Visit the red brick mansion where he lived his last 10 years and died. The cemetery here has many markers from which Dickens took the names for the people he cast in his stories.

Visit the City Museum in Eastgate House, open daily except Friday 14:00-17:30.

| Dep. Rochester | Frequent times from 05:56 to 22:32 |
| Arr. London (Vict.) | 60 minutes later |

London - Rye - London ABC 20

| Dep. London (Charing Cross) | Frequent times from 05:55 to 20:30 |
| Change from suburban train 90 minutes later, in Ashford. |
| Arr. Rye | 2 hours after departing London. |

Sights in **Rye**: This delightful little hilltop town was once an important seaport, but it is now 2 miles from the sea. See the 14th century city walls. The 14th century wood Monastery, now housing one of the town's 6 potteries.

It is a 10-minute walk up Conduit Hill to the 12th century Norman church and then to the oldest structure in Rye, the 13th century Ypres Tower, now the city Museum, open from Easter to the end of September, Monday-Saturday 10:30–12:30 and 14:15–17:30, Sunday 11:15–12:30.

| Dep. Rye | Frequent times from 05:47 to 21:38 |
| Change to Suburban train 30 minutes later, in Ashford. |
| Arr. London (Charing Cross) | 2 hours after departing Rye. |

London - Salisbury - Stonehenge - London 511

Most of these trains have light refreshments.

Dep. London (Wat.)	07:52 (1)	08:40 (2)	09:15 (1)	10:00 (4)	10:40 (5)	11:00 (4+8)
Arr. Salisbury	09:20	10:13 (3)	10:36	11:30	12:36	12:26

Sights in **Salisbury**: The Cathedral, with its tombs of Crusaders and one of the 4 existing copies of the Magna Carta. Buses operate between the Salisbury railstation and **Stonehenge** to view the mysterious oval of huge stones there, about 4,000 years old. The daily roundtrips are 10:45-14:44 and 12:45-14:44, plus Monday-Friday 14:45-16:39.

This is the most important prehistoric relic in Britain. How were these stupendous weights moved many miles from their quarry . . . and why ?

Dep. Salisbury	12:13 (4)	13:45 (4)	14:24 (5)	15:13 (6)	16:24 (7+9)
Arr. London (Wat.)	13:52	15:20	15:49	16:51	17:59

(1) Runs Saturday only. (2) Runs daily, except Saturdays and holidays. (3) Arrives 23 minutes later on Sunday. (4) Runs daily, except Sundays and holidays. (5) Runs Saturday and Sunday. (6) Runs Monday-Friday, except holidays. (7) Runs daily, except holidays. (8) Plus other departures from London at 12:40 (5) and 13:15 (4), arriving Salisbury 14:36 and 14:36. (8) Plus other departures from Salisbury at 17:18 (2), 17:43 (5), 18:24 (7), 19:20 (5), 19:54 (2), 20:00 (1), 20:39 (5) and 21:24 (5).

London - Salisbury - Exeter - London 511

As these schedules indicate, it is easy to visit both Salisbury and Exeter in one day.

Dep. London (Waterloo)	08:40	Dep. Exeter (St. Davids)	17:38 (2)
Arr. Salisbury	10:16 (1)	Dep. Exeter (Central)	17:43 (2)
Sightsee in Salisbury		Arr. London (Waterloo)	21:25
Dep. Salisbury	12:31		
Arr. Exeter (Central)	14:14 (1)		
Arr. Exeter (St. Davids)	14:19 (1)		

(1) Arrives 20 minutes later on Sunday. (2) Runs daily, except Sundays and holidays. Plus another departure from Exeter at 18:35 on Sunday, arriving London 22:16).

London - Stratford on Avon - London ABC page 182

Dep. London (Pad.)	07:15 (1)	08:32 (2)	09:20 (1)	10:36 (1)
Arr. Stratford	09:36	12:05	11:36	13:36
		* * *		
Dep. Stratford	12:00 (1)	14:00 (3)	15:38 (1)	16:15 (2)	17:06 (1+6)
Arr. London (Pad.)	14:50	16:33 (4)	18:52	19:01	19:43

(1) Runs daily, except Sunday. (2) Runs Sunday only. (3) Runs daily. (4) Arrives 17:27 on Sunday. (5) Runs Saturday only. (6) Plus other departures from Stratford at 18:38 (2), 19:35 (5) and 21:00 (1), arriving London 22:04, 22:06 and 23:41.

Many people prefer fully-escorted day tours to **Stratford** that start and end in London. Details are available from British Travel Centre, 12 Regent St.

A special "Shakespeare Connection" train departs from London's Euston station at 08:40 Monday-Friday, 08:30 on Saturday, and 09:40 on Sunday, arriving Coventry 10:35 Monday-Saturday, 12:15 on Sunday. A special bus transfers passengers from Coventry to Stratford-on-Avon, arriving there one hour after leaving Coventry. This bus stops near the Stratford office that books various local tours.

After many hours of leisurely sightseeing, passengers leave Stratford at 17:15 Monday–Saturday (18:20 on Sunday) for the trains departing Coventry at 18:10 (19:10 on Sunday) arriving London 19:28 (20:39 on Sunday).

Those wishing to attend a performance at the Royal Shakespeare Theater *cannot* purchase tickets for that night's performance until arriving at the theater and chance the possibility that all tickets have been sold. Those who attend the performance were once provided a bus at 23:30 for an 00:38 train from Coventry, arriving back in London at 02:32. *We could not confirm this at the end of 1991.)*

The "Shakespeare Connection" combination train-and-bus ticket can be purchased only in England — at either of British Rail Travel's central London offices (Regent Street or Oxford Street), or at London's Euston railstation.

There are many restaurants and pubs in Stratford, and visitors may picnic either by the theater or in the garden along the river.

It is a 10-minute walk from the Stratford railstation to Shakespeare's birthplace.

See the house of Mary Arden, his mother. The cottage of Anne Hathaway, his wife. Shakespeare's tomb in Trinity Church. The home of John Harvard, founder of America's great university.

There are afternoon performances at the Royal Shakespeare Theater on some Thursdays and Saturdays.

444

London - Torquay - London 510

Dep. London (Pad.)	07:45 (1)	08:02 (2)	08:20 (3)	09:20 (3)	09:35 (2+8)
Arr. Newton Abbot	10:40	-0-	11:26	12:32	-0-
Change trains.					
Dep. Newton Abbot	11:04	-0-	11:52	12:56	-0-
Arr. Torquay	11:05	11:33	12:02	13:07	12:38

Sights in **Torquay:** An 11-mile coastline that resembles a Mediterranean resort, palm trees and all. The British "Riviera". Pronounced "tor-kee". Stroll the walk along the formal gardens at the waterfront to the park, where concerts and dances are held in the Summer. Visit the Model Railroad and House Miniatures in the Victoria Arcade at the harbor.

See the collection of 17th century silver and 18th century glass at the Municipal Art Gallery and Museum in the 18th century building next to the ruins of the 12th century Torre Abbey. Nearby is the Model Village, open in Summer 09:00-22:00, in Winter 09:00 to dusk. The exhibits of archaeology, natural history and Devon folk life in the Museum of Natural History, open daily except Sunday from March through October 10:00–16:45, and Monday-Friday from November through February.

It is a 6-minute train ride (Table 520) from Torquay to **Paignton**, which has many bed-and-breakfast inns. Sights there include the restored 14th century Great Hall of Compton Castle, open May through October on Monday, Wednesday and Thursday 10:00–17:00. The ballroom filled with silver mirrors at Oldway House, called "a miniature Versailles", open Monday-Saturday 09:00–13:00 and 14:15–17:00, Sundays 14:00–17:00.

Dep. Torquay	15:24 (2)	15:43 (5)	16:35 (6)	16:58 (7)	18:16 (3+9)
Arr. Newton Abbot	-0-	15:54	-0-	17:10	18:27
Change trains.					
Dep. Newton Abbot	-0-	16:14	-0-	17:34	18:34
Arr. London (Pad.)	18:34	18:48	19:50	20:40	21:43

(1) Runs Monday-Friday, except holidays. Restaurant car. (2) Runs Saturday only. Direct train. No train change in Newton Abbot. (3) Runs Sunday only. (4) Runs daily, except Sunday. Direct train. No train change in Newton Abbot. (5) Runs Saturday only. (6) Runs Sunday only. Direct train. No train change in Newton Abbot. (7) Runs Saturday and Sunday. (8) Plus other London departures at 10:40 (4) and 10:50 (6), arriving Torquay 13:31 and 14:17. (9) Plus other Torquay departures at 18:55 (1) and 19:20 (3), arriving London 22:02 and 22:58.

London - Winchester - London ABC 59

All of these trains run daily.

Dep. London (Wat.)	Frequent times from 07:45 to 23:45
Arr. Winchester	60 minutes later (80 minutes later on Sunday)

Sights in **Winchester:** King Arthur's roundtable in the Great Hall at the Castle. The 11th century Cathedral, with the tombs of King Alfred, Jane Austen and Izaak Walton.

Dep. Winchester	Frequent times from 07:13 to 23:02
Arr. London (Wat.)	60 minutes later (80 minutes later on Sunday)

London - Windsor - London ABC 67

| Dep. London (Waterloo) | Frequent times from 06:42 to 23:16 |
| Arr. Windsor (Riverside) | 40–60 minutes later |

Sights in **Windsor**: Windsor Castle with its collection of Da Vinci drawings and, occasionally, members of the Royal Family. See the Changing of the Guard there, at 10:25. Queen Mary's Doll House. St. George's Chapel.

In the town, stroll down the 3-mile "Long Walk". See Eton College, where once it did not matter if you won or lost, in the days when observing niceties was more important than the final score.

| Dep. Windsor (Riverside) | Frequent times from 06:08 to 22:45 |
| Arr. London (Waterloo) | 40–60 minutes later |

London - York - London 570

Dep. London (Kings X)	06:00 (1)	07:00 (2)	07:30 (3)	08:00 (4)	08:30 (5)
Arr. York	08:28	08:58	09:36	09:43	10:29
Dep. London (Kings X)	08:45 (3)	09:00 (5)	09:30 (1)	10:00 (2)	10:30 (2+15)
Arr. York	10:38	10:53	11:34	11:51	12:19
		*	*	*	
Dep. York	14:38 (6)	14:50 (3)	15:04 (7)	15:25 (8)	15:48 (9)
Arr. London (Kings X)	16:45	16:50	17:04	17:32	17:59
Dep. York	16:02 (10)	16:17 (11)	16:34 (9)	17:12 (11)	17:44 (10+16)
Arr. London (Kings X)	18:27	18:30	18:55 (12)	19:05 (13)	20:18

(1) Runs daily, except Sundays and holidays. Light refreshments. (2) Runs daily, except Sundays and holidays. Restaurant car Monday–Friday. Light refreshments on Saturday. (3) Runs Monday–Friday, except holidays. Restaurant car. (4) Runs daily, except Sundays and holidays. Light refreshments on Saturday. (5) Runs Saturday only. Light refreshments. (6) Runs daily, except Sundays and holidays. (7) Runs Saturday only. (8) Runs daily, except Saturdays and holidays. (9) Runs daily, except holidays. (10) Runs Saturday and Sunday. (11) Runs daily, except Saturdays and holidays. Restaurant car Monday–Friday. (12) Arrives 30 minutes later on Sunday. (13) Runs Sunday only. (14) Runs Monday–Friday, except holidays. (15) Plus other London departures at 11:00 (2), 11:30 (2) and 12:00 (2). (16) Plus other York departures at 18:18 (11), 18:59 (3), 19:39 (11), 20:05 (2), 20:20 (7), 20:44 (13) and 21:41 (14).

Sights in **York**: Free walking tours in Summer leave from the fountain across from the Information Center (Exhibition Square) daily at 10:15, 14:15 and 19:15.

Founded by Romans in A.D. 71. Very crowded with tourists in July and August. Most of the interesting places are located within the one square mile that is encircled by 3 miles of ancient walls.

York Minister, the largest Gothic cathedral in Britain (open daily 07:30 to dusk) has fantastic stained glass. Its Great East Window is the size of a tennis court. It is advisable to use binoculars to study the detail on both the windows and the plaster work on the ceilings.

See the 14th and 15th century stained glass in All Saints Church, on North Street. The brass rubbings center at St. Williams College (outside the cathedral's Great East Window). Stroll along the top of the city walls for a great view of the ancient buildings that surround the cathedral.

Walk down "The Shambles". Visit the restored Guildhall on St. Helen's Square to see its modern stained glass and timbered roof. Castle Museum, Britain's largest folk museum, off Tower Street (open daily 09:30–18:30). The shrine commemorating the 12th century massacre of Jews at Clifford Tower, in the center of York.

Exhibits of Bronze Age, Iron Age and Roman-era remains, in the Yorkshire Museum on Museum Street (open Monday-Saturday 10:00–17:00, Sunday 13:00–17:00). The 25 old locomotives and many train cars (including Queen Victoria's ornate coach) at the National Railway Museum on Leeman Road.

There are special excursion trains from London, to the Railway Museum, for a few days in August, September, October and November each year. The all-day excursions include roundtrip train service from London and 4 hours touring the Museum.

SCENIC TRAIN TRIPS

There is much fine scenery on nearly every rail route in England. The next 3 train rides offer exceptional scenic views, as do several rail trips in Scotland (pages 451- 455).

London - Pwllheli - London   ABC page 160

There is excellent coastal scenery on this ride plus a splendid view of Harlech Castle.
This trip is too long as a one-way London roundtrip.

Dep. London (Euston)	07:30 (1)	08:30 (2)	09:10 (3)	09:40 (4)	11:00 (1)	13:40 (4+5)
Arr. Pwllheli	14:39	16:10	16:22	18:22	18:12	21:06

Sights in **Pwllheli**: This summer seaside resort is located on the southern side of the Lleyn Peninsula. The major attraction here is boating in **Tremadog Bay**.

Dep. Pwllheli	07:50 (1)	09:36 (1)	11:00 (4)	11:20 (1)	13:00 (1)	13:35 (4+6)
Arr. London (Euston)	14:28	16:58	18:01	18:28	20:02	20:39

(1) Runs daily, except Sunday. (2) Runs Saturday only. (3) Runs Monday–Friday. (4) Runs Sunday only. (5) Plus another London departure at 15:30 (2), arriving Pwellheli 22:15. (6) Plus other Pwllheli departures at 14:40 (1), 16:10 (4), 16:46 (3) and 17:25 (2), arriving London 23:08, 00:13, 02:42 and 02:47.

Leeds - Settle - Carlisle 562

The 62-mile Settle–Carlisle portion of this route is considered by many to be the most scenic train route in England. It goes through the **Pennine Hills** and the **Yorkshire Dales National Park**, close to the Lake district. This line has 14 tunnels and 21 viaducts, including the 104-foot-high Ribblehead Viaduct.

All of these trains have light refreshments, unless designated otherwise.

Dep. Leeds	09:46 (1)	10:47 (1)	13:03 (2)	15:03 (1)
Dep. Settle	10:57	11:47	14:09	16:10
Arr. Carlisle	12:50	13:30	15:51	17:53

Sights in **Settle**: A pretty town. Since 1429, a market has been held here every Tuesday.

Dep. Carlisle	15:04 (1)	16:32 (1)	17:10 (3)	18:14 (1)
Dep. Settle	17:09	18:10	18:52	19:55
Arr. Leeds	18:17	19:06	19:58	20:59

(1) Runs daily, except Sundays and holidays. (2) Runs daily. (3) Runs Sunday only. No light refreshments.

London - Windermere - London 550

The breathtaking scenery of England's "Lake country".

These trains run daily, except Sundays and holidays, unless designated otherwise.

Dep. London (Euston)	08:15	09:15	11:15	12:15	
Arr. Oxenholme	11:38	12:51	14:41	15:38	
Change trains.					
Dep. Oxenholme	12:05	13:02	15:10	15:40	
Arr. Windermere	12:26	13:23	15:31	16:01	
		* * *			
Dep. Windermere	13:27	14:40 (1)	15:35	17:40 (1)	17:44
Arr. Oxenholme	13:45	15:00	15:55	18:00	18:04
Change trains.					
Dep. Oxenholme	14:06	15:08	16:08	18:05	19:06 (2)
Arr. London (Euston)	17:34	19:09	19:35	21:42	22:28

(1) Runs Sunday only. (2) Restaurant car.

A DAY THROUGH WALES

There is a marvelous one-day circle train trip from London that takes you through the incredibly beautiful rural scenery in the heart of Wales, between Swansea and Shrewsbury. As shown below, this trip can be made either clockwise or counter-clockwise.

London - Swansea - Shrewsbury - London

530		541	
Dep. London (Pad.)	08:00	Dep. London (Euston)	07:30 (2)
Arr. Swansea	10:44 (1)	Arr. Shrewsbury	10:33
Change trains. 535		Change trains. 535	
Dep. Swansea	13:05	Dep. Shrewsbury	10:36 (2)
Arr. Shrewsbury	16:55	Arr. Swansea	15:22
Change trains. 541		Change trains. 530	
Dep. Shrewsbury	17:02	Dep. Swansea	15:32 (2)
Arr. London (Euston)	20:02 (1)	Arr. London (Pad.)	18:32

(1) Arrives 45 minutes later on Sunday. (2) Runs daily, except Sundays and holidays.

Sights in **Shrewsbury**: The 1,000-year-old castle. In **Wroxeter**, a short bus ride from here, are the reconstructed ruins of Roman baths built there 2,000 years ago.

RAIL CONNECTION WITH IRELAND via Wales

There is bus service between Swansea's railstation and its ferryport.

London - Swansea - Cork		Cork - Swansea - London	
530 Train		609 Ferry	
Dep. London (Pad.)	17:00 (1)	Dep. Cork	09:00 (2)
Arr. Swansea	20:04	Arr. Swansea	19:00
Change to ferry. 609		Change to train. 530	
Dep. Swansea	21:00 (2)	Dep. Swansea	20:00 (3)
Arr. Cork	07:00	Arr. London (Pad.)	00:16

(1) Runs daily, except holidays. (2) Early June to late September: runs daily. Late September to late June: see Cook's 1992 European Timetable. (3) Change trains in Cardiff.

MORE RAIL CONNECTIONS WITH IRELAND

London - Limerick (Shannon Airport) or Dublin (via Fishguard) 607

Dep. London (Paddington)	09:00 (1)	09:00 (4)	09:25 (5)	20:00 (6)
Arr. Fishguard (Harbour)	13:43	14:14	13:18	00:56
Change to ship.				
Dep. Fishguard (Harbour)	15:00 (2)	15:00 (2)	15:00 (2)	03:15 (2)
Arr. Rosslare (Harbour)	18:30	18:30	18:30	06:45
Change to train.				
Dep. Rosslare (Harbour)	19:40 (3)	19:40 (3)	19:40 (3)	07:55 (3)
Arr. Dublin (Connolly)	-0-	-0-	-0-	10:46
Arr. Limerick	23:25	23:25	23:25	-0-

* * *

Dep. Limerick	16:00 (3)	-0-	-0-
Dep. Dublin (Connolly)	-0-	18:05 (4)	18:30 (3)
Arr. Rosslare (Harbour)	19:30	21:00	21:25
Change to ship.			
Dep. Rosslare (Harbour)	21:40 (2)	21:40 (2)	21:40 (2)
Arr. Fishguard (Harbour)	01:10	01:10	01:10
Change to train.			
Dep. Fishguard (Harbour)	01:50 (3)	01:50 (4)	01:50 (3)
Arr. London (Paddington)	06:34	07:27	06:34

(1) Operates early September to late June. Runs Monday–Friday, except holidays. (2) Operates all year. Runs daily, except December 25 and 26. (3) Operates all year. Runs daily, except Sundays and holidays. (4) Operates all year. Runs Sunday only. (5) Late June to early September: runs daily, except Sundays and holidays. Early September to late June: runs Saturday only. (6) Operates all year. Runs daily, except holidays.

London - Dublin (via Holyhead) 605

Dep. London (Euston)	08:50 (1)	09:45 (2)	22:00 (3)
Arr. Holyhead	14:03	14:10	02:37
Change to ship.			
Dep. Holyhead	16:00	16:00	04:00
Arr. Dublin (Ferryport)	19:15	19:15	07:30

* * *

Dep. Dublin (Ferryport)	10:00 (4)	10:00 (5)	22:00 (5)
Arr. Holyhead	13:30	13:30	01:30
Change to train.			
Dep. Holyhead	14:30 (4)	16:10 (5)	02:30 (5+6)
Arr. London (Euston)	19:30	20:53	07:14

(1) Runs Sunday only. (2) Runs daily, except Sundays and holidays. Departs at 09:35 on Saturday. (3) Runs daily, except holidays. Departs at 21:45 on Saturday and Sunday. (4) Runs Sunday only. (5) Runs daily, except Sundays and holidays. (6) Carries a sleeping car.

RAIL CONNECTIONS WITH SCOTLAND

These are the schedules for rail travel between London (King's Cross railstation) and the capital of Scotland.

London - Edinburgh and Edinburgh - London   570

Seat reservation is advisable for all of these trains.

Dep. London	06:00 (1)	07:00 (2)	08:00 (3)	08:30 (4)	09:00 (2)
Arr. Edinburgh	11:10	11:38	12:03	13:24	13:39

Dep. London	09:30 (2)	10:00 (4)	10:30 (4)	11:00 (6)	11:30 (4)
Arr. Edinburgh	14:28	14:08 (5)	14:47	15:20	17:14 (5)

Dep. London	12:00 (4)	13:00 (4)	13:30 (4)	14:00 (7)	15:00 (4)
Arr. Edinburgh	16:20	17:27	18:08	18:24 (5)	19:02 (5)

Dep. London	16:00 (8)	17:00 (4)	18:00 (8)	18:30 (6)	
Arr. Edinburgh	20:28 (5)	21:10	23:33	23:16	

* * *

Dep. Edinburgh	06:00 (9)	06:30 (6)	07:00 (10)	08:00 (10)	09:00 (12)
Arr. London	10:48	10:50	11:50 (11)	12:38	13:38

Dep. Edinburgh	09:30 (13)	10:00 (14)	11:00 (14)	11:30 (16)	12:00 (12)
Arr. London	15:16	14:38 (15)	15:38 (15)	15:54	16:45

Dep. Edinburgh	12:30 (16)	13:00 (14)	13:30 (17)	14:00 (16)	15:00 (10)
Arr. London	16:50 (15)	17:32 (15)	18:22	18:30 (15)	19:05 (15)

Dep. Edinburgh	16:00 (6)	17:00 (16)	17:30 (4)	18:00 (13)	19:00 (6)
Arr. London	20:33	21:54 (15)	22:15 (5)	23:13	23:59

(1) Runs daily, except Sun. and holidays. Light refreshments. (2) Runs Sat. only. Light ref. (3) Runs daily, except Sun. and holidays. Light ref. on Sat. (4) Runs daily, except Sun. and holidays. Restaurant car Mon.–Fri. Light ref. on Sat. (5) Arrives 40 minutes later on Sat. (6) Runs Mon.–Fri., except holidays. Restaurant car (except the 19:00 departure from Edinburgh). (7) Runs daily, except holidays. Restaurant car Mon.–Fri. Light ref. Sat. and Sun. (8) Runs daily, except holidays. Light ref. Sat. and Sun. (9) Runs Sat. only. (10) Runs daily, except Sun. and holidays. Restaurant car Mon.–Fri. (11) Arrives 40 minutes earlier on Sat. (12) Runs daily, except Sun. and holidays. (13) Runs Sun. only. (14) Runs daily, except holidays. (15) Arrives 40–60 minutes later on Sun. (16) Runs daily, except holidays. Restaurant car Mon–Fri. (17) Runs Sat. and Sun.

SCOTLAND

The 2 rail trips north from Edinburgh (to Dundee–Aberdeen and to Perth–Inverness) are very scenic. There is also train service between Aberdeen and Inverness.

From Inverness, there is a rail route to Wick in northernmost Scotland, and to Kyle of Lochalsh on the west coast of Scotland. Other train routes to the same coastal area are from Glasgow to both Oban and to Mallaig. The other principal rail service in Scotland is between Edinburgh and Glasgow.

We list 36 one-day rail excursions in Scotland.

Edinburgh

The capital of Scotland. Most of the 25-acre railstation is under glass. Visit Edinburgh Castle, sitting on a cliff 270 feet above the city, on a site where there have been forts since the 6th century. A cannon has been fired from there every day since 1858. The Castle is open every day in the Summer: 09:30–18:00 Monday-Saturday, 11:00–18:00 on Sundays. The panoramic view of Edinburgh from the Castle is breathtaking.

At the Castle, see the hammer-beamed timbered ceiling in the Great Hall of James IV, the Scottish Crown Jewels, the small St. Margaret's Chapel, and the State Apartments, including the rooms once occupied by Mary Queen of Scots.

Below the Castle is the 37-acre Princess Street Gardens, with the city's main rail tracks running through it, at a lower level than the surface of the park.

Also visit the 17th century Palace of Holyrood House to see the Throne Room and also the portraits of 110 Scottish kings (painted by the same artist) in the gallery. You will notice that all 110 noses are the same ! Stroll through 648-acre Holyrood Park, which has 3 lakes.

Other interesting sights in Edinburgh: the paintings at both the National Gallery of Scotland and in the National Portrait Gallery. The National Museum of Antiquities. The collection of technology, art, archaeology, geology and natural history in the Royal Scottish Museum. The Museum of Childhood (historic books, toys and materials about child rearing), closed on Sundays. The adaptation of Athens' Temple of Theseus. The month-long International Festival of Music and Drama.

The pottery, handcrafted glass, textiles and woodwork at the Scottish Craft Center, in Acheson House, open daily except Sunday 10:00–17:00. The collection of Robert Burns, Sir Walter Scott and Robert Louis Stevenson manuscripts and memorabilia in the 17th century Lady Stair's House.

Edinburgh - Dundee - Aberdeen 600

This is a very scenic rail trip.

Dep. Edinburgh	06:35 (1)	08:40 (2)	09:15 (3)	10:20 (1)	10:55 (6)
Arr. Dundee	07:50	09:53 (2)	10:53 (4)	11:33 (5)	12:18
Arr. Aberdeen	09:09	11:15 (2)	12:05	12:50 (5)	13:32

Dep. Edinburgh	13:05 (3)	13:35 (3)	14:55 (8)	15:55 (9)	16:33 (9+11)
Arr. Dundee	14:30	14:42 (4)	16:06	17:13	17:45 (4)
Arr. Aberdeen	15:44 (7)	16:14	17:23	18:28	19:16

(1) Daily, except Sun. and holidays. (2) Runs daily, except holidays. Departs and arrives 15 minutes later on Sun. Light refreshments. (3) Runs daily, except holidays. Light refreshments Mon.–Sat. (4) Change trains in Dundee. (5) Arrives 20 minutes later on Sat. (6) Runs Sun. only. Light refreshments. (7) Arrives 20 minutes later on Sun. (8) Runs daily, except holidays. Light refreshments on Sun. (9) Runs daily, except Sun. and holidays. Light refreshments. (10) Runs Sun. only. (11) Plus other Aberdeen departures at 18:10 (9), 18:27 (9), 19:05 (10), 19:28 (9) and 21:00 (1), arriving Edinburgh 20:40, 21:23, 21:30, 22:23 and 23:27.

Sights in **Dundee**: A very ancient city, predating Roman occupation. Mountains of jam and preserves are processed here. Visit the Spalding Golf Museum in nearby Camperdown Park. The frigate "Unicorn," launched in 1824, now tied at Victoria Dock. The 4 castles: Dudhope, Claypotts, Broughty and Mains.

Sights in **Aberdeen:** A very popular tourist center and busy seaport. The center of Scotland's fishing industry (see the 07:00 fish market). Straddles 2 rivers. See the 15th century Cathedral of St. Machar. Streets that were laid out in the 13th and 14th centuries. The local history museum in the 17th century Provost Skene's House.

The 16th century Provost Ross's House. The 18th century St. Nicholas Church. Two very old bridges: the 14th century Brig o'Balgownie and the 16th century Old Bridge of Dee. The 19th century Music Hall. The 19th century Marischal College, considered the world's largest and finest granite building.

Edinburgh - Perth - Inverness 600

A very scenic train ride through the heart of the **Grampian Mountains**. Winter sports, including skiing, are the attraction at the **Aviemore** vacation resort.

Dep. Edinburgh	09:35 (1)	10:35 (2)	11:40 (3)	13:35 (4)	14:10 (5)	15:40 (3)
Dep. Perth	11:03 (1)	11:58	12:56	15:05	15:45	16:53
Dep. Aviemore	12:39	-0-	14:29	16:38	17:45	18:23
Arr. Inverness	13:20	-0-	15:09	17:16	18:30	19:04

* * *

Dep. Inverness	-0-	-0-	14:30 (3)	18:18 (6)	18:48 (3)	20:05 (3)
Dep. Aviemore	-0-	-0-	15:18	18:58	19:28	20:58
Arr. Perth	15:02 (5)	15:43 (2)	16:56	20:38	21:00	22:23
Arr. Edinburgh	16:20	17:03	18:22	21:53	22:12	23:36

(1) Runs daily, except holidays. light refreshments. On Sun., change trains in Perth. (2) Runs Sun. only. (3) Runs daily, except Sun. and holidays. Light refreshments. (4) Runs daily, except holidays. Change trains in Perth. Light refreshments. (5) Runs daily, except Sun. and holidays. (6) Runs Sun. only. Light refreshments.

Sights in **Perth**: A popular tourist center. There is much whiskey distilling and weaving of tartans here. Good Winter sports. Sailing and water skiing in the Summer. See the 360-degree panoramic color slide-show and hear the stereophonic presentation at the Round House waterworks. St. John's Kirk. The Perth Art Gallery and Museum, on George Street. A short distance from there, at North Post, visit the Fair Maid's House, an important locale in Sir Walter Scott's novel, "The Fair Maid of Perth".

Sights in **Inverness**: Located in the mountainous Highlands. Very cold Winters and cool Summers here. A popular tourist resort for hunting of grouse and deer, hiking, fishing, sailing, camping and Winter sports. Many whiskey distillers in this area. Visit the Castle. Stroll the garden paths along the River Ness. Nearby is Great Britain's highest mountain, Ben Nevis (4,406 feet).

Take a cruise on **Loch Ness,** and see if you can spot the "monster". Boats go from the lake through the **Caledonian Canal** and return to Inverness on cruises that take 2½ hours in the morning, 3 ½ hours in the afternoon, and 2½ hours in the evening.

Aberdeen - Inverness 595

Dep. Aberdeen	05:20 (1)	06:17 (1)	07:28 (2)	09:16 (2)	10:00 (3)	11:24 (2+6)
Arr. Inverness	07:38	08:45	09:42	11:32	12:14	13:40

Sight in **Inverness**: See description above this timetable.

Dep. Inverness	04:50 (1)	05:52 (2)	08:05 (2)	10:00 (4)	10:50 (2)	12:12 (4+7)
Arr. Aberdeen	07:04	08:15	10:25	12:11	13:08	14:24

(1) Runs daily, except Sundays and holidays. (2) Runs daily, except Sundays and holidays. Light refreshments. (3) Runs Sunday only. Light refreshments. (4) Runs daily. Light refreshments. (5) Runs daily, except holidays. Light refreshments. (6) Plus other Aberdeen departures at 13:14 (4), 15:24 (4), 17:14 (2), 18:05 (2), 19:45 (5) and 21:40 (4), arriving Inverness 15:24, 17:45, 19:28, 20:15, 22:16 and 23:50. (7) Plus other Inverness departures at 13:54 (2), 15:26 (5), 17:06 (4), 18:00 (2) and 20:40 (4), Arriving Aberdeen 16:10, 17:37, 19:22, 20:17 and 22:51.

Inverness - Wick 597

Change trains in Georgemas Junction 20 minutes before arriving and departing Wick. All of these trains have light refreshments.

Dep. Inverness	07:12 (1)	10:35 (2)	11:42 (1)	15:32 (1)	16:40 (2)	19:00 (1)
Arr. Wick	11:00	14:17	15:27	19:15	20:22	22:42

Sight in **Wick**: The northernmost tip of Scotland.

Dep. Wick	06:00 (1)	11:28 (3)	15:54 (3)	19:52 (1)
Arr. Inverness	09:52	15:18	19:52	23:47

(1) Runs daily, except Sundays and holidays. (2) Runs Sunday only. (3) Runs daily.

Inverness - Kyle of Lochalsh - Inverness 597

This is one of the most scenic train trips in Britain. The track climbs and descends, turns and twists through the Western **Ross Mountains** as it often goes along the shoreline of lovely lakes through the heart of the Highlands. In the Spring, there are fields of red and orange rhododendrons. The fields of purple heather can be seen all year.

In the high **Luib Summit** area there are forests and snowcapped mountains. It is only an 8-minute ferry-boat ride from Kyle to the **Isle of Skye**.

Dep. Inverness	06:45 (1)	10:15 (2)	11:15 (3)	12:27 (2)	18:10 (3)	18:42 (2)
Arr. Kyle	09:17	13:05	14:00	15:00	20:35	21:15

* * *

Dep. Kyle	06:50 (1)	10:30 (3)	11:35 (2)	15:05 (4)	17:05 (2)	-0-
Arr. Inverness	09:19	13:05	14:05	17:45	19:36	-0-

(1) Runs daily, except Sundays and holidays. (2) Runs daily, except Sundays and holidays. Light refreshments. (3) Runs Sunday only. Light refreshments. (6) Runs daily. Light refreshments.

Edinburgh - Dunbar - Edinburgh 570

Dep. Edinburgh   08:00 (1)   10:00 (2)   13:00 (1)   16:30 (3)   17:00 (1)   17:30 (1+7)
Arr. Dunbar   20-25 minutes later

Sights in **Dunbar**: A small fishing port, the birthplace of naturalist John Muir (128 High Street). See the Castle ruins at the harbor.

Take a 45-minute walk and visit the Old Harbor with its Lifeboat Museum, the roost for domesticated pigeons in Friar's Croft, and the Georgian houses (Castellau and Lauderdale). This walk is detailed in a guidebook available at the town's tourist information center in the 17th century Town House on High Street, open during Summer Monday-Saturday 09:00–19:00, Sunday 11:00–13:00.

Also visit the 1,667-acre John Muir Country Park, containing a wide variety of birds and plants. Near it are the restored 17th century Preston watermill and many old towns and villages: **Gifford, Haddington, Dirleton** and **North Berwick**. A list of hotels, guest houses and bed-and-breakfast places can be obtained by writing to the Dunbar Tourist Information Centre, if sufficient international reply coupons are enclosed.

Dep. Dunbar   07:55 (1)   09:48 (1)   11:06 (3)   12:42 (1)   14:55 (3)   15:58 (4+8)
Arr. Edinburgh 20-25 minutes later

(1) Runs daily, except Sundays and holidays. (2) Runs daily, except holidays. (3) Runs Sunday only. (4) Runs Saturday only. (5) Runs daily, except Saturday and holidays. (6) Runs Monday–Friday except holidays. (7) Plus other Edinburgh departures at 19:00 (1), 20:00 (3) and 21:00 (5). (8) Plus other Dunbar departures at 16:57 (6), 19:12 (4), 21:46 (3), 22:26 (4) and 22:46 (6).

Edinburgh - Glasgow - Edinburgh 590

Dep. Edinburgh   Frequent times from 05:50 to 23:30
Arr. Glasgow (Queen St.) 60–70 minutes later

Sights in **Glasgow**: A major seaport. Largest city in Scotland. See the great shipyards on the River Clyde.

The dozens of antique streetcars, motorcycles and trains (including King George VI's 72-foot-long railway coach, built in 1941 with wartime armor-plated shutters) in the Museum of Transport at Kelvin Hall on Albert Drive, open Monday-Saturday 10:00–17:00, Sunday 14:00–17:00. Nearby, the fine collection of weapons, paintings (Rembrandt, Monet), Mackintosh furniture and natural history exhibits in Kelvingrove Art Galleries and Museum.

The vast collection of paintings by James Abbott McNeil Whistler—the world's best collection—in the Hunterian Art Gallery at Glasgow University, open Monday-Friday 10:30–12:30 and 13:30–17:30, Saturday 09:30–13:00. The Gallery also features a reconstruction of 3 floors of the home of the great architect Charles Mackintosh.

Scottish genealogy at Roots Bureau in Stirling Library, on Royal Exchange Square. Many fine paintings in the Glasgow Art Gallery.

The more than 8,000 treasures of The Burrell Collection, in Pollok House: over 700 stained glass items (one of the world's best collections). Paintings by Rembrandt, Bellini, Memling, Degas, Manet. Excellent Chou Dynasty pieces. Neolithic burial urns. The more than 8-ton marble Warwick Vase, discovered in Rome in 1771. Also on view: jade, carpets, porcelain, silver, furniture, glass and gold. Open Monday-Saturday 10:00–17:00, Sunday 14:00–17:00.

Dep. Glasgow (Queen St.) Frequent times from 06:22 to 23:33
Arr. Edinburgh   60–70 minutes later

Glasgow - Oban - Glasgow 593

There is marvelous Highland scenery on this route.

All of these trains require changing trains in Crianlarich, unless designated otherwise.

Dep. Glasgow (Queen St.)	08:12 (1)	12:12 (2)	16:40 (3)	20:55 (4)
Arr. Oban	11:17	15:19	19:46	23:52

Sights in **Oban**: This has been a holiday resort for nearly a century, and a fishing port for even longer.

Dep. Oban	08:03 (5)	12:40 (3)	16:35 (6)	20:30 (5)
Arr. Glasgow (Queen St.)	11:10	15:55	19:40	00:32

(1) Runs daily, except Sundays and holidays. Light refreshments. (2) Runs daily, except holidays. light refreshments. (3) Runs daily. Light refresments. (4) Direct train. No train change in Crainlarich. Runs daily, except holidays. Light refreshments Sunday–Friday. (5) Runs daily, except Sundays and holidays. (6) Runs daily, except holidays. Light refreshments Monday–Saturday.

Glasgow - Fort William - Mallaig - Glasgow 593

A very scenic rail trip. The Fort William-Mallaig portion offers better views than an alternative auto route does of many lochs (lakes), glens (valleys) and bens (mountains) including Britain's highest, the 4,406-foot-high **Ben Nevis**.

All of these trains have light refreshments.

Dep. Glasgow (Queen St.)	08:12 (1)	12:12 (2)	16:40 (3)		
Arr. Fort William	11:48	15:51	20:22		
Arr. Mallaig	13:22	17:24	21:57		

* * *

Dep. Mallaig	06:00 (4)	06:40 (5)	10:35 (3)	14:25 (6)	18:20 (7)
Dep. Fort William	07:28	08:15	12:07	15:58	19:50 (7)
Arr. Glasgow (Queen St.)	11:00	11:42	15:55	19:40	00:45

(1) Runs daily, except Sun. and holidays. (2) Runs daily, except holidays. Mon.–Fri.: change trains in Fort Williams. (3) Runs daily. (4) Runs Mon.–Fri., except holidays. (5) Runs Sat. only. (6) Runs daily, except holidays. Mon.–Sat.: change trains in Fort Williams. (7) Runs Sat. only. Change trains in Crianlarich.

Glasgow - Ayr - Stranraer - Glasgow 591

A trip through the beautiful moorlands of southwest Scotland.

Dep. Glasgow (Cen.)	08:13 (1)	08:40 (2)	10:00 (3)	11:00 (3)	11:53 (1+6)
Dep. Ayr	09:00	09:27	10:50	11:50	12:40
Arr. Stranraer	10:25	10:52	-0-	-0-	14:08

Sights in **Ayr**: A resort. Many popular golf courses here.

Sights in **Stranraer**: A ferry port, for travel to Northern Ireland. A popular area for Summer sports: golf, swimming, fishing. See the 16th century Castle.

Dep. Stranraer	07:02 (4)	-0-	-0-	14:30 (5)	18:30 (5+7)
Dep. Ayr	08:27	09:45 (3)	10:45 (3)	15:56	20:12 (8)
Arr. Glasgow (Cen.)	09:11	10:34	11:34	16:45	21:02

(1) Runs daily, except Sun. and holidays. (2) Runs Sun. only. (3) Runs daily, except holidays. (4) Runs daily, except Sun. and holidays. (5) Runs daily, except holidays. Light refreshments. (6) Plus other Glasgow departures (that terminate in Ayr) at frequent times from 11:30 to 23:30....and departures which go to both Ayr and Stranraer at 12:55 (2), 15:37 (2) and 22:23 (4).   (7) Plus another Stranraer departure at 21:14 (4). (8) Plus other Ayr departures at frequent times from 05:45 to 23:00.

Chapter 8   CENTRAL and EASTERN EUROPE

EUROPEAN EAST PASS

First-Class-only unlimited train travel in Austria, Czechoslovakia, Hungary and Poland. The 1992 prices are: $160 (US) for any 5 days within 15 days, $259 for any 10 day within one month (such as June 3-July 2). Half-fare for children age 4–11. Children under 4 travel free. Sold in the U.S.A. and Canada by travel agencies and Rail Europe (offices listed under "France" on page 23).

ALBANIA

There are no rail connections between Albania and other countries. The really long train ride in little Albania is 96 miles, from Tirane to Vlore, taking nearly 5 hours.

Tirane   This is Albania's capital. There are 170 museums here. See the prehistoric and Illyrian objects and folk art in the Museum of National History, tracing the life of this area's peoples from ancient times to the 20th century. Many Moslem mosques and bazaars here. Tours of the textile factory and film studio are offered.

Durres   Albania's Adriatic port. Excellent sand beaches. Bus tours go to such interesting villages as Apollonia, Kruja (ruins of the 15th century Skanderbeg fortress), Shkodra (great Moslem mosques and bazaars), and Gjirokastra.

Vlore   An ancient seaport. The surrounding hills are covered with olive trees which supply the local olive oil refinery. The town is named after the Turk who declared Albania's independence in 1912, Ismail Kemal Bey Vlore.

Tirane - Durres - Vlore   and v.v.   949

Dep. Tirane	06:10	07:00	08:05	12:30	13:45	15:20	16:30	17:55	21:15
Arr. Durres	07:05	07:50	09:00	13:30	14:45	16:10	17:25	18:45	22:15
Arr. Vlore	-0-	-0-	13:15	-0-	-0-	-0-	-0-	22:30	-0-
				*	*	*			
Dep. Vlore	-0-	-0-	04:30	-0-	-0-	-0-	14:00	-0-	-0-
Dep. Durres	05:35	07:20	08:30	10:00	14:00	15:05	17:40	19:00	21:30
Arr. Tirane	06:40	08:25	09:35	11:05	15:00	16:10	18:50	20:10	22:35

BULGARIA

Children under 4 travel free. Half-fare for children 4–11 Children 12 and over must pay full fare.

BULGARIAN HOLIDAYS

January 1	New Year's Day	June 2	Memorial Day
May 1 and 2	Labor Day	Sept. 9 and 10	Liberation Day
May 24	Education Day	November 7	Revolution Day

SUMMER TIME

Bulgaria changes to Summer Time on the last Sunday of March, and converts back to Standard Time on the last Sunday of September.

ONE-DAY EXCURSIONS AND CITY-SIGHTSEEING

Here is 1 one-day rail trip that can be made comfortably from Sofia and 2 longer rides. Notes are provided on what to see at each destination. The number after the name of each route is the Cook's timetable.

Schedules for one other train route and international connections conclude this section.

Sofia

The capital of Bulgaria. See the beautiful icons at Alexander Nevsky Memorial Church. Relics from the Stone Age to the Roman Empire at the Archaeological Museum (closed Monday), in Bouyouk, the city's largest mosque.

The Byzantine 6th century Sancta Sophia Church. The 10th-14th century frescos in the brick Rotunda of St. Georgi Church (Sofia's oldest surviving building), in the courtyard of the Sheraton Hotel. The National Art Gallery (closed Tuesday).

The delicate murals in the medieval Boyanna Church, a 10-minute drive outside the city. There is an extensive art collection at the **Rila Monastery**, 74 miles from Sofia.

Sofia - Burgas - Sofia   962

Dep. Sofia	06:15 (1)	06:55 (2)	10:15 (3)	12:50(2)	14:15 (2)	16:00 (1)	22:10 (4+6)
Arr. Burgas	12:50	13:55	17:55	19:30	21:45	21:55	05:15

Sights in **Burgas**: A good beach resort.

Dep. Burgas	05:00 (1)	05:20 (2)	08:15 (3)	10:15 (2)	15:45 (2)	16:30 (1)	21:35 (4+7)
Arr. Sofia	11:10	12:35	16:05	17:37	22:50	23:00	05:00

(1) Reservation required. Restaurant car. (2) Light refreshments. (3) Restaurant car. (4) Operates early June to mid-September. Carries a sleeping car. Also has couchettes. (5) Carries a sleeping car. Light refreshments. (6) Plus another Sofia departure at 23:00 (5), arriving Burgas 05:45. (7) Plus another Burgas departure at 22:05 (5), arriving Sofia 06:00.

Sofia - Plovdiv - Sofia   962

Dep. Sofia	06:15 (1)	08:15 (2)	10:15 (3)	12:15 (4)	14:15 (4)	16:15 (5)	17:10 (1+6)
Arr. Plovdiv	08:31	10:43	12:50	14:48	16:45	18:15	19:24

Sights in **Plovdiv:** This city has been a commercial center for more than 2,000 years, serving the early caravans that moved between Europe, Asia and Africa. There are excellent exhibits of Thracian gold utensils in the Archaeological Museum. See the Bachkovo Monastery and, near it, the ruins of Tsar Ivan Asen II's fort. The Roman ruins. The Church of Constantine and Helena. The Turkish Imaret Djamiya.

Dep. Plovdiv	03:15	06:05	07:00 (5)	08:00 (1)	10:05 (4)	11:00 (2)	13:25 (3+7)
Arr. Sofia	06:00	08:42	09:00	10:20	12:35	13:35	16:05

(1) Reservation required. Restaurant car. (2) Second-class only. (3) Restaurant car. (4) Light refreshments. (5) Reservation required. First-class only. (6) Plus other Sofia departures at 18:50 (4) and 23:00 (4). (7) Plus other Plovdiv departures at 15:05 (4), 17:00 (2), 20:50 (1) and 03:15 (4).

Sofia - Varna - Sofia   962

Dep. Sofia	06:15 (1)	09:40 (2)	11:30 (3)	12:15 (3)	15:00 (1)	21:25 (4)	22:40 (4)
Arr. Varna	14:25	18:45	20:25	21:43	22:50	06:30	07:35

(Timetable continues on page 458.)

Sights in **Varna:** An ancient, lively and important seaport and a very popular beach resort.

See the relics of Greek, Roman, Byzantine, Turkish and Bulgarian eras in the Museum of Art and History (41 Boulevard Dimitar Blagoev), open daily except Monday 09:00–17:00 in Summer, 10:00–17:00 in Winter.Many museums and art galleries. The oldest gold ever found (from 3,500 years B.C.) is displayed there: jewelry and decorations from a burial site.

The Roman Bath. The cells and the chapel carved into the side of a chalk cliff at the 13th century Aladzha Monastery in **Druzhba**, a few miles to the north. It is open daily except Monday 10:00–17:00.

During the Summer, a hydrofoil service goes from Varna to Nesebar, Burgas and Sozopol. In **Nesebar** (a $7-U.S. taxi ride from Burgas), there are ruins of 13 churches dating back as early as the 9th century on this small islet at the end of a causeway. See the Church of John Aliturgetus and the 16th century St. Stephen's Church.

Dep. Varna	06:00 (1)	08:30 (3)	09:00 (2)	11:25 (3)	13:50 (1)	22:00 (4)	22:30 (4)
Arr. Sofia	14:05	17:45	18:02	20:45	22:20	06:40	07:35

(1) Reservation required. Restaurant car. (2) Restaurant car. (3) Light refreshments. (4) Carries a sleeping car. Light refreshments.

INTERNATIONAL ROUTES FROM BULGARIA

Sofia is the gateway for train travel to Yugoslavia (and on to Western Europe), Romania and Greece (and on to Turkey).

Sofia - Belgrade 945

There is great mountain scenery on the Dragomagoman-Crveni Krst portion of this route.

	86	65	87
Dep. Sofia	08:15 (1)	12:25 (2)	22:12 (4)
Set your watch back one hour.			
Arr. Belgrade (Belgrade)	15:40	19:18 (3)	05:59

(1) Restaurant car. (2) Operates late May to mid-October. Reservation required. Second-class only.
(3) Arrives at Belgrade's Centar railstation. (4) Carries a sleeping car. Also has couchettes.

Sofia - Bucharest

	960	960	89	960	960
Dep. Sofia	08:30 (1)	10:40	12:50	21:10 (2)	22:00 (3)
Arr. Bucharest (Nord)	19:05	20:46	23:25	07:05	08:41

(1) Second-class only. (2) Train has only sleeping cars. (3) Carries a sleeping car. Also has couchettes.

Sofia - Athens 89

There are 2 trains departing Sofia at 12:00. "Danubus Express" has only sleeping cars. "Transbalkan" carries a sleeping car, also has couchettes, and its coach is second-class only.

Dep. Sofia	12:00
Arr. Athens	05:10

CZECHOSLOVAKIA

A supplement is charged when traveling on Czechoslovakia's express trains, except for passengers holding tickets purchased outside the country.

Prague is the rail center for Czechoslovakia. International trains depart from both its Hlavni (Main) and Stred (Central) railstations. The city's 4 other stations are Holesovice, Liben, Masarykovo and Smichov (for suburban trains).

Reservations can be made at the office of CEDOK, the State Tourist Organization, a short walk from Hlavni station. The volume of rail service in Czechoslovakia is evidenced by the fact that its timetable book has 683 pages of tables.

CZECHOSLOVAKIAN HOLIDAYS

January 1	New Year's Day	May 9	Liberation Day
	Easter	October 28	Nationalization Day
	Easter Monday	December 25	Christmas Day
May 1	Labor Day	December 26	Additional Holiday

SUMMER TIME

Czechoslovakia changes to Summer Time on the last Sunday of March and converts back to Standard Time on the last Sunday of September.

CZECHOSLOVAKIA'S TRAIN PASS

See page 456 for information about the **European East Pass**.

ONE-DAY EXCURSIONS AND CITY-SIGHTSEEING

Here are 7 one-day rail trips that can be made comfortably from Prague, returning there in most cases before dinnertime. Notes are provided on what to see at each destination. The number after the name of each route is the Cook's timetable.

Details on 3 other rail trips recommended for exceptional scenery and schedules for international connections conclude this section.

Prague

Visit the 13th century Altneuschul (Old-New Synagogue), oldest surviving synagogue in Europe, now the state Jewish Museum. Nearby, the Old Jewish Cemetery (dating back to 1439). The clock with Hebraic numerals that runs counterclockwise, on the former Jewish Town Hall where rare books are stored now. The statue of John Huss at Staromestke Namesti (Old Town Square). The ceremony performed by the magnificent 15th century Astronomical Old Town Hall Clock. Dalibor Tower, a medieval prison.

See the beautiful frescos in the 18th century St. Nicolas Church. The complex of interesting buildings on Castle Hill: The picturesque fountains, courtyards and Gallery of the thousand-year old Hradcany Castle, closed Monday. The illuminated manuscripts and ancient globes in the library of Strahov Monastery, near Loretanski Square. The burial place of many Czech kings and the exhibit of crown jewels at St. Vitus Cathedral, in the Castle's third courtyard. The changing of the guard, outside the Cathedral.

The Art Gallery in the former Riding School. The Church and Monastery of St. George, with its Gallery of Bohemian Baroque Art. The Old Royal Palace's Vladislav Hall, so large that knights on horseback once jousted in it. The Clock Tower and the Diamond Monstrance in the Treasury at Baroque Church. The statue of the Infant Jesus of Prague, in the Church of Our Lady Victorious.

Also visit the 14th century Charles Bridge with its 30 statues of saints, straddling the Vltava River. The 14th century Tyn Cathedral. The 17th century Wallenstein Palace. The National Museum, closed Tuesday. Kinsky Palace.

The Prague House of Artists. The memorial to Mozart at Bertramka. The Laterna Magica. The tiny houses on Zlata Ulicka (Golden Lane). The 7 centuries of art exhibited in the 5 wings of the National Gallery, in Sternbeck Palace, closed Monday. Near Sternbeck is Lookout Point, a paved terrace that offers a good view of the city below. Then, see Belevedere, the royal Summer Palace, and visit the tiny museum across from it.

Ten minutes south, at **Pruhonice**, is one of the largest and most beautiful arboretums in Europe, open May–October. This 625-acre park features more than 1,200 trees, 900 varieties of roses, thousands of azaleas, tulips and rhododendrons and 18 water lily ponds.

Prague - Bratislava - Prague   87 + 880

Dep. Prague (Hole.)	00:08 (1)	01:10 (2)	05:57 (3)	07:38 (4)	09:10 (3+9)
Arr. Bratislava	05:10	06:30	11:11	12:59	14:12

Sights in **Bratislava**: An important Danube port in ancient Roman times. See the 14th–15th century castle. The Hussite House. The Old City Hall. The Cathedral. The palaces on Mirove Square, Michalska Street and Gottwald Square.

Dep. Bratislava	00:38 (1)	03:23 (6)	05:50 (7)	08:55	11:25 (3+10)
Arr. Prague (Hole.)	06:02 (5)	09:19	10:46 (5)	15:22 (5)	16:38

(1) Carries a sleeping car. Also has couchettes. (2) Operates mid-June to early September. Carries a sleeping car. Also has couchettes. (3) Restaurant car. (4) Light refreshments. (5) Arrives at Prague'Hlavni railstation. (6) Carries a sleeping only car. Also has couchettes. Light refreshments. (7) Reservation required. Restaurant car. (8) Train carries only sleeping cars. (9) Plus other Prague (Holesovice) departures at 10:09, 13:54 (3), 21:11 (1) and 22:52 (1), arriving Bratislava 15:09, 18:59, 02:18 and 04:56. (10) Plus other Bratislava departures at 12:15, 14:33, 17:28 (3), 18:20 (4), 20:18, 22:12 (1), 22:30 (8) and 23:45 (1), arriving Prague 17:14, 19:39, 22:39, 23:37, 01:40, 04:24, 06:44 (5) and 05:36 (5).

Prague - Brno - Prague   87 + 880

Dep. Prague (Hole.)	05:57 (1)	07:38 (2)	09:10 (1)	10:09
Arr. Brno	09:19	10:57	12:23	13:21

Sights in **Brno**: The folk-art exhibit of woodcarving, laces, pottery and costumes in the Moravian Museum. Brno Castle. Take a cruise on one of the underground rivers to see the Macocha and Sloup grottos. The outstanding 13th century Pernstejn Castle, near Brno.

Dep. Brno	14:02	16:22 (1)	19:19 (1)	20:20	22:14 (2)
Arr. Prague (Hole.)	17:14	19:39	22:39	23:37	01:40

(1) Restaurant car. (2) Light refreshments.

Prague - Ceske Budejovice - Prague   840

Dep. Prague (Hlavni)	07:48 (1)	Dep. Ceske Bude.	13:20	16:52 (2)	19:14
Arr. Ceske Bude.	11:03	Arr. Prague (Hlavni)	16:09	19:34	21:56

(1) Second-class only. (2) Change trains in Veseli at 17:24. Restaurant car 17:27 to 19:34.

Sights in **Ceske Budejovice**: This city appears the same now as it did in the Middle Ages. Visit the Budvar brewery.

Prague - Karlovy Vary - Prague   874

Dep. Prague (Hole.)	03:36 (1)	04:28	06:28 (2)	08:56 (3)	14:19 (2)	15:40 (2+7)
Arr. Karlovy Vary	07:42	08:36	09:48	13:00	17:51	19:58

Sights in **Karlovy Vary:** Once called Carlsbad, famous for its curative waters since 1347. Peter the Great, Beethoven, Mozart and England's Edward VII are among the celebrities that have come here to drink the elixir and use the monumental baths in their search for improved health. An international film festival is held here every July. Visit the Moser crystal glass factory. There is an interesting porcelain factory in nearby **Slakov**.

Dep. Karlovy Vary	04:08	09:20	17:36 (5)	18:27 (6)	18:58 (1)	23:41 (5)
Arr. Prague (Hole.)	08:25 (4)	13:49	20:54 (4)	22:41	22:53	04:49 (4)

(1) Reservation required. Carries a sleeping car. Also has couchettes. (2) Departs from Prague's Masarykovo railstation. Second-class only. (3) Restaurant car. (4) Arrives at Prague's Masarykovo railstation. (5) Second-class only. (6) Carries a sleeping car. Also has couchettes. (7) Plus other departures from Prague (Masarykovo) at 19:12 and 23:47 (5), arriving Karlovy Vary 23:09 and 23:47.

Prague - Liberec - Prague   876

Both of these trains are second-class only.

Dep. Prague (Masarykovo)	06:39	Dep. Liberec	17:25
Arr. Liberec	09:59	Arr. Prague (Masarykovo)	20:26

Sights in **Liberec:** This town is noted for its 17th century Reichenberg architecture. Walks in the encircling Jested Hills are recommended.

Prague - Marianske Lazne - Prague   870

Dep. Prague (Hla.)	04:05 (1)	08:47	11:20	13:04 (1)	16:55	18:53	20:45 (4)
Arr. Marianske	07:07	11:58	14:23	15:52	19:54	22:04	22:38

Sights in **Marianske Lazne**: Once called Marienbad, still a famous health spa.

Dep. Marianske	03:28 (2)	04:58	06:12	06:51	12:29	14:27 (1)	17:25 (5)
Arr. Prague (Hla.)	06:29	08:01 (3)	09:13	10:20	15:48	17:22	20:33

(1) Restaurant car. (2) Carries a sleeping car. Also has couchettes. (3) Arrives at Prague's Smichov railstation. (4) Plus another Prague departure at 23:40. (5) Plus another Marianske Lazne departure at 20:02 (1).

Prague - Plzen - Prague   870

Dep. Prague (Hlavni)	07:13 (1)	08:47	11:20	11:51 (2)	13:04 (1)
Arr. Plzen	08:52	10:37	13:08	13:28	14:42

Sights in **Plzen:** Visit the enormous Urquell brewery, where more than 200 million pints of beer are bottled annually. They have been producing beer here (hence "Pilsener") for over 800 years.

Dep. Plzen	13:58	14:34 (2)	15:43 (1)	16:35	18:43	19:43 (1)
Arr. Prague (Hlavni)	15:48	16:16	17:22	18:29	20:33	21:22

(1) Restaurant car. (2) Operates mid-June to mid-September. Restaurant car.

Prague - Tabor - Prague   840

Dep. Prague (Hlv.)	07:48	13:48	Dep. Tabor	14:12	17:22 (2)
Arr. Tabor	09:45	15:33	Arr. Prague (Hlv.)	15:44	18:52

(1) Restaurant car. (2) Plus other Tabor departures at 18:01 (1), 20:15 and 21:33.

Sights in **Tabor:** A museum town, preserved to immortalize the unusual Hussite 14th century reform movement which held that all people are brothers and equal.

SCENIC RAIL TRIPS

Bratislava - Kosice - Bratislava 885

Very good mountain scenery, through the Low and High Tatras Mountains.

Both of these trains have a restaurant car.

Dep. Bratislava	09:40	Dep. Kosice	06:30
Arr. Kosice	16:30	Arr. Bratislava	13:00

Poprad-Tatry to Stary Smokovec and Tatranska Lomnica

This spur off the Bratislava-Kosice route is the most scenic rail trip in Czechoslovakia. Forty minutes of the spectacular Tatras Mountains. Then, you can continue on to the **Tatranska Lomnica** ski resort and take a funicular to the top of 8,645-foot **Lomnicky Stit**.

885		887	
Dep. Bratislava	09:40 (1)	Dep. Tatranska Lomnica	12:15 (3)
Arr. Poprad-Tatry	16:27	Arr. Stary Smokovec	12:30 (3)
Change trains.		Change trains.	
887		Dep. Stary Smokovec	12:40 (2)
Dep. Poprad-Tatry	17:15 (2)	Arr. Poprad-Tatry	13:30 (2)
Arr. Stary Smokovec	18:05 (2)	Change trains.	
Change trains		885	
Dep. Stary Smokovec	18:15 (3)	Dep. Poprad-Tatry	14:02 (1)
Arr. Tatranska Lomnica	18:30 (3)	Arr. Bratislava	19:02

(1) Restaurant car. (2) Estimated. There are 26 departures each day. (3) Estimated. There are 20 departures each day (25 in Summer).

Strba - Strbske Pleso

This other spur off the Bratislava-Kosice line is a second great Tatras Mountain scenic rail trip. There are much Winter sports in the area around **Strbske Pleso**.

All of the Bratislava-Strba and v.v. trains have a restaurant car.

885			887		
Dep. Bratislava	06:30	09:40	Dep. Strbske Pleso	Frequent times	
Arr. Strba	11:24	14:45	Arr. Strba	13 minutes later	
Change trains.			Change trains		
887			885		
Dep. Strba	Frequent times		Dep. Strba	08:07	14:17
Arr. Strbske Pleso	13 minutes later		Arr. Bratislava	13:05	19:02

INTERNATIONAL ROUTES FROM CZECHOSLOVAKIA

Prague is Czechoslovakia's gateway to Berlin (and on to Copenhagen and all of Scandinavia), Budapest, Bucharest (and on to Athens), Nurnberg (and on to the rest of Western Europe), Vienna, and Warsaw (and on to Moscow).

Prague - Berlin 730

All of these trains require reservation, unless designated otherwise. All night trains carry a sleeping car and have couchettes. All day trains have a restaurant car.

Dep. Prague (Hlavni)	-0-	-0-	02:25	07:50	-0-
Dep. Prague (Holesovice)	00:37	02:05	-0-	08:05	10:14
Arr. Berlin (Licht.)	06:38	07:44	08:08	13:51	16:14

Dep. Prague (Hlavni)	12:20	15:54	-0-	-0-	-0-
Dep. Prague (Holesovice)	12:36	16:10	17:07	20:15	23:35
Arr. Berlin (Licht.)	18:14	21:44	22:44	02:14	05:19

Prague - Budapest - Bucharest 87

Dep. Prague (Holesovice)	00:08 (1)	02:04 (2)	05:57 (3)	07:38 (4)
Arr. Budapest (Nyugati)	08:28	-0-	-0-	16:25
Arr. Budapest (Keleti)	-0-	11:28	14:38	-0-
Arr. Bucharest (Nord)	-0-	-0-	-0-	10:05

Dep. Prague (Holesovice)	09:10 (3)	13:54 (3)	21:11 (5)	22:41 (6)
Arr. Budapest (Nyugati)	-0-	-0-	05:30	07:40
Arr. Budapest (Keleti)	17:27	22:12	-0-	-0-
Arr. Bucharest (Nord)	-0-	-0-	21:20	-0-

(1) Carries a sleeping car. Also has couchettes. Light refreshments. (2) Operates late June to early September. Carries a sleeping car. Also has couchettes. (3) Restaurant car. (4) Light refreshments. (5) Carries a sleeping car. Also has couchettes. Light refreshments until 24:00. (6) Departs from Prague's Hlavni railstation. Carries a sleeping car. Also has couchettes.

Prague - Nurnberg 870

Dep. Prague (Hlavni)	07:13 (1)	11:51 (2)	13:04 (3)	20:45 (4)	23:40 (4)
Arr. Nurnberg	13:52	17:30	19:03	02:52	05:47

(1) Train splits in Schirinding. Be sure to board a car in Prague marked "Nurnberg". Restaurant car. (2) Operates mid-June to mid-September. (3) Restaurant car. (4) Carries a sleeping car and couchettes.

Prague - Vienna 87

Dep. Prague (Hlavni)	00:06	03:00 (1)	06:18 (2)	14:51 (2)
Arr. Vienna (Franz Josefs Bf.)	06:07	08:35	12:07	20:07

(1) Carries a sleeping car. Also has couchettes. (2) Restaurant car.

Prague - Warsaw

	882	48
Dep. Prague (Hlavni)	19:59 (1)	22:55 (2)
Arr. Warsaw (Cen.)	06:10	11:30

(1) Reservation required. Carries a sleeping car. Also has couchettes. (2) This train carries only sleeping cars.

HUNGARY

Hungary became the 17th Eurailpass country in 1989.

Children under 4 travel free. Half-fare for children 4–11. Children 12 and older pay full fare.

Timetables (Hivatalos Menetrend) can be purchased at Hungary's main railstations. The larger stations in Hungary have food service.

Budapest's railstations are: Keleti (Eastern, for arrivals from and departures to Berlin, Prague and Vienna), Nyugati (Western, for arrivals from and departures to Berlin, Prague and Stockholm), and Deli (Southern, for arrivals from and departures to eastern Yugoslavia).

HUNGARIAN HOLIDAYS

January 1	New Year's Day	August 20	Constitution Day
	Easter	November 7	Revolution
	Easter Monday		Remembrance Day
April 4	Liberation Day	December 25	Christmas Day
May 1	Labor Day	December 26	Additional Holiday

SUMMER TIME

Hungary changes to Summer Time on the last Sunday of March and converts back to Standard Time on the last Sunday in September.

HUNGARY'S TRAIN PASSES

European East Pass: See page 456.

Hungarian Flexipass: First-class only, unlimited train travel. The 1992 adult prices are: $35 (US) for any 5 in 15 days, and $55 for any 10 days in a month (example June 3–July2). Half-fare for children age 5–14. Children under 5 travel free. Sold in North America by travel agencies and Rail Europe (U.S.A. and Canadian offices listed under "France" on page 23).

ONE-DAY EXCURSIONS AND CITY-SIGHTSEEING

Here are 4 one-day rail trips that can be made comfortably from Budapest, returning there in most cases before dinnertime. Notes are provided on what to see at each destination. The number after the name of each route is the Cook's timetable.

Schedules for international connections conclude this section.

Budapest

The capital of Hungary. Actually 2 cities, there is the dominant Buda on the west side of the Danube and the youthful Pest, extending east of the river.

Most museums here are closed on Monday.

In **Buda,** be sure to see the 112-acre garden island, Margit-ziget (Margaret Island). The Celtic and Roman ruins. The 250-foot Gothic tower at the 14th century Mathias Church. The view of the Danube and Pest from the tower of the nearby Fisherman's Bastion. The State Opera House. Heroes' Square. In Buda Castle, the medieval paintings and sculptures in the National Gallery and Art Museum in the Royal Palace, Castle Museum, and Budapest History Museum. The Railway Museum. The old stone fort. The display of pottery, weaving, wood-carving, embroidery and costumes in the Ethnographical Museum. The 13th century Coronation Church. The exhibits of pre-history, Roman, medieval and Turkish objects in the National Museum. The Aquincum Museum.

The tomb of the 16th century Turkish poet, Gul-Baba. The collection of medieval art in the museum at the Royal Palace.

The view of mountains, Buda Castle, Parliament, Pest and all of the Danube bridges from the top of the 770-foot hill called Gellerthegy. Take the cogwheel railway to the tops of Varhegy (Castle Hill) and Rozadomb (Hill of Roses).

In **Pest**: The 12th century church, Belvarosi Templom. Windowshop on Vaci Ucta. The great Zoo and Central Europe's largest amusement park, both in Varosliget Park. The city's best restaurants and shops are in Pest.

Budapest - Kecskemet - Szeged - Budapest   894

As these schedules show, it is possible to visit both Kecskemet and Szeged in the same day.
All these trains have buffet service, unless designated otherwise.

Dep. Budapest (Nyugati)	06:25 (1)	10:25	16:25 (1)	18:15
Arr. Kecskemet	07:43	11:40	17:40	19:45
Arr. Szeged	08:49	12:48	18:46	20:53

Sights in **Kecskemet**: Home of the ancient art of distilling barack (apricot brandy).
Sights in **Szeged**: Many Summer festivals.

Dep. Szeged	06:20 (1)	11:20	15:20	18:15 (1)
Dep. Kecskemet	07:23	12:25	16:25	19:24
Arr. Budapest (Nyugati)	08:42	13:48	17:50	20:45

(1) Reservation required.

Budapest - Lake Balaton (Siofok and Balantonszentgyorgy) and v.v.

It is a short train and bus ride to reach Hungary's most popular resort area, the 46-mile long **Lake Balaton**, circled with spas, motels and campgrounds along its 118 miles of shoreline. Great sailboating and fishing here. Frequent ferries link the many towns on both sides of the lake.

All of these trains have light refreshments, unless designated otherwise.
891

Dep. Budapest (Deli)	06:45 (1)	07:10	07:50 (2)	07:55 (3)	12:55 (6)
Arr. Siofok	08:11	08:36	09:10	09:53	14:22 (7)
Arr. Balatonszentgyorgy	09:06	09:45	-0-	11:46	15:33
		*	*	*	
Dep. Balatonszentgyorgy	06:13	06:49 (3)	11:47	-0-	14:48 (8)
Dep. Siofok	07:15	08:17	12:55	14:26 (4)	16:01 (9)
Arr. Budapest (Deli)	08:50	10:20	14:25	15:50	17:30

(1) Departs from Budapest's Keleti railstation. (2) Operates late June to late August. Reservation required. (3) Does not have light refreshments. (4) Reservation required. (5) Operates late June to late August. (6) Plus other Budapest departures at 14:00 (3), 17:15, 18:50 and 00:10 (5). (7) Plus other Siofok departures at 15:52 (3), 18:45, 20:37 and 01:40 (5). (8) Plus other Balatonszentgyorgy departures at 17:42, 20:20 and 02:18 (5). (9) Plus othe Siofok departures at 18:53, 19:46 (5), 21:14 and 03:24 (5).

Sights in **Siofok**: Many resort hotels and sidewalk cafes.

Sights in **Balatonszentgyorgy:** The attraction here is the curative carbonated water from the town's 11 mineral springs.

Sights in **Keszthely:** The Balaton Museum of the lake's natural history and the large collection of paintings and rare books in the Helicon Library at the 18th century Festetics mansion.

Sights in **Heviz:** The thermal waters. This has been famous as a health spa for more than 600 years.

INTERNATIONAL CONNECTIONS FROM HUNGARY

Budapest is Hungary's gateway for rail travel to Belgrade (and on to Athens and Istanbul), to Moscow, to Prague (and on to Berlin and Scandinavia), to Vienna (and on to the rest of Western Europe), and to Zagreb (and on to Italy).

Budapest - Belgrade 935

	88	86	82	87
Dep. Budapest (Keleti)	00:20 (1)	06:20 (2)	11:20 (3)	15:20 (2)
Arr. Belgrade	06:57	12:09	16:40	21:08

(1) Carries a sleeping car. Also has couchettes. (2) Restaurant car. (3) Reservation required.

Budapest - Moscow 88

Both of these trains carry only sleeping cars. Arrivals are on Day 3.

	88	
Dep. Budapest (Keleti)	20:15	23:50
Arr. Moscow (Kievski)	10:00	12:38

Budapest - Prague 87

	88	86	82	87
Dep. Budapest (Keleti)	08:05 (1)	11:10 (1)	14:00 (1)	-0-
Dep. Budapest (Nyugati)	-0-	-0-	-0-	15:05 (2)
Arr. Prague (Holesovice)	16:38	19:39	22:39	23:37
Dep. Budapest (Keleti)	-0-	18:35 (3)	-0-	-0-
Dep. Budapest (Nyugati)	17:00 (2)	-0-	21:25 (4)	23:50 (4+6)
Arr. Prague (Holesovice)	01:40	03:50	06:02 (5)	09:19

(1) Restaurant car. (2) Light refreshments. (3) Operates late June to early September. Carries a sleeping car. Also has couchettes. (4) Carries a sleeping car. Also has couchettes. (5) Arrives at Prague's Hlavni railstation. (6) Light refreshments 06:09 to 09:19.

Budapest - Vienna 890

All of these trains have a restaurant car, unless designated otherwise.

Dep. Budapest (Keleti)	06:00	08:30	09:50	12:30	13:30
Arr. Vienna (Westbf.)	09:20	11:50	12:57 (11)	15:50	17:00
Dep. Budapest (Keleti)	15:30	17:30	18:30 (2)	19:10 (3)	21:00 (4)
Arr. Vienna (Westbf.)	18:50	20:50	21:36 (1)	21:58 (1)	00:25 (5)

(1) Arrives at Vienna's Sudbahnhof railstation. (2) Reservation required. (3) Departs from Budapest's Deli railstation. (4) No restaurant car. (5) Arrives at Vienna's Hutteldorf railstation.

Budapest - Venice - Rome 88

Dep. Budapest (Keleti)	09:50	This train carries only sleeping cars. Early June to late
Arr. Venice (S.L.)	21:57	September: runs daily. Late September to early June: runs
Arr. Rome (Ter.)	08:20	daily, except Tuesday.

POLAND

Children under 4 travel free. Half-fare for children 4–11. Children 12 and over must pay full fare.

POLISH HOLIDAYS

January 1	New Year's Day	July 22	National Day
	Easter	November 1	All Saints' Day
	Easter Monday	December 25	Christmas Day
May 1	Labor Day	December 26	Additional Holiday
	Corpus Christi		

SUMMER TIME

Poland changes to Summer Time on the last Sunday of March and converts back to Standard Time on the last Sunday in September.

POLAND'S TRAIN PASSES

European East Pass   See page 456 for details.

Polrailpass   Sold worldwide by travel agencies and Rail Europe (see list of U.S. and Canadian offices under "France" on page 23). Unlimited *first*-class train travel.

The 1992 prices are: $35 (U.S.) for any 5 days within 15 days, $55 for any 10 days within a month (example: June 3 to July 2). Half-fare for children under 10.

ONE-DAY EXCURSIONS AND CITY-SIGHTSEEING

Here are 9 one-day rail trips that can be made comfortably from Warsaw, returning there in most cases before dinnertime. Notes are provided on what to see at each destination. The number after the name of each route is the Cook's timetable.

Warsaw

See the priceless collection of coins, jewelry, paintings and Polish crown jewels in 15 large rooms on the second floor of the rebuilt (1974) 16th century Royal Castle, destroyed during World War II. Also, see the Sigismund Column at the Castle.

Visit the churches, houses, Barbicon Wall, Blacha Palace and the ancient market in the reconstructed Old Quarter. The University in Casimir Palace. The reconstructed "Chopin Family Drawing Room" in the side wing of the former Raczynski Palace, closed Sunday. The very colorful changing of the guard (Sundays) in Victory Square.

Lazienki, the wonderful park with its enormous Chopin monument and Island Palace. Belvedere Palace, closed Monday. Wilanow Park and its 18th century Palace. Contem- porary art in Zacheta Museum, located in Malachowskiego Palace.

The Monument to the Heroes of the Ghetto. Marie Curie's House, closed Monday. The Archaeological Museum, closed Monday. The Lenin Museum, closed Monday.

During Summer, there are concerts on Sundays and holidays at nearby **Zelazowa Wola**, the birthplace of Chopin.

In the city center: The 37-story Palace of Culture and Science, highest building in Warsaw, and the view of the city and the Vistula River from the top of it. Amfora, a strolling street. The

National Philharmonic Hall. Warka, the museum devoted to General Pulaski and to the Polish emigration to America. The collection of picturesque folk costumes and hand-painted furniture and dishes in the Lowicz Museum.

The Zoological Gardens. The ancient Polish weapons at the Army Museum. The Jewish Historical Museum. The Curie Museum. The City Historical Museum.

Warsaw - Czestochowa - Warsaw 866

It is only a 2½-hour drive from Warsaw by taxi on Poland's best highway. The cost of a taxi roundtrip was about $100 (U.S.) in 1990.

Dep. Warsaw (Wsch.)	06:05 (1)	09:45
Dep. Warsaw (Cen.)	06:20	10:00
Arr. Czestochowa	09:40	13:13

Sights in **Czestochowa**: Four million people make a pilgrimage here to see the Black Madonna in the 14th century Jasna Gora Monastery. The cemetery here is 2,600 years old. There are no restaurants or lodging here.

Dep. Czestochowa	12:08 (1)	15:05 (1)	18:34 (1)
Arr. Warsaw (Cen.)	15:30	19:05	21:45
Arr. Warsaw (Wsch.)	14 minutes after arriving Centralna station		

(1) Light refreshments.

Warsaw - Gdansk - Gdynia - Warsaw 856

One-day roundtrips Warsaw-Gdansk, Warsaw-Gdynia and Gdansk-Gdynia (and v.v.) are possible.

Dep. Warsaw (Cen.)	05:42 (1)	06:02 (2)	08:57 (3)	12:27 (1)	15:12 (1+10)
Dep. Warsaw (Wsch.)	05:58	06:11	09:08	12:51	15:21
Arr. Gdansk	09:22	09:31	12:33	17:14	19:31
Arr Gdynia	09:49	09:59	13:00	17:47	20:05

*   *   *

Dep. Gdynia	00:08 (3)	01:31 (4)	04:19 (5)	05:30 (5)	06:20 (2+11)
Dep. Gdansk	00:41	02:07	04:51	06:00	06:45
Arr. Warsaw (Wsch.)	05:46	06:58	09:06	09:23	10:16
Arr. Warsaw (Cen.)	15 minutes after arriving Wschodnia railstation.				

(1) Light refreshments. (2) Reservation required. Light refreshments. (3) Operates late June to late August. Reservation required. Light refreshments. (4) Carries a sleeping car. Also has couchettes. Light refreshments. (5) Reservation required. Restaurant car. (6) Operates late June to late August. Carries a sleeping car. Also has couchettes. (7) Operates Late June to late August. Light refreshments. (8) Operates early June to late August. Reservation required. Light refreshments. (9) Carries a sleeping car. Light refreshments. (10) Plus other departures from Warsaw (Cen.) at 17:07 (5), 18:12 (5), 20:07 (1), 22:17 (6) and 23:42 (4), arriving Gdansk 20:37, 22:16, 00:20, 02:45 and 04:47 . . . and arriving Gdynia 21:09, 22:47, 00:55, 03:15 and 05:20.   (11) Plus other departures from Gdynia at 10:50 (1), 13:05 (1), 14:28 (7), 15:35 (3), 17:35 (5), 17:43 (2), 18:08 (8), 21:40 (9), 22:37 (6) and 22:47 . . . and other departures from Gdansk at 11:23 (1), 13:40 (1), 15:00 (7), 16:00 (3), 18:00 (5), 18:10 (5), 18:34 (8), 22:14 (9), 23:10 (6) and 23:22 . . . arriving Warsaw (Wsch.) 15:16, 18:16, 19:16, 19:26, 21:23, 21:36, 22:16, 02:31, 03:40 and 03:59.

Sights in **Gdansk**: A major Polish seaport. Called "Danzig" before World War II (when it was German). See the reconstructed Old Town. The immense Church of St. Mary. Town Hall. The Armory. Artus Mansion. The 600-pipe organ in nearby Oliwa.

Sights in **Gdynia**: A leading Polish seaport.

Warsaw - Krakow - Warsaw   865

Dep. Warsaw (Cen.)	06:10 (1)	06:42 (3)	09:25 (4)	16:25 (3)	17:45 (3+9)
Arr. Krakow (Gl.)	09:10 (2)	09:38	12:40	19:19	20:30

Sights in **Krakow:** Undamaged in World War II, it is one of Europe's most beautiful Medieval towns. See such historical monuments as Wawel Castle, with its priceless collection of tapestries. The unique 15th century carved wood altar in St. Mary's Church.

The very interesting library in the 14th century Jagiellonian University. The interior of the old Remuh Synagogue. The tombs of all of Poland's kings and queens, plus many national heroes and poets, in the 14th century Cathedral. The gold dome of Sigismund Chapel. There are 3 guided half-day bus tours: The Museum of Martyrdom at the death camp in **Oswiecim (Auschwitz)**. The underground sculptures, great hall, chapels, lakes and even tennis courts and a sanitarium in the 10th century salt mines at **Wieliczka**. The Ethnological Museum at **Zubrzyca Gorna**, a collection of houses typifying the lifestyles of several centuries of both peasants and wealthy people (primitive cooking utensils, elegant inlaid wood chests, furniture, etc.).

Dep. Krakow (Gl.)	02:20 (5)	05:51 (6)	06:21 (3)	07:10 (3)	08:35 (10)
Arr. Warsaw (Cen.)	05:30	08:54	09:05	10:00	13:55

(1) Res. required. Operates late June to early September. (2) Arrives at Krakow's Plaszow railstation. (3) Res. required. Restaurant car. (4) Restaurant car. (5) Carries a sleeping car and couchettes. Light refreshments. (6) Res. required. Light refreshments. (7) Operates late June to late September. (8) Carries a sleeping car and couchettes. (9) Plus other Warsaw departures at 19:00 (7), 19:40 (6), 21:50 (8), 22:10 (5) and 22:45 (5), arriving Krakow 22:15, 22:46, 01:36, 04:24 and 04:07. (10) Plus other Krakow departures at 14:55 (6), 18:20 (3), 23:10 (8), 23:28 (8) and 23:50 (8), arriving Warsaw (Cen.) 18:05, 21:05, 04:55, 05:05 and 06:25.

Warsaw - Lublin - Warsaw   863

Dep. Warsaw (Centralna)	00:37	-0-	06:47	08:42	09:47 (4)
Dep. Warsaw (Wschodnia)	00:47	02:50	06:57	08:57	09:57 (5)
Arr. Lublin	03:58	05:20	09:25	11:25	12:20

Sights in **Lublin:** One of Poland's oldest cities. Many outstanding churches. The Castle, above Lublin. The Gothic Krakowski Gate.

Dep. Lublin	01:05	06:30 (1)	07:13 (2)	09:30	14:00 (3+6)
Arr. Warsaw (Wschodnia)	04:35	09:02	09:27	12:02	16:52
Arr. Warsaw (Centralna)	04:49	-0-	09:37	12:17	17:32

(1) Light refreshments. (2) Reservation required. Light refreshments. (3) Reservation required. (4) Plus other Warsaw (Cen.) departures at 15:42 and 17:37 (2), arriving Lublin 18:19 and 19:53. (5) Plus other Warsaw (Wsch.) departures at 15:57, 17:47 (2) and 19:57 (1), arriving Lublin 18:19, 19:53 and 22:28. (6) Plus other Lublin departures at 14:00 (3), 15:30, 18:30 and 21:30, arriving Warsaw (Wsch.) 16:52, 18:02, 21:17 and 00:17.

Warsaw - Poznan - Warsaw   850

Dep. Warsaw (Wsch.)	06:00 (1)	06:20 (2)	06:30 (1)	09:30 (1)	13:10 (2)
Dep. Warsaw (Cen.)	15 minutes after departing Wschodnia station				
Arr. Poznan (Gl.)	09:43	10:36	09:53	12:56	17:58

Dep. Warsaw (Wsch.)	13:40 (2)	14:10 (2)	16:25 (3)	16:55 (3)	20:10 (2+8)
Dep. Warsaw (Cen.)	15 minutes after departing Wschodnia station				
Arr. Poznan (Gl.)	18:00	18:50	19:44	20:25	01:21

Sights in **Poznan:** Przemyslaw Castle. The sculptures at Dzialynski Castle. Gorki Palace. Parish Church. Franciscan Church. The State Ballet School. The stained-glass at the Church of the Holy Virgin. The Cathedral. The 12th century Church of St. John of Jerusalem.

Dep. Poznan (Gl.)	00:35 (4)	01:35 (5)	02:05 (6)	03:30 (7)	07:12 (3)
Arr. Warsaw (Cen.)	05:10	06:45	07:00	07:40	10:20
Arr. Warsaw (Wsch.)	14 minutes after arriving Centralna station				

Dep. Poznan (Gl.)	09:10	10:25	11:45 (1)	12:45 (2)	14:15 (1+9)
Arr. Warsaw (Cen.)	13:45	14:40	16:10	16:50	17:30
Arr. Warsaw (Wsch.)	14 minutes after arriving Centralna station				

(1) Res. required. Light refreshments. (2) Light refreshments. (3) Res. required. Restaurant car. (4) Operates early June to early September. Carries a sleeping car. Also has couchettes. (5) Carries a sleeping car. Also has couchettes. (6) Res. required. Carries a sleeping car. Also has couchettes. (7) This train carries only sleeping cars. (8) Plus other Warsaw (Wsch.) departures at 21:40 (4), 23:00 (6) and 23:10, arriving Poznan 02:10, 03:30 and 03:40. (9) Plus other Poznan departures at 17:05 (1), 18:00 (2) and 19:20 (2), arriving Warsaw (Wsch.) 20:24, 22:29 and 23:04.

Warsaw - Sopot - Warsaw   856

Dep. Warsaw (Cen.)	05:42 (1)	06:07 (2)	08:57 (3)	12:27 (1)	15:12 (1+8)
Dep. Warsaw (Wsch.)	10 minutes after departing Centralna station				
Arr. Sopot	09:35	10:12	12:48	17:34	19:51

Sights in **Sopot**: The International Music (Jazz) Festival, every August. This is a popular beach resort on the Baltic, with concerts on the half-mile pier.

Dep. Sopot	00:21 (4)	01:46 (4)	05:42 (5)	06:31 (2)	11:02 (1+9)
Arr. Warsaw (Wsch.)	05:46	06:58	09:23	10:16	15:16
Arr. Warsaw (Cen.)	15 minutes after arriving Wschodnia station				

(1) Light refreshments. (2) Reservation required. Light refreshments. (3) Operates late June to early September. Reservation required. Light refreshments. (4) Carries a sleeping car. Also has couchettes. Light refreshments. (5) Reservation required. Restaurant car. (6) Operates late June to early September. Carries a sleeping car. Also has couchettes. (7) Operates late June to early September. Reservation required. Light refreshments. (8) Plus other Warsaw (Cen.) departures at 16:47 (2), 17:07 (5), 18:12 (5), 20:07 (1), 21:17 (6) and 23:42 (4), arriving Sopot 20:41, 20:56, 22:35, 00:40, 03:03 and 05:08. (9) Plus other Sopot departures at 13:20 (1), 15:47 (3), 17:55 (2), 18:21 (7), 21:53 (1), 22:49 (6) and 23:00, arriving Warsaw (Wsch.) 18:16, 19:26, 21:36, 22:16, 02:31, 04:02 and 04:22.

Warsaw - Torun - Warsaw   862

Dep. Warsaw (Wsch.)	06:40 (1)	06:55 (2)	15:20 (1)	17:05 (3)	22:35
Dep. Warsaw (Cen.)	15 minutes after departing Wschodnia station				
Arr. Torun	09:55	11:10	19:00	20:10	02:15

Sights in **Torun:** A 13th century town on the banks of the Vistula River. This was the birthplace of Nicholas Copernicus in 1473. See the house where he was born. The instruments he used to determine that the earth revolves around the sun are exhibited there. Visit the ancient 3-story Town Hall. The Church of St. John contains one of the largest bells in Poland.

Dep. Torun	04:02	07:17 (3)	08:25 (1)	18:37 (1)
Arr. Warsaw (Cen.)	07:50	10:10	11:40	21:50
Arr. Warsaw (Wsch.)	15 minutes after arriving Centralna station			

(1) Light refreshments. (2) Operates early June to early September. (3) Reservation required. Restaurant car.

472

INTERNATIONAL CONNECTIONS FROM POLAND

Warsaw is Poland's gateway for rail travel to Berlin (and on to both Scandinavia and northwestern Europe), Moscow, and Vienna (and on to Italy, southeastern Europe and southwestern Europe).

Warsaw - Berlin

	850	23	17	850	850
Dep. Warsaw (Wsch.)	06:00 (1)	13:10 (2)	13:40 (2)	21:10 (3)	23:00 (4)
Dep. Warsaw (Cen.)	06:15	13:25	13:55	21:25	23:15
Arr. Berlin (Licht.)	-0-	-0-	-0-	-0-	08:50
Arr. Berlin (Hbf.)	13:58	22:28	22:50	08:09	-0-
Arr. Berlin (Fried.)	-0-	-0-	00:32	-0-	-0-
Arr. Berlin (Zoo)	-0-	23:14	00:44	08:50	-0-

(1) Reservation required. Light refreshments. (2) Second-class only. Light refreshments. (3) Carries only sleeping cars. (4) Carries a sleeping car. Also has couchettes.

Warsaw - Moscow

All of these trains carry only sleeping cars.

	900	900	900	900	23
Dep. Warsaw (Cen.)	09:22 (1)	11:37 (2)	13:52 (2)	14:57 (3)	16:57 (4+5)
Dep. Warsaw (Wsch.)	09:43	12:18	14:28	15:08	18:10

Set your watch forward one hour.

Arr. Brest	14:56	17:36	20:08	19:18	23:09

A short distance from the Brest railstation, the train is held for about 2 hours while the train's wheels are changed so as to conform to the wider Soviet track.

Dep. Brest	16:45	19:45	22:02	21:10	01:05 (4)
Arr. Moscow (Byel.)	06:55	10:08	11:48	10:55	15:17

(1) Operates early June to late September. Carries only sleeping cars. (2) Caries only sleeping cars. (3) Reservation required. Carries a sleeping car. Coach is second-class only. (4) Carries only sleeping cars. Has restaurant car Brest-Moscow. (5) Plus another Warsaw (Wsch.) departure at [table 47] 19:57 (2), arriving Moscow on Day 2 at 18:07.

Warsaw - Vienna

Both of these trains require reservation.

	866	48
Dep. Warsaw (Wschodnia)	07:40 (1)	20:00 (2)
Dep. Warsaw (Centralna)	07:55	20:15
Arr. Vienna (Sudbf.)	17:50	06:52

(1) Reservation required. Restaurant car. (2) Carries a sleeping car. Also has couchettes. Light refreshments 20:15-00:35.

ROMANIA

Children under 4 travel free. Half-fare for children –11. Children 12 and over must pay full fare.

Passengers who board a train that requires reservation whithout obtaining a reservation are charged a penalty fee.

To buy a Romanian timetable, ask for "Mersul Trenurillor".

ROMANIAN HOLIDAYS

January 1	New Year's Day	August 23	Liberation Day
January 2	Additional Holiday	August 24	Additional Holiday
May 1	Labor Day	December 30	Republic Day
May 2	Additional Holiday		

SUMMER TIME

Romania changes to Summer Time on the last Sunday of March and converts back to Standard Time on the last Sunday in September.

ONE-DAY EXCURSIONS AND CITY-SIGHTSEEING

Here are 7 one-day rail trips that can be made comfortably from Bucharest, returning there in most cases before dinnertime. Notes are provided on what to see at each destination. The number after the name of each route is the Cook's timetable.

Schedules for international connections conclude this section.

Bucharest

Most museums are closed on Monday.

See the lakes and fountains at Cismigiu Gardens on Gheorghiu-Dej Blvd. Great paintings at the National Art Museum in the Palace of the Republic. The lovely Athenaeum Concert Hall, and the Folk Art Museum, all on Calea Victoriei.

Near that museum, in Herastrau Park, is the city's major attraction, Village Museum (on Kisselef Ave.), featuring perfect replicas of 17th–20th century peasant homes, workplaces, shops, barns and churches, which have been moved from all over Romania to this site.

On Piata Victoriei, you will find the Statue of Soviet Heroes, the Geological Institute, the Natural Science Museum, and the Council of Ministers.

Other interesting places: The Zoo. A great collection of gold treasures and crown jewels in the Museum of Romanian History. The Technical Museum. The vast Northern Train Station, built in 1870 and restored in 1945, after World War II.

Guides at the Jewish Federation office (Strada Dmitri Rakovita 8) escort visitors to the well-preserved 200 year-old synagogue located at Strada Sfintul Veneri 9, and also to the kosher "soup kitchen" that is subsidized by American Jewish charities and to the Jewish Museum.

Bucharest - Brasov - Bucharest 950

All of these trains require reservation. These trains have a restaurant car, unless designated otherwise.

Dep. Bucharest (Nord)	06:45 (1)	07:35	09:30
Arr. Brasov	09:36	10:27	12:58

Sights in **Brasov:** Excellent Transylvania Mountain scenery in this area. See the 14th century Black Church. The Museum of History. The Art Museum. The Museum of the Romanian School. A popular Winter resort, **Poiana Brasov,** is 9 miles from here.

Dep. Brasov	12:11 (2)	15:18	17:40	18:02 (3)	20:17 (4)
Arr. Bucharest (Nord)	15:00	17:55	20:30	20:40	22:55

(1) Light refreshments. (2) No restaurant car. (3) Second-class only. No restaurant car. (4) Plus other Brasov departures at 21:24 (1) and 21:59, arriving Bucharest 23:59 and 00:36.

Bucharest - Constantza - Eforie - Mangalia   and v.v. 958

Dep. Bucharest (Nord)	06:05	07:10 (1)	08:35 (2)	10:10 (3)	14:00 (1+4)
Arr. Constantza	09:11	10:19	11:18	13:20	17:07
Dep. Constantza	09:23	-0-	11:33	-0-	17:27
Arr. Eforie (Nord)	09:43	-0-	11:53	-0-	17:55
Arr. Mangalia	10:29	-0-	12:40	-0-	19:00
		* * *			
Dep. Mangalia	05:05	-0-	-0-	16:30 (2+5)	-0-
Dep. Eforie (Nord)	06:00	-0-	-0-	17:19	-0-
Arr. Constantza	06:26	-0-	-0-	17:37	-0-
Dep. Constantza	06:45	13:20	16:50 (3)	17:49	18:00 (1)
Arr. Bucharest (Nord)	09:50	16:25	19:55	20:30	21:26

(1) Light refreshments. (2) Operates late June to late August. Restaurant car. (3) Restaurant car. (4) Plus another Bucharest departure at 18:50, arriving Mangalia 23:12.   (5) Plus other Mangalia departures at 17:25 (3) and 23:20, arriving Bucharest 22:00 and 04:15.

Sights: **Constantza** is a very large resort. See the Museum of Archaeology Parvan. The Open Air Museum of Archaeology. The Roman Mosaic. The Museum of the Black Sea. **Eforie** and **Mangalia** are popular Black Sea beach resorts.

Bucharest - Galati - Bucharest 957

Dep. Bucharest (Nord)	05:55	13:40	17:35
Arr. Galati	09:37	17:09	21:17

Sights in **Galati:** The most splendid array of birdlife in all of Europe.

Dep. Galati	06:09	15:05	19:00
Arr. Bucharest (Nord)	09:43	18:50	22:30

Bucharest - Sighisoara - Bucharest   950

All of these trains require reservation.

Dep. Bucharest (Nord)	06:45 (1)	07:35 (2)	09:20
Arr. Sighisoara	11:25	12:16	13:59

Sights in **Sighisoara**: The birthplace of Count Dracula. This is an interesting medieval fortress city. See the Museum of the Walled Town. Stroll through the old section.

Dep. Sighisoara	16:10	18:22 (2)	19:31
Arr. Bucharest (Nord)	20:40	22:55	23:59

(1) Light refreshments. (2) Restaurant car.

Bucharest - Sinaia - Bucharest   950

All of these trains require reservation.

Dep. Bucharest (Nord)	00:20 (1)	04:50 (2)	06:45 (1)	07:35 (2)	09:30 (2)
Arr. Sinaia	02:01	06:29	08:26	09:16	11:32

Dep. Bucharest (Nord)	13:02 (2)	18:45 (2)	20:00	21:00 (1)	23:00 (3)
Arr. Sinaia	14:43	20:26	21:48	22:43	00:41

Sights in **Sinaia**: This is a major Winter resort.

Dep. Sinaia	04:36	05:57	06:22 (1)	07:31 (1)	08:07
Arr. Bucharest (Nord)	06:25	07:45	08:05	09:13	10:05

Dep. Sinaia	10:18 (2)	13:20	16:16 (2)	18:45 (2)	19:00 (4)
Arr. Bucharest (Nord)	12:16	15:00	17:55	20:30	20:40

(1) Light refreshments. (2) Restaurant car. (3) Plus other Bucharest departures at 23:10 and 23:30, arriving Sinaia 00:54 and 01:14. (4) Plus other Sinaia departures at 21:15 (2), 22:21 (1) and 22:57 (2), arriving Bucharest 22:55, 23:59 and 00:36.

INTERNATIONAL ROUTES FROM ROMANIA

Bucharest is Romania's gateway for rail travel to Belgrade (and on to Yugoslavia's Adriatic cities), Budapest (and on to Western Europe), Kiev (and on to Moscow and Leningrad), and Sofia (and on to Athens and Istanbul).

Bucharest - Belgrade   954

This train requires reservation and carries a sleeping car.

Dep. Bucharest (Nord)   22:50

Set your watch back one hour.

Arr. Belgrade (Dunav)   10:40

Bucharest - Budapest   950

All of these trains require reservation.

Dep. Bucharest (Nord)   06:45 (1)   09:20 (2)   18:45 (3)   21:00 (1)   23:00(4+6)
    Set your watch back one hour.

Arr. Budapest (Nyugati)	-0-	22:57	-0-	12:16	14:00
Arr. Budapest (Keleti)	19:57	-0-	09:27	-0-	-0-

(1) Light refreshments. (2) Second-class only. Light refreshments. (3) Carries a sleeping car. Also has couchettes. Restaurant car. (4) Carries a sleeping car. Also has couchettes. Light refreshments. (5) Carries a sleeping car. Also has couchettes. (6) Plus another Bucharest departure at 23:10 (5), arriving Budapest (Keleti) 12:57.

Bucharest - Kiev - Moscow   89 + 955

All of these trains carry only sleeping cars.

Dep. Bucharest (Nord)	07:25	19:40	21:35	23:55
Arr. Ungeni	15:44	-0-	06:10 (1)	-0-
Arr. Vadu Siret	-0-	05:16 (1)	-0-	09:25 (1)

Ungeni and **Vadu Siret** are the Russian border stations where the wheels of the trains are changed to fit the wider Soviet rail gauge.

Dep. Ungeni	18:41	-0-	09:10	-0-
Dep. Vadu Siret	-0-	08:10 (2)	-0-	12:25 (2)
Arr. Kiev	07:56 (1)	18:56	22:16	23:13
Arr. Moscow (Kievski)	21:25	-0-	11:22 (3)	12:00 (3)

(1) Day 2. (2) Estimated. (3) Day 3.

Bucharest - Sofia - Istanbul

	89	960	960	87	960
Dep. Bucharest (Nord)	08:15 (1)	09:50 (3)	11:30 (4)	21:20 (5)	23:00 (6)
Arr. Sofia	19:20	21:05	21:52	08:20 (2)	09:20 (2)
Arr. Istanbul	10:50 (2)	-0-	-0-	-0-	-0-

(1) Bucharest-Sofia: only second-class coach cars. Sofia-Istanbul: only sleeping cars. (2) Day 2. (3) Operates early June to late October. Second-class only. (4) Second-class only. (5) Carries a sleeping car. Also has couchettes. (6) Carries only sleping cars.

RUSSIA   (U.S.S.R. — SOVIET UNION)

Children under 5 travel free. Half-fare for children 5-9. Children 10 and over must pay full fare.

Reservations are required for all trains.

There are 2 classes of train coach cars in Russia: Soft Class (upholstered seats, which convert to large 4-berth couchette compartments) and Hard Class (plastic or leather seats, which convert to bunks in 4-berth compartments or open non-compartment coaches). Bedding, including mattresses, is available at an extra charge for both classes.

Many of the important trains provide a third category of service: Sleeping Cars, with 2-berth compartments which have a folding table at the window, a closet and a speaker carrying both recorded music, which can be shut off, and announcements, which cannot be shut off. One car on the Trans Siberian Express is in this category. On these trains, conductors in each car serve tea to passengers.

Through sleeping cars going to Western Europe, Scandinavia, Greece, Turkey and Iran have single and double compartments in First Class and 3-berth compartments in second-class, all with full bedding included in the ticket price.

The only timetables available in Russia are printed in the Cyrillic alphabet.

Because Soviet rail tracks are 5 feet wide (along with Finland, whose rail system was constructed while Russians dominated that country), their passenger cars and compartments are considerably roomy. Good road maintenance and excellent engineers made Russian trains smooth-running in the early 1970's. Their quality declined in the 1980's, along with the Soviet's depressed economy.

As with all travel in Russia, your rail routes and travel dates must be predetermined and are limited to the provisions of the visa with which you enter the country.

All timetables show Moscow Time, even though Russia has 9 different time zones.

RUSSIAN HOLIDAYS

January 1	New Year's Day	May 9	Revolution Day
March 8	Women's Day	November 7	Victory Day (WW I)
May 1	Labor Day	November 8	Additional Holiday
May 2	Additional Holiday	December 5	Constitution Day

SUMMER TIME

The USSR changes to Summer Time the last Sunday of March and converts back to Standard Time on the last Sunday of September.

LONG-DISTANCE TRIPS FROM ST. PETERSBURG

Here are schedules for rail trips from St. Petersburg to 5 other interesting cities, with notes on what to see at each destination.

St. Petersburg (Leningrad)

Russia's most interesting city. The Hermitage Museum (closed Monday) has the world's largest exhibition of fine arts, over 2,500,000 articles. Visit the Summer Palace (open daily except Tuesday, May through November). See the 112 columns, gold cupola and priceless paintings and mosaics at St. Isaac's Cathedral (closed Tuesday, Wednesday and the last Monday of each month).

The park and palace at Petrodvorets. The Winter Palace. The 600-ton, 154-foot high Alexandrovskaya Column, marking Russia's victory over Napoleon. The Peter-Paul Fortress and Cathedral. The Summer Gardens of Peter the Great. The Museum of the History of Religion and Atheism, in Kazansky Cathedral (closed Wednesday).

The Monument to the Heroes of the Revolution, in the Field of Mars. The Central Museum, at the Marble Palace. The State Museum of the History of St. Petersburg (closed Wednesday). The State Museum of Russian Art, in Mikhailovsky Palace (closed Tuesday). The Arctic and Antarctic Museum (closed Monday and Tuesday).

In the Kunstkammer, the Peter the Great Museum of Anthropology and Ethnography and the Lomonosov Museum (closed Friday and Saturday). The Botanical Garden and Museum (the museum open only Wed., Sat. and Sun.). The Railway Museum.

Take an excursion to **Pushkin** to see the magnificent Yekaterinsky Palace (closed Tuesday and the last Monday of each month). In the Summer, hydrofoils cruise the **River Neva.**

St. Petersburg - Kiev and v.v.   914

| Dep. St. P. (Viteb.) | 11:57 | 21:20 (2) | Dep. Kiev | 09:46 (2) | 23:10 |
| Arr. Kiev | 18:06 (1) | 20:05 (1) | Arr. St. P. (Viteb.) | 10:10 (1) | 06:13 (3) |

(1) Day 2. (2) Operates June, July and August. (3) Day 3.

Sights in **Kiev:** The 11th century catacombs at the Pecherskaya Lavra Monastery. The frescos and mosaics at the 11th century St. Sophia Cathedral. The Golden Gate (Zolotiya Vorota) at the intersection of Sverlovskaya and Vladimirskaya. The Museum of Russian Art. The Museum of Western and Oriental Art.

Below are schedules for continuing on from Kiev to Odessa:

Kiev - Odessa and v.v.   910

| Dep. Kiev | 08:58 (1) | 21:15 (2) | Dep. Odessa | 15:35 (1) | 22:20 (2) |
| Arr. Odessa | 18:49 | 08:25 | Arr.Kiev | 01:23 | 08:58 |

(1) Carries a sleeping car. Restaurant car. (2) Carries a sleeping car.

Sights in **Odessa**: A sea resort and Russia'a largest port. See the beautiful Opera and Ballet Theater. The Potemkin Stairway, descending 455 feet from Primorsky Boulevard to the waterfront.

St. Petersburg - Moscow and v.v. 901

Dep. St. Petersburg (Mos.)	00:12 (1)	12:15 (2)	15:50	21:15 (3)
Arr. Moscow (St. P..)	08:40	17:14	21:40	04:59

Dep. St. Petersburg (Mos.)	23:00 (3)	23:33 (3)	23:59 (3)
Arr. Moscow (St. P.)	06:45	07:35	08:30

(1) Carries a sleeping car. Also has second-class couchettes. Restaurant car. (2) High-speed train. Runs Thursday only. (3) Carries a sleeping car. Also has second-class couchettes.

Sights in **Moscow**: See notes about sightseeing in Moscow under "Long- Distance Trips From Moscow"on page 480.

St. Petersburg - Murmansk and v.v. 918

Murmansk is the world's northernmost passenger rail terminus.

All of these trains have second-class couchettes and arrive on Day 2, unless designated otherwise.

Dep. St. Petersburg (Moskovski)	09:31 (1)	14:15 (2)	18:59
Arr. Murmansk	11:24	17:25	21:23

Sights in **Murmansk**: The largest city in the world north of the Arctic Circle. Founded in 1915 as a supply post in the First World War. Valuable in World War II as Russia's principal port for receiving war supplies from Britain and the U.S. Its ice-free harbor has made Murmansk a major ship repair center and commercial fishing base.

Dep. Murmansk	00:22 (2)	10:10	22:25 (1)
Arr. St. Petersburg (Moskovski)	04:32	12:42	23:52

(1) "Arktika". Carries a sleeping car and restaurant car. (2) Operates June 1 to August 31. Has only coach cars.

St. Petersburg - Tallinn and v.v. 913

Dep. St. Petersburg (Varshavski)	00:12 (1)	15:35 (2)	23:15 (1)
Arr. Tallinn	08:44	22:17	06:29

Sights in **Tallinn**: A fortified town for more than 2,000 years. Once the capital (1918-1940) of Estonia, before that country was annexed by Russia. In the walled Lower Town, see the 13th century Toom Church. The 13th century Great Guildhall. The 14th century Town Hall. Ruins of the 13th century fort built by invading Danes on Toompea Hill. The Gothic churches, Niguliste and Oleviste. The old castle.

Dep. Tallinn	16:11 (2)	22:53 (2)	23:55 (1)
Arr. St. Petersburg (Varshavski)	23:21	06:18	09:08

(1) Has only first and second-class coach cars that convert to couchettes. (2) Has only second-class coach cars that convert to couchettes.

LONG-DISTANCE TRIPS FROM MOSCOW

Here are schedules for rail trips from Moscow to 9 interesting cities, with notes on what to see at each destination.

Moscow

Most museums are closed on Monday.

See the Grand Kremlin Palace (closed Thursday). Red Square, with Lenin's Mausoleum, open daily except Monday and Friday. The 15th century Cathedrals: Uspensky, Blagoveshchensky and Archangelsky. The priceless jewelry,costumes, gold and silver objects, Faberge eggs, carriages and weapons in the Armory Museum (Oruzheinaya Palata).

The 16th century gigantic 38-ton canon, Czar Pushka. The 32-story Moscow University skyscraper. The Saturday and Sunday trading of birds and other pets on Kalitnikovskaya Street. The Bolshoi Theater. The Tretyakov Gallery, with its more than 50,000 paintings and sculptures. The Lenin State Library, containing over 19 million books, magazines and manuscripts in over 160 different languages.

The Zoo. The Lenin Museum. The Pushkin Museum of Fine Arts. The Museum of the Revolution. The marvelous decor of the Metro stations, particularly Komsomolskaya, Ploshchad, Revolutsi, Kropotkinskaya and Mayakovskaya.

Moscow's 9 railstations are: Byelorussian (trips to Warsaw, and on to Western Europe), Kazanski (to Tashkent and Samarkand), Kievski (to the city of Kiev and on to Eastern Europe), Kurski (to Sochi, and on to the Caspian Sea), Leningradski (to the city of Leningrad, and on to Helsinki), Paveletski (for which Cook's lists no trains), Riga (to the city of Riga and the Baltic area), Savelovski (for which Cook's lists no trains), and Yaroslavski (across Siberia to Russia's Far East area, and to Beijing).

Moscow - Kiev and v.v. 88 + 908 + 910

Only a few trains in each direction are day trains. Most of the night trains have first-class couchettes. A few of them carry a sleeping car.

It is advisable to bring your own food and beverages. Only a few trains carry a restaurant car. None of the trains have buffet or light refreshments.

Dep. Moscow (Kiev.)	15–18 trains every 24 hours
Arr. Kiev	12–15 hours later

Sights in **Kiev:** See notes about sightseeing in Kiev under "Leningrad- Kiev" on page 478.

Dep. Kiev	15–18 trains every 24 hours
Arr. Moscow (Kiev.)	12–15 hours later

Moscow - St. Petersburg and v.v. 901

Dep. Moscow (St. P.)	00:05	00:35 (1)	01:05 (2)	01:56 (3)	12:21 (4+6)
Arr. St. Petersburg (Mos.)	08:50	09:06	09:16	10:35	17:20

(1) Carries a sleeping car. Also has couchettes. Restaurant car. (2) Has first and second-class couchettes. (3) Has second-class couchettes. (4) High-speed train. Runs only on Friday. (5) Carries sleeping car. Also has second-class couchettes. (6) Plus other departures from Moscow at 17:20, 20:35 (3), 22:00 (5), 23:10 (5), 23:55 (5) and 23:59 (5), arriving St. Petersburg 23:10, 05:10, 05:48, 06:30, 07:32, 08:25 and 08:29.

Sights in **St. Petersburg:** See notes on page 478.

Moscow - Riga and v.v. 906

Dep. Moscow (Riga)	15:32 (1)	20:08 (2)	21:28 (2)
Arr. Riga	05:26	09:00	10:45

Sights in **Riga:** An important Baltic seaport. See the great pipe organ at the 13th-15th century Cathedral. The 14th century Riga Castle.

Dep. Riga	20:05 (2)	21:27 (2)	22:07 (1)
Arr. Moscow (Riga)	09:12	10:23	11:22

(1) Has second-class couchettes. (2) Carries sleeping car and first-class couchettes. Restaurant car.

Moscow - Sochi - Sukhumi and v.v. 923

Dep. Moscow (Kurski)	00:25 (1)	14:15 (3)	17:00 (1)	23:54 (5)	23:59 (1)
Arr. Sochi	09:27 (2)	01:01 (4)	22:22 (2)	08:13 (4)	08:42 (4)
Arr. Sukhumi	-0-	05:13	01:42 (4)	-0-	12:30 (4)
		* * *			
Dep. Sukhumi	01:55 (1)	03:00 (1)	13:54 (3)	22:16 (1)	-0-
Dep Sochi	05:36	06:21	18:29	03:01 (2)	09:48 (5)
Arr. Moscow (Kurski)	10:55 (2)	14:40 (2)	04:30 (4)	14:12 (4)	19:45 (2)

(1) Carries a sleeping car. Also has second-class couchettes. Restaurant car. (2) Day 2. (3) Operates late May to late September. Carries a sleeping car. Also has second-class couchettes. Restaurant car. (4) Day 3. (5) Carries a sleeping car. Also has first and second-class couchettes. Restaurant car.

Sights in **Sochi:** A popular Black Sea resort. Over 800 species of trees at the Dendrarium. Scenic Lake Ritsa is a 5-hour bus trip away.

Sights in **Sukhumi:** This is the heart of Russia's subtropical area: citrus fruits, tobacco, etc. See the monkey farm used by Russian scientists in their program of studying human behavior.

Moscow - Tashkent - Samarkand and v.v.

5031

Dep. Moscow (Kaz.)	00:15 (1)	12:03 (3)	13:56 (5)	22:15 (5)
Arr. Tashkent	18:35 (2)	04:10 (4)	04:25 (2)	07:55 (4)
Change trains. 5032				
Dep. Tashkent	15:20 (6)	16:20 (7)		
Arr. Samarkand	22:37	21:38		
	* * *			
Dep. Samarkand	01:56 (6)	02:51 (7)		
Arr. Tashkent	09:05	08:40		
Change trains. 5031				
Dep. Tashkent	11:40 (3)	14:20 (5)	23:10 (1)	04:50 (5)
Arr. Moscow (Kaz)	04:45 (8)	05:36 (9)	18:14 (8)	14:30 (9)

(1) Operates June 1 to August 31. Has only 2nd-class coaches and 2nd-class couchettes. Restaurant car. (2) Day 3 from Moscow. (3) Has 1st and 2nd-class couchettes.Restaurant car. (4) Day 4 from Moscow. (5) Carries a first-class sleeping car and 2nd-class couchettes. Restaurant car. (6) Train used by Intourist for foreign tourists. Second-class only. (7) Second-class only. Converts to 2nd-class couchettes. (8) Day 4 from Tashkent. (9) Day 3 from Tashkent.

Sights in **Tashkent:** This has been an important center of trade and handcraft on the major caravan route (the "silk road") between Europe and China and India for nearly 2,000 years.

There are many 15th and 16th century churches. Heavy Muslim cultural influence here. See: The Academy of Sciences. The Navoi Public Library. The Navoi Theater of Opera and Ballet.

Sights in **Samarkand:** One of the oldest cities in Central Asia. Alexander the Great captured Samarkand 2300 years ago. Heavy Turkish cultural influence here since the 6th century. Uninhabited from 1720 to 1770 due to an economic decline at that time caused by constant attacks by nomad tribes. The inception of train service in 1896 revived the city. See: The enormous colored domes of the 14th century mausoleums, decorated in marble and gold. The 14th century mosque. The ruins of a 16th century aqueduct.

Moscow - Volgograd - Rostov   —   Rostov - Moscow

Here is a great combination train and boat trip: a circle, from Moscow to Volgograd by train, and from Volgograd to Rostov by ship on the Volga-Don Canal. Then, return to Moscow by train.

5030

Dep. Moscow (Kaz.)	00:34 (1)	14:28 (3)	14:41 (3)	15:34 (4)
Arr. Volgograd (2)	06:52	10:52	12:23	13:30

(1) Second-class only. Restaurant car. (2) Day 2. (3) Train used by Intourist for foreign tourists. Carries a 2nd-class sleeping car and 2nd-class couchettes. Restaurant car. (4) Carries a 1st-class sleeping car and 2nd-class couchettes. Restaurant car.

Change to a ship for the Volgograd–Rostov cruise. Check Intourist for current Volga- Don Canal cruise timetables. The complete 2,000-mile ship trip runs from Moscow to Rostov. Change to a train in Rostov.

923 Train

Dep. Rostov	07:20 (1)	09:11 (3)	15:15 (3)	17:32 (3)	23:27 (4)
Arr. Moscow (Kur.) (2)	04:30	05:50	10:55	14:12	19:45

(1) Operates late May to late September. Carries a 1st-class sleeping car and 2nd-class couchettes. Restaurant car.   (2) Day 2. (3) Carries a 1st-class sleeping car and 2nd-class couchettes. Restaurant car. (4) Carries a 1st-class sleeping car and 1st-class couchettes. Restaurant car.

Sights in **Volgograd:** Renamed (from Stalingrad) after being destroyed during a 7-month battle in 1942–43. See: The enormous 63-mile canal. The huge industrial complex, particularly the Tractor Factory. But, most of all, the Soviet Union's Eternal Flame, memorial to their millions of World War II dead, in the Hall of Valor. All of those names are carved in its walls.

Sights in **Rostov:** Another post-World War II metropolis based on heavy industrial manufacturing. See the enormous theater on Teatralnaya Square. Window-shop Engels St.

Here is the reverse route for this circle trip:

923

Dep. Moscow (Kur.)	00:25 (1)	08:45 (1)	13:45 (1)	17:00 (1)	23:59 (1)
Arr. Rostov	20:43	04:59 (2)	10:35 (2)	12:17 (2)	20:25 (2)

(1) Carries a first-class sleeping car and second-class couchettes. Restaurant car. (2) Day 2.

Change to a ship for the Rostov-Volgograd cruise. Check Intourist for current Don Canal-Volga cruise timetables. Change to a train in Volgograd.

5030

Dep. Volgograd	07:02 (1)	12:45 (3)	13:30 (3)	16:37 (4)
Arr. Moscow (Kaz.) (2)	05:15	10:04	11:12	21:18

(1) Carries a first-class sleeping car and 2nd-class couchettes. Restaurant car. (2) Day 2 from Volgograd. (3) Train used by Intourist for foreign tourists. Carries a first-class sleeping car and 2nd-class couchettes. Restaurant car.   (4) Has only second-class coach and second-class couchettes. Restaurant car.

INTERNATIONAL ROUTES FROM RUSSIA

Here are the schedules for rail trips from St. Petersburg to Helsinki (and on to the rest of Scandinavia) and to Warsaw (and on to Western Europe).

Also, from Moscow to Bucharest (and on to the rest of Eastern Europe as well as to Athens and Istanbul), Khabarovsk (and on to Nakhodka, and from there to Yokohama and Hong Kong), Beijing, Tehran and Warsaw (and on to Western Europe).

St. Petersburg - Helsinki and Moscow-Helsinki 902

Both of these trains have first and second-class coach cars that convert to couchettes and a restaurant car.

Dep. St. Petersburg (Finlandsky)	-0-	10:25 (2)
Dep. Moscow (St. Petersburg)	21:30	-0-
Set your watch back one hour.		
Arr. Helsinki	12:54 (1)	16:54

(1) Day 2. (2) Reservation required.

St. Petersburg - Warsaw 911

Dep. St. Petersburg (Varshavski)	16:00 (1)	23:30 (3)
Arr. Grodno	09:15 (2)	14:57 (2)
Set your watch back one hour.		
Arr. Warsaw (Wschodnia)	14:49	20:35
Arr. Warsaw (Centralna)	15:02	21:17

(1) Carries only first and second-class sleeping cars. (2) Day 2. (3) Carries second-class sleeping cars. Also has second-class coaches that convert to bunks. Restaurant car St. Petersburg-Grodno.

Moscow - Warsaw - Berlin - Amsterdam

The long layover in Brest is to change train wheels to conform with Western Europe's narrower tracks.

23

Dep. Moscow (Byel.)	18:04 (1)	18:04 (5)			
Arr. Brest	08:03 (2)	08:03 (2)			
Dep. Brest	10:30	10:30			
Set your watch back one hour.					
Arr. Warsaw (Cen.)	13:47	13:17			
Arr. Berlin (Hbf.)	22:50	22:28			
Arr. Hannover	03:42 (3)	03:20 (3)			
Change trains. 67					
Dep. Hannover	06:33 (4)	08:33 (6)	10:33 (4)	12:33 (7)	14:33 (4)
Arr. Amsterdam (Cen.)	10:53	13:02	14:53	17:02	18:53

(1) "Oostende" portion of the Ost-West Express. Carries a first and second-class sleeping car and couchettes Berlin-Hannover. Restaurant car Moscow-Brest. (2) Day 2. (3) Day 3. (4) Light refreshments. (5) "Paris/Cologne" portion of the Ost-West Express. Same facilities as Footnote #1 — plus light refreshments Warsaw-Berlin. (6) Light refreshments. Change trains in Amersfoort. (7) Change trains in Amersfoort.

Moscow - Bucharest 955

All of these trains carry only sleeping cars.

Dep. Moscow (Kievski)	10:46	19:05	19:41
Arr. Bucharest (Nord)	22:45 (1)	08:15 (2)	07:36 (2)

(1) Day 2. (2) Day 3

Moscow - Beijing 5000

Both of these trains carry a first-class sleeping car. They also have first and second-class coaches that convert at night to berths and bunks, and a restaurant car.

Dep. Moscow (Yar.)	00:20 (1)	01:20 (4)
Dep. Irkutsk	03:51 (2)	05:59 (5)
Arr. Beijing	15:33 (3)	06:32 (6)

(1) Runs Wednesday only. Route is via Ulan Bator. (2) Day 3. (3) Day 6. (4) Route is via Shenyang. Late May to late September: runs Saturday and Sunday. Late September to late May: runs Saturday only. (5) Day 4. (6) Day 7.

Moscow - Warsaw - Berlin - Cologne - Paris

	900	80	23	62
Dep. Moscow (Byel.)	10:04 (1)	15:20 (3)	18:04 (4)	19:50 (5)
Dep. Brest	02:25 (2)	07:32 (2)	10:30 (2)	12:52 (2)
Set your watch back one hour.				
Arr. Warsaw (Wsch.)	04:12	09:45	12:19	15:15
Arr. Warsaw (Cen.)	04:37	10:17	13:17	15:47
Arr. Berlin (Hbf.)	13:51	19:18	22:28	-0-
Arr. Berlin (Zoo)	-0-	-0-	23:14	-0-
Arr. Cologne	-0-	-0-	-0-	09:58 (6)
Dep. Aachen	-0-	-0-	08:25 (4)	-0-
Arr. Paris (Nord)	-0-	-0-	13:04 (4)	-0-

(1) Operates early June to late September. Carries only sleeping cars. (2) Day 2. (3) Runs Friday only. Carries only sleeping cars. (4) This is the "Paris–Cologne" portion of the Ost-West Express. Carries a sleeping car. Also has couchettes. Light refreshments Moscow-Brest and Aachen-Paris. Arrives Aachen and Paris on Day3. (5) Carries only sleeping cars. (6) Day 3.

Moscow - Pyongyang 5000

Dep. Moscow (Yar.)	01:20 (1)	17:35 (3)
Arr. Shenyang	03:45 (2)	-0-
Arr. Pyongyang	15:55	13:19 (4)

(1) Runs Saturday only. Carries a first-class sleeping car. Also has first and second-class coaches that convert to berths. Restaurant car Moscow–Shenyang. (2) The following Friday. (3) Runs Thursday and Saturday. Carries a first-class sleeping car. Also has second-class coaches that convert to berths. (4) Day 9

Moscow - Tabriz - Tehran

5025		4500	
Dep. Moscow (Kurski)	19:05 (1)	Dep. Djulfa (Iran)	16:40 (3)
Arr. Djulfa (USSR)	09:33 (2)	Dep. Tabriz	21:15
Arr. Djulfa (Iran)	13:40	Arr. Tehran	11:00 (4)

(1) Runs Saturday only to Iranian Djulfa. Carries only sleeping cars. (2) Day 3 from Moscow (Tuesday). (3) Runs Tuesday only. Air-conditioned only in first-class coaches. No food or beverage. (4) Wednesday.

Moscow - Khabarovsk - Yokohama and v.v.

This is the eastward route of the Trans-Siberian Express. See page 617 for the Khabarovsk-Moscow westward schedule.

It is advisable to stopover in Novosibirsk (population 1,500,000) and Irkutsk on the 7½-day 5,118-mile-long Moscow-Khabarovsk trip. The Hotel Novosibirsk used to have better accommodations than were available in either Irkutsk or Khabarovsk. It is always recommended to bring toilet paper and soap when traveling on Soviet trains, including the Trans-Siberian Express.

Czar Nicholas officiated at the ceremony in Vladivostock when construction of the line began in 1891. Six separate sections were developed independently. Prisoners sent to Siberia were offered reduced sentences for working on the construction 8 months of work reduced a sentence by one year. By 1900 two unconnected sections had been completed: Moscow-Sretensk (east of Lake Baykal) and Khabarovsk-Vladivostock. Passengers traveled from Sretensk to Khabarovsk by river boat.

A line from Lake Baykal to Khabarovsk (the Chinese Eastern Railway, via Manchuria) was completed in 1903 and was much shorter than the present line. Russia lost it one year later, after the 1904 Russo-Japanese War, and had to begin building the present line from Baykal to Khabarovsk. Twelve years later the present Moscow-Vladivostock line, entirely on Russian territory, was completed and Russia began to develop Siberia.

It is necessary to check 1992 sailing dates of the Nakhodka-Yokohama (and v.v.) ships before determining dates on which to reserve Moscow or Nakhodka train departures.

925 (Train)		
Dep. Moscow		
(Yar.)	15:05 (1)	
Arr. Novosibirsk	10:29	Day 3
Arr. Irkutsk	16:13	Day 4
Arr. Khabarovsk	08:05 (2)	Day 7
Change trains.		
Dep. Khabarovsk	17:20 (3)	
Arr. Nakhodka	09:27	Day 8
Change to boat.		
5050		
Dep. Nakhodka	12:00 (4)	Day 8
Arr. Yokohama	15:00	Day 10

5050 (Boat)		
Dep. Yokohama	12:00 (4)	
Arr. Nakhodka	17:00	Day 3
Change to train.		
925		
Dep. Nakhodka	19:50 (5)	Day 3
Arr. Khabarovsk	12:02 (2)	Day 4
Change trains.		
Dep. Khabarovsk	13:09 (1+2)	Day 4
Arr. Irkutsk	14:32	Day 6
Arr. Novosibirsk	20:06	Day 7
Arr. Moscow		
(Yar.)	15:50	Day 9

(1) Carries a sleeping car. Also has second-class couchettes that convert to berths. Restaurant car. (2) Local time (7 hours later than Moscow). (3) Local time (7 hours later than Moscow). Runs only on days prior to sailings from Nakhodka to Yokohama. Carries a sleeping car. Also has second-class coaches that convert to berths. Restaurant car. (4) For specific sailing dates, check Far Eastern Shipping Co. (5) Local time (7 hours later than Moscow). Runs only on days that sailings from Yokohama arrive in Nakhodka. Carries a sleeping car. Also has second-class coaches that convert to berths. Restaurant car.

Sights in **Novosibirsk**: The Theater of Opera and Ballet, which is larger than Moscow's Bolshoi Theater. Take the 18-mile bus ride to **Akademgorodok**, the "Science Town", located along the Ob Sea, a man-made reservoir. There, top Soviet scientists and technicians live, work and shop in the USSR's most modern apartments, office buildings and stores.

Sights in **Irkutsk**: A large industrial city with no major tourist attraction. However, Irkutsk is the gateway for visiting the most unique place in the Soviet Union: **Lake Baykal**. Buses take tourists through a virgin forest to the shore of the world's deepest (6,365 feet) lake, 380 miles long and 12 to 50 miles wide, containing one-fifth of the fresh water on the earth's surface (four-fifths of the fresh water in the U.S.S.R.). Its waves sometimes measure over 15 feet.

Formed nearly 30,000,000 years ago by a rupture in the earth's crust, it is fed by 336 rivers and streams. There are 1,800 species of animals and plants in the lake. About three-quarters of them are found nowhere else in the world.

The day-trip includes a stop at the Limnological Museum, where hundreds of local flora and fauna are exhibited. The excursion to Baykal ends with a 90-minute hydrofoil ride from the Museum, up the **Angara River**, to Irkutsk.

Sights in **Khabarovsk**: Named after Yerofei Khabarov, a Slavak Daniel Boone who led a Cossack expedition to explore this area in the 17th century. Khabarovsk was first settled in 1858 by a handful of people living in tents along the banks of the **Amur River.**

When the Bolsheviks came into power in 1917, Khabarovsk was too far from Moscow for the embryonic Soviet regime to defend it, and the city was grabbed by Manchuria. Soviet rule here was re-established in 1922. By then, the old Khabarovsk had been reduced to ruins by the Manchurians. The city that exists today was started from scratch in 1922.

Its commercial air connections with Japan make Khabarovsk the Eastern gateway to the Soviet Union. Japanese tourism to Moscow and Leningrad begins and ends in Khabarovsk. The city is so geared to Japanese tourism and has so little tourism from elsewhere that several of its tourist brochures are printed only in the Japanese language.

There is a good museum here, with exhibits on the natural and political history of this area. The many 19th century wood and brick buildings are interesting. River boat excursions depart hourly from a dock that is across the park from the Intourist Hotel (one of the best hotels in Russia). **Vladivostok**, a major naval and long-range missile base, was opened to tourists in 1991 for the first time since the 1917 revolution.

Nakhodka

This is an overnight train trip from Khabarovsk, as shown in the timetable on page 485. It has one of the world's most beautiful harbors.

THE TRANS-SIBERIAN TIMETABLE

The times shown here are Moscow Time, considerably different than actual arrival and departure times as this 5,118-mile route covers 8 time zones.

For example, the real arrival time in Khabarovsk and Vladivostock is 7 hours *later* than the Moscow Time listed. Also the real departure time from Vladivostock and Khabarovsk (for the westward trip to Moscow) is 7 hours *earlier* than indicated.

The number of travel days is represented by capital letters: B = Day 2, C = Day 3 etc.

Moscow - Khabarovsk - Vladivostock   and v.v. 5020

Dep. Moscow (Yar.)	00:40 (1)	04:30 (2)	09:43 (3)	15:05 (4)
Dep. Kirov	19:59	05:10 B	01:27 B	04:00 B
Dep. Sverdlovsk	11:21 B	05:14 C	16:58	16:10
Dep. Omsk	02:37 C	07:11 D	05:44 C	03:13 C
Dep. Novosibirsk	12:25	20:00	15:42	10:44
Dep. Krasnoyarsk	01:58 D	14:08 E	05:25 D	22:31
Dep. Irkutsk	22:00	15:50 F	01:20 E	16:23 D
Dep. Ulan Ude	06:11 E	04:25 G	09:55	00:02 E
Dep. Chita	16:56	18:48	19:45	09:23
Dep. Skovorodino	15:00 F	20:00 H	17:12 F	05:20 F
Dep. Belogorsk	00:57 G	08:12 I	08:34 G	14:08
Arr. Khabarovsk	13:25	22:07	14:40	01:05 G
Arr. Vladivostock	-0-	17:10 J	05:10 H	13:30

* * *

Dep. Vladivostock	-0-	03:00 (3)	03:45 (2)	17:25 (4)
Dep. Khabarovsk	02:12 (5)	17:38 B	04:35 B	06:09 B
Dep. Belogorsk	12:48	06:14 C	20:04	16:52
Dep. Skovorodino	21:48	15:53	07:10 C	01:38 C
Dep. Chita	18:36 B	13:30 D	08:32 D	22:01
Dep. Ulan Ude	04:06 C	23:08	21:13	07:11 D
Dep. Irkutsk	11:51	07:21 E	09:00 E	14:42
Dep. Krasnoyarsk	06:08 D	03:51 F	14:38 F	08:23 E
Dep. Novosibirsk	18:24	17:17	08:42 G	20:21
Dep. Omsk	02:43 E	03:25 G	21:20	03:53 F
Dep. Sverdlovsk	14:34	17:07	-0-	14:57
Dep. Kirov	04:35 F	08:12 H	22:15 H	02:59 G
Arr. Moscow (Yar.)	18:50	22:55	01:40 J	15:50

(1) Second-class only. Restaurant car. (2) Second-class only. (3) Operates June 1 through August 31. Second-class only. (4) "Rossia" carries a first-class sleeping car. Restaurant car. (5) Runs Wednesday and Friday. Carries a first-class sleeping car. Also has second-class coaches that convert to berths.

YUGOSLAVIA

Children under 4 travel free. Half-fare for children 4–11. Children 12 and over must pay full fare,

Supplement is charged for internal express trains, except to passengers holding tickets that were issued outside Yugoslavia.

The 24,000,000 people here are divided into 24 ethnic groups, divided into 6 republics and 3 major religions (Eastern Orthodox, Roman Catholic and Muslim). The Adriatic Sea touches a deeply indented 3,800-mile-long coast and 725 islands.

Trains here are squalid, and their corridors are filled with passengers sitting on the floors.

YUGOSLAVIAN HOLIDAYS

January 1	New Year's Day	May 9	Victory Day (WWr II)
January 2	Additional Holiday	July 4	Veterans Day
May 1	Labor Day	November 29	Republic Day
May 2	Additional Holiday	November 30	Additional Holiday

SUMMER TIME

Yugoslavia changes to Summer Time on the last Sunday of March and converts back to Standard Time on the last Sunday of September.

ONE-DAY EXCURSIONS AND CITY-SIGHTSEEING

Here are 5 one-day rail trips that can be made comfortably from 3 major cities in Yugoslavia, returning to them in most cases before dinnertime. Notes are provided on what to see at each destination. The number after the name of each route is the Cook's timetable.

The 3 base cities are: Belgrade, Split and Zagreb.

This section concludes with details on 10 other rail trips (6 of which can be made as additional one-day roundtrip excursions) recommended for exceptional scenery, and ends with schedules for international connections.

Belgrade

The country's capital. Most of the museums are closed on Monday. See the collection of monuments to Serbian heroes in the Cathedral of the Holy Archangel Michael. The National Museum. The Kalemegdan Fortress and Park, with its Military Museum. Daman Pasha's Dome. The Museum of Medieval Frescos. The Ethnographic Museum. Many Turkish-style houses.

Split

This is a popular resort. See the 2,220-year old immense (7 acres) Palace of Diocletian, with its 7-foot thick, 72-foot high walls. Sacked in 615, only 3 of its 16 original towers remain. It is considered the largest and best preserved example of Roman palace architecture. Do not miss the fine frescos, marble pulpit and carvings in the Cathedral, which had been a mausoleum until it was converted to a church in 653. The Temple of Jupiter. The Museum of Ethnography in the Venetian Gothic Town Hall. The 12th century belfry at Our Lady of the Belfry Church.

Sarajevo

Turkish houses and mosques. The 16th century arched bridge over the Neretva River. The oriental handicrafts offered along Bascarsija, a row of small shops (silver, copper and other works).

Zagreb

One of Europe's largest collections of old European master painters is at the Strossmayer Gallery, 11 Zrinski Square, open 10:00–13:00. Also see the Ethnographic Museum at 14 Mazuranic Square, open daily except Monday 09:00–13:00 and also 17:00–19:00 on Tuesday, Wednesday and Thursday. Many medieval palaces. The Modern Gallery. St. Mark's Church.

St. Stephen's Cathedral. The art gallery and gambling casino at the Inter-Continental Hotel. The statues in the park at the Mirogoj cemetery. Ice skate at the rink on Salata Hill. Skiing is popular on nearby mountains. Buses from the main terminal on Drziceva Street go to thermal baths in **Stubicke Toplice, Krapinske** and **Catske**. Ten miles north of Zagreb are the popular hiking trails of Mount Sljeme, reached by cable car.

Take the funicular from Tomiceva Street to the top of Gradec, where you can visit the Primitive Art Gallery at Cirilometadska Ulica 3 (open 11:00–13:00 and 17:00–20:00) and the sculpture garden (a miniature version of the one next to Rodin's Paris home) of Ivan Mestrovic, a student of Rodin.

Belgrade - Zagreb - Belgrade 940

Dep. Belgrade	02:45 (1)	05:40 (2)	07:50	11:45 (3)	15:00 (2)
Arr. Zagreb	08:44	10:42	13:19	18:45	20:08

Dep. Belgrade	16:00 (3)	18:00	19:50	20:00 (4)	21:30 (4+8)
Arr. Zagreb	22:10	23:39	01:28	02:26	03:50

Sights in **Belgrade**: See notes about Belgrade on page 488.
Sights in **Zagreb**: See notes about sightseeing in Zagreb above, on this page.

Dep. Zagreb	01:10 (4)	02:00 (4)	03:20 (4)	05:40 (2)	07:40
Arr. Belgrade	06:14	06:45	08:32	09:45	12:48

Dep. Zagreb	10:40 (3)	15:40 (2)	16:00	19:40	22:40 (9)
Arr Belgrade	15:58	19:42	20:59	00:17 (5)	04:15

(1) Departs from Belgrade's Centar railstation. Carries a sleeping car. Also has couchettes. (2) Reservation required. First-class only. Light refreshments. (3) Light refreshments. (4) Carries a sleeping car. Also has couchettes. (5) Arrives at Belgrade's Centar railstation. (6) Reservation required. Carries a sleeping car. (7) Carries a sleeping car. Light refreshments. (8) Plus other Belgrade departures at 21:50 and 23:20 (7), arriving Zagreb 04:48 and 06:15. (9) Plus another Zagreb departure at 23:15 (7), arriving Belgrade 05:35.

Zagreb - Ljubljana - Zargreb 940

Dep. Zagreb	05:52 (1)	08:10 (2)	09:22	11:15 (3)
Arr. Ljubljana	08:15	10:17	11:45	13:15

Sights in **Ljubljana**: Sampling (free) hundreds of different Yugoslav wines at the Autumn Wine Fair. Interesting Baroque churches. The Castle. Several good museums.

Dep. Ljubljana	13:20	13:30 (3)	16:30	18:25 (1)	19:20 (5+7)
Arr. Zagreb	15:34	15:25	18:50	20:58 (4)	21:43

(1) Operates late May to late September. (2) Reservation required. Restaurant car. (3) Reservation required. First-class only. (4) Arrives at Zagreb's Zapad railstation. (5) Light refreshments. (6) Reservation required. (7) Plus other Ljubljana departures at 19:40 (2), 19:50 (1), 22:30 and 22:50 (6), arriving Zagreb 21:50, 22:10, 00:55 and 01:08.

LONG-DISTANCE RAIL TRIPS IN YUGOSLAVIA

Here are some longer trips in Yugoslavia to interesting destinations:

Belgrade - Split   and v.v.   934

Both of these trains carry sleeping cars have couchettes.

Dep. Belgrade	20:05	Dep. Split	20:32
Arr. Split	08:45	Arr. Belgrade	06:10

Sights in **Split:** See notes about sightseeing in Split on page 488.

Split - Zadar   and v.v.   934

All of the trains Knin-Zadar and v.v. are second-class only.

Dep. Split	06:20 (1)	11:05 (2)	14:45 (1)
Arr. Knin	08:52	13:24	17:00
Change trains.			
Dep. Knin	11:14	15:22	19:25
Arr. Zadar	13:07	17:23	21:18

Sights in **Zadar**: One of the most beautiful towns on the Adriatic. Many well-preserved Roman monuments here. See the 9th century St. Donat's Church. The 12th century Cathedral.

Dep. Zadar	06:40	10:14	14:45
Arr. Knin	08:36	12:29	16:18
Change trains.			
Dep. Knin	10:27 (1)	15:00 (2)	19:19 (1)
Arr. Split	12:25	17:00	21:30

(1) Reservation required. First-class only. Light refreshments. (2) Light refreshments.

Zagreb - Split   and v.v.   934

Between Sunja and Knin, this route passes through many gorges and the valley of the **Una River**. There is excellent scenery of thick forests as the train passes from one bank of the river to the other.

Dep. Zagreb	05:45 (1)	09:34 (2)	13:48 (1)	20:10 (3)	20:52 (4+6+8)
Arr. Split	12:26	17:00	21:30	05:30	05:58

Sights in **Split:** See notes about sightseeing in Split on page 488.

Dep. Split	06:20 (1)	11:05 (2)	14:45 (1)	18:30 (5)	19:55 (4+9)
Arr. Zagreb	14:18	19:07	21:37	02:11 (6)	04:44 (6)

(1) Reservation required. First-class only. Light refreshments. (2) Light refreshments. (3) Operates early June to late September. Runs daily. Has second-class couchettes Tuesday and Friday. (4) Operates early June to late September. Runs Monday–Friday. Carries only sleeping cars and couchettes cars. (5) Operates late June to early September. Carries a sleeping car. (6) Arrives/Departs Zagreb's Zapad railstation. (7) Carries a sleeping car. Light refreshments. (8) Plus other Zagreb departures at 21:05 (5+6) and 22:30 (7), arriving Split 05:18 and 06:39. (9) Plus other Split departures at 21:10 (7) and 22:00 (3), arriving Zagreb 05:28 and 07:13.

SCENIC RAIL TRIPS

Belgrade - Priboj - Bar and v.v. 942

This is the most scenic rail route in Yugoslavia. Steep canyons, turbulent rivers and mountains. The world's highest railway span, completed in 1976, is the 495-foot-high Mala Rijeka Bridge on this route.

The 325-mile line has 254 tunnels and 234 concrete and steel bridges. The trip climbs from the Danube to heights of 4,000 feet before descending to sea level on the Adriatic coast. The line from Priboj to Bar is narrow-gauge as the train descends to the valley of the **Rzav River**.

Dep. Belgrade	05:10 (1)	10:30 (2)	14:00 (1)	21:35 (3)	22:50 (4+5+6)
Dep. Priboj	08:43	14:17	17:43	01:39	02:53
Arr. Bar	12:19	18:00	21:14	05:27	06:46

Sights in **Bar**: A seaport and popular tourist resort.

Dep. Bar	05:05 (1)	09:50 (2)	14:10 (1)	20:20 (4)	21:35 (4+7)
Dep. Priboj	08:44	13:33	17:42	00:04	-0-
Arr. Belgrade	12:30	17:38	21:05	04:20 (5)	05:30

(1) Reservation required. First-class only. Light refreshments. (2) Light refreshments. (3) Carries a sleeping car. Light refreshments. (4) Operates early June to late September. Carries a sleeping car. Also has couchettes. (5) Depart/Arrive Belgrade's Centar railstation. (6) Plus another Belgrade departure at 23:00 (4), arriving Bar 07:17. (7) Plus another Bar departure at 22:15 (3), arriving Belgrade 06:38.

Belgrade - Vinkovci - Sarajevo - Ploce and v.v. 938

This Belgrade-Sarajevo portion of this route involves 120 tunnels and many bridges. It gives a view of the **Ovcar Gorge**, the **Kablar Mountains** and the **Zapadna River**. Many monasteries can be seen on the hillsides. The Vinkovci-Ploce portion has excellent mountain and river scenery.

Dep. Belgrade	06:30 (1)	10:20 (2)	15:10 (1)	22:00 (4)	23:35 (5)
Dep. Vinkovci	09:35	13:38	18:06	01:25	02:51
Arr. Sarajevo	13:20	18:10	22:03	06:10 (4)	07:24

Change trains.

Dep. Sarajevo	15:10 (1)	-0-	22:35 (3)	06:40 (4)	09:29 (2)
Arr. Ploce	17:54	-0-	01:36	09:42	12:35

Sights in **Sarajevo**: See notes about sightseeing in Sarajevo on page 489.

Dep. Ploce	-0-	05:30 (1)	08:50 (6)	18:55 (4)	-0-
Arr. Sarajevo	-0-	08:07	11:36	21:53 (4)	-0-

Change trains.

Dep. Sarajevo	06:27 (1)	11:50 (2)	15:15 (1)	22:20 (4)	23:00 (5)
Arr. Vinkovci	10:13	16:14	19:04	02:46	03:37
Arr. Belgrade	12:38	18:32	21:15	05:07	05:55

(1) Reservation required. First-class only. Light refreshments. (2) Light refreshments. (3) Second-class only. (4) Direct train. No train change in Sarajevo. Carries a sleeping car. Also has couchettes. Light refreshments. (5) Carries a sleeping car. Also has couchettes. (6) Restaurant car.

Ljubljana - Postojna - Ljubljana   930

The longest and most beautiful river cave of Europe is near **Postojna**, where the **Pivka River** flows through an underground passage.

Tourists, traveling through the cave on a small train, are able to see wonderful rows of stalactites and stalagmites, gigantic underground rooms, chasms and little lakes. A 16th century castle is at the entrance to the cave. Conducted tours are offered daily, every half-hour. June 1–September 1, from 08:30–16:00, plus 17:00 and 18:00. September 2 to May 31, from 09:30–13:30.

Because the cave is not deep, visitors can go a long distance through it. It extends 19 miles ! A narrow-gauge railway takes passengers more than one mile into the cave. Its terminal (Postojna Station) is larger than New York's Grand Central. English-speaking guides conduct tourists from it on a 1½-mile figure-eight walk. Great Mountain Room is more than 900-feet high.

Dep. Ljubljana	07:30	08:30(1)	09:30(2)	10:30	12:00	13:30	14:25(3)
Arr. Postojna	55-65 minutes later						

* * *

Dep. Postojna	11:55	12:10(4)	15:11	16:03(5)	17:25(3)	18:50(1)	19:23(6)
Arr. Ljubljana	55–65 minutes later						

(1) Operates early June to late September. Light refreshments. (2) Reservation required. Light refreshments. (3) Runs daily, except Saturday. (4) Light refreshments. (5) Runs daily, except Sundays and holidays. (6) Plus other Postojna departures at 20:56, 21:34 and 22:10.

Ljubljana - Jesenice - Sezana - Ljublana

There are many interesting ski resorts between Ljubljana and **Jesenice** in this region of the Slovenian Alps. **Kranj** is noted for fishing, water sports and mountain-eering. **Lesce-Bled** (Lake Bled) is popular both Summer and Winter.

All through this area there is fine scenery of evergreen forests and picturesque pastures. The most beautiful region of the Slovenian Alps is the route from Jesnice to Sezana.

All of these trains are second-class only.

940

Dep. Ljubljana	15:45 (1)
Dep. Kranj	16:09
Dep. Lesce-Bled	16:32
Arr. Jesenice	16:45
Change trains. 931	
Dep. Jesenice	16:54
Arr. Nova Gorica	18:36
Change trains.	

931

Dep. Nova Gorica	18:45
Arr. Sezana	19:45
Change trains.	
930	
Dep. Sezana	20:05
Arr. Ljubljana	21:58

(1) There are frequent departures from Ljubljana (to Jesenice) from 00:30 to 23:00.

Sarajevo - Dubrovnik and v.v. 938

The Mostar-Ploce portion of the trip from Sarajevo to Dubrovnik is one of the most beautiful train rides in Yugoslavia. The scenery is reminscent of Norway's fjords.

Dep. Sarajevo	05:44	06:05 (1)	06:40 (1)	09:29 (1)	15:10 (2+5)
Dep. Mostar	07:40	08:06	08:45	11:37	17:04
Arr. Ploce	08:31	09:12	09:42	12:35	17:54

Change to the local bus for the trip from Ploce to Dubrovnik.

Dep. Ploce	8 times per day
Arr. Dubrovnik	About 2 hours later

Sights in **Mostar**: Ruled by Turkey for more than 400 years, until the Austro-Hungarian occupation in 1878. Muslims constitute more than 40 of today's population.

Karadjoz Beg Dzamija is the oldest, largest and most splendid of the city's 24 mosques built in the 16th century. A muezzin calls the faithful to prayer every day at noon over a loudspeaker mounted at the top of its minaret.

Mostar was built on both sides of the **Neretva River.** Old houses are clustered along its banks. To see an elegant Turkish home, visit the 18th century Biscevic House (14 Biscevic Street), open daily 08:00–19:00. The Old Quarter is very Turkish, with an open-air market, a mosque and cobblestoned streets. See the arched bridge that the Turks built in 1566, using a mortar of eggs, butter and cheese !

Sights in **Dubrovnik**: One of Europe's most popular beach resorts. See the 4 ancient forts. The 15th century Rector's Palace. Prince's Court. St. Blaise's Cathedral. Sponza Palace. St. Vlah's Church. The Dominican and Franciscan Cloisters. The beautiful 600-year old pharmacy at St. Francis' Monastery. Shop on Stradun (a pedestrian mall) for sheepskin coats, coral jewelry, hand-woven rugs, filigree, lace, embroidery and leather items. Walk on the top of the city walls.

Bus

Dep. Dubrovnik	8 times per day
Arr. Ploce	About 2 hours later

Change to train.

Dep. Ploce	08:50 (3)	14:55 (1)	17:15 (1)	18:08	18:55 (1)
Dep. Mostar	09:47	15:53	18:24	19:12	19:59
Arr. Sarajevo	11:36	18:13	20:19	21:13	21:53

(1) Light refreshments. (2) Reservation required. First-class only. Light refreshments. (3) Restaurant car. (4) Second-class only. (5) Plus other Sarajevo departures at 17:10 (3) and 22:35 (4), arriving Ploce 19:54 and 01:30.

INTERNATIONAL ROUTES FROM YUGOSLAVIA

There are rail connections from Belgrade to Athens (and on to Istanbul), Bucharest (and on to Kiev and Moscow), Budapest (and on to Moscow, Prague, Vienna and Warsaw), Salzburg (and on to the rest of Western Europe and to Scandinavia), Sofia (and on to Athens and Istanbul), and to Venice (and on to the rest of Italy and Southern Europe).

Belgrade - Athens 970

Dep. Belgrade	07:35 (1)	21:45 (1)
Set your watch forward one hour.		
Arr. Athens (Larissa) (day 2)	05:45	18:45

(1) Carries a sleeping car. Also has couchettes.

Belgrade - Bucharest 954

Dep. Belgrade (Dunav)	18:00	Reservation required. Carries a sleeping car.
Set your watch forward one hour.		
Arr. Bucharest (Nord)	08:10	

Belgrade - Budapest 935

Day trains require reservation. The night train carries a sleeping car.

Dep. Belgrade	06:40	12:25	16:20	22:25
Arr. Budapest (Keleti)	13:13	18:18	22:43	05:13

Belgrade - Salzburg 940

Dep. Belgrade	15:00 (1)	15:20 (2)	18:00 (2)	19:35 (2+3)	21:30 (4)
Dep. Zagreb	20:20 (2)	22:00	00:05	01:20	04:50 (5)
Arr. Salzburg	04:15	05:53	09:48	08:50	12:15

(1) Reservation required. First-class only. Light refreshments. Change trains in Zagreb at 20:08. (2) Carries a sleeping car. Also has couchettes. (3) Departs from Belgrade's Centar railstation. (4) Carries a sleeping car. Also has couchettes. Change trains in Zagreb at 03:50. (5) Departs from Zagreb's Zapad railstation.

Belgrade - Sofia 945

Dep. Belgrade	09:00 (1)	12:50 (2)	21:55 (3)
Set your watch forward one hour.			
Arr. Sofia	18:00	22:10	07:20

(1) Departs from Belgrade's Centar railstation. Operates late May to late October. Reservation required. Second-class only. (2) Restaurant car. (3) Carries a sleeping car. Also has couchettes. Coach is second-class only.

Belgrade - Venice 930

Dep. Belgrade	07:50 (1)	20:00 (3)
Arr. Venice (S.L.)	22:19 (2)	11:38

(1) Reservation required. Light refreshments until 18:05. (2) Arrives at Venice's Mestre railstation. (3) Carries a sleeping car. Also has couchettes.

Chapter 9

THE MIDDLE-EAST

IRAN

Children under 7 travel free. Half-fare for children 7–13. Children 14 and over must pay full fare.

Five rail routes radiate from Tehran: (west to Tabriz (and on to both Russia and Turkey), south to Khorramshahr on the Persian Gulf (and on to Iraq), southeast to Zarand (with a spur to Isfahan, a popular tourist resort), and west to both Mashhad and Gorgan. A short line runs from Zahedan into Pakistan.

The country's oldest rail line has been operating only 60 some years. The rail service to Turkey was completed in 1971. Engineering and equipment are both highly modern.

Third-class has only wood or plastic seats. Sleeping cars and couchettes are avail-able on trains to Turkey and to the USSR.

Tehran

See the museums in the fantastic Shahyad Monument, built to commemmorate Iran's 2500th anniversary, only a few years ago. The 6-mile labyrinth of the city's Bazaar. The House of Strength. Gulistan Palace. The 19th century Sepahsalar Mosque. Shah Mosque. The Crown Jewels Museum in Markazi Bank.

The gardens and museums of Golestan Palace. The Ethnological Museum. The Archaeological Museum. The Mausoleum of Reza Shah The Great. The Marble Palace. The Decorative Art Museum. The National Art Museum.

Take a one-day excursion to the Shemshak ski resort or to see carpet-washing in the Cheshmeh Ali Stream.

Tehran - Esfahan 4510 Bus

Buses depart Tehran hourly   05:00–20:00, plus 12:45 and 14:00.
Buses depart Esfahan hourly   05:00–20:00.
                                      Journey time is 7 hours.

Sights in **Esfahan**: (This is the spelling used by Cook. Iranians spell it Isfahan.) A popular tourist resort.

See the blue enameled domes of the mosques. Visit the Ali Qapu Palace. View the breathtaking frescoes at the Palace of Four Columns. Visit ancient Friday Mosque and the Theological School. Browse through the Bazaar. Walk across the tiered bridges. Wonderful textiles, rugs and tiles can be purchased here. Esfahan carpets are magnificent.

Tehran - Gorgan 4503

Dep. Tehran	06:20	Dep. Gorgan	06:10
Arr. Gorgan	17:45	Arr. Tehran	17:50

Sights in **Gorgan:** This city was rebuilt after being destroyed in an earthquake during the 1930's.

Tehran - Kerman 4505

Both trains are air-conditioned and have a restaurant car.

Dep. Tehran	14:35	Dep. Kerman	14:20
Arr. Kerman	08:50 (1)	Arr. Tehran	08:20 (1)

(1) Day 2.

Sights in **Kerman**: Founded in the 3rd century and situated 5,738 feet above sea level. The largest carpet-exporting center of Iran.

See the 11th century mosque, Masjed-e-Malek. Visit the 18th century Qajar citadel, the many very old mosques and the ruins of a 3rd century castle. Browse through the large bazaar.

Tehran - Neyshabur - Meshhad 4504

There is excellent mountain scenery on this trip.

Dep. Tehran	10:10	12:50	15:30 (1)	16:45 (1)	18:00
Dep. Neyshabur	01:05	03:05	05:15	05:50	06:58
Arr. Meshhad	03:15	05:20	07:10	07:45	08:10

Sights in **Neyshabur:** This is the birthplace and burial site of Omar Khayyam, Persia's famous astronomer, mathematician and poet.

Sights in **Meshhad:** The holiest city in Iran, Shiite Muslims make pilgrimages to this city because Imam Ali Reza, their religious leader, was buried here in 817 in the great gold-domed shrine.

Also see: Gowhar Shad Mosque. The Tomb of Nader Shah. The Meshhad Museum.

Dep. Meshhad	10:45	13:30	14:30 (1)	15:10 (1)	22:25
Dep. Neyshabur	13:09	15:30	16:30	17:05	00:20
Arr. Tehran	04:45	05:05	05:30	06:05	13:25

(1) Air-conditioned. Carries first-class sleeping car.

Tehran - Tabriz 4500

There is interesting mountain scenery on this ride. Tabriz is the gateway for rail travel to Turkey (see "International Routes From Iran" on page 498).

All of these trains are air-conditioned in first-class.

Dep. Tehran	15:45	17:25
Arr. Tabriz	06:25	08:05

Sights in **Tabriz:** This is one of the major carpet producing areas in Iran. A popular Summer resort. Do not fail to see the fantastic 15th century Blue Mosque.

Dep. Tabriz	15:55 (1)	17:15	21:15 (2)
Arr. Tehran	07:00	07:55	11:00

(1) Runs daily, except Tuesday. (2) Runs Tuesday only.

Tabriz - Djulfa 4500

Both of these trains run only on Tuesday. Both are air-conditioned.

Dep. Tabriz	08:20		Dep. Djulfa (Iran)	16:40
Arr. Djulfa (Iran)	12:00		Arr. Tabriz	20:10

INTERNATIONAL ROUTES FROM IRAN

The gateway for train travel from Iran to Russia is Tehran. A line starting in Zahedan leads into Pakistan.

Tehran - Tabriz - Moscow
4500

Change your watch to Moscow time.

Dep. Tehran	15:45 (1)			
Dep. Tabriz	08:20 (2)			
Arr. Djulfa (Iran)	12:00	Dep. Djulfa (USSR)	18:49 (3)	
5025		Dep. Baku	08:00 (4)	
Dep. Djulfa (Iran)	16:30	Arr. Moscow (Kurski)	05:15 (5)	
Arr Djulfa (USSR)	16:45 (est.)			

(1) Runs daily. Air-conditioned in first-class. (2) Day 2. Runs Tuesday only Tabriz–Djulfa. (3) Carries a first-class sleeping car. Second class coaches convert to bunks. (4) Day 3 from Tehran. Restaurant car Baku–Moscow. (5) Day 5 from Tehran.

Zahedan - Quetta 5942
This is the rail route from Iran into Pakistan. The Zahedan railstation is 2 miles east of the city.

Dep. Zahedan	N/A (1)	N/A (1)
Dep. Mirjawa	N/A (2)	N/A (2)
Dep. Kuhi Taftan	15:15 (3)	14:35 (4)
Arr. Quetta	10:10 (5)	11:55 (5)

(1) Rail service Zahedan–Kuhi Taftan (84 km) has been suspended. It may be possible to go by taxi or unscheduled bus. There is bus service [Table 4510] 2 times in the morning and 2 times in the afternoon to Mirjawa on the Iran–Pakistan border. The journey time is one hour. (2) There has not been service between Mirjawa and Kuhi Taftan since 1983. Distance: 10 miles. (3) Runs Thursday only. (4) Runs Monday only. Restaurant car. (5) Day 2 from Kuhi Taftan.

IRAQ

Children under 4 travel free. Half-fare for children 4–9. Children 10 and over must pay full fare.

Iraqi trains have 3 classes of space: first, second and tourist. First-class and second-class seats convert into berths for overnight travel.

Baghdad

More than 100 mosques and minarets here, including the spectacular gold-domed Kazimayn Mosque. The 13th century Abbasid Palace and its museum. The 13th century Mustansiriyah law college. The selection of copper, cloth and silver in the many bazaars. The collection of Arabic history and literature at the Library of Waqfs.

The Central Library of Baghdad University. The Costumes and Ethnographic Museum. The Iraq Museum. The Iraq Natural History Museum. The Museum of Arab Antiquities. The National Museum of Modern Art. Nearby, the tombs of 2 imams.

Baghdad - Basra 4152

This scenic route follows the Tigris River to the Persian Gulf. Service was temporarily suspended in 1991 during the Gulf War.

Dep. Baghdad (West)
Arr. Basra (Ma'qil)

Sights in **Basra**: This is a prominent river harbor. Many date palm groves in this area.

Dep. Basra (Ma'qil)
Arr. Baghdad (West)

Baghdad - Mosul 4151

These trains are air-conditioned in all three classes. Overnight trains have first and second-class coach seats that convert to berths. These services are subject to confirmation.

Dep. Baghdad (West)	12:00	20:50	22:10 (1)
Arr. Mosul	19:00	05:06	05:49
		* * *	
Dep. Mosul	11:30	20:40	22:10 (1)
Arr. Bagdad (West)	18:50	05:30	05:40

(1) Carries a sleeping car.

Sights in **Mosul**: The ruins of ancient Nineveh are near here. The word "muslin" came from the production here once of fine cotton goods. See: The Great Mosque and its leaning minaret. The 13th century Red Mosque.

INTERNATIONAL ROUTES FROM IRAQ

There have been no international rail routes since the early 1980's..

ISRAEL

Children under 4 travel free. Half-fare for children 4–9. Children 10 and over must pay full fare.

Plan rail trips in Israel carefully to avoid the crowded conditions on public holidays and Friday afternoons and the suspension of nearly all transportation service from Friday sunset to Saturday sunset in conformance with the Jewish sabbath, which causes heavy traffic on Friday afternoon. Most museums and historical facilities are closed from 14:00 Friday until Sunday morning.

The country's principal train route is south from Haifa, to Tel Aviv. Its west–east line goes from Tel Aviv to Lod and Jerusalem.

There are *no* rail connections between Israel and countries adjacent to it.

The heaviest passenger train traffic in Israel is during August. Lightest is in February. Israel Railways urges tourists to make advance seat reservations at all times. Direct requests to: Traffic and Commercial Manager, Israel Railways, P.O. Box 44, Haifa, Israel.

Main Israeli Railstations

Haifa (Bat Galim) .... Telephone (04) 564564

Jerusalem .... Telephone (02) 717764 and (07) 733764

Netanya .... Telephone (053) 23470

Tel Aviv .... Telephone (03) 254271 and (03) 5421515

Haifa

This is Israel's main port. See the Bahai Shrine and Persian Gardens, open 09:00–12:00 (open in the afternoon for strolling). The Museum of Prehistory, a Nature Museum and Zoo complex, open Sunday-Thursday 08:00–14:00; Fridays 08:00–12:00; Saturdays 09:00–14:00.

The collection of Islamic folk art and costumes at the Museum of Ethnology, open 10:00–13:00 every day, plus 17:00–19:00 on Monday and Wednesday. The ClandestineImmigration Museum. The Carmelite Monastery. The Dagon Grain Museum. The Statue Garden.

Objects from 5,000 years of this area's maritime history, exhibited at the National Maritime Museum (198 Allenby Road), open Sunday-Thursday 10:00–16:00; Saturday 10:00–13:00. See the 4,000-year-old Egyptian funerary boat; a painting from 700 B.C. of a ship; ancient clay jars in which oil, wine and wheat were shipped to and from Israel; coins with maritime motifs from all over the world; rare 15th century maps; ship models; a 10th century Chinese jade astronomical device.

The Museum of Japanese Art on the summit of **Mt. Carmel** (89 Hanassi Avenue), open Sunday–Thursday 10:00–17:00; Saturday 10:00–14:00. (Israel's only subway is the one-mile "Carmelit" that goes to the top of Mt. Carmel.) Its exhibits include textiles, ceramics, metal objects, lacquers, scrolls and screens as well as 2,500 books and catalogs on Japanese art and culture. See the 18th and 19th century woodblock prints. The sliding, paper doors there create a perfect Japanese ambiance.

Israel's advancements in hi-tech and communications can be seen at the Institute of Technology (on Balfour Street), open Monday–Thursday 08:00–16:00; Friday 08:00–14:00. The program there includes an electronic newspaper and a 3-dimensional hologram exhibit. Nearby, see the exhibit of trains from the 19th century Turkish period, at the Railway Museum in the East Railway Station.

The paintings and drawings at the Museum of Ancient and Modern Art, open Sunday- Thursday 10:00–13:00 and 16:00–19:00; Friday and Saturday 10:00–13:00.

Tel Aviv

One of the oldest cities in the world, called Yafo 4,000 years ago.

See the photography and paintings (Van Gogh, Chagall, Vlaminck, Renoir, Utrillo, Degas) at the Tel Aviv Museum (27 Shaul Hamelech Boulevard), open Sunday–Thursday 10:00–22:00; Saturday 10:00–14:00 and 19:00–22:00. Its annex is the Helena Rubinstein Pavillion (7 Tarsat Boulevard), open Sunday–Thursday 09:00–13:00 and 17:00–19:00; Friday 09:00–11:00.

The animals at the 250-acre drive-through Safari Park, open Saturday–Thursday 09:00–15:00; Friday 09:00–13:00. The view from the observation terrace of the Shalom Building. The fascinating museum of the Jewish underground movement of the 1930's and 1940's, in the Bet Jabotinsky Building on King George Street.

The Museum of the Diaspora, recounting the cultural, social and religious events of those Jews who settled in different countries all over the world between 70 A.D. and the 20th century. Open Sunday, Monday, Tuesday and Thursday 10:00–17:00, Wednesday 10:00–21:00, closed Friday and Saturday. There are guided tours in English, Hebrew and many other languages. The exhibits are in the categories of Family, Community, Faith, Culture, Among The Nations, Return and Martyrdom. Located on the campus of Tel Aviv University, this museum is reached by Bus #25 from the beachfront hotels, or by taxi.

Models of 20 famous synagogues (including the 18th century one in Newport, Rhode Island and the one in Kai Feng Fu, the only known Jewish community in China) are part of the "Faith" exhibit. One of the dioramas in the "Community" section is an array of more than 100 figures re-enacting life in a 13th century German village.

The nearby Haaretz Museum complex consists of a planetarium, an archaeological dig, and exhibits of coins, folklore, science and technology. It is open Sunday–Thursday 09:00–16:00; Friday 09:00–13:00; Saturday 10:00–14:00.

Take a 20-minute bus ride to **Jaffa**, the ancient port, and browse in the artists' colony there. Nearly 100 commercial galleries there stay open until late night. The "Israel Experience", located in Old Jaffa, has 4 floors of craft shops, restaurants, a duty-free shop, and a tourist information center. A 40-minute slide show is presented there.

One-day bus tours from Tel Aviv go to the occupied **Golan Heights** (Thursday); the northwestern frontier at **Rosh Hanikra**, the Roman, Byzantine and Crusader ruins at Caesarea, and remains of the Crusaders at Acre (Tuesday, Friday and Sunday); Chris- tian holy sites (Monday, Wednesday and Saturday); and to the **Dead Sea** plus a 1,000-foot ascent by cable car to the **Masada** fortress, daily except Fridays (see more about Masada under "Jerusalem", page 506).

The Tel Aviv Marina offers boating, surfing and windsurfing. Nearby **Herzliya**, **Netanya** and **Caesarea** are popular beach resorts along Israel's Riviera. Take a guided tour of the Diamond Center in Netanya and shop for gems there.

Jerusalem

Bus #99 travels between 32 major tourist sites. A roundtrip ticket ($2 U.S.), sold at both the Central Bus Station and aboard the bus, allows getting on and off the bus all day.

The best way to see the Armenian, Christian, Jewish and Muslim quarters of the Old City is by walking. Brochures describing several walks, are available at the Ministry of Tourism (24 King George Street or at the Jaffa Gate).

Three-hour tours with an English speaking guide leave from the Tower of David courtyard at 09:00 and 14:00 Sunday–Friday and at 14:00 on Saturday.

There are other walking tours that include the ruins of the Second Jewish Temple (beneath the Dome of the Rock), the ramparts of the walls of the Old City, and a tunnel that reveals more of the Western Wall. Schedules for this walk can be obtained at the tour office at 34 Habad Street.

Visit the History of Jerusalem Museum in the restored ruins of the 2,000-year-old King David Fort, the Tower of David. This is just inside the Jaffa Gate in the Old City. Entry begins by crossing a 12th century moat, built by the crusaders. This museum's exhibits trace the city's history from its Canaanite origins to the present day.

The Dead Sea Scrolls are the highlight of the exhibits in the Israel Museum. This museum also has archaeological finds from the prehistoric era to the Middle Ages, a large collection of Jewish ceremonial art and artifacts, ancient coins, and a fine art collection. Four tours are offered: a 2-hour look at exhibits in the galleries, a 90-minute inspection of the ruins of the fort, a 40-minute look at the Old City, and rooftop views from the Citadel's towers.

This museum offers a sound-and-light show every evening April–October at 21:30 in English, at 22:30 in French and German (on alternate nights). The museum is open Sunday–Thursday 10:00–17:00, Friday and Saturday 10:00–14:00.

Don't fail to see the enormous diorama of the Jewish Second Temple, from the First Century. Also notable is the miniature of the 7th century Muslim Dome of the Rock. Statues of Crusader knights guard the entrance to a hall that is devoted to their reign over Jerusalem.

The Bezalel National Art Museum, Samuel Bronfman Biblical and Archaeological Museum, and Billy Rose Art Garden, all in the Israel Museum complex.

The Knesset (Israel's Parliament) and the President's Garden are opposite the Israel Museum.

A prominent satellite of the Israel Museum is the Rockefeller Museum, containing objects from prehistory to the Ottoman Empire: the skull of Galilee Man (100,000 B.C.), a carved wood beam from the 8th century al Aqsa Mo que, plaster pieces from the 8th century Islamic Hisham Palace, ivories from 12th century B.C. Armageddon, superlative Roman and Byzantine gold jewelry. The Rockefeller Museum is open Sunday–Thursday 10:00–17:00; Friday and Saturday 10:00–14:00.

Visit the Western (Wailing) Wall of the Temple Mount. The Dome of the Rock (Mosque of Omar). The al-Aqsa Mosque. The Church of the Holy Sepulchre. The 14 stations of the cross, along Via Dolorosa.

Shop at the nonprofit Benevolent Arts Workshop on Via Dolorosa for hand-embroidered dresses and tablecloths made by Christian Arab women. Next door to it, the Jerusalem Pottery sells what are said to be the best ceramics to be found in the Old City section: jars, plates and bowls decorated with Arabesque designs reproduced from 6th century mosaics and manuscripts.

Visit Hadrian's Arch and Roman Square, at Damascus Gate. The 6th century Nea Church. The archaeological park next to the City Museum at Jaffa Gate's Citadel. The 1,500-year-old artifacts in the Greek Orthodox Patriarchate Museum. Colorful oriental markets. The exhibits from the 1948–67 occupation at Tourjeman Post Museum in the Mandelbaum Gate area. The displays from the same period at the Cable Car Museum on Hebron Road.

Mount Zion, with the Tomb of the House of David, Cenacle (the room of the Last Supper), and the Abbey of the Dormition. The Tombs of the Sanhedrin. En Karem, birthplace of John the Baptist. The Chagall stained-glass windows, depicting the Tribes of Israel, at the Synagogue of the Hadassah Medical Center.

Don't fail to see the 24-foot-long Book of Isaiah, most ancient of the Dead Sea Scrolls. It is the centerpiece at the Shrine of the Book, where a beautiful copper scepter from 3,500 B.C. and the illuminated Italian Rothschild manuscript from 1470 are also exhibited.

See the 11th century mosaics and 17th century frescoes at the Monastery of the Holy Cross, open Monday–Thursday and Saturday 09:00–17:00, Friday 09:00–13:30, closed Sunday. The 30 dioramas telling the history of the Jewish people from 4,000 years ago to the re-establishment of Israel in 1948, Jewish ceremonial objects of all eras, and an 18th century carved ivory kiddush cup in the Wolfson Museum, open Sunday–Thursday 09:00-13:00, Friday 09:00–12:00.

Visit the Biblical Zoo. The Kennedy Memorial. The completely furnished, reconstructed mid-19th century Palestinian home (costumes, utensils, tools, and furniture used by Jews of that era) in the Old Yishuv Court Museum on Or Hahayim Street.

Yad Vashem Holocaust Memorial, open Sunday–Thursday 09:00–17:00 and Friday 09:00–13:00, commemorates the 6,000,000 Jews killed by the Nazis 1935–1944. Near its entrance is a grove of trees called "Garden of the Rightegous", memorializing individuals and groups who saved Jews during that period. More than

3,000 Christian families in France, Germany, Holland and Poland have been honored here. Inside, the names of the 22 largest death camps are stamped on a floor and there is a vault containing ashes recovered from camp gas chambers. There are also exhibits tracing the rise of Adolph Hitler, concluding with the Nuremberg war-criminal trials.

The L.A. Mayer Memorial Institute of Islamic Art, at 2 Hapalmach Street is open Sunday–Thursday 10:00–13:00 and 15:00–18:00, Saturday 10:00–13:00, closed Friday. It was founded by the Jewish granddaughter of a Lord Mayor of London, in honor of a Jewish professor of Islamic art. Its purpose is to acquaint non-Moslems with the heritage of Islam. The displays here of rugs, glassware, pottery, jewelry and calligraphy trace the history of Islamic art since the 7th century.

Two Islamic traditions are represented: the Eastern one that originated in Iraq and Iran, and the Western tradition that originated in Syria and Egypt. Among the exhibits are 12th and 14th century miniature paintings that illustrated manuscripts, an elegant Koran with beautiful calligraphy, bronze pieces inlaid with gold and silver thread, brilliantly-colored ceramic tiles that once ornamented mosques, and a collection of cameo glass, enameled glass and cut glass with geometric designs (7th to 19th centuries).

Southwest of the city are the ancient Jewish cemetery at the Mount of Olives and the Christian shrines at the Garden of Gethsemane. Below the Mount of Olives: Absalom's Pillar, the Tomb of Zechariah, and the toms of Bnei Hezir.

Northeast of the city are the Tombs of the Kings of Judah, the Garden Tomb, the Tomb of Simon the Just, the Cave of King Zedekiah (also known as Solomon's Quarries).

Masada is a 90-minute drive south. Buses leave daily, except Saturday and Jewish holy days, from the central Egged Bus Station (224 Yafo Road). The 4-minute cable-car ride to King Herod's palaces and fort on the top of the mountain runs every half-hour from 08:00 to 15:30.

After the fall of Jerusalem in 70 A.D., a group of Jewish zealots making the last attempt to revolt against the Romans barricaded themselves and held the mountain-top for 3 years against Roman siege. Masada has remained a symbol of heroism, and it is the modern scene of annual pilgrimages by young Israelis.

Tourists can inspect 2 large palaces, villas, bathhouses, storerooms, a fortified wall, the Herodian Synagogue (oldest synagogue in the world), cisterns and a 5th century Byzantine chapel.

All times shown here are Summer schedules.

Haifa - Tel Aviv 4004

Many of these trains have a buffet car. All trains are daily except Saturday unless noted.

Dep. Haifa (Merkaz)	05:54	06:24	07:24	08:24 (3)
Dep. Haifa (Bat Galim)	6 minutes later			
Arr. Tel Aviv (Arlozerov)	07:20	07:51	08:35	09:50

*   *   *

Dep. Tel Aviv (Arlozerov)	06:00	07:00	08:00	08:16 (1+4)
Arr. Haifa (Bat Galim)	07:27	08:29	09:07	09:33
Arr. Haifa (Merkaz)	6 minutes after departing Bat Galim station			

(1) Runs Sunday only. (2) Runs daily except Friday and Saturday. (3) Plus other departures from Haifa at 09:55, 10:58 (1), 11:24, 12:24, 13:24, 14:22, 15:24 (2), 16:24 (2), 17:24 (2) and 19:24 (2). (4) Plus other departures from Tel Aviv at 09:00, 10:30, 12:00, 13:00, 14:00, 15:00, 16:00 (2), 17:00 (2), 18:30 (2) and 20:00 (2).

Tel Aviv - Beersheva - Dimona

This train service has been suspended. Inquire locally for possible tours to Beersheva.

Sights in **Beersheva**: This modern desert town is the location where Abraham rested on his way south.

Haifa - Tel Aviv - Lod - Jerusalem 4005

This ride through the Judean wilderness, in operation since 1892, is the most scenic train trip and most exciting travel experience in Israel.

The train winds from the Mediterranean coast through orange groves before climbing into the Judean mountains, covered with pine and cypress trees. Then it passes **Zor'a** and **Eshtaol** and the **Valley of Sorek**, where Samson lived and met Delilah, according to the Bible.

Next, this route goes through a breach in the wall the Romans built around **Bittir** (called Beitar in biblical days), where Simeon Bar Kochba in 135 A.D. led the unsuccesful second Jewish revolt against the Romans, marking the beginning of the long Jewish diaspora.

All of these trains have buffet.

Dep. Haifa	06:54 (1)	Dep. Jerusalem	11:30 (2)	16:00 (3)
Dep. Tel Aviv (Ben.)	08:20	Dep. Lod	12:56	17:27
Dep. Lod	09:00	Arr. Tel Aviv (Ben.)	13:38	18:03
Arr. Jerusalem	10:35	Arr. Haifa	15:03	19:31

(1) Runs daily, except Saturday. (2) Runs Friday only. (3) Runs daily, except Friday and Saturday.

SAUDI ARABIA

Children under 4 travel free. Half-fare for children 4–11. Children 12 and over must pay full fare. Disabled passengers and those accompanying them travel at half-fare.

The only passenger rail route in Saudi Arabia is from the port of Dammam on the Persian Gulf to Riyadh, the inland capital. There are no train connections between Saudi Arabia and countries adjacent to it. The trains are modern air-conditioned diesels.

Dammam - Riyadh 4200

These trains are air-conditioned and have a restaurant car.

Dep. Dammam	07:30 (1)	14:45 (2)	Dep. Riyadh	07:55 (1)	15:10 (2)
Arr. Riyadh	11:38	18:53	Arr. Dammam	12:10	19:25

(1) Runs Monday, Tuesday, Saturday and Sunday.   (2) Runs Wednesday and Friday.

Sights in **Riyadh**: The Museum of Antiquities. The Zoo.

SYRIA

Children under 4 travel free. Half-fare for children 4–9. Children 10 and over must pay full fare.

When they were functioning, all of Syria's train routes became international connections. The rail lines in Syria which ceased operating after 1983 were the north-south standard-gauge from Kamechlie to Baghdad, the north-south standard-gauge from Halab (Aleppo) to Akkari (and on to Lebanon), the north-south special 3'5¼" gauge Hedjaz (also spelled "Hijaz") Railway from Dimashq (Damascus) to Deraa (and on to Jordan), a narrow-gauge from Dimashq (Damascus) to Beirut, and 2 short lines running north from Halab, one of which went to Karkamis (and on into eastern Turkey).

The only remaining passenger train services in 1991 were: (1) Halab-Fevzipasa (and on into central and western Turkey, en route to Ankara and Istanbul [table 4020] ,   (2) the route from Halab to Kamechlie [table 4075], and (3) Halab to Dimashq (Damascus) [table 4075].

Passenger train service was once possible from Europe, through Istanbul, via Turkey, Syria and Jordan all the way to Aqaba on the Red Sea. The interruption of service in Jordan from Amman to Ma'an, has made that intercontinental train travel impossible since 1917.

Halab (Aleppo)

Founded before 2,000 B.C. See the remains of the ancient Cathedral of St. Helena, converted into a mosque in the 12th century A.D. The 11th century minaret on the 8th century Great Umayyad Mosque. The ancient Citadel, built before the 13th century. Fantastic 16th and 17th century bazaars. The archaeological exhibits in the National Museum.

Dimashq (Damascus)

"The pearl of the east." Oldest inhabited city in the world, founded about 3,000 B.C. See the Great Umayyad Mosque. Al-Marjah Square, in the center of the city. The National Museum. The Qasr al-'Azm Museum. The Arab Academy, containing the national library. The fabulous orchards of the Ghutah.

Deraa

The ancient Greco-Roman ruins. The 13th century mosque.

Halab (Aleppo) - Haydarpasa - Istanbul 4020 + 4022

Dep. Halab	12:20 (1)
Arr. Fevzipasa	18:00
Dep. Fevzipasa	18:35 (2)
Arr. Haydarpasa	20:50 (3)

(1) June–September: runs Tuesday and Saturday. October–May: runs Saturday only. (2) Runs Tuesday, Thursday and Saturday all year. Carries sleeping car. (3) Day 2 from Fevzipasa.

When making connections for trains in Istanbul, allow 8 hours from arrival in Haydarpasa even though the boat trip from Haydarpasa to Istanbul is only a 20-minute ride. (See timetable on page 511.)

Halab - Kamechlie 4075

Dep. Halab	00:57 (1)	05:40 (2)	14:45 (2)	15:45 (2)
Arr. Kamechlie	09:05	13:17	22:40	23:25
		* * *		
Dep. Kamechlie	05:45 (2)	14:45 (2)	18:00 (1)	23:30 (2)
Arr. Halab	13:35	22:16	02:10	07:10

(1) Carries 1st and 2nd class sleeping cars. (2) Second-class only. Air-conditioned.

Halab - Dimashq (Damascus) 4075

Dep. Halab	02:10 (1)	15:15	23:50 (2)
Arr. Dimashq (Kadem)	09:25	21:50	07:15
		* * *	
Dep. Dimashq (Kadem)	00:01 (2)	15:35	18:35 (1)
Arr. Halab	07:20	21:50	00:57

(1) Carries a sleeping car and a restaurant car. (2) Carries a sleeping car. Light refreshments.

TURKEY

Children under 7 travel free. Half-fare for children 7–11. Children 12 and over must pay full fare.

The first-class sleeping cars here have single compartments. Second-class sleeping cars have 2-berth and 3-berth compartments. Some trains also have first-class 6-berth couchette cars or reclining-seat cars (designated "Pullman") for which a special fare is charged. Express and Mail trains charge higher fares than local trains. There is no air-conditioned space on Turkish trains.

Turkish trains in Asia are liable to cancellation or change.

Most of the train trips in Turkey for which we provide schedules are also the international rail routes to countries adjacent to Turkey. For that reason, we do not show a separate International Route list in this section.

Shoppers come to Turkey for alabaster (vases, lamps, chess sets), copper (trays, pitchers, bowls), inlaid wood (boxes, backgammon boards), leather and suede (coats, skirts, bags, briefcases), carpets, jewelry, ceramics and meerschaum (pipes, necklaces, bracelets).

TURKISH TRAIN DISCOUNTS

Students .... 10% discount.
Groups .... 30% discount for groups of 24 or more.
Roundtrips .... 20% discount for roundtrip tickets.
Sport Teams of 5 or more ...... 50% discount.

Ankara

Capital of the Turkish Republic. See: The Anitkabir, tomb of Mustafa Kemal Ataturk, father of modern Turkey. The collection of relics from prehistoric times until the present in the magnificent Ataturk Mausoleum, and the view of Ankara from there. The Museum of the National Assembly. The third century Roman Baths. The Columns of Julian. The Temple of Augustus.

The Byzantine Citadel. The finest collection of Hittite and pre-Hittite artifacts in Turkey can be seen in the Museum of Anatolian Civilizations. Visit the exhibits of ancient clothing, jewelry, manuscripts, tapestries, wood carving, musical instruments and weapons in the Ethnographic Museum.

Next to it is the Museum of Modern Art and Sculpture. Nearby, the Zoo at Ataturk's Farm. Ankara has several fine mosques: Haci Bayram, Alaettin, Ahielvan, Arslanhane and Yeni.

Istanbul

Colonized 2,600 years ago. First called Byzantium, then Constantinople. The city that links Europe and Asia. Haydarpasa is the eastern section of Istanbul.

See several exceptional mosques: The 17th century Blue Mosque (Sultanahmet), the rich tiles and stained-glass in the 16th century Suleymaniye, the enormous Fatih, the 15th century Eyup, the extraordinary jasper columns in the 15th century Beyazit, lovely tile decorations in the 17th century Yeni and in the 16th century Rustempasa.

One of the world's richest museums, Topkapi Sarayi, palace of sultans from the 15th to mid 19th century (open daily except Tuesday 09:00–17:00). The turbans, swords and tea cups encrusted with emeralds, rubies and diamonds as well as the satins embroidered with pearls will dazzle you. The kitchens there contain what is said to be the world's finest collection of Chinese porcelain.

The 19th century white marble Palace of Dolmabahce. Two other splendid palaces: Yildiz and Beylerbeyi. The blue and green tiled interior of the 15th century Cinili kiosk.

Istanbul's churches are outstanding: Ayasofia (St. Sophia), first built in 325, reconstructed in 532, later converted to a mosque, now a museum with fine Byzantine mosaics (closed Monday). The 4th century Church of St. Irene. The Byzantine frescoes and mosaics depicting the life of Christ and Old Testament scenes in the ancient Church of St. Saviour, now called Kaariye Mosque. The 14th century beautiful gilded mosaics in the old Church of St. Mary. The exquisite mosaics in the 12th century church, Pammakaristos (now called Fethiye Mosque).

The Summer open-air folklore performances at Rumeli Castle. The 4th century fortification. The Ramparts. Tour the great underground cistern, Yerebatan Sarayi. This storage facility, connected to the 4th century Aqueduct of Valens, supplied water to the Imperial Palace. It is built with 336 columns that have corinthian capitals.

Visit the Grand Bazaar. See the ancient Hippodrome of Constantinople, where chariot races took place. One of the 3 tall columns there was taken from the Egyptian Temple of Karnak. Another was removed from the Greek Temple of Apollo at Delphi.

The views of the Bosphorus from the luxury restaurant on Galata Tower and from the top of the Tower of Leander, and the view of Istanbul from the top of the white marble Beyazit Tower.

There are 2 incredibly beautiful fountains: Ahmet II (behind St. Sophia Cathedral) and the marble Tophane.

Istanbul has many excellent museums: The immense Greco-Roman collection at the Archaeological Museum (closed Monday). Next to it, the Assyrian, Babylonian, Sumerian and Hittite treasures in the Museum of Oriental Antiquities (closed Monday). The Museum of Mosaics (closed Tuesday).

The Museum of Turkish and Islamic Art(closed Monday). The Municipal Museum. The Naval Museum and the Military Museum (both closed Monday and Tuesday). During Summer, folk dances are performed at Gulhane Park every night except Sunday.

The spectacular view from the ancient fort at the first of the 96 gates along the 5th century 4-mile-long wall (15 feet thick by 35 feet high) that stretches from the Golden Horn to the Sea of Marmara.

Other interesting sights along the ancient wall are: the ancient spring of Zoodochos Pege near the Belgrade Gate, the Ottoman tombs outside the Edirne Gate, the 13th century Palace of Porphyrogenitus (tenanted in succession by Ottoman royalty, a Jewish poorhouse, a brothel, a pottery and a bottle works).

Also, the overwhelming panorama of dazzling mosaics and the monumental fresco of the Resurrection in the 14th century Church of St. Saviour in Chora.

Another wonder is the 4th century Aqueduct of Valens.

Istanbul - Haydarpasa (Boat Trip) 4042

Haydarpasa is the eastern section of Istanbul.

The boat departs both piers frequent times from 06:00 to 24:00 for the 20-minute journey. Allow at least 12 hours for making connections with trains.

Istanbul - Athens 974

Dep. Istanbul	22:25
Arr. Athens	23:16 Day 2

Istanbul - Edirne - Svilengrad - Sofia - Belgrade - Munich

	86 + 965	65 + 965
Dep. Istanbul (Sirkeci)	18:30 (1)	23:00 (4)
Dep. Svilengrad	02:35	07:05
Arr. Sofia	07:22	11:30
Dep. Sofia	08:15 (2)	12:25
Set your watch back one hour.		
Arr. Belgrade	15:40 (2)	19:18
Change trains.		
940		
Dep. Belgrade	18:00 (3)	19:35
Arr. Munich	09:48	10:56

(1) Has couchettes. (2) Restaurant car Sofia–Belgrade. (3) Carries a sleeping car. Also has couchettes. (4) Direct train. No train change in Belgrade. Reservation required. Operates early June to mid-October. Has second-class coaches and couchettes daily. Carries a sleeping car on Wednesday, Thursday and Sunday. (6) Restaurant car Svilengrad–Sofia.

Istanbul - Bandirma - Manisa - Izmir

Travel between Istanbul and Bandirma is by boat.

4041		4023	
Dep. Istanbul	09:30	Dep. Izmir (Basmane)	08:00 (2)
Arr. Bandirma (Quay)	13:45	Dep. Manisa	09:14
Change to train.		Arr. Bandirma (Quay)	14:00
4023		Change to boat	
Dep. Bandirma (Quay)	14:30 (1)	4041	
Dep. Manisa	19:18	Dep. Bandirma(Quay)	14:30
Arr. Izmir (Basmane)	20:38	Arr. Istanbul	18:45

(1) First-class only. (2) Third class only

(Sightseeing notes appear on page 512.)

Sights in **Manisa:** The 14th century Ulu Cami (Great Mosque) and the 16th century Muradiye Mosque.

Sights in **Izmir:** Third largest city in Turkey and its largest Aegean port. Once known as Smyrna. Walk along Ataturk Caddesi on the seafront.

See the elegant Moorish-style clock tower at Konak Meydani. The Bazaar. Three very attractive mosques: Kemeralti, Hisar and Sadirvan. Remains of the second-century Roman Agora. The Archaeological Museum in Culture Park. The magnificent view of the city from Velvet Castle, on Mount Pagos. The fortress of Kadifekale, built by one of Alexander the Great's generals.

Izmir - Ankara 4023

All of these trains have a restaurant car.

Dep. Izmir (Basmane)	18:00 (1)	21:00 (2)
Arr. Ankara	09:55	10:35

* * *

Dep. Ankara	18:20 (1)	20:00 (2)
Arr. Izmir (Basmane)	09:30	09:50

(1) Carries sleeping cars. (2) Reservation required. Supplement charged. First-class only. Has couchettes. The coach seats recline.

Izmir - Selcuk - Ephesus

In contrast to the train schedule shown below, there is also a more frequent guided bus service direct from Izmir to Ephesus and v.v. and it is only a 2-hour trip each way.

4026		Dep. Ephesus	Frequent times		
Dep. Izmir (Bas.)	08:10 (1)	Arr. Selcuk	15 minutes later		
Arr. Selcuk	09:51	Change to train.			
Change to mini-bus.		4026			
Dep. Selcuk	Frequent times	Dep. Selcuk	15:26	17:56	19:53
Arr. Ephesus	15 minutes later	Arr. Izmir	18:50 (2)	20:05 (2)	21:43

(1) Plus other departures from Izmir's Alsancak railstation at 08:45 and 09:40, arriving Selcuk 10:44 and 12:20.   (2) Arrives Izmir's Alsancak railstation

Sights in **Ephesus:** St. Paul preached here. The Virgin Mary spent her last days nearby. The Turkish Culture and Information office claims: "This vast ruined city has more to see than any other classical city anywhere. It is the grandest of ancient cities. Ephesus was famous as a center for worship of Artemis. The goddess' temple here was among the Seven Wonders of the World. The city is one of the Churches of the Revelation."

Fevzipasa - Halab (Aleppo) 4020 + 4022

Dep. Fevzipasa	11:45 (1)		Dep. Halab	12:20 (2)
Arr. Halab	17:01		Arr. Fevzipasa	18:00

(1) October–May: runs Friday only. June–September: runs Monday and Friday. (2) October–May: runs Saturday only. June–September: runs Tuesday and Saturday.

Ankara - Kars - Leninakan - Rostov - Kharkov - Moscow

4030		Change trains.		
Dep. Ankara	22:10 (1)	Set you watch to Moscow time.		
Dep. Kayseri	03:29 (2)	5025		
Dep. Erzurum	19:13	Dep. Leninakan	15:37 (4)	11:23 (8)
Arr. Kars	23:55	Arr. Rostov	05:07 (5)	17:12 (5)
Change trains.		Change trains.		
Dep. Kars	10:00 (3)	Dep. Rostov	08:09 (6)	17:22 (8)
Arr. Leninakan	14:50	Arr. Moscow (Kurski)	05:10 (7)	14:40 (7)

(1) Reservation required. Supplement charged. First class only. Restaurant car. Coach seats recline and there is a couchette car. (2) Day 2 from Ankara. (3) Day 3 from Ankara. Has only second-class coaches. Does *not* run on Friday in winter. (4) Train used by Intourist for foreign tourists. Second-class only. Compartments convert to 4 bunks. (5) Day 2 from Leninakan. (6) First-class only train used byIntourist for foreign tourists. Carries sleeping cars and restaurant car. (7) Day 3 from Leninakan. (8) Direct train. No train change in Rostov. Intourist train for foreign tourists. Carries a first-class sleeping car and a restaurant car.

Sights in **Kayseri:** Called Caesarea when it was the capital of a Roman province. See the Byzantine Citadel and, in it, the Faith Mosque. East of the Citadel, the 13th century Huand Mosque and College, and the geometric designs in the Baths of Princess Mahperi. Nearby, the beautifully decorated 13th century Doner Kumbet (Mausoleum). West of the Citadel is the interesting covered market. Also see the Archaeological Museum. The 13th century Koluk Mosque.

Sights in **Erzurum:** The Seljuk fort. The collonaded courtyard at the 12th century Ulu Cami Mosque. The Cifte Minareli Madrese Museum. The Hatuniye Medrese Mausoleum.

Sights in **Kars:** The 10th century Church of the Holy Apostles, now a museum. The ancient Georgian fort. The Kumbet Mosque. The 11th century Cathedral. The murals in the Church of St. Gregory. The Evliya Mosque.

Sights in **Rostov:** A post-World War II Russian metropolis, designed for heavy industrial manufacturing. See the enormous theater on Teatralnaya Square. Window-shop on Engels Street.

Sights in **Kharkov:** Almost totally reconstructed after World War II with wide streets. Sixth largest city in the USSR. Among the few old treasures that survived Nazi destruction are the 17th century Pokrovsky Cathedral, a belltower commemorating the 1812 victory over Napoleon, the 19th century Patriarchal Cathedral, and an 18th century theater. Modern sights include the large Park of Physical Culture, the Botanical Garden, several museums and a planetarium.

514

Ankara - Haydarpasa (Istanbul) 4027

All of these trains require reservation and have a restaurant car, unless designated otherwise.

Dep. Ankara	00:01 (1)	08:00 (2)	10:30 (3)	13:30 (4)	21:25 (5+8)
Arr. Haydarpasa	N/A	17:00	17:50	21:40	07:45

* * *

Dep. Haydarpasa	00:01 (1)	08:30 (2)	10:30 (3)	13:30 (4)	21:00 (5+9)
Arr. Ankara	N/A	17:25	17:50	21:45	08:10

(1) Supplement charged. Carries only first class sleeping cars. (2) No reservation required. Has only reclining-seat coaches. (3) First class only. Buffet car. (4) Supplement charged. Has only reclining-seat coaches. (5) Has couchettes. Coaches have reclining seat . (6) Carries only first-class sleeping cars. (7) Supplement charged. Has first-class couchettes and reclining-seat coaches. (8) Plus other departures from Ankara at 22:00 (6) and 22:50 (7) arriving Haydarpasa at 08:50 and 08:00. (9) Plus other departures from Haydarpasa at 22:00 (6) and 23:00 (7) arriving Ankara at 08:45 and 07:55.

Haydarpasa (Istanbul) - Ankara - Kayseri - Tatvan - Van

4027		4045 (Boat)	
Dep Haydarpasa	23:59 (1)	Dep Van Pier — Every 4 hours	
Arr Ankara	09:35	around the clock from 23:59.	
Change trains 4030		Arr Tatvan Pier 4 hours later	
Dep Ankara	10:40 (2)	Change to a train. 4030	
Dep Kayseri	18:52	Dep Tatvan Pier	08:25 (4)
Arr Tatvan Pier	17:55 (3)	Dep Kayseri	05:59 (5)
Change to a boat. 4045		Arr Ankara	15:05 (5)
Dep Tatvan Pier — Every 4 hours		Change trains. 4027	
around the clock from 02:00		Dep Ankara	21:25 (6+8)
Arr Van Pier 4 hours later		Arr Haydarpasa	07:45 (3)

(1) Reservation required. Supplement charged. Carries only first class sleeping cars and a restaurant car. (2) Runs Tuesday, Thursday and Sunday. (3) Day 2 from Ankara. (4) Runs Tuesday, Thursday and Saturday. (5) Day 2 from Tatvan. (6) Has first-class couchettes, and coaches with reclining seats. Restaurant car. (7) Reservation required. Supplement charged. (8) Plus other departures from Ankara at 22:00 (1) and 23:00 (6+7)....arriving Haydarpasa 08:45 and 07:55..

Sights in **Van:** This city is on a vast, salt lake. A famous trading place for carpets and rugs. See: The old fort. The 2 small Seljuk mosques. The 10th century Church of the Holy Cross, on an island in Lake Van, reached by frequent boats operated for tourists.

Samsun - Sivas 4025

Dep. Samsun	07:50 (1)	18:06 (2)	Dep. Sivas	07:30 (2)	20:55 (1)
Arr. Sivas	20:20	07:20	Arr. Samsun	19:48	09:30

(1) Runs Monday, Wednesday, Friday and Sunday. (2) Runs Tuesday, Thursday and Saturday.

Sights in **Samsun**: Birthplace of the Turkish Republic, in 1919. This is the largest Turkish port on the Black Sea.

Sights in **Sivas:** Excelent remains of 13th century Seljuq Turkish architecture. See the

11th century Great Mosque. The museum in the 13th century Blue Medrese (theological college). The mausoleum of Sultan Kay-Kaus I in the 13th century Medresesi. The intricately-carved facade and minarets of the Cifte Minare Medrese. The royal throne and other relics in the nearby Armenian Monastery of the Holy Cross.

Haydarpasa (Istanbul) - Mersin 4022

Dep. Haydarpasa	09:00 (1)	Dep. Mersin	21:30
Arr. Yenice	06:21 (2)	Arr. Yenice	22:15
Change trains.		Change Trains.	
Dep. Yenice	06:54	Dep. Yenice	22:30 (3)
Arr. Mersin	07:33	Arr. Haydarpasa	20:50 (4)

(1) Runs Tuesday, Thursday and Sunday. (2) Day 2 from Haydarpasa. (3) Runs Tuesday, Thursday and Saturday. Carries sleeping car. (4) Day 2 from Yenice.

Sights in **Mersin:** This is Turkey's principal port on the Mediterranean, surrounded by citrus groves. See Eski Cami (the Old Mosque) and Yeni Cami (the New Mosque). Crusaders' castles. Roman ruins.

Haydarpasa (Istanbul) or Ankara - Adana

	4022	4020
Dep. Haydarpasa	-0-	09:00 (3)
Dep. Ankara	19:00 (1)	-0-
Arr. Adana	06:15 (2)	06:55 (2)

Sights in **Adana:** This city was founded about 1,000 B.C. See: The second-century stone bridge, Tas Kopru. The 16th century Ulu (Great) Mosque. The 15th century Akca and Ramazanoglu mosques. The Archaelogical Museum.

	4022	4020
Dep. Adana	21:18 (4)	21:21 (5)
Arr. Ankara	09:15 (2)	-0-
Arr. Haydarpasa	-0-	20:50 (2)

(1) Reservation required. Supplement charged. First-class only. Runs Monday, Wednesday, Friday and Saturday. Carries a sleeping car . Also has couchettes. Restaurant car. (2) Day 2. (3) Runs Tuesday, Thursday and Sunday. Carries sleeping car. (4) Reservation required. Supplement charged. Runs Monday, Wednesday, Friday and Sunday. Carries a sleeping car. Also has couchettes. Restaurant car. (5) Runs Tuesday, Thursday and Saturday. Carries a sleeping car.

Haydarpasa (Istanbul) - Izmit 4027

Dep. Haydarpasa	08:30 (1)	09:00 (2)	13:30 (3)	17:30 (4)	20:00 (4+7)
Arr. Izmit	09:55	10:30	14:40	18:55	21:30

(Sightseeing, return trip and footnotes appear on page 516.)

Sights in **Izmit:** The remains of the ancient Roman walls. The Clock Tower. The Museum. The Pertev Pasha Mosque.

Dep. Izmit	04:41 (5)	06:01 (1)	06:21 (3)	07:32 (4)	08:19 (4+8)
Arr. Haydarpasa	06:30	07:45	08:00	09:15	10:00

(1) First class only. Restaurant car. (2) Runs Tuesday, Thursday and Sunday. (3) Reservation Required. Supplement charged. First class only. Restaurant car. (4) Restaurant car. (5) Supplement charged. First class only. Restaurant car. (6) Runs Monday, Wednesday and Friday. (7) Plus other departures from Haydarpasa at 21:00(4), 23:00(3) and 23:30(3). (8) Plus other departures from Izmit at 15:18(1), 19:04(6) and 20:08(3).

Haydarpasa (Istanbul) - Konya 4022

Dep. Haydarpasa	09:00 (1)	20:00 (2)	23:30 (3)
Arr. Konya	23:20	08:02	12:02

Sights in **Konya:** Inhabited since 3,000 B.C. This has been a holy Islamic city since the death there of the 13th century Mevlana Jalludin Rumi, founder of the Mevlevi order.

The legend is that when Mevlana walked by a goldsmith's shop one day, he heard "Allah" every time a worker hit the metal with a hammer. Mevlana whirled in ecstasy in the middle of the street. This started the tradition of the Whirling Dervishes. The 13th century Mevlana Mausoleum, ancient monastery of the Whirling Dervishes, decorated with greenish-blue tiles, is now a museum.

See the ebony pulpit, 42 Roman columns and sarcophagi of many sultans in the 13th century Alaeddin Mosque. Nearby, the 13th century Karaty College and the interesting ceramics in the ruins of the Seljuk Palace. The Museum of Wood and Stone Carving in the Minare Medrese (Koranic school).

The collection of Roman sarcophagi and statues in the Archaeological Museum, next to the Seljuk Sahip Ata Mosque. The 13th century Iplikci Mosque and Sircali College. The 16th century Selimiye Mosque. The collection of Islamic Art in the Koyunoglu Museum.

Dep. Konya	06:50 (4)	16:30 (3)	21:20 (2)
Arr. Haydarpasa	20:50	06:30	09:15

(1) Runs Tuesday, Thursday and Sunday. (2) Carries sleeping car and restaurant car. (3) Reservation required. Supplement charged. First-class only. Has couchettes and car with reclining seats. Restaurant car. (4) Runs Wednesday, Friday and Sunday.

Haydarpasa (Istanbul) - Adana - Fevzipasa - Halab (Aleppo) 4020

Dep. Haydarpasa	09:00 (1)	Dep. Fevzipasa	11:45 (3)
Arr. Adana	06:55 (2)	Arr. Halab	17:01 (4)
Dep. Adana	08:17 (3)		
Arr. Fevzipasa	11:24		
Change trains.			

(1) June–September: Runs Thursday and Sunday. October–May: runs Thursday only. (2) Day 2. (3) June–September: runs Friday and Monday. October–May: runs Friday only. (4) Arrives same day as departure from Fevzipasa.

Chapter 10

AFRICA

The longest rail trip on this continent is from Johannesburg, South Afriica to Dar es Salaam, Tanzania. This journey takes you through Botswana, Zimbabwe and Zambia. It can take up to 7 days, depending on the intervals between connections.

Here are the various segments and the pages in our book where they can be found.

ALGERIA

Children under 4 travel free. Half-fare for children 4–9. Children 10 and over must pay full fare.

The train lines here are standard-gauge. Algeria's rail system consists of one east-west route (connecting Tunisia with Morocco) from which there are 4 spurs heading north to Mediterranean ports (Annaba, Skikda, Bejaia and Tizi Ouzou) and 3 southern routes (Annaba–Tebessa, Constantine–Touggourt, and Mohammadia–Bechar, the last 2 going through the Atlas Mountains to the Sahara Desert).

Algiers

See the shops, cafes and unique narrow streets of the Kasbah. The Marechal Franchet d'Esperey Museum. The fabulous palaces (Summer and Winter) of the Governor-General. Many fine mosques. The view of little islands, harbor and city from Notre-Dame d'Afrique Church.

The splendid Jardin d'Essai du Hamma botanical gardens. The view from Saint-Raphael Park. Nearby, several good seashore resorts: **Moretti**, **Zeralda**, etc.

Constantine

Located on the eastern edge of the Kabylia mountain area. Rebuilt by the Roman emperor Constantine in AD 312, after the city was destroyed in the previous year. The ancient section of the city is on top of a steep rock. See: The spectacular gorges of the **Rhummel River**, which surround 3 sides of the city.

The elaborate Ahmed Bey Palace. Medina, the Moslem Quarter. The Gustav Mercier Museum. Nearby: restored ruins of ancient Roman towns: Tebessa, Timgad, Djemila. Several Berber villages.

There is much good Berber handicraft in this area: pottery, carved furniture, enamel-inlaid jewelry. Shoes and saddles made here are famous for exceptional leatherwork.

Transcontinental Algerian Rail Routes

The 3 services listed here and on page 519 are Algeria's only train connections with countries adjacent to it, Tunisia and Morocco.

Algiers - Constantine - Annaba - Tunis

2545

Dep. Algiers	07:05 (1)	14:00 (2)	19:00 (3)	21:05	22:00
Arr. Constantine	14:51	21:43	02:33	05:18	06:52
Dep. Constantine	-0-	-0-	02:43	05:28	-0-
Arr. Annaba	-0-	-0-	05:26 (3)	08:23	-0-

2550 + 2601

Dep. Annaba	09:30 (3)
Arr. Ghardimaou	13:24

Set your watch forward one hour.

Dep. Ghardimaou	14:23 (2)
Arr. Tunis	17:27

(1) Air-conditioned train. Buffet. (2) Buffet. (3) Direct train Algiers–Tunis. No train change in Annaba. Has couchettes. Light refreshments.

Sights in **Annaba:** This old city was settled by Phoenicians in the 12th century B.C. See: The narrow streets of the old town. The 11th century Sidi Bou Merouan Mosque. (Its columns were taken from Roman ruins.) The 18th century Salah Bey Mosque. The Place d'Armes. **Hippo Regius**, one mile south, was a rich city of Roman Africa until AD 300. Many of the archaeological finds from it are exhibited at the Hippo Museum.

Algiers - Oran 2542

Dep. Algiers	07:30 (1)	11:30 (1)	17:15 (1)	21:30	22:30 (2)
Arr. Oran	13:21	17:40	23:07	05:25	06:06

Sights in **Oran:** This city has 3 sections: La Blanca (the 16th century Spanish city on the hill), La Marine (near the Mediterranean) and La Ville Nouvelle (on the right bank of the Raz el-Ain River).

See: The Turkish Citadel, Santa Cruz. The early 19th century Cathedral of Saint-Louis. The fountain in the 18th century Place Emerat. The 18th century Porte de Canastel. The Great Mosque.

The Sidi al-Hawwari Mosque. Nearby, the Kasbah. Chateau Neuf, once the residence of the rulers and later the headquarters of the French colonial army. The harem of the rulers. The 18th century Jewish cemetery.

The Roman and Punic exhibits at the Municipal Museum. The collection of Islamic art in the Tlemcen Museum. The Aubert Library.

Dep. Oran	06:35 (1)	14:40 (1)	17:00 (1)	21:25	22:50 (2)
Arr. Algiers	12:30	20:25	22:52	05:22	05:44

(1) Buffet car. (2) Has couchettes. Light refreshments.

Algiers - Oran - Fez - Meknes - Rabat - Casablanca - Marrakech

2542		2510	
Dep. Algiers	22:30 (1)	Dep. Oujda	21:24 (3)
Arr. Oran	06:06	Dep. Fez	03:12
Change trains.		Dep. Meknes	04:00
2540		Dep. Rabat (Ville)	06:50
Dep. Oran	07:05	Arr. Casablanca (Port)	08:01
Arr. Maghnia	11:54	Change trains **and stations** !	
Dep. Maghnia	N/A (2)	2512	
Arr. Oujda	N/A	Dep. Casablanca (Voy.)	09:39 (4+5)
Change trains.		Arr. Marrakech	12:43

(1) Has couchettes. Light refreshments. (2) Service "temporarily" suspended in 1985. (3) Supplement charged. Air-conditioned. Carries sleeping car and couchettes. Light refreshments. (4) Supplement charged. Air-conditioned. Light refreshments. (5) Plus other departures from Casablanca at 12:08 (4) and 19:13 (4), arriving Marrakech 15:13 and 22:17.

Northern Algerian Rail Routes appear on Page 520

Northern Algerian Rail Routes

Here are the schedules for the 3 short spurs heading north from the transcontinental train route.

Constantine - Skikda 2547

Both of these trains are second-class only.

Dep. Constantine	06:00	17:40	Dep. Skikda	05:50	17:45
Arr. Skikda	07:25	19:05	Arr. Constantine	07:21	19:22

Sights in **Skikda:** Ruins of the largest Roman theater in Algeria. Roman antiquities in the City Museum.

Skikda - Annaba

2547

Dep. Skikda	05:50 (1)
Arr. Ramdane Djamal	06:36

Change trains. 2545

Dep. Ramdane Djamal	06:49
Arr. Annaba	08:23

* * *

These 1991 connections made this journey impractical that year.

Dep. Annaba	18:00	22:15
Arr. Ramdane Djamal	19:21	23:40

Change trains. 2547

Dep. Ramdane Djamal	07:02 (1)	18:42 (1)
Arr. Skikda	07:25	19:05

(1) Second-class only.

Algiers - Bejaia 2545

Dep. Algiers	05:55 (1)	08:00 (2)	14:00 (3)	14:55 (1)	19:00
Arr. Beni Mansour	-0- (1)	-0- (2)	16:55	-0- (1)	21:50
Change trains					
Dep. Beni Mansour	-0	-0-	17:30 (4)	-0-	22:05 (4)
Arr. Bejaia	11:19	12:44	19:07	20:25	23:35

* * *

Dep. Bejaia	05:50 (1)	13:20 (4)	14:45 (1)	16:17 (4)
Arr. Beni Mansour	-0- (1)	15:03	-0- (1)	17:54
Change trains.				
Dep. Beni Mansour	-0-	15:25 (3)	-0-	18:16 (3)
Arr. Algiers	11:20	18:28	20:11	21:20

(1) Direct train. No train change in Beni Mansour. (2) Second-class only. Direct train. No train change in Beni Mansour. (3) Buffet. (4) Second-class only.

Sights in **Bejaia:** There are many Roman ruins in this area.

Southern Algerian Rail Routes

The following schedules are for the 3 Algerian train lines going south from the transcontinental route.

Annaba - Souk Ahras - Tebessa 2550

All of these trains are second-class only.

Dep. Annaba	16:44	Dep. Tebessa	04:15
Arr. Souk Ahras	18:57	Arr. Souk Ahras	06:41
Change trains.		Change trains.	
Dep. Souk Ahras	19:22	Dep. Souk Ahras	06:42
Arr. Tebessa	21:49	Arr. Annaba	08:59

Sights in **Tebessa:** Founded by Romans in AD 71. Some of the finest Roman remains in Africa are in this area, including the 2nd century Arch of Caracalla. Only one mile to the north are the Roman ruins of the Temple of Minerva, thermal baths, and an amphitheater at the same site as a beautiful Christian basilica.

See the 6th century walled Byzantine Citadel, with 4 gates and 12 towers.

Carpets made here are among the best manufactured in Algeria.

Constantine - Biskra - Touggourt 2546

Dep. Constantine	05:45	18:00	Dep. Touggourt	00:45	12:30
Arr. Biskra	09:18	21:44	Arr. Biskra	04:56	16:46
Dep. Biskra	09:28	-0-	Dep. Biskra	05:06	16:56
Arr. Touggourt	14:43	-0-	Arr. Constantine	08:57	20:43

Sights in **Biskra:** An ancient Roman outpost, now a popular Winter resort. Five miles to the west is the hot sulphur spring famous for medicinal value, Hamman Salahin ("Bath of the Saints"). Many oases here.

Sights in **Touggourt:** A typical Saharan town. There are many dried mud buildings here. See the tremendous fortress minaret. The clock tower in the Kasbah. The tombs of the kings. Many date palms in this oasis. Nearby, the tomb of Sidi el-Hadj Ali.

Mohammadia - Bechar 2543

All of these trains are second-class only and carry a buffet car.

Dep. Mohammadia	08:10 (1)	18:35 (2)
Arr. Bechar	00:03	10:57
	* * *	
Dep. Bechar	05:40 (1)	15:40 (2)
Arr. Mohammadia	21:28	07:16

(1) Operates from mid-October to mid-April. (2) Operates from mid-April to mid-October.

Sights in **Bechar:** The city lies at the base of 1,600-foot high Djebel Bechar. Many date palm groves in this area. There are interesting covered narrow streets in the Arab section. Good leatherwork and jewelry are produced here.

ANGOLA

Children under 3 travel free. Half-fare for children 3–11. Children 12 and over must pay full fare.

The 3 parallel west–east rail lines in Angola start at seaports on the South Atlantic coastline and run inland. One of these, beginning in Lobito, connects at Dilolo with a train service in Zaire and ultimately provides also a train link with Zambia (at Ndola) and then on to Tanzania, Rhodesia, Mozambique, Botswana and South Africa. This route is part of the trans-African railway line.

Luanda - Malanje 3420

This line has 2 short spurs, one to Dondo and another to a hill station, Golungo Alta.

Dep. Luanda	06:00 (1)	08:45 (3)
Arr. N'Dalatando	12:24 (2)	13:35 (2)
Arr. Malanje	N/A	N/A

Sights in **Luanda**: The capital of Angola. A major harbor. See the Angola Museum. The Bunda Museum. The old Sao Miguel Fort. The 17th century Chapel of Nazareth. The Zoological Museum.

Sights in **Malanje**: The 350-foot high Duque de Braganca Falls. The Pungo Andongo stones, enormous black monoliths that figure in tribal legends. To the south, the Game Reserve.

Dep. Malanje	N/A (2)	N/A (2)
Dep. N'Dalatando	12:50 (1)	15:50 (4)
Arr. Luanda	19:42	21:00

(1) Runs daily, except Sunday and holidays. Restaurant car. Second and third-class only. (2) Service N'Dalatando–Malanje and v.v. was temporarily suspended in 1989. (3) Runs Tuesday and Thursday. Light refreshments. (4) Runs Thursday and Sunday. Light refreshments.

Luanda - Dondo 3420

These train carry only second-class and third-class space. All have light refreshments.

Dep. Luanda	13:50 (1)	14:05 (2)	Dep. Dondo	05:50 (3)	06:00 (4)
Arr. Dondo	19:50	20:05	Arr. Luanda	11:29	12:12

(1) Runs Monday–Friday, except holidays. (2) Runs Saturday only. (3) Runs Monday only. (4) Runs Tuesday–Saturday.

Luanda - Golungo Alta 3420

Dep. Luanda	06:00 (1)	Dep. Golungo Alta	07:30 (3)	08:30 (2)
Arr. Canhoca	11:38	Arr. Canhoca	08:40	11:05
Change trains.		Change trains.		
Dep. Canhoca	12:10 (2)	Dep. Canhoca	13:38 (1)	16:45 (4)
Arr. Golungo Alta	14:44	Arr. Luanda	19:42	21:00

(1) Runs daily, except Sundays and holidays. Restaurant car. Has only second-class and third-class space. (2) Runs Monday, Tuesday, Friday and Saturday. Has only second-class and third-class space. (3) Second-class only. Runs daily. (4) Runs Thursday and Sunday. Light refreshments.

Lobito - Dilolo - Lubumbashi

The 1,208-mile-long Benguela Railway is a major segment of Africa's only transcontinental rail line. When operating, there is service from Lobito (on the Atlantic Ocean) to Dilolo on the Zaire border, where the Benguela joins other lines that pass through the copper fields of Zaire and Zambia, terminating at the Indian Ocean cities of Beirain (Mozambique) and Dar es-Salaam (Tanzania).

Construction of the Benguela line took from 1903 to 1929.

There is outstanding scenery in the first 40 miles and an ascent from sea level to 6,000 feet in the first 250 miles, after which the train descends to 4,000 feet and goes through eucalyptus forests.

The country was once a colony of Portugal. A civil war began in Angola in 1975, when Portugal withdrew its troops and other government authorities. Passenger service over the complete Lobito–Dilolo route was first suspended in 1975 due to anti-government guerrillas attacking trains by bombing and derailing. The war ended in 1991.

3421

Dep. Lobito	N/A (1)	N/A (1)
Arr. Dilolo	N/A	N/A
Change trains 3206		
Dep Dilolo	00:01 (2)	03:30 (4)
Arr Lumbumbashi	05:05 (3)	06:05 (3)

(1) Since 1980, it has been reported that this service is in operation, circumstances permitting. Times have not been available. (2) Runs Saturday only. Has restaurant car. (3) Day 2 from Dilolo. (4) Runs Tuesdays only. Has deluxe class space, couchettes and a restaurant car.

Mocamedes - Lubango - Jamba - Menongue 3422

This train ascends from sea level to 5,000 feet on this route.

Dep. Mocamedes	22:55 (1)	Dep. Menongue	N/A (3)
Dep. Lubango	06:00 (2)	Dep. Jamba	06:00 (4)
Arr. Jamba	15:30 (3)	Dep. Lubango	15:40 (4)
Arr. Menongue	N/A (3)	Arr. Mocamedes	23:00

(1) Runs Thursday only. (2) Runs Friday only. (3) Service Jamba–Menongue has been "temporarily" suspended since prior to 1983. This train runs only "if circumstances permit". (4) Runs Saturday only.

524

BENIN

Previously called Dahomey.

Children under 4 travel free. Half-fare for children 4–9. Children 10 and over must pay full fare.

Cotonou - Ouidah - Segboroue 3022

All of these trains are second-class only.

Dep. Cotonou	09:13	18:00
Arr. Ouidah	10:33	19:25
Arr. Segboroue	-0-	20:21

Sights in **Ouidah**: This was a European slave trade center in the 18th century. See the 16th century Portuguese fort. The Cathedral. The streets lined with colorful blossoming plants and fruit trees. There is an interesting temple of the local traditional religion. Nearby coconut and coffee plantations.

Dep. Segboroue	05:08	-0-
Dep. Ouidah	05:52	11:36
Arr. Cotonou	07:36	12:50

Cotonou - Parakou 3020

All of these rains have light refreshments.

Dep. Cotonou	08:34 (1)	17:10 (2)
Arr. Parakou	17:40	07:00
	* * *	
Dep. Parakou	10:10 (1)	18:00 (3)
Arr Cotonou	19:47	06:30

(1) Runs daily. (2) Runs Friday only. Has couchettes. (3) Runs Sunday only. Has couchettes.

Sights in **Cotonou**: Many interesting markets. The Supreme Court. The National Assembly. Nearby are Abomey and Ouidah (see notes above).

Cotonou - Pobe 3021

Both of these trains are second-class only.

Dep. Cotonou	17:02	Dep. Pobe	06:00
Arr. Pobe	20:55	Arr. Cotonou	09:54

BOTSWANA

Children under 7 travel free. Half-fare for children 7–11. Children 12 and over must pay full fare.

First-class seats are upholstered. Second-class has harder seats and is more cramped. Third-class has wood seats. At night, first-class converts to 4-berth couchettes, second-class to 6 berths. There is a charge for bedding.

The one rail trip in landlocked Botswana (operated by Rhodesian Railways) leads north from Ramatlhabama near South Africa's border to Plumtree and into Rhodesia. It is one of the 2 routes from Johannesburg (South Africa) to Harrare (formerly Salisbury) in Zimbabwe (formerly Rhodesia).

The major tourist attraction here is wilderness preserves, comprising one-eighth of the country's area. They are: Chobe National Park, Moremi Game Reserve, Central Kalahari Game Reserve, Khutse Game Reserve, Gemsbok National Park and Makuasehube Game Reserve.

Johannesburg - Mafikeng - Plumtree - Harrare (Salisbury)

3475

Dep. Johannesburg	13:30 (1)	-0-	
Dep. Mafikeng	21:00	-0-	
Dep. Ramatlhabana	21:35	-0-	
Dep. Gaborone	01:09 (2)	18:30 (5)	
Dep. Plumtree	12:14	09:00 (6)	
Arr. Bulawayo	14:45	12:10	

Change trains.

3451

Dep. Bulawayo	20:00 (3)	21:00 (7)	08:00 (8)
Arr. Harrare	06:00 (4)	07:00 (4)	16:00

(1) Runs Tuesday only. Has first-class and second-class seats which convert to couchettes. Reservation required. Restaurant car Gaborone–Bulawayo. (2) Runs Wednesday only, day 2. (3) Runs Friday and Sunday only. Third-class only. (4) Day 2 from Bulawayo. (5) Runs daily. Has first, second and third-class seats. Buffet service until 06:00 day 2. (6) Day 2 from Gaborone. (7) Runs daily. Has first-class and second-class seats. Light refreshments. (8) Runs daily. Has second and third-class seats. Buffet car.

Sights in **Bulawayo**: See notes on page 582.

BURKINA FASO (UPPER VOLTA)

Landlocked Burkina Faso has one train route, from Ouagadougou to Bobo Dioulasso, and on to Abidjan (Ivory Coast). For schedules, see "Treichville–Abidjan–Bouake–Bobo Dioulasso–Ouagadougou" under Ivory Coast, on page 536.

CAMEROUN

Children under 3 travel free. Half-fare for children 3–9. Children 10 and over must pay full fare.

Only first-class has upholstered seats.

Douala - Nkongsamba 3131

Both of these trains are second-class only.

| Dep. Douala | 06:00 | Dep. Nkongsamba | 13:05 |
| Arr. Nkongsamba | 12:20 | Arr. Douala | 19:20 |

Sights in **Douala**: The 13,000-foot high Mount Cameroun, tallest mountain in West Africa. The beautiful view of the enormous bridge over the Wouri River.

Sights in **Nkongsamba**: Pleasant climate. A popular tourist resort. Many banana, coffee and palm-oil plantations.

Douala - Yaounde 3131

All of these trains have air-conditioning in first-class and a restaurant car, unless designated otherwise.

| Dep. Douala | 06:45 (1) | 07:50 (2) | 13:00 (3) | 19:00 (4) |
| Arr. Yaounde | 10:00 | 11:08 | 16:46 | 22:20 |

Sights in **Yaounde**: Capital of Cameroun. Many streams and shaded avenues. Nearby: The cocoa plantations in a very large forest. The Ekom Waterfalls and the Dschang health resort at the 4,000-foot high Bamileke Plateau. Nachtigal Falls. The Grottos of the Pygmies.

| Dep. Yaounde | 07:15 (1) | 07:20 (2) | 12:50 (3) | 18:35 (4) |
| Arr. Douala | 10:37 | 10:45 | 16:42 | 21:53 |

(1) Runs Monday–Friday, except holidays. (2) Runs Saturday, Sunday and holidays. (3) Runs daily. Does *not* have air-conditioning *or* a restaurant car. (4) Runs daily.

Yaounde - N'gaoundere 3130

| Dep. Yaounde | 07:10 (1) | 18:50 (2) |
| Arr. N'gaoundere | 17:42 | 06:30 |

* * *

| Dep. N'gaoundere | 07:20 (1) | 18:20 (2) |
| Arr. Yaounde | 18:00 | 05:26 |

(1) Second-class only. (2) Has first-class couchettes and second class coaches.

Sights in **N'gaoundere**: Big-game hunting and photography are the attractions here. There are large game reserves nearby.

CONGO

Children under 5 travel free. Half-fare for children 5–9. Children 10 and over must pay full fare.

The rail system in Congo starts at the South Atlantic seaport of Pointe Noire and runs inland to Loubomo, where it forms the two top arms of a"Y", one fork heading north to M'Binda, the other going east to **Brazzaville**, the nation's capital. Kinshasa, across the border in Zaire, has a rail line running to Matadi.

Pointe Noire

The country's main seaport is located on the coast of the Atlantic Ocean, at the end of the Congo–Ocean Railway. The railway was completed in 1934. The city grew rapidly after the port was opened five years later. This city of 200,000 has an international airport.

Brazzaville

This is the capital of the Congo. It is a major port, located in a luxuriant tropical forest on a broad section of the **Zaire River**. This city of 500,000, has an international airport. Visit the nearby scenic rapids.

Pointe Noire - Brazzaville 3170

This is the principal Congo–Ocean Railway.

Dep. Pointe Noire	06:00	12:45 (1)	19:10 (2)
Arr. Brazzaville	20:05	23:00	06:10 (3)
		* * *	
Dep. Brazzaville	06:20	12:30 (1)	18:45 (2)
Arr. Pointe Noire	20:40	22:15	05:20 (3)

(1) Reservation required. Buffet car. (2) Has first-class couchettes. Buffet car. (3) Day 2.

Pointe Noire - M'Binda 3170

Dep. Pointe Noire	06:00		Dep. M'Binda	05:10
Arr. Loubomo	11:13		Arr. Loubomo	12:56
Change trains.			Change trains.	
Dep. Loubomo	14:50		Dep. Loubomo	14:53
Arr. M'Binda	22:42		Arr. Pointe Noire	20:40

528

DJIBOUTI

This was formerly the northwestern corner of Somalia. Its only passenger rail service is the 63-mile portion of the line running from its Gulf of Aden seaport, Djibouti, to Ethiopia's Addis Abeba.

Djibouti - Dire Daoua - Addis Abeba 3251

Information about this journey will be found in the Ethopia train schedules on page 532.

Sights in **Djibouti City:** A major seaport on the Gulf of Aden. See the Palace, on Menelik Square. The Great Mosque, on Place Rimbaud, where a large camel market is conducted.

EGYPT

Children under 4 travel free. Half-fare for children 4–9. Children 10 and over must pay full fare.

Most Westerners prefer to visit Egypt November-March. Summer months are extremely hot.

Egyptian trains charge a supplement for traveling in air-conditioned cars. First-class sleeping cars have single-berth compartments. Second-class sleeping cars have 2-berth compartments. All sleeping cars are air-conditioned. Passengers in sleeping cars must pay 2 supplemental charges: for the sleeping-car and for air-conditioning.

From Cairo, there is one rail line south, to Sadd-el-Ali, where a connection can be made for train travel across the desert in Sudan. This is the only international rail route between Egypt and countries adjacent to it.

The 3 other Egyptian rail routes from Cairo are northwest to Alexandria, northeast to Ismailia (and on to Port Said), and east to Suez.

There is also train service along the Suez Canal, from the city of Suez to Ismailia. Egypt's Mediterranean coastal train trip is between Alexandria and Mersa Matruh.

EGYPTIAN HOLIDAYS

mid-April	Shams en-Nassim	July 23	Revolution Day
June 18	Evacuation Day	September 1	Arab Republic Day
mid-July	Feast of the Nile	December 23	Victory Day

Cairo

See the world's greatest collection of pharaonic treasures, covering the 30 dynasties of ancient Egypt from the dawn of civilization to the coming of the Romans, in the Egyptian Antiquities Museum at Tahrir Square, near the Nile Hilton Hotel. It is open daily 09:00–16:00 (closed Friday 11:15–13:30). The more than 3,000 world-famous treasures of Tutankhamun are on the second floor.

Egyptian life, as it was in the days of the pharaos, can be seen at The Pharaonic Village, on a 33-acre island in the Nile River, open daily 09:00–17:00.

This 2-hour excursion on a barge moves through canals showing activities of ancient daily life: sowing of seed, plowing, irrigation, harvesting, bee-keeping, construction of papyrus boats, brick-making, carpentry, home building and the making of linen, perfume, pottery, statues and papyrus. There is also a tour of a temple and the house of a nobleman.

There are marvelous views of the city from the top of the 12th century Citadel. Located inside the Citadel are both the Military Museum and the Jewel Palace (open 09:00–17:00), in which 19th century items are exhibited, including King Farouk's wedding throne.

Near the Citadel is the 14th century Mosque of Sultan Hussein, which has the tallest minarets in Cairo and is a veritable fortress. Adjacent is Rifai Mosque, worth seeing for its ornate, marble-inlaid floors. It contains the tomb of the last Shah of Iran. See the silver domes and ornate ceilings of the 19th century Mohammed Ali Mosque (also called the Alabaster Mosque for its marble interior).

The 600 stucco filigree windows (each with a different design) at the 9th century Mosque of Ibn Tulun, oldest in Cairo and noted as the world's finest example of pure Islamic architecture. It is near Anderson House, a museum on how a prosperous Cairo family would have lived in the 17th century (open daily except Friday 11:00–13:00).

In Old Cairo, visit the Coptic Museum that is open daily 09:00–6:00 (closed Friday 11:15–13:30), to see its ancient textiles, manuscripts, wood carvings and ivories.

Nearby, the 4th century Church of Abu Sarga (St. Sergius) where, according to legend, the Holy Family stayed when fleeing from Herod. The ancient El Muallaga Church. The 10th century gate, Bab Zuweilla.

The Papyrus Museum, in houseboats near the Sheraton Hotel, has an exhibit on making the early writing material. Nearby, the work of one of Egypt's best sculptors, in the Mukhtar Museum.

The ornate 10th century Al-Azhar Mosque is the oldest university in the Moslem world. Nearby is Wekalet el Ghouri, where local craft from different parts of Egypt are exhibited.

Cairo has several hundred mosques that are open to visitors except during Friday prayers. Women are not allowed to enter mosques after sunset.

See King Farouk's tomb, at El Rifai Mosque. The view of the city and the Nile from the revolving restaurant on the top of Cairo Tower. The Khan al-Khalili Market's tinsmiths, tentmakers, hand-hammered copper and brass trays, cotton caftans, and local inexpensive perfumes. The Ben Ezra Synagogue.

There are exceptional carved wood panels, hand-painted glass, carpets, coins, mosaics, weapons, pottery, copper and silver inlay, jewelry, manuscripts, calligraphy and Persian daggers at the Islamic Museum on Ahmed Maher Square (open same hours as the Egyptian Antiquities Museum). Thousands of bazaars in Cairo.

Cheops (the largest pyramid) and the Sphinx are in Giza, a 25-minute taxi ride from the center of Cairo. A visit to the pyramids at sunset is recommended and also the Sound and Light Pageant (19:30–20:30) in an outdoor theater at the Sphinx, where an English language commentary on the history of the pharaohs is performed daily except Tuesday and Sunday.

The state-owned MISR Travel has a full-day tour to the pyramids that cost $17 (U.S.) in 1991. MISR's U.S.A. office is 630 Fifth Ave., New York, NY 10111.

A one-hour sailboat ride in the evening on the Nile costs about $10. The boats leave from the Shepheards and Meridien hotels.

Alexandria

Egypt's most important port and second-largest city. A very popular beach resort.

Cairo - Alexandria - Cairo 2651

These trains require reservation and are air-conditioned.

Dep. Cairo (Main)	Frequent times from 06:20 to 21:53
Arr. Alexandria	2½–3½ hours later

* * *

Dep. Alexandria	Frequent times from 06:10 to 21:40
Arr. Cairo	2½–3½ hours later

Alexandria - El Alamein 2656

These trains have only second-class and third-class space.

Dep. Alexandria	06:35	10:00	13:40
Arr. El Alamein	09:43	13:15	17:03

* * *

Dep. El Alamein	10:46	14:18	15:46
Arr. Alexandria	14:30	17:10	19:25

Sights in **El Alamein:** There is a small museum commemorating General Montgomery's defeat of Field Marshal Rommel in one of the most famous battles of World War II. More than 8,000 soldiers are buried in large cemeteries in this area.

Cairo - Ismailia - Port Said 2652

These trains have only 2nd and 3rd-class space, unless designated otherwise.

Dep. Cairo (Main)	06:25 (1)	08:15 (2)	09:50 (1)	11:45	15:20 (1+3)
Dep. Ismailia	09:09	10:50	12:25	14:33	18:14
Arr. Port Said	10:30	12:10	-0-	15:50	19:35

* * *

Dep. Port Said	05:25 (1)	10:35 (2)	12:55 (1)	17:15 (1)	18:25 (2+4)
Dep. Ismailia	06:58	12:05	14:30	18:50	19:48
Arr. Cairo (Main)	09:45	14:35	17:10	21:45	-0-

(1) Air-conditioned in second-class. (2) Reservation required. Air-conditioned in first and second-class. Restaurant car. (3) Plus another departure from Cairo at 18:45 (1), arriving Ismailia 21:35...Port Said 23:00. (4) Plus another departure from Port Said at 19:40 (1), arriving Ismailia 21:05, arrivingCairo 23:45.

Sights in **Ismailia:** Many parks and gardens. The Suez Canal. The Sweet Water Canal, built in 1863 to provide thousands of canal workers with drinking water. There are several ancient ruins 10 miles west of here.

Sights in **Port Said:** This is Egypt's second most important seaport.

Cairo - Suez 2654

Dep. Cairo (Pont Limoun)	04:45 (1)	15:35 (1)	18:00 (2)
Arr. Suez	07:25	18:15	20:40

* * *

Dep. Suez	05:55 (1)	07:30 (2)	15:10 (1)
Arr. Cairo (Pont Limoun)	08:40	10:10	18:05

(1) Second and third-class only. (2) Reservation required. Air-conditioned train. Has first and second class coaches. Restaurant car.

Sights in **Suez:** The Canal and this city's 2 harbors. This is a departure point for pilgrimages to Mecca.

Cairo - Luxor - Aswan - El Sadd el Ali (the High Dam) 2655

Pyramids, ancient temples and camel trains can be seen on this route.

In 1991, the price for a reserved seat in an air-conditioned coach was only $21.90 (U.S.) for the 558-mile trip from Cairo to El Sadd el Ali. A sleeping compartment for one person Cairo-Luxor or Cairo-Aswan roundtrip was $194 (U.S.) and $252 for 2 persons. This included the ticket, compartment, dinner and breakfast.

The train's $2 lunch was not appetizing. Better to bring food from one's hotel.

Dep. Cairo (Main)	07:35 (1)	12:00 (1)	12:25 (2)	16:30 (2)
Arr. Luxor	18:20	23:30	01:00	07:30
Arr. Aswan	23:10	-0-	-0-	12:57
Arr. El Sadd el Ali	-0-	-0-	-0-	13:20
Dep. Cairo (Main)	18:40 (3)	19:00 (3)	20:30 (2)	21:05 (2)
Arr. Luxor	04:48	05:18	08:50	10:55
Arr. Aswan	09:15	09:40	14:12	-0-
Arr. El Sadd el Ali	-0-	-0-	14:35	-0-

* * *

Dep. El Sadd el Ali	-0-	-0-	-0-	-0-
Dep. Aswan	-0-	-0-	05:10 (1)	-0-
Dep. Luxor	04:15 (2)	05:30 (1)	10:20	15:35 (2)
Arr. Cairo (Main)	16:50	17:25	21:15	05:15
Dep. El Sadd el Ali	-0-	-0-	-0-	18:30 (2+4)
Dep. Aswan	15:00 (3)	16:00 (3)	18:40 (3)	19:35
Dep. Luxor	19:25	20:13	22:48	00:17
Dep. Cairo (Main)	05:55	06:40	08:40	13:50

(1) Reservation required. Air-conditioned train. Restaurant car. (2) Reservation required. Air-conditioned train. (3) Carries only air-conditioned sleeping cars, both 1st and 2nd-class. Restaurant car. (4) Plus another departure from El Sadd el Ali at 19:30 (2), departing Aswan 20:25, departing Luxor 01:08, arriving Cairo 13:50.

Janet Elliott Cain wrote us that in 1990 her sleeping compartment on a night-train Cairo-Luxor had a wash basin and the bed was fitted with starched and ironed sheets.

"The train was very nice," she said. "The sleeping cars, made in West Germany, were fairly new. Dinner and breakfast the next morning, both included in the ticket price, were served to my compartment. The scenery was lovely. At sunrise, the train crossed the Nile. I could see Arabs waking up from their rolled bedding on the sand and making campfires and coffee."

Sights in **Luxor:** In 2133 B.C. this was Thebes, capital of the Egyptian empire, and on the opposite side of the Nile it was Karnak, the "city of the dead", with the kings' mortuary temples. The obelisk now standing in Paris' Place de la Concorde was brought there by Napoleon from the Temple of Luxor. The ruins of the great temples of Karnak, Amon, Mont, Mut and Khons, and the complex of temples called Amon-Re are the interesting places to see here today. Also, the Colossi of Memnon, more than 60 tombs in the Valley of the Kings, burial grounds of the great pharaohs and their queens.

Sights in **Aswan**: A Winter resort. You can see the ancient quarries from which granite was taken for building the pharaohs' monuments. Four miles north is the Aswan High Dam, completed in 1970, one of the greatest engineering accomplishments in the world. It is 1½ miles long and has 180 sluices.

THE RAIL ROUTE TO SUDAN

Egypt's train connection with Sudan starts with a Nile boat trip from El Sadd el Ali to Wadi Halfa.

El Sadd el Ali - Wadi Halfa 2680

Dep. El Sadd el Ali	16:00 (1)	Dep. Wadi Halfa	16:00 (3)
Arr. Wadi Halfa	08:00 (2)	Arr. El Sadd el Ali	08:00 (2)

(1) Runs Monday and Saturday only. (2) Day 3. (3) Days of operation are not available.

Wadi Halfa - Khartoum 2700

This trip crosses the Nubian Desert.

Dep. Wadi Halfa	16:40 (1)	Arr. Khartoum	16:45	Day 2

(1) Runs Tuesday and Sunday only. Carries sleeping cars. Restaurant car.

ETHIOPIA

Children under 4 travel free. Half-fare for children 4–9. Children 10 and over must pay full fare.

Addis Abeba - Dire Daoua - Djibouti 3251

This ride descending from 8,000-foot high Addis Abeba to Dire Daoua is very scenic, similar to Colorado mountain scenery in the United States.

Notes about **Djibouti City** appear on page 528.

Dep. Addis Abeba	06:10	07:30	19:30 (1)
Arr. Dire Daoua	15:46	17:24	08:45
Change trains.			
Dep. Dire Daoua		19:30	
Arr. Djibouti		07:40	
	*	* *	
Dep. Djibouti		20:00	
Arr. Dire Daoua		06:55	
Change trains.			
Dep. Dire Daoua	06:00	07:30	19:30 (1)
Arr. Addis Abeba	16:27	17:27	08:50

(1) Carries a sleeping car.

Sights in **Addis Abeba**: The depiction of Africa's past struggles, present problems and future progress in the magnificent stained-glass window at All Africa Hall. The lavishly decorated National Palace. The mosaics, ceiling carvings and stained-glass at Holy Trinity Cathedral. The obelisk on Miazia 27 Square.

The Natural History Museum. The Imperial Lion House. The handicrafts for sale in the Empress Menen Handicraft School. The view of the city from Mount Entoto. Haile Selassie I Square. The National Museum's archaeology exhibits. The paintings in the Institute of Ethiopian Studies. The activities every Saturday at Mercato, the city's large marketplace. The heavy traffic of domestic animals on some of the downtown streets. The imperial lions in the small zoo at Jubilee Palace. Several other palaces. St. George's Cathedral.

Sights in **Dire Daoua**: The Mosque. The Muslim cemeteries. Prehistoric paintings in the nearby caves. The Palace.

GABON

Children under 4 travel free. Half-fare for children 4–11. Children 12 and over must pay full fare.

Under construction since 1980, the 293-mile track Ndjole–Franceville went into service at the end of 1986. Cost of the complete 403-mile Trans-Gabon route (Owendo-Ndjole–Franceville) was $3 billion (U.S.).

Scenery on this trip includes grasslands, the rushing rapids of the Ogooue River, and dense rain forests. A first-class ticket for the 10½-hour trip was $128 (U.S.) in 1988 ($85 for second-class).

All of the locomotives and passenger cars were new in 1987.

Owendo

A seaport and suburb of **Libreville**, the capital.

Owendo (Libreville) - Franceville 3160

All of these trains are air-conditioned and have buffet service.

Dep. Owendo	09:00 (1)	20:15 (2)		
Dep. Ndjole	12:06	23:21		
Arr. Franceville	19:39	06:25		
	*	*	*	
Dep. Franceville	09:40 (3)	12:40 (4)	20:10 (5)	21:15 (6)
Dep. Ndjole	16:26	19:39	03:22	04:05
Arr. Owendo	19:36	23:15	06:36	07:13

(1) Runs Tuesday and Saturday. (2) Runs Wednesday, Friday, Sunday and holidays. Has couchettes. (3) Runs Thursday only. (4) Runs Saturday, Sunday and holidays. (5) Runs Friday only. Has couchettes. (6) Runs Tuesday only. Has couchettes.

GHANA

Children under 3 travel free. Half-fare for children 3–11. Children 12 and over must pay full fare.

This country's rail system forms the letter "A", with the western arm running from the Atlantic seaport of Takoradi north to inland Kumasi, the eastern segment going from the port of Accra north to Kumasi, and the cross-arm extending from Tarkwa (on the western route) to the eastern route. The cross-arm is the Takoradi–Accra route.

First-class sleeping car compartments have one berth. Second-class has 4 berths per compartment.

Ghana's rail authorities advise travelers that its engines "are old and not wholly reliable" and therefore "breakdowns may occur during the course of travel." They also state: "The situation is being ameliorated but will definitely take some time."

Applicants for visas to travel in Ghana are required to purchase from the Ghana Consulate in their own country travel vouchers for use in purchasing food, lodging and transportation in Ghana. The price varies according to length of stay in Ghana.

Accra See the port longshoremen carrying crates and bundles on their heads. The spirited nightlife here. The Arts Council of Ghana. The Ethnological Museum. The Science Museum. Nearby: The enormous Volta Dam and, behind it, the largest manmade lake in the world, **Lake Volta**.

Takoradi - Tarkwa - Kumasi 3062

Dep. Takoradi	06:00 (1)	12:00 (1)	14:30 (3)	21:30 (4)
Dep. Tarkwa	N/A (2)	N/A (2)	N/A (2)	N/A (2)
Arr. Kumasi	13:45	20:15	21:57	05:15

Sights in **Tarkwa:** There is much mining here for gold, diamonds, manganese and bauxite. Because of the sand that is found in this area, there is a substantial glass industry here.

Sights in **Kumasi:** The "Garden City of West Africa". The Ashanti kings rule from here. The area is dense forest. See: The Ghana Regiment Museum in the old British fort. The museum, zoo and library at the Ashanti Cultural Center. Good textiles are available here.

Dep. Kumasi	06:00 (1)	11:40 (5)	14:30 (3)	21:30 (4)
Dep. Tarkwa	N/A (2)	N/A (2)	N/A (2)	N/A (2)
Arr. Takoradi	13:40	20:30	21:40	05:15

(1) Runs daily, except Sunday. (2) Times are not available. (3) Runs Sunday only. (4) Runs daily. Carries first and second-class sleeping cars. (5) Runs daily.

Takoradi - Tarkwa - Accra 3060

Dep. Takoradi	-0-	19:15 (2)	Dep. Accra	06:20 (1)	19:25 (2)
Dep. Tarkwa	05:20 (1)	N/A (3)	Arr. Tarkwa	18:35	N/A (3)
Arr. Accra	19:50	07:10	Arr. Takoradi	-0-	07:15

(1) Runs daily, except Sunday and holidays. (2) Carries first and second-class sleeping cars. (3) Time was not available in 1991.

Accra - Kumasi 3061

Dep. Accra	06:40 (1)	20:30 (2)	Dep. Kumasi	20:30 (2)
Arr. Kumasi	19:25	06:38	Arr. Accra	06:21

(1) Runs daily, except Sunday and holidays. (2) Carries first and second-class sleeping cars.

GUINEA

No discounts are allowed for children.

Guinea's 2 rail lines are from Conakry and Kamsar on the Atlantic seacoast to inland **Kankan** and **Sangaredi**.

Conakry - Kankan 2850

Dep. Conakry	07:00 (1)	Dep. Kankan	05:00 (2)
Arr. Kankan	13:00	Arr. Conakry	11:00

(1) Runs Wednesday only. (2) Runs Friday only.

Sights in **Conakry:** Good beaches. The Corniche, a lovely promenade along the seashore. The African exhibits at the Museum. The Mosque. The monument to anti-colonial martyrs. The picturesque Boulbinet fishing harbor. Nearby, the Botanical Garden in Camayenne.

Sights in **Kankan:** This was an 18th century caravan center. The ambience is very Moslem. Many mosques. Much wood, gold and ivory craftsmanship here. A center for trading in reptile skins, sesame, cattle, rice.

Kamsar - Sangaredi 2851

Both of these trains are second-class only.

Dep. Kamsar	11:50	Dep. Sangaredi	16:10
Arr. Sangaredi	15:15	Arr. Kamsar	19:50

IVORY COAST

Children under 4 travel free. Half-fare for children 4–9. Children 10 and over must pay full fare.

This country's single passenger rail route is the 725-mile narrow-gauge Abidjan–Niger Line (constructed by France), running from Abidjan on the shore of the Gulf of Guinea to Bouake, Bobo Dioulasso and then on to Ouagadougou in the grasslands of landlocked Burkina Faso (Upper Volta).

In the 1980's some of the turbine-powered trains had 38 first-class seats in an air-conditioned section of the locomotive. The back of each seat was fitted with a pull-down meal tray. Food could be purchased near Abidjan's railstation. Sandwiches and beverages were sold in a section of the locomotive. During the trip, a waiter sold a full hot lunch. At several stops, women vendors sold meat snacks, stews and fresh fruit. Is this still true ?

536

Treichville - Abidjan - Bouake - Bobo Dioulasso - Ouagadougou

This is the route from the Republic of Ivory Coast to Burkina Faso. People from several different tribes make this trip. Many of the women passengers wear very high-heeled shoes, colorful long dresses, turban-style hats.

The ride was said in 1981 to be quite smooth due to the modern rails and good roadbed. En route to Ougadougou, the train goes through a heavily-foliaged rain forest before arriving at **Dimbokro**. After leaving Dimbokro, the train travels alongside a village of dirt streets and many thatched-roof huts. Women can be seen in that village walking with lumber, large packages and trays balanced on their heads.

Next seen on the route are large banana plantations and a jungle with bright flowers. Adjacent to the Bouake railstation is a 66-room hotel built in 1975, with swimming pool and a restaurant that at least once featured French cuisine in a pleasant dining-room.

3100				
Dep. Treichville	06:00 (1)	08:30 (2)	15:00 (1)	
Dep. Abidjan	06:07	08:38	N/A (4)	
Dep. Dimbokro	09:20	12:33	19:08	
Arr. Bouake	11:25	14:58	21:40	
Dep. Bouake	-0-	15:20	-0-	
Arr. Bobo Dioulasso	-0-	02:35 (3)	-0-	
2740				
Dep. Bobo Dioulasso	-0-	03:05 (2)	06:30 (5)	14:45 (6)
Arr. Ouagadougou	-0-	09:35	11:30	21:05

(1) Air-conditioned train. Light refreshments. (2) Direct train Treichville–Ouagadougou. First class couchettes and first and second class coach cars. Has both a restaurant car and light refreshments. (3) Day 2. (4) Intermediate times are not available. (5) Air-conditioned first-class and ordinary second-class coaches. Light refreshments. (6) Light refreshments.

Sights in **Abidjan**: Chief port and largest city in the Republic of Ivory Coast. See: The exhibits of traditional Ivorian art in the National Museum. The handicrafts at Plateau Market in the enormous Square Bressoles. The 2-story bazaar in Treichville, a suburb. The Adme market. The extravagant President's Palace. The wonderful tropical rain forest, Parc National du Banco, north of the city.

Sights in **Bouake**: Many mosques here. Good textile products for sale. You cannot miss seeing the brilliant-colored clothing worn by the crowds at the open-air market.

Sights in **Bobo Dioulasso**: This is an Islamic center, with many clay mosques. There are good buys here in ivory and bronze products, also traditional jewelry.

Sights in **Ouagadougou**: This is the capital of Burkina Faso. The large street market is very interesting.

KENYA

Children under 3 travel free. Half-fare for children 3–15. Children 16 and over must pay full fare.

First-class compartments convert to 4 berths at night, second-class to 6 berths.

Kenya's one train line is from Mombasa on the Indian Ocean, inland to Nairobi. From there, the rail route forks, one tine running to Kisumu at Lake Victoria and a second tine going to Tororo on the Kenya–Uganda border, and to Kampala, in landlocked Uganda.

Passengers have a view of Tsavo National Park, teeming with African game. West of Nairobi, there are extraordinary views of flamingos and of tea and coffee plantations.

Mombasa - Nairobi - Kisumu 3270

Dr. Norbert Brockman, returning to the U.S.A. in 1990 after 5 years in East Africa, advises us that the Mombasa–Nairobi and v.v. service "is often sold-out, especially in Winter". Early reservations are essential.

Dr. Brockman wrote us that the trains on this route carry only sleeping cars "at modest cost" which Cook's Overseas Timetables do not note and that the food served in Kenyan restaurant cars is good, unlike most African trains.

Dep. Mombasa	17:00 (1)	19:00 (4)	Dep. Kisumu	17:00 (1)	18:30 (1)
Arr. Nairobi	08:02 (2)	08:30 (2)	Arr. Nairobi	05:42 (2)	07:45 (2)
Change trains.			Change trains.		
Dep. Nairobi	17:30 (1)	18:00 (1)	Dep. Nairobi	17:00 (1)	19:00 (4)
Arr. Kisumu	06:40 (3)	08:05 (3)	Arr. Mombasa	07:30 (5)	08:06 (5)

(1) Light refreshments. (2) Day 2. (3) Day 3 after departing Mombasa. (4) Restaurant car. (5) Day 3 after departing Kisumu.

Sights in **Mombasa:** More than 2,000 years old, Kenya's second-largest city (after Nairobi) sits on an offshore island, linked to the mainland by causeway, bridge and ferry. It has been an important seaport since Arab traders developed it in the 11th century.

See the Persian, Portuguese and medieval Chinese porcelain and other artifacts in the museum at the 2-acre, 16th century Fort Jesus, open daily. Behind the fort, on Treasury Street, there is an exhibit of elephant tusks, hippopotamus teeth and rhinocerous horns in the Game Department Ivory Room, where those items (confiscated from poachers or taken from dead animals on the game reserves) can be purchased legally at semi-annual auctions. The silver door at Lord Shiva Temple. The Moorish-style Anglican Memorial Cathedral, with its silver roof.

The stalls of ivory carvers, perfume makers, goldsmiths, spice merchants, tailors, tinsmiths, moneylenders and silk dealers in the winding, narrow streets of Old Town. Colorful articles from the Middle East, Persia, Pakistan and India are sold there. Vendors in the middle of Salim Road offer a large variety of African carvings and other goods. See the National Museum in the 16th century Fort Jesus, built by Portuguese to fend off Turks. In the modern part of the city, visit the African market in Mwembe Tayari to buy Swahili costumes. See the 16th century Manadhara/Mandhry Mosque. Sheikh Jundani Mosque. Kilindini Mosque. The 4 enormous sheet-metal elephant tusks forming an arch over Kilindini Road, the main street. Take a cruise of Kilindini Harbor.

Board a dhow at the quayside of the old port to bargain for brass chests, Arab silverware, Persian carpets, furniture, spices and dates. Take a short ferry-boat ride to the white-sand beaches south of Mombasa. North of the city, see the 20 acres of flowers and lawns in landscaped coral gardens at Nyali Beach. Go on a glass-bottomed boat to look at the colorful sea life.

Try the excellent world-record deep-sea fishing (marlin, sailfish, baracuda) and scuba diving. There are several special marine parks.

A few miles to the north are the 15th century Arab ruins at **Jumba La Mtwana**. Other Arab ruins are 10 miles south of **Malindi**, a colorful resort area where the largest (220 species) aviary in East Africa is located. In Malindi, see the Cross of Vasco da Gama, erected by the Portuguese explorer in 1499. It is a short airplane ride and ferry trip to **Lamu Island**, where there are no automobiles and the scene is the same as it was 200 years ago: robed peddlers riding donkeys on the dusty streets, prayers chanted from the mosques, dhows anchored along the ancient harbor, wood-carvers working on the street corners.

Sights in **Nairobi:** The capital of Kenya, Nairobi is the largest (800,000 population) city in East Africa. It is almost on the equator. However, it is one mile high, making for temperate climate.

See the treasures of Kenya's past and the exhibits of a vast number of birds, insects, mammals, fish, musical instruments, ornaments and tribal weapons in the National Museum of Kenya, a 15-minute walk from the center of Nairobi, open daily 09:30–18:00. Its exhibits include world-famous fossils from the Olduvai Gorge in Tanzania, remnants of earliest tool-making man, and remains of such remarkable prehistoric animals as a giant ostrich, an enormous rhinoceros, and a 2-million-year-old elephant which was brought into the museum by knocking down one of the walls.

Across the street from the museum is Snake Park. Its collection of 200 varieties of snakes, crocodiles and alligators is open daily 09:30–18:00. Visit the Sorsbie Art Gallery. Jeevanjee Gardens on Muindi Mbingu Street. The City Market is farther up that street.

See the trees and flowering plants in the 100-acre Arboretum. Tribal dances performed 14:30–16:00 Monday–Friday and 15:00–17:00 on Saturday and Sunday, as well as tribal jewelry, baskets and 16 replicas of tribal villages at the Bomas of Kenya cultural center. Near it, the lions, wildebeeste, ostriches, hartebeest, cheetahs, rhinos, buffalos, zebras and deer in the 44-square-mile Nairobi Game Park. Hunting in the area has been prohibited since 1977.

A fantastic collection of African railway relics at the Railway Museum, a 5-minute walk from the railstation. African and Western contemporary art at Paa-ya-Paa Gallery. The curios and exotic fruits, vegetables and fowers sold in Municipal Market. Jamia Mosque. The African exhibits at McMillan Memorial Library. The fascinating rust-red and white International House. At the Aquarium, a fine collection of marine life from the offshore coral reefs.

The tapestries, murals, tribal shields and the conference table made from 33 kinds of Kenya wood, in the National Assembly. The Tuesday morning coffee auction at Kahawa ("coffee") House. City Nurseries, with its enormous number of different species of bougainvillaea.

The old books and newspapers in the McMillan Memorial Library, open Monday–Friday 09:00–17:00; Saturday 09:00–13:00.

Sights in **Kisumu:** Kenya's third largest (300,000) city. There are many small fisheries here, on Lake Victoria.

Mombasa - Nairobi - Nakuru - Eldoret - Tororo - Kampala

3270

Dep. Mombasa	17:00 (1)	19:00 (3)	
Arr. Nairobi	08:02 (2)	08:30 (2)	
Change trains.			
Dep. Nairobi	15:00 (4)	17:30 (1)	18:00 (1)
Arr. Nakuru	20:35 (4)	22:30	00:20
Dep. Eldoret	04:25 (5)	-0-	-0-
Arr. Malaba	08:45 (6)	-0-	-0-

3285

Change trains. (6)

Dep. Tororo	07:00 (7)
Arr. Kampala	14:30

* * *

Dep. Kampala	08:00 (8)
Arr. Tororo	15:00 (6)

Change trains. (6)

3270

Dep. Malaba	16:00 (9)	-0-	-0-
Dep. Eldoret	21:00 (9)	-0-	-0-
Dep. Nakuru	03:35 (10)	00:50 (1)	02:25 (1)
Arr. Nairobi	08:45	05:42	07:45
Change trains.			
Dep. Nairobi	17:00 (1)	19:00 (3)	
Arr. Mombasa	07:30 (11)	08:06 (12)	

(1) Runs daily. Light refreshments. (2) Day 2. (3) Runs daily. Restaurant car. (4) Runs Tuesday, Friday and Saturday. Restaurant car. (5) Day 3. Runs Wednesday, Saturday and Sunday. Restaurant car. (6) There is frequent service by jitney-van Malaba–Tororo and v.v. (7) Runs Monday, Wednesday, and Friday. (8) Runs Tuesday, Thursday and Sunday. (9) Runs Wednesday, Saturday and Sunday. Restaurant car. (10) Day 2. Runs Thursday, Sunday and Monday. Restaurant car. (11) Day 3 from Malaba. (12) Day 2 from Nakuru.

Sights in **Nakuru:** The pelicans on the inland saline **Lake Nakuru**. Lake Nakuru National Park.

Sights in **Eldoret:** The temperate climate here is due to the 6,800-foot altitude, which attracted many European settlers in the period when this was an English colony.

Sights in **Kampala:** See notes about Kampala under "Tororo–Jinja–Kampala–Kasese" on page 576.

MADAGASCAR   (Malagsay Republic)

Children under 4 travel free. Half-fare for children 4–6. Children 7 and over must pay full fare.

Maximum health precautions are advisable, particularly against malaria. Tourists (mostly young Europeans) swarm to Madagascar at Christmas, Easter and in August. The most preferable tour season is September and October, when there is the least rain and while the lemurs are having babies.

Twenty nine species of lemurs thrive here (and only here) where there are no monkeys, the most virulent predator of lemurs wherever they are found in the rest of the world. The largest member of the lemur family, the Indri, can propel itself 30 feet backwards, turn in mid-air, and land facing the opposite direction it was facing before it leapt.

There are 3 short rail lines in north Madagascar: Antananarivo–Moramanga–Tamatave, Moramanga to Ambatosoratra, and Antananarivo to Antsirabe. (Antananarivo is also called Tananarive.)

The southern train route is Finanarantsoa to Manakara.

Antananarivo (Tana) - Moramanga - Toamasina (Tamatave) 3330

This is called "one of the world's great rail trips" by British travel writer Mark Ottaway, who also recommends Hilary Bradt's book "Guide to Madagascar".

In 1989, the train carried only one 54-seat first-class coach. Reservations are essential because the second-clas cars are very crowded and require standing for tickets in a line at the railstation as early as 2 hours before departure. The 1988 first-class price for this 13-hour ride was $8.00.

Of the thousands of Chinese coolies who worked on constructing this line 1910–1913, hundreds of them lost their lives. The train goes along the edge of cliffs overlooking raging rivers. From Antananarivo (also called "Tana"), the scenery on the ascent to **Anjiro** (not shown in Cook) includes patty fields and a forest.

Just before Anjiro, the track makes a very large hairpin bend and then descends through a green, bamboo rainforest and goes along the **Mangoro River**. The train's lunch stop at **Perinet** (also called **Andasibe**) allows passengers to dine in the Hotel de Gare there. Staying over in Perinet is recommended for viewing 9 species of lemurs and many reptiles and insects, including leeches. Perinet is *not* shown in Cook.

Shortly before nightfall, the train goes through palm tree groves and along the seacoast (too late to be able to see the view !).

Antananarivo: Capital of Madagascar. Also called "Tana". At 4,000 feet, the air here is fresh and clear. See the 19th century towered palaces of the Imerina kings on the royal estate, above the city. The exhibits of Malagsay culture and archaeology in the Organisation pour la Recherche Scientifique et Technique. The collection of lemurs and other Malagsay animals in the Zoo.

The Queen's Palace, called "Rova", open Tuesday-Saturday 14:00–17:00, Sunday 09:00–12:00 and 14:00–17:00. The Art and Archaeology Museum (17 Rue Docteur Villette)

The stupendous Friday outdoor market (called Zoma), on Independence Avenue. Thousands of booths and "blanket shops" offering leather goods, semiprecious stones, woven baskets, etc. This is the place to flex your bargaining muscles. Most items in this market are intended to sell for half the asking price, and buyers are expected to start bidding below that figure.

Take a taxi or bus 2½ miles from the center of town to the Natural History and Ethnology Museum, garden and zoo complex, called Tsimbazaza. A prize exhibit at the Museum is the skeleton of the "elephant bird", considerably larger than an ostrich and extinct for 800 years.

Sights in **Toamasina**: (Also called Tamatave.) This is the country's chief seaport, on the Indian Ocean. Stroll down tree-lined Avenue Poincare.

There is a wonderful beach and good snorkeling at **Nosy Tanikely**. Drive or fly to **Fort Dauphin** to visit the Berenty Lemur Reserve.

Dep. Antananarivo	06:00	09:10
Dep. Moramanga	09:56	13:00
Arr. Toamasina	17:30	-0-

* * *

Dep. Toamasina	05:30	-0-
Dep. Moramanga	12:53	08:55
Arr. Antananarivo	17:00	12:30

Moramanga - Ambatosoratra 3330

Dep. Moramanga	10:03	13:00
Arr. Ambatosoratra	15:20	17:28

Sights in **Ambatosorata**: Lake Alaotra.

Dep. Ambatosoratra	04:15	06:10
Arr. Moramanga	08:45	11:18

Antananarivo - Antsirabe 3330

This is a very scenic 92-mile ride to 4,000-foot high Antsirabe.

Dep. Antananarivo	05:20	06:10 (1)	11:30 (2)	13:30 (3)	17:15 (2)
Arr. Antsirabe	09:18	10:07	15:22	17:23	21:07

* * *

Dep. Antsirabe	04:50	05:40 (1)	11:05 (2)	13:00 (3)	16:00 (2)
Arr. Antananarivo	08:49	09:40	14:59	17:02	19:56

(1) Operates October 1 to April 30. Runs daily. (2) Runs Satursday, Sunday and holidays. (3) Runs Monday–Friday, except holidays.

Sights in **Antsirabe:** This is a thermal springs resort, situated under 8,674-foot high **Mt. Tsiafajavona**, the top of the Ankaratra volcanic mass. Attracted by the cool climate here, Norwegian missionaries founded this elegant city in 1872. It is actually cold here May-September. The former European area is to the right of the railstation. The Malagsay section with the town's market (Asabotsy) is to the left of the station.

Go a half-mile from the railstation, down the imposing grand avenue, to see the colonial-style (British) Hotel des Thermes.

Among the many short excursions from Antsirabe is the 3-mile one to the volcanic **Lake Andraikiba**. Another is 7 miles to **Lake Tritriva**, particularly interesting for ornithologists and botanists. Also, the 12-mile trip to **Betafo** to see **Lake Tatamarina** and the **Antafofo Waterfalls**.

Fianarantsoa (Fianar) - Manakara 3331

Even more scenic than the Antananarivo–Toamasina route.

Both of these trains are second-class only.

Dep. Fianarantsoa	07:00	Dep. Manakara	06:45
Arr. Manakara	12:30	Arr. Fianarantsoa	12:57

Sights in **Manakara**: The Antaimoro tribe migrated to this area more than 600 years ago. Although they are now Christian, they brought with them and continue to follow many Moslem customs: Arab style clothing and Arabic script. They adapted the script to the Malagsay language. The Antaimoro are located near **Vohipeno**, a village about 24 miles from Manakara.

MALAWI

Children under 3 travel free. Half-fare for children 3–13. Children 14 and over must pay full fare.

Landlocked Malawi's rail system consists of 2 routes that start at Chipoka on **Lake Malawi.** The first goes east, across Mozambique, to Nacala on the Indian Ocean. The other runs south through central Mozambique, ending at Beira (see page 548), another Indian Ocean seaport.

Chipoka - Nkaya - Nacala

3370		3345			
Dep.Chipoka	05:50 (1)	Dep. Entre Lagos	21:30 (2)		
Arr. Nkaya	11:30	Arr. Cuamba	00:41		
Change trains.		Change trains.			
3371		Dep. Cuamba	06:00 (3)	16:15 (4)	17:00 (5)
Dep. Nkaya	08:55 (2)	Arr. Nampula	18:23	03:36	05:21
Arr. Entre Lagos	13:35	Change trains.			
Change trains.		Dep. Nampula		04:00 (6)	16:00 (6)
		Arr. Nacala		11:58	23:58

(1) Runs daily with third class only.Wednesday and Saturday, also carries a second class coach. (2) Third-class only. (3) Runs Thursday only. Has first-class coach. (4) Runs Monday only. Carries first-class sleeping car and first-class coach. (5) Runs Wednesday and Saturday. Carries first-class sleeping car and first-class coach. (6) Runs daily. Has first-class coach.

Chipoka - Blantyre - Limbe - Inhaminga - Beira

3370		3343	
Dep. Chipoka	05:50 (1)	Dep. Dona Ana	N/A (4)
Dep. Blantyre	15:35	Arr. Inhaminga	N/A
Arr. Limbe	16:10	Change trains.	
Change trains.		Dep. Inhaminga	N/A (4)
Dep. Limbe	06:10 (2)	Arr. Beira	N/A
Arr. V.N. Fronteira	15:10 (3)		

(1) Runs daily with third class only.Wednesday and Saturday, also carries a second class coaches. (2) Day 2. Third class only. (3) Train currently terminates at Nsanje—which is 16 miles from V.N. Fonteira. From V.N. Fonteira to Dona Ana is a ½ mile walk along the railway track. (4) This service was suspended in 1985.

Sights in **Blantyre**: The Museum of Malawi. Jubilee Gardens. Rangely Gardens.

MALI

Children under 3 travel free. Half-fare for children 3–9. Children 10 and over must pay full fare.

The 2 rail lines in landlocked Mali are from its capital, Bamako, northeast only 33 miles to Koulikoro, and west to Kidira (and then on to Senegal).

The hot season is March to May. The rainy season is June to September.

Cholera, yellow fever, hepatitis, polio, meningitis, malaria and AIDS are widespread in Mali.

Bamako

This city is on the Niger River. See: The fine display of prehistoric-to-modern exhibits in the National Museum. The handicraft (weaving, jewelry, ironwork, sculpture, leatherwork) in Maison des Artisans (Artisans' House). The interesting marketplaces. The excellent Zoo. The Botanical Gardens.

Nearby, the forests at Lake Mandingues, La Boule National Game Reserve, Lake Ouegna, the Korounkorokale Grottoes, Oyako Waterfalls.

Bamako - Koulikoro 2761

Dep. Bamako	18:00		Dep. Koulikoro	05:45
Arr. Koulikoro	20:10		Arr. Bamako	08:15

Bamako - Kayes - Kidira - Dakar 2760

See page 553 for the complete schedule of this journey.

MAURITANIA

The only passenger rail service in Mauritania is a second-class, limited facility on an overnight iron-ore freight train that runs the 392 miles between **Nouadhibou**, a West African Atlantic fishing and freight port, and **Zouerate**, a mining town.

Nouadhibou-Zouerate 2800

Both of these trains are second-class only and have couchettes.

Dep. Nouadhibou	14:50		Dep. Zouerate	12:15
Arr. Zouerate	05:40		Arr. Nouadhibou	06:18

MOROCCO

Children under 4 travel free. Half-fare for children 4–10. Children 11 and over must pay full fare.

Moroccan trains are all standard gauge. A substantial supplement is charged for air-conditioned trains. The country's 3 classes of trains are: first-class, second-class and economy.

Morocco's rail system runs east from Marrakech to Casablanca and Rabat. It then forks at Sidi Kacem, one tine going to Tangier, the other to Oran (and on to Algeria).

MOROCCO's TRAIN PASS

Carte d'Abonnement   Unlimited travel on trains for one, 3, 6 or 9 months, or one year. Sold at sales offices of Maroccan Railways and at railstations. Prices not published.

Casablanca

Morocco's major seaport. See: The stained-glass at the white Cathedral of the Sacre Coeur. The gardens in the Park of the Arab League. Busy Muhammad V Square. The Municipal College of Fine Arts. Many good beaches.

Fes

Founded in the 9th century. See: The hundreds of columns and brilliant mosaics in the 9th century Qarawiyn Mosque (which can hold 20,000 people), oldest mosque in North Africa, housing the tomb of Idris II, but open only to Muslims.

However, the Attarine Medersa (prayer school), a former dormitory attached to the mosque, can be visited by non-Muslims and is worthwhile seeing for its Marinid decorative art.

The area around the mosque is interesting for its shops: silk, silver, incense, Moroccan leather with gold leaf, nougats, brass, books, copper objects, spices, beadwork, caftans and candles.

See how the rich Moroccans live, at the Museum of Moroccan Art in the 19th century Dar Batha Museum, which is also an ancient university (older than Oxford). The fascinating gate of the Andalusian Mosque. The charming 14th century Medersa Bou Inania (open to non-Muslims).

The Bon Jelud gardens. The multi-colored minaret on the Great Mosque, in the 13th century Fes Jalid complex. Nearby, the olive groves. The extremely high dam, Bin el Widane. The Royal Palace has not been open to the public since 1983.

Marrakech

A popular Winter resort. Good skiing at the nearby 8,000-foot Atlas Mountains. This area is a vast 30,000-acre date palm grove. See: Africa's most famous mosque: the 12th century Koutoubia, with its pale green 220-foot high minaret and the thrilling voice of its muezzin. The 16th century Sa'di Mausoleum. The 18th century Dar el-Beida Palace.

The Moorish gardens at the 19th century Bahia Palace. Marvelous fountains: El Mouasine and Eshrob ou Shouf. The fantastic scenes (dancers, acrobats, musicians, snake charmers, costumed water boys) in the tremendous square, Place Djemaa el-F'na.

The gardens of the Hotel Mamounia. The casino. The olive orchards of the walled 1,000-acre Agdal gardens and the Menara gardens, at the edge of which the Sahara Desert begins.

The costumes of the mountain and desert people, on a shopping visit. The green and blue tiles on the walls of the central court of the 16th century Medrassa of ben Yussef. The monumental palace, El-Badi, with its small museum and nesting storks. Take a ride around the Old City in a horse-drawn carriage.

Meknes

Founded in the 10th century. Stroll on narrow, ancient streets that veer off from the enormous square, Place El Hedim.

See the 25 miles of 17th century walls that circle the city. The heavily decorated gate, Bab Mansour El Aleuj. The large Royal Palace. The immense and beautiful stables and granary (once housing 12,000 horses and their feed) at Moulay Ismail's tomb. Many big gardens, irrigated by a 10-acre artificial lake, and several other large artificial lakes here. The shops with outstanding rugs.

The exhibits of silver jewelry, filigreed boxes, textiles, carpets, luxurious furniture and guns that have nielloed barrels and stocks that are inlaid with mother-of-pearl at Dar Jamai, open daily except Thursday 09:00–12:00 and 14:00–18:00.

The lovely tiles of the Nejjarine Fountain. The bronze doors of the 14th century Bou Inania Medersa (school for studying the Koran) and its beautiful courtyard, paved in marble and onyx. The building is open daily 09:00–12:00 and 15:00–18:00. Nearby, the ruins of the Roman Volubilis.

Rabat

This has been a military post since the 12th century. There are many splendid gardens here: Belvedere, Essai, Udayia, Triangle de Vue. See: The Kasbah. The 12th century Tour Hassan, largest Arabian minaret, once part of a now ruined mosque. The collection of Moroccan art in the King Muhammed V Memorial, and the view from its roof.

The Old Town. G'Naoua, the old fort. The Royal Palace, built in the 1950's. The Friday procession of the king, from his palace to Djamaa Abel Fez Mosque. Fine work is done here in carpets, blankets and leather handicrafts.

Near the Bou Regreg River, the collection of jewelry, costumes, weapons, carpets and pottery in the Museum of Moroccan Arts, located in the Andalusian Gardens. This 17th century building was originally a palace. It is open 08:30–12:00 and 16:00–18:00.

Shops featuring carpets, leatherware, brass, mosaics, thula-wood boxes, spices, clothes and jewelry line Rue des Consuls and Rue Souika. Visit the Museum of Traditional Arts, open 08:30–12:00 and 15:00–18:30. The 12th century Bab ar-Rouah (Gate of the Wind) and the Archaeological Museum. Nearby, the Roman ruins at Sala Colonia (Chellah).

Tangier

Excellent beaches. Extensive night life. See: Grand Socco, the colorful square in the Old Town, and the market stalls by walking through the twisting alleys to the Petit Socco.

Marrakech - Casablanca - Rabat - Meknes - Fes - Oran - Algiers

2512		
Dep. Marrakech	09:08 (1)	
Arr. Casablanca (Voy.)	12:04	
Change trains.		
2510		
Dep. Casablanca (Voy.)	12:45 (2)	
Dep. Rabat (Ville)	14:09	
Dep. Meknes	17:43	
Dep. Fes	19:00	
Arr. Oujda	00:58	
Change trains.		

2540				
Dep. Oujda	-0-	(3)	-0-	(3)
Arr. Maghnia	-0-		-0-	
Dep. Maghnia	05:45		15:44	
Arr. Oran	10:03		20:35	
Change trains.				
2542				
Dep. Oran	14:40 (4)		22:50 (5)	
Arr. Algiers	20:25		05:44	

(1) Supplement charged. Air-conditioned. Light refreshments. (2) Light refreshments. (3) Service Oujda to Maghnia was suspended in 1985, but is scheduled to resume in 1992. (4) Buffet car. (5) First and second-class couchettes. Light refreshments.

Oran - Algiers 2542

Dep. Oran	06:35 (1)	14:40 (1)	17:00 (1)	22:50 (2)
Arr. Algiers	12:30	20:25	22:52	05:44
		* * *		
Dep. Algiers	07:30 (1)	11:30 (1)	17:15 (1)	22:30 (2)
Arr. Oran	13:21	17:40	23:07	06:06

(1) Buffet car. (2) First and second class couchettes. Light refreshments.

Marrakech - Casablanca - Rabat

See Cook's Table 2511 for frequent departures from Casablanca's Port railstation, to Rabat and v.v..

*Although 2 timetables are used by Cook, most of these trains are direct Marrakech–Rabat and v.v., and they do **not** require changing trains in Casablanca unless designated otherwise.*

2512			
Dep. Marrakech	09:08 (1)	18:41 (1)	19:40 (2)
Arr. Casblanca (Voy.)	12:04	121:37	23:04 (3)
2510			
Dep. Casablanca (Voy.)	12:06	21:39	23:10 (2)
Arr. Rabat (Ville)	13:06	22:39	00:01
	* * *		

Dep. Rabat (Ville)	04:22 (2)	08:50 (1+5)	18:19 (1)	22:52 (6)
Arr. Casablanca (Voy.)	05:25	09:37	19:11	23:59 (3)
2512				
Dep. Casablanca (Voy.)	05:40 (4)	09:39 (1)	19:13	01:23
Arr. Marrakech	08:54	12:43	22:17	05:16

(1) Supplement charged. Air-conditioned. Light refreshments. (2) Operates early July to late September. (3) Change trains. (4) Operates from early July to late September. Has couchettes. (5) Depart from Rabat's Adgal railstation. (6) Light refreshments.

Marrakech - Casablanca - Meknes - Fes

2512

Dep. Marrakech	01:00	09:08 (1)	14:15 (1+2)	18:41 (1)
Arr. Casablanca (Voy.)	04:45	12:04	17:11 (2)	21:37
Change trains.				

2510

Dep. Casablanca (Voy.)	06:00 (3)	12:45 (3)	17:15 (1+2)	22:05 (3)
Dep. Meknes	10:38	17:43	21:14	02:35
Arr. Fes	11:33	18:50	22:05	03:28

* * *

Dep. Fes	00:42 (4)	07:22 (1+2)	10:10 (3)	12:05 (3+7)
Dep. Meknes	01:43	08:14	11:13	13:10
Arr. Casablanca (Voy.)	06:48	12:01 (2)	15:51	17:49
Change trains.				

2512

Dep. Casablanca (Voy.)	07:54	12:08 (1+2)	17:16 (5)	19:13 (1+8)
Arr. Marrakech	11:31	15:13	21:09	22:17

(1) Supplement charged. Air-conditioned. Light refreshments. (2) Direct train. No change in Casablanca. (3) Light refreshments. (4) Couchettes. Light Refreshments. (5) Second class only. (6) Arrive Casablanca *Port* station. *Change trains and stations.* (7) Plus another departure from Fes at 14:25 (1) arriving Casablanca 18:54 (6). (8) Plus another departure from Casablance (Voy.) at 01:23....arriving Marrakech at 05:16.

Casablanca - Rabat - Tangier 2510

Dep. Casablanca (Port)	07:15 (1)	12:27 (2)	17:57 (1)	23:10 (4+5)
Dep. Rabat (Ville)	08:16	13:26	18:53	00:10
Arr. Sidi Kacem	-0- (1)	15:00	-0- (1)	-0- (5)
Change trains.				
Dep. Sidi Kacem	-0- (1)	16:25 (3)	-0- (1)	-0- (5)
Arr. Tangier (Gare)	12:58	19:45	23:26	05:37

* * *

Dep. Tangier (Gare)	00:10 (5)	07:22 (1)	08:12 (3)	14:15 (6)	16:22 (1+7)
Arr. Sidi Kacem	03:25	-0- (1)	11:38	17:42	-0- (1)
Change trains.					
Dep. Sidi Kacem	05:07 (2)	-0- (1)	12:44 (3)	18:48 (2)	-0- (1)
Dep. Rabat (Ville)	06:50	11:52	14:34	20:43	21:11
Arr. Casablanca (Port)	08:01	12:51	15:51 (4)	21:47	22:12

(1) Direct train. No train change in Sidi Kacem. Supplement charged. Air-conditioned. Light refreshments. (2) Supplement charged. Air-conditioned. Light refreshments. (3) Light refreshments. (4) Depart/Arrive Casablanca's Voyageurs railstation. (5) Direct train. No change in Sidi Kacem. Operates early July to late September. Has couchettes. Light refreshments. (6) Operates early July to late September. Second-class only. (7) Plus another departure from Tangier at 23:30 (5), arriving Casablanca 05:25 (4).

MOZAMBIQUE

Children under 7 travel free. Half-fare for children 7–16. Children 17 and over must pay full fare.

This country's 3 major rail terminals are its Indian Ocean seaports: **Nacala**, **Beira** and **Maputo,** the capital.

Nacala - Nkaya - Chipoka

The Nacala–Cuamba rail line (second and third sections of the left-hand column) was undergoing reconstruction in 1991. The following schedules are subject to delays and alterations.

3345			Change trains.	
Dep. Nacala	04:00 (1)		3371	
Arr. Nampula	12:04		Dep. Entre Lagos	13:50 (4)
Change trains.			Arr. Nkaya	18:52
Dep. Nampula	15:30 (2)	17:10 (3)	Change trains.	
Arr. Cuamba	03:43	03:38	3370	
Change trains.			Dep. Nkaya	08:40 (5)
Dep. Cuamba		16:00 (4)	Arr. Chipoka	N/A
Arr. Entre Lagos		18:18		

(1) Runs daily. (2) Runs Monday, Wednesday and Saturday. Carries sleeping car on Monday and Saturday. (3) Runs Thursday only. Carries sleeping car. (4) Runs daily. Third-class only. (5) Runs daily with third class only. Also carries a second class coach on Tuesday and Friday. This rail line is currently under construction. Departures from Nkaya terminate in Salima at 14:59.

Beira - Sena - Dona Ana - Villa Nova Fronteira - Blantyre - Chipoka
3343 + 3370

The Beira–Dona Ana portion of this trip was suspended in 1984. When this train operates, passengers must walk ½ mile along the railway track from Dona Ana to Vila Nova Fronteira.

Sights in **Beira**: The ultra-modern railstation.

Beira - Machipanda - Mutare - Harare (Salisbury)

Rail service between Beira and Mutare has been suspended since 1977.

Inhambane - Inharrime 3342

Sights in **Inhambane:** This is a commercial seaport, on an inlet of the Indian Ocean.

This 55-mile trip runs in both directions on Monday, Wednesday, Thursday and Friday.

Dep. Inhambane	05:00	Dep. Inharrime	12:30
Arr. Inharrime	09:36	Arr. Inhambane	19:01

Maputo - Chicualacuala - Somabhula - Harare (Salisbury)

Maputo is the capital of Mozambique. A major seaport.

3344

Dep. Maputo	06:20 (1)	12:20 (1)
Arr. Magude	11:48 (2)	17:30 (2)
Arr. Chicualacuala	N/A	N/A

Change trains.

3452

Dep. Chicualacuala	N/A (3)
Dep. Mbizi	17:50 (4)
Arr. Somabhula	04:11

Change trains.

3451

Dep. Somabhula	10:34 (5)	22:49 (6)	00:01 (7)
Arr. Harare	16:00	06:00	07:00

(1) Second and third-class only. (2) Service Magude–Chicualacuala was temporarily suspended in 1988. (3) Service was suspended at the Zimbabwe border in 1981. It is 5km by road Chicuallacuala–Mbizi. (4) Third-class only. (5) Second and third-class only. Buffet car. (6) Runs Friday and Sunday. Third-class only. (7) Has a first-class coaches. Light refreshments.

Quelimane - Nicoadala - Mocuba 3340

Quelimane is a seaport on the Quelimane River. This town was established by Portuguese in 1761. A 78 square mile coconut plantation is located here.

All of these trains are second and third-class only, unless designated otherwise. All trains are subject to local confirmation.

Dep. Quelimane	03:00 (1)	03:30 (2)	07:00 (3)	13:00 (6)	18:30 (7)
Arr. Nicoadala	03:31	04:28	08:01 (4)	14:01	19:28
Arr. Mocuba	06:09	-0-	11:46 (5)	17:46	-0-

* * *

Dep. Mocuba	-0-	04:00 (6)	06:00 (8)	13:00 (9)	14:00 (10)
Dep. Nicoadala	04:45 (2)	07:50	09:50	15:28	17:50 (11)
Arr. Quelimane	05:43	08:46	10:46	16:09	18:46

(1) Runs Monday only. (2) Runs daily, except Sunday and holidays. Third-class only. (3) Runs Monday, Wednesday, Friday and Saturday. (4) Arrives 07:31 on Saturday. (5) Arrives 10:09 on Saturday. (6) Runs Saturday only. (7) Runs Monday–Friday, except holidays. Third-class only. (8) Runs Tuesday and Thursday. (9) Runs Monday and Saturday. *All times are 15 minutes later on Saturday.* (10) Runs Sunday and holidays only. (11) Plus another departure from Nicoadala at 19:45 (7), arriving Quelimane 20:43.

NIGERIA

Children under 3 travel free. Half-fare for children 3–13. Children 14 and over must pay full fare. First-class seats convert to couchettes at night.

Lagos - Ibadan - Ilorin - Minna - Kaduna - Zaria - Kano 3001

All of these trains have first and second-class coaches, first-class couchettes and a bufet car, unless designated otherwise.

Dep. Lagos (Ter.)	08:00 (1)	-0-	-0-	12:00 (5)	12:00 (7)
Dep. Ibadan	N/A	12:00 (2)	-0-	17:12	17:07
Arr. Llorin	17:25	17:06	-0-	22:16	22:24
Dep. Minna	-0-	04:25 (3)	-0-	09:15 (6)	09:35 (8)
Arr. Kaduna	-0-	08:35	-0-	13:17	13:42
Dep. Kaduna	-0-	08:45	12:05 (4)	13:27	-0-
Arr. Kano	-0-	14:05	17:25	18:35	-0-

* * *

Dep. Kano	07:30 (5)	08:30 (9)	18:30 (11)	-0-	-0-
Arr. Kaduna	12:45	14:00	08:30 (12)	-0-	-0-
Dep. Kaduna	-0-	14:10	08:40	-0-	00:35 (14)
Dep. Minna	-0-	18:05	12:55	-0-	04:25
Dep. Llorin	-0-	03:46 (10)	22:50	08:00 (1)	14:10
Arr. Ibadan	-0-	09:02	05:00 (13)	N/A	20:02
Arr. Lagos (Ter.)	-0-	15:00	-0-	17:35	03:00 (15)

(1) Runs daily. First-class only. Air-conditioned. Restaurant car. Intermediate time was not available. (2) Runs Tuesday and Thursday only. (3) Day 2. Runs Wednesday and Friday only. (4) Runs Sunday only. (5) Runs Monday only. (6) Day 2. Runs Tuesday only. (7) Runs Thursday and Saturday only. (8) Day 2. Runs Friday and Sunday only. (9) Runs Wednesday only. (10) Day 2. Runs Thursday only. (11) Runs Tuesday and Saturday only. (12) Day 2. Runs Wednesday and Sunday only. (13) Day 3. Arrives Thursday and Monday only. (14) Runs Wednesday and Sunday only. (15) Day 2. Arrives Thursday and Monday only.

Sights in **Lagos:** Capital of Nigeria. Second largest city in tropical Africa (after Kinshasa, Zaire). Settled more than 300 years ago. It is a complex of lagoons, sandbars and islands. The islands are: Iddo, Lagos, Ikoyi and Victoria. They are connected to each other and to the mainland by bridges. In a population of over 1,000,000 there are about 10,000 who are European, American or Asian.

See: the large harbor. The Zoo. The Iga Idungaran Palace, occupying 10 acres. The Obun Edo and Ebute Ero markets. The exhibit of Nigerian arts and crafts at the National Museum. The holy Qur'an Mosque. The Government Handicraft Center. The contemporary and historic sculptures in the Orhoghua Art Gallery. The Benin art in the Unikon Museum.

See the large harbor. The Zoo. The Iga Idungaran Palace, occupying 10 acres. The Obun Edo and Ebute Ero markets. The exhibit of Nigerian arts and crafts at the National Museum. The holy Qur'an Mosque. The Government Handicraft Center. The contemporary and historic sculptures in the Orhoghua Art Gallery. The Benin art in the Unikon Museum.

Sights in **Ibadan:** Many streams flow through this ancient city. There are teak forest reserves on the outskirts. Much weaving and pottery here. See the Iba Market. The 130-acre Agodi Garden. Four zoological and botanical gardens. The Central Mosque. Ansar ad-Din Mosque.

Sights in **Ilorin:** The Moorish-style concrete palace and the canopied Mallim Alimi Well, both near the Central Market. Traditional single-story, red-mud houses. The ancient mud wall. Much dyeing of cotton cloth with local indigo, weaving, pottery and leathergoods here. Nearby, the Borgu Game Reserve. There are roads from Ilorin to Ogbomosho, Kabba, Jebba and Kaiama.

Sights in **Minna:** This is a major collecting point for peanuts, cotton, indigo, yarns, tobacco, kola nuts, goats and chickens. Much raffia mats and baskets, brassware, pottery and woven and dyed cloth for sale here.

Sights in **Kaduna:** The name of the city is the word for "crocodile". See the stately Lugard Hall, in Muslim architecture, housing the state legislature. The Geological Survey of Nigeria headquarters. Much manufacturing here: explosives, furniture, soft drinks (kola nuts are collected in this area).

Sights in **Kano:** This city has been a tribal capital since the 11th century. A camel caravan center for many centuries. Kano was the greatest commercial power in West Africa in the 1820's, its leather and cotton goods shipped north, across the Sahara, by camel caravan to Morocco, Algeria and Tunisia where its red goatskin products were called "morocco leather".

The Encyclopedia Britannica carries a photo of tall pyramids built from peanuts harvested here. Kano is divided into 100 hamlets, each having its own mosque. See the Kurmi Market and Juma'at Mosque, both built in the 15th century. The 15th century Palace. Next to it, the Central Mosque (built in 1951), Nigeria's largest mosque. The collection of Hausa and Fulani artifacts at the museum in Gidan Makama ("Makama's House").

Lagos - Maiduguri   3000

Both of these trains have first-class couchettes and a buffet car.

Dep. Lagos (Ter.)	12:00	Sat.	Dep. Maiduguri	20:30	Mon.
Dep. Ibadan	17:07		Arr. Kaduna	00:05	Wed.
Dep. Kaduna	14:05	Sun.	Arr. Ibadan	20:00	
Arr. Maiduguri	16:10	Mon.	Arr. Lagos (Iddo)	03:00	Thurs.

Sights in **Maiduguri:** This city is on the historic pilgrimage path from Senegal to Mecca and is a major gathering center for many agricultural products. See: The Palace. The Mosque. The very large Monday market and the procession of nomads bringing crocodile skins, cattle hides, goats and sheep as well as finished leather products to the market by donkey and oxen. Chewing gum and peanut butter are manufactured here, and the tall pyramids of bagged peanuts is something to see.

Lagos - Jos 3000

This trip involves a short spur off the Lagos–Maiduguri line.

Both of these trains carry first and second-class coaches, first-class couchettes and a buffet car.

Dep. Lagos (Ter.)	12:00 Thursday only	Dep. Jos	15:00 Saturday only
Arr. Jos	00:50 Saturday	Arr. Lagos (Ter.)	03:00 Monday

Sights in **Jos:** Its high elevation makes this a cool resort. See the 60-acre park with the Zoo. The Arboretum. The open-air museum of traditional architecture. The Nok terra-cotta figurines and wood, brass, bronze and pottery artifacts in the Museum, the oldest in Nigeria. The Nok culture flourished in this area from 900 B.C. to 200 A.D.

Lagos - Kafanchan - Port Harcourt

All of these trains carry first and second-class coaches, first-class couchettes and a buffet car.

3000

Dep. Lagos (Ter.)	12:00 Thursday	12:00 Saturday
Arr. Kafanchan	21:00 Friday	21:50 Sunday

Change trains.

3002

Dep. Kafanchan	16:45 Tues. & Sun.	18:15 Monday
Arr. Port Harcourt	15:00 Wed. & Mon.	17:30 Tuesday

* * *

Dep. Port Harcourt	09:00 Mon. & Wed.	09:00 Saturday
Arr. Kafanchan	06:10 Tues. & Thurs.	06:20 Sunday

Change trains.

3000

Dep. Kafanchan	16:45 Tuesday	18:05 Saturday
Arr. Lagos (Ter.)	03:00 Thursday	03:00 Monday

Sights in **Port Harcourt:** Nigeria's second largest port. Much manufacturing here: cigarettes, tires, paper. Also offshore oil drilling.

SENEGAL

Children under 3 travel free. Half-fare for children 3–9. Children 10 and over must pay full fare. Senegal's 2 rail lines are the short ride from Dakar to St. Louis and the long route from Dakar to Kidira and on to Bamako in landlocked Mali.

The rainy season is June–September. The hot season is March–May. Nighttime temperatures are sometimes over 100 degrees Fahrenheit, overpowering hotel air-conditioners. Cholera, yellow fever, hepatitis, polio, meningitis, malaria and AIDS are widespread in Senegal.

Sights in **Dakar**: A major seaport. Capital of Senegal. About 1,000,000 population. There are good museums here on the sea, ethnography and archaeology. Also see: The Victorian railstation. The Zoo. The outstanding scarlet uniforms of the sentries at the President's Palace.

The green tile mosaics in the Moorish-style Great Mosque. The beautiful Church of Our Lady of Fatima in the Cathedral du Souvenir Africain. The making of leather-work, baskets, jewelry and woodwork at the Soumbedioune Artisnal Village. The collection of African art in the Museum of Dakar. The array of gold, silver, exotic musical instruments, produce, spices, jewelry and embroidered African garments sewn to order in a few minutes, all at the covered Sandaga central market. Nearby, the picturesque fishing village, Cayar.

Take the 20-minute ferry ride to Goree Island for a tour of the Slave House Museum. Goree was once the main port for the slave trade. You can see the cells where chained slaves were held before they were moved onto crowded ships.

Dakar - St. Louis 2811

Dep. Dakar	07:25 (1)	13:40 (2)	Dep. St. Louis	06:20 (2)	14:30 (1)
Arr. St. Louis	12:00	18:37	Arr. Dakar	11:02	19:10

(1) Runs Monday, Wednesday and Friday. (2) Runs daily

Dakar - Kidira - Bamako, (Mali) 2760 + 2810

Passengers are subjected to hot wind, dust and diesel smoke on this ride. In recent years the *non* air-conditioned train carried a mail car, 4 very old second-class coaches with wood slat seats, first-class coaches with padded seats dating from the 1950's (similar to a car on a commuter train in the western U.S.A.), and a restaurant car that had a small counter, a refrigerator and an old gas stove. At the end of the train were sleeping cars with dirty compartments, dirty linen, an openable window and an overhead fan.

Because the restaurant car had no tables, diners balanced the plate on their lap. Neither towels nor wash water was available. By the end of the trip, the train was filthy, and the stench from the toilets was very strong. A first-class ticket was $65 (U.S.) in 1990. A berth was an additional $35. Second-class (described as "abysmal") was $40.

Both of these trains carry sleeping cars and a restaurant car.

Dep. Dakar	08:00 (1)	Dep. Bamako	09:15 (1)
Dep. Kidira	N/A	Dep. Kayes	20:30
Dep. Kayes	03:20 (2)	Arr. Kidira	N/A
Arr. Bamako	14:30 (2)	Arr. Dakar	15:00 (2)

(1) Runs Wednesday and Saturday. (2) Day 2.

SOUTH AFRICA

Travel is free for children under 2 years old accompanied by an adult who has paid the full advertised ticket price. Half-fare for children 2–11 who either are traveling alone or when they travel with an adult who has paid a reduced ticket price. Children 12 and over must pay the full price.

Summer climate here is November to mid-April. The peak Summer holiday period is December 12 to January 30.

All major rail lines in South Africa are narrow-gauge (3'6") because so much track is over mountain terrain. However, carriages are only slightly narrower than those used on British, European and North American railways.

Reservations can be made up to 2 months in advance, with one exception: up to 11½ months for "Blue Train" (Pretoria-Johannesburg-Cape Town).

First-class coupes carry 2 passengers. First-class compartments carry 4. Second-class coupes carry 3, and second-class compartments accommodate 6. By paying a higher fare, one person can reserve a first-class coupe, and first-class compartments can be reserved for the use of 2 or 3 people.

Reservation is recommended for all night travel. On night trains, first -class compartments convert to 4 couchette berths and second-class to 6 berths. Passengers are charged for sterilized bedding, packed in a sealed canvas bag. The seal is broken in the passenger's presence, when the attendant makes up the berth. However, bedding and meals are included in the fare charged for Blue Train.

Holders of first-class tickets are permitted up to 100 pounds of free luggage.

A pocket timetable is available free from Spoornet (called South African Railways prior to 1990).

The country's extensive rail system connects inland Johannesburg with 5 seaports: Durban, East London, Port Elizabeth, Mossel Bay and Cape Town. There is train service from South Africa to 3 of the 4 countries adjacent to it: Zimbabwe (formerly Rhodesia), Botswana and South West Africa (Namibia). There was also train service from Johannesburg into Mozambique until guerrilla attacks forced it to cease. In 1989, that service terminated at Komatipoort, near the Mozambique border (table 3346).

The U.S.A. source for reservations on South Africa's main-line trains is: SARtravel Ltd, 1100 E. Broadway, Glendale, CA 91205. Telephones: (800) 727-7207 and (818) 549-1921.

Johannesburg

There are many museums here on archaeology, costumes, transportation, Judaica, geology, medicine and South African history. The railstation, largest in the African continent, has a splended railway museum. Among the exhibits there are models of locomotives and rolling stock from early days to modern times, and old restaurant car menus, tickets, signalling systems, uniforms and badges

See the collection of South African and European paintings (Manet, Monet, Pissaro, Van Gogh, Degas, Renoir, Rembrandt) at the Art Gallery. The Mosque. The Money Museum. Jan Smuts House. The Bensuan Museum of Photography. The Museum of History and Medicine. Replicas of the huts of many different South African tribes in the riverside African Village that is the central display of the Africana Museum.

Hermann Eckstein Park, a complex of a large zoo, the National Museum of Military History, and the Museum of Rock Art. The view of the city from the Carlton Panorama. Visit the Gold Museum at nearby Crown Mines, called "Gold Reef City".

Pretoria - Johannesburg - Pietermaritzburg - Durban

3520

Dep. Pretoria	Frequent times from 04:12 to 22:12				
Arr. Johannesburg	90 minutes later				

Change trains. 3510

Dep. Johannesburg	12:00 (1)	-0-	-0-	18:00 (5)	20:00 (6)
Dep. Pietermaritzburg	02:42 (2)	02:50 (3)	05:36 (4)	05:51 (2)	08:15 (2)
Arr. Durban	05:00	05:10	07:45	08:00	10:30

* * *

Dep. Durban	14:00 (1)	17:30 (7)	18:00 (5)	18:30 (8)	20:00 (4)
Dep. Pietermaritzburg	16:42	19:41	20:24	20:57	22:34
Arr. Johannesburg	05:35 (2)	-0-	07:45 (2)	-0-	10:20 (2)

Change trains. 3520

Dep. Johannesburg	Frequent times from 04:03 to 22:03
Arr. Pretoria	90 minutes later

(1) Runs Monday, Friday and Sunday. (2) Day 2. (3) Runs Monday only. (4) Runs Wednesday only. Restaurant car. (5) Runs daily. Restaurant car. (6) Runs Friday and Sunday. (7) Runs Thursday only. Restaurant car. (8) Runs Friday only.

Sights in **Pretoria:** The streets lined with jacaranda trees. Some of the oldest and most beautiful buildings in town are located around Church Square, the center of the city and the site of the first settlement in the region.

See Paul Kruger's house. The National Cultural History and Open Air Museum. The sunken gardens at Venning Park. The National Zoological Gardens. The Museum of Science and Technology, the only one of this kind on the African continent.

The Voortrekker Monument, commemorating the journey of the pioneers who fought Zulus in 1838. Made of marble and granite, its 27 panels depict the leaders of the battle. There are also 64 life-size ox wagons, the number that were present at the battle.

The collection of coins and minerals from around the world, at the South African Mint. The natural history exhibit at the Transvaal Museum. Works by South African artics at the Art Museum. The National Botanic Gardens.

Sights in **Pietermaritzburg:** Called "City of Flowers" for its many fine botanical gardens and parks. See the Voortrekker Museum. The Natal Museum.

The model native village in nearby Mountain Rise. Many nearby mountain resorts and game preserves, including the Natal Lion and Game Park (lions, giraffes, zebras, ostriches, rhinos and antelope).

Sights in **Durban:** This is South Africa's largest port and the country's major seaside resort, popular for sailing, swimming and deep-sea fishing in the Indian Ocean. Shop for brassware, ivory, carved masks and figurines, spices, fruits, beads, jewelry, gold, silver and semi-precious stones at the Indian Market.

Visit the fabled Orchid House in the Botanic Garden, a wooded area in the center of the city's business district. Also in the city center is the Old Fort, occupied by British soldiers during the Anglo-Boer War. See Snake Park. Japanese Water Gardens. The rose gardens in Jameson Park. The Oceanarium. The motorized cars, trains, ships and airplanes that move around and through a scaled-down (1/24th) reproduction of the city, called Minitown.

There are many nearby game and nature reserves: **Umfolzi** (the rare white rhino), **Hluhluwe** (black rhino), **Mkuzi** (for photographing wildlife congregating at waterholes), **Ndumu** (birdwatching) and **St. Lucia Estuary** (for birdwatching and to see hippos and crocodiles).

Johannesburg - Bloemfontein - East London 3508

All of these trains have an air-conditioned restaurant car.

Dep, Johannesburg	14:50	15:30 (2)
Dep. Bloemfontein	22:06	22:36
Arr. East London	10:45 (1)	-0-
	*	* *
Dep. East London	14:00	-0-
Arr. Bloemfontein	03:13 (1)	05:41 (3)
Arr. Johannesburg	11:00	13:00

(1) Day 2. (2) Runs Tuesday, Thursday and Sunday. (3) Runs Tuesday, Thursday and Saturday.

Sights in **Bloemfontein:** The beautiful 300-acre King's Park. The Franklin Game Reserve. Two astronomical observatories: Lamont-Hussey and Boyden Station. The enormous dinosaur and other fossils at the National Museum.

Sights in **East London:** The 80-acre Queen's Park. This Indian Ocean seaport's Museum has a coelacanth, a primeval fish. Beautiful beaches here. See the Victorian artifacts exhibited at the Gately House Historical Museum. Paintings by South African and English artists at the Ann Bryant Art Gallery.

Johannesburg - Bloemfontein - Port Elizabeth

Both of these trains have an air-conditioned restaurant car. Although 2 timetables are used by Cook's, these are direct trains. **There is no train change in Noupoort.**

3508		3523	
Dep. Johannesburg	15:30 (1)	Dep. Port Elizabeth	16:30 (3)
Dep. Bloemfontein	22:36	Arr. Noupoort	23:56
Arr. Noupoort	03:50 (2)	3508	
3523		Dep. Noupoort	00:30 (4)
Dep. Noupoort	04:10 (3)	Arr. Bloemfontein	05:41
Arr. Port Elizabeth	11:55	Arr. Johannesburg	13:00

(1) Runs Tuesday, Thursday and Sunday. (2) Day 2. (3) Runs Monday, Wednesday and Friday. (4) Runs Tuesday, Thursday and Saturday.

Sights in **Port Elizabeth:** Popular for swimming beaches and deep-sea fishing expeditions. Many fine parks, including St. George's Park. See Fort Frederick, built in 1799 to accommodate British troops. The milking of a puff adder's venom, at Snake Park. Dolphin performing in the oceanarium at Settler's Park Nature Preserve. Nearby is Addo Elephant National Park.

Climb the 204 steps to the top of the 52-meter-high Memorial Campanile for the View from the platform at the top, and hear the ring changes of its 23 bells, performed 3 times a day. Visit the King George VI Art Gallery. Enjoy the fine beaches with gigantic sand dunes at nearby coastal resorts: The Willows, Swartkops, Sea View, etc.

Take a one-day excursion on the narrow-gauge "Apple Express" hauled by a little steam locomotive. Used mainly to transport fruit from the Long Kloof orchards, it becomes a special sightseeing train only on the first Saturday of each month, except during the December holiday period when several additional days are added. Reservations are recommended for this popular $10 trip.

This very scenic 171-mile route is ablaze with wild flowers, fruit blossoms and the fragrance of ripe fruit. "Apple Express" departs Humewood Road Station (near Port Elizabeth's harbor) at 08:30, arriving Loerie at 12:05. The 12:50 departure from Loerie brings passengers back to Port Elizabeth at 16:30. At the railstation, the Humerail Museum has exhibits of the 2-foot gauge system.

Port Elizabeth - Mosselbaai (Mossel Bay) - Cape Town
(TRANSLUX TIMETABLE) 6010

Before it was suspended in late 1987, one of the most scenic train rides in South Africa was along "the Garden Route". Millions of flowers are always in bloom near Mosselbaai, which has the longest growing season of any area in the world due to mild climate and moderate rain. This trip also offers mountain and South Atlantic Ocean seashore scenery.

Bus service is provided by Translux. In 1991, we received its timetable (not carried in Cook) from the U.S.A. source for reservations on South Africa's main-line trains and buses: SARtravel Ltd., 1100 E. Broadway, Glendale, CA 91205. Telephones: (800) 727-7207 and (818) 549-1921.

Dep. P. Elizabeth (Elizabeth Hotel)	06:30	Dep. Cape Town	07:00
Dep. P. Elizabeth (Station)	07:00	Dep. Mosselbaai	11:50
Dep. Mosselbaai	14:00	Arr. P.Elizabeth (Station)	18:45
Arr. Cape Town	19:00	Arr. P. Elizabeth (Elizabeth Hotel)	19:00

Sights in **Mosselbaai:** A very nice seashore resort.

Sights in **Cape Town:** The 17th century houses in the Malay Quarter. The Municipal Botanic Garden, South African Library, Museum and National Gallery, all at what was once the garden of the East India Company. The Africana collection at both the Library of Parliament and the Castle.

Artwork spanning the centuries, at the Cultural History Museum. The South African Museum. The collection of paintings by South Africans in the Old Town House. DeWaal Park. The Military and Maritime Museum in the 17th century Castle of Good Hope. The National Gallery. The Flower Market. Groote Kerk (the "Great Church"). Koopmans de Wet House, a national monument which has exhibits of 18th century Colonial antiques.

See the view from View Point on Signal Hill. The marvelous coastal scenery, either by taking the Penny Ferry on a harbor tour around the Victoria Basin, the bus tour along Chapman's Peak Drive, or the 7-minute cable car ride to the top of Table Mountain.

The bus trip goes to the Kirstenbosch National Botanical Garden and through the Cape Nature Reserve to Cape Point, where the Atlantic and Indian Oceans meet.

Other bus tours go to the many wineries on the Stellenbosch Route and those in the Paarl district.

Pretoria - Johannesburg - Kimberley - Cape Town

This is the route of the wonderful, all first-class Blue Train, which provides 4 categories: "A" (a suite consisting of a bedroom with twin beds, private lounge and a bathroom with tub and toilet), "B" (compartment with one or 3 berths, with its own bathroom having a tub and toilet), "C"(compartment with one or 3 berths, private shower and toilet), and "D" (compartment with one or 2 berths that can be converted to 3 berths). There is only one "A"com- partment. Passengers traveling in a "D" compartment have use of a shower in the carriage.

The food is cordon bleu quality.

Blue Train is so popular that advance seat reservations are nearly always necessary. Due to the heavy demand for travel on this train, space on it can be reserved as much as 11 months in advance of travel date.

Air-conditioning with individual controls. Electrically operated venetian blinds sealed between windows. Suites equipped with refrigerator, wine rack and FM radio reception. Double insulation and advanced construction techniques make this train vibrationless and noiseless. The seats are upholstered in leather.

At 16:30, the "valet" brings tea and the afternoon newspaper.

The schedule provides daytime viewing in both directions of the scenic area through the Cape mountains and over the Hex River Pass between Touws River and Cape Town, during which the line descends or ascends 2,352 feet within one 36-mile section, into or out of De Doorns Valley.

	3500	3519
Dep. Pretoria	10:00 (1)	-0-
Dep. Johannesburg	11:30	12:30 (3)
Dep. Kimberley	19:06	21:03
Dep. De Aar	22:34	00:52 (2)
Arr. Cape Town	11:00 (2)	13:45

* * *

	3519	3500
Dep. Cape Town	09:20 (3)	10:50 (1)
Dep. De Aar	22:28	00:17 (2)
Dep. Kimberley	02:15 (2)	03:50
Dep. Johannesburg	10:00	11:00
Arr. Pretoria	-0-	12:02

(1) "Blue Train". Runs Monday, Wednesday and Friday. Has only sleeping cars. Suites and staterooms are available. Reservation required. Supplement charged. Air-conditioned. Restaurant car. (2) Day 2. (3) "Trans-Karoo Express". Air-conditioned restaurant car.

Sights in **Kimberley:** Many diamond mines in this area. See the exhibit of diamonds at the Mine Museum. Visit the De Beers Mine Observation Platform to view the mine that produces most of South Africa's diamonds. The block square, 14-story Harry Oppenheimer House. The Ernest Oppenheimer Memorial Garden.

The William Humphrey's Art Museum. The collection of Bushman artifacts in both the Dugglin-Cronin Bantu Gallery and in McGregor Memorial Museum.

Durban - Bloemfontein - Cape Town 3501

Both of these trains have an air-conditioned restaurant car.

Dep. Durban	17:30 (1)	Dep. Cape Town	18:50 (4)
Dep. Bloemfontein	09:45 (2)	Dep. Bloemfontein	15:46 (2)
Arr. Cape Town	06:15 (3)	Arr. Durban	07:45 (3)

(1) Runs Thursday only. (2) Day 2. (3) Day 3. (4) Runs Monday only.

Cape Town - Bitterfontein 3524

Dep. Cape Town	20:15 (1)	Dep. Bitterfontein	12:50 (3)
Arr. Klawer	06:42 (2)	Arr. Klawer	18:23
Change trains.		Change trains.	
Dep. Klawer	08:00 (3)	Dep. Klawer	19:20 (4)
Arr. Bitterfontein	12:39	Arr. Cape Town	06:00 (2)

(1) Runs Friday and Sunday. (2) Day 2. (3) Runs Monday only. (4) Runs Monday and Sunday.

Johannesburg - Harare (Salisbury)

The train route through Botswana to Zimbabwe.

3475		3451	
Dep. Johannesburg	13:30 (1)	Dep. Bulawayo	21:00 (3)
Dep. Mafikeng	21:00	Arr. Harare	07:00 (4)
Dep. Gaborone	01:09 (2)		
Arr. Bulawayo	14:45		
Change trains.			

(1) Runs Tuesday only. Reservation required. Restaurant car Gaborone–Bulawayo. Coach seats convert to couchettes. (2) Day 2. Runs Wednesday only. (3) Runs daily. Light refreshments. Coach seats convert to couchettes. (4) Day 2 after departing Bulawayo.

Johannesburg - De Aar - Keetmanshoop - Windhoek

One of the 2 train routes to South West Africa (Namibia).

"Trans-Karoo" is the only practical connection Johannesburg–DeAar and v.v. because of reservation restrictions imposed by "Blue Train" on passengers riding only this portion of its Johannesburg–Cape Town route.

Seats convert to couchettes on all of the overnight trains shown here.

3519			3600		
Dep. J'burg	12:30 (1)		Dep. Windhoek	12:00 (2)	18:45 (5)
Arr. De Aar	00:30		Arr. De Aar	17:10 (6)	06:27 (6)
Change trains.			Change trains		
3600			3519		
Dep. De Aar	00:55 (2)	02:00 (4)	Dep. De Aar	22:28 (1)	
Arr. Windhoek	08:05 (3)	13:10 (3)	Arr. J'burg	10:00 (7)	

(1) "Trans-Karoo". Runs daily. Air-conditioned restaurant car. (2) Runs Saturday only. Buffet. (3) Day 2 from De Aar (4) Runs Monday and Thursday. Light refreshments only on Monday.   (5) Runs Wednesday and Sunday. Light refreshments only on Wednesday. (6) Day 2 from Windhoek. (7) Day 3 from Windhoek.

Sights in **De Aar:** A major rail junction. Train buffs come here to see old steam trains. A very hot desert climate .

Sights in **Windhoek:** The capital of South West Africa (Namibia). Many hot springs in this area. Karakul (Persian lamb) graze here, and the furs are processed in this area. See the collection of very large meteorites in the State Museum. The lovely gardens around Christ Church. The 3 hilltop castles. Tourists come here for the Carnival (late April, early May) and the big Oktoberfest.

Cape Town - De Aar - Windhoek

The other train route to South West Africa (Namibia).

"Trans-Karoo" is the only practical connection Johannesburg–DeAar and v.v. because of reservation restrictions imposed by "Blue Train" on passengers riding only this portion of its Johannesburg–Cape Town route.

Seats convert to couchettes on all of the overnight trains shown here.

3519			3600		
Dep. Cape Town	09:20 (1)	18:50 (4)	Dep. Windhoek	12:00 (2)	18:45 (7)
Arr. De Aar	22:11	07:43	Arr. De Aar	17:10 (6)	06:27 (8)
Change trains.			Change trains		
3600			3501 + 3519		
Dep. De Aar	00:55 (2)	02:00 (5)	Dep. De Aar	00:52 (1)	17:00 (9)
Arr. Windhoek	08:05 (3)	13:10 (3)	Arr. Cape Town	13:45 (7)	06:15 (10)

(1) "Trans Karoo". Runs daily. Air-conditioned restaurant car. (2) Runs Saturday only. Buffet. (3) Day 2 from De Aar. (4) Runs Monday only. Restaurant car. (5) Runs Monday and Thursday. Has light refreshments only on Monday. (6) Day 2 from Windhoek. (7) Runs Wednesday and Sunday. Light refreshments only on Wednesday. (8) Day 3 from Windhoek. (9) Runs Friday only. Restaurant car. (10) Day 4 from Windhoek.

SOUTH WEST AFRICA (NAMIBIA)

These services were run by South African Railways until April, 1989, when the transitional Namibian goovernment took over complete control.

Travel is free for children under 2 years old accompanied by an adult who has paid the full advertised ticket price. Half-fare for children 2–11 when either traveling alone or with an adult who has paid a reduced ticket price. Children 12 and over must pay the full fare.

This is a former German colony, now subject to the administrative control and protection of South Africa. The key tourist attractions are **Etosha National Park** and the **Namib Desert**, said to be the world's oldest desert. Its unusual vegetation is supported only by occasional mists. A specialized world of plants, insects and reptiles has adapted to this environment.

Among the interesting sights in the Desert are the strange "Finger of God" rock formation, one of the most celebrated prehistoric rock paintings (near the tin-mining town of **Uis**, in the wild **Isisab Gorge**), and the 97-mile-long by 16-mile-wide superscenic **Fish River Canyon** which has a modern hot springs resort at **Ai-Ais**.

When the 80-by-30-mile **Etosha Park** is flooded annually, vast numbers of birds and game are attracted there.

Otavi - Windhoek - Keetmanshoop - De Aar

3607 (Bus)

Dep. Otavi	08:46 (1)	10:00 (2)	15:46 (3)	19:30 (4)
Arr. Windhoek	14:31	15:45	21:31	01:15

Change to train. 3600

Dep. Windhoek	18:45 (5)	12:00 (7)
Arr. De Aar	06:27 (6)	17:10 (8)

* * *

Dep. De Aar	00:55 (7)	02:00 (10)
Arr. Windhoek	08:05 (9)	13:10 (9)

Change to bus. 3607

Dep. Windhoek	07:00 (11)	09:30 (12)	10:00 (13)	14:00 (13)	16:35 (3+14)
Arr. Otavi	12:45	15:15	15:45	19:45	22:20

(1) Runs Monday and Wednesday. (2) Runs Monday and Friday (3) Runs Friday only. (4) Runs Monday and Sunday. (5) Runs Wednesday and Sunday. Light Refreshments on Wednesday only. (6) Day 3 from Windhoek. (7) Runs Saturday only. Buffet. (8) Day 2 from Windhoek. (9) Day 2 from De Aar. (10) Runs Monday and Thursday. Light refreshments on Monday only. (11) Runs Tuesday and Thursday only. (12) Runs Thursday only. (13) Runs Sunday only. (14) Plus another departure (on Thursday and Friday only) at 17:00, arriving Otavi 22:45.

Sights in **Windhoek:** The capital of South West Africa (Namibia). See notes about Windhoek under "Johannesburg-Windhoek" on page 560.

Walvisbaai - Swakopmund - Windhoek - Tsumeb

3602

Dep. Walvisbaai	18:15 (1)				
Dep. Swakopmund	19:42				
Arr. Windhoek	06:10 Day 2				

Change to bus.

3607

Dep. Windhoek	07:00 (2)	09:30 (3)	10:00 (4)	14:00 (4)	17:00 (5)
Dep. Otavi	12:45	15:15	15:45	19:45	22:45
Arr. Tsumeb	16:00	18:30	19:00	22:30	02:00

* * *

Dep. Tsumeb	07:00 (6)	14:00 (7)	18:15 (8)
Dep. Otavi	09:45	16:45	21:00
Arr. Windhoek	16:00	23:00	03:15 (9)

Change to train.

3602

Dep. Windhoek	19:10 (1)
Dep. Swakopmund	05:46 (10)
Arr. Walvisbaai	06:55

(1) Runs Tuesday, Friday and Sunday. (2) Runs Tuesday and Thursday. (3) Runs Thursday only. (4) Runs Sunday only. (5) Runs Thursday and Friday. (6) Runs Monday, Wednesday and Friday. (7) Runs Friday only. (8) Runs Monday and Sunday. (9) Day 2 from Tsumeb. (10) Day 2 from Windhoek.

Sights in **Swakopmund:** The government moves here from Windhoek, the capital, during the Summer (December and January) because it is cooler here than in Windhoek. This is South West Africa's principal seaside resort. Good fishing. See the exhibits of natural history, marine life and mineralogy in the Swakopmund Museum.

Sights in **Tsumeb:** The chief copper-mining center of this area. Lead, silver and vanadium are also mined here.

Luderitz - Keetmanshoop 3601

Dep. Luderitz	18:00 (1)	Dep. Keetmanshoop	18:30 (1)
Arr. Keetmanshoop	05:54 (2)	Arr. Luderitz	06:05 (2)

(1) Runs Friday and Sunday. (2) Day 2.

Sights in **Luderitz:** There is much diamond mining in this area. One cannot enter the prohibited area outside the town without a permit. Rock lobster fishing and processing is extensive here. See the small museum's collection of Bushman tools and other archaeological objects.

SUDAN

Children under 3 travel free. Half-fare for children 3–11. Children 12 and over must pay full fare.

Routes in Sudan are very dusty. Little vegetation is seen in Sudan. Grass fires engulf more than half the country every year.

Sudan's rail system links Port Sudan on the Red Sea with the inland capital, Khartoum. At Haiya, there are 2 possible train routes to Khartoum. A northern one goes via Atbara, and a southern route runs via Kassala.

There is rail service north from Khartoum to Wadi Halfa and, from there, on to the Nile and to Cairo by a combination of boat and train. This is the only rail connection between Sudan and a country adjacent to it. A short spur from this route goes west to Karima.

Two lines run south from Khartoum, one to Ed Damazine and the other to Kosti (from which there is a slow, 11-day boat trip to Juba) and to Babanusa.

A short spur runs from Kosti northwest to El Obeid. Two spurs continue from Babanusa. One goes northwest to Nyala, another southwest to Waw. (Service to Waw was suspended "temporarily" in 1985.)

Bur (Port) Sudan - Khartoum 2701   Via Atbara

Dr. Norbert Brockman, returning to the U.S.A. in 1990 after 5 years in East Africa, advised us that due to the civil war in Sudan, foreigners are not allowed to travel Bur Sudan–Khartoum.

All of these trains carry a sleeping car and a restaurant car.

| Dep. Bur Sudan | 18:00 (1) | 20:15 (3) | Dep. Khartoum | 08:15 (1) | 10:45 (5) |
| Arr. Khartoum | 06:00 (2) | 16:00 (4) | Arr. Bur Sudan | 06:00 (4) | 20:15 (4) |

(1) Runs Saturday only. (2) Day 3. (3) Runs Monday only. (4) Day 2. (5) Runs Thursday only.

Sights in **Khartoum:** It is very hot here. The temperature reaches more than 100 degrees Fahrenheit every month and goes as high as 117 degrees. The city was founded by Egyptians as an army camp in 1824. See the Republican Palace, the Sudan Museum. The Ethnographical Museum. The Natural History Museum. The Zoo, along the river. The meeting of the White Nile and Blue Nile, viewed from the White Nile Bridge. Across the bridge is the sister town, **Om Durman**, with its fabulous Mosque Square that holds 100,000 people. The silver Khalifa's Mosque. The Mahdi-Khalifiana Museum.

Sights in **Bur Sudan:** African Moslems stop here en route on their pilgrimage to Mecca. This is Sudan's principal port.

Bur (Port) Sudan - Khartoum 2703   Via Kassala

| Dep. Bur Sudan | 18:00 (1) | Dep. Khartoum | 13:00 (3) |
| Arr. Khartoum | 08:45 (2) | Arr. Bur Sudan | 09:05 (2) |

(1) Runs Friday only. (2) Day 3. (3) Runs Thursday only.

Khartoum - Ed Damazine 2702

Dep. Khartoum	17:00	Mon.	Dep. Ed Damazine	08:00	Wed.
Arr. Ed Damazine	11:20	Tues.	Arr. Khartoum	03:05	Thurs.

Khartoum - Kosti - El Obeid 2702

Both of these trains carry a sleeping car and a restaurant car.

Dep. Khartoum	17:50	Tues.	Dep. El Obeid	07:00	Thurs.
Dep. Kosti	08:25	Wed.	Dep. Kosti	17:50	Thurs.
Arr. El Obeid	17:30	Wed.	Arr. Khartoum	07:00	Fri.

Sights in **El Obeid:** Also called al-Ubayyid. Founded by Egyptians in 1821. The city was once encircled by a forest preserve, designed to alleviate frequent dust storms. The main activity here is trading in gum arabic.

Khartoum - Nyala 2702

Both of these trains carry a sleeping car and a restaurant car.

Dep. Khartoum	10:30	Mon.	Dep. Nyala	10:00	Thurs.
Arr. Nyala	10:30	Wed.	Arr. Khartoum	10:30	Sat.

Sights in **Nyala:** This is a trade center for gum arabic.

Khartoum - Kosti - Juba

2702 (Train)			2706 (Boat)		
Dep. Khartoum	10:30 (1)	17:50 (2)	Dep. Juba	N/A (3)	
Arr. Kosti	02:20	08:15	Dep. Malakal	N/A	
Change to boat.			Arr. Kosti	N/A (5)	
2706			Change to train		
Dep. Kosti	N/A (3)		2702		
Dep. Malakal	N/A		Dep. Kosti	17:50 (6)	20:35 (8)
Arr. Juba	N/A (4)		Arr. Khartoum	07:00 (7)	10:30 (7)

(1) Runs Monday only. Carries sleeping car and restaurant car. (2) Runs Tuesday only. Carries sleeping car and restaurant car.(3) Service was"temporarily" suspended in 1987. When running, service operates "about every 4 weeks". Schedules vary according to depth of water in river. Has a restaurant. (4) Arrives 8–11 days after departing Khartoum, depending on full moon periods. (5) Arrives 5–9 days after departing Juba, depending on full moon periods. (6) Runs Thursday only. Carries a sleeping car and restaurant car. (7) Day 2 after departing Kosti. (8) Runs Friday only. Carries a sleeping car and restaurant car,

Kosti - Babanusa 2702

Both of these trains carry a sleeping car and a restaurant car.

Dep. Kosti	02:30	Tues.	Dep. Babanusa	23:10	Thurs.
Arr. Babanusa	02:50	Wed.	Arr. Kosti	20:25	Fri.

Babanusa - Nyala 2702

Both of these trains carry a sleeping car and a restaurant car.

Dep. Babanusa	03:00 Wed.	Dep. Nyala	10:00 Thurs.
Arr. Nyala	10:30	Arr. Babanusa	23:00

Sights in **Nyala**: This is a trade center for gum arabic.

Babanusa - Waw 2705

This service was "temporarily" suspended in 1985.

Wadi Halfa - Khartoum 2700

Both of these trains carry a sleeping car and a restaurant car.

Dep. Wadi Halfa	16:40 (1)	Dep. Khartoum	16:40 (2)
Arr. Khartoum	16:45 Day 2	Arr. Wadi Halfa	15:40 Day 2

(1) Runs Tuesday and Sunday. (2) Runs Wednesday and Sunday.

Sights in **Wadi Halfa:** This area was the center of archaeological activities in the 1970's to save Egyptian monuments from being covered by the Aswan High Dam reservoir. Egyptian ruins from 2,000 B.C. (the ruins of Buchen) are across the river from Wadi Halfa. An Egyptian colony was here until the Roman invasion.

THE RAIL ROUTE TO EGYPT

Sudan's train connection with Egypt from Khartoum involves a Nile boat trip from Wadi Halfa to Sadd el Ali.

Khartoum - Wadi Halfa - El Sadd el Ali - Cairo

This trip crosses the vast Nubian Desert.

2700 (Train)		2680 (Boat—Nile Valley River Transport))		
Dep. Khartoum	16:40 (1)	Dep. Wadi Halfa	16:00 (3)	
Arr. Wadi Halfa	15:40 (2)	Arr. El Sadd el Ali	08:00 Day 3	
Change to boat.		Change to train.		
		2655		
		Dep. El Sadd el Ali	18:30 (4)	19:30 (4)
		Arr. Cairo (Main)	13:25 (5)	13:50 (5)

(1) Runs Wednesday and Sunday. Carries sleeping cars and a restaurant car. (2) Day 2 from Khartoum. (3) Days of operation are not currently available. (4) Runs daily. Reservation required. Air-conditioned train. (5) Day 2 from El Sadd el Ali.

Khartoum - Karima 2700

Dep. Khartoum	10:50 (1)	Dep. Karima	12:25 (1)
Arr. Karima	14:00 (2)	Arr. Khartoum	16:00 (2)

(1) Runs Wednesday and Sunday only (2) Day 2.

TANZANIA

Children under 3 travel free. Half-fare for children 3–13. Children 14 and over must pay full fare.

This country's rail system is the modern Tanzam Line that was completed in 1976, running from the seaport of Dar es Salaam to Tunduma (and on into Zambia, to Kapiri Mposhi), plus 2 routes going north from Dar es Salaam and 2 that head west from there. One of the northern lines connects Tanga, another of Tanzania's seaports, with Dar es Salaam.

The trains from Dar es Salaam to Kapiri Mposhi (see below) have first-class compartments that convert to 4 berths and second-class compartments that convert to 6 berths. On all other Tanzanian trains, first-class compartments convert to 2 berths.

There is also train-ferry service on Lake Victoria.

Tanzania has many excellent national parks, offering splendid viewing of monkeys, elephants, rhinos, antelopes, lions, zebras and giraffes: Arusha (45 minutes from Dar es-Salaam), Ngorongoro Crater, Lake Manyara, Tarangire, Mikumi, Gombe and the 5,000-square-mile Serengeti.

Dar es Salaam

Means "Haven of Peace" in Arabic. This is Tanzania's main Indian Ocean seaport. See the 1,700,000-year old skull at the National Museum, as well as abstract Makonde wood carving, Masai weapons, drums and Zanzibar chests and elaborately carved doors. The Botanical Gardens. The Askari Monument. The picturesque boats at Dhow Wharf. The Asian Bazaar, called "Uhindini".

An extensive complex of seaside resorts is located 15 miles to the north.

Dar es-Salaam - Kapiri Mposhi 3301

During this ride, the train climbs as high as 6,000 feet altitude. If you do not like curry and local maize cuisine, it is advisable to bring your own food for this 37–43 hours of travel.

Dr. Norbert Brockman, returning to the U.S.A. in 1990, after 5 years in East Africa, advised us that conditions on the Tanzanian portion of this route (Dar es Salaam to Tunduma) are inferior to the Zambian portion (Tunduma to Kapiri Mposhi). Poor service, running out of food, or food available only by paying a bribe. Also unclean conditions.

Dep. Dar es Salaam	09:54 (1)	16:30 (4)
Dep. Tunduma	11:22 (2)	13:04 (2)
Arr. Kapiri Mposhi	05:35 (3)	05:24 (3)

(1) Runs Friday only. Buffet. (2) Day 2. (3) Day 3. (4) Runs Tuesday only. Supplement charged. Restaurant car.

Dar es Salaam - Tanga 3315 Bus

Dep. Dar es Salaam	07:00	22:30	Dep. Tanga	07:30	22:30
Arr. Tanga	14:00	05:30	Arr. Dar es Salaam	14:30	05:30

Tanga - Korogwe - Moshi 3300

The Wednesday and Friday departures require laying-over 28 hours in Korogwe. The Sunday departure involves a 52-hour layover.

Dep. Tanga	19:30 (1)	Dep. Moshi	16:00 (1)
Arr. Korogwe	22:14	Arr. Korogwe	23:54
Change trains.		Change trains.	
Dep. Korogwe	02:47 (2)	Dep. Korogwe	04:00 (2)
Arr. Moshi	09:52	Arr. Tanga	06:47

(1) Runs Wednesday, Friday and Sunday. (2) Runs Friday, Sunday and Wednesday.

Dar es Salaam - Moshi

This trip goes to the southern foot of Mt. Kilimanjaro, highest mountain in Africa (over 19,000 feet).

	3300	3315	3315
Dep. Dar es Salaam	16:00 (1+2)	16:30 (3)	19:00 (3)
Arr. Moshi	09:52	04:30	07:00

                        *   *   *

	3315	3300	3315
Dep. Moshi	15:00 (3)	16:00 (4)	18:30 (3)
Arr. Dar es Salaam	03:00	11:20 (1)	06:30

(1) Departs/Arrives about 5 miles from Dar es Salaam's Tazara railstation. (2) Train. Runs Tuesday Thursday and Saturday. (3) Bus. (4) Train. Runs Wed., Fri. and Sun.

Dar es Salaam - Tabora - Mwanza 3300

This rail trip goes to Lake Victoria.

All of these trains carry a restaurant car.

Dep. Dar es Salaam	18:10 (1)	Dep. Mwanza	19:00 (5)
Arr. Tabora	18:43 (2)	Arr. Tabora	06:09 (6)
Change trains.		Change trains.	
Dep. Tabora	20:03 (3)	Dep. Tabora	06:40 (7)
Arr. Mwanza	06:26 (4)	Arr. Dar es Salaam	07:00 (4)

(1) Runs Tuesday, Wednesday, Friday and Sunday. (2) Day 2 from Dar es Salaam. (3) Runs Wednesday, Thursday, Saturday and Monday. (4) Day 2 from Tabora. (5) Runs Tuesday, Thursday, Friday and Sunday. (6) Day 2 from Mwanza. (7) Runs Wednesday, Friday, Saturday and Monday.

Dar es Salaam - Morogoro - Dodoma - Tabora - Kigoma 3300

Here are the schedules for the train ride to **Lake Tanganyika**. There is boat service across the lake, from **Kigoma** to **Kalemie (Zaire)**.

On this 900-mile trip, **Dodoma** and **Tabora** are fine stopping places en route, which at least until 1979 had good and picturesque railway hotels near both stations.

There is taxi service for the 5-mile trip from Kigoma to **Ujiji**. This is the village where on October 28, 1871, after many months of ordeal, Henry Stanley found Dr. David Livingstone. A small monument marks the site.

The Dar es Salaam departure and arrival is a railstation that is about 5 miles from Dar es Salaam's Tazara railstation.

Dep. Dar es Salaam	18:10 (1)		Dep. Kigoma	18:45 (5)
Dep. Morogoro	01:12 (2)		Arr. Tabora	05:23 (6)
Dep. Dodoma	08:38		Change trains.	
Arr. Tabora	18:43		Dep. Tabora	06:40 (7)
Change trains.			Dep. Dodoma	17:24 (7)
Dep. Tabora	21:00 (3)		Dep. Morogoro	00:40 (8+9)
Arr. Kigoma	06:56 (4)		Arr. Dar es Salaam	07:00

(1) Runs Tuesday, Wednesday, Friday and Sunday. Restaurant car. (2) Day 2 from Dar es Salaam. (3) Runs Wednesday, Thursday, Saturday and Monday. (4) Day 2 from Tabora. (5) Runs Tuesday, Thursday, Friday and Sunday. (6) Day 2 from Kigoma. (7) Runs Wednesday, Friday, Saturday and Monday. Restaurant car. (8) Runs Thursday, Saturday, Sunday and Tuesday. Restaurant car. (9) Day 3 from Kigoma.

From Dar es Salaam to **Morogoro** is only 7 hours by train. It took Stanley 29 days to walk this 121-mile distance. Here, as at many stations in Africa, one can buy hard-boiled eggs, peanuts, tea, oranges and samosas (spicy meat knishes) from vendors along the platform.

Sights in **Tabora:** Long avenues, shaded by mango trees that grew from seeds spitted by endless lines of slaves who were herded down these streets.

There is a small Livingstone museum in nearby **Kwihara** (reached by taxi from Tabora), where Stanley rested many weeks during his search for Livingstone in 1871.

Mpanda - Tabora - Kigoma 3300

This is the train route from Mpanda to **Lake Tanganyika.**

Dep. Mpanda	14:00 (1)		Dep. Kigoma	18:45 (5)
Arr. Tabora	03:23 (2)		Arr. Tabora	05:23 (6)
Change trains.			Change trains.	
Dep. Tabora	21:00 (3)		Dep. Tabora	19:40 (7)
Arr. Kigoma	06:56 (4)		Arr. Mpanda	10:44 (4)

(1) Runs Tuesday, Thursday and Saturday. (2) Day 2 from Mpanda. (3) Runs Monday, Wednesday Thursday and Saturday. (4) Day 2 from Tabora. (5) Runs Tuesday, Thursday, Friday and Sunday. (6) Day 2 from Kigoma. (7) Runs Monday, Wednesday and Friday.

TOGO

Children under 5 travel free. Half-fare for children 5–9. Children 10 and over must pay full fare.

Only one, spartan class is available, comparable to third-class in other African countries.

The official language in Togo is French.

Lome - Aneho 3055

The 1½-hour rail route was discontinued at the end of 1988, when it was replaced by a 29-mile bus service for which we have been unable to obtain departure times.

Sights in **Lome:** Luxury hotels on the beach of this popular resort. The German Cathedral. Nearby, Moslems wearing embroidered robes, selling beads, baskets and bracelets. Many stalls stocked with bolts of bright patterned cloth. Many French restaurants. See the fetish market (black roots, crudely carved dolls, iron objects, etc., all used in the local religion).

Lome - Kpalime 3051

Dep. Lome	06:30	14:45	Dep. Kpalime	06:10	12:45 (1)	13:20 (2)
Arr. Kpalime	11:30	18:53	Arr. Lome	10:30	17:45	17:25

(1)Runs Tuesday, Thursday and Saturday. (2)Runs Monday, Wednesday, Friday and Sunday.

Sights in **Kpalime:** The ride from Lome is through many small villages and tropical forest. Experience the Friday night frivolities before each Saturday's market day, where thousands of people from the outlying area come here to do their weekly shopping. Do not fail to see the famous fantastic kente cloth that has irridescent silk and cotton threads woven into geometric patterns.

Lome - Blitta 3050

Dep. Lome	05:45	07:22 (1)	
Arr. Blitta	11:45	18:30	
		* * *	
Dep. Blitta		05:10 (2)	12:30 (3)
Arr. Lome		16:50	18:30

(1) Runs Monday, Wednesday and Friday. (2) Runs Tuesday, Thursday and Saturday. (3) Runs Wednesday only.

TUNISIA

Children under 4 travel free. Children 4–9 pay 75.. Children 10 and over must pay full fare.

Because Tunisia is only 2 hours by air from Paris and one hour from Rome, it is a popular vacation place for Europeans.

Tunisia's rail system is 2 lines running west from Tunis (one to Bizerte and the other to Ghardimaou, and on to Algeria) and one heading south from Tunis, to Gabes. An 11-mile spur from Bir-bou-Rekba on this southern line goes to Hammamet and Nabeul.

The 3 classes of seats are luxury, first and second-class.

Tunis

There are more than 700 exceptional monuments to see here. The finest and largest collection of Roman mosaics in the world are on exhibit at the National Museum of the Bardo, as well as Punic, Byzantine, Arab and other Roman objects (open daily except Monday 09:00–12:00 and 14:00–17:30). Shop the native quarter for famous Kairouan rugs.

See the fantastic 9th century Great Mosque Zitouna (Mosque of the Olive Tree). A marvelous collection of illuminated Korans and other Arabic manuscripts in the National Library. The beautiful interior of the Zaouia (temple) of Sidi Mahrez. The marble and sculptured wood in the lovely Dar Ben Abdullah, an example of Tunis' many 19th century "great houses".

The Lapidary Museum of Sidi Bou Krissan. The valuable objects from Egypt, Persia and Turkey at the Dar Hussein Museum of Islamic Art, in an 18th century mansion. The 17th century Mosque of Hamouda Pasha. The 16th century Mosque El Youssefi (Mosque of the Kasbah). The Belvedere Zoo. The many beach resorts south of Tunis.

There are half-day tours to **Carthage** and **Sidi Bou Said**. A full-day tour goes to Dougga.

Dougga

It is a short drive from Tunis to Dougga. See the 2nd century B.C. Dougga Mausoleum, a prince's tomb. Many temples and an ancient Market Place, all very well preserved. The Comedie Francaise often performs in the large open-air theater. Dougga is Tunisia's largest archaeological site, one of the best-preserved Roman towns in Tunisia.

Kerkouane

This city is near Tunis. It is the only unmutilated Punic town, the only one that was not built upon by succeeding generations.

Thuburo Majus

Near both Tunis and Sousse. Many fabulous ruins here: temples, a Forum, and public buildings. An excellently preserved Roman town.

Utica

Near both Tunis and Bizerte. This was a Phoenician port in the 11th century B.C. Some vaults from that period and many fine Roman ruins can be seen here. The Museum has a fine collection of ancient jewels and funeral furniture.

Tunis - Bizerte 2602

All of these trains have light refreshments.

Dep. Tunis	05:50	11:40	16:05	18:20
Arr. Bizerte	07:29	13:06	17:41	19:56
		*	*	*
Dep. Bizerte	05:40	08:10	13:45	18:30
Arr. Tunis	07:16	09:35	15:20	20:07

Sights in **Bizerte:** A seaport and naval base. This city has been ruled by Punic, Roman, Byzantine, Arab and Turkish leaders. See: The Er-Rimel beach. The Old Port, with docks for fishing boats. Nearby there are many interesting villages: Tabarka, Utica, Raf-Raf, Ain Draham, Ghar El Melh (Porto Farina), Ras Djebel, Metline, Sounine, Aousdja, Zouaouine, El Alia, Kalaat El An-dalous, Sedjenane.

Tunis - Carthage 2603

It is a short ride from Tunis to **Carthage** on a 1908 wooden train which starts at Place d'Afrique in the center of Tunis and stops at several fashionable seaside resorts.

Get off at Carthage's Hannibal station to visit the birthplace of Hannibal. This city was founded in 814 B.C. There are many outstanding Punic and Roman ruins here. Plays, dances, musical performances and sound and light performances are presented every July and August in both the Roman Theater and in the Baths of Antonin.

See the very large and beautifully decorated 2nd century Roman baths, nearly 700 feet long. The National Museum of Carthage. The ancient Theater, built in a marble quarry. The pink marble columns and the mosaic floor (depicting birds in the leaves of a tree) at the Villa de la Voliere in the Carthage Antiquarium. The Basilica of St. Cyprian.

Get off at Carthage's Salammbo station to see The Tophet, now an open-air museum, where humans once were sacrificed.

Dep. Tunis (Nord)	Frequent times *except* 01:00 to 03:49
Arr. Carthage	38 minutes later
	* * *
Dep. Carthage	Frequent times *except* 01:15 to 03:49
Arr. Tunis (Nord)	38 minutes later

Tunis - Ghardimaou 2601

Dep. Tunis	06:30 (1)	11:10	12:58 (1)	14:25 (1)	16:50	18:40 (1)
Arr. Ghardimaou	09:27	14:12	15:49	17:26	20:18	21:32

* * *

Dep. Ghardimaou	03:40	07:00 (1)	10:20 (1)	13:22 (1)	14:23	16:40 (1)
Arr. Tunis	07:01	09:53	13:16	16:21	17:27	19:36

(1) Has air-conditioned luxury-class and first-class, for which a supplement is charged. Light refreshments.

Tunis - Ghardimaou - Algiers

Both of these trains are direct, with no train change in Annaba although Cook shows this trip as 2 timetables. Both trains have light refreshments.

2550		2545	
Dep. Tunis	11:10	Dep. Algiers	19:00 (1)
Dep. Ghardimaou	14:40	Dep. Constantine	02:43
Arr. Annaba	20:17	Arr. Annaba	05:26
2545		**2550**	
Dep. Annaba	22:15 (1)	Dep. Annaba	09:30
Dep. Constantine	01:06	Arr. Ghardimaou	13:24
Arr. Algiers	09:14	Arr. Tunis	17:27

(1) Has couchettes.

Tunis - Kairouan 2620 (Bus)

Dep. Tunis	06:00	07:00	08:00	09:00	10:00	15:00	16:30
Arr. Kairouan	4 hours later						

* * *

Dep. Kairouan	03:40	09:30	10:40	13:40	15:30	16:30	-0-
Arr. Tunis	4 hours later						

Sights in **Kairouan:** The unbelievably beautiful carved wood panels of the Minibar (pulpit) and gilded 9th century tiles in the massive 9th century Great Mosque of Okba Ibn Nafaa, the founder of Kairouan. The splendid collection of parchment manuscripts of the Koran, 9th century bookbindings, ceramics and glassware in the Museum of Islamic Art, opposite the Great Mosque.

The 17th century Zaouia of Abou Zamaa El Balaoui (Mosque of the Barber). The 9th century reservoirs, Bassins Aghlabides. Narrow streets that are 1,000 years old. The 9th century facade on the Mosque of Three Doors. The Museum of Rugs. The ruins of nearby Rakada.

Sights in **Rakada**: Taste the date cakes, dipped in honey. Famous piled rugs are made here. Also outstanding copperware: coffee and tea pots, jars, plates, cooking pots.

Tunis - Hammamet - Nabeul 2600

A one-day roundtrip from Tunis to Hammamet and/or Nabeul is possible, as these schedules indicate.

Dep. Tunis (East)	07:10 (1)	12:05 (1)	14:15 (3+4)	16:15 (5)
Arr. Bir-bou-Rekba	08:00	12:58	-0- (3)	17:17
Change trains.				
Dep. Bir-bou-Rekba	08:08 (2)	13:04 (2)	-0-	17:26 (6)
Arr. Hammamet	08:15	13:11	15:39	17:33
Arr. Nabeul	08:29	13:27	15:55	17:49

Dep. Tunis (East)	17:30 (1)	18:05 (3+7)	18:40
Arr. Bir-bou-Rekba	18:22	-0- (3)	19:40
Change trains			
Dep. Bir-bou-Rekba	18:30 (2)	-0-	19:50 (2)
Arr. Hammamet	18:37	19:30	19:57
Arr. Nabeul	18:53	19:48	20:15

Sights in **Hammamet:** A popular seashore resort. See: The medieval fortress. Fantastic gardens of flowers and fruit trees.

Sights in **Nabeul:** Many fine mosaics. Excellent straw and pottery porducts are made here.

Dep. Nabeul	05:30 (3)	06:28 (6)	07:35 (2)	08:35 (2)
Dep. Hammamet	05:49	06:47	07:52	08:52
Arr. Bir-bou-Rekba	-0- (3)	06:53	07:58	08:58
Change trains.				
Dep. Bir-bou-Rekba	-0-	06:58 (5)	08:07 (5+8)	09:01 (1)
Arr. Tunis (East)	07:16	08:04	09:04	09:56

Dep. Nabeul	12 :34 (2)	16:02 (2)	18:58 (2)
Dep. Hammamet	12:53	16:19	19:15
Arr. Bir-bou-Rekba	12:59	16:25	19:21
Change trains.			
Dep. Bir-bou-Rekba	14:03 (8+9)	16:30 (1)	19:45 (1)
Arr. Tunis (East)	15:01	17:25	20:44

(1) Reservation required. Air-conditioned. Has Luxury class. Light refreshments. (2) Second-class only. (3) Direct train. No train change in Bir-bou-Rekba. (4) Runs Friday and Saturday. (5) Runs daily, except Sundays and holidays. (6) Second-class only. Runs daily, except Sundays and holidays. (7) Runs Monday–Thursday. (8) Air-conditioned. Has a luxury class. Light refreshments. (9) Runs Sundays and holidays only.

Tunis - Sousse - El Djem - Sfax - Gabes - Jerba

2600 Train

Dep. Tunis (East)	07:10 (1)	12:05 (1)	13:05 (1)	14:10 (1+2)
Arr. Sousse	09:05	14:13	15:05	16:05
Dep. Sousse	09:15	-0-	15:15	16:15
Dep. El Djem	10:12	-0-	16:15	17:12
Arr. Sfax	10:58	-0-	17:02	17:58
Dep. Sfax	11:13	-0-	-0-	-0-
Arr. Gabes	13:33	-0-	-0-	-0-
Change to bus. Timetable 2620				
Dep. Gabes	02:15	-0-	-0-	-0-
Arr. Jerba	04:45	-0-	-0-	-0-

Dep. Tunis (East)	16:15 (3)	17:30 (1)	18:40	21:20 (1)
Arr. Sousse	18:47	19:29	21:10	23:18
Dep. Sousee	-0-	19:39	-0-	23:28
Dep. El Djem	-0-	20:43	-0-	00:28
Arr. Sfax	-0-	21:33	-0-	01:18
Dep. Sfax	-0-	-0-	-0-	02:02
Arr. Gabes	-0-	-0-	-0-	04:25

(1) Reservation required. Air-conditioned. Has Luxury class. Light refreshments. (2) Runs Saturday only. Light refreshments. (3) Runs daily, except Sundays and holidays.Tunis - Jerba 2620 (Bus)

Jerba - Gabes - Sfax - El Djem - Sousse - Tunis

2600 Train

Dep. Gabes	-0-	-0-	-0-	-0-
Arr. Sfax	-0-	-0-	-0-	-0-
Dep. Sfax	-0-	-0-	05:55 (1)	12:30 (1+5)
Dep. El Djem	-0-	-0-	06:46	13:18
Dep. Sousse	05:35 (3)	06:50 (4)	07:48	14:18
Arr. Tunis (East)	08:04	09:04	09:56	16:32

2620 Bus

Dep. Jerba	-0-	-0-	-0-	20:00
Arr. Gabes	-0-	-0-	-0-	22:30
Change to train. Timetable 2600				
Dep. Gabes	-0-	-0-	15:27 (1)	23:10 (1)
Arr. Sfax	-0-	-0-	18:00	01:30
Dep. Sfax	13:30 (1)	-0-	18:15	01:45
Dep. El Djem	14:18	-0-	19:02	02:36
Dep. Sousse	15:18	18:30 (1)	20:02	03:35
Arr. Tunis (East)	17:25	20:44	22:03	05:39

(1) Reservation required. Air-conditioned. Has Luxury class. Light refreshments. (2) Runs Saturday only.
(3) Runs daily, except Sundays and holidays. (4) Air-conditioned. Has luxury class. Light refreshments.
(5) Runs Sundays and holidays only.

Sights in **Sousse:** Exhibits of prehistoric objects as well as Punic, Roman and early Christian mosaics and statues at the Museum, in the Kasbah. The 9th century Ribat (fort), 2 rooms of which are devoted to exhibits of Islamic textiles, ceramics, miniatures, Koran manuscripts, jewelry and glassware. The 9th century Grand Mosque.

Sights in **Maktar:** Near Sousse. Outstanding Roman ruins: the Great Baths and Trajan's Triumphal Arch. Also Punic and Roman marble and bronze statues at the Museum.

Sights in **Mahdia:** Near Sousse. An important vacation resort. See the restored 10th century Mosque of Mahdia. Fantastic mosaics and Roman architecture. Fine wool embroidery is done here.

Sights in **Sbeitla:** Near Sousse. A truly magnificent ancient capital. See the Triumphal Arch, Forum, and the mosaics on the floor of an old Christian basilica.

Sights in **Moknine:** Near Sousse. This is a pottery center. Its little museum has ancient gold jewelry, still a specialty of local artisans. Much spectacular weaving is done here.

Sights in **Monastir:** A 25-minute train ride from Sousse. Visit the remarkably well-preserved 8th century Ribat, one of the largest Arab forts in North Africa, 3 rooms of which have exhibits of Islamic textiles, ceramics, miniatures, Koran manuscripts, jewelry and glassware.

Sights in **El Djem:** A marvelous 3rd century amphitheater, one of the largest and best preserved Roman colosseums. Near it are many statues, mosaics and bronze objects from the Punic, Roman and early Christian periods. Great wool embroidery here.

Sights in **Sfax;** Archaeological collections of mosaics, lamps and glass and bronze objects in the Municipal Museum.

Sights in **Gabes:** This town consists of 2 large villages: **Djara** and **Menzel.** It is a 3½ -mile oases along the seashore. There are many date palm groves here. Try the palm wine. Good palm leaf basket-work, jewelry and forged iron are offered in the shops of Djara. See the Sidi Driss Mosque. The Sidi Boulbaba Mosque is on the road to nearby Matmata.

Sights in **Matmata:** Near Gabes. People live here in holes, both to get out of the sun and because of the lack of building materials in this locale. However, the interior of some of these underground homes are beautifully furnished. One hotel, with a bar and restaurant, is completely underground.

Sights in **Zarzis:** Near Gabes. A dense green oasis resort, with a forest of 50-year old olive trees. There is exceptional fishing in nearby **Biban Lake**.

Sights in **Jerba:** This heavenly garden-oasis is one of Tunisia's most popular resorts. See the fine 3rd century mosaics. The massive white 15th century fort. La Ghriba, one of the oldest synagogues in the world. The magnificent Museum. Marvelous Thandicrafts (enameled jewelry, blankets) are sold in small shops.

UGANDA

Children under 3 travel free. Half-fare for children 3–13. Children 14 and over must pay full fare. First-class coach seats convert into couchette-type sleeping accommodations on overnight trips.

Landlocked Uganda's rail lines radiate from Tororo: northwest to Lira, west to Kasese, and southeast to Nairobi (and on to Mombasa).

Dr. Norbert Brockman, returning to the U.S.A. in 1990 after 5 years in East Africa, advised us that Ugandan trains "are filthy and overbooking is customary." On one ride he took, 12 people were issued a ticket for a 4-person compartment.

Tororo - Lira 3285

Although Thomas Cook shows these trains as "second and third-class", Dr. Brockman told us that the Tororo–Lira and v.v. trains have only third-class seats. "They usually refuse to sell tickets to foreigners. This line is frequently under guerilla attack or subject to robbery. It is very dangerous."

Dep. Tororo	15:30	Dep. Lira	14:30
Arr. Lira	12:15	Arr. Tororo	07:00

Tororo - Jinja - Kampala - Kasese 3285

This line touches the northern shore of Lake Victoria at Kampala.

Service between Kampala and Kasese is subject to local confirmation due to frequent flood damage on this route.

Dep. Tororo	07:00 (1)		Dep. Kasese	16:00 (5)	20:00 (4)
Dep. Jinja	11:27		Arr. Kampala	06:00 (3)	11:00 (7)
Arr. Kampala	14:30		Change trains.		
Change trains.			Dep. Kampala	08:00 (6)	
Dep. Kampala	15:00 (2)	19:00 (4)	Dep. Jinja	12:17	
Arr. Kasese	03:40 (3)	09:45 (3)	Arr. Tororo	15:00	

(1) Runs Monday, Wednesday and Friday. (2) Runs Monday, Wednesday and Friday. Has first-class seats that convert to couchettes. (3) Day 2. (4) Third-class only. (5) Runs Tuesday, Thursday and Saturday. Has first-class seats that convert to couchettes. (6) Runs Tuesday, Thursday and Sunday. (7) This arrival requires laying-over in Kampala in order to continue on to Jinja.

Sights in **Kampala:** The capital of Uganda. See the tombs of the kings of Baganda. The collection of African musical instruments in the Uganda Museum. Several Hindu temples. Rubaga Cathedral. The white Kibuli Mosque. The "apocalypse" ceiling of St. Francis' Chapel at Makerere University. The Botanical Garden in **Entebbe**, 20 miles away.

Tororo - Nairobi - Mombasa 3270

All of these trains have first and second-class coach seats that convert to berths.

Dep. Tororo	N/A (1)		Dep. Mombasa	17:00 (4)	19:00 (6)
Dep. Malaba	16:00 (2)		Arr. Nairobi	08:02 (7)	08:30 (7)
Arr. Nairobi	08:45 (3)		Change trains.		
Change trains.			Dep. Nairobi	15:00 (8)	
Dep. Nairobi	17:00 (4)	19:00 (6)	Arr. Malaba	08:45 (1+5)	
Arr. Mombasa	07:30 (5)	08:06 (5)	Arr. Tororo	N/A (1)	

(1) There is said to be frequent jitney-van service 18km (11 miles) on the road Tororo–Malaba and v.v. (2) Runs Wednesday, Saturday and Sunday. Restaurant car. (3) Day 2 from Malaba. (4) Runs daily. Light refreshments. (5) Day 2 from Nairobi. (6) Runs daily. Restaurant car. (7) Day 2 from Mombasa. (8) Runs Tuesday, Friday and Saturday. Restaurant car.

UPPER VOLTA (Burkina Faso)

Landlocked Upper Volta has one train route, from Ouagadougou to Bobo Dioulasso, and on to Abidjan (Ivory Coast). For schedules, see "Treichville–Bobo Dioulasso-Ouagadougou" under Ivory Coast, on page 536.

ZAIRE

Children under 3 travel free. Half-fare for children 3–9. Children 10 and over must pay full fare.

Zaire's trains have 4 classes: de luxe, first, second and third. Even de luxe and first-class are not comparable to European standards.

This country's rail system is Y-shaped, with Lubumbashi at the bottom of the vertical South-North line and Kamina at the point that one route goes northwest to Ilebo, where there is boat service to Kinshasa and train facility from there to the port of Pointe Noire on the coastline of Congo.

Another route goes northeast from Kamina to Kalemie (on the west shore of Lake Tanganyika), where there is boat service across the lake to Kigoma in Tanzania, and trains from Kigoma to Dar es-Salaam.

A third major rail line once ran west from Tenke (on the Lubumbashi–Kamina route) to Lobito on the coastline of Angola. This was a segment of Africa's only transcontinental rail line, running from Lobito on the Atlantic Ocean to the Indian Ocean cities of Beirain (Mozambique) and Dar es-Salaam (Tanzania).

There is boat service Matadi to Banana, on the Atlantic coast of Zaire. Construction started many years ago on a rail line to connect Banana, Boma and Matadi so as to provide a rail link between Banana and Kinshasa, the capital.

Rail facilities once operated also south from Lubumbashi to Kapiri Moshi and on through Zambia, Zimbabwe and Botswana into South Africa and all the way to Cape Town.

Lubumbashi - Tenke - Kamina 3201

Dep. Lubumbashi	09:00 (1)	12:00 (3)	22:00 (5)		
Dep. Tenke	17:15	21:40	23:20 (6)		
Arr. Kamina	06:00 (2)	12:30 (4)	04:20 (7)		
		*	*	*	
Dep. Kamina	04:30 (8)	05:20 (9)	08:50 (10)	14:20 (11)	16:00 (10+12)
Dep. Tenke	19:30	17:30	21:50	05:30 (4)	04:50 (4)
Arr. Lubumbashi	06:05 (4)	01:10 (4)	06:05 (4)	15:55	15:55

(1) Runs Monday, Thursday and Friday. Has deluxe, first and second-class seats. Also has couchettes. Restaurant car. (2) Day 2. Arrives 5:10 on Tuesday. (3) Runs Wednesday and Saturday. Restaurant car. (4) Day 2. (5) Runs Sunday only. (6) Day 2 from Lubumbashi. Runs Monday only. (7) Day 4 (Wednesday) after departing Lubumbashi on Sunday. (8) Runs Thursday only. Restaurant car. (9) Runs Wednesday only. Has deluxe and first-class seats. Also has couchettes. Restaurant car. (10) Runs Monday only. Has deluxe and first-class seats. Also has couchettes. Restaurant car. (11) Runs Sunday only. Restaurant car. (12) Plus another departure from Kamina at 18:00 Wednesday, departing Tenke 04:00 Thursday, arriving Lubumbashi 23:30 Thursday.

Kamina - Ilebo - Kinshasa - Brazzaville

This route involves a 4-day boat ride from Ilebo to Kinshasa.

3201				3218 (Boat)	
Dep. Kamina	08:00 (1)	14:30 (3)		Dep. Ilebo	15:00 (5)
Arr. Ilebo	17:00 (2)	03:35 (4)		Arr. Kinshasa	07:00 (6)
Change to boat.				Change to another boat.	
				3181	
				Dep. Kinshasa	N/A (7)
				Arr. Brazzaville	N/A (8)

(1) Runs Friday only. Has both de luxe and first-class seats. Also has couchettes. Restaurant car. (2) Arrives on Saturday. (3) Runs Sunday only. Restaurant car. (4) Arrives on Tuesday. (5) Runs Tuesday only. Reservation required. Restaurant on ship. (6) Arrives Saturday, Day 5. (7) Operates daytime only. Runs every 30 minutes. Exact times have not been available since prior to 1981. (8) Twenty minutes after departing Kinshasa.

Kinshasa - Matadi 3205

Completed in 1908, this line was the first Congo railroad.

All of these trains are second-class only.

Dep. Kinshasa	07:15 (1)	07:30 (2)		Dep. Matadi	06:00 (1)	06:30 (2)
Arr. Matadi	14:40	17:24		Arr. Kinshasa	15:55	13:50

(1) Runs Monday, Wednesday and Friday. (2) Runs Tuesday, Thursday and Saturday.

Sights in **Kinshasa:** The capital of Zaire. Formerly called Leopoldville, when this was the Belgian Congo. The largest city in Black Africa (1,400,000 population). See the National Museum and the Beaux Arts Academy. The central market is colorful .

Sights in **Matadi:** The Kikongo word for "stone". This is Zaire's principal port (a mile-long waterfront, cut in granite), 93 miles upstream from **Banana**, at the mouth of the Congo River, on the Atlantic coast. It is one of the largest harbors in Central Africa, the farthest point into Zaire that can be reached by oceangoing ships. .

Kamina - Kalemie - Kigoma - Tabora - Dar es Salaam

Kalemie, on the west shore of Lake Tanganyika, is a foreign trade transport center. This is the trip into Tanzania.

3200			3300	
Dep. Kamina	08:00 (1)		Dep. Kigoma	18:45 (5)
Arr. Kalemie	06:20 (2)		Arr. Tabora	05:23 (6)
Change to boat.			Change trains.	
3215			Dep. Tabora	06:40 (7)
Dep. Kalemie	16:30 (3)		Dep. Dodoma	17:24 (7)
Arr. Kigoma	07:00 (4)		Dep. Morogoro	00:40 (8)
Change to train.			Arr. Dar es Salaam	07:00 (9)

(1) Runs Saturday only. Has both de luxe and first-class seats. Also has couchettes. Restaurant car. (2) Arrives on Sunday. (3) Runs Monday only. Restaurant on ship. (4) Arrives on Tuesday. (5) Runs Tuesday, Thursday, Friday and Sunday. (6) Day 2 from Kigoma. (7) Runs Wednesday, Friday, Saturday and Monday. Restaurant car. (8) Runs Thursday, Saturday, Sunday and Tuesday. Restaurant car. (9) Day 3 from Kigoma. Day 2 from Tabora.

Lubumbashi - Ndola - Kapiri Mposhi 3400 + 3410
This is the route into Zambia.

See Kapiri Mposhi–Lubumbashi on page 581.

Lubumbashi - Sakania 3207

Dep. Lubumbashi	09:00 Wed.	Dep. Sakania	00:01 Thurs.
Arr. Sakania	21:00	Arr. Lubumbashi	15:00

ZAMBIA

Children under 3 travel free. Half-fare for children 3–15. Children 16 and over must pay full fare. First-class seats are upholstered. Second-class seats have leather covering.

On a map of landlocked Zambia, the outline of its rail system is a sloppy "Y", with Livingstone in the south at the bottom of the "Y". The right-arm runs east from Kapiri Mposhi to Tunduma and on into Tanzania. This is Zambia's portion of the Tanzam Railway, which terminates at the port of Dar es Salaam.

The left-arm of the "Y" goes from Kapiri Mposhi to Ndola and on into Zaire. A small spur runs off this route, from Ndola to Kitwe.

South of Livingstone is the border with Zimbabwe and a connection (before 1989) to Victoria Falls, and on to Bulawayo, a junction for continuing southwest to South Africa. There is also service from Bulawayo northeast to Harare (Salisbury). The train service to Mozambique has been "temporarily" suspended since 1977.

Livingstone - Victoria Falls - Bulawayo - Harare (Salisbury)

3453		3451	
Dep. Livingstone	N/A (1)	Dep. Harare	08:00 (4+8)
Arr. Victoria Falls	N/A	Arr. Bulawayo	16:10
Change trains.		Change trains.	
Dep. Victoria Falls	17:30 (2)	3453	
Arr. Bulawayo	07:05 (3)	Dep. Bulawayo	19:00 (2)
Change trains.		Arr. Victoria Falls	07:30 (3)
3451		Change trains.	
Dep. Bulawayo	08:00 (4+7)	Dep. Victoria Falls	N/A (1)
Arr. Harare	16:00	Arr. Livingstone	N/A

(1) Service Livingstone–Victoria Falls and v.v. was "temporarily" suspended in 1989. (2) Runs daily. First and second-class seats convert to couchettes. Buffet. (3) Day 2. (4) Second-class and third-class only. Light refreshments. (5) Runs Friday and Sunday. Third-class only. (6) Runs daily. First and second class seats convert to couchettes. Light refreshments. (7) Plus other departures from Bulawayo at 20:00 (5) and 21:00 (6), arriving Harare 06:00 (3) and 07:00 (3). (8) Plus other departures from Harare at 20:00 (5) and 21:00 (6), arriving Bulawayo 05:35 (3) and 06:40 (3).

Sights in **Livingstone:** This is the most popular tourist center in Zambia. See the flowers and aviary in Barotse Gardens. The Livingstone Museum's archaeological, historical and ethnological exhibits. Traditional dances, performed at Maramba Cultural Center. Visit the Railway Museum.

Nearby, Lake Kariba, Livingstone Game Park, Kafue National Park and Wankie National Park. Take a cruise on the Zambesi River.

The most important sight here is seen by taking an excursion to the nearby majestic Victoria Falls, which are more than 5,500 feet wide and have a minimum drop of 355 feet. The falls are the border between Zambia and Zimbabwe (formerly Rhodesia). There is a great view from Knife Edge Bridge. However, the best view is from the Zimbabwe side, looking at the two-thirds of the falls owned by Zambia.

Sights in **Victoria Falls:** See notes about Victoria Falls on page 582.

Livingstone - Lusaka - Kapiri Mposhi - Dar es Salaam

Dr. Norbert Brockman, returning to the U.S.A. in 1990 after 5 years in East Africa, advised us that the Zambian portion on the Tanzam Railway (Livingstone–Kapiri Mposhi) is superior to the Tanzanian portion (Kapiri Mposhi to Dar es-Salaam). Better food and service. Also cleaner conditions.

Much wildlife can be seen as the train passes through **Mkumi National Park**.

The train climbs as high as 6,000 feet altitude during this ride. If you do not like curry and local maize cuisine, it is advisable to bring your own food for this 37–43 hours of travel.

3400

Dep. Livingstone	07:00 (1)	20:30 (6)
Dep. Lusaka	21:58	08:10 (2)
Arr. Kapiri Mposhi (ZR)	05:03 (2)	13:14

Change trains *and railstations (about 1 mile apart)*.
3301

Dep. Kapiri Mposhi (New)	11:15 (3)	20:45 (7)
Dep. Tunduma	07:51 (4)	14:05 (4)
Arr. Dar es Salaam (TAZ)	09:12 (5)	11:53 (5)

*　　*　　*

Dep. Dar es Salaam (TAZ)	09:54 (3)	16:30 (7)
Dep. Tunduma	11:22 (8)	13:04 (8)
Arr. Kapiri Mposhi (New)	05:35 (9)	05:24 (9)

Change trains *and railstations (about 1 mile apart)*.
3400

Dep. Kapiri Mposhi (ZR)	11:59 (10)	02:16 (11)
Dep. Lusaka	17:04	09:19
Arr. Livingstone	04:04 (4)	23:52

(1) Reservation required. Runs Monday, Thursday, Friday and Sunday. Carries sleeping cars. Has first and second- class coaches. Buffet car. (2) Day 2 from Livingstone. (3) Runs Friday only. Buffet. (4) Day 2 from Kapiri Mposhi. (5) Day 3 from Kapiri Mposhi. (6) Res-

ervation required. Supplement charged. Runs Monday, Tuesday, Thursday and Friday. Carries sleeping cars. Has first and second-class coaches. Restaurant car. (7) Supplement charged. Runs Tuesday only. Restaurant car. (8) Day 2 from Dar es Salaam. (9) Day 3 from Dar es Salaam. (10) Supplement charged. Runs Monday, Wednesday, Thursday and Sunday. Carries a sleeping car. Coaches are second-class only. Restaurant car. (11) Reservation required. Runs Tuesday, Wednesday. Friday and Saturday. Carries a sleeping car. Coaches are first and second-class.

Sights in **Lusaka:** The capital of Zambia. Although the population is almost one million, the hotels and restaurants here are very primitive. See the large copper cross over the altar in the Anglican Cathedral of the Holy Cross. Luburma Central Market. The Tobacco Auction Floor. The 8-acre Twickenham Road Archaeological Site in **Olympia Park,** a suburb.

Nearby, Munda Wanga Park and Botanical Gardens, Kafue Gorge. The Ayrshire Farm Rock Engravings national monument. Blue Lagoon National Park.

Kapiri Mopshi - Ndola - Lubumbashi

This is the route into Zaire.

3400		
Dep. Kapiri Mposhi	05:13 (1)	13:24 (3)
Arr. Ndola	09:50	16:35
Change to bus.		
3410		
Dep. Ndola	N/A (2)	N/A (2)
Arr. Lubumbashi	N/A	N/A
	* *	*
Dep. Lubumbashi	N/A (2)	N/A (2)
Arr. Ndola	N/A	N/A
Change to train.		
3400		
Dep. Ndola	08:55 (4)	22:11 (5)
Arr. Kapiri Mposhi	11:59	02:16

(1) Reservation required. Runs Monday, Tuesday, Friday and Saturday. Buffet car. (2) Times have not been available since 1980. (3) Reservation Required. Supplement charged. Runs Tuesday, Wednesday, Friday and Saturday. (4) Reservation required. Supplement charged. Runs Monday, Wednesday, Thursday and Sunday. Restaurant car. (5) Reservation required. Runs Monday, Tuesday, Thursday and Friday. Buffet car.

Livingstone - Mulobezi 3401

This is a spur off the Victoria Falls-Kapiri Mposhi line.

Both of these trains are third-class only.

Dep. Livingstone	08:00 Sun.	Dep. Mulobezi	08:00 Mon.
Arr. Mulobezi	16:55	Arr. Livingstone	17:45

ZIMBABWE (formerly RHODESIA)

Children under 3 travel free. Half-fare for children 3–11. Children 12 and over must pay full fare. There are 3 classes of seats. First-class compartments convert to 4 berths at night and second-class to 6 berths. There is a charge for bedding.

There are rail connections between Harare (formerly Salisbury) in landlocked Zimbabwe and Zambia, Mozambique, Botswana and South Africa.

Sights in **Harare** (formerly Salisbury): The capital. See the Queen Victoria Memorial Library and Museum. The collection of talented African artisans in the National Gallery, open Monday-Friday 09:00–17:00. The more than 750 species of plants indigenous to Zimbabwe, in the National Botanic Gardens.

Sights in **Bulawayo:** The Railway Museum. The National Museum. Nearby, Cecil Rhodes' Tomb in the granite Matopo Hills, where cave paintings made 2,000 to 4,000 years ago can be viewed. The 75,000 specimens of mammals in the Natural History Museum. The 17th century Khami Ruins.

Sights in **Victoria Falls:** These spectacular falls are more than 5,500 feet wide and have a maximum drop of 355 feet, twice that of Niagara Falls. This is the border between Zimbabwe (formerly Rhodesia) and Zambia. The best view is from the Zimbabwe side, looking at the two-thirds of the falls that is in Zambia. Watch local artists carve soapstone at the African Craft Village.

Harare (Salisbury) - Bulawayo - Victoria Falls - Livingstone

The route to Zambia.
See schedules under "Livingstone-Harare" on page 579.

Harare (Salisbury) - Bulawayo - Mafikeng - Johannesburg

The route to Botswana and South Africa.

3451

Dep. Harare	08:00 (1)	20:00 (2)	21:00 (4)
Arr. Bulawayo	16:10	05:35 (3)	06:40 (3)
Change trains. 3475			
Dep. Bulawayo	11:05 (5)	11:10 (7)	
Arr. Gaborone	01:25 (6)	08:01	
Dep. Ramatlhabana	05:05	-0-	
Arr. Mafikeng	-0-	-0-	
Change trains. 3518			
Dep. Mafikeng	06:30 (6)	20:45 (8)	22:52 (8)
Arr. Johannesburg	12:45	04:55	05:22

(1) Runs daily. Second and third-class only. Buffet. (2) Runs Friday and Sunday. Third-class only. (3) Day 2. (4) Runs daily. Has first-class coaches. Light refreshments. (5) Reservation required. Runs Thursday only. Direct train to Johannesburg. No train change in Mafikeng. Has a first-class coach. Has restaurant car to Gaborone. (6) Reservation required. Runs Friday only. Direct train. No train change in Mafikeng. Has a first-class coach. Carries an air-conditioned restaurant car Mafikeng to Johannesburg. (7) Runs daily. Has a first-class coach. Buffet. (8) Runs Sunday only. Has a first-class coach.

Chapter 11   ASIA

BANGLADESH

Children under 3 travel free. Half-fare for children 3–9. Children 10 and over must pay full fare. Bangladesh offers 6 classes of train space: air-conditioned, first-class, executive, second-class, economy and third-class (which is tantamount to sixth-class). Air-conditioned class and first-class convert to 2-berths at night, second-class to 6 berths. "Express" and "Mail" trains charge a higher fare.

The principal cities in Bangladesh having train service are Chittagong and Dhaka.

Chittagong This is Bangladesh's largest port. See the slab believed to bear the imprint of Mohammed's foot, in the Qadam Mubarik Mosque. The Chandanpura Shahi Jame Mosque. The tortoises at the tomb of Hazrat Bayazid Bostami.

Dhaka (Dacca) The nearly 400-year old capital of Bangladesh. See the 17th Century Lalbagh Fort and the tomb of Pari Bibi. The 4 bazaars in the Chowk (old market). The 17th century Chowk Mosque. Other notable mosques: The Star, Kar Talab, Baidul Mukarram, and Sat Gumbad. The collection of coins, paintings, and stone, wood and metal sculptures in the Museum of Antiquities. There are many interesting archaeological digs at **Mainamati** and **Lalmai,** 5 miles west of **Comilla.**

Dhaka (Dacca) - Comilla - Chittagong 6602

Dep. Dhaka	06:30 (1)	08:00 (2+3)	09:00 (1)	12:20 (1+5)
Dep. Comilla	09:38	-0-	13:28	16:30
Arr. Chittagong	12:30	13:05	17:15	20:00
		* * *		
Dep. Chittagong	06:40 (2)	07:45 (1+3)	09:05 (1)	12:05 (1+6)
Dep. Comilla	-0-	10:31	12:35	14:59
Arr. Dhaka	11:45	13:55	17:35	19:10

(1) Supplement charged. Has first-class. Buffet. (2) Reservation required. Supplement charged. Has air-conditioned class and first-class. Restaurant car. (3) Runs daily, except Friday. (4) Supplement charged. Has air-conditioned class and first-class with seats that convert to berths. (5) Plus other departures from Dhaka at 15:00 (1+3), 16:30 (2) and 22:30 (4), arriving Chittagong 20:10, 21:35 and 07:15. (6) Plus other departures from Chittagong at 13:30 (1), 15:10 (2+3) and 22:30 (4), arriving Dhaka 19:35, 20:15 and 06:50.

Dhaka (Dacca) - Sylhet (via Akhaura) 6601 + 6602

All of these trains charge a supplement.

Dep. Dhaka	07:30 (1)	09:40 (2)	14:00 (3)	21:00 (4)	21:30 (5)
Arr. Sylhet	13:50	20:10	20:55	07:15	08:45

Sights in **Sylhet:** This is the tea estates area of the beautiful **Surma Valley.** Much small-game hunting here.

Dep. Sylhet	06:00 (6)	07:30 (7)	10:30 (2)	15:00 (1)	21:10 (4)	22:15 (8)
Arr. Dhaka	12:55	17:35	21:15	21:35	07:15	09:05

(1) Runs daily, except Wednesday. Has first-class and executive-class. Buffet. (2) Runs daily. Has first-class. Buffet. (3) Runs daily, except Saturday. Has first-class. (4) Runs daily. Has air-conditioned class and first-class that convert to berths. (5) Runs daily. Has first-class that converts to berths. Change trains in Akhaura at 01:00. (6) Runs daily, except Sunday. Has first-class. (7) Runs daily, except Tuesday. Has first-class. Change trains in Akhaura at 12:00. (8) Runs daily. Change trains in Akhaura at 04:15.

BURMA (MYANMAR)

Children under 3 travel free. Half-fare for children 3–9. Children 10 and over must pay full fare.

The 3 classes on Burmese trains are: upper-class (3 upholstered seats abreast), first-class (4 upholstered seats abreast), and ordinary-class (5 wood seats abreast), which we show as *first, second and third-class*.

Burma does not publish timetables. Those timetables that are posted at railstations are in Burmese script, including the numerals.

An English-speaking duty officer at the Information Office in Rangoon's railstation will assist foreigners with ticket purchases and will provide information about train connections.

Tickets may be purchased up to 3 days in advance of travel date, and it is usually necessary to make reservations 2 days in advance for First-Class space on the Rangoon–Mandalay ride. Lower class space is very unsatisfactory.

Only tea and soft drinks are served on Burma's trains. Vendors at many stations sell food. This is Burmese food and does not appeal to all Westerners. It is advisable to bring your own food and a container of water. Both Burma Airways and Tourist Burma's office in Rangoon arrange tours of Burma and a 3-hour guided tour of Rangoon.

Rangoon

The 320-foot high stupa of the enormous 2400-year old Shwe Dagon Pagoda is completely covered with gold leaf. Value of the 8,688 foot-square gold plates on the plantian bud at the top has been computed as over $2,500,000. There are 5,448 diamonds and more than 2,000 other precious stones at the top of the bud.

A 25-ton bell is located at one corner of the platform. The British took the bell, as a prize of war, and dropped it into the Rangoon River as they were attempting to load it onto a ship. Unable to raise the bell, the British abandoned it. Burmese workers raised it by tying enough bamboo poles to it until it floated.

The Shwe Dagon is said to be the most revered pagoda of the world's one billion Buddhists.

In central Rangoon, see: The 2300-year old Sule Pagoda. The National Museum. Burmese students learning their dances at the State School of music and Drama in Jubilee Hall. Bogyoke Market on Park Road, only a few minutes' walk from the town center, has many shops and stalle selling handcrafts. Also visit the Zoo, which has an excellent collection of monkeys. North of the city's center is the contemporary Kaba Aye Pagoda, built in 1956. In nearby **Regu**, a 2-hour auto ride, there is a 180-foot long reclining Buddha.

Rangoon - Mandalay   6700

The 06:00 departures are usually less crowded than the other departures.

All of these trains have first-class space.

Dep. Rangoon	06:00	11:45	18:15 (1)	21:00 (1)
Arr. Mandalay	20:00	07:15	07:00	10:40

* * *

Dep. Mandalay	06:00	11:10	18:15 (1)	21:00 (1)
Arr. Rangoon	20:00	07:40	08:00	10:40

(1) Carries a sleeping car.

Sights in **Mandalay:** This is one of Burma's youngest cities, existing since only 1857. Great Buddhist carvings here. Fine Burmese timber architecture. Many interesting monasteries, beautiful small pagodas.

Mandalay - Pagan 6720 Bus

Dep. Mandalay	04:00	Dep. Nyaungu	04:00 (1)
Arr. Nyaungu	14:00 (1)	Arr. Mandalay	14:00

(1) Taxi service was once available for the 7km ride Nyaungu–Pagan and v.v.

Sights in **Pagan:** Once a fantastic city of many millions and called City of Four Million Pagodas, before Kublai Khan sacked it in the 13th century. Now, there are splendid ruins of more than 5,000 structures to see: great temples and pagodas.

HERE ARE SCHEDULES FOR 3 OTHER LONG TRAIN TRIPS FROM MANDALAY:

Mandalay - Lashio 6701

This route has fine scenery. *Both trains have first-class space.*

Dep. Manadalay	05:10	Dep. Lashio	07:00
Arr. Lashio	17:00	Arr. Mandalay	19:40

Mandalay - Myitkyina 6701

All of these trains have first-class space. All arrivals are day 2.

Dep. Mandalay	15:00	16:00 (1)	Dep. Myitkyina	07:00	08:00 (1)
Arr. Myitkyina	15:00	17:25	Arr. Mandalay	07:00	09:50

(1) Carries sleeping car.

Mandalay - Thazi - Shwenyaung - Taunggyi 6700

All of these trains have first-class space.

Dep. Mandalay	06:00	Dep. Shweyaung	11:00	
Arr. Thazi	08:28	Arr. Thazi	21:30	
Change trains.		Change trains.		
Dep. Thazi	09:10	Dep. Thazi	03:34	05:10 (1)
Arr. Shwenyaung	16:35	Arr. Mandalay	07:15	07:00

(1) Plus other departures from Thazi at 07:50 and 17:05, arriving Mandalay 10:40 and 20:00.

It is an 11-mile taxi ride from **Shwenyaung** to **Taunggyi,** a hill station located at 4,712 feet.

HONG KONG

Children under 3 travel free. Half-fare for children 3–9. Children 10 and over must pay full fare.

This country owns the Kowloon-Canton Railway, which operates 40 passenger trains daily between Kowloon and Lo Wu, the border station for non-direct rail trips into the People's Republic of China. Nearly 2,000,000 people make this ride every year. There is ferry service from Hong Kong to Kowloon.

Prior to 1979, it had always been necessary to go through customs formalities in Lo Wu and then walk across the bridge spanning the Shum Chun River to the Chinese railstation on the north side of the river before boarding a second train in Shenzhen and proceeding to Guangzhou (Canton).

Since 1979, several trains per day make a direct ride from Hong Kong to Guangzhou and v.v., without requiring passengers to change trains in Lo Wu. These direct trains are operated by the People's Republic of China and are first-class only.

Hong Kong

See the art objects in Fung Ping Shan Museum at the University of Hong Kong. Take the cruise to Yaumati Typhoon Shelter to see the "floating people" who live their entire lives on small boats. Go on the bus tour to Aberdeen and several interesting villages. The bus also stops at the unique Tiger Balm Gardens.

Visit the Sung Dynasty village at Laichikok in Kowloon to see the architecture, costumes and food of the 10th–12th centuries. There are 3-hour guided group tours there Monday-Friday 10:00–13:00 (lunch included), 12:30–15:30 (lunch included), 15:00–18:00 (light snacks), and 17:30–20:00 (dinner). The village is also open to individuals on Saturdays and Sundays 12:30–17:00.

Eat at some of the 27 restaurants in the one-square-block called Food Street, in the Causeway Bay section everything from Sichuan to Cantonese, Taiwanese, Peking, Vietnamese, Indian, Pakistani, Indonesian, Japanese, Malaysan, Singapore, Sri Lanka . . . and European food.

Also visit the complex of food stalls located in Kowloon between the Star Ferry Terminal and the Peninsula Hotel. Shop for aphrodisiacs in the alleys behind Queen's Road Central.

Kowloon (Hong Kong) - Guangzhou (Canton) 5400

These trains require reservation, are first-class only, are air-conditioned and have light refreshments unless designated otherwise.

Dep. Kowloon (H. Hom)	08:15	09:00	12:25	14:25	16:25	18:05 (1)
Arr. Guangzhou	10:33	11:18	14:43	16:43	18:43	20:23
		*	*	*		
Dep. Guangzhou	08:30	10:20	12:20	14:20	16:27	18:30 (1)
Arr. Kowloon (H. Hom)	10:48	12:38	14:38	16:38	18:45	20:48

(1) Reservation not required

INDIA

Children under 5 travel free. Half-fare for children 5–11. Children 12 and over must pay full fare.

Every day, more than 10,000,000 people ride India's 11,000 trains, connecting 7,085 railstations. This is Asia's largest railway system.

The 5 classes of space on Indian Railways are: first-class air-conditioned, second- class air-conditioned, air-conditioned chair car, first-class, and second-class. First-class air-conditioned converts at night to 2 berths, second-class air-conditioned to 4 berths. First-class (not air-conditioned) compartments convert at night to 4, 5 or 6 berths. Second- class sleepercoaches convert into sleeping bunks between 21:00 and 06:00.

Foreign tourists can reserve air-conditioned classes and ordinary first-class space up to 180 days in advance of travel date. To determine which of the 7 rail offices in India you need contact for advance reservations, first communicate your itinerary to any Government of India Tourist Office. That office will advise you whether to direct your reservation order to the Central, Eastern, North Eastern, Northern, South Central, South Eastern or Western offices of Indian Railway.

Breaking of a journey at any station en route is permitted with single journey tickets when the entire trip is more than 200 miles, at the rate of one day for every 100 miles. However, the first break of journey cannot be made until the passenger has traveled at least 150 miles from his or her starting station.

There are restaurants at important railstations. The leading passenger trains have restaurant cars which offer both Indian and Western food. India Government Tourist Offices provide a "Tourist Timetable".

INDIA'S TRAIN PASS

Indrail Pass. Unlimited rail travel. Available to citizens of countries other than India and to those Indians residing outside India who hold valid passports. The bearer is not required to pay for reservations *but must make reservations.*

Even when full use of the pass is not made, having it avoids having to stand in long lines to buy tickets. Furthermore, on many trains that are ostensibly "sold-out", authorities somehow find seats for pass-holders.

Don't even consider the second-class pass. That class is usually so crowded that it is extremely uncomfortable. On the other hand, the highest-priced pass (air-conditioned) is frequently a waste of money because many routes don't have air-conditioned coaches.

The great advantage to the first-class pass is that both reservations and sleeping compartments are easier to obtain with it than with the second-class pass. Also, passengers having it can use comfortable first-class waiting rooms in the railstations.

The prices in U.S. dollars (children shown in parenthesis) in late **1991 were:**

	Air-conditioned		First-class		Second-class	
1 day	$ 65	(33)	$ 29	(15)	$ 12	(6)
7 days	220	(110)	110	(55)	55	(28)
15 days	270	(135)	135	(68)	65	(33)
21 days	330	(165)	165	(83)	75	(38)
30 days	410	(205)	205	(103)	90	(45)
60 days	600	(300)	300	(150)	135	(68)
90 days	800	(400)	400	(200)	175	(88)

Sold by Harri World Travel. In the U.S.A.: 30 Rockefeller Plaza, Room 21, New York, NY 10112. In Canada: Royal York Hotel, 100 Front St. W., Toronto, Ont. M5J 1E3.

Student Discounts

Students of educational institutions and art schools of foreign countries are allowed substantial discounts when traveling for educational purposes or when visiting places of artistic importance.

The letter of authority required in order to obtain this concession can be obtained from the Chief Commercial Superintendent in each major city upon presenting a passport and either a Student Identity Card or a letter from one's embassy certifying that the bearer is a student.

See the Deputy Superintendent at the railstation in order to obtain the address of the local C.C.I.

India's 4 principal cities (Bombay, Calcutta, Delhi and Madras) are connected by rail routes.

Bombay

This is a seaport. See the Zoo and the Victoria and Albert Museum at Victoria Gardens. The Mahatma Phule Market. Jehangir Art Gallery. The collection of Chinese jade and porcelain and the Tata Collection of paintings at The Prince of Wales Museum. The Rajabai Tower. Elephant Caves. Gateway of India.

Calcutta

A major seaport, although it is 100 miles from the Bay of Bengal. See the many alleys with shops called Bara Bazaar. The stone carvings in the India Museum. The large Nakhoda Mosque. The Botanical Gardens. The Kali Temple. The Jain Temple. The white tigers at the Zoo. The assortment of both great art objects and junk in the Marble Palace. The Victoria Memorial. Howrah Bridge. Belur Math. The National Library. The Philatelic Museum.

Delhi

See the 16th century Lodi Tombs. The Great Mosque. Teen Murtis House, once the home of Nehru and his daughter, Indira Gandhi. The Pearl Mosque. The 2200-year old Ashoka Pillar. The 17th century Red Fort. Humayun's Tomb. The view from the top of the 13th century 238-foot high, red sandstone Qutub Minar Tower.

The Zoo. The National Museum. For shopping, stroll Connaught Place and see the marvelous jewelry assortment (emeralds, diamonds, rubies and sapphires) in both the leading stores and at the Sundar Nagar Market. Visit the Central Cottage Industries Emporium on Janpath and the silver and cloth stores on Chandni Chowk.

The 43 locomotives and 17 coaches in New Delhi's enormous Rail Transport Museum (closed Monday), including the world's oldest (1855) and still operational steam locomotive. This museum also has a model train for children and a floating restaurant.

Madras

Visit the archaeological exhibit at the Government Museum on Pantheon Road near the Egmore railstation, open 09:00–17:00 daily except Fridays and holidays. In the first of the Museum's 3 buildings, see the miniature paintings of the Moguls and court processions. Also, 18th and 19th century carved ivory miniatures.

The second building, the Bronze Gallery, has 9th century Chola sculpture masterpieces. The third building displays ivory temple models, weapons, musical instruments, votive toys and wood carvings. Its major exhibit is 3rd and 4th century granite sculptures.

See the collection of weapons, chinaware and costumes in the Fort Museum. The view of the harbor from the top of the lighthouse. The fine beach. The South Indian bronzes at the National Art Gallery. Fort St. George, the oldest Anglican church in the Orient. San Thome Basilica, where the remains of the apostle Thomas are said to lie.

Bombay - Ahmadabad 6067

Dep. Bombay (Cen.)	06:00	07:45	17:00 (1)	18:25 (2)	19:00 (2+4)
Arr. Ahmadabad	15:30	20:50	01:00	03:30	04:15

Sights in **Ahmadabad:** Free guides are provided by the city, at Lal Darwaja, a few blocks from the Manek Chowk Bazaar. Spices, incense, brass, copper, hand-painted cottons, silver, jewelry, fruits and vegetables are sold in the streets of that bazaar. See the collection of rare 11th-16th century miniature paintings in the Sanskar Kendra Cultural Center.

The terra-cotta sculptures at the National Institute of Design. The exhibits of musical instruments, ceremonial costumes and jewelry at the Shreyas Folk Museum. The students practicing traditional dance, music and puppetry at the Darpana Academy. The 250 beautifully carved pillars at the lovely 15th century Jumma Masjid Mosque. The exquisite filligree marble windows at Sidi Said's Mosque. The promenades, boating, gardens and museums at **Lake Kankaria**.

Visit the **Sabarmati Ashram,** a colony of small cottages Gandhi established in 1915 and where he worked to promote Indian independence for the next 15 years.

Dep. Ahmadabad	05:00 (1)	07:10	07:40	20:15 (2)	22:00 (3+5)
Arr. Bombay (Cen.)	13:30	16:40	19:05	05:45	06:45

(1) Has second-class air-conditioned compartments that convert to berths. (2) Second-class only. (3) Has both first-class and second-class air-conditioned compartments that convert to berths. (4) Plus other departures from Bombay at 20:15 (1) and 21:30 (3), arriving Ahmadabad 05:40 and 06:30. (5) Plus another departure from Ahmadabad at 22:35 (1), arriving Bombay 08:05.

Bombay - Allahabad 6080

All arrivals are on day 2.

Dep. Bombay (Vict.)	05:00 (1)	06:40 (2)	19:35 (3)	21:10 (3)	23:55 (3)
Arr. Allahabad	05:10	08:15	23:10	20:45	23:50

Sights in **Allahabad** (City of God): The confluence of the Ganges, Jamuna and mythical Sarawati rivers. See the Pillar of Asoka at the 16th century fort. The Jami Masjid (Great Mosque). The Museum. The beautiful Victorian Nehru House.

Dep. Allahabad	08:20 (3)	11:10 (3)	15:10 (3)	16:50	21:05 (4)
Arr. Bombay (Vict.)	12:40	11:25	14:50	20:00 (2)	23:35

(1) Supplement charged (except Saturday) . Runs Monday, Wednesday, Thursday and Saturday. (2) Depart/Arrive Bombay's Dadar railstation. (3) Has second-class air-conditioned compartments that convert to bunks. (4) Supplement charged. Runs Tuesday, Thursday and Friday.

Bombay - Bangalore - Mysore

Bangalore - Mysore - Bangalore is an easy one-day excursion.
None of these trains are air-conditioned, unless designated otherwise.
6020

Dep. Bombay	08:45	17:50	20:45 (2)		
Arr. Miraj	20:00	05:00 (1)	06:10 (1)		
Change trains. Table 6155					
Dep. Miraj		13:30	06:25		
Arr. Bangalore		07:50 (1)	22:15		
Change trains. Table 6172					
Dep. Bangalore	07:25 (3)	10:45 (4)	22:30 (4)	14:00 (3)	16:45 (3)
Arr. Mysore	11:15	15:30 (5)	04:30 (5)	17:50	20:30

Sights in **Bangalore**: The palace of the Maharajah of Mysore. The 18th century Lal Bagh botanic garden. The Mysore Government Museum. The **Nandi Hill Station**, summer resort, 38 miles from here. The nearby **Hesaraghatta Lake**.

Sights in **Mysore**: Brindavn Gardens, at a dam, beautifully lighted at night.

Dep. Mysore	10:15 (3)	13:00	16:25 (3)	18:15 (3)
Arr. Bangalore	13:35	16:40	20:10	21:45
Change trains. Table 6155				
Dep. Bangalore	19:35	06:00 (6)		
Arr. Miraj	14:30 (6)	22:10		
Change trains. Table 6020				
Dep. Miraj	22:20 (2)	23:40	09:25	
Arr. Bombay	08:00 (7)	12:05 (7)	21:15	

(1) Day 2. from Bombay. (2) Has air-conditioned second-class that converts to bunks at night. (3) Restaurant car. (4) Second-class only. (5) Day 3 from Bombay. (6) Day 2 from Mysore. (7) Day 3 from Mysore.

Bombay - Calcutta 6105

Dep. Bombay (Vic.)	06:05 (1)	19:10 (3)	21:30 (5)
Arr. Calcutta (How.)	14:15 (2)	07:10 (4)	15:00 (4)

Sights in **Calcutta**: See notes about Calcutta on page 588.

Dep. Calcutta (How.)	12:15 (5)	13:25 (1)	20:15 (3)
Arr. Bombay (Vic.)	06:35 (4)	21:45 (2)	07:40 (4)

(1) Supplement charged. Runs daily. Has air-conditioned second-class that converts to bunks at night. Restaurant car. (2) Day 2. (3) Has air-conditioned first-class and second-class that convert to berths and bunks at night. Restaurant car. (4) Day 3. (5) Not air-conditioned.

Bombay - Madras 6095

Dep. Bombay (Victoria)	-0-	-0-	23:15 (1)
Dep. Bombay (Dadar)	14:25 (1)	19:50 (3)	23:30
Arr. Madras (Cen.)	16:35 (2)	19:50 (2)	05:45 (4)

Sights in **Madras**: See notes about Madras on page 588.

Dep. Madras (Cen.)	07:05 (5)	09:15 (1)	22:20 (1)
Arr. Bombay (Dadar)	07:05 (2)	12:00 (2)	04:28 (4)
Arr. Bombay (Victoria)	-0-	-0-	04:50

(1) Has air-conditioned second-class that converts to bunks at night. (2) Day 2. (3) Runs daily, except Monday and Saturday. Supplement charged. Has air-conditioned second-class that converts to bunks at night. (4) Day 3. (5) Supplement charged. Runs daily, except Wednesday and Friday. Has air-conditioned second-class that converts to bunks at night.

Bombay - New Delhi 6070

All of these trains charge a supplement. All arrivals are "Day 2" unless designated otherwise.

Dep. Bombay (Central)	08:25 (1)	11:30 (2)	17:00 (3)	21:15 (2)
Arr. New Delhi	04:45	10:25	09:15	19:30

Sights in **Delhi:** See notes about Delhi on page 588.

Dep. New Delhi	08:25 (2)	16:05 (3)	17:00 (2)	21:45 (1)
Arr. Bombay (Central)	07:00	08:35	15:00	18:10

(1) Has air-conditioned second-class that converts to bunks. Runs Monday, Thursday, Friday and Sunday from Bombay. Runs Tuesday, Wednesday, Friday and Saturday from New Delhi. (2) Has air-conditioned first and second-class that convert to berths and bunks. Restaurant car. (3) Reservation required. Restaurant car. Runs daily, except Saturday from Bombay. Runs daily, except Sunday from New Delhi. Has air-conditioned first and second-class that convert to berths and bunks, and also has air-conditioned chair car.

Bombay - Patna

6080

Dep. Bombay (Dadar)	05:13 (1)	06:40	19:50 (3)	21:25 (4)	23:55 (5)
Arr. Allahabad	05:10 (2)	08:15 (2)	23:15 (2+3)	20:45 (2)	23:50 (2)

Change trains. Table 6060

Dep. Allahabad	05:20 (6)	10:45	23:50 (3)
Arr. Patna	11:45	18:25	07:40 (7)

Sights in **Patna**: Many fine mosques. The collection of rare Arabic and Persian manuscripts in the Khudabuksh Oriental Library. An important Sikh temple.

Dep. Patna	05:00 (8)	07:30	13:30 (8)	23:25 (3)
Arr. Allahabad	10:55	15:55	20:00	07:45 (2+3)

Change trains. Table 6080

Dep. Allahabad	11:10 (9)	16:50	21:05 (10)	08:20 (3)
Arr. Bombay (Dadar)	10:53 (2)	20:00 (2)	23:03 (2)	12:10 (11)

(1) Supplement charged. Runs Monday, Wednesday, Thursday and Saturday. (2) Day 2. (3) Direct train. No change in Allahabad. Has air-conditioned second-class coach that converts to bunks. (4) Has air-conditioned second-class coach that converts to bunks. On Monday, Wednesday and Saturday also has air-conditioned first-class coach that converts to berths. (5) Departs from Bombay's Victoria railstation. Has air-conditioned second-class coach that converts to bunks. (6) Supplement charged. Has air-conditioned second-class coach. On Monday, Wednesday and Friday also has air-conditioned first-class coach. (7) Day 3 from Bombay. (8) Supplement charged. Has air-conditioned second-class. (9) Has air-conditioned second-class. (10) Supplement charged. Runs Tuesday, Thursday and Friday. (11) Day 3 from Patna.

Bombay - Pune 6095

The first double-deck passenger train in India started operating in 1978 on the 115-mile long Bombay–Pune line. Its coaches seat 148 (versus 90 in ordinary second-class coaches).

From Bombay to Pune, the train climbs 2,000 feet through the Western Ghat. There are extraordinary views of the Sahyadri mountain range from the high viaducts on this route.

Only trains that have air-conditioned compartments are listed here.

Dep. Bombay (Vic.)	06:00	07:55	12:35	14:25 (1)	15:35 (3)
Arr. Pune	3½–4½ hours later				

Sights in **Pune**: Many ancient palaces and temples. This route involves 25 tunnels and many high bridges and viaducts. Can be made as a one-day roundtrip. The very picturesque narrow-gauge Matheran Hill Railway is near this route and can be visited during the day.

Dep. Pune	00:33	01:03	02:18	03:28 (1)	04:00 (1+4)
Arr. Bombay (Vic.)	3½–4½ hours later				

(1) Depart/Arrive Bombay's Dadar railstation. (2) Supplement charged (3) Plus other Bombay departures at 19:50 (1+2), 20:45 (1+2), 21:55 and 23:15. (4) Plus other departures from Pune at 07:15 (2), 07:48 (1), 08:53, 16:15 and 18:45.

Calcutta - Allahabad 6060

| Dep. Calcutta (How.) | 09:15 (1) | 19:00 (3) | 20:00 (4) | 20:45 |
| Arr. Allahabad | 00:30 (2) | 09:05 (2) | 10:30 (2) | 15:55 (2) |

Sights in **Allahabad**: See notes under "Bombay-Allahabad" on page 589.

| Dep. Allahabad | 02:10 (5) | 10:45 | 18:00 (3) | 21:15 (6) |
| Arr. Calcutta (How.) | 18:00 | 06:10 (2) | 08:30 (2) | 13:15 (2) |

(1) Supplement charged. Has air-conditioned first and second-class compartments that convert to berths and bunks and also has air-conditioned chair car and restaurant car. (2) Day 2. (3) Supplement charged. Has air-conditioned first second-class compartments that convert to berths and bunks. Restaurant car. (4) Has air-conditioned second-class compartments that convert to bunks. (5) Supplement charged. Has air-conditioned first and second-class compartments that convert to berths and bunks. Also an air-conditioned chair car. (6) Has air-conditioned second-class compartments daily that convert to bunks.

Calcutta - New Jalpaiguri - Darjeeling

The New Jalpaiguri–Darjeeling narrow-gauge rail line was completed in 1881. It has been known as "the toy train".

This tortuous 53-mile route (crossing 550 bridges and making 6 switchbacks and 4 complete loops) takes more than 8 hours. The train moves so slowly that there are constant opportunities to take photos and to observe villages.

The scenic beauty along this route includes giant bamboos, ferns, mosses, orchids, magnolias, rhododendrons and many trees fig, oak, chestnut, birch, walnut.

The Jalpaiguri–Darjeeling (and v.v.) portion of this trip was temporarily suspended in 1991.

6112		6123	
Dep. Calcutta (Sealdah)	19:00 (1)	Dep. Darjeeling	N/A
Arr. New Jalpaiguri	08:30	Arr. New Jalpaiguri	N/A
Change trains.		Change trains.	
6123		6112	
Dep. New Jalpaiguri	N/A	Dep. New Jalpaiguri	18:45 (1)
Arr. Darjeeling	N/A	Arr. Calcutta (Sealdah)	08:45

(1) Has air-conditioned first and second-class compartments that convert to berths and bunks, and also has an air-conditioned chair car.

Sights in **Darjeeling**: At 7,000 feet, this is a cool and beautiful area. Many famous tea plantations. The town's name comes from the word "dorjee", the mystic thunderbolt of Indra, and "ling", meaning place.

There is a large population of Tibetans in Darjeeling. Many arts and crafts are sold at the Tibetan Refugee Center. The interesting items to purchase there are jewelry, carvings, colorful fabrics, carpets, prayer wheels. Nearby is the Zoo and the Museum of Himalayan Mountaineering.

Visit the shrines in the Mahakala Temple complex. Tour a factory that processes tea. Ride the longest cable chairlift in Asia, 5 miles to the village of **Singla**. Take a land-rover ride through spectacular forests to the very interesting Saturday market in **Kalimpong**. Go to the **Jaldapara** game sanctuary (about 120 miles away) to see rhinos and elephants. Excursions by 4-wheel-drive vehicles are made from Darjeeling to Nepal, Sikkim and Bhutan.

One can walk or take a jeep to **Tiger Hill** to see the sunrise. There is a hotel there. The preferred visit is to spend the night in Tiger Hill, see the sunrise the next morning (and a view of 4 countries: Nepal, Bhutan, Sikkim and India), and then catch the train from Darjeeling for the ride back to Calcutta.

Calcutta - Madras 6150

Dep. Calcutta (Howrah)	15:00 (1)	21:00 (3)	22:35 (5)
Arr. Madras (Central)	17:35 (2)	04:45 (4)	04:10 (4)

Sights in **Madras**: See notes about Madras on page 588.

Dep. Madras (Central)	07:20 (6)	08:10 (1)	22:30 (3)
Arr. Calcutta (Howrah)	13:45 (2)	11:15 (2)	06:30 (4)

(1) Supplement charged. Has air-conditioned second-class compartments that convert to bunks. Restaurant car. (2) Day 2. (3) Has air-conditioned second-class compartments that convert to bunks. (4) Day 3. (5) Supplement charged. Runs daily except Tuesday and Wednesday. Has air-conditioned second-class compartments that convert to bunks. (6) Supplement charged. Runs Monday, Wednesday, Thursday and Friday. Has air-conditioned second-class compartments that convert to bunks.

Calcutta - New Delhi 6060

The train passes through several different regions on this trip. Climate, language and clothing change every few hours.

Dep. Calcutta (Howrah)	09:15 (1)	16:30 (3)	19:00 (4)	20:45
Arr. New Delhi	10:40 (2)	09:50 (2)	-0-	-0-
Arr. Delhi	-0-	-0-	19:55 (2)	04:45 (5)

Sights in **Delhi**: See notes about Delhi on page 588.

Dep. Delhi	08:00 (4)	-0-	-0-	22:10
Dep. New Delhi	-0-	16:00 (1)	17:15 (3)	-0-
Arr. Calcutta (Howrah)	08:30 (2)	18:00 (2)	11:00 (2)	06:10 (5)

(1) Supplement charged. Has air-conditioned first and second-class compartments that convert to berths and bunks. Also an air-conditioned chair car. Restaurant car. (2) Day 2. (3) Reservation required. Supplement charged. From Calcutta: runs daily, except Wednesday and Saturday. From New Delhi: runs daily, except Thursday and Sunday. Has air-conditioned first and second-class compartments that convert to berths and bunks, and also an air-conditioned chair car. Restaurant car. (4) Supplement charged. Has air-conditioned first and second-class compartments that convert to berths and bunks. Restaurant car. (5) Day 3.

Delhi - Agra 6080

The 07:05 departure from New Delhi is "Taj Express". It is met on 09:50 arrival in Agra by an air-conditioned government-operated tourist bus and an official guide. Its tour includes the 17th century Taj Mahal and Fatehpur Sikri Fort. Avoid private guides. They *do not* provide as complete a tour as the government does. Another interesting sight in Agra is the tomb of Tmad-ud-Daulah. The bus brings you back to the Agra station for the 18:45 departure of "Taj Express", arriving back in New Delhi at 22:00.

As the schedules on page 594 indicate, it is not necessary to spend a night in Agra in order to see the Taj by moonlight.

Dep. New Delhi	06:15 (1)	07:05 (2)	08:00	10:50 (3)	12:00 (4)
Arr. Agra	08:05	09:50	12:10	13:40	14:35

Dep. New Delhi	12:50 (5)	15:00 (6)	16:20 (5)	18:40 (4)	19:30 (7+8)
Arr. Agra	15:45	18:35	19:23	21:35	22:15

* * *

Dep. Agra	01:25 (3)	05:40 (7)	06:30 (5)	08:01 (4)	09:40 (5)
Arr. New Delhi	07:10	09:05	10:30	11:55	13:00

Dep. Agra	11;28 (4)	15:18 (3)	16:20 (3)	17:30 (3)	18:45 (2+9)
Arr. New Delhi	14:30	20:20	20:10	21:05	22:00

(1) "Panchavati Express" runs daily Delhi–Agra-Bhopal (and v.v.). Its schedule is ideal for a day of sightseeing in Agra but a reservation is essential because only 3 of its 7 coaches (67 passengers each) allow a journey to Agra. This train has only air-conditioned chair cars. Seats recline and have a foot-rest. Each coach has 3 restrooms: 2 Indian style and one Western style. (2) "Taj Express". Reservation required. Has air-conditioned first-class compartments and air-conditioned chair car. Restaurant car. (3) Has air-conditioned second-class compartments. (4) Supplement charged. Has air-conditioned second-class compartments. Restaurant car or buffet. (5) Depart/Arrive Delhi's Hazrat Nizamuddin railstation. Has air-conditioned second-class compartments. (6) Runs Monday, Wednesday, Friday and Sunday. Has air-conditioned second-class compartments. (7) Supplement charged. Has air-conditioned second-class. (8) Plus other departures from New Delhi at 20:30 (5), 20:50 (3) and 23:20 (7)... arriving Agra 23:25, 00:40 and 01:52. (9) Plus another departure from Agra at 20:21 (1), arriving New Delhi 22:20.

Delhi - Ahmadabad 6036

Dep. Delhi	09:30	16:00	18:10 (2)	22:00 (3)
Arr. Ahmadabad	10:00 (1)	16:15 (1)	11:15 (1)	20:15 (1)

Sight in **Ahmadabad**: See notes under "Bombay–Ahmadabad" on page 589.

Dep. Ahmadabad	05:45	08:25 (3)	17:00 (2)	18:00
Arr. Delhi	05:30 (1)	07:30 (1)	10:00 (1)	19:00 (1)

(1) Day 2. (2) Supplement charged. Has air-conditioned second-class that converts to bunks. (3) Has air-conditioned first and second-class that convert to berths and bunks.

Delhi - Allahabad 6060

Dep. Delhi	-0-	08:00 (2)	-0-	-0-	18:45 (1+7)
Dep. New Delhi	06:30 (1)	-0-	12:30 (3)	16:10 (4)	-0-
Arr. Allahabad	15:20	17:50	23:25	02:20	04:10

Sights in **Allahabad**: See notes under "Bombay-Allahabad", page 589.

Dep. Allahabad	00:30 (4)	01:55 (3)	05:00 (3)	09:15 (2)	11:05 (1+8)
Arr. New Delhi	10:40	11:45	16:05	-0-	20:15
Arr. Delhi	-0-	-0-	-0-	19:55	-0-

(1) Supplement charged. Has air-conditioned second-class that converts to bunks. Restaurant car. (2) Supplement charged. Has air-conditioned first and second-class. Restaurant car. (3) Has air-conditioned second-class that converts to bunks. (4) Supplement charged. Has first and second-class that convert to berths and bunks, and an air-conditioned chair car. (5) Supplement charged. Daily: has air-conditioned second-class that converts to bunks. Monday, Wednesday and Friday: has air-conditioned first-class that converts to berths. (6) Supplement charged. Has air-conditioned first and second-class that convert to berths and bunks. (7) Plus other departures from New Delhi at 19:45 (5), 21:15 (3) and 22:00 (6), arriving Allahabad 05:10, 12:25 and 08:00. (8) Plus other departurse from Allahabad at 14:20 (3) and 21:00 (6), arriving New Delhi 06:15 and 06:50.

Delhi - Jaipur 6036

One of India's fastest trains, Pink City Express (colored pink), departs from a station that is a few miles away from the main Delhi station. Provide extra time to get there.

Dep. Delhi	06:00 (1)	09:30	13:00	18:10 (2)	22:00 (3)
Arr. Jaipur	11:15	17:40	20:45	23:35	04:50

Sights in **Jaipur**: This city is noted for the unusually colorful clothes worn by its people. See the pink Palace of the Winds.

Dep. Jaipur	00:30 (3)	04:35 (2)	06:45	10:40	17:00 (1)
Arr. Delhi	07:30	10:00	14:15	19:00	22:15

(1) "Pink City Express". Supplement charged. (2) Supplement charged. Has air-conditioned second-class compartments. (3) Has air-conditioned first-class and second-class compartments that convert to berths and bunks.

Delhi - Madras

6007 + 6080

Dep. New Delhi	12:00 (1)	15:00 (4)	18:40 (1)	22:30 (6)
Arr. Vijayawada	15:15 (2)	03:45 (5)	23:50 (2)	– 0 –
Change trains. Table 6150				
Dep. Vijayawada	19:40	04:10	23:59	– 0 –
Arr. Madras (Central)	06:10 (3)	12:35	07:00 (3)	07:50 (2)

Sights in **Madras:** See notes about sightseeing in Madras on page 588.

Dep. Madras (Central)	01:50 (7)	21:00 (6)	22:15 (1)	23:50 (9)
Arr. Vijayawada	10:30	– 0 –	05:00 (8)	10:30 (8)
Change trains. Tables 6007 + 6080				
Dep. Vijayawada	11:00	– 0 –	05:10	11:00
Arr. New Delhi	23:30	06:45	11:05	23:30

(1) Supplement charged. Has air-conditioned second-class that converts to bunks. Restaurant car or buffet. (2) Day 2 from New Delhi. (3) Day 2 from Vijayawada. (4) Runs Monday, Wednesday, Friday and Sunday. Has air-conditioned second-class that converts to bunks. (5) Day 3 from New Delhi. (6) Direct train ("Tamil Nadu Express"). No train change in Vijayawada. Supplement charged. Has air-conditioned first-class and second-class compartments that convert to berths and bunks and an air-conditioned chair car. Buffet. (7) Runs Saturday only. "Himsagar Express". Has air-conditioned 2nd class that converts to bunks. (8) Day 2 from Madras. (9) Runs Wednesday, Thursday and Sunday. Has air-conditioned 2nd class that converts to bunks.

Madras - Ernakulam - Cochin 6173

En route to Cochin, it is possible to leave the train in Ernakulum, sightsee there, and then later the same day take the trip of a few minutes to Cochin either by ferry boat or by bus across the bridge that connects the 2 cities.

Both trains have air-conditioned second-class compartments that convert to bunks.

Dep. Madras (Cent.)	19:40		Dep. Cochin	16:30
Arr. Ernakulam	08:55 day 2		Dep. Ernakulam	17:00
Arr. Cochin	09:20		Arr. Madras (Cent.)	06:15 day 2

Sights in **Ernakulam**: The week-long festival at the Siva temple, every January. Performances of the unusual Kathakali dance.

Sights in **Cochin:** This is actually a conglomerate of several islands and 3 cities. See the 16th century Santa Cruz Cathedral. The 16th century synagogue. The blue willow-patterned tiles on the floor of a second synagogue. The 16th century tomb of the great Spanish explorer Vasco de Gama. The Dutch Palace. Picturesque palm-lined beaches.

INTERNATIONAL ROUTES FROM INDIA

New Delhi is the gateway for train travel to Pakistan. The rail route to Sri Lanka (Ceylon) is via Madras and Rameswaram.

New Delhi - Amritsar - Lahore - Hyderabad - Karachi

All of these trains have second-class air-conditioned coaches that convert to bunks, unless designated otherwise.

6030

Dep. New Delhi	20:10 (1)	06:45 (2)	08:00	11:15 (3)	12:15 (11)
Arr. Amritsar	09:00	13:25	18:25	19:20	21:00

Change trains
6023

Dep. Amritsar	09:30
Arr. Lahore	13:35

Change trains
5910

Dep. Lahore	15:10 (4)	06:30 (6)	09:30 (8)	16:15 (9)	17:15 (10+12)
Dep. Hyderabad	06:35 (5)	19:53 (7)	02:53 (5)	08:00 (5)	-0-
Arr. Karachi (Can.)	09:05	22:05	05:30	10:25	18:30 (5)

(1)Restaurant car. (2) *No* air-conditioned second-class. Has air-conditioned chair car. (3) Supplement charged. Has air-conditioned first and second class. Restaurant car. (4) Has air-conditioned first-class and air-conditioned chair class. Restaurant car. (5) Day 2 from Lahore. (6) Supplement charged. Air-conditioned first-class that converts to berths. *No* air-conditioned second class. Has restaurant car *or* buffet. (7) Same day as Lahore departure. (8) Reservation required. Air-conditioned first class. Restaurant car. (9) *No* air-conditioned compartments. Restaurant car. (10) Has air-conditioned first-class. Restaurant car. (11) Plus other departures from New Delhi at 16:35 and 19:15(4), arriving Amritsar 05:30 and 06:15. (12) Plus another departure from Lahore at 19:35 (8), arriving Karachi 14:45.

Madras - Rameswaram - Talaimannar - Colombo Fort

6182		6300	
Dep. Madras (Egmore)	16:45	Dep. Talaimannar (Pier)	N/A (3)
Arr. Rameswaram	07:15 (1)	Dep. Talaimannar (City)	N/A
Change to ferry.		Arr Anuradhapura	N/A
6186		Change trains.	
Dep. Rameswaram (Port)	12:00 (2)	Dep. Anuradhapura	14:28 (4)
Arr. Talaimannar (Pier)	15:00	Arr. Colombo Fort	18:45
Change to train.			

(1) Day 2 from Madras. (2) Runs Monday, Wednesday and Friday. (3) Service was "temporarily" suspended in 1989. (4) Air-conditioned train.

INDONESIA

Children under 3 travel free. Half-fare for children 3–7. Children 8 and over must pay full fare. Cooks calls 2nd-class here "quite comfortable".

Nearly every train ride in Indonesia offers views of extinct volcanoes, mountains, water buffalo and rain forests.

Jakarta

The main railstation is Kota. See Bali dancing at Gedung Kesenian. The world's finest collection of Hindu-Javanese antiquities (coins, archaeological objects, Chinese ceramics) at the National Museum on Medan Merdeka. Its treasure room, containing Javanese gold ornaments from thousands of years ago, is open *only* on Sunday.

Do not miss seeing the morning activity at the Pasar Ikan, a large fish market. At the wharf, the unloading of spices, bananas, indigo and teak. The Maritime Museum, in what were once the warehouses of the old Dutch fort.

The National Mosque. The Museum Kota. Presidential Palace. The very tall National Monument. Spend an evening (plays, concerts, art exhibits, dances) at Taman Ismail Marzuki Cultural Complex, Jalan Cikini Raya 13. Go to the enormous park, Taman Mini, to see the exhibit (arts, crafts and building) from all the different islands of In- donesia. The interesting Dutch houses and the canals in Chinatown.

Ride out to **Bogoru** by bus or taxi to see the old Dutch palace (Merdeka Palace) and the fantastic 275-acre Botanical Garden: 10,000 species of trees and more than 500,000 other plants, including more than 100,000 orchid plants. Nothing in the world to compare with these gardens.

Before shopping for batik in the air-conditioned Aldiron Plaza, visit the Textile Museum on Jalan Satsuit Tubun and Keramik Museum on Fatahillah Square to learn how to differentiate between more than 300 types of Indonesian fabrics and many different styles of weaving. Across from the Keramik is the fantastic collection of puppets (Balinese, Javan, etc.) at Wayang Museum.

Browse in the flea markets along Jalan Surabaya: Chinese and European chinaware, Balinese wood sculptures, silver filigree from Jogjakarta, Javanese daggers. Shop for quality antiques at the stores on Jalan Kebon Sirih Timur Dalam, near the Hyatt Hotel. The specialty on Pasar Baru is fabrics. Check-out the art, curio and handicraft stalls in the 12-acre Indonesian Bazaar, next to the Hilton Hotel, open daily 10:00–18:00.

Visit the bird market (cockatoos and many other tropical birds) on Jalan Pramuka. The orchid markets, at Cipete and Cilandak. At Taman Fatahillah (a square in the center of Old Batavia) see: the Historical Museum in the 18th century Town Hall, the Wayang puppets in the Wayang Museum, and Balai Seni Rupa (the city art gallery).

Surabaja

There are 3 railstations. Trains for Jakarta depart from Gubeng. Trains for Bandung depart from Kota. Tasar Turi is the third railstation.

This is a major seaport. A 30-minute ferry-boat ride takes you to **Madura,** where the major attraction is the racing of bulls. Surabaja is a convenient point for visiting **Mount Bromo** and seeing live animals sacrificed in the boiling volcano crater there.

There are 2 routes from Jakarta to Surabaja.

Jakarta - Surabaja (via Cirebon) 7406

Dep. Jakarta (Kota)	12:10 (1+2)	16:00 (3)	16:30 (4)	17:53 (6+7)
Arr. Surabaja (Gubeng)	05:05	06:57	05:45 (5)	07:37 (5)

* * *

Dep. Surabaja (Gubeng)	14:15 (2)	16:10 (3)	16:30 (4+5)	17:30 (7)
Arr. Jakarta (Kota)	06:32 (1)	07:03	06:20	07:19 (6)

(1) Depart/Arrive Jakarta's Gambir railstation. (2) Third-class only. Restaurant car. (3) Reservation required. Has first-class sleeping cars and air-conditioned first-class coaches. Restaurant car. (4) First-class only. Air-conditioned train. Restaurant car. (5) Depart/Arrive Surabaja's Pasarturi railstation. (6) Depart/Arrive Jakarta's Pasarsenen railstation. (7) Third-class only. Buffet.

Jakarta - Surabaja (via Bandung) 7406

Dep. Jakarta (Kota)	05:25 (1)	09:35 (1)	11:10 (1)	13:40 (1)	15:15 (1)
Arr. Bandung	08:38	12:55	14:23	17:00	18:28

Change trains.

Dep. Bandung	05:25 (2)	17:30 (3)
Arr. Surabaja (Gubeng)	20:48	07:52

Sights in **Bandung**: This is a much nicer and cooler city than Jakarta. Quinine is derived from cinchona bark. This is the center of Indonesia's quinine industry, with many cinchona tree plantations here. There are also numerous tea plantations in this area, See the collection of crocodiles, birds and snakes at the Zoological Garden.

Dep. Surabaja (Gubeng)	05:26 (4)	17:50 (3)
Arr. Bandung	20:10	07:35

Change trains.

Dep. Bandung	05:00 (1)	06:15 (1)	09:10 (1)	10:45 (1)	18:15 (1)
Arr. Jakarta (Kota)	08:12	09:33	12:22	13:57	21:22

(1) Has first and second-class. Restaurant car. (2) Has second and third-class. Restaurant car. (3) Has first and second- class. Air-conditioned. Restaurant car. (4) Third-class only. Restaurant car.

Jakarta - Jogjakarta 7406

Dep. Jakarta (Gambir)	12:10 (1)	13:15 (2)	16:00 (3+4)	17:35 (5+7)
Arr. Jogjakarta	23:22	23:47	01:30	03:35

* * *

Dep. Jogjakarta	17:00 (1)	19:35 (5)	20:10 (2)	20:25 (1+8)
Arr. Jakarta (Gambir)	03:15	05:27	04:49	06:32

(1) Third-class only. Restaurant or buffet car. (2) Second and third-class only. Restaurant or buffet car. (3) Reservation required. Restaurant car. Carries a first-class sleeping car. Also has an air-conditioned first-class coach. (4) Depart/Arrive Jakarta's Kota railstation. (5) Second-class only. Restaurant car or buffet. (6) Depart/Arrive Jakarta's Pasarsenen railstation. (7) Plus other departures from Jakarta at 19:30 (5) and 20:00 (1+6), arriving Jogjakarta 05:20 and 07:00. (8) Plus other departures from Jogjakarta at 21:35 (3) and 22:22 (2), arriving Jakarta 06:54 and 07:42.

Sights in **Jogjakarta**: The batik schools, 2 museums, the mosques and the Sultan's Palace, all inside the walled Kraton complex. Be sure to see the carved teak pillars in the Bengsal Kencono (Golden Pavillion) and the gold pillars, gems and sacred weapons displayed in Gadjah Mada University. It is a short rickshaw ride to the village of **Kota Gede**, to see fine silver filigree being made.

Visit the shops stocked with excellent batik, along Jalan Tirtodipuran. The seated

Buddha at the Mendut Temple. Taman Siri, the Water Castle. Nearby is a bird market. Watch the complex dyeing of fabric at the Batik Research Center (Jalan Kusumanegara 2).

The dances at the 10th century Roro Djonggrang Temple, 10 miles from Jogjakarta.

There is an air-conditioned bus tour to the 9th century Borobudur, 35 miles from the city. The lower terraces of this low pyramid have 432 statues and 1,460 reliefs of the Buddha. It is a 15-mile trip to **Prambanam**, a temple complex dedicated to Shiva, Hindu deity.

Jogjakarta - Solo 7406

This is an easy one-day roundtrip.

Dep. Jogjakarta	02:05 (1)	03:35 (2)	09:15 (3)	14:05 (4)	23:22 (5+6)
Arr. Solo	03:23	04:52	11:04	15:36	00:43

Sights in **Solo:** A quite attractive village. Famous for its good batik cloth and its Sriwedai Amusement Park, which has a fine Zoological Garden.

Dep. Solo	10:01 (5)	14:59 (3)	17:41 (4)	18:10 (2)	18:50 (5+7)
Arr. Jogjakarta	11:25	17:03	20:08	19:33	20:23

(1) Has an air-conditioned first-class coach. Restaurant car. (2) Second-class only. Restaurant or buffet car. (3) Third-class only. (4) Second and third-class only. Restaurant car or buffet. (5) Third-class only. Restaurant car. (6) Plus another departure from Jogjakarta at 23:47 (4), arriving Solo 01:08. (7) Plus other departures from Solo at 21:00 (4) and 22:08 (1), arriving Jogjakarta 22:20 and 23:35.

Medan - Rantau Prapaet - Tanjon Balai 7400

The one rail route on Sumatra is across the bay from Penang. A one-day roundtrip from Medan to Tanjong Balai is possible.

All of these trains serve light refreshments and are second and / or third-class only.

Dep. Medan	07:30	09:30	14:45	22:00
Arr. Rantau Prapaet	-0-	16:07	-0-	-0-
Arr. Tanjong Balai	11:32	-0-	18:53	02:07

Sights in **Medan**: An ugly city of almost one million people. There are large oil palm and rubber tree plantations here. See the tamed Sumatran orangutans being trained so they can be returned to the jungle. Their "school" is in nearby **Mount Leuser Nature Reserve**, open to the public every afternoon.

To view rhinoceroses, elephants and tigers, go on the boat trip up the **Alas River,** into the rain forest.

Sights in **Rantau Prapaet:** A small resort. Visit the Saturday market for souvenirs. See the exhibitions of Batak music and dance every night at Hotel Prapaet.

Rantau Prapaet is the gateway to **Samosir Island** on large nearby 400-square-mile **Lake Toba** (twice the size of Lake Geneva). Only a short distance from the Equator, Samosir is 3,000-feet high and has a remarkably cool climate for its location. Take the ferry from Rantau Prapaet to see the unique Batak houses there, built without nails and up to 60 feet long. These windowless houses are decorated with incredible carvings and mosaics of humanlike figures, mythical birds, monsters, lizards and snakes. See the tomb of King Sidabutar. Walk the many paths that connect the island's villages.

Dep. Tanjong Balai	07:10	-0-	14:30	00:01
Dep. Rantau Prapaet	-0-	08:05	-0-	-0-
Arr. Medan	11:18	14:39	18:36	04:21

600

JAPAN

Children under 6 travel free. Half-fare for children 6–11. Children 12 and over must pay full fare. The 2 elements that are necessary for top quality rail service both exist in Japan: high population density and short distances.

In major cities, railstations have "Green Windows" where travel advice in English can be obtained.

Personnel who speak English and can render advice and information are also on duty at these offices of Japan National Tourist Organization:

Tokyo: 6-6 Yurakucho 1-Chome
Kyoto: Kyoto Tower Building, Higashi-Shiokojicho, Shimogyo-ku
Narita: The Terminal Building

Tickets for all Japanese trains which require reservation go on sale one month before travel day and can be purchased at Japanese Railways railstations and at major travel agencies throughout Japan.

Passengers are permitted to take 2 suitcases weighing a total of 44 pounds into their car and may also check 3 additional suitcases at a small fee for transit in the baggage car. Also, for little cost, arrangements can be made either to have baggage delivered from the train to one's residence or to be stored at a railstation. Although porters are available at all main railstations, they are very scarce.

Principal trains have restaurant cars. There are refreshment vendors on almost all other long-distance trains. Both Japanese and "Western" food are provided.

There are 4 classes of trains in Japan: Super-Express (Hikari and Kodama), Limited Express, Ordinary Express and Local. A surcharge is required for all types of express trains. When any express train arrives 2 hours or more late, the express surcharge is refunded at the destination.

Each express train has one or more "Green Cars". Seat reservations, at an additional charge, are required for space in a Green Car.

Sleeping cars have roomettes (for one person) and double compartments in Class "A" cars. Class "B" cars provide 2-berth and 3-berth compartments.

Combination tickets (for both hotel rooms and seats on bullet trains) can be purchased from either Japanese Railways or from Japan Travel Bureau. All of Japan's many privately owned trains are single-class and require seat reservations. Many of these trains serve resort areas.

Japan enacted in 1970 its "Law for Construction of Nationwide High-Speed Railways" calling for speeds up to 150 miles per hour on many routes. Completed in 1985, the 33.4-mile-long undersea Seikan Tunnel (world's longest) connects Tappi and Yoshioka, linking Hokkaido by rail with the rest of Japan. Passenger service began in 1988.

The hazardous 4½-hour ferry ride between Aomori and Hakodate (suspended an average of 80 days every year because of rough seas) was eliminated, and the 16-hour trip from Tokyo to Sapporo was reduced to 11 hours on bullet trains. Construction of the tunnel began in 1964. Its cost ($2.8 Billion) was more than 3 times the original estimate. It is actually a complex of 3 separate tunnels: the main one, plus narrower pilot and service tunnels. A 14.5-mile segment of the Seikan runs beneath the Tsugaru Strait, from Cape Tappi on Honshu Island to Yoshioka on Hokkaido Island.

At some locations the tunnel is 787 feet beneath the surface of the water and 328 feet beneath the seabed. There was one 4-month period that construction advanced only 120 feet.

Japan Railways Group surpasses all other rail systems in the world as to service and size. It operates more than 26,000 trains a day. Express trains between Tokyo and Osaka (345 miles) usually run at 125mph, sometimes going as fast as 137mph. Passengers can follow the trains' speed on speedometers located throughout the trains. On the stretch from Tokyo to Kyushu Island, some trains reach a speed of 156mph.

The most famous Japanese trains are its Shinkansen "bullet trains". The great "Hikari", leaving Tokyo every 15 or 20 minutes, runs the 345 miles from Tokyo to Osaka in 2 hours 26 minutes. The 455-mile run from Tokyo to Okayama is made in 3 hours 50 minutes. From Tokyo to Hakata (735 miles), it is only 5 hours 57 minutes.

Bullet trains, while traveling, have telephone service to 26 cities.

When we rode a bullet train both from Tokyo to Kyoto, and then the next day back to Tokyo, the speed was so great that it was difficult to focus on scenery or objects within 1,000 feet from the train. The interior was immaculately clean. It is one of the world's best travel experiences.

And the bullet trains are very safe. To guard against natural disasters, the Japanese installed seismoscopes, anemometers and rain gauges along the entire line. In case of an earthquake exceeding a certain intensity, the electrical current that runs the trains in the area concerned will automatically cut off.

If there are excessive rains or winds, the running speed of the train is restricted or the train is stopped. Each train window is made of double-layer glass with a dry air space between so as to minimize noise, wind pressure and moisture condensation, as well as guard against flying stones.

In planning a tour of Japan, keep in mind that the country is 4 major islands: Honshu (Tokyo and Kyoto), Shikoku (Takamatsu), Kyushu to the south (Hakata and Nagasaki), and Hokkaido, the wild northern land of Japan (Sapporo).

JAPAN'S TRAIN PASSES

Japan Railpass. *Cannot* be purchased in Japan. Unlimited travel on the trains, buses and ferries of the 6 Japanese rail companies (all of which also sell separate passes, which can be purchased only in Japan). Vouchers for Japan Railpass are sold only outside Japan, at offices of Japan Air Lines, Nippon Travel Agency and Japan Travel Bureau. After arriving in Japan, the voucher is exchanged for the pass at JR ticket counters at the New Tokyo International Airport (Narita) and at JR offices in Hakata, Hiroshima, Kumamoto, Kyoto, Nagoya, Niigata, Osaka, Sapporo, Sendai, Tokyo, Nishi Kagoshima and Yokohama.

Passengers must show the pass to board a train and also flash it again to get out of a station.

Travel must start within 3 months after the voucher is purchased. With a Japan Railpass there is no charge for seat reservations, which can be made only in Japan and at either any Travel Service Center or any railstation. Refundable at a 10% fee before the first day of use if presented at a Travel Service Center in a JR station that is designated to handle this pass.

The adult *first*-class prices in late 1991 were: Y-37,000 for 7 days, Y-60,000 for 14 days, and Y-78,000 for 21 days. Children 6-11: Y-18,500, Y-30,000 and Y-39,000. *Second*-class: Y-27,800, Y-44,200 and Y-56,000. For children 6-11: Y-13,900, Y-22,100 and Y-28,000.

Combinations (for example two 7-day passes, or a 7-day plus a 14-day pass) allow remaining several days in one city without depleting a pass.

Japan Tour Tickets. These cover a variety of routes listed by Japan Railways Group. Offering reduced-rate excursions, they can be obtained at principal Japanese railstations, or at the Kobe, Kyoto and Tokyo offices of Japan Travel Bureau, and also at all offices of Kinki Nippon Tourist.

Hiroshima

Rebuilt since 1955. All major sites can be reached by bus from the railstation: Shukkeien Garden, Hiroshima Castle, Asa Zoological Park, the Buddhist Fudoin Temple, the monuments at Peace Memorial Park and the interesting exhibits in the Peace Memorial Museum. It is a 25-minute train ride to Miyajimaguchi and then a 10-minute ferryboat ride from there to the magnificent landscape and 6th century Itsukushima Shrine of Miyajima (Shrine Island).

Kyoto

You will not see all worth seeing here in a few days. There are more than 200 Shinto shrines, over 1500 temples, plus 9 museums, 3 palaces and an imposing castle in Kyoto.

The 17th century Nijo Castle is first on everyone's list. Beautiful gold ceilings, wood sculptures, and murals to see at this complex.

Other sights in Kyoto: the 13th century 393-foot long Sanjusangendo (Hall of 33 Bays). The incredible halls at Nishi Hongan-ji. The 200-acre park in the center of Kyoto, with the Imperial Palace. The 3 large gardens of the 68-acre Shugaku-in. The 22 subtemples at Daitoku-ji, one of the city's many Zen temples. The Library, Zoo, Art Gallery and Heian Jingu Shrine, all in Okazaki Park. Hundreds of narrow streets, each with interesting shops, food stores and inns.

Kinkaku-ji (Temple of the Golden Pavilion). Ryoan-ji (Temple of the Peaceful Dragon). Kokedera (The Moss Temple), with many different types of moss in its lovely garden. The 17th century Kiyomizu (Clear Spring Temple). The view from the 8th century Kiyomizu Temple. The tallest (5-story) pagoda in Japan, at Toji Temple.

Osaka

The 16th century Osaka Castle, and its fine museum. Shitenno-ji Temple. Nishi Temple. Higashi Hongan-ji Temple. The Kabuki Theater. The view from the top of 338-foot high Tsutenkaku (Tower Leading to Heaven). The view from the top of the 340-foot high observation platform on Osaka Tower.

Sumiyoshi Taisha Shrine. Temmangu Shrine. The Bunraku puppet theater. The dozen different farmhouses with hundreds of utensils in the Museum of Japanese Farmhouses. The Japan Handicraft Museum. Ancient and modern art at the Municipal Art Museum in Tennoji Park, where the Zoo and Botanical Garden are also located.

The Electric Science Museum. The Transportation Museum. The Natural Science Museum. The Fujita Art Museum. A tourist specialty in Osaka is visiting factories: clothing, beverages, ice cream, chocolate, cameras, autos, bread, etc.

Tokyo

Schedules for the 60-minute train ride between Tokyo's Ueno Keisei station and Narita Airport appear under "Tokyo–Narita" on page 612.

There is monorail and bus service between Haneda Airport and the center of Tokyo. For train service to and from Narita Airport, see "Tokio – Narita" on page 612.

Several English language daily newspapers list entertainment events.

Any tour of Tokyo must focus on visiting the massive park surrounding the Palace, in the center of the city. Then see: The gardens at the Meiji Shrine. The enormous Zoo (open 09:30–16:30, closed Monday), the National Museum of Western Art, and the Tokyo National Museum (greatest collection in the world of Japanese art and archaeology), and the Shitamachi Museum, all in the 210-acre Ueno Park, next to Ueno Railstation.

Shitamachi features the lifestyle of common people in the 19th and early 20th centuries: a merchant's house, a candy shop, the house of a clog-maker, women's teeth-blackening utensils, early firefighting equipment. Closed Monday, Shitamachi is open other days 09:30–16:30.

Stroll the Ginza, particularly after dark to view the extraordinary illuminations. See the tremendous assortment of sealife very early in the morning at the wholesale fish market at Tsukiji (a 10-minute walk from the Ginza). See the elegant lobby of the Imperial Hotel. The Iris Garden (Shobu-en). The gardens at Shin-juku Gyoen. Kiyosumi Garden. The 60-acre Hama Rikyu Park. Buddhist art at Goto Museum. The collection of ancient Japanese and Chinese art in the Nezu Museum and at the Matsuoka Art Museum.

Koishikawa Botanical Garden. The Railway Museum. Ihinkan, a small museum of World War II memorabilia (human torpedos, warplanes, models of battleships) open daily 09:30–16:30. The gigantic paper lantern suspended from a gate made of 1700-year-old Japanese cypress, at the 7th century Asakusa Kannon Temple. Folkcrafts in Bingo-Ya. Kabuki-Za, the leading Kabuki theater.

The city's largest department stores have amusement parks and many restaurants on their roofs Several have undergrounds malls connected to Tokyo Railstation. The best in the Ginza are Matsuya, Mitsukoshi and Wako.

Hiroshima - Fukuoka (Hakata) 8000

All of these services are Bullet Trains which require reservation for first-class and are air-conditioned. Most have a restaurant car or light refreshments.

Dep. Hiroshima	Frequent times from 06:40 to 22:16
Arr. Fukuoka (Hakata)	90 minutes later

Sights in **Hakata**: Hakata is the railstation for Fukuoka. This twin-city is famous for Hakata dolls. Much nightlife here. Only a few miles from away, there is cormorant fishing at **Harazuru**.

Dep. Fukuoka (Hakata)	Frequent times from 6:00 to 21:46
Arr. Hiroshima	90 minutes later

Hiroshima - Kagoshima

All of the services Hiroshima–Fukuoka and v.v. are Bullet Trains which require reservation for first-class and are air-conditioned. Most have a restaurant car or light refreshments. All the Fukuoka–Kagoshima and v.v. trains require reservation for first-class and are air-conditioned. All have buffet or light refreshments.

8000

Dep. Hiroshima	Frequent times from 06:40 to 22:16					
Arr. Fukuoka (Hakata)	2 hours later					

Change trains. Table 8024

Dep. Fukuoka (Hakata)	07:00	08:00	09:13	10:17	11:17	12:17 (1)
Arr. Kagoshima (Nishi)	10:53	12:06	13:14	14:26	15:12	16:26

Sights in **Kagoshima**: Rebuilt since 1945. An old castle town, often called "Naples of the Orient". A good base for visiting the beautiful crater lake, many live volcanoes and the thick forests of **Kirishima-Yaku National Park**. See the view of **Kagoshima Bay** and **Sakurajima** (a volcanic island) from the hilltop Shiroyama Park. **Ibusuki Spa**, only one

(Timetables continues on page 604.)

hour by train from Nishi-Kagoshima station, is one of Japan's most popular hot springs resorts because of its lovely white seashore and the lush subtropical plants that surround it.

Dep. Kagoshima (Nishi)	06:41	07:15	08:35	09:10	10:12	11:15 (2)
Arr. Fukuoka (Hakata)	10:45	11:14	12:15	13:15	14:15	15:15

    Change trains.   8000

Dep. Fukuoka (Hakata)	Frequent times from 06:00 to 21:46
Arr. Hiroshima	90 minutes later

(1)Plus other departures from Fukuoka (Hakata) at 13:17, 14:17, 15:17, 16:17, 17:17, 18:16 and 19:16. (2) Plus other departures from Kagoshima at 12:17, 13:07, 14:48, 15:34, 16:19, 17:12 and 18:56.

Nishi-Kagoshima to Makurazaki (Government Timetable)

    The trip to the southern end of Japan's railway system

Dep. Nishi-Kagoshima	05:18	11:45	15:36	16:33	18:26	
Arr. Makurazaki	07:44	14:09	17:55	19:15	20:55	

    Sights in **Makurazaki**: A popular beach resort.

Dep. Makurazaki	05:00	06:35	07:48	14:14	17:59	19:42
Arr. Nishi-Kagoshima	07:23	09:15	09:49	17:03	20:30	22:17

Hiroshima - Kumamoto

All of the services Hiroshima–Fukuoka and v.v. are Bullet Trains which require reservation for first-class and are air-conditioned . Most have a restaurant car or light refreshments.

All the Fukuoka–Kumamoto and v.v. trains require reservation for first-class and have either buffet or light refreshments.

    8000

Dep. Hiroshima	Frequent times from 06:40 to 22:16
Arr. Fukuoka (Hakata)	90 minutes later

    Change trains.   8024

Dep. Fukuoka (Hakata)	Frequent times from 07:00 to 22:35
Arr. Kumamoto	90 minutes later

    Sights in **Kumamoto**: It is a short drive from here to marvelous Suizenji Park.

Dep. Kumamoto	Frequent times from 06:20 to 21:35
Arr. Fukuoka (Hakata)	90 minutes later

    Change trains.   8000

Dep. Fukuoka (Hakata)	Frequent times from 06:00 to 21:46
Arr. Hiroshima	90 minutes later

Hiroshima - Nagasaki

All of the services Hiroshima–Fukuoka and v.v. are Bullet Trains which require reservation for first-class and are air-conditioned . Most have a restaurant car or light refreshments.

All the Fukuoka–Nagasaki and v.v. trains require reservation for first-class and are air-conditioned. Most have buffet or light refreshments.

    8000

Dep. Hiroshima	Frequent times from 06:40 to 22:16
Arr. Fukuoka (Hakata)	90 minutes later

    Change trains.

There is great scenery of **Omura Bay** on the ride from Fukuoka (Hakata) to Nagasaki. Sit on the right-hand side for the best view in this direction.

8025						
Dep. Fukuoka (Hakata)	07:02	07:39	09:10	10:43	11:13	12:13 (1)
Arr. Nagasaki	09:05	10:00	11:21	12:51	13:29	14:16

Sights in **Nagasaki**: Japan's first contact with the Western world was here, as well as the country's early traffic with China. That explains both the Chinese and Catholic influence on this area. At Saints Martyrdom there is a chapel with twin towers reminiscent of Gaudi's Sagrada Familia church in Barcelona. This is the site of the crucifixion in 1597 of 6 foreign and 20 Japanese Christians for refusing to renounce their faith after Christianity was banned.

The local tradition is flying the huge kites that were first flown in China. Two other Chinese influences seen here even now are the annual June racing of large rowboats to the tempo of a drum that is beaten amidship and an annual October festival featuring Chinese-style costumes, floats and dragons.

See the Catholic Cathedral. (Nearly half of Japan's small Catholic population lives in this area.) The view of the city and harbor from Glover House, the place where Madame Butterfly (in Puccini's imagination) waited for Pinkerton to return. The exhibit at International Cultural Hall at Peace Park (daily 09:00–17:00), commemorating the August 9, 1945 atomic bomb blast. The 17th century Chinese Buddhist temple. The 33-foot high bronze torii at the Suwa Shrine. Much marvelous seacoast scenery in this area.

Dep. Nagasaki	06:30	08:08	09:14	09:39	10:28	11:04 (2)
Arr. Fukuoka (Hakata)	08:48	10:18	11:18	11:51	12:18	13:18

Change trains. 8000

Dep. Fukuoka (Hakata)	Frequent times from 06:00 to 21:46
Arr. Hiroshima	90 minutes later

(1) Plus other departures from Fukuoka (Hakata) at 12:43, 13:13, 14:13, 15:13, 16:13, 16:43, 17:13, 17:43, 18:13, 19:13, 20:13, 21:05 and 22:02. (2) Plus other departures from Nagasaki at 13:15, 13:37, 14:15, 14:37, 15:15, 15:41, 16:28, 17:32, 18:05, 19:32 and 20:25.

Kyoto - Gifu

All of the services Kyoto–Nagoya and v.v. are Bullet Trains which require reservation for first-class and are air-conditioned . Most have a restaurant car or light refreshments.

All the Nagoya–Gifu and v.v. trains require reservation for first-class, are air-conditioned and have light refreshments.

8000				8015			
Dep. Kyoto	07:37	08:17	11:21	Dep. Gifu	15:32	16:34	18:29
Arr. Nagoya	08:20	09:15	12:04	Arr. Nagoya	15:54	16:54	18:51
Change trains.				Change trains			
8015				8000			
Dep. Nagoya	08:40	09:40	12:40	Dep. Nagoya	16:11	17:16	19:11
Arr. Gifu	09:00	09:59	13:00	Arr. Kyoto	16:55	18:19	19:55

Sights in **Gifu**: There is large production of lovely paper lanterns and paper umbrellas here. Numerous hot springs resorts in this area. See the cormorant fishing, almost every night from mid-May to mid-October.

Kyoto - Kobe 8000

All of these services are Bullet Trains which require reservation for first-class and are air-conditioned . Most have a restaurant car or light refreshments.

Dep. Kyoto   Frequent times from 07:16 to 22:44
Arr. Kobe   32 minutes later

Sights in **Kobe**: This is Japan's largest seaport. See the Ikuta Shrine. Take a bus tour to Minatogawa Shrine and the ancient Temple in **Sumadera**. There are great cherry tree blossoms there every Spring. Equally beautiful maple tree foliage, every Autumn, at Zenshoji Temple. See the Hakutsuru Gallery of Oriental Art, near Mikage station. Visit the Zoo, Botanical Garden and all-girl opera at nearby **Takarazuka**.

Dep. Kobe   Frequent times from 06:12 to 21:18
Arr. Kyoto   32 minutes later

Kyoto - Okayama - Matsuyama -Uwajima

This ride to Shikoku Island includes traveling over the $8 Billion. Seto-Ohashi bridge that is 213-feet wide, has 4 highway lanes and 2 rail tracks. It crosses 5½ miles of water (the Inland Sea). Passengers can stare down at huge cargo ships.

All of the services Kyoto–Okayama and v.v. are Bullet Trains which require a reservation for first-class and are air-conditioned .

All the Okayama–Uwajima and v.v. trains require reservation for first-class, are air-conditioned and have light refreshments.

8000

Dep. Kyoto	09:20	10:12	12:16	13:40	15:12	16:12 (1)
Arr. Okayama	10:30	11:32	13:28	14:49	16:29	17:30

Change trains. Table 8022

Dep. Okayama	11:00	12:00	14:00	15:00	17:00	18:00 (2)
Arr. Matsuyama	14:07	15:10	17:06	18:14	20:13	21:10
Arr. Uwajima	-0-	17:01	-0-	-0-	-0-	22:56

Sights in **Matsuyama**: This is a popular hot springs resort. See the lovely maple trees in nearby Omogo Valley. There is a fine castle here. The local sport is bullfighting.

Sights in **Uwajima:** Near the railstation, the 17th century 3-storey dungeon at the 17th century Uwajima Castle. Also see Uwatsuhiko Shrine at the foot of Atago Park, and the view from the park. Visit Tenshaen, a beautiful garden.

Dep. Uwajima	-0-	06:46	-0-	-0-	-0-	12:43 (3)
Dep. Matsuyama	05:00	08:30	10:30	11:30	13:29	14:29
Arr. Okayama	08:16	11:34	13:32	14:34	16:32	17:33

Change trains. Table 8000

Dep. Okayama	08:43	12:03	13:43	14:43	16:43	17:43
Arr. Kyoto	09:52	13:16	14:51	15:51	17:51	18:51

(1) Plus another departure from Kyoto at 18:40, terminating in Matsuyama 22:53. (2) Plus another depature from Okayama at 20:00, terminating in Matsuyama 22:53. (3) Plus another departure from Uwajima at 14:22, departing Matsuyama 16:26, arriving Okayama 19:31 and Kyoto 20:52.

Kyoto - Nagoya 8000

All of these services are Bullet Trains which require reservation for first-class and are air-conditioned. Most have a restaurant car or light refreshments.

Dep. Kyoto   Frequent times from 06:17 to 21:52
Arr. Nagoya   40-50 Minutes later

Sights in **Nagoya:** The art objects in the recently re-built 5-story 17th century castle. The view of Nagoya from the top of the 350-foot high television tower. The modern Nittaiji Temple, a gift from Thailand. The 1700-year old Atsuta Shrine. The Tokugawa Art Museum. Shop for fine Noritake chinaware and Ando cloisonne.

It is only a 45-minute train ride to **Inuyama** to see the 16th century castle and the Kiso rapids there.

There is bus service every 20 minutes at the Nagoya station for the 1½-hour ride to the marvelous preservation park at **Meiji**, a 172-acre mountain village that has reproduced the lifestyle that existed in Japan at the end of the 19th century. Among the many monuments from the 1868–1912 era are: the railroad coach of the Meiji Emperor, the lobby of the original Frank Lloyd Wright Imperial Hotel (a Tokyo landmark for almost 50 years until it was demolished in the 1960's), a public bath, a merchant's townhouse, a teahouse, a Kabuki theater, antique railway machines, a hand-printing press, and textile spinning, weaving and threading machines. The village is open 10:00–17:00 March–October and 10:00–16:00 November–February.

Dep. Nagoya   Frequent times from 06:21 to 22:49
Arr. Kyoto   40–50 minutes later

Kyoto - Nara 8073

Dep. Kyoto   Frequent times from 08:30 to 22:50
Arr. Nara   30–40 minutes later

Sights in **Nara:** This is a very crowded tourist town. Weekends should be avoided. See the 1250-acre Nara Park and its temples.

Dep. Nara   Frequent times from 06:19 to 21:00
Arr. Kyoto   30–40 minutes later

Kyoto - Okayama 8000

All of these services are Bullet Trains which require reservation for first-class and are air-conditioned. Most have a restaurant car or light refreshments.

Dep. Kyoto   Frequent times from 07:16 to 22:38
Arr. Okayama   90 minutes later

Sights in **Okayama**: The bamboo groves, tea plantation, streams and ponds in the 28.5-acre Korakuen Park, one of Japan's finest gardens, established in 1700. Nearby, the lovely Kibitsu Shrine and the Saidaiji Temple. There is much extraordinary fruit in this area: white peaches, muscat grapes and unusual pears.

Dep. Okayama   Frequent times from 06:00 to 22:38
Arr. Kyoto   90 minutes later

Okayama - Matsuyama - Uwajima

See "Kyoto–Okayama–Matsuyama–Uwajima" on page 606.

Kyoto - Takamatsu

All of the services Kyoto–Okayama and v.v. are Bullet Trains which require reservation for first-class and are air-conditioned . Most have a restaurant car or light refreshments.

All the Okayama–Uwajima and v.v. trains require a reservation for first-class, are air-conditioned and have light refreshments.

8000

Dep. Kyoto	Frequent times from 07:16 to 22:38
Arr. Okayama	1½ hours later
Change trains. 8022	
Dep. Okayama	Frequent departures by local service.
Arr. Takamatsu	60 minutes later

Sights in **Takamatsu**: The museum of 12th century battle relics in **Yashima Temple**, 5 miles away. The outstanding Ritsurin Park and Zoo. The Kimpira Shrines, only a one-hour ride by electric train to **Kotohira**. Nearby **Kotobiki Park**.

Dep. Takamatsu	Frequent departures by local service.
Arr. Okayama	60 minutes later
Change trains. 8000	
Dep. Okayama	Frequent times from 06:00 to 22:38
Arr. Kyoto	1½ hours later

Kyoto - Toba 8090

All of these services are Bullet Trains which require reservation for first-class and are air-conditioned . Most have a restaurant car or light refreshments.

Dep. Kyoto	07:15 (1)	08:15	09:15	10:15	11:15	12:15	13:15 (2)
Arr. Toba	09:31	10:31	11:32	12:31	13:31	14:33	15:30

Sights in **Toba**: See women divers gathering oysters into which an irritant is inserted which starts the process of pearl formation. A program is presented at **Pearl Island**, near the waterfront. Then continue on to **Kashikojima**, where you will want to visit the Cultured Pearl Institute to see the exhibition there.

Dep. Toba	08:57	09:57	10:57	11:57	12:57	13:57	14:57 (3)
Arr. Kyoto	11:18	12:18	13:18	14:18	15:18	16:18	17:18

(1) No light refreshments. (2) Plus other departures from Kyoto at 14:15, 15:15, 16:15 and 18:15. (3) Plus other departures from Toba at 15:57, 16:57, 17:57 and 18:57 (1).

Kyoto - Tokyo 8000

All of these services are Bullet Trains which require reservation for first-class and are air-conditioned . Most have a restaurant car or light refreshments.

Dep. Kyoto	Frequent times from 06:17 to 21:17
Arr. Tokyo	2 hours and 40 minutes later

Sights in **Tokyo**: See notes about Tokyo on page 603.

Dep. Tokyo	Frequent times from 06:00 to 21:00
Arr. Kyoto	2 hours and 40 minutes later

Osaka - Himeji 8000

All of these services are Bullet Trains which require reservation for first-class and are air-conditioned . Most have a restaurant car or light refreshments.

Dep. Osaka (1)   Frequent times from 06:06 to 22:38
Arr. Himeji   40 minutes later

Sights in **Himeji:** The 5-story 17th century White Herron Castle.

Dep. Himeji   Frequent times from 06:59 to 22:34
Arr. Osaka (1)   40 minutes later

(1) Shin-Osaka, a commuter station.

Osaka - Kanazawa 8017

These trains have light refreshments.

Dep. Osaka (Umeda)   Frequent times from 07:05 to 20:05
Arr. Kanazawa   2 hours 35 minutes later

Sights in **Kanazawa:** A lovely castle city on Japan's seacoast. Mountain-climbing trips start from here. See Kenrokuen, the beautiful garden with ponds and waterfalls, next to the castle. Seisonkaku Villa (08:30–16:30, closed Wednesday), in the garden. Behind Seisonkaku is the Ishikawa Art Museum, which features Kutani ceramics. See artists painting intricate designs on silk at the Saihitsuan Yuzen Silk Center (09:00–12:00 and 13:00–16:30, closed Thursday).

Dep. Kanazawa   Frequent times from 06:10 to 19:55
Arr. Osaka (Umeda)   2 hours 35 minutes later

Osaka - Kobe 8000

All of these services are Bullet Trains which require reservation for first-class and are air-conditioned . Most have a restaurant car or light refreshments.

Dep. Osaka (1)   Frequent times from 06:00 to 23:03
Arr. Kobe   14 minutes later

Sights in **Kobe:** See notes under "Kyoto–Kobe" on page 606

Dep. Kobe   Frequent times from 06:12 to 23:18
Arr. Osaka (1)   14 minutes later

(1) Shin-Osaka, a commuter station.

Osaka - Nagoya 8000

All of these services are Bullet Trains which require reservation for first-class and are air-conditioned . Most have a restaurant car or light refreshments.

Dep. Osaka (1)   Frequent times from 06:00 to 21:35
Arr. Nagoya   60–70 minutes later

Sights in **Nagoya:** See notes under "Kyoto–Nagoya" on page 607.

Dep. Nagoya   Frequent times from 06:21 to 22:49
Arr. Osaka (1)   60–70 minutes later

(1) Shin-Osaka, a commuter station.

Osaka - Okayama 8000

All of these services are Bullet Trains which require reservation for first-class and are air-conditioned . Most have a restaurant car or light refreshments.

Dep. Osaka (1)   Frequent times from 06:00 to 22:35
Arr. Okayama   60–70 minutes later

Sights in **Okayama:** See notes under "Kyoto–Okayama" on page 607.

Dep. Okayama   Frequent times from 06:00 to 22:38
Arr. Osaka (1)   60–70 minutes later

(1) Shin-Osaka, a commuter station.

Osaka - Tottori 8018

All of these trains require reservation for first-class, have light refreshments (unless designated otherwise), and are air-conditioned.

| Dep. Osaka (Shin) | 09:32 | 12:20 (1) | 17:51 |
| Arr. Tottori | 13:50 | 16:34 | 22:22 |

Sights in **Tottori**: Many hotsprings here. See the sand dunes on the nearby shore.

| Dep. Tottori | 01:12 | 06:55 | 11:24 | 15:54 | 16:55 |
| Arr. Osaka (Shin) | 07:09 (1) | 10:56 (1) | 15:44 | 20:03 (1) | 21:12 |

(1) Depart/Arrive Osaka's Umeda railstation.

Osaka - Toyama 8017

All trains on this route have light refreshments and are air-conditioned.

| Dep. Osaka (Umeda) | Frequent times from 07:05 to 20:05 |
| Arr. Toyama | 3¼ –3½ hours later |

Sights in **Toyama**: Famous since the 17th century for its medical powders, pills, drugs and other pharmaceutical items.

| Dep. Toyama | Frequent times from 05:28 to 19:14 |
| Arr. Osaka (Umeda) | 3¼ –3½ hours later |

Tokyo - Hakone (Lake Ashi) 8049

Beautiful scenery on this easy one-day roundtrip.

Dep. Tokyo (Shinjuku)	07:30 then every 30 minutes from 09:30 to 18:30
	Sundays: as above + 08:00, 08:30, 09:00 and 19:00
Arr. Hakone-Yumoto	90 minutes later

Take a taxi or bus from Yumoto to the lake.

* * *

Dep. Hakone-Yumoto	09:13 then every 30 minutes from 10:43 to 20:13
	Sundays: as above + 20:43
Arr. Tokyo (Shinjuku)	90 minutes later

Sights in **Hakone**: A very popular resort, wedged between Mt. Fuji and Izu Peninsula. Volcanic topography, hot springs, historic relics and the beautiful scenery of deep glens, ravines and lovely **Lake Ashi**.

Odakyu Railways offers a "Hakone Pass" which includes the Tokyo-Hakone rail fare plus the Hakone Tozen Railway (30 minutes from Hakone–Yumoto to Gora), the Sounzan Cablecar (9 minutes from Gora to Sounzan), the Hakone Ropeway (33 minutes from Sounzan to Togendai), the Hakone Cruise Boat (30 minutes from Togendai to Moto–Hakone), a 20-minute walk from Moto–Hakone to Hakone–Machi, then the Hakone Tozen Bus (80 minutes from Hakone–Machi to the Atami railstation), and the train from Atami to Tokyo.

The 1991 price was Y-4,520 (Y-2,270 for children).

The unique craft in Hakone is elaborate inlaid and mosaic work made with cherry and camphor wood. Called "Hakone-Zaiku", the technique is used for dolls, toys, boxes and various accessories.

Tokyo - Kofu - Matsumoto 8011

All of these trains require reservation for first-class, have light refreshments, and are air-conditioned.

Dep. Tokyo (Shinjuku)	07:00	07:30	08:00	09:00	10:00	10:30 (1)
Arr. Kofu	08:33	09:05	09:34	10:37	11:34	12:06
Arr. Matsumoto	09:51	10:24	10:51	11:55	12:46	13:24

Sights in **Kofu:** Good views of the Japanese Alps. Fine Summer and Winter sports facilities. There are connections from Kofu to Lake Suwa.

Sights in **Matsumoto**: Great mountain scenery. Gateway to the Japanese Alps. See the Castle (open daily 08:30–17:00) and its 5-story donjon, from which there are magnificent views of the mountain peaks and the Utsukushigahara Plateau. At the Folklore Museum (open daily 09:00–16:30) there are over 50,000 exhibits on the archaeology, history, folklore and mountains of this area.

It is only 30 minutes by train from Matsumoto to Hotaka, and then a 7-minute walk from there to the Rokuzan Art Museum, open daily except Monday 09:00–17:00 April–October, 09:00–16:00 November–March. It features the sculptures of Rokuzan Ogiwara. He is called "the Rodin of the Orient".

A 40-minute walk from Hotaka's railstation, down a hiking road, leads to the very picturesque view of the country's largest Japanese horseradish farm-fields of green leaves of the "wasabi", surrounded by acacia and poplar trees.

Dep. Matsumoto	06:04	06:32	07:42	08:47	09:12	09:54 (2)
Dep. Kofu	07:22	07:49	09:04	10:04	10:29	11:06
Arr. Tokyo (Shinjuku)	09:11	09:24	10:35	11:35	12:05	12:35

(1) Plus frequent other Tokyo departures every hour 11:00–21:00. (2) Plus frequent other Matsumoto departures 10:47–19:42.

Tokyo - Kyoto - Osaka 8000

All of these services are Bullet Trains which require reservation for first-class and are air-conditioned . Most have a restaurant car or light refreshments.

Dep. Tokyo	Frequent times from 06:00 to 21:00
Arr. Kyoto	2¾ hours later
Arr. Osaka	15 minutes after departing Kyoto

Sights in **Kyoto**: See notes about Kyoto on page 602.

Sights in **Osaka**: See notes about Osaka on page 602.

Dep. Osaka	Frequent times from 06:00 to 21:00
Dep. Kyoto	Frequent times from 06:17 to 21:17
Arr. Tokyo	3 hours after departing Osaka

Tokyo - Mito 8008

All of these trains require reservation for first-class, have light refreshments and are air-conditioned.

Dep. Tokyo (Ueno)	Frequent times from 07:00 to 22:30
Arr. Mito	90 minutes later

Sights in **Mito**: Visit Kairaku-en Park, noted for its apricot blossoms, about one mile west of the railstation. The special flowering season is late February to mid-March.

(Timetable continues on page 612)

The beaches here are popular for swimming in Summer. See the orchid and hydrangea flowers at the Howaen Garden.

Dep. Mito	Frequent times from 07:31 to 21:15
Arr. Tokyo (Ueno)	60 minutes later

Tokyo - Narita 8012

The 90-minute taxi ride cost $140 (U.S.) in 1991, while the 60-minute train ride was $37 for first-class, $22 for second-class. The train has such amenities as private compartments, a self-service bar (in first-class), large restrooms and announcements in English. Reservation is required.

Here are the connections from 2 Tokyo railstations to the international jet airport that serves Tokyo. Departures are at frequent times whithin the time frame shown.

Dep. Tokyo (Ueno)	0630 — 18:00		Dep. Tokyo (Tokyo)	06:30 — 20:00
Arr. Narita	60 minutes later		Arr. Narita	53 minutes later
	* * *			* * *
Dep. Narita	09:20 — 22:00		Dep. Narita	07:45 — 21:45
AArr. Tokyo (Ueno)	60 minutes later		Arr. Tokyo (Tokyo)	53 minutes later

Sights in **Narita**: Located 40 miles from Tokyo and only 15 minutes by taxi from the international airport. Many Buddhist temples here. Visit the Historical Museum (08:30–16:00, closed Monday and national holidays) to see art objects relating to the 10th century Shinshoji Temple, located in front of the Museum, as well as archaeological and folkloric articles found in the northern part of the Boso Peninsula. Be sure to see the daily Goma cermenony at the Shinshoji. The Issaikyodo Temple is also worthwhile.

Nearby is the 45-acre Naritasan Park with flowering trees and plants, waterfalls and reflecting ponds. There are many country-inn restaurants on Monzen-Dori, Narita's narrow main street.

Tokyo - Niigata 8001

High-speed trains began operating in 1982 on this route through the 22.3km-long Daishimizu Tunnel. It is the world's second-longest, after Japan's 33.4-mile undersea Seikan Tunnel. At 200km (120 miles) per hour, the "bullet train" runs through the Daishimizu in 7 minutes.

All of these services are Bullet Trains which require reservation for first-class and are air-conditioned . Most have a restaurant car or light refreshments.

Dep. Tokyo (Ueno)	Frequent times from 06:16 to 21:10
Arr. Niigata	2¼–2½ hours later

Sights in **Niigata**: The leading Sea of Japan seaport.

Dep. Niigata	Frequent times from 06:22 to 21:25
Arr. Tokyo (Ueno)	2¼–2½ hours later

Tokyo - Nikko 8046

These trains are first-class only and require reservation.

Dep. Tokyo (Asakusa)	Frequent times from 07:20 to 20:10
Arr. Nikko	2 hours later

Sights in **Nikko**: A cool retreat from hot Tokyo in Summer. Beautiful foliage in Autumn. Fine Winter sports. Many mountain lakes in this area. Lake Chuzenji and Kegon Falls (nearly twice as high as Niagara Falls) are 30 minutes by bus, taxi or rental car from the railstation.

Dep. Nikko	Frequent times from 07:30 to 19:38
Arr. Tokyo (Asakusa)	2 hours later

Tokyo - Sendai 8002

All of these services are Bullet Trains which require reservation for first-class and are air-conditioned . Most have a restaurant car or light refreshments.

Dep. Tokyo (Ueno)	Frequent times from 06:00 to 21:20
Arr. Sendai	2 hours later

Sights in **Sendai:** The black-lacquered main building of the Osaki Hachiman Shrine, reminiscent of Tokugawa's mausoleum at Nikko. Near it, see Sendai's finest Buddhist temple, Rinnoji. Sendai Castle, built in 1602 by a feudal lord and residence for the next 270 years of 13 generations of his family.

The Star Festival (early August) is the most splendid display of color in Japan. Each year at that time, Sendai's streets are decorated with brilliant paper streamers. The celebration goes 24 hours. Also see the nearby Matsushima National Park. Nearly every night in August, you can see the Summer Dance Festival, illuminated by lanterns painted by school children. See many artcrafts and the portraits and old records of the ancient lords at the Municipal Museum (09:00–16:00, closed Monday). Only a 30-minute bus ride from Sendai are several pinetree mountain hot springs resorts with inns. Much beautiful foliage there. Skiing at nearby **Mt. Zao.**

Dep. Sendai	Frequent times from 06:13 to 21:22
Arr. Tokyo (Ueno)	2 hours later

Tokyo - Karuizawa 8010

All of these trains require reservation for first-class, are air-conditioned, and have light refreshments.

Dep. Tokyo (Ueno)	Frequent times from 07:00 to 21:00 plus 23:58
Arr. Karuizawa	2 hours later

Sights in **Karuizawa:** Japanese alpine scenery. There are connections in Karuizawa for **Lake Nojiri** and **Akakura**, where there is good skiing.

Dep. Karuizawa	Frequent times from 07:27 to 20:54 plus 01:44
Arr. Tokyo (Ueno)	2 hours later

Tokyo - Toyama 8010

All of these trains require reservation for first-class, have a restaurant car, and are air-conditioned, unless designated otherwise.

Dep. Tokyo (Ueno)	09:30	15:30	21:00 (1)
Arr. Toyama	14:44	20:48	04:49

Sights in **Toyama:** See notes under "Osaka–Toyama" on page 610.

Dep. Toyama	12:13	16:14	23:09 (1)
Arr. Tokyo (Ueno)	17:45	21:45	06:41

(1) Carries only second-class sleeping cars and second-class coaches.

Tokyo - Yokohama 8000

Dep. Tokyo	Frequent times from 06:06 to 22:44
Arr. Yokohama	17 minutes later

Sights in **Yokohama:** The Chinatown area. The boutiques in the Motomachi section. The 19th century garden, Sankei-en. A stroll outside Myohoji Temple. The thousands of Buddhas in the Taya Caves. The history written on the tombstones in the Foreign Cemetery.

Dep. Yokohama	Frequent times from 07:02 to 23:05
Arr. Tokyo	17 minutes later

HOKKAIDO TRAIN TRIPS

What Hokkaido offers tourists is wild, primitive scenery: great lakes, fierce animals, aborigines, large herds of cattle, a severe northern climate, fine Winter sports, scenic mountains and forests. The 5 main train routes on Hokkaido are: Hakodate–Sapporo, Sapporo–Abashiri, Sapporo–Kushiro, Abashiri–Kushiro and Sapporo–Wakkanai.

Hakodate

This is the starting point for rail trips to Japan's northernmost frontier. See the only Western castle in Japan: Goryokaku fortress, constructed in the form of a 5-pointed star. Take a cable car to see the view from the top of **Mt. Hakodate**.

Sapporo

Known as "Little Tokyo", this 1.3 million metropolis has marvelous skiing and is also a hot springs resort. Its most famous event is the annual February Show Festival, featuring 10-foot high snow sculptures of subjects ranging from Colonel Sanders to Donald Duck. Visit the **Shikotsu-Toya National Park**, **Akan National Park** (a reservation for Ainu aborigines) and **Daisetsuzan National Park**.

See the azalea and rose gardens and 2 small museums in the Hokkaido University Botanical Garden. The collection of Ainu handicrafts in the Batchelor Museum, founded by an English minister. The 2 underground shopping arcades: Pole Town (running from the Minami–Odori to the Susukino subway stations) and Aurora Town (from Odori-Sanchome to the TV tower).

Tokyo - Hakodate (via Sendai) - Sapporo 8028

All of these are overnight trains and are air-conditioned, carry only first and second class sleeping cars and a restaurant car..

Dep. Tokyo (Ueno)	16:50	17:17	19:03
Arr. Hakodate	04:24	04:52	06:38
Arr. Sapporo	08:53	09:23	10:57
		* * *	
Dep. Sapporo	17:18	18:11	19:19
Dep. Hakodate	21:46	22:39	23:41
Arr. Tokyo (Ueno)	09:20	10:12	11:12

Tokyo - Fukushima - Sapporo 8028 + Government Timetable

None of the "Northern Star" trains have coach cars. All of them carry only first and second-class sleeping cars and a restaurant car. All "Northern Star" trains have a shower in their "lobby car". They charged $2.00 in 1991 for 6 minutes of hot water plus 24 minutes to lounge in a bathrobe after the shower.

Dep. Tokyo (Ueno)	16:50 (1)	17:17 (1)	19:03 (1)	19:23
Dep. Fukushima	20:10	20:42	22:31	23:00
Arr. Sapporo	08:53	09:23	10:57	12:32

* * *

Dep. Sapporo	17:18 (1)	18:11 (1)	19:19 (1)	19:42
Dep. Fukushima	05:49	06:48	07:49	09:06
Arr. Tokyo (Ueno)	09:17	10:12	11:12	12:45

(1) "Northern Star".

Hakodate - Sapporo and Sapporo - Hakodate 8003

All of these trains require reservation for first-class, are air-conditioned, and have light refreshments unless designated otherwise.

Dep. Hakodate	01:37 (1)	07:16	08:57	10:12	12:13	13:37	15:00 (2)
Arr. Sapporo	06:18	11:01	12:35	13:41	15:50	17:22	18:46

* * *

Dep. Sapporo	07:00	08:00	09:53	11:30	13:00	15:00	17:00 (3)
Arr. Hakodate	10:41	11:43	13:42	15:19	16:42	18:44	20:41

(1) Second-class only. No light refreshments. (2) Plus other departures from Hakodate at 17:02 and 18:59, arriving Sapporo 20:49 and 22:43. (3) Plus other departures from Sapporo at 19:09 and 22:00 (1), arriving Hakodate 22:58 and 02:42.

Sapporo - Asahikawa - Abashiri 8003

All of these trains require reservation for first-class, are air-conditioned, and have light refreshments unless designated otherwise.

Dep. Sapporo	07:05	08:00 (1)	09:30	16:05	17:30	22:50 (2)
Arr. Asahikawa	08:41	09:33	11:05	17:41	19:08	01:15
Arr. Abashiri	12:24	– 0 –	14:48	21:21	22:55	06:22

Sights in **Abashiri**: Take a sightseeing bus or taxi to view the magnificent seacoast. See the unique igloo sculptures during February Snow Festival, including blocks of ice containing frozen fish.

Sights in **Asahikawa**: The aborigine Ainu village at **Chikabumi**, a few minutes away. Instead of stopping in Asahigawa, many tourists drive by rental car to the hot spring resorts a few hours away (**Shirogane** and **Sounkyo**), where there are good inns, skiing and beautiful mountain scenery. This is in the excellent Daisetsuzan National Park. There is excellent fishing in this area.

Dep. Abashiri	– 0 –	06:43	09:30	13:55	17:17	21:46 (2)
Dep. Asahikawa	07:10 (3)	10:35	13:12	17:40	21:00	04:20
Arr. Sapporo	08:43	12:09	14:46	19:14	22:34	06:34

(1) Plus other Sapporo – Asahikawa services (most second-class only) at frequent times 08:30 – 22:02. (2) Carries only second-class sleeping cars and second-class coaches. No light refreshments or air-conditioning. (3) Plus other Ashikawa – Sapporo services (most second-class only) at frequent times 10:00 – 20:00.

616

Sapporo - Kushiro 8003
All of these trains are first-class that require reservation, are air-conditioned, and have light refreshments unless designated otherwise.

| Dep. Sapporo | 08:08 | 09:57 | 11:14 | 12:14 (1) | 16:41 | 17:57 (3) |
| Arr. Kushiro | 12:52 | 14:46 | 16:12 | 19:28 | 21:10 | 22:40 |

* * *

| Dep. Kushiro | 07:30 | 09:09 | 10:34 | 13:27 | 15:24 | 17:13 (4) |
| Arr. Sapporo | 12:11 | 13:44 | 15:16 | 18:19 | 20:13 | 21:57 |

(1) Second-class coaches only. No air-conditioning. (2) Carries a sleeping car and a second-class coach. (3) Plus another departure from Sapporo at 23:00 (2), arriving Kushiro 06:10. (4) Plus another departure from Kushiro at 22:28 (2), arriving Sapporo 06:26.

Abashiri - Shari - Kushiro Government Timetables

Dep. Abashiri	06:44	09:57	10:59	12:48	13:56	15:40	18:02 (1)
Arr. Shari	07:23	10:35	11:43	13:40	14:35	16:23	18:47
Arr. Kushiro	10:00	12:56	-0-	-0-	-0-	19:16	21:27

Sights in **Shari**: Exhibits of this area's wildlife and geology, at the Shiretoko Museum, open April-September 08:30–17:00, October-March 09:00–16:00.

Sights in **Kushiro**: One of the bases for visiting **Akan National Park**.

Dep. Kushiro	06:15	-0-	08:55	-0-	-0-	-0-	14:52 (2)
Dep. Shari	08:43	09:40	11:10	13:05	14:46	16:27	17:11
Arr. Abashiri	09:23	10:58	11:48	13:45	15:34	17:12	17:51

(1) Plus other departures from Abashiri at 19:14 and 21:10, terminating in Shari 19:59 and 21:48. (2) Plus another departure from Kushiro at 17:33, departing Shari at 19:59, arriving Abashiri 20:38.

Sapporo - Asahikawa - Wakkanai 8003
The trip to Japan's northernmost rail terminal.

Dep. Sapporo	07:05 (1)	11:27 (2)	16:27 (2)	22:02 (3)
Dep. Asahikawa	08:49	13:17	18:19	00:20
Arr. Wakkanai	12:44	17:26	22:16	06:00

Sights in **Wakkanai**: Japan's northernmost city, situated on the west shore of Soya Bay. Because the Tsushima Current that touches it is warm, this port does not freeze in Winter. The main activity here is the processing of marine products. It is a 70-minute bus ride to the ruins of Soya Gokokuji Temple in **Cape Soya**, a small port village.

Dep. Wakkanai	07:51 (2)	12:56 (2)	16:06 (4)	22:06 (3)
Dep. Asahikawa	12:04	17:04	20:00	03:39
Arr. Sapporo	13:46	18:49	21:32	06:00

(1) Reservations required for first-class coaches. Light refreshments. Change trains in Asahikawa at 08:41. The Asahikawa–Wakkanai train is only second-class and has

light refreshments. (2) Only second-class. Light refreshments. (3) Carries a second-class sleeping car and second-class coach. (4) Only second-class. Change trains in Asahikawa at 19:57. The Asahikawa–Sapporo train has a first-class coach requiring reservation, is air-conditioned, and has light refreshments.

Sapporo - Oshamambe - Sapporo 8004

Called "an incredibly scenic route" in the Thomas Cook Overseas Timetable. An easy one-day roundtrip.

All of these trains are second-class.

Dep. Sapporo	08:01 (1)	11:04	14:14	15:44	18:52
Arr. Oshamambe	12:14	14:56	18:15	19:44	22:47

Sights in **Oshamambe**: The nearby **Lake Doya**.

Dep. Oshamambe	14:00	15:47 (1)	17:23 (1)	20:00	06:00 (2)
Arr. Sapporo	18:30	20:28	21:45	23:53	09:51

(1) Change trains in Otaru. (2) Plus other Oshamambe departures at 06:24, 08:45 and 10:32, arriving Sapporo 10:34, 13:50 and 15:06.

THE TRANS-SIBERIAN RAIL TRIP

This is the westward ride on the Trans-Siberian Express. See page 485 for the eastward Trans-Siberian schedule, sightseeing descriptions and historical notes.

Yokohama - Khabarovsk - Moscow

5050

Dep. Yokohama	12:00 (1)	Day 1
Arr. Nakhodka	17:00	Day 3

Set your watch back 8 hours to Moscow time.

Change to train. 5020

Dep. Nakhodka	12:50 (2)	Day 3
Arr. Khabarovsk	05:02	Day 4

Change trains.

5000 + 5020

Dep. Khabarovsk	06:09 (3)	Day 4
Dep. Ulan Ude	07:11	Day 6
Arr. Irkutsk	14:32	Day 6
Dep. Krasnoyarsk	08:23	Day 7
Arr. Omsk	03:38	Day 8
Arr. Sverdlovsk	14:42	Day 8
Arr. Moscow (Yar.)	15:50	Day 9

(1) For specific sailing dates, check a current Cooks "Overseas" Timetable. (2) Runs only on arrival days of ships from Yokohama. This train is used by Intourist for foreign tourists. Carries first-class sleeping car and restaurant car. Has only second-class coach cars. (3) This train ("Rossia") is used by Intourist for foreign tourists. Runs daily. Carries first-class sleeping cars. Has only second-class coach cars and a restaurant car.

The Khabarovsk arrival and departure times (as well as all the other Khabarovsk–Moscow times) are shown in "Moscow time". In Khabarovsk time, the actual arrival time in Khabarovsk from Nakhodka is 21:02 on Day 3, and the departure from Khabarovsk for Moscow is 22:09 on Day 3.

KAMPUCHEA (formerly called Khmer Republic and Cambodia)

The one rail route in Kampuchea links the seaport of Kompong Sam with the capital, Phnom Penh, and then extends westward from there to Aranyaprathet (just inside Thailand's border) and on to Bangkok.

Passenger service consists of one or 2 passenger cars attached to freight trains.

Phnom Penh - Kompong Sam 7101

Both of these trains are second-class only.

Dep. Phnom Penh	07:00	Dep. Kompong Sam	07:00
Arr. Kompong Sam	18:00	Arr. Phnom Penh	18:00

Sights in **Phnom Penh**: The diamond encrusted black derby at the Royal Museum in the Royal Palace. Also there: The Throne Hall, Silver Pagoda (with its solid silver floors and Golden Buddha), Pavilion of the Holy Sword, and the open-air Chanchhaya Hall, where royal ballets once were performed. Also see, nearby, The National Museum and the Khmer Art School, with its arts and handicrafts (silk sarongs, small figures of dancers and musicians, and silver carriages).

MALAYSIA

Children under 4 travel free. Half-fare for children 4–11. Children 12 and over must pay full fare.

The 3 classes of trains are: De Luxe (upholstered seats), Eksekutif (padded leather seats) and Ekonomi (cushioned plastic seats), shown in our footnotes as first, second and third-class.

There is passenger rail service from Kuala Lumpur to 2 Malayan seaports: Penang and Padang Besar on its westcoast. There is also train service from Kuala Lumpur south to Singapore.

The views through Malaysia include pepper-vine farms, rice paddies, colorfully clothed people at small railstations, water buffalo, and many different tree farms: rubber, banana, tapioca, coconut and palm oil nut (used in making soap and margarine).

MALAYSIA'S TRAIN PASS

Malayan Railway Pass   Unlimited train travel on all classes of coach on all rail lines within Peninsular Malaysia, including travel to and from Singapore. The 1992 prices are: 85 Malaysian Ringgit for 10 days, MR-175 for 30 days. Space in first-class air-conditioned coaches must be reserved. (The single air-conditioned coach operated between Kuala Lumpur and Singapore has seats for only 22 people.)

Reservations for first-class and second-class space can be made up to 3 months in advance of travel date from: Director of Commerce, Malayan Railway, Jalan Sultan Hishamuddin, Kuala Lumpur.

This pass is sold at stations in Butterworth, Johore Bahru, Kuala Lumpur, Padang Besar, Port Kelang, Rantau Panjang, Wakaf Bharu and Singapore.

Kuala Lumpur

The railstation, built in 1911, is an architectural jewel. See the marvelous collection of dioramas portraying primitive Malay life, costumes, ancient vehicles, silver, brass and weapons in the National Museum (Muzium Negara), open Saturday-Thursday 09:00–18:00; Friday 09:00–12:15 and 14:45–18:00.

The breathtaking modern Masjid Negara (National Mosque), measuring 5 acres and surrounded by 8 acres of gardens and reflecting pools. Its Grand Hall and encircling veranda accomodate 8,000 people.

Parliament House. Rubber and pewter factories. Tin mines. The old Central Mosque. The National Art Gallery, open Saturday-Thursday 10:00–18:00; Friday 09:00–12:15 and 14:45–8:00. The Zoo.

The Chan See Shu Yuen Society Temple. The Sunday Market (to be visited Saturday night) on Jalan Raja Muda Musa, to sample Malay food. The antiques and art in Wisma Loke, formerly the residence of a wealthy Chinese merchant, on Jalan Medan Tuanku.

Embroidery, tapestry, beadwork, teak furniture, ceramics and knitwear representative of Malaysia's 13 states and the federal district can be purchased at the 14 huts in the Karyaneka Handcraft Center, open daily 09:30–18:00.

The National Monument, featuring a group of bronze hero figures (sculpted by the American, Felix W. de Weldon, who made the Iwo Jima statue near Arlington National Cemetery). Open daily, 07:00–18:00, it is dedicated to those killed in World Wars I and II, as well as those who fell while fighting Communist insurgents in Malaysia during the 1950's.

The Batu Caves are 8 miles from Kuala Lumpu. The main sight there is a Hindu shrine more than a century old in a cavern at the top of 272 steps, alongside of which a rail car runs. Who walks the steps ? Thousands of pilgrims – on their knees and with skewers in their faces and bodies – as an annual penance. The caverns have large stalactites and stalagmites, as well as religious decorations and souvenir vendors.

Penang

An island, just off Butterworth. See the Snake Temple. Ayer Hitami Temple. Khoo Kongsi Temple. The view of the island from the top (2500 feet) of Penang Hill, reached by a funicular. Siva Temple. Goddess of Mercy Temple. The sociable monkeys at the Botanical Gardens. The shops on Campbell Street. The pagoda at Kek Lok Si Temple. Kapitan Kling Mosque.

Kuala Lumpur - Butterworth (Penang) - Padang Besar
7005

Dep. Kuala Lumpur	07:30 (1)	08:15 (2)	15:00 (3)	20:30 (4+7)
Arr. Butterworth	13:35	17:50	21:10	05:30
Change trains. 7050				
Dep. Butterworth	13:40 (6)			
Arr. Padang Besar	16:05			

* * *

Dep. Padang Besar	09:00 (6)			
Arr. Butterworth	12:25			
Change trains. 7005				
Dep. Butterworth	14: 15 (1)	20:30 (4)	22:00 (5)	07:45 (3+8)
Arr. Kuala Lumpur	20:15	05:30	06:40	13:45

(1) Has air-conditioned first and second-class coach cars. Buffet. (2) Has only second and third-class coach cars. Buffet car. (3) Reservation required. Has air-conditioned first and second-class coach cars. Buffet. (4) Has only second and third-class coach cars. (5) Carries air-conditioned sleeping cars. Also has non-airconditioned first and second-class coach cars. Buffet. (6) Has only second-class coach cars. (7) Plus another departure from Kuala Lumpur at 22:00 (5), arriving Butterworth 06:40. (8) Plus another departure from Butterworth at 08:30 (2), arriving Kuala Lumpur 17:50.

Kuala Lumpur - Gemas - Tumpat

7005			7006	
Dep. Kuala Lumpur	22:00 (1+2)		Dep. Tumpat	10:30 (3)
Arr. Gemas	01:30		Arr. Gemas	23:55
Change trains. Table 7006			Change trains. Table 7005	
Dep. Gemas	02:30 (3)		Dep. Gemas	03:09 (1)
Arr. Tumpat	15:30		Arr. Kuala Lumpur	07:00

(1) Carries an air-conditioned first-class sleeping car. Also has first and second-class coach cars. (2) There is also a departure at 20:30 which has a direct first-class coach car that is switched in Gemas to the same 02:30 departure from Gemas shown above. (3) Carries a second-class sleeping car to Gemas. Also has a first-class coach car that is switched in Gemas to an 01:51 departure to Kuala Lumpur that has only second-class coach cars.

INTERNATIONAL ROUTES FROM MALAYSIA

Butterworth is Malaysia's train gateway to Thailand. Kuala Lumpur is the starting point for rail trips to Singapore.

Butterworth - Bangkok 7050
This train carries an air-conditioned sleeping car and a restaurant car.

Dep. Butterworth	13:40		Arr. Bangkok	08:35 Day 2

Kuala Lumpur - Singapore 7005

Dep. Kuala Lumpur	07:30 (1)	08:30 (2)	14:00 (3)	20:30 (4)	22:00 (5)
Arr. Singapore	14:20	18:00	21:20	06:15	06:55

(1) Air-conditioned train. Buffet. (2) Has only second and third-class coaches. Buffet. (3) Reservation required. Has air-conditioned first and second-class coach cars. Buffet. (4) Carries second-class sleeping cars. Also has second and third-class coach cars. (5) Carries air-conditioned first-class sleeping cars. Also has first and second-class coach cars. Buffet.

NEPAL

Nepal's only passenger train service is the 31-mile Jaynagar–Bizalpura route. The main attraction for tourists in Nepal is guided treks into the Himalayas with Sherpa guides.

Jaynagar - Janakpurdham - Bizalpura 6200

Dep. Jaynagar	07:15	14:15	Dep. Bizalpura	08:00	13:30
Arr. Janakpurdham	09:10	16:10	Arr. Janakpurdham	09:30	15:00
Change trains.			Change trains.		
Dep. Janakpurdham	11:00	16:40	Dep. Janakpurdham	10:40	17:30
Arr. Bizalpura	12:30	18:10	Arr. Jaynagar	12:35	19:25

NORTH KOREA   (Dem. Rep. of Korea)

Children under 3 travel free. Half-fare for children 3–9. Children 10 and over must pay full fare.

Pyongyang - Chongjin 5205

All of these trains have a restaurant car.

Dep. Pyongyang	06:43 (1)	17:30 (2)	Dep. Chongjin	01:07	08:14 (3)
Arr. Chongjin	03:44	09:37	Arr. Pyongyang	21:23 (1)	23:15

(1) Depart/Arrive Pyongyang's West railstation. Second-class only. (2) Plus another Pyongyang departure at 19:50, arriving Chongjin 11:36. (3) Plus another Chongjin departure at 17:40, arriving Pyongyang 09:35.

Pyongyang - Dandong - Beijing (Pekin)

The scenery on this route is mostly rice paddies. The 16-car train from Pyonyang to Beijing is pulled by an electric engine. About half of the cars have sleeping facilities. These are occupied mainly by non-Koreans. The other cars have 4-seat benches. Passage between the 2 classes of cars is prevented by locked doors. A restaurant car is accessible to the first-class sleeping cars. In it, passengers can buy food, beer and Pullosul, a yellow liqueur containing an alcohol-preserved pit viper snake.

Before reaching the Chinese border, the train crosses the Yalu River. On the other side of the Yalu, a steam engine replaces the electric Korean locomotive. Chinese immigration officers board the train when it stops in **Dandong**, where a Chinese restaurant car replaces the Korean one. After reaching Beijing, there are connections by train from there to both Moscow and to Hanoi (and on from there to Ho Chi Minh City, formerly called Saigon).

5200		5300	
Dep. Pyongyang	12:00 (1)	Dep. Dandong	18:53 (2)
Arr. Dandong	16:23	Arr. Beijing	10:00
Change trains.			

(1) Runs Monday, Wednesday, Thursday and Saturday. Restaurant car. (2) Supplement charged.

Pyongyang -Moscow 5000

Dep. Pyongyang	12:00 (1)	12:50 (4)
Dep. Shenyang	07:22 (2)	– 0 –
Dep. Khabaruvsk	– 0 –	02:12 (5)
Arr. Moscow (Yaroslavski)	11:47 (3)	18:50 (6)

(1) Runs Saturday only. Carries first-class sleeping cars. Also has first-class coaches. (2) Day 2. (3) Day 7. (4) Runs Monday and Wednsday. Carries a first-class sleeping car. Also has a second-class coach. (5) Day 3, Moscow time. Local time is 06:12 on Day 2. (6) Day 8.

PAKISTAN

Children under 3 travel free. Half-fare for children 3–11. Children 12 and over must pay full fare. Most trains in Pakistan provide "special ladies' accommodation" which both male and female children under 12 may use if they are traveling with an adult female relative or companion.

There are 3 classes of train travel here: air-conditioned, first-class, and second-class. Air-conditioned class converts into sleeping compartments with 2 berths for night travel. First-class converts to 4 berths. Second-class converts to couchettes.

Advance application is recommended to reserve bedding rolls in air-conditioned class. Reservations are recommended for all overnight and long-distance journeys. Passengers in air-conditioned coaches on certain trains can obtain (at extra charge) bedding, soap, toilet paper and a towel.

The 3 major train routes in Pakistan are from Karachi: northeast to Lahore, north to Peshawar, and northwest to Quetta.

Karachi

See Burns Gardens. The Ghanshyam Art Center. The Zoo in Ghandi Gardens. The 270-acre Botanical Garden. The National Museum, with its Greco-Buddhist art, near Cantonment Railstation. Adamji Mosque. The Memorial Museum. Mamon Mosque. The Hindu Temple. Jahangir Park. You will find every thing from mangos to silver anklets in these typical Eastern bazaars: Juna, Khajoor, Jodia, Sarafa and Bahri.

Visit Fire Temple. Islamia College. "Mazaar", the Mausoleum of Quaid-E-Azam Mohammad Ali Jinnah, who guided Pakistan to independence. The Aquarium and amusement park, at Clifton.

This is a natural harbor. Half-day and full-day excursions can be made to many secluded swimming and fishing beaches, archaeological sites and bird sanctuaries. Only 17 miles away are the exquisitely carved gravestones of medieval kings, princes and Baluchi tribesmen.

Engraved red sandstone mausoleums over 600 years old, where some of the great Moghul governors are buried, can be seen at Makli Hill. The main attraction there is the Shah Jehan Mosque, one of the finest surviving works of Muslim architecture. It was built in 1644 by Jehan, the same emperor who constructed the TajMahal in India and, in 1632, the fabulous Shish Mahal in Lahore. Its series of 93 domes enables a prayer leader to be heard in every corner of the massive brick building. The Mosque's brick enamel and glazed tiles are unsurpassed.

An airplane excursion can be made to **Moenjodaro** (Mound of the Dead), a 25-acre split-level town, site of one of the earliest Asian civilizations. It had a covered sewage system, a huge public bath, a large granary, a religious seminary, and many private homes.

Karachi - Hyderabad 5910

Dep. Karachi (Can.)	06:30 (1)	07:15	08:00	09:10 (2)	10:50 (3+8)
Arr. Hyderabad	08:24	09:35	10:59	11:30	12:55

Sights in **Hyderabad**: Much lacquerware, ornamented silks and items of gold and silver are made here. See the large 18th century fort. The 1½ mile-long Shahi Bazaar, running from the fort to the Market Tower. The old palaces. The tombs of ancient rulers.

Dep. Hyderabad	02:53 (4)	03:17 (5)	03:55 (6)	05:35 (4)	06:05 (9)
Arr. Karachi (Can.)	05:30	06:20	06:40	08:35	08:55

(1) Supplement charged. Has air-conditioned coaches. Restaurant car. (2) Reservation required. Restaurant car. (3) Restaurant car. (4) Reservation required. Has air-conditioned coaches. Restaurant car. (5) Reservation required. Has air-conditioned coaches. (6) Has air-conditioned coaches. (7) Has air-conditioned coaches. Restaurant car. (8) Plus other departures from Karachi at 11:10 (4), 16:30 (7), 17:05 (6), 18:00 (5), 18:35 (6), 19:05 (4), 22:15 (4) and 22:30 (6). (9) Plus other departures from Hyderabad at 06:35 (7), 08:00 (3), 08:40 (5), 12:15 (2), 14:50 (5), 16:05, 17:20 and 19:53 (1).

Karachi - Lahore 5910

All of these trains have a restaurant car or buffet and have a coach that converts to berths, unless designated otherwise.

Dep. Karachi (Can.)	06:30 (1)	09:10 (2)	10:50 (3)	16:30	22:15 (4)
Arr. Lahore	22:05	04:15	05:05	09:55	18:10

*   *   *

Dep. Lahore	06:30 (1)	09:30 (4)	15:10 (3)	16:15	17:15 (3+5)
Arr. Karachi (Can.)	22:05	05:30	09:05	10:25	18:30

(1) Supplement charged. Has air-conditioned coach. (2) Reservationrequired. (3) Has air-conditioned coach. (4) Reservation required. Has air-conditioned coach. (5) Plus another departure from Lahore at 19:35 (2), arriving Karachi 14:45.

Sights in **Lahore**: Pakistan's second-largest city. Often called "the city of gardens". This is a busy rail center, with 10,000,000 passengers handled here every year.

See the complex of 16th–18th century palaces and halls inside Lahore Fort. The Shish Mahal (Palace of Mirrors) with its fretted screens, colored mirrors and marble, often called the most ornately decorated royal salon in the world. It was built in 1632 by the same Shah Jehan who built the great Mosque outside Karachi in 1644 and the Taj Mahal in India.

Also in the Fort, the museum of 18th and early 19th century maps, drawings and weapons. The small Moti Masjid Mosque. The royal apartments and throne room. The marble hall, Diwan-i-Khas.

At one of the world's largest places of worship, across from the Fort (on the other side of Hazuri Bagh Square), see the marble ornamentation at the 17th century Badshahi (Imperial) Mosque. Its courtyard, nearly 600-feet long, can hold 70,000 people praying at the same time. The view of Lahore from its minarets is worth climbing the more than 200 stairs to them.

Take the 2-mile walk from the Fort through many colorful bazaars (jewelry, leather, copper, brass, cloth). Also see the mirrored ceilings and glass mosaics in the mausoleum of the 18th century playboy, Maharajah Ranjit Singh. The ashes of his 4 wives and 7 concubines, cremated at his death, are also stored there. See the marvelous collection of Gandhara and Greco-Buddhist art (particularly the "starving Buddha") at the Lahore Museum.

Without fail, go 6 miles east of Lahore to the incredibly magnificent 40-acre **Shalimar Gardens**, one of the greatest gardens in the world. It was designed in the 17th century to rival the one of the same name at Srinigar in **Kashmir**.

Near Shalimar is Jehangir's Mausoleum, located in a 55-acre garden. The emperor Jehangir is resting in a white marble sarcophagus ornamented with mosaics of flowers and with the Arabic and Persian inscriptions that list the 99 attributes of God.

Karachi - Peshawar 5910

This is a 1,100-mile journey.

All of these trains require reservation, have first-class seats that convert to berths, and have a restaurant car.

Dep. Karachi (Canton.)	09:10	19:45 (2)	22:15 (4)
Arr. Peshawar (Canton.)	14:45 (1)	07:25 (3)	05:30 (3)

Sights in **Peshawar**: Stroll down the ancient Qissah Khawani Bazar (Street of Storytellers), with its stores selling dried fruits, rugs, sheepskin coats and lambskin (karacul) caps. In past centuries, travelers from Persia, Russia and Afghanistan sat in these narrow alleys and told stories of their journeys.

See the 17th century pure white Mahabat Khan Mosque. The 16th century Bala Hisar Fort. The shoes sold at Mochilara Bazaar. The central square, Chowk Yaad Gar. The former Buddhist Monastery, Gor Khatri. The famed **Khyber Pass**, 10 miles from Peshawar.

Dep. Peshawar (Canton.)	09:10	19:50 (2)	22:30 (4)
Arr. Karachi (Canton.)	14:45 (1)	08:35 (3)	05:35 (3)

(1) Day 2. (2) Has air-conditioned coach cars with seats that convert to berths. (3) Day 3. (4) Carries air-conditioned sleeping cars. Also has air-conditioned coach cars with seats that convert to berths.

Lahore - Peshawar 5910

All of these trains have a restaurant car or buffet, unless designated otherwise.

Dep. Lahore	04:45 (1)	18:40 (2)	21:25 (3)
Arr. Peshawar (Can.)	14:45	05:20	08:30
		* * *	
Dep. Peshawar (Can.)	09:10 (1)	18:30 (3)	22:30 (2)
Arr. Lahore	19:05	05:20	08:55

(1) Reservation required. (2) Reservation required. Carries air-conditioned sleeping cars. Also has air-conditioned coaches and first-class coaches, both of which convert to berths. (3) No food service. Has air-conditioned coach space and first-class seats, both of which convert to berths.

Peshawar - Landi Kotal 5904

This route is via the fabled Khyber Pass. Landi Kotal is 8 miles east of the Afghan border.

Pakistan did not publish schedules for this route 1984 – 1986 and during those years prohibited foreigners from traveling on it "until the political situation improves."

Schedules were available again 1987 – 1990, when the train ran (as it had done prior to 1984) only on Friday. This service was "temporarily suspended" in 1991.

When the train did operate, it was said that drug traffickers departing Peshawar at 9:00 had 2 hours (12:00 – 14:00) to conduct their business in Landi Kotal and arrived back in Peshawar at 17:05, "in time to have dinner with their families."

Dep. Peshawar (Cant.)	Dep. Landi Kotal
Arr. Landi Kotal	Arr. Peshawar (Cant.)

Sights in **Landi Kotal**: The "smuggler's bazaar", shops that are tucked away in rock caverns and along hilly sidestreets.

Karachi - Quetta 5940

All of these trains require reservation, have an air-conditioned coach that converts to berths at night, and carry a restaurant car.

Dep. Karachi (Can.)	11:35	Dep. Quetta	15:55
Arr. Quetta	07:55	Arr. Karachi (Can.)	12:30

Sights in **Quetta**: A popular Summer resort. This town developed around a fort occupied by British troops in 1876. It is a market center for western Afghanistan, eastern Iran and part of Central Asia. See: The Sandeman Library. The Geological Survey of Pakistan (there was severe earthquake damage here in 1935).

Lahore - Quetta

Although Cook uses 2 tables for this trip, all of the trains shown below are direct and there is no train changing in Rohri.

5910			5940		
Dep. Lahore	06:00 (1)	12:40 (3)	Dep. Quetta	11:20 (3)	18:45 (4)
Arr. Rohri	21:40	01:55 (2)	Arr. Rohri	21:15	04:50 (2)
5940			5910		
Dep. Rohri	22:05	02:20	Dep. Rohri	21:40	05:15
Arr. Quetta	08:45 (2)	12:35	Arr. Lahore	11:45 (2)	20:55

(1) Has air-conditioned class and first-class coaches that convert to berths. (2) Day 2 . (3) Reservation required. Carries an air-conditioned sleeping car. Also has air-conditioned class and first-class coaches that convert to berths. Restaurant car. (4) Has air-conditioned class and first-class coaches that convert to berths.

INTERNATIONAL ROUTES FROM PAKISTAN

The Pakistani rail gateway to Iran is Quetta. Lahore is the departure point for train travel to India.

Quetta - Zahedan 5942

Dep. Quetta	15:20 (1)	15:20 (4)
Arr. Kuhi Taftan	10:15 (2)	12:20 (2)
Dep. Mirjawa	N/A (3)	N/A (3)
Arr. Zahedan	N/A	N/A

(1) Runs Wednesday only. Restaurant car. (2) There has been no service Kuhi Taftan–Mirjawa (the Pakistan–Iran border) since 1984. Distance: 10 miles. (3) Rail service Mirjawa–Zahedan was suspended "temporarily" in 1985. There was bus service frequent times in the afternoon 1985–1987. Trip time: 1½ hours. (4) Runs Sunday only.

Lahore - Delhi - New Delhi 6023

Dep. Lahore	11:30
Arr. Amritsar	15:00

Change trains. 6006 + 6030

Dep. Amritsar	06:30	07:45 (1)	08:25 (2)	12:00 (3)	14:10 (4+7)
Arr. New Delhi	13:45	16:10	20:00	20:20	21:15

(1) Suplement charged. Has air-conditioned first and second-class coaches. Restaurant car. (2) Has air-conditioned second-class coaches. Restaurant car. (3) Has air-conditioned second-class coaches. (4) Supplement charged. Has air-conditioned chair car class. (5) Has air-conditioned second-class and ordinary first-class, both of which convert to berths. (6) Has air-conditioned first-class and second-class coaches, also ordinary first-class, all of which convert to berths. (7) Plus other departures from Amritsar at 16:00 (5), 20:45 (6) and 21:15 (5), arriving New Delhi 05:00, 08:15 and 11:45.

Sights in **Amritsar**: This is the holiest city of the Sikh Religion. Home of the wonderful Golden Temple.

PEOPLE'S REPUBLIC OF CHINA

Children under 1 meter tall travel free. Quarter-fare for children 1.00 to 1.29 meters. Children 1.30 meters and taller must pay full fare.

Short-distance trains have soft and hard (first and second-class) seat accommodations. Long-distance trains have first-class seats that convert to berths with complete bedding, and second-class seats that convert to hard bunks.

We learned on our rail trips (Shanghai-Changsha, Changsha-Guilin and Canton-Hong Kong) that Chinese trains do *not* provide drinking water, toilet paper, or soap, although each sleeping compartment is supplied with a thermos of hot water, tea and cups. There is enough storage space in each 4-person compartment for 6 large suitcases. Each berth has a reading lamp.

You can count on 2 things when touring China: the government will keep you on the go 10-14 hours every day, and you will be placed in a Friendship Store from one to 3 hours almost every day. These emporiums sell every possible souvenir you could want to bring home from China: jade, ivory, fabrics, furniture, porcelain, clothing, lacquerware, jewelry, books, etc.

Canton (Guangzhou, pronounced "Kwang-chow")

In the 64-acre Memorial Garden to the Martyrs (also called Red Uprising, the 1927 massacre of many Chinese Communist Party members by government soldiers), holding more than 5,000 bodies. Also: The Pavillion of Sino-Korean Friendship and the Memorial Pavillion. The Tomb of the 72 Martyrs, honoring leaders of the unsuccessful 1911 revolution, located at Huanghuagang (Yellow Flower Hill Park). The Sun Yat-sen Memorial Hall.

At the enormous Yuexiu Park, go to the top of the 600-year-old Zhen Hai Tower (also called Five-Storied Building) for a view of all of the city. Also located in this park are the Museum of Liberation and many other museums: prehistory, Ming Dynasty, the Manchu era, the Opium Wars, and one on the industrialization of Canton.

There is an excellent Chinese Orchid Garden at the west side of Yuexiu Park. The 82-acre Zoo, with more than 200 varieties of birds and animals, is considered one of the best in Asia and is famous for its Panda bears.

Other notable sights: the 6th century Lu Yung Temple (Temple of the Six Banyan Trees). The 7th century Huaisheng Mosque. The 4th century (B.C.) Kwang Shiao Temple. Many parks and lakes. The view from White Cloud Mountain. The Monument to the Struggle Against the British Invasion, at **Sanyuanli**, north of the city.

Beijing (Pekin)

It is said that everyone starts a tour of Beijing from the enormous Tiananmen Square (nearly 100 acres), where Chairman Mao Zedong first raised the flag of the People's Republic of China and initiated the contemporary era of China.

At the north side of the Square is Tian'anmen (Gate of Heavenly Peace), the entrance to the fabled Forbidden City, a 250-acre compound containing many palaces, museums, pavillions and gardens.

You walk first through the Upright Gate, then down Sightseer's Route to Meridian Gate and then through Gate of Supreme Harmony, next reaching the exhibits inside Hall of Supreme Harmony, followed by Hall of Complete Harmony, Hall of Preserving Harmony, Gate of Heavenly Purity, Palace of Heavenly Purity, Hall of Union, Hall of Earthly Peace, Gate of Earthly Peace, and finally reach hall of Imperial Peace, surrounded by the Imperial Garden.

East of Tiananmen Square are the Chinese History Museum and the Museum of the

Chinese Revolution. West of the Square is the Great Hall of the People. Its banquet room seats 5,000 people. A theater near it holds 10,000. At the south side of the Square is the magnificent Chairman Mao Memorial Hall and the Monument to the People's Heroes.

Other important sights in Beijing are: The large Zoo, featuring Giant Pandas. The 770-foot long white marble Marco Polo Bridge, spanning the Yungting River. The National Art Gallery. The fantastic 15th century Temple of Heaven, located in a complex measuring 16 square miles.

It is a 90-minute bus ride from Beijing to the Great Wall, the mightiest human construction in history. Although a special excursion train departs Beijing daily at 07:03 (arriving back in Beijing at 13:30), the train leaves passengers about ¼-mile from the Great Wall. Buses from Beijing take you directly to the section of the Great Wall at **Badaling** that was restored in 1957 for visitors.

Most of the 3,600-mile long wall was built 476–221 (B.C.), with more than another 100 years of work performed to restore and reinforce it in the 14th–15th century A.D.).

Seven miles from Beijing is the Summer Palace, set in a 700-acre park that includes the lovely Kunming Lake and many museums. The walk down the beautifully decorated "Long Corridor", along the lakeshore, is memorable.

Thirty miles from Beijing, the Ming Tombs cover an area of several square miles. The sculptured animals along the road leading to the exhibit tomb are very interesting.

Beijing - Tianjin - Harbin 5300

All of these trains have a first-class coaches and a restaurant car, unless designated otherwise.

Dep. Beijing	01:13 (1)	08:35	14:30 (2)	-0-	20:32 (3)
Dep. Tianjin bei	03:15	10:41	-0-	20:13	22:15 (6)
Arr. Harbin	22:54	06:17	06:46	15:27	14:45

Sights in **Tianjin:** see notes under "Shanghai – Bejing" on page 629.

Sights in **Harbin:** Called "Moscow of the East". It became a large Russian settlement when refugees surged here in 1917 to avoid capture by Soviet communists. The major annual event is the Ice Lantern Festival that runs all of January and February, when Harbin is filled with monumental ice sculptures.

Dep. Harbin	06:50	09:07	12:24 (2)	19:34 (2)	20:06 (2+7)
Dep. Tianjin bei	02:28	04:00 (4)	05:00	-0-	-0-
Arr. Beijing	04:10	-0-	06:32	11:55	10:47

(1) Depart/Arrive Beijing's Nan railstation. (2) Supplement charged. (3) Supplement charged. Late May to late September: runs Friday and Saturday. Late September to late May: runs Saturday only. (4) Depart/Arrive Tianjin's Xi railstation. (5) Terminates in Tianjin (xi railstation). (6) Plus another departure from Tianjin (xi railstation) at 01:02, arriving Harbin 20:03. (7) Plus other departures from Harbin at 20:36 (2), 00:14, 01:30 and 04:22...arriving Tianjin 10:20 (4), 19:54, 21:23 and 23:52 (5)...arriving Beijing -0-, 21:45, 23:10 (1) and -0-.

Canton (Guangzhou) - Changsha 5320

All of these trains charge a supplement and have a restaurant car.

Dep. Canton	19:01	21:05	23:00 (1)
Arr. Changsha	08:52	12:11	16:00
		* * *	
Dep. Changsha	17:00	19:13	22:52 (1)
Arr. Canton	07:30	09:05	15:55

(1) No supplement charged.

(Notes on sightseeing in Changsha appear on page 628)

Sights in **Changsha**: At the Hunan Provincial Museum, over 3,000 valuable artifacts from the Han Tomb excavations. Among the valuable relics from 2,100 years ago, you can view the well-preserved body of a woman. Also on exhibit, displayed in glass jars, are her vital organs.

Other exhibits include beautiful lacquerware, wind and stringed musical instruments, delicate silk fabrics, wood figurines in singing and dancing positions, silk paintings, huge colored wood coffins, bronzes over 3,000 years old, and porcelain pieces produced more than 1,000 years ago.

A tour of the Hunan Provincial Embroidery Factory is worthwhile not only to see the incredible work done there but also to experience the curiousity of the crowds of Chinese people who wait outside the factory to stare at tourists.

Canton (Guangzhou) - Kowloon - Hong Kong 5400

Prior to 1979, it had always been necessary to get off the train in Shenzhen, walk across the bridge spanning the Shum Chun River to the Lo Wu railstation on the south side of the river, and go through customs formalities there before boarding a second train and proceeding on to Kowloon and Hong Kong.

Since 1979, several trains per day make a direct ride from Hong Kong to Guangzhou and v.v. without requiring passengers to change trains inLo Wu. These direct trains are operated by the People's Republic of China and are first-class only.

There are frequent departures for the short ferry-boat ride from Kowloon to Hong Kong.

All of these trains are first-class only, require reservation, are air-conditioned and have light refreshments.

Dep. Canton	08:30	10:20	12:20	14:20	16:27	18:30
Arr. Kowloon (Hung Hom)	10:48	12:38	14:38	16:38	18:46	20:48

Canton - (Guangzhou) - Shanghai 5331

Both of these trains charge a supplement and have a restaurant car.

Dep. Canton	08:28	Dep. Shanghai	09:10
Arr. Shanghai	20:10 Day 2	Arr. Canton	20:06 Day 2

Sights in **Shanghai**: With more than 11,000,000 people, this is the second (after Mexico City) most populous city in the world. See Chung Shan Lu Street, on the waterfront, called "the Bund", with its European-style buildings, from the period when foreigners controlled the city. You will want to visit the Number One Department Store while strolling this famous street. Also see People's Park, once a race track.

The enormous People's Square. The goods displayed at the Industrial Exhibit, everything from jade to ship-building.

Next to the City God Temple are the Yueyuan Gardens and the Temple of the Town Gods and the Garden of the Purple Clouds of Autumn.

Do not miss the 3rd century pagoda, rebuilt in the 10th century, located in Lung Hua Park. The laughing Buddha in the temple there is a major attraction.

Visit the large natural exhibit Zoo in Si Jiao Park and the smaller Zoo in Fu Hsing Park. The vast collection of artwork in the Museum of Shanghai.

The white jade Buddha in the Jade Buddha Temple. The antiques for sale at the Antique and Curio Branch of Shanghai Friendship Store. The Children's Palace. Swan Lake in West Suburb Park.

Shanghai - Suzhou - Wuxi - Nanjing - Tianjin - Beijing 5330

At most stops on this route, passengers alight to buy local food items sold along the platforms. At Tianjin (Tientsin), the favorite is meat-filled dumplings that the Chinese regard as the best in their country.

The route actually originates in **Fuzhou (Foochow)**. Located in a critical military area, Fuzhou is closed to most foreigners.

Compartments are fitted with loudspeakers from which pour a steady combination of propaganda and music, the same as we experienced on the "Trans Siberia Express".

However, where the Soviet off-switch is in plain sight, the Chinese have placed theirs more obscurely under a small reading table.

The compartments on the Shanghai-Peking Express have a *fin de siecle* elegance: potted plants, porcelain cups, and tea bags. An acupuncturist is available for anyone requiring that service. As on most Chinese express trains, women workers are constantly scrubbing and mopping the interior. Boiling water is provided free in large thermos containers.

Each compartment has 4 berths. However, foreigners traveling in pairs are usually given an entire compartment. Early in the trip the train goes along the Grand Canal that was being used before Marco Polo saw it 6 centuries ago. It still has heavy boat traffic.

All of these trains have first-class seats that convert to berths (a supplement charged for bedding) and a restaurant car.

Dep. Shanghai	10:11 (1+2)	13:03 (2)	16:02 (1)	19:21	19:55 (1)
Dep. Suzhou	-0-	14:14	-0-	20:43	-0-
Dep. Wuxi	11:48	15:02	-0-	21:31	-0-
Dep. Nanjing	14:32	17:56	-0-	00:37 (3)	-0-
Arr. Tianjin (xi)	04:07 (3)	09:42 (3)	-0-	16:18	-0-
Arr. Beijing	05:45	11:40	09:01 (3)	18:25	12:54 (3)

* * *

Dep. Beijing	10:38 (1)	14:40 (1)	15:23	21:10	21:55 (1)
Dep. Tianjin (xi)	12:27	-0-	17:34	23:40	-0-
Dep. Nanjing	02:22 (3)	-0-	09:48 (3)	16:06 (3)	-0-
Dep. Wuxi	04:53	-0-	12:30	18:58	-0-
Dep. Suzhou	-0-	-0-	13:27	19:38	-0-
Arr. Shanghai	06:21 (2)	07:39 (3)	14:17 (2)	20:44	14:54 (3)

(1) Supplement charged. (2) Depart/Arrive Shanghai's Zhenru railstation. (3) Day 2.

Sights in **Tianjin:** China's third largest city, only a 2-hour train ride from Beijing. See the attractive lakes (with rowboats) and pavilions in the large "Water Park" (Shui Shang Gong Yuan).

The most important factories of handwoven carpets in China can be toured every day. Visits to them run about 90 minutes. A veteran weaver completes only 3 square inches a day. Carpets purchased there are shipped to the buyer's home.

This city is also popular for purchasing Chinese antiques (jade carvings and jewelry, porcelains, scroll paintings). Very good contemporary scroll paintings on silk can be purchased at the Yang Liu Qing Art Society.

See the collection of jade objects, stone rubbings, ceramics, bronzes and 1500 year-old calligraphy at the Museum of History, open daily 08:30–16:45. Hire a car to go to the nearby 17th century Qing Tombs, which the Chinese regard as more interesting and more beautiful than the Ming Tombs outside Pekin.

INTERNATIONAL ROUTES FROM
THE PEOPLE'S REPUBLIC OF CHINA

Here are the routes from Beijing to Russia and North Korea.

Beijing - Moscow 5000

These trains are used by Intourist for foreign travelers. All of them carry a sleeping car and a restaurant car.

Dep. Beijing	07:40 (1)	20:32 (3)
Arr. Moscow	12:15 (2)	11:47 (4)

(1) Runs Wednesday only. (2) Day 6, Monday. (3) Late May to late September: runs Friday and Saturday. Late September to late May: runs Saturday only. (4) Day 7, Friday.

Beijing - Dandong - Pyonyang - Chongjin

In Dandong, a Korean restaurant car replaces the Chinese one. It is accessble to the first-class sleeping cars. Passengers can buy food, beer and Pullosul, a yellow liqueur containing an alcohol preserved pit viper snake. An electric Korean locomotive replaces the Chinese steam engine, and the train crosses the **Yalu River**. About half of the cars have sleeping facilities. These are occupied mainly by non-Koreans. The other cars have 4-seat benches. Passage between the 2 classes of cars is prevented by locked doors.

5300		Change trains *and railstations..*		
Dep. Beijing	16:48 (1)	5205		
Arr. Dandong	08:07 (2)	Dep. Pyonyang	17:30 (4)	19:50 (4)
5200		Arr. Chongin	09:37 (5)	11:36 (5)
Dep. Dandong	09:35 (3)			
Arr. Pyongyang (West)	15:55			

(1) Runs Monday, Wednesday, Thursday and Saturday. Supplement charged for travel and for bedding. (2) Day 2. (3) Runs Tuesday, Thursday, Friday and Sunday. Restaurant car. Carries sleeping car on Friday. (4) Restaurant car. (5) Day 3 from Beijing.

PHILIPPINES

Children under 3 travel free. Half-fare for children 3–9. Children 10 and over must pay full fare.

The rail system on Luzon is 2 lines, north from Manila to San Fernando and south from Manila to Camalig.

Manila

See representations of the country's major regions (Visayas, Mindanao, Vigan and the Mountain Provinces) at the Philippine Village, next to the airport. Excellent souvenirs are sold there. Visit the complex of Cultural Center, Folks Art Theater and Convention Center.

The sidewalk cafes, Chinese and Japanese gardens, planetarium and the lagoon with "dancing" fountains, all in Rizal Park. The Rizal Monument in Luneta Park. Windowshop on Dasmarinas and Escolta streets.

Fort Santiago, San Augustine Church (which has artifacts from the era of Spanish rule) and Manila Cathedral, all in the 16th century walled city called Intramuros. Near it, Chinatown and the marble tombs in the Chinese cemetery. The Zoological and Botanical Garden.

The 18th century 12-foot wide Bamboo Organ of **Las Pinas** is only a few miles from Manila. Take a hydrofoil for the short trip to see the ruins of **Corregidor**, the famous World War II fort.

Manila - San Fernando 7700

| Dep. Manila (S. Laz.) | 17:35 (1) | Dep. San Fernando (P) | 05:30 (1) |
| Arr. San Fernando (P) | 19:27 | Arr. Manila (S. Laz.) | 07:55 |

(1) These trains are subject to local confirmation.

Manila - Camalig 7700

There are great views of **Mayon Volcano** between Naga and Camalig and of **Pagsanjan Falls and Rapids**.

All of these trains have a restaurant car.

Dep. Manila (S. Lazaro)	15:00 (1)	18:30 (3)	20:00 (4)	05:30 (5)
Arr. Naga	03:00 (2)	04:30 (2)	07:00 (2)	18:00 (2)
Arr. Camalig	N/A	N/A	N/A	N/A
	*	* *		
Dep. Camalig	N/A (2)	N/A (2)	N/A (2)	N/A (2)
Dep. Naga	05:30 (5)	16:30 (1)	18:30 (6)	20:00 (4)
Arr. Manila (S. Lazaro)	17:50	03:35	04:30	07:00

(1) Has only second-class coaches and third-class couchettes. (2) Service Naga–Camalig and v.v. was "temporarily" suspended in 1987. (3) Runs Monday, Wednesday and Friday. Has air-conditioned first-class coaches. (4) Has air-conditioned first-class coaches and non-airconditioned first-class couchettes. (5) Third-class only. (6) Runs Tuesday, Thursday and Saturday. Has air-conditioned first-class coaches and non-airconditioned first-class couchettes.

REPUBLIC OF CHINA (TAIWAN)

Children under 3 travel free. Half-fare for children 3–13. Children 14 and over must pay full fare.

Train tickets can be purchased at most major Taipei hotels as well as at the main railstation.

The 5 classes of trains are: First-class Air-conditioned, Air-conditioned, Air-conditioned Limited, Limited and Ordinary. Every train is entirely one of those classes. There is First-class Air-conditioned service from the northernmost part of Taiwan, at Keelung, extending south to Taipei and then along western Taiwain to Kaohsiung and Pingtung.

From Pingtung, local trains run to a fork at Chen-an. From Chen-an, one local spur goes to Tung-chiang and another to Fanh-liao. Another rail line runs from Keelung along the eastern side of the island, south to Hualien and Tai-tung Hai-an.

CHINESE HOLIDAYS

Jan.1	Founding of the Republic of China	Oct. 10	Double Tenth National Day
Jan. 2	Additional holiday	Oct. 25	Retrocession Day
Mar. 29	Youth Day	Oct. 31	Veterans' Day and
April 4	Tomb Sweeping Day and		birth of Chiang Kai-shek
	death of Chaing Kai-shek	Nov. 12	Dr. Sun Yat-sen's birthday
June	Dragon Boat Festival	Dec. 25	Constitution Day
Sept. 28	Confucius' Birthday also		
	Teacher's day		

Taipei

Among the leading sights to see in Taipei are the fabulous art treasures from mainland China in the National Palace Museum (open daily 09:00–17:00), the world's greatest collection of Chinese art since it was founded here in 1965. About 12,000 of its 620,000 objects are displayed on a 3–6 month rotation. They represent the last 5,000 years.

Its treasures include bronzes (cooking pots, bells, wine containers) used 1700–1200 B.C., paintings on silk and paper, 11th century opaque Ju vases, a 19th century translucent jade cabbage, ancient lacquer (14th to 20th century), 15th century blue-and-white porcelains, cloisonne, and miniature carvings from ivory, different kinds of wood and fruit stones. A store at the Museum sells good reproductions of the objects.

Also see the Monument of the Martyrs. The Memorial to Dr. Sun Yat Sen. Luan Shen Temple, and the street of food stores across from the Temple. The lobby and halls of the world's most extravagant and most beautiful hotel, The Grand Hotel, atop a hill that overlooks all of Taipei.

Chiang Kai-Shek Memorial Hall, a classical Chinese structure, honoring the country's first president. Lungshan Temple. Art objects and Chinese currency exhibited at the National Museum of History. Aboriginal artifacts at the Taiwan Provincial Museum.

"Window on China", 33 miles southwest of Taipei, features Lilliputian (1:25 scale) beautiful reproductions of many of China's historical sites, including the Temple of Heaven in Beijing.

Taipei - Taichung - Chiayi - Tainan - Kaohsiung 7800

We had the advantage of being escorted for 9 days in the Republic of China by the prominent Taiwan engineer and orchid expert, Mr. L. F. King, whose comments and knowledge illuminated everything we saw there. His kindness made our travels in Taiwan the most idyllic touring we have ever had in our travel throughout the world. We lost our good friend in 1986.

Taiwan's railstations and other of its public places have enormous mirrors. Personal appearance is very important to the Taiwanese, who like to inspect themselves when starting and ending a journey.

No one could become mussed on the air-conditioned, non-stop ride we made from Taipei to Taichung. A few minutes after leaving Taipei, Chinese-language and English-language newspapers were given to each passenger without charge. Next, an attendant brought hot, damp wash-cloths, and everyone washed face and hands. Meanwhile, recorded Western and Chinese music was played over the train's public address system.

Other train employees placed tea bags and hot water into large glasses that fit into holders along the wall, next to where one is sitting and within easy reach. More hot water was served frequently during the trip.

Mr. King, whose taste in art, orchids and food was impeccable, carried with him when he traveled a special blend of tea, which he brought on our trip in sufficient quantity for us so that we might have it to enjoy in place of the tea that the train serves. During the ride, he alerted us to various brick and ceramic factories, the construction of a new super-highway which his company was then building, and other interesting sights. Halfway to Taichung, the train goes along the Formosa Strait.

Vendors come through the train with sandwiches, candies and cigarettes. An hour before arriving in Taichung, a hot meal of pork, rice and a hardboiled egg flavored with tea could be purchased at one's seat for NT $58–$70 in 1991.

This train has airplane style seating, all passengers facing forward. Each car has separate lavatories for men and women. The 1991 price was NT $215–$320 for the all-first-class express train Taipei–Taichung, and NT $478–$711 Taipei–Kaohsiung.

Unless noted, all trains have air-conditioned coaches.

Dep. Taipei	08:00 (1)	09:00 (1)	10:00 (1)	11:00 (1)	12:00 (2)
Dep. Taichung	10:13	11:24	12:14	13:12	14:46
Dep. Chiayi	11:15	12:29	13:16	14:15	16:05
Dep. Tainan	11:53	13:00	13:54	14:53	16:58
Arr. Kaohsiung	12:22	13:38	14:23	15:22	17:40
		* * *			
Dep. Kaohsiung	08:00 (1)	09:30 (1)	10:00	11:00	12:00 (3)
Dep. Tainan	08:31	10:01	10:35	11:35	12:35
Dep. Chiayi	09:09	10:41	11:22	12:23	13:38
Dep. Taichung	10:13	11:51	12:43	13:45	14:44
Arr. Taipei	12:29	14:01	15:17	16:34	17:28

(1) Light refreshments. (2) Plus other departures from Taipei at 14:00 (1), 15:00, 16:40 (1), 19:00 (1) and 23:32. (3) Plus other departures from Kaohsiung at 14:17 (1), 15:25 (1), 16:35 (1), 17:00 , 19:15 and 23:00.

Sights in **Taichung**: Classical Chinese landscaping in the city-center 50-acre Chungshan Park. Primitive dwelling and artifacts representing each of the island's 9 major aborigine tribes are exhibited at the Aboriginal Culture Village.

In **Changhua**, 12 miles southwest of Taichung, see the Giant Buddha (72-feet tall, resting on a 14-foot-high lotus-shaped pedestal). An interior staircase leads to the head of the statue, from whose eyes (actually windows) there is a panoramic view of the area.

Sights in **Tainan**: Taiwan's oldest city. See the shrine to Koxinga (Cheng Chengkung), the Ming Dynasty loyalist who in 1661 restored Taiwan to Chinese rule after 37 years of Dutch occupation. The Confucian temple. Yitsai Castle.

Sights in **Kaohsiung**: Second-largest city in Taiwan (1,350,000). See the view of the city from Shou Shan, a hill topped by a martyr's shrine. This city is a gateway to several popular tourist attractions: Taiwan's newest Confucian Temple and the Dragon and Tiger Pagodas at **Lotus Lake**. The Chung Hsing Pagoda, one of Taiwan's best- known landmarks, at the nearby **Chen Ching Lake** resort area (aquariums, boating, fishing, hiking, golf, swimming).

Kaohsiung is also used as the base for trips to such other attractions as the picturesque bay at **Kenting National Park** and **Fo Kuang Shan** (Light of Buddha Mountain).

Taipei - Taichung - Sun Moon Lake

7800

Dep. Taipei	-0-	06:15	11:00	12:30 (1)
Arr. Taichung	-0-	08:59	13:02	14:57
Change to bus. (Government timetable)				
Dep. Taichung	08:00	09:50	14:20	16:20
Arr. Sun Moon Lake	10:00	11:50	16:20	18:30

One of Taiwan's 2 most famous tourist attractions is the incredibly beautiful Sun Moon Lake, a 50-mile trip from Taichung on the Golden Horse Bus. Motor launches offer cruises on the lake. Tourist sites include Wen Fu Temple and the Pagoda of Filial Piety.

The Handicraft Exhibition Hall is on this highway. Items of bamboo and rattan, lanterns, jewelry, lacquerware and toys can be purchased in this air-conditioned, 4-story building.

Dep. Sun Moon Lake	07:30	10:30	14:00	17:00
Arr. Taichung	09:30	12:30	16:00	19:00
Change to train. Table 7800				
Dep. Taichung	10:13	13:20	16:30	19:58 (2)
Arr. Taipei	12:29	15:58	19:21	22:47

(1) Plus other Taipei departures at 08:00, 09:00, 10:00, 11:00, 12:00, and frequent times from 13:55 to 23:32. (2) Plus other Taichung departures at 09:07, 09:51, 11:51, 12:43, 14:44, 15:16, 16:06, 21:31 and 02:47.

Here is an easy stopover in Taichung, en route from Taipei to Kaohsiung or vice versa, with a side-trip to Sun Moon Lake.

7800		7800	
Dep. Taipei	11:00 (1)	Dep. Kaohsiung	10:30 (2)
Arr. Taichung	13:02	Arr. Taichung	13:15
Take bus to Sun Moon Lake. 7810		Take bus to Sun Moon Lake. 7810	
Dep. Taichung	14:20	Dep. Taichung	14:20
Arr. Sun Moon Lake	16:20	Arr. Sun Moon Lake	16:20
Dep. Sun Moon Lake	17:00	Dep. Sun Moon Lake	17:00
Arr. Taichung	19:00	Arr. Taichung	19:00
Continue on, by train 7800		Continue on, by train. 7800	
Dep. Taichung	21:10 (1)	Dep. Taichung	19:58 (2)
Arr. Kaohsiung	23:29	Arr. Taipei	22:47

(1) Air-conditioned train. Light refreshments. (2) Air-conditioned train.

Chiayi - Alishan

This spur off the Kaohsiung-Taipei line has great Ali Shan Forest mountain scenery. The station at Alishan (7,461 feet) is the highest railstation in East Asia.

7800		7801	
Dep. Kaohsiung	09:00 (1)	Dep. Alishan	13:10
Arr. Chiayi	12:24	Arr. Chiayi	16:35
Change trains.		Change trains.	
7801		7800	
Dep. Chiayi	13:30	Dep. Chiayi	17:44 (1)
Arr. Alishan	16:55	Arr. Taipei	21:10

(1) Air-conditioned train. Light refreshments.

Sights in **Alishan**: People come to this forest recreation area for its smog-free mountain air and the spectacular view of the "Sea of Clouds" that rings 13,110-foot-high **Yushan** (Jade Mountain), the highest peak in Northwest Asia.

Taipei - New Hualien - Taitung 7802

A very scenic train ride down Taiwan's east coast.
All of these trains are air-conditioned.

Dep. Taipei	07:00 (1)	08:00	08:40 (1)	13:25 (1)	14:15 (3)
Arr. New Hualien	09:41	12:08	11:33	16:18	18:15 (4)
Arr. Taitung	12:16	15:39	-0-	-0-	21:21
		*	*	*	
Dep. Taitung	00:40	-0-	06:50 (1)	07:15	07:55 (5)
Dep. New Hualien	06:26	07:40	09:40	10:25	11:20 (6)
Arr. Taipei	10:15	11:28	12:34	14:05	15:05

(1) Light refreshments. (2) Terminates in New Hualien. (3) Plus other departures from Taipei at 15:15 (2). 17:05 (1), 17:50 (2), 19:30 (1+2), 23:10 and 23:58. (4) Plus other departures from New Hualien at 20:15 (1) and 03:24. (5) Plus other departures from Taitung at 10:05 (1), 15:10 and 16:10 (1). (6) Plus other departures from New Hualien at 13:05 (1), 13:40, 16:05 (1), 17:50 (1), 18:15 and 19:00 (1).

Sights in **Hualien:** It is only a 20-minute auto (or bus) ride from Hualien to the eastern end of Taiwan's most fantastic scenic subject: **Taroko Gorge.**

Spectacular marble mountains and, in the river along which you drive, marble boulders of various colors and patterns, larger than a sightseeing bus.

Within an hour, the road comes to a long, carved marble bridge. Do not drive over it. Instead, be sure you get out of your car and walk across this bridge in order to get a good view of a raging waterfall under the bridge and the massive boulders that have been polished by the extremely heavy and fast-falling watercourse.

The 3,000-foot-high cliffs along this 12-mile ride contain millions of tons of marble.

There are many marble factories on the outskirts of Hualien. We went through the largest, RSEA Marble Plant. It is well worth visiting. You can watch blocks of unpolished raw marble the size of a large automobile being sawed into smaller pieces and then see the smaller pieces being carved and buffed into ornamental vases, urns, tables, chairs, ash trays, wine glasses, lamps, chessboards, dragons, etc. The other great attraction in Hualien is the marvelous show presented 2 times during the day and once at night that features dancing and singing by very attractive, beautifully-costumed aborigine Taiwanese.

Sights in **Taitung**: This city faces the Pacific Ocean and has a subtropical temperature. Many orchids grow here. Crops include pineapple, oranges and sugarcane. There are many caves, waterfalls and lakes in this area.

SABAH

Extraordinary scenery of dense jungles, wild animals and high mountains is seen on the short rail trips in Sabah, one north from **Beaufort** and the other south from Beaufort.

Tenom - Beaufort - Tanjong Aru (Koto Kinabalu) 7014

Dep. Tenom	06:40 (1)	07:20 (2)	07:30 (3)	07:55 (4)	08:00 (3+6)
Arr. Beaufort	08:11	08:54	09:50	10:10	11:38
Arr. Tanjong Aru	-0-	-0-	12:30	-0-	14:37

Sights in **Tanjong Aru**: A marvelous beach resort that is next to Kota Kinabulu.

Sights in **Kota Kinabalu:** A modern seaport. The capital of Sabah.

See the museum complex on Old Palace Hill, a mile and a half from the center of the city. Its main building, in the style of a traditional longhouse, exhibits collections of ethnography, ceramics, history, archaeology and natural history with one display on headhunting (actively pursued here as late as 1915). Other exhibits include traditional uses of bamboo and a mounted Sumatra rhino, now almost extinct. There is also, in separate buildings, a Science Center, Conservation Center and an Art Gallery/Theater. Visit nearby Kinabalu National Park.

Dep. Tanjong Aru	-0-	-0-	-0-	8:00 (3)	11:00 (3+7)
Dep. Beaufort	06:45 (4)	08:25 (1)	10:50 (5)	12:00	13:55 (8)
Arr. Tenom	08:45	09:56	12:51	14:44	15:55

(1) Runs daily, except Sunday and holidays. First-class only. (2) Runs Sunday and holidays only. First-class only. (3) Runs daily, except Sunday and holidays. Third-class only. (4) Runs Sunday and holidays only. Third-class only. (5) Daily. Third-class only. (6) Plus another departure from Tenom at 12:10 (4), arriving Beaufort 14:30, Tanjong Aru 17:10 . . . and other departures from Tenom at 13:40 (3), 15:05 (4) and 16:00 (1), terminating in Beaufort 15:41, 17:10 and 17:30. (7) Plus another departure from Tanjong Aru at 11:20 (4), arriving Beaufort 14:30, Tenom 16:37. (8) Plus other departures from Beaufort at 14:30 (4), 15:05 (1) and 16:05 (2), arriving Tenom 16:37, 17:19 and 17:47.

SINGAPORE

The 3 classes of trains (operated by Malayan Railways) are De Luxe (upholstered seats), Eksekutif (padded leather seats), and Ekonomi (cushioned plastic seats), shown in our footnotes as first, second and third-class.

The long train ride from Singapore is to Kuala Lumpur, and on to Butterworth (Penang) and Bangkok. The short trip from Singapore is to Johore Bahru.

Singapore

A great seaport and the most modern city in Asia. See: the excellent exhibit of Malay culture at the National Museum. The view of the city and harbor from the top of Fort Canning Hill. The museum in the transformed 1854 courthouse, now called Empress Place. Songbirds in wood and wicker cages at various songbird cafes. Take a subway ride to the Eunos Station to see a market that tour buses don't reach.

The 50-foot tall, 300-ton statue of Buddha and other wonders in the Temple of 1,000 Lights in the Indian section, near Serangoon Road. The Thian Hock Keng Taoist temple.

The ornately-carved Sri Mariammon Hindu Temple. The wood and marble carvings in Sian Lim Sian Si temple. The orchids (some of which we contributed in 1975 from our then 28-year-old nursery) and the monkeys at the excellent Botanical Garden. The Chettiar Hindu temple. The Sultan Mosque. Twin Grove temple. Sakya Muni Gaya temple.

Take a one-hour cruise to see the hundreds of ships anchored in the world's fourth busiest harbor, only 77 miles north of the Equator. The cable car or ferry trip to **Sentosa Island**, to see its beaches, the museum of corals and shells, and the 18-hole golf course. A 3-hour out-of-town tour, visiting the nearby Malay villages, rubber and coconut plantations, temples and a crocodile farm.

Participate in the open-air eating that starts at 17:00 at the dozens of food stalls and pushcarts which vend Chinese, Indonesian and Malaysian delicacies at the Ras Singapura Food Centre (next door to the Singapore Arts and Crafts Centre) and also at Car Park on Orchard Road, near many hotels.

There are similar food facilities at Newton Eating Stalla, Albert Street, Hokkien Street and Bugis Street. Prawn fritters, fried pork, satay, beef curry, fish-head fried rice, carrot cake, exotic fruits, a rice dish called Nasi Goreng, and on and on. The gourmet can find in Singapore 9 styles of Chinese cuisine plus Thai, Indian, Malay, Italian, German, French and Japanese Food.

See the many Chinese and Indian shops on narrow, twisting Change Alley. The more than 7,000 birds of 350 species in aviaries (some so large that visitors can walk through them) in Jurong Bird Park. Near it, the elaborately landscaped Chinese and Japanese Gardens.

Also see the tremendous collection of jade from every important Chinese dynasty, in the House of Jade. The daily cultural show at Instant Asia. The exhibit of more than 3,000 fish and the many corals at Van Kleef Aquarium. Over 600 animals in the 70-acre Zoological Garden. Souvenirs and antiques in the stalls at Thieves' Market.

Singapore - Kuala Lumpur - Butterworth - Bangkok

Passengers must be at Singapore's railstation 30 minutes before departure time in order to complete customs formalities before boarding train.

7005

Dep. Singapore (5)	07:45 (1)	08:30 (2)	14:45 (4)	20:15 (6)	2 2 : 0 0
Arr. Kuala Lumpur	14:30	17:50	21:35	06:15	07:00
Change trains.					
Dep. Kuala Lumpur (2)	15:00 (1)	20:30 (3)	22:00 (5)	07:30 (4)	0 8 : 1 5
Arr. Butterworth	21:10	05:30	06:40	13:35	17:50
Change trains. 7050					
Dep. Butterworth				13:40 (7)	
Arr. Bangkok				08:35	

(1) Reservation required. Direct train. No train change in Kuala Lumpur. Has air-conditioned first and second-class coaches. Buffet. (2) Second and third-class only. Buffet. (3) Second and third-class only. (4) Has air-conditioned first and second-class. Buffet. (5) Carries air-conditioned first-class sleeping cars and non-air conditioned first and second-class coaches. Buffet. (6) Carries second-class sleeping cars and first and second-class coaches. (7) Carries air-conditioned first-class sleeping cars. Also has non-air conditioned second-class sleeping cars and second-class coaches. Restaurant car 16:53–08:35.

Singapore - Johor Bahru Bus 7019

Dep. Singapore	Frequent times from 06:30 to 23:59
Arr. Johor Bahru	40 minutes later

*   *   *

Dep. Johor Bahru	Frequent times from 06:30 to 23:30
Arr. Singapore	40 minutes later

Sights in **Johor Bahru**: Do not forget to bring your passport. This short trip takes you from the Republic of Singapore to Malaysia. See: The Hindu Mariamman Temple. The Sultan Suleiman Mosque. The Chinese Goddess of Mercy Temple. The National Museum collection of arts, crafts and Malaysian culture.

Singapore - Kota Bharu

Very beautiful jungle and high mountain scenery on this route.

7005 (Train)			7018 (Bus)		
Dep. Singapore	20:15 (1)		Dep. Kota Bharu	N/A (4)	N/A (4)
Arr. Gemas	01:51 (2)		Arr. Mentakab	N/A (4)	N/A (4)
Change trains. 7006			Change to train. 7006		
Dep. Gemas	02:30 (3)		Dep. Mentakab	21:32 (3)	10:00 (6)
Arr. Mentakab	04:42		Arr. Gemas	23:55	12:20
Change to bus. 7018			Change trains. 7005		
Dep. Mentakab	N/A (4)		Dep. Gemas	01:35 (2+5)	12:30 (7+9)
Arr. Kota Bharu	N/A		Arr. Singapore	06:55	18 :00

(1) Carries second-class sleeping cars and second-class coaches. (2) Day 2. (3) Carries a non-air condi-tioned sleeping car. Buffet. (4) This journey is a part of the Kota Bharu – Kuala Lumpur and v.v. bus service, for which Cook carried a separate timetable prior to 1988. The ride was 9 ½ hours. Neither Mentakab–Kota Bharu nor Kota Bharu–Mentakab departure times have been available since 1980. (5) Carries an air-conditioned sleeping car and a first-class coach. Buffet. (6) Third-class only. (7) Has a second-class coach. Buffet. (8) Reservation required. Has an air-conditioned first-class coach. Buffet. (9) Plus another Gemas departure at 16:45 (8), arriving Singapore 21:20.

SOUTH KOREA

Children under 6 travel free. Half-fare for children 6–12. Children 13 and over must pay full fare.

Seoul is the focal point for rail trips in South Korea, to 3 different seaports: Gangreung, Mokpo and Pusan.

Seoul

See: The Kyonghweru Banquet Hall and the Throne Hall in the 14th century Kyongbok (Great Happiness) Palace, rebuilt in 1867 after a 16th century Japanese invasion destroyed it (open Spring to Fall 09:00–18:00, Winter 09:00–17:00).

Nearby, the beautiful Pagoda, the National Folklore Museum (19th century houses, tools, pottery and artwork plus 14th century ceramic vases, dishes, statuary, bowls, incense burners), and Kwanghwa Gate. The collection of metal craft, pottery, paintings and sculpture in the National Museum.

The fantastic 78-acre Secret Garden in the 17th century Changdok (Illustrious Virtue) Palace, with its museum. This is the only palace in Seoul that can be entered only on a guided tour. English-speaking guides usually lead tours of Changduk Palace at 11:30, 13:30 and 15:30. Its beautiful garden has streams and lotus ponds among its pine, maple and cherry-blossom trees as well as flowers that bloom in different seasons.

Nearby, the Yun Kyung Dang residence, Changgyongwon (Garden of Bright Happiness), the Zoo and the Chongmyo Royal Ancestors' Shrine. In the center of Seoul, the Tok-su (Virtuous Longevity) Palace. The view from the 763-foot high hill in Namsan Park. The exhibits of music, dance, architecture and art at Korea House. The colorful Chogye-sa Buddhist Temple.

The great silks, jewelry, antiques, fresh fish and lacquerware on sale at the 2-mile-long East Gate Market. The folk dances and reproduction of rural Yi-dynasty lifestyles at Korean Folk Village, a one-hour drive south of Seoul.

The Korean Tourist Office provides information about one-day excursions to **Panmunjom**, the village that was the site of 1953 cease-fire talks at the end of the Korean War. The Freedom House there has a pagoda-style tower from which American soldiers watch movements on the Communist side of the 38th parallel.

Seoul - Mogpo 5503

Dep. Seoul (Main)	07:20 (1)	11:20 (2)	13:05 (3)	16:05 (4)	22:15 (5)
Arr. Mogpo	13:20	17:19	18:45	20:53	05:00
		* * *			
Dep. Megpo	08:20 (4)	09:30 (2)	11:20 (3)	15:05 (1)	21:45 (5)
Arr. Seoul (Main)	13:10	15:29	16:57	21:00	04:30

(1) Second-class only. (2) Has a first-class coach. (3) Second-class only. Air-conditioned. (4) Has an air-conditioned first-class coach and a restaurant car. (5) Carries a first-class sleeping car and a first-class coach.

Seoul - Chonju - Yosu 5502

Dep. Seoul (Main)	08:05 (1)	10:20 (2)	13:20 (2)	16:10 (3)	18:00 (1+5)
Dep. Chonju	11:25	14:01	17:02	19:27	21:06 (6)
Arr. Yosu	14:05	17:05	20:08	22:04	23:45
		* * *			
Dep. Yosu	07:35 (3)	08:40 (1)	10:15 (2)	13:30 (2)	16:30 (1+7)
Dep. Chonju	10:16	11:15	13:13	16:36	19:10 (8)
Arr. Seoul (Main)	13:36	14:25	16:50	20:22	22:30

(1) Air-conditioned. Has a first-class coach. Restaurant car. (2) Has a first-class coach. (3) Second-class only. Air-conditioned. (4) Carries first-class sleeping cars and a first-class coach. (5) Plus other departures from Seoul at 21:45 (2) and 22:45 (4), arriving Chonju 01:48 and 02:55, arriving Yosu 04:55 and 06:14. The 23:50 (4) Seoul departure terminates in Chonju 03:57. (6) Plus other departures from Chonju at 01:53 (2) and 03:00 (4), arriving Yosu 04:55 and 06:14. (7) Plus other departures from Yosu at 20:10 (2) and 22:05 (4), arriving Chonju 23:28 and 01:21, arriving Seoul 03:50 and 05:38. (8) Plus other departures from Chonju at 23:33 (2), 23:55 (4) and 01:26 (4), arriving Seoul 03:50, 04:08 and 05:38.

Sights in **Chonju:** The Tourist Information Office is in front of the railstation. This city is also spelled "**Gyeongiu**", "**Jeonju**" and "**Kyonju**". It is South Korea's most popular tourist resort and has been called "a museum without walls" because of the number of historical attractions here. See the ceramics, bejeweled sword hilts, elaborate gold jewelry, and the gold Silla crown and helmets in the National Museum, open daily 09:00–17:00.

On leaving the museum, turn left and go about one mile to the more than 200-year-old

Sungdok-jon Shrine. Then walk through the oldest part of Chonju, Choe Village. After that, take 2 succesive left turns to reach Chomsong-dae, a 7th century stone tower that was built as an observatory. Continuing on the same street takes you to Tumli Park, open daily 09:00–17:00. Its 20 ancient earth-mound tombs are interesting.

On the outskirts of Chonju are many interesting sculptures, temples and royal tombs. The hotels have rental cars for driving to many such nearby places of interest. See the 8th century Bulgugsa Temple, one of Korea's national treasures.

Seoul - Pusan (via Taejeon) 5501

Most of these trains are air-conditioned and have a restaurant car. Some overnight trains carry sleeping cars.

Dep. Seoul (Main)	Frequent times 06:10–19:30 and 21:30–23:55
Arr. Pusan	4–5 hours later

* * *

Dep. Pusan	Frequent times 06:00–18:45 and 21:30–23:55
Arr. Seoul (Main)	4–5 hours later

Sights in **Pusan**: This is South Korea's principal seaport. Many beaches, monasteries and hot springs resorts a few miles from here.

See the museums and temple at the Chung-Yol Shrine (open during daylight hours), where brightly-costumed dancers, singers and musicians perform. This Shrine honors 16th century patriots who resisted Japanese invaders.

The view of the city and harbor from the Pusan Observation Tower in Youngdusan (Dragonhead) Park. The enormous range of fish sold at "Visit The Fisheries" in the downtown dock area, amounting to an outdoor aquarium. The busy shopping center, called Kuk-Je to buy jewelry, silk items, masks and ginseng. The marvelous wood tile and the many carvings in Pomosa Temple.

The Zoo, Botanical Gardens and ancient fort in Kumgang Park. Pusan has the world's only United Nations Military Cemetery, where graves are decorated with the flags of the many nations that contributed soldiers to the battles in Korea in the 1950's. Visit **Boma-Sa** (15 miles north of Pusan), a temple complex with 30 buildings.

Seoul - Onyang 5502

All of these trains are second-class only and are air-conditioned.

Dep. Seoul (Main)	08:35	12:35	18:35
Arr. Onyang	09:56	13:58	19:53

Sights in **Onyang**: A major hot springs resort, surrounded by beautiful scenery.

Dep. Onyang	09:21	15:12	19:25
Arr. Seoul (Main)	10:43	16:37	20:49

SRI LANKA (CEYLON)

Children under 3 travel free. Half-fare for children 3–11. Children 12 and over must pay full fare.

Reservations can be made only up to 10 days before travel date. Contact the Government Railway Reservation Office, Fort Railway Station, Colombo.

Telephones: 434215 and 21281, extension 433 (extension 536 for information).

Among the sights to see in this tiny (270-mile by 140-mile) island off the southern tip of India are ancient palaces, shrines, temples, libraries and pleasure gardens.

The 3 train tour package that were offered in 1991 included bus transportation between hotel and railstation, all meals, hotel rooms, guides and city sightseeing.

They included the 4-day Nuwara Eliya Tour (Colombo-Kandy-Nuwara-Eliya) at $335 (U.S.) per person. **Nuwara Eliya** is a cool mountain resort (more than 6,000 feet altitude) from which a visit can be made to Hakgala Botanic Gardens and to a tea plantation to see the harvesting, blending and "proper" brewing of tea.

A 3-day Cultural Triangle Tour (Colombo-Anuradhapura-Polonnaruwa) was $162. A one-day Colombo-Kandy-Colombo roundtrip was $108.

Colombo

See the exhibit of stone and bronze sculptures at the Museum. Nearby, the performing elephants at the Zoo. Also a short distance away, the Buddhist murals in Kelaniya, at Raja Maha Vihara Temple.

Bentota, **Mount Lavinia** and **Negombo** are beach resorts a short distance from Colombo.

Colombo - Colombo Airport 6304

All of these trains are third-class only.

Dep. Colombo (Fort)	05:10		15:10
Arr. Colombo Airport	06:56		16:26
		*	* *
Dep. Colombo Airport	07:40		18:00
Arr. Colombo (Fort)	08:55		19:22 (1)

(1) Arrives at Colombo's Maradana railstation.

Colombo - Badulla 6305

Dep. Colombo (Fort)	05:55 (1)	09:45 (1)	20:15 (2)
Dep. Nanu Oya	13:31	15:40	03:56
Arr. Badulla	17:00	19:05	07:48

This extremely scenic rail trip is through mountains and tea plantations. The area at **Nanu Oya** (6,000 feet) is cool and green. **Badulla** is 5,000-foot altitude.

Dep. Badulla	05:55 (1)	08:50 (1)	17:45 (2)
Dep. Nanu Oya	09:36	12:44	22:06
Arr. Colombo (Fort)	15:23	20:00	05:40

(1) Carries a first-class observation car. Has second and third-class coaches. Buffet. (2) Carries first and second-class sleeping cars. Also has third-class couchettes (which Thomas Cook advises "should be avoided") and both second and third-class coaches. Buffet.

Colombo - Polonnaruwa - Batticaloa 6301

Both of these trains have buffet. Only second and third-class coach cars are carried.

Dep. Colombo (Fort)	06:05	Dep. Batticaloa	N/A (1)
Arr. Polonnaruwa	12:25 (1)	Arr. Polonnaruwa	12:25
Arr. Batticaloa	N/A	Arr. Colombo	18:20

(1) Service Polonnaruwa-Batticaloa and v.v. was temporarily suspended in 1989.

Sights in **Polonnaruwa**: The gigantic man-made lake (Parkrama Samudra). The ruins from this city's greatest era, in the 10th century.

Sights in **Batticaloa**: The singing fish.

Colombo - Kandy 6305

For the best views on this ride, sit on the right-hand side en route to Kandy, on the left-hand side when going to Colombo.

Only second and third-class coaches are carried on this line.

Dep. Colombo (Fort)	05:55 (1)	06:55 (2)	10:15 (3)	13:25	15:35 (2+5)
Arr. Kandy	08:54	09:30	13:36	16:35	18:05

* * *

Dep. Kandy	06:30 (2)	06:50	10:00	15:00 (2)	15:30 (3+6)
Arr. Colombo (Fort)	09:00	10:05	13:00	17:30	18:50

(1) Has a first-class observation car. Buffet. (2) Reservation required. Buffet. (3) Buffet. (4) Carries first and second-class sleeping cars. Also has third-class couchettes (which Thomas Cook says "should be avoided"). Buffet. (5) Plus other departures from Colombo at 16:20 and 20:15(3), arriving Kandy 19:25 and 23:55. (6) Plus other departures from Kandy at 17:05 (1) and 01:30 (4), arriving Colombo 20:00 and 05:40.

Sights in **Kandy**: The praying and ceremonies at the pink-domed Dalada Maligawa (Temple of the Tooth), so-named because it claims to have an authentic tooth of Buddha. A ceremony, during which the sacred relic can be viewed in a golden casket, occurs daily at approximately 11:00 and 18:30. Many fine art treasures are exhibited adjacent to the Temple, in the Archaeological Museum and National Museum.

See the jewelry and gems in the shops along the narrow streets of the Bazaar. The spices and great variety of fruits at the Market. Local brassware, lacquerware, carvings and silver items are displayed and sold at the Kandyan Arts and Crafts Centre. The Tea Factory. Elephants taking baths, nearly all afternoon. See wonderful orchids displayed at the 147-acre Botanical Gardens in nearby **Peradeniya**.

Kandy - Matale 6303

All of these trains are third-class only.

Dep. Kandy	04:25 (1)	05:25 (2)	06:55 (1)	13:40 (2)	14:18 (1)	16:55 (1+3)
Arr. Matale	06:08	06:52	08:09	15:00	15:39	17:57

* * *

Dep. Matale	04:53 (1)	05:30 (2)	06:56 (1)	08:15 (1)	10:20 (1)	13:55 (1+4)
Arr. Kandy	06:03	06:50	08:07	09:27	11:31	14:57

(1) Runs daily, except Sunday and holidays. (2) Runs Monday–Friday, except holidays. (3) Plus another departure from Kandy at 18:45 (1), arriving Matale 19:57. (4) Plus other departures from Matale at 15:10 (2) and 16:45 (1), arriving Kandy 16:22 and 18:06.

Colombo - Bentota - Galle - Matara 6306

This very scenic train ride, along Sri Lanka's coastline, offers many miles of palm-fringed beaches washed by turquoise ocean.

These trains have only second and third-class coach cars.

Dep. Colombo (Fort)	07:30	08:45 (1)	13:35 (2)	15:45	16:50 (2+6)
Dep. Bentota	09:04	– 0 –	15:03	– 0 –	18:23
Dep. Galle	10:22	11:23	16:28	18:15	20:00
Arr. Matara	11:40	12:15	17:52	19:10	– 0 –
		* * *			
Dep. Matara	– 0 –	– 0 –	– 0 –	05:40	07:05 (2+7)
Dep. Galle	03:50 (3)	04:40 (4)	05:00 (3)	06:46	08:25 (8)
Dep. Bentota	05:11	06:13	06:33	– 0 –	09:31
Arr. Colombo (Fort)	07:15	08:26	08:06 (5)	09:07	10:46

(1) Runs Saturday, Sunday and holidays. (2) Runs Monday–Friday, except holidays. (3) Runs daily, except Sunday and holidays. (4) Runs Sunday and holidays only. (5) Ar-rives 08:26 on Saturday. (6) Plus other departures from Colombo at 17:20 and 19:15, terminating in Galle 20:57 and 22:30. (7) Plus other departures from Matara at 13:25 and 15:57 (1), arriving Colombo 17:35 and 19:31. (8) Plus other departures from Galle at 08:40, 14:56 and 17:00 (1), arriving Colombo 12:20, 17:35 and 19:31.

Sights in **Bentota**: A seaside resort.

Sights in **Galle**: A Portuguese seaport before the Dutch seized it and then Sri Lanka's chief port until Colombo was developed in the 1880's.

Sights in **Matara:** An ancient fort town. See the old Dutch Reformed Church. Swim and snorkel at nearby **Polhena**.

Colombo - Negombo 6306

Dep. Colombo (Fort)	03:40 (1)	-0-
Dep. Colombo (Maradana)	03:45	10:40 (2)
Arr. Negombo	05:29	12:21

Sights in **Negombo**: A fishing port and beach resort. See the remarkable murals in Raja Maha Vihara, a famous temple. Visit the old Dutch fort.

Dep. Negombo	08:30 (2)	20:25 (1)
Arr. Colombo (Maradana)	10:20	23:10
Arr. Colombo (Fort)	-0-	-0-

(1) Runs Monday–Friday, except holidays. Third-class only. (2) Third-class only.

Colombo - Trincomalee 6301

Dep. Colombo (Fort)	06:05 (1)	Dep. Trincomalee	N/A (2)
Arr. Galoya	11:19	Arr. Galoya	N/A
Change trains.		Change trains.	
Dep. Galoya	N/A (2)	Dep. Galoya	13:16 (1)
Arr. Trincomalee	N/A	Arr. Colombo Fort	18:20

(1) Has only second and third-class coaches. Buffet. (2) Service Galoya–Trincomalee and v.v. was "temporarily" suspended in 1989.

Sights in **Trincomalee**: One of the world's finest natural harbors. The 17th century fort constructed by Portuguese invaders from the ancient Temple of a Thousand Columns.

Colombo - Anuradhapura - Jaffna 6300

The fantastic Elephant's Pass is on this route.

Dep. Colombo (Fort)	05:45 (1)	06:35 (3)	14:05 (3)
Arr. Anuradhapura	09:42 (2)	12:30 (2)	18:52 (2)
Arr. Jaffna	N/A	N/A	N/A

* * *

Dep. Jaffna	N/A (2)	N/A (2)	N/A (2)
Dep. Anuradhapura	05:05 (3)	14:28 (1)	15:40 (3)
Arr. Colombo (Fort)	09:40	18:45	20:43

(1) Air-conditioned train. Has a first-class coach. (2) Service Anuradhapura–Jaffna and v.v. was suspended "temporarily" in 1988. (3) Has only second-class and third-class coach seats.

Sights in **Anuradhapura**: Ruins of many ancient palaces and temples. The worl oldest documented tree, the sacred Sri Maha Bodhi. The 300-foot diameter dome of the Ruwanveliseya.

Sights in **Jaffna**: Many ancient ruins. An outstanding exhibit at the Archaeological Museum.

Colombo - Puttalam 6306

These trains have only third-class coach cars.

Dep. Colombo (Maradana)	03:45 (1)	10:40
Arr. Puttalam	09:01	15:20

* * *

Dep. Puttalam	05:35	16:30 (1)
Arr. Colombo (Maradana)	10:20	23:10

(1) Runs Monday–Friday, except holidays.

INTERNATIONAL ROUTE FROM SRI LANKA

There is ferry service from Talaimannar to Rameswaram in southern India. (Rail service is provided from Rameswaram to Bombay and Calcutta, via Madras.)

Colombo - Talaimannar - Rameswaram - Madras 6300

Dep. Colombo (Fort)	05:45 (1)	Dep. Anuradhapura	N/A (2)
Arr. Anuradhapura	09:43	Arr. Talaimannar (Pier)	N/A
Change trains			

(1) Air-conditioned train. Has a first-class coaches . (2) A connection in Anuradhapura for travel Colombo–Talaimannar has not been possible since 1989 due to the "temporary" suspension of the Anuradhapura–Tailamannar service .

6186 (Boat)		6182 (Train)		
Dep. Talaimannar Pier	09:00 (1)	Dep. Rameswaram	12:30 (2)	15:45 (2+3)
Arr. Rameswaram	12:00	Arr. Madras (Eg.)	06:00	06:15
Change to train.				

(1) Runs Tuesday, Thursday and Saturday. (2) Runs daily. (3) Plus another departure from Rameswaram at 17:20 (2), arriving Madras 16:05.

THAILAND

Children under 4 who are less than 100cm tall travel free. Half-fare for children 4–11 who are not more than 150cm tall. Children 12 and over must pay full fare.

Reservations in Thailand can be made 80 days before travel date. A supplement is charged for fast trains, sleeping berths and air-conditioned coaches.

The rail lines from Bangkok to Chiang Mai and to Nam Tok come close to Burma's border. The routes to Nong Khai and to Ubon Ratchathani go to Laos' border. The ride to Aranyaprathet is on the border of Kampuchea (Cambodia, Khmer) and ran to Phnom Penh prior to the 1976 closing of the frontier. Thailand's sixth rail route is to Butterworth (Penang) and then through the length of Malaysia to Singapore.

Bangkok

A boat ride on the klongs (canals) during peak activity in early morning to a floating market boats full of exotic tropical fruits and vegetables, plus cook-boats that prepare stir-fried dishes and a visit to the Royal Palace are the 2 major tourist attractions in Bangkok. The best place to hire a boat is at the pier in back of the Oriental Hotel.

Cruises on the Chao Phya River also start from there. The boats stop at Wat Arun (Temple of Dawn) and also to see the gilded royal barges (entry daily 08:30 – 15:30), of which the most spectacular one is about 130-feet-long, carved from a single teak log.

In the Royal Palace complex (open daily 08:00 – 17:00), see: Chakri Palace, the gold thrones in the Amarin, Dusit Hall, the Chapel of the Emerald Buddha. Nearby, the Temple of the 160-foot long Reclining Buddha (the most sacred object for Thai Buddhists). The exhibit of the history of this area since 4,000 B.C., at Southeast Asia's largest museum, the excellent Thai National Museum, open daily except Monday and Friday 09:00 – 16:00.

Also visit the Weekend Market at Pramane Ground. The Pasteur Institute Snake Farm. The collection of Thai paintings, pottery and Thai houses at Jim Thompson's House, open Monday–Saturday 08:00-17:00. Another collection of Thai art at Kamthiang House.

Suan Pakkad Palace. The Marble Temple, open daily 09:00–17:00.

Bangkok - Chiang Mai 7060 + Government timetable

"Sprinter" trains, introduced in 1991, have an air-conditioned locomotive car seating 72 passengers and an air-conditioned coach seating 80. Both feature adjustable seats, telephones and fax machines.

All of these trains have buffet.

Dep. Bangkok	06:40	08:10 (1+5)	Dep. Chiang Mai	06:30	08:10 (1+6)
Arr. Chiang Mai	19:55	19:00	Arr. Bangkok	20:35	19:10

(1) Sprinter train. (2) Carries a second-class sleeping car. (3) Supplement charged. Carries a second-class sleeping car. (4) Supplement charged. Carries a first-class sleeping car. (5) Plus other departures from Bangkok at 15:00 (2), 18:00 (3), 19:40 (4) and 22:00 (2), arriving Chiang Mai 05:15, 07:25, 08:05 and 11:55. (6) Plus other departures from Chiang Mai at 15:30 (2), 17:15 (3), 19:30 (4) and 20:45 (2), arriving Bangkok 05:30, 06:25, 08:25 and 10:40.

Sights in **Chiang Mai:** An abundance of Thai handicrafts are available here: lacquer- ware, woodcarving, pottery, weaving, batik cloth, silk and pottery. See: the 14th century temple, Wat Chian Man. The porcelain decorated 17th century Wat Koo Tao. The 14th century Wat Phra Singh. The beautiful bronze Buddha in Wat Kao Tue.

The view from the mountain-top Wat Doi Suthrep, 3500 feet above Chiang Mai. Climbing its 290 steep steps is an exertion on a hot, sultry day.

See the display of fruits and vegetables at Varoros Market. The 7 spires at Wat Ched Yod Temple. Take a tour outside the city to see local aborigines. Also, another tour, a 30-minute ride, to watch elephants perform logging work.

Bangkok - Thon Buri - River Khwae Bridge - Nam Tok 7067

This trip is through one of the most scenic areas of Thailand, abounding with wild orchids. The legendary wood bridge (rebuilt after World War II with steel and concrete) and original rail line were built by 18,000 Dutch and 700 U.S. prisoners, often forced by their Japanese captors to work 19 hours a day in tropical heat.

These prisoners were fed less than one pound of food a day, which the captives supplemented with tree fungus, rats, cats and dogs. Also conscripted to work on the construction were 200,000 Asian laborers. The deaths of 18,000 prisoners of war and 100,000 Asian workers occurred by the time the entire Bangkok-Nam Tok line was completed on October 25, 1943 — 15 months after construction began.

This is a special tourist train that requires reservation and has light refreshments.

On the return to Bangkok, the train stops at the allied cemetery in **Kanchanaburi.**

Dep. Bangkok (Hual.)	06:35	Dep. Nam Tok	14:40
Dep. River Khwae Bridge	09:57	Arr. Kanchanaburi	17:02
Arr. Nam Tok	11:30	Arr. Bangkok (Hual.)	19:35

Bangkok - Ubon Ratchathani 7065

All of these trains have only second and third-class coach cars and buffet service, unless designated otherwise..

Dep. Bangkok (Hual.	06:25	07:15	15:25	18:45	21:00 (1+3)
Arr. Ubon Ratchathani	16:45	20:35	04:35	05:20	07:40

* * *

Dep. Ubon Ratchathani	06:25	06:45	08:50 (2)	13:45	16:50 (4)
Arr. Bangkok (Hual.)	17:45	19:40	20:50	03:00	03:35

(1) Supplement charged. Carries first and second-class sleeping cars. Has air-conditioned second-class coaches. (2) No buffet. Third-class only. (3) Plus other departures from Bangkok at 22:45 and 23:25, arriving Ubon Ratchathani 09:35 and 12:25. (4) Plus other departures from Ubon Ratchathani at 17:45, 18:50 (1) and 23:00, arriving Bankok 04:35, 05:15 and 12:00.

Bangkok - Aranyaprathet 7059

These trains have only third-class coach cars.

Dep. Bangkok	06:00	13:10	Dep. Aranyaprathet	06:45	13:40
Arr. Aranyaprathet	11:00	18:15	Arr. Bangkok	11:50	18:35

Bangkok - Butterworth (Penang) - Kuala Lumpur - Singapore

7050

Dep. Bangkok	15:15 (1)			
Arr Butterworth	12:25 (2)			
Change trains. 7005				
Dep. Butterworth	14:15 (3)	22:00 (6)	07:45 (7)	08:30 (8)
Arr. Kuala Lumpur	20:15 (2)	06:40 (5)	13:45 (7)	17:50
Change trains.				
Dep. Kuala Lumpur	20:30 (4)	07:30 (3)	14:00 (7)	22:00 (6)
Arr. Singapore	06:15 (5)	14:20	21:20	06:55

(1) Runs daily. Carries air-conditioned sleeping cars. Has restaurant car until 07:04 on Day 2. (2) Day 2 from Bangkok. (3) Air-conditioned train. Buffet. (4) Carries only second-class coaches and second-class sleeping cars (5) Day 3 from Bangkok. (6) Carries air-conditioned first-class sleeping cars. Also has first and second-class coaches. Buffet. (7) Reservation required. Direct train. No train change in Kuala Lumpur. Has air-conditioned first and second-class coaches. Buffet. (8) Has only second-class and third-class coaches. Buffet.

VIETNAM

Children under 5 travel free. Half-fare for children 5–9. Children 10 and over must pay full fare.

Hanoi - Hue - Da Nang - Ho Chi Minh City 7305

All of these trains (unless designated otherwise) have couchettes and a restaurant car and the coach cars are second-class only.

Dep. Hanoi	08:00 (1)	10:00 (4)	13:00 (5)
Dep. Hue	04:32 (2)	08:06 (2)	10:57 (2)
Dep. Da Nang	08:35	12:02	15:26
Arr. Ho Chi Minh City	07:55 (3)	14:00 (3)	17:00 (3)

Sights in **Ho Chi Minh City**: Chinese, Japanese, Vietnamese, Cham and Khmer art objects in the National Museum. The Zoo. The Cho Ben Thanh Market. The Botanical Garden. The Flower Market. The Chinese temples in Cholon, the city's Chinatown suburb.

Sights in **Danang**: The Buddhist monastery at Marble Mountain.

Sights in **Hue:** Thai Hoa (Palace of the Full Peace). Dien Tho (Everlasting Longevity) Palace. The-Mieu Temple. Ngu Phung (Five Phoenix Building). Tin Tam (Serenity of Heart) Lake. The 7-story Phuoc Duyen Tower. The imperial tombs of the Nguyen emperors.

Dep. Ho Chi Minh City	08:00 (1)	10:00 (4)	13:00 (6)
Dep. Da Nang	08:22 (2)	12:14 (2)	15:12 (2)
Dep. Hue	11:42	15:50	18:40
Arr. Hanoi	07:55 (3)	14:00 (3)	17:00 (3)

(1) Runs Tuesday, Thursday and Saturday from Hanoi. Runs Wednesday, Friday and Sunday from Ho Chi Minh. Also carries a first-class sleeping car and a first-class coach. (2) Day 2. (3) Day 3. (4) Runs daily. (5) Runs Monday, Tuesday, Thursday and Saturday.

Hanoi - Haiphong 7300

Dep. Hanoi	05:00	08:00	12:00	17:50
Arr. Haiphong	09:25	12:30	16:25	21:50
		* * *		
Dep. Haiphong	05:10	11:00	14:20	18:10
Arr. Hanoi	09:45	15:25	18:45	22:10

Hanoi - Yen Bai and Lang Son 7300

Dep. Hanoi	05:30	13:20	19:10	22:50	23:30
Arr. Yen Bai	15:20	22:40	04:30	-0-	09:10
Arr. Lang Son	-0-	-0-	-0-	07:55	-0-
		* * *			
Dep. Lang Son	-0-	09:30	-0-	-0-	-0-
Dep. Yen Bai	07:00	-0-	11:00	17:10	18:30
Arr. Hanoi	16:30	18:55	20:45	02:50	04:50

INTERNATIONAL ROUTE FROM VIETNAM

There are no international trains.

648

Chapter 12

AUSTRALIA

Children under 4 travel free if space has not been reserved for them. Half-fare for children 4-15. Children 16 and over must pay full fare.

Summer here is December 1 to February 28. Winter is June 1 to August 31.

To make advance reservations, write to: Australian National Travel Centre, 132 No. Terrace, Adelaide, S.A. 5000, Australia. Telephone: (08) 231-7699.

The State Rail Authority of New South Wales offers more than 20 different special one-day train tours that leave Sydney between 07:40 and 09:20, arriving back in Sydney between 16:30 and 21:45.

Typical of a day's outing is the "Riverboat Postman Tour" which runs every Wednesday. An air-conditioned double-deck train takes you to **Hawkesbury River**, where you board the last Riverboat Mail Run operating in Australia. While enjoying the wonderful Hawkesbury River scenery, you are served a scrumptuous smorgasbord lunch. After leaving the boat at **Patonga**, passengers enjoy a bus tour of the Central Coast before boarding the train in **Gosford Station** for the journey back to Sydney.

Other one-day tours go to lakes, seashores, mountains, caves and sheep stations.

The 3 most outstanding train rides in Australia are luxurious and long.

"Indian Pacific", Australia's most elegant train, makes a 68-hour run between Sydney and Perth, a 2,461-mile journey from Australia's East Coast to its West Coast, and return. This trip involves 3 nights on board as the train crosses the rugged **Blue Mountains**, pastoral and grazing country, the wheat belt of South Australia, the arid **Nullarbor Plain**, the wheat belt between Kalgoorlie and the seacoast, and the **Darling Ranges**.

The portion of the trip on the Nullarbor Plain has the world's longest stretch of straight rail 287 miles without a curve.

Fully air-conditioned and sound-proofed, this train carries first and second-class sleeping cars and coach cars.

Two types of sleeping accommodations are available. Twinette cabins (2 berths) have private shower and toilet, wash basin, refrigerated water dispenser, and choice of radio or taped music. Roomettes (for one person) have all this, except they lack the private shower. However, there are shower rooms at both ends of the Roomette carriage.

This train has one deluxe compartment, a luxurious bed-sitting room with armchairs.

"Indian Pacific" carries a restaurant car, lounge car for first-class passengers (with piano, videotape programs, taped music and bar service), and a cafeteria club car that serves morning and afternoon teas, ice cream, sandwiches and liquor.

All food served on this train is prepared on board. The "Indian Pacific" is famous for its lavish breakfast: fruit juice, cereal, bacon and eggs, steak or sausage, potatoes, toast and beverage.

On this route, temperatures outside the train average 109 degrees Fahrenheit in February.

Overseas tourists are allowed up to 176 pounds of free luggage.

Reservations can and should be made one year in advance. Stops may be made at any station en route and journey resumed later at no extra cost, provided that the whole journey is completed within 2 months.

The second extraordinary Australian rail trip is the one made by "The Queenslander" and "Sunlander", the 1,043 miles from subtropical Brisbane across many coastal estuaries to Cairns, gateway to several Barrier Reef resorts. The roomette sleeping cars have shower facilities. This train is air-conditioned and has a Lounge Car for first-class sleeping berth passengers that has a bar, recorded music and a video.

The variety of landscapes is so interesting that the Queensland Government Travel Centre offers 5 and 6 day versions of this 37-hour trip (with 4 overnight stays en route to Brisbane, 5 nights en route to Cairns) so that all of the scenery can be observed during daylight.

The third exceptional Australian train service is "The Ghan" Adelaide to Alice Springs. It won the National Tourism Award in 1990 after it was refurbished. For details, see page 658.

AUSTRALIA'S TRAIN PASSES

All of the state railways offer separate train passes, valid for travel within their state borders.

Although sleeping berths and meals are included in the price of some Australian *tickets*, they are *not* covered by passes but can be obtained at additional cost.

Reservations are essential for travel on many days and should be made before arriving in Australia, for which a $25 (U.S.) deposit must accompany information that includes your name as it appears on your passport, your passport number and nationality, and a copy of your air ticket to Australia.

Use of the passes must start within 12 months from the date they are issued. The passes can be used from the first day of travel until midnight on the last day of validity.

Australpass   Unlimited first and budget-class travel on all Australian railways, including suburban and metropolitan lines.

Sold in most parts of the world by travel agencies and in the U.S. also by ATS/Tours, 100 N. First St., Suite 301, Burbank, CA 91502. Telephone: (800) 423-2880.

To order, send: a cashier's check, your name as it appears on your passport, a copy of your air ticket, and the number and nationality of your passport.

Until March of 1992, the *first*-class prices are: $573 (U.S.) for 14 days, $706 for 21 days, $872 for 30 days, $1,212 for 60 days, $1,394 for 90 days. A 7-day extension (available only in Australia) is $291.

Budget-class: $344 (U.S.), $444, $540, $772, $888 and $187.

Kangaroo Road 'n Rail Pass   Unlimited *train* and Greyhound *bus* travel. Sold by same sources as "Austrailpass" above and also by V/Line Travel, 589 Collins Street, Melbourne. Until March of 1992, the *first*-class prices are: $685 (U.S.) for 14 days, $822 for 21 days, and $1,004 for 28 days .

Budget-class: $432, $593, and $755.

Victoria Pass   Unlimited V/Line train *and* bus *first*-class travel throughout the state of Victoria for 14 consecutive days. This pass *does not* cover metropolitan trams, trains and buses. The adult price until March of 1992 is $99 (Aust.). For children age 4–16: $49 (Aust.).

Can be obtained from V/Line Travel, 589 Collins Street, Melbourne.

Sydney

Stop by Central Station and get a copy of the brochure which has details on 7 short, one-day rides by train, bus and/or ferry to such interesting destinations as Taronga Zoo, Manly Oceanarium and the Blue Mountains

See the view from the top of Centrepoint Tower, the highest point in the city. Take the guided tour of Sydney Opera House. Go on a walking tour around The Rocks, the oldest part of Sydney, after obtaining information from the Visitors' Centre at 104 George Street North. See the excellent collection of traditional and modern Australian and European art at Art Gallery of New South Wales, open Monday-Saturday 10:00-17:00, Sunday 12:00–17:00.

Visit the collection of Australian and European art at the Art Gallery of New South Wales. The exhibit of Aboriginal artifacts and relics in Australia Museum, College and William Streets, open Tuesday-Sunday 10:00–17:00 and on Monday 10:00–17:00. The Museum of Applied Arts and Sciences, Harris Street. The craft, gift and curio shops at Argyle Arts Center, open daily 10:00–18:00. Lush tropical plants and exotic trees at Royal Botanic Gardens, open daily 08:00 to sunset.

At Darling Harbour: The Aquarium (one of the world's largest), the National Maritime Museum, and the Museum of Contemporary Art.

The changing of the guard every Thursday at 13:30 at the ANZAC Memorial in beautiful Hyde Park. The panoramic 360-degree views of the city, the harbor and the Pacific Ocean from the Skywalk at the top of the Tower, on Australia Square. Australia's largest natural history collection, in the Australian Museum, Tuesday-Saturday 10:00–17:00, Sunday and Monday 12:00–17:00. Take a day tour to visit nearby sheep and cattle stations.

See the sharks and other Australian fish at Marineland. Take the ferry or hydrofoil from Circular Quay, also the departure point for visits to Taronga Zoo Park. There are many excellent beaches, easy to reach from the center of Sydney. Rail tours operate to Old Sydney Town, 44 miles to the north, where the settlement of 1810 has been re-created complete with convict dwellings, jail, church, shops and 2 old ships.

Adelaide

The collection of prints, drawings, sculpture, graphic arts, coins and paintings at the Art Gallery of South Australia, open 10:00–17:00. The Australian birds and animals in the South Australian Museum. The spectacular water-lilies at the Botanical Gardens. The view of Adelaide from Light's Vision. The sealife at Marineland. Australian native animals in nearby Cleland Wildlife Reserve, where visitors are allowed to hold koalas and feed kangaroos.

Winery tours in the nearby McLaren Vale and Barossa Valley wine districts. Coach and 4-wheel drive vehicle tours go from Adelaide to the **Andamooka** and **Coober Pedy** opal fields, often visiting Alice Springs and **Ayers Rock**.

Sydney - Adelaide - Kalgoorlie - Perth 9000

This is the air-conditioned "Indian Pacific". Reservation required. Restaurant car.

Dep. Sydney (Ter.)	13:30 (1)		Dep. Perth (East)	21:00 (2)	
Arr. Broken Hill	08:09	Day 2	Dep. Kalgoorlie	06:30	Day 2
Set watch back 30 minutes.			Set watch forward 1½ hours.		
Dep. Broken Hill	08:10		Arr. Adelaide (Kes.)	14:00	Day 3
Arr. Adelaide (Kes.)	17:00		Dep. Adelaide (Kes.)	14:40	
Dep. Adelaide (Kes.)	17:45		Arr. Broken Hill	23:59	
Set watch back 1½ hours.			Set watch forward 30 minutes.		
Arr. Kalgoorlie	20:45	Day 3	Dep. Broken Hill	01:00	Day 4
Arr. Perth (East)	07:00	Day 4	Arr. Sydney (Ter.)	19:28	

(1) Runs Monday, Thursday and Saturday. Carries first and second-class sleeping cars and a lounge car all 3 days. Also has a second-class coach on Monday and Thursday. (2) Runs Tuesday, Thursday and Sunday. Carries first and second-class sleeping cars and a lounge car all 3 days. Also has a second-class coach on Thursday and Sunday.

Sights in **Broken Hill**: This is the area of the dry, sunburnt "outback". The city is built over huge silver, lead and zinc deposits. Visits to mines can be arranged. Take an underground tour of Delprat's Mine. Also see the collection of coins, minerals, shells and Aboriginal artifacts at Carlton Gardens and Art Gallery. The restored Afghan Mosque, once used by the camel drivers imported to carry supplies through the region.

The unique School Of The Air conducts lessons via 2-way radio for children living in remote areas. It is open to visitors during school hours.

Scenic air tours operate from here to various nearby points of interest such as the diggings of the world's only source of black opals at **White Cliffs**, plus trips to **Kinchega National Park, Menindee Lakes** and several outback stations. Only 82 miles northeast are ancient Aboriginal rock carvings, at **Mootwingee**. The restored **Silverton ghost town** is also nearby.

Sights in **Kalgoorlie**: This famous goldrush town is still Australia's largest producer of gold. Tours of a mine can be arranged.

Sights in **Perth**: Wide sandy beaches on the Indian Ocean, with good surfing. Tours to wildflower and forest areas nearby from August to November, when it is Spring here. See the marvelous display of wildflowers in the 1,000-acre King's Park. London Court, a shopping area re-created as a 16th century English street. The folk museum of early pioneering days, Old Mill.

The exhibit of the large Blue Whale skeletons, meteorites, Aborigine culture and paintings in the Art Gallery of Western Australia, which has a major collection of comtemporary Australian art (open daily 10:00 – 17:00). The lovely Georgian-style Old Court House, in Stirling Gardens. The marvelous horses 37 miles away at El Caballo Blanco, where Andalusian dancing horses are bred. The 6,000-acre **Yanchep Park**, only 37 miles away, with its koalas, black swans, limestone caves and profusion of wildflowers.

The Maritime Museum and Art Center in nearby **Freemantle**, and the great views of the city and harbor from the Round House there. Trains depart Perth every 20 minutes for the 35-minute trip to this small, cosmopolitan seaport. Its uniqueness is that most of the buildings there were built shortly after it was settled in 1830.

Ferries make a 45-minute ride from Freemantle to the popular **Rottnest Island** resort, 12 miles offshore, at 7:00, 9:00 and 11:00. Ferries depart from the island at 15:00 and 17:00. There are one and 2-hour bus tours on Rottnest. Rental bicycles allow access to secluded coves and beaches. Skin-diving is popular there.

Adelaide - Mount Gambier 9032

All of these trains require reservation, are air-conditioned and are second-class only. This service is subject to local confirmation.

Dep. Adelaide (Keswick)	08:10 (1)	14:50 (2)	16:50 (3)
Arr. Mount Gambier	15:43	21:50	00:20

Sights in **Mount Gambier**: The remarkable Blue Lake. Australia's largest pine forests. Skin-diving in Little Blue Lake.

Dep. Mount Gambier	08:00 (1)	14:45 (2)	16:45 (3)
Arr. Adelaide (Keswick)	15:25	22:03	00:02

(1) Runs Monday-Friday, except holidays.   (2) Runs Sunday only.   (3) Runs Friday only.

EASTERN AUSTRALIA RAIL ROUTES

An extensive rail system in eastern Australia radiates west and north from Melbourne.

Melbourne

Opened in 1985, the Victorian Arts Centre consists of the 2,600-seat Concert Hall, the 2,000-seat State Theatre (for opera and dance), the 400-seat Studio (experimental theater), and the 850-seat Playhouse (plays and musicals). Two-hour tours of the Victorian Arts Centre are offered daily 10:00–17:00, except when there are matinee performances. These guided tours start at the Smorgon Family Plaza.

See the view from the top of the ICI Building, Nicholson Street, with a guide there pointing out the main features of the area. The largest plant collection in the Southern Hemisphere, at the Royal Botanical Gardens, open daily 08:30 to sunset. The Zoological Gardens in Royal Park. Treasury Gardens, near Parliament House. The superb collection of Australian trees, shrubs and plants at Maranoa Gardens in Balwyn.

Australia's largest art collection, at National Gallery, St. Kilda Road, open daily except Wednesday 10:00–17:00, Wednesday 10:00–21:00. Old Melbourne Gaol and Penal Museum, Russell Street. Institute of Applied Science Museum, Swanston Street. Australian birds, animals and minerals, as well as Aborigine artifacts, at the National Museum, Russell Street, open Monday-Saturday 10:00–17:00, Sunday 14:00–17:00.

The exhibit of Australian ceramics, weaving and hand-made jewelry in the Galaxy of Handicrafts, 99 Cardigan Street. Captain Cook's Cottage, in Fitzroy Gardens, honoring the discoverer of eastern Australia. Take a ride on one of Melbourne's trams.

See the Rhododendron garden at 100-acre Olinda. The demonstrations of sheep dogs working, sheep shearing, wool classing and freeze branding of cattle at **Grevisfield**, 24 miles from Melbourne. Take the bus to **Philip Island** to see the "Penguin Parade", a large number of Penguins coming onto the shore to feed their young.

Suburban electric trains run frequently from Melbourne's Flinders Street station for the 70-minute ride to Belgrave. Several different 2-hour roundtrip steam-train excursions on "Puffing Billy" offer fine mountain scenery on the 8-mile ride between **Belgrave** and beautiful **Emerald Lake Reserve.** A collection of early steam locomotives can be seen at the Steam Museum in **Menzies Creek**, one of the stops on that line.

See the collection of kangaroos, koalas, emus, wombats and platypuses at **Healesville Sanctuary**, 39 miles east of Melbourne.

Melbourne - Adelaide 9008 + 9032

This route includes wheat-growing areas, the 1,891-foot-long railway bridge spanning the Murray River, and the beautiful Mount Lofty Ranges.

Both trains require reservations, are air-conditioned, carry sleeping cars and a club car, and have light refreshments.

Dep. Melbourne (Spencer St.)	21:00	Dep. Adelaide (Kes.)	18:30
Arr. Adelaide (Kes.)	09:05	Arr. Melbourne (Spencer St.)	07:45

Melbourne - Sydney 9003 + 9027

The daytime train in both directions was discontinued in 1991.

Both of these trains require reservations, are air-conditioned, and carry a first-class sleeping car and a club car. Reservations are recommended for seating in the restaurant car.

Dep. Melbourne (Spencer St.)	20:00	Dep. Sydney (Terminal)	20:00
Arr. Sydney (Terminal)	08:55	Arr. Melbourne (Spencer St.)	09:00

Sydney - Canberra 9023

All of these trains require reservation, are air-conditioned and have light refreshments.

Dep. Sydney (Ter.)	07:05	17:05	Dep. Canberra	06:05	12:45
Arr. Canberra	12:05	22:30	Arr. Sydney (Ter.)	11:23	17:45

Sights in **Canberra**: This is the capital of Australia. Individual sightseeing here is easy with a day ticket on an Explorer Bus that allows getting on and off at all of the city's major attractions....or you can take the inexpensive city tour offered by the ACT Tourist Bureau, located in the Civic Center. See the modern art exhibit at National Library. The 6 tons of water jetting 450 feet into the air by the Captain Cook Memorial Water Jet on Lake Burley Griffin (10:00–12:00 and 14:00–16:00). The Sunday afternoon (14:45–15:30) concerts of the 53-bell carillon on **Aspen Island**.

The daily exhibits at the Indonesian Pavilion. The view of the marvelous surroundings of Canberra from Mt. Ainslie, Mt. Pleasant or Red Hill Lookout. All Saints' Anglican Church in a railway station that was built in 1868. Its bell is from an old locomotive.

The 98-acre Botanic Gardens, containing 6,000 native Australian plants representing 2,000 species. Parliament House, open to the public when in session. The coin museum at the Royal Australian Mint and seeing production of money there. An art gallery and the Museum of War Relics, at the Australian War Memorial. The Academy of Science.

The National Library. The Prime Minister's Lodge. The miniature village, called Cockington Green. The view from the revolving restaurant at the top of Telecom Tower on Black Mountain. Parliament House. The National Science and Technology Centre. High Court. The Australian National Gallery.

The **Tidbinbilla Nature Reserve** collection of kangaroos, emus and koalas is 24 miles from Camberra.

654

Melbourne - Bendigo - Swan Hill 9035

All of these trains are air-conditioned, and have buffet, unless designated otherwise.

Dep. Melb'rne (Spen.)	08:35 (1)	09:30 (3)	12:10 (1)	15:50 (4)	17:45 (5+11)
Arr. Bendigo	10:35	11:40	14:08	18:00	19:46
Dep. Kerang	12:29 (2)	13:33 (2)	-0-	-0-	21:20
Arr. Swan Hill	13:12	14:15	-0-	-0-	22:05

Sights in **Bendigo**: Central Deborah Gold Mine. Pottery Centre. Joss House. The Historical Museum and Art Gallery at nearby **Castlemaine**.

Sights in **Swan Hill**: The re-creation of pioneer days at the Folk Museum.

Dep. Swan Hill	-0-	-0-	06:40 (5)	12:40 (2)	14:15 (9+12)
Dep. Kerang	-0-	-0-	07:21	13:30 (8)	15:05
Dep. Bendigo	06:35 (4)	08:00 (7)	09:00	15:30	17:00 (13)
Arr. Melb'rne (Spen.)	08:50	10:04	11:00	17:30	19:03

(1) Runs daily, except Sundays and holidays. (2) Bus Kerang-Swan Hill and v.v.. (3) Runs Sundays and holidays only. (4) Runs daily, except Sundays and holidays. On Saturday runs 20 minutes later and has no buffet. (5) Reservation required. Runs daily, except Sundays and holidays. (6) Runs Saturday only. No buffet. (7) Runs Sundays and holidays only. No buffet. (8) Runs Monday–Friday except holidays. (9) Runs Saturdays, Sundays and holidays only. Bus Swan Hill- Kerang. Train Kerang-Melbourne. (10) Reservation required. Runs Sundays and holidays only. (11) Plus another departure from Melbourne at 16:30 (7) (terminating Bendigo at 18:55 (10) and 18:50 (10))...arriving Bendigo 21:05, Swan Hill 23:25. (12) Plus another departure from Swan Hill at 17:00 (10), arriving Melbourne 21:20. (13) Plus other departures from Bendigo at 08:00 (3), 11:20 (1), 18:30 (8) and 19:15 (10), arriving Melbourne 10:04, 13:19, 20:40 and 21:20.

Sydney - Brisbane 9018

Watch for the outstanding forest and river scenery between Sydney and Gosford en route to Brisbane. This area comes in view about 30 minutes after departing Sydney. The best way to see this area is by taking a ride on a suburban train from Sydney, returning to Sydney the same day.

Both of these trains require reservation, are air-conditioned and have a buffet.

Dep. Sydney (Ter.)	16:15	Dep. Brisbane (Roma)	07:40
Arr. Brisbane (Roma)	06:15	Arr. Sydney (Ter.)	21:40

Sights in **Brisbane**: The view from the observation platform of the clock tower at City Hall. Sub-tropical flowers and shrubs in the 50-acre Botanic Gardens, which provides moorings for visiting yachts. The simulated rainforest in Mount Coot-tha Botanic Gardens, open daily 08:00–17:00. (Australia's largest planetarium is also located there.)

The views from lookout points in Brisbane Forest Park. Brass-rubbing workshops Wednesday and Friday 10:00–15:00 at St. John's Cathedral, open daily 07:00–17:30. The collection of dolls and more than 700 different teddy bears at the Teddy Bear Land and Museum, 118 Edward St., open Monday-Friday 09:00–16:00, Saturday 08:30–12:00.

Queensland Art Gallery's fine collection of paintings, sculptures, photographs and prints, open daily 10:00–17:00 (until 20:00 on Wednesday). Many good ship models as well as an old frigate at Queensland Maritime Museum, open Wednesday 10:00–15:30, on Saturday and Sunday 10:00–16:30.

The exhibits at Queensland Museum (open daily 10:00–16:55) include dinosaurs, the only surviving World War I German tank and the airplane in which the first solo flight from England to Australia was made, in 1928. The lovely lake and the exotic animals, birds and plants at Alma Park Zoo and 32-acre Tropical Palm Gardens, open daily 09:00–17:00.

The 12,000 rose trees in bloom from September through November (and avenues of jacaranda and poinciana trees) in New Farm Park, along Brisbane River.

Brisbane's oldest home is Newstead House, built in 1846, open Monday-Thursday 11:00–15:00, Sunday 14:00–17:00. Several memorials, including the Australian-American Memorial, are located in its garden, now a public park. Nearby is the Miegunyah Folk Museum, another historic home, open Tuesday and Wednesday 10:30–15:00; Saturday and Sunday 10:30–16:00.

See the old buildings (hotel, store, slab hut, worker's cottage and a colonial mansion in 5 acres of natural forest) in Earlystreet Village, open Monday-Friday 09:30–16:30, Saturday and Sunday 10:30–16:30.

You can hold a koala and watch the kangaroos and wallabies at the Lone Pine Koala Sanctuary, open daily 09:30–17:00, reached by road or by taking a launch at Victoria Bridge. Another collection of Australian animals can be seen at Bunya Park Wildlife Sanctuary, open daily 09:30–17:00.

Brisbane's only Chinese temple, the Joss House, on Higgs Street (phone 262-5588 for an appointment). See the more than 5,000 toys, doll houses, model cars and planes, money boxes and teddy bears at Panaroo's Playthings, in nearby **Windsor**, open Wednesday, Thursday and Friday from 10:30–15:30, and on Saturdays, Sundays and holidays from 11:00–16:00.

Dozens of arts and crafts galleries. The collection of steam locomotives at the large Railway Museum, adjacent to the suburban Redbank station. The Australian Railway Historical Society runs several steam trains here.

"Southern Cross", the first airplane to cross the Pacific Ocean from California to Queensland (in 1928), displayed 24 hours at Brisbane Airport.

The Victorian opulence of the National Bank. The beauty of the Treasury Building and City Hall. Many tropical and sub-tropical parks and gardens. Shop in Queen Street Mall. Take the 2½-hour boat trip to **Moreton Island**, or a day cruise to **Stradbroke Island**.

Sydney - Lithgow - Sydney (Interurban schedule)

Marvelous Blue Mountain scenery on this easy one-day roundtrip by frequent suburban service. Departing Sydney, the best views are seen from the left side of the train as it climbs into the Blue Mountains.

Interurban trains depart from Sydney's Terminal railstation frequently for the 3-hour trip to Lithgow.

Sydney - Newcastle - Sydney 9017

It is an easy one-day roundtrip to take Australia's most scenic rail route. This line travels through the **Ku-ring-gai National Park**, the **Hawkesbury River** estuary (famous for its oyster farms), Australia's longest rail tunnel and the Lake Macquarie district. Departing Sydney, the best views of the Hawkesbury River estuary are from the *right side* of the train.

Dep. Sydney (Ter.)	Frequent departures from 05:00 to 23:25
Arr. Newcastle	2¼-3 hours later

*   *   *

Dep. Newcastle	Frequent departures from 06:02 to 23:25
Arr. Sydney (Ter.)	2¼-3 hours later

656

Brisbane - Rockhampton - Townsville - Cairns

All of these trains are air-conditioned.

	9016	9007	9004
Dep. Brisbane (Roma St.)	08:15 (1+2)	09:10 (4)	09:10 (5)
Arr. Rockhampton	18:00	19:45	20:35
Dep. Rockhampton	18:45 (2)	20:10	21:00
Arr. Townsville	09:20 (3)	10:30 (3)	11:20 (3)
Arr. Cairns	16:50	17:20	18:30

* * *

	9004	9007	9016
Dep. Cairns	07:00 (5)	08:15 (4)	10:00 (1+6)
Dep. Townsville	14:20	15:15	17:10
Arr. Rockhampton	04:40 (3)	05:15 (3)	07:30 (3)
Dep. Rockhampton	05:10	05:40	08:15 (1)
Arr. Brisbane (Roma St.)	16:25	16:25	18:00

(1) Change trains in Rockhampton. The Brisbane-Rockhampton and v. v. portion runs daily. Buffet Brisbane-Cairns and v.v.. (2) Rockhampton-Cairns runs only on peak holidays and on Monday if traffic warants. Buffet. (3) Day 2. (4) Reservation required. Supplement charged. Carries first-class sleeping cars and second-class coaches. Runs Brisbane-Cairns Sunday only. Runs Cairns-Brisbane Tuesday only. (5) Reservation required. Carries first and second-class sleeping cars and second-class coaches. Restaurant car. Runs Brisbane-Cairns Tuesday, Thursday and Saturday. Runs Cairns-Brisbane Monday, Thursday and Saturday. (6) Cairns-Rockhampton runs only on peak holidays and on Tuesday if traffic warrants. Buffet.

Sights in **Cairns**: Visitors can study coral gardens and colorful marine life from the Underwater Observatory or from a glass-bottomed boat at **Green Island**, only 17 miles from Cairns. The **Atherton Tableland Rainforest**, teeming with birdlife, is to the west of Cairns. Aerial tours of the **Great Barrier Reef** take tourists from Cairns along the jungle coastline and over many cattle stations. Twenty minutes by car north of Cairns' International Airport is the **Kewarra**, a resort on the Coral Sea beach.

Brisbane - Toowoomba 9014

The ascent through the Great Dividing Range offers outstanding scenery on this easy one-day roundtrip.

This service is by train from Brisbane–Ipswich and v.v. then by bus Ipswich–Toowoomba and v.v.

Dep. Brisbane (Cen.)	06:42 (1)	06:54 (2)	07:12 (3)	07:46 (4)	08:12 (4)
	09:12 (5)	10:12 (1)	12:12 (5)	13:12 (6)	13:42 (2)
	15:08 (2)	16:12 (3)	16:56 (2)	17:12 (1)	18:12 (5)
	19:12 (2)	20:12 (3)	21:12 (7)		
Dep. Brisbane (Roma)	2 minutes after departing Central station
Arr. Toowoomba	2¼–2½ hours later

Sights in **Toowoomba**: This is a garden city in the center of the very rich 8,500,000-acre Darling Downs agricultural area. A week-long Carnival of Flowers takes place here every September. The dense rainforest with many species of birds in **Ravensbourne National Park** is 28 miles from here.

Dep. Toowoomba	04:30 (5)	06:30 (2)	06:40 (1)	07:40 (5)	09:40 (5)
	10:40 (5)	12:40 (5)	14:55 (2)	15:40 (6)	16:40 (5)
	17:40 (2)	18:40 (3)			
Arr. Brisbane (Roma)	2¼–2½ hours later				
Arr. Brisbane (Cen.)	2 minutes after arriving Roma railstation.				

(1) Saturday only. (2) Monday–Friday except holidays. (3) Sundays and holidays only. (4) Daily except Sundays and holidays. (5) Daily. (6) Saturdays, Sundays and holidays only. (7) Friday only.

Rockhampton - Winton 9013

Both of these trains require reservation, are air-conditioned, carry a first-class sleeping car and a second-class coach, and have buffet. Both arrivals are day 3.

Dep. Rockhampton	18:45 (1)	Dep. Winton	14:45 (2)
Arr. Winton	12:20	Arr. Rockhampton	07:30

(1) Runs Tuesday and Friday. (2) Runs Wednesday and Saturday.

Sights in **Winton**: The Historical Museum. Qantilda Pioneer Place. Nearby, the Quarry Environmental Park.

Townsville - Mount Isa 9012

Both of these trains require reservation, are air-conditioned, carry a first-class sleeping car and second-class coach, and have buffet.

Dep. Townsville	18:00 (1)	Dep. Mount Isa	15:00 (2)
Arr. Mount Isa	11:50	Arr. Townsville	08:15

(1) Runs Wednesday and Sunday. (2) Runs Monday and Friday.

Sights in **Mount Isa**: Visit the National Trust Tent House. See mining memorabilia at the Underground Museum. The lifestyle of the Kalkadoon Aborigines. The Flying Doctor Base. The School of the Air, giving students in remote areas lessons by 2-way radio. Nearby, **Lake Moondarra**.

Visitors may inspect one of the world's richest copper, silver-lead and zinc mines.

Cairns - Kuranda - Cairns 9010

Kuranda is Australia's most northern rail terminal. This is one of the world's most scenic rail trips, through the most lush, tropical rain forests in Australia filled with tropical flowers. It is an easy one-day roundtrip through the Barron Gorge.

*Both of these are special tourist trains, hosted by a guide who comments on the history of the railway and the life along the line. The trains stop along the way for passengers to take photos and enjoy waterfall scenes. Included is lunch at **Tinaroo** (an orchid plantation) and a cruise on **Lake Barrine** for a different view of the rain forest. Special guided bus tours operate from Kuranda back to Cairns, riding through sugar-cane fields.*

The roundtrip price was $24 (Aust.) in 1991.

Dep. Cairns	09:00	Dep. Kuranda	12:00
Arr. Kuranda	10:30	Arr. Cairns	13:25

THE CENTRAL AUSTRALIAN RAIL ROUTE

Adelaide - Alice Springs 9005 + 9034

A standard-gauge train, "The Ghan" is the 1980 successor to the original narrow-gauge operation of the same name that ran from Port Pirie to Alice Springs from 1930 to 1980. The name is in tribute to the Afghan traders who in the 19th century carried passengers and goods on camels between Port Pirie and Oodnadatta, the end of the original rail line.

"The Ghan" requires a reservation, carries sleeping cars, coach cars and an entertainment car. Its restaurant car is available to sleeping car passengers. Light refreshments are available to all passengers.

The entertainment car has a souvenir shop, a book shop, 5 video monitors, electronic games, an area with card tables, and (most novel for a train car) 8 poker machines.

Dep. Adelaide (Keswick)	14:00 (1)	Dep. Alice Springs	17:10 (3)
Arr. Alice Springs	11:40 (2)	Arr. Adelaide (Keswick)	16:30 (4)

(1) May to October: runs Monday and Thursday. November to April: runs Thursday only. (2) Day 2 from Adelaide. (3) May to October: runs Tuesday and Friday. November to April: Runs Friday only. (4) Day 2 from Alice Springs.

Sights in **Alice Springs**: This is the ideal base for tours to the "Great Outback". It is a frontier town with modern homes and wide, tree-lined streets. Alice Springs is the headquarters for both the Royal Flying Doctor Service and the unique School of the Air, the sole means of education for those living in the deserted areas of Australia.

Visitors can listen to the children and the teachers, and visit the Flying Doctor facility.

See the museum in the Old Telegraph Station. Many art galleries and souvenir shops.

The Pitchi-Richi Bird Sanctuary, 2 miles from Alice Springs, has a collection of Aboriginal sculptures and implements, also Australian gemstones.

Take a tour to awe-inspiring **Ayers Rock** to see it change color at sunset and sunrise. Alice Springs is also the gateway to **Standley Chasm** and the Olgas.

Alice Springs - Darwin 9125 (Bus)

All arrivals are on Day 2.

Dep. Alice Springs	15:00	18:30 (1)	19:30
Arr. Darwin	08:30	11:45	16:00

Sights in **Darwin**: Tropical flowers, shrubs and trees in the jungle-like Botanical Gardens. The crocodiles and water buffaloes at Yarrawonga Park. The excellent Mandorah Beach.

Dep. Darwin	11:15	12:30 (1)	13:00
Arr. Alice Springs	05:30	06:15	09:00

(1) Service subject to confirmation.

WESTERN AUSTRALIAN ROUTES

Perth - Albany 9139 (Bus)

All of these buses require reservations.

Dep. Perth (Ter.)	09:00 (1)	09:00 (2)	15:00 (4)	18:00 (5)
Arr. Albany	15:25	16:15 (3)	20:50	23:50

Sights in **Albany**: A magnificent harbor. This is the starting point for tours through the Porongurup and Stirling mountain ranges for scenic walks and viewing marvelous wild-flowers August-November.

Dep. Albany	09:00 (6)	09:00 (7)	15:00 (4)	15:00 (8)	17:30 (5)
Arr. Perth (Ter.)	15:20	17:30	20:50	22:45	23:20

(1) Via Kojonup. Runs Monday, Tuesday, Thursday and Friday. (2) Via Katanning. Runs Monday, Thursday, Friday and Saturday. (3) Arrives Albany at 17:35 on Monday and Thursday, 16:55 on Friday. (4) Via Kojonup. Runs Wednesday and Sunday. (5) Via Kojonup. Runs Friday only. (6) Via Kojonup. Runs daily, except Wednesday and Sunday. (7) Via Katanning. Runs Thursday and Friday. Departs 09:15 on Thursday. (8) Via Katanning. Runs Sunday only.

Perth - Bunbury 9036

All of these trains require reservation, run daily except Sunday and holidays, and have a restaurant car unless designated otherwise.

Dep. Perth	10:00	19:00 (1)	Dep. Bunbury	06:30	15:40 (2)
Arr. Bunbury	12:20	21:20	Arr. Perth	08:50	18:00

(1) No restaurant car on Tuesday, Wednesday and Thursday. (2) Departs 15:55 Monday and Saturday

Sights in **Bunbury**: An important port. Good fishing and surfing here.

Perth - Fremantle 9037

These trains are second-class only.

Dep. East Perth	Mon.-Fri.	Frequent times	05:45 — 23:30
	Saturday	Frequent times	05:25 — 23:59
	Sun. and holidays	Frequent times	07:20 — 20:10
Arr. Fremantle		35 minutes later	

* * *

Dep. Fremantle	Mon.-Fri	Frequent times	05:45 — 23:30
	Saturday	Frequent times	05:25 — 23:59
	Sun. and holidays	Frequent times	07:20 — 20:10
Arr. East Perth		35 minutes later	

Sights in **Fremantle**: This is Western Australia's principal port. See the Maritime Museum and Art Center. The great views of the city and harbor from The Round House.

Perth - Kalgoorlie

All of these trains require reservation, are air-conditioned, first-class only, and have a restaurant car.

The "Prospector" trains are among Australia's fastest, making their 407-mile (655km) trip in 6-7½ hours. Stewardesses bring hot meals to the passengers' seats: lunch at 12:30, dinner at 18:30.

"Indian Pacific" is described on page 648. "Trans Australian" is described on page 649.

	9034	9034	9034	9034	9000
Dep. East Perth	09:00 (1)	15:35 (2)	15:40 (3)	18:00 (4)	21:00 (5)
Arr. Kalgoorlie	16:35	21:35	23:00	24:00	06:00

Sights in **Kalgoorlie:** See notes about sightseeing in Kalgoorlie, under "Sydney-Port Pirie-Kalgoorlie-Perth" on page 651.

	9034	9034	9034	9034	9000
Dep. Kalgoorlie	06:45 (2)	08:15 (1)	15:10 (3)	17:50 (4)	21:00 (4)
Arr. East Perth	12:50	15:40	22:35	00:15	07:00

(1) "Prospector". Runs Monday–Thursday in both directions. (2) "Prospector". Runs Friday only Perth-Kalgoorlie. Runs Saturday only Kalgoorlie-Perth. (3) "Prospector". Runs Friday and Sunday in both directions. (4) "Prospector". Runs Saturday only Perth-Kalgoorlie. Runs Thursday only Kalgoorlie-Perth. (5) "Indian Pacific". Runs Tuesday, Thursday and Sunday Perth-Kargoolie. Runs Monday, Wednesday and Saturday Kargoolie-Perth.

TASMANIA

Australia's island state, 150 miles south of mainland Victoria, measures 190 miles from east to west and 180 miles from north to south. Visitors can inspect historic homes and folk museums, stay at old inns, see the ruins of old penal colonies, enjoy fine beaches, swimming and excellent mountain and rural scenery.

Tasmania's one rail route ceased operating in 1978. It ran north from **Hobart** to **Launceston** and then west to **Devonport** and **Wynyard**.

Chapter 13

NEW ZEALAND

Children under 4 travel free. Half-fare for children 4-14. Children 15 and over must pay full fare. Sleeping cars have 2-berth compartments.

The country is 2 islands: North Island and South Island. There is ferry service between the 2 islands, connecting Wellington (at the southern tip of North Island) with Picton (the north tip of South Island).

NEW ZEALAND'S TRAIN PASS

Intercity Travelpass

Available worldwide from travel agencies. Also available in New Zealand at train and bus depots, offices of Intercity Travel, and travel agencies. In the U.S.A.: from New Zealand Central Reservations Office, Suite 1270, 6033 West Century Blvd., Los Angeles, CA 90045.

Unlimited travel on all trains, buses (except suburban ones) and inter-island ferries. Not transferable or refundable. Half-fare for children 4-14 years old. Children under 4 travel free.

The single-class prices until October 31, 1992 (subject to major currency fluctuations) are: $209 (U.S.) for any 8 days within 14 days, $259 for any 15 days within 22 days, and $347 for any 22 days within 30 days.

NORTH ISLAND RAIL ROUTES

The rail system on North Island is 4 lines running north from Wellington.

Auckland

Walking tours are so popular here that the city publishes 2 brochures: "Go Strolling in Your Lunch Hour" and "Coast to Coast Walking". (It is only an 8-mile walk from the Pacific Ocean on the east side of Auckland to the Tasman Sea on the west side of the city.) All interesting sights are outlined in a free map, and the routes are marked clearly.

See: The sculptures and fountains in Queen Elizabeth II Square. Parnell Rose Gardens. Westhaven Marina. The view of Waitemata Harbor from the War Memorial Museum (open daily 10:00 – 17:00), which has a good collection of Maori artifacts, native New Zealand animals and plants, and relics of both wars.

Heritage Park. The exhibits and Pioneer Village at the Museum of Transport and Technology, reached by double-decker buses from and to major downtown hotels. The outstanding collection of mammals, fish, reptiles and birds (including the local non-flying Kiwi) at the Zoo.

Marvelous views of Auckland, its beaches and harbors as well as many streams and waterfalls, at Centennial Memorial Park. See the Cathedral of the Holy Trinity. The Waitakere Scenic Reserve. The view of the city from Mt. Eden, a dormant volcano. The Emily Nixon Garden of Memories. The views of Hauraki Gulf from

Musick Point. Tour the Earth Satellite Tracking Station. Travel in a clear tunnel through the huge Underwater World aquarium (open daily 09:00 – 21:00). Swim in the thermal pools at nearby **Waiwera**.

Take a 2-day motorcoach tour to **Waitomo** (to see its caves and Glowworm Grotto) and to **Rotorua**, an interesting place with thermal swimming pools, the beautiful Government Gardens, the Maori Arts and Crafts Institute (a school for young woodcarvers and weavers), trout fishing, the Whakarewarewa Maori Village, St. Faith's Maori Church, TeWairoa (an excavated Maori village), the exhibits of sheepshearing, wool spinning, working sheep dogs and performing rams at Agrodome, the hand-fed trout at Rainbow Springs, and the overall Polynesian ambiance.

Visit some of the 19 wineries in West Auckland's Henderson Valley.

Hamilton

This is only 68 miles by bus from Rotorua (see notes above about sights in Rotorua and timetable below for training to Hamilton).

Wellington

Many fine beaches here. See the view of the city, harbor and Hutt Valley from the 548-foot high Mount Victoria. The 62-acre Botanical Gardens. Lady Norwood Rose Gardens. The Zoological Gardens. The crafts at the New Zealand Display Center. Conducted tours of the marble-faced House of Parliament. Freyberg Tepid Pool.

Government Building, one of the largest wood structures in the Southern Hemisphere. The South Pacific manuscripts and maps in Turnbull Library. The collection of Maori exhibits at Dominion Museum and National Art Gallery. Nearby, the Carillon and Hall of Memories. The Carter Observatory. Many fine beaches.

Take the cable car from Lambton Quay 397 feet up to Kelburn Park.

Wellington - Hamilton - Auckland 9750

This scenic trip includes the breathtaking Raurimu Spiral, rivers, forests, seascapes and 3 high volcanoes: Ngauruhoe (7,515 feet), Ruapehu (9,175) and Tongariro (6,517).

The morning departure from both Wellington and Auckland is "Silver Fern". Passengers on it can have morning and afternoon teas, lunch, softdrinks and liquor served to their seats, airline style.

The night departures from both cities are "Northerner". Light refreshments are available through the night. Reservations for the night trains can be made as much as 6 months before travel date.

Both "Silver Fern" and "Northerner" require reservations and are first- class only.

Dep. Wellington	08:20 (1)	20:45 (2)	Dep. Auckland	08:30 (1)	21:15 (2)
Dep. Hamilton	16:39	06:00	Dep. Hamilton	10:18	23:20
Arr. Auckland	18:30	08:15	Arr. Wellington	18:40	08:30

(1) "Silver Fern". Supplement charged. Runs daily, except Sundays and holidays. Air-conditioned train. Buffet. (2) "Northerner". Runs daily, except Saturday. Light refreshments.

Wellington - Palmerston North - Napier - Gisborne 9750

This route includes the scenic shoreline of Hawkes Bay (Wairoa–Gisborne). These trains stop for refreshments at Palmerston North and Napier. South of Gisborne, the track crosses an airport runway, a popular "shot" for photographers.

These trains require reservation, are first-class only and have buffet.

Dep. Wellington	08:00	Dep. Gisborne	09:30 (1)
Dep. Palmerston North	10:08	Dep. Wairoa	11:25
Dep. Napier	13:30	Dep. Napier	14:30
Dep. Wairoa	16:30 (1)	Dep. Palmerston North	17:54
Arr. Gisborne	18:15	Arr. Wellington	20:00

(1) Wairoa–Gisborne and v.v. is by bus service.

Sights in **Napier**: The exhibit of dolphins, sea lions, sea leopards, penguins and other animals and sea birds at Marineland. The assortment of birds in the Botanic Gardens. The fine swimming and fishing beaches. The beautiful Sunken Garden and lovely Golden Mile Park, along the shore.

Wellington - Masterton 9750

All of these trains are second-class only.

Dep. Wellington	14:27 (1)	16:10 (1)	16:27 (2)	17:36 (1)	19:27 (3)	21:27 (4)
Arr. Masterton	16:00	17:52	18:00	19:14	21:00	23:00

* * *

Dep. Masterton	05:54 (1)	06:36 (1)	08:57 (5)	16:57 (3)	17 :57 (4)
Arr. Wellington	07:41	08:19	10:27	18:27	19:34

(1) Runs Monday–Friday, except holidays. (2) Runs Saturday only. (3) Runs Sundays and holidays only. (4) Runs Friday only. (5) Runs daily, except Sundays and holidays.

Wellington - Palmerston North 9750

All of these trains require a reservation , are first-class only and have buffet, unless designated otherwise.

Dep. Wellington	08:00	08:20 (1)	20:45 (2)
Arr. Palmerston North	09:58	10:13	22:52

* * *

Dep. Palmerston North	06:09 (3)	16:36 (1)	17:54
Arr. Wellington	08:30	18:40	20:00

(1) "Silver Fern". Supplement charged. Runs daily, except Sundays and holidays. Air-conditioned train. Passengers can have morning and afternoon teas, lunch, soft-drinks and liquor served to their seats, airline style. (2) "Northerner". Runs daily, except Saturday. Light refreshments are available through the night. (3) "Northerner". Runs daily except Saturday. Light refreshments.

SOUTH ISLAND RAIL ROUTES

A ferry service connects North Island and South Island.

The rail system on South Island is one route along the South Pacific shoreline due south from Picton via Christchurch and terminating in Invercargill, plus a single cross-island line running from Christchurch to Greymouth.

Bus and taxi service is available between Wellington's railstation and its pier.

Wellington - Picton - Christchurch

The notable scenery on this ride includes views of man-made lakes of Grassmere Saltworks, ocean surf, many attractive beaches, and the Kaikoura mountain range.

These ferries carry both automobiles and passengers. They have food and beverage service.

9780 (Bus)

Dep. Wellington (Railst'n)	07:25 (1)	09:25	15:25	18:05 (3)
Arr. Wellington (Ferry Ter.)	07:40	09:40	15:40	18:20
Change to ferry.				
Dep. Wellington (Ferry Ter.)	08:00	10:00	16:00	18:40
Arr. Picton	11:00	13:20	19:00	22:00
Change to train. Table 9800				
Dep. Picton		14:00 (2)		
Dep. Kaikoura		16:22		
Arr. Christchurch		19:25		

* * *

Dep. Christchurh			08:10 (2)	
Dep. Kaikoura			11:10	
Arr. Picton			13:30	
Change to ferry. Table 9780				
Dep. Picton	05:40 (4)	12:00 (1)	14:20	19:45 (4+6)
Arr. Wellington (Ferry Ter.)	09:00	15:00	17:40	22:45
Change to bus.				
Dep. Wellington (Ferry Ter.)	09:10	15:10	17:50	22:55
Arr. Wellington (Railst'n)	15 minutes after departing from Ferry Terminal			

(1) Runs daily, except Monday and Tuesday. (2) Reservation required. First-class only. Has a parlor car Monday and Friday in both directions. Snacks can be purchased during a refreshment stop in Kaikoura. (3) Runs daily, except Sunday. (4) Runs daily, except Monday. (5) Runs Monday only. (6) Plus another departure from Picton at 22:20 (5), arriving Wellington's Ferry Terminal (no bus service) 01:20.

Sights in **Christchurch:** Takahe, the carved Maori meeting house. The beautiful Botanical Gardens in Hagley Park. The mementos from Captain Cook's 3 voyages, displays on Antarctica explorations, and the exhibit of Maori articles (including a 47-foot wood war canoe) in the Canterbury Museum on the side of Hagley Park. Cathedral Square. The view from Summit Road. Take a hydrofoil boat tour through **Waimakariri Gorge**.

Christchurch - Timaru - Dunedin - Invercargill 9800

Invercargill is the most southerly rail terminal in the world – latitude 46 degrees.

There is fine scenery of the South Pacific coastline and the Canterbury Plains on this ride. Looking to the west, one can see the New Zealand Alps. Other views: rivers, sheep runs and wheatfields.

The schedules below are for "Southerner", a first-class only, luxury train with buffet service. Reservations are required. These trains run Monday–Friday, except holidays.

Seats can be reserved up to 6 months prior to travel date. As you board, you are given a folder about the journey, with a map and notes on points of interest en route.

A hostess will serve morning and afternoon teas and light meals to anyone who is physically unable to eat in the buffet car and to mothers traveling with young children. Arrangements can be made to have a rental car or taxi waiting for one's arrival. In the smoking carriage, passengers are served wine, cocktails and liquor at their seat.

Dep. Christchurch	07:45	Dep. Invercargil	09:50
Dep. Timaru	09:53	Dep. Dunedin	13:20
Dep. Dunedin	13:20	Dep. Timaru	16:44
Arr. Invercargill	16:50	Arr. Christchurch	18:55

Sights in **Timaru**: A large port. A great beach. Good fishing in this area. Nearby, the National Park with its many mile-high mountains.

Sights in **Dunedin**: Attractive old stone buildings such as the Railstation. The enjoyable miles of beaches. The Kauri wood, Italian marble and Venetian glass in Larnach Castle, perched on top of a 1,000-foot-high hill on Otago Peninsula, and the view from it. Originally the 19th century mansion of a wealthy banker, the castle is now a hotel.

The Jacobean-style Olveston House. Glenfalloch Woodland Gardens. A Maori village. Penguin Place. Nearby, Mount Aspiring National Park and several lovely lakes: **Manapouri**, **Te Anau**, **Ohau**, **Pukaki** and **Tekakpo**.

Sights in **Invercargill**: The view of the city from the seventh floor of the Kelvin Hotel. The collection of Maori exhibits and art gallery at the Southland Centennial Museum in the 200-acre Queen's Park, located in the center of Invercargill. The park features a display of native and exotic trees and plants, a group of statues for children, a large sunken rose garden surrounded by flowering prunus and cherry trees, and a special iris garden. At the eastern side of this park is a wide variety of tropical plants, a large pond containing aquatic plants and fish, a large lily pond, and a well-stocked aviary, all in the Steans Memorial Winter Garden.

Also see the City Gardens, along the Otepuni stream that runs through the center of Invercargill. Rose Gardens. The display of provincial history in the Southland Centennial Museum and Art Gallery. The 85-acre Waihopai Scenic Reserve. The City Art Gallery in the 60-acre Anderson Park. The 25-mile long sandy Oreti Beach, fine for swimming.

Christchurch - Arthur's Pass - Greymouth 9800

This is the most scenic rail trip in New Zealand. After departing Christchurch, the train climbs to 2,500 feet at Arthur's Pass before going through the 5½-mile Otira Tunnel. Some grades are as great as 4 on this steep ride. On the approach to Greymouth, there are splendid views of the Tasman Coast.

These trains require reservation, are first-class only, and carry a parlor car Monday and Friday.

Dep. Christchurch	07:30	Dep. Greymouth	13:25
Dep. Arthur's Pass	10:28	Dep. Arthur's Pass	15:51
Arr. Greymouth	12:35	Arr. Christchurch	18:40

Sights in **Greymouth**: Visit a coal mine. Take a jet-boat ride up the Taramakau River to the Kaniere gold dredge and see the little museum of the gold-rush days at **Hokitaka**. Trout fishing at nearby **Brunner**.

Kingston - Fairlight 9802

A special 6-mile steam train trip Kingston–Fairlight on "Kingston Flyer" to the south shore of **Lake Wakatipu** operates only on a charter basis. The operator, Kingston Flyer Company, gives only a 48-hour notice prior to days there is service.

Kenneth Gordon wrote us in 1989 about this popular excursion: "It was fun ! "

Chapter 14

NORTH AMERICA

Winter in North America is from December 21 to March 20. Summer is from June 21 to September 20.

CANADA

Children under 5 not occupying a separate seat travel free with each passenger 18 or older. Half-fare for children 5–11. Children 12 and over must pay full fare.

The national Canadian passenger train network is called "VIA RailCanada". Since the Spring of 1992, all trains operating between Vancouver and Toronto were completely refurbished, including showers on all sleeping cars. "Silver & Blue Class" service, introduced in April of 1992, includes upgraded amenities such as enhanced restaurant car services.

For reservations and information, contact a travel agency.

Canada's other train systems are: Algoma Central Railway, British Columbia Railway, Ontario Northland Railway, Quebec North Shore & Labrador Railways, and Toronto Hamilton & Buffalo Railway.

The Canrailpass described below is valid only on VIA routes.

CANADA'S TRAIN PASSES

Must be purchased before you arrive in Canada. Sold at travel agencies worldwide outside Canada. Valid for 30 consecutive days from the first day of travel.

If a trip involves the use of a pass either completely on High-Season days or on a combination of High-Season *and* Low-Season days, then a High-Season pass must be used.

Coach seats can be upgraded at additional charge to a sleeping compartment with upper and/or lower berths, for which early reservation is advisable.

Low Seasons (overlapping the annual edition of Eurail® Guide) are November 1, 1991 to April 25, 1992....and also November 1, 1992 to April 25, 1993. High Season is April 26, 1992 to October 31, 1992.

"Youths" are passengers under 25 years old.

Systemwide Canrailpass

Unlimited travel throughout all of Canada.

The 1991–1992 and 1992 –1993 Low Season prices are: $299 (Can.) for adults, $249 for youths, High Season: $439 and $399.

Eastern Canrailpass

Unlimited travel in the area extending from Halifax west to Toronto.

The 1991–1992 and 1992 –1993 Low Season prices are: $179 (Can.) for adults, $159 for youths, High Season: $269 and $219.

Montreal

See the 23,400-pound bell ("Le Gros Bourdon") and marvelous stained-glass windows in the Notre Dame Basilica, completed in 1829 and resembling Westminster Abbey. The bell requires 12 men when it is tolled manually and can be heard for 15 miles. It is operated electrically now.

The pipe organ there, one of the largest in North America, has 4 keyboards, 84 stops, 30 pedals and 6,800 pipes (the tallest is 12 feet). Also look at the carved, gilded wood interior of the church. See the gifts from Louis XIV in the tiny museum next to the Chapel.

Visit the magnificent St. Joseph's Oratory (open daily 06:00–22:00), one of the world's largest ecclesiastical buildings, completed in 1974. It is a complex with escalators that includes a lower church which seats 1,000 and a 4,000-seat basilica. (Its spectacular cupola is a copy of the one at St. Peter's in Rome. The cupola is 506 feet above street level and, because this church is atop Mount Royal, it is the highest point in Montreal.)

See the 30 stained-glass windows (all with biblical scenes) in Erskine and American Church, open daily 09:00–16:30.

The colection of arms, costumes, prints, paintings, photographs, documents and books at the David M. Stewart Museum on Ile Ste. Helene, open Tuesday-Sunday 10:00-17:00. Some of the many exceptional exhibits there: a floor map of the Atlantic Ocean, a scale model of Montreal as it was in 1760, and a spectacular large-scale model of the 18th century 70-gun French ship Le Jupiter.

A collection of furniture, glass, textiles and ceramics from 1935 to the present, at the Chateau Dufresne/Montreal Museum of Decorative Arts, at 2929 Jeanne d'Arc Avenue, open Thursday-Sunday 12:00–17:00.

The colonial-era costumes, maps, guns, engravings, paintings and wood sculptures as well as objects from China, India and the West Indies at Chateau de Ramezay at 280 Notre-Dame Street, open Tuesday-Sunday 10:00–16:30. It is considered by some to be the most interesting museum in Montreal.

The 34 galleries (exhibiting 19th century French impressionists, 18th century British portraits, works of early and contemporary Canadian artists) in the Museum of Fine Arts, at 1379 Sherbrooke Street West, open daily except Monday 11:00–17:00.

An ethnographic representation of costumes, decorative and folk art, paintings, prints, drawings and photos pertaining to Canada's various Indian tribes, in McCord Museum, at 690 Sherbrooke Street West, open Wednesday-Sunday 11:00–17:00.

Examples of 17th and 18th century furniture, furnishings, religious art and secular art in San Gabriel House, at 2146 Favard Street, with guided tours Tuesday–Saturday 12:30 and 15:00. On Sunday at 13:30, 14:30 and 15:30.

The Sulpician Seminary, built in 1685, the oldest building in Montreal. The oldest wood clock in North America is exhibited there.

The interesting 60-minute audiovisual history of the city, at the Montreal History Center, 335 Place d'Youville. The Place des Arts complex of concert and theater halls. The vast underground shopping malls in the ultramodern center of the city, called Place Ville-Marie. Take the short trip to Mount Royal.

Ottawa

During July and August, 80-minute guided bus tours start at Confederation Square daily every half-hour from 11:00 to 17:00.

The Gothic-styled buildings on Parliament Hill are dominated by a 302-foot-high Peace Tower, which has a 53-bell carillon. Free guided tours of the complex are conducted every 20 minutes 08:30–16:30. Free guided tours of Parliament are offered 09:00–11:00 and 13:00–17:00. During Summer, a changing-of-the-guard ceremony can be seen daily at 10:00.

See the superb Canadian and European art (some of the latter dating back to the 13th century) at the National Gallery, open during Summer months Monday-Saturday 10:00–18:00, Sundays and holidays 10:00–14:00. The National Arts Center.

The Arboretum at the Central Experimental Farm. The Governor General's Residence. Hog's Back Falls, located in the city. The Royal Canadian Mint. The display of weapons and uniforms at the Canadian War Museum, open daily 10:00–17:00. The Indian Burial Grounds. The Centennial Cabin Museum. The Old Depot Museum.

The antique skis at the Canadian Ski Museum, open daily 11:00–16:00. The National Postal Museum at 365 Laurier Street sells first-day covers. The Currency Museum in the Bank of Canada at 245 Sparks Street is open daily except Monday.

The Museum of Science and Technology at 1867 St. Laurent Blvd. is open daily 10:00–20:00. See floral displays, hundreds of types of trees, and Clydesale horses pulling wagons at the 1200-acre experimental farm south of Carling Avenue, near Carlton University.

Take the 5½-mile cruise on the Rideau Canal. It operates 6 times a day (starting at 10:00) July through September. Board near the Conference Center on Confederation Square. In Winter, this 123-mile-long canal is one of the longest ice-skating rinks in the world.

Visit the food shops and stands at Byward Market, near Notre Dame Basilica.

Quebec City

Guided walking tours start from the lobby of the Chateau Frontenac Hotel, the first of 3 daily tours beginning at 09:30 (10:00 on Saturday and Sunday). Across the street from the entrance of the hotel, there is a 30-minute audiovisual recreation of the 6 sieges to which the city was subjected (Musee du Fort, at 10 Rue Ste.-Anne).

Nearby at (69 Rue Ste.-Anne, across from City Hall), Eskimo weaving and stone carving are sold at Aux Multiples.

Shop for handmade jewelry, wood sculptures, leather clothing and pottery in the Quartier Petit Champlain, an old section of town that is near the river. See the collection of antique furniture in Chevalier House, at Place Champlain

Stroll on the Plains of Abraham. See the changing of the guard every morning at 10:00, at the 37-acre Citadel. Take the 4-hour cruise on the St. Lawrence Seaway. A 3-week Winter Carnival, ends on the night of Mardi Gras.

Toronto

A major port. See: The astounding view from the top of Canadian National's Tower, the tallest (1,800 feet) free-standing structure in the world. City Hall.

The George R.Gardiner Museum of Ceramic Art displays 2,000 pieces ranging from pre-Columbian pottery to 18th century porcelain (Meissen, Worcester, etc.). Located at 111 Queen's Park, it is open daily except Monday 10:00–17:00.

Across the street from the Gardiner is the Royal Ontario Museum, second-largest museum in North America (after New York's Metropolitan). It has an outstanding Chinese collection (complete temple clay wall paintings, the only Ming tomb complex in the Western Hemisphere), several extraordinary dioramas showing 13 dinosaurs in dramatic movement, an exceptional collection of Egyptian mummies — and its "Mediterranean World", a chronological depiction of the beginnings of Judaism, Christianity and Islam, starting with a 2,040 B.C. Sumerian clay that records the sale of 4 sheep.

The Royal Ontario Museum opens daily at 10:00, closing at 18:00 Monday–Wednesday, Saturday and Sunday. It closes at 20:00 on Thursday and Friday. Exhibits on space, communication and other technologies at the Ontario Service Center, open daily 10:00–18:00. The Marine Museum of Upper Canada. Fort York. Casa Loma Castle. The 19th century MacKenzie House, home of Toronto's first mayor. McLaughlin Planetarium. Black Creek Pioneer Village.

The Ontario Place recreation complex, at the waterfront. The fine paintings at the Art Gallery of Ontario (Monet, Degas, Gainsborough, Renoir, Picasso), more than 100 sculptures and 500 prints by Henry Moore, and a cross-section of 17th-20th century Canadian art. It is open Tuesday–Sunday at 11:00, closing at 17:30 on Tuesday, Friday, Saturday and Sunday, and at 21:00 on Wednesday and Thursday.

The Hockey Museum. Ride the special train through the 710-acre Metro Zoo for a view of the 4,000 animals exhibited there. Take a one-hour tour (beginning 10:00 most days) of the gigantic Skydome baseball park.

Board a ferry behind the Harbour Castle Hilton, at the foot of Bay Street, for a 10-minute ride to the Toronto Islands, a small archipelago of 19th century resorts that are now public parks. The most popular is a 612-acre complex of amusement rides, bike paths, parks, beaches and lagooons.

Go on one of the boats that tour the harbor, departing from next to the Hilton Hotel. Some of these have dinner-dancing cruises.

Vancouver

See: The Zoo and the killer whales in 1,000-acre Stanley Park. The view while walking across Capilano Suspension Bridge. The exhibit of the history of British Columbia from the ice age to today, at the Centennial Museum. The Shakespearean Gardens. Nitobe Gardens. Chinatown. The bazaar of saris, spices and sweets, glass bangles and gold jewelry in Little India, at the end of Main Street.

On the waterfront near the 1100 block of Chestnut Street: the Vancouver Museum, the Maritime Museum and the shows presented in the MacMillan Planetarium. One of the world's finest collections of Northwest Coast Indian art in the Museum of Anthropology at the University of British Columbia.

Halifax - Montreal 27

These trains require reservation are air-conditioned, carry sleeping cars, have ordinary coaches and a restaurant car, and start both journeys daily, except Tuesday. Arrive day 2.

Dep. Halifax	13:00	Dep. Montreal (Cen.)	18:45
Dep. Truro	14:25	Set watch forward 2 hours.	
Dep. Moncton	18:05	Dep. Moncton	11:40
Set watch back 2 hours.		Dep. Truro	14:45
Arr. Montreal (Cen.)	08:35	Arr. Halifax	16:15

Moncton - Saint John 27

Both of these trains require reservation, are air-conditioned, and have both ordinary coaches and a restaurant car.

Dep. Moncton	18:05 (1)	Dep. Saint John	09:30 (2)
Arr. Saint John	19:55	Arr. Moncton	11:20

(1) Runs monday, Thursday and Saturday. (2) Runs Tuesday, Friday and Sunday.

Montreal - Ottawa 22

All of these trains are air-conditioned and have buffet or light refreshments.

| Dep. Montreal (Cen.) | 07:20 (1) | 09:30 (2) | 13:05 (3) | 16:30 (4+6) |
| Arr. Ottawa (Union) | 09:29 | 11:32 | 15:22 | 18:40 |

Sights in **Ottawa**: See notes about Ottawa on page 669.

| Dep. Ottawa (Union) | 07:05 (1) | 08:50 (2) | 14:45 (3) | 17:10 (3+7) |
| Arr. Montreal (Cen.) | 09:14 | 10:50 | 16:52 | 19:15 |

(1) Runs Monday–Friday, except holidays. (2) Runs Saturdays, Sundays and holidays. (3) Runs daily. (4) Runs Sundays and holidays only. (5) Runs daily except Sundays and holidays. (6) Plus other departures from Montreal at 17:50 (5) and 19:40 (4), arriving Ottawa 19:49 and 21:58. (7) Plus another departure from Ottawa at 19:20 (4), arriving Montreal 21:50.

RAIL ROUTES FROM TORONTO

Toronto - Brantford - Toronto 18

All of these trains are air-conditioned and have buffet or light refreshments.

| Dep. Toronto (Union) | 09:05 | 13:00 | 16:30 | 17:15 (4) |
| Arr. Brantford | 10:14 | 14:12 | 17:38 | 18:19 |

Sights in **Brantford:** The home of Alexander Graham Bell, with the world's first telephone business office. The history of Brant County, from Paleo-Indian culture to the days of the Six Nations Indians and Canadian pioneers, in the Brant Historical Museum. The exhibit of Woodland Indian artifacts at the Wood and Indian Museum.

| Dep. Brantford | 10:49 (1) | 12:49 (2) | 14:27 (3) | 17:26 (5) |
| Arr. Toronto (Union) | 12:15 | 14:20 | 16:00 | 18:50 |

(1) Runs Saturday, Sunday and holidays. (2) Runs Monday–Friday except holidays. (3) Runs Monday, Friday and Sunday. (4) Plus another departure from Toronto at 19:00, arriving Brantford 20:05. (5) Plus another departure from Brantford at 20:27, arriving Toronto 21:50.

Toronto - Montreal 23

All of these trains require reservation, are air-conditioned and have buffet, unless designated otherwise.

| Dep. Toronto (Union) | 07:35 (1) | 11:10 | 12:40 | 15:45 (3) |
| Arr. Montreal (Cen.) | 12:30 | 16:45 | 17:25 | 20:15 |

*   *   *

| Dep. Montreal (Cen.) | 07:35 (1) | 10:25 | 12:25 | 15:45 (4) |
| Arr. Toronto (Union) | 12:20 | 16:00 | 17:10 | 20:15 |

(1) Runs daily, except Sundays and holidays. (2) Runs Friday and Sunday. (3) Plus other departures from Toronto at 16:50 and 18:10 (2), arriving Montreal 22:15 and 23;15. (4) Plus other departures from Montreal at 17:05 and 18:15 (2), arriving Toronto 22:25 and 23:20.

Toronto - Ottawa 23

All of these trains are air-conditioned and have buffet.

| Dep. Toronto (Union) | 08:10 (1) | 12:00 (2) | 17:30 (3) |
| Arr. Ottawa (Union) | 12:19 | 16:25 | 21:29 |

*   *   *

| Dep. Ottawa (Union) | 07:30 (1) | 12:25 (2) | 17:00 (3) |
| Arr. Toronto (Union) | 12:10 | 16:50 | 20:59 |

(1) Reservation required. Runs daily, except Sundays and holidays. (2) Runs daily.
(3) Reservation required. Runs daily.

Toronto - Winnipeg - Saskatoon - Edmonton - Vancouver 1 + 5

The spectacular scenery of 3 mountain ranges (Rockies, Selkirks and Coast), many ancient glaciers, large lakes and waterfalls attracts many tourists to this route.

Both of these trains require reservation, are air-conditioned, carry sleeping cars, ordinary coaches, a domecar and a restaurant car. An Amtrak bus provides transfer between the Vancouver and Seattle railstations. See page 718.

Dep. Toronto (Union)	23:30 (1)	Dep. Vancouver	21:30 (5)
Dep. Winnipeg	12:15 (2)	Set watch forward one hour.	
Dep. Saskatoon	22:35	Arr. Edmonton	23:00 (6)
Set watch back one hour.		Dep. Edmonton	23:45
Arr. Edmonton	06:30 (3)	Set watch forward one hour.	
Dep. Edmonton	08:00	Dep. Saskatoon	07:00 (7)
Set watch back one hour.		Arr. Winnipeg	18:00
Arr. Vancouver	08:00 (4)	Arr. Toronto (Union)	07:30 (8)

(1) Runs Tuesday, Thursday and Saturday. (2) Day 3 from Toronto: Thursday, Saturday and Monday. (3) Day 4 from Toronto: Friday, Sunday and Tuesday. (4) Day 5 from Toronto: Saturday, Monday and Wednesday. (5) Runs Monday, Thursday and Saturday. (6) Day 2 from Vancouver: Tuesday, Friday and Sunday. (7) Day 3 from Vancouver: Wednesday, Saturday and Monday. (8) Day 5 from Vancouver: Friday, Monday and Wednesday.

NORTHERN CANADIAN RAIL ROUTES

In addition to train service in Nova Scotia, to be covered later in this section, there are 12 rail routes on the mainland extending north from Canada's transcontinental lines.

Sept Iles - Schefferville 26

Indians are charged lower fares on these trains.

Both of these trains have light refreshments.

Dep. Sept Iles	08:00 (1)	Dep. Schefferville	08:00 (2)
Arr. Schefferville	19:15	Arr. Sept Iles	19:15

(1) Runs Thursday only. (2) Runs Friday only.

Montreal - Quebec City 28

All of these trains are air-conditioned and have buffet, unless designated otherwise.

Dep. Montreal (Cen.)	07:15 (1)	13:00	17:55 (2)
Arr. Quebec (Palais)	10:20	16:10	21:05

* * *

Dep. Quebec (Palais)	06:45 (3)	08:00 (4)	11:50	17:45 (2)
Arr. Montreal (Cen.)	09:55	11:10	15:00	21:10

(1) Runs daily. Buffet Monday–Friday. Light refreshments Saturdays, Sundays and holidays. (2) Runs daily. Buffet Sunday–Friday. Light refreshments on Saturday. (3) Runs Monday–Friday, except holidays. (4) Runs Saturdays, Sundays and holidays.

Montreal - Hervey - Jonquiere 24

These trains are air-conditioned and have light refreshments.

Dep. Montreal (Cen.)	14:15 (1)	Dep. Jonquiere	11:05 (2)	13:25 (3)
Dep. Hervey	17:25	Dep. Hervey	16:50	19:15
Arr. Jonquiere	23:10	Arr. Montreal (Cen.)	20:05	22:25

(1) Runs Monday, Wednesday and Friday. (2) Runs Tuesday and Thursday. (3) Runs Sunday only.

674

Montreal - Hervey - Senneterre - Tascheau - Cochrane 24

All of these trains are air-conditioned.

Dep. Montreal (Cent.)	18:30 (1+2)	20:30 (1+5)
Dep. Hervey	21:59	23:59
Arr. Senneterre (3)	08:30	10:30
Change trains.		
Dep. Senneterre	09:05 (4)	11:05 (6)
Arr. Taschereau	11:07	13:02
Arr. Cochrane	-0-	16:40

* * *

Dep. Cochrane	10:55 (7)	-0-
Dep. Taschereau	14:20	19:15 (4)
Arr. Senneterre	16:30	21:25
Change trains.		
Dep. Senneterre	17:20 (1+7)	22:15 (1+4)
Dep. Hervey (3)	03:02 (8)	07:57 (9)
Arr. Montreal (Cent.)	06:20	11:15

(1) Carries a sleeping car and a coach. Light refreshments.   (2) Runs Monday and Wednesday. (3) Day 2. (4) Runs Tuesday and Thursday. (5) Runs Friday only. (6) Runs Saturday only. (7) Runs Sunday only. (8) Runs Monday only. (9) Runs Wednesday and Friday.

Toronto - North Bay - Cochrane - Moosonee Ontario Northland Rly. Timetable

"Polar Bear Express" makes one-day excursion roundtrips into the Canadian wilderness daily except Friday, from late June to early September, to **Moosonee**, a trading post since 1673.

For 1992 prices and overnight hotel reservations (Polar Bear Lodge or Moosonee Lodge), contact Ontario Northland Railway, 65 Front Street West, Toronto, Ontario, Canada M5J 1E6.

The prices at the end of 1991 were: $42 (Can.) for passengers 12 and older, $21 for children 5–11, free for children under 5. The Senior Discount (65 and older) was 50%. A Family Price (covering mother, father and all dependent children under age 22) was $104.

It is very, very important to bring insect repellent.

Before reserving train tickets, be sure to first have a room reservation in Moosonee at either Polar Bear Lodge or Moosonee Lodge.

All of these trains are air-conditioned.

Dep. Toronto (Union)	12:00 (1)		Dep. Moosonee	09:00 (4)	17:15 (2)
Dep. North Bay (C.N.)	17:00		Arr. Cochrane	14:30	21:20
Arr Cochrane	22:00		Change trains.		
Change trains.			Dep. Cochrane		08:50 (1)
Dep. Cochrane	08:30 (2)	10:10 (3)	Arr. North Bay (C.N.)		13:50
Arr. Moosonee	12:50	15:45	Arr. Toronto (Union)		18:35

(1) Reservation required. Runs daily except Saturday. Restaurant car. (2) "Polar Bear Express". Reservation required. Operates late June to early September. Runs daily except Friday. Restaurant car. (3) Operates late June to early September. Runs Tuesday and Thursday. Has buffet. (4) Operates late June to early September. Runs Wednesday only. Has buffet.

Sault Ste. Marie - Hearst 13

The marvelous scenery on the one-day (08:00–17:00) Agawa Canyon sightseeing excursion train operated by Algoma Central Railway. Fall foliage is particularly outstanding, attracting up to 1,500 people daily. About 86,000 passengers make the ride during the late May to mid-October operation. The views of the Montreal River from a 130-foot high and 1,550-foot long bridge and of hundreds of lakes are some of the interesting sights on this ride.

Comments are broadcast on the train's public address system. Before making the return ride to Sault Ste. Marie, passengers have time to climb to lookout points above the canyon and walk into the canyon. Hot lunches are sold on the train. The Canadian meat pie and strawberry shortcake are favorites.

All of these trains are air-conditioned.

Dep. Sault Ste. Marie	08:30 (1)	09:30 (2)
Dep. Eton	12:29	13:50
Arr. Hearst	17:50	19:15

*　*　*

Dep. Hearst	07:15 (1)	08:15 (2)
Dep. Eton	12:29	13:50
Arr. Sault Ste. Marie	16:30	18:10

(1) Operates mid-October to late May. *From Sault*—Runs Friday, Saturday and Sunday. *From Hearst*—Runs Saturday, Sunday and Monday. From early January to late March, a restaurant car is carried Saturday and Sunday from Sault to Eton and v.v. (2) Operates late May to mid-October. *From Sault*—Runs daily except Monday. *From Hearst*—Runs daily except Tuesday. A restaurant car is carried Wednesday–Sunday from Sault to Eton and v.v.

Winnipeg - Hudson Bay - Churchill 10

This is a mind-boggling train trip, 1,055 miles from Winnipeg to the chilly, distant Churchill. Check VIA Rail Canada for a possible escorted 6-day "Hudson Bay Explorer Tour", a package that provides 2 nights in Churchill and includes rail fare, berth, all meals, and a tour of the surrounding area plus a day trip to **Eskimo Point**, an Inuit community.

These trains require reservation, carry sleeping cars and a restaurant car, and are air-conditioned.

Dep. Winnipeg (C.N.)	21:55(1)		Dep. Churchill	21:00 (2)	
Dep. Dauphin	01:50	Day 2	Dep. Gillam	05:10	Day 2
Dep. Hudson Bay	06:40		Dep. Thompson	11:40	
Arr. The Pas	09:35		Arr. The Pas	19:05	
Dep. The Pas	10:50		Dep. The Pas	20:20	
Dep. Thompson	19:20		Dep. Hudson Bay	21:25	
Dep. Gillam	01:25	Day 3	Dep. Dauphin	04:20	Day 3
Arr. Churchill	08:20		Arr. Winnipeg (C.N.)	08:00	

(1) Runs Tuesday, Thursday and Sunday. (2) Runs, Tuesday, Thursday and Saturday.

Sights in **Churchill:** This is the only town in the world that is located on a polar bear migratory route. They can be seen here during September and October. Seals can be viewed here May-June and white beluga whales from mid-June to mid-September.

The grain elevator in Churchill fills ships from all over the world. See the restored 18th century stone Fort Prince of Wales, built by the Hudson's Bay Company over a 40-year period. The Eskimo Museum. Indian (Inuit) carvings are sold in several craft stores here.

Extended daylight in late June and early July (20 hours long) brings a great number of bird species to this area. Over 125 species breed here.

Arrangements to tour outlying areas by van or small bus can be made after arriving in Churchill. Boat trips are offered for spotting whales. There are flights to **Eskimo Point**, an Inuit settlement, where visitors can eat caribou and seal blubber as well as buy crafts.

Sights in **The Pas**: See notes under "Winnipeg - Lynn Lake" on page 677.

Sights in **Thompson**: The huge International Nickel Company mining complex.

Sights in **Flin Flon**: The beautiful scenery at **Beaver Lake**.

Hudson Bay - Prince Albert - Saskatoon - Regina Bus

When going west across Canada and detouring north to Churchill, it is not necessary to return to Winnipeg in order to rejoin the transcontinental line. One can return from Churchill to the cross-country train line on a different route than that taken to Churchill by changing to a bus at Hudson Bay and proceeding from there to Prince Albert, Saskatoon and Regina. The train from Prince Albert to Saskatoon was replaced by bus in 1982.

When going east across Canada, the detour to Churchill can start at Regina, and one can return from Churchill by continuing from Hudson Bay on to Winnipeg, rather than returning to Regina.

88				
Dep. Hudson Bay		05:45 (1)		
Arr. Prince Albert		10:25		
Change buses.				
Dep. Prince Albert	09:30	10:30	14:00	18:00
Arr. Saskatoon	12:25	12:45	15:50	19:55
Change buses. 99				
Dep. Saskatoon	08:00	13:30	17:30	20:00
Arr. Regina	10:55	16:30	20:25	22:55

* * *

Dep. Regina	08:00	13:30	17:30	19:30
Arr. Saskatoon	10:55	16:25	20:25	22:25
Change buses. 88				
Dep. Saskatoon	14:00	17:25	18:00	09:00
Arr. Prince Albert	15:50	20:40	20:05	10:55
Change buses.				
Dep. Prince Albert	19:30			
Arr. Hudson Bay	00:35			

(1)Runs daily. Departs 06:25 on Monday, Wednesday and Friday.

Saskatoon - Winnipeg 5

Both of these trains require reservation, are air-conditioned and carry a sleeping car and a restaurant car.

Dep. Saskatoon	07:00 (1)	Dep. Winnipeg	12:15 (2)
Arr. Winnipeg	18:00	Arr. Saskatoon	21:50

(1) Runs Tuesday, Thursday and Sunday. (2) Runs Monday, Thursday and Saturday.

Winnipeg - Hudson Bay - The Pas - Lynn Lake

Bring food with you on the rides from The Pas to Lynn Lake and v.v. These trains have *no* food service. The days in early April when we made the trip, the temperature was below zero Fahrenheit. The area north of Winnipeg was under 4 feet of snow.

10		12	
Dep. Winnipeg (C.N.)	21:55 (1+2)	Dep. Lynn Lake	07:30 (4)
Dep. Dauphin	01:50 (3)	Arr. The Pas	17:35
Dep. Hudson Bay	06:40 (3)	Change trains. #10	
Arr. The Pas	09:35 (3)	Dep. The Pas	20:20 (1+5)
Change trains. #12		Dep. Hudson Bay	21:25
Dep. The Pas	11:00 (3)	Dep. Dauphin	04:20 (6)
Arr. Lynn Lake	21:15	Arr. Winnipeg (C.N.)	08:00

(1) Reservation required. Air-conditioned train. Carries a sleeping car and a restaurant car. (2) Runs Tuesday, Thursday and Sunday. (3) Runs Wednesday, Friday and Monday. Day 2 from Winnipeg. (4) Runs Tuesday, Thursday and Saturday. Requires staying overnight in The Pas before taking the train the next day to Hudson Bay. (5) Runs Wednesday, Friday and Sunday. Day 2 from Lynn Lake. (6) Runs Thursday, Saturday and Monday. Day 3 from Lynn Lake.

Sights in **The Pas:** The hand-carved pews and the Ten Commandments in the Cree Indian language. The Museum. The Cathedral of Our Lady of the Sacred Heart.

The Pas, and most of the land north of it, is a massive reservation for Indians, a few of whom trap for furs.

The train from The Pas to Lynn Lake will stop at any point to let passengers board or get off. On our ride, it stopped in a completely deserted area so that a very old Indian man whose house could be seen on a hill a mile away from the track could get off. As the train started, we could see him beginning his long walk from the track to his house, on the other side of a frozen lake.

Our train for the 233-mile ride from The Pass to Lynn Lake was 23 freight cars, 2 passenger cars and a caboose, hauled by 4 locomotives. Only a few of the seats were filled, mostly by Indians.

The track goes alongside more than 20 very large lakes after the 12:35 departure from Cranberry Portage, and nearly all of this route is heavily forested. Much ore is transported out of here in open gondola freight cars.

Some cabins of fur trappers are only a few feet from the rail track.In Winter, you can also see the snowmobile paths leading from the train track into the forest, to trapper cabins located away from the rail line.

From October to May, while there is snow on the ground, tracks of moose, deer, lynx, foxes and rabbits can be seen for hundreds of miles, only a few feet from the railway track.

In June, July and August, the splendid fishing and wilderness camping in the **Lynn Lake** area attract many tourists. It is possible to camp and hike only a short distance from either the rail track or from the well-traveled highway running between Lynn Lake and **Pukatawagan**.

Edmonton - Jasper - Prince George - Prince Rupert 5

There is very beautiful scenery between **Burns Lake** and Prince Rupert.

All of these trains require reservation, carry air-conditioned sleeping cars and coaches, and have a restaurant car.

Dep. Edmonton	08:00 (1)	
Arr. Jasper	14:50	
Change trains.		
Dep. Jasper	18:10 (2)	20:10 (4)
Arr. Prince George	00:30 (3)	02:30 (3)
Dep. Prince George	01:00	03:00
Arr. Prince Rupert	14:00	15:45

Dep. Prince Rupert	10:30 (5)	11:30 (7)
Arr. Prince George	23:30	00:20
Dep. Prince George	23:59	00:50 (6)
Arr. Jasper	08:15 (6)	09:00
Change trains		
Dep. Jasper	17:35 (1)	
Arr. Edmonton	23:00	

(1) Runs Tuesday, Friday and Sunday. (2) Operates early May to early June. Runs Tuesday, Friday and Sunday. (3) Day 2 from Jasper. (4) Early June to late September: runs Monday, Wednesday and Friday. Late September to early June: runs Tuesday, Friday and Sunday. (5) Operates early May to early June. Runs Monday, Thursday and Saturday. (6) Day 2 from Prince Rupert. (7) Early June to late September: runs Tuesday, Wednesday and Friday. Late September to early June: runs Monday, Thursday and Saturday.

Sights in **Prince Rupert**: This area has many fjords, mountains and islands. Prince Rupert, the world's third largest natural harbor, is on **Kaien Island**. The rail line here from Prince George required 10,000,000 pounds of dynamite.

See 10,000 years of history (a flourishing Tsimshian society lived here 4,000 years ago) exhibited at the Museum of Northern British Columbia. The totems and flower gardens in Service Park. Take a gondola ride to the top of Mt. Hays. Go on a sightseeing cruise around the harbor and to the **Charlotte Islands**, or a sightseeing flight on an amphibious airplane.

Vancouver - Whistler - Lillooet - Prince George BC Timetable

This is one of the most scenic rail trips in Canada. The train travels north along the fjord-like coast of Howe Sound before climbing alongside the massive rock cliffs and rushing whitewater of the steep and heavily-timbered Cheakamus Canyon to **Alta Lake**. After stopping at the resort village of **Whistler**, the route continues to **Pemberton**, where snow-capped mountains stand above the lush forests and farmland of the Pemberton Valley. From here, the track negotiates a narrow path. The waters of Anderson and Seton Lakes are on one side, towering rock walls on the other side. Then, the track drops down into the historic gold-rush town of **Lillooet** in the Fraser River Valley.

In the Fall, this route offers red, yellow and green foliage. In the Spring, there is a profusion of flowering trees and shrubs. From Lillooet, the rail route heads north along Fraser Canyon and provides marvelous vistas while climbing toward the Cariboo Plateau, where the landscape is green forests and rolling ranchland.

"Cariboo Class" is deluxe service available for traveling to and from Prince George. It includes spacious seating and full meal service. Coach passengers may purchase light snacks to eat at their seat. Both "Cariboo Class" and coach seats requires advance reservation. Reservation is not required for coach seat passengers not going north of Lillooet. The 1992 "Cariboo Class" prices in Canadian dollars are: $206.00 for adults, $164.50 for seniors (60 and over), $144.00 children 2-11 and $111.00 children under 2. For Coach-class: $133.50, $100.50, $66.50, $33.00 and Free.

Whistler and Lillooet are popular for a day-trip from North Vancouver. Getting off in Whistler allows 8 hours for golfing on a championship course, windsurfing on **Alta Lake**, hiking on good trails, or simply exploring the village. A package available in Summer months includes a gondola ride to the top of a montain, lunch at the peak, and touring the valley in the afternoon.

Those wanting a longer train ride can go to Lillooet, stop there for 2 hours, leisurely tour the Museum's exhibits of relics from early prospecting days, re-board and be back in North Vancouver at day's end.

For reservations, write to: BC RAIL Passenger Services, P.O. Box 8770, Vancouver, B.C. V6B 4X6, Canada. Or, phone (604) 631-3500.

Or you can use the following schedule on your own.

Both of these trains are air-conditioned.

Dep. North			Dep. Prince	
Vancouver	07:00 (1)	07:30 (2)	George (BCR)	07:00 (3)
Arr. Whistler	09:34	10:04	Dep. Lillooet	15:20
Arr. Lillooet	12:30	13:00	Dep. Whistler	18:10
Arr. Prince			Arr. North	
George (BCR)	20:30	21:00	Vancouver	20:35

(1) Operates mid-September to late June. Runs daily North Vancouver-Lillooet. Runs Wednesday, Friday and Sunday Lillooet-Prince George. (2) Operates late June to mid-September. Runs daily North Vancouver-Prince George. (3) Mid-September to late June: runs Monday, Thursday and Saturday Prince George-Lillooet. Runs daily Lillooet-North Vancouver. Late June to mid-September: runs daily Prince George-North Vancouver.

THE ROUTES OF THE "ROCKY MOUNTAINEER"

Great Canadian Railtour Company Ltd. operates 2–day train journeys over more than 600 miles of fantastic Canadian Rockies scenery late May to early October In order to not miss any of the scenery, passengers travel in the company's private railcars during daylight and stay overnight in Kamloops.

The company's passenger cars are fitted with reclining seats, tray tables, pictures windows and a non-smoking environment. Smoking is permitted only in designated areas.

Breakfast and lunch both days (and a dinner on the eastbound Banff-Calgary ride) are served to passengers at their seats, with emphasis on such famous Canadian food as British Columbia salmon and Alberta beef.

The Vancouver-Kamloops route goes through the beautiful Fraser Valley and along the Fraser and Thompson rivers and Kamloops Lake.

There is a choice of 2 different routes to and from Kamloops.

The first of these (Kamloops-Jasper) goes across the rolling plateaus of the North Thompson River and offers views of the Gate of Hell Canyon, the snowy peaks of the Monashee Mountains, Pyramid Falls cascading 300 feet down Mount Cheadle, the glaciers of the Albreda Icefield, the highest mountain in the Canadian Rockies (12,972–feet–high Mount Robson), and the sparkling waters of Moose Lake and Yellowhead Lake.

It is only 4 hours by bus or car from Jasper to Edmonton.

The second route (Kamloops-Banff-Calgary) has scenery of the ranchland of the South Thompson River Valley, shining Shuswap Lake, the towering peaks and glistening glaciers of Glacier National Park, the "Spiral Tunnels" that go through Cathedral Mountain and Mount Ogden, Yoho National Park, the green Bow River, and the "Stampede" city of Calgary.

The 2 eastbound routes:

Dep. Vancouver	07:45		Dep. Vancouver	07:45
Arr. Kamloops	17:05		Arr. Kamloops	17:05
Overnight in Kamloops.			Overnight in Kamloops.	
Dep. Kamloops	08:00		Dep. Kamloops	07:30
Set your watch			Set your watch	
forward one hour.			forward one hour.	
Arr. Jasper	17:55		Arr. Banff	18:45
			Arr. Calgary	21:00

The 2 westbound routes:

Dep. Calgary	07:00		Dep. Jasper	09:00
Dep. Banff	09:20		Set your watch	
Set your watch			forward one hour.	
forward one hour.			Arr. Kamloops	16:55
Arr. Kamloops	18:20		Overnight in Kamloops.	
Overnight in Kamloops.				
Dep. Kamloops	07:30		Dep. Kamloops	07:30
Arr. Vancouver	16:55		Arr. Vancouver	16:55

"Rocky Mountaineer" tour includes assigned train seating, breakfast and lunch both days, a light dinner eastbound Banff-Calgary, complimentary snacks and non-alcoholic beverages, one night of hotel accommodation (including room tax) in Kamloops, roundtrip bus transfers in Kamloops train–hotel and hotel–train, and an information package.

For 2 weeks in Spring and 2 weeks in Fall, the tour operates only its Vancouver-Banff-Calgary route (with a discount of about 15% from the price during its 16–week

"Regular Season") on these 1992 departure dates from Vancouver: May 24 and 28; June 2; September 27; and October 1 and 6.

From Calgary: June 9, 14, 18, 23 and 28; July 2, 7, 12, 16, 21, 26 and 30; August 4, 9, 13, 18, 23 and 27; and September 1, 6, 10, 15, 20 and 24.

During its 16–week "Regular Season", the company operates both the Vancouver-Jasper and the Vancouver-Banff-Calgary routes on these 1992 departures from Vancouver: June 7, 11, 16, 21, 25 and 30; July 5, 9, 14, 19, 23 and 28; August 2, 6, 11, 16, 20, 25 and 30; and September 3, 8, 13, 17 and 23.

From Calgary: June 9, 14, 18, 23 and 28; July 2, 7, 12, 16, 21, 26 and 30; August 4, 9, 13, 18, 23 and 27; and September 1, 6, 10, 15, 20 and 24.

For prices, brochures and any information, contact Great Canadian Railtour Company Ltd., Dept. "E", Suite 104, 340 Brooksbank Ave., North Vancouver, B.C., Canada V7J 2C1. Telephone (U.S.A. and Canada, except Vancouver): (800) 665-7245. From Vancouver: (604) 278-7757. Fax: (604) 669-6192.

Halifax - Truro - Sydney Bus 132

The route north from Halifax connects in North Sydney with the ferry service to Port aux Basques, Newfoundland. (Table 51)

Dep. Halifax	08:00	09:10 (1)	13:30	18:00 (1)
Dep. No. Sydney	-0-	16:11	20:21	23:55
Arr. Sydney	15:50	16:45	20:45	00:05

Sights in **Halifax**: Tours by double-decker buses and 2-hour cruises are available. Also free guided walking tours.

See the Old Town Clock that was installed in 1803 by the Duke of Kent (son of George III, and later the father of Queen Victoria). A harsh military leader, he severely punished soldiers under his rule who were late in starting a duty assignment by flogging and hanging. When his men protested that they could not know the time because they did not have watches, he gave them this 4-faced clock on Citadel Hill. It can be seen from everywhere in Halifax.

Visit the exhibits of marine objects from the eras of sail and steam, at the Maritime Museum on Water Street. It is a short walk from there to the restaurants and craft shops at Historic Properties, a compound of restored 18th century buildings on the waterfront.

See the formal Victorian gardens on Spring Garden Road, called Public Gardens.

Dep. Sydney	08:00 (1)	12:00	14:15	18:00 (1)
Dep. No. Sydney	08:25	-0-	-0-	18:25
Arr. Halifax	15:15	17:30	21:50	00:10

(1) Runs daily except Saturday.

BUS SERVICE IN NEWFOUNDLAND

Here is the daily cross-island bus service, connecting with the arrival of the ferry from Nova Scotia, and its return trip.

Port aux Basques - St. John's Bus 142

Dep. Port aux Basques	08:00	Dep. St. John's	08:00
Dep. Gander Airport	17:45	Dep. Gander Airport	13:10
Arr. St. John's	22:30	Arr. Port aux Basques	22:55

SPECIAL CANADIAN TRAIN EXCURSIONS

North Vancouver - Squamish - North Vancouver 4

This is an easy one-day roundtrip (27 miles each way), featuring a steam locomotive tour of scenic Howe Sound. Scenery on this trip includes forests, waterfalls and the seacoast. **Squamish** is a logging town. Visitors can shop there for Indian arts and crafts and see the 1,000-foot cascade of **Shannon Falls**, logging and sports shows, musical performances and sidewalk markets. There is an optional tour by airplane of the nearby glacier and an optional bus tour of the area.

A combination train-and-boat one-day excursion has been operated since 1982 by Harbour Ferries, #1 North Foot of Denman Street, Vancouver B.C. V6G 2W9, Canada. Their phone is (800) 663-1500. Operates from late May to late September Wednesday–Sunday.

Passengers have the option of either going from Vancouver to Squamish by Royal Hudson Steam Train and returning to Vancouver by luxury ferry (10:00–16:30) or the reverse (09:30–16:00).

For the do-it-yourself train-only roundtrip, a bus departs from the downtown Vancouver bus depot at 09:00, making several stops on the way to the excursion train (front of the Hudson Bay Department Store, front of The Royal Bank, etc.). Look for the bus that displays a sign reading "Train Connection".

Here are the schedules for the ordinary train service that operates late June to early September and runs daily, except Monday and Tuesday.

Dep. North Vancouver	08:00	Dep. Squamish	19:39
Arr. Squamish	09:10	Arr. North Vancouver	21:00

Victoria - Courtenay - Victoria 3

Good views of Vancouver Island scenery as this line winds along sheer cliffs high above Finlayson Arm, en route to Malahat Summit. There are spectacular vistas from many high trestles before the train begins its descent along Shawnigan Lake, en route to **Nanaimo**.

The station 13 minutes before arriving **Courtenay** is **Union Bay.** Many prefer to get off the train there in order to have a more leisurely lunch than is possible when going all the way to Courtenay.

A 2-day circle-trip can be made by taking the bus ferry Vancouver-Victoria (with a night in Victoria), and then the next day the Victoria-Nanaimo train and the Nanaimo- Vancouver ferry.

Dep. Victoria	08:15	Dep. Courtenay	13:15
Arr. Courtenay	12:50	Arr. Victoria	17:45

Toronto - Niagara Falls - Toronto 18

All of these trains are air-conditioned.

Dep. Toronto (Union)	09:30 (1)	17:40	
Arr. Niagara Falls (Canada)	11:30	19:40	
	*	*	*
Dep. Niagara Falls (Canada)	06:30 (2)	07:50 (3)	18:25 (1)
Arr. Toronto (Union)	08:25	09:45	20:25

(1) Buffet. (2) Runs Monday–Friday, except holidays. (3) Runs Saturdays, Sundays and holidays.

INTERNATIONAL ROUTES FROM CANADA

The gateways for travel from Canada to the United States are: Montreal (to Boston, New York and south along the eastern U.S. seaboard), Toronto (to Buffalo and on to New York City or Cleveland, or to Detroit and on to Chicago), and Vancouver (to Seattle).

Montreal - New York City 210

Both of these trains are air-conditioned and have a buffet car..

Dep. Montreal (Cen.)	10:00	Dep. New York (Penn)	10:45
Arr. New York (Penn)	20:03	Arr. Montreal	20:45

Toronto - Niagara Falls - Buffalo - New York (or Cleveland and Chicago)

18		186	
Dep. Toronto (Union)	09:30 (1)	Dep. Buffalo (Depew)	03:56 (2)
Dep Niagara Falls (Can.)	11:30	Arr. Cleveland	
Dep. Niagara Falls (U.S.A.)	12:45	(Lakefront)	07:01
Arr. Buffalo (Depew)	13:32	Arr. Toledo	09:14
Arr. New York (Penn)	21:18	Arr. Chicago (Union)	13:03

(1) Air-conditioned train. Buffet. (2) Reservation required. Carries sleeping car. Also has Slumbercoach and coach cars. Restaurant car.

Toronto - Windsor - Detroit 18

Take a taxi from Windsor to Detroit through the International Tunnel.

All of these trains are air-conditioned.

Dep. Toronto (Union)	09:05 (1)	13:00 (1)	16:30 (1)	17:15 (2)	19:00 (3)
Arr. Windsor	13:35	17:25	20:55	21:30	23:35

(1) Light refreshments daily. Buffet daily, except Saturday. (2) Runs Thursdays, Sundays and holidays. Buffet. (3) Runs daily. Buffet.

Vancouver - Seattle Bus 580

In 1981, this train service was replaced by bus transportation for connection between the Montreal-Vancouver train and the Seattle-Los Angeles train.

Dep. Vancouver	07:00	08:00	09:15	11:00	13:30	15:00	20:30
Arr. Seattle	10:30	11:30	13:30	15:30	17:00	18:15	00:30

MEXICO

Children under 5 travel free when accompanied by a parent. Half-fare for children 5–11. Children 12 and over must pay full fare.

There are 4 classes of service: Star (exceptional first-class only), Special First-Class, first-class and second-class.

Mexico's passenger trains are operated by Ferrocarriles Nacionales de Mexico (NdeM).

Its routes along the U.S. border originate from Juarez (El Paso), Piedras Negras, Mexicali (Calexico), Nogales, Nuevo Laredo (Laredo), and Matamoros (Brownsville), all of these providing service to Mexico City. Other N de M gateways to Mexico City are Tampico, Veracruz, Coatzacoalos, Oaxaca, Uruapan, Durango, Manzanillo and Guadalajara.

All Mexican railway schedules use the same time as U.S. Central Standard Time (same as Chicago).

Several U.S. and Mexican tour operators offer escorted private train tours of Mexico. Check your travel agent for details. Because Mexican railways do not pay travel agents a commission, an agent who assists you in obtaining train reservations is entitled to a fee of 15% of the ticket price. *Advance reservations are advisable.*

Mexico City

Largest population of any city in the world: more than 20,000,000. Its altitude of 7,350 feet (2,240 meters) limits activity for many tourists. Cool and dry weather except during the May-September rainy season.

Railways link Mexico City with 5 Gulf of Mexico seaports (Matamoros, Tampico, Veracruz, Coatzacoalcos and Campeche) and 4 Pacific ports (Los Mochis, Mazatlan, Manzanillo and Ciudad Hidalgo).

Most museums here are open daily except Monday 10:00–17:00. See the Diego Rivera murals that depict the course of Mexican history from the time of the Aztecs to the 1917 Mexican Revolution, at the National Palace on the main square, Plaza Mayor (also called "Zocalo"). Also, dozens of lovely Rivera frescoes can be seen at the Ministry of Education (30 Avenida Brasil).

See the extraordinary Aztec treasures at Museo del Templo Mayor (Great Temple), at 1 Avenida Argentina.

A wealthy German immigrant acquired 9,000 craftworks and art from the 16th century: ceramics, timepieces, furniture, gold and silver objects, and textiles. The best of these are displayed at Museo Franz Mayer (45 Avenida Hidalgo).

The art, sculpture, movies and scale models of ancient cities at the National Museum of Anthropology and History in the 1,500-acre Chapultepec Park (open 10:00–18:00) are the major attractions. You will see the results of more than 15,000 discovery sites, including the 167-ton statue of Tlatloc, the Aztec rain god, and a 30-ton Aztec calendar stone.

All the major Indian tribes of Mexico Maya, Toltec, Olmec and Aztec are represented at this fabulous museum (jewelry, paintings, furniture, sculpture). Guided tours are conducted in many languages, including English.

Also see the Museum of Modern Art, open 11:00–19:00. The 16th century Basilica de Guadalupe, most sacred shrine in Mexico. The mariachi bands in Plaza de Garibaldi. The daily markets, Centro de Abastos and San Juan. Window-shop the displays of silver jewelry on Juarez and Madero Streets. The shops in Zona Rosa. The textiles at the Londres Street Market. Visit the Cathedral, oldest and largest church in Latin America. The National Pawnshop (Monte de Piedad). Palacio Nacional. The Palace of Fine Arts. The good collection of European paintings at the School of Fine Arts. Plaza Mexico, the largest bullfighting ring in the world. Jai Alai at Fronton Mexico. The almost 1,000-acre Bosque de Chapultepec.

There are several splendid one-day excursions from Mexico City. It is only 40 miles to the pre-Aztec pyramids at **Teotihuacan**. Take the short ride to **Cuernavaca** and the Popocatepetl and Ixtaccihuati national parks. Do not miss seeing the floating gardens at **Xochimilco**.

Unless indicated otherwise, Mexico City departure and arrival times are for its Buenavista railstation.

U.S. RAIL GATEWAYS TO MEXICO
Brownsville-Matamoros or Laredo-Nuevo Laredo
to
Monterrey and Mexico City

Take a taxi from Brownsville, to Matamoros or from Laredo, to Nuevo Laredo.

	1023	1023	1003	1002
Dep. Matamoros	06:50	14:00 (2)	-0-	-0-
Dep. Nuevo Laredo	-0-	-0-	15:15 (1+3)	18:55 (3+4)
Arr. Monterrey	23:55	18:50	19:00 (3)	23:30 (3+4)
Change trains.				
Dep. Monterrey	19:50 (1)	19:50 (1)	19:50 (1+3)	00:01 (3+4)
Arr. Saltillo	-0-	-0-	-0-	02:35
Arr. Mexico City	10:00	10:00	10:00	19:00

* * *

	1002	1023	1003	1023
Dep. Mexico City	09:00 (3+4)	09:00 (5)	18:00 (1+3)	18:00 (1)
Dep. Saltillo	00:13 (3+4)	-0-	-0-	-0-
Arrive Monterrey	02:20 (3+4)	02:20	08:10 (3)	08:10
Change trains.				
Dep. Monterrey	02:50 (3+4)	06:00	08:30 (1+3)	08:40 (2)
Arr. Nuevo Laredo	07:20	-0-	12:15	-0-
Arr. Matamoros	-0-	13:05	-0-	13:30

(1) Star service. Air-conditioned train. Carries 1st-class sleeping car (with berths, roomettes and bedrooms) and Special First-Class coach. Restaurant car. (2) Star service. Reservation required. Has Special 1st-class air-conditioned coaches. Light Refreshments. (3) Direct train. No train change in Monterrey. (4) Reservation required. Has air-conditioned Special 1st-class coach Nuevo Laredo-Saltillo (and v.v.). Light refreshments. (5) Reservation required. Has air-conditioned 1st and 2nd-class coach cars. Light refreshments.

Sights in **Matamoros**: The cannon, walls and turrets of old Fort Mata, site of the Casa Mata Museum. The Cathedral. The leather, jewelry and souvenirs for sale in the city's 2 street markets. The handwork of Tamaulipas artisans on sale at the Arts and Crafts Center, near the International Bridge.

Sights in **Monterrey**: Founded in 1579. See the collection of rare books in Indian languages and more than 2,000 editions of Don Quixote in many languages at the regional museum in the 200-year-old El Obispado, originally a bishop's palace. The painting and sculpture gallery in the Casa de la Cultura arts center, formerly a railstation. Sunday bullfights and Mexican-style rodeos. Sampling free cerveza at the Carta Blanca brewery. The 18th century Cathedral in Plaza Zaragosa, where band concerts are performed. El Obispado (the Bishop's Palace), once occupied by Pancho Villa.

Nuevo Laredo - Monterrey - San Luis Potosi - Mexico City 1023

Many package tours of Mexico (transportation, hotels, sightseeing, entertainment and meals) start and end in Laredo. Check your travel agent for details. Several connections can be made from Monterrey.

Both of these trains are air-conditioned, carry a first-class sleeping car and a Special First-class coach.

Dep. N. Laredo	15:15 (1)	18:55 (2)	Dep. Mexico City	09:00 (2)	18:00 (1)
Arr. Monterrey	19:00	23:30	Dep. S. L. Potosi	17:38	00:11
Dep. Monterrey	19:50	00:01	Arr. Monterrey	02:20	08:10
Dep. S. L. Potosi	04:00	10:35	Dep. Monterrey	02:50	08:30
Arr. Mexico City	10:00	19:00	Arr. N. Laredo	07:20	12:15

(1) Star service [table 1003]. Restaurant car. (2) Reservation required [table 1002]. Light refreshments.

Monterrey - Torreon - Durango 1016

Dep. Monterrey	08:10	Dep. Durango	07:00
Arr. Torreon	14:42	Arr. Torreon	11:30
Dep. Torreon	15:12	Dep. Torreon	12:05
Arr. Durango	20:10	Arr. Monterrey	18:50

Sights in **Torreon**: Many wineries. The famous Willie's ice cream. Charcoal-broiled baby goat is a regional specialty here.

Sights in **Durango**: Very popular for hunting game (wolves, bears, deer, ducks). The 17th century Cathedral. The iron-water spring. The Government Palace. Sunday concerts in Plaza de Armas. The display of handblown glass, ceramics, textiles and sculpture at the Arts and Crafts School in Guardiana Park

San Luis Potosi - Tampico 1023

Between Cardenas and Valles, the track follows a small stream that widens into a rushing river. Watch to the left for the spectacular Micos Waterfall.

Both of these trains carry a Special First-class coach and have light refreshments.

Dep. San Luis Potosi	07:50	Dep. Tampico	06:30
Arr. Tampico	20:47	Arr. San Luis Potosi	20:14

Sights in **San Luis Potosi**: The frescoes at the modern railstation. The Cathedral. The ornate tower of San Agustin Church. The suspended glass boat and the beautiful white and blue tiled dome of San Francisco Church. The Capilla de Aranzazu in the museum behind San Francisco Church. The lovely altar and pulpit of Carmen Church, as well as its tiled dome.

Sights in **Tampico**: Great sea and river fishing here. **Playa de Miramar**, nearby, is a popular beach resort.

El Paso - Ciudad Juarez - Mexico City 1004 + 1016

Passengers transferring from or to Amtrak in El Paso have to make their own provision for crossing the border. There is taxi service. At Chihuahua, there is a connection for taking the "Copper Canyon Ride" to Los Mochis (see page 688). At Torreon, a feeder line runs to Durango. At Irapuato, there is a connection for Guadalajara and Guanajuato (see page 689).

Both of these "Star Service" trains require reservation, have an air-conditioned first-class sleeping car, Special First-class coach, and (Zacatecas–Mexico City and v.v.) a restaurant car.

Dep. Ciudad Juarez	22:00		Dep. Mexico City	20:00	
Arr. Chihuahua	03:15	Day 2	Dep. Irapuato	02:30	Day 2
Dep. Chihuahua	03:45		Dep. Zacatecas	09:50	
Arr. Torreon	12:00		Arr. Torreon	17:10	
Dep. Torreon	12:40		Dep. Torreon	17:45	
Dep. Zacatecas	20:25		Arr. Chihuahua	01:20	Day 3
Dep. Irapuato	03:45	Day 3	Dep. Chihuahua	01:45	
Arr. Mexico City	09:30		Arr. Ciudad Juarez	06:45	

Sights in **Ciudad Juarez:** The statues of Abraham Lincoln and Mexico's counterpart of him, Benito Juarez. Visit the Museum of Art and History in Juarez Cultural Center. Bullfights. Dog and thoroughbred horse racing.

Sights in **Chihuahua City**: Our favorite sight here is the museum at Quinta Gameros, an old private residence. Its decor and furnishings are extraordinary. Visit the dungeon of Miguel Hidalgo, Mexico's George Washington, at the beautiful Federal Palace. The colonial Cathedral, built from 1724 to 1826 because Indian wars interrupted its construction. Quinta Luz, Pancho Villa's home, now a museum about him and his exploits. The 18th century Chihuahua Aqueduct, completed in 1764. Some of its arches are 59 feet high.

The murals in Governor's Palace, depicting the history of Chihuahua. Plaza de la Constitucion. Tarahumara Indians in colorful costumes roaming the streets. Chihuahua dogs. Benito Juarez Palace. There is much hunting and fishing here.

Interesting side trips can be made to **Santa Eulalia,** oldest mining town in northern Mexico; **Aldama,** a picturesque town in the center of an important fruit producing area; **Camargo,** famed for its hot springs; and **La Boquilla Dam,** one of the largest artificial lakes in the world and a fisherman's paradise.

Sights in **Zacatecas:** It is over 8,000-feet-high here. See the images of St. Peter and St. Francis, made from hummingbird feathers, in the Church de Nuestra Senora Guadalupe, and the hundreds of paintings there as well as the Christ on the Cross made of corn-stalks and the porcelain Virgin Mary. The Church of Santo Domingo.

The Temple of San Augustin. The ancient aqueduct. The outstanding wrought-iron in Pension Tacuba. The thousands of carved figures and designs on the main facade of the marvelous Cathedral. You can visit the tremendous El Bote Silver Mine by obtaining a permit and guide at the Tourist Office. Also, it is only a 30-mile drive south to **La Quemada** to see the prehistoric **Chicomoztoc Ruins**.

Torreon - Durango

These are the schedules for making a detour from Torreon to Durango, en route from Ciudad Juarez to Mexico City.

1004 + 1016			1015		
Dep. Ciudad Juarez	22:00 (1)		Dep. Durango	07:00 (3)	
Arr. Torreon	12:00 (2)		Arr. Torreon	11:20	
Change trains.			Change trains		
1015			1004 + 1016		
Dep. Torreon	15:20 (3)		Dep. Torreon	12:40 (1)	
Arr. Durango	20:10		Arr. Mexico City	09:30 (4)	

(1) Reservation required. Carries an air-conditioned first-class sleeping car. Has a Special First-class coach. (2) Day 2 from Ciudad Juarez. (3) Has first and second-class coaches. (4) Day 2 from Durango.

Sights in **Torreon** and **Durango**: See notes under "Monterry–Durango" on page 686.

Durango - Regocijo 1018

Considered by many to be the most beautiful rail trip in Mexico. An easy one-day excursion that provides great mountain scenery. Be sure to see the last 3 miles going into Regocijo from the rear of the last car.

Both of these trains run Tuesday and Thursday.

Dep. Durango	06:30	Dep. Regocijo	11:55
Arr. Regocijo	11:30	Arr. Durango	16:37

El Paso - Ciudad Juarez - Chihuahua - Los Mochis

This is the Copper Canyon ride. It offers some of the most spectacular scenery in Mexico. Highest point of the journey is 8,071 feet at **Los Ojitos.**

For best views Chihuahua–Los Mochis, sit on the left side. Completed only in 1961, the rail line to Los Mochis crosses 39 very tall bridges and passes through 8½ miles of 86 tunnels (one is 4,134 feet long) as it crosses the Sierra Tarahuamara mountain range. The bridge over **Septentron River** is 335 feet high. At several points, the route is so rugged that the track must double back in a complete circle.

Scenery includes spectacular deserts, mountains, pine forests and semi-tropical landscape. The journey begins as the line leaves the plateau west of Chihuahua City and climbs into the Sierra Madres. The aborigine Tarahuamara Indians can be observed from Creel to Divisadero. They are the most primitive people in North America, many of them living in caves, some of which can be visited at Creel and at Divisadero.

Delays in the 13-hour journey occur several times a year. Breaking the trip by over-nighting at Creel, Bahuichivo or Divisadero is advisable.

In **Creel**, the Hotel Nuevo (near the railstation) or the picturesque Copper Canyon Lodge (a 30-minute ride by the lodge's bus) will arrange many different short tours by pick-up truck or station wagon. Within 6 miles, there are vast forests, swimming and fishing in mountain lakes, waterfalls and archaeological sites. Hotel tours go to **Cuzarare** (12 miles), **Norogachi** (48 miles), **Basihuare** (24 miles) and **Sisoguichi** (18 miles).

Halfway between Chihuahua and Los Mochis, the train comes into **Divisadero**. Meaning "look-out point", Divisadero stands on the rim of **Urique Canyon**. The train stops here for 20 minutes of viewing down 6,000 feet into the canyon. We recommend overnighting here at the comfortable Cabanas Divisadero, perched on the very rim of the Canyon.

Then the train proceeds into a mile-long tunnel, making a 360-degree turn inside the mountain so that when it emerges from the tunnel and passes a 400-foot waterfall it is heading back in the direction from which it entered the tunnel.

Sights in **Los Mochis**: Fields of safflower. The Botanical Garden. Fifteen miles away is the harbor of **Topolobampo**. Excellent deep-sea fishing there.

Take a bus or taxi from El Paso to Ciudad Juarez.

1004 + 1016			
Dep. Ciudad Juarez	07:00 (1)	22:00 (2)	-0-
Arr. Chihuahua	11:50	03:15	-0-
Change trains. 1006 + 1013			
Dep. Chihuahua	-0-	07:00 (3)	08:00 (1)
Dep. Creel	-0-	11:45	13:21
Dep. Divisadero	-0-	12:57	15:00
Set your watch back one hour.			
Arr. Los Mochis	-0-	19:00	21:44

The Los Mochis departure times shown in Cook are confusing, because they are one hour later than the time used throughout the city. **It is 06:00 at your hotel in Los Mochis when the 07:00 train departs Los Mochis for Chihuahua !** One needs to leave one's Los Mochis hotel at 05:15 for the very long ride to the railstation so as not to miss the "07:00" departure !

Dep. Los Mochis	-0-	07:00 (3+4)	08:00 (1+4)	-0-
Set your watch forward one hour.				
Dep Divisadero	-0-	12:53	14:41	-0-
Dep. Creel	-0-	14:20	16:23	-0-
Arr. Chihuahua	-0-	19:05	21:39	-0-
Change trains. 1004 + 1016				
Dep. Chihuahua	-0-	-0-	01:45 (2)	17:35 (1)
Arr. Ciudad Juarez	-0-	-0-	06:45	22:35

(1) Light refreshments. (2) Reservation required. Star service. Air-conditioned train. Carries first-class sleeping cars and Special First-class coaches. (3) Reservation required. Star service. Air-conditioned train has only Special First-class coaches. Restaurant car. (4) One hour earlier in the city of Los Mochis. Railstation is on Central time. Los Mochis is on Pacific time.

Ciudad Juarez - Irapuato - Mexico City

Here are the schedules for making a detour from Irapuato to Guadalajara en route from Ciudad Juarez to Mexico City.

All of these trains require reservations and are air-conditioned.

1004 + 1016			Change trains. 1026		
Dep. Ciudad Juarez	22:00 (1)		Dep. Irapuato	03:59 (4)	
Dep. Chihuahua	03:45 (2)		Arr. Guadalajara	08:10	
Dep. Torreon	12:40		Change trains. 1008 + 1026		
Dep. Zacatecas	20:25		Dep. Guadalajara	19:30 (5)	20:55 (4)
Dep. Leon	02:07 (3)		Dep. Irapuato	00:42 (6)	01:37 (6)
Arr. Irapuato	03:40		Arr. Mexico City	07:05	08:10

(1) Star Service. Carries first-class sleeping cars and Special First-class coaches. Restaurant car Zacatecas-Irapuato. (2) Day 2. (3) Day 3. (4) Star service. Carries first-class sleeping cars and Special First-class coachs. Restaurant car. Domecar. (5) Has only first and second-class coaches. Light refreshments. (6) Day 4.

Irapuato - Guanajuato 1016 + 1030

Another interesting detour from the Ciudad Juarez-Mexico City route. Sightseeing requires staying overnight in Guanajuato.

These "Star Service" trains require reservations and are air-conditioned.

Dep. Irapuato	12:15	Dep. Guanajuato	14:30
Dep. Silao	13:05	Dep. Silao	15:10
Arr. Guanajuato	13:25	Arr. Irapuato	16:00

Sights in **Guanajuato**: Many ornate 17th century churches that were endowed by the wealth of the richest silver mine in the world. Visit the former residence of the man who owned that mine. There is much late Renaissance architecture here.

The evolution of the career and the style of Diego Rivera is traced in nearly 100 paintings , lithographs and sketches exhibited in the house where Rivera spent his infancy, now a museum. Included are a watercolor of a Greek bust he painted when he was 12 and a caricature of John Foster Dulles.

See the ghoulish exhibit of mummified corpses at the Panteon Museum. An old underground aqueduct that is now used as a subterranean road. The Palace of the Governor.

Nogales - Mazatlan - Guadalajara - Mexico City 1008 + 1012 + 1026

These four "Star Service" trains require reservation and have air-conditioned special and first-class coaches

Dep. Nogales	14:20		Dep. Mexico City	20:40 (1)	
Dep. Mazatlan	06:55	Day 2	Arr. Guadalajara	08:10	Day 2
Arr. Guadalajara	19:05		Change trains.		
Change trains.			Dep. Guadalajara	09:15	
Dep. Guadalajara	20:55 (1)		Dep. Mazatlan	19:05	
Arr. Mexico City	08:10	Day 3	Arr. Nogales	11:05	Day 3

(1) Carries first-class sleeping cars, a restaurant car and a dome car.

Sights in **Mazatlan:** A marvelous seashore resort. Ride a 3-wheel "pneumonia" past the hotels, boutiques and shopping centers that line the seaside Avenida de Mar. Prize billfish and marlin are caught here. Much hunting for wild boar, deer, rabbit, ducks, quail and pheasant in the nearby mountains.

Sights in **Guadalajara:** The 16th century Cathedral, surrounded by 4 plazas in the shape of a cross. The Cabanas Institute arts center and its marvelous Orozco murals, at the former Orphanage. Near there, the sculpture and fountains at the new Plaza Tapatia. Municipal Palace. The State Museum. The Library. Mercado Libertad, Mexico's largest public market. Casa de las Artesianas de Jalisco, a state-run arts and crafts exhibition and shop.

Guadalajara - Manzanillo 1024

This sensational ride down the steep sides of the Sierra Madre is very uncomfortable, dusty and hot, unless the air-conditioned train is used.

Dep. Guadalajara	09:00 (1)	10:00 (2)	Dep. Manzanillo	06:00 (2)	13:00 (1)
Arr. Manzanillo	16:00	18:16	Arr. Guadalajara	14:45	20:00

(1) Reservation required. Star service. Air-conditioned train. Has Special First-Class and ordinary first-class coaches. Buffet. (2) Not air-conditioned. Light refreshments.

Sights in **Manzanillo:** Mexico's principal Pacific seaport. Excellent beaches and great deep-sea fishing here. Much hunting in the nearby hills. The fabulous Las Hadas resort complex.

THE CALIFORNIA GATEWAY

The California connection with rail travel to Mexico City begins by walking or driving from Calexico across the border to Mexicali and taking the short line from Mexicali to Benjamin Hill, where a connection can be made with the Nogales- Guadalajara line.

Mexicali - Benjamin Hill - Mazatlan - Guadalajara - Mexico City 1008 + 1012

Both of these "Star Service" trains require reservation and have air-conditioned Special First-class and first-class coaches.

Dep. Mexicali	09:00		Dep. Mexico City	20:40 (1)	
Arr. Benjamin Hill	16:25		Arr. Guadalajara	08:10	Day 2
Through cars switched here.			Change trains.		
Dep Benjamin Hill	16:40		Dep. Guadalajara	09:15	
Dep. Mazatlan	06:55	Day 2	Dep. Mazatlan	19:05	
Arr. Guadalajara	19:05		Arr. Benjamin Hill	08:45	Day 3
Change trains.			Through cars switched here.		
Dep Guadalajara	20:55 (1)		Dep. Benjamin Hill	09:00	
Arr. Mexico City	08:10	Day 3	Arr. Mexicali	16:30	

(1) Carries a first-class sleeping car, a restaurant car and a dome car.

Mazatlan - Tepic (San Blas) - Guadalajara 1012

It is a one-hour bus ride from Tepic to San Blas.

All of these train are "Star Service", require reservation, are air-conditioned and have a restaurant car.

Dep. Mazatlan	06:55 (1)	23:40 (2)	Dep. Guadalajara	09:15 (1)	19:00 (2)
Dep. Tepic	12:25	04:45	Dep. Tepic	14:05	00:20
Arr. Guadalajara	19:05	11:05	Arr. Mazatlan	19:00	05:00

(1) Has a Special First-class and an ordinary first-class coach. (2) First-class only.

Sights in **San Blas**: A popular resort.

Mexico City - Morelia - Patzcuaro - Uruapan 1035

Excellent Michoacan farm scenery is viewed on this ride.

Dep. Mexico City	06:55 (1)	22:00 (2)	Dep. Uruapan	06:35 (1)	19:15 (2)
Dep. Morelia	17:32	06:31	Dep. Patcuaro	09:05	21:41
Dep. Patzcuaro	18:56	07:57	Dep. Morelia	10:33	23:04
Arr. Uruapan	21:05	10:10	Arr. Mexico City	20:50	07:17

(1) Light refreshments. Has an ordinary first-class coach. (2) Star service. Resveration required. Air-conditioned train. Carries a first-class sleeping car. Has Special First-class and ordinary first-class coaches. Domecar. Light refreshments.

Sights in **Morelia**: Many of the structures in this 16th century city date from the 17th century. Visit the twin-towered, 200-foot-high Cathedral built between 1640 and 1744, the tallest in Mexico. One of Mexico's most splendid, its high altar's tremendous silver font and the enormous gold crown on a crucified Christ are worth seeing.

The tourist office, 2 blocks west of the Cathedral, in the Palacio de Clavijero, on Nigromante, has information about city bus tours.

Visit the Morelos Museum. The arcade with 50 candy stalls. The city aqueduct's 250 arches. Cuauhtemoc Park. The carved flowers, gilded columns and painted statues in the Sanctuario del Guadalupe. The Conservatorio de las Rosas, a 17th century convent, the oldest musical school in North America. Next door to it, the dancing and art displays at Casa de la Cultura which houses a small museum of pre-colonial artifacts.

See the exhibits at the Museum of Michoacan, near the main plaza. The Cardenas mural in the Palace of Justice. Regional crafts at Casa de Artesianas. Another display of handcraft articles from various parts of this state copperware from **Vila Escalante**, stringed instruments from **Paracho**, lacquer trays and cups from **Uruapan** at the 16th century Convent of San Francisco. The 18th century aqueduct.

Sights in **Patzcuaro**: Many 16th century buildings around Plaza Grande, a large green park. See the 16th century church, La Compania. One block from it, craftsmen's studios and shops at House of 11 Patios.

Tarascan Indians bring lacquer, copper, wood and paper-mache items to the Friday market-day.

See the large mural in the Public Library, depicting this region from prehistoric times to the 1910 revolution. The museum of folk art at the site of the 16th century San Nicolas College, before it moved to Morelia. Satisfy your sweet tooth at Joaquinita's Chocolate Supremo.

The 14-mile-long **Lake Patzcuaro,** famous for tasty whitefish, is 2½ miles from the city center. A ferryboat goes to **Janitzio**, largest island on the lake, which has many restaurants specializing in fish and a gigantic statue of Jose Morelos. He was the hero of Mexican independence from France and was shot in 1815.

A good place to shop for pottery and straw items and to rest is at the ruins of **Tzintzuntzan**, capital of the Tarascan Empire, near the lake's eastern shore – a 7-mile drive from Patzcuaro.

Sights in **Uruapan**: It is one mile high here. Founded in 1540. Tjarascan Indians are native to this area. Their crafts, including outstanding lacquerware, are exhibited and sold at the Gutapara Museum, next to the crafts market and on the ground floor of the Hotel Mansion de Cupatitzio, a 16th century structure noted for its lovely patio. See the jungle foliage of Eduardo Ruiz National Park (called "Cupatitzio"), a garden of tropical plants, rustic walks and bubbling streams along both banks of the **Cupatitzio River**.

Tzararacua Falls is 7 miles south, along the river.

See the daily market that runs along Constitucion, starting at Calzada Benito Juarez, and ending at the plaza. The crafts market is one block before reaching the plaza. Excellent lacquerware there: wood chests, small boxes, trays. Try the crispy barbequed pork at the Antojitos food stalls.

Monterrey - Tampico 1022

Both of these trains have light refreshments.

| Dep. Monterrey | 08:00 | Dep. Tampico | 07:48 |
| Arr. Tampico | 17:55 | Arr. Monterrey | 18:50 |

ROUTES SOUTH OF MEXICO CITY

There are 4 principal train routes south from Mexico City: to Veracruz, Oaxaca, Merida and Ciudad Hidalgo.

Mexico City - Veracruz

The excellent tropical mountain scenery on this route, including **Orizaba Volcano** (Mexico's tallest), warrants taking this trip during daylight. It is necessary to bring your own food. Box lunches can be purchased on the lower level of Mexico City's Buenavista Railstation.

	1044	1043	1000	1043
Dep. Mexico City	07:18 (1)	07:34 (2)	21:15 (3)	22:02 (2)
Arr. Veracruz	19:25	19:00	07:00	07:30

Sights in **Veracruz**: A very picturesque resort. See the excellent 17th century Palacio Municipal. Look for the silver-decorated tortoise-shell jewelry that is a specialty here. The beautiful Isla de Sacrificios beach. Take the bus marked "Ulua" to see the 16th century San Juan de Ulua Castle on **Gallega Island** (reached by a road).

	1044	1043	1000	1043
Dep. Veracruz	07:25 (1)	08:00 (2)	21:25 (3)	22:00 (2)
Arr. Mexico City	19:45	19:12	07:37	08:07

(1) Takes the route **via Jalapa**. Light refreshments. (2) Takes the route **via Orizaba**. Light refreshments. (3) Star service. Reservation required. Air-conditioned train. Carries a first-class sleeping car. Has a Special First-class coach and an ordinary first-class coach. Domecar. Light refreshments.

Mexico City - Puebla - Oaxaca 1042

Both of these "Star Service" trains require reservation, are air-conditioned, and carry a first-class sleeping car, Special First-class and ordinary first-class coaches and a restaurant car.

Dep. Mexico City	19:00	Dep. Oaxaca	19:00
Arr. Puebla	23:28	Arr. Puebla	04:00
Arr. Oaxaca	09:30	Arr. Mexico City	09:20

Sights in **Puebla**: The beautiful tiles at the Patio de los Azulejos. The great view of many snow-capped volcanoes from the top of Avenida Internacional, and a similar view from the Cathedral's bell-tower.

The marvelous onyx and marble statues, marble floors and gold leaf decor in the Cathedral. Nearby, Casa del Alfenique (Sugar Candy House). The outstanding museum of Mexican history near the forts of Guadalupe and Loreto. The sensational 16th century Talavera tiles in the Museo de Santa Rosa. The 17th century Church of San Cristobal.

The courtyard and tiled entrance at the Consejo de Justicia. The Cinco de Mayo civic center. The 16th century theater, oldest in the western hemisphere. The collection of Talavera pottery and Chinese porcelain in the Museo de Bello. The onyx and souvenir stores on Plaza Parian. The fascinating architecture, Indian statues in Santa Maria de Tonantzintla Church, and the excavated pyramid at nearby **Cholula.**

Sights in **Oaxaca**: Pronounced "wah–HAH–kah". The arcaded Zocalo Plaza, with the 16th century Cathedral built of pale green stone and, nearby, the fantastic gold leaf and the national museum in Santo Domingo Church. The Saturday Indian market. Do not miss seeing the sculpture and ironwork in the 17th century La Soledad Church. See the view from the monument to Juarez on Cerro de Fortin.

Shop for woolen zarapes, gold and silver jewelry, blankets made from cane, green and black pottery, embroidered blankets and clothing, rugs, etc. The Regional Museum has exhibits of Zapotec Indian treasures from the nearby Monte Alban tombs and Mixtec art from **Mitla**, another archaeological site on the outskirts of Oaxaca.

Mexico City - Palenque - Campeche - Merida 1001 + 1047

Stopovers en route at Palenque and Campeche (to see Mayan ruins) can be arranged. Short excursions from Merida to Uxmal and Chichen-Itza are recommended. A first-class bus to Uxmal leaves Merida for this one-hour drive at 8:00, 9:00, 12:00, 13:00 and 17:00. Departures from Uxmal for the ride back to Merida are at 9:30, 12:30, 13:30, 17:30 and 19:30. Price in 1991 was 4,500 Pesos.

A bus for the 1½-hour drive to Chichen Itza departs Merida at 08:45 and departs Chichen Itza at 15:00 for the ride back to Merida. Price in 1991 was 13,300 Pesos.

A special tour bus to 5 archaeological zones (including Uxmal and Chichen Itza) departs Merida at 8:00, arriving back there at 17:00. Price in 1991 was 25,000 Pesos

Both of the trains below carry a first-class sleeping car, have both ordinary first and second-class coach cars, and have light refreshments. (See sightseeing notes on page 694.)

Dep. Mexico City	18:30	Dep. Merida	20:00
Dep. Coatzacoalcos	13:10 (1)	Dep. Campeche	01:27 (1)
Dep. Palenque	19:45	Dep. Palenque	08:37
Dep. Campeche	03:00 (2)	Dep. Coatzacoalcos	15:20
Arr. Merida	06:00	Arr. Mexico City	09:15 (2)

(1) Day 2.   (2) Day 3.

Sights in **Coatzacoalcos:** An important river and ocean port.

Sights in **Palenque**: Interesting Mayan ruins of stone buildings from the 7th and 8th centuries constructed without the aid of the wheel, metal tools, or beasts of burden are located only 5 miles from this lovely orchard village.

Palenque originally covered about 20 square miles. The area visited today is only slightly more than 30 acres, which the jungle would engulf within a month if it were not constantly cleared of growth.

One of the ruins, the pyramid-like Temple of the Inscriptions, was built into the side of a hill. Visitors can descend 65 feet below its entrance to the tomb of a Mayan ruler and see the 12½ -foot long carved stone slab that once covered a sarcaphagous.

Or, visitors can climb up 69 steep and narrow steps to the top, 75 feet above the ground, to see pillars remaining from a temple. The pillars are decorated with bas-reliefs of priests holding up offerings to both the sun and to the god of maize (corn). Inside the portico, 3 enormous, carved stone panels have the hieroglyphics for which the temple is named (Temple of the Inscriptions) recording the ancestry and accession to the throne of the ruler who was interred inside it.

A palace complex covers about the area of a typical American block. It has underground passages that lead to ancient chambers, latrines and steam baths. The fireflies in this area are so large that a newspaper can be read by the light of a few captured ones.

Sights in **Campeche**: A fortified city, walled in the 17th century for protection from marauding pirates. See the white and vermillion painted wood altars in the 16th century San Francisquito Church. The excellent museum. The rocky seacoast. The museums at the 18th century San Miquel Fort. About 25 miles by road, the Edzna pyramid.

Sights in **Merida:** It is great to sightsee here in a horse-drawn carriage (about $3.00 U.S. per hour). See the marvelous wrought-iron on the mansions on Paseo de Montejo. The entire history of Mexico in bas-relief at the massive Monument of the Flags. Casa Montejo, home of the man who founded this city in 1542. Exhibits of pre-Columbian Yucatan in the Museum of Archaeology.

The 16th century Cathedral, built from stones of Mayan ruins found on the site. Buy souvenirs at the tremendous public market (traditional Yucatan costumes, embroidered cotton smocks, huaraches, hammocks, mountains of fruit). Maps and advice can be obtained from the English-speaking employees of the Tourist Office on Zocalo Plaza. Take the short bus ride to Progreso Beach to swim and to eat fish, turtle and shrimp. Try the mild regional Yucatan cuisine.

Sights in **Uxmal**: Ruins of the perfectly-proportioned 11th century Mayan buildings that are decorated with intricate stone carvings. One week here might be adequate there is that much to see here.

Sights in **Chichen Itza**: The best-preserved Mayan City, spread over an area of 6 square miles, occupied from 1,000 B.C. to the 15th century A.D.

The structural features of El Castillo, the 75-foot high grand pyramid atop which is a large temple extending another 15 feet higher, have chronological elements that measure days of the year as well as the Spring and Fall equinoxes. For the Mayans, March 21 was considered the best day to plant corn and September 21 the best day to harvest it.

INTERNATIONAL CONNECTIONS FROM MEXICO

All the schedules for rail travel between Mexico and the United States appear at the start of this section.

The only train connection from Mexico to Guatemala is very difficult, and we advise against attempting this trip until the conditions improve. There is no acceptable lodging in either primitive Ciudad Hidalgo or in equally primitive Tecun Uman, the Guatemalan city on the other side of the border. Furthermore, there is a 16-hour overnight layover and no place for tourists to stay. The final obstacle is that *passengers attempting to transfer from Ciudad Hidalgo to Tecun Uman must walk more than one mile* in great heat and mucho dust, and a substantial toll charge is exacted to cross the border bridge !

Mexico City - Tapachula - Ciudad Hidalgo - Guatemala City

1000 + 1043		1043	
Dep. Mexico City	21:15 (1)	Dep. Tapachula	13:15 (5)
Arr. Veracruz	07:00 (2)	Arr. Ciudad Hidalgo	14:35
Change trains. 1043		Change trains. 1150	
Dep. Veracruz	09:05 (3)	Dep. Tecun Uman	06:00 (6)
Arr. Tapachula	08:45 (4)	Arr. Guatemala City	18:00
Change trains.			

(1) Star service. Reservation required. Air-conditioned. Carries first-class sleeping cars and both Special First-class and ordinary first-class coach cars. Domecar. Light refreshments. (2) Day 2. (3) Has ordinary first and second-class coach cars. Light refreshments. (4) Day 3 from Mexico City. (5) Second-class only. (6) Runs Wednesday, Friday and Sunday. Second-class only.

Sights in **Tapachula:** The extinct Taconah Volcano that towers above the city. Fifteen miles south is the *Puerto Madero* beach resort.

Information and Reservations

Because few travel agents book Mexican train travel, you will find the following sources of information and reservations helpful. The name of the city from which a trip originates indicates the contact for reservations in the list below.

CHIHUAHUA
Chihuahua Pacific Railway
P.O. Box 46 Chihuahua, Chih., Mexico
TEL: 13-09-93

CIUDAD JUAREZ
National Railways of Mexico
P.O. Box 2200 El Paso, TX. 79951
TEL: 13-48-82

GUADALAJARA
Pacific Railroad Calle Tolsa No. 336
Guadalajara, Jal., Mexico
TEL: 12-51-86

MEXICALI Sonora-Baja California Rly.
P.O. Box 231 Calexico, CA. 92231
TEL: 57-23-86 and 57-21-01

MEXICO CITY
National Railways of Mexico
Buenavista Station
06358 Mexico, D.F.
TEL: 547-5819, 547-3190 and 547-4114

NOGALES
Pacific Railroad Calle Internacional
No. 10 Nogales, Son., Mexico
TEL: 2-00-24

NUEVO LAREDO
National Railways of Mexico
Passenger Station Nuevo Laredo,
Tamps., Mexico
TEL: 2-80-97 and 2-01-34
or
P.O. Box 595 Laredo, TX. 78042

UNITED STATES OF AMERICA

Children under 2 travel free. Half-fare for children 2–15 in coach-class only, when accompanied by a person 18 or older. Children 12 and over must pay full fare when traveling alone.

The classes of train service in the U.S.A. are: compartments convertible to various sleeping accomodations, Slumbercoach (a high-density sleeping car), Club (Parlor) car, Custom, and ordinary coach.

On some day trains, first-class service consists of reserved-seat club cars with 2 seats on one side of the aisle and one seat on the other side.

Night trains have variable first-class sleeping compartments. Most are complete with private wash and toilet facilities. All have doors that can be locked. All sleeping spaces must be reserved in advance.

Trains *east* of the Mississippi River feature roomettes for one person. The seat used during the day folds over at night, making room for a bed that is lowered from a recess in the wall.

Bedrooms are available in 2 different daytime styles, one with a 2-person divan, the other with 2 chairs. At night, the porter makes up one upper bed and one lower bed. Each is 30 inches wide.

The Bedroom Suite results when the dividing partition between 2 adjoining bedrooms is removed. Accommodates up to 4 persons and has 2 wash basins and 2 toilets.

A Slumbercoach costs much less than other sleeping spaces. Rooms for one or 2 persons are available. Much smaller than other sleeper spaces. A double slumbercoach has one upper and one lower bed (each less than 27 inches wide) and private toilet and washbasin. Singles also have private toilet and washbasin.

West of the Mississippi River, 2-level Superliner sleeping cars have deluxe, economy, family and special bedrooms. Deluxe sleeps 2 persons and has private wash, shower and toilet facilities. Economy accommodates one or 2 persons but *does not* have either private wash basin or toilet. Family bedroom sleeps 3 adults and 2 children. Special bedrooms with private wash basin and toilet are available for handicapped persons.

Coaches have 2 seats on each side of the aisle. These seats are adjustable to a semi-reclining position, similar to airplane reclining seats. Most long-distance trains have reserved-seat coaches with reclining seats and leg rests for overnight journeys.

All Amtrak trains are air-conditioned. Most long-distance trains carry a restaurant car. Some short-distance trains have a snack bar or lounge car with counter food service. Most Amtrak long-distance trains operating west of Chicago carry 2-level Superliner observation-lounge cars with large wrap-around windows for viewing the scenery.

Amtrak's fares are shown in its free publications, available at Amtrak or by writing to: Amtrak Distribution Center, P.O. Box 7717, Itasca, Ill. 60143, U.S.A.

Trains in the U.S.A. run through 4 time zones: Eastern, Central, Mountain and Pacific. There is a one-hour difference between each adjacent time zone. Summer schedules are in effect from the second Sunday of April to and including the last Saturday of October.

U.S.A. TRAIN FARES

All Aboard America coach fares can be used either for one-way or roundtrip travel. Prices September 13, 1991 - May 21, 1992 are: a trip within one region of the U.S. $179, 2 regions $229, 3 regions (transcontinental) $259. Subject to change after this edition was printed at the end of 1991, the prices after May 21, 1992 were expected to be $189, $269, and $339. (This fare has some restrictions and "is in limited inventory".) Half-fare for children 2 –15.

Eastern Region: East Coast west to Chicago, Milwaukee or New Orleans. Western Region: West Coast east to El Paso, Wolf Point (Montana) or Denver. Central Region: everything between the 2 other regions.

The trip itinerary must be set at the time the All Aboard America fare is purchased. Sleeping accommodations are extra. The trip can start any day of the week but must be completed within 45 days. Stopover is allowed at 3 cities between origin and completion.

$7 Return Fare   Available September 13, 1991 to May 21, 1992. Roundtrip must be completed within 45 days. When the outbound ticket is $65 or more, the cost of the return ticket is $7.

Sleeping Car Tickets   The price for a first-class sleeping car ticket includes meals that may be selected from the restaurant car menu (salad, entree, and choice of coffee, tea or milk), a morning wake- up with a complimentary newspaper, and a stationery and information packet. See notes on page 701 regarding reservation of sleeping car space.

Senior Citizens and Handicapped Persons Discount.   Ten percent off the lowest available roundtrip coach fare Monday–Thursday for those who prove they are 62 or older and those who offer certification from a physician, a government agency or an organization of handicapped persons that the applicant is handicapped. Not available to a passenger using the All Aboard America or the $7 return fares. Not offered on many days in holiday periods

Packaged Tours.   Amtrak offers more than 400 different packaged tours (some escorted, some independent), that include transportation and, in some cases, hotels.

"Amtrak's America" travel planner and tour books can be obtained from travel agents or by writing to: Amtrak Distribution Center, P.O. Box 7717, Itasca, Ill. 60143, U.S.A.

Both National U.S.A. Rail Pass and Region U.S.A. Rail Pass are sold outside North America. Citizens of the U.S.A and Canada are not eligible to buy them. These passes offer unlimited stopovers and 45 days of unlimited coach travel on all Amtrak trains other than Metroliners and Auto Trains. Unlike passes in Europe which (except for Spain) do not require obtaining a ticket, these passes must be presented prior to boarding an Amtrak train in order to obtain the actual ticket that Amtrak requires.

High-Season fares are in effect May 22 – September 15, 1992.

Reservation should be made as much in advance of travel day as possible. Coach seats can be upgraded by paying an additional fee for reserved-seat club car or for sleeping car space. Travelers wanting more information should write to: Amtrak International Sales, 60 Massachusetts Ave., N.E., Washington, D.C. 20002, U.S.A.

National U.S.A. Rail Pass.   The 1992 high-season prices are: $349 for adults, $175 for children 2–15. Low-season: $299 and $150. For all U.S.A. passes, children under 2 not occupying a separate seat travel free.

East Region U.S.A. Rail Pass.   The area from Chicago and New Orleans to Atlantic Coast cities. The 1992 high-season prices are: $199 for adults, $100 for children 2–15. Low-season: $189 and $95.

Mississippi-West Region U.S.A. Rail Pass.   The area from the Pacific Coast as far east as Chicago and New Orleans. The 1992 high-season prices are: $269 for adults, $135 for children 2–15. Low-season: $239 and $120.

Far West Region U.S.A. Rail Pass.   Travel within Arizona, Colorado (west of Denver), Idaho, Oregon, Montana (west of Glacier Park), Nevada, New Mexico, Utah and Washington. The 1992 High-season prices are: $199 for adults, $100 for children 2–15. Low-season: $189 and $95.

Florida Region U.S.A. Rail Pass.   Travel in Florida. The 1992 high-season prices are: $79 for adults, $39.50 for children 2-15. Low-season: $69 and $34.50.

TRAVEL PLANNER

The 1992 free 90-page booklet features Amtrak's travel packages to 70 major destinations and includes a dozen escorted tours. It gives a complete explanation of Amtrak's routes, equipment and service.

A copy of "Travel Planner" can be obtained by writing to: Amtrak's Distribution Center, P.O. Box 7717, Itasca, IL 60143, U.S.A. An international edition, "Amtrak's USA" is available at the same address.

Notes for sightseeing in 9 principal U.S. cities appear below.

Boston

The collection of Oriental and Egyptian art at the Museum of Fine Arts. The splendid Italian Renaissance paintings in the Isabella Stewart Gardner Museum. The many outstanding museums of science and industry at Harvard University. The elegant 19th century architecture of the Boston Public Library, which has many fine murals.

The New England Aquarium. Arnold Arboretum. The Massachusetts Institute of Technology. The Museum of Science and the Hayden Planetarium, both in Science Park. The Christian Science Mother Church. Take the Bay Cruise.

Many historic places are open to the public: Boston Massacre Site. Old South Church. Bunker Hill. The Tea Party Site. Boston Common. Haymarket Square. The Paul Revere House. The ship "Old Ironsides". Old South Meeting House. King's Chapel. Benjamin Franklin's birthplace.

Chicago

The Field Museum of Natural History. Shedd Aquarium, world's largest collection of sealife. Adler Planetarium. The collection of Near East art at Chicago University's Oriental Institute and, near it, a World War II submarine and the Apollo-8 spacecraft in the enormous Museum of Science and Industry. Lincoln Park Zoo. The Picasso statue at Civic Center Plaza. The Chagall mosaic at First National Bank Plaza. The Museum of Contemporary Art. The exhibit of impressionist art at the splendid Art Institute of Chicago. Sightseeing motorcoach tours leave from Union Station.

Los Angeles

You cannot depend on public transportation to sightsee in Los Angeles. To do so by taxi is extremely expensive. Car rental is the solution. See Olvera Street across from the 1939 railstation, which is an Art Moderne version of the white churches that Spanish missionaries built throughout California, replete with beautifully landscaped patios. This is where the city began.

See the incomparable Music Center complex of 3 outstanding theaters and the City Mall, leading from it to City Hall and the Civic Center of city, county, state of California and Federal buildings.

The marvelous Victorian interior of the 19th century Bradbury Building (elegant tile work and paneling, ornate cast-iron stairways, and open-cage elevators that rise from a marble floor), open daily except Sunday 10:00–17:00. The Coliseum, site of the 1932 Olympics and also where the 1984 ceremonies and many games were held. Near it, a splendid Natural History Museum.

Heading west on Wilshire Boulevard toward the Pacific Ocean, the Los Angeles County Museum of Art at 5905 Wilshire Blvd., open Tuesday-Friday 10:00–17:00, Saturday and Sunday 10:00-18:00, closed Monday. A 2-minute walk from it, the Page Museum of prehistoric mammals and birds at the La Brea Tar Pits. Nearby, Farmers' Market for the finest fruits, vegetables, meats and seafood in the world, also restaurants serving Mexican, Chinese, Italian and American food.

In the **Hollywood** area: The interesting forecourt at the Chinese Theater, with foot-prints and handprints of Hollywood's greatest stars from Mary Pickford to Sylvester Stallone. The major musical events at the Hollywood Bowl all Summer.

The many wealthy residential estates in **Beverly Hills, Bel Air, Westwood and Brentwood**. The Alcoa "Century City" complex, between Beverly Hills and Westwood. Window-shop the row of high-priced stores on Rodeo Drive in Beverly Hills. Visit the University of California at Los Angeles campus, in Westwood.

The expanse of great beaches on the Pacific Ocean shoreline, from **Santa Monica** north to **Malibu** and **Oxnard**, and south to **Newport Beach, Laguna Beach, La Jolla** and **San Diego**. The spectacular array of private yachts at both **Marina Del Rey** (near Los Angeles International Airport) and at **Newport Beach-Balboa**, a one-hour drive south of Los Angeles International Airport.

Take the guided tours of both Universal Studios in **Universal City** and the National Broadcasting Company in **Burbank**.

Hearst's Castle in **San Simeon** is a 5-hour drive north by auto (or by Amtrak to **San Luis Obispo**) from Los Angeles. Disneyland, in **Anaheim**, is a one-hour drive south by auto, as is **San Pedro** which has the Queen Mary and Howard Hughes' "Spruce Goose" gigantic airplane.

In **Pasadena**, 20 minutes by car from the Los Angeles Civic Center, there is more to see than can be done in a single day. See 18th century art (including Gainsborough's "Blue Boy") at the Huntington Library, Art Gallery and Botanical Garden (1151 Oxford Road, San Marino, adjacent to Pasadena), open daily except Monday 13:00–6:30. The Norton Simon Museum at 411 W. Colorado Blvd., open Thursday-Sunday 12:00–18:00, has a much larger and more diverse art collection than the Huntington.

The Pacific Asia Museum (46 No. Los Robles Ave.) is the only museum in Southern California specializing in Far Eastern art. It is open Wednesday-Sunday 12:00–17:00. Visit Gamble House (4 Westmoreland Place), a combination of an Alpine chalet and a Japanese temple, to see its Tiffany stained-glass door and original furnishings from 1908, the year it was built. Open Tuesday and Thursday 10:00–15:00 and every Sunday (except when a major holiday falls on a Sunday) 12:00–15:00.

Entry to the William Wrigley Italian Renaissance Mansion (391 So. Orange Grove Blvd.) is allowed late January to late September on Wednesdays. See other old mansions on Arroyo Terrace. A very wide collection of paintings from the early Renaissance, early tapestries, and modern art at the Norton Simon Museum of Art (411 W. Colorado Blvd.).

Free tours of the California Institute of Technology are guided by students Monday, Wednesday and Friday at 15:00, and on Tuesday and Thursday at 11:00, starting from the school's public relations office (315 So. Hill St.). Lasting 60–90 minutes, this tour visits many laboratories, including Cal Tech's world-famous seismology lab.

A collection of Indian artifacts is exhbited at the Southwest Museum (234 Mission Dr.), open Tuesday-Saturday 11:00–17:00, Sundays (except holidays) 13:00–17:00. Art from the Far East can be seen at the Pacific Asia Museum (46 No. Los Robles Ave.).

The Rose Bowl Stadium. The 165-acre Descanso Gardens, noted for its collection of 600 varieties of camellias, at the Los Angeles Arboretum (301 No. Baldwin Ave.) in nearby **Arcadia**, near Santa Anita Racetrack.

New York City

The Statue of Liberty. The United Nations complex. The view from the top of the Empire State Building. The New York Stock Exchange. The Rockefeller Center complex. The Metropolitan Museum of Art, greatest art museum in the United States. The Whitney Museum of American Art. The Solomon R. Guggenheim Museum. The American Museum of Natural History.

The International Center of Photography. Central Park, but never after dark. The Museum of the City of New York. The Cathedral of St. John the Divine(largest Protestant church in the world), far more interesting than St. Patrick's, but often neglected by tourists. The 10,000-pound bronze statue of the archangel Michael was placed on Peace Fountain there in 1985.

The exhibits and movies at the U.S.A.'s first capitol, at 26 Wall Street. The museum of Revolutionary War relics and Washington memorabilia at Fraunces Tavern. Guided tours at the Federal Reserve Bank. Chinatown. The Bronx Zoo and Botanical Garden.

Philadelphia

The Liberty Bell and Independence Hall, on Independence Square. Stroll down Elfreth's Alley, one of America's oldest streets, to the Betsy Ross House. Nearby, the grave of Benjamin Franklin. See the hundreds of fine portraits at The Historical Society of Pennsylvania.

The War Library and Museum. Rosenbach Museum. The Pennsylvania Academy of Fine Arts. The Academy of Natural Sciences. The Rodin Museum, largest collection of Rodin sculptures outside Paris. The Philadelphia Museum of Art. The 388-acre food industry park (stores, warehouses, processing plants) called Food Distribution Center. Performances of the Philadelphia Orchestra at the Academy of Music. The Civic Center Museum. The Franklin Institute of Science Museum. The University Museum.

San Francisco

Fisherman's Wharf. Watch them making chocolate at nearby Ghirardelli Square. The Maritime Museum. The Chinese Museum. The treasures for sale at Gump's store. Chinatown. North Beach. The Presidio. Golden Gate Bridge. The Arboretum and the spectacular exhibits of Far Eastern art at the de Young Memorial Museum, both in the 1,017-acre Golden Gate Park. Fleischacker Zoo, one of the world's best zoos. The pyramidal Transamerica Building. San Francisco Museum of Art. Nob Hill and the cable car ride from there, down California Street.

Seattle

A 90-second monorail ride starts from Fourth Avenue and Pine, ending at the 74-acre Seattle Center (an amusement park, Pacific Science Center, Modern Art Pavilion, Center House Food Bazaar) for a magnificent view of the city, Puget Sound and mountains from the observation deck of the 607-foot high tripod Space Needle tower.

The Aquarium at Waterfront Park. The marvelous seafood, fruits and vegetables in Pike's Farmers' Market, at the waterfront. The 200-acre Arboretum. A tour of Boe-ing's 747 assembly plant (phone 206-342-4801 for reservations and directions). The Seattle Art Museum. The more than 1,000,000 used books, for sale at Shorey Bookstore. The granite sculptures at Myrtle Edwards Park. The crafts in the specialty shops at Pioneer Square. Take the 2½-hour sightseeing cruise of Puget Sound, from Pier 51 (at 10:30 and 13:00). Or, go on the ferry-boat ride, starting at the foot of Marion Street.

Washington, D.C.

See the 1908 Beaux Arts railstation, restored in 1988, open 24 hours.

Then visit the many great museums in the Smithsonian Institution complex: The exhibit of balloons, dirigibles, primitive propellor airplanes and on to the Apollo II space ship in the Air & Space wing. The several displays (dinosaurs, Hope Diamond and other gems, etc.) in the Natural History Museum. The numerous old machines and clothing in the Museum of History & Technology. The marvelous French Impressionist and Italian Renaissance paintings at the National Gallery of Art. The sculptures and mobiles in the circular Hirschorn Museum. The collection of art in the Freer Gallery.

Most of these museums are open 10:00–17:30.

See Congress in session. Tours of the House of Representatives and the Senate operate every 15 minutes from 09:00–15:45 daily, starting from the Rotunda. Walk up the 897 steps to the top of the 555-foot high Washington Monument obelisk, open 09:00–17:00 daily (also 20:00–24:00 in the Summer). The Reflecting Pool in West Potomac Park. The Jefferson Memorial, open 24 hours. The Lincoln Memorial, always open.

The National Zoo. The National Arboretum, with its large display of azaleas, daffodils and magnolias. The eternal-flame tomb of John F. Kennedy, the Greek Revival Arlington House, and the Tomb of the Unknowns, all in Arlington National Cemetery.

The largest collection of books, maps, newspapers, documents and manuscripts in the world, at the Library of Congress (guided tours Monday-Friday 09:00–16:00.)

See the art collections at Corcoran Gallery, Phillips Collection, the National Portrait Gallery and the National Collection of Fine Arts. Take a tour of Federal Bureau of Investigation, every 15 minutes (09:15–16:15, Monday-Friday) at 13th Street and Penn- sylvania Avenue. There is a 25-minute tour of the Bureau of Engraving & Printing (where money is not printed as fast as it is spent) Monday-Friday 08:00–11:30 and 12:30–14:00.

Visit the White House for a 40-minute tour Tuesday-Saturday, 10:00-12:00. Tour the Supreme Court when the Court is not in session, Monday-Friday 09:00-16:30 and, when it is in session, 10:00-14:30. Take the short guided bus trip to Mt. Vernon.

AMTRAK RESERVATION and INFORMATION TELEPHONE NUMBER

1 (800) 872-7245

Amtrak will accept both sleeper and coach reservations up to 11 months in advance, Travelers need to make sleeping car reservations well in advance of travel date, because sleeping space is very limited. Coach travel in Summer should also be reserved well in advance. Although the phone number above is a 24-hour service, it may be easier to reach a reservation agent either early in the morning or late at night.

If a sleeping accommodation is cancelled less than 48 hours before departure time, the cancellation fee (depending on its price) is $10–$150.

For those who want to take daytime sightseeing tours and/or to travel only during the day and stay in hotels along the way at night, Amtrak's tour operator (open Monday–Friday 09:00–17:00 Central Time) will reserve sightseeing tours and/or rooms in those hotels in which Amtrak buys blocks of rooms. U.S.A. telephone: (800) 321-8684. Canadian telephone: (800) 321-9885.

TRANSCONTINENTAL RAIL ROUTES

There is a rail route from New York City to Chicago. From Chicago, there are 4 different train routes to the West Coast of the United States.

Another route to the West is from New York City, the long ride via New Orleans.

NEW YORK ROUTES WEST

New York - Albany - Buffalo - Cleveland - Chicago 186

This route can also be started in Boston, by connecting in Albany. (See "Boston–Albany" below.)

These trains require reservations, run daily, are air-conditioned, and carry sleeping cars, Slumbercoach, ordinary coach and a restaurant car.

Dep. New York (Penn.)	19:10	Dep. Chicago (Union)	18:25
Dep. Albany	22:28	Set your watch forward one hour.	
Dep. Buffalo (Depew)	03:56	Dep. Cleveland	02:11
Dep. Cleveland	07:11	Dep. Buffalo (Depew)	05:27
Set your watch back one hour.		Arr. Albany	10:22
Arr. Chicago (Union)	13:03	Arr. New York (Penn..)	13:50

Sights in **Cleveland**: Sea World. The Cleveland Museum of Art. Blossom Music Center. A cruise along the Lake Erie shore on the Goodtime Sightseeing Boat. Playhouse Square Theater Complex. The NASA Lewis Research Visitors Center. The Cleveland Health Education Museum.

Boston - Albany - Chicago 186

These trains require reservations, run daily, are air-conditioned, and carry sleeping cars, slumbercoach and ordinary coach. Restaurant car.

Dep. Boston (South)	16:20	Dep. Chicago (Union)	18:25
Arr. Albany	21:35	Dep. Albany	10:58 (1)
Arr. Chicao (Union)	13:03 (1)	Arr. Boston (South)	15:58

(1) Day 2.

Detroit - Chicago 227

All of these trains run daily, are air-conditioned, have an ordinary coach and serve light refreshments.

Dep. Detroit (Michigan Ave.)	07:30	11:45	17:25
Arr. Chicago (Union)	11:59	16:10	21:40

* * *

Dep. Chicago (Union)	07:45 (1)	08:15 (2)	14:45	17:50
Arr. Detroit (Mich. Ave.)	14:09	14:35	21:05	00:15

(1) Runs daily, except Sunday. (2) Runs Sunday only.

Sights in **Detroit**: Belle Isle. Cranbrook Educational Community. Greenfield Village & Henry Ford Museum. Renaissance Center. University Cultural Center. The Zoological Park.

New York - Pittsburgh - Chicago 185 + 225

This route can be started in Washington (see next timetable) with a connection in Pittsburgh.

These trains require reservations, are air-conditioned, and carry a sleeping car, a slumbercoach. an ordinary coach and a restaurant car.

Dep. New York (Penn.)	14:05	Dep. Chicago (Union)	20:15
Dep. Philadelphia		Set watch forward one hour.	
(30th Street)	16:10 (1)	Dep. Pittsburgh (Penn.)	07:40
Dep. Pittsburgh (Penn.)	00:11	Arr. Philadelphia	
Set your watch back one hour.		(30th Street)	15:16 (2)
Arr. Chicago (Union)	09:29	Arr. New York (Penn.)	17:25

(1) Stops only for passengers boarding train. (2) Stops only for passengers getting off train.

Sights in **Pittsburgh**: Gateway Clipper. Nationality Classrooms. Kennywood Park. Station Square. Carnegie Institute. Buhl Science Center. Duquesne Incline. Fort Pitt Blockhouse. Heinz Hall.

Washington - Pittsburgh - Chicago 220

These trains require reservation, are air-conditioned and carry sleeping cars, ordinary coach cars and a restaurant car..

Dep. Washington (Union)	16:05	Dep. Chicago (Union)	16:30
Dep. Pittsburgh	23:32	Dep. Pittsburgh	03:15
Arr. Chicago (Union)	08:25	Arr. Washington (Union)	10:27

New York - New Orleans - Houston - Los Angeles

A long (3,417 miles) but interesting route from New York to the West Coast is via New Orleans, where there is a 20-hour layover on the trip West and more than 11 hours when going from Los Angeles to New York. Passengers were once allowed to occupy sleeping space on the train during each overnight stop, but now must make other provision.

A few miles west of **El Paso,** watch for "The Christ of the Rockies", a 27-foot high statue at the top of the 4,756-foot Sierra de Cristo Rey mountain.

Between Phoenix and Los Angeles, "Sunset Limited" rides at the lowest altitude of the Amtrak system: 231 feet (70 meters) *below* sea level, near Niland, California.

Sights in **Philadelphia:** see page 700.

Sights in **Baltimore**: The National Aquarium. HarborPlace. The view from the Observation Level of the World Trade Center. Ft. McHenry. The Maryland Science Center and Planetarium. The 18th century U.S. Frigate Constellation. The B & O Railroad Museum. Lexington Market. The Zoo.

Sights in **Washington**: see page 701.

Sights in **Atlanta**: Cyclorama and the Zoo, both in Grant Park. The Toy Museum. Fernbank Science Center. Swan House. Wren's Nest. Stone Mountain Park. White Water Parks.

Sights in **New Orleans**: Mardi Gras. Jazz on Bourbon Street and the Spanish-French architecture in the French Quarter. Visit the 1831 Hermann-Grima Historical House (820 St. Louis Street) and take a 20-minute guided tour of one of the earliest and best examples of early American architecture in the French Quarter. Its interior and garden have been restored authentically.

See Absinthe House. Audubon's Little House. Boat tours of the harbor. The view from the top of the 400-foot high International Trade Mart, at the foot of Canal Street.

Audubon Park and Zoo. The Cabrini Doll Museum. French Market. The Casta Hove Museum. The Cathedral of St. Louis. The Museum of Art.

Sights in **Houston**: The Astrodome. Johnson Space Center. Astroworld. The Museum of Natural Science. Hermann Park & Zoo. The downtown underground shopping center.

Sights in **Phoenix**: Desert Botanical Gardens. The Heard Museum. The Phoenix Art Museum. The Zoo. The Pueblo Museum and Indian Ruins. The Gila River Indian Arts and Crafts Center.

Sights in **Los Angeles**: see page 698.

These trains require reservation, are air-conditioned and carry a sleeping car, an ordinary coach and a restaurant car.

213 + 223			244		
Dep. New York (Penn.)	14:25 (1)		Dep. Los Angeles	22:50 (5)	
Dep. Philadelphia (30th St.)	16:02 (1+2)		Set watch forward one hour.		
Dep. Baltimore (Penn.)	17:33 (1+2)		Dep. Phoenix	07:20 (6)	Day 2
Dep. Washington(Union)	18:50 (1+2)		Set watch forward one hour.		
Arr. Atlanta (Peachtree St.)	08:30 (1) Day 2		Dep. El Paso	17:40	
Dep. Atlanta (Peachtree St.)	08:45 (1)		Dep. San Antonio		
Set your watch back one hour.			(East Commercial St.)	06:35 (7)	Day 3
Arr. New Orleans	19:20		Dep. Houston	11:10	
Change trains.			Arr. New Orleans	19:50	
244			Change trains.		
Dep. New Orleans	14:15 (3) Day 3		213 + 223		
Dep. Houston	22:35		Dep. New Orleans	07:00 (1)	Day 4
Dep. San Antonio			Set watch forward one hour.		
(East Commercial St.)	03:40 (4) Day 4		Arr. Atlanta (Peachtree St.)	19:15	
Dep. El Paso	14:05		Dep. Atlanta (Peachtree St.)	19:40 (1)	
Set your watch back one hour.			Arr. Washington (Union)	09:20 (8)	Day 5
Dep. Phoenix	22:31		Arr. Baltimore (Penn.)	10:45 (8)	
Set your watch back one hour.			Arr. Philadelphia (30th St.)	12:18 (8)	
Arr. Los Angeles	07:00	Day 5	Arr. New York (Penn.)	14:08 (8)	

(1) Runs daily. (2) Stops only for passengers boarding. (3) Runs Monday, Wednesday and Saturday. Has special facilities for disabled passengers. (4) Runs Tuesday, Thursday and Sunday. (5) Runs Tuesday, Friday and Sunday. (6) Runs Wednesday, Saturday and Monday. (7) Runs Thursday, Sunday and Tuesday. (8) Stops only for passengers getting off.

CHICAGO ROUTES WEST

Here are the schedules for the 5 train services west from Chicago.

Chicago - Minneapolis - Spokane - Seattle (or Portland) 194 + 241

West of Minneapolis, the train passes waterfalls, dams, forests and Indian reservations.

These trains run daily, require reservations, are air-conditioned and carry sleeping cars, ordinary coaches, a restaurant car and an entertainment car, and have special facilities for disabled passengers.

From Spokane, one section goes to Portland, another section to Seattle.

Dep. Chicago (Union)	15:15		Dep. Portland	15:55 (3)	
Dep. Milwaukee	16:51		Dep. Seattle	16:20 (3)	
Dep. Minneapolis	00:35	Day 2	Dep. Spokane	00:10	
Dep. Fargo	05:06		Set your watch forward one hour.		
Set your watch back one hour.			Dep. Glacier Park	08:55 (1)	Day 2
Dep. Glacier Park	19:32 (1)		Set your watch forward one hour.		
Set your watch back one hour.			Dep. Fargo	01:30	Day 3
Arr. Spokane	02:25 (2)	Day 3	Dep. Minneapolis	07:10	
Arr. Seattle	10:45 (2)		Arr. Milwaukee	14:01	
Arr. Portland	10:15 (2)		Arr. Chicago (Union)	15:40	

(1) Stops in Glacier Park only from late May to early September. (2) From Spokane, one section goes to Portland, another section to Seattle. Buffet car Spokane–Portland and v.v. (3) One section starts in Portland, another section in Seattle. The 2 sections combine in Spokane.

Chicago - Denver - Salt Lake City - Reno - Oakland - San Francisco 189

Many regard the Denver-Salt Lake City portion of this route, with marvelous views of the Rocky Mountains, to be the most scenic train ride in the U.S.A. The train reaches an altitude of 9,239 feet, the highest point of any rail line in the U.S.A., when going through the 6.2-mile-long Moffat Tunnel.

These trains run daily, require reservations, are air-conditioned and carry sleeping cars, ordinary coaches, a restaurant car and an entertainment car, and have special facilities for disabled passengers.

Dep. Chicago (Union)	14:55		Dep. San Francisco	10:05 (1)	
Dep. Omaha	23:44		Dep. Oakland	10:40	
Set your watch back one hour.			Dep. Reno	17:00	
Dep. Denver (Union)	09:00	Day 2	Set watch forward one hour.		
Dep. Salt Lake City	00:20	Day 3	Dep. Salt Lake City	05:35	Day 2
Set your watch back one hour.			Dep. Denver	21:10	
Arr. Reno	09:22		Set watch forward one hour.		
Arr. Oakland	17:00 (1)		Dep. Omaha	07:04	Day 3
Arr. San Francisco	17:35		Arr. Chicago (Union)	16:25	

(1) Bus service Oakland-San Francisco and v.v.

Sights in **Salt Lake City**: The temple and tabernacle of the Mormon Church, in 10-acre Temple Square, at the center of the city.

Visitors can attend recitals on the 11,000-pipe tabernacle organ in a building considered acoustically perfect since it is entirely wood, even to the wood nails that were used in its construction. Performances are offered Monday–Friday at 12:00; on Monday, Tuesday and Wednesday at 19:30; and on Saturday and Sunday at 16:00.

Every day except Sunday, more than 5,000 people of every faith use the Mormon Genealogical Library (50 East North Temple St.), containing statistics on more than one *billion* people who lived and died in 60 countries since 1538. It is open Monday 07:30–18:00, Tuesday-Thursday 07:30–22:00, and Saturday 07:30–17:00.

Chicago - St. Louis - Dallas - San Antonio - Los Angeles 188

These trains require reservations, are air-conditioned, carry sleeping cars, ordinary coaches and have special facilities for disabled passengers.

These trains run daily between Chicago and San Antonio with a restaurant car to Dallas, then a buffet car to San Antonio (and v.v.). See footnotes for days of operation between San Antonio–Los Angeles and v.v.

Dep. Chicago (Union)	17:45 (1)		Dep. Los Angeles	22:50 (3)	
Dep. St. Louis	00:20	Day 2	Set watch forward one hour.		
Dep. Dallas	14:49		Dep. Phoenix	07:20	Day 2
Dep. Fort Worth	16:37		Set watch forward one hour.		
Arr. San Antonio	23:45		Dep. El Paso	17:40	
Dep. San Antonio	03:40 (2)	Day 3	Arr. San Antonio	06:05 (3)	Day 3
Dep. El Paso	14:25		Dep. San Antonio	07:05	
Set your watch back one hour.			Dep. Fort Worth	14:35	
Dep. Phoenix	22:31		Dep. Dallas	16:10	
Set your watch back one hour.			Dep. St. Louis	07:35	Day 4
Arr. Los Angeles	07:00	Day 4	Arr. Chicago (Union)	14:20	

(1) Departures on Tuesday, Friday and Sunday continue on to Los Angeles. (2) Departs San Antonio for Los Angeles on Thursday, Sunday and Tuesday. Carries an entertainment car and a restaurant car. (3)Departs Tuesday, Friday and Sunday for San Antonio and Chicago. Carries a restaurant and entertainment car to San Antonio. (3) Arrive San Antonio Thursday, Sunday and Tuesday.

Chicago - Kansas City - Albuquerque - Los Angeles 187 + 248

At Flagstaff, there is bus service to the Grand Canyon (see page 718).

These trains run daily, require reservations, are air-conditioned, carry sleeping cars, ordinary coaches, a restaurant car and an entertainment car, and have special facilities for disabled passengers.

Dep. Chicago (Union)	17:00		Dep. Los Angeles	20:30	
Dep. Kansas City	01:05	Day 2	Set watch forward one hour.		
Dep. Dodge City	07:20		Dep. Flagstaff	06:57	Day 2
Set your watch back one hour.			Dep. Albuquerque	13:45	
Dep. Albuquerque	17:10		Set watch forward one hour.		
Dep. Flagstaff	21:24		Dep. Dodge City	00:42	Day 3
Set your watch back one hour.			Dep. Kansas City	07:40	
Arr. Los Angeles	08:10	Day 3	Arr. Chicago (Union)	15:50	

Chicago - New Orleans 183

These trains run daily, require reservations, are air-conditioned, carry sleeping cars, ordinary coaches, a restaurant car and a domecar.

Dep. Chicago (Union)	18:45		Dep. New Orleans	15:05	
Dep. Memphis	05:25	Day 2	Dep. Memphis	22:45	
Arr. New Orleans	13:15		Arr. Chicago (Union)	09:50	Day 2

EASTERN SEABOARD TRAIN ROUTES

Boston - New York City - Philadelphia - Washington 202

Note: There are departures not listed here (see Cook's Table 213) from New York City to Washington at frequent times 06:00–21:20 and from Washington to New York City 05:50–22:20.

All of the trains listed below are air-conditioned, have light refreshments, and have ordinary coaches, unless designated otherwise.

Dep. Boston (South)	Arr. New York (Penn.)	Arr. Philadelphia (30th St.)	Arr. Washington (Union)
07:15	12:55	14:43	16:42
07:30 (1)	12:06	13:42	15:40
09:28 (2)	14:01	15:46	17:44
10:20 (2)	15:01	16:53	18:48
13:35 (2)	18:10	19:59	21:59
14:20	20:11	21:54	00:03
15:25 (2)	20:11	21:54	00:03
16:30 (3)	20:52	22:48	00:47
17:30 (4)	21:59	23:57	01:48
22:10 (5)	03:02	05:41	07:55
-0-	07:24 (6)	09:52	11:45
-0-	09:14 (2)	11:12	13:12

Washington - Philadelphia - New York City - Boston 220

Dep. Washington (Union)	Dep. Philadelphia (30th St.)	Dep. New York (Penn.)	Arr. Boston (South)
03:40 (7)	05:44	08:07	13:17
07:20 (2)	09:08	11:06	15:56
10:20 (2)	12:10	14:06	18:55
12:10 (1)	13:58	15:48	20:32
13:20	15:10	17:15	23:15
14:20 (2)	16:10	18:19	23:09
15:20 (2)	17:15	19:11	23:59
22:20 (5)	00:33	03:20	08:35
-0-	07:20 (4)	09:17	14:04
-0-	07:35 (3)	09:17	14:01
-0-	-0-	06:37 (3)	11:09

(1) Parlor car. Buffet car. (2) Parlor car. (3) Runs Monday–Friday except holidays. Parlor car. (4) Runs Saturdays, Sundays and holidays. Parlor car. (5) Carries sleeping cars. (6) Carries a sleeping car. Buffet car. (7) Runs daily, except Monday.

New York - Philadelphia - Washington - Miami

These trains run daily, require reservations, are air-conditioned, and carry sleeping cars, slumbercoaches, ordinary coaches and a restaurant car.

	184	182
Dep. New York (Penn.)	08:35	16:33 (3)
Dep. Philadelphia (30th St.)	10:18 (1)	18:19 (1)
Dep. Washington (Union)	13:15 (1)	21:30 (1)
Arr. Miami	12:05 (2)	18:35 (2)

Sights in **Miami**: Metrozoo (12400 SW 152 St.), open daily 10:00–17:30. The nearly one square mile of orchids at Orchid Jungle (26715 SW 157 St.), open daily 08:30–17:30. Viscaya, a 50-room Italian Renaissance palace built in 1914 with a large formal garden (3251 S. Miami Ave.), open daily 09:30–16:30.

The collection of Oriental, American and European art in the Lowe Art Museum at the University of Miami in Coral Gables. The acquarium and performing dolphins at Seaquarium (4400 Rickenbacker Causeway), open 09:00–17:00. Nearby is Planet Ocean. Many uncaged tropical birds at Parrot Jungle (11000 SW 157 Ave.). The serpents and snakes at Serpentarium (12655 So. Dixie Hwy.).

"Little Havana", a 20-block section on Eighth Street. Monkey Jungle (14805 SW 157 Ave.). The 83 acres of tropical plants and trees from around the world in Fairchild Tropical Gardens (10901 Old Sutler Rd.), open 09:30–16:30.

	182	184
Dep. Miami	09:45	14:40
Arr. Washington (Union)	06:48 (2+4)	13:40 (2+4)
Arr. Philadelphia (30th St.)	09:32 (4)	16:43 (4)
Arr. New York (Penn.)	11:33	18:51

(1) Stops only for passengers boarding train. (2)Day 2. (3) Restaurant car New York–Orlando and v.v.. Buffet car entire trip. (4) Stops only to allow passengers to get off train.

WESTERN TRAIN ROUTES

Los Angeles - Las Vegas - Salt Lake City 191

"Desert Wind" eastbound connects in Salt Lake City with "Zephyr" heading east to Denver and Chicago. "Zephyr" westbound from Chicago and Denver connects in Salt Lake City with "Desert Wind" heading west to Las Vegas and Los Angeles.

These trains require reservations, are air-conditioned, carry sleeping cars, ordinary coaches, a restaurant car and an entertainment car, and have special facilities for disabled passengers.

Dep. Los Angeles	12:00	Dep. Salt Lake City	00:40
Arr. Las Vegas	18:55	Set watch back one hour.	
Set watch forward one hour.		Arr. Las Vegas	07:35
Arr. Salt Lake City	04:10 Day 2	Arr. Los Angeles	14:55 Day 2

Sights in **Las Vegas**: Many gambling casinos. Nearby, **Boulder Dam** and **Lake Mead**.

Los Angeles - San Diego 252

Amtrak has a one-day independent tour package from Los Angeles to **San Diego** and return, which includes rail fare, transfers between the San Diego railstation and the exceptional San Diego Zoo (Balboa Park), admission to the Zoo, a 40-minute guided bus tour of the 128-acre wildlife facility, and a ride on the Zoo's aerial tram.

Other San Diego area attractions: Sea World, open daily 09:00–17:00. Old Town. Seaport Village. The large harbor. Four missions. Wild Animal Park. It is a 20-minute auto drive to Tijuana, across the border.

These trains have both a first-class and an ordinary coach, are air-conditioned and have light refreshments.

Dep. Los Angeles	06:15	07:45	10:50	12:45	14:45	16:45	18:20	21:05
Arr. San Diego	09:05	10:35	13:37	15:30	17:30	19:35	21:05	23:47
			*	*	*			
Dep. San Diego	05:13	06:20	09:50	11:45	14:45	16:50	18:45	21:05
Arr. Los Angeles	07:53	09:06	12:37	14:30	17:32	19:37	21:35	23:45

Los Angeles - Oakland (San Francisco) - Portland - Seattle 192

A very scenic route: seacoast, forests, snow-capped mountains. On the northward route, views of the Cascade mountain range come into sight before reaching Portland, and the descent into the Willamet Valley is spectacular. The largest herd of llamas in Oregon often can be seen near Salem.

These trains run daily, carry sleeping cars, ordinary coaches, a restaurant car, an entertainment car, are air-conditioned and have special facilities for disabled passengers.

Dep. Los Angeles	09:50		Dep. Seattle	10:40	
Arr. Oakland	20:45 (1)		Arr. Portland	14:50	
Dep. Oakland	21:15		Dep. Portland	15:10	
Arr. Portland	14:25	Day 2	Arr. Oakland	08:23 (1)	Day 2
Dep. Portland	14:40		Dep. Oakland	08:53	
Arr. Seattle	18:50		Arr. Los Angeles	19:40	

(1) Bus service to/from San Francisco connects with arrival/departure.

Sights in **Portland**: The Oregon Historical Society's Museum (1230 SW Park Ave.), open Monday-Saturday 10:00–16:45. Nearby, the Portland Art Museum, open Tuesday-Sunday at 12:00. The Washington Park Zoo. Japanese Gardens. Washington Park International Rose Test Gardens. Western Forestry Center. The Oregon Museum of Science and Industry. Pittock Mansion. The Grotto at the Sanctuary of Our Sorrowful Mother.

Portland - Seattle

Here are all the schedules for this route, in addition to the trains shown on page 709.

These trains run daily, are air-conditioned, have an ordinary coach, and have special facilities for disabled passengers, unless designated otherwise.

	264	195	192
Dep. Portland	08:00 (1)	14:10 (2)	14:40 (2)
Arr. Seattle	12:00	18:10	18:50

* * *

	195	192	264
Dep. Seattle	08:00 (2)	10:40 (2)	17:30 (1)
Arr. Portland	12:10	14:50	21:30

(1) Light refreshments. (2) Reservation required. Restaurant car.

Portland - Spokane 194

This is a spur off the Seattle-Spokane-Chicago route. The train passes through the historic Columbia River Gorge, following the path of the Lewis and Clark expedition. Unfortunately, the best scenery is passed during night hours. The train unites in Spokane with the Seattle-Chicago service.

Both of these trains run daily, require reservation, are air-conditioned, carry sleeping cars, ordinary coaches and an entertainment car, have buffet service and have special facilities for disabled passengers.

Dep. Portland	15:55	Dep. Spokane	03:10
Arr. Spokane	23:00	Arr. Portland	10:15

Denver - Boise - Portland - Seattle 195

These trains run daily, are air-conditioned, carry sleeping cars, ordinary coaches and a restaurant car and have special facilities for disabled passengers.

Dep. Denver	10:15	Dep. Seattle	08:00
Dep. Boise	03:25	Dep. Portland	12:30
Set your watch back one hour.		Set your watch forward one hour.	
Arr. Portland	14:00	Dep. Boise	23:45
Arr. Seattle	18:10	Arr. Denver	17:00

San Francisco - Oakland - Reno 189 + 250

These trains require reservations, are air-conditioned, have ordinary coaches, carry a restaurant car, and have special facilities for disabled passengers.

Bus			Train	
Dep. San Francisco			Dep. Reno	09:22
(Transbay Ter.)	11:15	(est.)	Arr. Oakland	17:00
Arr. Oakland	11:35		Change to bus.	
Change to train.			Dep. Oakland	17:15 (est.)
Dep. Oakland	10:40		Arr. San Francisco	
Arr. Reno	17:00		(Transbay Ter.)	17:35

Sights in **Reno**: Many gambling casinos. See Harrah's collection of vintage autos. Harold's Club gun collection. Ponderosa Ranch. Fleischmann Planetarium. The Nevada Historical Society Museum. Nearby are Virginia City, Carson City, some gold-mining ghost towns and beautiful Lake Tahoe.

SCENIC RAIL TRIPS

The schedules for these 8 scenic train rides appear earlier in this section.

Denver - Salt Lake City (189)   This route reaches a height of more than 9,000 feet and provides marvelous views of the Rocky Mountains (page 705).

Denver - Seattle (195)   This route goes through 2 of the most scenic river valleys in North America: the Snake River Valley in southern Idaho and the Columbia River Valley through Oregon and Washington State (page 710).

Oakland - Reno (189 + 250)   Excellent mountain scenery of the High Sierra can be seen on this portion of the Oakland-Ogden ride (page 711).

Los Angeles - Seattle (192)   Very fine views of the Pacific seacoast, forests and snow-capped mountains (page 709).

Raton Pass (187 + 248)   Crossing the Colorado-New Mexico state line (Chicago-Albuquerque-Los Angeles route), the train goes over the 7,588-foot high Raton Pass (page 706).

Glacier National Park (194 + 241)   Fifty-six miles of glaciers and soaring peaks can be seen as the Chicago-Fargo-Seattle route passes through Glacier National Park (page 705).

New York City - Albany (186)   The train follows the beautiful Hudson River for 142 miles on this trip (page 702).

AlaskaPass

Allows unlimited travel throughout Alaska on the trains, ferries and buses operated by Alaska Marine Highway and Alaska Railroad; in both Alaska and in Canada's Yukon Territory by the services of Alaskon Express Motorcoaches; in the Yukon Territory by Greyhound Lines of Canada and Norline Coaches; and in Canada's British Columbia by the services of BC Ferries, BC Rail, Greyhound Lines of Canada, and Island Coach Lines.

Sold by travel agencies worldwide and AlaskaPass Inc. (P.O. Box 897, Haines, Alaska 99827-0897, U.S.A. Telephone: (800) 248-7598. From outside the U.S.A , call (907) 766-3145). The prices valid May 31 to September 15, 1992 are: $429 (U.S.) for 8 days, $569 for 15 days, $699 for 22 days, and $799 for 30 days. Children 3-11: $289, $379, $469 and $529.

An off-season pass (September 16–May 30) is offered for 8 days at $461.50, and 15 days at $541.50. This pass is offered at $100 discount for persons 65 and older. Children 3-11: $311.50 and $361.50. In off-season, one flight between Juneau and Anchorage on Alaska Airlines is included.

Flexible AlaskaPass

For any 12 days of travel within 21 days, the 1992 price is $589. Any 21 out of 45 days: $849. Children 3–11: $399 and $569.

TWO ALASKAN SCENIC RAILROADS

White Pass and Yukon Route

In the early 1980's, Skagway was practically a ghost town. Passengers from the few cruise ships that then stopped there a few hours were limited to wandering streets that were dismal in those days, haunting its "frontier" bars, and selecting cheap souvenirs before their ship weighed anchor.

The explosive revival of Skagway since 1983 has been matched by the increased volume of cruise ships calling at this port—over 240 ships carrying more than 150,000 passengers every year in the late 80's, compared to 30,000 passengers during 1973.

The U.S. National Park Service spent millions of dollars restoring several pioneer buildings, and the city paved many streets. Private businesses restored or built a dozen more 1898-style structures along Skagway's 7-block-long "Historic District".

The town became in the 1980's a living museum of the Klondike gold-rush that erupted one century earlier. Many artists migrated here and have transformed the town into "the Carmel of the North". Shops and galleries sell gold nugget jewelry, carved Alaskan ivory, jade sculptures, native wood carvings and much more.

The Klondike Highway connects Skagway with the Alaska Highway.

After gold was discovered in the Klondike Valley, early prospectors reached Skagway by ship and carried their outfits the 40-mile walk (mostly uphill) to **Lake Bennett**, proceeding from there by boat on the **Yukon River** to the gold field. It soon became impossible to provide the growing population in the Klondike with adequate supplies.

Construction of the famous narrow-gauge (36-inch) privately owned railroad began in May of 1898 and was one of the most difficult railroad projects ever engineered. Supplies had to be brought 1,000 miles on small coastal steamers from Seattle. There was no heavy construction equipment. Workers had only horses, shovels and black powder to cut through barriers of solid rock.

The track reached **White Pass** in February of 1899 and **Whitehorse** in July of 1900. This railroad had a colorful history as a major carrier for the enormous amount of construction material used to build the Alaska Highway during World War II, and supplying mines in the Yukon until its trains ceased running in 1982 when plunging world metal prices closed the major mines, the railroad's principal source of revenue.

Daily scheduled passenger service resumed in 1989, with trains operating late May through late September from Skagway to Fraser, British Columbia, on the Klondike Highway. At Fraser, the train connects with motorcoaches that go north to Whitehorse. Similarly, southbound travelers can go by bus from Whitehorse to Fraser and transfer there for the Fraser–Skagway train. The 1992 one-way train/bus fare for adults is $92, roundtrip $160.

There are neither public eating nor lodging facilities in Fraser. Passengers wanting to stop there or to overnight at either Fraser or Lake Bennett must bring their own equipment: tents, sleeping bags, food, camp stove and water. Bennett is the stop for hiking the Chilkoot Trail.

The 12-mile Fraser-Bennett ride, called "Chilkoot Trail Service", is a track motorcar that operates mid-June to mid-September. The 1992 price is $15.

Rivaling many of the most scenic train trips in Europe, the Skagway–Fraser route offers views of the original "trail of '98" Dead Horse Gulch (where 3,000 pack animals died while carrying prospector's supplies), Bridal Veil Falls, and Inspiration Point. Over 36,000 people rode the line when a limited excursion was operated in 1988. The railroad carried nearly twice that number during its first complete season, in 1989.

Another ride, particularly suited for cruise-ship passengers who have only part of a day ashore, is the short roundtrip shown below that features the most scenic portion of the Skagway–Fraser ride, going only to the summit of White Pass and then returning to Skagway.

Skagway - White Pass - Skagway 270

A few minutes after leaving Skagway, watch out the right-hand side of the train for the very small goldrush graveyard, only a few feet to the side of the track. The train climbs along the edge of mountains for an hour before reaching a plateau at the summit. This ascent of 2,885 feet is made in only 21 miles, with a grade of 4 at one point. During the ascent, there is a great view looking down at Skagway and up at the snow-topped mountains.

The final stretch, into Bennett, has excellent scenery, including many cold-blue indigo ponds and dwarfed pine trees. Other sights en route are the 100-ton granite Black Cross Rock, Bridal Veil Falls, Dead Horse Gulch (where 3,000 pack animals died while carrying the prospectors' supplies) and Beaver Lake.

Now deserted, except for a few Parks Canada Rangers and Summer rail employees, Bennett was where more than 10,000 men built rafts and crude boats in 1898 to get themselves and their equipment up the Yukon River to the Klondike gold fields. Highest point on the complete Skagway-Whitehorse route is 2,916 feet, at Log Cabin, B.C.

This is the 1991 schedule. For more information, contact White Pass & Yukon Route, P.O. Box 435, Skagway, Alaska 99840. Telephone from the U.S.A.: (800) 343-7373. Telephone from British Columbia, Yukon Territory, or Northwest Territories: (800) 478-7373. The telephone to call from other locations: (907) 983-2217.

The 1992 roundtrip price is: $69 for adults, $34.50 for children under 12.

These trains operate in 1992 from late May to late September, running daily. Reservation is required.

| Dep. Skagway | 09:00 | 13:30 | Dep. White Pass | 10:25 | 15:15 |
| Arr. White Pass | 10:15 | 15:05 | Arr. Skagway | 11:45 | 16:10 |

714

Skagway - Fraser - Bennett or Whitehorse WP&YR Timetable

The 1992 one-way price is $72 for passengers 13 and older, $36.50 for children up to 12 years old.

Reservation required. This service operates late May to late September.

Dep. Skagway	07:45 (1)	13:00 (2)	Dep. Whitehorse	-0-	08:30 (6)
Arr. Fraser	09:25 (2)	14:35 (3)	Dep. Bennett	13:15 (4)	-0-
Arr. Bennett	11:15	-0-	Dep. Fraser	14:55 (5)	10:25 (5)
Arr. Whitehorse	-0-	18:30	Arr. Skagway	16:39	12:10

(1) Train.   (2) Change to rail motorcar.   (3) Change to a bus.   (4) Rail motorcar.   (5) Change to train.   (6) Bus.

ALASKA RAILROAD

Reservations are required at least 2 weeks in advance of travel date. Write: P.O. Box 107500, Anchorage, Alaska 99510, U.S.A. Telephone: (907) 265-2685 or (800) 544-0552.

Mt. McKinley (Denali National Park) Rail Route

Completed in 1923, the Alaska Railroad's 356-mile line from Fairbanks to Anchorage with Vistadome cars ranks among the world's most exotic train journeys (see timetable on page 716). Fairbanks is only 160 miles south of the Arctic Circle. In Summer, there are 20 hours of daylight every day here.

Also riding along with the Alaska Railroad passenger cars are private luxury domecars owned by Princess Cruises & Tours and by Gray Line of Alaska (owned by Holland America Line-Westours Inc.). Seating in these domecars is offered as part of cruise/tour packages to Alaska.

This railway, first surveyed in 1914, provides access to North America's highest mountain, Mt. McKinley (20,320 feet). Construction began in 1915. The temperature on this route ranges from 100(F) in Summer to -70 (F) in Winter.

The Fairbanks–Anchorage line affords many interesting travel possibilities: (1) an easy one-day roundtrip Anchorage–Talkeetna (site for viewing Mt. McKinley)–Anchorage, (2) another easy one-day roundtrip Fairbanks–Denali National Park–Fairbanks, (3) the complete ride from Fairbanks to Anchorage (and vice versa), and (4) the complete Fairbanks-Anchorage or Anchorage–Fairbanks ride with a stopover at the **Denali National Park** resort.

Inside the 3,030 square mile national park are 3 other prominent mountains: Mt. Foraker (17,000 feet), Mt. Hunter (14,960 feet) and Mt. Russell (11,500 feet). On some Summer days, Mt. McKinley and Mt. Foraker are clearly visible from Anchorage, more than 150 miles to the South.

Headquarters for park activities is the McKinley Park Station Hotel, built in 1972 and operated by a private firm, with accommodations for 275 guests. The hotel is open from late May to late September. A highway links the hotel with such points of interest as Sable Pass, Polychrome Pass, Caribou Pass, Toklat Creek, Igloo Creek, Camp Eilson, Wonder Lake, Camp Denali and Richardson Highway.

Hotel and Park Tour reservations can be made through ARA Outdoor World Ltd.: 825 W. 8th Ave., Anchorage, Alaska 99501, U.S.A. Telephone: (907) 276-7234.

Caribou, giant Alaska moose, 33 other mammals and 112 kinds of birds comprise the animal life in the park. There are grizzly bears and 200-pound mountain sheep to be seen there. Salmon and trout abound in the nearby lakes, streams and rivers.

The hotel offers 2 guided tours. One starts at 06:00, so as to have maximum opportunity to observe wildlife. For late sleepers, a second tour starts at 15:00.

Both the Park Station Hotel and other hotels just outside the Denali Park entrance provide free transportation from them to the train station and to the free shuttle bus, which runs through the park on an hourly basis.

Pack trips in and around the park are available.

Some of the interesting points along the route from Fairbanks to Anchorage are: **College**, where the northernmost institution of higher education in the world is located, the University of Alaska. **Dunbar**, from which trails lead to a goldmining district. (It is F 70 degrees below zero here in the Winter.) **Clear**, a military post. Mountain sheep, between **Healy** and **Denali National Park**. **Honolulu**, with many beaver dams, on the western side of the track. Hurricane Gulch, which the train crosses on a bridge that is 296 feet above the creek. From Mt. McKinley Station to Chulitna, there are (weather permitting) splendid views of Mt. McKinley, and then such views again from Curry to Nancy.

Fairbanks - Denali National Park - Anchorage AR Timetable

One hundred thousand people ride this route every year.

Going south (from Fairbanks), for the best views sit on the left side until Denali Park, on the right side Denali Park-Anchorage. The reverse is advised when going north (from Anchorage). About 60 miles south of Fairbanks, the train travels over the **Tanana River** on the 700-foot high Mears Memorial Bridge, one of the longest single-span bridges in the world. Before the completion of this bridge in 1923, passengers had to cross the river on a ferry.

Fifty miles after leaving the town of **Nenana**, passengers begin to view the 600-mile-long Alaska Range. Its peaks are snow-covered all year. The track clings to the side of cliffs as it goes along the Nenana River Canyon.

Most passengers overnight at **Denali National Park** in order to take a 7-hour narrated bus tour which affords glimpses of **Mount McKinley**, (tallest mountain in North America) and the area's wildlife (caribou, Dall sheep, grizzly bears, wolves, foxes, birds, etc.). For reservations at the Park's 10 hotels and lodges, use a travel agency or contact Denali National Park Central Reservations and Travel, 519 W. 4th Ave., Anchorage, Alaska 99501, U.S.A. Telephone: (907) 274-5366.

Moose are often spotted near **Honolulu Pass**, halfway between Fairbanks and Anchorage. The view is marvelous while crossing the 918-foot-long, 296-foot-high bridge over **Hurricane Gulch**: waterfalls and a river in an immense glacial valley.

Approaching Anchorage, the train goes through the **Matanuska Valley**, where extraordinary vegeatables (70-pound cabbages, radishes the size of a baseball !) thrive in the 19 hours of daylight during Summer.

Late May to mid-September: runs daily in both directions. Mid-September to late May: Runs only Saturday Anchorage–Fairbanks. Runs only Sunday Fairbanks–Anchorage. Both of these trains have a restaurant car, a vistadome and private domecars.

Dep. Anchorage	08:30	Dep. Fairbanks	08:30
Arr. Denali Park	15:45	Dep. Denali Park	12:15
Arr. Fairbanks	20:30	Arr. Anchorage	20:30

PORTAGE - WHITTIER SHUTTLE

South of Anchorage, the town of Whittier was built during World War II to serve as a deepwater port for the military. The only ground access to Whittier is by rail.

Much of the 12-mile Portage-Whittier track is inside 2 long tunnels. The train passes popular Portage Glacier en route to Whittier, now serving as a port for cruise ships. Another use of the train is to board in Whittier dayboats which take passengers to both Columbia Glacier and College Fjord. The train carries passengers in gallery railcars and- vehicles on flatcars.

Portage - Whittier AR Timetable

About 200,000 people take this 30-minute ride along the **Portage Glacier** every year.

Phone Alaska Railroads for times (907) 265-2685. *Late May to mid-September: runs daily, at least 4 roundtrips per day. Mid-September to late May: runs Wednesday, Friday, Saturday and Sunday, 2 roundtrips on each of those days. These trains carry vehicles.*

A sightseeing boat offers cruises on **Prince William Sound** from Whittier to **Valdez.** Scenery along the way includes **Columbia Glacier**, a spectacular colony of black-legged kittiwakes, whales, porpoises, sea otters and sea lions.

SEWARD ROUTE

This 114-mile ride from Anchorage to Seward has spectacular scenery, winding along the Saltwater Turnagain Arm and offering views of the only bore tides in North America (a continuous wave that covers miles of mudflats as contrasted with waves that "break" with a crash and move up and down a beach as the tide changes).

Sighting American bald eagles and mountain goats is common during the first 60 miles of the route. After passing Portage, the train climbs through steep mountains, allowing vistas of river gorges and 3 large glaciers, also alpine meadows, waterfalls, moose and black bears. From Seward, a deepwater port founded in 1903, you can take a dayboat to **Kenali Fjords National Park** to view whales and puffins.

Anchorage - Seward AR Timetable

Operates late May to early September. Runs daily. These trains have light refreshments.

At Portage, the track climbs to high country, passes a few miles from Skookum Glacier, and then skirts the banks of the sparkling **Placer River**. There is a good chance to see moose grazing in the meadows near **Moose Pass**.

| Dep. Anchorage | 07:00 | Dep. Seward | 18:00 |
| Arr. Seward | 11:00 | Arr. Anchorage | 22:00 |

Anchorage

Alaska's largest city (240,000 population). Named for Captain Cook having anchored his ships here in 1778. See the National Park Service movies 12:15 and 14:30 at the NPS Information Center at 540 West Fifth Ave. Subjects covered in the film are park lands, Alaskan history and the northern environment (Canada and Alaska).

Also see the traditional prospector's log cabin, which houses the Visitor Information Center at Fourth Ave. and "F" Street. The 139-foot high Sitka spruce flagpole at the City Hall. Many Eskimo, Aleut and Athabascan Indian artifacts at the Anchorage Museum of History and Art, 121 West Seventh Ave. The Oscar Anderson House. Eklutna Russian Orthodox Church. **Lake Hood,** one of the largest seaplane bases in the world. The Alaska Aviation Heritage Museum. Take a tour of the Crow Creek Gold Mine.

There are good buys here in fox, mink, seal, beaver, muskrat, wolf and coyote furs. Also Eskimo carvings (scrimshaw) in whalebone, walrus ivory, jade and soapstone.

INTERNATIONAL ROUTES FROM THE UNITED STATES

All of the schedules for train trips to Mexico appear earlier in this chapter, in the section on "Mexico" (pages 685–690).

The U.S. gateways for train trips to Canada are: Boston, New York, Detroit and Seattle.

Boston - New London - Montreal

These trains run daily, require reservations, are air-conditioned and have ordinary coaches.

202		196	
Dep. Boston (South)	18:10 (1)	Dep. New London	23:15 (2)
Arr. New London	19:55	Arr. Montreal (Cen.)	10:45
Change trains.			

(1) Parlor car. Light refreshments. (2) Carries sleeping cars and a buffet car.

New York - Montreal 210

This train runs daily, is air-conditioned, has both first-class and ordinary coaches and has buffet.

Dep. New York (Penn.)	10:45
Arr. Montreal (Central)	20:45

New York - Toronto 18

There is excellent Hudson River scenery for 142 miles after leaving New York City. For best views, sit on the left side of the train when going to Toronto, on the right side when going to New York City. The train crosses the gorge below Niagara Falls.

These trains run daily, are air-conditioned, have ordinary coaches and have buffet service.

Dep. New York (Penn.)	08:45	Dep. Toronto	09:30
Dep. Niagara Falls (USA)	17:14	Dep. Niagara Falls (USA)	12:45
Arr. Toronto	20:25	Arr. New York (Penn.)	21:18

Detroit - Windsor - Toronto 18

Take a taxi from Detroit through the International Tunnel to Windsor.

These trains are air-conditioned, have a parlor car and ordinary coaches.

Dep. Windsor (Walkerville)	06:05 (1)	07:50 (2)	09:50 (3)	11:40 (4+6)
Arr. Toronto (Union)	10:30	12:15	14:20	16:00

(1) Runs daily, except Sunday and holidays. Light refreshments on Saturday, buffet on Sunday. (2) Runs Saturday, Sunday and holidays only. (3) Runs Monday–Friday, except holidays. Buffet. (4) Runs Monday, Friday and Sunday. Buffet Monday–Friday. Light refreshments on Sunday. (5) Runs daily. Light refreshments. Also has buffet daily, except Saturday. (6) Plus other departures from Windsor at 14:30 (5) and 17:25 (5), arriving Toronto 18:50 and 21:50.

Seattle - Vancouver Bus 580

In 1981, this train service was replaced by bus transportation between Amtrak's Seattle terminal and VIA Rail Canada's station in Vancouver, allowing for connection with the Vancouver–Toronto train (see page 672 for timetable).

Dep. Seattle	06:00	09:30	12:02	13:00	13:45	16:30	18:30
Arr. Vancouver	10:15	14:00	15:20	16:30	18:40	20:45	22:30

* * *

Dep. Vancouver	07:00	08:00	09:15	11:00	13:30	15:00	20:30
Arr. Seattle	10:30	11:30	13:30	15:30	17:00	18:15	00:30

ADDENDUM

Schedules appear on page 706 for the Chicago–Albuquerque–Los Angeles route, including a stop at **Flagstaff**. There are guided tours at Grand Canyon.

Here are the bus services between Flagstaff and the Grand Canyon.

Flagstaff - Grand Canyon Bus 540

Dep. Flagstaff	07:00	08:45	16:00
Arr. Grand Canyon	09:05	10:50	17:30

* * *

Dep. Grand Canyon	09:45	-0-	17:45
Arr. Flagstaff	11:25	-0-	19:30

SKUNK RAILWAY

This California route is one of the most popular steam train rides in the U.S.A.

Fort Bragg - Willits - Fort Bragg 267

Dep. Fort Bragg	09:20 (1)	13:35 (2)	
Arr. Willits	11:30	17:20	

* * *

Dep. Willits	08:50 (1+2)	13:20 (3)	13:45 (2)
Arr. Fort Bragg	12:20	15:30	16:00

(1) "Skunk" train. (2) Operates mid-June to early September. (3) Operates early January to mid-June and mid-September to late December.

Chapter 15

CENTRAL AMERICA and WEST INDIES

In Central America, a train scheduled to run on a certain day may actually leave a day later.

COSTA RICA

Children under 3 travel free. Half-fare for children 3–10. Children 11 and over must pay full fare.

There are no train connections from Costa Rica to adjacent countries. It is possible to travel by train in Costa Rica from the Caribbean (Limon) to the Pacific Ocean (Puntarenas). En route, the train passes through Cartago and San Jose, the country's capital.

The peak tourist season is December–April.

Cartago

See the tiny (under 6 inches tall) statue of the legendary Indian Black Virgin, in the Basilica of Our Lady of the Angels. Pilgrims come from all over Central America to see La Negrita.This is the location where a primitive structure was built in 1715 on the place where the Virgin Mary is believed to have appeared to a peasant girl. The Sunday market is an interesting event. Take the short bus trip to see the crater of the **Mount Irazu Volcano**. Its eruption in 1723 destroyed the original town.

Limon

Millions of bunches of bananas are exported from this seaport every year. See the gardens in Vargas Park. It rains 300 days each year on the jungle and forest near the Caribbean coast.

San Jose

The capital of Costa Rica. See: The National Theater, with its statues, gold-decorated foyer and marble staircases. The excellent collection of pre-Columbian (as far back as 10,000 B.C.) ceramic and stone vases, figurines, tools and other antiques in the National Museum, open daily except Monday, 09:00–17:00. Thousands of pre-Columbian jade birds, ornaments, musical instruments and human figures at the Jade Museum (in the Insurance Building on Calle 17), open daily except Monday, 10:00–16:00. The National Liquor Factory, in Parque Espana. Frescoes of Costa Rican life in the Salon Dorado at the old La Sabana Airport, now an enormous park.

See the colored glassware and carved wood pieces sold at the government craft center, next to Soledad Church. One of the world's largest collections of insects, displayed at the University of Costa Rica. The leather goods for sale at Caballo Blanco on Moravia Church Plaza. There are all-day bus tours to the Monteverde Cloud Forest, a 4,000-acre biological reserve. Cool at its 4,500-foot altitude, the reserve has 2,000 species of plants and 320 of birds.

The 19th and 20th century paintings and sculptures in the Museum of Costa Rican Art, at the former International Airport Terminal. The food and curios at the indoor Central Market. The miles of broad white-sand beaches at Manuel Antonio Beach Park, a 4-hour drive. Take a bus trip to the volcanoes, Poas and Irazu.

San Jose - Cartago - Limon 1401

NOTE: This narrow-gauge trip departs from and arrives back at the San Jose railstation that is located on the *northeast* side of Parque Nacional !

There is extraordinary scenery on this 102-mile train trip, which takes about 7 hours partly because of the nature of the route (scores of tunnels, bridges and hairpin curves as you descend 5,000 feet to sea level) and partly due to the fact that there are 52 scheduled stops in addition to some unscheduled ones.

It cost thousands of lives (yellow fever, dysentery, beriberi) to build this line between 1871 and 1890.

In the area of the 20 miles leading into Limon, it has rained as much as 35 inches in a 30-hour period.

When it opened (years before the construction of the Panama Canal), this track shortened the trip to Europe from the west coast of Central and South America by 3 months. **Tres Rios**, the first stop on the ride from San Jose, is in the heart of the coffee country. Then come dense rain forest jungles, swamps, banana plantations, waterfalls, hibiscus, poinciana trees, sugar cane, the rampaging **Reventazon River**, coconut trees, orchids and many other wildflowers. The train makes one 3,000-foot descent in 30 minutes.

One can visit a Chinese general store during a 5-minute stop in **Batan**, a Chinese community. **Turrialba** has many coffee plantations. **Gualpiles** and **Siquirres** serve banana plantations. White, sandy beaches along the Caribbean come into view during the last 12 miles, before arriving in Limon.

En route, Indian vendors offer hot coffee, watermelon slices, cashews, corn on the cob, mangoes, hard-boiled eggs, cold chicken and guava juice. There is a 26-minute airplane flight (about $10) you can take for the return to San Jose. However, the last flight of the day may be prior to the train's arrival in Limon.

Dep. San Jose (Atlan.)	N/A (1)	Dep. Limon	N/A (1)
Dep. Cartago	N/A (1)	Dep. Cartago	N/A (1)
Arr. Limon	N/A (1)	Arr. San Jose (Atlan.)	N/A (1)

(1) Time was not available in 1991. Travel time in 1990 was: one hour San Jose-Cartago, 6 hours Cartago-Limon. The trains ran daily.

San Jose - Puntarenas 1400

NOTE: This train departs from and arrives back at the San Jose railstation that is located at the *south* end of the city !

These trains are second-class only.

Dep. San Jose (Pac.)	06:15 (1)	06:30 (2)	Dep. Puntarenas	06:00	15:00 (3)
Arr. Puntarenas	09:15	09:30	Arr. San Jose (Pac.)	09:00	18:00

(1) Runs Saturdays, Sundays and holidays. (2) Plus another San Jose departure at 15:00.
(3) Plus another Puntarenas departure at 18:30 (1).

Sights in **Puntarenas:** Good sea bathing and fishing (shark and tuna) here. An inexpensive boat ride ($1.00) takes you on Sunday mornings to San Lucas Island, with its great El Coro beach. Because it is a penal colony, your guide on San Lucas will be an English-speaking prisoner !

CUBA

Children under 5 travel free. Half-fare for children 5–11. Children 12 and over must pay full fare.

The categories of Cuban trains are: Especial, Primera Especial, Primera and Segunda. Especial requires reservation, is air-conditioned and has reclining seats. Primera Especial is air-conditioned, with reclining seats. (Segunda is tantamount to fourth-class.)

The 4 rail trips from Habana are west to Pinar del Rio and Guane, a short trip east to Matanzas, and the route southeast to both Cienfuegos and to Santiago de Cuba.

Habana

This is the largest, most cosmopolitan and most beautiful city in the Caribbean.

See: El Morro Castle. The view from the tower of the city's oldest fort, La Fuerza. Marvelous gardens in Parque Central. Vermay paintings in El Templete on Plaza Carlos Manuel Cespedes. The patio at the former palace of the Captain's General, on the west side of the Plaza Cespedes.

The lovely interior of La Merced Church. The view from the east tower of the Cathedral. The National Museum in Palacio de Bellas Artes. The Botanical Gardens on Avenida Allende. The Museum of Natural Sciences, in the Capitol building. The Museum of the Revolution, in the Presidential Palace. The statues and mausoleums in the outstanding Colon Cemetery.

Ernest Hemingway's home, maintained as it was when he lived there in 1960. The art gallery, carnival rides, equestrian center and restaurants in the enormous Lenin Park. The tremendous monument to Jose Marti, a leader of the last century's revolution against Spain, in the Plaza of the Revolution, competing with the enormous picture on a government building of Che Guevara, who helped Fidel Castro overthrow Batista in this century.

Santiago de Cuba

See The Colonial Museum.

Habana - Pinar del Rio - Guane 1511

Dep. Habana (Central)	05:25 (1)	-0-
Dep. Habana (Tulipan)	-0-	17:00 (2)
Arr. Guane	14:12	22:26
	* * *	
Dep. Guane	02:00 (2)	04:35 (1)
Arr. Habana (Tulipan)	07:49	-0-
Arr. Habana (Central)	-0-	14:19

(1) Fourth-class only.   (2) Primera Especial-class only. Air-conditioned. Reclining seat. Light refreshment.

Habana - Matanzas 1510

All of these trains are fourth-class only.

Dep. Habana (C.B.)	04:50	07:58	11:40	14:57	18:12	21:23
Arr. Matanzas	07:26	10:38	14:17	17:38	20:49	23:59

* * *

Dep. Matanzas	04:45	07:56	11:45	14:55	18:12	21:25
Arr. Habana (C.B.)	07:23	10:40	14:20	17:40	20:40	23:55

Habana - Cienfuegos 1512

Dep. Habana (Tulipan)	06:58 (1)	07:24 (2)	23:00 (1)
Arr. Cienfuegos	12:33	16:45	04:27

* * *

Dep. Cienfuegos	07:48 (2)	15:05 (1)	23:43 (1)
Arr. Habana (Tulipan)	16:24 (2)	20:48	05:18

(1)Primera Especial-class only. Air-conditioned. Reclining seats. Light refreshments.
(2)Fourth-class only. Depart/Arrive Habana's Central railstation.

Habana - Santiago de Cuba 1515

Dep. Habana (Central)	00:40 (1)	18:10 (3)
Arr. Santiago de Cuba	N/A (2)	07:55

* * *

Dep. Santiago de Cuba	12:40 (1)	18:15 (3)
Arr. Habana (Central)	05:00	08:08

(1) First-class only. Light refreshments. (2) Time has not been available since 1989.
(3) Especial-class only. Reservation required. Air-conditioned train. Reclining seats.
Restaurant car.

EL SALVADOR

Uprisings here ended all passenger train service in 1989.

The principal train line in El Salvador was from Cutuco, a seaport on the Pacific Ocean, to inland San Salvador. The only international rail route from El Salvador was a continuation of the Cutuco–San Salvador line into Guatemala. Because El Salvador is largely 2 rows of volcanoes, many volcanoes may be seen on the trips listed here.

Cutuco

This is a popular resort for swimming and fishing.

San Salvador

See Casa Presidencial. The Zoo. Many beautiful parks. The view from the top of **Mount Chulul**, looking through 2 tremendous vertical rocks called Puerta del Diablo (Devil's Door). Recommended short excursions: to **Panchimalco and Lake Iloopango,** the crater of San Salvador Volcano, Izalco Volcano and **Atescol Park, Ichanmichen Park, Lake Coatepeque, and Cerro Verde.**

Cutuco - San Salvador

Dep. Cutuco	Dep. San Salvador
Dep. San Miguel	Dep. San Vicente
Dep. Zacatecoluca	Dep. Zacatecoluca
Dep. San Vicente	Dep. San Miguel
Arr. San Salvador	Arr. Cutuco

Sights in **San Miguel:** Fine parks. The statues and fountains at Chinameca Church.

Sights in **Zacatecoluca**: Inchanmichen, the garden park.

Sights in **San Vicente**: El Pilar, the most unique church in El Salvador.

Three other rail routes in El Salvador were: San Salvador–San Jeronimo, San Salvador–Ahuachapan, and San Salvador–Sonsonate.

San Salvador - San Jeronimo

Dep. San Salvador	Dep. San Jeronimo
Arr. San Jeronimo	Arr. San Salvador

San Salvador - Ahuachapan

Dep. San Salvador	Dep. Ahuachapan
Arr. Texis Junction	Arr. Texis Junction
Change trains.	Change trains.
Dep. Texis Junction	Dep. Texis Junction
Arr. Ahuachapan	Arr. San Salvador

Sights in **Ahuachapan**: The Atehuezian waterfalls. Many geysers. Two lakes draw visitors: Laguna Verde and Apaneca.

San Salvador - Sonsonate

Dep. San Salvador	Dep. Sonsonate
Arr. Sonsonate	Arr. San Salvador

Sights in **Sonsonate:** The Sunday market (dairy products, tropical fruits, hides). El Pilar Church. The white porcelain cupola on the Cathedral. It is a 30-minute bus ride from Sonsonate to the fine beaches at **Acajutla**, El Salvador's main seaport.

INTERNATIONAL ROUTE FROM EL SALVADOR

Here is the route from El Salvador to western Guatemala.

San Salvador - San Jeronimo - Anguiatu - Zacapa - Guatemala City

200		
Dep. San Salvador	N/A	
Arr. San Jeronimo	N/A	(1)
Change trains.		
000		
Dep. Anguiatu	N/A	(2)
Arr. Zacapa	N/A	
Stay overnight in Zacapa.		

1151		
Dep. Zacapa	N/A	(3)
Arr. Guatemala City	N/A	

(1) Walk or take bus or taxi ½-mile to Anguiatu. (2) Service from Anguiatu to Zacapa was suspended in 1986. (3) Ran Wednesday, Friday and Sunday.

GUATEMALA

Children under 3 travel free. Half-fare for children 3–11. Children 12 and over must pay full fare.

It is possible to travel in Guatemala by train from the Caribbean (Puerto Barrios) to the Pacific Ocean (Tecun Uman).

Guatemala City

See Mayan treasures in the Archaeological Museum in La Aurora Park, open daily except Monday. A very large collection of Mayan figurines, masks and pottery at Popol Vuh Museum (9 Calle 3-62), open daily except Sunday. Museo Ixchel (4 Avenue 6-27) has a good exhibit of Indian textiles and clothing, open daily except Monday.

The murals, stained-glass and tiled patios and fountains in the National Palace, near Central Park. Next door is the Metropolitan Cathedral. The gold and mahogany altar at Cerro del Carmen Church, and the splendid view of the city from the gardens there.

The marvelous assortment of fabrics at the Central Market. The Botanical Gardens. The Zoo. The National Museum of History and Fine Arts. A display of products made in Guatemala, at the Popular Arts and Handicrafts Center (10 Avenue and 11 Calle). The fish-shaped Templo de la Expiacion. These churches: La Merced, San Francisco, Santa Domingo, Las Capuchinas, and Santa Rosa.

The slide lecture on Mayan archaeology, every night at 19:00 Camino Real Hotel, 9 Calle 4-69.

Take a local bus to the western side of the city to see the Mayan ruins of Kaminal Juyu (Valley of Death). It is a short bus ride to see these nearby Indian villages: **Chinautla, San Pedro Sacatepequez** and **San Juan Sacatepequez**.

Visit nearby (28 miles) **Antigua** to see many colonial churches, plazas, fountains and walled palaces where 70,000 people lived before Antigua was destroyed by earthquake in the 18th century. One of the many giant volcanos here is still very active.

Visit nearby (90 miles) **Chichicastenango** for fabulous bargains in strawgoods, fabrics (tablecloths, napkins, etc.) and pottery at the extraordinary Thursday and Sunday markets.

Visit nearby (134 miles) **Quirigua** to see excellent remains of the Mayan Old Empire. Visit nearby 50-square-mile **Lake Atitlan** to see its beautiful setting amid mountains and volcanos. The lake's color changes constantly.

Guatemala City - Puerto Barrios 1151

This route goes through many banana plantations and dense jungles. Watch for 3 volcano cones, a short distance from Guatemala City. *The train to Puerto Barrios usually runs 2–6 hours late, and the return is often one day late.*

Dep. Guatemala City	07:15 (1)		Dep. Puerto Barrios	06:00 (2)
Dep. Rancho	11:26		Dep. Zacapa	13:10
Dep. Zacapa	13:38		Dep. Rancho	15:52
Arr. Puerto Barrios	21:15		Arr. Guatemala City	20:00

(1) Runs Tuesday, Thursday and Saturday. (2) Runs Wednesday, Friday and Sunday.

Sights in **Zacapa**: En route from Guatemala City, a stop is made here for dining at the railstation. This is the junction for the train service to and from El Salvador.

Sights in **Puerto Barrios:** Nearby beaches (Escabas and Santo Tomas de Castilla) are very popular.

Guatemala City - Esquintla - Mazatenango - Tecun Uman 1150

Dep. Guatemala City	07:30 (1)		Dep. Tecun Uman	06:00 (2)
Dep. Escuintla	10:17		Dep. Mazatenango	10:20
Dep. Mazatenango	14:39		Dep. Escuintla	14:45
Arr. Tecun Uman	19:15		Arr. Guatemala City	18:00

(1) Runs Tuesday, Thursday and Saturday. (2) Runs Wednesday, Friday and Sunday.

Sights in **Escuintla**: Famous for fruits and medicinal baths. Nearby are giant sculptures in La Democracia (an archeological park) and the 13th century ruins at **Mixco Viejo**.

Sights in **Mazatenango**: The production of tropical fruits, coffee, sugar and cacao.

726

INTERNATIONAL ROUTE FROM GUATEMALA

This is the train connection from Guatemala to Mexico.

Guatemala City - Tecun Uman - Ciudad Hidalgo - Mexico City 1150

Dep. Guatemala City	07:30 (1)	Arr. Tecun Uman	19:15

It is possible, although very difficult, to travel by train from from Guatemala City into southern Mexico. The reasons we always advise against attempting this trip until conditions improve are:

There is no acceptable lodging in either primitive Tecun Uman or in equally primitive Cuidad Hidalgo, the 2 border cities where a transfer is necessary.

Further, there is an *overnight* interval of 14 hours between arriving in Tecun Uman and departing from Ciudad Hidalgo for Tapachula and on to Veracruz and Mexico City.

The final obstacle is that passengers attempting this transfer have to walk more than a mile in great heat and mucho dust from Tecun Uman to Ciudad Hidalgo, and pay a substantial toll charge to cross the border bridge.

1043		1000 + 1043	
Dep. Ciudad Hidalgo	08:30 (2)	Dep. Veracruz	21:25 (5)
Arr. Tapachula	09:50	Arr. Mexico City	07:37 (6)
Change trains.			
Dep. Tapachula	15:10 (3)		
Arr. Veracruz	14:20 (4)		
Change trains.			

(1) Runs Tuesday, Thursday and Saturday. Second-class only. (2) Runs daily. Second-class only. (3) Runs daily. Light refreshments. (4) Day 2. (5) "Star" service train. Reservation required. Runs daily. Air-conditioned train. Carries a sleeping car a Primera Especial-class coach, and a domecar. Light refreshments. (6) Day 3 from Ciudad Hidalgo.

HONDURAS

Children under 3 travel free. Half-fare for children 3-11. Children 12 and over must pay full fare.

The country's rail lines serve banana plantations and 2 seaports.

Puerto Cortes

Honduras' main port. Very hot climate here. Take the bus ride to see the castle at **Omoa**.

San Pedro Sula

This is the gateway (by air or bus) for travel to Tegucigalpa. Terribly hot here. The population is cosmopolitan: North American, Irish, Cuban, Russian. Fabulous Mayan ruins are located at **Copan**, 112 miles by road from San Pedro Sula.

Tela

This seaport ships mountains of bananas. See United Fruit Company's experimental farm in nearby **Lancetilla**.

San Pedro Sula - La Ceiba - Tela - Baracoa - Puerto Cortes 1250

The run between La Ceiba and Tela is a very scenic 2-hour ride through banana plantations and jungle.

Dep. San Pedro Sula	-0-	07:00 (2)	-0-	15:00 (2)
Dep. La Ceiba	N/A (1+2)	-0-	N/A (1)	-0-
Dep. Tela	06:00	-0-	13:45	-0-
Arr. Baracoa	07:45	08:05	16:05	16:15
Arr. Puerto Cortes	-0-	09:15	17:15	-0-
	*	* *		
Dep. Puerto Cortes	-0-	07:00	15:15 (2)	-0-
Dep. Baracoa	07:45 (2)	08:15	16:15	16:15 (2)
Dep. Tela	-0-	10:30	-0-	18:00
Arr. La Ceiba	-0-	N/A (1)	-0-	N/A (1)
Arr. San Pedro Sula	09:00	-0-	17:30	-0-

(1) Time has not been available since 1980.   (2) Carries second-class and third-class coaches only.

JAMAICA

Children under 3 travel free. Half-fare for children 3–11. Children 12 and over must pay full fare.

Jamaica has 3 rail lines: one from Kingston to Port Antonio, one from Kingston to Montego Bay, and a short line for one-day excursions from Montego Bay to the Appleton Rum Distillery.

Kingston

The capital and commercial center of Jamaica. Shopping for duty-free items is the key tourist attraction here. See: The carvings and historical items at the Institute of Jamaica. The Royal Botanical Gardens at **Hope**, only a few minutes away, a fine collection of tropical plants, including many orchids.

Montego Bay

Also popular for its duty-free goods. Take the glass-bottom boat to see the beautiful coral gardens. Much deep-sea fishing, sailing, water skiing, golf and tennis here.

Spanish Town

There is much fine 18th century English architecture here. See a broad canvas of Jamaican history and interesting ethnic exhibits at the Museum. The Cathedral.

Kingston - Spanish Town - Montego Bay 1550

This is a very scenic trip on trains that do not have air-conditioning. The route is through mountains, dense jungles, many sugarcane and banana plantations, tropical rain forests, farms, swamps and crocodile breeding-grounds. Vendors selling snacks are usually on board.

Service between Spanish Town and Montego Bay has not operated since 1989 because of hurricane damage to that part of the line that year. All of the trains below run Monday–Friday except holidays and are second-class only.

Dep. Kingston	06:50	08:30	15:40	16:55	17:15 (1)
Arr. Spanish Town	07:18	09:00	16:10	17:22	17:43
Arr. Montego Bay	-0-	-0-	-0-	-0-	-0-
		* * *			
Dep. Montego Bay	-0-	-0-	-0-	-0-	-0-
Dep. Spanish Town	06:03	06:52	07:20	07:50	09:15 (2)
Arr. Kingston	30 minutes later				

(1) Plus another departure from Kingston at 17:45, arriving Spanish Town 18:11. (2) Plus another departure from Spanish Town at 16:20, arriving Kingston 16:50.

SPECIAL TRAIN TOURS

Guides and calypso bands accompany all tours. Transportation is included from one's Montego Bay hotel to the railstation and, at end of tour, from the railstation back to hotels.

The Appleton Express

A very scenic route. The distillery, founded in 1825, is located beside the Black River, in a picturesque valley.

The $55 (U.S.) price for this tour in 1991 included riding in air-conditioned coaches, a bar coach open all day, touring the Ipswich caves, sampling Appleton rums during the tour of the distillery, and a leisurely lunch.

For advance reservations contact Ragus Tours Ltd., P.O. Box 989, Montigo Bay, Jamaica, West Indies. Telephone: (809) 952-3692.

The Jamaica Tourist Board has advised us since 1990 that these trains run Tuesday, Thursday and Friday despite Cook's contrary information. Depart Montego Bay 08:50, arrive Appleton 11:30. Depart Appleton 13:35, arrive back in Montego Bay 15:45.

Catadupa Chu Chu

Hurricane damage in late 1989 caused this tour to cease operating since then for repairs.

This tour included train stops in **Cambridge** and **Catadupa**. The return to Montego Bay was by bus, with a stop in **Seaford Town**.

Mandeville Rail Tour

Hurricane damage in late 1989 caused this tour to cease operating since then for repairs.

This tour included the train stopping in **Balaclava** (to order shirts, dresses, skirts and blouses from light-weight fabrics in dazzling colors and wild designs). At **Williamsfield**, passengers transferred to a bus that toured **Mandeville**. The return train ride stopped in Balaclava to pick up clothes that were ordered that morning.

NICARAGUA

Children under 3 travel free. Half-fare for children 3–10. Children 11 and over must pay full fare. Nicaraguan trains have only one class of coach.

The only rail route in Nicaragua once went from Corinto on the Pacific Ocean to Leon, Managua, and then to Granada on the shore of Lake Nicaragua. It now runs only from Leon to Granada. There are no rail connections between Nicaragua and adjacent countries.

Corinto

Nicaragua's main seaport.

Leon

See: The largest Cathedral in Central America. Ancient streets and buildings. The 16th century Subtiava Church. Do not miss the iron cannon at the old colonial bridge, Guadalupe. En route from Leon to Managua, there is a short spur to El Sauce, for which timetables are not available.

Managua

Most of this city was totally destroyed in the 1972 earthquake and has been in the process of being rebuilt since then. Be sure to stroll through the beautiful Parque Central (fountains, statues, stately trees). See the Cathedral and the nearby National Palace.

Masaya

Much Indian handicrafts here.

Granada

This city is at the end of the 114-mile rail line that once began in Corinto. Boats leave from the center of Granada for excursions to islands on Lake Nicaragua, one of the world's most unique phenomenon.

The area of this lake was once part of the Pacific Ocean. Volcano lava formed a fill, separating this area from the ocean, but not until after salt-water species of fish had been cut off from the ocean. Over millions of years, the water changed slowly from salt-water to fresh-water, allowing the sea life time to adapt to the new environment. The only fresh-water sharks in the world inhabit this lake.

Sights to see in Granada: The Jalteva and San Francisco churches. The turtles and baby crocodiles in the fountains at Parque Central. A very interesting cemetery. Ride in a horse-drawn carriage.

Leon - Managua - Masaya - Granada 1300

Dep. Leon	04:30 (1)	05:00	09:15 (2)	12:00 (1)	15:30 (3)
Arr. Managua	06:30	07:20	12:40	14:00	17:50
Change trains.					
Dep. Managua	-0-	08:00	13:30 (2)	-0-	18:00 (2)
Dep. Masaya	-0-	09:10	14:40	-0-	19:12
Arr. Granada	-0-	09:50	15:20	-0-	19:55

* * *

Dep. Granada	05:20 (4)	05:50 (6)	11:00 (3)	15:30 (3)
Dep. Masaya	06:00	06:30	11:40	16:10
Arr. Managua	07:10	07:40	12:40	17:10
Change trains.				
Dep. Managua	07:25 (5)	08:00 (6)	12:45 (7)	18:00 (3+10)
Arr. Leon	09:15	11:05	15:00	20:20

(1) Runs daily. Supplement charged. Light refreshments. (2) Runs daily. Light refreshments. (3) Runs daily. (4) Runs daily, except Sundays and holidays. Light refreshments. (5) Runs daily, except Sundays and holidays. Supplement charged. Light refreshments. (6) Runs Sundays and holidays only. Light refreshments. (7) Runs Saturdays, Sundays and holidays. (8) Runs Sundays and holidays only. (9) Runs Monday–Friday, except holidays. (10) Plus other departures from Managua at 09:30 (8), 11:00 (9) and 17:00 (1). arriving Leon 11:30, 13:20 and 19:00.

PANAMA

Children under 5 travel free. Half-fare for children 5–14. Children 15 and over must pay full fare. A supplement is charged both children and adults for air-conditioned space.

It was once possible to travel by train from the Caribbean (Colon) to the Pacific Ocean (Panama City) in 90 minutes. There are on this trip excellent views of the jungle, the canal and the ships passing through the Canal. Sit on the left side for the best view. There are no rail connections between Panama and adjacent countries.

A. T. Peters told us in 1985 that the statement by Cook about air-conditioning is inaccurate: "There is *no air-conditioning* in any car, and many seats are missing. Some of the remaining seats are damaged.

"Delays while waiting for the canal passage are 5 times longer than they were before Panama took over operating the railway. Trains often depart later than scheduled and arrive late even when they depart on time."

Panama City

Stroll down Paseo de las Bovedas and see the view from there of the Bay of Panama and the islands offshore (Flamenco, Naos and Perico). See the President's Palace, called Palacio de las Garzas. The egrets there are worth the visit. The gold altar and famous organ in San Jose Church.

The view of the bay from the top of La Cresta. Inca and Spanish treasures in the National Museum. The monument dedicated to the Canal, at Plaza de Francia. Instituto Bolivar. The 17th century Cathedral, facing Plaza de la Independencia.

Panama City - Colon 1500

Dep. Panama City	04:40 (1)	06:45 (1)	08:30 (2)	12:35 (2)	15:20 (1+3)
Arr. Colon	90 minutes later				

Sights in **Colon**: This is one of the world's busiest ports. See the statues on Paseo Centenario. The Cathedral. The Casino. Many nightclubs. Shop for English bone china, ivory, furniture and perfume on Front Street.

There are 3 good excursions from Colon: To Gatun Locks and the nearby jungle. To Fort San Lorenzo, at the mouth of the Chagres River. And a boat trip to the San Blas archipelago.

The old Spanish ruins at the city of **Portobello** are *not within walking distance of Colon, and the road to them is impassable after a heavy rain.*

Dep. Colon	04:40 (1)	06:40 (2)	06:55 (1)	10:45 (2)	15:35 (1+4)
Arr. Panama City	90 minutes later				

(1) Runs Monday–Friday, except holidays. (2) Runs Saturday only. (3) Plus other departures from Panama City at 17:40 (1) and 17:50 (2). (4) Plus other departures from Colon at 16:00 (2) and 17:25 (1).

Concepcion - Puerto Armuelles 1502

Dep. Concepcion	08:30	13:30	Dep. Puerto Armuelles	13:30
Arr. Puerto Armuelles	11:30	16:30	Arr. Concepcion	16:30

Chapter 16
SOUTH AMERICA

Winter in South America (south of Colombia and Venezuela) is from June 21 to September 20. Summer is from December 21 to March 20.

In South America, a train scheduled to run on a particular day may actually leave a day later. In planning trips based on information in this chapter, readers are advised to consider the fact that throughout Eastern Europe, Asia, Africa and Latin America, second-class space is usually primitive and almost always extremely crowded. It is best to reserve first-class space when traveling these areas by train.

As is true of countries in Western Europe, train schedules and ticket prices are always subject to change. **Departure and arrival times should be re-checked at each leg of a trip.** Where changes have occurred, usually the changes will be slight and have little effect on one's itinerary. Re-checking will help you reach a railstation before your train departs.

Another point that has been repeated throughout this book is that many cities all over the world have 2 or more railstations.

Throughout this book, we have taken pains to tell you the name of the railstation (in parentheses immediately after the name of a city) whenever a city has more than one railstation, so you will not miss a departure by going to the wrong station.

ARGENTINA

Children under 3 travel free. Half-fare for children 3–11. Children 12 and over must pay full fare. The 3 classes of coach cars are: air-conditioned class, first-class and second- class.

There are 27,000 miles of rail service in Argentina, radiating out from Buenos Aires.

The 6 major rail routes from Buenos Aires are to Rosario (from where one branch continues to Tucuman and Jujuy, via Cordoba, and a second goes to Tucuman and Jujuy via La Banda), the transcontinental route to Mendoza (and on to Valparaiso, Chile, the most exciting rail trip in South America before Mendoza–Valparaiso was substituted by bus in 1980), and the lines to Santa Rosa, Mar del Plata, Posadas and to Bahia Blanca (from where one branch continues to Zapala and a second branch goes to San Carlos de Bariloche, gateway to the Lake District).

The connection with Uruguay (and on to Brazil) involves using hydrofoil boat service from Buenos Aires to Colonia and then bus service from Colonia to Montevideo, from where rail service resumes.

There is also connection by rail from Buenos Aires to Asuncion, Paraguay.

ARGENTINA'S TRAIN PASS

Argempass *Not* transferable. Unlimited first-class train travel. Sold only in Argentina, at railway booking offices. Can be upgraded for sleeping car accommodation by paying the supplemental charge for sleeper space. The validity period begins on the first day the pass is used and ends at 24:00 on the final day.

The 1991 adult prices were: 1,487,700 Australs for 30 days, A-2,500,500 for 60 days, and A-3,449,200 for 90 days. Children 3-12 years old: A-743,900, A-1,250,800 and A-1,724,600.

There is a small charge for obtaining a refund before starting to use the pass. When a 60-day pass has been used any part of the first 30 days, it can be returned to the Argentine Railways for a refund that results in the passenger paying only for a 30-day pass.

TICKET DISCOUNTS

Group 10%–25% for 10–25 persons.
Family 25% for 3 or more persons in the same family.
Youth 25% for persons 13–30 years old.
Senior Citizens 25% for women 55 years of age or older, and for men 60 years of age or older.

Buenos Aires

This is an enormous city with a population of 11,000,000. A 3-hour bus tour costs only $7 and is advisable before starting independent sightseeing.

The railstations here and the routes they serve are: Constitucion (southern), Lacroze (northeastern Paraguay), Once (western), Puente Alsina, Retiro (Chile and Bolivia), and Velez Sarsfield (northwestern).

Stroll the magnificent Avenida 9 Julio. See Colon Opera House. The Museum of Modern Art. The statues, formal gardens and 2 lakes in Palermo Park and the nearby Zoological and Botanical Gardens. The excellent statues and paintings in the Cathedral. See and hear the inimitable tango in San Telmo, the oldest section of the city, where an antiques market takes place every Sunday.

Eva Peron's mausoleum, in Recoleta Cemetery. The collection of gaucho artifacts, silver and iron objects, musical instruments and tapestries in the Museo de Motivos de Jose Hernandez (Avenida de Libertador 2373). The tapestries and antiques at the Museum of Decorative Arts and the National Museum of Oriental Art (both at Ave. de Libertador 1902).

Argentina's largest art collection, in the Museo de Bellas Artes (Ave. de Libertador 1437), open daily 08:30–19:00. The Natural Sciences Museum (Avenida Angel Gallardo 470). The outstanding collection of colonial silver in the Isaac Fernandez Blanco Museum of Spanish-American Art (Suipacha 1422), open daily 14:00–19:00. El Pilar Church (Junin 1904). The Municipal Museum. The Numismatic Museum at the Banco Central.

Buenos Aires - Rosario 2266

Dep. B.A. (Retiro)	07:00 (1)	09:30 (2)	13:00 (3)	16:30 (4)	18:00 (5+7)
Arr. Rosario (Norte)	11:10	14:35	17:30	20:45	22:15

Sights in **Rosario**: The Juan B. Castagnino Municipal Museum and the Provincial Historical Museum, both in Parque Independencia. The Cathedral (Calle 25 de Mayo). Stroll on Boulevard Orono. The Monument of The Flag, along the river bank.

Dep. Rosario (Norte)	02:25 (6)	04:20 (5)	05:50 (4)	07:00 (1)	08:00 (5+8)
Arr. B.A. (Retiro)	07:10	09:05	10:35	11:40	12:50

(1) Runs daily. Air-conditioned first-class. Light refreshments. (2) From Buenos Aires — Runs Monday and Saturday. From Rosario — Runs Tuesday and Sunday. Has second-class only. (3) From Buenos Aires — Runs Tuesday, Thursday and Saturday. From Rosario — Runs Wednesday, Friday and Saturday. Air-conditioned first-class. Buffet. (4) From Buenos Aires — Runs Tuesday and Friday. From Rosario — Runs Monday and Thursday. Supplement charged. Carries an air-conditioned first-class sleeping car and first-class coach. Restaurant car. Cinema car. (5) Runs daily. Air-conditioned first-class. Restaurant car. (6) Runs Monday, Wednesday and Friday. Air-conditioned first-class. (7) Plus other departures from Buenos Aires at 19:00 (1), 21:00 (5) and 23:00 (6), arriving Rosario 23:10, 01:20 amd 03:25. (8) Plus other departures from Rosario at 13:00 (3), 17:00 (2) and 19:00 (1), arriving Buenos Aires 17:45, 22:20 and 23:40.

Buenos Aires - Rosario - Tucuman - Salta or Jujuy 2261

Dep. Buenos Aires			Dep. Jujuy	07:12 (4)	08:05 (5)
(Retiro)	08:45 (1)		Dep. Salta	-0-	08:10
Dep. Rosario (Oeste)	14:20		Arr. Tucuman		
Dep.			(Norte)	15:10 (4)	17:08
Alta Cordoba	22:02		Dep.		
Dep. Tucuman			Alta Cordoba		09:27 (6)
(Norte)	13:52 (2)	15:05 (3)	Dep. Rosario (Oeste)		16:28
Arr. Salta	22:17	-0-	Arr. Buenos Aires		
Arr. Jujuy	22:42	23:34	(Retiro)		21:15

(1) Runs Wednesday, Friday and Sunday. Buffet Buenos Aires–Tucuman. Train divides in Guemes, one section going to Salta and the other section to Jujuy. (2) Day 2 from Buenos Aires. (3) Departs from Tucuman's GM railstation. Runs Tuesday and Friday. Buffet. (4) Runs Thursday and Sunday. Arrives at Tucuman's GM railstation. (5) Runs Wednesday, Friday and Sunday. Buffet Tucuman–Buenos Aires. Train starts as 2 sections, one in Jujuy, the other in Salta. The 2 sections combine in Guemes. (6) Day 2 from Tucuman.

Sights in **Cordoba**: Founded in 1573, it is Argentina's second largest city. Climate here is temperate all year.

See the outline of the front of the 17th century Cathedral, in white stone on the pavement in front of the Cathedral. A block from the Cathedral is the Compania de Jesus (Jesuit) Church, constructed in 1649. It is one of the finest examples of colonial architecture and is the oldest ecclesiastical building in Argentina.

Also see the College of Monserrat. The 17th century university. The Historical and Colonial Museum in the Viceroy's House, on Calle Rosario. The lovely doorway at the Church and Convent of Santa Teresa, on Calle Independencia. The cedar vault and cupola in the 17th century La Merced Church, on Calle Rivadavia. The serpent collection at the excellent Zoological Garden, and the view of Cordoba from there. The Museum of Fine Arts at the Plaza Centenario. The Academy of Fine Arts, near the Plaza Velez Sarsfield. Sacred Heart Church.

Sights in **Tucuman**: Government Palace. At Plaza Independencia: The Church of San Francisco, the Cathedral, Government Palace, and the statue of Liberty, surrounded by orange and palm trees. The Museum at Casa Historica, on Calle Congresso, and the *"son et lumiere"* programs presented there every night.

The menhir stone in beautiful Parque 9 de Julio. The herbarium, animals and insects in the Instituto Miguel Lillo. The lovely Parque Avellaneda and Parque Quebrada de Lules. The Folklore Museum. The Anthropological Museum at 25 de Mayo 492. Nearby: the outstanding Villa Nougues residential area.

Sights in **Salta**: The 16th century images of Cristo del Milagro and the Virgin Mary, in the Cathedral. The Museum of Colonial History and Fine Arts, at Caseros 575. The historical museum, Cabildo, at Caseros 549. Shopping for handicraft, particularly onyx. The view of Salta from Cerro San Bernardo, a short walk or drive. There is train service from Salta to Resistencia, Posadas, La Paz and Antofagasta.

Sights in **Jujuy**: The superb wood pulpit in the Cathedral at Plaza Belgrano. The Palacio de Tribunales. Parque San Martin. Nearby: numerous ancient Franciscan, Dominican and Jesuit churches.

Here is the second route between Rosario and Tucuman.

Buenos Aires - Rosario - Tucuman (via La Banda) 2266

Dep. B.A. (Retiro)	16:30 (1+2)	18:00 (4)
Arr. Rosario (Norte)	20:45	22:15
Dep. Rosario (Norte)	21:00	22:30
Arr. Tucuman (GM)	10:20 (3)	13:00 (3)
	* * *	
Dep. Tucuman (GM)	16:30 (2+5)	18:00 (4)
Arr. Rosario (Norte)	05:35 (3)	07:50 (3)
Dep. Rosario (Norte)	05:50	08:00
Arr. B.A. (Retiro)	10:35	12:50

(1) Runs Tuesday and Friday. (2) Supplement charged. Carries an air-conditioned sleeping car and an air-condiioned first-class coach. Restaurant car. Cinema car. (3) Day 2. (4) Runs daily. Has an air-conditioned coach. Restaurant car. (5) Runs Wednesday and Sunday.

Buenos Aires - Rojas 2263

All of these trains are third-class only.

Dep. Buenos Aires (Lacroze)	06:15 (1)	19:20 (2)	20:15 (3)
Arr. Rojas	10:58	23:50	00:50
	* * *		
Dep. Rojas	05:00 (4)	16:45 (3)	
Arr. Buenos Aires (Lacroze)	09:30	21:18	

(1) Runs Saturday only. (2) Runs Monday–Friday, except holidays. (3) Runs Sundays and holidays only. (4) Runs daily, except Sundays and holidays.

Buenos Aires - Rosario - Cordoba 2264

Dep. Buenos Aires (Retiro)	09:30 (1)	21:00 (2)
Dep. Rosario (Norte)	14:50	01:30
Arr. Cordoba	22:55	09:20
	* * *	
Dep. Cordoba	08:40 (1)	20:30 (2)
Arr. Rosario (Norte)	16:40	03:55
Arr. Buenos Aires (Retiro)	22:20	09:05

(1) Runs Monday and Saturday. Second-class only. (2) Carries air-conditioned first-class sleeping cars and first-class coaches. Restaurant car.

Buenos Aires - Daireaux 2268

These trains are third-class only and have light refreshments.

Dep. Buenos Aires (P. Con.)	07:25 (1)	18:50
Arr. Daireaux	18:47	06:24
	* * *	
Dep. Daireaux	11 :45 (2)	20:35
Arr. Buenos Aires (P. Con.)	23:22	08:20

(1) Runs Saturday only. (2) Runs Sunday only.

Buenos Aires - Las Flores - Quequen Necochea 2272

These trains have air-conditioned coaches and light refreshments.

Dep. Buenos Aires (P. Con.)	23:00 (1)		Dep. Quequen Necochea	22:45 (3)
Dep. Las Flores	01:20 (2)		Arr. Las Flores	06:16 (4)
Arr. Quequen Necochea	08:55		Arr. Buenos Aires (P. Con.)	09:07

(1) Runs Monday, Wednesday and Friday. (2) Runs Tuesday, Thursday and Saturday. (3) Runs Tuesday, Thursday and Sunday. (4) Runs Wednesday, Friday and Monday.

Buenos Aires - Rufino - San Rafael 2267

Schedules shown were effective in 1990. Timetable was not available in 1991.

These trains have an air-conditioned coach and a restaurant car.

Dep. Buenos Aires (Retiro)	22:00 (1)		Dep. San Rafael	17:30 (3)
Dep. Rufino	04:48 (2)		Arr. Rufino	05:25 (4)
Arr. San Rafael	16:30		Arr. Buenos Aires (Retiro)	11:45

(1) Runs Tuesday and Friday. (2) Runs Wednesday and Saturday. (3) Runs Thursday and Sunday. (4) Runs Friday and Monday.

Buenos Aires - Venado Tuerto 2277

These trains run Monday–Friday except holidays, are third-class only and have light refreshments.

Dep. Buenos Aires (Retiro)	19:15		Dep. Venado Tuerto	03:10
Arr. Venado Tuerto	02:05		Arr. Buenos Aires (Retiro)	10:00

Buenos Aires - Zapala 2275

Dep. Buenos Aires	10:00 (1)		Dep. Zapala	16:15 (3)
Dep. Bahia Blanca	20:34		Arr. Neuquen	20:15
Arr. Neuquen	08:30 (2)		Change trains.	
Change trains.			Dep. Neuquen	20:45 (1)
Dep. Neuquen	08:50 (3)		Arr. Bahia Blanca	08:30 (1+2)
Arr. Zapala	13:00		Arr. Buenos Aires	20:10

(1) Carries an air-conditioned first-class sleeping car and air-conditioned first-class coach. Restaurant car. (2) Day 2. (3) Runs daily, except Sundays and holidays. Has an air-conditioned first-class coach.

Sights in **Zapala**: The Copahue Volcano and mineral baths in **Copahue National Reservation**, at the Chilean border, which can be visited from Zapala by bus. The animal and bird sanctuary in Laguna Blanca National Park. There is bus transportation from Zapala to **Lake Huechulafquen**.

Buenos Aires - Santa Fe - Resistencia 2261

Both of these trains have a second-class coach and buffet.

Dep. Buenos Aires (Ret.)	10:00 (1)	Dep. Resistencia	09:45 (3)
Dep. Santa Fe	20:40	Dep. Santa Fe	10:15 (2)
Arr. Resistencia	20:27 (2)	Arr. Buenos Aires (Ret.)	20:17

(1) Runs Tuesday, Thursday and Saturday. (2) Day 2. (3) Runs Monday, Thursday and Saturday.

Sights in **Santa Fe**: The 17th century La Merced Church on Plaza Mayo. Nearby, Casa de Gobierno. The marvelous 17th century San Francisco Church. Across from it, the Provincial Historical Museum. The Rosa Galisteo de Rodriguez Museum of Fine Arts on Calle General.

Buenos Aires - Santa Rosa 2273

Both trains have an air-conditioned coach and a restaurant car.

Dep. Buenos Aires (Once)	21:00 (1)	Dep. Santa Rosa	15:56 (2)
Arr. Santa Rosa	13:14	Arr. Buenos Aires (Once)	08:15

(1) Runs Monday, Wednesday and Friday. (2) Runs Wednesday, Friday and Sunday.

Buenos Aires - Bahia Blanca - San Carlos de Bariloche 2274 + 2281

All of these trains carry an air-conditioned sleeping car, an air-conditioned coach and a restaurant car.

	2274	2281
Dep. Buenos Aires (P. Con.)	10:00	22:00 (1)
Arr. Bahia Blanca (Sud)	20:19	08:52 (2)
Dep. Bahia Blanca (Sud)	-0-	09:20 (3)
Arr. San Carlos de Bariloche	-0-	09:57 (4)

Sights in **Bahia Blance:** The statues and lakes in Parque de Mayo. The Zoological Garden in Parque Independencia.

Sights in **San Carlos de Bariloche**: This is the biggest ski area in South America (7 different chairlifts). Similar to an Alpine village. Much mountain climbing here, also. See the collection of Indian artifacts in the Nahuel Huapi Museum. Take the cable car from Cerro Cathedral. Many tours of Argentina's Lake District orginate in Bariloche.

	2274	2281
Dep. San Carlos de Bariloche	-0-	21:00 (6)
Arr. Bahia Blanca (Sud)	-0-	21:00 (6)
Dep. Bahia Blanca (Sud)	08:45	21:30 (7)
Arr. Buenos Aires (P. Con.)	20:10	07:57 (8)

(1) Runs Wednesday and Sunday. (2) Day 2. (3) Runs Thursday and Monday. (4) Day 2 from Bahia Blanca. (4) Day 2 from Bahia Blanca. Day 3 from Buenos Aires. (5) Runs Tuesday and Friday. (6) Day 2 from San Carlos de Bariloche. (7) Runs Wednesday and Saturday. (8) Day 2 from Bahia Blanca. Day 3 from San Carlos de Bariloche.

THE PATAGONIAN EXPRESS

The southernmost rail trip in the Western Hemisphere is this spur from the Buenos Aires-Bariloche line — the ride from Ingeniero Jacobacci to **Esquel**, a ranch town that attracts skiers in September and October. There are 70 mph cyclones here in July and August. During harvest period, that train operates at different times and on different days than the schedule published by Argentina.

Buenos Aires - Ingeniero Jacobacci - Esquel - San Carlos de Bariloche

Detouring to Esquel en route from Buenos Aires to San Carlos de Bariloche *requires a 4-night stay in Esquel (Friday, Saturday, Sunday and Monday) and a 7-hour layover in Ingeniero G. Jacobacci on a Tuesday, on the way to San Carlos de Bariloche.*

Detouring to Esquel en route from San Carlos de Bariloche to Buenos Aires *requires a 2-night stay in Ingeniero G. Jacobacci (Wednesday and Thursday), a 4-night stay in Esquel (Friday, Saturday, Sunday and Monday), and a 3½-hour layover in Ingeniero G. Jacobacci on the way to San Carlos de Bariloche.*

2281		2281	
Dep. Buenos Aires (P. Con.)	22:00 (1+2)	Dep. San Carlos de Bariloche	20:20 (2+7)
Arr. Ingeniero G. Jacobacci	04:49 (3)	Arr. Ingeniero G. Jacobacci	01:14
Change trains.		Change trains.	
2278		2278	
Dep. Ingeniero G. Jacobacci	07:00 (4+5)	Dep. Ingeniero G. Jacobacci	07:00 (4+5)
Arr. Esquel	20:19	Arr. Esquel	20:19
Dep. Esquel	08:30 (5+6)	Dep. Esquel	08:30 (5+6)
Arr. Ingeniero G. Jacobacci	22:03	Arr. Ingeniero G. Jacobacci	22:03
Change trains.		Change trains.	
2281		2281	
Dep. Ingeniero G. Jacobacci	04:59 (2+7)	Dep. Ingeniero G. Jacobacci	01:24 (2+8)
Arr. San Carlos de Bariloche	09:57	Arr. Buenos Aires (P.Con.)	07:57 (9)

(1) Runs Wednesday and Sunday. (2) Carries an air-conditioned sleeping car and frst-class coach. Restaurant car. (3) Day 3 — Friday and Tuesday. (4) Runs Friday only. Light refreshments. (5) Second-class only. Light refreshments. (6) Runs Tuesday only. (7) Runs Tuesday and Friday. (8) Runs Wednesday and Saturday. (9) Day 2 from Ingeniero G. Jacobacci — Thursday and Sunday.

Sights in **Bariloche**: Developed as a recreation center at the beginning of the 20th century. Known internationally for its fashionable ski slopes operated June–September. The town has a wide range of hotels

The chocolate shops that line the 200 block of Mitre Street include Del Turista, a chocolate supermarket.

THE LAKE DISTRICT BUS CONNECTION

Bariloche - Puerto Montt 2353

Dep. Bariloche	07:00 (1)	10:00 (2)	Dep. Puerto Montt	08:30 (1)	10:30 (2)
Arr. Puerto Montt	N/A	N/A	Arr. Bariloche	N/A	N/A

(1) Runs early September to late May, daily except Sunday. Arrive to same day. (2) Runs early April to late August, Monday–Friday except holidays. There is an overnight stop at Penulla.

The interesting lakes in the Bariloche area are: **Argentino, Nahuel Huapi, Correntoso, Espejo, Traful, Gutierrez, Mascardi, Futulafquen, Meliquina, Falkner, Villarino, Epulafquen** and **Tromen**. There is outstanding trout fishing in many of these lakes.

Take the 35-mile ride by auto around Lake Nahuel Huapi.

ADDENDUM

Buenos Aires - Mar del Plata 2280

All of these trains have an air-conditioned coach and a restaurant car, unless designated otherwise.

Dep. B.A. (P.Con.)	08:00	15:30	18:30 (1)	19:45 (2)	23:45
Arr. Mar del Plata	13:20	20:46	23:19	02:28	05:06

Sights in **Mar del Plata**: Five miles of attractive sandy beaches. A very large casino.

Dep. Mar del Plata	09:00	15:15	18:40 (3)	21:20 (4)	23:30
Arr. B.A. (P.Con.)	14:46	20:42	23:28	04:18	05:02

(1) Supplement charged. Runs Friday only. (2) Runs Monday, Wednesday and Friday. Second-class only. Light refreshments. (3) Supplement charged. Runs Sunday only. (4) Runs Tuesday, Thursday and Sunday. Second-class only. Light refreshments.

INTERNATIONAL ROUTES FROM ARGENTINA

Argentina's gateways for rail travel to Bolivia, central Brazil, northern Chile and southern Peru are Tucuman and Salta.

From Tucuman, there is rail service to La Paz (with spurs to Potosi, Sucre and Cochabamba), to Santa Cruz (and on across Brazil to Sao Paulo, Brasilia and Rio de Janeiro), and also a beautiful valley ride to Antofagasta.

Buenos Aires is the starting point for 2 train trips to southern Chile, Paraguay and Uruguay (and on to southern Brazil).

Tucuman - La Paz

2261		
Dep. Tucuman (GM)	15:05 (1)	
Arr. La Quiaca	09:28 (2)	
1900		
Dep. La Quiaca	09:30 (3)	-0-
Dep. Villazon	15:30 (3)	14:10 (5)
Arr. La Paz	09:38 (4)	10:50 (4)

(1) Runs Tuesday and Friday. Buffet. (2) Arrive Wednesday and Saturday. (3) Runs Wednesday and Saturday. Cook's timetable indicates nearly 6 hours to travel 3 kilometers by train from La Quiaca, across the border, to Villazon. In prior years, passengers were advised to walk from La Quiaca to Villazon. Restaurant car Villazon-La Paz. (4) Day 2 from Villazon. (5) Runs Tuesday and Friday. Restaurant car.

Salta - Yacuiba - Santa Cruz

2261		1907			
Dep. Salta	20:15 (1)	Dep. Yacuiba	08:50 (2)	18:20 (3)	22:00 (4)
Arr. Yacuiba	16:00	Arr. Santa Cruz	22:25	10:45	06:32
Change trains.					

(1) Runs Monday only. Light refreshments. (2) Supplement charged. Runs Tuesday, Thursday and Saturday. Restaurant car. (3) Runs Wednesday and Sunday. (4) Sup. charged. Runs Monday, Wednesday, Friday and Sunday. First-class only. Restaurant car.

Tucuman - Antofagasta

This is a very scenic valley train ride.

2261 Train		Change to bus.	
Dep. Tucuman (Norte)	13:52 (1)	2465 Bus	
Arr. Guemes	20:26	Dep. Salta	N/A (3)
Change trains.		Arr. Socompa	N/A
Dep. Guemes	08:35 (2)	Arr. Antofagasta	N/A (4)
Arr. Salta	10:33		

(1) Runs Monday, Thursday and Saturday . (2) Runs Friday only. (3) Times have not been available since 1981. (4) Arrival 18 hours after departure from Salta since 1981.

Buenos Aires - Mendoza - Valparaiso - Santiago

Before it was discontinued in 1980, the Mendoza-Los Andes portion of this rail trip was the most exciting train ride in South America.

Altitudes (in feet) En Route

ASCENT		DESCENT	
Mendoza	2,518	Caracoles (tunnel exit)	10,420
Paso de los Andes	3,069	El Portillo	9,408
Blanco Encalda	3,502	El Juncal	7,321
Cacheuta	4,080	Guardia Vieja	5,397
Portrerillos	4,443	Rio Blanco	4,764
Guido	4,957	Salta del Soldado	4,141
Uspallata	5,741	San Pablo	3,174
Rio Blanco	7,000	Los Andes	2,669
Zanjon Amarillo	7,236	Valparaiso	-0-
Punta de las vacas	7,852		
Puente del Inca	8,915		
Las Cuevas	10,331		
Tunnel Entrance	10,452	(the summit is 13,082.)	

Breakfast was served at the railstation in Mendoza before boarding a narrow-gauge train that went through a scenic valley to Paso de Los Andes. There is much snow in this area from May to November. The ride from Puente del Inca to Las Cuevas was by rack railway. It is a deep descent from Las Cuevas to Portillo.

At Llay Llay there is a fork, and one branch of the train route went to Santiago, the other to Valparaiso.

All of the trains Buenos Aires–Mendoza and v.v. have an air-conditioned first-class coach and a restaurant car.

2270 Train
Dep. Buenos Aires	20:30 (1)	20:30 (2)	21:30 (3)		
Arr. Mendoza	09:30	10:35	14:00		
Change to bus. 2300					
Dep. Mendoza	08:30	10:00	11:30	11:50	13:00 (4)
Dep. Puente del Inca	Times for this portion of the journey have not been available				
Dep. Los Andes	since 1980.				
Set your watch back one hour.					
Arr. Santiago	14:30	16:00	17:30	17:50	19:00
Change buses. 2465					
Dep. Santiago	Frequent times from 04:00 to 20:30				
Arr. Valparaiso	2 hours later.				

(1) Supplement charged. Runs Thursday and Sunday. Carries an air-conditioned sleeping car and a cinema car. (2) Runs Friday only. (3) Carries air-conditioned sleeping car. (4) Plus direct buses Mendoza–Valparaiso departing 08:00 and 10:30, arriving 10 hours later.

Sights En Route

Mendoza is a large, modern city, having been completely rebuilt after it was destroyed by earthquake and fire in 1861. Its profusion of gardens make the city extremely beautiful. A 24-hour stopover here is well worthwhile. Do not miss seeing the public park with the splendid monument to Jose de San Martin, the liberator of Chile and Peru. It has an incredible collection of statues and bas-reliefs. Then walk to the lake and streams in the nearby Zoological Gardens.

Also see: The San Martin Museum (Av. General San Martin). The exhibit of Argentine animals and plants in the Moyano Museum of Natural History (Calle Belgrano). The beautiful Romanesque Law Courts building. Window- shop on Calle Las Heras.

There is a splendid all-day bus trip to see the famous Christ the Redeemer statue, which cannot be seen on the train trip. Great scenery on this ride, with a stop for lunch at **Las Cuevas**. Particularly recommended for those not making the complete train trip to Chile.

From **Cacheuta**, the train follows an old Spanish trail called Camino de los Andes. After **Uspallata**, a desolate and vast plain comes into view. There are many rushing mountain streams in the area of **Rio Blanco**. Next in sight is Aconcagua, highest (22,834 feet) mountain in the Western hemisphere.

Puente del Inca is a popular Winter sports resort, attracting the largest crowds of visitors from November to May. It is named for the natural stone bridge spanning the Mendoza River and is one of South America's most marvelous sights. This city is also popular as a base for excursions by foot and horseback to many high valleys in the Andes.

Next in sight is the Horcones River, before arriving at **Las Cuevas** on the Chilean border. This is another popular ski resort.

Extremely good rock scenery can be seen after emerging from the tunnel at **Caracoles**. Next, you will see the Aconcagua River. Here, on the Pacific side of the Andes, the ground is covered by foliage, including many flowers.

Portillo, another Andean ski resort, has many attractive lodges and hotels. The views from the ski lifts and at the 10,824-foot peak are so superb, it's worthwhile visiting here even if you don't ski. The best ski weather is from mid-August to mid-September.

Only 4,000 people are allowed to use this facility each season. Of these, there are 3,000 who have permanent privilege. The few hundred newcomers are culled from over 8,000 applicants, permitting entry only to those who come here on a package tour (check the tour desk of Braniff International). There is much farming in the valley that continues from Portillo to Valparaiso.

Buenos Aires - Puerto Montt

For this transcontinental train trip across southern Argentina, please refer to separate schedules earlier in this section for (1) Buenos Aires-Bahia Blanca [page 737], (2) Bahia Blanca-San Carlos de Bariloche [page 737], and (3)Bariloche-Puerto Montt [page 739].

Buenos Aires - Posadas - Encarnacion - Asuncion

The trip from Buenos Aires to Asuncion is a very rough ride, 930 miles through dense brush and jungle.

The inconveniences include hard wood seats, stifling heat, swarms of mosquitoes and much dust. The locomotive on this portion of the route was buit in 1912. The train is said to be the oldest train in South America. From Encarnacion to Asuncion at night the station platforms at villages along the route are lined with people who, sitting at tables while eating and singing, enjoy watching the train pass by.

Be sure to have an inexpensive (about $1.00)"through ticket" before departing Buenos Aires. Passengers without it are required to leave the train at Posadas, carry their luggage to the auto ferry pier, take the auto ferry across the river, and re-board the train on the other side of the river, in Encarnacion. With a "through ticket", passengers can remain on the train as it is carried across the river and then change trains.

Cook's timetables do not show that the 41½-hour, once-a-week train that departs Buenos Aires at 15:00 on only Tuesday carries one non-airconditioned second-class coach car that is transfered in Posadas to the Posadas-Asuncion train. The 1991 price for it was 350,000 Australes per person.

2260		2230	
Dep. Buenos Aires (F. Lacroze)	15:00 (1)	Dep. Posadas	12:30 (3)
Arr. Posadas	10:17 (2)	Set your watch back one hour	
Change trains.		from April 1 to September 30	
		Dep. Encarnacion	15:30 (4)
		Arr. Asuncion	08:35 (5)

(1) Runs Tuesday only. Carries an air-conditioned sleeping car and an air-conditioned first-class coach. Restaurant car. (2) Day 2 from Buenos Aires. (3) Runs Wednesday only. (4) Restaurant car Encarnacion-Asuncion. (5) Day 3 from Buenos Aires.

Sights in **Posadas**: Make the 210-mile bus trip to see one of South America's most impressive sights, Iguazu Falls, much grander than Victoria Falls or Niagara Falls. The biggest flow is August to November.

Buenos Aires - Corrientes 2260

Both of these trains run daily and carry air-conditioned first-class sleeping cars and a restaurant car.

Dep. B. A. (F. Lacrose)	15:00	Dep. Corrientes	15:30
Arr. Corrientes	12:20	Arr. B. A. (F. Lacroze)	12:40

Sights in **Corrientes:** The Colonial Historical and Fine Arts Museum. The Church of La Cruz. Government Palace on Plaza 25 de Mayo. The Cathedral.

Buenos Aires - Montevideo Hydrofoil Boat 2211

Dep. Buenos Aires	07:50	08:30	10:50	11:30	14:50	18:00 (1)
Arr. Colonia	One hour later. Bus service Colonia-Montevideo					
Arr. Montevideo	11:50	12:00	14:50	15:00	18:50	21:30

(1) Plus other Buenos Aires departures at 21:00 and 21:50, arriving Montevideo 00:30 and 01:50.

Buenos Aires - Rio de Janeiro Bus 2300

Dep. Buenos Aires	14:00 (1)	18:00 (3)
Arr. Rio de Janeiro	10:00 (2)	14:00 (2)

(1) Runs Tuesday and Friday. (2) Day 3. (3) Runs daily.

BOLIVIA

Children under 3 travel free. Half-fare for children 3–11. Children 12 and over pay full fare. All of Bolivia's scant 1,400 miles of railway are narrow-guage, one metre wide.

La Paz

This is the world's highest capital (11,735-foot altitude). See the collection of colonial and contemporary art at the National Art Museum, across from the Cathedral, in the Palace of the Condes do Arana, open Tuesday–Friday 09:30–12:00 and 14:30–18:30, Saturday 10:00–12:30. Next to the Art Museum is the Presidential Palace.

Two blocks away is the Ethnographic and Folklore Museum (916 Calle Ingavi), with exhibits of the culture of several Indian groups. It is open Monday–Friday 08:30–11:30 and 14:30–17:45. Then, it is a 3-block walk to Calle Jaen, on which many other museums are located. Among these are: The collection of native handicraft, furniture and art in Casa de Murillo, home of the hero of Bolivia's War of Independence . . . the collection of Inca and pre-Columbian gold and silver ornaments at Museo de Metales Preciosos . . . and the exhibit of local customs at Museo Costumbrista. All 3 museums are open Tuesday–Friday 09:30–12:00 and 14:30–18:30, Saturday and Sunday 10:00–12:30.

Window-shop on Calle Comercio. See the Central Food Market, largest one in South America. Visit the House of Culture. Stroll Calle Sagarnaga, called "Street of the Indians" to examine the assortment of handicrafts sold there. The view of La Paz from Monticulo Park. Walk on The Prado (Avenida 16 de Julio) and on Avenida Buenos Aires. See ancient Indian arts and crafts in The National Museum (Calle Don Bosco 93).

The baroque Spanish architecture of the 16th century Church of San Francisco. Next to it, the handicrafts (musical instruments, weavings) in a shop sponsored by the church, open Monday–Friday 10:00–13:00 and 14:30–19:00, only in the morning on Sat. and Sun. On nearby Calle Linares, see the women who wear bowler hats while selling medicinal herbs. The 3rd–12th century stone monoliths and figures in Tiwanacu Prehistoric Park.

For $5, you can have a seat and beverages (snacks and meals are extra) at any one of several "penas" halls where Indian groups perform with native musical intruments. Penas are open Thursday–Saturday after 21:00. Several performances are offered each night.

Go to the **Tiahuanco** ruins, 49 miles from La Paz.

La Paz - Cochabamba 1900

All of these trains have first-class coaches, for which a supplement is charged.

Dep. La Paz	08:00 (1)	21:00 (2)	Dep. Cochabamba	08:00 (3)	20:30 (4)
Arr. Cochabamba	16:43	05:40	Arr. La Paz	17:14	05:48

(1) Runs Mon. and Wed.. (2) Runs Fri. only. (3) Runs Tues. and Thurs.. (4) Runs Sun. only.

Sights in **Cochabamba:** This is the most comfortable area in Bolivia, a mere 8,500 feet altitude. See: The former home of tin baron Simon Patino, now a museum. The several museums in the Palace of Culture. Colorful stalls in the Municipal Market.

La Paz - Potosi - Sucre 1902

This train ride over the Andes is both the highest meter-gauge track in the world (15,705 feet at El Condor, between Rio Mulato and Potosi), **and it is also the world's highest passenger train run on any gauge**.

All of these trains charge a supplement and have a first-class coach.

Dep. La Paz	16:10 (1)	18:00 (3)	Dep. Sucre	15:30 (4)	18:50 (5)
Arr. Potosi	06:37 (2)	04:52 (2)	Dep. Potosi	22:00	23:30
Arr. Sucre	13:10	09:25	Arr. La Paz	12:40 (2)	10:39 (2)

(1) Runs Wednesday only. Buffet. (2) Day 2. (3) Runs Tuesday and Saturday. (4) Runs Thursday only. Buffet. (5) Runs Wednesday and Sunday.

Sights in **Potosi:** In 1650, when its population was 160,000 (now only 90,000), this was one of the most important cities in the world. Many tourists find it difficult to acclimate to the thin air of its 15,000-foot altitude. Most stores and offices are closed 14:00–15:30.

See the silver and silk statue of Christ in San Francisco Cathedral. The silver altar in the 16th century San Lorenzo Church. Only 4 blocks away is the Mercado Artesiana, where exceptional handmade weavings, belts, antiques, silverware and ponchos are sold.

Half-day tours of the tin mine are offered weekdays at 09:00, starting at the headquarters of COMIBOL. The mine can be reached by taxi or by taking the 07:45 bus from Plaza 10 de Noviembre. After the tin mine tour, you can see the nearby ancient Inca hot springs.

Do not fail to visit the Royal House of Money, built in 1773, for a 2-hour tour of this enormous ancient mint near the Plaza 10 de Noviembre.

A guide there charges only 10 U.S. cents for a 3-hour tour that includes seeing 8-foot-high wood gears and wheels originally operated by slaves, a display of thousands of coins that were made here for Spain and for many Latin American countries (many custom-made for wealthy residents who used them for wedding souvenirs), numerous colonial paintings, and a collection of sculpture and exquisite furniture. Coins that were minted here several centuries ago and also elegant silverware made in this area can be purchased from small stands near the entrance to the market on Calle Oruro.

Visit the small shops near the mint, on Calle Bustillos. See the array of tropical fruits at the market on Calle Bolivar.

Sights in **Sucre:** This city is 10,300 feet high. The Tourist Office cannot arrange for English-speaking guides. Hire one at a travel agency to take you on a tour of the 17th century San Felipe Neri Church and to take you to the roof of that church for a view of numerous roofs made of ceramic blocks that are bonded by silver from the Potosi mines.

The Cathedral is famed for its statue of the Virgin, covered by a multimillion-dollar garment of gold, diamonds, emeralds and pearls that were donated by wealthy people from 1538 to 1825. See the desks, paintings and books inlaid with mother-of-pearl, at the museum next to the Cathedral. Visit the House of Liberty, where Bolivia was founded, the place where its constitution was completed, open 11:00–12:00 and 15:00–17:00.

See the weavings, colonial paintings and furniture, and archaeological objects at the University Museum (Calle Bolivar 698), open Monday-Friday 08:30–12:00 and 14:00–18:00, Saturday and Sunday 09:00–12:00. The marvelous 16th and 17th century architecture. The ancient University of San Francisco Xavier. The Palace of Justice. Guided tours of the Monastery of La Recoleta (in Spanish language) are conducted 10:00–12:00 and 14:00–17:00.

INTERNATIONAL ROUTES FROM BOLIVIA

La Paz - La Quiaca - Jujuy - Tucuman or Buenos Aires

On this 1500-mile route to Argentina, please note the 6-hour wait at La Quiaca, involving a search for drugs by Argentine customs officials before they allow the train to proceed to Tucuman.

1900			
Dep. La Paz	19:00 (1)		
Set watch forward 1 hour.			
Arr. Villazon	13:05 (2)		
Arr. La Quiaca	15:30		
Change trains.			

2261		
Dep. La Quiaca	21:20 (3)	21:20 (3)
Arr. Jujuy	07:02 (4)	07:02 (4)
Change trains only for Buenos Aires.		
Dep. Jujuy	07:12 (5)	08:05 (6)
Arr. Tucuman (GM)	15:10	17:03
Dep. Tucuman (Norte)	-0-	17:13
Dep. Alta Cordoba	-0-	09:27 (7)
Dep. Rosario (Oeste)	-0-	16:28
Arr. Buenos Aires (Re.)	-0-	22:15

(1) Runs Friday only to La Quiaca. Restaurant car La Paz-Villazon. (2) Day 2 from La Paz....Saturday. (3) Runs Wednesday and Saturday. Buffet La Quiaca-Tucuman. (4) Day 3 from La Paz....Sunday. (5) Runs Sunday and Thursday. Buffet. (6) Runs Sunday, Wednesday and Friday. Buffet. (7) Day 4 from La Paz. Runs Monday, Thursday and Saturday. Buffet.

The route to Peru is via Cuzco

La Paz - Cuzco - Lima

1910 Bus		
Dep. La Paz	08:00 (1)	
Arr. Puno	17:00	
Change to train.		
1800		
Dep. Puno	06:55 (2)	
Arr. Cuzco	17:35 (3)	
1820 Bus		
Dep. Cuzco	N/A (4)	
Arr. Huancavelica	N/A (4)	

Change to train.		
1801		
Dep. Huancavelica	07:00 (5)	13:00 (5)
Arr. Huancayo	10:10	16:10
Change trains.		
1802		
Dep. Huancayo		N/A (6)
Arr. Lima (Des.)		N/A

(1) Runs daily. (2) Runs daily except Sundays and holidays. Departs 09:20 on Saturday. Buffet. (3) Arrives 19:50 on Saturday. (4) Time has not been available since 1980. (5) First-class only. Runs daily, except Sundays and holidays. (6) Train service was temporarily suspended in 1991. Bus service (8 hours) is available . Departure times for buses were not available in 1991.

There are 2 rail routes from La Paz to Chile: southwest to Arica, and south to Antofagasta.

La Paz - Charana - Arica 1901

Marvelous Andean scenery while riding on an excellent train. Passengers are amazed by the elegant complimentary service of tea, sandwiches and cookies on individual silver trays. You travel on 30 miles of rack and pinion track during a portion of this 270-mile trip. The highest place on this route is 14,000 feet at **General Lagos**.

Both of these trains charge a supplement and have first-class coaches.

Dep. La Paz	07:00 (1)	Dep. Arica	09:30 (2)
Dep. Charana	11:17	Dep. Charana	15:35
Arr. Arica	19:06	Arr. La Paz	20:04

(1) Runs monday, Wednesday and Friday. (2) Runs Tuesday, Thursday and Saturday.

The best scenery is at the start of the trip, during the ascent from La Paz. The Chilean border is only 5 minutes from **Charana**, at **Visviri**, where the passport control procedure takes more than one hour. Many herds of llamas roam here. Because military installations are nearby, photo-taking is not permitted at the frontier area.

Seventy miles before reaching Arica, the track plunges from 11,000 feet to sea level. The scenery on this stretch is a jumble of brown lava rocks.

La Paz - Antofagasta 1900

From La Paz to Ollague, for more than 22 hours, the train is constantly at more than 12,000-feet altitude.

Conections in 1991 made this trip impractical.

Dep. La Paz	Dep. Uyuri
Arr. Uyuri	Arr. Antofagasta
Change trains.	

Santa Cruz - Sao Paulo - Rio de Janeiro

There is great jungle scenery on the Santa Cruz-Puerto Suarez portion of this train trip to Brazil.

1907

Dep. Santa Cruz	12:40 (1)	13:35 (3)	18:00 (4)	
Arr. Puerto Suarez	06:49 (2)	08:05 (2)	06:17 (2)	
Change trains. 2011				
Dep. Corumba	07:00 (5)			
Arr. Bauru	16:00 Day 2 from Corumba			
Change trains. 2015				
Dep. Bauru	23:37 (6)	04:18 (8)	07:48 (9)	13:29 (9)
Arr. Sao Paulo (Luz)	06:00 (7)	10:45	14:52	20:01
Change trains. 2012				
Dep. Sao Paulo (Luz)				23:00 (10)
Arr. Rio de Jan. (D.Ped.)				08:30

(1) Supplement charged. Runs Tuesday and Saturday. Has a first-class coach. Restaurant car. (2) Day 2 from Santa Cruz. It is 11km (7 miles) from Puerto Suarez to Corumba. (3) Runs Thursday and Sunday. (4) Supplement charged. Runs Monday, Wednesday and Friday. Has a first-class coach. Buffet. (5) Runs Monday, Wednesday and Friday. Carries a sleeping car. Restaurant car. (6) Supplement charged. Runs daily. Carries a sleeping car. Restaurant car. (7) Day 2 from Bauru. (8) Second-class only. Runs daily. Restaurant car. (9) Second-class only. Runs daily. Restaurant car. (10) Reservation required. Air-conditioned train. Carries a sleeping car. Has a first-class coach. Lounge car. Restaurant car.

Santa Cruz - Yacuiba - Pocitos - Salta

Another train route to Argentina.

1907				2261	
Dep. Sta. Cruz	10:00 (1)	11:55 (2)	18:30 (3)	Dep. Pocitos	15:20 (5)
Arr. Yacuiba	19:22 (4)	20:25 (4)	10:00 (4)	Arr. Salta	10:33

(1) Runs Tuesday, Thursday and Saturday. Has a first-class coach. Restaurant car. (2) Runs Monday, Wednesday, Friday and Saturday. First-class only. Restaurant car. (3) Runs Thursday and Sunday. Has a first-class coach. (4) It is 4km Yacuiba to Pocitos. (5) Runs Thursday only. Has a first-class coach. Light refreshments. There are also buses [Table 2300] that depart Salvador Mazza station daily at 14:00, 21:00, 21:30 and 23:00, arriving Salta 21:30, 04:30, 05:00 and 06:30.

Sights in **Salta**: See page 734.

BRAZIL

Children under 3 travel free. Half-fare for children 3–9. Children 10 and over must pay full fare.

Nearly all (91%) of Brazil's 23,000 miles of rail lines are located within 300 miles of its shoreline on the Atlantic Ocean. Brazil employs 5 different rail gauges. However, most of its tracks are one metre.

Belo Horizonte

See the odd-shaped church at Pampulha, on the edge of the city. Palacio de Liberdade, in Praca de Liberdade. The City Museum. The collection of lamps, photographs, tools, maps and crystal in the Tassini Museum. The 2,000 varieties of trees in the Municipal Park gardens. The marble and glass Museum of Modern Art. The Governor's Palace. The enormous (110,000 seats) soccer stadium. The Fantastic rock shapes in the 22 million-year-old Lapinha Cavern.

Brasilia

See the tomb of Kubitschek, the former president of Brazil who campaigned in 1955 on the pledge to transform what had been until then an uninhabited and remote area into the the country's new capital, which Brasilia has been since 1960.

Walk a short distance from that monument to the Trelliswork Tower and take the elevator there to its 250-foot high observation deck for a panoramic view of the entire city.

Next, go to the National Cathedral and then to the Three Powers Plaza, at which a colorful flag-lowering ceremony highlighted by a military band and a parade by the honor guard takes place every Tuesday at sundown.

Also see the lovely water gardens at the Ministry of Foreign Affairs, the most beautiful structure in Brazil. Across from it, the Palacio de Justica. The blue glass Church of Dom Bosco. Great sculptures throughout the city. The view at night of the white marble federal buildings, sparkling in the glow of spotlights.

The unique housing units, each containing expensive apartments, buildings for middle-income workers, and a complete shopping center. The National Cathedral. Nearby, the 18 buildings that are each for a different government department. Planalto Palace, where the President's office is located. Alvorada Palace, residence of the President. Arcos Palace. The Metropolitan Cathedral. The 600-foot-long Gallery of States shopping mall, featuring handicrafts from each of Brazil's 22 states. Take the 50-mile drive around Paranoa.

The Museum. The Hall of Mirrors, scene of formal state receptions. The exquisite interior of Alvorada Palace. The National Theater.

Rio de Janeiro

Perhaps the most beautiful city in the world. Take the funicular from Rua Cosme Velho 513 to see the incredible 100-foot-high 700-ton statue, Christ The Redeemer, at the 2400-foot-high top of Corcovado, and the view of the city from there. The ride starts at 513 Rua Cosme Velho every hour from 08:00–20:00. It is a short walk from the Cosme Velho station to the 5 marvelous colonial-style houses in the little square called Largo do Boticario.

Confeitaria Colombo, founded in 1884, is a double-tiered restaurant noted for both its food and decor. Diners are surrounded by gigantic ceiling-high mirrors mounted in hand-wrought Brazilian rosewood frames. There is a stained-glass skylight, and additional illumination is provided by light bulbs set in tulip-petal sconces.

Ride the cablecar from Praia Vermelha (in Botafogo) to the top of Sugar Loaf for the fine view of Rio's beaches from there. (Among the city's 16 marvelous beaches, the best-known are Ipanema, Copacabana and Sao Conrado.)

See the concrete and steel Candelaria Cathedral (styled after Mayan temples). Next to the Cathedral is a stop for the city's last streetcar. Ride it for a one-hour roundtrip on its route through the hilly Santa Teresa residential area.

Sao Bento Monastery. The Church of Penha. Gloria Church. The Museum of Modern Art on Avenida Presidente Vargas. The Museum of Fine Arts (Avenida Rio Branco 100). The Natural History Museum. The collection of movie theaters, called Cinelandia.

The photos, jewels and costumes of the great Brazilian entertainer of the 1930's, at the Carmen Miranda Museum. The collection of weaving, stone works, leather and ceramics in the Indian Museum (Rua das Palmeira).

Gems and precious stones at the Museum of Geology and Mineralogy (Avenida Pasteur 404). The Museum of Villa-Lobos (Rua da Imprensa 16). The Museum of the Republic (Rua do Catete 153) in the granite and rose-colored marble Catete Palace. The Museum of Sacred Arts. The Museum of Pictures and Sound. The Municipal Theater.

The enormous collection of flora at the Botanical Gardens (Rua Jardim Botanico), open 08:00–17:00. Founded in 1808, the gardens contain 135,000 plants and trees.

The National Library (Avenida Rio Branco). Fine colonial art in the Convent of Santa Antonio. The Church of Candelaria. Early phones, in the Telephone Museum (63 Rua Dois de Dezembro, Catete). The National Museum in the Quinta da Boa Vista Park at Sao Cristovao (with one of the world's best collections of birds, reptiles and insects) open daily except Monday 10:00–16:45. The nearby Zoo is open daily except Monday 09:00–16:00.

Take bus # 206 from Largo da Carioca to Silvestre. Visit Ipanema, Barra da Tijuca and Leblon beaches.

Salvador

Called "Bahia" by Brazilians. English-speaking guides are available at the Tourist Office at Praca da Se. To its left is the 18th century Archbishop's Palace. On the other side of the Tourist Office is the 18th century Holy House of Mary Church.

See the Sao Damaso Seminary. The absolutely beautiful Church of Sao Francisco Convent, filled with gold-leaf decorations. The picturesque market near Praca Cairu. Take the ride on the Lacerda elevator, from Praca Cairu to Praca Municipal to see the Government Palace and Municipal Library, and to window-shop on Rua Chile.

The 17th century furniture in Sao Bento Church. The Instituto Geografico e Historico. Sao Pedro Fort. The Zoo, in the Botanical Gardens at Ondina. The view from Ondina Hill. The 16th century Basilica Cathedral and the church of St. Peter of the Clerics, in the square of Terreiro de Jesus. The silver altar and the tiles in the Museum of Sacred Art in the 17th century Santa Teresa Church.

Do not miss seeing Largo do Pelourinho, on Alfredo de Brito Street. The 17th century Convent of the Desterro, most beautiful of all of Brazil's convents.

Dique, the 17th century artificial lake below the Tororo steps. The blue tiles inside University Rectory, en route to Lagoa do Abaete. The beach at Itaparica. The lofty coconut trees at Itapoa Beach. The forts of Santa Maria and Sao Diogo. Igreja da Graco, Salvador's first church. The stalls of fish, pork, beef and tropical fruits at the Agua de Meninos market.

The Fratelli Vita glassblowing factory. The fort of Mont Serrat and, nearby, Mont Serrat Church. The Cacao Institute, for a look at the processing of chocolate from seed to candy.

Sao Paulo

Largest city in Latin America. See the view while standing on the bridge that spans Avenida Anhangabau. The Municipal Theater, across from Praca Ramos de Azevedo. Instituto Butantan, South America's largest snake farm. Nearby, the collection of antique pottery and furniture in Casa do Bandeirante.

Stroll through huge, lake-dotted Ibirapuera Park, with its statues, Japanese Pavillion (an exact copy of Japan's Katura Palace), the various museums (Science, Aeronautics and Technical Arts) in the History Pavillion, contemporary art in the Pavillion Pereira, and the Planetarium. Visit Praca de la Republica. Walk along Praca do Patriarca, the Times Square of Brazil. Window-shop on Rua Augusta.

The Zoological Park (Avenida Miguel Estefeno), considered to be the world's largest. Nearby, the world-famed orchid collection (over 35,000 species). To visit the orchids and Zoo, take Bus # 546 from Praca da Liberdade or from Anhangabau.

There is an outstanding collection of Renoir, Lautrec, Rembrandt, Frans Hals, and many modern Brazilian painters, at the Art Museum (Avenida Paulista 1578). See the Sound and Image Museum (Avenida Europa 158). South America's largest cathedral, in Cathedral Plaza. Liberdade, the city's oriental district (rock gardens, herb stores and many restaurants).

The Museum of Brazilian Art (Rua Alagoas 903), with its collection of copies of all the statues and monuments in the buildings and parks of Brazil. The Museum of Sacred Art in Convento da Luz. The State Art Collection (Avenida Tiradentes 141).

The collection of Indian artifacts at Casa do Sertanista (Avenida Francisco Morato 2200).

If you want to learn to dance the samba, there are 44 samba schools here. Sao Paulo's annual Carnival features their students.

ROUTES IN NORTHERN BRAZIL

Sights in **Fortaleza**: The best lobsters in Brazil. The museum and shops in the Tourist Center. Excellent beaches. Good textiles are sold here, including exquisite handmade laces. Handicrafts from all over the Northeast area of Brazil are sold in the shopping mall at the old city prison on Rua Monsenhor Tabosa, also along the beachfront at night.

Fortaleza - Teresina 2130 Bus

This was a very scenic rail trip until service was discontinued in 1987. It has been an 8-hour bus trip since then.

Fortaleza - Crato 2130 Bus

This is a 9 hour bus trip. Inquire locally for departure times.

Recife - Caruaru 2130 Bus

| Dep. Recife | Frequent times from 05:50 to 19:30 |
| Arr. Caruaru | 2 hours later |

*   *   *

| Dep. Caruaru | Frequent times from 05:00 to 19:30 |
| Arr. Recife | 2 hours later |

Sights in **Recife**: Long, beautiful beaches. Many sugarcane plantations. Named for the reefs along its coastline. Called "the Venice of Brazil" because it is on 3 rivers.

Start walking at the 3-story, old prison on Rua Floriano Peixoto which has housed the state of Pernambuco's House of Culture since 1973. The displays there of this region's folk art include jewelry, ceramics, leatherwork, woodcuts and the handmade lacework for which this area is famous. Former cells have been converted into boutique shops and snack bars.

Then visit the 17th century, lavishly gilded Capela Dourada (with its gold carved altar) on Rua Imperador Pedro II, one of the most important examples of this area's religious art.

Go down cobblestoned alleys to the nearby 17th century square called Patio de Sao Pedro where the 18th century Baroque church, Sao Pedro dos Clerigos, is located. This square, with its small outdoor cafes, is a popular gathering place at sunset. Other churches to see are the 18th century Convento de Sao Francisco, Madre de Deus, and Conceicao dos Militares, and the 17th century Santo Antonio.

Everything from dried snakeskins to cassette tapes is sold at the crowded San Jose Market. Visit the Museum of Sugar and Alcohol. The oldest church in Brazil, the 16th century San Cosme e Damiao, is in nearby **Igaracu**.

Many of the town's best restaurants and small hotels are on the boulevard that runs along what is considered the finest beach in the area, at **Boa Viagem** (an island suburb, 10 miles south of Recife). It is a small version of Rio de Janeiro's Ipanema.

Many who visit Recife are attracted to the faithful reproduction of Jerusalem at **Nova Jerusalem**, 115 miles to the west.

Olinda, a seaport 5 miles north, is the arts and crafts capital of this region and has been called "the most idyllic place in Brazil". There are marvelous old mansions here, decorated with silver, gold and brilliant Portuguese ceramic tiles. It has a nice sand beach, and water sports are popular here (sailing, scuba diving, water skiing).

Don't fail to visit the display of colorful costumes, masks and musical instruments used in religious festivals at the Museum of Northeast Man, in the Casa Forte neighborhood. It also has anthropological and historical exhibits on this region's many centuries of sugarcane production.

See the view of Olinda from the hill called "Alto de Se", where a seminary is located. As you walk down winding roads from there, you come to the beautiful 16th century church of St. Francis and to the Museum of Sacred Arts, which has exhibits of both popular paintings and Baroque sculptures.

Also in Olinda, visit the Ribeira Market, originally an 18th century slave market and now a center for the exhibition and sale of folk arts and crafts.

Sights in **Caruaru**: Great leather, straw articles and pottery bargains at the Wednesday and Saturday markets.

Barra Mansa - Ribeirao Vermelho 2013

Both of these trains have a restaurant car.

Dep. Barra Mansa	07:50	Dep. Ribeirao Vermelho	05:50
Arr. Ribeirao Vermelho	16:55	Arr. Barra Mansa	14:55

Belo Horizonte - Montes Claros - Monte Azul 2008

All of these trains have a restaurant car. The overnight trains (Belo Horizonte–Montes Claros and v.v.) carry sleeping cars.

Dep. Belo Horizonte	19:00 (1)	Dep. Monte Azul	06:45 (4)
Arr. Montes Claros	08:45 (2)	Arr. Montes Claros	14:00
Change trains.		Change trains	
Dep, Montes Claros	10:15 (3)	Dep. Montes Claros	19:35 (5)
Arr. Monte Azul	17:35	Arr. Belo Horizonte	09:40 (6)

(1) Runs Saturday only. (2) Arrives Sunday. (3) Runs Sunday, Wednesday and Friday. (4) Runs Monday, Wednesday and Friday. (5) Runs Friday only. (6) Arrives Saturday

Itabira - Vitoria 2007

Both of these trains have a buffet car.

Dep. Itabira	08:00	Dep. Vitoria (Nolasco)	07:20
Arr. Vitoria (Nolasco)	19:37	Arr. Itabira	19:02

Sights in **Vitoria**: A beautiful seaport. Marvelous beaches.

Porto Santana - Serra do Navio 2001

All of these trains are second-class only.

Dep. Porto Santana (Macapa)	07:01 (1)	12:31 (2)	20:31 (3)
Arr. Serra do Navio	11:47	16:56	00:27
	* * *		
Dep. Serra do Navio	07:01 (4)	14:01 (1)	19:30 (2)
Arr. Porto Santana (Macapa)	12:25	19:25	23:40

(1) Runs Tuesday and Thursday. (2) Runs Friday only. (3) Runs Sunday only. (4) Runs Monday only.

Bauru - Campo Grande - Corumba 2011

Both of these trains run Monday, Wednesday and Friday. Both carry a sleeping car and a restaurant car.

Dep. Bauru	13:00	Dep. Corumba	07:00
Arr. Campo Grande	08:20	Arr. Campo Grande	18:10
Dep. Campo Grande	08:45	Dep.Campo Grande	18:35
Arr. Corumba	20:00	Arr. Bauru	16:00

ROUTES IN SOUTHERN BRAZIL

Curitiba - Foz do Iguacu 2130 (Bus)

Dep. Curitiba	11 time a day from 06:45 to 23:30
Arr. Foz do Iguacu	10 hours later

* * *

Dep. Foz do Iguacu	12 time a day from 06:30 to 21:30
Arr.Curitiba	10 hours later

Sao Paulo - Panorama 2015

All of these trains are second-class only.

Dep. Sao Paulo			Dep. Panorama	06:30 (3)	21:05 (2)
(Luz)	08:25 (1)	16:50 (2)	Arr. Sao Paulo		
Arr. Panorama	22:41	06:23	(Luz)	20:01	10:45

(1) Restaurant car until 17:17. (2) Light refreshments. (3) Restaurant car 11:42–20:01.

Sao Paulo - Presidente Prudente 2016

Both of these trains carry an air-conditioned first-class sleeping car and a second-class coach. Both have buffet..

Dep. S. Paulo (Prestes)	16:00	Dep. Pres. Prudente	18:15
Arr. Pres. Prudente	07:17	Arr. S. Paulo (Prestes)	10:05

Sao Paulo - Porto Alegre Bus 2130

Dep. Sao Paulo	14:00	15:00	18:00	19:00	20:00
Arr. Porto Alegre	08:00	09:00	12:00	13:00	14:00

Sights in **Porto Alegre**: A marvelous modern seaport city, at the junction of 5 rivers. The environment here is very Germanic. See: Farroupilha Park. The Zoological Gardens. The Julio de Castilhos Museum. Rua dos Andradas, a strolling street.

Dep. Porto Alegre	11:00	12:45	14:00	15:00	16:00	18:00 (1)
Arr. Sao Paulo	05:00	06:45	08:00	09:00	10:00	12:00

(1) Plus other departures from Porto Alegre at 18:30, 20:30 and 22:00, arriving Sao Paulo Day 2 at 12:30, 14:30 and 16:00.

Brasilia - Araguari - Campinas 2018 + 2020

Dep. Brasilia	20:25 (1)	-0-	Dep. Campinas	09:30 (4)	12:05 (1)
Dep. Araguari	05:45 (2)	09:00 (3)	Arr. Araguari	21:35	23:36
Arr. Campinas	17:05	21:04	Arr. Brasilia	-0-	08:55 (5)

(1) Reservation required. Supplement charged Araguari-Campinas and v.v.. From Brasilia: runs Friday only. From Campinas: runs Sunday only. Carries a sleeping car. Has a parlor car and a first-class coach. (2) Day 2. Supplement charged. (3) Runs daily, except Saturday. Restaurant car. (4) Runs daily, except Sunday. Restaurant car. (5) Day 2. Monday only.

Santa Maria - Porto Alegre 2021

Both of these trains have a restaurant car.

Dep. Santa Maria	08:00 (1)		Dep. Porto Alegre (Pestana)	08:00 (2)
Arr. Porto Alegre (Pestana)	16:00		Arr. Santa Maria	16:00

(1) Runs Tuesday, Thursday and Sunday. (2) Runs Monday, Wednesday and Friday.

BRAZIL'S MOST SCENIC RAIL TRIPS

Curitiba - Paranagua (originating in Sao Paulo)

This railroad was built in the 19th century to haul coffee and cotton from mountain plantations to the port of Paranagua. It takes 3-4 hours to travel this tortuous 70-mile route. One of the 3 trains that were in service in 1990 carried a modern, air-conditioned coach. One of the others, named Gralha Azul (Blue Chatterbox), is more desirable because its windows are open, allowing passengers to lean out and photograph waterfalls, villages and wildflowers.

On the spectacular ride from Curitiba to the coastal town of Paranagua, the train descends from 3,000 feet to sea level. Along the way, there is great mountain, canyon, waterfall and jungle scenery. A one-way ticket in recent years was $3.50 (U.S.)

As the schedules below indicate, a same-day roundtrip Curitiba-Paranagua-Curitiba is easy.

Bus 2130			
Dep. Sao Paulo	Frequent times.		
Arr. Curitiba	6 hours later.		
Change to train.	2022		
Dep. Curitiba	07:00 (1)	08:00 (2)	08:30 (3)
Arr. Paranagua	10:30	11:55	11:20
		* * *	
Dep. Paranagua	15:30 (3)	16:30 (1)	
Arr. Curitiba	18:05	20:20	
Change to bus.	2130		
Dep. Curitiba	Frequent times.		
Arr. Sao Paulo	6 hours later.		

(1) Runs Saturdays, Sundays and holidays. Second-class only. (2) Runs Monday–Friday, except holidays. Second-class only. (3) Reservation required. Runs Saturdays, Sundays and holidays. Air-conditioned first-class only. Light refreshments.

Sights in **Curitiba**: This is Brazil's melting-pot: Italian, Polish, German, Slav, Japanese and Syrian settlers galore. See: The Cathedral, patterned after the one in Barcelona. The Civic Center. The tropical fish collection at the Aquarium in Passeio Publico, a public park in the center of the city. The Coronel David Carneiro Museum. The Paranaense Museum, in the old city hall.

Trips to **Iguacu Falls** originate from here. It has been calculated that 500,000 gallons of water crash every second (30,000,000 gallons every minute !) over the 1½ -mile long line of 275 separate waterfalls.

The roar can be be heard 5 miles away. The perpetual mist creates constant rainbows.

Because most of the falls are on the Argentine side, the best views are from the Brazilian side. There are hotels on both sides of the falls, and there are inexpensive airplane flights that circle the falls several times and also take passengers 12 miles below the falls to where the Iguacu and Upper Parana rivers meet. . . and also to Itaipu Dam – more than 620 feet high and about 7 miles long and to the 550-square-mile lake that was created by the dam.

These rivers form the borders of Brazil, Argentina and Paraguay in this area. Local bus and ferry services connect all of the tourist centers that surround the falls: Brazil (**Foz do Iguacu** and **Porto Meira**), Argentina (**Puerto Iguazu** and **Puerto Canoas**), Paraguay (**Puerto Strossner** and **Puerto Pointe France**).

Sights in **Paranagua**: Much of Brazil's coffee is shipped from this seaport. See: The Museum of Archaeology and Popular Art in the wonderful Colegio dos Jesuitas building. The fascinating market near the waterfront. The Church of Sao Benedito. The 17th century fountain. Nearby, the Nossa Senhora do Rocio shrine. Take the one-hour boat trip to see the 18th century Nossa Senhora dos Orazeres Prazeres fort. Shop here for crafts. Try the seafood.

Sao Paulo - Santos 2130

One of the rail wonders of the world was experienced before 1986 on the 50-mile trip from Sao Paulo to Santos. At 5 separate locations, the entire train was lifted by wire cables from one elevation to another until the train reached the top of the 2300-foot high Serra do Mar escarpment.

Train service was "temporarily" suspended in July, 1985. The bus schedules are:

Dep. Sao Paulo (Luz)	Frequent times from 00:01 to 23:50
Arr. Santos	1 hour later

*   *   *

Dep. Santos	Frequent times from 00:01 to 23:30
Arr. Sao Paulo (Luz)	1 hour later

Sights in **Sao Paulo**: See notes about Sao Paulo on page 750.

Sights in **Santos**: A very popular holiday resort and Brazil's most active seaport. Many monuments in the various parks: Praca da Republica, Praca Rui Barbosa, Praca Jose Bonifacio. Night-life activities in the Gonzaga area.

INTERNATIONAL ROUTES FROM BRAZIL

Rio de Janeiro - Buenos Aires Bus 2130

Arrival in Buenos Aires is on Day 3.

Dep. Rio de Janeiro	13:30
Arr. Buenos Aires	11:30

Rio de Janeiro - Sao Paulo - Montevideo

2012 Train

Dep. Rio de J. (D.Pedro)	23:00 (1)				
Arr. Sao Paulo (Luz)	08:05 (2)				

Change to bus. 2130

Dep. Sao Paulo	14:00 (2)	15:00 (2)	18:00 (2)	19:00 (2)	22:00 (4)
Arr. Porto Alegre	08:00 (3)	09:00 (3)	12:00 (3)	13:00 (3)	-0- (4)

Change buses.

Dep. Porto Alegre		20:00	21:00 (6)	22:00	-0- (4)
Arr. Montevideo		06:00 (5)	07:00 (5)	08:00 (5)	05:30 (7)

(1) Reservation required. Air-conditioned first-class only. Carries a sleeping car, a restaurant car and a lounge car. (2) Day 2 from Rio de Janeiro. (3) Day 2 from Sao Paulo. (4) Direct bus. No bus change in Porto Alegre. (5) Day 2 from Porto Alegre. (6) Runs Thursday only. (7) Day 3 from Sao Paulo.

Sao Paulo - Bauru - Corumba - Santa Cruz - La Paz

2015

Dep. Sao Paulo (Luz)	08:25 (1)	12:00 (1)	16:50 (2)	23:00 (3)
Arr. Bauru	15:20	19:00	23:28	05:10

(1) Restaurant car. (2) Light refreshments. (3) Supplement charged. Carries a sleeping car, only first-class coaches, and a restaurant car.

Change trains. 2011

You cross the Mato Grosso mountain range going from Bauru to Corumba.

Dep. Bauru	13:00 (1)
Arr. Corumba	20:00 Day 2 from Bauru.

(1) Runs Monday, Wednesday and Friday. Carries a sleeping car and a restaurant car.

Take a bus or taxi 11km (7 miles) to Puerto Suarez.
Change trains. 1907

Dep. Puerto Suarez	09:00 (1)	11:00 (2)	12:20 (3)
Arr. Santa Cruz	21:19	06:11	07:40

Change to bus. 1910

Dep. Santa Cruz	06:00	16:00	16:30	17:00	17:30
Arr. Cochabamba	18:30	04:30	05:00	05:30	06:00

Change to train. 1900

Dep. Cochabamba	20:30 (4)				08:00 (5)
Arr. La Paz	05:48				17:14

(1) Supplement charged. Runs Tuesday, Thursday and Saturday. Buffet. (2) Supplement charged. Runs Wednesday and Sunday. Restaurant car. (3) Runs Monday and Friday. (4) Supplement charged. Runs Sunday only. (5) Supplement charged. Runs Tuesday and Thursday.

Sao Paulo - Antofagasta

1907

Arr. Santa Cruz from Sao Paulo	21:19 (1)	06:11 (3)	07:40 (5)

(See preceding timetable, page 757)

Change trains.
1907

Dep. Santa Cruz	10:00 (2)	11:55 (4)	18:30 (6)
Arr. Yacuiba	19:22	20:25	10:00 (7)

Change trains.
2261

Dep. Yacuiba	14:00 (8)
Arr. Salta	10:33 (9)

Change to bus.
2465

Dep. Salta	N/A (10)
Arr. Antofagasta	N/A

(1) Arrives Tuesday, Thursday and Saturday. (2) Supplement charged. Runs Tuesday, Thursday and Saturday. Restaurant car. (3) Arrives Monday and Thursday. (4) Supplement charged. First-class only. Restaurant car. Runs Monday, Wednesday, Friday and Saturday. (5) Arrives Tuesday and Saturday. (6) Runs Thursday and Sunday. (7) Day 2 from Santa Cruz. (8) Runs Thursday only. Light refreshments. (9) Arrives Friday. (10) The days that buses run and their departure/arrival times for this 18-hour journey are not available. The fact that Antofagasta–Salta time have been available occasionally since 1989 verifies that there *is* service.

Rio de Janeiro - Santiago Bus 2130

Dep. Rio de Janeiro	18:00	Mon., Wed., Thurs. and Fri.
Arr. Santiago	18:00	Day 4

CHILE

Children under 1m.20 tall travel free. Children 1m.20 and taller must pay full fare.

From September to March, first-class train tickets in Chile are difficult to obtain. It is advisable to reserve space far in advance of travel date through a prominent travel agency in Santiago or Antofagasta.

Train service runs from Antofagasta to Puerto Montt, on the shore of the Gulf of Ancud. Feeder lines branch off the main north-south line, eastward to great resorts at **Lake Villarrica**, **Lake Panguipulli**, **Lake Ranco**, **Lake Puyehul** and **Lake Llanquihue**. The Lake District is the area east of the rail line from **Temuco** to Puerto Montt. The connecting point is **Puerto Varas**.

The average width of Chile is a scant 120 miles, ranging from 312 miles at its widest to 56 miles at its narrowest..

Antofagasta

There are many beautiful beaches, parks and plazas in this city.

Arica

Founded 1570 on the site of a pre-Columbian community. Arica belonged to Peru until captured by Chile in 1897. An important transportation hub: Chile's northernmost seaport, an international airport, a rail terminal for trains from Peru and Bolivia, and located on the Pan-American highway.

Santiago

See the Presidential Palace. The view of the city from the terrace of Castillo Gonzalez on Santa Lucia Hill in the center of the city, site of its founding in 1541. A museum, chapel and fountains are on the top of this 226-foot-high hill.

The Popular Arts Museum in Castillo Hidalgo. The 19th century European furnishings and decorations in the Cousino Palace (Dieciocho 438), open daily except Monday 10:00–13:00.

The Cathedral, near Plaza de Armas, with its fine painting of The Last Supper. These churches: Santo Domingo, San Francisco (location of the Colonial Art Museum, open daily except Monday 10:00–13:00), San Augustin, La Merced, Santa Ana, Recoleta Dominica and Recoleta Franciscana.

The foods and souvenirs (saddles, baskets, ceramics, dolls, rugs) in the central market. The collection of both foreign and national art at the National Art Museum in Parque Forestal. The National Library and the Historical Museum, both in the same building at Alameda, between Miraflores and McIver streets.

The Natural History Museum and Modern Art Museum, both in the Quinta Normal. The exhibit of Indian textiles, pottery and funerary masks in the Chilean Museum of Pre-Columbian Art at Bandera 361, open daily except Monday 10:00–18:00.

Take the funicular to the top of San Cristobal Hill (and enjoy tastings at the Wine Museum there) for a spectacular view of Santiago, stopping on the ascent to see the Zoo that is about one-third of the way up.

Valparaiso

See the Beaux Arts Museum. Severin Public Library. The view from Miradero O'Higgins, in Alto del Puerto.

Take the 20-minute ride to the beaches at **Vina del Mar,** called "The Pearl of the Pacific" and "The Garden City". Also in Vina: The Academy and Museum of Fine Arts in the Quinta Vergara, the Naval History Museum, and the Municipal Casino.

Valparaiso - Santiago - Chillan -Cabrero - Concepcion

Marvelous scenery: fertile farms (first colonized by Germans in the early 19th century), snow-capped mountains, shimmering lakes, mile after mile of wildflowers, vineyards and pine forests.

The 3-hour train service Valparaiso–Santiago was replaced in 1987 by 1½-hour bus service after a fire destroyed most of the train cars.

2465 Bus

Dep. Valparaiso (Puerto)	Frequent times from 06:10 to 21:30
Arr. Santiago (Mapocho)	2 hours later

Change to train . . . and to Alameda station.

2430

Dep. Santiago (Alameda)	08:30 (1)	09:00 (2)	13:30 (1)	23:00 (3)
Arr. Chillan	13:30	14:34	18:26	03:45
Arr. Concepcion	17:25	18:15	22:20	07:30

* * *

Dep. Concepcion	08:30 (1)	13:00 (1)	22:00 (3)
Dep. Chillan	12:12	16:45	01:35
Arr. Santiago (Alameda)	17:30	21:50	07:10

Change to bus . . . and to Mapocho station

2465

Dep. Santiago (Mapocho)	Several times from 04:05 to 20:30
Arr. Valparaiso (Puerto)	2 hours later

(1) Has an air-conditioned "supersalon" coach. Buffet. (2) First-class only. Service is subject to local confirmation. (3) Carries sleeping cars, air-conditioned parlor car, video bar and has light refreshments.

Sights in **Chillan**: The thermal hot springs here have attracted tourists for over 150 years. Skiing (June–October) became popular after a ski lift and hotel here were remodeled in 1984. The top of the chairlift is 8,200 feet above the resort. Of the 6 ski runs, the main slope has a vertical drop of 2,300 feet. A learner's slope drops only 98 feet over a 1,312-foot-long run.

The resort, Termas de Chillan, will pickup visitors at the railstation, airport and bus terminal by prior arrangement.

Crafts in wood, leather and iron, also pottery, ponchos and hats are made and sold here.

Sights in **Concepcion**: The Pedro del Rio Zanartu Museum. The view of the city from Cerro Amarillo. A lovely view from Cerro Caracol of valleys and **Bio-Bio**, Chile's largest river.

Santiago - Cartagena 2427

These trains operate only from December 15 to March 15. This service is subject to local confirmation.

Dep. Santiago (Alameda	07:15 (1)	Dep. Cartagena	19:30 (2)
Arr. Cartagena	09:50 (1)	Arr. Santiago (Alameda)	22:05 (2)

(1) 30 minutes later on Sunday.   (2) 30 minutes earlier on Sunday.

Arica - Santiago Bus 2465

Rail passenger service for this 1,300-mile trip, basically a freight train with limited passenger accommodation, is considered to be so appalling that the state railway refuses to publish information about the journey.

Here is the schedule for the bus trip.

Dep. Arica	08:00	09:30	10:30	18:00	22:00
Arr. Santiago	15:30 (1)	17:00 (1)	18:00 (1)	01:30 (2)	05:30 (2)
		*	*	*	
Dep. Santiago	09:00	11:00	18:00		
Arr. Arica	16:30 (1)	18:30 (1)	01:30 (2)		

(1) Day 2. (2) Day 3.

Antofagasta - Santiago Bus 2465

All arrivals are on Day 2.

Dep. Antofagasta	06:00	10:45	11:00	15:00	18:00	18:40	19:00 (1)
Arr. Santiago	03:30	08:15	08:30	12:30	15:30	16:10	16:30
			*	*	*		
Dep. Santiago	09:00	10:00	11:00	15:00	18:00	19:00	
Arr. Antofagasta	06:30	07:30	08:30	12:30	15:30	16:30	

(1) Plus other departures from Antofagasta at 21:00 and 21:30, arriving Santiago Day 2 at 18:30 and 19:00.

Antofagasta - Arica Bus 2465

Dep. Antofagasta	00:01	01:15	19:00	20:00	21:00		
Arr. Arica	12:00	13:15	07:00	08:00	09:00		
			*	*	*		
Dep. Arica	08:00	09:30	10:30	18:00	20:30	21:00	22:00
Arr. Antofagasta	20:00	21:30	22:30	06:00	08:30	09:00	10:00

Santiago - Puerto Montt 2430

See description of Puerto Montt area under "Bariloche–Puerto Montt" on page 739.

Dep. Santiago (Ala.)	18:30 (1)	21:30 (2)	Dep. Puerto Montt	N/A (2)	N/A (1)
Arr. Puerto Montt	14:00	N/A (3)	Arr. Santiago (Ala.)	06:30	07:30

(1) Carries first-class sleepings cars, air-conditioned parlor car, video car and a restaurant car. (2) Light refreshments. (3) Time was not available in 1991.

LAKE DISTRICT BUS CONNECTIONS

Puerto Montt - San Carlos de Bariloche 2300

This bus service is available only to group tours.

SPECIAL ONE-DAY ANDEAN SCENIC TRAIN TRIP

Valparaiso - Los Andes 2426

Here is an exciting one-day glimpse by train at the overwhelming Andes mountain range.

All of these trains are first-class only.

Dep. Valparaiso	08:05 (1)	N/A (2)	14:30 (3)	18:00 (4)
Arr. Los Andes	11:00	N/A	17:25	20:55

* * *

Dep. Los Andes	07:40 (4)	15:50 (1)	N/A (2)	17:35 (3)
Arr. Valparaiso	10:35	18:45	N/A	20:30

(1) Runs Saturdays, Sundays and holidays. (2) Special tourist train. Light refreshments. Has no fixed schedule. January and February: runs Sundays and holidays. Runs on most national and regional holidays throughout the year. (3) Runs Monday-Friday, except holidays. (4) Runs daily.

Santiago - Los Andes Bus 2465

Since 1985, only bus service has been offered between Santiago and the Los Andes resort.

Dep. Santiago	09:00	Dep. Los Andes	15:00
Arr. Los Andes	11:00	Arr. Santiago	17:00

INTERNATIONAL ROUTES FROM CHILE

There is train service from both Arica and Antofagasta to La Paz. One can cross the continent by rail from Antofagasta to Sao-Paulo. Until 1980, there was transcontinental train service all the way, from Valparaiso to Buenos Aires.

Valparaiso (Santiago) - Mendoza - Buenos Aires

The Los Andes-Mendoza portion of this rail trip was the most exciting train ride in South America before the train was replaced by bus in 1980.

Altitudes (in feet) En Route

ASCENT		DESCENT	
Valparaiso	-0-	Tunnel Exit	10,452
Los Andes	2,669	Las Cuevas	10,331
San Pablo	3,174	Puente del Inca	8,915
Salto del Soldado	4,141	Punta de las Vacas	7,852
Rio Blanco	4,764	Zanjon Amarillo	7,236
Guardia Vieja	5,397	Rio Blanco	7,000
El Juncal	7,321	Uspallata	5,741
El Portillo	9,408	Guido	4,957
Caracoles (tunnel entrance)	10,420	Portrerillos	4,443
(The summit is 13,082.)		Cacheuta	4,080
		Blanco Encalda	3,502
		Paso de los Andes	3,069
		Mendoza	2,518

On the trans-Andean train ride that operated until 1980, there were great amounts of snow Los Andes–Mendoza from May to November. It was a steep descent from Portillo (a Winter sports resort) to Las Cuevas, another ski resort. Then, it was a rack railway from Las Cuevas to Puente del Inca. The ride from Puente del Inca to Mendoza was by narrow-gauge, through a scenic valley.

Since 1980, only bus service has been offered to Mendoza.

Valparaiso - Mendoza - Buenos Aires 2465 Bus

Dep. Valparaiso	07:00	08:00	08:30
Set your watch forward one hour.			
Arr. Mendoza	17:00	18:00	18:30

Santiago - Mendoza - Buenos Aires 2465 Bus

Dep. Santiago	07:00	08:00	08:30	09:00	12:00
Set your watch forward one hour.					
Arr. Mendoza	14:00	15:00	15:30	16:00	19:00

2270 Train

Dep. Mendoza	16:00 (1)	18:55 (2)	20:15 (3)
Arr. Buenos Aires (Re.)	08:30	09:30	09:30

(1) Carries first-class air-conditioned sleeping cars, first-class air-conditioned coaches, and a restaurant car. (2) Runs Sunday only. Has first-class air-conditioned coaches and a restaurant car. (3) Runs Monday and Friday. Carries first-class air-onditioned sleeping cars, first-class air-conditioned coaches, a restaurant car and a cinema car.

Sights En Route

The train traveled through a fertile valley until beginning the ascent to **Portillo**, a popular ski resort with many hotels. Mountain slopes on the Pacific side of the Andes are covered with foliage, including many flowers. You saw the Aconcagua River and excellent rock scenery before entering the tunnel at Caracoles. See notes about skiing at Portillo, earlier in this chapter under "Buenos Aires–Valparaiso".

The next arrival was at **Las Cuevas**, another popular ski resort. After leaving Las Cuevas, you had a view of the **Horcones River** before arriving at **Puente del Inca**, a popular Winter sports resort area, attracting the greatest crowds from November to May. It is named for its natural stone bridge spanning the **Mendoza River** and is one of South America's most marvelous sights. This city is also popular as a base for excursions by foot and horseback to many high valleys in the Andes: Los Penitentes, Laguna de los Horcones, etc.

After leaving Puente del Inca, **Aconcagua** was next in sight. It is the highest (22,834 feet) mountain in the western hemisphere. Many rushing mountain streams could be seen in the area of **Rio Blanco**. Then, a desolate and vast plain came into view before reaching **Uspallata**. The train followed an old Spanish trail called Camino de los Andes between Upsallata and **Cacheuta**.

The next stop was **Mendoza**. If you left Valparaiso or Santiago on a Saturday, a 36-hour stopover here was well worthwhile, continuing on to Buenos Aires the following Monday.

See notes about sightseeing in Mendoza on page 742.

ROUTES TO BOLIVIA, BRAZIL AND PERU

There are 4 rail routes from Chile to Bolivia: Mendoza north to Tucuman and then on from there to either La Paz or Santa Cruz; Antofagasta–La Paz; and Arica–La Paz.

The one rail route from Chile to Brazil is from Antofagasta to Sao Paulo.

The bus ride to Peru is Santiago–Arica–Lima.

Mendoza - Tucuman

2465 Bus

Arr. Mendoza	(by bus from Valparaiso or Santiago, schedules on page 763).		
Change buses.			
2300			
Dep. Mendoza	13:00	14:00 (1)	20:30
Arr. Tucuman	09:00	10:00	16:30

(1) Runs Monday and Friday.

Tucuman - La Quiaca - La Paz

2261			1900		
Dep. Tucuman (GM)	15:05 (1)		Dep. Villazon	14:10 (2)	15:30 (3)
Arr. La Quiaca	09:28 (3)		Arr. La Paz	10:50	09:40
Walk 3km across border.					

(1) Runs Tuesday and Friday. Buffet. (2) Runs Tuesday and Friday. Restaurant car. (3) Direct train Tucuman-La Qiaca-La Paz on Friday, arriving La Quiaca Saturday and not requiring walk across border La Quiaca-Villazon. Runs both Saturday and Wednesday Villazon-La Paz. Restaurant car Villazon-La Paz.

Tucuman - Salta - Pocitos - Yacuiba - Santa Cruz

2261			
Dep. Tucuman (Norte)	13:52	Runs Monday, Thursday and Saturday.	
Arr. Guemes	20:26		
Change trains.			
Dep. Guemes	20:57	Runs Monday, Thursday and Saturday.	
Arr. Salta	22:17		
Change trains.			
Dep. Salta	20:15	Runs Monday only. Light Refreshments.	
Arr. Yacuiba	16:00	Tuesday	
Change trains.			
1907			
Dep. Yacuiba	08:50 (1)	18:20 (2)	22:00 (3)
Arr. Santa Cruz	22:25	10:45	06:32

(1) Supplement charged. Runs Tuesday, Thursday and Saturday. Has a first-class coach. Restaurant car. (2) Runs Wednesday and Sunday. (3) Supplement charged. Runs Monday, Wednesday, Friday and Sunday. First-class only. Restaurant car.

Antofagasta - La Paz 1900

Bus		Train	
Dep. Antofagasta	N/A (1)	Dep. Calama	N/A (1)
Arr. Calama	N/A (1)	Arr. La Paz	N/A (1)
Change to train.			

(1) Time was not available in 1991.

It is easy to understand why this train trip of 705 miles takes 36 hours. The first 18 miles out of Antofagasta, there is an ascent of 1,800 feet as the route crosses the **Atacama Desert**. In the next 211 miles, the train climbs to the summit of the Chilean section of the ride: 13,000 feet above sea level, at **Ascotan**.

There is generally a 3 to 4-hour wait at **Ollague** (the Chile-Bolivia border) while Bolivian customs officers go through the train to check passports and inspect baggage.

One of the most unusual sights on this trip occurs on the second day, just before reaching **Poopo**. Thousands of flamingos can be seen on a lake that is 12,000 feet above sea level.

Santiago - Lima Bus

2465		1820	
Dep. Santiago	09:00 Tues. & Fri .	Dep. Lima	09:30 Wed. & Sun.
Arr. Lima	09:00 Day 3.	Arr. Santiago	09:30 Day 3.

Arica - Charana - La Paz 1901

There are 30 miles of rack and pinion track during this 270-mile rail trip. During the first 70 miles after departing Arica, the track climbs from sea level to 11,000 feet. The scenery on this stretch is a jumble of brown lava rocks. The highest place on this route is 14,000 feet, at **General Lagos**. The Bolivian border is only 5 minutes from Charana, at Visviri, where the passport control procedure takes more than one hour. Many herds of llamas roam here. Because military installations are nearby, photo-taking is not permitted at the frontier area.

The best scenery is during the last portion of the trip, on the 1,000-foot *descent* into the highest capital in the world. La Paz is nearly 12,000 feet above sea level. During the last 6 miles, a series of loops traveled very slowly, there is excellent scenery of 3 tremendous Andean peaks: Illampu (21,490 feet), Illimani (21,315 feet) and Huayna–Potosi (20,407 feet) if there are no clouds or fog.

Dep. Arica	09:30 (1)	23:00 (2)	Dep. La Paz	07:00 (5)	22:00 (6)
Arr. Charana	-0-	08:00 (3)	Arr. Charana	-0-	05:55 (3)
Change trains.			Change trains.		
Dep. Charana	-0-	09:10 (4)	Dep. Charana	-0-	09:30 (7)
Arr. La Paz	20:04	18:40	Arr. Arica	19:06	18:00

(1) Runs Tuesday, Thursday and Saturday. Supplement charged. Direct train. No train change in Charana. Has first-class coaches. (2) Second-class only. Runs only on the second and fourth Tuesday of each month. (3) Arrives Wednesday. (4) Runs Wednesday only. (5) Runs Monday, Wednesday and Friday. Suplement charged. Direct train. No train change in Charana. Has first-class coaches. (6) Runs Tuesday only. (7) Second-class only. Runs only on the second and fourth Wednesday of each month.

Antofagasta - Salta - Yacuiba - Bauru - Sao Paulo

2465 Bus			
Dep. Antofagasta	15:00 (1)		
Arr. Salta	09:00 (2)		
Change to train.			
2261			
Dep. Salta	20:15 (3)		
Arr. Yacuiba	16:00 (4)		
Change trains.			
1907			
Dep. Yacuiba	22:00 (5)		
Arr. Santa Cruz	06:32 (6)		

Change trains.
1907 Train
Dep. Santa Cruz 18:00 (7)
Arr. P. Suarez 06:17 (8)
It is 11km (7 miles) to Corumba.
Change trains.
2011
Dep. Corumba 07:00 (9)
Arr. Bauru 16:00 (10)

(1) Runs Wednesday and Saturday. (2) Day 2 from Antofagasta (Thursday and Sunday). (3) Runs Monday only. Light refreshments. (4) Day 2 from Salta (Tuesday). (5) First-class only. Supplement charged. Runs Monday, Wednesday, Friday and Sunday. Restaurant car. (6) Day 2 from Yacuiba. (7) Supplement charged. Runs Wednesday, Friday and Monday. Buffet. (8) Day 2 from Santa Cruz. Train has not continued to Corumba since 1981. (9) Runs Monday, Wednesday and Friday. (10) Day 2 from Corumba.

All of these trains run daily.

2015				
Dep. Bauru	04:18 (1)	07:48 (2)	13:29 (2)	23:37 (3)
Arr. Sao Paulo (Luz)	10:45	14:52	20:01	06:00

(1) Light refreshments. (2) Restaurant car. (3) Supplement charged. Carries a sleeping car and a restaurant car.

COLOMBIA

The 5 classes of trains are: Lujo, Rapido, Expreso, Turisto and Ordinario. Children under 2 travel free. Half-fare for children 2–9 on Ordinario trains; 25% discount on Turisto trains; no discount on Lujo, Rapido or Expreso trains.

This is the only South American country with a coast on both the Atlantic and Pacific oceans. There is no train service between Colombia and adjacent countries, only a few short internal narrow-gauge rail routes.

Bogota

Capital of Colombia. Founded in 1538 at 8,460-feet altitude. Population is nearly 5,000,000. See 20,000 pre-Colombian gold items and the world's largest emerald in the Museo del Oro in Santander Park on Carrera 7. It is an indescribable thrill to stand in the totally dark room on the

Gold Museum's third floor and instantly see more than 10,000 gold objects when the lights are switched on.

Of the city's more than 300 churches, be sure to see the ceiling of Islamic designs in La Concepcion, Bogota's oldest church (late 16th century). The panelled ceiling and the main altar in the very beautiful Moorish-style 17th century San Francisco Church. The carved oak-and-cedar altar in the 18th century La Tercera Church.

The colonial paintings by Vasquez and the columns inlaid with turquoise in the lovely El Sagrario Chapel, next door to the Cathedral. The outstanding stained-glass in the Church of Maria del Carmen. The 16th century Veracruz Church. Also visit San Diego, San Augustin, San Ignacio and Santa Ines churches.

See exceptional art and history collections at the National Museum. The Museum of Natural History and the sidereal projection room, both in the City Planetarium. Take the cable car to the top of Montserrate, 2000 feet above the city, for a spectacular view of Bogota. Seeing the pilgrims climb the mountain on their knees during Holy Week is a fantastic spectacle.

Nearby is Yequendama Falls, set in lush jungle foliage. Quinta de Bolivar, the villa given to the liberator by a wealthy man, now a museum of Napoleonic-style furniture and Bolivar relics. Its gardens are decorated with busts of heroes and heavy bronze cannons used in the country's War of Independence (1810).

The Palace of San Carlos. The Municipal Palace. The coin presses and wood balconies in the Mint House Museum. The pre-Colombian pottery in the mansion of the Marques de Jan Jorge. The incredible carved ceiling in the Presidential Palace. The Museum of July 20, 1810 (Independence Day). The Museum of Folk Art. The excellent collection of paintings in the Museum of Colonial Art. Teatro Colon. Luis Angel Arango Library.

Exceptional art and history collections at the National Museum. Many rare coins at Casa de la Moneda. Rare manuscripts at Hierba Buena Literary Museum. The craft-work at the Handicrafts and Traditional Arts Museum. Religious art at the Theological Seminary Museum. The elegant police uniforms. The ramshackle huts in the suburbs.

Shop for emeralds, reptile leatherwork (alligator, crocodile, snake) and beautiful linen shirts. The handicrafts of more than 1,000,000 artisans are sold at Artesanias de Colombia. Stroll the cobbled streets of the La Candelaria area to see the 17th century colonial homes with red tile roofs, overhanging balconies and interior patios. Celebrate the tradition of afternoon "Chocolate Santaferreno".

Medellin

The 17th century churches: San Benito, La Veracruz, San Jose and the Old Cathedral. The cattle auctions on Tuesday and Thursday. The South American animals and birds in the Zoo. The Museum of Folk Art. The Museo Zea. The Botanical Garden, with its world-famous collection of orchids.

Santa Marta

This was the first European city in South America. It is now a banana center. Founded in 1525, it is Colombia's important commercial Atlantic seaport. Simon Bolivar, South America's great liberator, died here. You can visit the plantation where he lived his last days, 3 miles southeast of the city.

Also see: The Gaira and Rodadero beaches, the Cathedral and the Church of San Francisco. Visit the two nearby fishing villages, **Taganga** and **La Concha** and the marine biology institute at Punta de Betin.

Bogota - Barrancabermeja - Santa Marta 1702

Some meal stops are made during this trip. Most of the journey offers great jungle, river and mountain scenery. Particularly scenic is the descent at **Puerto Salgar** to the **Magdalena River**.

Both of these trains charge a supplement and carry a sleeping car and restaurant car December 1 to March 31.

Dep. Bogota	08:00	Mon. only	Dep. Santa Marta	07:00	Wed. only
Dep. Barrancabermeja	22:22		Dep. Barrancabermeja	21:24	
Arr. Santa Marta	12:46	Day 2.	Arr. Bogota	12:29	Day 2.

Sights in **Barrancabermeja**: The Cathedral of the Sacred Heart of Jesus.

Medellin - Santa Marta 1702

Both of these trains charge a supplement all year. They carry a sleeping car and a restaurant car December 1 – March 31.

Dep. Medellin	12:10 (1)	Dep. Santa Marta	07:00 (2)	
Dep. Barrancabermeja	22:22	Dep. Barrancabermeja	21:24	
Arr. Santa Marta	12:46 Day 2.	Arr. Medellin	07:47	Day 2.

(1) Runs Monday only. (2) Runs Wednesday only.

Barrancabermeja - Bucaramanga 1720 Bus

It took 8 hours to travel by train the 89-mile-long Barrancabermeja- Bucaramanga spur off the Bogota–Santa Marta line before rail service was replaced by 3-hour bus service in mid-1989.

Times have not been available since 1988.

Dep. Barrancabermeja	N/A	Dep. Bucaramanga	N/A
Arr. Bucaramanga	N/A	Arr. Barrancabermeja	N/A

Bogota - Grecia - Medellin 1702

Dep. Bogota	N/A (1)	Dep. Medellin (Car.)	07:00 (3)
Arr. Grecia (P. Berrio)	N/A	Arr. Grecia (P. Berrio)	13:23
Change trains.		Change trains.	
Dep. Grecia (P. Berrio)	01:23 (2)	Dep. Grecia (P. Berrio)	N/A (1)
Arr. Medellin (Car.)	05:54	Arr. Bogota	N/A

(1) Service Bogota–Grecia has not operated since 1989. (2) Runs Tuesday and Friday. First-class only. (3) Runs daily. Third-class only.

Girardot - Neiva 1700

Both of these trains are third-class only.

Dep. Girardot	07:00 Saturday	Dep. Neiva	16:00 Sunday
Arr. Neiva	11:55	Arr. Girardot	20:43

Cauca Valley Scenic Train Rides

There are 2 beautiful short rail trips in the scenic Cauca Valley.

Cali - Armenia 1705

Both of these trains are first-class only.

Dep. Cali	13:15	Dep. Armenia	06:30
Arr. Armenia	18:25	Arr. Cali	11:40

Sights in **Cali**: See relics of the city's last Royal Sheriff in the colonial ranchhouse called Canasgordas. The Museum of Natural History. Plaza de Caicedo, with the Cathedral and National Palace. There are great views of Cali from San Fernando Mountain. See the 3,000 different types of orchids at "El Orquideal". There is excellent deep-sea fishing at **Buenaventura**, a 2-hour ride from Cali.

Sights in **Armenia**: A modern city. See Quindio University.

Cali - Cartago 1705

Dep. Cali	06:10 (1)	07:55 (2)	09:30 (3)	11:50 (1)	17:00 (1)
Arr. Cartago	09:43	12:09	13:36	15:18	20:23

Sights in **Cartago**: Many fine colonial buildings. See Casa de Los Virreyes (House of the Viceroys).

Dep. Cartago	04:50 (3)	06:25 (1)	10:20 (1)	12:45 (2)	16:35 (1)
Arr. Cali	08:56	09:51	13:46	17:25	19:58

(1) Runs daily. Third-class only. (2) Runs Saturday and Sunday. Second-class only. Light refreshments. (3) Runs daily. First-class only.

ECUADOR

Children under 3 travel free. Half-fare for children 3–11. Children 12 and over must pay full fare. There is no train service between Ecuador and adjacent countries.

The 288-mile ride from Guayaquil (Duran Alfaro) to Quito is one of the world's most thrilling train trips and advance reservations are essential. The former antique bus on rail wheels that provided 30 uncomfortable wood seats was replaced in 1980 by a new autoferro that has 43 upholstered seats.

No food is sold en route. There is time for breakfast in a restaurant at the first of many stops where food and beverages can be purchased.

The ride begins with a 20-minute ferryboat trip from Guayaquil to Duran. The train ascends a 5.5 percent gradient, climbing in one 50-mile stretch (Bucay-Palmira) from 975 feet to 10,600 feet. At a point called "Devil's Nose", there is a double switchback zig-zag, carved out of a rock mountain.

Highest point on the route is 11,841 feet, at **Urbina**. Watch for **Mt. Chimborazo**, rising an additional 8,000 feet above the train. This 12-hour train trip involves hundreds of bridges and tunnels. You can make the return trip by airplane in 35 minutes. A popular stopover is at Riobamba.

Here are the stations and their altitudes:

MILES FROM GUAYAQUIL		ALTITUDE IN FEET	MILES FROM GUAYAQUIL		ALTITUDE IN FEET
0	Guayaquil	15	142	Luisa	10,379
14	Yaguachi	20	150	Riobamba	9,020
21	Milagro	42	170	Urbina	11,841
31	Naranjito	100	178	Mocha	10,346
43	Barranganeta	300	186	Cevallos	9,100
54	Bucay	975	196	Ambato	8,435
72	Huigra	4,000	219	San Miguel	8,645
76	Chunchi	4,875	227	Latacunga	9,055
81	Sibambe	5,925	239	Lasso	10,375
89	Alausi	8,553	250	Cotopaxi	11,653
95	Tixan	9,200	263	Machachi	10,118
103	Palmira	10,626	266	Aloag	9,090
112	Guamote	10,000	273	Tambillo	9,891
132	Cajabamba	10,388	288	Quito	9,375

Guayaquil - Quito 1751

Service Alausi–Riobamba (and v.v.) was suspended in early 1984 while the line was being repaired after landslides. It had not resumed in 1991.

Dep. Guayaquil (Duran)	06:25 (1)		Dep. Quito	09:30 (3)
Dep. Milagro	07:15		Dep. Latacunga	N/A (4)
Dep. Sibambe	10:40		Dep. Ambato	N/A (4)
Arr. Alausi	11:08 (2)		Arr. Riobamba	13:49 (2)
Dep. Riobamba	13:00 (3)		Dep. Alausi	08:56 (1)
Dep. Ambato	N/A (4)		Dep. Sibambe	09:22
Dep. Latacunga	N/A (4)		Dep. Milagro	12:39
Arr. Quito	17:56		Arr. Guayaquil (Duran)	13:30

(1) Second-class only. From Guayaquil runs Thursday–Sunday. From Alausi, runs Friday–Monday. (2) Service Alausi-Riobamba and v.v. has been suspended since a 1984 landslide. (3) Runs when required. (4) Trains did not stop here in 1991.

On the route from Guayaquil to Quito, Indian women meet the train's arrival in **Milagro**, hawking fruits and native bread. Lush foliage can be seen after leaving **Bucay**. Then the train ascends the Chanchan River gorge as it appraoches **Huigra** and finally climbs 1,000 feet above the river, up the Devil's Nose (Nariz del Diablo).

Many small Indian mountain villages line the track en route to **Sibambe**. In **Alausi,** a resort village, bus connections to Quito are available. At **Palmira**, there is a view of many high mountain peaks: Altar, Carihuairazo, Chimborazo, Sangay and Tungurahua. Next, the train skirts the shoreline of **Lake Colta** before coming into Riobamba.

Highest point of the trip (11,841 feet) is shortly after leaving Riobamba, at **Urbina Pass**. The Indian market at **Ambato** is worth visiting. It is the "garden city" of Ecuador: many flowers and fruits.

Nine volcanoes can be seen from **Latacunga,** a town of 23,000 people at 9,055 feet altitude. Sights here are the Museum of Popular Art, the Cathedral and the Indian market.

Guayaquil

This is the largest city (800,000 population) in Ecuador as well as the country's financial and commercial center. See: The City Museum. La Rotunda. Government Palace. San Carlos Fort. The Municipal Tower. The tombs and monuments at "White City", the major cemetery. Santo Domingo Church. Colon Park.

Do not miss the view of the city from El Mirador, or a visit to the world's largest balsa wood factory.

Riobamba

There are wonderful views from here of the peaks of Altar, Tungurahua and Chimborazo, an inactive volcano that at 20,577 feet tall is Ecuador's highest peak. Visit the Saturday fair, in 9 different plazas (leather articles, rope sandals, embroidered belts, etc.).

The exhibits of precious stones, silver, gold, 16th century furnishings from the Spanish conquest, and paintings of religious subjects by Ecuadorian Indians who were taught by European missionaries are the attractions in the Museum of Religious Art. See the woven rugs and tapestries in nearby **Guano.**

Quito

Ecuador's capital. It is 9,300-feet high here. See the marvelous sculptures at the San Francisco Convent. The gold leaf in La Compania Church. Fine art in the Cathedral. The campus at the Central University. The National Palace.

The view of Quito and the snow-covered cone of 19,347-foot high Cotopaxi (world's highest active volcano) from the patio restaurant at the top of the 600-foot high Panecillo Hill. Inside the 100-foot monument there to the Virgin of Quito are stairs leading to a landing that has other excellent views of the area around the city. The experience can be enjoyed at night as well as day since the restaurant is open Monday–Saturday until 24:00, Sunday until 22:00.

Colonial homes about 400 years old along La Ronda, reached by walking downhill from the intersection of Venezuela and Rocafuerte. The exhibits of Andean and jungle civilizations at the Museo de Banco Central (10 de Agosto and Briseno). The natural science collection at Casa de Cultura (Patria and 12 de Octubre).

Some of Ecuador's best art, in the Municipal Art and History Museum at the Real de Lima. Stroll through two suburbs: Guapulo and San Roque.

You can stand on the equator by taking a 15-mile auto trip north of Quito, where you can place one foot in the northern hemisphere and the other in the southern hemisphere. The 90-feet-high Equator Monument (at latitude 0-0-0) is near the village of **San Antonio de Pichincha**. The exact site is called "Mitad del Mundo"— the Middle of the World. The monument is a stone obelisk. A metallic ball, representing the earth, sits on top of the obelisk.

Every year at noon on the days of the vernal and autumnal equinoxes (near March 21 and September 22), the sun is directly overhead so that neither the monument nor peoples visiting it cast a shadow. Because the force of gravity is weaker at the Equator than anywhere else, everybody weighs less there.

There is a splendid view of the mountains from the monument's observation deck. Take the elevator up, but *walk* down from the deck. Each of the 9 levels features information and exhibits about different Indian tribes.

Popular attractions near the monument are **San Pablo Lake** and shopping in a village called **Calderon**.

Take the very scenic 2½-hour $1.20 bus ride to **Otalvo**, particularly on Friday in order to see the early-morning opening of the Saturday market with its many concessions (merchandise, food, beverages) and the colorful Indian costumes worn there.

Sibambe - Cuenca 1752

Both of these trains are first-class only.

| Dep. Cuenca | 06:00 | Dep. Sibambe | 13:20 |
| Arr. Sibambe | 12:09 | Arr. Cuenca | 19:33 |

Sights in **Cuenca**: Founded by Spaniards in the 16th century on the ruins of the residence of a former Inca ruler. The major tourist attraction here is the Indian market.

See the 16th century La Concepcion Convent and the 17th century Las Carmelitas Descalzas Convent. The Municipal Museum.

Quito - San Lorenzo 1750

Dep. Quito	N/A (1)	Dep. San Lorenzo	06:55
Arr. Ibarra	N/A	Arr. Ibarra	14:00
Change trains.		Overnight in Ibarra.	
Dep. Ibarra	07:00	Dep. Ibarra	N/A (1)
Arr. San Lorenzo	13:56	Arr. Quito	N/A

(1) Service Quito–Ibarra and v.v. has been suspended most of the time since 1982.

Sights in **San Lorenzo**: Ecuador's second rail-connected seaport, linked by train service (via Quito) with the other port, Guayaquil, before a 1984 landslide damaged the Riobamba-Alausi section of the Quito-Guayaquil route (page 770).

PARAGUAY

Children under 3 travel free. Half-fare for children 3–9. Children 10 and over must pay full fare.

Paraguay's only rail routes are from Asuncion to Encarnacion and San Salvador to Abai. Its only passenger train service to an adjacent country is the extension from Encarnacion to Argentina.

Asuncion

The capital of Paraguay. Linked by rail (via Encarnacion) with Buenos Aires. Most of the sights can be seen by starting at the Customs House and going from it down Calle El Paraguayo Independiente. You will first come to Government Palace, styled after the Louvre in Paris.

Next, the Congressional Palace on Plaza Constitucion. During the legislature's April-December session, the public is allowed to observe the debates there. The 19th century Cathedral is on the same Plaza. Two blocks away, on Calle Chile, is the Pantheon of Heroes, the national shrine designed to emulate the Invalides in Paris.

See the Gran Hotel del Paraguay. The view of Asuncion from Parque Carlos Antonio Lopez. Window-shop on Calle Palma. Take a ride on one of the old trolleys, maintained for tourists as are those in San Francisco, CA.

It is a 45-minute train or bus ride to nearby **Trinidad,** where a Botanical Garden, a Museum of Natural History and a pathetic Zoo are located. Eighteen miles east by road is **Itaugua**, famous for the "spiderweb" lace made there, called *nanduti*.

Encarnacion

A busy port on the Alto Parana River. Posadas, on the Argentine side of the river, is a base for taking auto or airplane trips to see the **Iguazu Falls**, most spectacular from August to November. See notes about the falls under "Curitiba", on page 755. Local bus and ferry services connect both of the tourist centers surrounding the falls: **Puerto Strossner** and **Foz de Iguacu**.

Asuncion - Foz do Iguaco Bus 2250

Dep. Asuncion	00:15	01:00	02:00	07:30	23:15
Arr. Puerto Strossner	05:05	05:50	06:50	12:20	04:05
Arr. Foz do Iguacu	05:45	06:30	07:30	13:00	04:45
		*	*	*	
Dep. Foz do Iguacu	07:00	11:00	12:30	14:30	20:00
Dep. Puerto Strossner	07:40	11:40	13:10	15:10	20:40
Arr. Asuncion	12:30	16:50	18:00	20:00	01:30

Asuncion - San Salvador - Encarnacion - Posadas - Buenos Aires

The 40-hour Asuncion-Buenos Aires trip is a very rough ride, 930 miles through dense brush and jungle. The inconveniences include hard wood seats, stifling heat, swarms of mosquitoes and much dust. The locomotive was built in 1912, and the train is said to be the oldest in South America.

At night, from Asuncion to Encarnacion, the station platforms at villages along the route are lined with people who enjoy watching the trains pass by while sitting at tables, eating and singing.

Cook's timetables do not show that the 4½-hour once-a-week train that departs Asuncion at 18:00 on only Tuesday carries one non-airconditioned second-class coach car that is transferred in Posadas to the Posadas-Asuncion train. The 1991 price for it was 350,000 Argentine australes.

Both of these train carry a restaurant car.

2230			2260	
Dep. Asuncion	18:00	Tuesday	Dep. Posadas	17:30 (1)
Dep. San Salvador	00:40	Wednesday	Arr. Buenos Aires	
Arr. Encarnacion	09:20		(F. Lacroze)	12:40 (2)
Arr. Posadas	12:00			
Change trains.				

(1) Runs daily. Carries air-conditioned first-class sleeping cars and air-conditioned first-class coach cars. (2) Day 2 from Posadas.

San Salvador - Abai 2231

Dep. San Salvador	01:30	Sat.	Dep. Abai	07:30	Sun.
Arr. Abai	05:40		Arr. San Salvador	11:45	

PERU

Children under 4 travel free. Half-fare for children 4–11. Children 12 and over must pay full fare.

Many rail routes in Peru are at such high altitudes that several trains provide passengers with free oxygen. Details on trips follow a description of interesting sights in 6 cities which can be visited by train.

Buffet-Class is far superior to first and second-class cars, which are dominated by animals (on the seats, below them, and on overhead racks).

Demand for Buffet Class (which includes breakfast and lunch served to passengers at their seats) is limited and in great demand. Reservations can be made only from 09:00 to 11:00 on the morning prior to the trip day.

Arequipa

This is called "The White City" because it is built mostly of white volcanic rock. It lies at the foot of 19,200-foot high El Misti Volcano. See: the beautiful furniture in the 17th century Santa Cataline Convent, reflecting medieval architecture and life. The flowery Plaza de Armas. The colonial residences: Casa del Moral, Casa Ricketts and Casa Gibbs. Leatherwork is a specialty here. At an altitude of 7,500 feet, much lower than Cuzco, Arequipa has a splendid climate.

Cuzco

The oldest continually inhabited city in the Americas, dating from either the 10th or 11th century. November to March is the rainy season. This is the popular tourist spot in Peru the rest of the year. At 11,400 feet altitude, it is often cold here in what was once the capital of the Inca Empire. A tea made from leaves of the coca plant is usually helpful for relieving altitude sickness.

There are many Inca remains in this area. See: the famous stone of Twelve Angles, in the walls of the Palace of Inca Roca. Main Square, where Incas held their celebrations and ceremonies.

Stroll Callejon Loreto, a perfectly preserved Inca street. Visit the unusually quiet Indian market. The base of the ancient Temple of the Sun, now in the foundation of the Church of Santa Domingo. The gold and bejeweled pulpit, also the nearly 400 paintings from the Cuzco school, in the 17th century Cathedral. The House of the Chosen Women, now the Convent of Santa Catalina. Five colonial churchs are interesting: El Triunfo, La Merced, Santa Domingo, Jesuite, and Jesus and Maria.

Also see the excellent murals, carved altars and paintings in La Compania de Jesus, Cuzco's most beautiful church. The magnificent main altar in Belen de los Reyes Church, outside the city. The Inca stonework throughout the city's streets. The prominent colonial residences: La Casa de Garcilaso de la Vega Inca, La Casa de los Marqueses de Buenavista, La Casa de Diego Maldonado, and La Casa de Concha.

The museums: Art, Anthropological and Archaeological, Culture, Larco Herrera, and Viceregal. Nearby is an ancient fort: Puca Pucara (the "red fort").

Take a taxi 12 miles to **Pisac,** an Inca complex so vast that it takes more than a week to explore it completely. The Sunday market there is an outstanding event.

En route to Pisac, stop one mile from Cuzco at the enormous **Sacsayhuaman** (pronounced "sexy woman") with its 3 tremendous parallel walls. Some of its stones weigh an estimated 300 tons each and were placed without mortar so precisely that a knife blade cannot be wedged between them. Stand at the edge of the cliff there for a splendid view of Cuzco, below.

Also stop a few minutes at **Tambo Machay**, the Inca Baths. See the ruins of **Quenko**, **Tambomachay** and **Pucara**.

The great excursion from Cuzco is the trip to Machu-Picchu, the large ancient Inca city-fortress. Details for that train ride appear on page 778.

Huancayo

Located where an Inca highway once existed, in a wide valley at 10,696 feet altitude. Sunday fairs is the event that attracts tourists here (herbs, fruits, embroidered skirts and petticoats, vegetables, furs, silver jewelry, gourds, etc.). This is the most famous market in Peru, attracting both Peruvian and Bolivian Indians.

Juliaca

Great woolen goods, leather items and alpaca knits are offered in the Sunday and Monday markets in the enormous Plaza Melgar.

Lima

Shopping for silver and gold jewelry, alpaca and llama furs, and colonial antiques is a key tourist activity in Lima.

See much fine 16th and 17th century colonial architecture. Torre Tagle Palace and these churches: Santa Domingo (one block west of Government Palace), La Merced (on Jiron de la Union, 2 blocks from Plaza de Armas), San Francisco (one block east of Government Palace), San Augustin (2 blocks from Plaza de Armas), and San Pedro (2 blocks east and one block south of Plaza de Armas).

The curved mahogany ceiling in the main hall at the Court of the Inquisition. The city's famous bullring. Plaza San Martin, a lovely park. The centuries-old, 15-minute ritual of Changing of the Guard at Government Palace, daily except Sunday at 13:00.

The Museum of Art (5,000 years of Peruvian culture) in the 1868 Exposition Palace on Paseo Colon. Pre-Hispanic relics (back to 500 B.C.) in the Museum of Anthropology and Archaeology, and the adjoining Museum of the Republic, both at Plaza Bolivar. The Museum of Peruvian Culture at 650 Alfonso Ugarte Ave.

Colonial paintings, furniture and costumes in the Museum of Vice-royalty in the Quinta de Presa mansion. The Museum of Italian Art on Paseo de la Republica. The gold and silver collection at the Rafael Larco Herrera Museum. The mosaic tiles at **La Punta**, along the beach. The Military Museum at Fort Felipe Real. Shop for alpaca fur coats and silver filigree.

The most ornately decorated colonial churches here are San Francisco and Santo Domingo. The cavernous cathedral is plainer than them, and disappointing. There is good surfing at the nearby **Herradura**, **Punta Hermosa** and **Ponta Rocas** suburbs.

See the fantastic gold and silver items in the Gold Museum at **Monterrico**, another suburb. The 3½-hour tour (operated every day by Lima Tours, located near Hotel Bolivar) to the nearby **Pachacamac** ruins. Sunday afternoon fights in the Plaza de Acho bullring.

Puno (and Lake Titicaca)

It is cold and windy here, at 12,648 feet. The legend is that the Sun God created the first Inca king and his queen on the Island of the Sun in Lake Titicaca, on Peru's western border with Bolivia.

Today, 37-pound trout are the monarchs of a lake that is more than 2 miles above sea level, 35 miles wide and 95 miles long. There are many hydrofoil boat excursions to small "floating islands" of reeds, populated by Uru Indians.

Lima - Huancayo 1802

Even in Peruvian Summer (January, February, March), the weather on this trip is very cold. Pickpockets and bag-slashers are a menace on this trip.

For an optimum experience, depart Lima on Saturday morning, spend that night in Huancayo, see the weekly Indian market there on Sunday (silver, llama wool blankets, hides, etc.), and return to Lima on Monday morning.

The Lima-La Oroya portion of this train journey is the highest standard gauge rail trip in the world (built in 1893 and reaching a height of 15,681 feet at **Calera**, the world's highest railstation) and carries a staff doctor. The descent to 10,696-foot high Huancayo becomes a relief ! The altitude is so debilitating that most passengers sleep or take oxygen inhalation.

WARNING ! There are usually long lines for the tickets that cannot be purchased until the day of travel. Seating in the first-class buffet car requires reservation. Many passengers in the regular first-class and second-class coach cars have to stand. It is advisable to get tickets and reservations through a Peruvian travel agency in Lima. The price in 1991 was $5 (U.S.) for Buffet-Class (see description of "Buffet" on page 775), $4 for first-class. Children : $3 and $2.

A breakfast of sandwiches and coffee or tea is served in the first-class buffet car soon after departing Lima.

Not shown in Cook's timetable, the first stop out of Lima is the former resort, **San Bartolome** (5,000 feet altitude). Fruit sellers go through the train there during the period that the locomotive is moved to the rear of the train so as to maneuver the first of 20 switchbacks that enable the train to zig-zag 2,000 feet up the mountain in 17 minutes.

At the early part of the trip is **Chosica**, a popular Winter resort. Then, the train goes through scenic valleys and passes by Indian farmhouses and rustic railstations where Indian women sell fruits and flowers.

The track follows the **Rimac River** as it crosses 59 bridges, goes through 66 tunnels and makes 22 switchbacks. The "descent" into Huancayo is along small wheat farms.

At **Rio Blanco** (11,400 feet), the train doctor leaves the "downhill" Huancayo-Lima train to board the Lima-Huancayo train. Service of a tasty, hot lunch, then begins.

The elevation signs at succeeding stations are fascinating: **Chicla** 12,135 feet; **Casapalca** 13,500 feet. There are few animals on the windswept, barren plateau at 14,500 feet. After **Ticlio**, the train goes through a 4,000-foot-long tunnel (15,700 feet) and stops at 15,681-foot-high **Galera**, where the brakes are tested before beginning the descent to **La Oroya** (12,500 feet).

During the 75 miles from La Oroya to Huancayo, the train follows the **Rio Mantano** as it rushes downhill to the Amazon.

Service has been temporily suspended since 1990.

Dep. Lima (Desamparados)	Dep. Huancayo
Dep. La Oroya	Arr. La Oroya
Arr. Huancayo	Arr. Lima (Desamparados)

La Oroya - Cerro de Pasco 1803

Although Cook carries this timetable, the Peru Tourist Office advised us in 1991 that this service has been suspended since 1990.

Dep. La Oroya	Dep. Cerro de Pasco
Arr. Cerro de Pasco	Arr. La Oroya

Sights in **Cerro de Pasco**: At 14,232-feet altitude, this is one of the world's highest towns. There are many metal mines here (copper, gold, zinc, lead). The town was rebuilt in the early 1970's.

Huancayo - Huancavelica 1801

The Peru Tourist Office advised us in 1991 that this first-class only train runs daily except Sunday, and that the price of a ticket was $2.50 (U.S.) for adults, $1.25 for children.

Dep. Huancayo	07:00	Dep. Huancavelica	07:00 13:00
Arr. Huancavelica	10:10	Arr. Huancayo	10:10 16:10

Cuzco to Machu-Picchu and Inca City PTO timetable

One of the most popular train journeys in Peru is from Cuzco to Machu-Picchu, paralleling the turbulent Urubamba River. The 5,000-foot descent from Cuzco through the verdant jungle is considered by many as one of the most scenic rail trips in the world. The other attraction, of course, is seeing the incredible 15th century Inca ruins at **Machu Picchu**, an 8,000-foot high plateau surrounded by snow-covered mountains, unknown until discovered in the early 20th century by Hiram Bingham, a Yale University professor.

In his book "The Lost City of the Incas", Bingham wrote: "I know of no other place in the world that can compare to this sight."

Reserve a window seat on the left going to Machu Picchu, and on the right for the return ride (and be sure it is the seat that faces forward) overlooking the Urubama River. A cart comes through the train with coffee, tea, gingerale and cookies.

At a village called **Purchoi** (not shown on Cooks Timetable), large-kerneled sweet corn can be purchased. Watch in this area for coveys of green parrots. In the Urubama Valley, you will see hundreds of Inca-built terraces still being farmed. The train goes through dense jungles.

At some train stops, native women go through the train, selling tortillas. En route, the train goes through a fertile valley at **Ollantaytambo**.

The ruins, called **Inca City,** are open daily 06:30—7:00. It is estimated that 500-1,000 people lived here in about 250 houses made of rock and clay mortar.

The buses that provide transportation 5 miles from the **Puente Ruinos** railstation 1,000 feet up to Inca City have been inadequate for many years, and some tourists have to wait unsheltered as long as 2 hours (sometimes in heavy rain). In such frequent instances, visitors don't reach the ruins until noon and have only 90 minutes for exploring there — far too little time.

Because of this chronic problem, it is highly advisable to reserve at least 3 months in advance of arrival a room at the 25-room Machu-Pichu Pueblo Hotel, near the Puente Ruinos railstation. That way, the entire afternoon on arrival day can be used to visit the ruins, before returning to Cuzco the next day.

Reservations can be made the day before travel and are essential. A roundtrip in 1991 cost $42 (U.S.), including the 25-minute bus service for the 5-mile ascent from Puente Ruinos to Inca City plus admission to the ruins.

All of these trains have a parlor car.

Dep. Cuzco (S.Pedro)	06:00	09:00
Dep. Machu-Picchu	09:30	12:40
Arr. Puente Ruinos	09:40	12:50
	* * *	
Dep. Puente Ruinos	13:50	17:20
Dep. Machu-Picchu	14:00	17:30
Arr. Cuzco (S.Pedro)	18:00	21:00

Juliaca - Arequipa PTO timetable

The train passes along many grain fields. Highest place on the route is 14,688-feet high **Crucero Alto**. After it, all water flows toward the Pacific Ocean.

Many tall mountains can be seen as well as grazing vicunas, sheep, llamas and alpacas. The train descends in 189 miles from Juliaca (12,500 feet) to Arequipa (7,500 feet).

(Timetable appears on page 780.)

All of these trains have a restaurant car or buffet.

Dep. Juliaca	08:35	10:55	21:15
Arr. Arequipa	16:50	19:00	06:00

* * *

Dep. Arequipa	08:45	21:00
Arr. Juliaca	17:45	05:50

INTERNATIONAL ROUTES FROM PERU

Rail + Boat connection was available prior to 1985 from both Cuzco and Arequipa to Bolivia. Puno, on the shore of Lake Titicaca, is 12,648 feet high.

The extremely scenic Cuzco-Juliaca route along the heights of the Andes is close to the main, centuries-old Inca highway, which required a month by foot. At the Juliaca railstation, Indian women sell colorful knitted garments.

The train reaches an altitude of 14,000 feet at **La Raya** (not shown in Cook's timetable). After going downhill to the lush **Vilcanota River Valley**, it ascends to a bleak mesa and then plunges down the other side of the Andes to Puno.

A first-class roundtrip ticket in 1991 was only $14 (U.S.) for this 11-hour, 232-mile train trip.

These are Peru Tourist Office timetables.

Cuzco-Juliaca-Puno

Dep. Cuzco	07:30 (1)
Arr. Juliaca	16:35
Arr. Puno	17:35

(1) Runs daily, except Sunday.

Arequipa-Puno

Dep. Arequipa	21:00
Dep. Juliaca	06:20
Arr. Puno	07:20

Puno - Guaqui - La Paz

The Puno–Guaqui boat has been limited to only freight since 1985, when passenger service was "temporarily" suspended.

1810 Boat		1903 Train		
Dep. Puno		Dep. Guaqui	15:40 (1)	17:55 (2)
Arr. Guaqui		Arr. La Paz	20:00	20:15
Change to train.				

(1) Runs Wednesday only. (2) Runs Thursday only.

URUGUAY

All passenger train service in Uruguay was suspended in November, 1987. Children under 3 traveled free. Half-fare was charged for children 3–9. Children 10 and over had to pay full fare.

Montevideo was the hub for Uruguay's 1,874 miles of rail service. The 4 lines from there went to Colonia, Mercedes, Rio Branco and Rivera. A branch off the line to Rivera led to Salto and Artigas.

Colonia

See the Municipal Museum. The Mansion of the Viceroy. The beautiful plaza. The Parochial Church.

Montevideo

Peak tourist season here is January and February. The major attraction is the city's big beaches. See the enormous marble Legislative Palace. The National Historical Museum (Rincom 437). Plaza Independencia and the nearby Natural History Museum (Buenos Aires 652). The large lake and National Fine Arts Museum in Rodo Park.

The Oceanography and Fish Museum (Rambla Republica de Chile 4215). The Zoo on Avenida de Rivera. The Military Museum (Montevideo Hill), and the view from there. The Pre-Columbian Museum (Mateo Vidal 3249). The collection of paintings and sculptures at the Joaquin Torres Garcia Museum (Constitujente 1467). The outstanding Rose Garden (850 varieties) and Municipal Museum of Fine Arts and History, both in El Prado Park. The Sunday morning flea market on Calle Tristen Narvaja, across from the University's statue of David.

The many fine statues in Batlle y Ordonez Park. The Cathedral, on Plaza Constitucion. Stroll down Avenida 18 de Julio. East of Plaza Zabala, see the Customs House, the Bolsa (Stock Exchange) and Banco de la Republica. Lunch at the stand-up bars (barbecued meats, fruits, soups, sandwiches, fish) at Mercado del Puerto, at the waterfront. Then walk to the breakwater at Punta Santa Teresa to see ships coming into port, or walk along the beaches bordered by Rio de Plata

The nearby **Punta del Este beach** resort, during the peak season (mid- December to mid-March). The Casa Pueblo Museum, featuring the work of Uruguayan painter Carlos Paez Vilaro, the Picasso of South America. Night life centers at the local gambling casino. Stroll Avenida Gorlero to see its antique shops, notable for American and European Art Nouveau items from the early years of this century. Take a boat to **Isla de Lobos** to see the seal colony there.

Rivera

See: Canapiru Dam. Plaza Internacional. Stroll the street which is the border with Brazil. On the other side of the street is the Brazilian city **Santa Ana do Livramento**.

Salto

See: Lovely Solari Park. The walkway along the Uruguay River.

INTERNATIONAL ROUTES FROM URUGUAY

Montevideo - Buenos Aires 2211

Dep. Montevideo by Bus	06:15	07:30	09:15	13:15	14:00	16:15 (1)
Arr. Colonia	09:05	09:45	12:05	16:05	16:15	19:05
Dep. Colonia (Hydrofoil)	09:20	10:00	12:20	16:20	16:30	19:20
Arr. Buenos Aires	60 minutes later					

(1) Plus another departure from Montevideo at 17:00, arriving Buenos Aires 20:30.

Montevideo - Porto Alegre - Sao Paulo Bus

2220

Dep. Montevideo	20:00	22:00
Arr. Porto Alegre	06:00	08:00

Change buses.

2130

Dep. Porto Alegre	11:00	14:00	15:00	16:00	18:00	18:30	20:30 (1)
Arr. Sao Paulo	05:00	08:00	09:00	10:00	12:00	12:30	14:30

(1) Plus another departure from Porto Alegre at 22:00, arriving Sao Paulo 16:00.

VENEZUELA

Children under 3 travel free. Half-fare for children 3–11. Children 12 and over must pay full fare.

There is no train service between Venezuela and adjacent countries. The only rail service for which timetables are available is the 105-mile route from Puerto Cabello to Barquisimeto.

Puerto Cabello - Barquisimeto 1650

These trains run only Saturdays, Sundays and holidays.

Dep. Puerto Cabello	06:00	16:00
Arr. Barquisimeto	08:45	18:45

* * *

Dep. Barquisimeto	06:00	16:00
Arr. Puerto Cabello	08:45	18:45

Sights in **Puerto Cabello**: A heavily industrialized city.

Sights in **Barquisimeto**: A collecting point for sugar, cacao, cereals, coffee and cattle.

Chapter 17

EURAIL® GUIDE ROUTE CHART

In view of the fact that there are over 100,000 miles of railroad lines in just the 17 Eurailpass countries, it would be impossible to list every conceivable trip one could make by train in Western Europe. We do provide you in this chapter a list of 734 trips that most people touring Europe might make, showing the travel time and first-class fare for each.

The list of ticket prices enables our readers (a) first, to compute the cost of ordinary tickets for an itinerary and (b) then, to compare that total cost with one or a combination of the train passes described in Eurail® Guide.

We have condensed route descriptions by listing them only in alphabetical priority. For example, the first route is Aix-en-Provence to Marseille. If you were looking for the trip from Marseille to Aix-en-Provence, you would refer to the name that has alphabetical priority: Aix-en-Provence. Similarly, the trip Rome-Paris will be found as Paris-Rome, etc.

The rates listed are first-class fares, in U.S. dollars. To compute second- class fares, figure 66 % of the first-class fare shown. While this will not always be the exact second-class fare, it will be very close to it.

Also remember that European train fares, like the prices of all other European goods and services, are subject to change relative to the exchange rates for U.S. dollars and other non-European currencies.

On the other hand, once a Eurailpass, France Railpass, GermanRail Flexipass, or any other train pass has been issued to you, you are protected from the devaluation of your currency increasing the cost of your train transportation — another hidden plus to having a pass.

All the fares listed in this chapter are subject to a seat reservation fee of $3 (U.S.) per person (if you want to be sure of having a seat). This charge is made whether traveling with a ticket or with Eurailpass. However, a Eurailpass holder does not have to pay the *supplement* that is charged in addition to the ticket price when riding on some EuroCity or TGV trains, ranging from $3 (U.S.) to $8.

Keep in mind that on trips which involve both a Eurailpass country and also a country not covered by Eurailpass such as Vienna-Athens (via non-Eurailpas Yugo-slavia), the passenger holding a Eurailpass has to purchase a ticket for the non-Eurailpass portion of that trip.

Because Paris has 6 different railstations, we indicate in parenthesis after the name "Paris" the name of the Paris railstation at which a train is departing or arriving.

EURAIL® GUIDE ROUTE CHART

1992 first-class train fares, *not* including seat reservation fee.

	Travel Time	Fare
AIX-EN-PROVENCE		
Marseille	½	8.00
ALBORG		
Copenhagen	6 ½	47.00
ALGECIRAS		
Cordoba	4 ½	34.00
Granada	5	33.00
Madrid	11 ½	82.00
Malaga	4	27.00
Seville	6	38.00
ALICANTE		
Valencia	2	21.00
ALKMAAR		
Amsterdam	½	7.00
AMSTERDAM		
Antwerp	2 ½	32.00
Basel (via Roosendaal)	9 ½	120.00
Berlin	8 ½	112.00
Bremen	4	68.00
Brussels	3 ½	38.00
Cologne (Koln)	3	49.00
Copenhagen (Kobenhavn)	13	171.00
Dusseldorf	2 ½	43.00
Frankfurt	6	95.00
Hamburg	6	92.00
Hannover	5 ½	71.00
Heidelberg	6 ½	107.00
Hoek Van Holland	2	20.00
Luxembourg (via Roosendaal)	5	68.00
Milan	15 ½	241.00

Munich (Munchen)	12	179.00
Paris (Nord)	5 ½	83.00
Rome	21	309.00
Rotterdam	1	16.00
Salzburg	13	210.00
Utrecht	½	7.00
Vienna (Wien)		
(via Passau)	15	231.00
Wiesbaden	6	87.00
Zurich	11	190.00

ANDALSNES

Oslo	7	92.00

ANDERMATT

Brig	2	34.00
Chur	2 ½	41.00
Luzern	2	34.00
Zurich	2	44.00

ANTWERP

Brussels	1	8.00
Paris (Nord)	3 ½	53.00
Rotterdam	1 ½	19.00

AOSTA

Milan	3 ½	24.00
Turin (Torino)	1 ½	16.00

ARHUS

Copenhagen (Kobenhavn)	4 ½	44.00

ARLES

Marseille	1	15.00
Nimes	½	9.00

AROSA

Chur	1	11.00
Zurich	3	50.00

ASSISI
Florence (Firenze)	3	22.00
Rome	2 ½	22.00

ATHENS
Patras	3	24.00
Thessaloniki	9	46.00

AVIGNON
Barcelona	6 ½	64.00
Cannes	3 ½	46.00
Carcassonne	2 ½	38.00
Geneva	4 ½	54.00
Lourdes	7	67.00
Lyon	2 ½	35.00
Marseille	1	20.00
Nice	4	49.00
Nimes	1	10.00
Paris (Lyon)	7	88.00
Port Bou	4	45.00

BADEN-BADEN
Basel	2	38.00

BARCELONA
Bilboa	9 ½	81.00
Carcassonne	6	45.00
Geneva	12	103.00
Genoa	13 ½	115.00
Lourdes	10	77.00
Lyon	10	86.00
Madrid	8	80.00
Marseille	8	72.00
Nice	10	93.00
Paris (Austerlitz)	11 ½	130.00
Rome	20	171.00
Seville	13	111.00
Toulouse (Via Port Bou)	7	57.00
Valencia	4	41.00
Vigo	18 ¼	128.00
Zaragoza	3 ½	43.00

BARI

Bologna	7 ½	70.00
Brindisi	1 ½	14.00
Messina	9	70.00
Milan	10	96.00
Naples	4	35.00
Pescara	3 ½	32.00
Rome	6	59.00
Taranto	1 ½	14.00
Turin (Torino)	13	107.00
Venice	13	86.00

BASEL

Bern	1	34.00
Brig	3	67.00
Brussels	7	84.00
Bucharest (Partly covered by Eurailpass)	29	290.00
Budapest	16	181.00
Cologne (Koln)	6	110.00
Copenhagen (Kobenhavn)	15	259.00
Florence (Firenze)	10	122.00
Frankfurt	3	73.00
Geneva	3 ½	67.00
Genoa	9	103.00
Hamburg	9	182.00
Hannover	7 ½	145.00
Heidelberg	3	60.00
Innsbruck	6	83.00
Interlaken	2 ½	52.00
Lausanne	2 ½	54.00
Locarno	4 ½	73.00
Luxembourg	4	52.00
Luzern	1 ½	29.00
Milan	6	86.00
Montreux	3	60.00
Paris (Est)	6	67.00
Rome	13	154.00
Rotterdam (via Brussels)	9	155.00
Salzburg	9	119.00
Strasbourg	1	22.00
Venice	10	114.00
Vienna (Wien)	12	149.00
Wiesbaden	4	75.00
Zurich	1	32.00

BAYONNE

Hendaye	1	8.00
Madrid	6 ½	79.00

BAYREUTH

Nurnberg	1 ½	19.00

BERGEN

Bodo	26 ½	215.00
Flam	3 ½	35.00
Goteborg	12	160.00
Myrdal	2 ½	31.00
Oslo	7	94.00
Trondheim	14 ½	150.00
Voss	1 ½	20.00

BERLIN

Bremen	5 ½	67.00
Brussels	10	140.00
Cologne (Koln)	7	107.00
Copenhagen (Kobenhavn)	12	62.00
Dusseldorf	6 ½	98.00
Frankfurt/Main	7	76.00
Hamburg	4 ½	36.00
Hannover	4	40.00
Leipzig	2 ½	18.00
Luxembourg	11	152.00
Malmo	9 ½	60.00
Munich (Munchen)	9	103.00
Nurnburg	7	68.00
Oslo	19 ½	179.00
Paris (Nord)	14	179.00
Rotterdam	10	114.00
Stockholm	17	148.00
Vienna (Wien) (Sudbf.) via Prague	14	77.00

BERN

Brig	2	46.00
Geneva	2	52.00
Interlaken	1	22.00
Lausanne	1	30.00
Lugano	4 ½	71.00
Luzern	1 ½	29.00
Milan	4 ½	66.00

Montreux	3 ½	54.00
Paris (Lyon) via Verrieres	5	95.00
Zurich	1 ½	46.00

BILBAO

Hendaye	4 ¼	32.00
Madrid	6	62.00
Vigo	14 ½	88.00
Zaragoza	4 ½	38.00

BODEN

Haparanda	2	37.00
Narvik	7	92.00
Stockholm	16	127.00

BODO

Goteborg	24 ½	230.00
Oslo	19	172.00
Trondheim	11 ½	127.00

BOLOGNA

Florence (Firenze)	1 ½	11.00
Genoa	4 ½	32.00
Innsbruck	6 ½	50.00
Milan	2 ½	24.00
Naples	6 ½	70.00
Paris (Lyon)	10	171.00
Ravenna	1 ½	10.00
Rimini	1 ½	14.00
Rome	3 ¼	48.00
Turin (Torino)	4 ½	38.00
Venice	2	19.00
Verona	1 ½	14.00

BONN

Cologne (Koln)	½	8.00
Frankfurt (Main)	2	39.00
Koblenz	1	11.00

BORDEAUX

Geneva	10	95.00
Hendaye	3	36.00
Lourdes	3 ½	41.00
Lyon	9	78.00
Marseille	7	82.00
Nice	12	105.00
Paris (Austerlitz)	5	72.00
Toulouse	3 ½	39.00
Tours	3 ½	49.00

BREMEN

Budapest	19 ½	237.00
Cologne (Koln)	3	69.00
Copenhagen (Kobenhavn)	6 ½	103.00
Dusseldorf	3	61.00
Essen	2 ½	53.00
Frankfurt/Main	6	98.00
Hamburg	2	25.00
Hannover	1	25.00
Heidelberg	7	115.00
Munich (Munchen)	8 ½	156.00
Stuttgart	8 ½	136.00
Vienna (Wien)	14	208.00

BRIG

Chur	4 ½	63.00
Interlaken	1 ½	39.00
Lausanne	1 ½	46.00
Zermatt	1 ½	37.00

BRUGGE

Brussels	1 ½	14.00

BRUSSELS

Budapest	20 ½	248.00
Calais	3	34.00
Cologne (Koln)	2 ½	36.00
Copenhagen (Kobenhavn)	13	208.00
Frankfurt	5 ½	83.00
Ghent	½	9.00
Hamburg	8	130.00
Liege	1	15.00
Luxembourg	3	32.00

Munich (Munchen)	10	166.00
Paris (Nord)	3	47.00
Rotterdam	2	25.00
Vienna (Wien) (via Nurnberg)	15	219.00
Zurich	13	116.00

BUCHS

Innsbruck	3	27.00
Zurich	1 ½	38.00

BUDAPEST

Cologne (Koln)	18	210.00
Frankfurt/Main	15 ½	166.00
Hamburg	19 ½	248.00
Milan	16 ½	136.00
Munich (Munchen)	11	107.00
Paris (Est)		
via Munich	21	255.00
via Basel	25	248.00
Rome	25	174.00
Trieste	15	107.00
Venice	13	112.00
Vienna (Wien)	4	34.00
Zurich	18	163.00

CADIZ

Madrid	8	80.00
Seville	2	17.00

CALAIS

Paris (Nord)	3 ½	44.00
Strasbourg	9 ½	76.00

CANNES

Florence (Firenze)	11	54.00
Geneva	9	85.00
Genoa	3	30.00
Marseille	2	30.00
Milan	7 ½	43.00
Nice	1	7.00
Paris (Lyon)	7	120.00
Rome	13	86.00
San Remo	3	13.00

CARCASSONNE

Lourdes	4	40.00
Marseille	4	48.00
Nice	7	70.00
Paris (Austerlitz)	8	94.00
Port Bou	2 ½	26.00
Toulouse	1	15.00

CHAMONIX-MONT BLANC

Geneva	2 ½	19.00
Grenoble	2 ¼	36.00
Martigny (Second-class only)	3	24.00
Paris (Lyon)	8	87.00

CHARTRES

Paris (Montparnasse)	1	15.00

CHERBOURG

Paris (St. Lazare)	3 ½	52.00

CHUR

St. Moritz	2 ½	38.00
Zurich	1 ½	41.00

COLOGNE (KOLN)

Copenhagen (Kobenhavn)	10	173.00
Dortmund	1	24.00
Dusseldorf	½	11.00
Essen	1	17.00
Frankfurt	2 ½	46.00
Hamburg	5	95.00
Hannover	3	63.00
Koblenz	1	19.00
Luxembourg (Via Koblenz)	4	45.00
Luzern	7 ½	138.00
Mainz	2	38.00
Mannheim	3	53.00
Milan	12	192.00
Munich (Munchen)	7	129.00
Paris (Nord)	7	75.00
Rotterdam	3 ½	45.00
Salzburg	8 ½	161.00
Stuttgart	4 ½	81.00
Vienna (Wien)	12	181.00

Wiesbaden	2	38.00
Zurich	7 ½	141.00

COIMBRA
Lisbon	2 ½	19.00

COMO
Lugano	½	10.00
Luzern	4	64.00
Milan	1	6.00
Venice	4	35.00
Zurich	4	72.00

COPENHAGEN (KOBENHAVN)
Frankfurt	10 ½	184.00
Fredrickshavn	7	47.00
Hamburg (via Puttgarden)	5	80.00
Helsinki (Partly by Ship)	23 ½	172.00
Hoek Van Holland	12	175.00
Kristiansand (Ship)	15 ½	87.00
Luxembourg (via Koln)	13 ½	221.00
Malmo (Hydrofoil)	½	19.00
(Not covered by Eurailpass.)		
Milan	22 ½	341.00
Munich (Munchen) (via Berlin)	19	166.00
Narvik	31	147.00
Odense	3	29.00
Oslo	10 ½	137.00
Paris (Nord)	15	247.00
Rome	30	409.00
Rotterdam	14 ½	173.00
Stockholm (via Hassleholm)	8	117.00
Trondheim (via Goteborg)	19	226.00
Venice	24	320.00
Vienna (Wien)	20	295.00
Wiesbaden	13	194.00

CORDOBA
Granada	3 ½	27.00
Madrid	5	49.00
Malaga	2 ½	21.00
Seville	1	15.00

DAVOS
St. Moritz	1 ½	26.00
Zurich	3	56.00

DIJON

Lausanne	3	43.00
Lyon	2	23.00
Paris	2	46.00
Strasbourg (via Belfort)	4	49.00

DORTMUND

Paris (Nord)	7	98.00

DUSSELDORF

Essen	½	8.00
Frankfurt/Main	3	54.00
Hamburg	4	86.00
Hannover	3	58.00
Munich (Munchen)	11	137.00
Paris (Nord)	6	82.00

FLAM

Myrdal (2nd class fare)	1	7.00
Oslo	6 ½	79.00

FLORENCE (FIRENZE)

Geneva	10	122.00
Genoa	4	27.00
Innsbruck	8	55.00
Lausanne	9	108.00
Livorno	1 ½	14.00
Luzern	9	105.00
Marseille	12	82.00
Milan	3	35.00
Munich (Munchen)	10	85.00
Naples	5 ¼	59.00
Nice	11	49.00
Paris		
(Lyon) via Iselle	15	176.00
(Lyon) via Pisa	18	143.00
(Lyon) via Turin (Torino)	18	132.00

Perugia	2 ½	19.00
Pisa	1 ½	10.00
Ravenna	3	16.00
Rome	2 ¼	35.00
Siena	2 ½	11.00
Turin (Torino)	6	48.00
Venice	3	30.00
Vienna (Wien)	13	104.00

FRANKFURT/MAIN

Hamburg	5 ½	110.00
Hannover	3 ½	73.00
Heidelberg	1	19.00
Innsbruck	7 ½	121.00
Luxembourg	4 ½	59.00
Mainz	½	8.00
Mannheim	1	17.00
Nurnberg	2 ½	49.00
Paris (Est)	7	100.00
Rotterdam	6	91.00
Salzburg	7	117.00
Stuttgart	2 ½	43.00
Vienna (Wien)	9	137.00
Wiesbaden	½	11.00
Zurich	5	104.00

FREDRICKSHAVN

Hamburg	7 ½	86.00
Oslo (Ship) (Not covered by Eurailpass.)	10	93.00
Stockholm (Ship) (Not covered by Eurailpass.)	7 ½	103.00

GARMISCH-PARTENKIRCHEN

Innsbruck	1 ½	13.00
Munich (Munchen)	1 ½	21.00

GAVLE

Stockholm	2	39.00

GENEVA

Genoa		
via Milan	7 ½	95.00
via Turin (Torino)	7	62.00
Grenoble	3 ½	26.00
Grindelwald	3 ½	70.00
Gstaad	2 ½	50.00
Interlaken (via Bern)	3	65.00
Lausanne	½	24.00
Locarno	4 ½	90.00
Lourdes	10	106.00
Luzern	3 ½	68.00
Lyon	3	26.00
Marseille (via Lyon)	6 ½	66.00
Milan	6	84.00
Montreux	1	32.00
Nice (via Lyon)	10 ½	88.00
Paris (Lyon)	6	76.00
Rome	9 ¼	148.00
Turin (Torino)	5	55.00
Venice	8	116.00
Zurich	3	76.00

GENOA

Lausanne	7	81.00
Luzern	7 ½	86.00
Marseille	7 ½	57.00
Milan	2	19.00
Monaco-Monte Carlo	3	21.00
Munich (Munchen)	11 ½	96.00
Naples	8 ½	80.00
Nice	3 ½	25.00
Paris (Lyon) (via Torino)	12	114.00
Pisa	2 ½	19.00
Rome	7	59.00
Salzburg	14	102.00
San Remo	2	16.00
Turin (Torino)	2 ½	19.00
Venice	7	43.00

GOTEBORG

Copenhagen (Kobenhavn)	4 ½	67.00
Hamburg	10	137.00
Helsingborg	3	53.00
Kalmar	5	74.00
Oslo	5	79.00
Stockholm	4 ½	89.00
Trondheim	21	150.00

GRANADA

Madrid	6 ½	55.00
Malaga	3	21.00
Seville	4 ½	32.00
Valencia	8	75.00

GRAZ

Vienna (Wien)	3 ½	32.00

GRENOBLE

Lyon	2	21.00
Marseille	5 ½	46.00

GRINDELWALD

Interlaken (Not covered by Eurailpass)	1	9.00
Zurich (Only partially covered by Eurailpass)	3 ½	65.00

HAMBURG

Hannover	2	37.00
Heidelberg	7	128.00
Helsinki (Partly by Ship)	33	214.00
Luxembourg	8 ½	143.00
Munich (Munchen)	8 ½	167.00
Oslo	15 ½	207.00
Paris (Nord)	11	169.00
Rotterdam	6 ½	94.00
Salzburg	10	197.00
Stockholm	13	187.00
Stuttgart	8	148.00
Vienna (Wien)	13	219.00

HANNOVER		
Munich (Munchen)	6	131.00
Paris (Nord)	10	138.00
Rotterdam	5	73.00
Wurzburg	4	74.00
HAPARANDA		
Helsinki	12	79.00
HEIDELBERG		
Koblenz	2	38.00
Luzern	4 ½	88.00
Mainz	1	19.00
Munich (Munchen)	4	73.00
Nurnberg	4	53.00
Paris (Est)	7	90.00
Rothenburg ("Castle Road" Bus)	3	48.00
Stuttgart	1	23.00
Wiesbaden	1 ½	21.00
HELSINKI		
Kuopio	6	53.00
Oslo (Partly by Ship)	22	172.00
Oulu	7 ½	70.00
Stockholm (Ship)	12 ½	55.00
Turku	3	26.00
HENDAYE		
Lisbon	17	102.00
Lourdes	3 ½	28.00
Madrid	7	71.00
Paris (Austerlitz)	8	96.00
Zaragoza	4 ¼	37.00
HOEK VAN HOLLAND		
Innsbruck	13	214.00
Munich (Munchen)	12	179.00
Rotterdam	½	5.00

INNSBRUCK

Kitzbuhel	1	17.00
Luzern	6	70.00
Milan	6 ½	50.00
Munich (Munchen)	4	34.00
Paris (Est)	21	150.00
Rome	12	93.00
Salzburg	4	38.00
Venice	5	45.00
Verona	5	34.00
Vienna (Wien)	8	79.00
Zurich	5	65.00

INTERLAKEN

Lausanne	2	50.00
Luzern	2	23.00
Milan	5	62.00
Montreux	3	50.00
Paris (Lyon) via Verrieres	8 ½	111.00
Zurich	3	60.00

KARLSTAD

Oslo	3	56.00
Stockholm	3 ½	69.00

KLAGENFURT

Salzburg	4	35.00
Venice	4 ½	37.00
Vienna (Wein)	6	49.00

KLOSTERS

Zurich	2 ½	50.00

KOBLENZ

Luxembourg	2 ½	32.00
Munich (Munchen)	6 ½	111.00
Paris (via Reims)	7 ½	85.00
Vienna (Wien)	10	163.00
Wiesbaden	1	19.00

KONSTANZ
Zurich	1	27.00

KRISTIANSAND
Oslo	5	76.00
Stavanger	3 ½	52.00

LAUSANNE
Locarno	4	79.00
Lugano	5 ½	90.00
Luzern	3	56.00
Milan	4 ½	70.00
Montreux	½	8.00
Paris (Lyon)	4	80.00
Rome	13 ¼	134.00
Venice	8 ½	102.00
Zurich	2 ½	65.00

LE HAVRE
Paris (St. Lazare)	2 ½	34.00

LIEGE
Luxembourg	3	25.00
Paris (Nord)	4	54.00

LINZ
Salzburg	2	20.00
Vienna (Wien)	2	29.00

LISBON
Madrid (Atocha)	9	69.00
Paris (Austerlitz)	25	198.00
Porto	4	27.00
Santiago de Compostela	9	48.00
Seville	12	48.00
Vigo	9	39.00

LIVORNO
Pisa	½	2.00
Rome	3	35.00

LOCARNO
Lugano	1	14.00
Luzern	3	54.00
Milan	1	29.00
Zurich	3 ½	67.00

LOURDES

Madrid	12	99.00
Nice	12	97.00
Paris (Austerlitz)	8 ½	99.00
Toulouse	2 ½	28.00

LUGANO

Luzern	3	56.00
Milan	1 ½	15.00
Venice	6	43.00
Zurich	3 ½	67.00

LUXEMBOURG

Marseille	10	104.00
Metz	1	12.00
Munich (Munchen)	9	134.00
Nurnberg	7	107.00
Paris (Est)	4	57.00
Salzburg (via Strasbourg)	11	150.00
Strasbourg	3	34.00
Stuttgart (via Strasbourg)	6	70.00
Vienna (Wien)	13	194.00
Zurich	5	84.00

LUZERN

Milan	4 ½	69.00
Montreux	5 ½	63.00
Munich (Munchen)	6 ½	99.00
Paris (Est)	10	96.00
Rigi	1 ½	41.00
Rome	12 ¼	137.00
Venice	8	97.00
Vienna (Wein)	13	136.00
Zurich	1	23.00

LYON

Marseille	4	50.00
Milan	4 ½	63.00
Nice	5	72.00
Paris (Lyon)	4	65.00
Strasbourg	6	61.00
Turin (Torino)	4 ½	47.00
Tours	7	60.00

MADRID

Malaga	7	70.00
Pamplona	8 ½	49.00
Paris (Austerlitz)	13	167.00
Port Bou	10	94.00
Rome	34	246.00
San Sebastian	7	69.00
Santiago de Compostela	7 ½	74.00
Seville	5	63.00
Toledo	1 ¼	9.00
Valencia	5 ½	45.00
Vigo	8	74.00
Zaragoza	3	37.00

MAINZ

Munich (Munchen)	5	92.00
Paris	7	95.00

MALAGA

Seville	3 ½	26.00

MALMO

Stockholm	6	105.00

MARSEILLE

Milan	11	70.00
Nice	3	35.00
Paris (Lyon)	8	100.00
Port Bou	4 ½	53.00
Rome	15	113.00
Toulouse	5	57.00
Venice	17	102.00

MILAN

Montreux	4	60.00
Munich (Munchen)	8 ½	80.00
Naples	6 ¼	91.00
Nice	6	38.00
Padua	3	27.00
Paris (Est) via Chiasso	9	153.00
Paris (Lyon) via Vallorbe	7 ½	144.00
Rome	5 ¼	70.00

Stuttgart	9	119.00
Turin (Torino)	2	19.00
Trieste	6	48.00
Venice	3	30.00
Verona	1 ½	16.00
Vienna	15 ½	104.00
Zurich	4 ½	77.00

MONTREUX

Paris (Lyon)	6 ½	87.00
Zurich	3	68.00

MOSJOEN

Oslo	14	144.00

MUNICH (MUNCHEN)

Nurnberg	½	41.00
Oberammergau	2	19.00
Paris (Est)	10	148.00
Rome	13 ¼	123.00
Rotterdam	11	175.00
Salzburg	2	32.00
Stuttgart	3	49.00
Venice (via Innsbruck)	9	72.00
Vienna (Wien)	6	78.00
Wiesbaden	5	94.00
Zurich	5	83.00

MYRDAL

Oslo	5 ½	71.00

NANCY

Paris (Est)	3	50.00

NAPLES

Nice	14	102.00
Paris (Lyon)		
via Rome-Florence	20 ¼	235.00
via Rome-Pisa	23 ½	189.00
Reggio Calabria	5 ½	54.00
Rome	2	24.00

Taranto	5	35.00
Turin (Torino)	10	96.00
Venice	8 ¼	86.00
Vienna (Wien)	18 ¼	163.00

NARVIK

Oslo	33	166.00
Stockholm	22	137.00

NICE

Paris (Lyon)	11 ½	123.00
Rome (via Pisa)	11 ½	81.00
Turin (Torino)	4 ½	36.00
Venice	11 ½	70.00

OSLO

Stavanger	8 ½	113.00
Stockholm	6 ½	117.00
Trondheim	7	107.00
Voss	5 ½	80.00

PALERMO

Paris (Lyon)	32	217.00
Rome	13	102.00

PARIS

Port Bou (Austerlitz)	12	111.00
Rheims (Est)	2	24.00
Rome (Lyon) via Pisa	17	170.00
Rouen (St. Laz.)	1 ½	22.00
Salzburg (Est) (via Munich)	11 ½	180.00
San Sebastian (Austerlitz)	9 ½	98.00
Stockholm (Nord)	25	354.00
Strasbourg (Est)	4 ½	65.00
Stuttgart (Est)	7 ½	100.00
Toulouse (Austerlitz)	7	85.00
Tours (Aust.)	2	35.00
Trieste (Lyon)	15 ½	187.00
Turin (Torino) - (Lyon)	11	98.00
Venice (Lyon) via Vallorbe	13	176.00
Vienna (Wein) - (Est)	15	194.00
Zurich (Est)	7 ½	99.00

PERUGIA

Rome	3	24.00

PISA

Rome	3 ½	38.00
Siena	2 ½	14.00

RATTVIK

Stockholm	3	61.00

RAVENNA

Rimini	1	6.00
Venice	3	22.00

RIMINI

Venice	3 ½	30.00

ROME

Siena	4 ½	30.00
Trieste	7	80.00
Turin (Torino)	7	75.00
Venice	5 ¼	64.00
Vienna (Wien)	19 ¼	142.00
Zurich	8 ¼	145.00

ROTTERDAM

Vienna (Wein)	19	227.00

SALZBURG

Trieste	7 ½	51.00
Venice	7 ½	56.00
Vienna (Wien)	4	46.00
Villach	3	29.00
Zurich	8 ½	101.00

ST. MORITZ

Zurich	5	68.00

STOCKHOLM

Trondheim	12 ½	137.00
Turku (ship)	12 ½	28.00
Uppsala	1	17.00

STUTTGART

Vienna (Wien)	9	126.00
Zurich	4	57.00

TRIESTE
    Venice | 2 ½ | 19.00
    Vienna (Wien) | 10 | 75.00

TURIN (Torino)
    Venice | 5 | 48.00

VENICE
    Verona | 2 | 14.00
    Vienna (Wien) | 10 | 80.00
    Zurich | 7 | 108.00

VIENNA (WIEN)
    Zurich | 12 | 131.00

INDEX OF CITIES, RESORTS AND SCENIC PLACES

1992

JANUARY
S	M	T	W	T	F	S
			1	2	3	4
5	6	7	8	9	10	11
12	13	14	15	16	17	18
19	20	21	22	23	24	25
26	27	28	29	30	31	

MAY
S	M	T	W	T	F	S
					1	2
3	4	5	6	7	8	9
10	11	12	13	14	15	16
17	18	19	20	21	22	23
24	25	26	27	28	29	30
31						

SEPTEMBER
S	M	T	W	T	F	S
		1	2	3	4	5
6	7	8	9	10	11	12
13	14	15	16	17	18	19
20	21	22	23	24	25	26
27	28	29	30			

FEBRUARY
S	M	T	W	T	F	S
						1
2	3	4	5	6	7	8
9	10	11	12	13	14	15
16	17	18	19	20	21	22
23	24	25	26	27	28	29

JUNE
S	M	T	W	T	F	S
	1	2	3	4	5	6
7	8	9	10	11	12	13
14	15	16	17	18	19	20
21	22	23	24	25	26	27
28	29	30				

OCTOBER
S	M	T	W	T	F	S
				1	2	3
4	5	6	7	8	9	10
11	12	13	14	15	16	17
18	19	20	21	22	23	24
25	26	27	28	29	30	31

MARCH
S	M	T	W	T	F	S
1	2	3	4	5	6	7
8	9	10	11	12	13	14
15	16	17	18	19	20	21
22	23	24	25	26	27	28
29	30	31				

JULY
S	M	T	W	T	F	S
			1	2	3	4
5	6	7	8	9	10	11
12	13	14	15	16	17	18
19	20	21	22	23	24	25
26	27	28	29	30	31	

NOVEMBER
S	M	T	W	T	F	S
1	2	3	4	5	6	7
8	9	10	11	12	13	14
15	16	17	18	19	20	21
22	23	24	25	26	27	28
29	30					

APRIL
S	M	T	W	T	F	S
			1	2	3	4
5	6	7	8	9	10	11
12	13	14	15	16	17	18
19	20	21	22	23	24	25
26	27	28	29	30		

AUGUST
S	M	T	W	T	F	S
						1
2	3	4	5	6	7	8
9	10	11	12	13	14	15
16	17	18	19	20	21	22
23	24	25	26	27	28	29
30	31					

DECEMBER
S	M	T	W	T	F	S
		1	2	3	4	5
6	7	8	9	10	11	12
13	14	15	16	17	18	19
20	21	22	23	24	25	26
27	28	29	30	31		

1993

JANUARY
S	M	T	W	T	F	S
					1	2
3	4	5	6	7	8	9
10	11	12	13	14	15	16
17	18	19	20	21	22	23
24	25	26	27	28	29	30
31						

MAY
S	M	T	W	T	F	S
						1
2	3	4	5	6	7	8
9	10	11	12	13	14	15
16	17	18	19	20	21	22
23	24	25	26	27	28	29
30	31					

SEPTEMBER
S	M	T	W	T	F	S
			1	2	3	4
5	6	7	8	9	10	11
12	13	14	15	16	17	18
19	20	21	22	23	24	25
26	27	28	29	30		

FEBRUARY
S	M	T	W	T	F	S
	1	2	3	4	5	6
7	8	9	10	11	12	13
14	15	16	17	18	19	20
21	22	23	24	25	26	27
28						

JUNE
S	M	T	W	T	F	S
		1	2	3	4	5
6	7	8	9	10	11	12
13	14	15	16	17	18	19
20	21	22	23	24	25	26
27	28	29	30			

OCTOBER
S	M	T	W	T	F	S
					1	2
3	4	5	6	7	8	9
10	11	12	13	14	15	16
17	18	19	20	21	22	23
24	25	26	27	28	29	30
31						

MARCH
S	M	T	W	T	F	S
	1	2	3	4	5	6
7	8	9	10	11	12	13
14	15	16	17	18	19	20
21	22	23	24	25	26	27
28	29	30	31			

JULY
S	M	T	W	T	F	S
				1	2	3
4	5	6	7	8	9	10
11	12	13	14	15	16	17
18	19	20	21	22	23	24
25	26	27	28	29	30	31

NOVEMBER
S	M	T	W	T	F	S
	1	2	3	4	5	6
7	8	9	10	11	12	13
14	15	16	17	18	19	20
21	22	23	24	25	26	27
28	29	30				

APRIL
S	M	T	W	T	F	S
				1	2	3
4	5	6	7	8	9	10
11	12	13	14	15	16	17
18	19	20	21	22	23	24
25	26	27	28	29	30	

AUGUST
S	M	T	W	T	F	S
1	2	3	4	5	6	7
8	9	10	11	12	13	14
15	16	17	18	19	20	21
22	23	24	25	26	27	28
29	30	31				

DECEMBER
S	M	T	W	T	F	S
			1	2	3	4
5	6	7	8	9	10	11
12	13	14	15	16	17	18
19	20	21	22	23	24	25
26	27	28	29	30	31	